i-Ready® Classroom Mathematics

Teacher's Guide

Grade 8 • Volume 2

NOT FOR RESALE

978-1-7280-1309-1

North Billerica, MA 01862

5 6 7 8 9 10 11 12 13 14 15 22 21

BTS21
801147

Curriculum Associates®

Contents

Program Overview A10

Program Resources A10

Pacing Guidance for the Year A12

Volume 1

UNIT 1 Geometric Figures
Rigid Transformations and Congruence 1a

UNIT 2 Geometric Figures
Transformations, Similarity, and Angle Relationships 79a

UNIT 3 Linear Relationships
Slope, Linear Equations, and Systems 173a

UNIT 4 Functions
Linear and Nonlinear Relationships 345a

Volume 2

UNIT 5 Integer Exponents
Properties and Scientific Notation 445a

UNIT 6 Real Numbers
Rational Numbers, Irrational Numbers, and the Pythagorean Theorem 555a

UNIT 7 Statistics
Two-Variable Data and Fitting a Linear Model 693a

Data Sets DS1

Cumulative Practice CP17

Interactive Glossary/Glosario Interactivo GL1

Supporting Research B1

Content Focus in the Common Core State Standards B7

Correlations B9

Common Core State Standards (CCSS) Correlations by Standard B9

Common Core State Standards (CCSS) Correlations by Lesson B14

Standards for Mathematical Practice Correlations to Lessons B17

Lesson Correlations to Standards for Mathematical Practice B17

Unit Review Correlations B19

Acknowledgments B22

UNIT 1

Geometric Figures

Rigid Transformations and Congruence

Unit Planning

Unit Resources 1a
Unit Overview 1c
Lesson Progression 1e
Connect Mathematics and Language Development 1g
Professional Learning: Supporting Math and Academic Vocabulary Development 1g
Differentiation for English Language Learners: Language Expectations 1h
Math Background 1i
Rigid Transformations 1i
Types of Rigid Transformations 1j
Working with Rigid Transformations 1m
Standards for Mathematical Practice in Every Lesson 1q

Unit Opener 1
Prepare for Unit 1 2

LESSON 1 **Understand Rigid Transformations and Their Properties** 3a
8.G.A.1, 8.G.A.1a, 8.G.A.1b, 8.G.A.1c, 8.G.A.2
Focus: M SMP 2, 3, 5, 6, 7

LESSON 2 **Work with Single Rigid Transformations in the Coordinate Plane** 15a
8.G.A.3, 8.G.A.1a, 8.G.A.1b, 8.G.A.1c, 8.G.A.2
Focus: M SMP 1, 2, 3, 4, 5, 6, 7

LESSON 3 **Work with Sequences of Transformations and Congruence** 43a
8.G.A.2, 8.G.A.3, 8.G.A.1a, 8.G.A.1b, 8.G.A.1c
Focus: M SMP 1, 2, 3, 4, 5, 6, 7

MATH IN ACTION **Rigid Transformations in the Coordinate Plane** 65a
Animating a Logo | Shattering a Jewel | Forming a Key
8.G.A.1a, 8.G.A.2, 8.G.A.3
Focus: M SMP 1, 2, 3, 4, 5, 6, 7, 8

Self Reflection 74
Vocabulary Review 75
Unit Review 76
Unit Game | Literacy Connection 76–77
Unit Assessment 78b

Unit 1 Themes

- Rigid transformations are slides, flips, or turns that change the location or orientation of a figure but not its size or shape. You can use the coordinate plane to explore how transformations affect the coordinates of a figure's vertices.
- You can use rigid transformations to make sense of congruence and understand why corresponding sides and angles of congruent figures have the same measure.

Standards in boldface indicate the standards covered by the majority of the lesson content.

See page B7 for correlation tables that provide more details about Major Focus lessons.

M = Lessons that have a major focus in the Common Core State Standards
S = Lessons that have a supporting focus in the Common Core State Standards
A = Lessons that have an additional focus in the Common Core State Standards

UNIT 2

Geometric Figures

Transformations, Similarity, and Angle Relationships

Unit Planning

Unit Resources 79a
Unit Overview 79c
Lesson Progression 79g
Connect Mathematics and Language Development 79i
Professional Learning: Establishing Classroom Environments That Support Mathematical Discourse for ALL Learners 79i
Differentiation for English Language Learners: Language Expectations 79j

Math Background 79k
Dilations 79k
Angle Relationships and Parallel Lines 79m
Angle Relationships in Triangles 79o

Unit Opener 79
Prepare for Unit 2 80

LESSON 4 **Understand Dilations and Similarity** 81a
8.G.A.4
Focus: M **SMP** 2, 3, 6, 7

LESSON 5 **Perform and Describe Transformations Involving Dilations** 93a
8.G.A.3, 8.G.A.4
Focus: M **SMP** 1, 2, 3, 4, 5, 6, 7, 8

LESSON 6 **Describe Angle Relationships** 115a
8.G.A.5, 8.G.A.2
Focus: M **SMP** 1, 2, 3, 4, 5, 6

LESSON 7 **Describe Angle Relationships in Triangles** 137a
8.G.A.5, 8.G.A.2, 8.G.A.4
Focus: M **SMP** 1, 2, 3, 4, 5, 6

MATH IN ACTION **Dilations, Similarity, and Angle Relationships** 159a
Building Nesting Boxes | Toolboxes | Designing Shelves
8.G.A.3, 8.G.A.4, 8.G.A.5
Focus: M **SMP** 1, 2, 3, 4, 5, 6, 7, 8

Self Reflection 168
Vocabulary Review 169
Unit Review 170
Unit Game | Literacy Connection 170–171
Unit Assessment 172b

Unit 2 Themes

- A dilation is a transformation that can enlarge or reduce a figure. You can use what you know about scale drawings to understand dilations and similar figures.
- You will use what you know about transformations to discover relationships between angles formed by a pair of parallel lines and a line that intersects them.
- Knowing about types of angle pairs will help you explore angle relationships in triangles. You will also learn how to use angle measures to show that two triangles are similar.

Standards in boldface indicate the standards covered by the majority of the lesson content.

See page B7 for correlation tables that provide more details about Major Focus lessons.

M = Lessons that have a major focus in the Common Core State Standards
S = Lessons that have a supporting focus in the Common Core State Standards
A = Lessons that have an additional focus in the Common Core State Standards

UNIT 3

Unit 3 Themes

- A linear equation in two variables has a graph that is a straight line. Knowing about proportional relationships can help you make sense of the slope and y-intercept of a line.
- Linear equations in one variable can have one solution, no solution, or infinitely many solutions.
- A system of linear equations is a group of related linear equations where a solution makes all the equations true at the same time. You can use what you know about solving equations to solve systems of equations.

Standards in boldface indicate the standards covered by the majority of the lesson content.

See page B7 for correlation tables that provide more details about Major Focus lessons.

M = Lessons that have a major focus in the Common Core State Standards

S = Lessons that have a supporting focus in the Common Core State Standards

A = Lessons that have an additional focus in the Common Core State Standards

Linear Relationships

Slope, Linear Equations, and Systems

Unit Planning

Unit Resources 173a

Unit Overview 173c

Lesson Progression 173g

Connect Mathematics and Language Development 173i

Professional Learning: Teacher Talk Moves That Engage Students in Discourse and Mathematical Thinking 173i

Differentiation for English Language Learners: Language Expectations 173j

Math Background 173k

Slope of a Line 173k

One-Variable Linear Equations 173m

Systems of Linear Equations 173o

Unit Opener 173

Prepare for Unit 3 174

LESSON 8 **Graph Proportional Relationships and Define Slope** 175a
8.EE.B.5, **8.EE.B.6**, 8.G.A.4, 8.G.A.5
Focus: M SMP 1, 2, 3, 4, 5, 6, 7

LESSON 9 **Derive and Graph Linear Equations of the Form $y = mx + b$** 197a
8.EE.B.6, 8.EE.B.5, 8.EE.C.7b, 8.F.A.3
Focus: M SMP 1, 2, 3, 4, 5, 6, 7

LESSON 10 **Solve Linear Equations in One Variable** 225a
8.EE.C.7, **8.EE.C.7b**, 8.G.A.5
Focus: M SMP 1, 2, 3, 4, 5, 6

LESSON 11 **Determine the Number of Solutions to One-Variable Equations** 247a
8.EE.C.7, **8.EE.C.7a**, 8.EE.C.7b
Focus: M SMP 1, 2, 3, 4, 5, 6, 7, 8

LESSON 12 **Understand Systems of Linear Equations in Two Variables** 269a
8.EE.C.8, **8.EE.C.8a**, **8.EE.C.8b**, 8.EE.C.7a, 8.EE.C.7b, 8.EE.C.8c, 8.F.B.4
Focus: M SMP 2, 3, 4, 7

LESSON 13 **Solve Systems of Linear Equations Algebraically** 281a
8.EE.C.8, **8.EE.C.8b**, 8.EE.C.7a, 8.EE.C.7b, 8.EE.C.8a, 8.EE.C.8c, 8.F.B.4
Focus: M SMP 1, 2, 3, 4, 5, 6, 7

LESSON 14 **Represent and Solve Problems with Systems of Linear Equations** 309a
8.EE.C.8, **8.EE.C.8c**, 8.EE.C.7b, 8.EE.C.8a, 8.EE.C.8b, 8.F.B.4
Focus: M SMP 1, 2, 3, 4, 5, 6

MATH IN ACTION **Linear Relationships and Systems of Equations** 331a
Coral Nursery | Analyzing Growth Data | Designing an Experiment
8.EE.B.5, 8.EE.C.7a, 8.EE.C.7b, 8.EE.C.8a, 8.EE.C.8b, 8.EE.C.8c
Focus: M SMP 1, 2, 3, 4, 5, 6, 7, 8

Self Reflection 340

Vocabulary Review 341

Unit Review 342

Unit Game | Literacy Connection 342–343

Unit Assessment 344b

UNIT 4

Functions

Linear and Nonlinear Relationships

Unit Planning

Unit Resources 345a
Unit Overview 345c
Lesson Progression 345g
Connect Mathematics and Language Development 345i
Professional Learning: Knowing and Valuing Every Learner: Culturally Responsive Mathematics Teaching 345i
Differentiation for English Language Learners: Language Expectations 345j

Math Background 345k
Functions 345k
Linear and Nonlinear Functions 345l
Equations of Linear Functions 345n
Comparing Functions 345o
Analyzing Relationships Qualitatively 345p

Unit Opener 345
Prepare for Unit 4 346

LESSON 15 **Understand Functions** 347a
8.F.A.1, 8.F.A.3, 8.EE.B.6
Focus: M **SMP** 1, 2, 3, 7, 8

LESSON 16 **Use Functions to Model Linear Relationships** 359a
8.F.B.4, 8.EE.B.6, 8.F.A.2, 8.F.A.3, 8.F.B.5, 8.SP.A.3
Focus: M **SMP** 1, 2, 3, 4, 5, 6, 7

LESSON 17 **Compare Different Representations of Functions** 387a
8.EE.B.5, 8.F.A.2, 8.F.A.1, 8.F.A.3, 8.F.B.4, 8.F.B.5
Focus: M **SMP** 1, 2, 3, 4, 5, 6

LESSON 18 **Analyze Functional Relationships Qualitatively** 409a
8.F.B.5, 8.F.B.4
Focus: M **SMP** 1, 2, 3, 4, 5, 6, 7

MATH IN ACTION **Functional Relationships** 431a
Planning a Car Chase | Budgeting for Background Actors | Choosing a VFX Company
8.EE.B.5, 8.F.A.1, 8.F.A.2, 8.F.A.3, 8.F.B.4, 8.F.B.5
Focus: M **SMP** 1, 2, 3, 4, 5, 6, 7, 8

Self Reflection 440
Vocabulary Review 441
Unit Review 442
Unit Game | Literacy Connection 442–443
Unit Assessment 444b

Unit 4 Themes

- A function is a rule that assigns exactly one output to each input. You can use what you know about relationships between two variables to help you understand functions.
- You can use tables, graphs, equations, and verbal descriptions to model, evaluate, and compare characteristics of linear functions.
- You can describe a function qualitatively based on its graph, even when no scale values are shown.

Standards in boldface indicate the standards covered by the majority of the lesson content.

See page B7 for correlation tables that provide more details about Major Focus lessons.

M = Lessons that have a major focus in the Common Core State Standards
S = Lessons that have a supporting focus in the Common Core State Standards
A = Lessons that have an additional focus in the Common Core State Standards

UNIT 5

Integer Exponents

Properties and Scientific Notation

Unit Planning

Unit Resources 445a
Unit Overview 445c
Lesson Progression 445g
Connect Mathematics and Language Development 445i
Professional Learning: The Process of English Language Learning and What to Expect 445i
Differentiation for English Language Learners: Language Expectations 445j

Math Background 445k
Properties of Integer Exponents 445k
Very Large and Very Small Quantities 445n
Operations with Scientific Notation 445o

Unit Opener 445
Prepare for Unit 5 446

LESSON 19 **Apply Exponent Properties for Positive Integer Exponents** 447a
8.EE.A.1
Focus: M SMP 1, 2, 3, 4, 5, 6, 7, 8

LESSON 20 **Apply Exponent Properties for All Integer Exponents** 469a
8.EE.A.1
Focus: M SMP 1, 2, 3, 4, 5, 6, 7, 8

LESSON 21 **Express Numbers Using Integer Powers of 10** 491a
8.EE.A.3, 8.EE.A.1, 8.EE.A.4
Focus: M SMP 1, 2, 3, 4, 5, 6, 7, 8

LESSON 22 **Work with Scientific Notation** 513a
8.EE.A.4, 8.EE.A.1, 8.EE.A.3
Focus: M SMP 1, 2, 3, 4, 5, 6, 7

MATH IN ACTION **Scientific Notation and Properties of Exponents** 541a
Planetary Orbits | Insulating Blankets | Satellites
8.EE.A.1, 8.EE.A.3, 8.EE.A.4
Focus: M SMP 1, 2, 3, 4, 6, 7, 8

Self Reflection 550
Vocabulary Review 551
Unit Review 552
Unit Game | Literacy Connection 552–553
Unit Assessment 554b

Unit 5 Themes

- You can explore operations with powers and discover patterns that help you understand and apply properties of exponents.
- A very large or very small quantity can be expressed as a product of a number and a power of 10. You can use what you know about properties of exponents to operate with numbers in this form.

Standards in boldface indicate the standards covered by the majority of the lesson content.

See page B7 for correlation tables that provide more details about Major Focus lessons.

M = Lessons that have a major focus in the Common Core State Standards
S = Lessons that have a supporting focus in the Common Core State Standards
A = Lessons that have an additional focus in the Common Core State Standards

UNIT 6

Real Numbers

Rational Numbers, Irrational Numbers, and the Pythagorean Theorem

Unit Planning

Unit Resources 555a
Unit Overview 555c
Lesson Progression 555g
Connect Mathematics and Language Development 555i
Professional Learning: Bridging Funds of Knowledge to the Mathematics Classroom 555i
Differentiation for English Language Learners: Language Expectations 555j

Math Background 555k
Understanding Real Numbers 555k
Square Roots and Cube Roots 555l
Rational and Irrational Numbers 555m
Connecting Irrational Numbers to Geometry 555n

Unit Opener 555
Prepare for Unit 6 556

LESSON 23 **Find Square Roots and Cube Roots to Solve Problems** 557a
8.EE.A.2
Focus: M **SMP** 1, 2, 3, 4, 5, 6, 7

LESSON 24 **Express Rational Numbers as Fractions and Decimals** 579a
8.NS.A.1, 8.EE.C.7b
Focus: M **SMP** 1, 2, 3, 4, 5, 6, 7, 8

LESSON 25 **Find Rational Approximations of Irrational Numbers** 595a
8.NS.A.1, 8.NS.A.2, 8.EE.A.2
Focus: M **SMP** 1, 2, 3, 4, 5, 6, 7, 8

LESSON 26 **Understand the Pythagorean Theorem and Its Converse** 617a
8.G.B.6, 8.EE.A.2
Focus: M **SMP** 2, 3, 4, 5, 6, 7

LESSON 27 **Apply the Pythagorean Theorem** 629a
8.G.B.7, 8.G.B.8, 8.NS.A.2, 8.EE.A.2, 8.G.B.6
Focus: M **SMP** 1, 2, 3, 4, 5, 6, 7

LESSON 28 **Solve Problems with Volumes of Cylinders, Cones, and Spheres** 657a
8.G.C.9, 8.NS.A.2, 8.G.B.7
Focus: M **SMP** 1, 2, 3, 4, 5, 6, 7

MATH IN ACTION **Irrational Numbers, the Pythagorean Theorem, and Volume** 679a
Installing a Wind Turbine | Designing a Food-Waste Digester | Fencing a Solar Farm
8.NS.A.2, 8.EE.A.2, 8.G.B.7, 8.G.C.9
Focus: M **SMP** 1, 2, 3, 4, 5, 6, 7, 8

Self Reflection 688
Vocabulary Review 689
Unit Review 690
Unit Game | Literacy Connection 690–691
Unit Assessment 692b

Unit 6 Themes

- An irrational number cannot be written as a terminating or repeating decimal. You can use what you know about working with rational numbers to solve problems with irrational numbers in topics like algebra and geometry.
- The side lengths of a right triangle have a special relationship. You can use this relationship and what you know about triangles to determine unknown side lengths.
- You can use what you know about pi and the area of circles to solve real-world problems about the volumes of cylinders, cones, and spheres.

Standards in boldface indicate the standards covered by the majority of the lesson content.

See page B7 for correlation tables that provide more details about Major Focus lessons.

M = Lessons that have a major focus in the Common Core State Standards
S = Lessons that have a supporting focus in the Common Core State Standards
A = Lessons that have an additional focus in the Common Core State Standards

UNIT 7

Statistics

Two-Variable Data and Fitting a Linear Model

Unit Planning

Unit Resources 693a
Unit Overview 693c
Lesson Progression 693g
Connect Mathematics and Language Development 693i
Professional Learning: Discourse as a Tool for Learning the Language of Mathematics 693i
Differentiation for English Language Learners: Language Expectations 693j

Math Background 693k
Bivariate Data 693k
Bivariate Quantitative Data 693l
Bivariate Categorical Data 693o

Unit Opener 693
Prepare for Unit 7 694

LESSON 29 **Analyze Scatter Plots and Fit a Linear Model to Data** 695a
8.SP.A.1, 8.SP.A.2, 8.F.B.5
Focus: M **SMP** 1, 2, 3, 4, 5, 6

LESSON 30 **Write and Analyze an Equation for Fitting a Linear Model to Data** 723a
8.SP.A.3, 8.F.A.3, 8.F.B.4, 8.SP.A.1, 8.SP.A.2
Focus: M **SMP** 1, 2, 3, 4, 5, 6

LESSON 31 **Understand Two-Way Tables** 745a
8.SP.A.4
Focus: S **SMP** 1, 2, 3, 5, 7

LESSON 32 **Construct and Interpret Two-Way Tables** 757a
8.SP.A.4
Focus: S **SMP** 1, 2, 3, 4, 5, 6, 7

MATH IN ACTION **Representing Data** 779a
Internet Users | Age Groups | Emissions, GDP, and Urban Population
8.SP.A.1, 8.SP.A.2, 8.SP.A.3, 8.SP.A.4
Focus: S **SMP** 1, 2, 3, 4, 5, 6, 7

Self Reflection 788
Vocabulary Review 789
Unit Review 790
Unit Game | Literacy Connection 790–791
Unit Assessment 792b

Unit 7 Themes

- You will build on what you know about one-variable data displays by constructing and analyzing two-variable data displays.
- Knowing about linear equations will help you model a linear pattern in a two-variable data set and use your model to make predictions.
- You will organize and interpret two-variable categorical data and describe possible associations between the variables using relative frequencies.

Standards in boldface indicate the standards covered by the majority of the lesson content.

See page B7 for correlation tables that provide more details about Major Focus lessons.

M = Lessons that have a major focus in the Common Core State Standards
S = Lessons that have a supporting focus in the Common Core State Standards
A = Lessons that have an additional focus in the Common Core State Standards

Program Resources

i-Ready Classroom Mathematics provides a wealth of instructional resources to support teachers in effective implementation, including assessment tools and support for differentiated instruction. The online Teacher Toolbox provides complete access to all grade-level resources.

Student

Component	Print	Online	Spanish
Student Worktext	■	■	■
Interactive Learning Games		■	■
Digital Math Tools powered by Desmos		■	
Multilingual Glossary		■	■
Interactive Glossary	■	■	■
Family Resource Center: Family Letters	■	■	■
Family Resource Center: Unit Flow and Progression Videos*		■	

*Closed-captioned in English and Spanish

Teacher

Component	Print	Online	Spanish
Instruction and Practice			
Teacher's Guide	■	■	■
Lesson PowerPoint® Slides		■	■
Interactive Tutorials		■	
Digital Math Tools powered by Desmos		■	
Digital Practice (available 2021)		■	
Fluency and Skills Practice **		■	■
Activity Sheets		■	■
Unit Games		■	■
Literacy Connections		■	■
Discourse Cards	■	■	■
Cumulative Practice	■	■	■

**Available as editable Word® documents or as a student workbook

Teacher *continued*

Component	Print	Online	Spanish
Assessment			
Adaptive Diagnostic Assessment		■	■
Lesson Quizzes**	■	■	■
Unit Assessments**	■	■	■
Assessment Practice Tests	■	■	■
Assignable Comprehension Checks		■	■
Reports			
Diagnostic Assessment Reports		■	
Prerequisites Report		■	
Comprehension Check Reports		■	
Learning Games Reports		■	
Differentiated Instruction on the Teacher Toolbox			
Tools for Instruction		■	■
Math Center Activities		■	■
Enrichment Activities		■	■
Implementation			
Pacing Guidance for the Year	■	■	
Unit Pacing and Unit Resources	■	■	
Common Core State Standards (CCSS) Correlations	■	■	
Standards for Mathematical Practice (SMP) Correlations	■	■	
WIDA PRIME V2 Correlation		■	
Connect Mathematics and Language Development	■	■	
Lesson Progressions	■	■	
Math Background	■	■	■
Unit Flow and Progression Videos*		■	
Lesson 0		■	■
Manipulatives List		■	

*Closed-captioned in English and Spanish **Editable Word document available

Pacing Guidance for the Year

The chart below provides pacing for *i-Ready Classroom Mathematics*. Use these guidelines flexibly alongside district calendars to ensure program completion.

M = major standards of a grade
S = supporting standard

		Session 45–60 min.	Focus
Diagnostic Assessment*		2	
Unit 1 Geometric Figures: Rigid Transformations and Congruence			
Lesson 0**	Lessons for the First Five Days *Recommended*	5	
Lesson 1	Understand Rigid Transformations and Their Properties	3	M
Lesson 2	Work with Single Rigid Transformations in the Coordinate Plane	5	M
Lesson 3	Work with Sequences of Transformations and Congruence	4	M
Math in Action	Rigid Transformations in the Coordinate Plane *Flexibly Scheduled*	2	M
Unit 1 Unit Assessment or Digital Comprehension Check		1	
Unit 1 Total Days		**20**	

		Session 45–60 min.	Focus
Unit 2 Geometric Figures: Transformations, Similarity, and Angle Relationships			
Lesson 4	Understand Dilations and Similarity	3	M
Lesson 5	Perform and Describe Transformations Involving Dilations	4	M
Lesson 6	Describe Angle Relationships	4	M
Lesson 7	Describe Angle Relationships in Triangles	4	M
Math in Action	Dilations, Similarity, and Angle Relationships *Flexibly Scheduled*	2	M
Unit 2 Unit Assessment or Digital Comprehension Check		1	
Unit 2 Total Days		**18**	

		Session 45–60 min.	Focus
Unit 3 Linear Relationships: Slope, Linear Equations, and Systems			
Lesson 8	Graph Proportional Relationships and Define Slope	4	M
Lesson 9	Derive and Graph Linear Equations of the Form $y = mx + b$	5	M
Lesson 10	Solve Linear Equations in One Variable	4	M
Lesson 11	Determine the Number of Solutions to One-Variable Equations	4	M
Lesson 12	Understand Systems of Linear Equations in Two Variables	3	M
Lesson 13	Solve Systems of Linear Equations Algebraically	5	M
Lesson 14	Represent and Solve Problems with Systems of Linear Equations	4	M
Math in Action	Linear Relationships and Systems of Equations *Flexibly Scheduled*	2	M
Unit 3 Unit Assessment or Digital Comprehension Check		1	
Unit 3 Total Days		**32**	
Practice Test or Diagnostic Assessment		**2**	

		Session 45–60 min.	Focus
Unit 4 Functions: Linear and Non-Linear Relationships			
Lesson 15	Understand Functions	3	M
Lesson 16	Use Functions to Model Linear Relationships	5	M
Lesson 17	Compare Different Representations of Functions	4	M
Lesson 18	Analyze Graphs of Functional Relationships Qualitatively	4	M

*The Diagnostic takes two days to administer. See i-Ready Classroom Central for information on when to administer.
**Lesson 0 is on the Teacher Digital Experience. See the Classroom Resources tab on the Teacher Toolbox.

		Session 45–60 min.	Focus
Unit 4 Functions: Linear and Non-Linear Relationships *continued*			
Math in Action	Functional Relationships *Flexibly Scheduled*	2	M
Unit 4 Unit Assessment or Digital Comprehension Check		1	
Unit 4 Total Days		19	
Unit 5 Integer Exponents: Properties and Scientific Notation			
Lesson 19	Apply Exponent Properties for Positive Integer Exponents	4	M
Lesson 20	Apply Exponent Properties for All Integer Exponents	4	M
Lesson 21	Express Numbers Using Integer Powers of 10	4	M
Lesson 22	Work with Scientific Notation	5	M
Math in Action	Scientific Notation and Properties of Exponents *Flexibly Scheduled*	2	M
Unit 5 Unit Assessment or Digital Comprehension Check		1	
Unit 5 Total Days		20	
Unit 6 Real Numbers: Rational Numbers, Irrational Numbers, and the Pythagorean Theorem			
Lesson 23	Find Square Roots and Cube Roots to Solve Problems	4	M
Lesson 24	Express Rational Numbers as Fractions and Decimals	3	M
Lesson 25	Find Rational Approximations of Irrational Numbers	4	M
Lesson 26	Understand the Pythagorean Theorem and Its Converse	3	M
Lesson 27	Apply the Pythagorean Theorem	5	M
Lesson 28	Solve Problems with Volumes of Cylinders, Cones, and Spheres	4	M
Math in Action	Irrational Numbers, the Pythagorean Theorem, and Volume *Flexibly Scheduled*	2	M
Unit 6 Unit Assessment or Digital Comprehension Check		1	
Unit 6 Total Days		26	
Unit 7 Statistics: Two-Variable Data and Fitting a Linear Model			
Lesson 29	Analyze Scatter Plots and Fit a Linear Model to Data	5	M
Lesson 30	Write and Analyze an Equation for Fitting a Linear Model to Data	4	M
Lesson 31	Understand Two-Way Tables	3	S
Lesson 32	Construct and Interpret Two-Way Tables	4	S
Math in Action	Representing Data *Flexibly Scheduled*	2	S
Unit 7 Unit Assessment or Digital Comprehension Check		1	
Unit 7 Total Days		19	
Practice Test or Diagnostic Assessment		2	

When to Administer a Lesson Quiz *or* Comprehension Check

Lesson Quizzes or Comprehension Checks are to be given flexibly throughout the pacing of *i-Ready Classroom Mathematics*. A few options for implementation are:

- **At the start of the Explore session** Before starting a new lesson, provide the Lesson Quiz cr Comprehension Check from the previous lesson.
- **At the end of the Refine session** After the completion of the Refine session, provide the Lesson Quiz or Comprehension Check to assess student understanding.
- **In place of the Refine session** If the various data points from the duration of the lesson show student growth and success, provide the Lesson Quiz or Comprehension Check in place of the Refine session activities.

Print Resources

Reach all students using these print resources that support instruction, practice, assessment, and differentiation.

Resources can be found in the Student Worktext or Teacher's Guide or downloaded from the Teacher Toolbox section in the Teacher Digital Experience.

In-Class Instruction and Practice

Teacher's Guide
- Learning Progression
- ELL Language Expectations
- Connect to Culture
- Discussion Prompts and Instructional Support

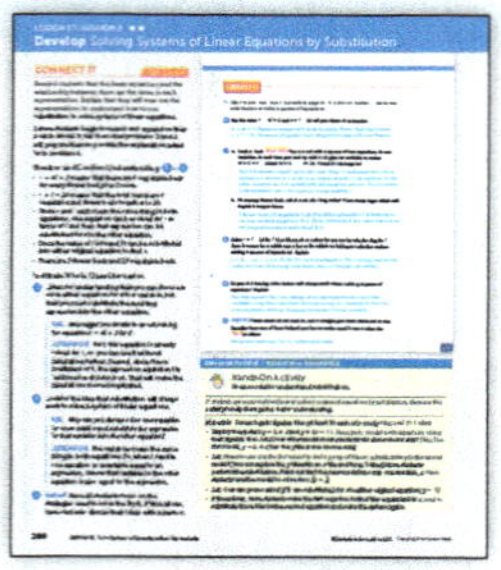

Student Worktext
Use the blue pages for in-class instruction and practice.

Instruction Page

Independent Practice for School or Home

Teacher's Guide
- Additional Practice
- Cumulative Practice

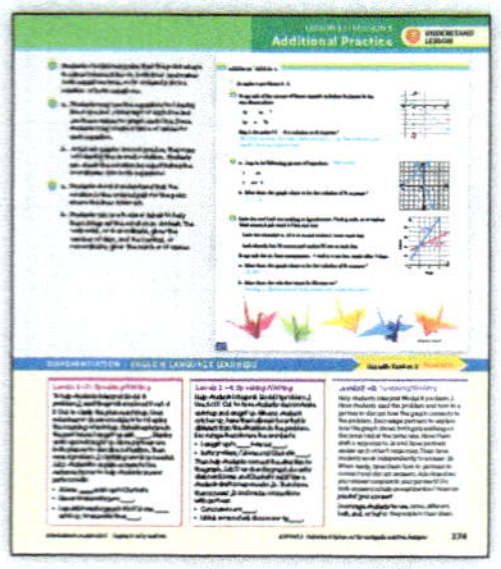

Student Worktext
Use the green pages for independent practice.
- Additional Practice
- Cumulative Practice

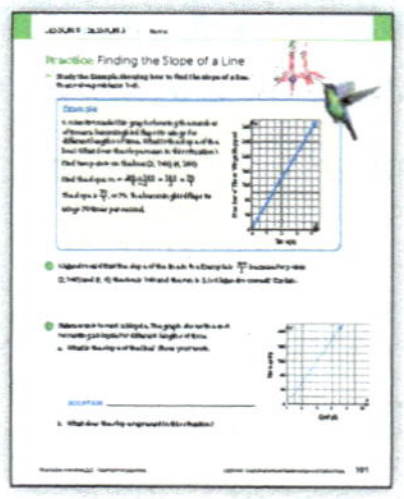

Additional Practice Page

Teacher Toolbox
- Fluency and Skills Practice
- Unit Game
- Cumulative Practice

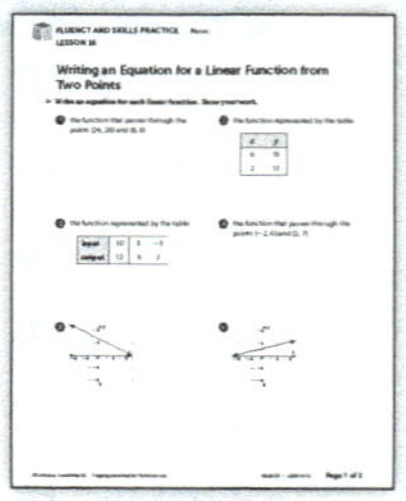

Fluency and Skills Practice

Assessments and Reports

Teacher's Guide
- Starts
- Support Whole Group/Partner Discussion
- Ask/Listen Fors
- Common Misconceptions
- Error Alerts
- Close: Exit Ticket

Student Worktext
- Self Checks
- Apply It
- Reflect Questions
- Self Reflection
- Math Journal Questions
- Unit Review

Self Check

Teacher Toolbox
- Editable Lesson Quizzes
- Editable Unit Assessments

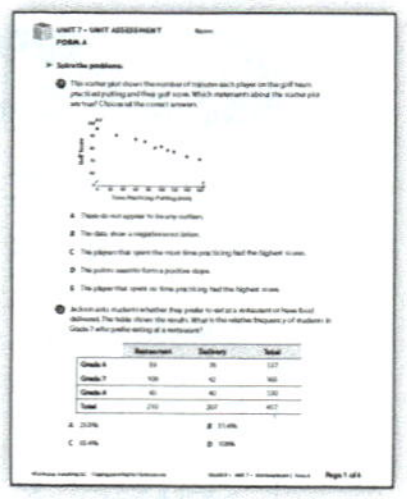

Unit Assessment

Differentiation

Before the Unit/Lesson: Prerequisites Report
Recommended resources to support students' learning needs are highlighted in the Prerequisites report.

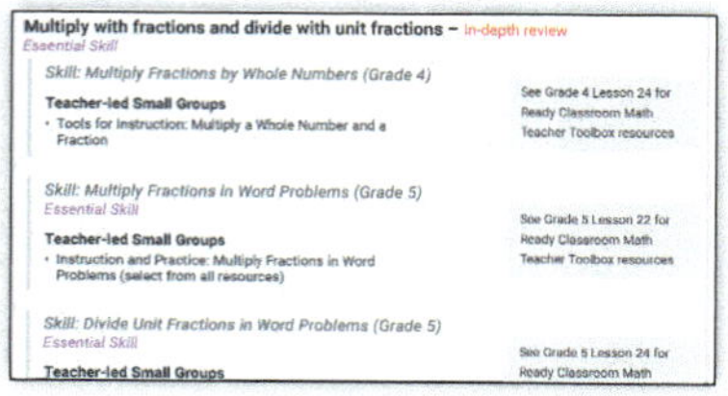

Prerequisites Report: Resources

During the Lesson: Teacher's Guide
- Hands-On Activities or Visual Models
- Deepen Understanding
- ELL Differentiated Instruction
- Refine Sessions

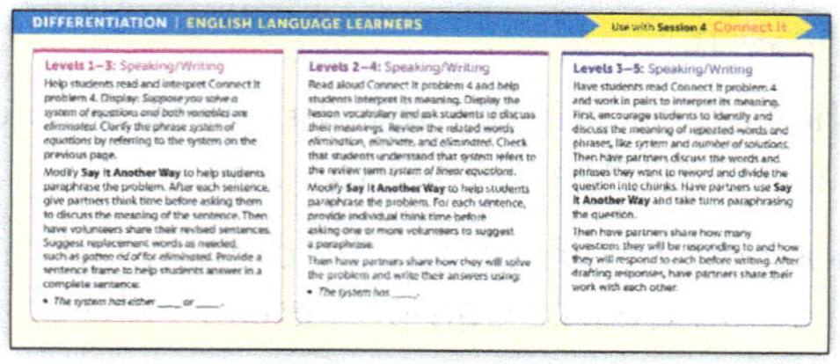

ELL Differentiated Instruction

After the Lesson: Teacher Toolbox
- Reteach: Tools for Instruction
- Reinforce: Math Center Activities
- Extend: Enrichment Activities

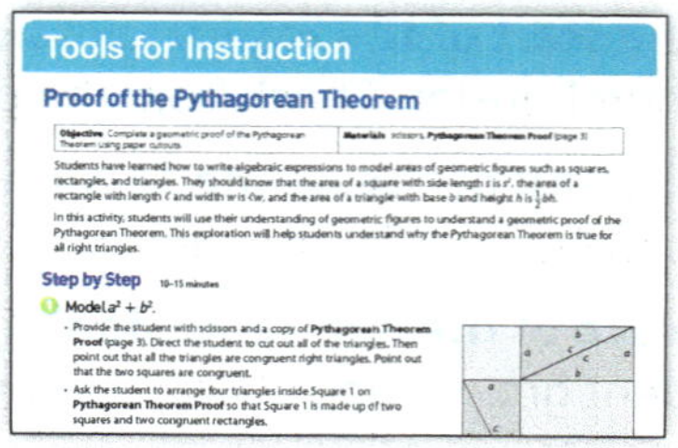

Reteach: Tools for Instruction

Digital Resources

Engage students with digital resources that provide interactive instruction, practice, assessment, and differentiation.

Resources can be found in the Student Digital Experience and the Teacher Digital Experience.

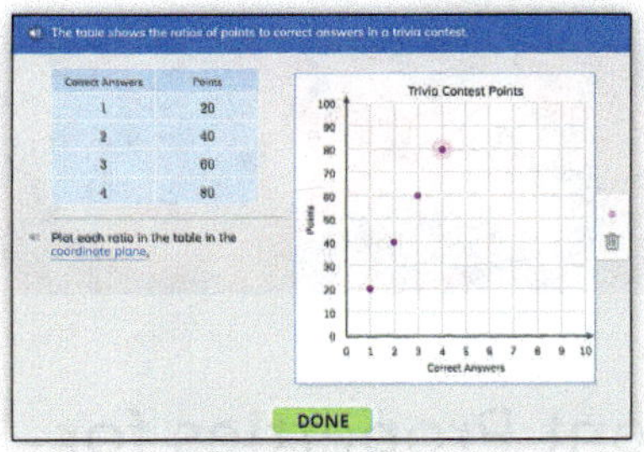

Interactive Tutorials

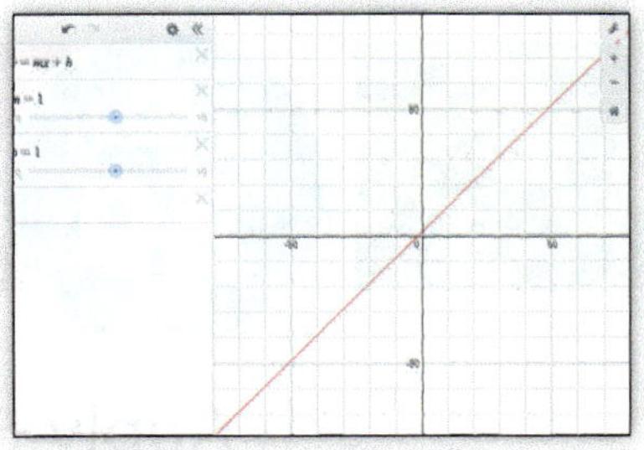

Digital Math Tools powered by Desmos

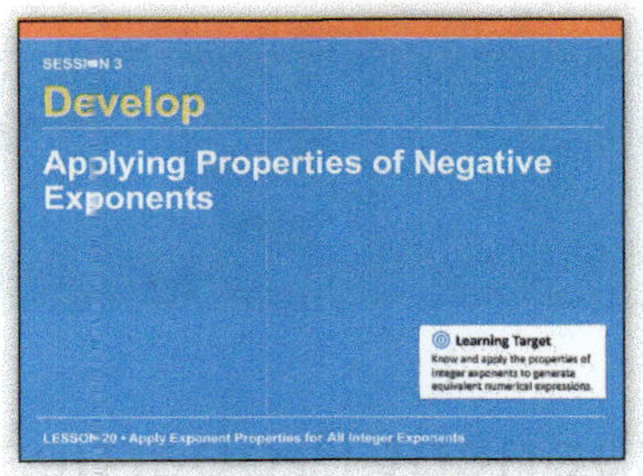

PowerPoint® Slides

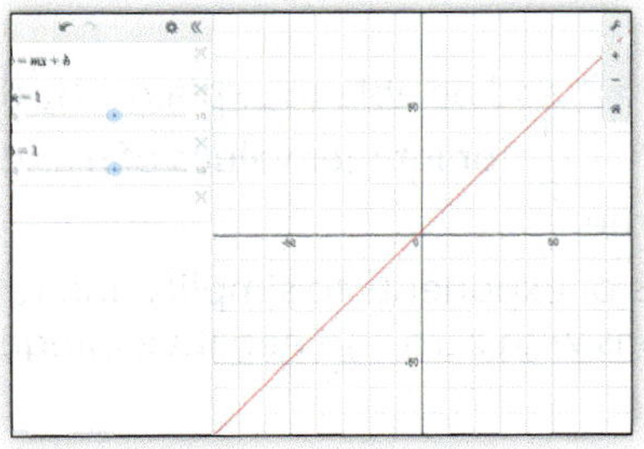

Digital Math Tools powered by Desmos

Learning Games

Digital Practice

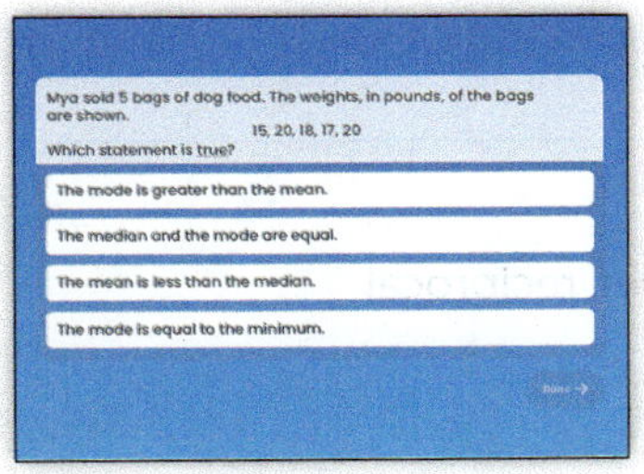

Diagnostic

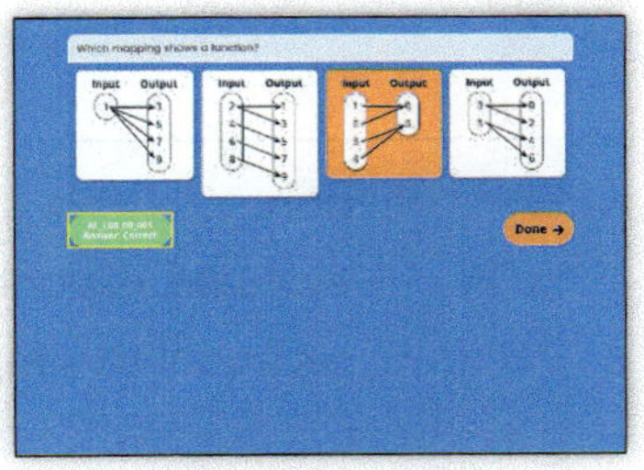

Lesson and Unit Comprehension Checks

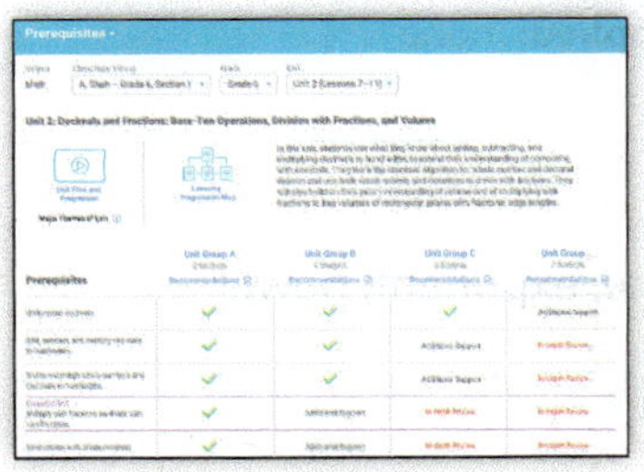

Prerequisites Report

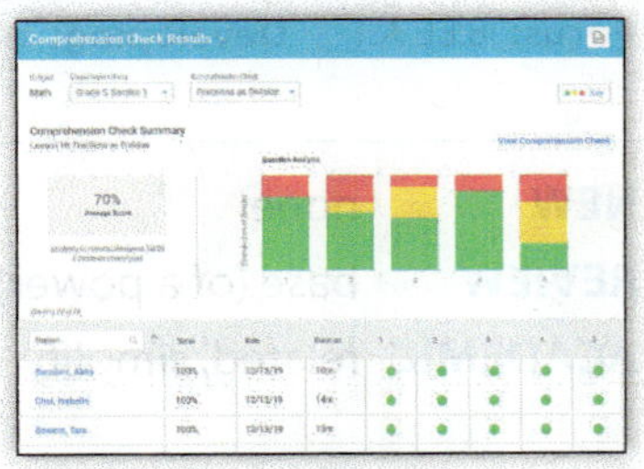

Comprehension Check Reports

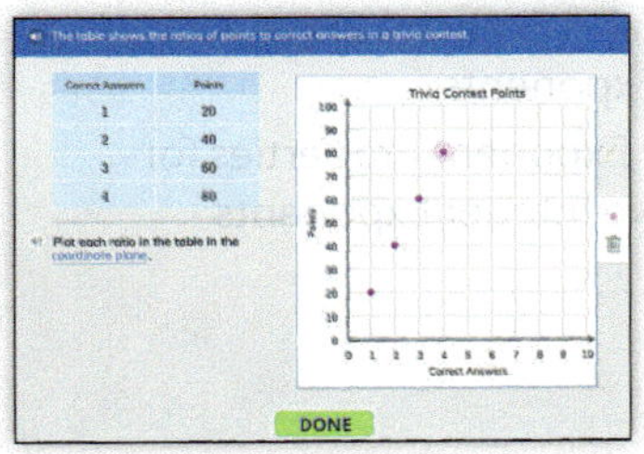

Interactive Tutorials

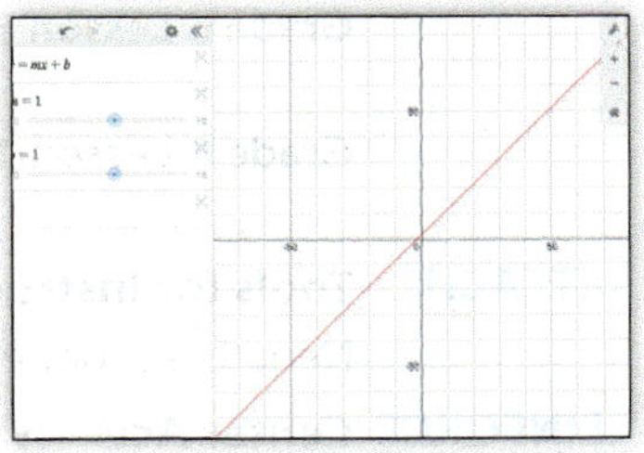

Digital Math Tools powered by Desmos

Learning Games

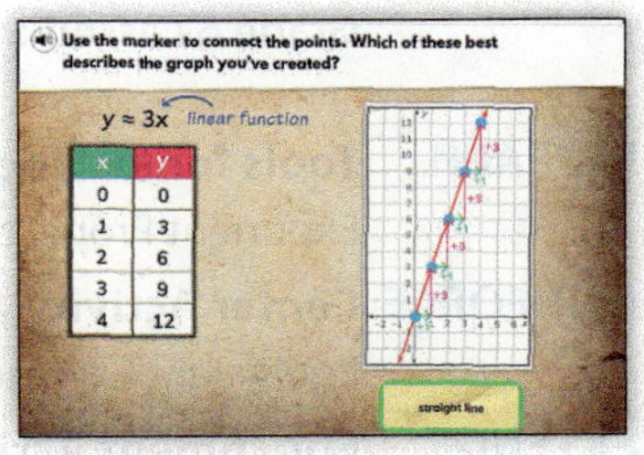

Optional Add-On: *i-Ready Personalized Instruction*

Microsoft PowerPoint® is a registered trademark of Microsoft Corporation.

UNIT 5

Integer Exponents

Properties and Scientific Notation

Before the Unit
- Self Check
- Prepare for Exponent Properties and Scientific Notation

After the Unit
- Math in Action
- Self Reflection
- Vocabulary Review
- Unit Review & Performance Task
- Unit Assessment, Forms A and B
- Digital Comprehension Checks

LESSON 19

Apply Exponent Properties for Positive Integer Exponents

PACING: 4 sessions

OBJECTIVES
- Understand these properties of positive integer exponents:
  power of a power: $(a^m)^n = a^{mn}$
  product of powers: $a^m a^n = a^{m+n}$
  quotient of powers: $\frac{a^m}{a^n} = a^{m-n}$
  power of a product: $(ab)^m = a^m b^m$
  power of a quotient: $\left(\frac{a}{b}\right)^m = \frac{a^m}{b^m}$.
- Apply the properties of positive integer exponents to simplify expressions and to generate equivalent expressions.

STANDARDS

Focus: 8.EE.A.1 | **Developing:** none | **Applied:** none

VOCABULARY

NEW none
REVIEW base (of a power), evaluate, exponent, power
ACADEMIC related, simplify

LESSON-LEVEL DIFFERENTIATION

PREPARE **Ready Prerequisite Lessons**
Grade 5 Lesson 7 — Understand Powers of 10
Grade 6 Lesson 5 — Write and Evaluate Expressions with Exponents

RETEACH **Tools for Instruction**
Exponent Properties

REINFORCE **Center Activity**
Equivalent Exponential Expressions

EXTEND **Enrichment Activity**
Power-ful Stuff

See the Lesson Overview for additional session-level differentiation.

LESSON 20

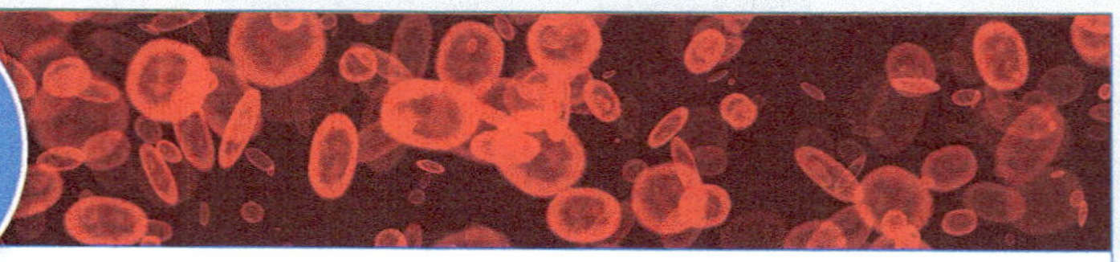

Apply Exponent Properties for All Integer Exponents

PACING: 4 sessions

OBJECTIVES
- Understand that $a^0 = 1$ and be able to explain why this is true.
- Understand that $a^{-n} = \frac{1}{a^n}$ for integer values of n and be able to explain why this is true.
- Apply the properties of exponents to simplify and rewrite numerical expressions with zero and negative integer exponents.

STANDARDS

Focus: 8.EE.A.1 | **Developing:** none | **Applied:** none

NEW none
REVIEW evaluate, exponent, power, reciprocal
ACADEMIC set equal to, simplify

PREPARE **Ready Prerequisite Lessons**
Grade 5 Lesson 7 — Understand Powers of 10
Grade 6 Lesson 5 — Write and Evaluate Expressions with Exponents
Grade 8 Lesson 19 — Apply Exponent Properties for Positive Integer Exponents

RETEACH **Tools for Instruction**
Negative Exponents

REINFORCE **Center Activity**
Expressions with Integer Exponents

EXTEND **Enrichment Activity**
Grow and Shrink

See the Lesson Overview for additional session-level differentiation.

LESSON
21

Express Numbers Using Integer Powers of 10

PACING: 4 sessions

OBJECTIVES

- Write numbers expressed as a single digit times an integer power of 10 in standard form, and vice versa.
- Write estimates for quantities using a single digit times an integer power of 10.
- Compare quantities expressed as a single digit times an integer power of 10.

STANDARDS

Focus: 8.EE.A.3 | **Developing:** 8.EE.A.4 | **Applied:** 8.EE.A.1

NEW none
REVIEW integers, power of 10, round
ACADEMIC express, mass

PREPARE **Ready Prerequisite Lessons**
Grade 5 Lesson 6 Understand Decimal Place Value
Grade 5 Lesson 7 Understand Powers of 10
Grade 8 Lesson 20 Apply Exponent Properties for All Integer Exponents

RETEACH **Tools for Instruction**
Compare and Estimate with Powers of 10

REINFORCE **Center Activity**
Comparing Quantities with Powers of 10

EXTEND **Enrichment Activity**
Metric Maze

See the Lesson Overview for additional session-level differentiation.

NOTES

. . . continued

Integer Exponents

Properties and Scientific Notation

LESSON 22

Work with Scientific Notation

PACING: 5 sessions

OBJECTIVES

- Express numbers in scientific notation.
- Add, subtract, multiply, and divide with numbers expressed in scientific notation.
- Choose appropriate units for measurements of large or small quantities.
- Interpret scientific notation that has been generated by technology.

STANDARDS

Focus: 8.EE.A.4 | **Developing:** none | **Applied:** 8.EE.A.1, 8.EE.A.3

VOCABULARY

NEW scientific notation
REVIEW absolute value, power of 10
ACADEMIC contiguous, molecule

LESSON-LEVEL DIFFERENTIATION

PREPARE **Ready Prerequisite Lessons**
Grade 7 Lesson 14 Use the Four Operations with Negative Numbers
Grade 8 Lesson 20 Apply Exponent Properties for All Integer Exponents
Grade 8 Lesson 21 Express Numbers Using Integer Powers of 10

RETEACH **Tools for Instruction**
Add and Subtract with Scientific Notation

REINFORCE **Center Activity**
Use Scientific Notation Vocabulary

EXTEND **Enrichment Activity**
Humans and Ants

See the Lesson Overview for additional session-level differentiation.

Math in Action

Math Lessons from the Real World

Planetary Orbits | Insulating Blankets | Satellites

PACING: 2 sessions

KEY SKILLS

- Add and subtract numbers expressed in scientific notation.
- Multiply and divide numbers expressed in scientific notation.
- Apply the relationship between distance, rate, and time to solve problems.
- Apply the formula for circumference of a circle.

STANDARDS

Focus: 8.EE.A.1, 8.EE.A.3, 8.EE.A.4

Digital Resources

- Unit and Lesson Comprehension Checks
- Comprehension Check Reports
- Prerequisites Report
- Digital Tools powered by Desmos®
- Interactive Tutorials
- Learning Games (available 2020)
- Digital Practice (available 2021)

i-Ready

A personalized instruction path helps students fill prerequisite gaps and build up grade-level skills.

NOTES

Which lessons are students building upon?

	Grade 5, Lesson 7 Understand Powers of 10 5.NBT.A.2 →	**Grade 6, Lesson 5** Write and Evaluate Expressions with Exponents 6.EE.A.1, 6.EE.A.2c →
Grade 5, Lesson 7 Understand Powers of 10 5.NBT.A.2 →	**Grade 6, Lesson 5** Write and Evaluate Expressions with Exponents 6.EE.A.1, 6.EE.A.2c →	**Grade 8, Lesson 19** Apply Exponent Properties for Positive Integer Exponents 8.EE.A.1 →
Grade 5, Lesson 6 Understand Decimal Place Value 5.NBT.A.1 →	**Grade 5, Lesson 7** Understand Powers of 10 5.NBT.A.2 →	**Grade 8, Lesson 20** Apply Exponent Properties for All Integer Exponents 8.EE.A.1 →
Grade 7, Lesson 14 Use the Four Operations with Negative Numbers 7.NS.A.3, 7.EE.B.3 →	**Grade 8, Lesson 20** Apply Exponent Properties for All Integer Exponents 8.EE.A.1 →	**Grade 8, Lesson 21** Express Numbers Using Integer Powers of 10 8.EE.A.3 →

In this unit . . .

Lesson 19
Apply Exponent Properties for Positive Integer Exponents
8.EE.A.1

Lesson 20
Apply Exponent Properties for All Integer Exponents
8.EE.A.1

Lesson 21
Express Numbers Using Integer Powers of 10
8.EE.A.3

Lesson 22
Work with Scientific Notation
8.EE.A.4

Which lessons are students preparing for?

Grade 8, Lesson 20
Apply Exponent Properties for All Integer Exponents
8.EE.A.1

Algebra
Arithmetic with Polynomials and Rational Expressions
HSA.APR.A.1

Grade 8, Lesson 21
Express Numbers Using Integer Powers of 10
8.EE.A.3

Number and Quantity
The Real Number System
HSN.RN.A.1

Grade 8, Lesson 22
Work with Scientific Notation
8.EE.A.4

Number and Quantity
Quantities
HSN.Q.A.1

Number and Quantity
Quantities
HSN.Q.A.1

Number and Quantity
Quantities
HSN.Q.A.2

Professional Learning

The Process of English Language Learning and What to Expect

Adapted from *Teaching Mathematics to English Language Learners*, by Dr. Gladis Kersaint

Gladis Kersaint, Ph.D.
Dr. Kersaint is the Dean of the Neag School of Education at the University of Connecticut and a respected scholar in mathematics education whose research focuses on equity, mathematical discourse, and effective teaching and learning of at-risk students.

Below are the five principles for creating effective second language acquisition-rich learning environments based on evidence-based practice. (Erben, Castaneda, and Ban, 2008)

Principle 1

Give ELLs many opportunities to read, write, listen to, and discuss oral and written English and mathematics texts expressed in a variety of ways. Classroom practices that have been found to improve academic literacy development include:

- modeling reading comprehension through think-alouds.
- giving explicit strategy instruction in context.
- providing instruction to help students read and write mathematics.
- providing mathematics assignments that require students to read and write.
- providing ELLs opportunities to use the language of mathematics to process new information.

Principle 2

Draw attention to and provide instruction related to the language structures of English (both grammar and vocabulary use) and mathematics.

Principle 3

Give ELLs classroom time to use their English productively while learning mathematics.

- When ELLs are engaged in talk, they make communication modifications that help language become more comprehensible.

Principle 4

Give ELLs opportunities to notice their errors and to correct their English while learning mathematics.

- Offer explicit correction through rewording.
- Request clarification.
- Provide metalinguistic clues.
- Provide repetitions.

Principle 5

Construct activities that maximize opportunities for ELLs to interact with others in English.

- Student engagement is the key to academic success; vary the types of instructional tasks.
- Provide students with linguistic stems, frames, and questions that provide opportunities for rich and rigorous discussions with English-speaking peers.

Develop Academic Language

Use the suggestions in *Develop Academic Language* to expose all students, especially ELLs, to academic sentence structures, vocabulary, and elements of discourse.

DEVELOP ACADEMIC LANGUAGE

WHY? Support students as they build onto their responses to the Discuss It question.

HOW? Encourage students to listen for ideas they agree with during whole-class discussion. Have students share their ideas about what is the same about the equations. Explain that one way to add to, or build on, someone's explanation is to give another example that shows that the idea makes sense. Use: *I also think ____ and I can add onto this idea by ____.*

Differentiation: English Language Learners

Use the Differentiation charts to plan for specific opportunities for ELLs at different levels of English proficiency to read, write, listen to, and discuss mathematical ideas.

DIFFERENTIATION | ENGLISH LANGUAGE LEARNERS — Use with **Session 1** Connect It

Levels 1–3: Speaking/Writing

Prepare students to talk and write about Connect It problem 2. Read the problem aloud. Review the phrases *winning record* and ____ *out of* ____ *games*. Guide students to indicate which number represents a *part* and which number represent the *whole*. Use **Co-Constructed Word Bank** and include these phrases if students do not mention them.

Facilitate a small-group discussion about the table of equivalent ratios. Encourage students to use terms from the word bank in their responses. Provide frames to help students write their answers:

- *[Name] wins ____ out of ____. This is ____.*
- *The friend with the best ____ is ____.*

Levels 2–4: Speaking/Writing

Prepare students to talk and write about Connect It problem 2. Read the problem and help students discuss the meaning of *winning record*. Ask: *What does a winning record tell?* Create a **Co-Constructed Word Bank** with these and other words from the problem. Then have them turn to partners to talk about the problem. Ask: *What do the friends keep track of? How do they compare their winning records? How do you find each percent? What do you do to compare?* Allow think time for students to process ideas and complete the problem. Guide students to use *won* to explain their answers:

- *[Student name] has the best winning record because [student name] won ____.*

Levels 3–5: Speaking/Writing

Prepare students to talk and write about Connect It problem 2. Have students work with a partner to make sense of the problem and talk about the meaning of *winning record*. Then have partners begin a **Co-Constructed Word Bank** of important words that might be used to talk and write about the problem. Compile the terms into a class bank. Allow think time for students to discuss the problem. Then have them work on problems 2a–c individually. Use **Stronger and Clearer Each Time** to help students respond to problem 2d. When students finish drafting, explaining, and revising their answers, have them share the verbs they used to explain.

Differentiation for English Language Learners

Language Expectations

The chart below shows examples of what English learners at different levels of English language proficiency can do in connection with one of the Common Core State Standards (CCSS) addressed in this unit. As you plan for this unit, use these examples of language expectations to help you differentiate instruction to meet the needs of English learners.

Standard 8.EE.A.4 Perform operations with numbers expressed in scientific notation, including problems where both decimal and scientific notation are used. Use scientific notation and choose units of appropriate size for measurements of very large or very small quantities. Interpret scientific notation that has been generated by technology.

LANGUAGE DOMAINS	BEGINNING	INTERMEDIATE		ADVANCED/ADVANCED HIGH	
	Level 1	Level 2	Level 3	Level 4	Level 5
LISTENING	With a partner, match the word forms of numbers expressed in scientific notation and/or standard form to the number forms in visual models by using teacher modeling and a place-value chart.	With a partner, match oral descriptions of numbers expressed in scientific notation and/or standard form to the number forms in visual models by using visual examples and a place-value chart.	With a partner, categorize numbers by scientific notation and/or standard form based on oral descriptions by using visual examples and a place-value chart.	Categorize numbers by scientific notation and/or standard form based on class discussions or oral explanations by using visual examples and a place-value chart.	Categorize numbers by scientific notation and/or standard form based on complex oral discourse by using visual examples.
SPEAKING	Identify a strategy to express a standard-form number in scientific notation by showing the computations. Justify the strategy in a partner discussion in English and/or the home language.	Describe a strategy to express a standard-form number in scientific notation by referring to computations. Justify the strategy in a partner discussion in English and/or the home language.	Describe a strategy to express a standard-form number in scientific notation by referring to computations. Justify the strategy in a partner discussion using word banks.	Justify a strategy to express a standard-form number in scientific notation by referring to computations in a partner discussion and using sentence starters.	Justify a strategy to express a standard-form number in scientific notation by referring to computations in a partner discussion.
READING	Based on highlighted key words and pictures, judge whether a word problem involves very large or very small numbers by using a bilingual dictionary and peer support.	With a partner, identify context words in a word problem and judge whether the problem involves very large or very small numbers by using a bilingual dictionary.	With a partner, identify context words in a word problem and judge whether the problem involves very large or very small numbers by using a dictionary and visual support.	Judge whether a word problem involves very large or very small numbers by identifying the problem context by using a dictionary and visual support as needed.	Judge whether a word problem involves very large or very small numbers by identifying the problem context by using a dictionary as needed.
WRITING	Use models, numbers, and symbols to record the order of steps to perform operations with numbers written in scientific notation. Then label the steps with teacher assistance.	With a partner, describe the order of steps to perform operations with numbers written in scientific notation by using sequence words and an illustrated list of math terms.	Describe the order of steps to perform operations with numbers written in scientific notation by using sentence starters and an illustrated list of math terms.	Describe the order of steps to perform operations with numbers written in scientific notation by using a Co-Constructed Word Bank with math terms and sequence words.	Describe and explain the order of steps to perform operations with numbers written in scientific notation.

Models, Progressions, and Teaching Tips

As you plan lessons, use this information to unpack the learning progressions and make connections between key concepts.

Unit Themes

The major themes of this unit are:

- You can explore operations with powers and discover patterns that help you understand and apply properties of exponents.
- A very large or very small quantity can be expressed as a product of a number and a power of 10. You can use what you know about properties of exponents to operate with numbers in this form.

Prior Knowledge

Students will build on prior understandings of exponents and powers of 10.

Students should:

- understand place value, powers of 10, and how to round numbers.
- be able to write and evaluate expressions with whole-number exponents.
- be fluent in all operations with rational numbers.

Watch the video
See the flow and progression of math concepts in this unit come to life with tips and insights on using models and making connections.

Properties of Integer Exponents

INSIGHTS ON . . .

Powers with the Same Base

✔ Students use repeated reasoning to discover that to multiply powers with the same base, they can keep the base and add the exponents. Similarly, to divide powers with the same base, they can keep the base and subtract the exponents.

✔ Students may check their answers by evaluating powers separately and then performing the multiplication or division.

EXAMPLE To find $3^2 \cdot 3^3$, evaluate powers and multiply 9 by 27 to get 243. This is equal to 3^5.

✔ Common Misconception Students may think that a product of powers with the same base can be found by multiplying the exponents or by multiplying bases and adding exponents. Provide students with simple examples to show why this does not work.

✔ In Grade 8, students mostly work with numerical exponential expressions. This work will prepare students for working with algebraic exponential expressions in later grades.

Students develop understanding of **products of powers** with the same base . . .

$$3^2 \cdot 3^3 = (3 \cdot 3)(3 \cdot 3 \cdot 3)$$
$$= 3^5$$
$$= 3^{2+3}$$

. . . and extend that understanding to **quotients of powers** with the same base.

$$\frac{4^6}{4^2} = \frac{4 \cdot 4 \cdot 4 \cdot 4 \cdot 4 \cdot 4}{4 \cdot 4}$$
$$= \frac{4 \cdot 4}{4 \cdot 4} \cdot \frac{4 \cdot 4 \cdot 4 \cdot 4}{1}$$
$$= 4^4$$
$$= 4^{6-2}$$

Properties of Integer Exponents *(continued)*

INSIGHTS ON . . .

Power of a Power

- ✔ When raising a power to a power, students discover they can keep the base and multiply the exponents.
- ✔ Students attend to precision when working with negative bases. They may check their work by reasoning that when a negative number is raised to an even exponent, the value is positive. When a negative number is raised to an odd exponent, the value is negative.

  EXAMPLE $(-3)^2$ means $(-3)(-3)$, which equals 9. $(-3)^3$ means $(-3)(-3)(-3)$, which equals -27. $(-3)^4$ means $(-3)(-3)(-3)(-3)$, which equals 81. The values of the powers alternate between positive and negative.
- ✔ **Common Misconception** Students may believe -2^4 is equal to $(-2)^4$. Explain that -2^4 refers to the opposite of 2^4, while $(-2)^4$ means to use -2 as a factor four times. The value of -2^4 is -16, while the value of $(-2)^4$ is 16.

Students learn that to evaluate a **power of a power**, the exponents are multiplied, . . .

$$(10^4)^2 = (10 \cdot 10 \cdot 10 \cdot 10)(10 \cdot 10 \cdot 10 \cdot 10)$$
$$= 10^8$$
$$= 10^{4 \cdot 2}$$

. . . and apply this idea to evaluate expressions with **positive bases** and with **negative bases**.

$$(5^2)^2 = 5^{2 \cdot 2} = 5^4 = 625$$

$$[(-4)^3]^2 = (-4)^{3 \cdot 2} = (-4)^6 = 4{,}096$$

INSIGHTS ON . . .

Powers with the Same Exponent

- ✔ Students already know how to use order of operations to evaluate a power of a product. For example, to evaluate $(-4 \cdot 2)^3$, they can multiply -4 by 2 and then cube the product. Now they discover another way to evaluate such expressions: They can raise each factor to the power and then multiply the two results.
- ✔ **Common Misconception** Students may think that *power* refers only to the exponent. Use precise language to explain.

  EXAMPLE In 2^3, 2 is the base, 3 is the exponent, and 2^3 is the power. Even though phrases such as "two to the third *power*" make it sound as if the exponent *is* the power, remind students that the word *power* actually refers to the base and the exponent as a whole.

Students learn that with a **power of a product**, the exponent applies to each factor . . .

$$(-4 \cdot 2)^3 = (-4 \cdot 2)(-4 \cdot 2)(-4 \cdot 2)$$
$$= (-4 \cdot -4 \cdot -4)(2 \cdot 2 \cdot 2)$$
$$= (-4)^3 \cdot 2^3$$

. . . and with the **power of a quotient**, it applies to the dividend and divisor.

$$\left(\frac{3}{4}\right)^5 = \frac{3}{4} \cdot \frac{3}{4} \cdot \frac{3}{4} \cdot \frac{3}{4} \cdot \frac{3}{4}$$
$$= \frac{3 \cdot 3 \cdot 3 \cdot 3 \cdot 3}{4 \cdot 4 \cdot 4 \cdot 4 \cdot 4}$$
$$= \frac{3^5}{4^5}$$

Properties of Integer Exponents *(continued)*

INSIGHTS ON . . .

Zero and Negative Exponents

- ✔ Many students will be surprised to learn that when a nonzero value is raised to the zero power, the result is 1. Students might expect the result to be 0 since any number times 0 equals 0. However, raising a number to the 0 power does not actually involve multiplication by 0. The concept of a zero exponent becomes clear to students when they repeatedly divide a power by its base and see how the value changes.
- ✔ After students discover that a value raised to the zero power equals 1, they extend the pattern to learn how to evaluate powers with negative exponents.
- ✔ Clarify for students that a number without an exponent has an understood exponent of 1, not zero. For example, 5 is the same as 5^1.
- ✔ **Common Misconception** Students may think that if the exponent is negative, the value of the power will be negative. When students look for and make use of structure, they see that this is not true.

  EXAMPLE 2^{-2} equals the reciprocal of 2^2, which is $\frac{1}{2^2}$. Note that 2^{-2} is not the same as -2^2 or as $(-2)^2$.
- ✔ **Common Misconception** Look for students who think that because $2^0 = 1$, it must be true that $(-2)^0 = -1$. By starting with $(-2)^2$ and repeatedly dividing by the base, -2, students can see $(-2)^2$ is 4, $(-2)^1$ is -2, and $(-2)^0$ is 1.
- ✔ Students may use digital tools to explore patterns in exponents. However, they must attend to precision when entering expressions into calculators.

  EXAMPLE When keying in $3^{2 \cdot 3}$, enter parentheses around $2 \cdot 3$. Otherwise, the calculator might compute $3^2 \cdot 3$.
- ✔ Students consolidate their learning by applying properties of exponents to simplify complicated expressions such as $\frac{(75^{-6} \cdot 31^0)^{-3}}{75^{10} \cdot 31^{-9}}$. They find that the properties may be applied in different orders. As long as they are used correctly, the resulting forms of the expressions will be equivalent to one other.

Students extend patterns to understand **zero and negative exponents** when the **base is positive** . . .

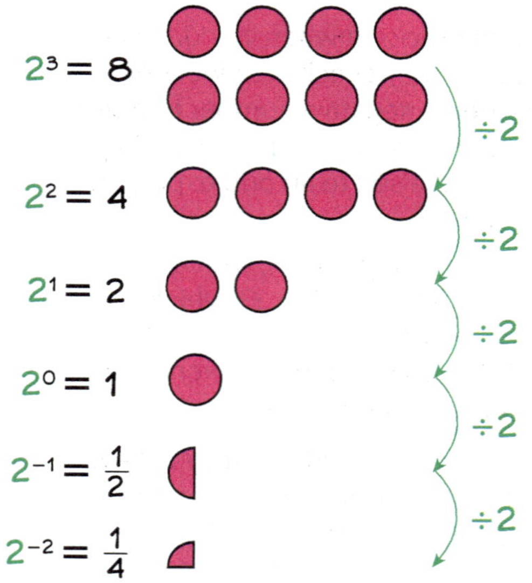

. . . and when the **base is negative**.

Power	Value
$(-2)^3$	-8
$(-2)^2$	4
$(-2)^1$	-2
$(-2)^0$	1
$(-2)^{-1}$	$\frac{1}{(-2^1)}$, or $\frac{1}{2}$
$(-2)^{-2}$	$\frac{1}{(-2^2)}$, or $\frac{1}{4}$

÷(−2) ÷(−2) ÷(−2) ÷(−2) ÷(−2)

Very Large and Very Small Quantities

INSIGHTS ON . . .

Integer Powers of 10

- ✔ Before students use scientific notation to express very large and small numbers, they work with numbers expressed as a single digit times an integer power of 10.
- ✔ When students use a single digit times an integer power of 10 to express a number, encourage them to check their work by rewriting their answer in standard form.
- ✔ To approximate a number as a single digit times a power of 10, first round it to the greatest place value with a nonzero digit. Then rewrite the rounded number as a single digit times a power of 10.
- ✔ **Common Misconception** A phrase such as *move the decimal point* may help students remember how to multiply by a power of 10, but be sure they have a conceptual understanding of the process. Each time a number is multiplied or divided by 10, the digits shift one place left or right. So, although students move the decimal point to find the product, it is the digits that are actually moving. The decimal point is always in the same position—between the ones and tenths places.

Students use **integer powers of 10** to express very large and very small numbers . . .

$$2{,}000{,}000{,}000 = 2 \times 1{,}000{,}000{,}000 = 2 \times 10^9$$

$$0.00003 = \frac{3}{100{,}000} = 3 \times \frac{1}{10^5} = 3 \times 10^{-5}$$

. . . and **approximate** numbers as a product of a single digit and a power of 10.

62,000 is close to 60,000 or 6×10^4.

0.0078 is close to 0.0080 or 8×10^{-3}.

INSIGHTS ON . . .

Comparing with Powers of 10

- ✔ Students then learn to make sense of very large and very small numbers by comparing quantities expressed as single digits times integer powers of 10.
- ✔ Students understand that when two positive quantities are each written as a single digit times a power of 10, the quantity with the greater power of 10 has the greater value. For example, any single digit times 10^4 is greater than any single digit times 10^3. This is because ten-thousands are much greater than thousands.
- ✔ Students compared quantities multiplicatively when they studied ratios and proportionality. Now, they apply this understanding to compare two quantities that are each expressed using powers of 10.

Students reason about exponents to compare numbers written as a single digit times a **power of 10** . . .

$$3 \times 10^{-5} > 9 \times 10^{-6}$$

. . . and use **multiplicative comparison** to describe the relationship between two quantities.

8×10^5 is how many times as great as 4×10^3?

$$8 \div 4 = 2$$

$$10^5 \div 10^3 = 10^2$$

So, 8×10^5 is 2×10^2, or 200 times as great as 4×10^3.

Very Large and Very Small Quantities *(continued)*

INSIGHTS ON . . .

Scientific Notation

- ✔ Students transition from quantities expressed as a single digit times a power of 10 to scientific notation, which expresses a quantity as a decimal greater than or equal to 1, but less than 10, times a power of 10.
- ✔ As a convention, numbers expressed in scientific notation use the × symbol rather than a dot to indicate multiplication. This helps to prevent confusion between the multiplication symbol and a decimal point.
- ✔ When entering numbers in scientific notation into a calculator, students may use the EE key. Depending on the technology, results in scientific notation may be expressed using a power of 10 or with an E symbol.
- ✔ **Common Misconception** Students may believe that the *E* in a technology display means *error*. Explain that it is just an abbreviation for *times ten to the power of*.

Students **use scientific notation** to represent very large and very small quantities . . .

$$8{,}367{,}000{,}000{,}000{,}000 = 8.367 \times 10^{15}$$

$$0.00000000000000097 = 9.7 \times 10^{-16}$$

. . . and **interpret scientific notation** that has been generated by technology.

3.45E12	means	3.45×10^{12}
5.8E−9	means	5.8×10^{-9}

Operations with Scientific Notation

INSIGHTS ON . . .

Adding and Subtracting with Scientific Notation

- ✔ To add and subtract numbers given in scientific notation, students use what they know about place value to understand why they may first need to rewrite one or both numbers to make the powers of 10 the same.
- ✔ **Error Alert** Watch for students who rewrite 5.63×10^5 as 0.563×10^4. Point out that changing 10^5 to 10^4 is equivalent to dividing by 10, so the other factor, 5.63, must be multiplied by 10 to ensure the value does not change.
- ✔ The result of a computation with numbers in scientific notation may not itself be in scientific notation. Students may need to rewrite it so the decimal factor is greater than or equal to 1 but less than 10.

Students **add** and **subtract** numbers in scientific notation by rewriting them using the **same power**.

$$(5.63 \times 10^5) - (2.52 \times 10^4)$$

using 10^4 → $(56.3 \times 10^4) - (2.52 \times 10^4)$

$$= 53.78 \times 10^4$$

$$= 5.378 \times 10^5$$

using 10^5 → $(5.63 \times 10^5) - (0.252 \times 10^5)$

$$= 5.378 \times 10^5$$

Operations with Scientific Notation *(continued)*

INSIGHTS ON . . .

Multiplying and Dividing with Scientific Notation

- ✔ Scientific notation simplifies multiplication and division of very large and very small numbers. It allows students to work with the nonzero digits and think about the place values of those digits separately.
- ✔ When multiplying or dividing with scientific notation, the numbers do not need to be expressed using the same power of 10. Point out how this is different from addition and subtraction. Students connect this idea to computation with fractions, where a common denominator is needed for addition and subtraction but not for multiplication and division.
- ✔ Students apply the commutative and associative properties to help them multiply and divide quantities expressed in scientific notation. They multiply or divide the decimal parts and then use the properties of exponents to multiply or divide the powers of 10.
- ✔ **Error Alert** Watch for students who may incorrectly apply recently learned properties of integer exponents. For example, when dividing powers with the same base, students may divide the exponents instead of subtracting them.

Students extend their understanding of operations with scientific notation to include **multiplication** . . .

$$(3.5 \times 10^{-3}) \times (3.2 \times 10^{5})$$
$$= (3.5 \times 3.2) \times (10^{-3} \times 10^{5})$$
$$= 11.2 \times 10^{2}$$

. . . and **division.**

$$\frac{8.58 \times 10^{5}}{2.2 \times 10^{2}}$$
$$= \frac{8.58}{2.2} \times \frac{10^{5}}{10^{2}}$$
$$= 3.9 \times 10^{3}$$

Future Learning

Students will move on to apply their understanding of integer exponents and scientific notation to solve problems.

Students will:

- solve problems involving square roots and cube roots.
- use exponential expressions to calculate volume of figures.
- extend the properties of whole-number exponents to fractional exponents.
- work with nonlinear functions, including exponential functions.

Unit Big Ideas

This unit introduces students to operations with powers, comparing integer powers of ten, and expressing and operating with numbers in scientific notation. Students preview the skills they will be learning in this unit and assess what they know and do not know about them. Students record their progress after completing each lesson and reflect on their learning at the end of the unit.

The major themes of this unit are:

- You explore operations with powers and discover patterns that help you understand and apply properties of exponents.
- A very large or very small quantity can be expressed as a product of a number and a power of ten. You can use what you know about properties of exponents to operate with numbers in this form.

Self Check

- Take a few minutes to have each student independently read through the list of skills. Ask students to consider each skill and check the box if it is a skill they think they already have.
- Remind students that these skills are likely to all be new to them and that over time, they will be able to check off more and more skills.

Support Whole Class Discussion

Engage students in a discussion about the skills with questions such as:

- *Which skills seem related to something you already know?*
- *Which skills do you think you would use in your everyday life? Why?*

Support Growth Mindset

At the end of the unit, have students review the skills on the **Student Book Self Reflection** page and work in pairs to respond to the prompts. Encourage students to revisit the work they did in each lesson.

Unit 5

Integer Exponents

Properties and Scientific Notation

Self Check — Before starting this unit, check off the skills you know below. As you complete each lesson, see how many more skills you can check off!

I can . . .	Before	After
Simplify expressions with two or more powers using exponent properties.		
Apply exponent properties to rewrite or simplify expressions with zero and negative integer exponents.		
Express, estimate, and compare quantities using integer powers of 10.		
Perform operations with numbers in scientific notation.		
Work with scientific notation to solve problems.		
Listen carefully during discussion in order to understand and explain another person's ideas.		

445

Unit Skills	Lesson
Simplify expressions with two or more powers using exponent properties.	19, 20, 21, 22
Apply exponent properties to rewrite or simplify expressions with zero and negative integer exponents.	20, 21, 22
Express, estimate, and compare quantities using integer powers of 10.	21
Perform operations with numbers in scientific notation.	22
Work with scientific notation to solve problems.	22
Listen carefully during discussion in order to understand and explain another person's ideas.	19–22

Prepare for Unit 5

- Read the directions and the headings in the boxes, or have a student do so. Call on volunteers to explain the task in their own words.
- Allow time for students to write what they know about cubes in the graphic organizer.
- Have students work with a partner to share their ideas. Give students time to revise and add onto what they have written in their graphic organizers. Circulate and validate responses and clarify any misconceptions.
- After most students have finished, debrief with a whole class discussion.

Build Academic Vocabulary

- Display academic terms that will be used throughout this unit when discussing word problems and possible solutions: *property* and *simplify*. Students will likely have some prior knowledge of the terms from math learning in previous grade levels or other content areas. Use the **Academic Vocabulary** routine described in Unit 1 Professional Learning to provide explicit instruction and active engagement.
- Additional academic vocabulary for each lesson is listed in the Lesson Overview. The cognate chart at right includes the Spanish cognates for academic vocabulary introduced in the unit and in each lesson. To support students whose primary language is Spanish, use the **Cognate Support** routine described in Unit 1 Professional Learning
- Support students as they move from informal language to formal academic language by using the **Collect and Display** routine. Have students refer to the chart during discussion and writing.

UNIT 5 **Prepare for Exponent Properties and Scientific Notation**

➤ **You have learned to use reasoning about powers, exponents, and factors. Write what you know about the term *cube* in the boxes. Share your ideas with a partner and add new information to the boxes as needed.**

Possible answers:

Numerical Expressions
- 4^3
- $4 \times 4 \times 4$
- 64

How to Say the Expression
- 4^3 is *four cubed*
- $4 \times 4 \times 4$ is *four times four times four*
- 64 is *sixty-four*

cube

Related Words
- power
- exponent
- base
- cubic
- volume
- repeated multiplication

446

Cognates for Academic Vocabulary in Unit 5

ACADEMIC WORD	SPANISH COGNATE	ACADEMIC WORD	SPANISH COGNATE
related	*relacionado(a)*	mass	*masa*
simplify	*simplificar*	contiguous	*contiguo(a)*
express	*expresar*	molecule	*molécula*

Overview | Apply Exponent Properties for Positive Integer Exponents

MATH FOCUS

Focus Standard

8.EE.A.1 Know and apply the properties of integer exponents to generate equivalent numerical expressions.

STANDARDS FOR MATHEMATICAL PRACTICE (SMP)

SMP 1, 2, 3, 4, 5, and 6 are integrated into the Try-Discuss-Connect routine.*

This lesson provides additional support for:

2 Reason abstractly and quantitatively.

7 Look for and make use of structure.

8 Look for and express regularity in repeated reasoning.

* See page 1o to learn how every lesson includes these SMP.

Objectives

Content Objectives

- Understand these properties of positive integer exponents:

  power of a power: $(a^m)^n = a^{mn}$

  product of powers: $a^m a^n = a^{m+n}$

  quotient of powers: $\frac{a^m}{a^n} = a^{m-n}$

  power of a product: $(ab)^m = a^m b^m$

  power of a quotient: $\left(\frac{a}{b}\right)^m = \frac{a^m}{b^m}$
- Apply the properties of positive integer exponents to simplify expressions and to generate equivalent expressions.

Language Objectives

- Understand the terms *base, exponent,* and *power* and use them to describe the properties for positive integer exponents.
- Use the definition of *power* to explain in writing why a property of exponents is true.
- Use the properties of exponents to justify strategies and solutions during partner and class discussion.
- Interpret word problems by applying the properties of exponents to write and simplify expressions with positive integer exponents.

Prior Knowledge

- Understand the parts of a power.
- Rewrite powers as products with repeated factors.

Vocabulary

Math Vocabulary

There is no new vocabulary. Review the following key terms.

base (of a power) in a power, the number that is used as a repeated factor.

evaluate to find the value of an expression.

exponent in a power, the number that shows how many times the base is used as a factor.

power an expression with a base and an exponent.

Academic Vocabulary

related connected in some way to one or more other things.

simplify to make easier to work with or understand.

Learning Progression

In Grade 5, students multiplied and divided by powers of 10 and explored the patterns of products and quotients.

In Grade 6, students evaluated expressions involving whole-number exponents. Students worked fluently with products of numbers, applying the associative and commutative properties as appropriate.

In this lesson, students learn properties of exponents and explain why each property is true for positive integer exponents. They use the properties to evaluate, simplify, and rewrite expressions.

Later in Grade 8, students will learn the meanings of zero and negative exponents and will apply properties they learn in this lesson to expressions involving all integer exponents.

Pacing Guide

Items marked with ↖ are available on the **Teacher Toolbox**.

	MATERIALS	DIFFERENTIATION
SESSION 1 **Explore** Exponent Properties for Positive Integer Exponents (35–50 min)		
• **Start** (5 min) • **Try It** (5–10 min) • **Discuss It** (10–15 min) • **Connect It** (10–15 min) • **Close: Exit Ticket** (5 min) **Additional Practice** (pages 451–452)	Presentation Slides ↖	**PREPARE** Interactive Tutorial ↖ **RETEACH or REINFORCE** Visual Model
SESSION 2 **Develop** Applying Properties for Powers with the Same Base (45–60 min)		
• **Start** (5 min) • **Try It** (10–15 min) • **Discuss It** (10–15 min) • **Connect It** (15–20 min) • **Close: Exit Ticket** (5 min) **Additional Practice** (pages 457–458)	Presentation Slides ↖	**RETEACH or REINFORCE** Visual Model **REINFORCE** Fluency & Skills Practice ↖ **EXTEND** Deepen Understanding
SESSION 3 **Develop** Applying Properties for Powers with the Same Exponent (45–60 min)		
• **Start** (5 min) • **Try It** (10–15 min) • **Discuss It** (10–15 min) • **Connect It** (15–20 min) • **Close: Exit Ticket** (5 min) **Additional Practice** (pages 463–464)	**Math Toolkit** grid paper, straightedges Presentation Slides ↖	**RETEACH or REINFORCE** Visual Model **REINFORCE** Fluency & Skills Practice ↖ **EXTEND** Deepen Understanding
SESSION 4 **Refine** Applying Exponent Properties for Positive Integer Exponents (45–60 min)		
• **Start** (5 min) • **Monitor & Guide** (15–20 min) • **Group & Differentiate** (20–30 min) • **Close: Exit Ticket** (5 min)	**Math Toolkit** Have items from previous sessions available for students. Presentation Slides ↖	**RETEACH** Visual Model **REINFORCE** Problems 4–9 **EXTEND** Challenge **PERSONALIZE** i-Ready
Lesson 19 Quiz ↖ or **Digital Comprehension Check**		**RETEACH** Tools for Instruction ↖ **REINFORCE** Math Center Activity ↖ **EXTEND** Enrichment Activity ↖

Overview | Apply Exponent Properties for Positive Integer Exponents

Connect to Culture

➤ **Use these activities to connect with and leverage the diverse backgrounds and experiences of all students. Engage students in sharing what they know about contexts before you add the information given here.**

SESSION 2 ■ ■ □ □

Try It Ask students to share what they know about bacteria. A colony of bacteria is a mass of microorganisms. Some strains of bacteria can be harmful but many others can be beneficial to our health. Bacteria colonies can have different shapes, sizes, colors, and surface textures. For example, bacteria called P. luminescens glow a bright green. When the bacteria get into a human wound, the green glow is usually a sign that the wound will heal. Given certain conditions, bacteria can grow very quickly and change appearance as they grow. Listeria, for instance, grows a comet tail when it gets inside an animal cell. Listeria uses that tail to move around inside the cell. The study of bacteria helps those in medical research understand how bacteria grow in various conditions. This research may eventually lead to cures for illnesses.

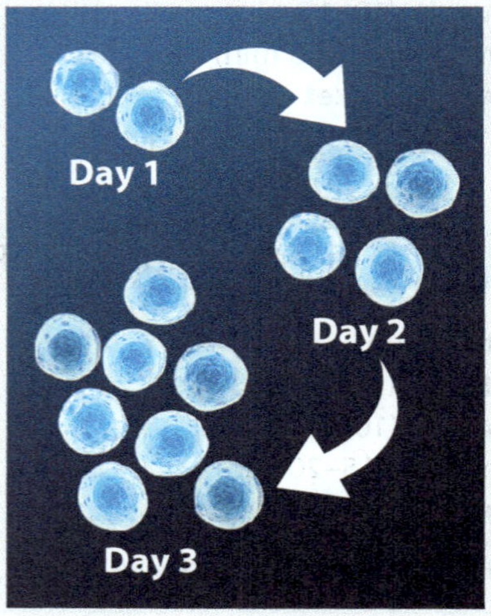

SESSION 3 ■ ■ ■ □

Try It Diwali is a five-day celebration of the Hindu religion in India. The holiday is a joyful time that involves special foods, bright lights, and loud noises. Families that celebrate Diwali often make rangolis. These designs are a family tradition, typically made with rice, sand, or flower petals. Making a rangoli brings families together as a way to spend time with one another. Ask students who have had experiences celebrating Diwali or making a rangoli to share their experiences with the class.

SESSION 4 ■ ■ ■ ■

Apply It **Problem 8** Ask any students who have had experience making homemade modeling clay to share their recipes with the class. While modeling clay can be made in huge quantities by a manufacturer, it can also be made at home with common ingredients. One recipe uses flour, salt, water, and food coloring. Once those ingredients are mixed together, the clay hardens in a refrigerator overnight. Another recipe uses cornstarch, baking soda, and water. Using these household ingredients saves money since store-bought clay could be expensive.

Connect to Family and Community

➤ **After the Explore session, have students use the Family Letter to let their families know what they are learning and to encourage family involvement.**

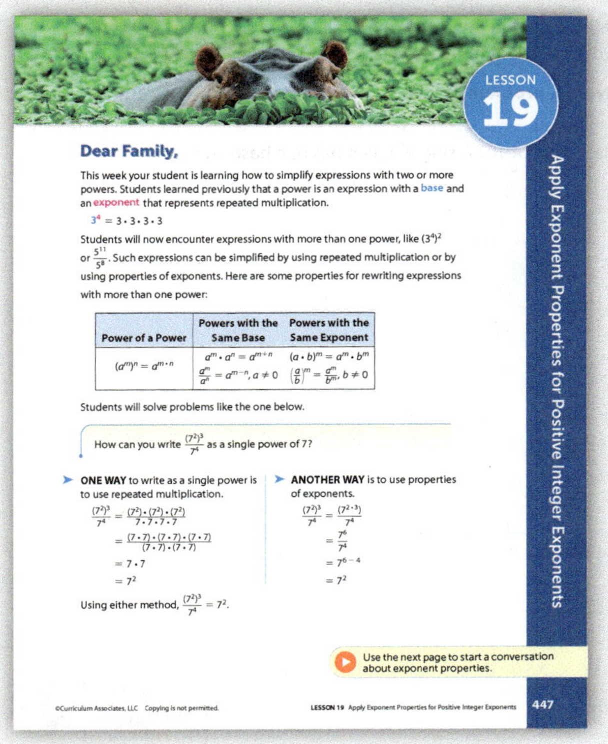

LESSON 19

Apply Exponent Properties for Positive Integer Exponents

Dear Family,

This week your student is learning how to simplify expressions with two or more powers. Students learned previously that a power is an expression with a base and an exponent that represents repeated multiplication.

$3^4 = 3 \cdot 3 \cdot 3 \cdot 3$

Students will now encounter expressions with more than one power, like $(3^4)^2$ or $\frac{5^{11}}{5^8}$. Such expressions can be simplified by using repeated multiplication or by using properties of exponents. Here are some properties for rewriting expressions with more than one power:

Power of a Power	Powers with the Same Base	Powers with the Same Exponent
$(a^m)^n = a^{m \cdot n}$	$a^m \cdot a^n = a^{m+n}$ $\frac{a^m}{a^n} = a^{m-n}, a \neq 0$	$(a \cdot b)^m = a^m \cdot b^m$ $\left(\frac{a}{b}\right)^m = \frac{a^m}{b^m}, b \neq 0$

Students will solve problems like the one below.

How can you write $\frac{(7^2)^3}{7^4}$ as a single power of 7?

➤ **ONE WAY** to write as a single power is to use repeated multiplication.

$$\frac{(7^2)^3}{7^4} = \frac{(7^2) \cdot (7^2) \cdot (7^2)}{7 \cdot 7 \cdot 7 \cdot 7} = \frac{(7 \cdot 7) \cdot (7 \cdot 7) \cdot (7 \cdot 7)}{(7 \cdot 7) \cdot (7 \cdot 7)} = 7 \cdot 7 = 7^2$$

➤ **ANOTHER WAY** is to use properties of exponents.

$$\frac{(7^2)^3}{7^4} = \frac{(7^{2 \cdot 3})}{7^4} = \frac{7^6}{7^4} = 7^{6-4} = 7^2$$

Using either method, $\frac{(7^2)^3}{7^4} = 7^2$.

Use the next page to start a conversation about exponent properties.

©Curriculum Associates, LLC Copying is not permitted. LESSON 19 Apply Exponent Properties for Positive Integer Exponents 447

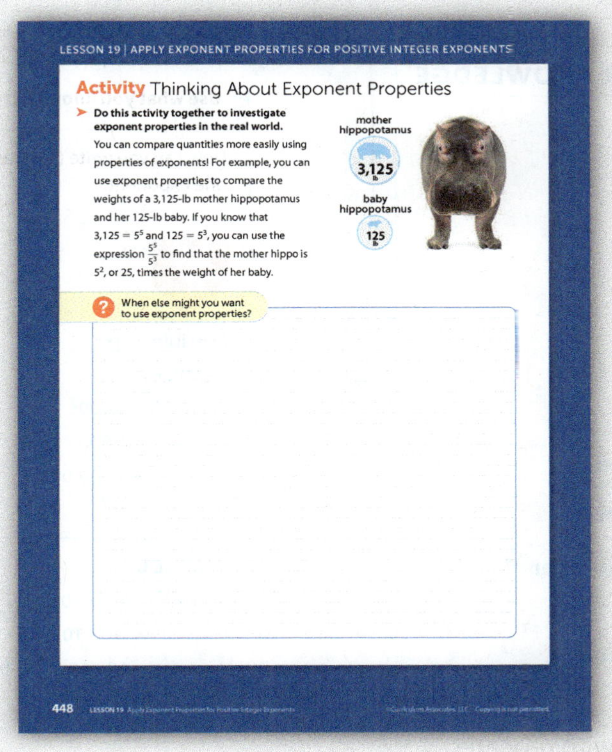

LESSON 19 | APPLY EXPONENT PROPERTIES FOR POSITIVE INTEGER EXPONENTS

Activity Thinking About Exponent Properties

➤ **Do this activity together to investigate exponent properties in the real world.**

You can compare quantities more easily using properties of exponents! For example, you can use exponent properties to compare the weights of a 3,125-lb mother hippopotamus and her 125-lb baby. If you know that $3{,}125 = 5^5$ and $125 = 5^3$, you can use the expression $\frac{5^5}{5^3}$ to find that the mother hippo is 5^2, or 25, times the weight of her baby.

When else might you want to use exponent properties?

448 LESSON 19 Apply Exponent Properties for Positive Integer Exponents ©Curriculum Associates, LLC Copying is not permitted.

Connect to Language

➤ **For English language learners, use the Differentiation chart to scaffold the language in each session. Use the Academic Vocabulary routine for academic terms before Session 1.**

DIFFERENTIATION | ENGLISH LANGUAGE LEARNERS — Use with **Session 1** **Connect It**

MATH TERM

A *product* is the result of multiplication.

A *factor* is a number that is multiplied.

ACADEMIC VOCABULARY

Repeated means occurring several times.

Levels 1–3: Reading/Speaking

Help students interpret Connect It problem 2. Read the problem as students follow along. Help them make sense of phrases by displaying them in a chart. Display *power of a power* and *single power*. Have partners find examples of each in the problem and identify the base and exponents in the expressions. Then display *product of repeated factors* and *repeated multiplication* and provide examples.

Have partners talk about the table in problem 2c. Ask them to identify the base and exponent in any expressions with exponents. Help them connect the exponents to the number of factors.

Levels 2–4: Reading/Speaking

Help students use a **Co-Constructed Word Bank** to make sense of Connect It problem 2. Read the problem with students and ask them to select words and phrases to include in the word bank. If needed, suggest *base, exponent, power, product of repeated factors, repeated multiplication*, and *square the expression*. Review meanings with students.

Next, have partners discuss the expressions in problem 2c using terms from the word bank. Prompt students to explain what they noticed or assumed about the expressions, what they decided to do as a result, and why.

Levels 3–5: Reading/Speaking

Have students use a **Co-Constructed Word Bank** to make sense of Connect It problem 3. Have students read the problem with partners and discuss words and phrases to include in the word bank. If needed, suggest *product of repeated factor* and *square the expression*. Have students discuss the meanings.

Have students reason about the expressions that complete the table in problem 2c. Prompt students to explain to partners what they noticed or assumed about the given expressions, what they decided to do as a result, and why. Remind students to use precise terms.

Explore Exponent Properties for Positive Integer Exponents

Purpose

- **Explore** the idea that a power raised to an exponent can be written as a single power.
- **Understand** that the expression $(a^m)^n$ can be written as a^{mn}.

START CONNECT TO PRIOR KNOWLEDGE

Which One Doesn't Belong?

A: 5^2	B: $2 \cdot 2 \cdot 2 \cdot 2$
C: $3 \cdot 3 \cdot 3$	D: $7 \cdot 3$

Possible Solutions

A is the only exponential expression.

B is the only product with even factors.

C is the only product with an odd number of factors.

D is the only product of different factors.

WHY? Support students' facility with repeated multiplication and exponents.

TRY IT SMP 1, 2, 4, 5, 6

Make Sense of the Problem

Before students work on Try It, use **Say It Another Way** to help them make sense of the problem. They should understand that an expression written as a single power of 10 means the base is 10 and there is a single exponent.

DISCUSS IT SMP 2, 3, 6, 7

Support Partner Discussion

After students work on Try It, have them respond to Discuss It with a partner. Listen for understanding that:

- 10 to the third power squared means *10 to the third power* is multiplied by itself.
- there are 6 repeated factors of 10.

Explore Exponent Properties for Positive Integer Exponents

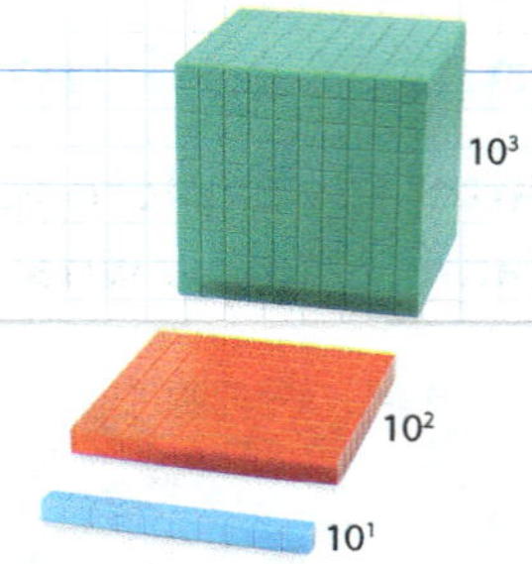

Previously, you learned how to evaluate powers. In this lesson, you will learn ways to simplify expressions involving two or more powers.

➤ **Use what you know to try to solve the problem below.**

How can you write $(10^3)^2$ as a single power of 10? A single power has one base and one exponent.

TRY IT

Possible work:

SAMPLE A

$(10^3)^2 = 1{,}000^2$
$= 1{,}000 \cdot 1{,}000$
$= 1{,}000{,}000$
$= 10^6$

SAMPLE B

$(10^3)^2 = 10^3 \cdot 10^3$
$= (10 \cdot 10 \cdot 10) \cdot (10 \cdot 10 \cdot 10)$
$= 10 \cdot 10 \cdot 10 \cdot 10 \cdot 10 \cdot 10$
$= 10^6$

DISCUSS IT

Ask: How did you find the exponent in your answer?

Share: I found the exponent by . . .

Learning Target SMP 1, SMP 2, SMP 3, SMP 4, SMP 5, SMP 6, SMP 7, SMP 8
Know and apply the properties of integer exponents to generate equivalent numerical expressions.

Common Misconception Listen for students who think that a power refers to the exponent only. As students share their strategies, encourage them to ask questions of one another to bring out the fact that a power includes both a base and an exponent.

Select and Sequence Student Strategies

Select 2–3 samples that represent the range of student thinking in your classroom. Here is one possible order for class discussion:

- 10^3 calculated and squared; result written as a power of 10
- (misconception) answer includes only the exponent
- expression written as repeated multiplication and then as a power of 10
- reasoning used to conclude that $(10^3)^2$ has 6 factors of 10

Facilitate Whole Class Discussion

Call on students to share selected strategies. Remind students that one way to agree and build on ideas is to give another example that shows that the strategy makes sense.

Guide students to **Compare and Connect** the representations. If everyone has something to say, use turn and talk before calling on students to share.

ASK *How was the way [student name] found the single power of 10 similar to the way [student name] found the single power of 10? How was it different?*

LISTEN FOR Each strategy involved using 10 as the base and an exponent for the number of factors. One student calculated the value of the expression and then wrote that value as a power of 10. Another reasoned about the number of factors of 10 without performing any calculations.

CONNECT IT

SMP 2, 4, 5

1 Look Back Look for understanding that using exponents is shorthand for repeated multiplication. A single power of 10 is a power with 10 as a base and a single exponent applied to that base.

DIFFERENTIATION | RETEACH or REINFORCE

Visual Model

Use repeated factors to model writing a power of a power as a single power.

If students are unsure about writing a power of a power as a single power, then use this activity to help them visualize the concept.

- Display the expression $(10^4)^3$.
- Ask: *What does the exponent 3 mean?* [10^4 is used as a factor 3 times.]
- Invite a student to rewrite the expression using multiplication with 10^4 as the factor.
- Ask: *What does the exponent 4 mean on each factor of 10^4?* [10 is used as a factor 4 times for each factor.]
- Invite another student to rewrite the expression, replacing each 10^4 with $10 \cdot 10 \cdot 10 \cdot 10$.
- Ask: *How many factors of 10 are there?* [12]
- Ask: *What is the value of the expression written as a single power of 10?* [10^{12}]
- Ask: *How does the exponent, 12, relate to the two exponents in the original expression?* [12 is the product of the two exponents, 3 and 4.]

LESSON 19 | SESSION 1

CONNECT IT

1 Look Back What is $(10^3)^2$ rewritten as a single power? How did you get your answer?
10^6; Possible answer: I rewrote the powers as repeated multiplication and counted the number of 10s in the product.

2 Look Ahead An expression like $(10^3)^2$ is called a power of a power. Recall that a power is an expression with a base and an exponent. You can write a power as repeated multiplication of the base when the exponent is a positive integer. The exponent tells how many times the base is used as a factor. For example, $(-3)^2 = (-3) \cdot (-3)$.

a. Write 10^3 as a product of repeated factors. $10 \cdot 10 \cdot 10$

b. Square the expression you wrote in problem 2a. Write the answer as repeated multiplication. How does the number of repeated factors change?
$(10 \cdot 10 \cdot 10)^2 = 10 \cdot 10 \cdot 10 \cdot 10 \cdot 10 \cdot 10$; The number of factors doubles from 3 to 6.

c. Complete the table.

Power of a Power	Written as Repeated Factors	Single Power
$(10^2)^5$	$(10 \cdot 10) \cdot (10 \cdot 10) \cdot (10 \cdot 10) \cdot (10 \cdot 10) \cdot (10 \cdot 10)$	10^{10}
$(10^4)^2$	$(10 \cdot 10 \cdot 10 \cdot 10) \cdot (10 \cdot 10 \cdot 10 \cdot 10)$	10^8
$(10^3)^3$	$(10 \cdot 10 \cdot 10) \cdot (10 \cdot 10 \cdot 10) \cdot (10 \cdot 10 \cdot 10)$	10^9

d. Look at each row of the table in problem 2c. How are the exponents in the first column related to the exponent in the third column?
The exponent in the third column is the product of the two exponents in the first column.

3 Reflect How could you write $((-5)^7)^3$ as a single power of -5? Explain.
$(-5)^{21}$; Possible explanation: $(-5)^7$ is the product of 7 factors of -5. That product raised to the third power is equal to 3 groups of 7, or 21 factors of -5.

450

2 Look Ahead Review the meaning of *power* with students. Explain that $(10^3)^2$ is a *power of a power* because the base, 10^3, is a power.

Point out the parentheses in the expression $(-3)^2$, and ask why they are needed to indicate that -3 is the base. Discuss how $(-3)^2$ is different from -3^2. If necessary, explain that $(-3)^2$ means *raise -3 to the 2nd power*, while -3^2 means *raise 3 to the 2nd power and then take the opposite of the result*.

Students should notice that, for each example in the table, the exponent of the single power is the product of the two exponents. In general, 10^m has m factors of 10, so $(10^m)^n$ has n groups of m factors of 10, which is $m \cdot n$ factors of 10 in all. So, $(10^m)^n = 10^{mn}$.

CLOSE | EXIT TICKET

3 Reflect Look for understanding that there will be 21 factors of -5 in the final product, so the expression as a single power of -5 is $(-5)^{21}$.

Common Misconception If students write an answer of -5^{21}, then discuss the difference between -5^{21} and $(-5)^{21}$. Point out that the question asks for a power of -5, so $(-5)^{21}$ is the correct answer.

Prepare for Applying Exponent Properties for Positive Integer Exponents

Support Vocabulary Development

Assign **Prepare for Applying Exponent Properties for Positive Integer Exponents** as extra practice in class or as homework.

If you have students complete this in class, then use the guidance below.

Ask students to consider the term *power*. Ensure they understand that a power has both a base and an exponent.

Have students work in pairs to complete the graphic organizer. Invite pairs to share their completed organizers, and prompt a whole-class comparative discussion of the definitions, known facts, and examples given.

Have students look at the powers in problem 2 and discuss with a partner which part of the expression is the factor and which part indicates how many times that factor is repeated.

Problem Notes

1. Students should understand that a power is an expression with a base and an exponent that represents repeated multiplication. Student responses might include examples with whole-number, decimal, or fraction bases.

2. In problem 2a, $\frac{1}{3}$ is used as a factor three times. In problem 2b, 10 is used as a factor four times. In problem 2c, 0.8 is used as a factor twice.

LESSON 19 | SESSION 1 Name:

Prepare for Applying Exponent Properties for Positive Integer Exponents

1 Think about what you know about powers and exponents. Fill in each box. Use words, numbers, and pictures. Show as many ideas as you can.
Possible answers:

power

What Is It?
an expression with a base and an exponent that represents repeated multiplication

What I Know About It
The base is the number being multiplied. The exponent tells how many times the base is used as a factor.
x^2 is read "x squared."
x^3 is read "x cubed."

Examples
$\left(\frac{1}{2}\right)^4 = \frac{1}{2} \cdot \frac{1}{2} \cdot \frac{1}{2} \cdot \frac{1}{2} = \frac{1}{16}$
$(2.5)^2 = (2.5)(2.5) = 6.25$

Examples
$9^2 = 9 \cdot 9 = 81$
$3^4 = 3 \cdot 3 \cdot 3 \cdot 3 = 81$

Examples
$5^1 = 5$
$19^1 = 19$
$1^6 = 1 \cdot 1 \cdot 1 \cdot 1 \cdot 1 \cdot 1 = 1$
$0^5 = 0 \cdot 0 \cdot 0 \cdot 0 \cdot 0 = 0$

2 Write each power as a product of repeated factors. Then evaluate the power.

a. $\left(\frac{1}{3}\right)^3$
$\frac{1}{3} \cdot \frac{1}{3} \cdot \frac{1}{3} = \frac{1}{27}$

b. 10^4
$10 \cdot 10 \cdot 10 \cdot 10 = 10{,}000$

c. $(0.8)^2$
$(0.8) \cdot (0.8) = 0.64$

451

REAL-WORLD CONNECTION

To describe the strength of earthquakes, scientists use the Richter scale. The Richter scale is based on powers of 10. An increase of 1 on the scale means a 10-times increase in earthquake strength. For example, an earthquake measuring 4.0 on the Richter scale is 10 times as powerful as an earthquake measuring 3.0 on the scale and 10^2, or 100, times as powerful as an earthquake measuring 2.0 on the scale. Ask students to think of other real-world examples when using properties for positive integer exponents might be useful.

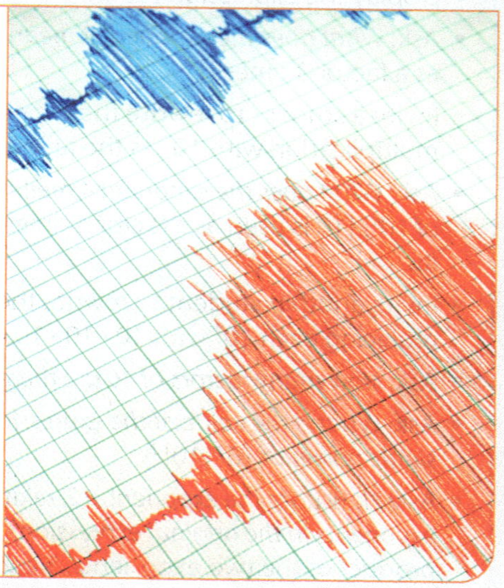

Additional Practice

3 Problem 3 provides another look at writing a power of a power of 10 as a single power of 10. This problem is similar to the problem where $(10^3)^2$ was written as a single power of 10. This problem asks for the expression $(10^2)^4$ to be written as a single power of 10.

Students may calculate the value of 10^2, raise the result to the fourth power, and then write the final result as a power of 10. Or, they may write 10^2 as $10 \cdot 10$ and then write $(10 \cdot 10)^4$, first as repeated multiplication and then as a power of 10.

Suggest that students use **Say It Another Way** to help them make sense of the problem.

LESSON 19 | SESSION 1

3 **a.** How can you write $(10^2)^4$ as a single power of 10? Show your work.

Possible work:

$$(10^2)^4 = 10^2 \cdot 10^2 \cdot 10^2 \cdot 10^2$$
$$= (10 \cdot 10) \cdot (10 \cdot 10) \cdot (10 \cdot 10) \cdot (10 \cdot 10)$$
$$= 10 \cdot 10 \cdot 10 \cdot 10 \cdot 10 \cdot 10 \cdot 10 \cdot 10$$
$$= 10^8$$

SOLUTION 10^8

b. Check your answer to problem 3a. Show your work.

Possible work:

$$(10^2)^4 = 100^4$$
$$= 100 \cdot 100 \cdot 100 \cdot 100$$
$$= 10{,}000 \cdot 10{,}000$$
$$= 100{,}000{,}000$$
$$= 10^8$$

452

DIFFERENTIATION | ENGLISH LANGUAGE LEARNERS

Use with **Session 2** Connect It

Levels 1–3: Speaking/Writing

Help students prepare to write responses to Connect It problem 3. Read the problem with students and help them identify the two expressions. Ensure students understand that the expressions are equivalent. Provide time for students to reason about the expressions and model their ideas. Call on students to share and record their models. Help students write responses by summarizing the models with short sentences.

Adapt **Stronger and Clearer Each Time** by pairing students with more proficient English speakers. Ask students to read responses to partners, pausing frequently to refer to their models. Have partners review responses together and clarify ideas as needed.

Levels 2–4: Speaking/Writing

Have students prepare and write responses to Connect It problem 3. Ask students to read the problem and use **Say It Another Way** to confirm understanding. Then call on students to suggest precise math terms they might use in written responses. If needed, suggest *equal groups, factors, product, multiply/multiplied by, repeated multiplication, power, exponent,* and *same base.*

Have students pre-write their responses using precise math terms. Then have students use **Stronger and Clearer Each Time** to discuss and revise responses. Ask partners to take turns explaining ideas, pausing to refer to models, and checking that their ideas make sense. Then have partners revise as needed.

Levels 3–5: Speaking/Writing

Have students prepare and write responses to Connect It problem 3. Ask partners to read the problem in pairs and discuss what they notice about the expressions. Encourage students to use mathematical models to show why the product of two powers can be written as a single power. Then have students draft responses independently.

Have students use **Stronger and Clearer Each Time** to explain ideas to partners and revise written responses. Have students take turns explaining ideas and offering feedback. Remind students that a good explanation describes what they did and why they decided to do it. Encourage students to refine responses after each pairing.

Develop Applying Properties for Powers with the Same Base

Purpose

- **Develop** strategies for simplifying products of powers and quotients of powers.
- **Recognize** that when powers have the same base, the exponents are added when the powers are multiplied, and the exponents are subtracted when the powers are divided.

START CONNECT TO PRIOR KNOWLEDGE

Same and Different

A	B
2^6	$2 \cdot 2 \cdot 2 \cdot 2 \cdot 2 \cdot 2$
C	**D**
$(2^3)^2$	$(2^2)^3$

Possible Solutions

A is the only expression with one exponent.

A, C, and D are all expressions with exponents.

C and D are both powers of powers.

All are equivalent to 2^6, or 64.

WHY? Support students' facility with working with repeated multiplication, powers, and powers of powers.

DEVELOP ACADEMIC LANGUAGE

WHY? Use active and passive voice to talk about exponents and powers.

HOW? Read Model It and have students tell how *they* can write the powers. Point out how the emphasis is on who does the action. (*you*) Then ask questions to help them restate: *How can 2^7 be written? And 2^4?* Guide students to tell where the emphasis is (*written*). Encourage them to use similar structures as they work on Connect It problem 3.

TRY IT SMP 1, 2, 4, 5, 6

Make Sense of the Problem

See ***Connect to Culture*** to support student engagement. Before students work on Try It, use **Say It Another Way** to help them make sense of the problem. Come to a consensus as a class about the correct details of the problem. It is important that students understand what the base and exponent of the power represent in the problem context.

Develop Applying Properties for Powers with the Same Base

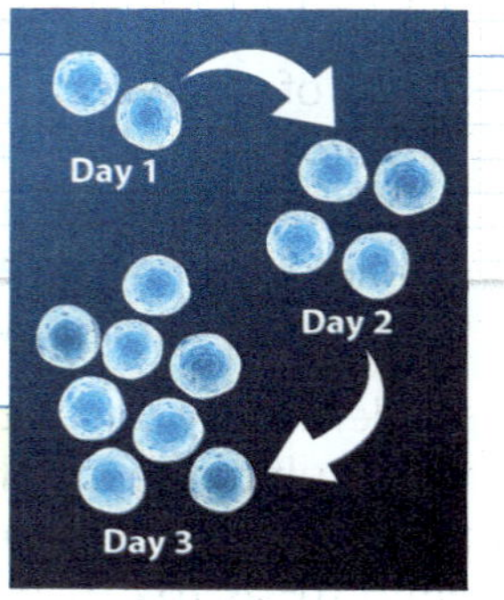

➤ **Read and try to solve the problem below.**

One population of single-celled bacteria doubles each day. On Day *x*, the population of the colony is 2^x. How many times as large is the population of the colony on Day 7 than on Day 4?

TRY IT

Possible work:

SAMPLE A

Day	Number
1	2
2	4
3	8
4	16
5	32
6	64
7	128

$\frac{\text{Number on Day 7}}{\text{Number on Day 4}} = \frac{128}{16} = 8$

There are 8 times as many bacteria on Day 7 than on Day 4.

SAMPLE B

Population on Day 7: $2^7 = 2 \cdot 2 \cdot 2 \cdot 2 \cdot 2 \cdot 2 \cdot 2$
$= 128$

Population on Day 4: $2^4 = 2 \cdot 2 \cdot 2 \cdot 2$
$= 16$

$\frac{\text{Population on Day 7}}{\text{Population on Day 4}} = \frac{128}{16} = 8$

The population is 8 times larger on Day 7.

DISCUSS IT

Ask: How did you use powers and exponents to solve the problem?

Share: I used powers and exponents when I . . .

DISCUSS IT SMP 2, 3, 5, 6

Support Partner Discussion

After students work on Try It, encourage them to respond to Discuss It with a partner. If students need support in getting started, prompt them to ask each other questions such as:

- *What power represents the number of bacteria on Day 4?*
- *What power represents the number of bacteria on Day 7?*
- *How can you compare the populations on those two days?*

Common Misconception Listen for students who subtract the populations for Day 7 and Day 4. As students share their strategies, discuss what it means to find how many times as large one number is as another. Provide a simpler example, such as *10 is ____ times as large as 2*. Have a volunteer explain why solving the Try It problem means finding what factor the Day 4 population must be multiplied by to get the Day 7 population.

Select and Sequence Student Strategies

Select 2–3 samples that represent the range of student thinking in your classroom. Here is one possible order for class discussion:

- table of powers of 2 used to find solution
- (misconception) subtracted Day 4 population from Day 7 population
- powers evaluated to find Day 4 and Day 7 populations and quotient of results calculated
- quotient of powers written and simplified

Facilitate Whole Class Discussion

Call on students to share selected strategies. Prompt students to check whether their explanations are clear by asking their classmates for questions.

Guide students to **Compare and Connect** the representations. During the discussion, have students turn and talk with a partner.

ASK *How did the strategies use powers of 2? Did all the strategies find the value of the powers?*

LISTEN FOR All the strategies used the fact that the population on Day 4 was 2^4 and the population on Day 7 was 2^7. Some strategies found the value of these powers, and some just used the fact that they represent repeated multiplication of 2.

Model It

If students presented these models, have students connect these models to those presented in class.

If no student presented at least one of these models, have students first analyze key features of the models, and then connect them to the models presented in class.

ASK *How are the two Model It strategies the same? How are they different?*

LISTEN FOR Both use the fact that the Day 4 population is 2^4, and both divide to compare the two populations. The first starts with the Day 4 population, doubles it until Day 7, and then divides the result by the Day 4 population. The second writes the Day 7 population as 2^7 and then divides this by the Day 4 population.

For the table, prompt students to think about how they could simplify the quotient. Ask: *What factors in the numerator and denominator are common factors?*

For the quotient of powers, prompt students to consider how the quotient is simplified. Ask: *Why can you rewrite the quotient as a product of factors of $\frac{2}{2}$ and 2?*

➤ **Explore different ways to divide powers with the same base.**

One population of single-celled bacteria doubles each day. On Day x, the population of the colony is 2^x. How many times as large is the population of the colony on Day 7 than on Day 4?

Model It

You can start with the population on Day 4.

Double the population each day after that until Day 7.

Day	Population
4	2^4
5	$2 \cdot 2^4$
6	$2 \cdot 2 \cdot 2^4$
7	$2 \cdot 2 \cdot 2 \cdot 2^4$

The relationship between the population on Day 7 and the population on Day 4 is $\frac{(2 \cdot 2 \cdot 2) \cdot 2^4}{2^4}$.

Model It

You can write each power as repeated multiplication of the same factor.

$$\frac{\text{population on Day 7}}{\text{population on Day 4}} = \frac{2^7}{2^4} = \frac{2 \cdot 2 \cdot 2 \cdot 2 \cdot 2 \cdot 2 \cdot 2}{2 \cdot 2 \cdot 2 \cdot 2} = \frac{2}{2} \cdot \frac{2}{2} \cdot \frac{2}{2} \cdot \frac{2}{2} \cdot 2 \cdot 2 \cdot 2$$

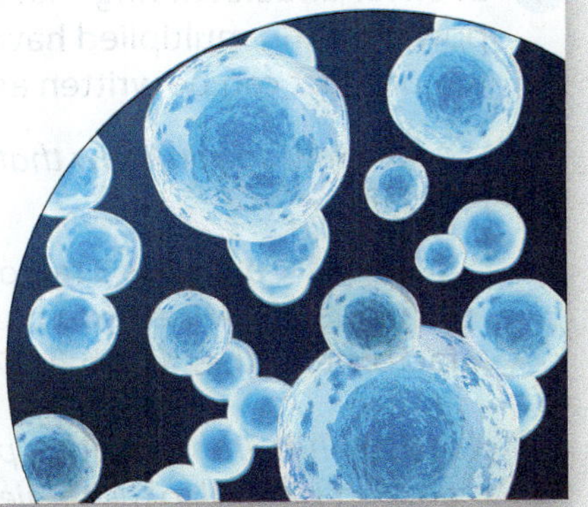

DIFFERENTIATION | EXTEND

SMP 2

Deepen Understanding

Reasoning Quantitatively about Constant Versus Exponential Growth

Prompt students to think about how doubling the population each day compares to adding 2 to the population each day.

ASK *A different colony of bacteria starts with 2 bacteria on Day 1, and then increases by 2 bacteria each day. What would the population be on Day 2? On Day 3? On Day x?*

LISTEN FOR It would be 4 on Day 2, 6 on Day 3, and $2x$ on Day x.

ASK *Look at the first step in the second Model It. What expression could you write to show the population on Day 7 divided by the population on Day 4 for this new colony?*

LISTEN FOR You could write $\frac{2 \cdot 7}{2 \cdot 4}$.

ASK *What is the value of this expression? That is, how many times as large is the colony on Day 7 as on Day 4?*

LISTEN FOR $\frac{7}{4}$, or 1.75; The population is 1.75 times as large on Day 7 as on Day 4.

ASK *How does the growth in the two colonies from Day 4 to Day 7 compare?*

LISTEN FOR The original colony grows much faster. It increases 8 times, while the population of the new colony does not even double.

Develop Applying Properties for Powers with the Same Base

CONNECT IT

SMP 2, 4, 5, 6, 7, 8

Remind students that the quantities and the relationships between them are the same in each representation. Explain that they will now use those relationships to reason about how to multiply and divide powers with the same base.

Before students begin to record and expand on their work in Model It, tell them that problem 2 will prepare them to provide the explanation asked for in problem 3.

Monitor and Confirm Understanding 1

- The power 2^3, which is $\frac{2^7}{2^4}$, represents the relationship between the Day 7 and Day 4 populations.
- The Day 7 population is 2^3, or 8, times as large as the Day 4 population.
- When you simplify $\frac{2^7}{2^4}$ you get 2^3. You can subtract the original exponents: $7 - 4 = 3$.

Facilitate Whole Class Discussion

2 Look for understanding that because the powers being multiplied have the same base, the product can be written as a single power.

> **ASK** *How do you know that $2^3 \cdot 2^4$ is equal to 2^7?*
>
> **LISTEN FOR** 2^3 has 3 factors of 2, and 2^4 has 4 factors of 2. When you multiply all the factors together, you have 7 factors of 2.

> **ASK** *What are some other powers whose product is equal to the single power 2^7?*
>
> **LISTEN FOR** 2^2 times 2^5 or 2^1 times 2^6. Any powers of 2 with exponents that add to 7 will have a product of 2^7.

3 Look for understanding of why the exponent of the single power of -6 is equal to the sum of the exponents in the factors.

> **ASK** *What are two other powers of -6 that can be multiplied to get $(-6)^{38}$?*
>
> **LISTEN FOR** Any powers with exponents that add to 38 will have a product of $(-6)^{38}$, for example, $(-6)^{30} \cdot (-6)^8$.

4 **Reflect** Have all students focus on the strategies used to solve the Try It. If time allows, have students discuss their ideas with a partner.

CONNECT IT

➤ **Use the problem from the previous page to help you understand how to multiply and divide powers with the same base.**

1 **a.** What single power of 2 represents the relationship between the population of the colony on Day 7 and the population on Day 4? Use your answer to complete the equation. How many times as large is the population of the colony on Day 7 than on Day 4?

$\frac{2^7}{2^4} =$ 2^3; 8 times as large

b. Look at the equation you completed in problem 1a. How are the exponents on the left side of the equation related to the exponent on the right side?

Possible answer: The exponent 3 is the difference of the exponents in the numerator and the denominator on the left side, $7 - 4$.

2 **a.** Look at the first **Model It**. The table shows the population of the colony on Day 7 as $(2 \cdot 2 \cdot 2) \cdot 2^4$. How can you write this expression as a product of two powers? $2^3 \cdot 2^4$

b. What power represents the population of the colony on Day 7? Write an equation by writing your answer to problem 2a equal to this power.

2^7; $2^3 \cdot 2^4 = 2^7$

c. How are the exponents in your equation related?

Possible answer: The exponent in the single power answer is 7. It is the sum of the exponents of the powers in the product $3 + 4$.

3 Explain why you can write the product $(-6)^{23} \cdot (-6)^{15}$ as the single power $(-6)^{38}$.

Possible explanation: The power $(-6)^{23}$ can be written as the product of 23 factors of -6 and the power $(-6)^{15}$ can be written as the product of 15 factors of -6. Since $23 + 15 = 38$, when the two quantities are multiplied, the result is the product of 38 factors of -6.

4 **Reflect** Think about all the models and strategies you have discussed today. Describe how one of them helped you better understand how to multiply and divide powers with the same base.

Responses will vary. Check student responses.

455

DIFFERENTIATION | RETEACH or REINFORCE

Visual Model

Simplify quotients of powers.

If students are unsure about simplifying quotients of powers, then use this activity to solidify the concept.

- Display the expression $\frac{3^6}{3^2}$.
- Point to the exponent 6 in the numerator. Ask: *What does the exponent 6 in the numerator mean?* [3 is used as a factor 6 times.]
- Point to the exponent 2 in the denominator. Ask: *What does the exponent 2 in the denominator mean?* [3 is used as a factor 2 times.]
- Invite a student to rewrite the expression, showing the powers in the numerator and denominator as multiplication with 3 as the repeated factor.
- Ask: *How many factors of 3 can be divided out of the numerator and denominator?* [2]
- Invite a student to cross out two factors of 3 in both the numerator and denominator.
- Ask: *What is the value of the remaining expression written as a single power of 3?* [3^4]
- Ask: *How does the exponent of 3^4 compare to the exponents in the original expression?* [It is the difference of the exponents.]

Apply It

For all problems, encourage students to use a model to support their thinking. Some students may be able to work directly with the properties of exponents, while others may need to write out the repeated multiplication.

5 $\frac{7^4 \cdot 7^8}{7^2} = \frac{7^{4+8}}{7^2} = \frac{7^{12}}{7^2} = 7^{12-2} = 7^{10}$,
so any expression equivalent to 7^{10} is correct.

A is correct.

B is correct. $7^4 \cdot 7^4 \cdot 7^2 = 7^{4+4+2} = 7^{10}$

D is correct. $(7^2)^5 = 7^{2 \cdot 5} = 7^{10}$

E is correct. $\frac{7^{15}}{7^5} = 7^{15-5} = 7^{10}$

C is not correct. This answer is found by multiplying the exponents in the numerator and then dividing by the exponent in the denominator.

F is not correct. This answer is found by adding all the exponents.

6 If students have trouble seeing how they can write an equation to solve for *n*, ask: *For two powers of 23 to be equal, what must be true about the exponents?* Students should see that the powers will be equal if the exponents are equal. So, once each side is written as a single power of 23, the problem can be solved by setting the exponents equal to each other and solving for *n*.

LESSON 19 | SESSION 2

Apply It

Use what you learned to solve these problems.

5 Which expressions are equal to $\frac{(7^4 \cdot 7^8)}{7^2}$? Select all that apply.

- (A) 7^{10}
- (B) $7^4 \cdot 7^4 \cdot 7^2$
- C 7^{16}
- (D) $(7^2)^5$
- (E) $\frac{7^{15}}{7^5}$
- F 7^{14}

6 Write each side of the equation as a single power. Then write and solve an equation to find the value of *n*. Show your work.

$23^8 \cdot 23^n = (23^5)^3$

Possible work:

$23^{8+n} = 23^{5 \cdot 3}$

$23^{8+n} = 23^{15}$

$8 + n = 15$

$n = 7$

SOLUTION $n = 7$

7 Evaluate the expression $\left(\frac{(-2)^3}{-2}\right)^3$. Show your work.

Possible work:

$\left(\frac{(-2)^3}{(-2)^1}\right)^3 = ((-2)^{3-1})^3$

$= ((-2)^2)^3$

$= (-2)^6$

$= 64$

SOLUTION 64

456

CLOSE EXIT TICKET

7 Students' solutions should show an understanding of:

- how to evaluate a quotient of powers and a power of powers.
- how to determine the sign of the result when a negative base is raised to an exponent.

Error Alert If students simplify the expression inside the parentheses, $\frac{(-2)^3}{-2}$, as $(-2)^3$, then remind them that a number without an exponent has an unwritten exponent of 1, not 0. So, $\frac{(-2)^3}{-2} = \frac{(-2)^3}{(-2)^1} = (-2)^2$.

Practice Applying Properties for Powers with the Same Base

Problem Notes

Assign **Practice Applying Properties for Powers with the Same Base** as extra practice in class or as homework.

1. Students may apply the properties of exponents or rewrite each power using repeated multiplication and then simplify. ***Basic***

2. Students may set up and evaluate an expression as was done in the bacteria colony problem from the Try It. ***Medium***

3. Students should demonstrate understanding that you can only multiply powers by adding the exponents if the powers have the same base. ***Medium***

LESSON 19 | SESSION 2 Name:

Practice Applying Properties for Powers with the Same Base

➤ **Study the Example showing how to simplify an expression involving powers that have the same base. Then solve problems 1–5.**

Example

Rewrite the expression $\frac{(6^9 \cdot 6^4)}{6^{11}}$ as a single power.

$$\frac{(6^9 \cdot 6^4)}{6^{11}} = \frac{6^{9+4}}{6^{11}}$$
$$= \frac{6^{13}}{6^{11}}$$
$$= 6^{13-11}$$
$$= 6^2$$

1. Rewrite each expression as a single power.

   a. $(-4)^6(-4)^5$ $(-4)^{11}$

   b. $13^7 \cdot 13^2$ 13^9

   c. $\frac{9^{14}}{9^7}$ 9^7

   d. $\frac{(-24)^5}{-24}$ $(-24)^4$

2. A certain type of bacteria reproduces so that after x hours there are 15^x cells. What single power represents the size relationship between the cell population after 24 hours and the cell population after 8 hours? Show your work.

   Possible work:

   $$\frac{15^{24}}{15^8} = 15^{24-8} = 15^{16}$$

   SOLUTION 15^{16}

3. Cody tried to rewrite the expression $2^9 \cdot 3^4$ as a single power. His work is shown below. What was Cody's mistake?

   $$2^9 \cdot 3^4 = 6^{9+4}$$
   $$= 6^{13}$$

   Possible answer: The exponents cannot be added unless the bases are the same.

Vocabulary

power
an expression with a base and an exponent.

457

Fluency & Skills Practice

Applying Properties for Powers with the Same Base

In this activity, students rewrite expressions involving powers with the same base as a single power, and they evaluate such expressions. They also determine the value of x that makes a given equation true.

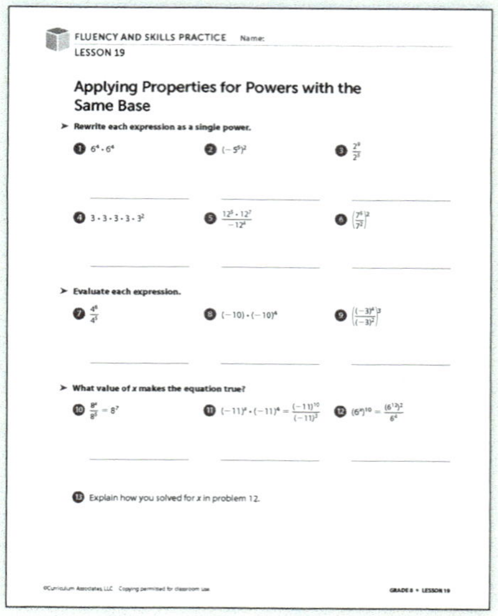

Additional Practice

4 **a.** Students may rewrite the 2 as 2^1 before simplifying the expression. ***Basic***

b. Students should understand that a negative base raised to an odd exponent yields a negative answer. ***Basic***

c. Students may feel more comfortable writing the numerator and denominator with repeated multiplication and replacing each $\frac{-11}{-11}$ with 1. ***Medium***

d. Students may multiply the exponents to rewrite the power of a power in the numerator, or they may write out the repeated multiplication. ***Medium***

e. Students may rewrite the expression inside the parentheses as a single power to get the power of a power $(10^5)^2$. ***Medium***

f. Students may rewrite the expression inside the parentheses as a single power to get the power of a power $(4^2)^2$. ***Medium***

5 **a.** Students may write each side of the equation as a single power of −5 and then set the exponents equal. ***Medium***

b. Students need to simplify a power of a power, a product of powers, and a quotient of powers to rewrite each side as a single power of 8. Then they can set the exponents equal. ***Challenge***

c. On the left side, students may rewrite $7^5 \cdot 7^n$ as 7^{5+n}. Then they can apply the distributive property to the exponents to rewrite $(7^{5+n})^4$ as 7^{20+4n}. ***Challenge***

LESSON 19 | SESSION 2

4 Evaluate each expression.

a. $2(2^5)$ 64

b. $(-10)^4(-10)^3$ −10,000,000

c. $\frac{(-11)^3(-11)^6}{(-11)^7}$ 121

d. $\frac{(3^2)^7}{3^{10}}$ 81

e. $(10^2 \cdot 10^3)^2$ 10,000,000,000

f. $\left(\frac{4^7}{4^5}\right)^2$ 256

5 What value of *n* makes the equation true? Show your work.

a. $\frac{(-5)^{11}}{(-5)^n} = (-5)^2 \cdot (-5)^1$

Possible work:

$11 - n = 2 + 1$

$11 - n = 3$

$n = 8$

SOLUTION $n = 8$

b. $8^9 \cdot 8^4 = \frac{(8^n)^3}{8^2}$

Possible work:

$9 + 4 = 3n - 2$

$15 = 3n$

$5 = n$

SOLUTION $n = 5$

c. $(7^5 \cdot 7^n)^4 = \left(\frac{7^{16}}{7^n}\right)^3$

Possible work:

$(7^{5+n})^4 = (7^{16-n})^3$

$4(5 + n) = 3(16 - n)$

$20 + 4n = 48 - 3n$

$7n = 28$

$n = 4$

SOLUTION $n = 4$

458

DIFFERENTIATION | ENGLISH LANGUAGE LEARNERS

Use with **Session 3** **Apply It**

Levels 1–3: Reading/Listening

Help students make sense of Apply It problem 7. Adapt **Three Reads** by reading the problem as students follow along.

For Read 1, use **Act It Out**. Bounce a rubber ball and show how it bounces. Draw a line to represent the drop height and arrows to represent the ball dropping and bouncing several times. Add labels: *drop height, bounce 1, bounce 2*, etc.

After Read 2, clarify *fraction* and *fourth bounce*. Ask: *What fraction is in the problem? What number does* fourth *refer to?* Have partners make a sketch or table to show what they are trying to find out.

After Read 3, ask: *What expression will you solve? What will x be?*

Levels 2–4: Reading/Listening

Help students make sense of Apply It problem 7 using **Three Reads**.

For Read 1, use **Act It Out**. Bounce a rubber ball several times. Have students discuss what happens to the height of the bounce over time. Ask students to sketch the problem context.

After Read 2, ask students to discuss *fraction* and ensure they understand that it refers to a part of a whole. Have students use their sketches to show what they are trying to find out.

After Read 3, have students label their sketches with the important quantities and relationships. Have partners discuss how they can solve the problem.

Levels 3–5: Reading/Listening

Have students make sense of Apply It problem 7 using **Three Reads**. Display the questions students will answer before each read. Then provide individual think time for students to sketch, model, or pre-write their ideas. Have students turn to talk with partners and then share their ideas with the class.

Encourage students to listen for understanding during discussions. Remind students that when something is unclear during a discussion, they can try to paraphrase and then check whether they understood the speaker's ideas. Suggest students use:

- *I think ____ said ____.*
- *Did I understand you correctly?*

Develop Applying Properties for Powers with the Same Exponent

Purpose

- **Develop** strategies for simplifying powers of products and powers of quotients.
- **Recognize** that the exponent is applied to each factor of a product and to both the dividend and divisor of a quotient.

START CONNECT TO PRIOR KNOWLEDGE

Always, Sometimes, Never

A The value of a power with a negative base is negative.

B A product of powers with the same base can be written as a single power.

C To divide powers with the same base, divide the bases and the exponents.

Solutions

A is sometimes true.

B is always true.

C is never true.

WHY? Support students' understanding of powers and properties of exponents.

DEVELOP ACADEMIC LANGUAGE

WHY? Support students as they justify their solutions using definitions, properties, and what they already know.

HOW? Review that one way to justify a solution is to use definitions, properties, and what you already know to support your thinking. As students explain their strategies, encourage them to draw on what they already know about calculating area and applying properties for the same exponent.

TRY IT SMP 1, 2, 4, 5, 6

Make Sense of the Problem

See ***Connect to Culture*** to support student engagement. Before students work on Try It, use **Three Reads** to help them make sense of the problem, giving students a chance to turn and talk with a partner before sharing the answers to each question. *What is the problem about?* [the area of two rangoli designs] *What are you trying to find out?* [how the two areas compare] *What are the important quantities and relationships?* [15 in., triple]

Develop Applying Properties for Powers with the Same Exponent

➤ **Read and try to solve the problem below.**

Rani makes a special design called a rangoli for Diwali. Her design is square with a side length of 15 in. Rani then makes a larger rangoli by tripling this side length. How many times as large is the area of the new rangoli than the area of the original rangoli?

TRY IT Math Toolkit grid paper, straightedges

Possible work:

SAMPLE A

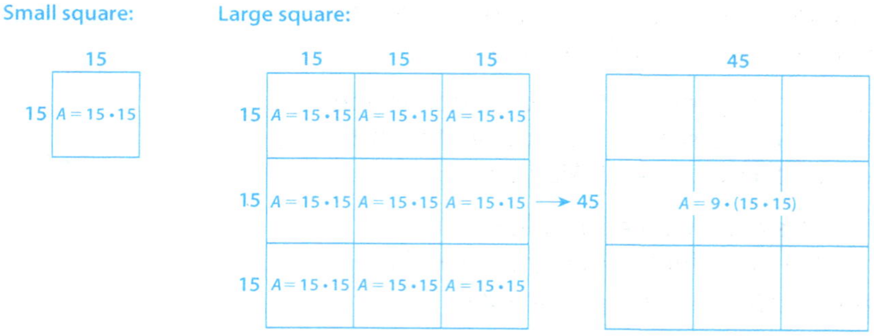

The area of the new rangoli is 9 times the area of the original rangoli.

SAMPLE B

Original rangoli:

side length = 15 in.; area = 15^2 in.^{2} = 225 in.^{2}

New rangoli:

side length = 15 • 3 = 45 in.; area = 45^2 in.^{2} = 2,025 in.^{2}

2,025 ÷ 225 = 9

The new rangoli is 9 times as large.

DISCUSS IT

Ask: What was your first step in solving the problem?

Share: The first thing I did was . . .

459

DISCUSS IT SMP 2, 3, 6

Support Partner Discussion

After students work on Try It, encourage them to respond to Discuss It with a partner. If students need support in getting started, prompt them to ask each other questions such as:

- *Why did you choose the strategy you used?*
- *Did you calculate the area of the original rangoli?*
- *Why might a sketch be helpful when solving this problem?*

Common Misconception Listen for students who think that tripling the side length triples the area. As students share their strategies, if a drawing of the original rangoli and the new rangoli is not presented, ask a student to make one. Students should see that the area of the new rangoli is 9 times the area of the original. Discuss that the new area can be found by calculating (3 • 15)(3 • 15), which is (3 • 3)(15 • 15), so the original area 15 • 15 is multiplied by 9.

Select and Sequence Student Strategies

Select 2–3 samples that represent the range of student thinking in your classroom. Here is one possible order for class discussion:

- a drawing that shows the new area is 9 times the original area
- (misconception) incorrect conclusion that tripling the side length triples the area
- original and new areas calculated and divided
- $\frac{(3 \cdot 15)(3 \cdot 15)}{(15 \cdot 15)}$ written and simplified
- factors of $(3 \cdot 15)(3 \cdot 15)$ rearranged as $3^2 \times 15^2$

Facilitate Whole Class Discussion

Call on students to share selected strategies. Remind students to use definitions, properties, and what they already know to support their strategy.

Guide students to **Compare and Connect** the representations. To emphasize a key idea, call on a couple of other students to rephrase so that it can be explained in more than one way.

ASK *What are some of the different ways these strategies compared the areas?*

LISTEN FOR Strategies may have used drawings, calculated each area and divided, or written an expression for the area of a square with side lengths $3 \cdot 15$ and then rearranged the factors.

Model It

If students presented these models, have students connect these models to those presented in class.

If no student presented at least one of these models, have students first analyze key features of the models, and then connect them to the models presented in class.

ASK *What is the main difference between the strategies used in the two models shown?*

LISTEN FOR The first Model It divides to compare the areas, and the second Model It writes the area of the new rangoli in terms of the area of the original.

For the fraction, prompt students to think about why the products of the factors are not calculated. Ask: *How is leaving the numerator and denominator as products of factors helpful?*

For the power expression, prompt students to notice how rearranging the factors is useful for understanding the relationship between the areas. Ask: *What do $3 \cdot 3$ and $15 \cdot 15$ represent in the context of this situation?*

➤ **Explore different ways to find the power of a product.**

Rani makes a special design called a rangoli for Diwali. Her design is square with a side length of 15 in. Rani then makes a larger rangoli by tripling this side length. How many times as large is the area of the new rangoli than the area of the original rangoli?

Model It

You can use a fraction to compare the areas.

original rangoli side length (in.): 15

new rangoli side length (in.): $3 \cdot 15$

$$\frac{\text{area of new rangoli (in.}^2\text{)}}{\text{area of original rangoli (in.}^2\text{)}} = \frac{(3 \cdot 15)(3 \cdot 15)}{15 \cdot 15} = \frac{(3 \cdot 3)(15 \cdot 15)}{15 \cdot 15} = \frac{3 \cdot 3}{1} \cdot \frac{15 \cdot 15}{15 \cdot 15}$$

Model It

You can use a power expression for the area of the new rangoli.

The area of the original rangoli is $15 \cdot 15$. Find the area of the new rangoli in terms of the area of the original rangoli.

area of new rangoli (in.^{2}): $(3 \cdot 15)^2$

$$(3 \cdot 15)^2 = (3 \cdot 15) \cdot (3 \cdot 15) = (3 \cdot 3) \cdot (15 \cdot 15)$$

DIFFERENTIATION | EXTEND

SMP 8

Deepen Understanding
Using Repeated Reasoning to Understand Powers of a Product

Prompt students to think about the relationship between the quantities in this situation.

ASK *How does the area of the new rangoli compare to the original?*

LISTEN FOR The area of the new rangoli is 9 times as large as the area of the original.

ASK *How would the area of the new rangoli compare to the original area if each side length was doubled?*

LISTEN FOR The area of the new rangoli would be 4 times as large as the original area.

ASK *How would the areas compare if each original side length was quadrupled?*

LISTEN FOR The area of the new rangoli would be 16 times as large as the original area.

ASK *What conjecture can you make about how the area of a square changes when each side length changes by the same factor?*

LISTEN FOR The area of the new square becomes larger than the original area by the square of the factor by which the side lengths are changed.

Develop Applying Properties for Powers with the Same Exponent

CONNECT IT

SMP 2, 4, 5, 6

Remind students that the quantities and the relationships between them are the same in each representation. Explain that they will now use those relationships to reason about how to find powers of products and powers of quotients.

Before students begin to record and expand on their work in Model It, tell them that problem 2 will prepare them to provide the explanations asked for in problem 3.

Monitor and Confirm Understanding 1

The area of the large rangoli is 9 times as large as the area of the small one.

Facilitate Whole Class Discussion

2 Look for understanding of how the idea that $(a \cdot b)^n = a^n \cdot b^n$ is used in reverse to solve problem 2c.

ASK *Explain how you figured out how to write $18^3 \cdot 35^3$ as a power of a product.*

LISTEN FOR There are 3 factors of 18 and 3 factors of 35. I can group the factors so there are three groups of $18 \cdot 35$, which is $(18 \cdot 35)^3$.

3 Look for understanding that just as the exponent is distributed to each factor in a power of a product, it is distributed to both the numerator and denominator of a power of a quotient.

ASK *Do you think the parentheses around the fraction are important? Explain.*

LISTEN FOR Yes; without the parentheses, only the numerator would be raised to the power.

4 **Reflect** Have all students focus on the strategies used to solve the Try It. If time allows, have students discuss their ideas with a partner.

CONNECT IT

➤ **Use the problem from the previous page to help you understand powers of products and powers of quotients.**

1 How many times as large is the area of the new rangoli than the area of the original rangoli?
The area of the new rangoli is 9 times as large.

2 **a.** The second **Model It** shows that $(3 \cdot 15)^2 = (3 \cdot 3) \cdot (15 \cdot 15)$. Rewrite the right side of the equation as a product of two powers. $3^2 \cdot 15^2$

b. How can you write an expression equivalent to $(a \cdot b)^n$ as a product of two powers? Explain why the expressions are equivalent.
$a^n \cdot b^n$; When written as repeated multiplication, both expressions have n factors of a and n factors of b.

c. The expression $(3 \cdot 15)^2$ is a power of a product. How can you write the expression $18^3 \cdot 35^3$ as the power of a product? $(18 \cdot 35)^3$

3 **a.** The side length of the original rangoli in feet is 1.25, or $\frac{5}{4}$. The area of this rangoli in square feet can be written as a power of a quotient.

$\left(\frac{5}{4}\right)^2 = \frac{5}{4} \cdot \frac{5}{4} = \frac{5 \cdot 5}{4 \cdot 4}$

Rewrite $\frac{5 \cdot 5}{4 \cdot 4}$ as a quotient of two powers. $\frac{5^2}{4^2}$

b. Write the expression $\left(\frac{5}{4}\right)^6$ as a quotient of two powers. Show that the expressions are equivalent by writing the powers as repeated multiplication.
$\frac{5^6}{4^6}$; $\left(\frac{5}{4}\right)^6 = \frac{5}{4} \cdot \frac{5}{4} \cdot \frac{5}{4} \cdot \frac{5}{4} \cdot \frac{5}{4} \cdot \frac{5}{4}$, and $\frac{5^6}{4^6} = \frac{5 \cdot 5 \cdot 5 \cdot 5 \cdot 5 \cdot 5}{4 \cdot 4 \cdot 4 \cdot 4 \cdot 4 \cdot 4}$

4 **Reflect** Think about all the models and strategies you have discussed today. Describe how one of them helped you better understand powers of products and powers of quotients.
Responses will vary. Check student responses.

461

DIFFERENTIATION | RETEACH or REINFORCE

Visual Model

Apply an exponent to a product.

If students are unsure about how to apply an exponent to a product, then use this activity to demonstrate the process.

- Display the expression $(4 \cdot 5)^3$.
- Ask: *What does the exponent 3 mean in this case?* [$(4 \cdot 5)$ is used as a factor 3 times.]
- Invite a student to rewrite the expression as repeated multiplication of $(4 \cdot 5)$.
- Ask: *Are the parentheses needed in this expression? Explain.* [No; You can multiply in any order, so they are not needed.] Rewrite the expression without parentheses.
- Ask: *Can you rearrange the factors so all the 4s are together and all the 5s are together? Why?* [Yes; You can use the commutative property to reorder the factors.]
- Invite a student to rewrite the expression.
- Ask: *How many factors of 4 are there?* [3] *How many factors of 5 are there?* [3]
- Ask: *How can you rewrite this new expression as the product of a power of 4 and a power of 5?* [$4^3 \cdot 5^3$]

Apply It

For all problems, encourage students to use a model to support their thinking. Allow some leeway in precision; some students may show more steps than others.

5 Students may write both 8^4 and 7^4 as repeated multiplication, rearrange the factors into groups of $8 \cdot 7$, write a power of this product, and then multiply $8 \cdot 7$ to get a base of 56.

6 $\frac{(12 \cdot 17^4)^5}{17^{10}} = \frac{12^5 \cdot 17^{20}}{17^{10}} = 12^5 \cdot 17^{10}$, so any expression equivalent to $12^5 \cdot 17^{10}$ is correct.

B is correct. $\left(\frac{12 \cdot 17^4}{17^2}\right)^5 = \frac{12^5 \cdot 17^{20}}{17^{10}} = 12^5 \cdot 17^{10}$

C is correct.

D is correct. $(12 \cdot 17^2)^5 = 12^5 \cdot 17^{10}$

A is not correct. Students who chose this answer likely applied the power of a product property to get $12^5 \cdot 17^{20}$, but then divided the exponents of 17, getting $20 \div 10 = 2$, instead of subtracting them to get $20 - 10 = 10$.

E is not correct. Students who chose this answer likely added the exponents 4 and 5, getting 17^9, instead of multiplying them to get 17^{20}.

F is not correct. Students who chose this answer likely did not raise 12 to the 5th power.

Apply It

➤ **Use what you learned to solve these problems.**

5 How can you write $8^4 \cdot 7^4$ as a single power? Show your work.

Possible work:

$8^4 \cdot 7^4 = (8 \cdot 7)^4$

$= 56^4$

SOLUTION 56^4

6 Which expressions are equal to $\frac{(12 \cdot 17^4)^5}{17^{10}}$? Select all that apply.

A $12^5 \cdot 17^2$

B $\left(\frac{12 \cdot 17^4}{17^2}\right)^5$

C $12^5 \cdot 17^{10}$

D $(12 \cdot 17^2)^5$

E $\frac{12^5 \cdot 17^9}{17^{10}}$

F $\frac{12 \cdot 17^{20}}{17^{10}}$

7 When a rubber ball is dropped on a particular surface, it bounces back to $\frac{8}{10}$ of its drop height. The ball's height after bounce x is $\left(\frac{8}{10}\right)^x$ times its drop height. What fraction of its drop height will the ball bounce up to after its fourth bounce? Show your work.

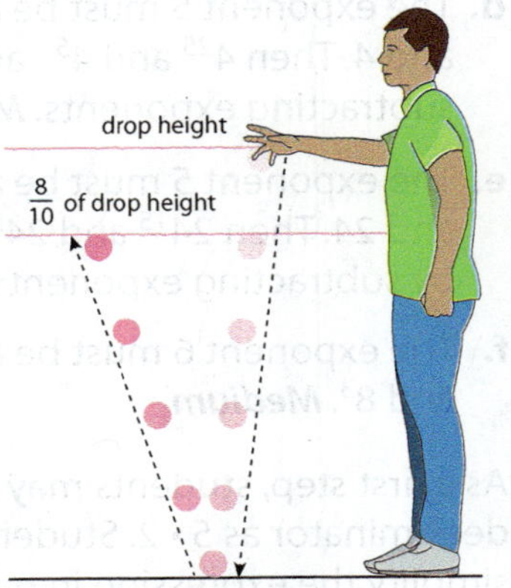

Possible work:

$\left(\frac{8}{10}\right)^4 = \frac{8^4}{10^4}$

$= \frac{4{,}096}{10{,}000}$

SOLUTION It will bounce up to $\frac{4{,}096}{10{,}000}$ of its drop height.

CLOSE EXIT TICKET

7 Students' solutions should show an understanding of:

- substituting 4 for x because x represents the number of times the ball bounces. There were 4 bounces.
- applying the power of a quotient property to simplify the expression.

Error Alert If students write $\frac{8^4}{10}$ and give the answer $\frac{4{,}096}{10}$, then have them look at the expression for bounce height in the problem. Point out that the entire fraction is raised to the exponent x, not just the numerator. You might also ask if it makes sense for the height after the fourth bounce to be more than 400 times the drop height.

Practice Applying Properties for Powers with the Same Exponent

Problem Notes

Assign **Practice Applying Properties for Powers with the Same Exponent** as extra practice in class or as homework.

1 **a.** The exponent 3 must be applied to both $(-10)^3$ and 6. Then, rewriting the power of a power gives the expression $(-10)^9 \cdot 6^3$. *Medium*

b. The exponent 3 must be applied to both 3^2 and 5. Then, rewriting the power of the power in the numerator gives $\frac{3^6}{5^3}$. *Medium*

2 **a.** *Basic*

b. *Basic*

c. The exponent 2 must be applied to both 32^5 and 3. Then 3^{10} and 3^2 can be combined by adding exponents. *Medium*

d. The exponent 5 must be applied to 4^5, 9^7, and 4. Then 4^{25} and 4^5 can be combined by subtracting exponents. *Medium*

e. The exponent 5 must be applied to 7^4, 24^3, and 24. Then 24^{15} and 24^5 can be combined by subtracting exponents. *Medium*

f. The exponent 6 must be applied to both 15^9 and 8^3. *Medium*

3 As a first step, students may rewrite the denominator as $5 \cdot 2$. Students can then simplify the expression in parentheses as $5^3 \cdot 2^3$ and apply the exponent 3 to the product to get $5^9 \cdot 2^9$, which is equal to 10^9, or 1,000,000,000. *Challenge*

LESSON 19 | SESSION 3 Name:

Practice Applying Properties for Powers with the Same Exponent

➤ **Study the Example showing how to evaluate an expression that involves powers with the same exponent. Then solve problems 1–6.**

Example

Evaluate the expression $\left(\frac{(-3)}{2^4}\right)^2$.

$$\left(\frac{(-3)}{2^4}\right)^2 = \frac{(-3)^2}{(2^4)^2} = \frac{9}{2^8} = \frac{9}{256}$$

1 Evaluate the expression.

a. $((-10)^3 \cdot 6)^3$ $-216{,}000{,}000{,}000$

b. $\left(\frac{3^2}{5}\right)^3$ $\frac{729}{125}$

2 Rewrite each expression as a product of two powers or a quotient of two powers.

a. $(6 \cdot 13)^8$ $6^8 \cdot 13^8$

b. $\left(\frac{9}{14}\right)^7$ $\frac{9^7}{14^7}$

c. $3^{10}(32^5 \cdot 3)^2$ $3^{12} \cdot 32^{10}$

d. $\left(\frac{4^5}{9^7 \cdot 4}\right)^5$ $\frac{4^{20}}{9^{35}}$

e. $\left(\frac{7^4 \cdot 24^3}{24}\right)^5$ $7^{20} \cdot 24^{10}$

f. $\left(\frac{15^9}{8^3}\right)^6$ $\frac{15^{54}}{8^{18}}$

3 What is the value of the expression $\left(\frac{5^4 \cdot 2^4}{10}\right)^3$? Show your work.

Possible work:

$$\left(\frac{5^4 \cdot 2^4}{10}\right)^3 = \left(\frac{10^4}{10}\right)^3 = (10^{4-1})^3 = (10^3)^3 = 10^9$$

SOLUTION 1,000,000,000

Vocabulary

power
an expression with a base and an exponent.

463

Fluency & Skills Practice

Applying Properties for Powers with the Same Exponent

In this activity, students rewrite expressions involving powers with the same exponent as a single power, and they rewrite such expressions as the product of two powers or the quotient of two powers.

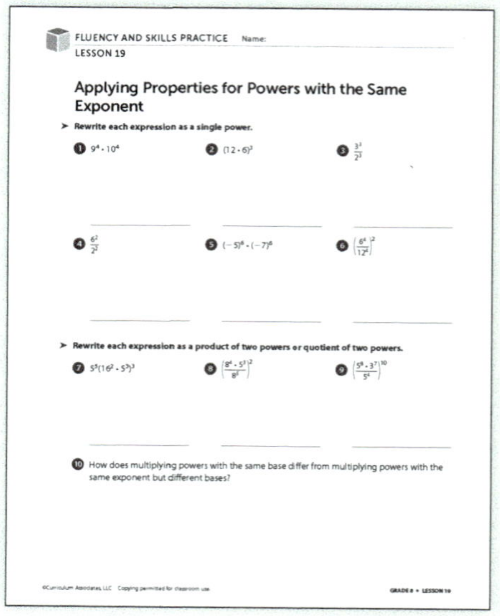

Additional Practice

4 **a.** Students may first use substitution to replace x with 3, rewriting the expression as $\left(\frac{3}{4}\right)^3$. They can rewrite this as $\frac{3^3}{4^3}$ and evaluate to get $\frac{27}{64}$. ***Medium***

b. Students may first use substitution to replace x with 3, rewriting the expression as $\left(\frac{2}{3}\right)^3$. They can rewrite this as $\frac{2^3}{3^3}$ and evaluate to get $\frac{8}{27}$. ***Medium***

c. Students may first use substitution to replace x with 3, rewriting the expression as $\left(\frac{3}{10}\right)^3$. They can rewrite this as $\frac{3^3}{10^3}$ and evaluate to get $\frac{27}{1{,}000}$. ***Medium***

5 Students should recall that the volume of a cube with edge length s is s^3. So the tripled side length, $3 \cdot 25$, is being raised to a power of 3. By rewriting $(3 \cdot 25)^3$ as $3^3 \cdot 25^3$, students can see that the volume of the sculpture is 3^3, or 27, times as large as the volume of the model. ***Medium***

6 After rewriting, students may recognize that the numerators are equal, so the denominators must be equal as well. Because both denominators are powers of 7, they will be equal if the exponents are equal. ***Challenge***

LESSON 19 | SESSION 3

4 When a ball is dropped, the height it reaches after it bounces is a fraction of its original drop height. The expression shown for each ball gives the fraction of the drop height that the ball reaches after x bounces. What fraction of its original height does each ball bounce up to after the third bounce?

a. basketball: $\left(\frac{3}{4}\right)^x$ $\frac{27}{64}$

b. tennis ball: $\left(\frac{2}{3}\right)^x$ $\frac{8}{27}$

c. softball: $\left(\frac{3}{10}\right)^x$ $\frac{27}{1{,}000}$

5 Moses is creating a large cube sculpture for a city park. He first makes a smaller cube to use as a rough model of his sculpture. The edge lengths of the model are each 25 in. The edge lengths of the sculpture will be 3 times the model's edge lengths. How many times as large is the volume of the sculpture than the volume of the model? Show your work.

Possible work: $\frac{(3 \cdot 25)^3}{25^3} = \frac{3^3 \cdot 25^3}{25^3}$

$= 3^3$

$= 27$

SOLUTION The volume of the sculpture is 27 times as large as that of the model.

6 What value of n makes the equation true? Show your work.

$$\left(\frac{19^8}{7^n}\right)^4 = \left(\frac{19^4}{7^3}\right)^8$$

Possible work:

$\frac{19^{32}}{7^{4n}} = \frac{19^{32}}{7^{24}}$

$4n = 24$

$n = 6$

SOLUTION $n = 6$

464

DIFFERENTIATION | ENGLISH LANGUAGE LEARNERS

Use with Session 4 **Apply It**

Levels 1–3: Writing/Speaking

Help students discuss and write responses to Apply It problem 3. Review that *equivalent expressions* have the same value. Have students identify the equivalent expression and share their solution strategies. Record models and statements for students to reference later on.

Next, say: *Caitlin chose C. Is C the correct answer? How do you know?* Prompt students to refer to the recorded models and statements to identify possible mistakes. Help partners write explanations using these sentence frames:

- *I think Caitlin made a mistake in the ____ step.*
- *She might have ____. She should have ____.*

Levels 2–4: Writing/Speaking

Have partners read Apply It problem 3 and discuss solution strategies. Provide time for students to identify the equivalent expression. Then ask students to turn to partners and take turns explaining strategies. Encourage students to use words like *first*, *next*, and *because* to help others follow their explanations. Then, have partners discuss reasons why Caitlin might have gotten her answer before constructing a written explanation. Ask students to refer to their models to help explain possible mistakes and to suggest strategies to correct it:

- *Caitlin might have made a mistake by ____.*
- *She should have ____.*

Call on volunteers to share their explanations.

Levels 3–5: Writing/Speaking

Have partners read Apply It problem 3 and discuss solution strategies. Provide time for students to identify the equivalent expression and then turn to partners to compare solution strategies. Ask partners to discuss reasons someone could have chosen C. Prompt students to use properties of exponents to identify when they think someone might have made an error and to justify their own strategies.

Have students construct their written responses by identifying Caitlin's possible mistake and using what they know about the properties of exponents to suggest corrections. Encourage students to reread their responses and revise if needed.

Refine Applying Exponent Properties for Positive Integer Exponents

Purpose

- **Refine** strategies for simplifying expressions with positive integer exponents by using properties of exponents.
- **Refine** understanding of how the properties work by rewriting powers as products of repeated factors.

START CHECK FOR UNDERSTANDING

Evaluate the expression.

$\left(\frac{(-2)}{3^3}\right)^2$

Solution

$\frac{4}{729}$

WHY? Confirm students' understanding of simplifying expressions with positive integer exponents using properties of exponents, identifying common errors to address as needed.

MONITOR & GUIDE

Before students begin to work, use their responses to the **Start** to determine those who will benefit from additional support. Use the **Error Analysis** table below to guide remediation.

Have all students complete the Example and problems 1–3, using Consider This and Pair/Share as appropriate. Observe and monitor their reasoning and guide or redirect students as needed.

Refine Applying Exponent Properties for Positive Integer Exponents

➤ **Complete the Example below. Then solve problems 1–10.**

Example

Write the expression $\frac{6^2 \cdot 24^9}{4^9}$ as a single power.

Look at how you could combine powers with the same exponent.

$\frac{6^2 \cdot 24^9}{4^9} = 6^2 \cdot \left(\frac{24}{4}\right)^9$

$= 6^2 \cdot 6^9$

$= 6^{2+9}$

SOLUTION 6^{11}

CONSIDER THIS . . . How are the bases of the powers in the numerator related to the base of the power in the denominator?

PAIR/SHARE What is the value of the expression?

Apply It

1 What is the value of n? Show your work.

$22^n \cdot 22^6 = (22^8)^3$

Possible work:

$22^{n+6} = 22^{8 \cdot 3}$

$n + 6 = 8 \cdot 3$

$n + 6 = 24$

$n = 18$

SOLUTION $n = 18$

CONSIDER THIS . . . How can you rewrite each side of the equation as a single power?

PAIR/SHARE Suppose the left side of the equation was $(22^n \cdot 22)^6$. How would the solution change?

START ERROR ANALYSIS

If the error is . . .	Students may . . .	To support understanding . . .
$-\frac{4}{729}$	have simplified the numerator as -2^2 instead of $(-2)^2$.	Prompt students to pay attention to the use of parentheses, especially with negative bases. Ask: *How do you evaluate -2^2 and $(-2)^2$?* [The power -2^2 is the opposite of the product of 2 factors of 2, so $-2^2 = -4$. The power $(-2)^2$ is the product of 2 factors of -2, so $(-2)^2 = 4$.]
$\frac{4}{243}$	have added the exponents when raising 3^3 to the second power.	Ask students to write each power as repeated multiplication of the same factor to help them evaluate the expression.
$-\frac{2}{729}$	have only distributed the exponent of 2 to the denominator.	Remind students that the exponent of 2 should be *distributed* to the numerator AND denominator of the expression.

Example

Guide students in understanding the Example. Ask:

- *What does it mean for an expression to be written as a single power?*
- *Which powers in the numerator and denominator have the same exponent?*
- *How can you rewrite the quotient of powers that have the same exponent as a single power?*

Help all students focus on the Example and responses to the questions by having members of the class paraphrase or summarize the answers to see if they understand. Have them check with the speaker to see if they got the ideas right.

Look for understanding that because the base of 24 in the numerator and the base of 4 in the denominator have the same exponent, these powers can be combined into a single power.

Apply It

1 Students may add exponents to write $22^n \cdot 22^6$ as a single power and multiply exponents to write $(22^8)^3$ as a single power. Once both sides of the equation are powers of 22, students can set the exponents equal and solve. Students may use substitution to check their solution. *DOK 2*

2 Students may first apply the exponent 2 to both the numerator and denominator and then rewrite the power of products in the resulting numerator as a product of powers. Then they may subtract the exponents of powers that have the same base in the numerator and denominator. *DOK 2*

3 **D is correct.** Apply the exponent of 3 to the powers 15^4 and 7^6: $\frac{(15^4 \cdot 7^6)^3}{15^2} = \frac{(15^{4 \cdot 3} \cdot 7^{6 \cdot 3})}{15^2} = \frac{(15^{12} \cdot 7^{18})}{15^2}$. Subtract the exponents of the base of 15 in the numerator and denominator: $\frac{(15^{12} \cdot 7^{18})}{15^2} = 15^{12-2} \cdot 7^{18} = 15^{10} \cdot 7^{18}$.

A is not correct. This answer would result if the exponent 3 were applied only to 7^6 and the exponents were added instead of multiplied.

B is not correct. This answer would result if the exponent 3 was not applied to the power 15^4.

C is not correct. This answer would result if the exponent 3 were added to the exponents 4 and 6 instead of being multiplied by them.

DOK 3

LESSON 19 | SESSION 4

2 Rewrite $\left(\frac{5^7(-3)^4}{5^6}\right)^2$ as a product of two powers. Show your work.

Possible work:

$$\left(\frac{5^7(-3)^4}{5^6}\right)^2 = (5^{7-6}(-3)^4)^2$$
$$= (5(-3)^4)^2$$
$$= 5^2(-3)^{4 \cdot 2}$$
$$= 5^2(-3)^8$$

SOLUTION $5^2(-3)^8$

CONSIDER THIS . . . How can you combine powers that have the same base?

PAIR/SHARE What is the value of the expression inside the large parentheses?

3 Which expression is equivalent to $\frac{(15^4 \cdot 7^6)^3}{15^2}$?

A $15^2 \cdot 7^9$

B $15^2 \cdot 7^{18}$

C $15^5 \cdot 7^9$

Ⓓ $15^{10} \cdot 7^{18}$

Caitlin chose C as the correct answer. How might she have gotten that answer?

Possible answer: Caitlin may have added the exponent of 3 to the other exponents in the numerator. She should have multiplied instead.

CONSIDER THIS . . . Which exponents do you need to work with first?

PAIR/SHARE Think of another expression involving powers that is equivalent to the expression in the problem.

466

GROUP & DIFFERENTIATE

Identify groupings for differentiation based on the **Start** and problems 1–3. A recommended sequence of activities for each group is suggested below. Use the resources on the next page to differentiate and close the lesson.

Approaching Proficiency

- **RETEACH** Visual Model
- **REINFORCE** Problems 4, 7, 9

Meeting Proficiency

- **REINFORCE** Problems 4–9

Extending Beyond Proficiency

- **REINFORCE** Problems 4–9
- **EXTEND** Challenge

Have all students complete the **Close: Exit Ticket.**

Resources for Differentiation are found on the next page.

Refine Applying Exponent Properties for Positive Integer Exponents

Apply It

4 **B, D, and E are correct.**

$\frac{8^5 \cdot 10^{15}}{10^9 \cdot 8^2} = 8^{5-2} \cdot 10^{15-9} = 8^3 \cdot 10^6$

$8 \cdot 10^4 \cdot (8 \cdot 10)^2 = 8^{1+2} \cdot 10^{4+2} = 8^3 \cdot 10^6$

$\left(\frac{8 \cdot 10^5}{10^3}\right)^3 = 8^3 \cdot 10^{3(5-3)} = 8^3 \cdot 10^6$

A is not correct. This answer is equal to $8^3 \cdot 10^9$.

C is not correct. This answer is equal to $8^4 \cdot 10^6$.

DOK 2

5 **a.** Multiply exponents n and 2. Set the exponents equal to each other. So, $n = 4$.

b. If $n = 4$, the left side is $(-5)^3 \cdot (-5)^4$, or $(-5)^7$.

c. If $n = 4$, the left side is equal to 19^3 and the right side is equal to 19^4.

d. If $n = 4$, the left side is equal to $(3 \cdot 4)^2$, which is 12^2, or 144.

e. Rewriting the left side gives $\frac{4}{25}$. If $n = 4$, the right side is also $\frac{4}{25}$.

DOK 2

6 The expression is equivalent to $(-99)^{2n}$. Because $2n$ is an even number, the expression is equal to the product of an even number of negative factors, so it must be positive. *DOK 3*

7 Add the exponents in the numerator and multiply the exponents in the denominator. Then, subtract the exponents of the resulting powers. *DOK 1*

---

4 Which expressions are equivalent to $8^3 10^6$? Select all that apply.

A $(8 \cdot 10^3)^3$

(B) $\frac{8^5 \cdot 10^{15}}{10^9 \cdot 8^2}$

C $\frac{(8 \cdot 10)^6}{8^2}$

(D) $8 \cdot 10^4 \cdot (8 \cdot 10)^2$

(E) $\left(\frac{8 \cdot 10^5}{10^3}\right)^3$

5 Tell whether $n = 4$ makes the equation true.

	Yes	No
a. $(7^n)^2 = 7^8$	●	○
b. $(-5)^3 \cdot (-5)^n = (-5)^{12}$	○	●
c. $\frac{19^4}{19} = 19^n$	○	●
d. $(3n)^2 = 144$	●	○
e. $\left(-\frac{2}{5}\right)^2 = \frac{n}{25}$	●	○

6 Explain why the number $(-99)^n(-99)^n$ is positive.

Possible answer: The expression equals $(-99)^{2n}$, which can be rewritten as $((-99)^2)^n$. The power $(-99)^2$ is positive because the product of two negative numbers is positive. A positive number raised to any power must be positive, so $((-99)^2)^n$ is positive.

7 What is the value of the expression $\frac{5^{18} \cdot 5^6}{(5^{10})^2}$? Show your work.

Possible work: $\frac{5^{18+6}}{5^{10 \cdot 2}} = \frac{5^{24}}{5^{20}}$

$= 5^4$

SOLUTION 625

467

DIFFERENTIATION

RETEACH

Visual Model

Write expressions equivalent to a given expression that include exponents.

Students approaching proficiency with properties of exponents will benefit from writing expressions equivalent to a given expression that includes exponents.

- Display the expression $3^4 \cdot 5^6$.
- Display the expression $3 \cdot 3 \cdot 3 \cdot 3 \cdot 5 \cdot 5 \cdot 5 \cdot 5 \cdot 5 \cdot 5$ and ask students to explain whether it is equivalent to $3^4 \cdot 5^6$.
- Display the template $\frac{3^{\square}}{3^{\square}} \cdot \frac{5^{\square}}{5^{\square}}$ and tell students the goal is to write an expression equivalent to $3^4 \cdot 5^6$.
- Ask: *How is the template similar to the final expression? How is it different?* [It is the same because it has factors of 3 multiplied by factors of 5. It is different because the factor of 3 and 5 is written as a quotient in the template.]
- Ask: *How can quotients of powers with the same base be simplified?* [Subtract the exponents.]
- Explain that to use the template, substitute a number for the exponents in the numerator and denominator of each fraction. The difference of each pair of exponents should equal the exponents in the original expression.
- Ask: *What numbers could be substituted into the quotients to get a result of $3^4 \cdot 5^6$?* [Possible answer: for the base of 3: 7 and 3; for the base of 5: 8 and 2]
- Have students work in pairs to write their own expression on the board.
- Repeat this process using the following templates: $3^{\square} \cdot 3^{\square} \cdot 5^{\square} \cdot 5^{\square}$; $(3^{\square})^{\square} \cdot (5^{\square})^{\square}$.

Refine

8 See ***Connect to Culture*** to support student engagement. Doubling the edge length makes the volume 2^3, or 8, times as great, so Paulo needs 8 times as much clay, or 8 oz. ***DOK 3***

9 Students may first add the exponents inside the parentheses to get 9^4. Then multiply exponents to get 9^{20}, or 20 factors of 9. ***DOK 1***

CLOSE EXIT TICKET

10 **Math Journal** Look for understanding of how to rewrite a power of a power by multiplying the exponents and how to rewrite the quotient of powers with the same base by subtracting the exponents.

Error Alert If students write 1^3 as the single power in problem 10b, then they correctly found the exponent but incorrectly divided the bases, instead of keeping 20 as the base. Have these students write the numerator and denominator as products of repeated factors of 20.

End of Lesson Checklist

INTERACTIVE GLOSSARY Support students by suggesting they discuss the everyday meaning of *related* with a partner. Ask them to connect this to what they mean when they talk about how bases of powers are related.

SELF CHECK Have students review and check off any new skills on the Unit 5 Opener.

LESSON 19 | SESSION 4

8 Paulo used clay to make the cube shown. He wants to make a larger cube with an edge length that is twice as long. How many ounces of clay does he need to make this larger cube? Show your work.

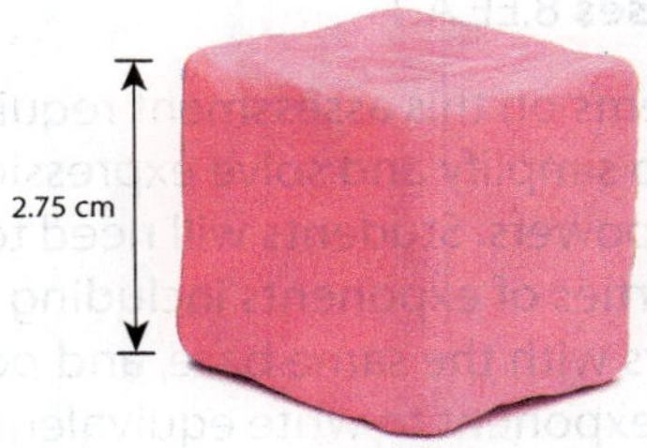

1 ounce of clay

Possible work:

The original cube has volume 2.75^3 cm^3. The larger cube has volume $(2 \cdot 2.75)^3$, or $2^3 \cdot 2.75^3$, cm^3. This is 2^3, or 8, times the volume of the original cube. The original cube uses 1 oz of clay, so the larger cube uses 8 times that, or 8 oz.

SOLUTION He needs 8 oz of clay.

9 The expression $(9^3 \cdot 9)^5$ written as repeated multiplication has 20 factors of 9.

10 **Math Journal** Rewrite each expression as a single power. Use repeated factors to explain your answers.

a. $(38^5)^2$

38^{10}; Possible explanation: The expression 38^5 can be written as $38 \cdot 38 \cdot 38 \cdot 38 \cdot 38$. When this product is squared, or multiplied by itself, it can be written as $(38 \cdot 38 \cdot 38 \cdot 38 \cdot 38)(38 \cdot 38 \cdot 38 \cdot 38 \cdot 38)$. The product of 10 factors of 38 can be written as 38^{10}.

b. $\frac{20^6}{20^3}$

20^3; Possible explanation: The expression $\frac{20^6}{20^3}$ can be written as $\frac{20 \cdot 20 \cdot 20 \cdot 20 \cdot 20 \cdot 20}{20 \cdot 20 \cdot 20}$, or $\frac{20 \cdot 20 \cdot 20}{20 \cdot 20 \cdot 20} \cdot 20 \cdot 20 \cdot 20$. The fraction $\frac{20 \cdot 20 \cdot 20}{20 \cdot 20 \cdot 20}$ equals 1, so the expression equals the product of three factors of 20, or 20^3.

End of Lesson Checklist

- ☐ **INTERACTIVE GLOSSARY** Write a new entry for *related*. Explain why you might want to know how bases are *related* when rewriting an expression involving powers.
- ☐ **SELF CHECK** Go back to the Unit 5 Opener and see what you can check off.

468

REINFORCE

Problems 4–9

Evaluate expressions using properties of exponents.

Students meeting proficiency will benefit from additional work with simplifying expressions with positive integer exponents using properties of exponents by solving problems in a variety of formats.

- Have students work on their own or with a partner to solve the problems.
- Encourage students to show their work.

EXTEND

Challenge

Evaluate complex expressions.

Students extending beyond proficiency will benefit from solving for an unknown exponent by using properties of exponents.

- Have students work with a partner to solve this problem: *Find the value of x in* $3^4 = 9^x$.
- If students need help getting started, suggest they write 9 as a power using 3 as a base.
- Repeat, this time using the equations $125^2 = 5^x$ and $4^6 = 8^x$.

PERSONALIZE

i-Ready

Provide students with opportunities to work on their personalized instruction path with *i-Ready* Online Instruction to:

- fill prerequisite gaps.
- build up grade-level skills.

Lesson Quiz

TESTED SKILLS

Assesses 8.EE.A.1

Problems on this assessment require students to be able to simplify and solve expressions with two or more powers. Students will need to recognize the properties of exponents including power of a power, powers with the same base, and powers with the same exponent to write equivalent expressions. They will apply properties of exponents to find a value of an exponent that makes an equation true. They will also apply properties of exponents to find the numeric value of an expression with more than one power. Students will also need to be familiar with evaluating a power, solving one-variable equations, and repeated multiplication.

Alternately, teachers may assign the **Digital Comprehension Check** online to assess student understanding of this material.

Error Alert Errors may result if students:

- add exponents instead of subtract when applying powers with the same base property to simplify an expression with a denominator.
- multiply the exponents instead of add when applying powers with the same base property to simplify an expression.
- multiply only one exponent inside parentheses by the exponent outside the parentheses when applying the power of a power property.

Problem Notes

1. Students could solve the problem by applying properties of exponents.

   (2 points)

   DOK 2 | 8.EE.A.1

2. Students could recognize that the powers have the same base, apply the properties of exponents, and then simplify both sides of the equation to solve for n.

   (2 points)

   DOK 1 | 8.EE.A.1

LESSON 19 • QUIZ Name: ____________

➤ **Solve the problems.**

1 Sabrina uses 2 oz of clay to make the cube shown. She wants to make a larger cube with an edge length that is twice as long. How many ounces of clay does she need to make the larger cube? Show your work. *(2 points)*

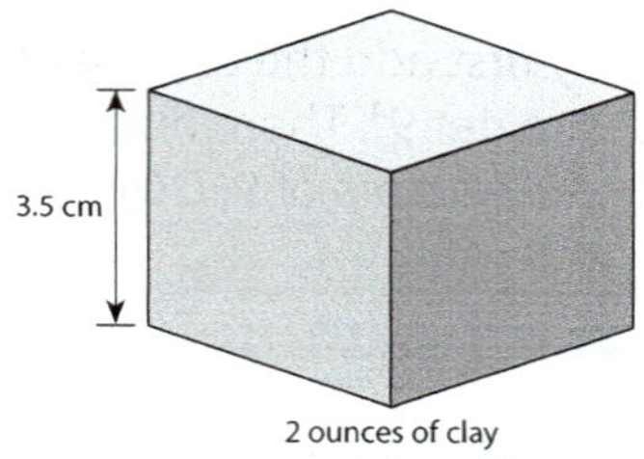

Possible student work: 2 ounces of clay makes a cube with a volume of $(3.5)^3$ cm^3. The volume of the larger cube is $(2 \cdot 3.5)^3$ cm^3.

$x = (2 \cdot 3.5)^3$
$= 2^3 \cdot 3.5^3$
$= 8 \cdot 3.5^3$

$2 \cdot 8 = 16$ ounces

SOLUTION 16 ounces

2 What value of n makes the equation true? Show your work. *(2 points)*

$$\frac{(-4)^{10}}{(-4)^n} = (-4)^2 \cdot (-4)^2$$

Possible student work:

$10 - n = 2 + 2$
$10 - n = 4$
$n = 6$

SOLUTION 6

Short Response Scoring Rubric

Points	Expectations
2	Response has the correct solution(s) and includes well-organized, clear, and concise work demonstrating thorough understanding of mathematical concepts and/or procedures.
1	Response contains mostly correct solution(s) and shows partial understanding of mathematical concepts and/or procedures.
0	Response shows no attempt at finding a solution and no effort to demonstrate an understanding of mathematical concepts and/or procedures.

3 (2 points)

DOK 1 | 8.EE.A.1

4 **B is correct.** Students could solve the problem by applying the power of a power property of exponents to simplify the numerator and then apply powers with the same base property of exponents to find the equivalent expression.

A is not correct. This answer represents ignoring the denominator 18^3 when simplifying the expression.

C is not correct. This answer represents adding the exponent in 18^7 to 3 and adding the exponent in 5^9 to 3 instead of applying the power of a power property of exponents.

D is not correct. This answer represents forgetting to apply the power of a power property of exponents by subtracting 3 from the exponent in 18^7 and also adding the exponent in 5^9 to 3.

(1 point)

DOK 1 | 8.EE.A.1

5 (1 point)

DOK 1 | 8.EE.A.1

LESSON 19 • QUIZ Name:

3 What value of n makes the equation true? Show your work. *(2 points)*

$$7^7 \cdot 7^5 = \frac{(7^n)^4}{7^4}$$

Possible student work:

$7^7 \cdot 7^5 = \frac{7^{4n}}{7^4}$

$7^{7+5} = 7^{4n-4}$

$7 + 5 = 4n - 4$

$16 = 4n$

$4 = n$

SOLUTION 4

4 Which expression is equivalent to $\frac{(18^7 \cdot 5^9)^3}{18^3}$? *(1 point)*

A $18^{21} \cdot 5^{27}$

(B) $18^{18} \cdot 5^{27}$

C $18^{10} \cdot 5^{12}$

D $18^4 \cdot 5^{12}$

5 What is the value of the expression $\frac{7^{12} \cdot 7^9}{(7^6)^3}$? Record your answer on the grid. Then fill in the bubbles. *(1 point)*

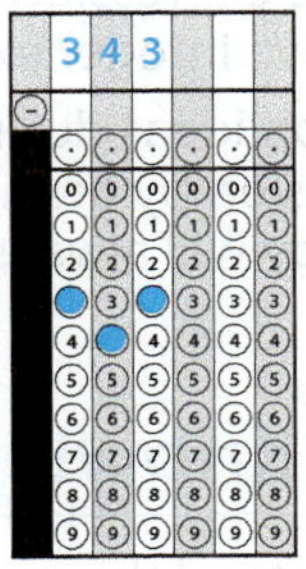

DIFFERENTIATION

RETEACH Tools for Instruction

Students who require additional support for prerequisite or on-level skills will benefit from activities that provide targeted skills instruction.

GRADE 8

- **Lesson 19** Exponent Properties

REINFORCE Math Center Activity

Students who require practice to reinforce concepts and skills and deepen understanding will benefit from small group collaborative games and activities (available in on-level, below-level, and above-level versions).

GRADE 8

- **Lesson 19** Equivalent Exponential Expressions

EXTEND Enrichment Activity

Students who have achieved proficiency with concepts and skills and are ready for additional challenges will benefit from group collaborative games and activities that extend understanding.

GRADE 8

- **Lesson 19** Power-ful Stuff

LESSON 20

Overview | Apply Exponent Properties for All Integer Exponents

MATH FOCUS

Focus Standard

8.EE.A.1 Know and apply the properties of integer exponents to generate equivalent numerical expressions.

STANDARDS FOR MATHEMATICAL PRACTICE (SMP)

SMP 1, 2, 3, 4, 5, and 6 are integrated into the Try-Discuss-Connect routine.*

This lesson provides additional support for:

1 Make sense of problems and persevere in solving them.

7 Look for and make use of structure.

8 Look for and express regularity in repeated reasoning.

* See page 1o to learn how every lesson includes these SMP.

Objectives

Content Objectives

- Understand that $a^0 = 1$ and be able to explain why this is true.
- Understand that $a^{-n} = \frac{1}{a^n}$ for integer values of n and be able to explain why this is true.
- Apply the properties of exponents to simplify and rewrite numerical expressions with zero and negative integer exponents.

Language Objectives

- Explain why $a^0 = 1$ is true by referring to tables and models to support reasoning.
- Connect the expressions a^{-n} and $\frac{1}{a^n}$ by showing how each expression represents the solution to a word problem.
- Understand the lesson vocabulary and use it to explain how the properties of exponents can be used to simplify and rewrite expressions with zero and negative integer exponents.
- Build on ideas during partner and class discussion by giving reasons why a strategy will always or sometimes work.

Prior Knowledge

- Understand the properties of exponents for positive integer exponents.
- Work fluently to simplify and rewrite numerical expressions with positive integer exponents.

Vocabulary

Math Vocabulary

There is no new vocabulary. Review the following key terms.

evaluate to find the value of an expression.

exponent in a power, the number that shows how many times the base is used as a factor.

power an expression with a base and an exponent.

reciprocal for any nonzero number a, the reciprocal is $\frac{1}{a}$. The reciprocal of any fraction $\frac{a}{b}$ is $\frac{b}{a}$. Zero does not have a reciprocal. The reciprocal of a number is also called the *multiplicative inverse* of that number.

Academic Vocabulary

set equal to to write an equation by connecting two expressions with an equal sign.

simplify to make easier to work with or understand.

Learning Progression

In Grade 5, students multiplied and divided by powers of 10.

In Grade 6, students evaluated expressions involving whole-number exponents.

Earlier in Grade 8, students learned the properties of exponents for positive integer exponents and used those properties to generate equivalent numerical expressions.

➤

In this lesson, students learn the meanings of zero and negative integer exponents and apply the properties of exponents to simplify and rewrite numerical expressions involving zero and negative integer exponents.

➤

Later in Grade 8, students will use both positive and negative integer exponents to write and compare numbers in scientific notation. They will also perform operations with numbers in scientific notation.

Pacing Guide

Items marked with [icon] are available on the Teacher Toolbox.

	MATERIALS	DIFFERENTIATION
SESSION 1 **Explore** Exponent Properties for Zero Exponents (35–50 min)		
• **Start** (5 min) • **Try It** (5–10 min) • **Discuss It** (10–15 min) • **Connect It** (10–15 min) • **Close: Exit Ticket** (5 min) **Additional Practice** (pages 473–474)	Presentation Slides	**PREPARE** Interactive Tutorial **RETEACH or REINFORCE** Visual Model
SESSION 2 **Develop** Applying Properties of Negative Exponents (45–60 min)		
• **Start** (5 min) • **Try It** (10–15 min) • **Discuss It** (10–15 min) • **Connect It** (15–20 min) • **Close: Exit Ticket** (5 min) **Additional Practice** (pages 479–480)	Presentation Slides	**RETEACH or REINFORCE** Visual Model **Materials** For display: completed table from Session 1 Connect It problem 1 with three empty rows added **REINFORCE** Fluency & Skills Practice **EXTEND** Deepen Understanding
SESSION 3 **Develop** Applying Properties of Integer Exponents (45–60 min)		
• **Start** (5 min) • **Try It** (10–15 min) • **Discuss It** (10–15 min) • **Connect It** (15–20 min) • **Close: Exit Ticket** (5 min) **Additional Practice** (pages 485–486)	Presentation Slides	**RETEACH or REINFORCE** Visual Model **Materials** For each student: 2 sticky notes **REINFORCE** Fluency & Skills Practice **EXTEND** Deepen Understanding
SESSION 4 **Refine** Applying Exponent Properties for All Integer Exponents (45–60 min)		
• **Start** (5 min) • **Monitor & Guide** (15–20 min) • **Group & Differentiate** (20–30 min) • **Close: Exit Ticket** (5 min)	Presentation Slides	**RETEACH** Visual Model **REINFORCE** Problems 4–8 **EXTEND** Challenge **PERSONALIZE** i-Ready
Lesson 20 Quiz or **Digital Comprehension Check**		**RETEACH** Tools for Instruction **REINFORCE** Math Center Activity **EXTEND** Enrichment Activity

Overview | Apply Exponent Properties for All Integer Exponents

Connect to Culture

➤ **Use these activities to connect with and leverage the diverse backgrounds and experiences of all students. Engage students in sharing what they know about contexts before you add the information given here.**

SESSION 1 ■ □ □ □

Try It Microalgae are small organisms found in many water sources. They are too small to be seen with the unaided human eye. Microalgae are beneficial to the food chain for fish and other water creatures. The food chain extends from these microalgae through the fish to humans. When humans eat fish, the nutritional benefits these organisms provide, such as proteins, carbohydrates, and lipids, are ingested. Some microalgae produce fuel that can be used to power cars or even airplanes. Ask students to share any facts they know about microalgae from their studies in science.

SESSION 2 ■ ■ □ □

Try It Ask students whether they have ordered dim sum from a Chinese restaurant. If so, have them share the characteristics of this type of food with the class. Dim sum is a Cantonese word that refers to small bits of food that were traditionally served in baskets or small plates. In China, dim sum is served with tea and is enjoyed with family and friends. In the United States, dim sum is a style of eating in which restaurant patrons choose small plates of food from an assortment that is presented on a cart. Most often, the food is accompanied by hot tea.

SESSION 4 ■ ■ ■ ■

Apply It **Problem 8** Ask students if they know what it means for a car's value to *depreciate*. Many experts say that as soon as a new car is driven off the lot at the dealership, it loses about 10% of its value. Then, in the first year, it may lose another 15–25% of its value. This is due to the wear and tear on the engine parts of the car as well as nicks and scratches on the body of the car. Depreciated, or decreased, values can be estimated by online calculators. The formulas used to make these calculations involve the age, mileage, and physical appearance of the car.

Connect to Family and Community

➤ **After the Explore session, have students use the Family Letter to let their families know what they are learning and to encourage family involvement.**

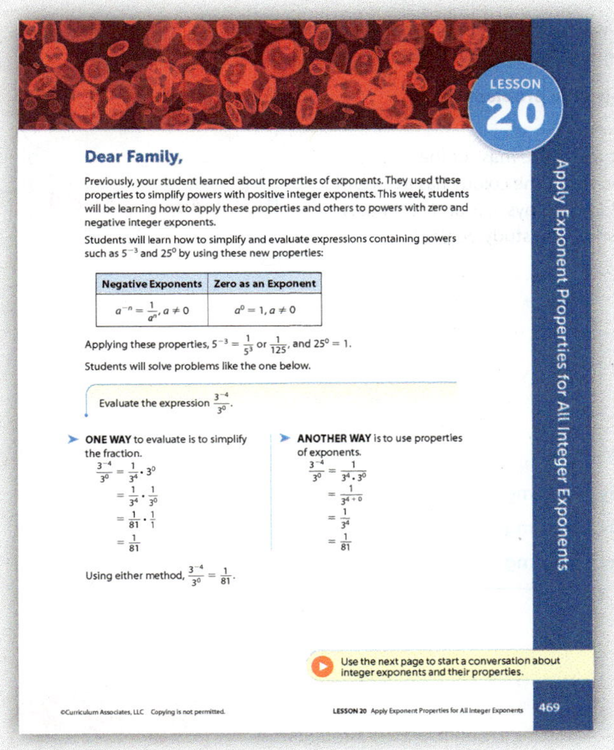

LESSON 20

Dear Family,

Previously, your student learned about properties of exponents. They used these properties to simplify powers with positive integer exponents. This week, students will be learning how to apply these properties and others to powers with zero and negative integer exponents.

Students will learn how to simplify and evaluate expressions containing powers such as 5^{-3} and 25^0 by using these new properties:

Negative Exponents	Zero as an Exponent
$a^{-n} = \frac{1}{a^n}, a \neq 0$	$a^0 = 1, a \neq 0$

Applying these properties, $5^{-3} = \frac{1}{5^3}$ or $\frac{1}{125}$, and $25^0 = 1$.

Students will solve problems like the one below.

Evaluate the expression $\frac{3^{-4}}{3^0}$.

➤ **ONE WAY** to evaluate is to simplify the fraction.

$$\frac{3^{-4}}{3^0} = \frac{1}{3^4} \cdot 3^0 = \frac{1}{3^4} \cdot \frac{1}{3^0} = \frac{1}{81} \cdot \frac{1}{1} = \frac{1}{81}$$

➤ **ANOTHER WAY** is to use properties of exponents.

$$\frac{3^{-4}}{3^0} = \frac{1}{3^4 \cdot 3^0} = \frac{1}{3^{4+0}} = \frac{1}{3^4} = \frac{1}{81}$$

Using either method, $\frac{3^{-4}}{3^0} = \frac{1}{81}$.

Use the next page to start a conversation about integer exponents and their properties.

Apply Exponent Properties for All Integer Exponents

©Curriculum Associates, LLC Copying is not permitted. LESSON 20 Apply Exponent Properties for All Integer Exponents 469

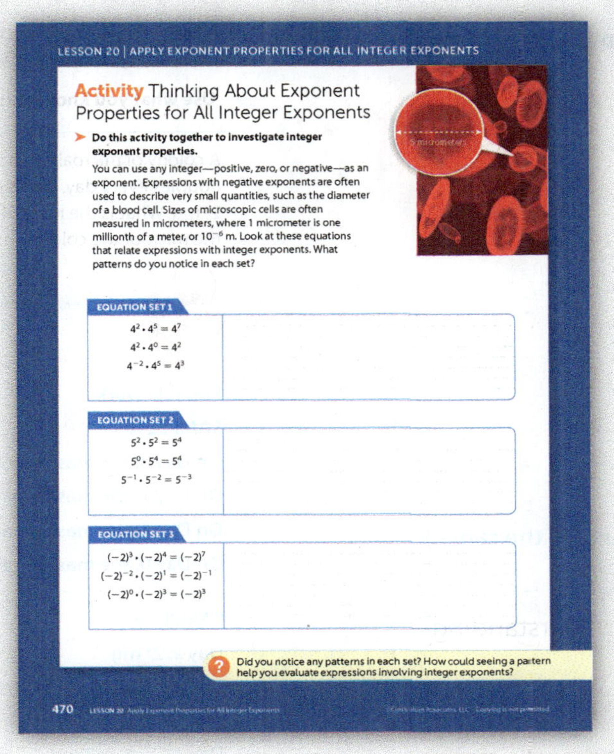

LESSON 20 | APPLY EXPONENT PROPERTIES FOR ALL INTEGER EXPONENTS

Activity Thinking About Exponent Properties for All Integer Exponents

➤ **Do this activity together to investigate integer exponent properties.**

You can use any integer—positive, zero, or negative—as an exponent. Expressions with negative exponents are often used to describe very small quantities, such as the diameter of a blood cell. Sizes of microscopic cells are often measured in micrometers, where 1 micrometer is one millionth of a meter, or 10^{-6} m. Look at these equations that relate expressions with integer exponents. What patterns do you notice in each set?

EQUATION SET 1

$4^2 \cdot 4^5 = 4^7$
$4^2 \cdot 4^0 = 4^2$
$4^{-2} \cdot 4^5 = 4^3$

EQUATION SET 2

$5^2 \cdot 5^2 = 5^4$
$5^0 \cdot 5^4 = 5^4$
$5^{-1} \cdot 5^{-2} = 5^{-3}$

EQUATION SET 3

$(-2)^3 \cdot (-2)^4 = (-2)^7$
$(-2)^{-2} \cdot (-2)^1 = (-2)^{-1}$
$(-2)^0 \cdot (-2)^3 = (-2)^3$

Did you notice any patterns in each set? How could seeing a pattern help you evaluate expressions involving integer exponents?

470

Connect to Language

➤ **For English language learners, use the Differentiation chart to scaffold the language in each session. Use the Academic Vocabulary routine for academic terms before Session 1.**

DIFFERENTIATION | ENGLISH LANGUAGE LEARNERS Use with **Session 1** **Connect It**

MATH TERM

In a fraction, the *numerator* is the number above the line in a fraction and the *denominator* is the number below the line.

In a power, the *base* is the number that is used as a repeated factor.

A *single power* is a power with one base and one exponent.

Levels 1–3: Reading/Speaking

Help students make sense of Connect It problem 2. Display the expressions and ask students to tell what they notice. Record any statements related to the parts or values of the expressions. Reword using the math terms or the lesson vocabulary terms *power* or *exponent*, if appropriate.

Read the problem with students and help them connect to their statements. Encourage students to use *numerator* and *denominator* to write responses for problem 2a. For problem 2c, ask for examples of nonzero bases. Then ask: *How are the expressions the same?* Help students use mathematical language to respond.

Levels 2–4: Reading/Speaking

Have students read Connect It problem 2 and make sense of mathematical language. As they read, ask students to circle mathematical words and phrases and add them to a **Co-Constructed Word Bank**. If needed, suggest *the value of each expression* and *nonzero base*. Then encourage students to add other words they can use to describe the expressions, like the Math Terms. Clarify meanings as needed.

Have students evaluate the expressions and write them as single powers before asking students to turn to partners to discuss. Encourage students to use terms from the Word Bank.

Levels 3–5: Reading/Speaking

Support students as they make sense of Connect It problem 2. Ask students to discuss the meanings of the math terms and the lesson vocabulary terms *power* and *exponent*. Then ask them to use the terms to tell what they notice about the expressions. Encourage students to make connections between the expressions using what they know about fractions and powers.

Next, have students read the problem and draft responses independently. Then ask students to turn to partners and compare responses. If partners disagree, suggest they come up with a way to test whether a strategy makes sense.

Explore Exponent Properties for Zero Exponents

Purpose

- **Explore** the idea that exponents are not always positive.
- **Understand** that a power with a nonzero base and an exponent of 0 has a value of 1.

START CONNECT TO PRIOR KNOWLEDGE

Always, Sometimes, Never

A To rewrite a quotient of powers, you can divide exponents.

B To rewrite a power of a power, you can multiply exponents.

C To rewrite a product of powers, you can add exponents.

Solutions

A is never true.

B is always true.

C is sometimes true. (The bases must be the same.)

WHY? Support students' facility understanding the properties of exponents.

TRY IT SMP 1, 2, 4, 5, 6

Make Sense of the Problem

See ***Connect to Culture*** to support student engagement. Before students work on Try It, use **Three Reads** to help them make sense of the problem. After the first read, ask students to explain what the situation is about. After the second read, ask students to paraphrase what they need to find out. Then after the third read, have students describe the relationships in the problem.

DISCUSS IT SMP 2, 3, 6, 7, 8

Support Partner Discussion

After students work on Try It, have them respond to Discuss It with a partner. Listen for understanding of:

- how to evaluate the expression 2^x for $x = 3$, $x = 2$, and $x = 1$.
- the pattern from each day to the previous one.
- how to work backward from Day 3 to Day 0.

LESSON 20 | SESSION 1

Explore Exponent Properties for Zero Exponents

Previously, you learned how to work with positive exponents and their properties. In this lesson, you will learn about exponents that are not positive.

➤ **Use what you know to try to solve the problem below.**

A colony of microalgae is being studied. The mass of the colony doubles every day. On Day x of the study, the colony has a mass of 2^x mg. What is the mass of the colony on Days 3, 2, and 1? What is the mass of the colony on Day 0, when the study begins?

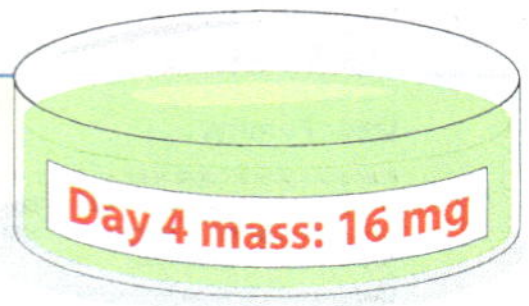

TRY IT

Possible work:

SAMPLE A

On Day 3, the mass is 2^3 mg = 8 mg.

On Day 2, the mass is half of Day 3, or 8 mg ÷ 2 = 4 mg.

On Day 1, the mass is half of Day 2, or 4 mg ÷ 2 = 2 mg.

On Day 0, the mass is half of Day 1, or 2 mg ÷ 2 = 1 mg.

SAMPLE B

Day x: 2^x mg

Day 3: $2^3 = 2 \cdot 2 \cdot 2 = 8$; 8 mg

Day 2: $2^2 = 2 \cdot 2 = 4$; 4 mg

Day 1: $2^1 = 2$; 2 mg

Day 0: $2^0 = 1$ (half of 2^1); 1 mg

DISCUSS IT

Ask: How did you find the mass for each day?

Share: I found the mass by . . .

Learning Target SMP 1, SMP 2, SMP 3, SMP 4, SMP 5, SMP 6, SMP 7, SMP 8

Know and apply the properties of integer exponents to generate equivalent numerical expressions.

Common Misconception Listen for students who think that the mass on Day 0, 2^0, is 0 because the exponent is 0. As students share their strategies, have them discuss the fact that, because each day the mass is half of the mass of the day before, the mass can never be 0 mg.

Select and Sequence Student Strategies

Select 2–3 samples that represent the range of student thinking in your classroom. Here is one possible order for class discussion:

- evaluating 2^3 to find the mass on Day 3 and then repeatedly dividing by 2 to find the mass on Days 2, 1, and 0
- (misconception) incorrectly stating that $2^0 = 0$, so the mass on Day 0 is 0
- evaluating 2^3, 2^2, 2^1, and using a pattern to determine 2^0

Facilitate Whole Class Discussion

Call on students to share selected strategies. Remind students to describe what they did and why they decided to do it.

Guide students to **Compare and Connect** the representations. Reword any unclear statements, or ask a student to do so, so that others understand. Confirm with the speaker that the rewording is accurate.

ASK *How did these strategies use patterns to find the mass on Day 0?*

LISTEN FOR Some strategies used the pattern of repeated division by 2 to work backward from Day 3 to Day 0. Others evaluated 2^x for $x = 3, 2,$ and 1, and then observed a pattern that could be used to find 2^0.

CONNECT IT

SMP 2, 4, 5, 8

1 Look Back Look for understanding that the mass on Day 3 was 8 mg, which means the mass on Day 2 was 4 mg, and the mass on Day 1 was 2 mg. Based on this pattern, the mass on Day 0 was 1 mg.

DIFFERENTIATION | RETEACH or REINFORCE

Visual Model

Use a pattern to understand why a power with an exponent of 0 equals 1.

If students are unsure about why a power with an exponent of 0 equals 1, then use this activity to help them understand why this is true.

- Display a two-column table with the column heads 4^x and *Value* and four empty rows. Fill in the 4^x column with the values 4^3, 4^2, and 4^1, in that order. Leave the last row empty.
- Point to 4^3. Ask: *What is the value of 4^3? How did you find it?* [64; I multiplied $4 \cdot 4 \cdot 4$.]
- Write 64 in the first row under *Value*.
- Repeat to fill in the values of 4^2 and 4^1.
- Ask: *How do the powers change as you read down the 4^x column?* [The exponents decrease by 1.]
- Point to the empty cell in the 4^x column.
- Ask: *What should I write here to continue the pattern?* [4^0]
- Ask: *How do the values of the power change as you read down the Value column?* [Each value is the previous value divided by 4.]
- Point to the empty cell in the *Value* column.
- Ask: *What should I write here to continue the pattern? Why?* [1; It is equal to $4 \div 4$.]
- Repeat with decreasing powers of 10.

LESSON 20 | SESSION 1

CONNECT IT

1 Look Back Complete the table to show the mass of the colony on Days 3, 2, 1, and 0. How did you get your answers?

Possible explanation: I multiplied to find 2^3, 2^2, and 2^1. Then I used the pattern I saw in the table to find the value of 2^0.

x	2^x	Mass (mg)
3	2^3	8
2	2^2	4
1	2^1	2
0	2^0	1

2 Look Ahead Consider the expressions shown.

$\frac{2^5}{2^5}$ $\qquad \frac{10^8}{10^8}$ $\qquad \frac{25^{13}}{25^{13}}$

a. What is the value of each expression? How do you know?

All three expressions are equal to 1. Possible explanation: The value of the numerator equals the value of the denominator in each fraction, so they all equal 1.

b. Write each expression as a single power.

$\frac{2^5}{2^5} = 2^{5-5} = 2^0$; $\frac{10^8}{10^8} = 10^{8-8} = 10^0$; $\frac{25^{13}}{25^{13}} = 25^{13-13} = 25^0$

c. The value of any power with a nonzero base and an exponent of 0 is 1. How do your answers to problems 2a and 2b show that this is true?

Possible answer: Each of the three expressions given is equivalent to 1 and equivalent to a power with an exponent of 0.

3 Reflect Write an equation showing the expression $6^3 \cdot 6^0$ as a single power. How does your answer show that $6^0 = 1$?

$6^3 \cdot 6^0 = 6^{3+0} = 6^3$; Possible answer: The value of 6^3 does not change when multiplied by 6^0, so 6^0 must be equal to 1.

472

2 Look Ahead Point out that the quotient of powers property can be used to show that a power with a nonzero base and an exponent of 0 has a value of 1. Students should recognize that the base and exponent of the powers in the numerator and denominator are the same. When the quotient of powers property is applied, the result is a power with the same base and an exponent of 0. Because the numerator and denominator of the original fraction are the same, that power is equal to 1.

CLOSE EXIT TICKET

3 Reflect Look for understanding that the product of powers property leads to the conclusion that $6^0 = 1$. The same reasoning can show that any power with a nonzero base and a zero exponent is equal to 1.

Error Alert If students write the single power as 6^0, then they may have multiplied the exponents 3 and 0 instead of adding them. Ask students to explain how to multiply powers with the same base. Students should recall that, when powers with the same base are multiplied, you can add the exponents.

Prepare for Applying Exponent Properties for All Integer Exponents

Support Vocabulary Development

Assign **Prepare for Applying Exponent Properties for All Integer Exponents** as extra practice in class or as homework.

If you have students complete this in class, then use the guidance below.

Ask students to consider the term *exponent*. Remind them to draw on their previous knowledge of powers to help them consider the term.

Have students work individually to complete the graphic organizer. Invite students to share their completed organizers, and prompt a whole-class comparative discussion of the related words, definitions, and examples students provided.

Have students look at the powers in problem 2 and discuss with a partner what two numbers make up the power. Be sure students understand that the exponent in a power is applied to the entire base, and when a negative sign is part of a base, it must be enclosed inside parentheses.

Problem Notes

1. Students should understand that in a power, the exponent shows how many times the base is used as a factor in a repeated multiplication expression. Student responses might include examples with positive or negative bases.

2. In problem 2a, the exponent 7 indicates that the base 10 is used as a factor 7 times. In problem 2b, the exponent 1 indicates that the base 18 is used as a factor once. In problem 2c, the exponent 4 indicates that the base -5 is used as a factor 4 times. Discuss with students why the power has a positive value even though the base is negative. Make sure students know the difference between $(-5)^4$ and -5^4.

LESSON 20 | SESSION 1 Name:

Prepare for Applying Exponent Properties for All Integer Exponents

1. Think about what you know about powers and exponents. Fill in each box. Use words, numbers, and pictures. Show as many ideas as you can. Possible answers:

exponent

What is it?
in a power, the number that shows how many times the base is used as a factor

Related Word
power: an expression with a base and an exponent

Related Word
base: in a power, the number that is used as a repeated factor

Example
In 999^3, the exponent is 3 and the base is 999.
$999^3 = 999 \times 999 \times 999$

Example
In 32^1, the exponent is 1.

Example
In 3^{54}, the exponent is 54.

2. Evaluate the power. What is the exponent in the expression?

a. 10^7
10,000,000; 7

b. 18^1
18; 1

c. $(-5)^4$
625; 4

473

REAL-WORLD CONNECTION

A meter contains 100 centimeters. So, a centimeter is $\frac{1}{100}$ of a meter, or 10^{-2} m. A meter contains 1,000 millimeters. So, a millimeter is $\frac{1}{1,000}$ of a meter, or 10^{-3} m. There are smaller metric units too. For example, a nanometer is 1 billionth of a meter, or 10^{-9} m. These tiny measurements are used in nanotechnology where scientists are working to make mechanical devices smaller than a single human blood cell. These devices could have uses in fiber optics, sensors, and electronics. Ask students to think of other real-world examples when applying properties of integer exponents might be useful.

Additional Practice

3 Problem 3 provides another look at using a pattern to find the value of a power with an exponent of 0. This problem is similar to the problem about the mass of a microalgae colony doubling every day. In both problems, an exponential expression for the mass of a colony on Day *x* is given and students must find the mass of the colony on Day 0. In this problem, the mass of the colony triples every day.

Students may want to use a table to solve.

Suggest that students use **Three Reads** to help them determine what the problem is about, what they are trying to find out, and what the important quantities and relationships are.

3 A colony of amoebas is being studied. The mass of the colony triples every day. On Day *x* of the study, the colony has a mass of 3^x mg.

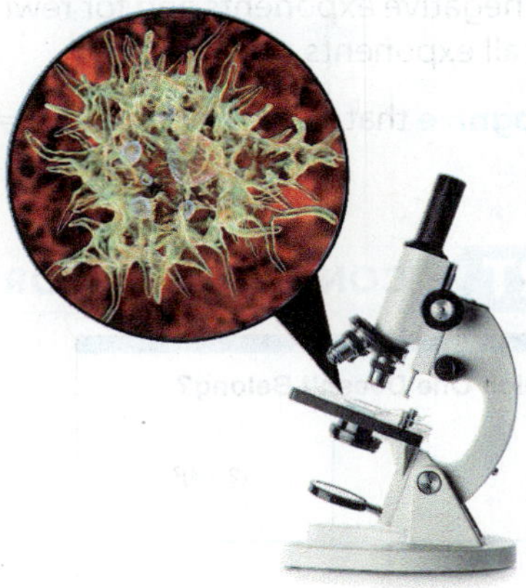

a. What is the mass of the colony on Days 3, 2, and 1? What is the mass of the colony on Day 0, when the study begins? Show your work.

Possible work:

On Day 3, the mass is 3^3 mg = 27 mg.

On Day 2, the mass is one-third of Day 3, or 27 mg ÷ 3 = 9 mg.

On Day 1, the mass is one-third of Day 2, or 9 mg ÷ 3 = 3 mg.

On Day 0, the mass is one-third of Day 1, or 3 mg ÷ 3 = 1 mg.

SOLUTION Day 3: 27 mg; Day 2: 9 mg; Day 1: 3 mg; Day 0: 1 mg

b. Check your answer to problem 3a. Show your work.

Possible work:

Day 3: $3^3 = 3 \cdot 3 \cdot 3 = 27$; 27 mg

Day 2: $3^2 = 3 \cdot 3 = 9$; 9 mg

Day 1: $3^1 = 3$; 3 mg

Day 0: $3^0 = 1$ (one-third of 3^1); 1 mg

DIFFERENTIATION | ENGLISH LANGUAGE LEARNERS

Use with **Session 2** Apply It

Levels 1–3: Speaking/Writing

Prepare students to construct written responses to Apply It problem 7. Use **Notice and Wonder** to help students preview and discuss the pattern. Provide words they can use to help their statements, like *pattern, dots, fraction, decreases by, divided by,* and *division*. Then encourage students to wonder about how the pattern relates to powers. Record statements. Next, help students read the problem and connect to their statements. Ask students to write what the pattern shows using:

- *The pattern shows that the value is divided by ____ when an exponent decreases by ____.*
- *The value of a power will be ____ when the exponent is ____. One example is ____.*

Levels 2–4: Speaking/Writing

Help students prepare to construct written responses to Apply It problem 7. Use **Notice and Wonder** to help students preview and discuss the pattern. Allow time for partner discussion, then call on volunteers to share their ideas. Encourage other students in the class to agree and add on to observations using math terms and patterns.

Read the problem with students and help them connect to their earlier discussion. Ask students to explain in writing what the pattern shows about the value of powers when the exponent is 0 and when it is negative. Encourage students to use the equations to support their conclusions.

Levels 3–5: Speaking/Writing

Have students prepare to construct written responses to Apply It problem 7. Ask partners to use **Notice and Wonder** to discuss the pattern. Call on students to share their ideas. If needed, encourage students to consider how the pattern might relate to powers and exponents and to draw conclusions from the patterns. Prompt students to build on ideas they agree with by giving reasons that a strategy will always work or will work only sometimes.

Have students read the problem. Ask students to write responses independently. Encourage students to refer to the pattern and equations as they provide reasons to explain how they know their conclusions are reasonable.

Develop Applying Properties of Negative Exponents

Purpose

- **Develop** strategies for evaluating expressions with zero and negative exponents and for rewriting expressions so that all exponents are positive.
- **Recognize** that $a^{-m} = \frac{1}{a^m}$ and $\frac{1}{a^{-m}} = a^m$.

START CONNECT TO PRIOR KNOWLEDGE

Which One Doesn't Belong?

A: $(2^2)^3$	B: $(2 \times 4)^2$
C: $2^4 \times 2^2$	D: 4^3

Possible Solutions

A is the only power of a power.

B is the only power of a product.

C is the only product of powers.

D is the single power of a base.

WHY? Support students' facility with properties of exponents.

DEVELOP ACADEMIC LANGUAGE

WHY? Support students as they agree with and build on the ideas of others.

HOW? Explain to students that they can build on a strategy or solution they agree with by describing ways to test the idea. During partner talk, encourage students to identify ideas they agree with and build on those ideas by thinking of ways they might test the idea. Suggest the sentence frame:

I could test this idea by ___.

TRY IT SMP 1, 2, 4, 5, 6

Make Sense of the Problem

See ***Connect to Culture*** to support student engagement. Before students work on Try It, use **Say It Another Way** to help them make sense of the problem. Have one partner read the problem, then instruct the other partner to paraphrase the problem. The first partner should indicate agreement with the paraphrasing or ask questions to clarify their understanding.

Develop Applying Properties of Negative Exponents

Read and try to solve the problem below.

A Chinese restaurant calculates that there are 2^{14} ways to order dim sum by choosing from the dishes they offer. They also calculate that there are 2^{10} ways to order dim sum from another restaurant in town. They want to advertise that the other restaurant offers only a small fraction of the possibilities that they do. Evaluate the expression $\frac{2^{10}}{2^{14}}$ to find that fraction.

TRY IT

Possible work:

SAMPLE A

$$\frac{2^{10}}{2^{14}} = \frac{1{,}024}{16{,}384}$$
$$= \frac{1}{16}$$

SAMPLE B

$$\frac{2^{10}}{2^{14}} = \frac{2 \cdot 2 \cdot 2 \cdot 2 \cdot 2 \cdot 2 \cdot 2 \cdot 2 \cdot 2 \cdot 2}{2 \cdot 2 \cdot 2 \cdot 2 \cdot 2 \cdot 2 \cdot 2 \cdot 2 \cdot 2 \cdot 2 \cdot 2 \cdot 2 \cdot 2 \cdot 2}$$
$$= \frac{2 \cdot 2 \cdot 2 \cdot 2 \cdot 2 \cdot 2 \cdot 2 \cdot 2 \cdot 2 \cdot 2}{2 \cdot 2 \cdot 2 \cdot 2 \cdot 2 \cdot 2 \cdot 2 \cdot 2 \cdot 2 \cdot 2} \cdot \frac{1}{2 \cdot 2 \cdot 2 \cdot 2}$$
$$= \frac{1}{2 \cdot 2 \cdot 2 \cdot 2}$$
$$= \frac{1}{16}$$

DISCUSS IT

Ask: How did you work with the exponents?

Share: I used the exponents when I . . .

475

DISCUSS IT SMP 2, 3, 6, 7

Support Partner Discussion

After students work on Try It, encourage them to respond to Discuss It with a partner. If students need support in getting started, prompt them to ask each other questions such as:

- *What properties do you know about exponents that might apply here?*
- *How could you rewrite the expression in a simpler way?*
- *Is the fraction less than or greater than 1? How do you know?*

Common Misconception Listen for students who rewrite the expression as 2^{-4} and assume its value is negative because the exponent is negative. As students share their strategies, ask if a negative answer is reasonable in the context of the situation. Discuss other ways the expression can be rewritten in order to find its value.

Select and Sequence Student Strategies

Select 2–3 samples that represent the range of student thinking in your classroom. Here is one possible order for class discussion:

- powers evaluated and resulting fraction simplified
- **(misconception)** assumption that 2^{-4}, the result of using the quotient of powers property, has a negative value
- powers rewritten as a product of repeated factors and then common factors eliminated
- power in denominator rewritten as $2^{10} \cdot 2^4$ and then common factor 2^{10} eliminated

Facilitate Whole Class Discussion

Call on students to share selected strategies. Prompt students to understand more about the problem by connecting it with others they have solved.

Guide students to **Compare and Connect** the representations. To help students collect their ideas, ask them to turn and talk about how their strategy was the same as or different from the strategies that were presented.

ASK *What are some different ways of simplifying the fraction given in the problem?*

LISTEN FOR Evaluate the powers and then simplify the result. Write out the repeated multiplication in the numerator and denominator and divide out common factors. Rewrite the 2^{14} as a product with a factor of 2^{10} and then divide out the common factors.

Model It

If students presented these models, have students connect these models to those presented in class.

If no student presented at least one of these models, have students first analyze key features of the models, and then connect them to the models presented in class.

ASK *How are these models alike? How are they different?*

LISTEN FOR Both use a property of exponents to rewrite the expression, but the properties and the resulting expressions are different.

For the model that rewrites the fraction, prompt students to consider how this method was chosen. Ask: *There are many ways to write the denominator as a product. Why do you think this particular way was chosen?*

For the model that subtracts the exponents, prompt students to think about properties of exponents. Ask: *Why are the exponents subtracted?*

LESSON 20 | SESSION 2

➤ Explore different ways to write powers.

A Chinese restaurant calculates that there are 2^{14} ways to order dim sum by choosing from the dishes they offer. They also calculate that there are 2^{10} ways to order dim sum from another restaurant in town. They want to advertise that the other restaurant offers only a small fraction of the possibilities that they do. Evaluate the expression $\frac{2^{10}}{2^{14}}$ to find that fraction.

Model It

You can simplify the fraction.

$$\frac{2^{10}}{2^{14}} = \frac{2^{10}}{2^{10} \cdot 2^4}$$
$$= \frac{2^{10}}{2^{10}} \cdot \frac{1}{2^4}$$
$$= 1 \cdot \frac{1}{2^4}$$
$$= \frac{1}{2^4}$$

Model It

You can use what you know about exponents to write the expression as a single power.

$$\frac{2^{10}}{2^{14}} = 2^{10-14}$$
$$= 2^{-4}$$

476

DIFFERENTIATION | EXTEND SMP 7

Deepen Understanding
Using Structure to Simplify the Expression

Prompt students to consider how they could rewrite the fraction using powers of 4 and then simplify it.

ASK *The numerator and denominator are powers with a base of 2. How can you use the fact that $2^2 = 4$ to rewrite these powers with a base of 4 instead?*

LISTEN FOR $2^{10} = (2^2)^5$, which equals 4^5 and $2^{14} = (2^2)^7$, which equals 4^7.

ASK *So, the fraction is equivalent to $\frac{4^5}{4^7}$. What do you get when you simplify this fraction? How does the result compare to the result for the powers of 2?*

LISTEN FOR You get $\frac{1}{4^2}$, which is equal to $\frac{1}{16}$. The result is the same.

ASK *Could you rewrite the fraction using only powers with a base of 8? Explain.*

LISTEN FOR No. $8 = 2^3$. 2^{10} is the same as 3 groups of 2^3 with one 2 left over. 2^{14} is the same as 4 groups of 2^3 with two 2s left over.

Develop Applying Properties of Negative Exponents

CONNECT IT

SMP 2, 4, 5, 6

Remind students that the quantities and the relationships between them are the same in each representation. Explain that they will now use those relationships to reason about how to work with negative exponents.

Before students begin to record and expand on their work in Model It, tell them that problems 2 and 3 will prepare them to provide the answers asked for in problem 4.

Monitor and Confirm Understanding 1 – 2

- An exponent in the denominator of a fraction is evaluated in the same manner as other exponents, so $\frac{1}{2^4} = \frac{1}{16}$.
- $\frac{1}{2^4}$ can be written as $\frac{2^0}{2^4}$. Using the quotient of powers property, $\frac{2^0}{2^4} = 2^{0-4} = 2^{-4}$. So, $2^{-4} = \frac{1}{2^4}$.

Facilitate Whole Class Discussion

3 Look for understanding that $\frac{1}{2^{-4}}$ can be written as a division problem and then simplified to get 2^4.

ASK *After you write $\frac{1}{2^{-4}}$ as $1 \div 2^{-4}$, what should you do as the next step?*

LISTEN FOR I can write $1 \div 2^{-4}$ as $1 \div \frac{1}{2^4}$ and then divide by multiplying by the reciprocal.

4 Look for understanding that a power with a negative exponent can be rewritten as 1 over a power with the same base and opposite exponent.

ASK *Can a power with a positive base and a negative exponent ever be negative? Why?*

LISTEN FOR No, because you can rewrite the power as 1 over a power with the same base and the opposite, positive exponent. Since the power in the denominator is positive, the fraction will be positive too.

5 **Reflect** Have all students focus on the strategies used to solve the Try It. If time allows, have students discuss their ideas with a partner.

CONNECT IT

➤ **Use the problem from the previous page to help you understand how to work with negative exponents.**

1 Look at the last line of the first **Model It**. What fraction will the restaurant use in their advertisement?

$\frac{1}{16}$

2 The equation shown is written by setting the last expressions of the two **Model Its** equal to one another.

$$\frac{1}{2^4} = 2^{-4}$$

You can show that this equation is true. Begin with $\frac{1}{2^4}$ and rewrite the numerator as a power of 2. Then use what you know about exponents to rewrite the expression as a single power.

$$\frac{1}{2^4} = \frac{2^?}{2^4}$$

$$\frac{1}{2^4} = \frac{2^0}{2^4}$$

$$= 2^{0-4}$$

$$= 2^{-4}$$

3 Use $2^{-4} = \frac{1}{2^4}$ to show that $\frac{1}{2^{-4}} = 2^4$.

Possible answer: $\frac{1}{2^{-4}}$ is the same as $1 \div 2^{-4}$ or $1 \div \frac{1}{2^4}$. $1 \div \frac{1}{2^4} = 1 \cdot 2^4$ or 2^4.

4 Rewrite each expression using only positive exponents.

$10^{-8} = \frac{1}{10^8}$ $(-5)^{-3} = \frac{1}{(-5)^3}$ $\frac{1}{17^{-1}} = 17^1$ or 17

5 **Reflect** Think about all the models and strategies you have discussed today. Describe how one of them helped you better understand how to work with negative exponents.

Responses will vary. Check student responses.

477

DIFFERENTIATION | RETEACH or REINFORCE

Visual Model

Use a pattern to develop understanding of negative exponents.

If students are unsure about negative exponents, then use this activity to build a pattern that demonstrates the relationship between the exponent and the value of the power.

Materials For display: completed table from Session 1 Connect It problem 1 with three empty rows added

- Prompt students to review the table and recall how they used it to understand powers with 0 exponents.
- Ask: *What patterns do you notice in the table?* [The *x*-values decrease by 1 each time, the exponent in the second column is the same as the *x*-value from the first column, the values are divided by 2 as you move down the table.]
- Have one or more volunteers complete the blank rows one cell at a time.
- After each row is completed, ask: *What are the contents of the row?* [first blank row: −1, $2^{-1} = \frac{1}{2}$; second blank row: −2, $2^{-2} = \frac{1}{4}$; third blank row: −3, $2^{-3} = \frac{1}{8}$]
- Display $2^{-m} =$ ______ and have students complete the rule. $\left[\frac{1}{2^m}\right]$

Apply It

For all problems, encourage students to use a model to support their thinking. Encourage students to look for patterns to connect expressions to the properties of exponents.

6 **A, C, and D are correct.** Students may solve the problem by using properties of exponents to rewrite each of the answer choices to tell whether it is equivalent to the given expression.

B is not correct. This answer could be rewritten with a numerator of 17^{-5}, but the denominator would be 29^{-3}.

E is not correct. This answer could be rewritten with a denominator of 29^3, but the numerator would be 17^5.

F is not correct. This answer could be rewritten with a denominator of 29^3, but the numerator would be 17^5.

7 Students should notice that each time the exponent decreases by 1, the number of dots and the value of the power is divided by 2. Students should continue this pattern for negative exponents.

Apply It

➤ **Use what you learned to solve these problems.**

6 Which expressions are equivalent to $\frac{17^{-5}}{29^3}$? Select all that apply.

(A) $\frac{1}{17^5 \cdot 29^3}$

B $\frac{29^3}{17^5}$

(C) $17^{-5} \cdot 29^{-3}$

(D) $\left(\frac{17^5}{29^{-3}}\right)^{-1}$

E $17^5 \cdot 29^{-3}$

F $\frac{29^{-3}}{17^{-5}}$

7 Fill in the missing exponents to complete the pattern. Use the pattern to explain how to evaluate 0 and negative exponents.

$2^3 = 8$ $2^2 = 4$ $2^1 = 2$ $2^{0} = 1$ $2^{-1} = \frac{1}{2}$ $2^{-2} = \frac{1}{4}$

Possible explanation: When the exponents for the powers of 2 decrease by 1, the value of the power is divided by 2. I know $2^1 = 2$, so $2^{1-1} = 2^0 = 2 \div 2 = 1$. So while 2^n means multiplying by n factors of 2, 2^{-n} means dividing 1 by 2, n times.

8 Rewrite the expression $\frac{9^{-8} \cdot 3^0}{2^{-1}}$ using only positive exponents. Show your work.

Possible work:

$$\frac{9^{-8} \cdot 3^0}{2^{-1}} = \frac{9^{-8} \cdot 1}{2^{-1}}$$
$$= \frac{2^1}{9^8}$$

SOLUTION $\frac{2^1}{9^8}$ or $\frac{2}{9^8}$

CLOSE **EXIT TICKET**

8 Students' solutions should show an understanding that:

- a nonzero base raised to a power of 0 is always 1.
- a power with a negative exponent is the same as 1 over the power with the same base and the opposite exponent.
- 1 over a power with a negative exponent is equal to the same power with the opposite exponent.

Error Alert If students write an incorrect expression, then suggest they first write the expression as a product, $9^{-8} \cdot 3^0 \cdot \frac{1}{2^{-1}}$ and rewrite each factor separately.

Practice Applying Properties of Negative Exponents

Problem Notes

Assign **Practice Applying Properties of Negative Exponents** as extra practice in class or as homework.

1. **a.** *Basic*

   b. Since -2 is raised to a positive power, this factor can stay in the numerator. ***Medium***

   c. Students may discover a shortcut. They can change negative exponents in the numerator to positive exponents and move the power to the denominator and change negative exponents in the denominator to positive exponents and move the power to the numerator. ***Medium***

   d. Students may use the shortcut described in the problem 1c note. ***Medium***

2. Students may use properties of exponents to rewrite each of the answer choices with positive exponents and then recognize that a fraction with a lesser numerator than denominator will be between 0 and 1. Since there are no negative bases, all expressions have a value greater than 0.

   B is correct. This answer is equivalent to $\frac{4^2}{5^7}$, which is less than 1.

   C is correct. This answer is equivalent to $\frac{1}{5^3 \cdot 4^6}$, which is less than 1.

   E is correct. This answer is equivalent to $\frac{1}{4^3 \cdot 5^9}$, which is less than 1.

   A is not correct. This answer is equivalent to $\frac{5^3}{4^3}$, which is greater than 1.

   D is not correct. This answer is equivalent to $\frac{5^3}{4^2}$, which is greater than 1.

   Medium

LESSON 20 | SESSION 2 Name:

Practice Applying Properties of Negative Exponents

➤ **Study the Example showing how to rewrite expressions involving negative exponents. Then solve problems 1–4.**

Example

Rewrite the expression using only positive exponents.

$$\frac{14^0 \cdot 15^{-9}}{2^{-5} \cdot 99^3} = \frac{1 \cdot 15^{-9}}{2^{-5} \cdot 99^3} \quad \leftarrow \quad 14^0 = 1$$

$$= \frac{2^5}{15^9 \cdot 99^3} \quad \leftarrow \quad 15^{-9} = \frac{1}{15^9};\ \frac{1}{2^{-5}} = 2^5$$

1. Rewrite each expression using only positive exponents.

   a. $6^{-10} \cdot 41^{-4} \cdot 11^{-13}$ $\quad \frac{1}{6^{10} \cdot 41^4 \cdot 11^{13}}$

   b. $\frac{(-2)^7 \cdot 19^{-3}}{31^{-1}}$ $\quad \frac{(-2)^7 \cdot 31^1}{19^3}$

   c. $15^0 \cdot 8^{-6} \cdot 23^5$ $\quad \frac{23^5}{8^6}$

   d. $\frac{3^{25} \cdot 16^0}{5^{-9} \cdot 52^{-3}}$ $\quad 3^{25} \cdot 5^9 \cdot 52^3$

2. Which expressions have a value between 0 and 1? Select all that apply.

   A $\left(\frac{4}{5}\right)^{-3}$

   (B) $5^{-7} \cdot 4^2$

   (C) $\frac{5^{-3}}{4^6}$

   D $\frac{4^{-2}}{5^{-3}}$

   (E) $4^{-3} \cdot 5^{-9}$

479

Fluency & Skills Practice

Applying Properties of Negative Exponents

In this activity, students practice rewriting expressions involving zero and negative exponents as expressions with only positive exponents.

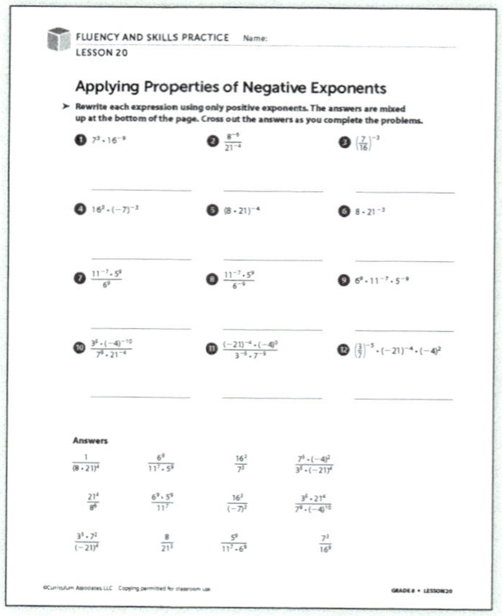
FLUENCY AND SKILLS PRACTICE Name:
LESSON 20
Applying Properties of Negative Exponents

Additional Practice

3 **a.** *Basic*

b. *Basic*

c. Students may rewrite the expression as $1 \cdot \frac{1}{10^5}$, or just $\frac{1}{10^5}$, and then evaluate it. *Medium*

d. Students may solve the problem by recognizing that 27 is equal to 3^3. So, 27^{-2} is equal to $(3^3)^{-2}$, or 3^{-6}. Students may then use the quotient of powers property to simplify. ***Challenge***

4 **a.** Students may rewrite the left side of the equation as $\frac{1}{13^n}$ and then see that n must equal -2. ***Medium***

b. Students may rewrite the right side of the equation as $\frac{1}{35^9}$ and then see that n must equal 9. ***Medium***

LESSON 20 | SESSION 2

3 Evaluate each expression.

a. $\left(\frac{1}{4}\right)^{-3}$ 64

b. $\left(\frac{7}{8}\right)^{-2}$ $\frac{64}{49}$

c. $6^0 \cdot 10^{-5}$ $\frac{1}{100{,}000}$

d. $\frac{3^{-5}}{27^{-2}}$ 3

4 What value of n makes the equation true? Show your work.

a. $13^{-n} = \frac{1}{13^{-2}}$

Possible work:

$13^{-n} = \frac{1}{13^{-2}}$

$13^{-n} = 13^2$

$-n = 2$

$n = -2$

SOLUTION $n = -2$

b. $\frac{1}{35^n} = 35^{-9}$

Possible work:

$\frac{1}{35^n} = 35^{-9}$

$35^{-n} = 35^{-9}$

$-n = -9$

$n = 9$

SOLUTION $n = 9$

480

DIFFERENTIATION | ENGLISH LANGUAGE LEARNERS

Use with **Session 3** **Discuss It**

Levels 1–3: Speaking/Listening

Support Discuss It by helping students describe their solution strategies. First, review *evaluate* with students. Help students make a word bank with terms to describe parts of the expression, like *power, base, exponent, parenthesis, fraction bar, division line, factor,* and *quotient*. Then ask students to add terms that describe steps for evaluating expressions, like *divide, multiply, add, subtract, rewrite, simplify,* and *eliminate*. Support understanding with examples.

Next, ask students to work with partners to identify the first step of their solution strategy using words from the word bank. Ask partners to compare their first steps and tell whether they were the same or different.

Levels 2–4: Speaking/Listening

Support Discuss It by helping students describe their solution strategies using mathematical language. Before partner discussions, ask students to brainstorm a list of math terms related to evaluating an expression with powers. Call on volunteers to share terms as you write them on the board. Include *expression, parentheses, eliminate, powers, bases, exponents,* and *operations* if students do not suggest these.

Read Discuss It with students. Have partners describe the first steps in their strategies. Reinforce that clear explanations use complete sentences and precise vocabulary. Encourage partners to explain whether their strategies were the same or different.

Levels 3–5: Speaking/Listening

Have students prepare for Discuss It by identifying mathematical language they can use in their discussions. Before partner discussions, ask students to brainstorm a list of math terms related to evaluating an expression with powers. Call on volunteers to share terms like *simplify the expression, combine the powers,* and *eliminate the parentheses*.

Next, have partners read Discuss It and explain the first step in their strategies. Encourage students to listen to explanations and tell whether they used the same or a different strategy. If the strategies were different, have students explain how they thought about the problem differently.

Develop Applying Properties of Integer Exponents

Purpose

- **Develop** strategies for using properties of exponents to generate expressions equivalent to numerical expressions involving zero and negative exponents.
- **Recognize** that the properties of exponents hold true for powers with zero and negative exponents.

START CONNECT TO PRIOR KNOWLEDGE

Which One Doesn't Belong?

A: $\frac{1}{(2^3)^2}$	B: 7^0
C: $\left(-\frac{3}{4}\right)^3$	D: 4^{-5}

Possible Solutions

A is the only expression that contains a power of a power.

B is the only expression whose value is a whole number.

C is the only expression whose value is negative.

D is the only power with a negative exponent.

WHY? Support students' facility in working with powers involving zero and negative exponents.

DEVELOP ACADEMIC LANGUAGE

WHY? Recognize the meaning of *so that* and *as* in mathematical expressions.

HOW? Explain that the terms are used to state characteristics of mathematical expressions or representations. Have students find the terms in Model It and Connect It problem 1. Ask: *How do you need to rewrite the powers? And the expressions?* Challenge students to use both terms to answer each question. (Example: *I need to rewrite the powers so that they have . . .; I need to rewrite the powers as powers with . . .*)

TRY IT SMP 1, 2, 4, 5, 6

Make Sense of the Problem

Before students work on Try It, use **Notice and Wonder** to help them make sense of the problem. Emphasize the responses that are relevant to evaluating the expression.

LESSON 20 | SESSION 3

Develop Applying Properties of Integer Exponents

Read and try to solve the problem below.

Adriana and Katrina are evaluating the expression shown. Adriana thinks the value is between 0 and 1, while Katrina thinks the value is greater than 1.

Evaluate the expression. Who is correct?

TRY IT

Possible work:

SAMPLE A

$$\left(\frac{81^{-2}}{27^{-3}}\right)^5 = \left(\frac{27^3}{81^2}\right)^5$$
$$= \left(\frac{27 \cdot 27 \cdot 27}{81 \cdot 81}\right)^5$$
$$= \left(\frac{27 \cdot 27 \cdot 27}{(27 \cdot 3) \cdot (27 \cdot 3)}\right)^5$$
$$= \left(\frac{27}{(3 \cdot 3)}\right)^5$$
$$= \left(\frac{27}{9}\right)^5$$
$$= 3^5$$
$$= 243$$

Katrina is correct.

SAMPLE B

$$\left(\frac{81^{-2}}{27^{-3}}\right)^5 = \left(\frac{27^3}{81^2}\right)^5$$
$$= \left(\frac{19{,}683}{6{,}561}\right)^5$$
$$= 3^5$$
$$= 243$$

Katrina is correct.

DISCUSS IT

Ask: What was your first step?

Share: The first thing I did was . . .

DISCUSS IT SMP 1, 2, 3, 6, 7

Support Partner Discussion

After students work on Try It, encourage them to respond to Discuss It with a partner. If students need support in getting started, prompt them to ask each other questions such as:

- *Why did you decide to do that step first?*
- *How do you know that the value is positive?*
- *Is there a different way you could have started evaluating the expression?*

Error Alert Be aware that some students may get the correct answer with incorrect work. For example, some students may rewrite the expression in the parentheses as 3^1 by dividing the bases and subtracting the exponents of the expression. You can use a simpler expression such as $\frac{8^{-2}}{2^{-2}}$ to show that this strategy will not always work $\left(\frac{1}{8} \neq 1\right)$. Then ask these students what must be true about the bases in order to rewrite a quotient of powers as a single power. Students should recall that the bases must be the same. The result will be a single power with the same base and an exponent equal to the difference of the exponents.

Select and Sequence Student Strategies

Select 2–3 samples that represent the range of student thinking in your classroom. Here is one possible order for class discussion:

- expression in parentheses rewritten with positive exponents as first step
- power of a quotient property applied to eliminate parentheses as first step
- numerator and denominators rewritten with base 3 as first step

Facilitate Whole Class Discussion

Call on students to share selected strategies. Remind students that they can ask questions about strategies that are not clear.

Guide students to **Compare and Connect** the representations. Ask students to reword statements using mathematical terms or properties when appropriate.

ASK *How are the strategies alike and how are they different?*

LISTEN FOR They all use the properties of exponents, but in different orders.

Model It

If students presented these models, have students connect these models to those presented in class.

If no student presented at least one of these models, have students first analyze key features of the models, and then connect them to the models presented in class.

ASK *When is the exponent of 5 from the original expression applied in each model?*

LISTEN FOR In the first model, it is applied to the powers in the numerator and denominator in the very first step. In the second model, it has still not been applied in the last step shown.

For the model that eliminates parentheses, prompt students to consider the properties of exponents used.

- *What reasoning is used to get from line 2 to 3?*
- *Why is this step important?*

For the model that rewrites powers with a base of 3, prompt students to consider the importance of the first line of the solution.

- *Why is it important to know the factors of 81 and 27?*
- *What is the benefit of this model?*

➤ **Explore different ways to work with integer exponents.**

Adriana and Katrina are evaluating the expression shown. Adriana thinks the value is between 0 and 1, while Katrina thinks the value is greater than 1.

Evaluate the expression. Who is correct?

Model It

You can begin by eliminating the parentheses.

$$\left(\frac{81^{-2}}{27^{-3}}\right)^5 = \frac{81^{-10}}{27^{-15}}$$
$$= \frac{27^{15}}{81^{10}}$$
$$= \frac{27^{15}}{(3 \cdot 27)^{10}}$$
$$= \frac{27^{15}}{3^{10} \cdot 27^{10}}$$
$$= \frac{27^{5}}{3^{10}}$$
$$= \frac{(3^3)^{5}}{3^{10}}$$
$$= \frac{3^{15}}{3^{10}}$$

Model It

You can rewrite the powers so that they have the same base.

$$\left(\frac{81^{-2}}{27^{-3}}\right)^5 = \left(\frac{(3^4)^{-2}}{(3^3)^{-3}}\right)^5$$
$$= \left(\frac{3^{-8}}{3^{-9}}\right)^5$$
$$= (3^{-8-(-9)})^5$$
$$= (3^{-8+9})^5$$
$$= (3^1)^5$$

DIFFERENTIATION | EXTEND

SMP 1

Deepen Understanding
Persevering in Simplifying an Expression

Prompt students to consider different ways to simplify the expression.

ASK *A student applies the exponent 5 to the fraction after the second step of the second Model It. What would the expression look like? What could the student do next?*

LISTEN FOR $\frac{3^{-40}}{3^{-45}}$; The student could divide the powers by subtracting the exponents or rewrite the expression so it has only positive exponents.

ASK *At this same step, another student rewrites the expression in parentheses so it has positive exponents. What would the expression look like? What could the student do next?*

LISTEN FOR $\left(\frac{3^9}{3^8}\right)^5$; The student could divide the powers by subtracting the exponents or could apply the exponent 5 to the powers in the numerator and denominator.

ASK *Why do either of these two methods and the method shown in the Model It result in the same final expression?*

LISTEN FOR When properties of exponents are used correctly, the resulting forms of the expressions are equivalent to one another.

Develop Applying Properties of Integer Exponents

CONNECT IT

SMP 2, 4, 5, 6

Remind students that the original expression is the same in each representation. The steps used to simplify it are different. Explain that they will now use those representations to reason about how to simplify exponential expressions.

Before students begin to record and expand on their work in Model It, tell them that problem 4 will prepare them to provide the explanation asked for in problem 5.

Monitor and Confirm Understanding 1 – 3

- The last expressions in both Model Its are equivalent to 3^5, which has a value of 243.
- A power with a base greater than 1 and a positive integer exponent is always greater than 1.

Facilitate Whole Class Discussion

4 Look for understanding that because the powers in the numerator and denominator do not have the same base, it is difficult to determine whether the expression has a value less than or greater than 1.

ASK *If the powers had the same base, how could you tell if the fraction is greater than 1? What if the bases were different, but the exponents were the same?*

LISTEN FOR If the bases are the same, then the power with the greater exponent is greater. If that power is in the numerator, the fraction is greater than 1. If the exponents are the same, then the power with the greater base is greater. If that power is in the numerator, the fraction is greater than 1.

5 Look for the idea that there may be several different ways to simplify an expression involving multiple exponents.

ASK *What benefit did you get from seeing multiple approaches for simplifying an exponential expression?*

LISTEN FOR It helped me see that there is more than one way to solve these problems, and it helped me understand when to use some of the properties I had not been using.

6 **Reflect** Have all students focus on the strategies used to solve the Try It. If time allows, have students discuss their ideas with a partner.

CONNECT IT

➤ **Use the problem from the previous page to help you understand how to work with integer exponents.**

1 Look at the last expression of each **Model It**. Rewrite each expression as a single power. Do they both simplify to the same power? Explain.

3^5; 3^5; Yes; Possible explanation: $\frac{3^{15}}{3^{10}} = 3^{15-10} = 3^5$ and $(3^1)^5 = 3^{1 \cdot 5} = 3^5$

2 What is the value of the expression? Who is correct? 243; Katrina

3 Do you need to find the exact value of the expression in order to tell whether it is less than or greater than 1? Explain.

No; Possible explanation: I could tell that the expression was greater than 1 when I saw that it simplified to a positive power of 3.

4 a. What is the simplest form of the expression you could write without changing the bases of any of the powers? How would you evaluate this expression?

$\frac{27^{15}}{81^{10}}$; Possible answer: I would have to calculate each power.

b. Can you tell whether the expression in problem 4a is less than or greater than 1? Why or why not?

Possible answer: I cannot tell whether the numerator is less than or greater than the denominator. The base in the numerator is less than the base in the denominator, but the exponent in the numerator is greater than the exponent in the denominator.

5 Did you or your classmates evaluate the expression in a different way than shown in the **Model Its**? Which ways seem simpler or more efficient? Explain.

Possible answer: Yes, many ways apply the same rules, but in a different order. I prefer to eliminate parentheses, but my partner likes to rewrite powers using the same base.

6 **Reflect** Think about all the models and strategies you have discussed today. Describe how one of them helped you better understand how to solve the **Try It** problem.

Responses will vary. Check student responses.

483

DIFFERENTIATION | RETEACH or REINFORCE

Visual Model

Identify multiple ways to simplify exponential expressions.

If students are always using repeated factors or are struggling with simplifying powers, then use this activity to help them see entry points for other properties.

Materials For each student: 2 sticky notes

- Display the expression $\left(\frac{16^{-3}}{64^{-2}}\right)^{-4}$. Tell students the goal is to identify as many different first steps for simplifying this expression as possible.
- Have students write two possible first steps, one on each note.
- One at a time, have students place these on a wall. If their first step is the same as another student's, they should place it on top of the other student's.
- If students only come up with a couple of different first steps, then suggest some.
- Choose various first steps and have volunteers complete the simplification.
- Ask: *Why do you think it is important to use different ways to simplify exponential expressions?* [Some properties make simplifying an expression simpler than others.]

Apply It

For all problems, encourage students to use exponent properties to support their thinking.

7 **A** **is correct.** This answer is equivalent to $\frac{1}{29^6 \cdot 54^3}$, which is between 0 and 1.

B **is correct.** This answer is equivalent to $\frac{29^2}{54^2}$, which is between 0 and 1.

D **is correct.** This answer is equivalent to $\frac{1}{54^2} \cdot 1$, or just $\frac{1}{54^2}$, which is between 0 and 1.

C is not correct. This answer has 1 in the denominator and a positive base with a positive exponent in the numerator after applying the power of a power property.

E is not correct. Although this number has a greater number in the denominator when simplified, the exponent in the numerator is much larger, so the value will be greater than 1.

8 Students may also evaluate the expression using these steps:

$$\begin{aligned} 24^{-3} \cdot 6^4 &= \frac{1}{24^3} \cdot 6^4 \\ &= \frac{6^4}{24^3} \\ &= \frac{6^4}{(4 \cdot 6)^3} \\ &= \frac{6^4}{4^3 \cdot 6^3} \\ &= \frac{6}{4^3} \\ &= \frac{6}{64} \\ &= \frac{3}{32} \end{aligned}$$

LESSON 20 | SESSION 3

Apply It

➤ **Use what you learned to solve these problems.**

7 Which expressions have a value between 0 and 1? Select all that apply.

A $\left(\frac{54}{29^{-2}}\right)^{-3}$

B $(54^2 \cdot 29^{-2})^{-1}$

C $\left(\frac{54^{-7}}{29^0}\right)^{-3}$

D $54^{-2}(29^3 \cdot 54^{-1})^0$

E $\frac{54^{-2} \cdot 29^5}{29^{-7} \cdot 54^2}$

8 Evaluate the expression $24^{-3} \cdot 6^4$. Show your work

Possible work:

$$\begin{aligned} 24^{-3} \cdot 6^4 &= (4 \cdot 6)^{-3} \cdot 6^4 \\ &= 4^{-3} \cdot 6^{-3} \cdot 6^4 \\ &= 4^{-3} \cdot 6^1 \\ &= \frac{6^1}{4^3} \\ &= \frac{6}{64} \\ &= \frac{3}{32} \end{aligned}$$

SOLUTION $\frac{3}{32}$

9 Rewrite the expression $\frac{(75^{-6} \cdot 31^0)^{-3}}{75^{10} \cdot 31^{-9}}$ with no parentheses and using only positive exponents. Show your work.

Possible work and answer:

$$\begin{aligned} \frac{(75^{-6} \cdot 31^0)^{-3}}{75^{10} \cdot 31^{-9}} &= \frac{75^{18} \cdot 31^0}{75^{10} \cdot 31^{-9}} \\ &= 75^{18-10} \cdot 31^{0-(-9)} \\ &= 75^8 \cdot 31^9 \end{aligned}$$

SOLUTION $75^8 \cdot 31^9$

484

CLOSE EXIT TICKET

9 Students' solutions should show an understanding of how to apply the properties of exponents to simplify an exponential expression involving zero and negative integer exponents.

Error Alert If students move a power from the numerator to the denominator or vice versa without changing the sign of the exponent, ask them if $\frac{1}{5^1} = \frac{5^1}{1}$. These fractions are not equivalent. Remind students that when a power is moved within a fraction this way, the sign of the exponent must also be changed.

Practice Applying Properties of Integer Exponents

Problem Notes

Assign **Practice Applying Properties of Integer Exponents** as extra practice in class or as homework.

1 **a.** Students may solve the problem by multiplying exponents or by simplifying inside the parentheses first. ***Basic***

b. Students may solve the problem by adding exponents or by rewriting the expression with all positive exponents first. ***Basic***

c. Students may solve the problem by rewriting 3^0 as 1, then raising 8^2 to the power of -2. ***Medium***

d. Students may solve the problem by adding exponents in the numerator first, and then distributing the negative exponent. ***Challenge***

2 **a.** Students may solve the problem by adding the exponents inside the parentheses, applying the –2 exponent, and then adding the exponents of the two remaining expressions with base 39. ***Medium***

b. Students may solve the problem by subtracting exponents of powers with the same base, and then rewriting any expressions with negative exponents. Other students may prefer to write the expression with all positive exponents first. ***Medium***

c. Students may solve the problem by multiplying exponents to eliminate the parentheses, then adding exponents of powers with the same base, and then rewriting any expressions with negative exponents. ***Medium***

d. Students may solve the problem by adding exponents in the denominator, then subtracting exponents of powers with the same base, then multiplying exponents, and finally rewriting the expression with a positive exponent. ***Medium***

LESSON 20 | SESSION 3 Name:

Practice Applying Properties of Integer Exponents

Study the Example showing how to evaluate expressions involving integer exponents. Then solve problems –4.

Example

Evaluate the expression $\frac{(4^{-3} \cdot 9^0)^2}{4^{-5}}$.

$\frac{(4^{-3} \cdot 9^0)^2}{4^{-5}} = \frac{4^{-6} \cdot 9^0}{4^{-5}}$ ← $(4^{-3})^2 = 4^{-6}$; $(9^0)^2 = 9^0$

$= \frac{4^{-6}(1)}{4^{-5}}$ ← $9^0 = 1$

$= \frac{4^5}{4^6}$ ← $4^{-6} = \frac{1}{4^6}$; $\frac{1}{4^{-5}} = 4^5$

$= \frac{1}{4}$ ← $(4^{5-6}) = 4^{-1}$

1 Evaluate each expression.

a. $(12^0)^4$ 1

b. $7^{-4} \cdot 7^4$ 1

c. $(3^0 \cdot 8^2)^{-2}$ $\frac{1}{4{,}096}$

d. $\left(\frac{5^{-4} \cdot 5^7}{10^2}\right)^{-1}$ $\frac{4}{5}$

2 Rewrite each expression using only positive exponents.

a. $39^{-5}(39^{-6} \cdot 39)^{-2}$ 39^5

b. $\frac{11^{-3} \cdot 40^{-2}}{40^6 \cdot 11^{-8}}$ $\frac{11^5}{40^8}$

c. $16^{-10} \cdot 16^4(16^{-5})^2$ $\frac{1}{16^{16}}$

d. $\left(\frac{21^2}{21^{-9} \cdot 21^5}\right)^{-7}$ $\frac{1}{21^{42}}$

485

Fluency & Skills Practice

Applying Properties of Integer Exponents

In this activity, students use the properties of exponents to evaluate numerical expressions and to rewrite expressions using only positive exponents. They also reflect on whether the order in which they apply the properties is important.

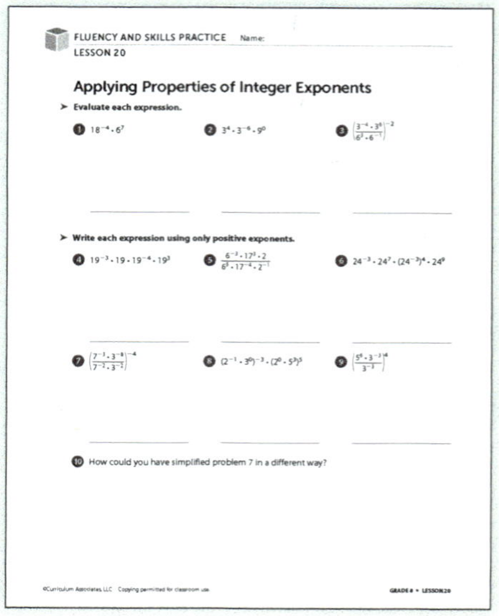

FLUENCY AND SKILLS PRACTICE Name:
LESSON 20

Applying Properties of Integer Exponents

Evaluate each expression.

Write each expression using only positive exponents.

How could you have simplified problem 7 in a different way?

Additional Practice

3 **a.** Students should recognize that the base should have stayed as $\frac{2}{5}$. ***Medium***

b. Students may also solve the problem by applying the negative exponent first and expanding the numerator and denominator to eliminate common factors. ***Medium***

4 **a.** Students may simplify until there is a power with a base of 8 on each side, and then set the exponents equal to each other and solve. ***Medium***

b. Students may check their work by substituting their answer for *n* and simplifying the original expression. ***Medium***

LESSON 20 | SESSION 3

3 Glen rewrote an expression as shown. $\left(\frac{2}{5}\right)^4\left(\frac{2}{5}\right)\left(\frac{2}{5}\right)^{-3} = \left(\frac{8}{125}\right)^2$

a. What was Glen's mistake?

Possible answer: Glen multiplied the bases together.

b. Rewrite the expression correctly as a single power. Show your work.

Possible work: $\left(\frac{2}{5}\right)^4\left(\frac{2}{5}\right)\left(\frac{2}{5}\right)^{-3} = \left(\frac{2}{5}\right)^{4+1-3}$

$= \left(\frac{2}{5}\right)^2$

SOLUTION $\left(\frac{2}{5}\right)^2$

4 What value of *n* makes the equation true? Show your work.

a. $(8^{-n})^5 = \frac{8}{8^{-14}}$

Possible work:

$(8^{-n})^5 = \frac{8}{8^{-14}}$

$8^{-5n} = 8^{1-(-14)}$

$8^{-5n} = 8^{15}$

$-5n = 15$

$n = -3$

SOLUTION $n = -3$

b. $\left(\frac{3^4}{3^n}\right)^2 = 3^6$

Possible work:

$\left(\frac{3^4}{3^n}\right)^2 = 3^6$

$3^{2(4-n)} = 3^6$

$2(4 - n) = 6$

$8 - 2n = 6$

$-2n = -2$

$n = 1$

SOLUTION $n = 1$

486

DIFFERENTIATION | ENGLISH LANGUAGE LEARNERS

Use with Session 4 **Apply It**

Levels 1–3: Listening/Writing

Have students identify the correct answer for Apply It problem 3. Then help students participate in Pair/Share and prepare to write responses. First, show the meaning of *change* by writing a number and then changing it to a new number. Then ask students make changes to generate other equivalent expressions, using models to show their ideas. Have students turn to partners and explain their ideas by referring to their models. Encourage students to listen for understanding.

Next, have partners consider Benjamin's choice and tell why the equation is *not* equivalent. Help partners write short sentences to explain their ideas.

Levels 2–4: Speaking/Writing

Have students identify the equivalent expression in Apply It problem 3. Then provide support to help students discuss Pair/Share and prepare to write responses. Ask: *What are some ways you can change an expression with powers?* Have students explain their ideas to partners. Remind students that they can ask questions about ideas that are not clear during partner discussions. For example:

- *What do you mean by ____?*

Next, ask students to explain in writing why Benjamin might have made a mistake. Suggest students justify by describing the changes that would have made the expression equivalent.

Levels 3–5: Speaking/Writing

Have students identify the equivalent expression in Apply It problem 3. Then, support students as they discuss Pair/Share and justify their written responses. Provide think time for students to read Pair/Share and consider changes they can make to the expressions. Have students explain their ideas to partners. Prompt students to check their understanding by trying to paraphrase partners' ideas. Suggest they ask questions about ideas that are unclear.

Next, ask students to explain in writing why Benjamin might have made a mistake. Prompt students to use definitions, properties, and what they already know as they justify their explanations.

Refine Applying Exponent Properties for All Integer Exponents

Purpose

- **Refine** strategies for generating equivalent numerical expressions for expressions with zero and negative integer exponents.
- **Refine** understanding of the properties of exponents as applied to zero and negative exponents.

START CHECK FOR UNDERSTANDING

Rewrite the expression as a single power using only positive exponents.

$\left(\frac{16^{-3}}{8^{-2}}\right)^4$

Solution

$\frac{1}{2^{24}}$

WHY? Confirm students' understanding of generating equivalent numerical expressions for expressions with negative integer exponents, identifying common errors to address as needed.

MONITOR & GUIDE

Before students begin to work, use their responses to the **Start** to determine those who will benefit from additional support. Use the **Error Analysis** table below to guide remediation.

Have all students complete the Example and problems 1–3, using Consider This and Pair/Share as appropriate. Observe and monitor their reasoning and guide or redirect students as needed.

LESSON 20 | SESSION 4

Refine Applying Exponent Properties for All Integer Exponents

➤ **Complete the Example below. Then solve problems 1–9.**

Example

Esteban has some money in a savings account that earns interest each year. The amount of money in his account x years from now will be $250(1.05)^x$. How much money is in the account right now? How much was in the account 1 year ago?

Look at how you could use 0 and negative exponents.

Right now is 0 years from now, so $x = 0$. The amount of money now is $250(1.05)^0 = 250(1)$.

1 year ago is −1 year from now, so $x = -1$. The amount of money 1 year ago is $250(1.05)^{-1} = \frac{250}{1.05}$.

SOLUTION now: \$250; 1 year ago: \$238.10

CONSIDER THIS . . . Do positive or negative *x*-values represent the past?

PAIR/SHARE How do you know which amount of money should be greater?

Apply It

1 What value of n makes the equation true? Show your work.

$\frac{85^n}{85^6} = 85^{-6}$

Possible work:

$\frac{85^n}{85^6} = 85^{-6}$

$85^{n-6} = 85^{-6}$

$n - 6 = -6$

$n = 0$

SOLUTION $n = 0$

CONSIDER THIS . . . Write an equation that you can solve for *n*.

PAIR/SHARE How would the problem change if the powers had different bases?

487

START ERROR ANALYSIS

If the error is . . .	Students may . . .	To support understanding . . .
-2^{24}	have assumed that the value of a power is negative because the exponent is negative.	Prompt students to rewrite each power as a product of repeated factors and divide out common factors.
$\frac{1}{2^4}$	have divided the bases instead of rewriting the powers with the same base.	Prompt students to rewrite the powers so that they have the same base before applying properties of exponents.
$\frac{1}{2^6}$	have correctly evaluated the expression inside parentheses, $\frac{16^{-3}}{8^{-2}}$ but then forgot to apply the exponent of 4 outside parentheses.	Ask students to explain each step they took to get them to see they still have to apply the exponent outside the parentheses.

Example

Guide students in understanding the Example. Ask:

- *Why does $x = 0$ represent right now?*
- *Why does $x = -1$ represent 1 year ago?*
- *Would any x-values lead to a negative amount of money in the account?*
- *How can you use properties of zero and negative exponents to solve this problem? How else could you solve the problem?*

Help all students focus on the Example and responses to the questions by asking questions to clarify something they do not understand or asking for more information.

Look for understanding that *right now* is represented by the integer 0 and *1 year ago* is represented by the integer −1. Also, look for understanding that $a^0 = 1$ and $a^{-n} = \frac{1}{a^n}$.

Apply It

1 Students may notice that 85^{-6} can be rewritten as $\frac{1}{85^6}$, which means that $85^n = 1$. Therefore, n must equal 0. *DOK 1*

2 Students may solve the problem by rewriting 15^{-3} as $(3 \cdot 5)^{-3}$, and then writing that as a product of two powers, $3^{-3} \cdot 5^{-3}$. Then they can apply properties of exponents because there will be powers in the numerator and denominator that have the same base. *DOK 1*

3 **C is correct.** Students may solve the problem by writing 4^{-9} as a power with a positive exponent, which is $\frac{1}{4^9}$.

A is not correct. This answer is equivalent to 4^8.

B is not correct. This answer has a value of 1 because $(4^9)^0 = 4^{9 \cdot 0} = 4^0 = 1$.

D is not correct. This answer is equivalent to 4^9.

DOK 3

LESSON 20 | SESSION 4

2 Evaluate the expression $\frac{3^2 \cdot 5^{-7}}{15^{-3}}$. Show your work.

Possible work:

$$\frac{3^2 \cdot 5^{-7}}{15^{-3}} = \frac{3^2 \cdot 5^{-7}}{3^{-3} \cdot 5^{-3}}$$
$$= 3^{2-(-3)} \cdot 5^{-7-(-3)}$$
$$= 3^{2+3} \cdot 5^{-7+3}$$
$$= 3^5 \cdot 5^{-4}$$
$$= \frac{3^5}{5^4}$$
$$= \frac{243}{625}$$

SOLUTION $\frac{243}{625}$

CONSIDER THIS . . . How can you rewrite 15^{-3} as a product of two powers?

PAIR/SHARE Could you tell whether the expression was less than or greater than 1 before evaluating the powers?

3 Which expression is equivalent to 4^{-9}?

A $4^9 \cdot 4^{-1}$

B $(4^{-9})^0$

Ⓒ $\frac{1}{4^9}$

D $\frac{4^9}{4^0}$

Benjamin chose A as the correct answer. How might he have gotten that answer?

Possible answer: Benjamin may have thought that when powers that have the same base are multiplied, the exponents should also be multiplied. Instead, the exponents should be added.

CONSIDER THIS . . . How can you combine powers that have the same base?

PAIR/SHARE How can you change each of the other expressions so that they are all equivalent to 4^{-9}?

488

GROUP & DIFFERENTIATE

Identify groupings for differentiation based on the **Start** and problems 1–3. A recommended sequence of activities for each group is suggested below. Use the resources on the next page to differentiate and close the lesson.

Approaching Proficiency
- **RETEACH** Visual Model
- **REINFORCE** Problems 4, 6, 7

Meeting Proficiency
- **REINFORCE** Problems 4–8

Extending Beyond Proficiency
- **REINFORCE** Problems 4–8
- **EXTEND** Challenge

Have all students complete the **Close: Exit Ticket**.

Resources for Differentiation are found on the next page.

Refine Applying Exponent Properties for All Integer Exponents

Apply It

4 **A** **is correct.** Subtract the exponents to get $28^{-5-(-2)} = 28^{-3}$.

C **is correct.** Write $\frac{1}{28^{-3}}$ as a power with a positive exponent, 28^3. Then multiply the exponents, $(28^3)^{-1} = 28^{3 \cdot -1} = 28^{-3}$.

F **is correct.** This expression is equivalent to $7^{-3} \bullet 4^{-3}$, which is $(7 \bullet 4)^{-3}$, or 28^{-3}.

B is not correct. This answer is 28^3.

D is not correct. This answer is equivalent to $7^3 \bullet 4^3$, which is equivalent to $(7 \bullet 4)^3$ or 28^3.

E is not correct. This answer is 28^{-2+5}, or 28^3.

DOK 2

5 Students may also solve by reasoning that $\left(\frac{a}{b}\right)^{-1}$ is equivalent to $1 \div \left(\frac{a}{b}\right)^1$ or $1 \div \frac{a}{b}$, which is $1 \bullet \frac{b}{a}$, or just $\frac{b}{a}$. *DOK 3*

6 Students may write both sides of the equation as single powers of 42 and equate the exponents. *DOK 1*

7 **a.** Write $\frac{1}{7^{-4}}$ as a power with a positive exponent, 7^4.

b. Add exponents, $7^2 \bullet 7^{-2} = 7^{2+(-2)} = 7^0$, or 1.

c. Multiply exponents, $(7^2)^{-2} = 7^{2 \cdot (-2)} = 7^{-4}$.

d. $\left(\frac{1}{7^4}\right)^{-1}$ can be written as $\frac{1}{7^{-4}}$, or 7^4.

DOK 2

---

4 Which expressions are equivalent to 28^{-3}? Select all that apply.

(**A**) $\frac{28^{-5}}{28^{-2}}$ **B** $28^0 \cdot 28^3$ (**C**) $\left(\frac{1}{28^{-3}}\right)^{-1}$

D $(7^{-3} \cdot 4^{-3})^{-1}$ **E** $28^{-2} \cdot 28^5$ (**F**) $\frac{7^{-3}}{4^3}$

5 Angel says that raising a fraction to the power of −1 is the same as finding the reciprocal of the fraction. Do you agree? Explain.

Yes; Possible explanation: The expression $\left(\frac{a}{b}\right)^{-1}$ can be written as $\frac{a^{-1}}{b^{-1}}$, which is equivalent to $\frac{1}{a} \div \frac{1}{b} = \frac{b}{a}$.

6 What value of n makes the equation true? Show your work.

$$\frac{42^n}{42} = \frac{1}{42^{-8}}$$

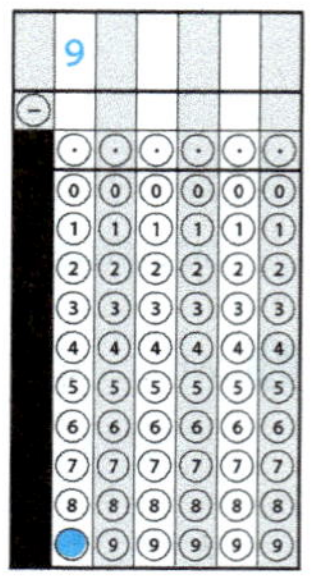

Possible work:

$42^{n-1} = 42^8$

$n - 1 = 8$

$n = 9$

7 Tell whether each expression is equivalent to 7^4, 7^{-4}, or *Neither*.

	7^4	7^{-4}	Neither
a. $\frac{1}{7^{-4}}$	●	○	○
b. $7^2 \cdot 7^{-2}$	○	○	●
c. $(7^2)^{-2}$	○	●	○
d. $\left(\frac{1}{7^4}\right)^{-1}$	●	○	○

489

DIFFERENTIATION

RETEACH

Visual Model

Use a table to understand negative exponents.

Students approaching proficiency with understanding the property of negative exponents will benefit from using a table to demonstrate the meaning of negative exponents.

- Display a table with two columns and seven rows. Label the first column *Power* and the second column *Value*. Fill in the first column with $4^3, 4^2, 4^1, 4^0, 4^{-1}, 4^{-2}, 4^{-3}$.
- In the second column, ask volunteers to write the repeated factors and the value of the first three powers. [$4 \bullet 4 \bullet 4 = 64$; $4 \bullet 4 = 16$; $4 = 4$]
- Ask: *What is the value of 4^0?* [1] Write the value in second column of the table.
- Ask: *What pattern do you notice in the values as you move from the top to the bottom of the table?* [Each value is one-fourth the value of the row above.] *How can you use the value in the first row to find the value in the second row?* [Divide the value by 4.] *Can you apply this rule to find the value in the third row? Explain.* [Yes, $16 \div 4 = 4$.]
- Ask: *If you continue applying the pattern, what is the value of 4^{-1}?* $\left[\frac{1}{4}\right]$ Repeat for 4^{-2} and 4^{-3}. Complete the table with the values of these powers.
- Have students look at the first three rows of the table. Ask: *What do positive exponents mean?* [They tell you how many times to use the base as a factor.]
- Ask: *What does the negative exponent mean in 4^{-1}?* [It means to divide by 4 once.] Repeat for 4^{-2} and 4^{-3}.
- Have students look at the last three rows of the table. Ask: *What do negative exponents mean?* [They tell you how many times to divide by the base.]

8 See ***Connect to Culture*** to support student engagement.

a. Students may reason that *right now* is represented by the integer 0. They may substitute 0 for *x* and simplify. ***DOK 2***

b. Students may reason that *one year ago* is represented by the integer −1. They may substitute −1 for *x* and simplify. ***DOK 2***

CLOSE EXIT TICKET

9 **Math Journal** Look for understanding that the value of the expression inside parentheses is greater than 1 and, when raised to a power of −1, has a value between 0 and 1.

Error Alert If students say the expression is not between 0 and 1, then be sure they understand that raising an expression to the power of −1 means finding the reciprocal of the expression.

End of Lesson Checklist

INTERACTIVE GLOSSARY Support students by suggesting they look back at the first Model It in Session 2, which shows the steps of simplifying an expression. Then have students explain in their own words what it means to simplify an expression.

SELF CHECK Have students review and check off any new skills on the Unit 5 Opener.

---

8 The value of Serafina's car is decreasing by 10% each year. Its value in dollars *x* years from now will be $12{,}000\left(\frac{9}{10}\right)^x$.

a. How much is the car worth right now? Show your work.

Possible work:

$12{,}000\left(\frac{9}{10}\right)^0 = 12{,}000(1)$

$= 12{,}000$

SOLUTION The car is worth $12,000 now.

b. How much was the car worth one year ago? Show your work.

Possible work:

$12{,}000\left(\frac{9}{10}\right)^{-1} = 12{,}000\left(\frac{10}{9}\right)$

$= \frac{120{,}000}{9}$

$\approx 13{,}333.33$

SOLUTION The car was worth about $13,333.33 one year ago.

9 **Math Journal** Explain how to find if the value of the expression $\left(\frac{26^3}{15^{-8}}\right)^{-1}$ is between 0 and 1. Do you have to find the exact value of the expression?

No; Possible explanation: When written with only positive exponents, the expression inside the parentheses becomes $26^3 \cdot 15^8$, which is greater than 1. This expression is then raised to the power of −1, which is the same as finding the reciprocal of the number.

$\frac{1}{26^3 \cdot 15^8}$ is < 0 and > 1.

End of Lesson Checklist

- ☐ **INTERACTIVE GLOSSARY** Find the entry for *simplify*. Write a new entry for *simplify*. Tell what you do when you *simplify* an expression.
- ☐ **SELF CHECK** Go back to the Unit 5 Opener and see what you can check off.

REINFORCE

Problems 4–8

Solve problems involving zero and negative exponents.

Students meeting proficiency will benefit from additional work with properties of exponents as applied to zero and negative exponents by solving problems in a variety of formats.

- Have students work on their own or with a partner to solve the problems.
- Encourage students to show their work.

EXTEND

Challenge

Solve problems with negative bases and negative exponents.

Students extending beyond proficiency will benefit from evaluating expressions with negative bases and negative exponents.

- Have students work with a partner to solve the problem: *Evaluate* $(-2)^{-3}$.
- Some students may find it helpful to first rewrite the expression with a positive exponent and then rewrite it using repeated factors.
- Repeat, using these expressions: $(-3)^{-4}$, $\left(-\frac{1}{2}\right)^{-2}$, $\left(-\frac{1}{4}\right)^{-3}$.

PERSONALIZE

i-Ready

Provide students with opportunities to work on their personalized instruction path with *i-Ready* Online Instruction to:

- fill prerequisite gaps.
- build up grade-level skills.

Lesson Quiz

TESTED SKILLS

Assesses 8.EE.A.1

Problems on this assessment require students to apply properties of exponents to powers with negative integer exponents and powers with zero integer exponents. Students will write powers with negative exponents as powers with positive exponents. They will simplify and evaluate expressions with integer exponents and use properties of exponents to recognize equivalent expressions. Students will also need to be familiar with properties of exponents including power of a power, powers with the same base, and powers with the same exponent.

Alternately, teachers may assign the **Digital Comprehension Check** online to assess student understanding of this material.

Error Alert Errors may result if students:

- add exponents instead of multiplying when applying the properties of exponents.
- add exponents instead of subtracting when applying the properties of exponents.
- forget to change the sign of the exponent when rewriting a power with a negative exponent.

Problem Notes

1 (2 points)

DOK 1 | 8.EE.A.1

2 Students could solve this problem by writing and simplifying an expression for the reciprocal of a fraction and writing and simplifying another expression for the fraction raised to the −1. The student should recognize that the two expressions are equal.

(2 points)

DOK 2 | 8.EE.A.1

3 **A is correct.** Students could solve the problem by writing $-n$ equal to $-(-6)$ and solving for the value of n.

B is not correct. This answer represents writing $-n$ equal to the numerator of the fraction, 1.

C is not correct. This answer represents writing n equal to the numerator of the fraction, 1.

D is not correct. This answer represents writing $-n$ equal to -6 instead of $-n$ equal to $-(-6)$.

(1 point)

DOK 1 | 8.EE.A.1

LESSON 20 • QUIZ | Name:

➤ **Solve the problems.**

1 Rewrite the expression using only positive exponents. Show your work. *(2 points)*

$5^{-12} \cdot 32^{-3} \cdot 9^{-15}$

Possible student work: $\frac{1}{5^{12}} \cdot \frac{1}{32^3} \cdot \frac{1}{9^{15}} = \frac{1}{5^{12} \cdot 32^3 \cdot 9^{15}}$

SOLUTION $\frac{1}{5^{12} \cdot 32^3 \cdot 9^{15}}$

2 Ira says that the reciprocal of a fraction is equal to the fraction raised to the power of −1. Is Ira correct? Explain your answer. *(2 points)*

SOLUTION Yes; Possible explanation: $\frac{1}{\frac{a}{b}} = 1\left(\frac{b}{a}\right) = \frac{b}{a}$ and $\left(\frac{a}{b}\right)^{-1} = \frac{1}{\frac{a}{b}} = \frac{b}{a}$; therefore, $\frac{1}{\frac{a}{b}} = \left(\frac{b}{a}\right)^{-1}$.

3 Which value of n makes the equation true? *(1 point)*

$15^{-n} = \frac{1}{15^{-6}}$

(A) −6

B −1

C 1

D 6

Multiple Select Scoring Rubric	
Points	**Expectations**
2	All answers are correct
1	1 incorrect answer
0	2 or more incorrect answers

Short Response Scoring Rubric	
Points	**Expectations**
2	Response has the correct solution(s) and includes well-organized, clear, and concise work demonstrating thorough understanding of mathematical concepts and/or procedures.
1	Response contains mostly correct solution(s) and shows partial understanding of mathematical concepts and/or procedures.
0	Response shows no attempt at finding a solution and no effort to demonstrate an understanding of mathematical concepts and/or procedures.

4 Students could solve this problem by understanding that the time *right now* is 0 years from now and then evaluate the expression at $x = 0$. The expression raised to the 0 power is equal to 1.

(2 points)

DOK 2 | 8.EE.A.1

5 **C, D, F are correct.** Students could solve the problem by applying the properties of exponents to evaluate each expression, and then identify the expressions equivalent to 24^{-7}.

A is not correct. This answer represents adding exponents instead of subtracting when applying the properties of exponents.

B is not correct. This answer represents multiplying unlike bases and then adding the exponents when applying the properties of exponents.

E is not correct. This answer represents subtracting the exponents instead of adding when applying the properties of exponents.

(2 points)

DOK 1 | 8.EE.A.1

LESSON 20 • QUIZ | Name:

4 The value of Huda's business computer is decreasing by 15% each year. Its value, in dollars, x years from now will be $3{,}000\left(\frac{17}{20}\right)^x$. How much is the computer worth now? Show your work. *(2 points)*

Possible student work: $3{,}000\left(\frac{17}{20}\right)^0 = 3{,}000(1) = 3{,}000$

SOLUTION $3,000

5 Which expressions are equivalent to 24^{-7}? Choose all the correct answers. *(2 points)*

A $\frac{24^{-3}}{24^{-4}}$

B $3^{-2} \cdot 8^{-5}$

(C) $\left(\frac{1}{24^{-7}}\right)^{-1}$

(D) $\frac{8^{-7}}{3^7}$

E $24^7 \cdot 24^0$

(F) $(24^3 \cdot 24^4)^{-1}$

DIFFERENTIATION

RETEACH Tools for Instruction

Students who require additional support for prerequisite or on-level skills will benefit from activities that provide targeted skills instruction.

GRADE 8
- **Lesson 20** Negative Exponents

REINFORCE Math Center Activity

Students who require practice to reinforce concepts and skills and deepen understanding will benefit from small group collaborative games and activities (available in on-level, below-level, and above-level versions).

GRADE 8
- **Lesson 20** Expressions with Integer Exponents

EXTEND Enrichment Activity

Students who have achieved proficiency with concepts and skills and are ready for additional challenges will benefit from group collaborative games and activities that extend understanding.

GRADE 8
- **Lesson 20** Grow and Shrink

LESSON 21

Overview | Express Numbers Using Integer Powers of 10

MATH FOCUS

Focus Standard

8.EE.A.3 Use numbers expressed in the form of a single digit times an integer power of 10 to estimate very large or very small quantities, and to express how many times as much one is than the other.

See Unit 5 Overview for developing and applied standards.

STANDARDS FOR MATHEMATICAL PRACTICE (SMP)

SMP 1, 2, 3, 4, 5, and 6 are integrated into the Try-Discuss-Connect routine.*

This lesson provides additional support for:

1 Make sense of problems and persevere in solving them.

7 Look for and make use of structure.

8 Look for and express regularity in repeated reasoning.

* See page 1o to learn how every lesson includes these SMP.

Objectives

Content Objectives

- Write numbers expressed as a single digit times an integer power of 10 in standard form, and vice versa.
- Write estimates for quantities using a single digit times an integer power of 10.
- Compare quantities expressed as a single digit times an integer power of 10.

Language Objectives

- Explain solution strategies using numbers expressed in standard form and as single digits times an integer power of 10.
- Use lesson vocabulary and *less than, greater than, times as many,* and *as great as* to write and talk about problems that involve expressing, estimating, and comparing quantities using powers of 10.

Prior Knowledge

- Understand place value of whole numbers and decimals and rounding numbers to any place.
- Explain patterns in the number of zeros and the placement of the decimal point in the product when a number is multiplied or divided by a power of 10.
- Use integer exponents to denote powers of 10.
- Apply properties of exponents to generate equivalent expressions.

Vocabulary

Math Vocabulary

There is no new vocabulary. Review the following key terms.

integers the set of whole numbers and their opposites.

power of 10 a number that can be written as a product of 10s. For example, 100 and 1,000 are powers of 10 because $100 = 10 \times 10$ and $1{,}000 = 10 \times 10 \times 10$.

round to approximate the value of a number by finding the nearest ten, hundred, or other place value.

Academic Vocabulary

express to show or represent by a sign or symbol.

mass the amount of matter in an object.

Learning Progression

In Grade 5, students learned about place value of very large and very small numbers and rounded numbers to any place. Students also used exponents to represent powers of 10 and observed and explained patterns in the number of zeros and the placement of the decimal point when a number is multiplied or divided by a power of 10.

Earlier in Grade 8, students learned and explained the properties of integer exponents and used these properties to generate equivalent expressions.

In this lesson, students convert numbers expressed as a single digit times an integer power of 10 to standard form, and vice versa. They write estimates for quantities using a single digit times an integer power of 10 and compare quantities expressed in this form.

Later in Grade 8, students will learn the definition of scientific notation and will add, subtract, multiply, and divide numbers given in scientific notation.

Pacing Guide

Items marked with ✱ are available on the **Teacher Toolbox**.

	MATERIALS	DIFFERENTIATION
SESSION 1 **Explore** Using Integer Powers of 10 (35–50 min)		
• **Start** (5 min) • **Try It** (5–10 min) • **Discuss It** (10–15 min) • **Connect It** (10–15 min) • **Close: Exit Ticket** (5 min) **Additional Practice** (pages 495–496)	Presentation Slides ✱	**PREPARE** Interactive Tutorial ✱ **RETEACH or REINFORCE** Visual Model
SESSION 2 **Develop** Estimating Quantities Using Integer Powers of 10 (45–60 min)		
• **Start** (5 min) • **Try It** (10–15 min) • **Discuss It** (10–15 min) • **Connect It** (15–20 min) • **Close: Exit Ticket** (5 min) **Additional Practice** (pages 501–502)	Presentation Slides ✱	**RETEACH or REINFORCE** Visual Model **REINFORCE** Fluency & Skills Practice ✱ **EXTEND** Deepen Understanding
SESSION 3 **Develop** Comparing Quantities Involving Integer Powers of 10 (45–60 min)		
• **Start** (5 min) • **Try It** (10–15 min) • **Discuss It** (10–15 min) • **Connect It** (15–20 min) • **Close: Exit Ticket** (5 min) **Additional Practice** (pages 507–508)	Presentation Slides ✱	**RETEACH or REINFORCE** Visual Model **Materials** For display: 10 hundreds flats, 4 thousands cubes **REINFORCE** Fluency & Skills Practice ✱ **EXTEND** Deepen Understanding
SESSION 4 **Refine** Expressing Numbers Using Integer Powers of 10 (45–60 min)		
• **Start** (5 min) • **Monitor & Guide** (15–20 min) • **Group & Differentiate** (20–30 min) • **Close: Exit Ticket** (5 min)	Presentation Slides ✱	**RETEACH** Visual Model **REINFORCE** Problems 4–8 **EXTEND** Challenge **PERSONALIZE** i-Ready
Lesson 21 Quiz ✱ or **Digital Comprehension Check**		**RETEACH** Tools for Instruction ✱ **REINFORCE** Math Center Activity ✱ **EXTEND** Enrichment Activity ✱

Overview | Express Numbers Using Integer Powers of 10

Connect to Culture

➤ **Use these activities to connect with and leverage the diverse backgrounds and experiences of all students. Engage students in sharing what they know about contexts before you add the information given here.**

SESSION 1 ■ □ □ □

Try It Ask students who have ever collected coins to share their experiences with the class. There are four production facilities, called *mints*, in the United States that manufacture coins. They are located in Philadelphia, Pennsylvania; San Francisco, California; Denver, Colorado; and West Point, New York. Each mint stamps its coins with a letter that indicates where the coins were made. These coins are shipped to Fort Knox, Kentucky, where they are distributed and put into circulation.

SESSION 2 ■ ■ □ □

Try It Ask if any students have eaten foods made with soybeans such as tofu, soy milk, or edamame. People who eat little to no meat may eat foods made from soybeans since they are high in protein. Young soybeans that have not yet ripened are called *edamame*, and can be served as a snack. Soy milk, which can be used as a beverage or in cooking, is an alternative for those who are lactose intolerant because, unlike cow's milk, soy milk does not contain lactose. Soy sauce is also commonly used in cooking.

SESSION 3 ■ ■ ■ □

Try It Have students share their experiences with attending fireworks displays. The Fourth of July is a holiday in the United States celebrating the Declaration of Independence. For many people, it marks the moment when America was born as a country. John Adams, the second president of the United States, decided to celebrate America's Independence Day with fireworks. The first official July 4th fireworks display, hosted by the president in Philadelphia, Pennsylvania, included 13 fireworks to symbolize the 13 colonies. Since then, communities and cities around the country host fireworks displays to celebrate July 4 each year.

CULTURAL CONNECTION

Alternate Notation In the United Kingdom and some Latin American countries, the way in which numbers are read aloud is a bit different. Instead of changing the number name as the place value becomes 1,000 times as large, they change the name as the place value becomes 1,000,000 times as large. Encourage students who have experience with this kind of system for number names to share what they know with the class.

U.S.	Power of 10	UK and Latin America
1 million	10^6	1 million
1 billion	10^9	1 thousand million
1 trillion	10^{12}	1 billion

Connect to Family and Community

➤ **After the Explore session, have students use the Family Letter to let their families know what they are learning and to encourage family involvement.**

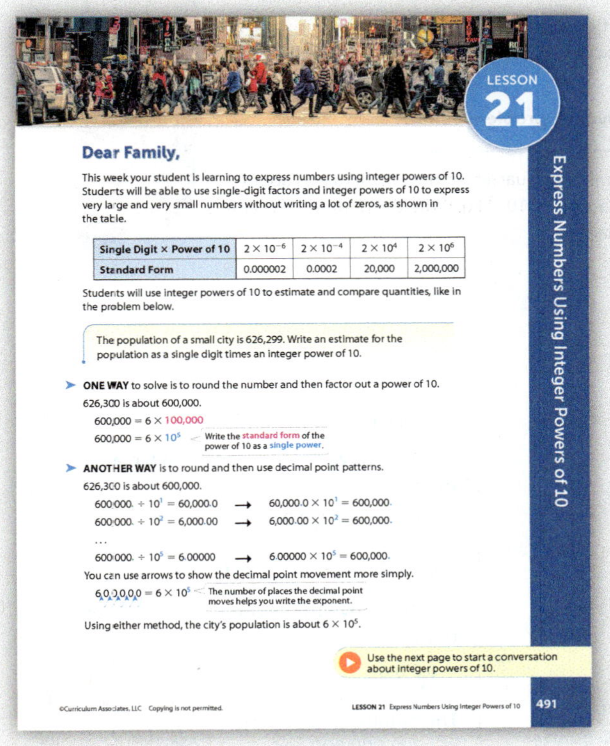

LESSON 21

Express Numbers Using Integer Powers of 10

Dear Family,

This week your student is learning to express numbers using integer powers of 10. Students will be able to use single-digit factors and integer powers of 10 to express very large and very small numbers without writing a lot of zeros, as shown in the table.

Single Digit × Power of 10	2×10^{-6}	2×10^{-4}	2×10^{4}	2×10^{6}
Standard Form	0.000002	0.0002	20,000	2,000,000

Students will use integer powers of 10 to estimate and compare quantities, like in the problem below.

The population of a small city is 626,299. Write an estimate for the population as a single digit times an integer power of 10.

➤ **ONE WAY** to solve is to round the number and then factor out a power of 10.

626,300 is about 600,000.

$600{,}000 = 6 \times 100{,}000$

$600{,}000 = 6 \times 10^5$ — Write the standard form of the power of 10 as a single power.

➤ **ANOTHER WAY** is to round and then use decimal point patterns.

626,300 is about 600,000.

$600{,}000. \div 10^1 = 60{,}000.0 \rightarrow 60{,}000.0 \times 10^1 = 600{,}000.$

$600{,}000. \div 10^2 = 6{,}000.00 \rightarrow 6{,}000.00 \times 10^2 = 600{,}000.$

...

$600{,}000. \div 10^5 = 6.00000 \rightarrow 6.00000 \times 10^5 = 600{,}000.$

You can use arrows to show the decimal point movement more simply.

$600000 = 6 \times 10^5$ — The number of places the decimal point moves helps you write the exponent.

Using either method, the city's population is about 6×10^5.

Use the next page to start a conversation about integer powers of 10.

©Curriculum Associates, LLC Copying is not permitted. LESSON 21 Express Numbers Using Integer Powers of 10 491

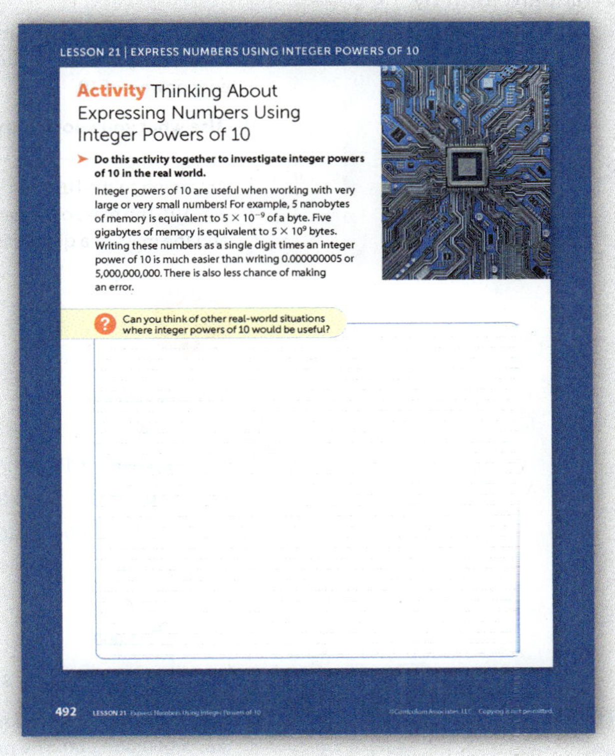

LESSON 21 | EXPRESS NUMBERS USING INTEGER POWERS OF 10

Activity Thinking About Expressing Numbers Using Integer Powers of 10

➤ **Do this activity together to investigate integer powers of 10 in the real world.**

Integer powers of 10 are useful when working with very large or very small numbers! For example, 5 nanobytes of memory is equivalent to 5×10^{-9} of a byte. Five gigabytes of memory is equivalent to 5×10^9 bytes. Writing these numbers as a single digit times an integer power of 10 is much easier than writing 0.000000005 or 5,000,000,000. There is also less chance of making an error.

Can you think of other real-world situations where integer powers of 10 would be useful?

492 LESSON 21 Express Numbers Using Integer Powers of 10 ©Curriculum Associates, LLC Copying is not permitted.

Connect to Language

➤ **For English language learners, use the Differentiation chart to scaffold the language in each session. Use the Academic Vocabulary routine for academic terms before Session 1.**

DIFFERENTIATION | ENGLISH LANGUAGE LEARNERS Use with **Session 1** **Connect It**

Levels 1–3: Reading/Speaking

Support students as they interpret Connect It problem 2. Read the first paragraph as you point to the single digit, times symbol, and power of 10 for each of the two quantities in the diagram. Repeat, but this time have students point. Point to relevant parts as you ask: *Why is this a power of 10? Why is this an integer exponent?* Provide sentence frames:

- *This is a ____ because the base is ____.*
- *This is an ____ because the number is an ____.*

Read problem 2a. Help students identify the digit, times symbol, power of 10, and integer exponent in each case. Explain that *standard form* is the usual way to write a number. Have students complete the table. Repeat for problem 2b.

Levels 2–4: Reading/Speaking

Support students as they interpret Connect It problem 2. Read the first paragraph as you point to the single digit, times symbol, and power of 10 for one of the quantities in the diagram. Repeat, but have students point using the other quantity. Then have them read the quantities and labels. Help students explain *power of 10* and *integer exponent*. Provide sentence starters:

- *A power of 10 has ____.*
- *An integer exponent is ____.*

Have partners read problem 2a. Partners take turns reading a number and identifying its parts. Next, explain that *standard* means *usual*. Call on volunteers to tell the meaning of *standard form* and complete the table. Repeat for problem 2b.

Levels 3–5: Reading/Speaking

Support students as they interpret Connect It problem 2. Have students read the first paragraph and point to the single digit, times symbol, and power of 10 for each of the two quantities in the diagram. Then have them read the quantities and labels. Call on volunteers to explain *power of 10* and *integer exponent*.

Have partners discuss the meaning of *standard form*. Then have them read and complete problem 2a. Allow time for partners to connect. Ask them to compare the numbers and corresponding notations in different rows on the table. Encourage them to use the terms *single digit, power,* and *integer exponent* in their conversations. Then have them work on problem 2b and repeat.

Explore Using Integer Powers of 10

Purpose

- **Explore** the idea that a single digit times an integer power of 10 offers a shorthand way of writing very large or very small numbers.
- **Understand** that you can convert a number from a single digit times an integer power of 10 to standard form by looking at the exponent in the power of 10 and moving the decimal point appropriately.

START CONNECT TO PRIOR KNOWLEDGE

Same and Different

A: 10^5	B: 10,000
C: 0.001	D: 10^{-3}

Possible Solutions

All are powers of 10.

A and D have exponents.

B and C are in standard form.

C and D have the same value and are less than 1.

A and B are greater than 1.

WHY? Support students' facility at recognizing powers of 10 in various forms.

TRY IT SMP 1, 2, 4, 5, 6

Make Sense of the Problem

See ***Connect to Culture*** to support student engagement. Before students work on Try It, use **Say It Another Way** to help them make sense of the problem. Be sure students understand that standard form is a form of a number that uses only digits to represent the number, and no operations.

DISCUSS IT SMP 1, 2, 3, 6, 7

Support Partner Discussion

After students work on Try It, have them respond to Discuss It with a partner. Listen for understanding that:

- when you multiply by a power of 10 with a positive exponent, the exponent indicates the number of places to move the decimal point right.
- when you multiply by a power of 10 with a negative exponent, the absolute value of the exponent indicates the number of places to move the decimal point left.

Explore Using Integer Powers of 10

Previously, you learned about properties of integer exponents. In this lesson, you will learn how to express and estimate quantities using integer powers of 10.

➤ **Use what you know to try to solve the problem below.**

According to the U.S. Mint, the number of quarters minted in 2018 was about 2×10^9. The mass of a quarter is about 6×10^{-3} kg. Write the number of quarters and the mass of a quarter in standard form.

TRY IT

Possible work:

SAMPLE A

10^9 is a power of 10 with 9 zeros.

So, $2 \times 10^9 = 2 \times 1{,}000{,}000{,}000$

$= 2{,}000{,}000{,}000$

$10^{-3} = \frac{1}{10^3}$

$= \frac{1}{1{,}000}$

So, $6 \times 10^{-3} = \frac{6}{1{,}000}$ or 0.006

The number of quarters minted in 2018 was 2,000,000,000. The mass of a quarter is 0.006 kg.

SAMPLE B

2×10^9: move the decimal point 9 places to the right

2 000000000

$6 \times 10^{-3} = 6 \times \frac{1}{10^3}$ or $6 \div 10^3$

$6 \div 10^3$: move the decimal point 3 places to the left

0.006

The number of quarters is 2,000,000,000 and the mass is 0.006 kg.

DISCUSS IT

Ask: How did you use the exponents in the powers of 10 to help you solve the problem?

Share: I used the exponents to . . .

Learning Target SMP 1, SMP 2, SMP 3, SMP 4, SMP 5, SMP 6, SMP 7, SMP 8
Use numbers expressed in the form of a single digit times an integer power of 10 to estimate very large or very small quantities, and to express how many times as much one is than the other.

Common Misconception Listen for students who think that when 10 is raised to a negative exponent, its value is negative. As students share their strategies, be sure they understand that multiplying by 10^{-3} is equivalent to multiplying by $\frac{1}{10^3}$, or dividing by 10^3. Ask students whether $\frac{1}{10^3}$ and 10^3 are positive or negative. Students should recognize that they are positive and understand that multiplying or dividing a positive number by a positive number will always give a positive result. Also, remind students that the decimal point does not actually move within a number—it always comes after the ones place—but appears to move as the number is multiplied or divided by powers of 10.

Select and Sequence Student Strategies

Select 2–3 samples that represent the range of student thinking in your classroom. Here is one possible order for class discussion:

- powers of 10 written in standard form and then factors multiplied
- (misconception) strategies that interpret the 10^{-3} as a negative number
- decimal points moved to the right or left the number of places indicated by the exponent

Facilitate Whole Class Discussion

Call on students to share selected strategies. Prompt students to build on to ideas they agree with by giving other examples that show the strategy makes sense.

Guide students to **Compare and Connect** the representations. To prompt students to use precise academic language, call on volunteers to reword vague or unclear statements.

ASK *Why is multiplying 6 by 10^9 the same as moving the decimal point 9 places to the right?*

LISTEN FOR When you multiply 6 by 10 repeatedly, you get 60, then 600, then 6,000 and so on. The decimal point moves one place to the right each time. After 9 times, the decimal point will have moved 9 places right.

CONNECT IT

SMP 2, 4, 5

1 Look Back Look for understanding that a positive exponent on the power of 10 means the decimal point moves to the right and a negative exponent means the decimal point moves to the left.

DIFFERENTIATION | RETEACH or REINFORCE

Visual Model

Find a pattern when multiplying by a power of 10.

If students need practice writing the standard form of a single-digit factor times a power of 10, then use this activity to reinforce understanding.

- Display a table with columns labeled *Product*, *Standard Form*, and *Number of Places*. Fill in the first column with 5 multiplied by increasing integer powers of 10: 5×10^0, 5×10^1, 5×10^2, and so on, up to 5×10^6.
- Have students take turns writing the product in standard form and identifying the number of places the decimal point has moved from its place in 5 to its place in the product for each row.
- Ask: *What pattern do you observe?* [Multiplying by a power of 10 with a positive exponent moves the decimal point right the number of places equal to the exponent.]
- Make a new table for 5×10^{-1}, 5×10^{-2}, and so on to 5×10^{-6} and repeat the process above.
- Ask: *What pattern do you observe?* [Multiplying by a power of 10 with a negative exponent moves the decimal point left the number of places equal to the absolute value of the exponent.]

CONNECT IT

1 Look Back What is standard form for the number of quarters minted in 2018 and the mass of a quarter? Explain how you solved the problem.

2,000,000,000; 0.006 kg; Possible explanation: I used what I know about multiplication and division by powers of 10 to move the decimal point in the given quantities.

2 Look Ahead The given quantities in **Try It** are examples of a single digit times a power that has a base of 10 with an integer exponent. These powers are called integer powers of 10.

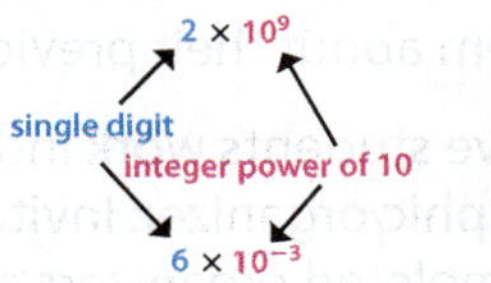

Writing numbers as a single digit times an integer power of 10 is a way to express very large or very small numbers without writing a lot of zeros.

a. Write each of these large numbers in standard form.

Single Digit × Power of 10	Standard Form
4×10^5	400,000
4×10^6	4,000,000
4×10^7	40,000,000

b. Write each of these small numbers in standard form.

Single Digit × Power of 10	Standard Form
9×10^{-4}	0.0009
9×10^{-5}	0.00009
9×10^{-6}	0.000009

3 Reflect Suppose you are given a number that is written as a single digit times an integer power of 10. How can you write it in standard form?

Possible answer: I can write the power of 10 in standard form and then multiply it by the single digit.

2 Look Ahead Point out that a single digit times an integer power of 10 with a positive exponent is a way to express very large numbers, and a single digit times an integer power of 10 with a negative exponent is a way to express very small numbers. Students should be able to generalize a pattern that helps them write a single digit times a power of 10 in standard form.

CLOSE EXIT TICKET

3 Reflect Look for understanding that an integer power of 10 with a positive exponent represents a product of factors of 10, and an integer power of 10 with a negative exponent represents a product of factors of $\frac{1}{10}$ (or repeated division by 10).

Common Misconception Look for students who think the negative exponent indicates the number of zeros after the decimal point in the standard form of the number. For example, these students think that 6×10^{-4} is equivalent to 0.00006. Remind them that multiplying by 10^{-4} is the same as dividing by 10 four times. So, the decimal point should move 4 places left. Then, ask them to count the number of places the decimal point moves from 6 to 0.00006.

Prepare for Expressing Numbers Using Integer Powers of 10

Support Vocabulary Development

Assign **Prepare for Expressing Numbers Using Integer Powers of 10** as extra practice in class or as homework.

If you have students complete this in class, then use the guidance below.

Ask students to consider the term *integer*. Remind them about their previous work with integers.

Have students work individually to complete the graphic organizer. Invite students to share their completed organizers and prompt a whole-class comparative discussion of the examples and non-examples students provided.

Have students look at the statement and question in problem 2 and discuss with a partner what they would have to provide in their explanations if they agree with the statement and what they would have to provide if they disagree. Students should understand that only one counterexample is required to disprove the statement.

Problem Notes

1. Students should understand that the set of integers are the whole numbers and their opposites. Students should recognize that integers can be positive, negative, or zero. Student responses might include examples of a positive integer, a negative integer, and 0. Their non-examples might include fractions and decimals.

2. The sum of two integers is always an integer. The difference of two integers is always an integer. The product of two integers is always an integer. However, the quotient of two integers is not always an integer. For example, $1 \div 2 = 0.5$, which is not an integer.

LESSON 21 | SESSION 1 Name:

Prepare for Expressing Numbers Using Integer Powers of 10

1. Think about what you know about numbers. Fill in each box. Use words, numbers, and pictures. Show as many ideas as you can.

Possible answers:

What Is It?
The integers are the whole numbers and their opposites.

What I Know About It
Integers can be positive, negative, or zero.
Integers and their opposites are the same distance from 0 on a number line but are on opposite sides of 0.

integers

Examples
$-17, -5, 0, 3, 42$

Non-Examples
$-3.5, -\frac{1}{2}, 4.001, 8\frac{2}{3}$

2. A student says that the sum, difference, product, and quotient of two integers are always integers. Do you agree? Explain.

No; Possible explanation: The student is correct about the sum, difference, and product, but the quotient of two integers is not always an integer. For example, 2 and 3 are integers, but $\frac{2}{3}$ is not an integer.

REAL-WORLD CONNECTION

Computer storage systems use the unit *byte* to quantify how much data they can store. The amount of data that systems can hold has increased tremendously over the years. The guidance computers used for the 1969 Apollo 11 moon landing had a capacity of 4×10^3 bytes of data. In the 1980s, 3.5-inch floppy disks were used to store data. These disks were able to hold 1.44 megabytes, or 1.44×10^6 bytes of data, which is 360 times as much as the Apollo 11 computers! Now, many personal computers can hold 2 terabytes, or 2×10^{12} bytes of data. Ask students to think of other real-world examples when writing numbers as a single digit times an integer power of 10 might be useful.

Additional Practice

3 Problem 3 provides another look at writing two numbers given as a single digit times an integer power of 10 in standard form. This problem is similar to the problem about the number of quarters minted in 2018 and the mass of a quarter. In both problems, a very large number and a very small number are written in standard form. This problem asks students to express the length and thickness of a wire made from 1 ounce of gold in standard form.

Suggest that students use **Say It Another Way** to make sure they can paraphrase the intent of the question and to confirm their answers.

3 One ounce of gold can be made into a wire that is 8×10^4 m long and 5×10^{-6} m thick.

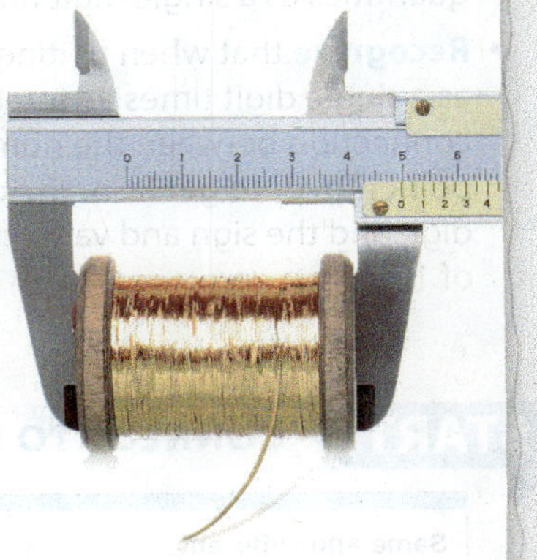

a. Write the length and thickness of the wire in standard form. Show your work.

Possible work:

10^4 is a power of 10 with 4 zeros.

So, $8 \times 10^4 = 8 \times 10{,}000$
$= 80{,}000$

$10^{-6} = \frac{1}{10^6}$
$= \frac{1}{1{,}000{,}000}$

So, $5 \times 10^{-6} = \frac{5}{1{,}000{,}000}$ or 0.000005

SOLUTION The wire is 80,000 m long and 0.000005 m thick.

b. Check your answer to problem 3a. Show your work.

Possible work:

8×10^4: move the decimal point 4 places to the right

8 0 0 0 0

$5 \times 10^{-6} = 5 \times \frac{1}{10^6}$ or $5 \div 10^6$.

$5 \div 10^6$: move the decimal point 6 places to the left

0.0 0 0 0 0 5

The length is 80,000 m and the thickness is 0.000005 m.

DIFFERENTIATION | ENGLISH LANGUAGE LEARNERS

Use with Session 2 **Apply It**

Levels 1–3: Reading/Writing

Use a **Co-Constructed Word Bank** to support students as they work on Apply It problem 6. Read the problem. Have students circle the definition of *light year*. Then have them find the amount in the picture. Next, have students circle words they can use to talk about the problem. Add the words to the bank and explain as needed. Encourage students to share cognates they know. (For example, cognates for *astronomers, distance, estimate, number, miles, digit, integer,* and *galaxy*.) Support students as they write an estimate in standard form and as a single digit times an integer power of 10:

- *There are about _____ in a light year.*

Levels 2–4: Reading/Writing

Use a **Co-Constructed Word Bank** to support students as they work on Apply It problem 6. Read the problem with students. Have them circle the definition of *light year*. Then have them find the amount in the picture. Next, discuss words students can use to talk about the problem. Add the words to the bank. Encourage students to share cognates or synonyms they know. Next, have them write an estimate in standard form and as a single digit times an integer power of 10:

- *There are about _____.*

Help students read the answer and rephrase:

- *The light travels about _____ in one year.*

Levels 3–5: Reading/Writing

Use a **Co-Constructed Word Bank** to support students as they work on Apply It problem 6. Have students read the problem. Call on volunteers to read the definition and the amount in the picture. Next, have students suggest words to add to the bank. Encourage them to include cognates and synonyms. Next, have students write an estimate in standard form and as a single digit times an integer power of 10.

Have students read the answer and rephrase each other's responses. Have students discuss their choice of words and phrases.

Develop Estimating Quantities Using Integer Powers of 10

Purpose

- **Develop** strategies for writing estimates for given quantities as a single digit times an integer power of 10.
- **Recognize** that when writing an estimate for a quantity as a single digit times an integer power of 10, there is a connection between the number of places the decimal point moves to get from the original quantity to a single digit and the sign and value of the exponent in the power of 10.

START CONNECT TO PRIOR KNOWLEDGE

Same and Different

A: 1,217 rounds to 1,000	B: 1,217 rounds to 1,220
C: 1,434 rounds to 1,000	D: 1,434 rounds to 1,430

Possible Solutions

The original numbers for A and B are the same.

The original numbers for C and D are the same.

A and C show rounding to the nearest thousand.

B and D show rounding to the nearest ten.

A, C, and D are rounded down but B is rounded up.

WHY? Support students' facility with rounding.

DEVELOP ACADEMIC LANGUAGE

WHY? Understand dense commands.

HOW? Read Apply It problem 8 and help students understand the command: *Write an estimate for/ the smallest diameter of a grain of silt/ as a single digit times an integer power of 10.* Point to each part as you say: *You need to write an estimate. What will you estimate? How do you have to write that amount?* Allow time for students to answer. Then have them explain the command.

TRY IT — SMP 1, 2, 4, 5, 6

Make Sense of the Problem

See ***Connect to Culture*** to support student engagement. Before students work on Try It, use **Three Reads** to help them make sense of the problem. Record student responses after each read. Look for understanding of the phrase *single digit times an integer power of 10.*

Develop Estimating Quantities Using Integer Powers of 10

➤ **Read and try to solve the problem below.**

Claudia's family has a soybean farm. They plant 175,000 soybeans on each acre of the farm. Each soybean weighs about 0.0057 oz. Write an estimate for both the number of soybeans per acre and the weight of a soybean as a single digit times an integer power of 10.

TRY IT Possible work:

SAMPLE A

Round 175,000 to 200,000. Round 0.0057 to 0.006.

$2 \times 10^0 = 2 \times 1 = 2$	$6 \times 10^0 = 6 \times 1 = 6$
$2 \times 10^1 = 2 \times 10 = 20$	$6 \times 10^{-1} = 6 \times 0.1 = 0.6$
$2 \times 10^2 = 2 \times 100 = 200$	$6 \times 10^{-2} = 6 \times 0.01 = 0.06$
$2 \times 10^3 = 2 \times 1{,}000 = 2{,}000$	$6 \times 10^{-3} = 6 \times 0.001 = 0.006$
$2 \times 10^4 = 2 \times 10{,}000 = 20{,}000$	
$2 \times 10^5 = 2 \times 100{,}000 = 200{,}000$	

The family plants about 2×10^5 soybeans per acre.

Each soybean weighs about 6×10^{-3} oz.

SAMPLE B

175,000 rounds to 200,000; 0.0057 rounds to 0.006.

For 200,000, try 2×10^6. This is $2 \times 1{,}000{,}000 = 2{,}000{,}000$.

There is 1 zero too many. So, $200{,}000 = 2 \times 10^5$.

For 0.006, try 6×10^{-2}. This is $6 \times \frac{1}{10^2} = \frac{6}{100}$ or 0.06.

The denominator should be 1,000. So, $0.006 = 6 \times 10^{-3}$.

The estimates are 2×10^5 soybeans and 6×10^{-3} oz.

DISCUSS IT

Ask: How can you state what the problem is asking in your own words?

Share: The problem asks . . .

497

DISCUSS IT — SMP 2, 3, 6

Support Partner Discussion

After students work on Try It, have them explain their work and then respond to Discuss It with a partner. Look for understanding of:

- what it means to write an estimate of a number.
- what it means to write a number as a single digit times an integer power of 10.

Common Misconception Listen for students who think the exponent in the power of 10 can be found by counting the number of zeros in the standard form of the number. As students share their strategies, discuss how 0.003 has 2 zeros after the decimal point, but is equivalent to 3×10^{-3}, not 3×10^{-2}. Encourage students to focus on counting the number of places that the decimal point needs to move, rather than the number of zeros.

Select and Sequence Student Strategies

Select 2–3 samples that represent the range of student thinking in your classroom. Here is one possible order for class discussion:

- 2 and 6 multiplied by increasing and decreasing powers of 10, respectively, until the product is in correct standard form
- (misconception) zeros counted to identify the exponent of the power of 10
- rounded numbers factored as a single digit times a power of 10 in standard form, then the power of 10 is rewritten in exponential form
- decimal point patterns used to write rounded numbers as a single digit times a power of 10

Facilitate Whole Class Discussion

Call on students to share selected strategies. Prompt students to check their understanding by trying to paraphrase the speaker's ideas. They can ask questions about ideas that are unclear.

Guide students to **Compare and Connect** the representations. To engage all students, ask them to turn and talk to discuss the struggles they overcame while working on this problem.

ASK *What are some different ways to determine the correct power of 10 to show in the product?*

LISTEN FOR Write the single digit part and then guess-and-check different powers of 10 or think about how many places you need to move the decimal point to get from the single digit to the original number. Or, factor out the single digit and then write the other factor as a power of 10.

Model It

If students presented these models, have students connect these models to those presented in class.

If no student presented at least one of these models, have students first analyze key features of the models, and then connect them to the models presented in class.

ASK *How are the two models different?*

LISTEN FOR The first uses factoring to find a power of 10. The second uses decimal patterns.

For the factored model, prompt students to consider the relationships shown. Ask: *Why are the second factors powers of 10?*

For the decimal point pattern model, prompt students to consider the relationships between the exponents and the decimal point movement. Ask: *How does multiplying or dividing a whole number by a power of 10 change the number?*

LESSON 21 | SESSION 2

Explore different ways to write estimates for quantities using integer powers of 10.

Claudia's family has a soybean farm. They plant 175,000 soybeans on each acre of the farm. Each soybean weighs about 0.0057 oz. Write an estimate for both the number of soybeans per acre and the weight of a soybean as a single digit times an integer power of 10.

Model It

You can round and then factor out a power of 10.

Round to the greatest place value with a nonzero digit:

175,000 is about 200,000   0.0057 is about 0.006

Rewrite the rounded number as the product of a single nonzero digit and a power of 10.

$200{,}000 = 2 \times 100{,}000$ $0.006 = 6 \times 0.001$

Write the standard form of the power of 10 as a single power.

Model It

You can use what you know about decimal point patterns after you round.

Recall that every time you multiply or divide a number by 10, the decimal point moves one place. For example:

$200{,}000. \div 10^1 = 20{,}000.0 \rightarrow 20{,}000.0 \times 10^1 = 200{,}000.$

$200{,}000. \div 10^2 = 2{,}000.00 \rightarrow 2{,}000.00 \times 10^2 = 200{,}000.$

Similarly:

$0.006 \times 10^1 = 00.06$

$0.006 \times 10^2 = 000.6$

Continue until there is a single nonzero digit to the left of the decimal point. This is the single-digit factor.

The absolute value of the exponent in the power of 10 is equal to the number of places the decimal point moves to get the single-digit factor. The sign of the exponent is determined by whether the original number is greater or less than 1.

$2{,}0{,}0{,}0{,}0{,}0 = 2 \times$ <u>10^5</u> $0.0{,}0{,}6 = 6 \times$ <u>10^{-3}</u>

498

DIFFERENTIATION | EXTEND

SMP 7

Deepen Understanding
Using Structure to Relate Multiplication and Division Equations

Prompt students to think about how the equations before and after the arrows are related. Discuss the idea that the multiplication *undoes* the division.

ASK *Look at how the division equations before the arrows are related to the multiplication equations after. How does the multiplication undo the division?*

LISTEN FOR Each division equation divides 200,000 by a power of 10 to get a new number in which the decimal point has moved. The multiplication equation multiplies that new number by the same power of 10 to get 200,000 back.

ASK *Now look at the multiplication equation that shows 0.006 multiplied by 10^1. What division equation undoes this multiplication equation? How can you rewrite the division as multiplication by a power of 10 with a negative exponent?*

LISTEN FOR $0.06 \div 10^1 = 0.006$; $0.06 \times 10^{-1} = 0.006$

ASK *Now look at the equation that shows 0.006 multiplied by 10^2. What division equation undoes this multiplication equation? How can you rewrite the division as multiplication by a power of 10 with a negative exponent?*

LISTEN FOR $0.6 \div 10^2 = 0.006$; $0.6 \times 10^{-2} = 0.006$

Develop Estimating Quantities Using Integer Powers of 10

CONNECT IT

SMP 2, 4, 5, 6, 7, 8

Remind students that the quantities and the relationships between them are the same in each representation. Explain that they will now use those quantities to reason about how to write estimates for quantities using integer powers of 10.

Before students begin to record and expand on their work in Model It, tell them that problems 1–3 will prepare them to provide the explanation asked for in problem 4.

Monitor and Confirm Understanding 1 – 3

- When the number is rounded to the greatest place value with a nonzero digit, the rounded number will have one nonzero digit. That is the digit used in the estimate.
- Moving the decimal point one place to the right is the same as multiplying by 10. Moving the decimal point one place to the left is the same as dividing by 10. The absolute value of the exponent of 10 is a count of how many times the decimal point is moved to get from the standard form to the single digit.
- The sign of the exponent of 10 is positive when the original number is greater than 1 and negative when it is less than 1.

Facilitate Whole Class Discussion

4 Look for understanding of the connection between the standard form of the rounded number and the exponent of 10 when it is rewritten as a single digit times a power of 10.

ASK *How can considering the number of places you move the decimal point to get from the standard form to the single digit help you determine the exponent for the power of 10? What else do you need to consider?*

LISTEN FOR The number of places tells you how many times you multiply or divide by 10, so it is the absolute value of the exponent of 10. You also need to think about whether the original number is greater or less than 1. If the original number is greater than 1, then the exponent will be positive. If it is less than 1, it will be negative.

5 **Reflect** Have all students focus on the strategies used to solve the Try It. If time allows, have students discuss their ideas with a partner.

CONNECT IT

➤ **Use the problem from the previous page to help you understand how to write estimates for quantities using integer powers of 10.**

1 Look at the first **Model It**. Why do you round each number to the greatest place value with a nonzero digit?

Possible answer: We are estimating with a single digit times a power of 10, so the single digit must be a good estimate for the quantity.

2 Look at the second **Model It**. Why does moving the decimal point help you find the correct exponent for the power of 10?

Possible answer: Each time you move the decimal point one place, you are multiplying or dividing by 10. The absolute value of the exponent keeps track of the number of times the decimal point moves. The sign depends on whether you are multiplying by 10 (original number $>$ 1) or dividing by 10 (original number $<$ 1).

3 **a.** Fill in the powers of 10 in the second **Model It**. How do you know whether the exponent in the power of 10 is positive or negative?

See second Model It. Possible answer: If the original number is greater than 1, the exponent is positive. If it is less than 1, the exponent is negative.

b. Write an estimate for both the number of soybeans per acre and the weight of a soybean as a single digit times an integer power of 10.

2×10^5 soybeans; 6×10^{-3} oz

4 How can you write an estimate for a number as a single digit times an integer power of 10?

Possible answer: First round to the greatest place value with a nonzero digit. Then move the decimal point to get a single digit. The number of places you move the decimal point and whether the original number is greater than or less than 1 tells you the exponent in the power of 10.

5 **Reflect** Think about all the models and strategies you have discussed today. Describe how one of them helped you better understand how to solve the **Try It** problem.

Responses will vary. Check student responses.

499

DIFFERENTIATION | RETEACH or REINFORCE

Visual Model

Use patterns to write numbers as a single digit times a power of 10.

If students are unsure how to write a number as a single digit times a power of 10, then use this activity to solidify the concept.

- Display a table with columns titled *Number, Single Digit Times a Power of 10, Number of Places Moved*. Fill the first column with 5; 50; 500; 5,000; 50,000; and 500,000.
- Have students take turns writing each number as a single digit times a power of 10, and identifying the number of places the decimal point has moved from its place in the original number to its place in the single digit, 5.
- Ask: *What pattern do you observe?* [Each time the number is 10 times as great, the decimal point must move one more place to the left to get the single digit. The number of places matches the exponent.]
- Make a new table with the same column heads and with the numbers 0.5, 0.05, 0.005, and so on to 0.000005, in the *Number* column. Repeat the steps above.
- Ask: *What pattern do you observe?* [Each time the number is divided by 10, the decimal point must move one more place to the right to get the single digit. The number of places matches the absolute value of the exponent.]

Apply It

For all problems, encourage students to use a model to support their thinking. Remind students that estimates should be rounded to the greatest place value with a nonzero digit.

6 Students may also solve the problem by counting the number of places the decimal point must move to get from the standard form of 6 trillion to the single digit 6. Because the decimal point moves 12 places and the original number is greater than 1, the exponent of 10 is 12.

7 **A is correct**. Students may solve the problem by rounding to 800,000, factoring out an 8, and then writing the single digit times the power of 10.

B is not correct. This answer may have resulted from rounding 809,762 to 900,000 instead of 800,000.

C is not correct. This answer uses the number of digits in the original number as the exponent.

D is not correct. This answer may have resulted from rounding 809,762 to 900,000 instead of 800,000, and using the number of digits in the original number as the exponent.

Apply It

➤ **Use what you learned to solve these problems.**

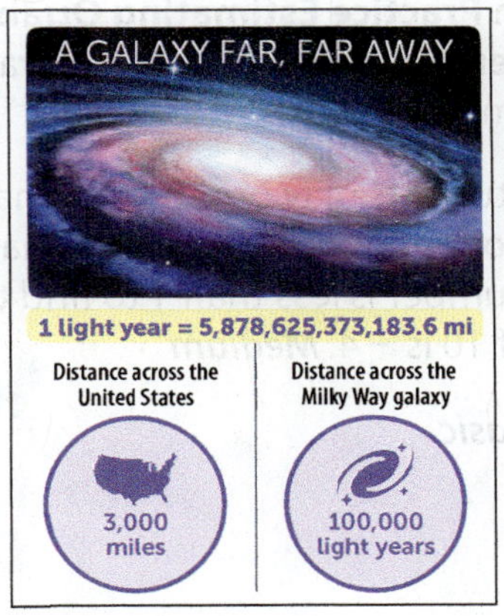

6 Astronomers use light years to measure large distances. A light year is the distance light travels in one year. Write an estimate for the number of miles in a light year as a single digit times an integer power of 10. Show your work.

Possible work:

5,878,625,373,183.6 is about 6,000,000,000,000.

$6{,}000{,}000{,}000{,}000 = 6 \times 1{,}000{,}000{,}000{,}000$

$= 6 \times 10^{12}$

SOLUTION There are about 6×10^{12} mi in a light year.

7 The population of a city is 809,762. Which is the best estimate for the population?

- (A) 8×10^5
- B 9×10^5
- C 8×10^6
- D 9×10^6

8 Silt is like sand but with smaller grains. The smallest diameter of a grain of silt is 0.0000039 m. Write an estimate for the smallest diameter of a grain of silt as a single digit times an integer power of 10. Show your work.

Possible work:

0.0000039 is about 0.000004.

$0.000004 = 4 \times 10^{-6}$

SOLUTION The smallest diameter is about 4×10^{-6} m.

CLOSE EXIT TICKET

8 Students' solutions should show an understanding of:

- how to round to the greatest place value with a nonzero digit.
- how to determine the correct power of 10.

Error Alert If students write 4×10^6, then ask them to write 10^6 in standard form and multiply it by 4. Discuss the fact that when the original number is less than 1, the exponent of 10 will be negative. If necessary, remind students that multiplying by an integer power of 10 with a negative exponent is the same as dividing the number by 10 repeatedly, which will give a number that is less than the original number.

Practice Estimating Quantities Using Integer Powers of 10

Problem Notes

Assign **Practice Estimating Quantities Using Integer Powers of 10** as extra practice in class or as homework.

1. Students may use the fact that the decimal point moves 4 places and that the original number is less than 1 to find that the exponent of 10 is −4. ***Medium***
2. ***Basic***

LESSON 21 | SESSION 2 Name:

Practice Estimating Quantities Using Integer Powers of 10

➤ **Study the Example showing how to write an estimate for a quantity as a single digit times an integer power of 10. Then solve problems 1–5.**

Example

The average mass of one grain of rice is 0.000029 kg. Write an estimate for the average mass of one grain of rice as a single digit times an integer power of 10.

Round 0.000029 to the greatest place value with a nonzero digit.

0.000029 is about 0.00003

Rewrite 0.00003 as a single nonzero digit times a power of 10.

$0.00003 = 3 \times 0.00001$

Write the standard form of the power of 10 as a single power.

$0.00001 = 10^{-5}$

The average mass of one grain of rice is about 3×10^{-5} kg.

1. The average thickness of a chicken eggshell is 0.000356 m. Write an estimate for the average thickness of a chicken eggshell as a single digit times an integer power of 10. Show your work.

   Possible work: 0.000356 is about 0.0004.

   $0.0004 = 4 \times 0.0001$

   $= 4 \times 10^{-4}$

   SOLUTION The average thickness is about 4×10^{-4} m.

2. A news podcast has 77,000 subscribers. Write an estimate for the number of subscribers as a single digit times an integer power of 10. Show your work.

   Possible work: 77,000 is about 80,000.

   $80000 = 8 \times 10^4$

   SOLUTION The number of subscribers is about 8×10^4.

Fluency & Skills Practice

Estimating Quantities Using Integer Powers of 10

In this activity, students are given a very large or a very small number and an estimate for the number written as a single digit times an integer power of 10. They either determine that the estimate is correct or write the correct estimate.

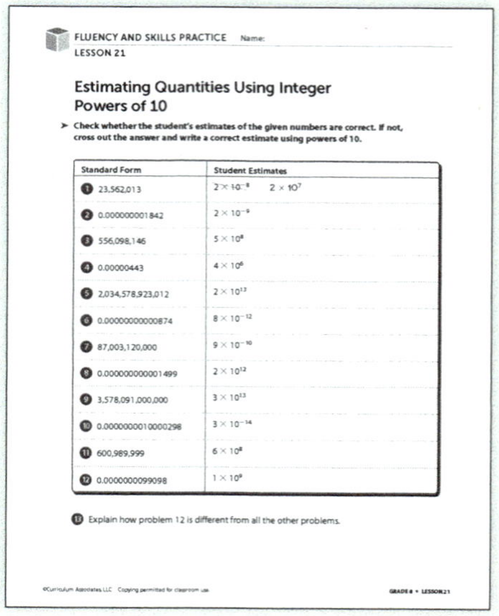
FLUENCY AND SKILLS PRACTICE Name:
LESSON 21

Estimating Quantities Using Integer Powers of 10

➤ **Check whether the student's estimates of the given numbers are correct. If not, cross out the answer and write a correct estimate using powers of 10.**

Standard Form	Student Estimates
1 23,562,013	~~2×10^{-8}~~ 2×10^7
2 0.000000001842	2×10^{-9}
3 556,098,146	5×10^8
4 0.00000443	4×10^6
5 2,034,578,923,012	2×10^{13}
6 0.0000000000874	8×10^{-12}
7 87,003,120,000	9×10^{-10}
8 0.000000000001499	2×10^{12}
9 3,578,091,000,000	3×10^{13}
10 0.0000000010000298	3×10^{-14}
11 600,989,999	6×10^8
12 0.0000000099098	1×10^9

13 Explain how problem 12 is different from all the other problems.

©Curriculum Associates, LLC Copying permitted for classroom use. GRADE 8 • LESSON 21

Additional Practice

3 **a.** Students should recognize that the greatest place value with a nonzero digit is the tenths place, so the number should have been rounded to the nearest tenth. ***Challenge***

b. Students may also find the power of 10 by noting that the decimal point moved one place and the value of the original number is less than 1. ***Medium***

4 Students may solve the problem by rounding the original number and then factoring out a power of 10. ***Medium***

5 **a.** Students may solve the problem by rounding the original number, writing the rounded number as a single digit times a power of 10, and then comparing to the answers provided. ***Medium***

b. Students should recognize that using the methods from the session to estimate provides a more accurate estimate than either of the estimates in problem 5a. ***Challenge***

LESSON 21 | SESSION 2

3 A standard baseball has a mass of 0.148835 kg. A student was asked to write an estimate for the mass as a single digit times an integer power of 10. The student's work is shown at the right.

0.148835 is about 0.05.
$0.05 = 5 \times 0.01$
$= 5 \times 10^{-2}$
The mass is about 5×10^{-2} kg.

a. Explain the student's error.

The student rounded incorrectly. He or she should have rounded the mass to the greatest place value with a nonzero digit, which is the tenths place. 0.148835 is about 0.1.

b. Show how to solve the problem correctly.

$0.1 = 1 \times 10^{-1}$

The mass is about 1×10^{-1} kg.

4 According to a recent survey, the number of pet dogs and cats in the United States is about 183,900,000. Write an estimate for the number of pet dogs and cats as a single digit times an integer power of 10. Show your work.

Possible work: 183,900,000 is about 200,000,000.

$200{,}000{,}000 = 2 \times 10^{8}$

SOLUTION The number of pet dogs and cats is about 2×10^{8}.

5 **a.** Which is a better estimate for 682,000: 6×10^{5} or 7×10^{6}? Explain.

6×10^{5}; Possible explanation: 6×10^{5} is 600,000 and 7×10^{6} is 7,000,000. So, 6×10^{5} is closer to the given value than 7×10^{6}.

b. Is there a better way to write an estimate for 682,000 as a single digit times an integer power of 10? Explain.

Yes; you can round 682,000 to 700,000. This is 7×10^{5}, and this is closer to 682,000 than either of the choices in problem 5a.

502

DIFFERENTIATION | ENGLISH LANGUAGE LEARNERS

Use with Session 3 **Connect It**

Levels 1–3: Listening/Speaking

Support students as they prepare to respond to Connect It problem 5. Use **Act It Out** with objects to review the meaning of *quantity*. Next, read the problem. Have students turn to partners to describe the quantities they need to compare. Ask: *What do you compare first? What do you do next? Which quantity is greater?*

Then, have students draft their responses to the problem. Provide sentence frames:

- *First, I compare ____.*
- *If ____ are the same, I compare ____.*
- *The quantity with ____ is ____.*

Levels 2–4: Listening/Speaking

Support students as they prepare to respond to Connect It problem 5. Use **Act It Out** with objects to have students demonstrate *quantity*. Next, read the problem with students. Have students turn to partners to describe the quantities they need to compare. Ask: *What do you do first? What do you do next? Which quantity is greater?* Then have students discuss how they can find how many times as great. Encourage them to use sequence words to explain. Have them meet with other partners to connect and compare strategies before drafting their responses. Ask: *How are the strategies the same? How are they different?*

Levels 3–5: Listening/Speaking

Support students as they prepare to respond to Connect It problem 5. Have students turn to partners to read the problem. Encourage them to share words they can use to compare and words they can use to describe their steps. Allow time for students to work on the problem and draft their responses. Then have them meet with other partners to connect and compare strategies. Remind students to identify similarities and differences between their steps. If time allows, have students add details to build on ideas or explain if they disagree with any of the steps.

Develop Comparing Quantities Involving Integer Powers of 10

Purpose

- **Develop** strategies for comparing two quantities given as a single digit times an integer power of 10.
- **Recognize** that you can compare quantities written as a single digit times an integer power of 10 by comparing the digits and comparing the powers of 10.

START CONNECT TO PRIOR KNOWLEDGE

Always, Sometimes, Never

A 7×10^n is greater than 7×10^{-n}.

B 2×10^n is less than 2 if $n < 0$.

C 2×10^n is greater than 6×10^n.

Solutions

A is sometimes true.

B is always true.

C is never true.

WHY? Support students' facility with reasoning about single digits times powers of 10.

DEVELOP ACADEMIC LANGUAGE

WHY? Support students in using precise mathematical language.

HOW? Using precise mathematical language is a skill that develops over time. When working on Try It, encourage students to use *expecting, powers of ten,* and *times as many* as they discuss their responses. Encourage partners to rephrase each other's responses using precise mathematical language.

TRY IT

SMP 1, 2, 4, 5, 6

Make Sense of the Problem

See ***Connect to Culture*** to support student engagement. Before students work on Try It, use **Three Reads** to help them make sense of the problem. Have students use the routine in pairs to answer the questions.

Develop Comparing Quantities Involving Integer Powers of 10

Read and try to solve the problem below.

The people planning Fourth of July fireworks in City A expect 3×10^5 people to attend. The people planning Fourth of July fireworks in City B expect 6×10^4 people to attend. Which city is expecting more people to attend the fireworks? How many times as many people are expected in that city?

TRY IT

Possible work:

SAMPLE A

City A: $3 \times 10^5 = 3 \times 100{,}000$
$= 300{,}000$

City B: $6 \times 10^4 = 6 \times 10{,}000$
$= 60{,}000$

$300{,}000 \div 60{,}000 = 5$

City A is expecting 5 times as many people as City B.

SAMPLE B

City A: $3 \times 10^5 = 30 \times 10^4$

City B: 6×10^4

Since the powers of 10 are the same now, compare 30 and 6.

$30 \div 6 = 5$

City A is expecting more people. They are expecting 5 times as many people.

DISCUSS IT

Ask: What did you do first to solve this problem?

Share: The first thing I did was . . .

503

DISCUSS IT

SMP 1, 2, 3, 4, 5, 6

Support Partner Discussion

After students work on Try It, encourage them to respond to Discuss It with a partner. If students need support in getting started, prompt them to ask each other questions such as:

- *How can you compare the numbers when the exponents are different?*
- *Did you rewrite one or both of the numbers in order to compare them?*
- *What operations are involved when finding how many times as many?*

Common Misconception Listen for students who compare only the first factor of each expression without considering the different powers of 10. As students share their strategies, have them write both numbers in standard form. Point out that the power of 10 indicates the place value of the nonzero digit in the number. The power 10^4 indicates that 6×10^4 is 6 *ten thousands,* while 10^5 indicates that 3×10^5 is 3 *hundred thousands.*

Select and Sequence Student Strategies

Select 2–3 samples that represent the range of student thinking in your classroom. Here is one possible order for class discussion:

- numbers written in standard form for comparison, and then divided
- (misconception) first factors compared without considering powers of 10
- powers of 10 compared to determine which is greater; then powers and factors divided, and results multiplied to find how many times as great
- numbers rewritten to have the same power of 10 and compared; then the new first factors divided to find how many times as great

Facilitate Whole Class Discussion

Call on students to share selected strategies. Remind students that one way to agree and build on ideas is to add details to help listeners understand more about the strategy or solution.

Guide students to **Compare and Connect** the representations. Allow time for students to think by themselves before starting the discussion.

ASK *Which factor, the single digit or the power of 10, is more significant when comparing values? Why?*

LISTEN FOR the power of 10; When comparing the two single-digit factors, the difference will only be another single digit. When comparing powers of 10, each difference of 1 in the exponent corresponds to a factor of 10.

Model It

If students presented these models, have students connect these models to those presented in class.

If no student presented at least one of these models, have students first analyze key features of the models, and then connect them to the models presented in class.

ASK *What is the difference between the Model Its?*

LISTEN FOR The first compares the powers of 10 to figure out which number is greater. The second determines how many times as great.

For the model comparing only powers of 10, prompt students to consider why 10^5 is greater. Ask: *What are 10^5 and 10^4 in standard form?*

For the model determining the number of times as great, prompt students to think about why the quotients must be multiplied. Ask: *Why do you need to find $\frac{1}{2} \times 10$ to find out how many times as great 3×10^5 is?*

➤ Explore different ways to compare quantities involving integer powers of 10.

The people planning Fourth of July fireworks in City A expect 3×10^5 people to attend. The people planning Fourth of July fireworks in City B expect 6×10^4 people to attend. Which city is expecting more people to attend the fireworks? How many times as many people are expected in that city?

Model It

You can compare the powers of 10 and the single digits to find which quantity is greater.

When both quantities are written as a single digit times a power of 10, the quantity with the greater power of 10 is greater.

City A	City B
3×10^5	6×10^4

10^5 is greater than 10^4.

Model It

You can compare the powers of 10 and the single digits to find how many times as great one quantity is than the other.

Divide the single-digit factors. Divide the powers of 10.

City A	City B
3×10^5	6×10^4

3 is $\frac{1}{2}$ as great as 6.

10^5 is 10 times as great as 10^4.

Then multiply the quotients.

$\frac{1}{2} \times 10$

DIFFERENTIATION | EXTEND

SMP 1

Deepen Understanding

Making Sense of Statements Comparing Numbers Involving Powers of 10

Prompt students to refer to the diagram as they make sense of the numbers given.

ASK *How were the digits 3 and 6 compared? How were the powers of 10 compared?*

LISTEN FOR 3 was divided by 6. 10^5 was divided by 10^4.

ASK *What does the product of these quotients reveal?*

LISTEN FOR City A expects 5 times as many people as City B.

ASK *What is the result of changing the order in which the single-digit factors and powers of 10 are divided? What would the product of these quotients reveal?*

LISTEN FOR The first quotient would be 2 and the second would be $\frac{1}{10}$. City B expects $\frac{1}{5}$ as many people as City A.

ASK *How does the order in which the single-digit factors and powers of 10 are divided help you interpret the meaning of the results in context?*

LISTEN FOR The quotient tells how many times as great the quantity in the dividend is compared to the quantity in the divisor.

Develop Comparing Quantities Involving Integer Powers of 10

CONNECT IT

SMP 2, 3, 4, 5, 6, 7, 8

Remind students that the quantities and the relationships between them are the same in each representation. Explain that they will now use those representations to reason about how to compare quantities involving integer powers of 10.

Before students begin to record and expand on their work in Model It, tell them that problems 1–4 will prepare them to provide the explanation asked for in problem 5.

Monitor and Confirm Understanding 1 – 4

- When two numbers are each written as a single digit times a power of 10 and the powers of 10 are different, then the number with the greater exponent on the power is greater.
- If the powers of 10 are the same, then the number with the greater single-digit factor is greater.
- To determine the number of times as great, both the single-digit factor and the power of 10 must be compared.
- City A is expecting 5 times as many people as City B.

Facilitate Whole Class Discussion

5 Look for understanding that to determine which number is greater, the powers of 10 should be compared first. Then, if the powers are the same, the single digits should be compared. To determine how many times as great one number is compared to the other, both the single digits and the powers of 10 must be divided and the quotients multiplied.

ASK *How did you determine which numbers should be the dividends and which should be the divisors?*

LISTEN FOR The single digit and power of 10 from the greater number should be the dividends, and the single digit and power of 10 from the lesser number should be the divisors.

6 **Reflect** Have all students focus on the strategies used to solve the Try It. If time allows, have students discuss their ideas with a partner.

CONNECT IT

➤ **Use the problem from the previous page to help you understand how to compare quantities involving integer powers of 10.**

1 Look at the first **Model It**. The first quantity's power of 10 is greater. Why can you also conclude that the first quantity is greater?
Possible answer: A number with a greater power of 10 will be greater since it must have a nonzero digit in a greater place value.

2 How can you decide which quantity is greater if the powers of 10 are the same?
Compare the numbers that are multiplied by the power of 10. The greater number is the greater quantity.

3 Look at the second **Model It**. Why do you have to compare both the single digits and the powers of 10 to determine how many times as great one quantity is than the other?
Comparing only the digits or only the powers doesn't compare the whole quantities.

4 Which city is expecting more people to attend the fireworks? How many times as many people? City A is expecting more people; 5 times as many.

5 How can you compare two quantities written as a single digit times an integer power of 10? How can you find how many times as great one quantity is than the other?
Possible answer: Compare the powers of 10. The quantity with the greater power of 10 is greater. If the powers of 10 are the same, compare the single digits. The quantity with the greater single digit is greater. To find how many times as great, divide the single digits and divide the powers of 10 in each quantity. Then multiply the quotients.

6 **Reflect** Think about all the models and strategies you have discussed today. Describe how one of them helped you better understand comparing quantities with integer powers of 10.
Responses will vary. Check student responses.

505

DIFFERENTIATION | RETEACH or REINFORCE

Visual Model

Use a model to understand comparing numbers written as single digits times a power of 10.

If students are unsure about comparing numbers written as a single digit times a power of 10, work through a model with powers of 10 less than 10,000.

Materials For display: 10 hundreds flats, 4 thousands cubes

- Enlist student help to build models for 4×10^3 and 8×10^2 using base-ten blocks.
- Ask: *Which model represents the greater number? How can you tell?* [4×10^3; there are more unit cubes that make 4 thousands cubes than 8 hundreds flats.]
- Ask: *What do you notice about the greater number?* [The exponent on the power is greater.]
- Enlist student help to build models for 3×10^2 and 7×10^2 using base-ten blocks.
- Ask: *Which model represents the greater number?* [7×10^2]
- Ask: *What do you notice about this number compared to the other number?* [The exponents on the power of 10 are the same, but the single-digit factor is greater.]

Apply It

For all problems, encourage students to use a model to support their thinking.

7 Students may also solve the problem by writing the numbers in standard form and comparing or by rewriting 8×10^5 as 800×10^3 and comparing 800 to 4.

8 **A is correct**. Students may solve the problem by writing 20 as 2×10^1 and then dividing 4 by 2 and 10^6 by 10^1.

B is not correct. This answer has the correct single digit but incorrect power of 10.

C is not correct. This answer is the result of assuming Midville's population is 20 times as great as Elmwood's and then choosing the incorrect power of 10.

D is not correct. This answer is the result of assuming that Midville's population is 20 times as great as Elmwood's.

Apply It

➤ **Use what you learned to solve these problems.**

7 A movie star's social media account has 8×10^5 subscribers. An athlete's social media account has 4×10^3 subscribers. How many times as many subscribers are there to the movie star's account than to the athlete's account? Show your work.

Possible work:

8 is 2 times as great as 4. 10^5 is 100 times as great as 10^3.

$2 \times 100 = 200$

SOLUTION The movie star has 200 times as many subscribers.

8 The population of Elmwood is about 4×10^6. This is about 20 times the population of Midville. Which of the following could be the population of Midville?

(A) 2×10^5

B 2×10^6

C 8×10^6

D 8×10^7

9 A deer's hair has a diameter of about 4×10^{-4} m. A dog's hair has a diameter of about 8×10^{-5} m. Which animal's hair has a greater diameter? How many times as great? Show your work.

Hair diameter: 4×10^{-4} m

Hair diameter: 8×10^{-5} m

Possible work:

10^{-4} is greater than 10^{-5}, so the diameter of the deer's hair is greater. 4 is $\frac{1}{2}$ as great as 8. 10^{-4} is 10 times as great as 10^{-5}.

$\frac{1}{2} \times 10 = 5$

SOLUTION The diameter of a deer's hair is 5 times as great as the diameter of a dog's hair.

CLOSE EXIT TICKET

9 Students' solutions should show an understanding that:

- 4×10^{-4} is greater because it has the power of 10 with the greater exponent.
- to find out how many times as great, the single-digit factor and power factor for the deer should be divided by the corresponding factors for the dog and then multiplied.

Error Alert If students say the diameter of the dog's hair is greater and divide the numbers in the opposite order, then ask them to compare the exponents on the powers. Ask: *Which is greater, −4 or −5?* Students should recognize that −4 is greater, so the deer's hair has the greater diameter. You might also ask students to compare 1×10^4 and 9×10^3 in standard form to make the point that a greater power of 10 always indicates the greater number even if the difference between the single-digit factors is as large as possible.

Practice Comparing Quantities Involving Integer Powers of 10

Problem Notes

Assign **Practice Comparing Quantities Involving Integer Powers of 10** as extra practice in class or as homework.

1. Because the powers of 10 are the same, students may compare the numbers by comparing the single-digit factors. ***Medium***

2. Students may also solve the problem by rewriting 9×10^{-11} as 90×10^{-12} and then comparing 90 to 3. ***Medium***

LESSON 21 | SESSION 3 Name:

Practice Comparing Quantities Involving Integer Powers of 10

➤ **Study the Example showing how to compare quantities involving integer powers of 10. Then solve problems 1–5.**

Example

Linda is comparing densities of materials. The density of red oak is about 2×10^{-2} pound per cubic inches. The density of stainless steel is about 3×10^{-1} pound per cubic inches. Which material has a greater density? How many times as great?

Both numbers are written as a single digit times a power of 10, so compare the powers of 10. 10^{-1} is greater than 10^{-2}, so the density of stainless steel is greater than the density of red oak.

Compare the single digits and the integer powers of 10.

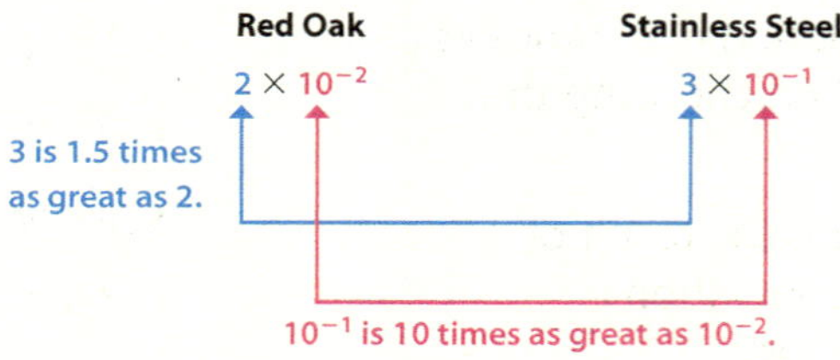

$1.5 \times 10 = 15$

The density of stainless steel is 15 times as great as that of red oak.

1. Use information from the Example. The density of brick is about 7×10^{-2} lb per in.^{3}. Which material has a greater density, brick or red oak? How do you know?

   Brick; Possible explanation: The powers of 10 are the same. The single digit for brick is greater than the single digit for red oak.

2. Which number is greater: 3×10^{-12} or 9×10^{-11}? How many times as great? Show your work.

   Possible work: 10^{-11} is 10 times as great as 10^{-12}, so 9×10^{-11} is greater. 9 is 3 times as great as 3. $3 \times 10 = 30$

   SOLUTION 9×10^{-11} is 30 times as great.

507

Fluency & Skills Practice

Comparing Quantities Involving Integer Powers of 10

In this activity, students determine whether a number written as a single digit times an integer power of 10 is greater than a given number, and if so, how many times as great.

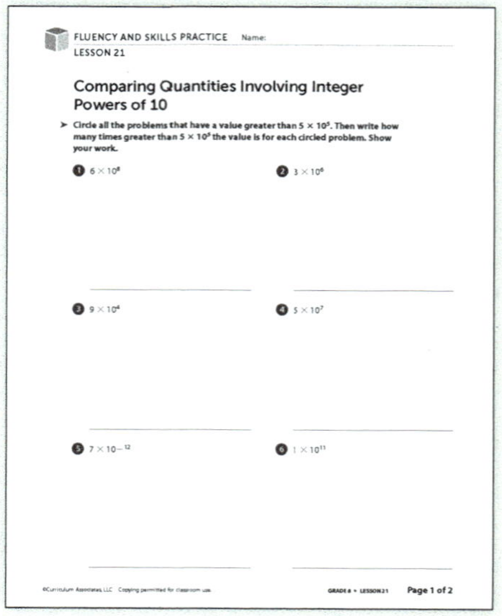

FLUENCY AND SKILLS PRACTICE Name:
LESSON 21

Comparing Quantities Involving Integer Powers of 10

➤ Circle all the problems that have a value greater than 5×10^5. Then write how many times greater than 5×10^5 the value is for each circled problem. Show your work.

1. 6×10^8
2. 3×10^6
3. 9×10^4
4. 5×10^7
5. 7×10^{-12}
6. 1×10^{11}

©Curriculum Associates, LLC Copying permitted for classroom use. GRADE 8 • LESSON 21 Page 1 of 2

Additional Practice

3 **a.** *Basic*

b. Students may also solve the problem by rewriting 2×10^7 as 20×10^6 and then comparing 20 and 5. ***Medium***

4 Students may also solve the problem by writing the number for New Mexico in standard form, comparing, and then dividing the greater number by the lesser number. ***Challenge***

5 Students may also solve the problem by writing the numbers in standard form, comparing, and then dividing the greater number by the lesser number. ***Challenge***

LESSON 21 | SESSION 3

3 The Boston Public Library has about 2×10^7 books. The Dallas Public Library has about 5×10^6 books.

a. Which library has a greater number of books? How do you know?

Boston Public Library; the power of 10 is greater.

b. How many times as many books? Show your work.

Possible work:

2 is 0.4 of 5. 10^7 is 10 times as great as 10^6.

$0.4 \times 10 = 4$

SOLUTION The Boston Public Library has 4 times as many books.

4 The 2019 population of California was 39,776,830. The 2019 population of New Mexico was about 2×10^6. How many times as large was the population of California than the population of New Mexico in 2019? Show your work.

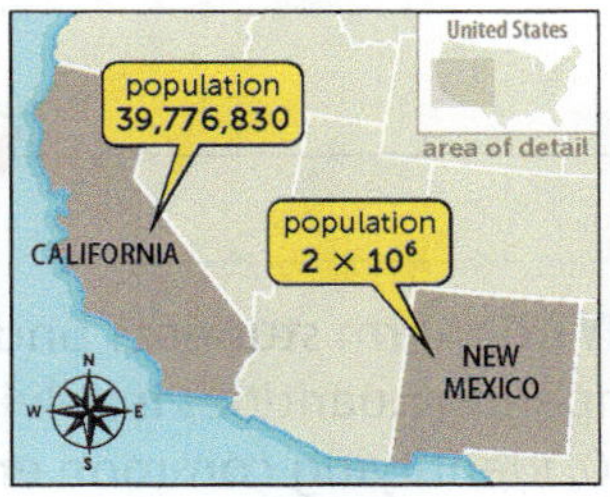

Possible work: 39,776,830 is about 40,000,000 or 4×10^7.

4 is 2 times as great as 2. 10^7 is 10 times as great as 10^6.

$2 \times 10 = 20$

SOLUTION The population of California was 20 times as large.

5 A geologist is studying a sample of chalk and a sample of marble. The chalk sample has a mass of 8×10^{-2} kg. The marble sample has a mass of 2×10^2 kg. Which sample has a greater mass? How many times as great? Show your work.

Possible work:

10^2 is greater than 10^{-2}, so the marble sample has a greater mass.

2 is $\frac{1}{4}$ as great as 8. 10^2 is 10,000 times as great as 10^{-2}.

$\frac{1}{4} \times 10,000 = 2,500$

SOLUTION The marble sample's mass is 2,500 times as great.

508

DIFFERENTIATION | ENGLISH LANGUAGE LEARNERS

Use with **Session 4** **Apply It**

ACADEMIC VOCABULARY

Greatest means the largest amount or measure.

Least means the smallest amount or measure.

Levels 1–3: Reading/Writing

Modify **Three Reads** to help students respond to Apply It problem 4. Read the first sentence. Help students connect the text with the table. Ask: *What foods are listed in the table? What does g mean? What are the quantities in the right column?* Display the Academic Vocabulary and read the second sentence. Ask: *How will you order the foods?* Have partners work on the problem. Provide a sentence frame:

- *The foods from* ____ *to* ____ *are* ____.

Levels 2–4: Reading/Writing

Modify **Three Reads** to help students respond to Apply It problem 4. Read the problem with students. Help them connect the text with the table. Ask: *What does the sentence tell about the table? What do you see in each column?* Then display the Academic Vocabulary. Have students use the vocabulary to tell what they need to do. Next, have students turn to partners to reread the problem and discuss. Ask: *What is the order of foods from greatest to least? How did you find the answer?* Encourage students to use sequence words to explain their responses.

Levels 3–5: Reading/Writing

Modify **Stronger and Clearer Each Time** to help students respond to Apply It problem 4. Display the Academic Vocabulary and have students read the problem. Invite them to explain how the text connects to the table. Then have them work on the problem and draft an answer. Allow time for students to decide how they will explain. Next, have students turn to partners to share their work and explain the answers. Ask students to check whether their partners used sequence words and *greatest* and *least* to explain their responses.

Refine Expressing Numbers Using Integer Powers of 10

Purpose

- **Refine** strategies for writing estimates for quantities using a single digit times an integer power of 10.
- **Refine** understanding of estimating and comparing quantities by writing them as a single digit times an integer power of 10.

START CHECK FOR UNDERSTANDING

The weight of a car is 4×10^3 pounds. The weight of a semi-truck is 8×10^4 pounds. How many times as great is the weight of the semi-truck than the car?

Solution

20

WHY? Confirm students' understanding of comparing quantities involving integer powers of 10, identifying common errors to address as needed.

MONITOR & GUIDE

Before students begin to work, use their responses to the **Start** to determine those who will benefit from additional support. Use the **Error Analysis** table below to guide remediation.

Have all students complete the Example and problems 1–3, using Consider This and Pair/Share as appropriate. Observe and monitor their reasoning and guide or redirect students as needed.

Refine Expressing Numbers Using Integer Powers of 10

➤ **Complete the Example below. Then solve problems 1–9.**

Example

Last year, Company A earned about 3×10^5 dollars. Company B earned about 7×10^8 dollars. About how many times as much did Company B earn than Company A?

Look at how you could solve the problem by comparing the single digits and the powers of 10.

Company A: 3×10^5

Company B: 7×10^8

7 is about 2 times as great as 3.

10^8 is 1,000 times as great as 10^5.

SOLUTION Company B earned about 2,000 times as much as Company A.

CONSIDER THIS . . . The phrase *About how many times . . .* means you can solve the problem by estimating.

PAIR/SHARE How would your answer be different if the income for Company A was 3×10^6 dollars?

Apply It

1. The height of the statue of Abraham Lincoln at the Lincoln Memorial in Washington, DC, is 5.7912 m. Write an estimate for the height of the statue as a single digit times an integer power of 10. Show your work.

   Possible work:

   5.7912 is about 6.

   $6 = 6 \times 1$

   $= 6 \times 10^0$

   SOLUTION The height of the statue is about 6×10^0 m.

CONSIDER THIS . . . The integer exponent in the power of 10 can be positive, negative, or zero.

PAIR/SHARE How can you check that your estimate for the height is correct?

509

START ERROR ANALYSIS

If the error is . . .	Students may . . .	To support understanding . . .
2	have only divided the single digits.	Prompt students to compare both the single digits and the powers of 10. Remind students they must divide the single-digit factors, divide the powers of 10, and then multiply the quotients.
10	have only divided the powers of 10.	Ask students if they compared both the single digits and the powers of 10. Remind students they must divide the single-digit factors, divide the powers of 10, and then multiply the quotients.
5	have divided the single-digit factors and powers of 10 in an inconsistent order and then multiplied.	Remind students that when both quantities are written as a single digit times a power of 10, the quantity with the greater power of 10 is greater. Therefore, prompt students to divide the single digit and the power of 10 of the greater number by the corresponding single digit and power of 10 of the lesser number. Then multiply the quotients.

Example

Guide students in understanding the Example. Ask:

- *Which company earned the greater amount? How do you know?*
- *7 is about how many times as great as 3?*
- *10^8 is how many times as great as 10^5?*

Help all students focus on the Example and responses to the questions by asking them to explain why they think their answers are correct.

Look for understanding that Company B earned more because their earnings have the greater power of 10. Also, look for understanding of how to estimate how many times as much by comparing both the single digits and the powers of 10.

Apply It

1 Students should notice that the decimal point does not need to be moved to get a single digit, and therefore they should multiply the single digit by 1. Ask: *How do you write 1 as a power of 10?* [10^0] *DOK 2*

2 Students may also solve this problem by writing all the lengths in standard form and comparing them. *DOK 2*

3 **D is correct.** Rounding 0.00438 to the nearest thousandth gives 0.004. You can move the decimal point 3 places to get a whole number, so, since the original number is less than 1, the exponent of 10 is −3.

A is not correct. The single digit and the exponent are incorrect.

B is not correct. The exponent is incorrect.

C is not correct. The single digit is incorrect.

DOK 2

2 The table shows the approximate lengths of some rivers in the United States. Which of the rivers is the longest? Show your work.

River	Length (m)
Copper	500,000
Missouri	4×10^6
Ohio	2,000,000
Porcupine	9×10^5
Rio Grande	3×10^6

Possible work:

Copper: $500{,}000 = 5 \times 10^5$

Ohio: $2{,}000{,}000 = 2 \times 10^6$

$10^6 > 10^5$, so the Missouri, Ohio, and Rio Grande are longer than the Copper and Porcupine.

$4 > 2$, so the Missouri is longer than the Ohio.

$4 > 3$, so the Missouri is longer than the Rio Grande.

SOLUTION The Missouri River is longest.

CONSIDER THIS . . . How can you use powers of 10 to help order the numbers?

PAIR/SHARE What can you say about the single digit and the power of 10 for any river longer than those in the table?

3 The volume of a small spoon is 0.00438 L. Which is the best estimate for the volume?

A 5×10^{-2} L

B 4×10^{-2} L

C 5×10^{-3} L

D 4×10^{-3} L

Tiana chose C as the correct answer. How might she have gotten that answer?

Possible answer: Tiana rounded 0.00438 up to 0.005, but she should have rounded it down to 0.004.

CONSIDER THIS . . . You can think of this problem as comparing 0.00438 to the numbers written as a single digit times a power of 10.

PAIR/SHARE How would your answer change if the volume were 0.00431 L?

510

GROUP & DIFFERENTIATE

Identify groupings for differentiation based on the **Start** and problems 1–3. A recommended sequence of activities for each group is suggested below. Use the resources on the next page to differentiate and close the lesson.

Approaching Proficiency
- **RETEACH** Visual Model
- **REINFORCE** Problems 4, 5, 7

Meeting Proficiency
- **REINFORCE** Problems 4–8

Extending Beyond Proficiency
- **REINFORCE** Problems 4–8
- **EXTEND** Challenge

Have all students complete the **Close: Exit Ticket.**

Resources for Differentiation are found on the next page.

Refine Expressing Numbers Using Integer Powers of 10

Apply It

4 Students may also solve this problem by writing all the numbers in standard form and comparing them or by rewriting the numbers so they all have the same power of 10 and then comparing the whole-number factors. *DOK 2*

5 **A, C, and D are correct.** For the numbers to fall within the given range, if the exponent of the power of 10 is -5, then the single digit must be greater than 6. If the exponent of the power of 10 is -4, then the single digit must be less than 3.

B is not correct. This number is less than 6×10^{-5}.

E is not correct. This number is greater than 3×10^{-4}.

F is not correct. This number is greater than 3×10^{-4}.

DOK 2

6 **a.** Any power of 10 is positive, so the product is never negative.

b. Any power of 10 is positive, so if p is positive, then $p \times 10^{-2}$ will be positive.

c. If $m = 1$, $5 \times 10^m = 50$ and $50^m = 50$. If m is an integer other than 1, 5×10^m is not equal to 50^m.

d. $q \times 10^{-1}$ is the same as $q \div 10$ because q is a positive number less than 10. So, this quotient will be less than 1.

DOK 3

4 The table shows the number of grams of vitamin A in a 100-gram serving of several foods. List the foods from the greatest amount of vitamin A to the least. Show your work.

Food	Vitamin A (g)
Beef liver	6×10^{-3}
Egg	7×10^{-5}
Red grapefruit	1×10^{-4}
Salmon	2×10^{-4}
Sweet potato	2×10^{-3}

Possible work:

The greatest power of 10 in the table is 10^{-3}.

$6 > 2$, so beef liver has the most vitamin A, then sweet potato.

The next greatest power of 10 is 10^{-4}.

$2 > 1$, so next is salmon, then red grapefruit.

The least power of 10 is 10^{-5}, which is egg.

SOLUTION beef liver, sweet potato, salmon, red grapefruit, egg

5 Which of the following values are between 6×10^{-5} and 3×10^{-4}? Select all that apply.

(**A**) 8×10^{-5}

B 5×10^{-5}

(**C**) 1×10^{-4}

(**D**) 7×10^{-5}

E 5×10^{-4}

F 7×10^{-4}

6 Tell whether each statement is *Always*, *Sometimes*, or *Never* true.

	Always	Sometimes	Never
a. If n is an integer, then 3×10^n is negative.	○	○	●
b. If p is a positive single-digit number, then $p \times 10^{-2}$ is positive.	●	○	○
c. If m is an integer, then 5×10^m equals 50^m.	○	●	○
d. If q is a positive single-digit number, then $q \times 10^{-1}$ is greater than 1.	○	○	●

511

DIFFERENTIATION

RETEACH

Visual Model

Compare quantities involving integer powers of 10.

Students approaching proficiency with comparing quantities involving integer powers of 10 will benefit from using this activity to think about the process.

- Display: *Is 5×10^2 or 1×10^3 greater? How many times as great is it?*
- Ask: *Should you first compare the single digits or powers of 10?* [powers of 10]
- Ask: *Which number is greater? How do you know?* [1×10^3; It has the greater exponent.]
- Display: *1 is ____ times as great as 5.*
- Ask: *How do you compare the single digits?* [Divide the single digit of the greater number by the single digit of the lesser number.]
- Invite a student to complete the sentence on the board. [1 is $\frac{1}{5}$ times as great as 5.]
- Display: *10^3 is ____ times as great as 10^2.*
- Ask: *How do you compare the powers of 10?* [Divide the power of 10 of the greater number by the power of 10 of the lesser number.]
- Invite a student to complete the sentence on the board. [10^3 is 10 times as great as 10^2.]
- Ask: *How do you use the comparisons of the single digits and the powers of 10 to compare the two original numbers?* [Multiply the quotients $\frac{1}{5}$ and 10. Since $\frac{1}{5} \times 10 = 2$, you know that 1×10^3 is 2 times as great as 5×10^2.]

7 **a.** Students should round each number and then move the decimal point 4 places. Both numbers are greater than 1, so the power of 10 is 10^4. *DOK 1*

b. Because the powers of 10 are the same, students can compare the single-digit factors. *DOK 2*

8 The standard form of 3×10^9 and 30×10^8 represent the same number. *DOK 3*

CLOSE EXIT TICKET

9 **Math Journal** Look for understanding of how to round the number and how to determine the power of 10. Because the number is greater than 1, the exponent of 10 is the number of places the decimal point is moved to get a single-digit number.

Error Alert If students use an exponent of 6 for the power of 10, then ask them to count the number of places they move the decimal point to get a single digit.

End of Lesson Checklist

INTERACTIVE GLOSSARY Support students by suggesting they look through their work in the lesson to see how various numbers were *expressed*.

SELF CHECK Have students review and check off any new skills on the Unit 5 Opener.

LESSON 21 | SESSION 4

7 Kwame compares the number of people that can be seated in two stadiums. Stadium A can seat 82,933 people. Stadium B can seat 29,005 people.

a. Write an estimate for the seating capacity of each stadium as a single digit times a power of 10.

Stadium A: 8×10^4 Stadium B: 3×10^4

b. About how many times as great is the seating capacity of Stadium A than the seating capacity of Stadium B? Show your work.

Possible work:

8 is about 3 times as great as 3. The powers of 10 are the same in both quantities.

SOLUTION The seating capacity of Stadium A is about 3 times as great.

8 Eldora was asked to determine which is greater, 5×10^8 or 3×10^9, and how many times as great it is. Her work is shown here. Is she correct? Explain her strategy if she is correct. Explain her error if she is not correct.

5×10^8	3×10^9
↓	↓
5×10^8	30×10^8

$30 > 5$, so 3×10^9 is greater.
$30 \div 5 = 6$, so 3×10^9 is 6 times as great.

Yes; Possible explanation: First Eldora wrote 3×10^9 as 30×10^8. Now it has the same power of 10 as 5×10^8, so she can just compare the numbers multiplied by the powers of 10.

9 **Math Journal** Choose a 6-digit whole number. Each digit in the number should be different. Explain how to write an estimate for the number as a single digit times an integer power of 10.

Possible answer: 293,851; Round the number to the greatest place value with a nonzero digit. 293,851 is about 300,000.

$300,000 = 3 \times 10^5$ So, 3×10^5 is an estimate for 293,851.

End of Lesson Checklist

☐ **INTERACTIVE GLOSSARY** Write a new entry for *express*. Tell what you do when you *express* a quantity as a single digit times an integer power of 10.

☐ **SELF CHECK** Go back to the Unit 5 Opener and see what you can check off.

512

REINFORCE

Problems 4–8

Solve problems by comparing quantities involving integer powers of 10.

Students meeting proficiency will benefit from additional work with quantities involving integer powers of 10 by solving problems in a variety of formats.

- Have students work on their own or with a partner to solve the problems.
- Encourage students to show their work.

EXTEND

Challenge

Solve problems comparing negative quantities involving integer powers of 10.

Students extending beyond proficiency will benefit from comparing negative quantities with integer powers of 10.

- Have students work with a partner to solve this problem: *Which number is greater, -5×10^3 or -8×10^4? How many times as great is it?*
- Repeat, this time comparing -3×10^{-4} and -6×10^{-2}.

PERSONALIZE

i-Ready

Provide students with opportunities to work on their personalized instruction path with *i-Ready* Online Instruction to:

- fill prerequisite gaps.
- build up grade-level skills.

Lesson Quiz

TESTED SKILLS

Assesses 8.EE.A.3

Problems on this assessment require students to be able to express numbers using integer powers of 10. Students will compare and estimate quantities by rounding the number and factoring the power of 10 or rounding and then using decimal patterns. Students will compare numbers written in powers of 10 to identify the greater value, express how many times greater one number is than another, and determine the best estimate. Students will also need to be familiar with exponents.

Alternately, teachers may assign the **Digital Comprehension Check** online to assess student understanding of this material.

Error Alert Errors may result if students:

- incorrectly place the decimal point when rewriting a number in standard form.
- round incorrectly.
- place emphasis on the single digit instead of the power of 10 when comparing numbers represented as powers of 10.

Problem Notes

1 **A is correct.** Students could solve the problem by rounding to 0.002 and then applying decimal patterns to write the point 3 places to the right.

B is not correct. This answer represents counting the number of zeros between the decimal point and the digit 2.

C is not correct. This answer represents counting the number of zeros between the decimal point and the digit 2 and not understanding that the exponent is negative because the original number is less than 1.

D is not correct. This answer represents not understanding that the exponent is negative because the original number is less than 1.

(1 point)

DOK 1 | 8.EE.A.3

2 Students could also recognize that the power of 10 is greater for Monique's high school.

(2 points)

DOK 1 | 8.EE.A.3

LESSON 21 • QUIZ | Name:

➤ **Solve the problems.**

1 The mass of a dime is about 0.002268 kg. Which is the best estimate of the mass? *(1 point)*

A 2×10^{-3} (circled)

B 2×10^{-2}

C 2×10^{2}

D 2×10^{3}

2 The total number of students who have attended Lacey's high school since it first opened is about 4×10^4 students. The total number of students who have attended Monique's high school since it first opened is about 3×10^5 students. Which school has a greater number of students who have attended? Show your work. Explain your reasoning. *(2 points)*

Possible student work: $4 \times 10^4 = 40{,}000$, and $3 \times 10^5 = 300{,}000$

SOLUTION Monique's high school; Possible explanation: 300,000 students have attended Monique's high school and 40,000 students have attended Lacey's high school. Since 300,000 > 40,000, Monique's high school has the greater number of students who have attended.

3 Which is a better estimate for 891,000: 8×10^5 or 9×10^6? Explain your reasoning. *(2 points)*

SOLUTION 8×10^5; Possible explanation: 8×10^5 is 800,000, and 9×10^6 is 9,000,000. So, 8×10^5 is closer to the given value than 9×10^6.

GRADE 8 • LESSON 21 • Express Numbers Using Integer Powers of 10 **Page 1 of 2**

Multiple Select Scoring Rubric

Points	Expectations
2	All answers are correct
1	1 incorrect answer
0	2 or more incorrect answers

Short Response Scoring Rubric

Points	Expectations
2	Response has the correct solution(s) and includes well-organized, clear, and concise work demonstrating thorough understanding of mathematical concepts and/or procedures.
1	Response contains mostly correct solution(s) and shows partial understanding of mathematical concepts and/or procedures.
0	Response shows no attempt at finding a solution and no effort to demonstrate an understanding of mathematical concepts and/or procedures.

3 Students could solve the problem by rewriting each estimate in standard form and then comparing each number to 891,000 using place value.

(2 points)

DOK 2 | 8.EE.A.3

4 Students could also solve the problem by rounding the population of Chicago to 2.7 million people and rewriting the population of Austin as 0.9 million people. Then they could divide 2.7 by 0.9 to determine that the population of Chicago is 3 times greater than Austin.

(2 points)

DOK 2 | 8.EE.A.3

5 **A, D, E are correct.** Students could solve the problem by writing each number in standard form and then comparing the numbers using place value to determine the expressions with values between 6×10^{-6} and 5×10^{-5}.

B is not correct. This answer represents a value less than 6×10^{-6}.

C is not correct. This answer represents a value greater than 5×10^{-5}.

(2 points)

DOK 2 | 8.EE.A.3

LESSON 21 • QUIZ | Name:

4 The 2018 population of Chicago, Illinois, was 2,720,546 people. The 2018 population of Austin, Texas, was about 900,000 people. How many times greater was the population of Chicago than Austin? Show your work. *(2 points)*

Possible student work:

2,720,546 is about 2,700,000, or 2.7×10^6.

900,000 is 9×10^5.

2.7 is 0.3 of 9, and 10^7 is 10 times greater than 10^6.

$0.3 \times 10 = 3$

SOLUTION The population of Chicago is 3 times greater.

5 Which of the following values are between 6×10^{-6} and 5×10^{-5}? Choose all the correct answers. *(2 points)*

(A) 4×10^{-5}

B 5×10^{-6}

C 6×10^{-5}

(D) 7×10^{-6}

(E) 8×10^{-6}

DIFFERENTIATION

RETEACH Tools for Instruction

Students who require additional support for prerequisite or on-level skills will benefit from activities that provide targeted skills instruction.

GRADE 8

- **Lesson 21** Compare and Estimate with Powers of 10

REINFORCE Math Center Activity

Students who require practice to reinforce concepts and skills and deepen understanding will benefit from small group collaborative games and activities (available in on-level, below-level, and above-level versions).

GRADE 8

- **Lesson 21** Comparing Quantities with Powers of 10

EXTEND Enrichment Activity

Students who have achieved proficiency with concepts and skills and are ready for additional challenges will benefit from group collaborative games and activities that extend understanding.

GRADE 8

- **Lesson 21** Metric Maze

LESSON 22

Overview | Work with Scientific Notation

MATH FOCUS

Focus Standard

8.EE.A.4 Perform operations with numbers expressed in scientific notation, including problems where both decimal and scientific notation are used. Use scientific notation and choose units of appropriate size for measurements of very large or very small quantities (e.g., use millimeters per year for seafloor spreading). Interpret scientific notation that has been generated by technology.

See Unit 5 Overview for developing and applied standards.

STANDARDS FOR MATHEMATICAL PRACTICE (SMP)

SMP 1, 2, 3, 4, 5, and 6 are integrated into the Try-Discuss-Connect routine.*

This lesson provides additional support for:

2 Reason abstractly and quantitatively.

7 Look for and make use of structure.

* See page 1o to learn how every lesson includes these SMP.

Objectives

Content Objectives

- Express numbers in scientific notation.
- Add, subtract, multiply, and divide with numbers expressed in scientific notation.
- Choose appropriate units for measurements of large or small quantities.
- Interpret scientific notation that has been generated by technology.

Language Objectives

- Justify that a number is written in scientific notation by describing its properties.
- Use the lesson vocabulary to explain how to add, subtract, multiply, and divide with numbers expressed in scientific notation.
- Interpret a problem context by reasoning about the appropriate unit size for measurements.
- Explain how a number generated by technology can be expressed in scientific notation using *exponent* and *power of 10.*
- Use counterexamples to show reasons for disagreeing with a speaker's strategy.

Prior Knowledge

- Write numbers expressed as a single digit times an integer power of 10 in standard form, and vice versa.
- Compare quantities expressed as a single digit times an integer power of 10.

Vocabulary

Math Vocabulary

scientific notation a way of expressing a number as a product in the form $n \times 10^a$, where a is an integer and n is a decimal number such that $1 \leq n < 10$.

Review the following key terms.

absolute value a number's distance from 0 on the number line. Absolute value is never negative.

power of 10 a number that can be written as a product of 10s. For example, 100 and 1,000 are powers of 10 because $100 = 10 \times 10$ and $1{,}000 = 10 \times 10 \times 10$.

Academic Vocabulary

contiguous without interruption or next to one another.

molecule the smallest possible particle of a substance.

Learning Progression

In Grade 6, students used the order of operations to evaluate expressions with exponents and explained patterns in the placement of the decimal point after multiplying or dividing by powers of 10.

In Grade 7, students performed operations with exponents in real-world problems.

Earlier in Grade 8, students wrote numbers as a single digit times an integer power of 10 in standard form, and vice versa. They wrote estimates for quantities using a single digit times an integer power of 10 and compared numbers written in this form.

➤

In this lesson, students learn about scientific notation. They convert between standard form and scientific notation and perform operations with numbers expressed in scientific notation. They also choose appropriate units to represent quantities and interpret scientific notation outputs given by technology, such as calculators and spreadsheets.

➤

Later in Grade 8, students will calculate volume, which will require them to work with exponential expressions.

In high school, students will use properties of exponents to interpret expressions for exponential functions, including functions representing exponential growth or decay.

Pacing Guide

Items marked with ✦ are available on the **Teacher Toolbox**.

Session	MATERIALS	DIFFERENTIATION
SESSION 1 **Explore** Scientific Notation (35–50 min) • **Start** (5 min) • **Try It** (5–10 min) • **Discuss It** (10–15 min) • **Connect It** (10–15 min) • **Close: Exit Ticket** (5 min) **Additional Practice** (pages 517–518)	Presentation Slides ✦	**PREPARE** Interactive Tutorial ✦ **RETEACH or REINFORCE** Visual Model
SESSION 2 **Develop** Writing Numbers in Scientific Notation (45–60 min) • **Start** (5 min) • **Try It** (10–15 min) • **Discuss It** (10–15 min) • **Connect It** (15–20 min) • **Close: Exit Ticket** (5 min) **Additional Practice** (pages 523–524)	Presentation Slides ✦	**RETEACH or REINFORCE** Visual Model **REINFORCE** Fluency & Skills Practice ✦ **EXTEND** Deepen Understanding
SESSION 3 **Develop** Adding and Subtracting with Scientific Notation (45–60 m n) • **Start** (5 min) • **Try It** (10–15 min) • **Discuss It** (10–15 min) • **Connect It** (15–20 min) • **Close: Exit Ticket** (5 min) **Additional Practice** (pages 529–530)	Presentation Slides ✦	**RETEACH or REINFORCE** Visual Model **REINFORCE** Fluency & Skills Practice ✦ **EXTEND** Deepen Understanding
SESSION 4 **Develop** Multiplying and Dividing with Scientific Notation (45–60 min) • **Start** (5 min) • **Try It** (10–15 min) • **Discuss It** (10–15 min) • **Connect It** (15–20 min) • **Close: Exit Ticket** (5 min) **Additional Practice** (pages 535–536)	Presentation Slides ✦	**RETEACH or REINFORCE** Visual Model **REINFORCE** Fluency & Skills Practice ✦ **EXTEND** Deepen Understanding
SESSION 5 **Refine** Working with Scientific Notation (45–60 min) • **Start** (5 min) • **Monitor & Guide** (15–20 min) • **Group & Differentiate** (20–30 min) • **Close: Exit Ticket** (5 min)	Presentation Slides ✦	**RETEACH** Visual Model **REINFORCE** Problems 4–10 **EXTEND** Challenge **PERSONALIZE** i-Ready
Lesson 22 Quiz ✦ or **Digital Comprehension Check**		**RETEACH** Tools for Instruction ✦ **REINFORCE** Math Center Activity ✦ **EXTEND** Enrichment Activity ✦

Overview | Work with Scientific Notation

Connect to Culture

➤ **Use these activities to connect with and leverage the diverse backgrounds and experiences of all students. Engage students in sharing what they know about contexts before you add the information given here.**

SESSION 1 ■ □ □ □ □

Try It Ask students who are familiar with the concept of astronomical units to share what they know. Since Earth's orbit around the sun is not a perfect circle, the distance from Earth to the sun is different at different times of the year. The average distance from Earth to the sun is 149,597,870.7 km, which is about 92,955,807.3 miles. In astronomy, this distance is used as a unit of measure called an *astronomical unit.* Using astronomical units allows distances in space to be expressed relative to the distance from Earth to the sun. For example, the average distance from Saturn to the sun is 9.6 astronomical units. This means that the average distance from the sun to Saturn is 9.6 times the average distance from the sun to Earth.

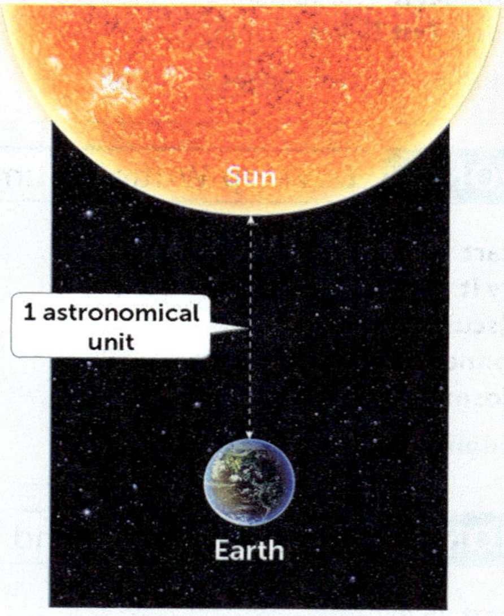

SESSION 2 ■ ■ □ □ □

Try It Almost 97% of all water on Earth is in oceans, seas, and bays. Ask students to think of other places on Earth water can be located. About 2% of Earth's water is found in glaciers and ice caps. Less than 1% of all water on Earth is fresh water in rivers, lakes, and smaller tributaries. Another very small percent is water vapor found in the atmosphere. About 71% of Earth's surface is covered with water. However, there are also several places on Earth where water is held underground.

SESSION 3 ■ ■ ■ □ □

Try It Ask students if they know what it means to be part of the 48 contiguous states. Some think of these states as the ones within North America between Mexico and Canada. Others think of these states as the United States minus Alaska and Hawaii. In 1867, the territory of Alaska was bought from Russia for a little over $7 million. In 1898, Hawaii was annexed as a United States territory. These last two states to join the United States became official states in 1959.

SESSION 4 ■ ■ ■ ■ □

Try It Have students share other information they might know about seafloor spreading from their studies in science. Seafloor spreading is a natural process that occurs as Earth's core pushes heat up through layers of Earth. Over time, the ocean floor moves plates of Earth apart along underwater mountains and trenches. Seafloor spreading occurs at different rates. The Mid-Atlantic Ridge is a slow spreading process that separates plates in the Atlantic Ocean. The East Pacific Rise is a faster-moving process that separates plates in the Pacific Ocean.

SESSION 5 ■ ■ ■ ■ ■

Apply It **Problem 8** The Dakota Territory was formed in 1861 and included North Dakota and South Dakota and parts of Wyoming and Montana. It was expected that this territory would join the United States as a single state once it had a population of more than 60,000 and a state constitution. However, political differences among the populations of the southern and northern parts of the territory resulted in two different states being formed. Ask students who have ever visited or lived in either of the Dakotas to describe their experiences.

Connect to Family and Community

➤ **After the Explore session, have students use the Family Letter to let their families know what they are learning and to encourage family involvement.**

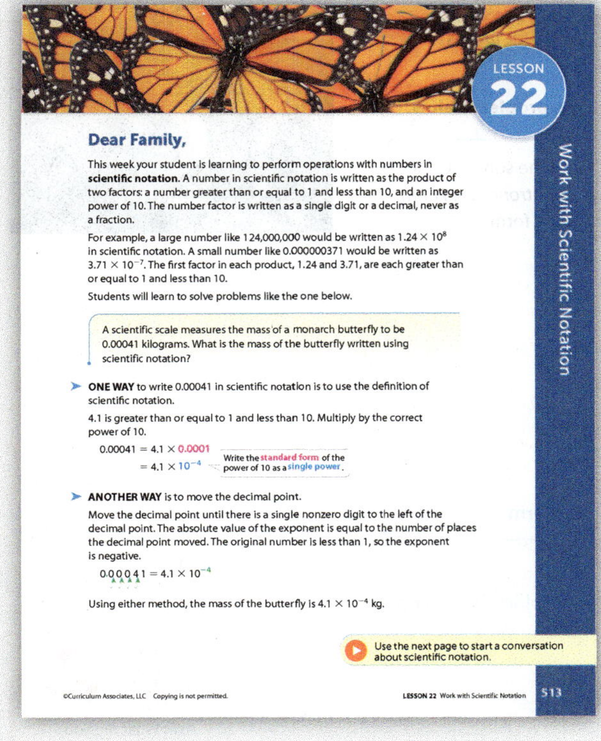

LESSON 22

Work with Scientific Notation

Dear Family,

This week your student is learning to perform operations with numbers in **scientific notation.** A number in scientific notation is written as the product of two factors: a number greater than or equal to 1 and less than 10, and an integer power of 10. The number factor is written as a single digit or a decimal, never as a fraction.

For example, a large number like 124,000,000 would be written as 1.24×10^8 in scientific notation. A small number like 0.000000371 would be written as 3.71×10^{-7}. The first factor in each product, 1.24 and 3.71, are each greater than or equal to 1 and less than 10.

Students will learn to solve problems like the one below.

A scientific scale measures the mass of a monarch butterfly to be 0.00041 kilograms. What is the mass of the butterfly written using scientific notation?

➤ **ONE WAY** to write 0.00041 in scientific notation is to use the definition of scientific notation.

4.1 is greater than or equal to 1 and less than 10. Multiply by the correct power of 10.

$0.00041 = 4.1 \times 0.0001$

$= 4.1 \times 10^{-4}$ — Write the standard form of the power of 10 as a single power.

➤ **ANOTHER WAY** is to move the decimal point.

Move the decimal point until there is a single nonzero digit to the left of the decimal point. The absolute value of the exponent is equal to the number of places the decimal point moved. The original number is less than 1, so the exponent is negative.

$0.00041 = 4.1 \times 10^{-4}$

Using either method, the mass of the butterfly is 4.1×10^{-4} kg.

Use the next page to start a conversation about scientific notation.

©Curriculum Associates, LLC Copying is not permitted. LESSON 22 Work with Scientific Notation 513

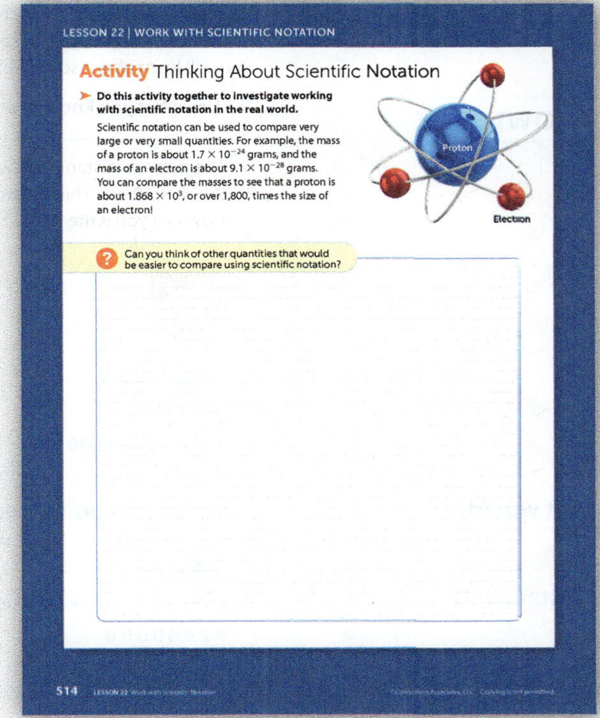

LESSON 22 | WORK WITH SCIENTIFIC NOTATION

Activity Thinking About Scientific Notation

➤ **Do this activity together to investigate working with scientific notation in the real world.**

Scientific notation can be used to compare very large or very small quantities. For example, the mass of a proton is about 1.7×10^{-24} grams, and the mass of an electron is about 9.1×10^{-28} grams. You can compare the masses to see that a proton is about 1.868×10^3, or over 1,800, times the size of an electron!

Can you think of other quantities that would be easier to compare using scientific notation?

514

Connect to Language

➤ **For English language learners, use the Differentiation chart to scaffold the language in each session. Use the Academic Vocabulary routine for academic terms before Session 1.**

DIFFERENTIATION | ENGLISH LANGUAGE LEARNERS

Use with **Session 1** **Connect It**

Levels 1–3: Speaking/Writing

Help students respond to Connect It problem 3. Read the problem and have students circle the two things they need to compare. Use **Act It Out** to provide examples of each form. Then, have students turn to partners. Make a T-chart with the headings *Scientific Notation* and *Single Digit Times an Integer Power of 10.* Have partners say words or phrases that describe each form. Allow time for students to review the completed chart. Then, help them draft a response to the problem:

- *The number forms are similar because they both have* _____.
- *The number forms are different because* _____.

Levels 2–4: Speaking/Writing

Help students respond to Connect It problem 3. Read the problem and have students say what they need to compare. Call on volunteers to write an example of each form. Then, have students turn to partners. Make a T-chart with the headings *Scientific Notation* and *Single Digit Times an Integer Power of 10.* Ask partners to say words or phrases that describe each form. Then use **Stronger and Clearer Each Time.** Suggest students use *similar, different, and, both,* and *but* in their drafts. Then, have them meet with other partners to share and explain. Help partners comment on the drafts. Ask: *What words did your partner use to compare? Did your partner use the word* both*? When?*

Levels 3–5: Speaking/Writing

Help students respond to Connect It problem 3. Have students read the problem and say what they need to compare. Call on volunteers to write an example of each form. Then, have students turn to partners. Ask students to take turns describing each form. Then use **Stronger and Clearer Each Time.** Have students circle comparison words they used in their drafts. Then have them meet with partners to share and explain. Invite other partners to provide feedback. Remind them to be specific about the part they think is not correct, for example: *I think you need to change the word* _____ *because you are describing* _____ *instead of* _____.

Explore Scientific Notation

Purpose

- **Explore** the idea that very large or very small numbers can be expressed in scientific notation and that numbers in this form can be converted to standard form, and vice versa.
- **Understand** that scientific notation is useful for representing a very large or very small number concisely.

START CONNECT TO PRIOR KNOWLEDGE

Which Would You Rather?

A: Go on vacation 10^2 miles from home.

B: Go on vacation 10^3 miles from home.

C: Go on vacation 10^4 miles from home.

Possible Solutions

A because it is the closest to home and it would take the least time to get there.

B because it is most likely in a different state and I would get to see new things.

C because it is the farthest from home and most likely in another country.

WHY? Support students' facility on what powers of 10 represent.

TRY IT SMP 1, 2, 4, 5, 6

Make Sense of the Problem

See ***Connect to Culture*** to support student engagement. Before students work on Try It, use **Say It Another Way** to help them make sense of the problem. Students used the term *standard form* in earlier lessons but may need a reminder that a number in standard form only uses numerical digits. It does not have any operations or exponents.

DISCUSS IT SMP 2, 3, 6

Support Partner Discussion

After students work on Try It, have them respond to Discuss It with a partner. Listen for understanding of:

- the meaning of the power 10^7.
- how multiplying by an integer power of 10 affects the placement of the decimal point.

Explore Scientific Notation

Previously, you learned how to use powers of 10 to write estimates of very large and small numbers. In this lesson, you will learn about scientific notation.

➤ **Use what you know to try to solve the problem below.**

The average distance between Earth and the sun is about 9.296×10^7 mi. This distance is called an *astronomical unit*. How can you write 9.296×10^7 in standard form?

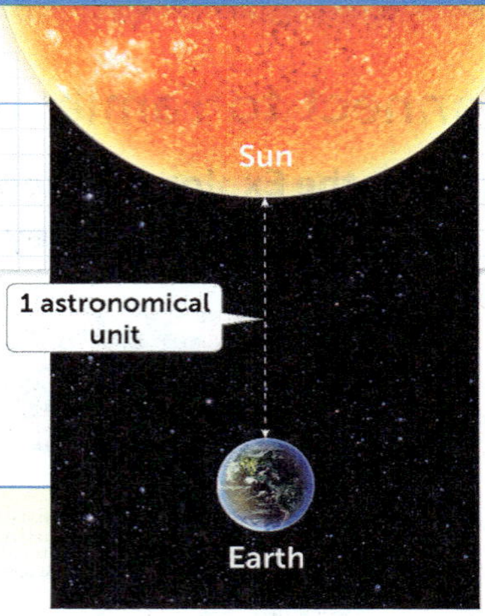

TRY IT

Possible work:

SAMPLE A

$10^7 = 10{,}000{,}000$

$9.296 \times 10{,}000{,}000 = 92{,}960{,}000$

9.296×10^7 is 92,960,000 in standard form.

SAMPLE B

9.296×10^7: move the decimal point 7 places to the right

9 2 9 6 0 0 0 0

$9.296 \times 10^7 = 92{,}960{,}000$

DISCUSS IT

Ask: What did you do first to write 9.296×10^7 in standard form?

Share: I knew . . . so I . . .

Learning Target SMP 1, SMP 2, SMP 3, SMP 4, SMP 5, SMP 6, SMP 7
Perform operations with numbers expressed in scientific notation, including problems where both decimal and scientific notation are used. Use scientific notation and choose units of appropriate size for measurements of very large or very small quantities. Interpret scientific notation that has been generated by technology.

Common Misconception Listen for students who think the standard form is 92,960,000,000. These students wrote the nonzero digits followed by 7 zeros. As students share their strategies, ask them to describe the pattern in how the decimal point moves when a number is multiplied by a power of 10. You might have them start with 9.296 and multiply by 10 seven times, observing that the decimal point moves one place right each time.

Select and Sequence Student Strategies

Select 2–3 samples that represent the range of student thinking in your classroom. Here is one possible order for class discussion:

- 10^7 written as a product of seven factors of 10; the first factor multiplied by one 10 at a time
- (misconception) number written as 92,960,000,000
- power of 10 written in standard form and then factors multiplied
- decimal point in 9.296 moved seven places to the right

Facilitate Whole Class Discussion

Call on students to share selected strategies. To prompt students to use precise academic language, call on volunteers to reword vague or unclear statements.

Guide students to **Compare and Connect** the representations. Prompt students to connect two different strategies by explaining how each gives the same solution.

ASK *Did each strategy result in the same standard form of the number? Was any student's method more efficient than another?*

LISTEN FOR Any correct strategy gives the same standard form. Students may consider the strategy of moving the decimal point more efficient than methods involving calculations.

CONNECT IT SMP 2, 4, 5

1 Look Back Look for understanding that the decimal point moves 7 places to the right when 9.296 is multiplied by 10^7. So, in the standard form of the number, 92,960,000, there are 7 digits after the first 9.

DIFFERENTIATION | RETEACH or REINFORCE

Visual Model

Model the movement of a decimal point.

If students are unsure about how to rewrite a number expressed in scientific notation in standard form, then use this activity to reinforce the process.

- Display the number 3.572×10^6.
- Ask: *What is the exponent of the power of 10?* [6]
- Ask: *How many places must the decimal point move to write this number in standard form?* [6]
- Ask: *In what direction will the decimal point move? How do you know?* [right; The exponent of the power of 10 is positive, so both factors are greater than 1 and the product will be greater than either of the factors.]
- Draw U-shaped arcs under each digit starting at the decimal point and moving right. Count each arc as you draw. After the third arc, ask: *I ran out of digits. What do I need to do to draw more arcs?* [Write zeros.] Write several zeros after the 2.
- Finish drawing 6 arcs and point to the end of the last arc. Ask: *Now that I have 6 arcs, what belongs here?* [a decimal point]
- Ask: *Where should the commas be placed in this number?* [after the 3 and after the 2; 3,572,000]

LESSON 22 | SESSION 1

CONNECT IT

1 Look Back What is 9.296×10^7 written in standard form? Explain how you found your answer.

92,960,000; Possible explanation: I took 9.296 and moved the decimal point 7 places to the right to match the exponent in the power of 10.

2 Look Ahead The number 9.296×10^7 is written in a form called **scientific notation.** Scientific notation is often used to write equivalent forms of very large or very small numbers. Numbers written in scientific notation are written as a product of two factors:

a decimal number ≥ 1 and < 10 → 9.296×10^7 ← an integer power of 10

In scientific notation, the number factor is never written as a fraction.

a. Are 3.01×10^{-8} and 7.25×10^1 both written in scientific notation? Explain.

Yes; both are written as a product of a decimal number greater than or equal to 1 and less than 10 and an integer power of 10.

b. Are 42.655×10^{-5}, 0.6×10^6, and 2.539×3^5 written in scientific notation? Explain.

No; 42.655 and 0.6 are not greater than or equal to 1 and less than 10. In 2.539×3^5, 3^5 is not an integer power of 10.

c. Desiderio says that 4.13×10^0 is not written in scientific notation. Explain why Desiderio is incorrect.

4.13 is greater than or equal to 1 and less than 10 and is multiplied by an integer power of 10. Zero is an integer.

3 Reflect How are numbers written in scientific notation and numbers written as a single digit times an integer power of 10 similar? How are they different?

Both forms are written as a product of two factors, a number greater than or equal to 1 and less than 10 and an integer power of 10. In scientific notation the number factor can be a decimal as well as a single digit. Also, scientific notation is an equivalent form of a number and not just an approximation.

516

2 Look Ahead Explain that scientific notation is a condensed way to write very large or very small numbers. Ask a volunteer to rephrase the definition of *scientific notation*. Support student understanding by pointing out that the first factor in a number in scientific notation must be at least 1, but not as great as 10. It must have a single nonzero digit before its decimal point. The second factor must be an integer power of 10. Be sure students can explain why each example in problem 2b is not in scientific notation.

CLOSE EXIT TICKET

3 Reflect Look for understanding that both notations express a number as a number greater than or equal to 1 but less than 10 times an integer power of 10. However, in scientific notation, the first factor can be a decimal.

Common Misconception Look for students who think any number written as a whole number times an integer power of 10 is in scientific notation. Show these students numbers such as 34×10^3 and 105×10^5 and reinforce why those numbers are not in scientific notation.

Prepare for Working with Scientific Notation

Support Vocabulary Development

Assign **Prepare for Working with Scientific Notation** as extra practice in class or as homework.

If you have students complete this in class, then use the guidance below.

Ask students to consider the term *power of 10*. Remind them of their earlier work with powers and that a power must have a base and an exponent.

Have students work individually to complete the graphic organizer. Invite students to share their completed organizers, and prompt a whole-class comparative discussion of the parts of a power and the examples of powers of 10 that students generated.

Have students look at the number in standard form given in problem 2 and discuss with a partner how they would write that number as the product of a single digit and a power of 10.

Problem Notes

1. Students should understand that a power of 10 is a number that can be written as a product of several factors of 10 or $\frac{1}{10}$. Student responses might include the patterns in powers of 10. Students should recognize that when a power of 10 represents a number greater than 1, the exponent in the power is positive, and when the power of 10 represents a number less than 1, the exponent in the power of 10 is negative. If a power of 10 is equal to 1, its exponent is 0.

2. Students may calculate the product they wrote to check to that their work is correct.

LESSON 22 | SESSION 1 Name:

Prepare for Working with Scientific Notation

1. Think about what you know about powers. Fill in each box. Use words, numbers, and pictures. Show as many ideas as you can.
Possible answers:

power of 10

What Is It?
a number that can be written as a product or quotient of 10s

What I Know About It
Powers of 10 have patterns. The exponent tells how many 10s are multiplied or divided.
The base in a power of 10 is always 10. The exponent in a power of 10 can be positive, zero, or negative.

Examples
Powers of 10 that are ≥ 1:

$1 = 10^0$
$10 = 10^1$
$100 = 10^2$
$1{,}000 = 10^3$
$10{,}000 = 10^4$
$100{,}000 = 10^5$
$1{,}000{,}000 = 10^6$

Examples
Powers of 10 that are < 1:

$0.1 = 10^{-1}$
$0.01 = 10^{-2}$
$0.001 = 10^{-3}$
$0.0001 = 10^{-4}$
$0.00001 = 10^{-5}$
$0.000001 = 10^{-6}$
$0.0000001 = 10^{-7}$

2. How can you write 5,000,000 as a product of a single digit and a power of 10?
5×10^6

517

REAL-WORLD CONNECTION

Astronomers use scientific notation to describe distances between planets, stars, and other objects in space. These distances are often so large that it is unrealistic to describe them in standard form. For example, the distance between Saturn and the sun is 8.908×10^8 miles. Similarly, chemists use scientific notation to describe very small measurements such as the mass of atoms. For example, the mass of a hydrogen atom is 1.6727×10^{-27} kg. Ask students to think of other real-world examples when using numbers in scientific notation might be useful.

Additional Practice

3 Problem 3 provides another look at converting a number from scientific notation to standard form. This problem is similar to the problem about the average distance between Earth and the sun. In both problems, a number given in scientific notation must be written in standard form. This problem asks for the average distance from Neptune to the sun to be written in standard form.

Students may want to write out the power of 10 in standard form before multiplying. They may also choose to move the decimal point in the first factor to the right based on the exponent of the power to find the product.

Suggest that students use **Say It Another Way** to make sure they understand the problem. Review what it means for a number to be written in standard form. Remind students to place commas in their answer in the appropriate places.

LESSON 22 | SESSION 1

3 On average, Neptune is about 2.795×10^9 mi from the sun.

a. How can you write 2.795×10^9 in standard form? Show your work.

Possible work:

$2.795 \times 10^9 = 2.795 \times 10 \times 10 \times 10 \times 10 \times 10 \times 10 \times 10 \times 10 \times 10$

$= 2{,}795{,}000{,}000$

SOLUTION 2,795,000,000

b. Check your answer to problem 3a. Show your work.

Possible work:

2.795×10^9: move the decimal point 9 places to the right

2 7 9 5 0 0 0 0 0 0

$2.795 \times 10^9 = 2{,}795{,}000{,}000$

DIFFERENTIATION | ENGLISH LANGUAGE LEARNERS

Use with **Session 2** Apply It

ACADEMIC VOCABULARY

Mass is the amount of matter in an object.

Matter is the thing or substance that forms objects.

Levels 1–3: Reading/Speaking

Support students as they interpret Apply It problem 7. Review the lesson Math Vocabulary. Help students identify the base, exponent, and power in $n \times 10^a$. Next, display the definitions of *mass* and *matter.* Read the problem. Have students read the mass of each animal. Then have students turn to partners to write the numbers in scientific notation. Provide a sentence frame to help them write and state the answers:

- *The mass of the ____ is about ____.*

Levels 2–4: Reading/Speaking

Support students as they interpret Apply It problem 7. Review the lesson Math Vocabulary. Have students use *base, exponent,* and *power* to describe $n \times 10^a$. Next, display *mass* and *matter.* Read the problem with students. Have them turn to partners to write the numbers in scientific notation.

Allow time for partners to compare the numbers in scientific notation to the original numbers. Then help them connect by telling what is different and what is the same.

Levels 3–5: Reading/Speaking

Support students as they interpret Apply It problem 7. Review the lesson Math Vocabulary. Have students use *base, exponent,* and *power* to describe $n \times 10^a$. Next, display *mass* and *matter.* Have students read the problem and write the numbers in scientific notation. Allow time for students to compare the numbers in scientific notation to the original numbers. Then have them meet with partners and explain how the numbers connect.

Develop Writing Numbers in Scientific Notation

Purpose

- **Develop** strategies for converting a number from standard form to scientific notation.
- **Recognize** that when converting between standard form and scientific notation, there is a connection between the number of places and direction the decimal point moves and the exponent of the power of 10 in scientific notation.

START CONNECT TO PRIOR KNOWLEDGE

Same and Different

A: 2.18×10^{-2}	B: 0.0218
C: $2.18 \times \frac{1}{10^2}$	D: $2.18 \times \frac{1}{100}$

Possible Solutions

All values are equivalent.

A is in scientific notation.

B is in standard form.

C and D have factors that are fractions.

A and C include exponents.

WHY? Support students' facility with recognizing relationships between different ways to express the same value.

DEVELOP ACADEMIC LANGUAGE

WHY? Reinforce understanding of *repeatedly . . . until . . .* in the context of scientific notation.

HOW? Read the second Model It. Help students understand the second sentence. Circle *repeatedly* and *until*. Explain that *repeatedly* describes how an action will be done. Ask: *What is the action?* Then say: Until *signals at what point you will stop the action*. Point to relevant parts in the sentence as you ask: *What do you need to move? How will you move the decimal point? When do you stop?*

TRY IT SMP 1, 2, 4, 5, 6

Make Sense of the Problem

See ***Connect to Culture*** to support student engagement. Before students work on Try It, use **Notice and Wonder** to help them make sense of the problem. Have students turn and talk with a partner about what they wondered.

LESSON 22 | SESSION 2 ■ ■ □ □ □

Develop Writing Numbers in Scientific Notation

➤ **Read and try to solve the problem below.**

Almost 97% of all water on Earth is in oceans, seas, and bays. Together, they hold about 1,338,000,000 cubic kilometers of water. What is 1,338,000,000 written in scientific notation?

TRY IT

97% of all water on Earth

Possible work:

SAMPLE A

1.338 is greater than or equal to 1 and less than 10.

1,338,000,000

There are 9 place values after the 1, so the power of 10 will have 9 zeros: 10^9.

1,338,000,000 written in scientific notation is 1.338×10^9.

SAMPLE B

1.338 is greater than or equal to 1 and less than 10.

Guess: $1.338 \times 10^{10} = 1.338 \times 10{,}000{,}000{,}000$

$= 13{,}380{,}000{,}000$

13,380,000,000 is greater than 1,338,000,000 by a factor of 10. Subtract 1 from the exponent.

Guess: $1.338 \times 10^9 = 1.338 \times 1{,}000{,}000{,}000$

$= 1{,}338{,}000{,}000$

$1{,}338{,}000{,}000 = 1.338 \times 10^9$

DISCUSS IT

Ask: How do you know your answer is reasonable?

Share: I know the number . . .

519

DISCUSS IT SMP 2, 3, 6

Support Partner Discussion

After students work on Try It, encourage them to respond to Discuss It with a partner. If students need support in getting started, prompt them to ask each other questions such as:

- *How did you know where to place the decimal point?*
- *How did you know what number to use as the exponent for the power of 10?*
- *How did you know whether the exponent was positive or negative?*

Common Misconception Listen for students who count only the zeros when the number is in standard form to determine the exponent of the power of 10. As students share their strategies, encourage them to check their answer by multiplying the first factor in the scientific notation of the number repeatedly by 10. If they do not arrive at the standard form given in the problem, then tell them to adjust their exponent.

Select and Sequence Student Strategies

Select 2–3 samples that represent the range of student thinking in your classroom. Here is one possible order for class discussion:

- decimal point placed between 1 and 3 to find first factor; number of place values after the 1 in original number used to find exponent of 10 in the power
- (misconception) wrote first factor and counted only the number of zeros in the standard form to find the exponent of the power of 10
- decimal point placed between 1 and 3 to find first factor; second factor written first in standard form and then as a power of 10
- decimal point placed between 1 and 3 to find first factor; decimal point pattern used to determine power of 10

Facilitate Whole Class Discussion

Call on students to share selected strategies. Encourage students to give reasons to explain why their answer is reasonable, given the context.

Guide students to **Compare and Connect** the representations. Allow time for students to think by themselves before starting the discussion.

ASK *What are some ways to find the power of 10?*

LISTEN FOR You can use the number of place values after 1 in the original number as the exponent. You can count the places you move the decimal point. You can write a product with 1.338 as one factor and then count the zeros in the other factor to determine the exponent of 10.

Model It

If students presented these models, have students connect these models to those presented in class.

If no student presented at least one of these models, have students first analyze key features of the models, and then connect them to the models presented in class.

ASK *How does each model find the power of 10?*

LISTEN FOR The first writes the power in standard form, then as a single power. The other uses decimal patterns.

For the definition approach, ask students about the power of 10.

- *How do you know the second factor is correct?*
- *Why can this factor be written as a power of 10?*

For the decimal point pattern, prompt students to think about how the decimal points moves. Ask: *When counting movements of the decimal point, when should you stop?*

LESSON 22 | SESSION 2

Explore different ways to write a large number in scientific notation.

Almost 97% of all water on Earth is in oceans, seas, and bays. Together, they hold about 1,338,000,000 cubic kilometers of water. What is 1,338,000,000 written in scientific notation?

Model It

You can use the definition of scientific notation.

Scientific notation is written as a product of two factors:

a decimal number ≥ 1 and < 10 $\times$ an integer power of 10

1.338 is greater than or equal to 1 and less than 10. Multiply by the correct power of 10.

1,338,000,000 = 1.338 × 1,000,000,000

Write the standard form of the power of 10 as a single power.

Model It

You can use what you know about decimal point patterns to move the decimal point.

Repeatedly move the decimal point one place until there is a single nonzero digit to the left of the decimal point.

The absolute value of the exponent in the power of 10 is equal to the number of places the decimal point moves.

The sign of the exponent depends on whether the original number is greater than or less than 1.

1 3 3 8 0 0 0 0 0 0 = 1.338 × 10^9

Glaciers, ice caps, and permanent snow hold 1.74% of Earth's total water.

520

DIFFERENTIATION | EXTEND

SMP 2

Deepen Understanding

Reasoning Abstractly About the Sign of the Exponent of the Power of 10 When Writing Numbers in Scientific Notation

Prompt students to think about the sign of the exponent of the power of 10 as the decimal point is being moved.

ASK *What is the power of 10 when the number in the Try It is written in scientific notation? Why is the exponent of the power of 10 positive when the decimal point has been moved to the left to make a lesser number?*

LISTEN FOR 10^9; Each time the decimal point is moved one place to the left, that represents dividing by 10. To keep the value of the number the same, it is necessary to also multiply by 10 for each movement.

ASK *Suppose the given number in standard form is 0.001338. What would the power of 10 be in scientific notation? Why is the exponent on the power of 10 negative when the decimal point must be moved to the right to make a greater number?*

LISTEN FOR 10^{-3}; Each time the decimal point is moved one place to the right, that represents multiplying by 10. To keep the value of the number the same, it is necessary to also divide by 10, or multiply by 10^{-1}, for each movement.

Develop Writing Numbers in Scientific Notation

CONNECT IT

SMP 2, 4, 5, 6

Remind students that the quantities and the relationships between them are the same in each representation. Explain that they will now use those representations to reason about how to write very large and very small numbers in scientific notation.

Before students begin to record and expand on their work in Model It, tell them that problem 2 will prepare them to provide the description asked for in problem 3.

Monitor and Confirm Understanding 1

- 1,338,000,000 is written 1.338×10^9.
- The exponent can be found from the first Model It by counting zeros in 1,000,000,000. It can be found from the second Model It by noting that the decimal point moves 9 places and that the original number is greater than 1.

Facilitate Whole Class Discussion

2 Look for the idea that to convert from standard form to scientific notation, you can move the decimal point to find a value between 1 and 10. The number of places you move and whether the original number is less than or greater than 1 tells you the exponent of the power of 10.

ASK *What pattern do you notice in the table?*

LISTEN FOR Each time the decimal point moves to the left one place in the standard form, the integer value of the exponent in the scientific notation decreases by 1.

3 Look for understanding of why the exponents of the powers of 10 are positive or negative.

ASK *When the scientific notation for a number has a power of 10 with a negative exponent, how does the value of the number compare to the value of the first factor? Why?*

LISTEN FOR It is less than the first factor; multiplying by a power of 10 with a negative exponent is like repeatedly dividing by 10.

ASK *When the scientific notation for a number has a power of 10 with a positive exponent, how does the value of the number compare to the value of the first factor? Why?*

LISTEN FOR It is greater than the first factor; multiplying by a power of 10 with a positive exponent is like repeatedly multiplying by 10.

4 **Reflect** Have all students focus on the strategies used to solve the Try It. If time allows, have students discuss their ideas with a partner.

CONNECT IT

➤ **Use the problem from the previous page to help you understand how to write very large and very small numbers in scientific notation.**

1 Look at both **Model Its**. Fill in the power of 10 in the second **Model It**.
What is 1,338,000,000 written in scientific notation? See Model It; 1.338×10^9

2 **a.** Use patterns to complete the table.

Standard Form	Scientific Notation
13.003	1.3003×10^1
1.3003	1.3003×10^0
0.13003	1.3003×10^{-1}
0.013003	1.3003×10^{-2}
0.0013003	1.3003×10^{-3}

b. To write 0.000013003 in scientific notation, how many places will you move the decimal point to get the number factor? Explain.
5; The number factor must be greater than or equal to 1 and less than 10.

c. To write 0.000013003 in scientific notation, will the exponent of the power of 10 be positive or negative? Explain.
Negative; 0.000013003 is less than 1.

d. Write 0.000013003 in scientific notation. 1.3003×10^{-5}

3 Suppose you are writing the number *a* in scientific notation. Write *positive, zero,* or *negative* to complete each sentence.

If $a \geq 10$, the power of 10 has a ___positive___ exponent.

If $a < 1$, the power of 10 has a ___negative___ exponent.

If $1 \leq a < 10$, the power of 10 has a ___zero___ exponent.

4 **Reflect** Think about all the models and strategies you have discussed today. Describe how one of them helped you better understand how to solve the **Try It** problem.
Responses will vary. Check student responses.

521

DIFFERENTIATION | RETEACH or REINFORCE

Visual Model

Find a pattern to write numbers in scientific notation.

If students are unsure about the process of converting from standard form to scientific notation, then use this activity to help them understand the process.

- Display the numbers 24,500; 2,450; 245; 24.5; 2.45; 0.245; 0.0245; and 0.00245.
- Ask: *How can you move the decimal point in 24,500 to make a value between 1 and 10? What is that value?* [Draw four U-shaped arcs left from the decimal point; 2.45]
- Ask: *What exponent will you use for the power of 10? Explain.* [4; The decimal point was moved 4 places. Since 24,500 is greater than 1, the exponent is positive.]
- Ask: *What is 24,500 in scientific notation?* [2.45×10^4]
- Help volunteers write each of the remaining numbers in scientific notation.
- Ask: *How can you find the first factor of a number to write it in scientific notation?* [Write the first nonzero digit followed by a decimal point and the remaining digits to the right.] *How do you know what exponent to use for the power of 10?* [Move the decimal point to make the correct first factor. The exponent is the number of places moved. Use negative for numbers < 1 and positive for numbers > 1.]

Apply It

For all problems, encourage students to check their answers. Allow students to use the method that makes the most sense to them when converting to scientific notation.

5 Students may move the decimal point so that it lies between 9 and 7 and count the places to determine the exponent of 10.

6 **A** **is correct.** 5.8 is greater than or equal to 1 and less than 10; 9 is an integer.

C **is correct.** 5.8 is greater than or equal 1 and less than 10; -4 is an integer.

F **is correct.** 5.008 is greater than or equal to 1 and less than 10; -3 is an integer.

B is not correct because 58 is not less than 10.

D is not correct because 50.8 is not less than 10.

E is not correct because 0.58 is not greater than or equal to 1.

Apply It

➤ **Use what you learned to solve these problems.**

5 The chance that 10 flips of a coin result in heads every time is 0.0009765625. Write 0.0009765625 in scientific notation. Show your work.

Possible work:

$0.0009765625 = 9.765625 \times 0.0001$

$= 9.765625 \times 10^{-4}$

SOLUTION 9.765625×10^{-4}

6 Which numbers are written in scientific notation? Select all that apply.

(A) 5.8×10^{9}

B 58×10^{9}

(C) 5.8×10^{-4}

D 50.8×10^{9}

E 0.58×10^{-3}

(F) 5.008×10^{-3}

7 The mass of a mouse is about 30 g. The mass of an African elephant is about 6 million g. Write both 30 and 6 million in scientific notation. Show your work.

Possible work:

$30 = 3 \times 10$

$= 3 \times 10^{1}$

6 million = 6,000,000

= 6 0 0 0 0 0 0

$= 6 \times 10^{6}$

SOLUTION $30 = 3 \times 10^{1}$; 6 million $= 6 \times 10^{6}$

CLOSE **EXIT TICKET**

7 Students' solutions should show an understanding of:

- how to write 6 million in standard form.
- the process of converting from standard form to scientific notation.

Error Alert If students write the incorrect scientific notation for 6 million, then ask them to write the number in standard form. If the standard form is correct, then ask them to explain to a partner the steps for converting to scientific notation.

Practice Writing Numbers in Scientific Notation

Problem Notes

Assign **Practice Writing Numbers in Scientific Notation** as extra practice in class or as homework.

1. Students may use a guess-and-check method and choose an integer exponent for their power of 10 in the scientific notation, multiplying the factors to check whether they get the original number and then adjusting the exponent accordingly. ***Medium***

2. **a.** Since the original number is less than 1, the exponent will be negative. ***Basic***

   b. Since the original number is greater than 1, the exponent will be positive. ***Basic***

3. Students may use decimal point patterns to find the exponent of 10. ***Medium***

Practice Writing Numbers in Scientific Notation

➤ **Study the Example showing how to write a number in scientific notation. Then solve problems 1–8.**

Example

Bacteria are very small organisms that are found nearly everywhere on Earth. They live in Arctic snow and inside humans. One type of bacteria is about 0.0000079 in. long, which is about 0.00020066 mm. Write both lengths using scientific notation.

0.0000079 in. = 7.9×10^{-6} in.

0.00020066 mm = 2.0066×10^{-4} mm

1. A larger kind of bacteria is about 0.00039 in. long. Write this length using scientific notation.

   0.00039 in. = 3.9×10^{-4} in.

2. **a.** Will the exponent of the power of 10 be positive or negative when writing 0.00000008 in scientific notation? How do you know?

   Negative; 0.00000008 is less than 1.

   b. Will the exponent of the power of 10 be positive or negative when writing 20 billion in scientific notation? How do you know?

   Positive; 20 billion is greater than 1.

3. A model of a 1960s sports car is 254 mm long. The real car is 5,200 mm long. Write the length of the real car using scientific notation.

   5.2×10^3 mm

Vocabulary

scientific notation
a way of expressing a number as a product in the form $n \times 10^a$, where a is an integer and n is a decimal number such that $1 \le n < 10$.

Fluency & Skills Practice

Writing Numbers in Scientific Notation

In this activity, students practice writing numbers in scientific notation.

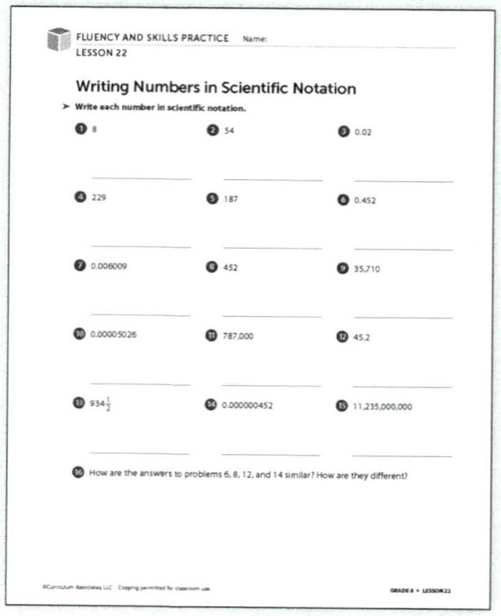
FLUENCY AND SKILLS PRACTICE Name:
LESSON 22

Writing Numbers in Scientific Notation

➤ **Write each number in scientific notation.**

1. 8
2. 54
3. 0.02
4. 229
5. 187
6. 0.452
7. 0.006009
8. 452
9. 35,710
10. 0.00005026
11. 787,000
12. 45.2
13. $934\frac{1}{2}$
14. 0.000000452
15. 11,235,000,000
16. How are the answers to problems 6, 8, 12, and 14 similar? How are they different?

©Curriculum Associates, LLC Copying permitted for classroom use. GRADE 8 • LESSON 22

Additional Practice

4 Students need to write the mixed number as a decimal before trying to convert to scientific notation. ***Medium***

5 Students should notice that the zero between the 4 and 5 is a digit that needs to be included in the first factor of the number when it is written in scientific notation. ***Medium***

6 **C is correct.** 9.1 is greater than or equal to 1 and less than 10; −4 is an integer; 9.1×10^{-4} is equivalent to $0.00091 \approx 0.000909$.

A is not correct. This answer is not in scientific notation because 909 > 10.

B is not correct. This answer is not in scientific notation because 91 > 10.

D is not correct. This answer is equivalent to 0.000091, which is not an accurate approximation of 0.000909.

Medium

7 Students may recognize that because 6 is already greater than 1 and less than 10, they do not need to move the decimal point. So, the exponent of 10 is 0. ***Challenge***

8 **a.** Students may use decimal point patterns to find the exponent of 10. ***Basic***

b. Students may refer to the definition of scientific notation to support their explanations. ***Medium***

LESSON 22 | SESSION 2

4 Write $3{,}901\frac{1}{4}$ in scientific notation.

$3{,}901\frac{1}{4} = 3{,}901.25$

$= 3.90125 \times 10^3$

5 Anders made a mistake while writing 4,050,000 in scientific notation. His work is shown. What error did Anders make? What is the correct answer?

$4{,}050{,}000 = 4.5 \times 1{,}000{,}000$

$= 4.5 \times 10^6$

Anders wrote the first number as 4.5 instead of 4.05. The correct answer is 4.05×10^6.

6 The length of a cell is 0.000909 mm. Which of the following is the best estimate of the length written using scientific notation?

A 909×10^{-4} mm

B 91×10^{-4} mm

(C) 9.1×10^{-4} mm

D 9.1×10^{-5} mm

7 Write the number 6 in scientific notation.

6×10^0

8 The circumference of Earth at the equator is about 131,300,000 ft.

a. What is 131,300,000 written in scientific notation?

1.313×10^8

b. Explain how you know your answer to problem 8a is written in scientific notation.

1.313 is greater than or equal to 1 and less than 10, and 1.313 is multiplied by an integer power of 10.

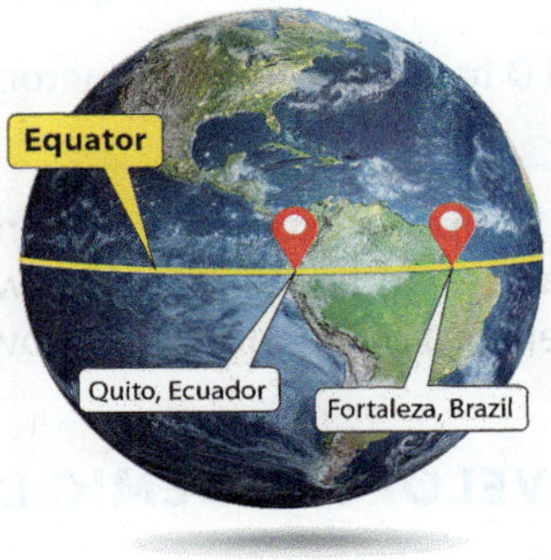

524

DIFFERENTIATION | ENGLISH LANGUAGE LEARNERS

Use with **Session 3** **Apply It**

Levels 1–3: Reading/Speaking

Use **Act It Out** with drawings and a map to help students interpret Apply It problem 9. Help students identify south and southeast on a map. Then read the first sentence. Draw a river flowing south. Read the second sentence and draw the river turning southeast. Have students tell what number to use to label each section. Then ask: *Are the numbers written in scientific notation?* Read the question. Point to the sections in the drawing and ask: *How do you find the total length?* Help students talk about the steps:

- *To find the total length, I have to ____.*
- *Then, I need to ____.*

Levels 2–4: Reading/Speaking

Use **Act It Out** with drawings and a map to help students interpret Apply It problem 9. Have students identify south and southeast on a map. Then help them read the first sentence. Draw a river flowing south. Help students read the second sentence. Invite them to draw the river turning southeast. Have volunteers label the sections. Then ask: *What type of notation is this?* Read the question and ask: *How do you find the total length?* Have students talk about the steps. Encourage other students to ask questions:

- *Do you need to ____?*
- *How do you ____?*

Levels 3–5: Reading/Speaking

Use **Act It Out** with drawings and a map to have students interpret Apply It problem 9. Have students identify south and southeast on a map. Then have them read the first two sentences. Allow time for students to make drawings that represent the situation. Remind them to use labels. Then have them read the rest of the problem. Have students use sequence words and *because* to describe and explain the steps. Encourage other students to ask questions about the steps. Allow time for students to consider the answers and say whether they agree. If they disagree, invite them to explain why.

Develop Adding and Subtracting with Scientific Notation

Purpose

- **Develop** strategies for adding and subtracting numbers in scientific notation, including choosing units of appropriate size.
- **Recognize** that numbers written in scientific notation need not be converted to standard form in order to add or subtract them.

START CONNECT TO PRIOR KNOWLEDGE

Same and Different

A: 34.7×10^5	B: 3.47×10^{-4}
C: 3.47×10^6	D: 34.7×10^{-5}

Possible Solutions

All have two factors, one being a power of 10.

B and C are in scientific notation.

B and D have the same value, as do A and C.

A and D have the same first factor, as do B and C.

WHY? Support students' recognizing similarities and differences between numbers written as a decimal times a power of 10.

DEVELOP ACADEMIC LANGUAGE

WHY? Support students' use of counterexamples when explaining why they disagree with an idea or solution.

HOW? Tell students that an effective way to disagree with a strategy can be to give a counterexample that illustrates the error. Model how to do this. As students discuss solution strategies to Try It with a partner, invite them to use the speaker's strategy but with numbers that show there is an error. Have students reflect on using this approach.

TRY IT SMP 1, 2, 4, 5, 6

Make Sense of the Problem

See ***Connect to Culture*** to support student engagement. Before students work on Try It, use **Three Reads** to help them make sense of the problem. Be sure students understand the meaning of the word *contiguous*.

Develop Adding and Subtracting with Scientific Notation

➤ **Read and try to solve the problem below.**

The 48 contiguous states have an area of about 3.12×10^6 mi². The area of Alaska is about 6.63×10^5 mi². How many fewer square miles in area is Alaska? Write your answer using scientific notation.

TRY IT

Possible work:

SAMPLE A

$3.12 \times 10^6 - 6.63 \times 10^5 = 3{,}120{,}000 - 663{,}000$
$= 2{,}457{,}000$
$= 2.457 \times 10^6$

Alaska has 2.457×10^6 fewer square miles.

SAMPLE B

$3.12 \times 10^6 - 6.63 \times 10^5 = (3.12 \times 1{,}000{,}000) - (6.63 \times 100{,}000)$
$= (31.2 \times 100{,}000) - (6.63 \times 100{,}000)$
$= (31.2 - 6.63) \times 100{,}000$
$= 24.57 \times 100{,}000$
$= 2.457 \times 1{,}000{,}000$
$= 2.457 \times 10^6$

Alaska is smaller by 2.457×10^6 mi².

DISCUSS IT

Ask: How did you know which operation to use?

Share: The problem is asking . . .

525

DISCUSS IT SMP 2, 3, 6, 7

Support Partner Discussion

After students work on Try It, encourage them to respond to Discuss It with a partner. If students need support in getting started, prompt them to ask each other questions such as:

- *What words in the problem statement helped you decide which mathematical operation to use?*
- *What do you have to do to the quantities in the problem before you can perform the operation?*

Common Misconception Listen for students who think they should compare the numbers using division instead of subtraction. As students present their strategies, ask them to read the question and consider what it means to find *how many fewer* one number is than another. If necessary, have them consider a simpler example: *Ms. Diaz has 28 students in her class. Mr. Chang has 24 students in his class. How many fewer students does Mr. Chang have?*

Select and Sequence Student Strategies

Select 2–3 samples that represent the range of student thinking in your classroom. Here is one possible order for class discussion:

- numbers converted to standard form and subtracted; then difference converted to scientific notation
- (misconception) numbers compared using division
- 3.12×10^6 converted to $31.2 \times 100{,}000$ or 31.2×10^5 and then difference calculated
- 6.63×10^5 converted to $0.663 \times 1{,}000{,}000$ or 0.663×10^6 and then difference calculated

Facilitate Whole Class Discussion

Call on students to share selected strategies. To emphasize key ideas, ask another student to rephrase the strategy a little differently so that students can hear the explanation in another way.

Guide students to **Compare and Connect** the representations. Encourage listeners to ask questions if they need further explanation for clarification.

ASK *What do all of the correct strategies have in common?*

LISTEN FOR All the strategies required writing the two numbers in the same form before subtracting them.

Model It

If students presented these models, have students connect these models to those presented in class.

If no student presented at least one of these models, have students first analyze key features of the models, and then connect them to the models presented in class.

ASK *How are the solutions in both Model Its similar?*

LISTEN FOR In both Model Its, one number is rewritten so that it has the same power of 10 as the other number.

For the strategy that writes both numbers using 10^5, prompt students to focus on the other factor. Ask: *How does reducing the exponent of the power from 6 to 5 affect the placement of the decimal point in the other factor? Why?*

For the strategy that writes both numbers using 10^6, prompt students to focus on the other factor. Ask: *How does increasing the exponent of the power from 5 to 6 affect the placement of the decimal point in the other factor? Why?*

LESSON 22 | SESSION 3

➤ **Explore different ways to add and subtract with numbers written in scientific notation.**

The 48 contiguous states have an area of about 3.12×10^6 mi². The area of Alaska is about 6.63×10^5 mi². How many fewer square miles in area is Alaska? Write your answer using scientific notation.

Model It

You can rewrite both areas with the power 10^5 and subtract.

Use the distributive property to rewrite the difference as a product of two factors.

$$(3.12 \times 10^6) - (6.63 \times 10^5) = (31.2 \times 10^5) - (6.63 \times 10^5)$$
$$= (31.2 - 6.63) \times 10^5$$

Factor out the common factor, 10^5.

Model It

You can rewrite both areas with the power 10^6 and subtract.

Use the distributive property to rewrite the difference as a product of two factors.

$$(3.12 \times 10^6) - (6.63 \times 10^5) = (3.12 \times 10^6) - (0.663 \times 10^6)$$
$$= (3.12 - 0.663) \times 10^6$$

Factor out the common factor, 10^6.

Denali National Park, Alaska

526

DIFFERENTIATION | EXTEND

SMP 2

Deepen Understanding
Relating Numbers with the Same Power of 10 to Like Terms

Prompt students to think about the similar ties between numbers with powers of 10 with the same exponent and like terms.

ASK *Can you add or subtract 11x and 5x? Why or why not? Can you add or subtract 9x and 7xy? Why or why not?*

LISTEN FOR Yes, because they are like terms. No, because they are not like terms.

ASK *In both Model Its, what had to take place in order for you to subtract the areas?*

LISTEN FOR One of the numbers had to be converted so that the exponents of the powers of 10 were the same in both numbers. Then the common power, 10^5 in the first Model It and 10^6 in the second, was factored out of the expression using the distributive property.

ASK *How are numbers with the same power of 10 related to like terms?*

LISTEN FOR Variable terms can only be added or subtracted when the variable part shows the same variables to the same powers, just as numbers in scientific notation can only be added or subtracted when they are converted to equivalent numbers with the same power of 10.

Develop Adding and Subtracting with Scientific Notation

CONNECT IT

SMP 2, 4, 5, 6

Remind students that the quantities and the relationships between them are the same in each representation. Explain that they will now use those representations to reason about how to add and subtract numbers written in scientific notation.

Before students begin to record and expand on their work in Model It, tell them that problem 4 will prepare them to provide the explanation asked for in problem 5.

Monitor and Confirm Understanding 1 – 3

- The solution from the first Model It, 24.57×10^5, must be rewritten as 2.457×10^6 so it is in scientific notation.
- The solution from the second Model It, 2.457×10^6, is already in scientific notation.

Facilitate Whole Class Discussion

4 Students should refer to the Model Its and try to perform addition using the power 10^5 and using the power 10^6.

ASK *Did you have to make any adjustments with either of your sums in order to represent them in scientific notation?*

LISTEN FOR When I rewrite both areas using 10^5, I have to rewrite the sum, 37.83×10^5, as 3.783×10^6.

5 Look for understanding that numbers in scientific notation can be added or subtracted, even if the powers of 10 differ.

ASK *What first step is necessary in order to add or subtract numbers in scientific notation that have different powers of 10?*

LISTEN FOR One of the numbers must be rewritten so it has the same power of 10 as the other. Once the powers of 10 are equal, then the numbers can be added or subtracted using the distributive property.

6 **Reflect** Have all students focus on the strategies used to solve the Try It. If time allows, have students discuss their ideas with a partner.

CONNECT IT

➤ **Use the problem from the previous page to help you understand how to add and subtract numbers written in scientific notation.**

1 Look at the first **Model It**. Complete the solution and write your answer using scientific notation. How many fewer square miles in area is Alaska?

$(31.2 - 6.63) \times 10^5 = 24.57 \times 10^5 = 2.457 \times 10^6$; 2.457×10^6 mi^2

2 Look at the second **Model It**. Complete the solution and write your answer using scientific notation. How many fewer square miles in area is Alaska?

$(3.12 - 0.663) \times 10^6 = 2.457 \times 10^6$; 2.457×10^6 mi^2

3 Why does the second **Model It** require one less step when you complete the solution?

Possible answer: When you find the difference using 10^6 as the power of 10 for both numbers, the result is already written in scientific notation. When you use 10^5 as the power of 10, you have to rewrite the difference to write it in scientific notation.

4 Suppose you want to know the sum of the areas. Add the areas using the methods from both **Model Its**. Write your answers using scientific notation. Do the methods also work for addition? Explain.

3.783×10^6 mi^2; Yes, both methods give the same sum.

5 What must be true about numbers written in scientific notation before you can add or subtract? Explain.

Possible answer: The powers of 10 must be the same so that you can apply the distributive property, and then add or subtract the number factors.

6 **Reflect** Think about all the models and strategies you have discussed today. Describe how one of them helped you better understand how to add or subtract numbers written in scientific notation.

Responses will vary. Check student responses.

527

DIFFERENTIATION | RETEACH or REINFORCE

Visual Model

Rewrite numbers given in scientific notation in order to add them.

If students are unsure how to adjust one of the addends given in scientific notation so the first factors can be added, then use this model to help them better understand the process.

- Display the addition problem $(2.39 \times 10^{10}) + (5.7 \times 10^8)$. Ask: *Which number should you rewrite so you can add the two numbers?* [either one]
- Ask: *What mathematical operation would you use to change 10^{10} to 10^8?* [division; Divide by 10^2, or 100.] Write $\div$ *100* above 10^{10}.
- Discuss that whatever operation is used to change one factor, the inverse operation should be used with the other factor to leave the product unchanged. Ask: *If you divide 10^{10} by 100, what do you have to do to 2.39 to leave the product unchanged?* [Multiply it by 100.] Write $\times$ *100* above 2.39.
- Ask: *What is the result of multiplying 2.39 by 100?* [239] *What is the number 2.39×10^{10} rewritten as a number times a power of 10 with an exponent of 8?* [239×10^8]
- Repeat the steps to demonstrate how to rewrite the number 5.7×10^8 as a number times a power of 10 with an exponent of 10. [0.057×10^{10}]
- Have students perform both additions to see they get the same sum. [2.447×10^{10}]

Apply It

For all problems, encourage students to use a model to support their thinking.

7 In this problem, the two numbers being subtracted have negative exponents, but the strategy is the same: rewrite one number so that both numbers have the same power of 10.

a. Lincoln changed 10^{-10} to 10^{-8}. Because this is equivalent to multiplying by 10^2, or 100, he needed to divide the other factor, 2.63, by 100.

b. Students consider how they could change the other number so that both numbers have an exponent of −10. In this case, they change 10^{-8} to 10^{-10}. This is equivalent to dividing by 100, so they must multiply the other factor, 5.7, by 100.

8 **B is correct.** Students may solve this by writing 105 g as 0.0105×10^4 g and then subtracting 0.0105×10^4 from 9.2×10^4 to get 9.1895×10^4 grams. In order to express this amount in kilograms, they have to divide by 1,000, or 1×10^3, because there are 1,000 g in 1 kg. The result is $9.1895 \times 10^1 = 91.895 \approx 92$ kg.

A is not correct. A student who selected this answer may have used the number in standard form without converting from grams to kilograms.

C is not correct. A student who selected this answer may have divided by 10 instead of 1,000 when converting from grams to kilograms.

D is not correct. Students who selected this answer did not convert their calculation from grams to kilograms.

Apply It

➤ **Use what you learned to solve these problems.**

7 Lincoln finds the difference of 5.7×10^{-8} and 2.63×10^{-10}. His work is shown to the right.

$$(5.7 \times 10^{-8}) - (2.63 \times 10^{-10}) = (5.7 \times 10^{-8}) - (0.0263 \times 10^{-8})$$
$$= (5.7 - 0.0263) \times 10^{-8}$$
$$= 5.6737 \times 10^{-8}$$

a. Did Lincoln use the distributive property correctly? Explain.

Yes; 5.7 and 0.0263 are both multiplied by 10^{-8}, so Lincoln can use the distributive property to factor out 10^{-8}.

b. Suppose Lincoln decides not to rewrite 2.63×10^{-10}. How can he rewrite 5.7×10^{-8} instead to solve the problem?

$5.7 \times 10^{-8} = 570 \times 10^{-10}$

8 A panda has a mass of 105 g when born. It has a mass of 9.2×10^4 g when fully grown. Which is the best estimate of the difference in kilograms between the panda's mass when fully grown and at birth?

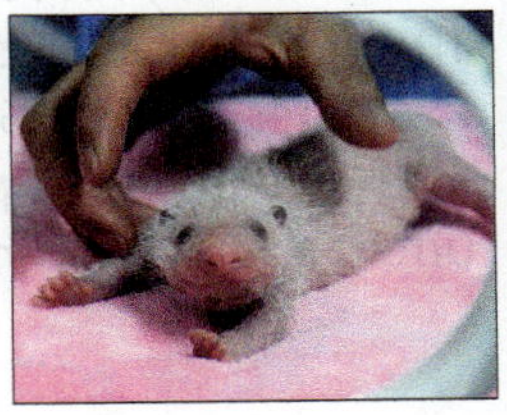

A 9.2 kg

(B) 92 kg

C 9,200 kg

D 92,000 kg

9 A river starts by flowing south for about 1.1×10^7 ft. Then it flows southeast for about 3.2×10^6 ft before it empties into the ocean. What is the length of the river? Write your answer using scientific notation. Show your work.

Possible work:

$$(1.1 \times 10^7) + (3.2 \times 10^6) = (11 \times 10^6) + (3.2 \times 10^6)$$
$$= (11 + 3.2) \times 10^6$$
$$= 14.2 \times 10^6$$
$$= 1.42 \times 10^7$$

SOLUTION The length of the river is about 1.42×10^7 ft.

CLOSE **EXIT TICKET**

9 Students' solutions should show an understanding that:

- the two lengths should be added.
- the numbers should be rewritten so they have the same exponent in the power of 10.
- the answer must be written in correct scientific notation.

Error Alert If students give the answer 14.2×10^6, then ask them to restate the definition of scientific notation. If necessary, have them find the definition in the student worktext. Then, ask the students to rewrite the answer in the correct form.

Practice Adding and Subtracting with Scientific Notation

Problem Notes

Assign **Practice Adding and Subtracting with Scientific Notation** as extra practice in class or as homework.

1. Students may solve this problem by adding the mass of an oxygen atom to the mass of the water molecule from the example. ***Basic***

2. **a.** To complete the partially worked problem using -24 as the power of 10, students may notice that the answer needs to be expressed as a power of -23 in order to be in scientific notation. ***Medium***

   b. Students may reason that changing 10^{-24} to 10^{-23} is the same as multiplying by 10, so the other factor, 1.67, must be divided by 10 so the value of the product will be unchanged. ***Medium***

LESSON 22 | SESSION 3 Name:

Practice Adding and Subtracting with Scientific Notation

➤ **Study the Example showing how to add numbers written in scientific notation. Then solve problems 1–5.**

Example

A water molecule is made of two hydrogen atoms and one oxygen atom. A hydrogen atom has a mass of about 1.67×10^{-24} g. An oxygen atom has a mass of about 2.66×10^{-23} g. Write the mass of a water molecule using scientific notation.

hydrogen atom + hydrogen atom + oxygen atom

$(1.67 \times 10^{-24}) + (1.67 \times 10^{-24}) + (2.66 \times 10^{-23})$

$= (1.67 \times 10^{-24}) + (1.67 \times 10^{-24}) + (26.6 \times 10^{-24})$

$= (1.67 + 1.67 + 26.6) \times 10^{-24}$

$= 29.94 \times 10^{-24}$

$= 2.994 \times 10^{-23}$

The mass of a water molecule is about 2.994×10^{-23} g.

1. Look at the Example. A hydrogen peroxide molecule has two oxygen atoms and two hydrogen atoms. What is the mass of one molecule of hydrogen peroxide? Write your answer using scientific notation. 5.654×10^{-23} g

2. **a.** Use the information from the Example. Complete the steps to find how many grams as great the mass of one oxygen atom is than the mass of one hydrogen atom.

   $(2.66 \times 10^{-23}) - (1.67 \times 10^{-24}) = (\underline{26.6} \times 10^{-24}) - (1.67 \times 10^{-24})$

   $= (\underline{26.6} - \underline{1.67}) \times 10^{-24}$

   $= \underline{24.93} \times 10^{-24}$

   $= \underline{2.493} \times 10^{-23}$

   The mass of an oxygen atom is $\underline{2.493 \times 10^{-23}\text{ g}}$ as great.

   b. Write the two masses using a different power of 10 that would still allow you to subtract the two numbers.

   Possible answer: 2.66×10^{-23} g; 0.167×10^{-23} g

Vocabulary

scientific notation

a way of expressing a number as a product in the form $n \times 10^a$, where a is an integer and n is a decimal number such that $1 \leq n < 10$.

529

Fluency & Skills Practice

Adding and Subtracting with Scientific Notation

In this activity, students add and subtract numbers written in scientific notation.

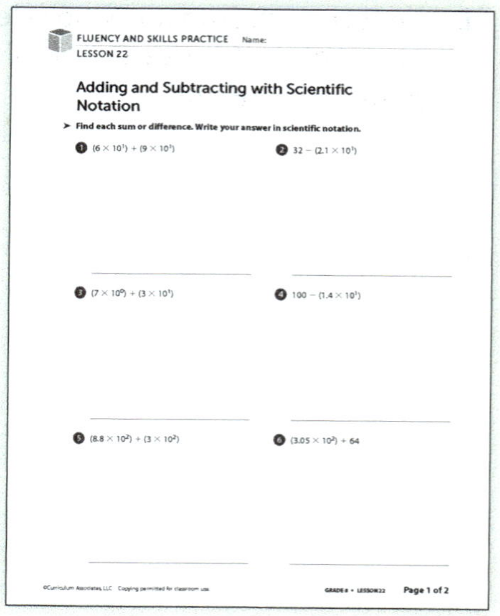
FLUENCY AND SKILLS PRACTICE Name:
LESSON 22

Adding and Subtracting with Scientific Notation

➤ Find each sum or difference. Write your answer in scientific notation.

1. $(6 \times 10^1) + (9 \times 10^1)$
2. $32 - (2.1 \times 10^1)$
3. $(7 \times 10^0) + (3 \times 10^1)$
4. $100 - (1.4 \times 10^1)$
5. $(8.8 \times 10^2) + (3 \times 10^2)$
6. $(3.05 \times 10^2) + 64$

©Curriculum Associates, LLC Copying permitted for classroom use. GRADE 8 • LESSON 22 Page 1 of 2

Additional Practice

3 **a.** Students may write both numbers in scientific notation or write both numbers in standard form. If they choose standard form, they will need to convert the sum to scientific notation. ***Basic***

b. Students should recognize that they should use the population of Kansas City, Missouri, which is 4.9×10^5. Students may also perform the calculation by rewriting both numbers with the power 10^6. ***Medium***

4 ***Basic***

5 Students may rewrite the numbers with the power 10^{14} or 10^{10}. Students may choose to add the first two numbers and then subtract the third number from the sum. ***Challenge***

LESSON 22 | SESSION 3

3 The population of Kansas City, Missouri, is about 4.9×10^5. The population of Kansas City, Kansas, is about 153,000.

a. What is the combined population of the two cities? Write your answer using scientific notation. Show your work.

Possible work:

$(4.9 \times 10^5) + (1.53 \times 10^5) = (4.9 + 1.53) \times 10^5$

$= 6.43 \times 10^5$

SOLUTION The population is about 6.43×10^5.

b. The state of Missouri has a population of a little more than 6 million people. About how many people live in Missouri, but not in Kansas City, Missouri? Write your answer using scientific notation. Show your work.

Possible work: 6 million $= 6 \times 10^6$

$(6 \times 10^6) - (4.9 \times 10^5) = (60 \times 10^5) - (4.9 \times 10^5)$

$= (60 - 4.9) \times 10^5$

$= 55.1 \times 10^5$

$= 5.51 \times 10^6$

SOLUTION About 5.51×10^6 people live in Missouri, but not in Kansas City, Missouri.

4 Two numbers are written in scientific notation. What must be true of their powers of 10 before you can add or subtract the numbers using scientific notation?

Their powers of 10 must be equal.

5 Evaluate $(7.5 \times 10^{12}) + (2.2 \times 10^{14}) - (3 \times 10^{10})$. Write your answer in scientific notation. Show your work.

Possible work:

$(7.5 \times 10^{12}) + (2.2 \times 10^{14}) - (3 \times 10^{10})$

$= (7.5 \times 10^{12}) + (220 \times 10^{12}) - (0.03 \times 10^{12})$

$= (7.5 + 220 - 0.03) \times 10^{12}$

$= 227.47 \times 10^{12}$

SOLUTION 2.2747×10^{14}

530

DIFFERENTIATION | ENGLISH LANGUAGE LEARNERS

Use with **Session 4** **Apply It**

Levels 1–3: Listening/Speaking

Support students as they talk about Apply It problem 6. Begin a **Co-Constructed Word Bank** with the word *entomologist*. Have students repeat the word. Say: *Entomologists study insects.* Add the Spanish cognates *entomólogo* and *entomóloga* if appropriate. Have students add other cognates they know. Then read the problem. Have students circle and repeat words they can use to talk about the problem (*estimates, territory, divides, average*). Include and discuss *section* and *equal-sized*. Ask: *What can you tell about the sizes of equal-sized sections?* (They are the same.) Then have partners work on the problem. Ask: *How do you find the number of ants in each section? What word gives you the clue?* [divide]

Levels 2–4: Listening/Speaking

Support students as they talk about Apply It problem 6. Begin a **Co-Constructed Word Bank** with the word *entomologist*. Have students repeat the word. Say: *The part* entomo- *refers to insects. What does an entomologist do?* Have students share cognates they know. Then help them read the problem. Have students identify words they can use to talk about the problem. Model pronunciation as needed. Then have students repeat. Include and discuss *section* and *equal-sized*. Invite volunteers to explain the phrase *equal-sized sections*. Then have students turn to partners to work on the problem. Ask: *What do you need to find? How will you do that? What word gives you a clue?*

Levels 3–5: Listening/Speaking

Use **Say It Another Way** to help students talk about Apply It problem 6. Have students read the problem. Invite volunteers to pronounce and explain *entomologist*. Then have volunteers take turns saying the problem another way. Encourage other students to comment by adding details to complete the information or suggesting changes to make the paraphrase more accurate. Then have students work on the problem. Allow time for students to meet with partners and connect strategies. Have them discuss whether they used the same or different strategies and whether their answers were the same.

Develop Multiplying and Dividing with Scientific Notation

Purpose

- **Develop** strategies for multiplying and dividing numbers in scientific notation, including choosing units of appropriate size.
- **Recognize** that numbers written in scientific notation can be multiplied and divided using properties of exponents learned earlier in this unit.

START CONNECT TO PRIOR KNOWLEDGE

Same and Different

A: $(2.45 \times 10^5) + (3.9 \times 10^5)$	B: $(4.3 \times 10^3) + (0.005 \times 10^3)$
C: $(70.53 \times 10^{-2}) - (3.1 \times 10^{-1})$	D: $(5.43 \times 10^{-3}) - (4 \times 10^{-1})$

Possible Solutions

A and D have both numbers written in scientific notation.

B and C have just one number written in scientific notation.

A and B can be added as is.

C and D need to written with the same power of 10 before subtracting.

WHY? Support students' recognizing when powers of 10 are in scientific notation, and when they can be added or subtracted.

DEVELOP ACADEMIC LANGUAGE

WHY? Understand *must be true* and *also true*.

HOW? Read Connect It problem 4. Discuss the meaning of *must be true*. Call on volunteers to paraphrase the first question using *needs to happen*. Then discuss the meaning of *also true*. Invite other volunteers to use *also applies* to paraphrase the second question. Then have students use the phrases to describe what needs to happen and if the same applies when multiplying or dividing.

TRY IT

SMP 1, 2, 4, 5, 6

Make Sense of the Problem

See ***Connect to Culture*** to support student engagement. Before students work on Try It, use **Three Reads** to help them make sense of the problem. Remind students to listen for key details and important numbers as the problem is being read.

LESSON 22 | SESSION 4

Develop Multiplying and Dividing with Scientific Notation

➤ **Read and try to solve the problem below.**

Over time, the ocean floor moves apart along underwater mountains and trenches. The Mid-Atlantic Ridge moves an average of 3.5×10^{-2} m per year. The East Pacific Rise has moved about 6.6×10^6 m in 60 million years.

How many meters has the Mid-Atlantic Ridge moved in 60 million years? Write your answer using scientific notation.

About how many times as many meters has the East Pacific Rise moved than the Mid-Atlantic Ridge in 60 million years?

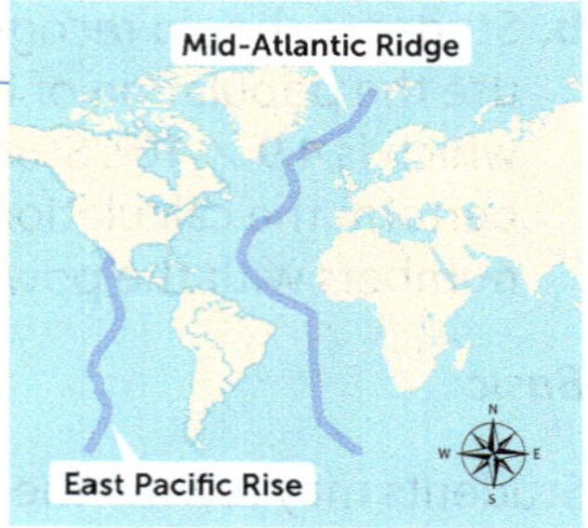

TRY IT

Possible work:

SAMPLE A

$(3.5 \times 10^{-2}) \times (60{,}000{,}000)$

$= (3.5 \times 0.01) \times (60{,}000{,}000)$

$= 0.035 \times 60{,}000{,}000$

$= 2{,}100{,}000$

$= 2.1 \times 10^6$

The Mid-Atlantic Ridge has moved about 2.1×10^6 m.

$(6.6 \times 10^6) \div (2.1 \times 10^6)$

$= (6.6 \times 1{,}000{,}000) \div (2.1 \times 1{,}000{,}000)$

$= 6{,}600{,}000 \div 2{,}100{,}000$

≈ 3.1

The East Pacific Rise has moved about 3.1 times as many meters.

SAMPLE B

60 million $= 6 \times 10^7$

$(3.5 \times 10^{-2}) \times (6 \times 10^7)$

$= (3.5 \times 0.01) \times (6 \times 10{,}000{,}000)$

$= (3.5 \times 6) \times (0.01 \times 10{,}000{,}000)$

$= 21 \times 100{,}000$

$= 2{,}100{,}000$

about 2.1×10^6 m

$(6.6 \times 10^6) \div (2.1 \times 10^6)$

$= \frac{6.6 \times 10^6}{2.1 \times 10^6}$

$= \frac{6.6 \times 1{,}000{,}000}{2.1 \times 1{,}000{,}000}$

$= \frac{6.6}{2.1}$

≈ 3

about 3 times as many

DISCUSS IT

Ask: How can you state what the problems is asking in your own words?

Share: The problem asks . . .

531

DISCUSS IT

SMP 2, 3, 6

Support Partner Discussion

After students work on Try It, encourage them to respond to Discuss It with a partner. If students need support in getting started, prompt them to ask each other questions such as:

- *How did you know what operation to use to answer the first question?*
- *How did you decide what operation to use to answer the second question?*

Error Alert If students incorrectly apply the properties of exponents, then ask them to explain how to multiply and divide powers with the same base and how to raise a power to a power. Then, have them review and correct their work.

Select and Sequence Student Strategies

Select 2–3 samples that represent the range of student thinking in your classroom. Here is one possible order for class discussion:

- convert numbers to standard form before performing the multiplication or division
- write all numbers in scientific notation and apply properties of exponents to perform calculations

Facilitate Whole Class Discussion

Call on students to share selected strategies. Prompt students to describe what they noticed or assumed about the problem and what they decided to do as a result.

Guide students to **Compare and Connect** the representations. Have students turn and talk about what is similar in the strategies before resuming the class discussion.

ASK *How do the strategies show different ways of working with powers of 10?*

LISTEN FOR Some strategies used standard form for all the numbers. Others used scientific notation for all the numbers. Some used numbers in both forms.

Model It

If students presented these models, have students connect these models to those presented in class.

If no student presented at least one of these models, have students first analyze key features of the models, and then connect them to the models presented in class.

ASK *What is similar about these models?*

LISTEN FOR They both use numbers written in scientific notation to perform the calculations.

For the multiplication problem, prompt students to recognize that 60 million was converted to scientific notation. Ask: *Why is 60 million equal to 6×10^7?*

For the division problem, prompt students to note how the problem includes the phrase *about how many times*. Ask: *What symbol is used to indicate that the result of the calculation is not an exact amount?*

LESSON 22 | SESSION 4

➤ **Explore different ways to multiply and divide numbers written in scientific notation.**

Over time, the ocean floor moves apart along underwater mountains and trenches. The Mid-Atlantic Ridge moves an average of 3.5×10^{-2} m per year. The East Pacific Rise has moved about 6.6×10^6 m in 60 million years.

How many meters has the Mid-Atlantic Ridge moved in 60 million years? Write your answer using scientific notation.

About how many times as many meters has the East Pacific Rise moved than the Mid-Atlantic Ridge in 60 million years?

Model It

You can multiply using properties of integer exponents to answer the first question.

60 million $= 6 \times 10^7$

$$(3.5 \times 10^{-2}) \times (6 \times 10^7) = (3.5 \times 6) \times (10^{-2} \times 10^7)$$
$$= 21 \times 10^{-2+7}$$
$$= 21 \times 10^5$$
$$= 2.1 \times 10^6$$

Model It

You can divide using properties of integer exponents to answer the second question.

$$(6.6 \times 10^6) \div (2.1 \times 10^6) = \frac{6.6 \times 10^6}{2.1 \times 10^6}$$
$$= \frac{6.6}{2.1} \times \frac{10^6}{10^6}$$
$$\approx 3 \times 10^{6-6}$$

532

DIFFERENTIATION | EXTEND

SMP 7

Deepen Understanding
Using Structure in Number Names to Relate to Powers of 10

Prompt students to think about how exponential forms of 1 thousand, 1 million, 1 billion, and 1 trillion can be used to write numbers in scientific notation.

ASK *How do you write 1 thousand as a power of 10? What about 1 million? 1 billion? 1 trillion? What is the pattern in the exponents in these powers?*

LISTEN FOR 10^3, 10^6, 10^9, 10^{12}; The exponents are increasing multiples of 3.

ASK *How can you use the idea that 1 million is 10^6 to write 60 million in scientific notation?*

LISTEN FOR I can write it first as 60×10^6, and then convert it to scientific notation by dividing 60 by 10 and multiplying 10^6 by 10 to get 6×10^7.

ASK *How could you write 600 million in scientific notation? What about 60 billion?*

LISTEN FOR 600 million is 600×10^6, or 6×10^8. 60 billion is 60×10^9, or 6×10^{10}.

ASK *What is 6,000 million in scientific notation? How would you ordinarily say this number?*

LISTEN FOR 6,000 million $= 6{,}000 \times 10^6 = 6 \times 10^9$; 6 billion

Develop Multiplying and Dividing with Scientific Notation

CONNECT IT

SMP 2, 4, 5, 6

Remind students that the quantities and the relationships between them are the same in each representation. Explain that they will now use those representations to reason about how to multiply and divide numbers written in scientific notation.

Before students begin to record and expand on their work in Model It, tell them that problem 3 will prepare them to provide the explanation asked for in problem 4.

Monitor and Confirm Understanding 1 – 2

- The Mid-Atlantic Ridge has moved 2.1×10^6 m in 60 million years.
- The East Pacific Rise has moved about 3 times as many meters as the Mid-Atlantic Ridge in 60 million years.

Facilitate Whole Class Discussion

3 Look for understanding of how the product of powers and quotient of powers properties were used in the computations.

4 Look for understanding that the properties for multiplying and dividing powers only require that the powers have the same base, not the same exponent.

ASK *What generalizations can you make about adding, subtracting, multiplying, and dividing when numbers are given in scientific notation?*

LISTEN FOR When you add or subtract, the numbers need to have the same power of 10. Then, to find the sum or difference, you add or subtract the first factors and use the same power of 10. When you multiply or divide, you do not need the same power of 10. To multiply, you just multiply all the factors; you add the exponents to find the product of the powers of 10. To divide, you divide the first factors and divide the powers of 10 by subtracting the exponents.

5 **Reflect** Have all students focus on the strategies used to solve the Try It. If time allows, have students discuss their ideas with a partner.

CONNECT IT

➤ **Use the problem from the previous page to help you understand how to multiply and divide numbers written in scientific notation.**

1 Look at the first **Model It**. How many meters has the Mid-Atlantic Ridge moved in 60 million years?

The Mid-Atlantic Ridge has moved about 2.1×10^6 m.

2 Look at the second **Model It**. Complete the solution. About how many times as many meters has the East Pacific Rise moved than the Mid-Atlantic Ridge during this time?

$3 \times 10^0 = 3$; The East Pacific Rise has moved about 3 times as many meters.

3 What properties of integer exponents are used in the **Model Its**? How are the properties used?

When you multiply powers with the same base, you add exponents. So, to multiply 10^{-2} and 10^7, you add the exponents -2 and 7 to get 10^5. When you divide powers with the same base, you subtract exponents. So, to divide 10^6 and 10^6, you subtract the exponents 6 and 6 to get 10^0.

4 What must be true about the powers of 10 when adding or subtracting numbers written in scientific notation? Is this also true when multiplying or dividing numbers written in scientific notation? Explain.

To add or subtract, the powers of 10 must be the same. This is not true for multiplying or dividing since you can use properties of integer exponents to perform the operations.

5 **Reflect** Think about all the models and strategies you have discussed today. Describe how one of them helped you better understand how to solve the **Try It** problem.

Responses will vary. Check student responses.

533

DIFFERENTIATION | EXTEND

Visual Model

Break down multiplying numbers in scientific notation.

If students are unsure about the concept of multiplying numbers in scientific notation, then use this activity to help solidify their understanding.

- Display $(2.5 \times 10^5) \times (3 \times 10^3)$. Ask: *Why can you multiply the first factors and then multiply the second factors?* [You can multiply factors in any order.]
- Then display $(2.5 \times 3) \times (10^5 \times 10^3)$. Ask: *What is the product of the first factors?* [7.5] *What is the product of the powers of 10?* [$10^{5+3} = 10^8$] *What is the product of the original expression?* [7.5×10^8] *Is this product in scientific notation? Explain.* [Yes, $1 \le 7.5 < 10$.]
- Repeat the process for $(1.5 \times 10^4) \times (9 \times 10^6)$ to find the product 13.5×10^{10}. Ask: *Is this product in scientific notation? Explain.* [No, $13.5 > 10$.]
- Ask: *How can you adjust the product so that it is in scientific notation?* [Divide the first factor by 10 and multiply the power of 10 by 10 to write 1.35×10^{11}.]
- Ask: *Why do you both divide and multiply by 10?* [If you just divide to make the first factor 1.35 and do not multiply by 10, the value of the product changes.]

Apply It

For all problems, encourage students to use a model to support their thinking.

6 Students may also leave 23 in standard form:
$\frac{1.5 \times 10^9}{23} \approx 0.065 \times 10^9 = 6.5 \times 10^7$.

7 a. Students should recognize what *scale factor* means. In this case the scale factor 2×10^{-8} is the number you must multiply the actual distance by to get the distance on the map.

b. Students should recognize that kilometers are not an appropriate unit of distance for a web design; a much smaller unit of length is needed.

Apply It

➤ **Use what you learned to solve these problems.**

Ant hills can grow to be several feet high.

6 An entomologist estimates there are 1.5 billion ants in the territory he studies. He divides the territory into 23 equal-sized sections. On average, how many ants are in each section? Show your work. Write your answer using scientific notation.

Possible work: $(1.5 \times 10^9) \div 23 = \frac{1.5 \times 10^9}{2.3 \times 10^1}$
$\approx 0.65 \times 10^8$
$= 6.5 \times 10^7$

SOLUTION There are about 6.5×10^7 ants in each section.

7 The driving distance from Casablanca, Morocco, to Gaborone, Botswana, is about 1.1×10^4 km. A GPS map of Africa has a scale factor of 2×10^{-8}.

a. Multiply the actual distance by the scale factor to find how long a web designer should make this distance on the map. Write your answer using scientific notation. Show your work.

Possible work: $(1.1 \times 10^4) \times (2 \times 10^{-8}) = (1.1 \times 2) \times (10^4 \times 10^{-8})$
$= 2.2 \times 10^{-4}$

SOLUTION The distance should be 2.2×10^{-4} km.

b. Rewrite your answer to problem 7a using a more appropriate unit for the web designer to use on the map. Possible answer:
There are 1×10^5 cm in 1 km: $(1 \times 10^5) \times (2.2 \times 10^{-4})$
$= (1 \times 2.2) \times (10^5 \times 10^{-4})$
$= 2.2 \times 10^1$
$= 22$; 22 cm

8 Find the product of (5×10^{-16}) and (1.7×10^9). Write your answer in scientific notation. Show your work. Possible work:
$(5 \times 10^{-16}) \times (1.7 \times 10^9) = (5 \times 1.7) \times (10^{-16} \times 10^9)$
$= 8.5 \times 10^{-16+9}$
$= 8.5 \times 10^{-7}$

SOLUTION 8.5×10^{-7}

CLOSE **EXIT TICKET**

3 Students' solutions should show an understanding of how to apply the properties of exponents to multiply numbers written in scientific notation.

Error Alert If students divide the numbers, then remind them that the term *product* is used to indicate the result of multiplication.

Practice Multiplying and Dividing with Scientific Notation

Problem Notes

Assign **Practice Multiplying and Dividing with Scientific Notation** as extra practice in class or as homework.

1 Students should realize this is a division problem, for which the numerator is the greater of the two areas, the area of Colorado. They should also understand that since the word *about* was used in the question, their answer will be an approximation. ***Medium***

2 Although students should gradually become accustomed to using scientific notation to perform calculations, some may still use standard form, computing (320,000,000) × (1,100,000,000,000) and then converting the product to scientific notation. ***Medium***

 Name:

Practice Multiplying and Dividing with Scientific Notation

➤ **Study the Example showing how to multiply numbers written in scientific notation. Then solve problems 1–5.**

Example

Colorado's shape is almost a rectangle. It measures about 2×10^6 ft long by 1.478×10^6 ft wide. What is the estimated area of the state? Write your answer using scientific notation.

$$(2 \times 10^6) \times (1.478 \times 10^6) = (2 \times 1.478) \times (10^6 \times 10^6)$$
$$= 2.956 \times 10^{6+6}$$
$$= 2.956 \times 10^{12}$$

The area of Colorado is approximately 2.956×10^{12} ft^2.

1 Look at the Example. The area of Rhode Island is about 43.07 billion square feet. About how many times as great is the area of Colorado than the area of Rhode Island? Show your work.

Possible work: 43.07 billion $= 4.307 \times 10^{10}$

$$\frac{2.956 \times 10^{12}}{4.307 \times 10^{10}} = \frac{2.956}{4.307} \times \frac{10^{12}}{10^{10}}$$
$$\approx 0.686 \times 10^{12-10}$$
$$= 0.686 \times 10^2$$

SOLUTION The area of Colorado is about 68.6 times as great.

2 The water in Earth's oceans has a volume of about 3.2×10^8 cubic miles. There are about 1.1×10^{12} gallons in 1 cubic mile. How many gallon jugs would it take to hold all the ocean water on Earth? Show your work. Write your answer using scientific notation.

Possible work:

$$(3.2 \times 10^8) \times (1.1 \times 10^{12}) = (3.2 \times 1.1) \times (10^8 \times 10^{12})$$
$$= 3.52 \times 10^{20}$$

SOLUTION It would take about 3.52×10^{20} gallon jugs.

> **Vocabulary**
> **scientific notation**
> a way of expressing a number as a product in the form $n \times 10^a$, where a is an integer and n is a decimal number such that $1 \le n < 10$.

Fluency & Skills Practice

Multiplying and Dividing with Scientific Notation

In this activity, students multiply and divide numbers written in scientific notation.

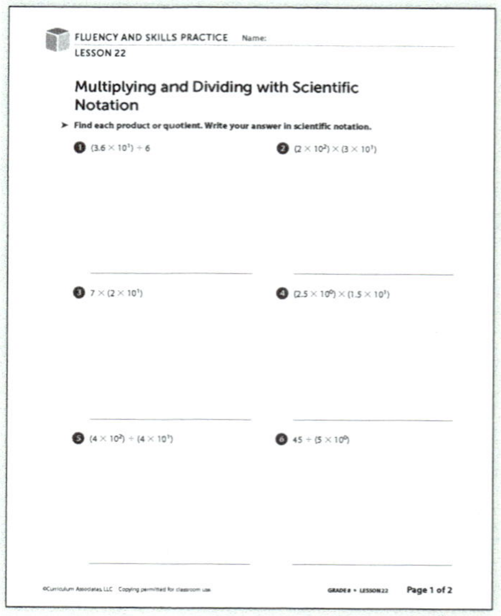
FLUENCY AND SKILLS PRACTICE Name:
LESSON 22

Multiplying and Dividing with Scientific Notation

➤ Find each product or quotient. Write your answer in scientific notation.

Additional Practice

3 Students should recognize that they need to divide the mass of an oxygen atom by the mass of a hydrogen atom. ***Medium***

4 Students should see these statements as applications of the properties of exponents for the product of powers and the quotient of powers. ***Basic***

5 **a.** Students may multiply the dimensions of Section A to find its area. ***Medium***

b. Students may divide the area of Section B by its known width to find the unknown length. ***Medium***

c. Students may determine that the assistant added the exponents as if it were a multiplication problem rather than a division problem. ***Challenge***

LESSON 22 | SESSION 4

3 A hydrogen atom has a mass of about 1.67×10^{-24} g. An oxygen atom has a mass of about 2.66×10^{-23} g. About how many times as great is the mass of an oxygen atom than the mass of a hydrogen atom? Show your work.

Possible work: $\frac{2.66 \times 10^{-23}}{1.67 \times 10^{-24}} = \frac{2.66}{1.67} \times \frac{10^{-23}}{10^{-24}}$

$\approx 1.59 \times 10^{-23-(-24)}$

$= 1.59 \times 10^{1}$

$= 15.9$

SOLUTION The mass of an oxygen atom is about 16 times as great.

4 Write *add* or *subtract* to complete each sentence.

When multiplying two numbers written in scientific notation, you can add the exponents of the powers of 10.

When dividing two numbers written in scientific notation, you can subtract the exponents of the powers of 10.

5 Look at the blueprint for a new mall.

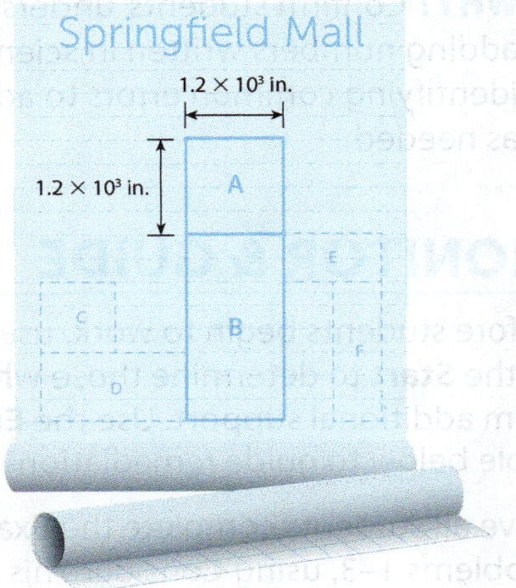

a. What is the area of Section A, written using scientific notation?

1.44×10^6 in.^{2}

b. Section B has area 2.88×10^6 in.^{2}. What is the unknown length of Section B, written using scientific notation?

2.4×10^3 in.

c. The builder's assistant solved problem 5b and got 2.4×10^9 in. What mistake do you think the assistant made?

Possible answer: The assistant may have added the exponents $6 + 3 = 9$ instead of subtracting them.

536

DIFFERENTIATION | ENGLISH LANGUAGE LEARNERS

Use with **Session 5** **Apply It**

Levels 1–3: Reading/Writing

Modify **Three Reads** to help students interpret Apply It problem 8. Read the three statements. Explain that *roughly* means *almost, close to.* Have students look at the picture and describe the shapes:

- *The shape of ____ is ____ a rectangle.*

Have students label the picture with the dimensions they know about each state. Then read the question. Have students tell what they need to find out. Explain that *combined* means total. Then read the complete problem. Allow time for students to work on the problem. Then have them turn to partners to review.

Levels 2–4: Reading/Writing

Modify **Three Reads** to help students interpret Apply It problem 8. Read the three statements with students. Explain that *roughly* means *almost, close to.* Have students look at the picture and describe the shapes. Ask students to label the picture with the dimensions they know about each state. Then have them read the question. Have students tell what they need to find out. Then read the complete problem. Allow time for students to work on the problem. Then have them turn to partners to review. Encourage partners to share the word or words that gave them clues to answer the problem.

Levels 3–5: Reading/Writing

Modify **Three Reads** to help students interpret Apply It problem 8. Have students read the three statements. Invite volunteers to explain the meaning of *roughly*. Then ask other students to paraphrase the first sentence. Next, have students tell what they know about each state.

Have students read the question and tell what they need to find out. Then ask them to read the complete problem. Allow time for students to work on the problem. After some think time, have students review and compare strategies with partners. Encourage them to explain their strategies by connecting to key words in the problem.

Refine Working with Scientific Notation

Purpose

- **Refine** strategies for writing numbers in scientific notation.
- **Refine** understanding of performing operations with numbers written in scientific notation.

START CHECK FOR UNDERSTANDING

There are 5.3×10^5 microbes in one test tube and 3.9×10^6 microbes in another. What is the total number of microbes in both test tubes? Write your answer using scientific notation.

Solution

4.43×10^6

WHY? Confirm students' understanding of adding numbers written in scientific notation, identifying common errors to address as needed.

MONITOR & GUIDE

Before students begin to work, use their responses to the **Start** to determine those who will benefit from additional support. Use the **Error Analysis** table below to guide remediation.

Have all students complete the Example and problems 1–3, using Consider This and Pair/Share as appropriate. Observe and monitor their reasoning and guide or redirect students as needed.

LESSON 22 | SESSION 5

Refine Working with Scientific Notation

➤ **Complete the Example below. Then solve problems 1–11.**

Example

Jia's classmates send an average of 85 text messages per day. At this rate, how many texts would all of the eighth graders in the U.S. send in a year? There are about 3,500,000 eighth graders in the U.S. Jia uses her calculator to multiply $85 \times 365 \times 3{,}500{,}000$ and gets the result 1.086E+11. What does this answer mean?

Look at how you can use scientific notation to analyze the answer.

$85 \times 365 \times (3.5 \times 10^6) = (3.1025 \times 10^4) \times (3.5 \times 10^6)$

$= 1.086 \times 10^{11}$

E+11 means the exponent on the power of 10 is positive 11.

SOLUTION 1.086E+11 means 1.086×10^{11}.

CONSIDER THIS . . . Many calculators use a special notation to display answers that are longer than 10 digits.

PAIR/SHARE What do you think 1.086E−11 means?

Apply It

1 Complete the table. Then use scientific notation to find the difference in the masses of a giraffe and a giant squid. Show your work.

Insect or Animal	Average Mass (g) Standard Form	Average Mass (g) Scientific Notation
Ant	0.004	4×10^{-3}
Hummingbird	3.6	3.6×10^0
House cat	4,500	4.5×10^3
Giant squid	200,000	2×10^5
Giraffe	1,190,000	1.19×10^6

Possible work: $(1.19 \times 10^6) - (2 \times 10^5) = (11.9 \times 10^5) - (2 \times 10^5)$

$= 9.9 \times 10^5$

SOLUTION The difference in mass is 9.9×10^5 g.

CONSIDER THIS . . . How could you use patterns in powers of 10 to help complete the table?

PAIR/SHARE How many times as great is the mass of a giraffe than the mass of a giant squid?

537

START ERROR ANALYSIS

If the error is . . .	Students may . . .	To support understanding . . .
9.2×10^6 or 9.2×10^5	have added the first factors without making sure both numbers were written with the same power of 10.	Prompt students to use what they know about decimal point patterns to move the decimal point of one of the numbers written in scientific notation so that both numbers have the same power of 10 before they add the number factors.
44.3×10^5	have written both numbers with the power 10^5, but neglected to rewrite the sum in scientific notation.	Prompt students to recall the definition of scientific notation. Remind them that scientific notation is the product of two factors: a number greater than or equal to 1 and less than 10 and an integer power of 10. Help students realize that their final answer is not written in scientific notation.
3.37×10^6	have written both numbers with the power 10^6, but subtracted the first factors instead of adding them.	Ask students to carefully read the question and determine which operation to use to solve the problem.

Refine

Example

Guide students in understanding the Example. Ask:

- *Why did Jia multiply the average number of text messages sent per day, 85, by 365? What does 365 represent?*
- *How can you write the number of eighth graders in scientific notation?*
- *How do you multiply numbers in scientific notation?*
- *How does the product written in scientific notation compare to the result on the calculator?*

Help all students focus on the Example and responses to the questions by rewording any unclear statements so that all students understand. Confirm with the speaker that the rewording is accurate.

Look for understanding that E+11 on a calculator screen represents multiplying by a power of 10 with a positive exponent of 11.

Apply It

1. Students should use the definition of scientific notation to complete the table. Numbers in scientific notation are written as the product of two factors: a number greater than or equal to 1 and less than 10 and an integer power of 10. To subtract, the powers of 10 must be the same. Students may choose to rewrite the mass of the squid so the power is 10^6. *DOK 2*

2. Students may add the three side lengths. They may choose to rewrite the side lengths so all have the power 10^{13}. This method will yield a sum that is already written in scientific notation. *DOK 1*

3. **B is correct.** $(7.5 \times 10^{18}) \div (4 \times 10^{11}) = (7.5 \div 4) \times 10^{18-11} = 1.875 \times 10^7$.

   A is not correct. This answer is the result of dividing the first factors of each number.

   C is not correct. This answer is the estimate of the amount of grains of sand on Earth.

   D is not correct. This answer is the result of dividing the first factors of each number and adding the exponents of the powers of 10 instead of subtracting them.

   DOK 3

LESSON 22 | SESSION 5

2 What is the perimeter of the triangle written using scientific notation? Show your work.

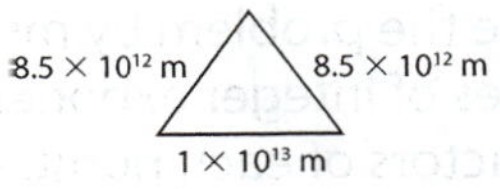

Possible work:

$2(8.5 \times 10^{12}) + (1 \times 10^{13})$
$= (17 \times 10^{12}) + (1 \times 10^{13})$
$= (17 \times 10^{12}) + (10 \times 10^{12})$
$= 27 \times 10^{12}$

CONSIDER THIS . . . The triangle has two equal sides, so there is more than one way to find the triangle's perimeter.

PAIR/SHARE How would your work change if the triangle were equilateral rather than isosceles?

SOLUTION The perimeter is 2.7×10^{13} m.

3 Scientists estimate there are about 7.5×10^{18} grains of sand on Earth. They estimate there could be as many as 4×10^{11} stars in the Milky Way galaxy. How many times as many grains of sand are there on Earth than stars in the galaxy?

A 1.875

B 1.875×10^7 (circled)

C 7.5×10^{18}

D 1.875×10^{29}

Amelia chose D as the correct answer. How might she have gotten that answer?

Possible answer: Amelia may have added the exponents 18 and 11 instead of subtracting them.

CONSIDER THIS . . . How do you know if the exponents on the powers of 10 need to be the same in order to solve this problem?

PAIR/SHARE How can you check your answer?

538

GROUP & DIFFERENTIATE

Identify groupings for differentiation based on the **Start** and problems 1–3. A recommended sequence of activities for each group is suggested below. Use the resources on the next page to differentiate and close the lesson.

Approaching Proficiency

- **RETEACH** Visual Model
- **REINFORCE** Problems 4, 5, 9

Meeting Proficiency

- **REINFORCE** Problems 4–10

Extending Beyond Proficiency

- **REINFORCE** Problems 4–10
- **EXTEND** Challenge

Have all students complete the **Close: Exit Ticket**.

Resources for Differentiation are found on the next page.

Refine Working with Scientific Notation

Apply It

4 Students may solve the problem by multiplying, using the properties of integer exponents. Multiply the first factors of each number to find the first factor of the product, then add the exponents of the powers of 10 to find the power of 10. ***DOK 1***

5 When people are traveling, distance is typically measured in miles or kilometers. Students must give the distance in standard form. ***DOK 2***

6 When changing 10^{13} to 10^{12}, Kevin divided by 10, so he had to multiply the other factor by 10 to compensate. When changing 10^{12} to 10^{13}, Muna multiplied by 10, so she had to divide the other factor by 10 to compensate. ***DOK 2***

7 **A** **is correct.** E–09 means the exponent of the power of 10 is negative 9.

C **is correct.** $(6.7 \times 10^{-9}) - (3.9 \times 10^{-11}) = (6.7 \times 10^{-9}) - (0.039 \times 10^{-9}) = 6.661 \times 10^{-9}$

D **is correct.** To find the exponent of the product of the powers of 10, add the exponents.

B is not correct. E–11 means the exponent of the power of 10 is negative 11.

E is not correct. Addition of exponents is used to multiply two powers of 10. To add, change one number to the same power of 10 and then factor out the power of 10 using the distributive property.

DOK 3

---

4 Scientists estimate there are about 7.5×10^{18} grains of sand on Earth. The mass of one grain of sand is about 1.1×10^{-13} kg. What is the mass of all the sand on Earth? Write your answer using scientific notation.

$(7.5 \times 10^{18}) \times (1.1 \times 10^{-13}) = 8.25 \times 10^{18 + (-13)}$

$= 8.25 \times 10^{5}$

The mass of all the sand on Earth is 8.25×10^{5} kg.

5 A student determines he lives 2.5×10^{5} cm from school. What might be a better way to communicate this distance to a friend? Choose an appropriate unit and write the answer using standard form.

Possible answer: $(2.5 \times 10^{5}) \div (1 \times 10^{5}) = 2.5$

The distance is 2.5 km.

6 To add 8.5×10^{12} and 2.7×10^{13}, Muna and Kevin write different first steps. Who is correct? Explain.

Muna's First Step	Kevin's First Step
$(8.5 \times 10^{12}) + (27 \times 10^{12})$	$(0.85 \times 10^{13}) + (2.7 \times 10^{13})$

They are both correct; Possible explanation: To add numbers in scientific notation, the powers of 10 must be equal. Muna rewrites the second number to have a power of 10^{12} and Kevin rewrites the first number to have a power of 10^{13}.

7 Which statements are true about the spreadsheet? Select all that apply.

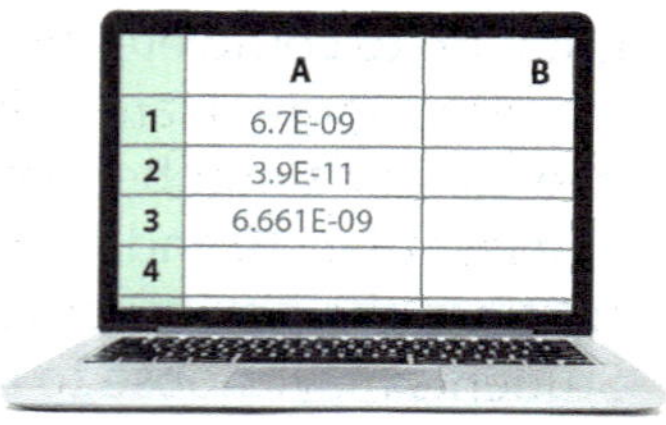

(A) Cell A1 shows the number 6.7×10^{-9}.

B Cell A2 shows the number 3.9×10^{11}.

(C) Cell A3 shows the difference of cell A1 minus cell A2.

(D) To find the product of cells A1 and A2, you would add the exponents $-9 + (-11)$.

E To find the sum of cells A1 and A2, you would add the exponents $-9 + (-11)$.

539

DIFFERENTIATION

RETEACH

Visual Model

Divide with numbers in scientific notation.

Students approaching proficiency with dividing numbers in scientific notation will benefit from visualizing the process.

- Display the expression $(5.25 \times 10^{6}) \div (1.5 \times 10^{2})$.
- Invite a student to write the expression as a single fraction.
- Ask another student to rewrite the expression as the product of two fractions, one dividing the two first factors and the other dividing the two powers of 10.
- Ask: *What is the quotient of the first factors? How did you find this value?* [3.5; Divide 5.25 by 1.5.]
- Ask: *What is the quotient of the powers of 10? How did you find this value?* [10^{4}; Subtract the exponents of the powers of 10 to find the exponent of the quotient.]
- Ask: *Why can you subtract the exponents of the powers of 10 to find their quotient?* [The powers of 10 have the same base, 10.]
- Ask: *What is the quotient of the original expression? How did you use the quotient of the first factors and the quotient of the powers of 10 to find the quotient of the original expression?* [3.5×10^{4}; Multiply the quotient of the first factors by the quotient of the powers of 10.]
- Discuss the process for dividing numbers written in scientific notation. Elicit from students that to divide numbers in scientific notation, divide the first factors and then divide the powers of 10. Then multiply the quotients. Remind them to check that their final answer is in scientific notation.

8 See ***Connect to Culture*** to support student engagement. To add the areas, the powers of 10 must be the same. *DOK 2*

9 To write a number greater than 1 and less than 10 in scientific notation, students must use a power of 10 equal to 1. *DOK 1*

10 $(2.3 \times 10^{71}) \times n = 4.6 \times 10^{71}$; To find n, students may divide both sides by 2.3×10^{71}. *DOK 2*

CLOSE EXIT TICKET

11 **Math Journal** Look for understanding that when adding or subtracting numbers in scientific notation, the powers of 10 must be the same, and when multiplying or dividing numbers in scientific notation, the properties of integer exponents are used.

Error Alert If students find the difference in volumes to be 3.63×10^2, then be sure they understand that the powers of 10 must be the same to subtract.

End of Lesson Checklist

INTERACTIVE GLOSSARY Support students by suggesting they use colored pencils to write each part of a number in scientific notation: a number greater than or equal to 1 and less than 10, 10, and an integer exponent. Have students list restrictions.

SELF CHECK Have students review and check off any new skills on the Unit 5 Opener.

LESSON 22 | SESSION 5

8 North Dakota is roughly shaped liked a rectangle. The state is about 5.45×10^5 m long and 3.4×10^5 m wide. South Dakota has an area of about 1.997×10^{11} m^2. What is the estimated combined area of the two states? Write your answer using scientific notation. Show your work. Possible work:

$$(5.45 \times 10^5) \times (3.4 \times 10^5) = 18.53 \times 10^{10}$$
$$= 1.853 \times 10^{11}$$
$$(1.853 \times 10^{11}) + (1.997 \times 10^{11}) = 3.85 \times 10^{11}$$

SOLUTION The combined area is about 3.85×10^{11} m^2.

9 Write a number that is greater than 1 and less than 10 in scientific notation. Possible answer: 4×10^0

10 4.6×10^{71} is the product of 2.3×10^{71} and what number?

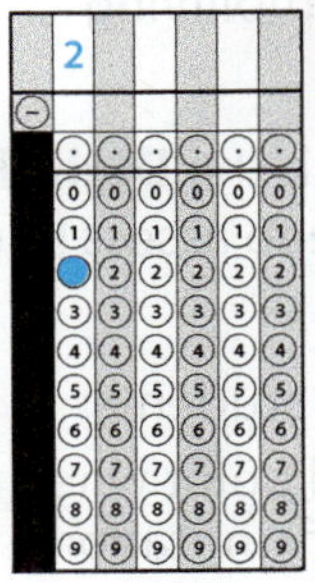

11 **Math Journal** Use the table to write an addition, subtraction, or division word problem. Then solve your problem. Write your answer using scientific notation. Possible answer:

Lake	Volume (m^3)
Superior	1.21×10^{13}
Erie	4.84×10^{11}

What is the difference in volume of the two lakes?

$$(1.21 \times 10^{13}) - (4.84 \times 10^{11}) = (121 \times 10^{11}) - (4.84 \times 10^{11})$$
$$= 116.16 \times 10^{11}$$
$$= 1.1616 \times 10^{13}$$

The difference in volume is 1.1616×10^{13} m^3.

End of Lesson Checklist

- ☐ **INTERACTIVE GLOSSARY** Find the entry for *scientific notation*. Write a definition and give examples of numbers written in scientific notation.
- ☐ **SELF CHECK** Go back to the Unit 5 Opener and see what you can check off.

540

REINFORCE

Problems 4–10

Solve problems involving scientific notation.

Students meeting proficiency will benefit from additional work with performing operations with scientific notation by solving problems in a variety of formats.

- Have students work on their own or with a partner to solve the problems.
- Encourage students to show their work.

EXTEND

Challenge

Solve problems involving scientific notation by performing multiple operations.

Students extending beyond proficiency will benefit from using multiple operations to solve problems involving scientific notation.

- Have students work with a partner to solve this problem: *Simplify the expression* $(2.5 \times 10^2) \times [(2.4 \times 10^4) + (2.8 \times 10^5)] \div (1.6 \times 10^3)$. *Write the answer in scientific notation.*
- Encourage students to think about and use the order of operations to simplify the expression.
- Repeat with other expressions, such as $[(5.7 \times 10^4) - (3.8 \times 10^3)] \div (3.5 \times 10^2) \times (4.2 \times 10^3)$.

PERSONALIZE

i-Ready

Provide students with opportunities to work on their personalized instruction path with *i-Ready* Online Instruction to:

- fill prerequisite gaps.
- build up grade-level skills.

LESSON 22
Lesson Quiz

TESTED SKILLS
Assesses 8.EE.A.4

Problems on this assessment require students to be able to perform operations with numbers in scientific notation. Students will rewrite numbers so both numbers have the same power of 10 before adding and subtracting and correctly place the decimal point to express numbers in scientific notation. Students will compare numbers in scientific notation to determine the greater value and combine operations to solve problems. Students will also need to be familiar with the properties of exponents and simplifying expressions.

Alternately, teachers may assign the **Digital Comprehension Check** online to assess student understanding of this material.

Error Alert Errors may result if students:
- incorrectly place the decimal point when rewriting numbers in scientific notation.
- add or subtract incorrectly when simplifying expressions.
- multiply exponents instead of adding when applying the properties of exponents.

Problem Notes
1 **Part A**

(2 points)

DOK 1 | **8.EE.A.4**

Part B

Students could solve the problem by applying decimal patterns to write the decimal point one place to the left in 8.8×10^{-4}, so the exponent in both powers of 10 is -3.

(2 points)

DOK 1 | **8.EE.A.4**

LESSON 22 • QUIZ Name:

➤ **Solve the problems.**

1 A hummingbird nest has two eggs. Egg A has a weight of 8.8×10^{-4} lb, and Egg B has a weight of 2.2×10^{-3} lb.

PART A

How many pounds greater is the weight of Egg B than Egg A? Write your answer in scientific notation. Show your work. *(2 points)*

Possible student work:

$(2.2 \times 10^{-3}) - (8.8 \times 10^{-4}) = (22.0 \times 10^{-4}) - (8.8 \times 10^{-4})$

$= (22.0 - 8.8) \times 10^{-4} = 1.32 \times 10^{-3}$

SOLUTION 1.32×10^{-3} lb

PART B

Write the two weights using a different power of 10 that would still allow the numbers to be subtracted. Show your work. *(2 points)*

Possible student work:

$8.8 \times 10^{-4} = 8.8 \times 10^{-1} \times 10^{-3} = 0.88 \times 10^{-3}$

2.2×10^{-3}

SOLUTION Possible answer: 0.88×10^{-3} and 2.2×10^{-3}

Short Response Scoring Rubric

Points	Expectations
2	Response has the correct solution(s) and includes well-organized, clear, and concise work demonstrating thorough understanding of mathematical concepts and/or procedures.
1	Response contains mostly correct solution(s) and shows partial understanding of mathematical concepts and/or procedures.
0	Response shows no attempt at finding a solution and no effort to demonstrate an understanding of mathematical concepts and/or procedures.

2 Students could solve the problem by rewriting each number to have the same power of 10 and then simplifying the expression.

(2 points)

DOK 2 | **8.EE.A.4**

3 **A is correct.** Students could solve the problem by multiplying 4.3 by 1.1 and then adding the exponents 11 and 4 to determine the mass of all beads in the inventory.

B is not correct. This answer represents multiplying the powers of 10 exponents instead of adding.

C is not correct. This answer represents adding 4.3 and 1.1 instead of multiplying.

D is not correct. This answer represents adding 4.3 and 1.1 and then multiplying the powers of 10 exponents.

(1 point)

DOK 2 | **8.EE.A.4**

4 Students could also solve this problem by writing each number in standard form, finding the total area of the two fields, and then writing the area in scientific notation.

(2 points)

DOK 2 | **8.EE.A.4**

LESSON 22 • QUIZ | Name:

2 Evaluate $(8.7 \times 10^{13}) + (1.2 \times 10^{15}) - (2 \times 10^{11})$. Write your answer in scientific notation. Show your work. *(2 points)*

Possible student work: $(8.7 \times 10^{13}) + (1.2 \times 10^{15}) - (2 \times 10^{11})$

$= (8.7 \times 10^{13}) + (120 \times 10^{13}) - (0.02 \times 10^{13})$

$= (8.7 + 120 - 0.02) \times 10^{13}$

$= 128.68 \times 10^{13}$

$= 1.2868 \times 10^{15}$

SOLUTION 1.2868×10^{15}

3 Elizabeth owns a jewelry-making company. She estimates there are about 4.3×10^{11} beads in her inventory. The mass of one bead is 1.1×10^{4} mg. What is the mass of all beads in her inventory? *(1 point)*

A 4.73×10^{15} mg

B 4.73×10^{44} mg

C 5.4×10^{15} mg

D 5.4×10^{44} mg

4 The soccer field at a high school is 1.08×10^{2} m long and 6.58×10^{1} m wide. The football field has an area of about 4.462×10^{3} square meters. What is the estimated combined area of the two fields? Write your answer using scientific notation. Show your work. *(2 points)*

Possible student work: $(1.08 \times 10^{2}) \times (6.58 \times 10^{1}) = 7.11 \times 10^{3}$

$(7.11 \times 10^{3}) + (4.46 \times 10^{3}) = 11.57 \times 10^{3}$

$= 1.157 \times 10^{4}$

SOLUTION 1.157×10^{4} square meters

DIFFERENTIATION

RETEACH Tools for Instruction

Students who require additional support for prerequisite or on-level skills will benefit from activities that provide targeted skills instruction.

GRADE 8

- **Lesson 22** Add and Subtract with Scientific Notation

REINFORCE Math Center Activity

Students who require practice to reinforce concepts and skills and deepen understanding will benefit from small group collaborative games and activities (available in on-level, below-level, and above-level versions).

GRADE 8

- **Lesson 22** Use Scientific Notation Vocabulary

EXTEND Enrichment Activity

Students who have achieved proficiency with concepts and skills and are ready for additional challenges will benefit from group collaborative games and activities that extend understanding.

GRADE 8

- **Lesson 22** Humans and Ants

Overview | Scientific Notation and Properties of Exponents

MATH FOCUS

Focus Standards

8.EE.A.1, 8.EE.A.3, 8.EE.A.4

STANDARDS FOR MATHEMATICAL PRACTICE (SMP)

This lesson provides support for:

1 Make sense of problems and persevere in solving them.

3 Construct viable arguments and critique the reasoning of others.

6 Attend to precision.

Additional SMP

2, 4, 7, 8

Lesson at a Glance

In this lesson, students apply multiple skills from the unit to solve real-world problems related to space. Problems involve applying properties of exponents to perform calculations with numbers written in scientific notation.

Key Skills

- Add and subtract numbers expressed in scientific notation.
- Multiply and divide numbers expressed in scientific notation.
- Apply the relationship between distance, rate, and time to solve problems.
- Apply the formula for circumference of a circle.

Pacing Guide

Items marked with are available on the **Teacher Toolbox**.

	MATERIALS
SESSION 1 (45–60 min)	
Planetary Orbits	
Study an Example Problem and Solution (20–30 min) Example Problem (10–15 min) | One Student's Solution (10–15 min) **Try Another Approach** (25–30 min) Plan It (5 min) | Solve It (15–20 min) | Reflect (5 min)	For each student: Activity Sheet *Solution Sheet*
SESSION 2 (45–60 min)	
Insulating Blankets	
Discuss Models and Strategies (20–30 min) Plan It and Solve It (15–25 min) | Reflect (5 min)	For each student: Activity Sheet *Solution Sheet*
Satellites	
Persevere On Your Own (25–30 min) Solve It (20–25 min) | Reflect (5 min) **DIFFERENTIATION** **RETEACH** Extra Support **EXTEND** Challenge	For each student: Activity Sheet *Solution Sheet*

Purpose

- **Examine** a problem that involves multiplying and dividing numbers written in scientific notation.
- **Analyze** a sample solution to identify what makes it a good solution.
- **Demonstrate** that the problem has more than one approach and more than one solution.

Study an Example Problem and Solution

Planetary Orbits

Make Sense of the Problem

Present the Planetary Orbits problem and use **Three Reads** to help students make sense of it. For each read, have a different volunteer read aloud each section of information.

After the first read, be sure students recognize that, although a planet's orbital speed is constantly changing, the values in the table can be used to determine the average speed for each planet.

ASK *Why do you think the distances and times in the table are given in scientific notation?*

LISTEN FOR They are given in scientific notation because the numbers are very large. If they were written in standard form, they would take up a lot of space and be difficult to work with.

After the second read, listen for students to articulate that they need to find the distance the planet of their choice will travel along its orbit in 7 Earth days, or one week.

After the third read, have students identify the important quantities and relationships in the problem, including any quantities that involve student choice. Ensure that students understand that student choice means there can be multiple correct solutions to the problem.

Invite students to share their ideas about how they might use concepts from the unit to solve this problem. Allow them to describe different approaches, but do not implement any strategies.

ASK *Do you think you will need to use operations with numbers in scientific notation? Which operations do you think you will have to use? Why?*

LISTEN FOR I think I will need to multiply and divide numbers in scientific notation. The problem involves distance, time, and speed, which are related by multiplication and division.

Math in Action | SESSION 1

Scientific Notation and Properties of Exponents

Math IN Action

SMP 1 Make sense of problems and persevere in solving them.

Study an Example Problem and Solution

➤ **Read this problem involving scientific notation. Then look at one student's solution to this problem on the following pages.**

Planetary Orbits

Jamal attends an event about careers in the space industry. He meets with an astronomer who talks about a planet's orbital period, which is the amount of time it takes the planet to orbit the sun once.

Read the information about the orbits of the planets in our solar system. Choose a planet and use its data to determine about how far it would travel along its orbit in 7 Earth days. Use an appropriately sized unit.

Planetary Orbits in Our Solar System

A planet's orbit around the sun is not an exact circle, so its distance from the sun changes as it orbits.

A planet's distance from the sun affects its orbital speed. The closer a planet is to the sun, the faster it moves.

Although a planet's orbital speed is constantly changing, you can use the average speed to estimate how far it travels over a given period of time.

	Mercury	Venus	Earth	Mars	Jupiter	Saturn	Uranus	Neptune
Length of Orbit (meters)	3.6×10^{11}	6.8×10^{11}	9.4×10^{11}	1.4×10^{12}	4.9×10^{12}	9.0×10^{12}	1.8×10^{13}	3.7×10^{13}
Orbital Period (seconds)	7.6×10^{6}	1.9×10^{7}	3.2×10^{7}	5.9×10^{7}	3.7×10^{8}	9.3×10^{8}	2.6×10^{9}	5.2×10^{9}

541

CONNECT TO CONTEXT

Planetary Orbits Ask students to share what they know about the orbits of Earth and the other planets in our solar system. Earth completes one revolution, or orbit, around the sun about every 365 days, the duration of a year on Earth. The planets orbit the sun because of the sun's gravitational pull. Refer to the problem, which states that a planet's orbit is not a perfect circle. Optionally, work with a science teacher at your school to help students further explore planetary orbits.

Appropriate Precision Explain that, because a planet's speed varies throughout its orbit, students will use the average speed to determine how far the planet travels in 7 days. Also, point out that the orbit lengths and orbital periods in the table are rounded values. As a result, the distances students find will be estimates, rather than precise values.

One Student's Solution

Read through the sample solution to the Planetary Orbits problem together, one section at a time. Point out that the Notice That boxes provide important information about this student's solution.

Problem-Solving Checklist

Explain to students that they will use the Problem-Solving Checklist on this page to identify what makes this a good solution.

- Have students look at the sample solution to find and circle where the student wrote known, or given, information.
- Then have students underline where the student wrote what they need to find.
- As a class, find and box where the student showed their work.
- Finally, ask students to put a checkmark next to the place where the student checked their solution.
- Tell students that they can use this checklist as a model when they write their own solutions for this problem and for other problems.

Facilitate Whole Class Discussion

Support students in analyzing and discussing the steps of the sample solution in order to better understand it.

ASK *How does the student determine the distance Jupiter travels in 1 second?*

LISTEN FOR The student divides the length of the orbit in meters by the time it takes Jupiter to complete the orbit in seconds.

ASK *How does the student divide the two numbers, which are both given in scientific notation?*

LISTEN FOR The student divides the two decimal factors and the two powers of 10 separately, and then multiplies the quotients. To divide the powers of 10, the student subtracts the exponents.

Discuss how the student uses estimation to check that the rate is reasonable.

ASK *What does the student do to estimate Jupiter's rate of travel?*

LISTEN FOR The student rounds 4.9 to the nearest whole number, 5, to get 5×10^{12} meters and rounds 3.7 to the nearest whole number, 4, to get 4×10^{8} seconds. Then, the student divides these rounded values.

UNIT 5 Math in Action | SESSION 1

One Student's Solution

Problem-Solving Checklist

- ☐ Tell what is known.
- ☐ Tell what the problem is asking.
- ☐ Show all your work.
- ☐ Show that the solution works.

First, I have to choose a planet to analyze.

I will choose Jupiter because it is the largest planet. Because a planet travels at different speeds on different days, based on its distance from the sun, I will figure out on average how far Jupiter moves along its orbit over 7 Earth days.

Then, I will calculate about how far Jupiter travels in 1 second.

The data in the table tell me that Jupiter's orbit is 4.9×10^{12} meters long, and it takes Jupiter 3.7×10^{8} seconds to make 1 trip around the sun.

I can divide distance by time to find the rate. I can use properties of exponents to divide:

$$\frac{4.9 \times 10^{12}}{3.7 \times 10^{8}} = \frac{4.9}{3.7} \times \frac{10^{12}}{10^{8}}$$
$$\approx 1.3243 \times 10^{12-8}$$
$$= 1.3243 \times 10^{4}$$

Jupiter travels about 1.3243×10^{4} meters per second.

NOTICE THAT . . . $4.9 \div 3.7$ results in a repeating decimal. In this case, it does not make sense to use more than 4 digits since the power of 10 is 4. $1.3243 \times 10^{4} = 13{,}243$

Next, I will use estimation to check that the rate I found is reasonable.

The length of Jupiter's orbit is about 5×10^{12} meters. The orbital period is about 4×10^{8} seconds.

I can use properties of exponents to divide:

$$\frac{5 \times 10^{12}}{4 \times 10^{8}} = \frac{5}{4} \times \frac{10^{12}}{10^{8}}$$
$$= 1.25 \times 10^{12-8}$$
$$= 1.25 \times 10^{4}$$

Jupiter travels about 1.25×10^{4} meters per second. This is close to the rate I found using more precise calculations, so I feel confident that rate is reasonable.

542

Prompt students to discuss how to compare the estimate with the more precise answer.

ASK *How does the student's estimate show that the answer found using more precise calculations is reasonable?*

LISTEN FOR Both the estimate and the more precise answer have the same power of 10, and the first factors are both between 1 and 1.5. So, the two numbers are close enough for the student to be confident that the answer found using more precise calculations is reasonable.

Prompt students to consider the steps used to calculate the number of seconds in 7 Earth days.

ASK *How does the student calculate the number of seconds in 7 Earth days?*

LISTEN FOR First, the student calculates the number of hours in 7 Earth days by multiplying 7 and the number of hours in a day, 24. Then the student calculates the number of minutes in 7 Earth days by multiplying that number of hours by the number of minutes in an hour, 60. Finally, the student calculates the number of seconds in 7 Earth days by multiplying that number of minutes by the number of seconds in a minute, 60.

ASK *Why does the student use multiplication to calculate the distance Jupiter travels in 7 days?*

LISTEN FOR The rate gives the distance Jupiter travels in 1 second. It will travel this distance for each of the seconds in 7 Earth days, so the correct operation is multiplication.

Have students discuss the use of estimation and appropriate precision from the sample solution.

ASK *How does the student use estimation to check the reasonableness of the final answer?*

LISTEN FOR The student multiplies the previous estimate of the distance Jupiter travels in 1 second by an estimate of the number of seconds in 7 Earth days. The student compares this result to the result of the more precise calculation. Because both answers have the same power of 10 and first factors that are close, the solution is reasonable.

After discussing the sample solution, have a volunteer summarize the steps taken to solve the problem.

ASK *How can you summarize the steps in the sample solution?*

LISTEN FOR Choose a planet to analyze. Find the distance the planet travels in 1 second, and use estimation to check that it is reasonable. Calculate the number of seconds in 7 Earth days. Multiply the distance the planet travels in 1 second by the number of seconds in 7 Earth days to find the distance traveled in 7 Earth days. Check the reasonableness of the answer using estimation.

Math in Action

Next, I will calculate the number of seconds in 7 Earth days.

There are 24 hours in a day, and $7 \times 24 = 168$.

So, there are 168 hours in 7 days.

There are 60 minutes in an hour, and $168 \times 60 = 10{,}080$.

So, there are 10,080 minutes in 7 days.

There are 60 seconds in a minute, and $10{,}080 \times 60 = 604{,}800$.

So, there are 604,800 seconds in 7 days.

I can write 604,800 in scientific notation as 6.048×10^5.

> **NOTICE THAT . . .** Because I know how far Jupiter travels in 1 second, I need to know how many seconds are in 7 days.

Now, I can multiply to find out about how far Jupiter travels in 7 Earth days.

I can multiply rate and time to find the distance.

$$(1.3243 \times 10^4)(6.048 \times 10^5) = (1.3243 \times 6.048)(10^4 \times 10^5)$$
$$= 8.0093664 \times 10^9$$

Jupiter travels about 8.0093664×10^9 meters in 7 Earth days.

Finally, I can check my answer using estimation.

6.048×10^5 seconds is about 6×10^5 seconds.

I will use my estimated rate of 1.25×10^4 meters per second.

$(6 \times 10^5)(1.25 \times 10^4) = 7.5 \times 10^9$

7.5×10^9 is close to 8.0093664×10^9.

Since I got similar answers using estimation and more precise calculations, I feel confident my answer is correct.

> **NOTICE THAT . . .** The first factors in both numbers (7.5 and 8.0093664) are close to 8. Both numbers have the same power of 10.

543

Math in Action

Try Another Approach

Planetary Orbits

Materials For each student: Activity Sheet *Solution Sheet*

Facilitate Whole Class Discussion

After reviewing the sample student solution on the previous pages, prompt students to look for different approaches to solve the problem.

ASK *What are some different steps you could use to solve the problem?*

LISTEN FOR I could select a different planet. I could find the distance the planet travels in 1 day and then multiply that distance by 7. I could change the numbers to standard form and then do the calculations. I could rewrite the numbers so they have the same power of 10 and then divide the decimal parts.

Plan It

Facilitate Whole Class Discussion

Read the Plan It questions from the next page aloud. Prompt students to discuss how they will approach and solve this problem in another way.

ASK *How can you convert the orbital period from a measure in seconds to a measure in days?*

LISTEN FOR I can find the number of seconds in a day, and then divide the orbital period by this number. This would give me the orbital period as a number of days, rather than as a number of seconds.

ASK *What properties of exponents do you think you will use to solve this problem? Why?*

LISTEN FOR Because distance, speed, and time are related by multiplication and division, I will probably use the product of powers and quotient of powers properties.

UNIT 5 Math in Action | SESSION 1

Try Another Approach

There are many ways to solve problems. Think about how you might solve the Planetary Orbits problem in a different way.

Planetary Orbits

Jamal attends an event about careers in the space industry. He meets with an astronomer who talks about a planet's orbital period, which is the amount of time it takes the planet to orbit the sun once.

Read the information about the orbits of the planets in our solar system. Choose a planet and use its data to determine about how far it would travel along its orbit in 7 Earth days. Use an appropriately sized unit.

Problem-Solving Checklist

- ☐ Tell what is known.
- ☐ Tell what the problem is asking.
- ☐ Show all your work.
- ☐ Show that the solution works.

Planetary Orbits in Our Solar System

A planet's orbit around the sun is not an exact circle, so its distance from the sun changes as it orbits.

A planet's distance from the sun affects its orbital speed. The closer a planet is to the sun, the faster it moves.

Although a planet's orbital speed is constantly changing, you can use the average speed to estimate how far it travels over a given period of time.

	Mercury	Venus	Earth	Mars	Jupiter	Saturn	Uranus	Neptune
Length of Orbit (meters)	3.6×10^{11}	6.8×10^{11}	9.4×10^{11}	1.4×10^{12}	4.9×10^{12}	9.0×10^{12}	1.8×10^{13}	3.7×10^{13}
Orbital Period (seconds)	7.6×10^{6}	1.9×10^{7}	3.2×10^{7}	5.9×10^{7}	3.7×10^{8}	9.3×10^{8}	2.6×10^{9}	5.2×10^{9}

544

Solve It

Problem-Solving Tips

Introduce the Problem-Solving Tips as ideas students may use to explain their thinking. Remind them to also use the Problem-Solving Checklist to make sure their answer is complete.

Have students write their own complete solutions on a copy of Activity Sheet *Solution Sheet* or a blank sheet of paper.

Reflect

As they work, have students share their thinking with a partner and discuss the Reflect questions.

As time permits, have students explain their solutions to the class.

Possible Solution

I decided to analyze Earth because that is where I live. Because a planet travels at different speeds on different days based on its distance from the sun, I will figure out on average how far Earth moves along its orbit over 7 days. The data in the table tells me that Earth's orbit is 9.4×10^{11} m, and it takes Earth 3.2×10^7 seconds to make 1 trip around the sun.

I want to change the orbital period to days. First, I will find the number of seconds in 1 day. There are 24 hours in a day. Because there are 60 minutes in each hour and 60 seconds in each minute, there are $24 \cdot 60 \cdot 60$, or 86,400, seconds in 1 day. In scientific notation, this is 8.64×10^4 seconds. To find Earth's orbital period in days, I can divide:

$$\frac{3.2 \times 10^7}{8.64 \times 10^4} \approx 0.370 \times 10^3$$

Earth's orbital period is 3.70×10^2 days, which is 370 days. I know this is reasonable because there are 365 days in 1 Earth year.

Now, I can divide to find how far Earth travels in 1 day.

$$\frac{9.4 \times 10^{11}}{3.7 \times 10^2} \approx 2.54 \times 10^9$$

Earth travels about 2.54×10^9 m in 1 day.

Finally, I can multiply by 7 to find how far Earth travels in 7 days.

$$7 \times 2.54 \times 10^9 = 17.78 \times 10^9$$

17.78×10^9 is the same as 1.778×10^{10}. Earth travels about 1.778×10^{10} m in 7 days.

Math in Action

Plan It

Answer these questions to help you start thinking about a plan.

a. How could you solve this problem without determining how far the planet travels in 1 second?

b. How will the properties of exponents help you solve this problem?

Solve It

Find a different solution for the Planetary Orbits problem. Show all your work on a separate sheet of paper. You may want to use the Problem-Solving Tips to get started.

PROBLEM-SOLVING TIPS

Key Terms

scientific notation	standard form	exponent
product	quotient	base
power		

Models You may want to use . . .

- properties of exponents to multiply and divide numbers written in scientific notation.
- scientific notation to write very large or very small numbers.

Questions

- Do the units of your final answer make sense? Would another unit be more appropriate?
- How far does the planet you chose travel on an average day?

Reflect

Use Mathematical Practices As you work through the problem, discuss these questions with a partner.

- **Use Models** How can using scientific notation and the properties of exponents help you solve this problem?
- **Reason Mathematically** Does it make sense for the planet to travel farther in 1 second or 1 day?

545

Scoring Rubric (4 points)

Points	Expectations
4	The solution and explanation are clear and complete, with no errors. All work is shown. The final approximation of the distance traveled in 7 Earth days is reasonable, and the degree of precision is appropriate.
3	The solution is complete, with one or two errors. Solution steps are correct, but not all work is shown, or the work is disorganized. The estimate of the distance traveled in 7 Earth days is reasonable.
2	All parts of the task were attempted. Some of the solution steps may not be appropriate for the problem. There are some errors in the calculations that involve scientific notation or the application of the properties of exponents.
1	Some parts of the task were not attempted. The solution and explanations are unclear and incomplete. Many calculations are incorrect. The distance traveled in 7 Earth days is missing or incorrect.

Purpose

- **Understand** two new open-ended, multi-step problems involving operations with scientific notation and properties of exponents.
- **Choose** appropriate models and strategies to plan for and solve the problems.

Discuss Models and Strategies

Insulating Blankets

Materials For each student: Activity Sheet *Solution Sheet*

Make Sense of the Problem

Present the Insulating Blankets problem and use **Three Reads** to help students make sense of it. Have different volunteers take turns reading aloud each section of information.

ASK *What is this problem about?*

LISTEN FOR It is about determining the thickness, in inches, of a blanket used to insulate spacecraft from damaging heat and radiation from the sun.

Invite volunteers to point out what is known and what they need to figure out.

ASK *What do you need to include in your plan and solution?*

LISTEN FOR The plan needs to include the number of pairs of reflector and separator layers that will be used, as well as the choices for the thicknesses of these layers and of the inner and outer covers. The solution will need to include the total thickness of the blanket.

Ensure that students understand what is meant by *15–20 total pairs of reflector-separator layers.*

ASK *If you choose 16 pairs, then how many reflector layers will you use? How many separator layers will you use?*

LISTEN FOR I will use 16 reflector layers and 16 separator layers.

UNIT 5 Math in Action | SESSION 2 ■■

Discuss Models and Strategies

➤ **Read the problem. Write a solution on a separate sheet of paper. Remember, there can be lots of ways to solve a problem.**

Problem-Solving Checklist

- ☐ Tell what is known.
- ☐ Tell what the problem is asking.
- ☐ Show all your work.
- ☐ Show that the solution works.

Insulating Blankets

An aerospace engineer explains that insulating blankets protect spacecraft from damaging heat and radiation from the sun. He tells Jamal that the blankets are constructed using several layers of special materials. Read the information about the design of these blankets.

Jamal notices that the blankets seem very thin and wonders how thick one might be. Use the specifications below to describe a blanket for a spacecraft. Then find the thickness of the blanket.

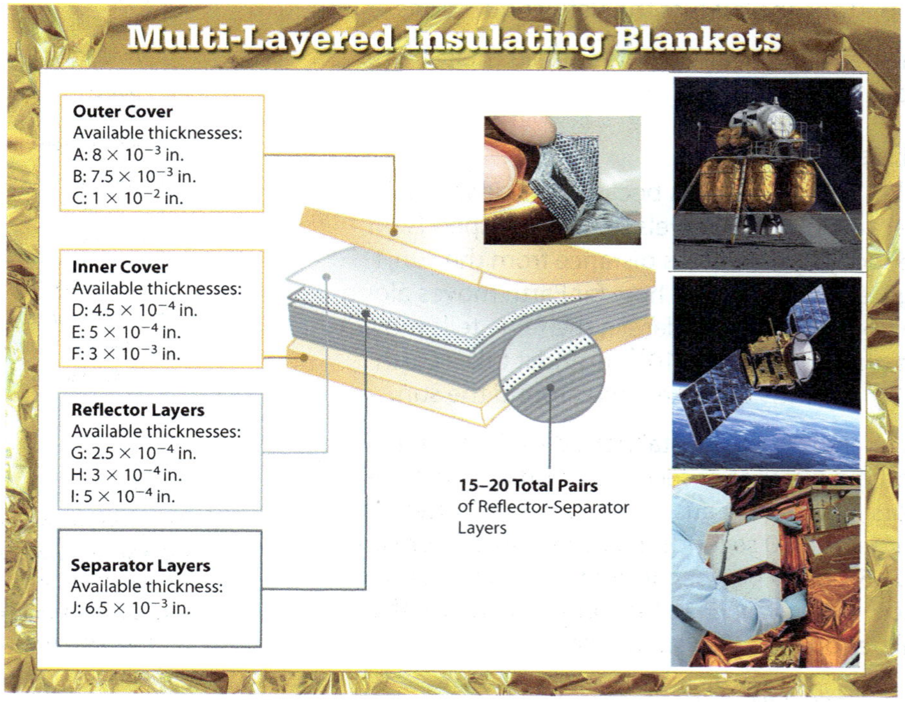

546

Discuss possible steps, ways to organize the information, and techniques that might be helpful. Invite students to take notes.

ASK *How might the diagram help you organize the information?*

LISTEN FOR It has the available thicknesses categorized by cover and layer types, as well as the number of each that is required. This will help me write equations to solve the problem.

CONNECT TO CONTEXT

Insulating Blankets These blankets are referred to as MLI, which stands for multilayer insulation. They are used to provide thermal protection to spacecraft and launch vehicles. The layers of these blankets are made of a combination of thin films, foils, and fabrics. There are different grades of insulating blankets, dependent upon the temperatures in which protection is required. The blankets can provide protection from temperatures ranging from 300°C to temperatures exceeding 1,000°C.

Materials used in these blankets are the same materials used in "space blankets," the shiny, metallic blankets often found in first aid kits and used in emergency or survival situations. Ask a student who has seen one of these blankets to describe what they look like.

Plan It and Solve It

Problem-Solving Checklist & Tips

Have students use various resources, including the Problem-Solving Checklist and the Problem-Solving Tips, as they begin to plan a solution.

Support Student Work

Have students work in pairs to discuss their preliminary solution strategies and the Reflect questions. Discuss a variety of approaches as a class. Let students revise their plans and discuss again with a partner.

When students are confident that their plans make sense, have them write a complete solution on a copy of Activity Sheet *Solution Sheet* or a blank sheet of paper.

Reflect

As they work, have students share their thinking with a partner and discuss the Reflect questions.

As time permits, have students explain their solutions to the class.

Possible Solution

I chose thicknesses that have the same power of 10 when it was possible, to make my calculations simpler. I chose: Outer Cover, Thickness A; Inner Cover, Thickness F; Reflector Layer, Thickness I; Separator Layer, Thickness J.

I will use 20 pairs of reflector and separator layers and rewrite the thicknesses so they have the same power of 10. Then I will add to find the total thickness of one pair.

$$5 \times 10^{-4} + 6.5 \times 10^{-3} = 0.5 \times 10^{-3} + 6.5 \times 10^{-3}$$
$$= 7 \times 10^{-3} \text{ in.}$$

I can multiply the result by 20 to find the total thickness of all the pairs of reflector and separator layers.

$$20 \times 7 \times 10^{-3} = 140 \times 10^{-3} \text{ in.}$$

Rather than converting this number to correct scientific notation, I will leave it in this form to make calculations easier. I add on the thicknesses of both covers to find the total thickness of the blanket.

$$8 \times 10^{-3} + 3 \times 10^{-3} + 140 \times 10^{-3} = 151 \times 10^{-3} \text{ in.}$$

I will write my final answer in scientific notation as 1.51×10^{-1} in.

The thickness of my blanket is approximately 0.15 in.

Math IN Action

Plan It and Solve It

➤ **Find a solution to the Insulating Blankets problem.**

Write a detailed plan and support your answer. Be sure to include:

- the thicknesses of the inner and outer covers you will use.
- the thicknesses of the reflector and separator layers you will use.
- the number of pairs of reflector and separator layers in your blanket.
- the total thickness of the blanket.

PROBLEM-SOLVING TIPS

Key Terms

scientific notation	standard form	power
product	quotient	sum
properties of exponents	factor	

Models You may want to use . . .

- properties of exponents to simplify an expression.
- decimal point patterns to rewrite numbers so that all numbers in an expression have the same power of 10.

Questions

- What is the total thickness of 1 reflector layer and 1 separator layer? What is the total thickness of all the reflector and separator layers in the blanket?
- Will you use scientific notation or standard form to do your calculations?

Reflect

Use Mathematical Practices As you work through the problem, discuss these questions with a partner.

- **Make Sense of Problems** What operations will you use to determine the total thickness of the insulating blanket?
- **Make an Argument** Does it make sense to write your final answer in scientific notation or standard form? Why?

Insulating "space blankets" are often given to runners at the end of a long-distance race to help regulate body temperature.

547

Scoring Rubric (4 points)

Points	Expectations
4	The solution and explanation are clear and complete, with no errors. The thicknesses of the covers, reflector, and separator layers and the number of pairs of inner layers are stated. All of the work to find the total thickness of the blanket is shown.
3	The solution is complete, with one or two errors. Properties of exponents may not always be used correctly, but the answers given are reasonable. The total thickness of the blanket is stated.
2	All parts of the task were attempted. Some layers were not included, or an incorrect number of reflector and separator layers was chosen. The calculations may have been done incorrectly.
1	The solution is not complete. The number of reflector and separator layers or the chosen thicknesses are not stated. The calculations are incomplete or incorrect.

Persevere On Your Own

Satellites

Materials For each student: Activity Sheet *Solution Sheet*

Make Sense of the Problem

Present the Satellites problem and use **Three Reads** to help students make sense of it. Have different volunteers take turns reading aloud each section of information. Encourage students to carefully examine the diagram to determine which pieces of information they will need to solve the problem. Point out that there are three orbits shown. Each callout gives information about a type of satellite with that orbit.

CONNECT TO CONTEXT

Satellites Ask students to share what they know about satellites. They are likely aware that Earth has satellites orbiting around it but may not realize that there are thousands of them! Satellites are launched into space to perform specific functions. There are nine different types of satellites. The type that is most widely used is the navigation satellite, which is used to provide GPS (Global Positioning System) directions. Students may also be familiar with communication satellites. Satellite television providers have a fleet of Geostationary Communications Satellites to deliver high-definition television programming to homes and businesses.

UNIT 5 Math in Action | SESSION 2

Persevere On Your Own

Problem-Solving Checklist
- ☐ Tell what is known.
- ☐ Tell what the problem is asking.
- ☐ Show all your work.
- ☐ Show that the solution works.

➤ **Read the problem. Write a solution on a separate sheet of paper.**

Satellites

Jamal meets a satellite technologist. She explains to Jamal that satellites travel faster the closer they are to Earth, just as planets move faster the closer they are to the sun. Jamal wonders how long it takes for a satellite to complete one orbit around Earth.

The satellite technologist shows Jamal this diagram, which gives information about the orbits of three types of satellites. Choose one type of satellite and calculate the time it takes to complete one orbit of Earth.

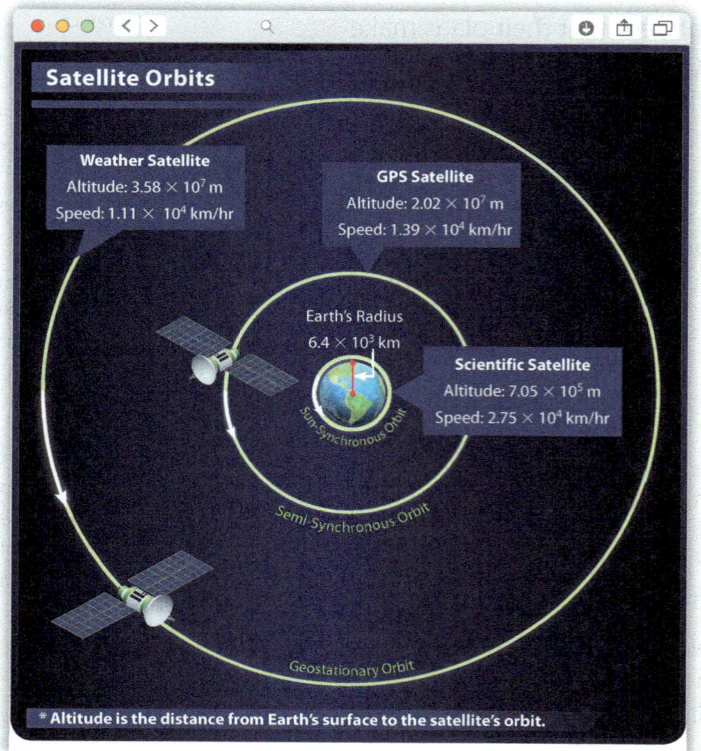

* Altitude is the distance from Earth's surface to the satellite's orbit.

548

DIFFERENTIATION | Use with Satellites

RETEACH

Extra Support

Examine the diagram to gather important information.

- Ask: *In addition to the speed of the satellite, what do you need to know to find how long it takes the satellite to orbit Earth once?* [the distance it travels in one orbit]
- Point out that the length of an orbit is the circumference of a circle.
- Ask: *What information do you need before you can calculate the length of an orbit?* [the radius or diameter of the orbit]
- Ask: *How can you use the information in the diagram to find the radius of an orbit?* [Add the altitude to Earth's radius.]
- Ask: *What do you notice about the units for the altitudes and Earth's radius?* [Altitudes are in meters; the radius is in kilometers.]
- Ask: *Why does it make sense to convert the measure in meters to a measure in kilometers?* [The speeds are in kilometers per hour.]

EXTEND

Challenge

Solve a different problem.

Refer to the satellite diagram. How much more quickly does the fastest satellite orbit Earth than the slowest satellite?

Possible Solution

The fastest satellite is the scientific satellite, and the slowest satellite is the weather satellite. Using the circumference formula, the orbit distance for the scientific satellite is 4.49×10^4 km, and the orbit distance for the weather satellite is 2.65×10^5 km. To find the time each orbit takes, I can divide the distance by the speed.

Scientific: $\frac{4.49 \times 10^4}{2.76 \times 10^4} \approx 1.63 \times 10^0$ Weather: $\frac{2.65 \times 10^5}{1.11 \times 10^4} \approx 2.39 \times 10^1$

It takes the scientific satellite about 1.6 h to orbit. It takes the weather satellite about 24 h. The scientific satellite takes about 22.4 fewer hours.

Solve It

Remind students that there are many different ways to solve a problem.

Invite them to look back at the Problem-Solving Checklist to help them get started. They might also want to look at the Problem-Solving Tips on other pages to get some ideas for how to start.

Have students write their complete solution on a copy of Activity Sheet *Solution Sheet* or a blank sheet of paper.

Reflect

Have students work with a partner to share their thinking and discuss the Reflect questions.

As time permits, have students explain their solutions to the class.

Possible Solution

I will use the GPS satellite.

I need to find the distance for one orbit of Earth. I will find the radius of the GPS satellite's orbit by adding its altitude to Earth's radius. I will first convert the altitude from meters to kilometers: 2.02×10^4 km. Then I will add it to Earth's radius.

$$2.02 \times 10^4 + 6.4 \times 10^3 = 2.02 \times 10^4 + 0.64 \times 10^4$$
$$= 2.66 \times 10^4 \text{ km}$$

I will use the radius of the orbit to find the circumference of the GPS satellite's orbit. I will use 3.14 as an approximation of π.

$$C = 2\pi r$$
$$\approx 2(3.14)(2.66 \times 10^4)$$
$$\approx 16.7 \times 10^4$$
$$= 1.67 \times 10^5$$

The circumference of the orbit is about 1.67×10^5 km.

The speed of the GPS satellite is 1.39×10^4 km/h.

To find the time one orbit takes, I divide the distance by the speed.

$$\frac{1.67 \times 10^5}{1.39 \times 10^4} \approx 1.2 \times 10^{5-4}$$
$$= 1.2 \times 10^1$$
$$= 12$$

It takes about 12 h for the GPS satellite to orbit Earth.

Math in Action

Solve It

➤ **Find a solution to the Satellites problem.**

- Calculate the distance one type of satellite will travel to complete one orbit. (The formula for the circumference of a circle with radius r is $C = 2\pi r$.)
- Determine how long it will take the satellite to complete one orbit.

Reflect

Use Mathematical Practices After you complete the problem, choose one of these questions to discuss with a partner.

- **Be Precise** What units did you use when doing your calculations? What units did you use to give your final answer?
- **Persevere** What models or strategies did you use to determine your answer?

A satellite dish is a bowl-shaped antenna that transmits and receives information from a communication satellite.

549

Scoring Rubric (4 points)	
Points	**Expectations**
4	The solution and explanation are clear and complete, with no errors. The satellite's altitude and Earth's radius are used to find the radius of the satellite's orbit. The circumference is correctly calculated and divided by the satellite's speed to find the time. All work is shown.
3	The solution is complete, with one or two errors. Work is shown and organized. Calculations of the radius of the satellite's orbit, circumference, or time to complete one orbit may have minor errors, but the answers given are reasonable.
2	All parts of the task were attempted. Some, but not all, explanations are provided. There are errors in the calculations of the radius of the satellite's orbit, circumference, or time to complete one orbit.
1	The solution is incomplete. The explanation is incomplete or inaccurate. Calculations of the radius of the satellite's orbit, circumference, or time to complete one orbit are incorrect or missing.

Self Reflection

Have students review the skills on the **Self Reflection** page and work in pairs to respond to the prompts. Encourage students to revisit the work they did in each lesson in order to help develop growth mindset.

- Remind students that this is the same list of skills that they saw on the **Self Check** page at the beginning of the unit.
- Tell students that revisiting the list of skills is an opportunity for them to reflect on their learning and progress during the unit.
- Have students read through the list of skills independently and then work in pairs to respond to the prompts. Encourage students to revisit the work they did in each lesson as they think about how to respond to the prompts.
- Discuss students' responses to the prompts as a class if time permits. Tell students that they will build on these skills in later lessons during the year and/or in other grade levels.

UNIT 5 Self Reflection

In this unit you learned to . . .

Skill	Lesson
Simplify expressions with two or more powers using exponent properties.	19, 20, 21, 22
Apply exponent properties to rewrite or simplify expressions with zero and negative integer exponents.	20, 21, 22
Express, estimate, and compare quantities using integer powers of 10.	21
Perform operations with numbers in scientific notation.	22
Work with scientific notation to solve problems.	22
Listen carefully during discussion in order to understand and explain another person's ideas.	19–22

Think about what you have learned.

➤ **Use words, numbers, and drawings.**

1. One topic I could use in my everyday life is __________ because . . .

2. Something I know well is . . .

3. One thing I still need to work on is . . .

550

Vocabulary Self-Assessment

- Students have interacted with and used unit math and academic vocabulary throughout the unit in listening, speaking, reading, and writing. Use this activity to review the terms and help students check their understanding of the definitions.
- Have students read the vocabulary terms and put a check mark by the terms they can use in speaking and writing. Students can look up words they do not know in the Interactive Glossary or the Academic Glossary in the Teacher Toolbox.

Problem Notes

1. Encourage students to explain the reasoning they used to determine whether to use standard form or scientific notation.
2. Check student understanding by asking why one exponent is positive and the other exponent is negative.
3. Students may provide examples of simplifying expressions and evaluating expressions. Encourage students to use complete sentences in their responses.

If time allows, this is a good opportunity to have students work in pairs to read and provide feedback on responses. Feedback should focus on the word meaning, accuracy, and clarity of the response.

UNIT 5 Vocabulary Review

Review the unit vocabulary. Put a check mark by items you can use in speaking and writing. Look up the meaning of any terms you do not know.

Math Vocabulary		Academic Vocabulary
☐ absolute value	☐ power of 10	☐ express
☐ base (of a power)	☐ standard form	☐ mass
☐ evaluate	☐ scientific notation	☐ molecule
☐ exponent		☐ simplify

Use the unit vocabulary to complete the problems.

1. Tell whether you would most likely use standard form or scientific notation to represent each quantity.
   a. The diameter of a basketball in inches standard form
   b. The distance from Earth to Mars in miles scientific notation
   c. The world population scientific notation

2. Select a positive number greater than 10,000,000 and a positive number less than 0.000001. Express both numbers in standard form and in scientific notation. Use *scientific notation* and *standard form* to label your numbers. Possible answers:
   Standard form: 25,678,000 and 0.00000002506
   Scientific notation: 2.5678×10^7 and 2.506×10^{-8}

3. Explain what you do when you simplify an expression. How is it the same or different from what you do when you evaluate an expression?
   Possible answer: You simplify an expression by combining like terms or using properties of operations in order to have the fewest terms possible. You evaluate an expression by finding its value. For some expressions, simplifying and evaluating result in the same expression or value.

4. Label this expression with at least three math or academic vocabulary terms.

   1.685×10^4
   scientific notation (whole expression); base (10); exponent (4); power of 10 (10^4)

551

Problem Notes

1 **A, B, D are correct.** Students could solve the problem by applying properties of exponents to simplify each expression and then determine if the expression is equivalent to $7^4 \cdot 9^8$.

C is not correct. This answer represents raising 9^4 to the fourth power, making the expression equivalent to $7^4 \cdot 9^{16}$ instead of $7^4 \cdot 9^8$.

E is not correct. This answer represents dividing 7^8 by 7^2, making the expression equivalent to $7^6 \cdot 9^8$ instead of $7^4 \cdot 9^8$.

DOK 1 | **8.EE.A.1**

2 **D is correct.** Students could solve the problem by applying properties of exponents to simplify each expression and then determine if the expression is equivalent to 3^{-5}.

A is not correct. This answer is equivalent to $3^{5-0} = 3^5$ instead of $3^{0-5} = 3^{-5}$.

B is not correct. This answer is equivalent to $3^{5 \cdot 0} = 3^0$ instead of $3^{0-5} = 3^{-5}$.

C is not correct. This answer is equivalent to $3^{5-1} = 3^4$ instead of $3^{5(1)} = 3^{-5}$.

DOK 1 | **8.EE.A.1**

3 Students could solve the problem by comparing the single digits, 1 and 2. Since both are multiplied by a base of 10, compare the exponents, 1 and −3, to determine which sample has the greater mass.

DOK 2 | **8.EE.A.3**

UNIT **5** Unit Review

➤ **Use what you have learned to complete these problems.**

1 Which expressions are equivalent to $7^4 \cdot 9^8$? Choose all the correct answers.

(**A**) $7 \cdot 9^5 \cdot (7 \cdot 9)^3$

(**B**) $\left(\frac{7 \cdot 9^6}{9^4}\right)^4$

C $(7 \cdot 9^4)^4$

(**D**) $\frac{7^5 \cdot 9^{12}}{9^4 \cdot 7}$

E $\frac{(7 \cdot 9)^8}{7^2}$

2 Which expression is equivalent to 3^{-5}?

A $\frac{3^5}{3^0}$

B $(3^5)^0$

C $3^5 \cdot 3^{-1}$

(**D**) $\frac{1}{3^5}$

3 A geology class is studying a sample of rock and a sample of dry sponge. The rock sample has a mass of 1×10^1 kg. The dry sponge sample has a mass of 2×10^{-3} kg. Which sample has a greater mass? How many times greater? Show your work.

Possible student work: 10^1 is greater than 10^{-3}, so the rock sample has a greater mass than the sponge sample.

1 is $\frac{1}{2}$ as great as 2. 10^1 is 1,000 times greater than 10^{-3}.

$\frac{1}{2} \times 1{,}000 = 500$

SOLUTION The mass of the rock sample is 500 times greater than the mass of the dry sponge sample.

4 Find the perimeter of the triangle using scientific notation. Write your answers in the blanks.

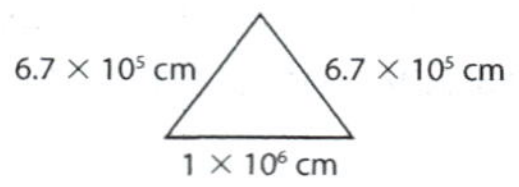

$2(6.7 \times 10^5) + (1 \times 10^6) = (13.4 \times 10^5) + (1 \times 10^6)$

$= (13.4 \times 10^5) + (10 \times \underline{10^5})$

$= \underline{23.4} \times 10^5$

$= \underline{2.34} \times 10^{\underline{6}}$

552

SMP 2, 5, 6, 7, 8

Unit Game

8.EE.A.1

Power Play

Materials For each player: Recording Sheet, Game Board, 20 counters; For each pair: 2 sets of Integer Cards

WHY Reinforce using properties of integer exponents to generate equivalent exponential expressions.

HOW Players use Integer Cards to build exponential expressions and then generate equivalent exponential expressions using integers on the Game Board.

- Reinforce that students should add counters to the Game Board for the integers in the equivalent expression only.
- After students finish the game, ask them to share strategies they used. Ask questions such as: *What properties of integer exponents did you use to write equivalent exponential expressions? What strategies did you use to cover up spaces on your Game Board?*

ELL Support Review the vocabulary in the directions by demonstrating a turn and explaining the meaning of the words equivalent, exponential expression, and discard pile.

Challenge When making an equivalent expression, use only positive exponents.

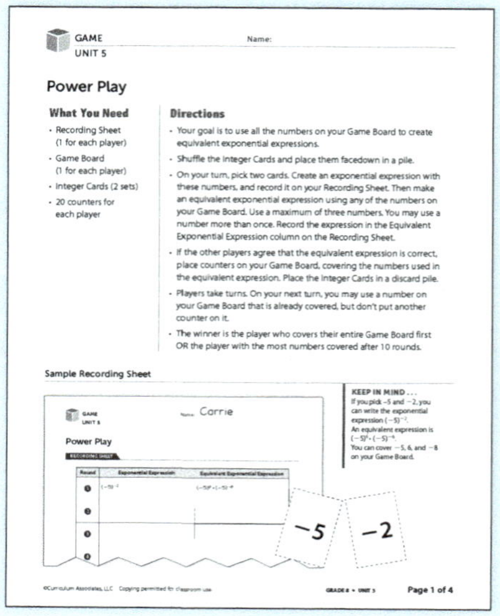

4 DOK 2 | 8.EE.A.4

5 Students could also solve the problem by using the properties of exponents to simplify the expression in a different order. For example,
$$\frac{2^3 \cdot 7^{-8}}{14^{-5}} = \frac{2^3 \cdot 7^{-8}}{2^{-5} \cdot 7^{-5}} = \frac{2^3 \cdot 2^5}{7^8 \cdot 7^{-5}} = \frac{2^8}{7^3} = \frac{256}{343}.$$
DOK 1 | 8.EE.A.1

6 **C, D, E are correct.** Students could solve the problem by determining the values of 7×10^{-6} and 6×10^{-5}. Then students compare the single digits and the integer powers of 10 in each expression to the values of 7×10^{-6} and 6×10^{-5}.

A is not correct. This answer is less than 7×10^{-6}.

B is not correct. This answer is greater than 6×10^{-5}.

F is not correct. This answer is greater than 6×10^{-5}.

DOK 2 | 8.EE.A.3

7 *DOK 2* | 8.EE.A.4

---

5 Evaluate the expression $\frac{2^3 \cdot 7^{-8}}{14^{-5}}$. Show your work.

Possible student work:
$$\frac{2^3 \cdot 7^{-8}}{14^{-5}} = \frac{2^3 \cdot 7^{-8}}{2^{-5} \cdot 7^{-5}}$$
$$= 2^{3-(-5)} \cdot 7^{-8-(-5)}$$
$$= 2^8 \cdot 7^{-3}$$
$$= \frac{2^8}{7^3}$$
$$= \frac{256}{343}$$

SOLUTION $\frac{256}{343}$

6 Which of the following values are between 7×10^{-6} and 6×10^{-5}? Choose all the correct answers.

A 6×10^{-6}

B 8×10^{-5}

(C) 9×10^{-6}

(D) 4×10^{-5}

(E) 8×10^{-6}

F 7×10^{-5}

7 The mass of one grain of sand is about 6.7×10^{-7} kg. An hourglass is estimated to contain 2.1×10^4 grains of sand. What is the mass of the sand in the hourglass? Write your answer using scientific notation. Show your work.

Possible student work:
$$(6.7 \times 10^{-7}) \times (2.1 \times 10^4) = 14.07 \times 10^{-7+4}$$
$$= 14.07 \times 10^{-3}$$
$$= 1.407 \times 10^{-4}$$

SOLUTION 1.407×10^{-4} kg

553

Literacy Connection

Science Fiction

Materials "The War of the Worlds," Literacy Connection Problems

Summary In this excerpt from "The War of the Worlds," the narrator finds Martians who have landed on Earth and died from bacteria.

Math Connection In H.G. Wells' story, there are no bacteria on Mars and so "our microscopic allies" are able to overthrow the invaders. After reading the story, students use what they have learned about exponents and powers of 10 to solve real and fictional problems about bacteria growth and traveling from Mars to Earth.

- Have students read the passage.
- Distribute the literacy connection problems. After reading the directions aloud, direct students to turn and talk about problem 1. Check for understanding.
- Have students work independently to complete the remaining problems. Encourage them to use manipulatives or to draw pictures to solve each problem.
- Circulate and monitor while students work.
- Ask volunteers to share and discuss their solutions with the class.

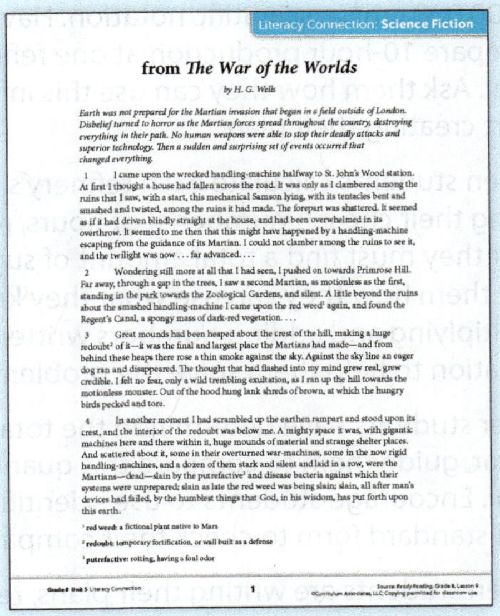
Literacy Connection: Science Fiction
from The War of the Worlds
by H. G. Wells

Unit Review

Purpose

Apply understanding of operations with numbers expressed in scientific notation in order to design a production plan.

MATH FOCUS

DOK 3

Standards 8.EE.A.3 and 8.EE.A.4

MONITOR & GUIDE

SMP 1, 2, 4, 6

Make Sense of the Problem

Before students work on the Performance Task, use **Three Reads** to help them make sense of the problem. During Read 1, ask students to focus on the context of the problem. Collect student responses, such as *There are three refineries producing sugar and filling grocery store sugar orders.* During Read 2, have students identify what they are trying to find out. Students might discuss creating plans that include daily production, amount of sugar needed, and mass of sugar. During Read 3, ask students to identify important quantities that will help them solve the problem. Highlight student responses mentioning hourly production, maximum production hours of the refineries, and mass of a cubic centimeter of sugar. Point out measurement units, such as cubic centimeters and kilograms. Remind students that although they can choose the number of hours the refineries produce sugar each day, it must be 10 hours or less.

Facilitate Problem Solving

Have students complete the task independently, with partners, or in small groups.

If students need additional support as they get started, guide them to rewrite 3,000,000 cm^3 and 5,000,000 cm^3 in scientific notation. Have them compare 10-hour production at one refinery to the goal. Ask them how they can use this information to start creating their plan.

When students calculate each refinery's production using their chosen number(s) of hours, remind them that they must find a total amount of sugar as well. Ask them how they can use what they know about multiplying and adding numbers written in scientific notation to help them solve the problem.

After students have determined the total amount of sugar, guide them to compare this quantity to the goal. Encourage students to use scientific notation and standard form to check their comparisons.

When students are writing their plans, remind them to calculate the total mass of sugar.

UNIT 5 Unit Review

Performance Task

➤ **Answer the questions and show all your work on separate paper.**

A company that harvests and produces sugar has three refineries. The table shows how much sugar each refinery can produce in one hour.

Refinery	Hourly Production (cm^3)
A	1.6×10^5
B	2.1×10^5
C	2.4×10^5

Each refinery can produce sugar for a maximum of 10 h each day. Also, a cubic centimeter of sugar has a mass of 8.5×10^{-4} kg.

The company receives large orders from national grocery stores. It must produce between 3,000,000 cm^3 and 5,000,000 cm^3 of sugar each day to fill the orders.

Create a plan for the refineries to produce the amount of sugar needed to fill the grocery store orders. Describe the following in your plan:

- how much sugar, in cubic centimeters, will be produced in one day;
- how many hours each refinery will produce sugar;
- total mass of sugar produced using your one-day plan.

Use scientific notation for your calculations.

Checklist

Did you . . .

- ☐ create a complete plan, including how much sugar is produced, how many hours each refinery produces sugar, and the total mass of the sugar?
- ☐ check your calculations to be sure they are accurate?
- ☐ make sure your plan meets the required conditions?

Reflect

Use Mathematical Practices After you complete the task, choose one of the following questions to answer.

- **Use Reasoning** How can you use what you know about scientific notation to make sure your plan uses powers of 10 correctly?
- **Be Precise** How could you test your solution to make sure it answers the task?

554

Problem Notes

Students should demonstrate understanding of performing operations with numbers written in scientific notation.

Students may choose different numbers of operation hours. Accept all plans that use 10 hours or less and produce an amount of sugar within range of the goal.

Students should recognize that cubic centimeters must be converted to kilograms to find total mass, using the conversion factor supplied in the task.

Student plans should include hours of production at each refinery, total production in cubic centimeters, total mass in kilograms, and proof that the plan meets the goal.

Reflect

Use Reasoning Look for explanations that describe writing numbers in scientific notation and checking operations performed with numbers in scientific notation.

Be Precise Look for explanations that describe comparing plans to required conditions, checking calculations for accuracy, and making sure the total amount of sugar is within range of the goal.

4-Point Solution

First, I used scientific notation to write the amount of sugar needed to fill the orders:

$3{,}000{,}000 \text{ cm}^3 = 3.0 \times 10^6 \text{ cm}^3$ and $5{,}000{,}000 \text{ cm}^3 = 5.0 \times 10^6 \text{ cm}^3$

Then I checked each refinery's production for 8 hours:

Refinery A: $8 \times (1.6 \times 10^5) = (8 \times 1.6) \times 10^5 = 12.8 \times 10^5 = 1.28 \times 10^6 \text{ cm}^3$

Refinery B: $8 \times (2.1 \times 10^5) = (8 \times 2.1) \times 10^5 = 16.8 \times 10^5 = 1.68 \times 10^6 \text{ cm}^3$

Refinery C: $8 \times (2.4 \times 10^5) = (8 \times 2.4) \times 10^5 = 19.2 \times 10^5 = 1.92 \times 10^6 \text{ cm}^3$

Next, I added the sugar production of all three refineries:

$(1.28 \times 10^6) + (1.68 \times 10^6) + (1.92 \times 10^6) = 4.88 \times 10^6 \text{ cm}^3$

And I made sure the total amount is between $3.0 \times 10^6 \text{ cm}^3$ and $5.0 \times 10^6 \text{ cm}^3$:

$3.0 \times 10^6 < 4.88 \times 10^6 < 5.0 \times 10^6$, or $3{,}000{,}000 < 4{,}880{,}000 < 5{,}000{,}000$

Finally, I calculated the total mass of sugar produced:

$$(4.88 \times 10^6) \times (8.5 \times 10^{-4}) = (4.88 \times 8.5) \times (10^6 \times 10^{-4})$$
$$= 41.48 \times 10^2 = 4.148 \times 10^3 \text{ kg}$$

One-Day Plan:

Production time for Refinery A is 8 hours, to produce $1.28 \times 10^6 \text{ cm}^3$ of sugar.

Production time for Refinery B is 8 hours, to produce $1.68 \times 10^6 \text{ cm}^3$ of sugar.

Production time for Refinery C is 8 hours, to produce $1.92 \times 10^6 \text{ cm}^3$ of sugar.

All three refineries will produce a total of $4.88 \times 10^6 \text{ cm}^3$ of sugar in a day, which has a mass of 4.148×10^3 kg.

Scoring Rubric

Points	Expectations
4	The student's response is accurate and complete. The student creates a plan that describes how many hours each refinery produces sugar and how much sugar is produced in one day. They also calculate the total mass of sugar produced in a day.
3	The student's strategy and process are correct, but there are minor miscalculations. A plan is written that shows how many hours each refinery produces sugar, the total amount of sugar produced, and the mass of sugar.
2	The response contains several mistakes in the calculations. The student may have attempted to address all parts of the problem, but the response is incorrect and/or incomplete.
1	The student's response is incorrect and incomplete. The response does not address all the questions or requirements.

DIFFERENTIATION | EXTEND

If students have more time to spend on this problem or require an additional challenge, then use this extension to have them revisit their plan to match new criteria for sugar orders.

The national grocery stores double their sugar orders. Revisit your plan to determine if the refineries can produce double the amount of $3{,}000{,}000 \text{ cm}^3$ to $5{,}000{,}000 \text{ cm}^3$ of sugar each day to fill this order.

Solution

- Double the amount of $3{,}000{,}000 \text{ cm}^3$ to $5{,}000{,}000 \text{ cm}^3$:
  $(2 \times 3.0 \times 10^6) = 6.0 \times 10^6 \text{ cm}^3$ and $(2 \times 5.0 \times 10^6) = 10.0 \times 10^6 = 1.0 \times 10^7 \text{ cm}^3$
- Check each refinery's production for 10 hours:
  Refinery A: $10 \times (1.6 \times 10^5) = (10 \times 1.6) \times 10^5 = 16 \times 10^5 = 1.6 \times 10^6 \text{ cm}^3$
  Refinery B: $10 \times (2.1 \times 10^5) = (10 \times 2.1) \times 10^5 = 21 \times 10^5 = 2.1 \times 10^6 \text{ cm}^3$
  Refinery C: $10 \times (2.4 \times 10^5) = (10 \times 2.4) \times 10^5 = 24 \times 10^5 = 2.4 \times 10^6 \text{ cm}^3$
- Add the sugar production for all three refineries:
  $(1.6 \times 10^6) + (2.1 \times 10^6) + (2.4 \times 10^6) = 6.1 \times 10^6 \text{ cm}^3$
- Make sure the total amount is between $6.0 \times 10^6 \text{ cm}^3$ and $1.0 \times 10^7 \text{ cm}^3$:
  $6.0 \times 10^6 < 6.1 \times 10^6 < 1.0 \times 10^7$, or $6{,}000{,}000 < 6{,}100{,}000 < 10{,}000{,}000$

If production time is 10 hours a day, all three refineries will produce $6.1 \times 10^6 \text{ cm}^3$ of sugar.

Problem Notes

Form A is shown. *See* ***Teacher Toolbox*** *for Form B.*

1 **B is correct.** Students could solve the problem by simplifying the expression as $\frac{11^{12} \cdot 6^{18}}{11^3} = 11^{12-3} \cdot 6^{18} = 11^9 \cdot 6^{18}$.

A is not correct. This answer represents adding the exponents (12 + 3) of the base 11 instead of subtracting (12 − 3).

C is not correct. This answer represents adding the exponent 2 to the exponents inside the parentheses instead of multiplying.

D is not correct. This answer represents only applying the power 2 to 6^9 in the numerator.

(1 point)

DOK 1 | 8.EE.A.1

2 **B, C, E are correct.** Students could solve the problem by using properties of exponents to determine if each expression can be rewritten as 42^{-5}.

A is not correct. This answer is equivalent to 42^5. Students subtracted the exponents and misinterpreted the exponent in the difference to be negative.

D is not correct. This answer is equivalent to 42^5 instead of 42^{-5}. Students misinterpreted the exponent in the product to be negative.

F is not correct. This answer is equivalent to 42^5. Students did not apply the −1 exponent properly.

(2 points)

DOK 1 | 8.EE.A.1

3 **a.** A base of 10 with a negative exponent is the same as the reciprocal of that base of 10 with the opposite, positive exponent. This resulting reciprocal is positive, so 2 times a positive number is positive.

b. 10^5 is a positive number. A negative value of q times a positive number is always negative.

c. If $m = 1$, then $6 \times 10^{-1} = \frac{6}{10^1} = \frac{6}{10}$. If $m = -1$, then $6 \times 10^{-(-1)} = 6 \times 10^1 = 60$.

d. 10^{-3} can be written as $\frac{1}{10^3}$, which is less than 1. A positive single-digit number multiplied by $\frac{1}{10^3}$ will be less than 1.

(2 points)

DOK 2 | 8.EE.A.3

4 Students can use the distributive property to rewrite the product and the difference as $(6.12 \times 10^5) \times (4.5 \times 10^5) = (6.12 \times 4.5) \times (10^5 \times 10^5) = 27.54 \times 10^{10} = 2.754 \times 10^{11}$ m².

(2 points)

DOK 2 | 8.EE.A.4

5 (2 points)

DOK 1 | 8.EE.A.1

UNIT 5 • UNIT ASSESSMENT Name:

FORM A

➤ **Solve the problems.**

1 Which expression is equivalent to $\frac{(11^6 \cdot 6^9)^2}{11^3}$? *(1 point)*

A $11^{15} \cdot 6^{18}$

(B) $11^9 \cdot 6^{18}$

C $11^5 \cdot 6^{11}$

D $11^3 \cdot 6^{18}$

2 Which expressions are equivalent to 42^{-5}? Choose all the correct answers. *(2 points)*

A $42^{-3} \cdot 42^8$

(B) $\frac{42^{-7}}{42^{-2}}$

(C) $\frac{6^{-5}}{7^5}$

D $42^0 \cdot 42^5$

(E) $\left(\frac{1}{42^{-5}}\right)^{-1}$

F $\left(\frac{6^{-5}}{7^5}\right)^{-1}$

UNIT 5 • UNIT ASSESSMENT Name:

FORM A continued

3 Tell whether each statement is always, sometimes, or never true.

Choose *Always, Sometimes,* or *Never* for each statement. *(2 points)*

	Always	Sometimes	Never
a. If n is a negative integer, then 2×10^n is negative.	○	○	●
b. If q is a negative single-digit number, then $q \times 10^5$ is negative.	●	○	○
c. If m is an integer, then 6×10^{-m} equals 60^{-m}.	○	●	○
d. If p is a positive single-digit number, then $p \times 10^{-3}$ is less than 1.	●	○	○

4 Colorado is roughly shaped like a rectangle. The state is about 6.12×10^5 m long and 4.5×10^5 m wide. Wyoming has an area of about 2.6×10^{11} m². What is the estimated difference of area between the two states? Write your answer using scientific notation. Show your work. *(2 points)*

Possible student work:

Area of Colorado: $(6.12 \times 10^5) \times (4.5 \times 10^5) = 27.54 \times 10^{10}$
$= 2.754 \times 10^{11}$ m²

$(2.754 \times 10^{11}) - (2.6 \times 10^{11}) = 0.154 \times 10^{11}$
$= 1.54 \times 10^{10}$ m²

SOLUTION The difference in area is about 1.54×10^{10} m².

5 What is the value of m? Write your answers in the blanks. *(2 points)*

$18^m \cdot 18^5 = (18^3)^4$

$18^{\underline{m} + 5} = 18^{3 \cdot \underline{4}}$

$m + 5 = \underline{3} \cdot 4$

$m + 5 = 12$

$m = \underline{7}$

6 (1 point)

DOK 1 | **8.EE.A.1**

7 Students could first identify the food items with the least powers of 10 and then compare the base for each expression. Students could also write each expression in standard form and compare values.

(2 points)

DOK 2 | **8.EE.A.3**

8 Students could rewrite the expression using another power of 10, as long as the final answer is written in scientific notation. For example, $(1.58 \times 10^{15}) - (9.82 \times 10^{13}) + (7.9 \times 10^{11}) =$ $(1.58 \times 10^{15}) - (0.0982 \times 10^{15}) + (0.00079 \times 10^{15}) = 1.48259 \times 10^{15}$.

(2 points)

DOK 2 | **8.EE.A.4**

9 (2 points)

DOK 1 | **8.EE.A.3**

UNIT 5 • UNIT ASSESSMENT | Name:

FORM A continued

6 What value of n makes the equation true? Record your answer on the grid. Then fill in the bubbles. *(1 point)*

$$\frac{38^n}{38} = \frac{1}{38^{-6}}$$

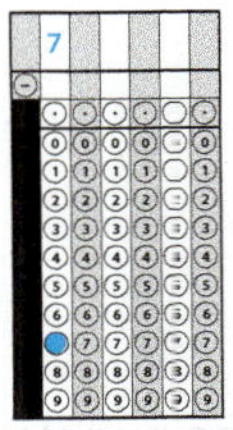

7 The table shows the number of grams of vitamin B_{12} in a 100-gram serving of several foods. List the foods from the least amount of vitamin B_{12} to the greatest. Show your work. *(2 points)*

Food	Vitamin B_{12} (g)
Chicken breast	3×10^{-7}
Low-fat milk	1×10^{-6}
Trout	5×10^{-6}
Clams	8×10^{-5}
Eggs	6×10^{-7}

Possible student work:

The least power of 10 in the table is 10^{-7}.

$3 < 6$, so chicken breast has the least amount of B_{12}, then eggs.

The next least power of 10 is 10^{-6}.

$1 < 5$, so low-fat milk, then trout.

The greatest power of 10 is 10^{-5}, which is clams.

SOLUTION chicken breast, eggs, low-fat milk, trout, clams

UNIT 5 • UNIT ASSESSMENT | Name:

FORM A continued

8 Evaluate $(1.58 \times 10^{15}) - (9.82 \times 10^{13}) + (7.9 \times 10^{11})$. Show your work. *(2 points)*

Possible student work:

$(1.58 \times 10^{15}) - (9.82 \times 10^{13}) + (7.9 \times 10^{11})$

$= (158 \times 10^{13}) - (9.82 \times 10^{13}) + (0.079 \times 10^{13})$

$= (158 - 9.82 + 0.079) \times 10^{13}$

$= 148.259 \times 10^{13}$

SOLUTION 1.48259×10^{15}

9 The height of the United States Capitol Building in Washington, DC, is 288 ft. Estimate the height of the building as a single digit times an integer power of 10. Write your answers in the blanks. *(2 points)*

288 ft ≈ 300 ft

$300 = 3 \times$ 100

$=$ 3 $\times 10^{2}$ ft

Problem Notes

10 **a.** $6^8 \cdot 6^{-8} = 1$

b. $(6^4)^{-2} = 6^{-8}$

c. $\left(\frac{1}{6^8}\right)^{-1} = 6^8$

d. $\frac{1}{6^8} = 6^{-8}$

(2 points)

DOK 1 | **8.EE.A.1**

11 **B is correct.** Students could solve the problem by first dividing $\frac{4.5 \times 10^{12}}{5.7 \times 10^{10}} = \frac{4.5}{5.7} \times \frac{10^{12}}{10^{10}} \approx 0.789 \times \frac{10^{12}}{10^{10}}$. Next, students use their knowledge of properties of exponents to subtract the exponents. $0.789 \times 10^{12-10} = 0.789 \times 10^2$. Finally, students rewrite the expression with a single power of 10. $0.789 \times 10^2 = 7.89 \times 10^1$.

A is not correct. This answer represents adding exponents instead of subtracting when dividing Neptune's distance by Mercury's distance from the sun, then rewriting the expression 0.789×10^{22} with a single power of 10: 7.89×10^{21}.

C is not correct. This answer represents dividing Mercury's distance by Neptune's distance, $(5.7 \times 10^{10}) \div (4.5 \times 10^{12})$.

D is not correct. This answer represents dividing 5.7 by 4.5 and subtracting the exponents.

(1 point)

DOK 2 | **8.EE.A.4**

12 Students could also solve the problem by rewriting the power in the denominator with a negative exponent: $\frac{4^{22} \cdot 4^5}{4^{24}} = 4^{22} \cdot 4^5 \cdot 4^{-24} = 4^{(22+5-24)} = 4^3$.

(2 points)

DOK 1 | **8.EE.A.1**

13 Students could also solve the problem by using the associative property. First, divide the single digits: $\frac{9}{4} \approx 2$. Next, divide the power of 10 values: $\frac{10^4}{10^4} = 1$. Finally, multiply the quotients: $2 \times 1 = 2$.

(2 points)

DOK 2 | **8.EE.A.3**

14 (2 points)

DOK 1 | **8.EE.A.4**

UNIT 5 • UNIT ASSESSMENT Name:

FORM A continued

10 Tell whether each expression is equivalent to 6^8, 6^{-8}, or neither.

Choose 6^8, 6^{-8}, or *Neither* for each statement. *(2 points)*

	6^8	6^{-8}	Neither
a. $6^8 \cdot 6^{-8}$	○	○	●
b. $(6^4)^{-2}$	○	●	○
c. $\left(\frac{1}{6^8}\right)^{-1}$	●	○	○
d. $\frac{1}{6^8}$	○	●	○

11 The average estimated distance Mercury is from the sun is 5.7×10^{10} m. The average estimated distance Neptune is from the sun is 4.5×10^{12} m. About how many times farther is Neptune from the sun than Mercury? *(1 point)*

A 7.89×10^{21}

(B) 7.89×10^1

C 1.27×10^{-2}

D 1.27×10^2

UNIT 5 • UNIT ASSESSMENT Name:

FORM A continued

12 What is the value of the expression $\frac{4^{22} \cdot 4^5}{(4^6)^4}$? Show your work. *(2 points)*

Possible student work:

$$\frac{4^{22} \cdot 4^5}{(4^6)^4} = \frac{4^{27}}{(4^6)^4} = \frac{4^{27}}{4^{24}} = 4^3 = 64$$

SOLUTION 64

13 Jackson compares the number of people in two cities. City A has a population of 92,100 people. City B has a population of 40,615 people. Estimate the number of people in each city as a single digit times a power of 10. How many times greater is the population of City A than the population of City B? Show your work. *(2 points)*

Possible student work:

City A: 9×10^4 City B: 4×10^4

9 is a little more than 2 times greater than 4. The powers of 10 are the same in both quantities.

SOLUTION The population of City A is a little more than 2 times greater than the population of City B.

14 Complete the equation to show 9.3×10^{65} is equal to the product of a single digit and a value represented as a power of 10. Write your answers in the blanks. *(2 points)*

$9.3 \times 10^{65} =$ __3__ $\times (3.1 \times 10^{\underline{65}})$

Scoring Guide

For the problems in the Unit 5 Unit Assessments (Forms A and B), the table shows:

- depth of knowledge (DOK) level
- points for scoring
- lesson assessed by each problem
- standard addressed

Problem	DOK	Points	Lesson	Standard
1	1	1	19	8.EE.A.1
2	1	2	20	8.EE.A.1
3	2	2	21	8.EE.A.3
4	2	2	22	8.EE.A.4
5	1	2	19	8.EE.A.1
6	1	1	20	8.EE.A.1
7	2	2	21	8.EE.A.3
8	2	2	22	8.EE.A.4
9	1	2	21	8.EE.A.3
10	1	2	20	8.EE.A.1
11	2	1	22	8.EE.A.4
12	1	2	19	8.EE.A.1
13	2	2	21	8.EE.A.3
14	1	2	22	8.EE.A.4

Scoring Rubrics

Short Response Scoring Rubric

Points	Expectations
2	Response has the correct solution(s) and includes well-organized, clear, and concise work demonstrating thorough understanding of mathematical concepts and/or procedures.
1	Response contains mostly correct solution(s) and shows partial understanding of mathematical concepts and/or procedures.
0	Response shows no attempt at finding a solution and no effort to demonstrate an understanding of mathematical concepts and/or procedures.

Multiple Select, Fill-in-the-Blank, and Choice Matrix Scoring Rubric

Points	Expectations
2	All answers are correct
1	1 incorrect answer
0	2 or more incorrect answers

Print Resources

Reach all students using these print resources that support instruction, practice, assessment, and differentiation.

Resources can be found in the Student Worktext or Teacher's Guide or downloaded from the Teacher Toolbox section in the Teacher Digital Experience.

In-Class Instruction and Practice

Teacher's Guide

- Learning Progression
- ELL Language Expectations
- Connect to Culture
- Discussion Prompts and Instructional Support

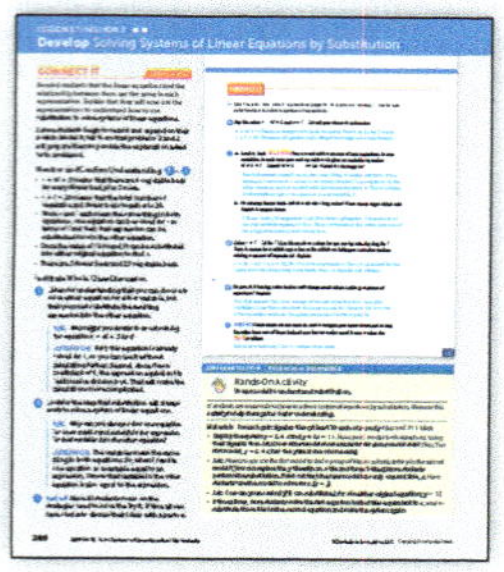

Student Worktext

Use the blue pages for in-class instruction and practice.

Instruction Page

Independent Practice for School or Home

Teacher's Guide

- Additional Practice
- Cumulative Practice

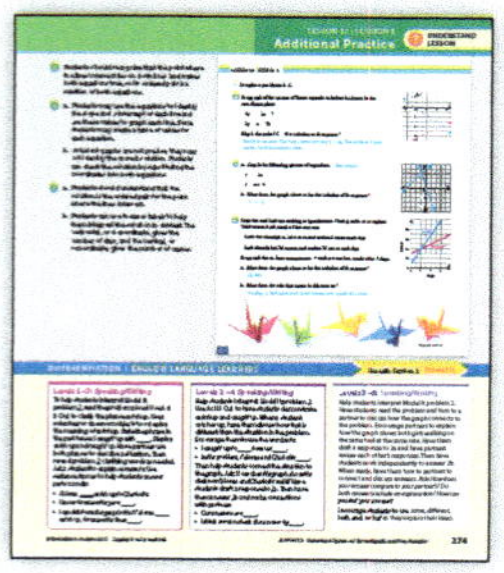

Student Worktext

Use the green pages for independent practice.

- Additional Practice
- Cumulative Practice

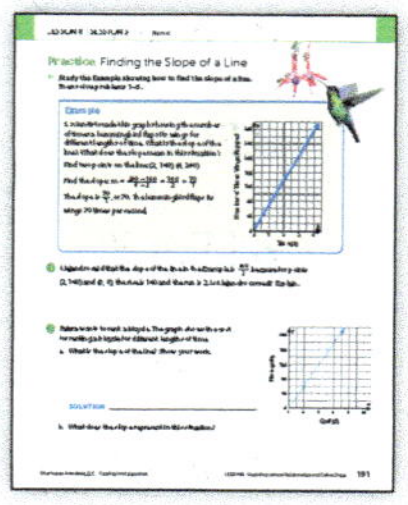

Additional Practice Page

Teacher Toolbox

- Fluency and Skills Practice
- Unit Game
- Cumulative Practice

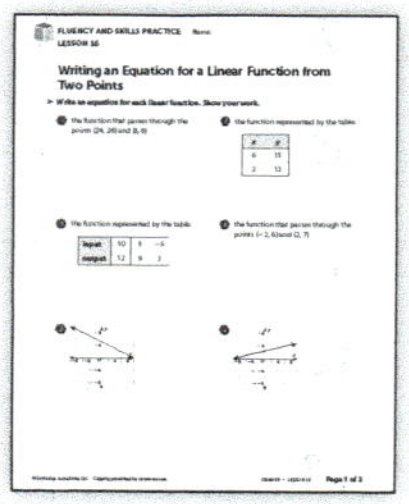

Fluency and Skills Practice

Assessments and Reports

Teacher's Guide

- Starts
- Support Whole Group/Partner Discussion
- Ask/Listen Fors
- Common Misconceptions
- Error Alerts
- Close: Exit Ticket

Student Worktext

- Self Checks
- Apply It
- Reflect Questions
- Self Reflection
- Math Journal Questions
- Unit Review

Self Check

Teacher Toolbox

- Editable Lesson Quizzes
- Editable Unit Assessments

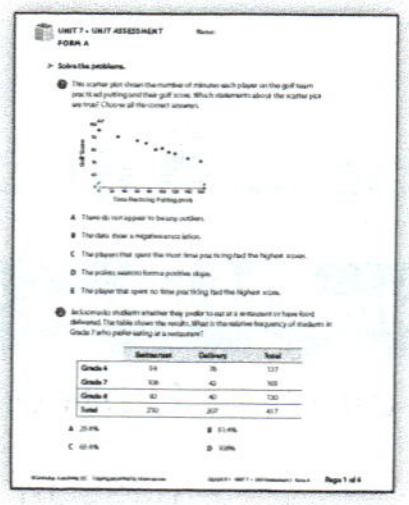

Unit Assessment

Differentiation

Before the Unit/Lesson: Prerequisites Report

Recommended resources to support students' learning needs are highlighted in the Prerequisites report.

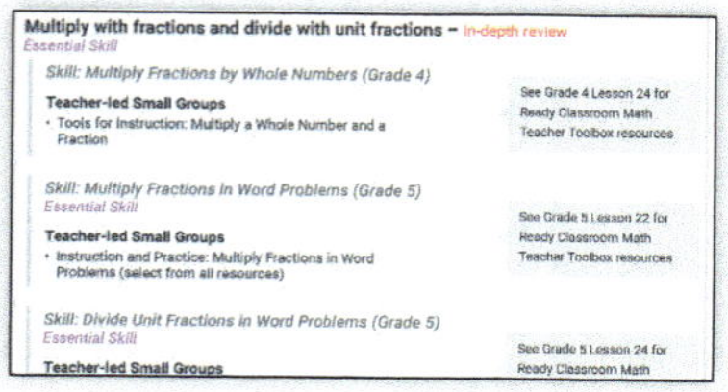
Multiply with fractions and divide with unit fractions – In-depth review

Prerequisites Report: Resources

During the Lesson: Teacher's Guide

- Hands-On Activities or Visual Models
- Deepen Understanding
- ELL Differentiated Instruction
- Refine Sessions

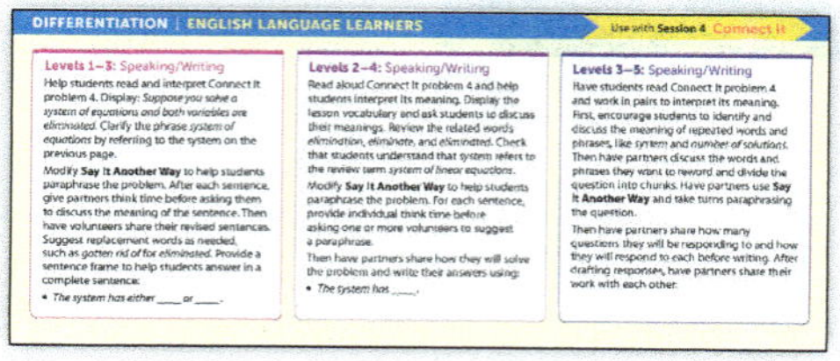
DIFFERENTIATION | ENGLISH LANGUAGE LEARNERS

ELL Differentiated Instruction

After the Lesson: Teacher Toolbox

- Reteach: Tools for Instruction
- Reinforce: Math Center Activities
- Extend: Enrichment Activities

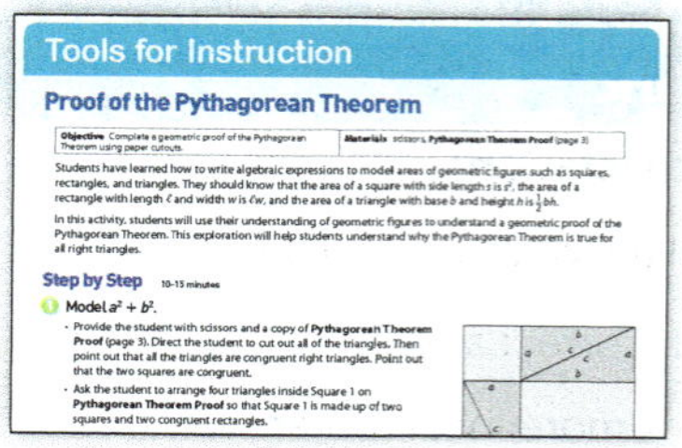
Tools for Instruction

Proof of the Pythagorean Theorem

Reteach: Tools for Instruction

Digital Resources

Engage students with digital resources that provide interactive instruction, practice, assessment, and differentiation.

Resources can be found in the Student Digital Experience and the Teacher Digital Experience.

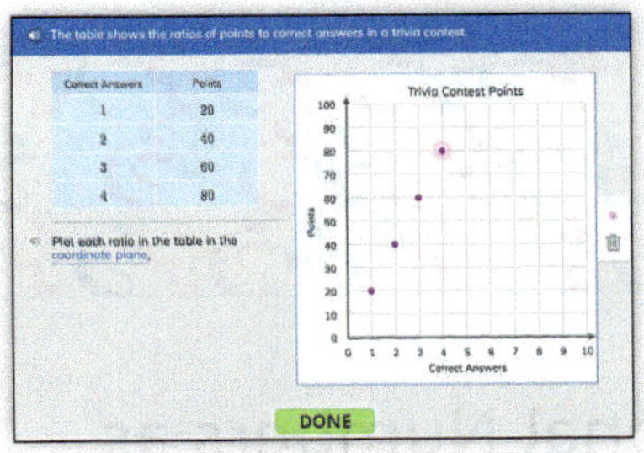

Interactive Tutorials

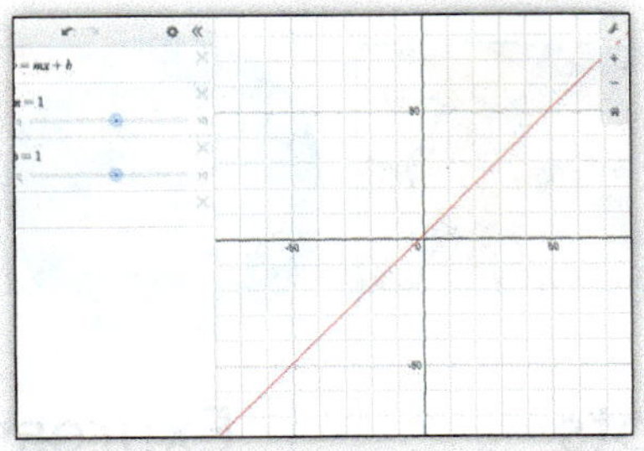
Digital Math Tools powered by Desmos

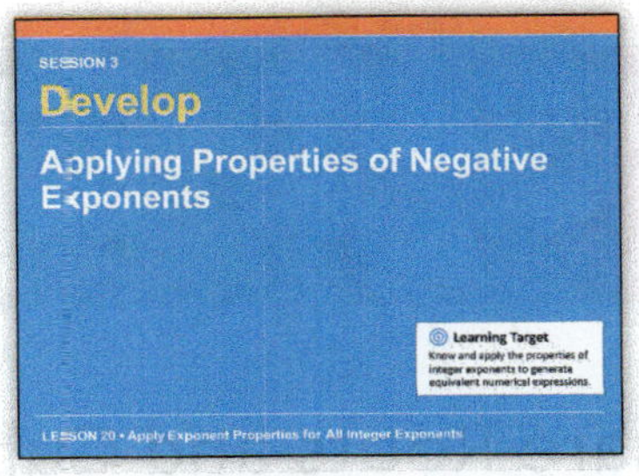

PowerPoint® Slides

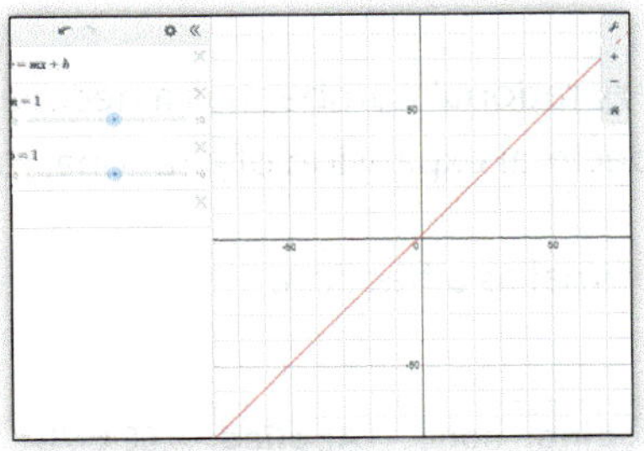
Digital Math Tools powered by Desmos

Learning Games

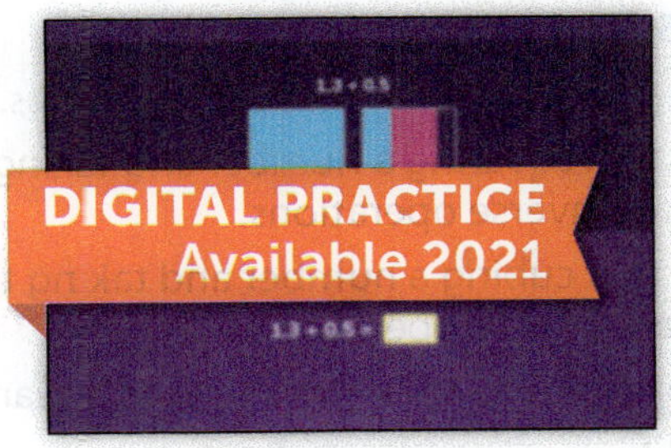

Digital Practice

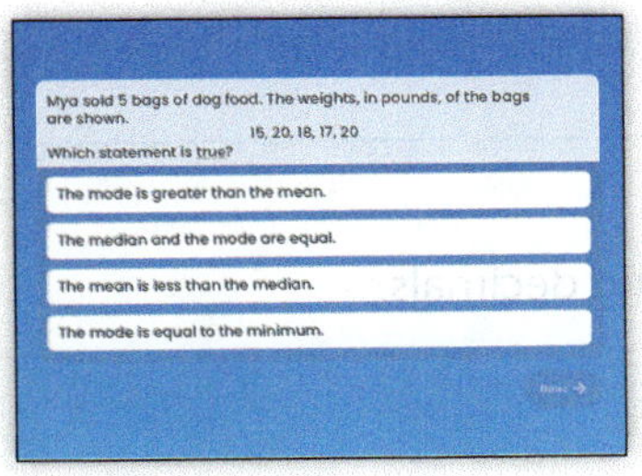

Diagnostic

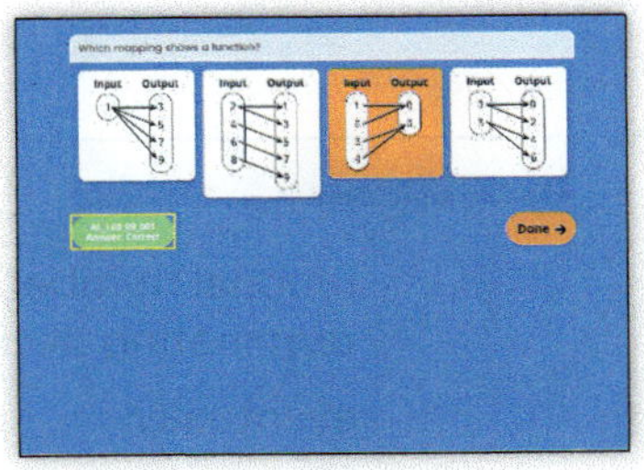

Lesson and Unit Comprehension Checks

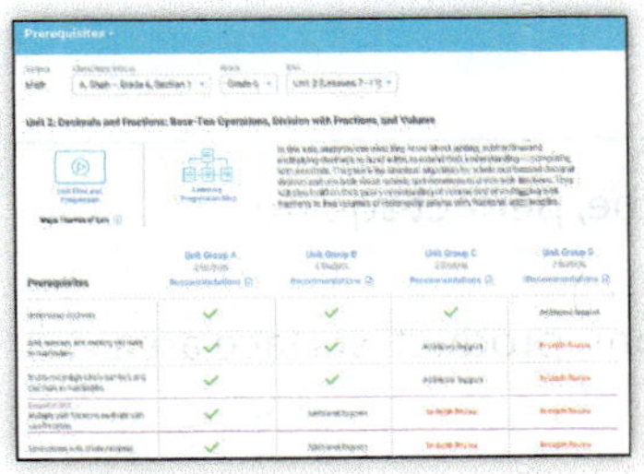
Prerequisites Report

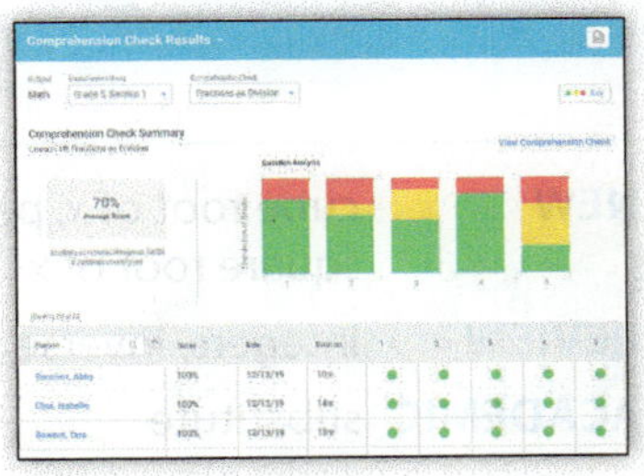
Comprehension Check Reports

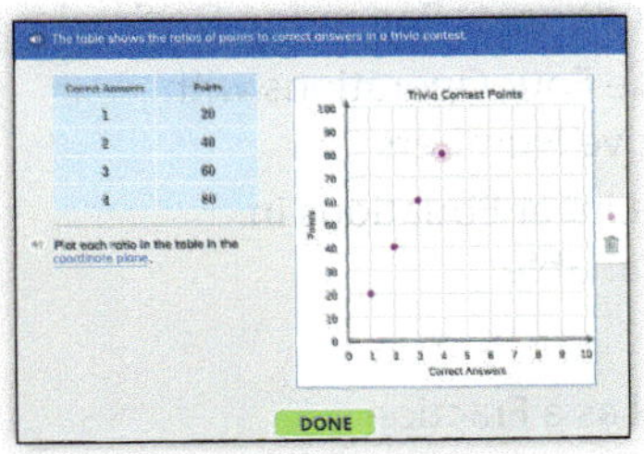

Interactive Tutorials

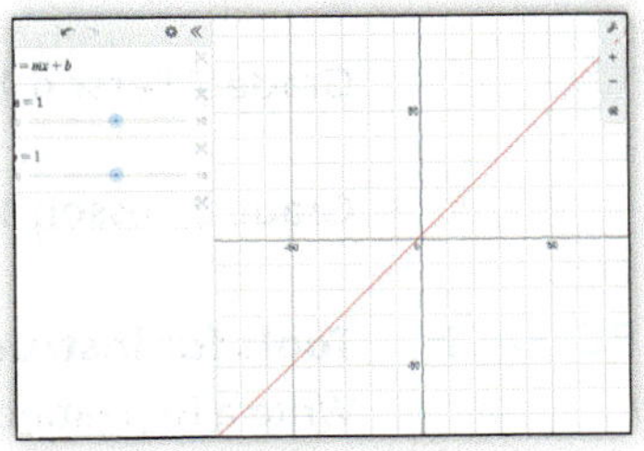
Digital Math Tools powered by Desmos

Learning Games

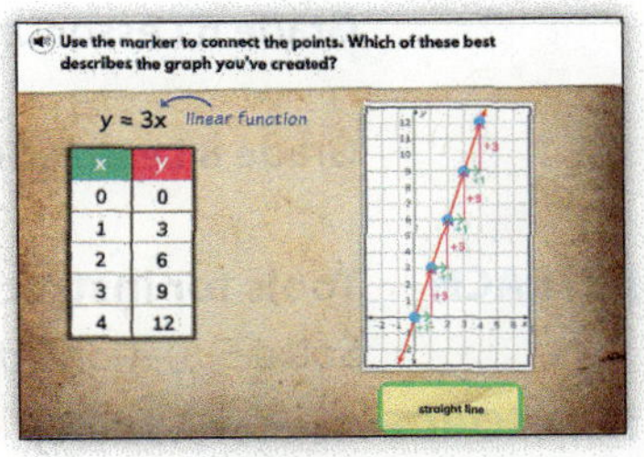

Optional Add-On: *i-Ready Personalized Instruction*

Microsoft PowerPoint® is a registered trademark of Microsoft Corporation.

UNIT 6

Real Numbers

Rational Numbers, Irrational Numbers, and the Pythagorean Theorem

Before the Unit
- Self Check
- Prepare for Rational and Irrational Numbers

After the Unit
- Math in Action
- Self Reflection
- Vocabulary Review
- Unit Review & Performance Task
- Unit Assessment, Forms A and B
- Digital Comprehension Checks

LESSON 23

Find Square Roots and Cube Roots to Solve Problems

PACING: 4 sessions

OBJECTIVES
- Recognize perfect squares and perfect cubes.
- Recognize that squaring a number and taking the square root of a number are inverse operations.
- Recognize that cubing a number and taking the cube root of a number are inverse operations.
- Solve problems that involve finding the square root or cube root of a number.

STANDARDS

Focus: 8.EE.A.2 | **Developing:** none | **Applied:** none

VOCABULARY

NEW cube root of *x*, perfect cube, perfect square, square root of *x*

REVIEW integers, inverse operations, product, surface area

ACADEMIC substitute

LESSON-LEVEL DIFFERENTIATION

PREPARE **Ready Prerequisite Lessons**
- **Grade 6 Lesson 20** Understand Solutions of Equations
- **Grade 6 Lesson 21** Write and Solve One-Variable Equations
- **Grade 8 Lesson 10** Solve Linear Equations in One Variable

RETEACH **Tools for Instruction**
Solve Equations Using Square and Cube Roots

REINFORCE **Center Activity**
Four Square Roots and Cube Roots in a Row

EXTEND **Enrichment Activity**
The Root of It

See the Lesson Overview for additional session-level differentiation.

LESSON 24

Express Rational Numbers as Fractions and Decimals

PACING: 3 sessions

OBJECTIVES
- Understand that every rational number has a decimal expansion.
- Recognize that the decimal expansion of a rational number repeats eventually.
- Write a repeating decimal as a fraction.

STANDARDS

Focus: 8.NS.A.1 | **Developing:** none | **Applied:** 8.EE.C.7b

VOCABULARY

NEW none

REVIEW rational number, repeating decimals, terminating decimals

ACADEMIC eventually

LESSON-LEVEL DIFFERENTIATION

PREPARE **Ready Prerequisite Lessons**
- **Grade 7 Lesson 13** Express Rational Numbers as Terminating or Repeating Decimals
- **Grade 7 Lesson 14** Use the Four Operations with Negative Numbers
- **Grade 8 Lesson 10** Solve Linear Equations in One Variable

RETEACH **Tools for Instruction**
Write a Repeating Decimal as a Fraction

REINFORCE **Center Activity**
Convert Repeating Decimals

EXTEND **Enrichment Activity**
Terminate or Repeat?

See the Lesson Overview for additional session-level differentiation.

LESSON 25

Find Rational Approximations of Irrational Numbers

PACING: 4 sessions

OBJECTIVES

- Distinguish between rational and irrational numbers.
- Understand that every irrational number has a decimal expansion, and therefore all rational and irrational numbers have decimal expansions.
- Approximate the value of an irrational number or irrational expression.
- Compare and order rational and irrational numbers and locate them on a number line.

STANDARDS

Focus: 8.NS.A.1, 8.NS.A.2, 8.EE.A.2	**Developing:** none	**Applied:** none

NEW	irrational number, real numbers
REVIEW	perfect square, pi (π), rational number, repeating decimals, square root of x, terminating decimals
ACADEMIC	approximate (adjective), approximate (verb), approximation, exact

PREPARE	**Ready Prerequisite Lessons**	
	Grade 7 Lesson 13	Express Rational Numbers as Terminating or Repeating Decimals
	Grade 8 Lesson 23	Find Square Roots and Cube Roots to Solve Problems
	Grade 8 Lesson 24	Express Rational Numbers as Fractions and Decimals
RETEACH	**Tools for Instruction**	
	Approximate and Order Irrational Numbers	
REINFORCE	**Center Activity**	
	Irrational Go Between	
EXTEND	**Enrichment Activity**	
	That's So Irrational	

See the Lesson Overview for additional session-level differentiation.

NOTES

. . . continued

Rational Numbers, Irrational Numbers, and the Pythagorean Theorem

LESSON 26

Understand the Pythagorean Theorem and Its Converse

PACING: 3 sessions

OBJECTIVES

- Understand how the side lengths of a right triangle are related.
- Explain geometric and algebraic proofs of the Pythagorean Theorem.
- Explain a proof of the converse of the Pythagorean Theorem.
- Use the side lengths of a triangle to determine whether it is a right triangle.

STANDARDS

Focus: 8.G.B.6 | **Developing:** none | **Applied:** 8.EE.A.2

VOCABULARY

NEW converse of the Pythagorean Theorem, hypotenuse, legs (of a right triangle), Pythagorean Theorem

REVIEW congruent (≅), right triangle, square, square root of x

ACADEMIC proof, prove

LESSON-LEVEL DIFFERENTIATION

PREPARE **Ready Prerequisite Lessons**

- **Grade 7 Lesson 25** Solve Problems Involving Area and Surface Area
- **Grade 7 Lesson 29** Draw Plane Figures with Given Conditions
- **Grade 8 Lesson 23** Find Square Roots and Cube Roots to Solve Problems

RETEACH **Tools for Instruction**
Proof of the Pythagorean Theorem

REINFORCE **Center Activity**
Use Pythagorean Theorem Vocabulary

EXTEND **Enrichment Activity**
Semicircles Instead of Squares

See the Lesson Overview for additional session-level differentiation.

LESSON 27

Apply the Pythagorean Theorem

PACING: 5 sessions

OBJECTIVES

- Apply the Pythagorean Theorem to determine unknown side lengths in right triangles in real-world and mathematical problems, in two and three dimensions.
- Identify and use Pythagorean triples.
- Use the Pythagorean Theorem to find the distance between two points in the coordinate plane.

STANDARDS

Focus: 8.G.B.7, 8.G.B.8 | **Developing:** none | **Applied:** 8.NS.A.2, 8.EE.A.2, 8.G.B.6

VOCABULARY

NEW none

REVIEW multiple, Pythagorean Theorem, right rectangular prism

ACADEMIC consider

LESSON-LEVEL DIFFERENTIATION

PREPARE **Ready Prerequisite Lessons**

- **Grade 6 Lesson 28** Solve Problems in the Coordinate Plane
- **Grade 8 Lesson 25** Find Rational Approximations of Irrational Numbers
- **Grade 8 Lesson 26** Understand the Pythagorean Theorem and Its Converse

RETEACH **Tools for Instruction**
Pythagorean Theorem and Rectangular Prisms

REINFORCE **Center Activity**
Find Pythagorean Triples

EXTEND **Enrichment Activity**
Spiral of Theodorus

See the Lesson Overview for additional session-level differentiation.

LESSON 28

Solve Problems with Volumes of Cylinders, Cones, and Spheres

PACING: 4 sessions

OBJECTIVES

- Understand relationships between the volumes of cylinders, cones, and spheres.
- Use formulas to find volumes of cylinders, cones, and spheres.
- Find volumes of composite solids by adding or subtracting volumes of cylinders, cones, and spheres.
- Apply the Pythagorean Theorem to find an unknown dimension of a cone.
- Use a given volume and the appropriate volume formula to find the radius or height of a cylinder, cone, or sphere.

STANDARDS

Focus: 8.G.C.9 | **Developing:** none | **Applied:** 8.NS.A.2, 8.G.B.7

NEW	cone, sphere
REVIEW	cylinder, prism, radius (of a circle), vertex, volume
ACADEMIC	circular, cylindrical, spherical

PREPARE **Ready Prerequisite Lessons**
Grade 7 Lesson 26 Solve Problems Involving Volume
Grade 8 Lesson 25 Find Rational Approximations of Irrational Numbers
Grade 8 Lesson 27 Apply the Pythagorean Theorem

RETEACH **Tools for Instruction**
Volume of Cylinders and Cones

REINFORCE **Center Activity**
Use Volume Vocabulary for Cylinders, Cones, and Spheres

EXTEND **Enrichment Activity**
Double Up

See the Lesson Overview for additional session-level differentiation.

Math in Action

Math Lessons from the Real World

Installing a Wind Turbine | Designing a Food-Waste Digester | Fencing a Solar Farm

PACING: 2 sessions

KEY SKILLS

- Use the Pythagorean Theorem to find unknown side lengths of right triangles.
- Find rational approximations for irrational numbers.
- Use volume formulas for a cylinder and a cone.
- Calculate with rational numbers that are expressed as fractions and decimals.
- Apply the perimeter and area formulas for a square to solve problems.

STANDARDS

Focus: 8.NS.A.2, 8.EE.A.2, 8.G.B.7, 8.G.C.9

Digital Resources

- Unit and Lesson Comprehension Checks
- Comprehension Check Reports
- Prerequisites Report
- Digital Tools powered by Desmos®
- Interactive Tutorials
- Learning Games (available 2020)
- Digital Practice (available 2021)

i-Ready

A personalized instruction path helps students fill prerequisite gaps and build up grade-level skills.

Real Numbers

Rational Numbers, Irrational Numbers, and the Pythagorean Theorem

Which lessons are students building upon?

Grade 6, Lesson 20 Understand Solutions of Equations 6.EE.B.5	**Grade 6, Lesson 21** Write and Solve One-Variable Equations 6.EE.B.7	**Grade 8, Lesson 10** Solve Linear Equations in One Variable 8.EE.C.7b
Grade 7, Lesson 13 Express Rational Numbers as Terminating or Repeating Decimals 7.NS.A.2d, 7.EE.B.3	**Grade 7, Lesson 14** Use the Four Operations with Negative Numbers 7.NS.A.3, 7.EE.B.3	**Grade 8, Lesson 10** Solve Linear Equations in One Variable 8.EE.C.7b
Grade 7, Lesson 13 Express Rational Numbers as Terminating or Repeating Decimals 7.NS.A.2d, 7.EE.B.3	**Grade 8, Lesson 23** Find Square Roots and Cube Roots to Solve Problems 8.EE.A.2	**Grade 8, Lesson 24** Express Rational Numbers as Fractions and Decimals 8.NS.A.1
Grade 7, Lesson 25 Solve Problems Involving Area and Surface Area 7.G.B.6	**Grade 7, Lesson 29** Draw Plane Figures with Given Conditions 7.G.A.2	**Grade 8, Lesson 23** Find Square Roots and Cube Roots to Solve Problems 8.EE.A.2
Grade 6, Lesson 28 Solve Problems in the Coordinate Plane 6.NS.C.8, 6.G.A.3	**Grade 8, Lesson 25** Find Rational Approximations of Irrational Numbers 8.NS.A.1, 8.NS.A.2, 8.EE.A.2	**Grade 8, Lesson 26** Understand the Pythagorean Theorem and Its Converse 8.G.B.6
Grade 7, Lesson 26 Solve Problems Involving Volume 7.G.B.6	**Grade 8, Lesson 25** Find Rational Approximations of Irrational Numbers 8.NS.A.1, 8.NS.A.2, 8.EE.A.2	**Grade 8, Lesson 27** Apply the Pythagorean Theorem 8.G.B.7, 8.G.B.8

In this unit . . .

Lesson 23
Find Square Roots and Cube Roots to Solve Problems
8.EE.A.2

Lesson 24
Express Rational Numbers as Fractions and Decimals
8.NS.A.1

Lesson 25
Find Rational Approximations of Irrational Numbers
8.NS.A.1, 8.NS.A.2, 8.EE.A.2

Lesson 26
Understand the Pythagorean Theorem and Its Converse
8.G.B.6

Lesson 27
Apply the Pythagorean Theorem
8.G.B.7, 8.G.B.8

Lesson 28
Solve Problems with Volumes of Cylinders, Cones, and Spheres
8.G.C.9

Which lessons are students preparing for?

In this unit	Preparing for	Preparing for
Lesson 23	**Grade 8, Lesson 27** Apply the Pythagorean Theorem 8.G.B.7, 8.G.B.8	**Algebra** Reasoning with Equations and Inequalities HSA.REI.B.4b
Lesson 24	**Grade 8, Lesson 25** Find Rational Approximations of Irrational Numbers 8.NS.A.1, 8.NS.A.2, 8.EE.A.2	**Number and Quantity** The Real Number System HSN.RN.B.3
Lesson 25	**Grade 8, Lesson 28** Solve Problems with Volumes of Cylinders, Cones, and Spheres 8.G.C.9	**Algebra** Reasoning with Equations and Inequalities HSA.REI.B.4a
Lesson 26	**Grade 8, Lesson 27** Apply the Pythagorean Theorem 8.G.B.7, 8.G.B.8	**Geometry** Similarity, Right Triangles, and Trigonometry HSG.SRT.B.4
Lesson 27	**Geometry** Similarity, Right Triangles, and Trigonometry HSG.SRT.C.8	**Geometry** Expressing Geometric Properties with Equations HSG.GPE.B.7
Lesson 28	**Geometry** Geometric Measurement and Dimension HSG.GMD.A.1	**Geometry** Geometric Measurement and Dimension HSG.GMD.A.3

Professional Learning

Bridging Funds of Knowledge to the Mathematics Classroom

Adapted from *Reimagining the Mathematics Classroom*, coauthored by Dr. Mark Ellis

Mark Ellis, Ph.D.
Dr. Ellis is a Professor of Education at California State University, Fullerton, and a highly regarded scholar and teacher of K–12 mathematics education. He is best known for his collaborative work with educators in developing strategies that help students understand mathematics concepts, supporting instruction around new standards, and addressing issues of equity in mathematics education.

What Are Funds of Knowledge?

Students bring with them "funds of knowledge," that is, out-of-school experiences from their homes and communities. These funds of knowledge include:

- linguistic and ethnic patterns of interaction.
- aspects of familial and community knowledge and lived experiences.
- behaviors, beliefs, and artifacts of the communities of the students in the classroom (Ensign, 2003).

In mathematics, "students bring with them ways of thinking and reasoning with and about quantities and quantitative contexts—as well as ways of interacting and communicating—that serve as a foundation upon which to build their understanding of mathematics." (Ellis, 2018).

Accessing Funds of Knowledge

Students must see mathematics as part of their lives and identities, and teachers must make students' experience and reasoning the center of the process of learning mathematics. Tapping into students' funds of knowledge connects students to the content with relevant authentic situations. Teachers can access and elicit their students' funds of knowledge and connect that knowledge with mathematics concepts and skills development.

Community Relevance and Lived Experiences

One simple way to collect information about your students' funds of knowledge is to survey families about topics such as the following:

- **Home Language** What is the student's home language?
- **Family Occupations** What variety of jobs, trades, or skills are represented in the student's family? How do any of them require the use of math?
- **Family Activities** What types of activities or hobbies do the student and his or her family enjoy?
- **Family Traditions** Are there special events or holidays the student's family engages in or celebrates?
- **Family Chores** Does the student have chores he or she is responsible for, such as helping with dishes, clearing the table after meals, or doing laundry?

Connect to Culture

Connect to Culture in the Teacher's Guide for each lesson offers suggestions for tapping into students' funds of knowledge and connecting that knowledge to *Try It* and other problems in the lesson.

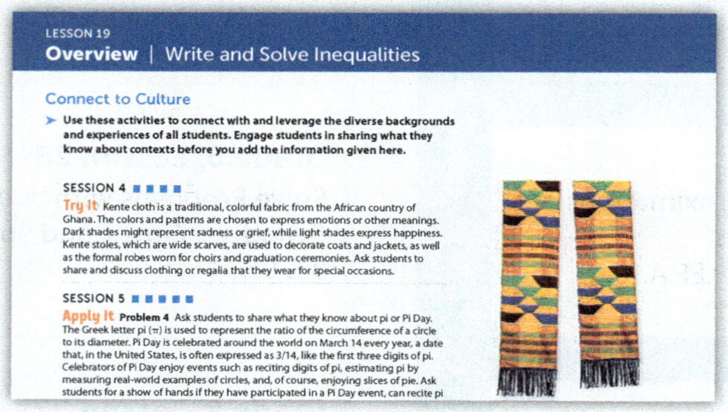

LESSON 19
Overview | Write and Solve Inequalities

Connect to Culture

➤ **Use these activities to connect with and leverage the diverse backgrounds and experiences of all students. Engage students in sharing what they know about contexts before you add the information given here.**

SESSION 4

Try It Kente cloth is a traditional, colorful fabric from the African country of Ghana. The colors and patterns are chosen to express emotions or other meanings. Dark shades might represent sadness or grief, while light shades express happiness. Kente stoles, which are wide scarves, are used to decorate coats and jackets, as well as the formal robes worn for choirs and graduation ceremonies. Ask students to share and discuss clothing or regalia that they wear for special occasions.

SESSION 5

Apply It **Problem 4** Ask students to share what they know about pi or Pi Day. The Greek letter pi (π) is used to represent the ratio of the circumference of a circle to its diameter. Pi Day is celebrated around the world on March 14 every year, a date that, in the United States, is often expressed as 3/14, like the first three digits of pi. Celebrators of Pi Day enjoy events such as reciting digits of pi, estimating pi by measuring real-world examples of circles, and, of course, enjoying slices of pie. Ask students for a show of hands if they have participated in a Pi Day event, can recite pi

Family Letter

Use the *Family Letter*—which provides background information, math vocabulary, and an activity—to keep families apprised of what their child is learning and to open an opportunity for students and families to engage with and talk about the mathematics of the unit.

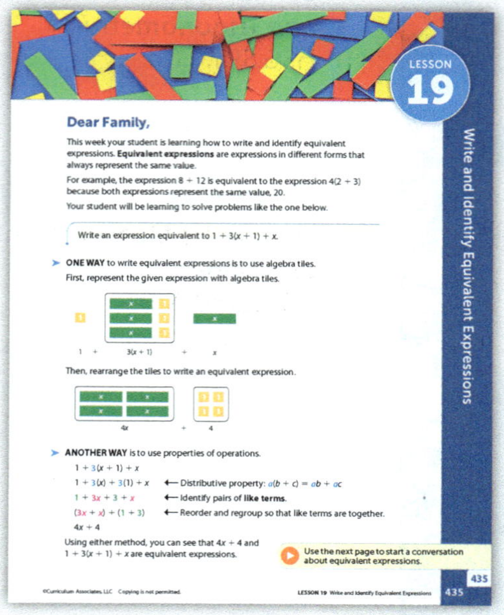

LESSON 19

Write and Identify Equivalent Expressions

Dear Family,

This week your student is learning how to write and identify equivalent expressions. **Equivalent expressions** are expressions in different forms that always represent the same value.

For example, the expression $8 + 12$ is equivalent to the expression $4(2 + 3)$ because both expressions represent the same value, 20.

Your student will be learning to solve problems like the one below.

Write an expression equivalent to $1 + 3(x + 1) + x$.

➤ **ONE WAY** to write equivalent expressions is to use algebra tiles.

First, represent the given expression with algebra tiles.

$1 + 3(x + 1) + x$

Then, rearrange the tiles to write an equivalent expression.

$4x + 4$

➤ **ANOTHER WAY** is to use properties of operations.

$1 + 3(x + 1) + x$
$1 + 3(x) + 3(1) + x$ ← Distributive property: $a(b + c) = ab + ac$
$1 + 3x + 3 + x$ ← Identify pairs of **like terms**.
$(3x + x) + (1 + 3)$ ← Reorder and regroup so that like terms are together.
$4x + 4$

Using either method, you can see that $4x + 4$ and $1 + 3(x + 1) + x$ are equivalent expressions.

Use the next page to start a conversation about equivalent expressions.

©Curriculum Associates, LLC Copying is not permitted. LESSON 19 Write and Identify Equivalent Expressions 435

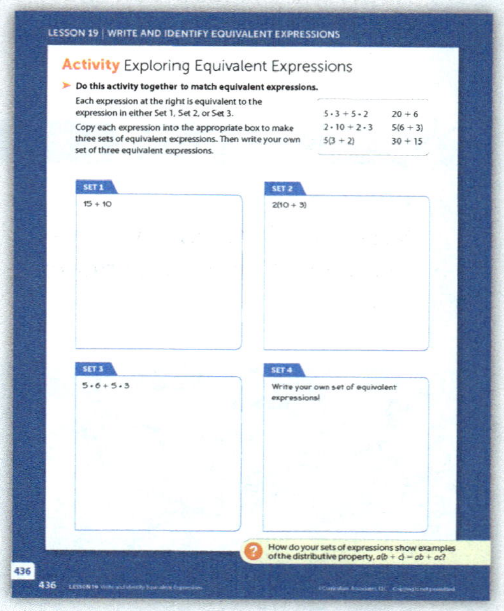

LESSON 19 | WRITE AND IDENTIFY EQUIVALENT EXPRESSIONS

Activity Exploring Equivalent Expressions

➤ **Do this activity together to match equivalent expressions.**

Each expression at the right is equivalent to the expression in either Set 1, Set 2, or Set 3.

Copy each expression into the appropriate box to make three sets of equivalent expressions. Then write your own set of three equivalent expressions.

$5 \cdot 3 + 5 \cdot 2$	$20 + 6$
$2 \cdot 10 + 2 \cdot 3$	$5(6 + 3)$
$5(3 + 2)$	$30 + 15$

SET 1
$15 + 10$

SET 2
$2(10 + 3)$

SET 3
$5 \cdot 6 + 5 \cdot 3$

SET 4
Write your own set of equivalent expressions!

How do your sets of expressions show examples of the distributive property, $a(b + c) = ab + ac$?

436

Differentiation for English Language Learners

Language Expectations

The chart below shows examples of what English learners at different levels of English language proficiency can do in connection with one of the Common Core State Standards (CCSS) addressed in this unit. As you plan for this unit, use these examples of language expectations to help you differentiate instruction to meet the needs of English learners.

Standard 8.G.B.7 Apply the Pythagorean Theorem to determine unknown side lengths in right triangles in real-world and mathematical problems in two and three dimensions.

LANGUAGE DOMAINS	BEGINNING Level 1	INTERMEDIATE Level 2	INTERMEDIATE Level 3	ADVANCED/ADVANCED HIGH Level 4	ADVANCED/ADVANCED HIGH Level 5
LISTENING	In partner discussion, understand more about a strategy used to find an unknown side length in a right triangle by selecting questions from a list of simple modeled sentences. (e.g., *What did you do?*)	In partner discussion, understand more about a strategy used to find an unknown side length in a right triangle by asking simple *Wh-* questions using sentence frames. (e.g., *What does ____ mean?*)	In partner and small-group discussions, understand more about a strategy used to find an unknown side length in a right triangle by asking questions using a list of sentence starters. (e.g., *Can you explain ____?*)	In partner and small-group discussions, follow oral explanations of strategies used to find an unknown side length in a right triangle and ask clarifying questions using prompts.	In partner, small-group, and class discussions, follow oral explanations of strategies used to find an unknown side length in a right triangle and ask clarifying questions to build understanding.
SPEAKING	Explain how the Pythagorean Theorem can be used to find the unknown side length in a figure by responding to *Yes/No* questions.	Explain how the Pythagorean Theorem can be used to find the unknown side length in a figure by using simple sentence frames with a word bank.	Explain how the Pythagorean Theorem can be used to find the unknown side length in a figure by using sentence starters in partner discussion.	Explain why the Pythagorean Theorem justifies a strategy for finding the unknown side length in a figure by using sentence starters in small groups.	Explain how the Pythagorean Theorem justifies a strategy for finding the unknown side length in a figure after rereading the theorem in small groups.
READING	Follow along as a partner reads a written explanation of the reasoning he or she used to find an unknown side length of a right triangle. Work with the partner to connect short pieces of information to a model or drawing.	Follow along as a partner reads a written explanation of the reasoning he or she used to find an unknown side length of a right triangle. Work with the partner to connect the steps to a model or drawing.	Read a partner's written explanation of the reasoning he or she used to find an unknown side length of a right triangle. Work with the partner to check the reasoning by connecting the steps to a model or drawing.	With a partner, check the work of another classmate's written explanation of the reasoning he or she used to find an unknown side length of a right triangle by connecting the steps to a model or drawing.	Check the work of another classmate's written explanation of the reasoning he or she used to find an unknown side length of a right triangle by connecting the steps to a model or drawing.
WRITING	With a partner, use an illustrated word bank to label right triangles in a drawing of a three-dimensional figure. Describe how to find an unknown side length with teacher support.	With a partner, use a word bank to label right triangles in a drawing of a three-dimensional figure. Describe how to find an unknown side length by following a writing sample.	With a partner, describe how to find an unknown side length of a right triangle in a drawing of a three-dimensional figure by using a list of math terms and academic vocabulary.	Describe how to find an unknown side length of a right triangle in a drawing of a three-dimensional figure after brainstorming useful math terms and academic vocabulary in small groups.	Describe how to find an unknown side length of a right triangle in a drawing of a three-dimensional figure after discussing ideas with partners.

Models, Progressions, and Teaching Tips

As you plan lessons, use this information to unpack the learning progressions and make connections between key concepts.

Unit Themes

The major themes of this unit are:

- An irrational number cannot be written as a terminating or repeating decimal. You can use what you know about working with rational numbers to solve problems with irrational numbers in topics like algebra and geometry.
- The side lengths of a right triangle have a special relationship. You can use this relationship and what you know about triangles to determine unknown side lengths.
- You can use what you know about pi and the area of circles to solve real-world problems about the volumes of cylinders, cones, and spheres.

Prior Knowledge

Students will build on prior understandings of working with rational numbers.

Students should:

- be able to perform long division.
- be able to find squares and cubes of numbers.
- be able to move flexibly between fraction and decimal representations of rational numbers.
- be able to recognize terminating and repeating decimals.
- be able to find the volume of a rectangular prism.

Watch the video
See the flow and progression of math concepts in this unit come to life with tips and insights on using models and making connections.

Understanding Real Numbers

INSIGHTS ON . . .

Rational and Irrational Numbers

- ✔ Students learn that numbers can be rational or irrational and that both of these sets of numbers are subsets of the set of real numbers.
- ✔ Irrational numbers are numbers that cannot be expressed as the quotient of two integers. The decimal expansion of an irrational number does not terminate or repeat.

  EXAMPLE The number π is an irrational number because it is a nonrepeating decimal that does not terminate.
- ✔ In this unit, students find exact and approximate values for rational and irrational numbers and expressions when solving real-world problems.

Students develop an understanding of **rational** and **irrational numbers** and learn how to work with them.

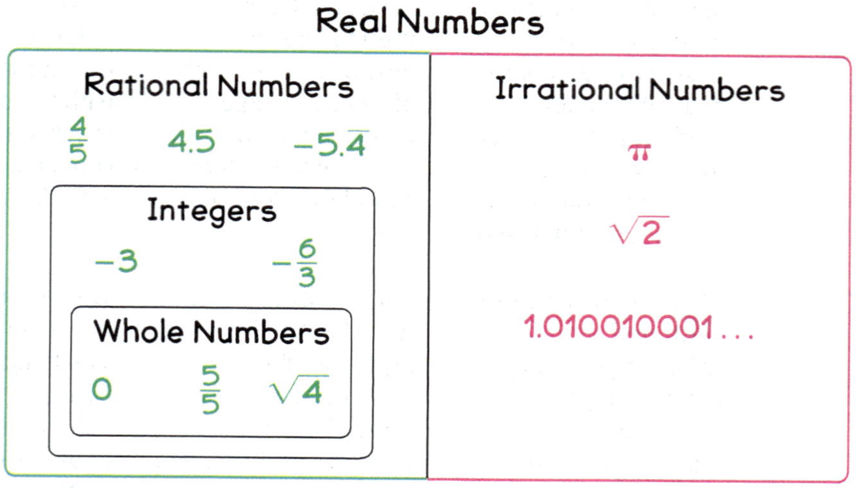

Square Roots and Cube Roots

INSIGHTS ON . . .

Understanding Square and Cube Roots

- ✔ Students are introduced to square roots by finding the side lengths of squares with given areas. They learn that the square root of a number *x* is a number that when squared, is equal to *x*.
- ✔ Students connect a cube root to the edge length of a cube with a given volume. The cube root of a number *x* is a number that when cubed, is equal to *x*.
- ✔ Just as multiplication and division are inverse operations, squaring and taking the square root and cubing and taking the cube root are pairs of inverse operations. Students use this fact to help them solve equations.

Students develop an understanding of the inverse relationship between **squares** and **square roots** and between **cubes** and **cube roots**.

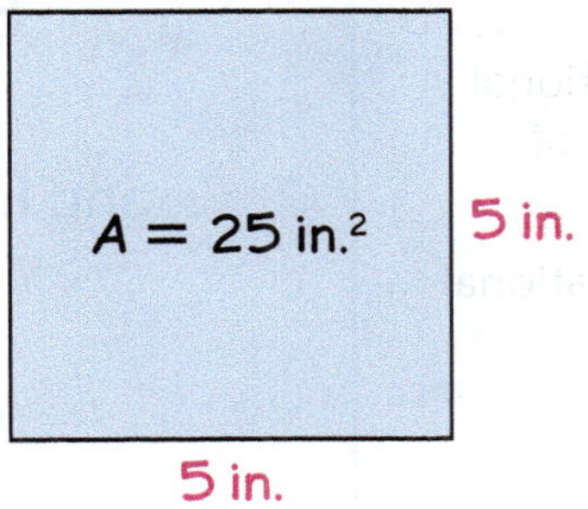

$5^2 = 25$

$\sqrt{25} = 5$

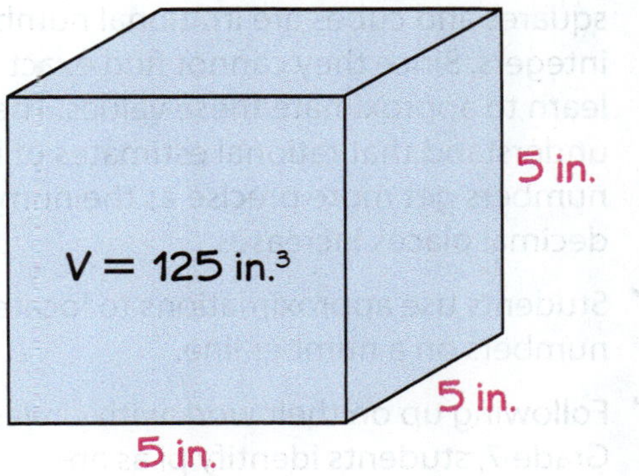

$5^3 = 125$

$\sqrt[3]{125} = 5$

INSIGHTS ON . . .

Finding Roots of Perfect Squares and Perfect Cubes

- ✔ Students use tables of squares and cubes to find roots of perfect squares and cubes.

  EXAMPLE To find the cube root of 64, find 64 in the x^3 row. Then find the value of *x* that corresponds to 64. The *x*-value 4 corresponds to 64, so $\sqrt[3]{64} = 4$.
- ✔ Using what they know about integer operations, students see that every positive number has two square roots. Students use a problem's context to decide whether one or both of the roots make sense for the solution. They also learn that the square root sign implies only the positive square root. To indicate both roots, the ± sign must be written in front of the radical.
- ✔ Students use what they know about multiplication of positive and negative numbers to see that a positive number has just one cube root, which is positive.

Students use tables to find roots of **perfect squares** and **perfect cubes** . . .

What is $\sqrt[3]{64}$?

x	1	2	3	4	5	6
x^2	1	4	9	16	25	36
x^3	1	8	27	64	125	216

. . . and **solve equations** involving **roots.**

$$t^2 = \frac{9}{25}$$

$$t = \pm\sqrt{\frac{9}{25}}$$

$$t = \pm\frac{3}{5}$$

Rational and Irrational Numbers

INSIGHTS ON . . .

Approximating Irrational Numbers

- ✔ Students learn that the roots of nonperfect squares and cubes are irrational numbers, not integers. Since they cannot find exact roots, they learn to approximate these values. They understand that rational estimates of irrational numbers get more precise as the number of decimal places increases.
- ✔ Students use approximations to locate irrational numbers on a number line.
- ✔ Following up on their work with circles in Grade 7, students identify pi as an irrational number with an approximate value of 3.14, or $\frac{22}{7}$. They may use this approximation to estimate the area and circumference of circles, or they may use the symbol π to express the exact values.

  EXAMPLE The area of a circle with a radius of 3 units can be expressed exactly as 9π units^2 or approximated as $(9)(3.14) = 28.26$ units^2.

Students use perfect squares and cubes to **approximate square and cube roots** to the nearest whole number . . .

Between which two integers is $\sqrt{2}$?

Since $1^2 = 1$ and $2^2 = 4$, $1 < \sqrt{2} < 2$.

. . . and **improve their approximations** by estimating to more decimal places.

What is $\sqrt{2}$ to the nearest tenth?

x	1.1	1.2	1.3	1.4	1.5	1.6
x^2	1.21	1.44	1.69	1.96	2.25	2.56

2 is closer to 1.96 than 2.25, so $\sqrt{2}$ is closer to 1.4 than 1.5.

INSIGHTS ON . . .

Writing Repeating Decimals as Fractions

- ✔ In Grade 7, students used long division to write fractions as decimals, including repeating decimals. They build on these skills in Grade 8 to express rational numbers in different forms.

  EXAMPLE Since $\frac{1}{9} = 0.\overline{1}$, it makes sense that $\frac{5}{9} = 5 \cdot \frac{1}{9} = 0.\overline{5}$.
- ✔ Students learn to write and solve equations to express repeating decimals as fractions. To use the equation strategy effectively, students multiply both sides of the equation by the same power of 10. The power should correspond to the number of repeating digits. If there is one repeating digit, multiply by 10^1; if there are two, multiply by 10^2. This makes the subtraction simpler and results in whole-number answers.

Students use **equations** to write repeating decimals as fractions.

Write $0.\overline{3}$ as a fraction.

$$x = 0.\overline{3}$$

$$10 \cdot x = 0.\overline{3} \cdot 10$$

$$10x = 3.\overline{3}$$

$$10x - x = 3.\overline{3} - 0.\overline{3}$$

$$9x = 3$$

$$x = \frac{1}{3}$$

Connecting Irrational Numbers to Geometry

INSIGHTS ON . . .

The Pythagorean Theorem and Its Converse

- ✔ In Grade 7 and earlier in Grade 8, students found unknown angle measures of triangles. In this unit, they continue their work with triangles as they find unknown side lengths, which can include irrational numbers.
- ✔ Giving rise to one of the most famous equations in mathematics, the Pythagorean Theorem is an important relationship that will resurface throughout students' mathematical careers. Students begin their exploration of the theorem as they make sense of and explain algebraic and geometric proofs.
- ✔ The Pythagorean Theorem states that if a and b are the lengths of the legs of a right triangle and c is the length of the hypotenuse, then $a^2 + b^2 = c^2$. This means that if you know the lengths of any two sides of a right triangle, then you can find the length of the third side.
- ✔ The converse of the Pythagorean Theorem states that if a triangle has sides with lengths a, b, and c and $a^2 + b^2 = c^2$, then the triangle is a right triangle. This means that if the three side lengths of a triangle make the equation true, then you can be sure the triangle is a right triangle.
- ✔ Students will benefit from illustrations and discussions with their peers as they make sense of the Pythagorean Theorem. Ask students what the square grids show and have them draw connections between the models.
- ✔ After making sense of the Pythagorean Theorem, students make use of the theorem in a variety of applications, such as finding diagonal distances in the coordinate plane. In later grades, students extend this application of the theorem as they develop a formula for the distance between any two points in the coordinate plane.

Students explore **the Pythagorean Theorem** . . .

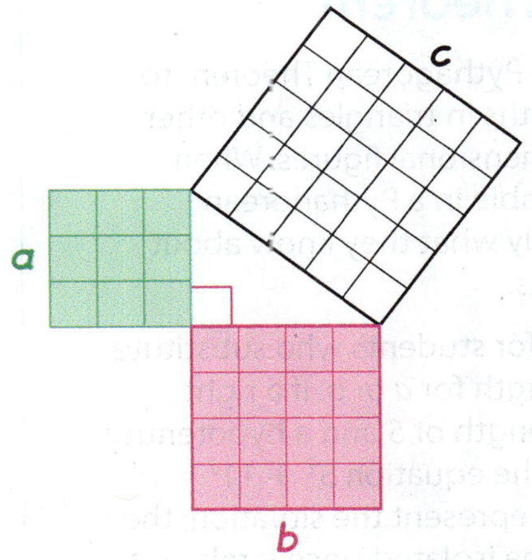

Pythagorean Theorem:
If a triangle is right, then $a^2 + b^2 = c^2$.

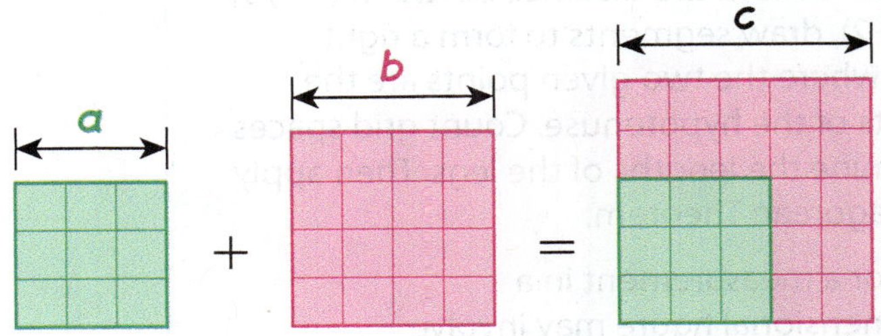

. . . and **its converse**.

Converse:

If $a^2 + b^2 = c^2$, then the triangle is right.

A triangle has side lengths 12, 15, and 18.
Is it a right triangle?

$12^2 + 15^2 = 18^2$?

$144 + 225 = 324$

$369 = 324$ ← false

The triangle is not a right triangle.

Connecting Irrational Numbers to Geometry *(continued)*

INSIGHTS ON . . .

Applying the Pythagorean Theorem

- ✔ Students apply the Pythagorean Theorem to find unknown lengths in triangles and other two- and three-dimensional figures. When solving for the variable in a Pythagorean equation, they apply what they know about finding square roots.
- ✔ **Error Alert** Watch for students who substitute the hypotenuse length for *a* or *b*. If a right triangle has a leg length of 5 and a hypotenuse length of 11, then the equation $5^2 + 11^2 = c^2$ does not correctly represent the situation; the square of 11 must be isolated since it relates to the longest side.
- ✔ To find the distance between two points that are not on a horizontal or vertical line, students may apply the Pythagorean Theorem.

  EXAMPLE To find the distance between $(-1, 3)$ and $(3, -2)$, draw segments to form a right triangle, where the two given points are the endpoints of the hypotenuse. Count grid spaces to determine the lengths of the legs. Then apply the Pythagorean Theorem.
- ✔ Solving for a measurement in a three-dimensional figure may involve using the Pythagorean Theorem twice. Support students by highlighting the two different triangles they need to work with. To help students visualize the diagonal of a rectangular prism, you can show them a box, such as a tissue box, with one face cut off.

  EXAMPLE To find the length of the diagonal of a rectangular prism, first determine the length of the diagonal of the prism's base. Then use that value to find the length of the diagonal of the whole prism.
- ✔ When the side lengths of a right triangle are all whole numbers, the lengths form a Pythagorean triple. For example, one common Pythagorean triple is 3, 4, 5. Multiplying all three numbers in a Pythagorean triple by the same factor produces another Pythagorean triple. Encourage students to look for and make use of structure by keeping their eyes open for common Pythagorean triples when they solve right triangle problems.

Students use the **Pythagorean Theorem** to solve real-world problems **in two dimensions** . . .

What is the unknown side length?

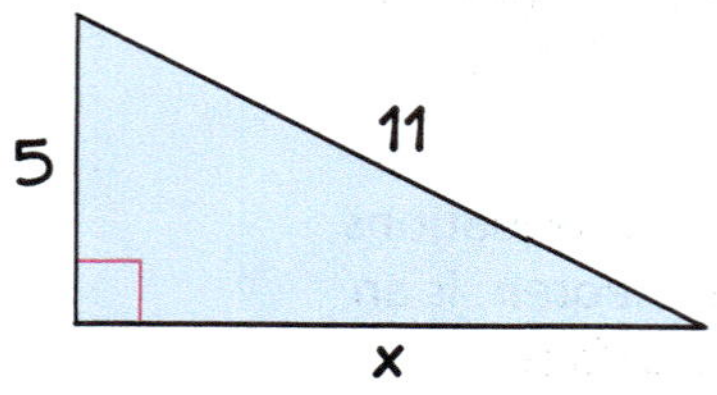

$$x^2 + 5^2 = 11^2$$
$$x^2 + 25 = 121$$
$$x^2 = 96$$
$$x = \sqrt{96}$$

What is the distance between $(-1, 3)$ and $(3, -2)$?

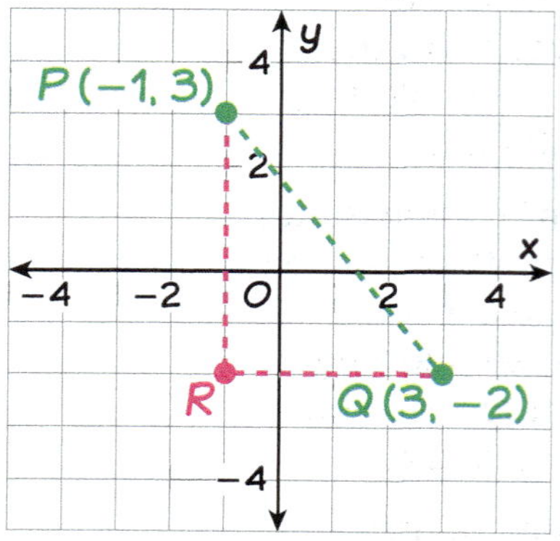

$$4^2 + 5^2 = c^2$$

. . . and **three dimensions.**

What is the length of the diagonal of the prism?

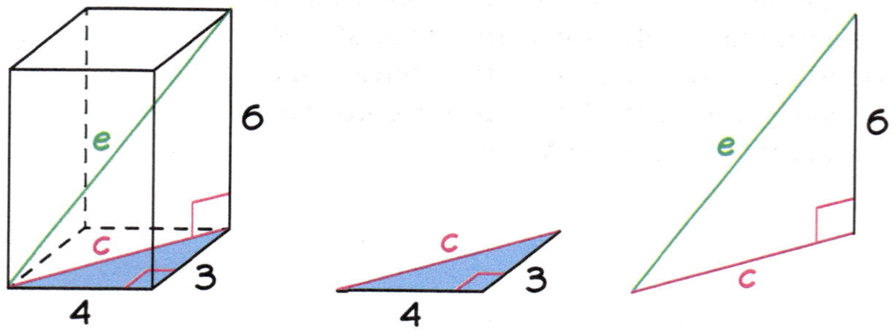

$$3^2 + 4^2 = c^2$$

$$c^2 + 6^2 = e^2$$

Connecting Irrational Numbers to Geometry *(continued)*

INSIGHTS ON . . .

Volume of Cylinders, Cones, and Spheres

- ✔ Students explore the relationships between the volumes of cylinders, cones, and spheres. They discover that, if a cylinder and a cone have the same radius and height, then the volume of the cone is $\frac{1}{3}$ that of the cylinder. And, if the radius and height of a cylinder are both equal to the radius of a sphere, then the volume of the sphere is $\frac{4}{3}$ that of the cylinder. Building this conceptual understanding will help students learn and remember the volume formulas.
- ✔ Students may benefit from hands-on exploration. Pouring rice from a cone into a cylinder with the same base and height can help students make sense of the relationship between the volumes of the figures. It will take exactly 3 cones of rice to fill the cylinder.
- ✔ Since cylinders, cones, and spheres all have curved surfaces, their volumes all relate to π. Students use rational approximations of the irrational number π to estimate the volumes of these figures. When they know the volume and solve for the radius, they apply what they know about finding square and cube roots.
- ✔ Students solve real-world problems involving composite solids that require them to apply more than one volume formula. Encourage students to attend to precision and keep their work organized when managing several steps.

Students explore the relationship between **volumes** of **cylinders, cones,** and **spheres . . .**

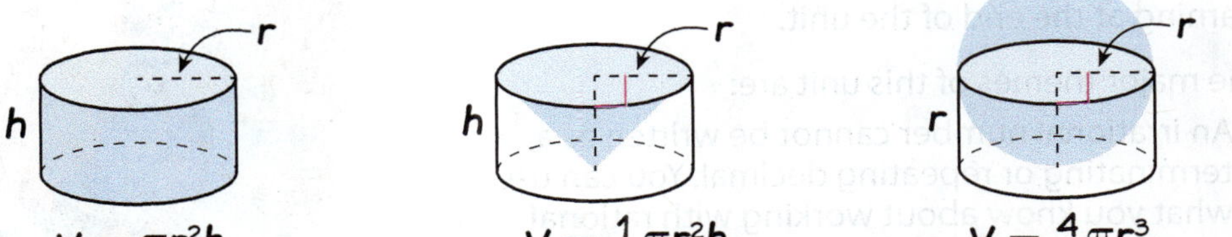

$V = \pi r^2 h$ $\quad V = \frac{1}{3}\pi r^2 h$ $\quad V = \frac{4}{3}\pi r^3$

. . . and solve real-world problems involving **exact** and **approximate values.**

What is the volume?

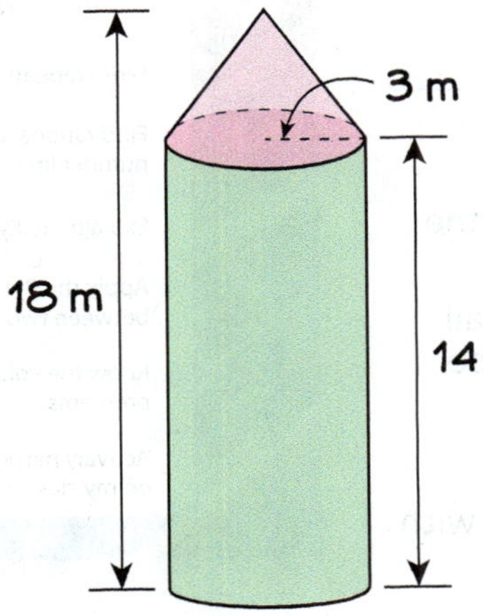

Cone:

$V \approx \frac{1}{3}(3.14)(3^2)(4)$

$V \approx 37.68$

Cylinder:

$V \approx 3.14(3^2)(14)$

$V \approx 395.64$

$V = 138\pi \text{ m}^3$ or $V \approx 433.32 \text{ m}^3$

Future Learning

Students will move on to extend their understanding of real numbers.

Students will:

- solve quadratic equations.
- use properties of rational and irrational numbers to solve problems.
- prove theorems about triangles.
- further explore triangles to learn about trigonometric functions.
- give informal arguments for the volume formulas of figures.

Real Numbers

Unit Big Ideas

This unit introduces students to irrational numbers, Pythagorean Theorem and its converse, and finding the volume of cylinders, cones and spheres. Students preview the skills they will be learning in this unit and assess what they know and do not know about them. Students record their progress after completing each lesson and reflect on their learning at the end of the unit.

The major themes of this unit are:

- An irrational number cannot be written as a terminating or repeating decimal. You can use what you know about working with rational numbers to solve problems with irrational numbers in topics like algebra and geometry.
- The side lengths of a right triangle have a special relationship. You can use this relationship and what you know about triangles to determine unknown side lengths.
- You can use what you know about pi and the area of circles to solve real-world problems about the volumes of cylinders, cones, and spheres.

Self Check

- Take a few minutes to have each student independently read through the list of skills. Ask students to consider each skill and check the box if it is a skill they think they already have.
- Remind students that these skills are likely to all be new to them and that over time, they will be able to check off more and more skills.

Support Whole Class Discussion

Engage students in a discussion about the skills with questions such as:

- *Which skills seem related to something you already know?*
- *Which skills do you think you would use in your everyday life? Why?*

Support Growth Mindset

At the end of the unit, have students review the skills on the **Student Book Self Reflection** page and work in pairs to respond to the prompts. Encourage students to revisit the work they did in each lesson.

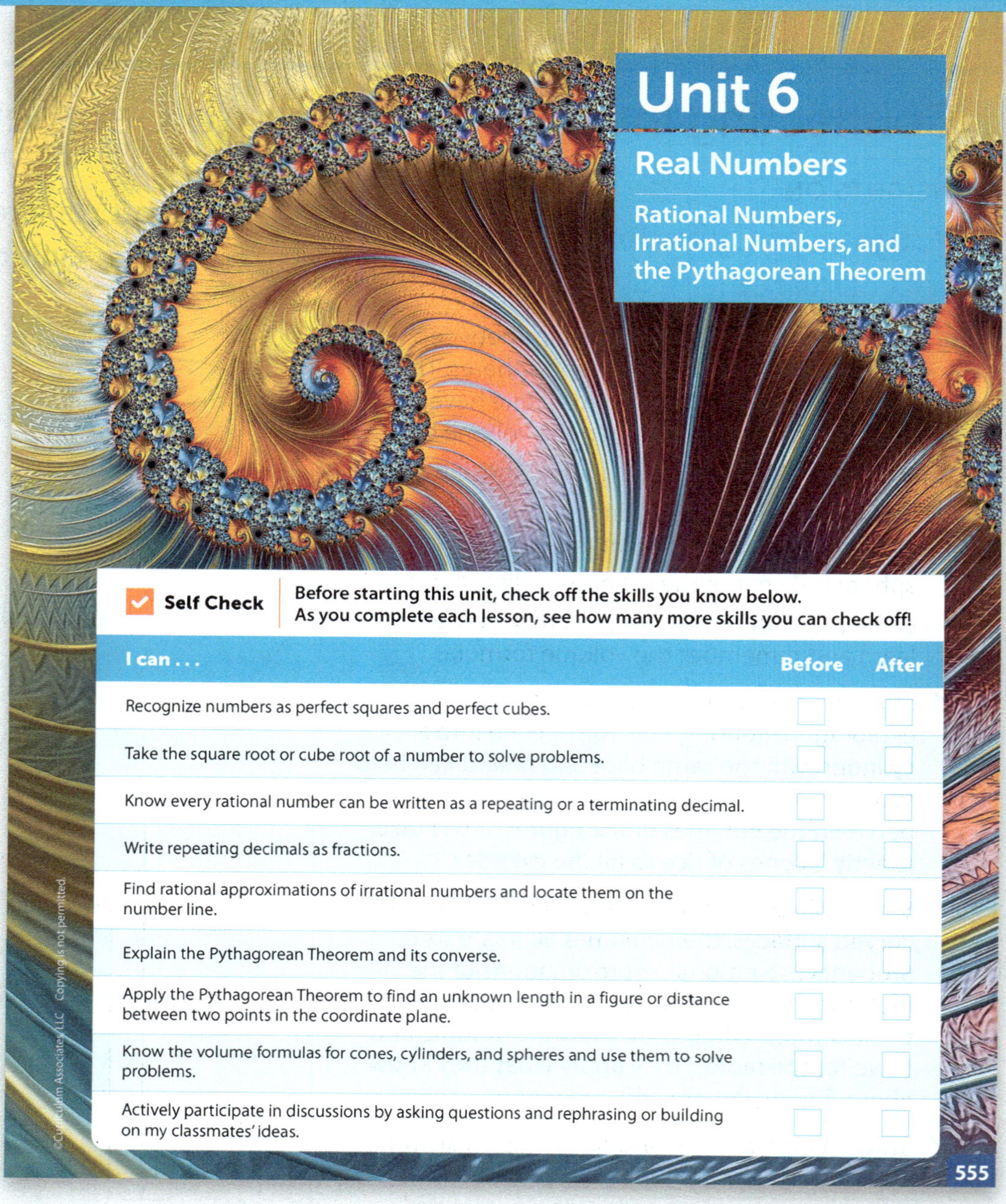

Unit 6

Real Numbers

Rational Numbers, Irrational Numbers, and the Pythagorean Theorem

Self Check | Before starting this unit, check off the skills you know below. As you complete each lesson, see how many more skills you can check off!

I can . . .	Before	After
Recognize numbers as perfect squares and perfect cubes.		
Take the square root or cube root of a number to solve problems.		
Know every rational number can be written as a repeating or a terminating decimal.		
Write repeating decimals as fractions.		
Find rational approximations of irrational numbers and locate them on the number line.		
Explain the Pythagorean Theorem and its converse.		
Apply the Pythagorean Theorem to find an unknown length in a figure or distance between two points in the coordinate plane.		
Know the volume formulas for cones, cylinders, and spheres and use them to solve problems.		
Actively participate in discussions by asking questions and rephrasing or building on my classmates' ideas.		

Unit Skills	Lesson
Recognize numbers as perfect squares and perfect cubes.	23
Take the square root or cube root of a number to solve problems.	23
Know every rational number can be written as a repeating or a terminating decimal.	24
Write repeating decimals as fractions.	24
Find rational approximations of irrational numbers and locate them on the number line.	25
Explain the Pythagorean Theorem and its converse.	26
Apply the Pythagorean Theorem to find an unknown length in a figure or distance between two points in the coordinate plane.	27, 28
Know the volume formulas for cones, cylinders, and spheres and use them to solve problems.	28
Actively participate in discussions by asking questions and rephrasing or building on your classmates' ideas.	23–28

Prepare for Unit 6

- Read the directions and the headings in the chart, or have a student do so. Call on volunteers to explain the task in their own words.
- Have students continue the pattern to fill in the missing parts of the chart.
- Have students work with a partner to share their ideas and write answers to the questions.
- Circulate and validate responses and clarify any misconceptions.
- After most students have finished, debrief with a whole class discussion.

Build Academic Vocabulary

- Display academic terms that will be used throughout this unit when discussing word problems and possible solutions: *eliminate* and *approximate*. Students will likely have some prior knowledge of the terms from math learning in previous grade levels or other content areas. Use the **Academic Vocabulary** routine described in Unit 1 Professional Learning to provide explicit instruction and active engagement.
- Additional academic vocabulary for each lesson is listed in the Lesson Overview. The cognate chart at right includes the Spanish cognates for academic vocabulary introduced in the unit and in each lesson. To support students whose primary language is Spanish, use the **Cognate Support** routine described in Unit 1 Professional Learning
- Support students as they move from informal language to formal academic language by using the **Collect and Display** routine. Have students refer to the chart during discussion and writing.

UNIT 6 Prepare for Rational and Irrational Numbers

➤ **Continue the pattern below by drawing the figures for Steps 4 and 5. Express the total number of unit squares as an addition expression, a sum, and a power.**

	Squares	Addition Expression	Sum	Power
Step 1		1	1	1
Step 2		1 + 3	4	2^2
Step 3		1 + 3 + 5	9	3^2
Step 4	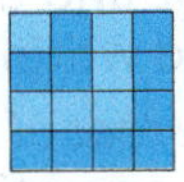	1 + 3 + 5 + 7	16	4^2
Step 5	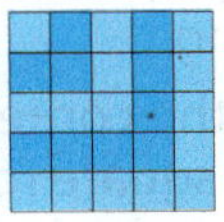	1 + 3 + 5 + 7 + 9	25	5^2

Meet with a partner and compare your answers. Discuss the answers on which you disagree. You may revise or add to your work. With your partner, answer the following two questions.

1. What relationship do you see between the step number and the power?
   The power is the step number squared.
2. What relationship do you see between the step number and the sum?
   The sum is the square of the step number.

Cognates for Academic Vocabulary in Unit 6

ACADEMIC WORD	SPANISH COGNATE	ACADEMIC WORD	SPANISH COGNATE
approximate	*aproximado(a)*	exact	*exacto(a)*
circular	*circular*	consider	*considerar*
consider	*considerar*	proof	*prueba*
cylindrical	*cilíndrico(a)*	prove	*probar*
eliminate	*eliminar*	substitute	*sustituir*

Overview | Find Square Roots and Cube Roots to Solve Problems

MATH FOCUS

Focus Standard

8.EE.A.2 Use square root and cube root symbols to represent solutions to equations of the form $x^2 = p$ and $x^3 = p$, where p is a positive rational number. Evaluate square roots of small perfect squares and cube roots of small perfect cubes. Know that $\sqrt{2}$ is irrational.

STANDARDS FOR MATHEMATICAL PRACTICE (SMP)

SMP 1, 2, 3, 4, 5, and 6 are integrated into the Try-Discuss-Connect routine.*

This lesson provides additional support for:

2 Reason abstractly and quantitatively.

7 Look for and make use of structure.

8 Look for and express regularity in repeated reasoning.

* See page 1o to learn how every lesson includes these SMP.

Objectives

Content Objectives

- Recognize perfect squares and perfect cubes.
- Recognize that squaring a number and taking the square root of a number are inverse operations.
- Recognize that cubing a number and taking the cube root of a number are inverse operations.
- Solve problems that involve finding the square root or cube root of a number.

Language Objectives

- Understand the terms *perfect square* and *perfect cube* and use them accurately in speech and writing.
- Use *square root of x* and *cube root of x* to identify operations when speaking and writing.
- Interpret the context of word problems involving square roots or cube roots to determine whether the solution is positive or negative.

Prior Knowledge

- Evaluate expressions with exponents.
- Use the formula for the area of a square, $A = s^2$.
- Use the formula for the volume of a cube, $V = s^3$.

Vocabulary

Math Vocabulary

cube root of *x* the number that when cubed is equal to *x*.

perfect cube the product when an integer is used as a factor three times.

perfect square the product of an integer and itself.

square root of *x* the number that when multiplied by itself is equal to *x*.

Review the following key terms.

integers the set of whole numbers and their opposites.

inverse operations operations that undo each other. For example, addition and subtraction are inverse operations, and multiplication and division are inverse operations.

product the result of multiplication.

surface area the sum of the areas of all the faces of a three-dimensional figure.

Academic Vocabulary

substitute to replace one thing with another.

Learning Progression

In Grade 6, students evaluated expressions containing exponents. They also used formulas for areas of squares and volumes of cubes.

In Grade 7, students solved multi-step problems involving rational numbers.

➤

In this lesson, students recognize perfect squares and perfect cubes and use the concept of inverse operations to find square roots and cube roots. Students solve equations that involve finding the square root or cube root of a number to solve real-world problems.

➤

Later in Grade 8, students will learn that square roots of whole numbers that are not perfect squares are irrational numbers, and so their values cannot be expressed exactly as repeating or terminating decimals.

Pacing Guide

Items marked with ✱ are available on the **Teacher Toolbox**.

	MATERIALS	DIFFERENTIATION
SESSION 1 **Explore** Square Roots (35–50 min)		
• **Start** (5 min) • **Try It** (5–10 min) • **Discuss It** (10–15 min) • **Connect It** (10–15 min) • **Close: Exit Ticket** (5 min) **Additional Practice** (pages 561–562)	**Math Toolkit** grid paper, paper squares, unit tiles Presentation Slides ✱	**PREPARE** Interactive Tutorial ✱ **RETEACH or REINFORCE** Hands-On Activity **Materials** For each pair: 16 unit tiles
SESSION 2 **Develop** Finding a Square Root to Solve Problems (45–60 min)		
• **Start** (5 min) • **Try It** (10–15 min) • **Discuss It** (10–15 min) • **Connect It** (15–20 min) • **Close: Exit Ticket** (5 min) **Additional Practice** (pages 567–568)	**Math Toolkit** grid paper, paper squares, unit tiles Presentation Slides ✱	**RETEACH or REINFORCE** Hands-On Activity **Materials** For each group: 100 unit tiles **REINFORCE** Fluency & Skills Practice ✱ **EXTEND** Deepen Understanding
SESSION 3 **Develop** Finding a Cube Root to Solve Problems (45–60 min)		
• **Start** (5 min) • **Try It** (10–15 min) • **Discuss It** (10–15 min) • **Connect It** (15–20 min) • **Close: Exit Ticket** (5 min) **Additional Practice** (pages 573–574)	**Math Toolkit** unit cubes Presentation Slides ✱	**RETEACH or REINFORCE** Hands-On Activity **Materials** For each group: 125 unit cubes **REINFORCE** Fluency & Skills Practice ✱ **EXTEND** Deepen Understanding
SESSION 4 **Refine** Finding Square Roots and Cube Roots to Solve Problems (45–60 min)		
• **Start** (5 min) • **Monitor & Guide** (15–20 min) • **Group & Differentiate** (20–30 min) • **Close: Exit Ticket** (5 min)	Presentation Slides ✱	**RETEACH** Hands-On Activity **Materials** For each pair: 64 unit cubes **REINFORCE** Problems 4–8 **EXTEND** Challenge **PERSONALIZE** i-Ready
Lesson 23 Quiz ✱ or **Digital Comprehension Check**		**RETEACH** Tools for Instruction ✱ **REINFORCE** Math Center Activity ✱ **EXTEND** Enrichment Activity ✱

Connect to Culture

➤ **Use these activities to connect with and leverage the diverse backgrounds and experiences of all students. Engage students in sharing what they know about contexts before you add the information given here.**

SESSION 1 ■ □ □ □

Prepare For **Problem 3** Ask students if they have a special family quilt. If so, have them describe the quilt to others in the class. Many families make quilts out of squares that have meaningful patches inside each square. These patches may include words or graphics that help families recall special vacations, milestones, or close relatives. The squares are stitched together to form a larger square, which can be used as a wall hanging or a blanket.

SESSION 2 ■ ■ □ □

Try It Ask students if they have ever seen the Rio Grande Gorge Bridge. If any have, ask them to explain what makes the bridge so famous. This bridge is part of United States Highway 64 near Taos, New Mexico. It has been featured in several popular movies. It was placed on the National Register of Historic Places in 1997. The bridge, which is between 550 and 650 feet above the Rio Grande River, is one of the most visited tourist attractions in northern New Mexico. Visitors can stand on platforms and look at spectacular views of the river and terrain below.

SESSION 3 ■ ■ ■ □

Try It A fossil is any part of a plant or animal (or an impression of one) that existed in the past and has been found in the soil. Because fossils are delicate, they need to be stored properly to preserve their features. In a museum, rooms where fossils are stored must have proper heating and cooling systems. The containers that hold fossils must be resistant to fire, water, and insects. Ask students to share any experiences they have had seeing fossils in a museum, and ask if they remember how those fossils were stored or displayed for the public to see.

SESSION 4 ■ ■ ■ ■

Apply It **Problem 4** Ask students who have made candles to explain the process and describe their experiences. Candles are made by melting wax and then shaping it into a mold of a certain shape around a wick, which ignites the candle. Some do-it-at-home candle makers add colors and fragrances to their candles.

Connect to Family and Community

➤ **After the Explore session, have students use the Family Letter to let their families know what they are learning and to encourage family involvement.**

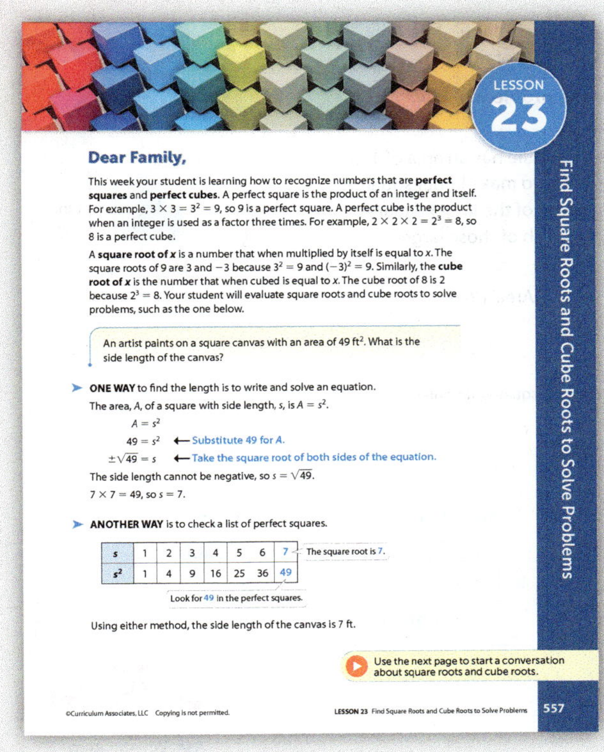

LESSON 23

Find Square Roots and Cube Roots to Solve Problems

Dear Family,

This week your student is learning how to recognize numbers that are **perfect squares** and **perfect cubes**. A perfect square is the product of an integer and itself. For example, $3 \times 3 = 3^2 = 9$, so 9 is a perfect square. A perfect cube is the product when an integer is used as a factor three times. For example, $2 \times 2 \times 2 = 2^3 = 8$, so 8 is a perfect cube.

A **square root of *x*** is a number that when multiplied by itself is equal to *x*. The square roots of 9 are 3 and −3 because $3^2 = 9$ and $(-3)^2 = 9$. Similarly, the **cube root of *x*** is the number that when cubed is equal to *x*. The cube root of 8 is 2 because $2^3 = 8$. Your student will evaluate square roots and cube roots to solve problems, such as the one below.

An artist paints on a square canvas with an area of 49 ft^2. What is the side length of the canvas?

➤ **ONE WAY** to find the length is to write and solve an equation.

The area, *A*, of a square with side length, *s*, is $A = s^2$.

$A = s^2$

$49 = s^2$ ← Substitute 49 for *A*.

$\pm\sqrt{49} = s$ ← Take the square root of both sides of the equation.

The side length cannot be negative, so $s = \sqrt{49}$.

$7 \times 7 = 49$, so $s = 7$.

➤ **ANOTHER WAY** is to check a list of perfect squares.

s	1	2	3	4	5	6	7
s^2	1	4	9	16	25	36	49

The square root is 7.

Look for 49 in the perfect squares.

Using either method, the side length of the canvas is 7 ft.

Use the next page to start a conversation about square roots and cube roots.

©Curriculum Associates, LLC Copying is not permitted.

LESSON 23 Find Square Roots and Cube Roots to Solve Problems 557

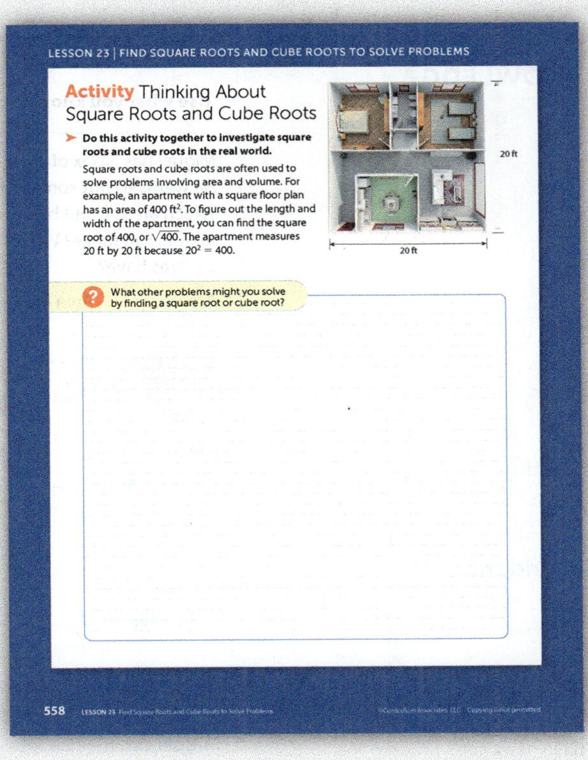

LESSON 23 | FIND SQUARE ROOTS AND CUBE ROOTS TO SOLVE PROBLEMS

Activity Thinking About Square Roots and Cube Roots

➤ **Do this activity together to investigate square roots and cube roots in the real world.**

Square roots and cube roots are often used to solve problems involving area and volume. For example, an apartment with a square floor plan has an area of 400 ft^2. To figure out the length and width of the apartment, you can find the square root of 400, or $\sqrt{400}$. The apartment measures 20 ft by 20 ft because $20^2 = 400$.

What other problems might you solve by finding a square root or cube root?

558 LESSON 23 Find Square Roots and Cube Roots to Solve Problems ©Curriculum Associates, LLC Copying is not permitted.

Connect to Language

➤ **For English language learners, use the Differentiation chart to scaffold the language in each session. Use the Academic Vocabulary routine for academic terms before Session 1.**

DIFFERENTIATION | ENGLISH LANGUAGE LEARNERS

Use with **Session 1** **Connect It**

Levels 1–3: Listening/Writing

Help students respond in writing to Connect It problem 1. First, display these frames to help students write their solutions:

- *Miguel can make ____ possible square(s).*
- *Miguel can make a square with an area of ____ sq in. and a side length of ____ in.*

Next, use an adaptation of **Stronger and Clearer Each Time** to help students write their solution strategies. Ask: *Did you draw, use unit tiles, write an expression, or use another strategy?* Have students turn to partners to respond. Ask volunteers to share strategies and record for reference. Have students write their responses, using the recorded sentences as appropriate, and read their responses to partners.

Levels 2–4: Listening/Writing

Help students prepare and write responses for Connect It problem 1 using an adaptation of **Stronger and Clearer Each Time**. First, work with students to brainstorm active past-tense verbs that they could use to describe their strategies, such as *noticed, decided, sketched, arranged, wrote, counted,* and *used.* Ask students to review and label their work with the verbs they want to use. Ask: *What did you notice about the problem? What did you decide to do as a result? What did you do first? What did you do next?* Have students draft their responses before sharing with partners. Suggest students ask questions to clarify meanings of verbs or ask for more details when needed. After partner discussions, have students revise their writing as needed.

Levels 3–5: Listening/Writing

Have students prepare and write responses for Connect It problem 1 using an adaptation of **Stronger and Clearer Each Time**. Ask questions to help students think about their strategies: *What did you notice about the problem? What did you decide to do as a result? What did you do first?* Ask students to draft their explanations and then take turns explaining their strategies to partners. Reinforce that an effective way to listen is to paraphrase the speaker's ideas and check for understanding using sentences like:

- *I think you said ____. Is that correct?*
- *Let me see if I understood. Did you say ____?*

After partner discussions, have students revise their writing as needed.

Explore Square Roots

Purpose

- **Explore** the idea that for some whole numbers, you can find a value whose square is equal to that whole number.
- **Understand** that the square root of a given number is a value that when squared is equal to the given number.

START CONNECT TO PRIOR KNOWLEDGE

Same and Different

25 (A)	36 (B)
49 (C)	100 (D)

Possible Solutions

All are equal to a whole number times itself.

A and C are odd. B and D are even.

A and C have three factors, including 1 and the number itself.

B and D have more than three factors.

WHY? Support students' facility with recognizing the factors of numbers.

TRY IT SMP 1, 2, 4, 5, 6

Make Sense of the Problem

Before students work on Try It, use **Three Reads** to help them make sense of the problem. After the first read, ask what the problem is about. After the second read, ask a student what the problem is asking students to do. Finally, have students pair up. Have one partner read the problem to the other. Ask: *What are the important quantities and relationships in the problem?*

DISCUSS IT SMP 2, 3, 6

Support Partner Discussion

After students work on Try It, have them respond to Discuss It with a partner. Listen for understanding of:

- methods to model or visualize the squares.
- methods to determine the side lengths of the squares given the area of the squares.

Explore Square Roots

Previously, you learned about powers of numbers. In this lesson, you will learn about square roots and cube roots of numbers.

➤ **Use what you know to try to solve the problem below.**

Miguel has a box of small square tiles. Each tile has an area of 1 in.^{2}. He wants to put some of the tiles together to make larger squares. Which areas listed below are possible areas of the larger squares Miguel can make? What side length will each of those larger squares have?

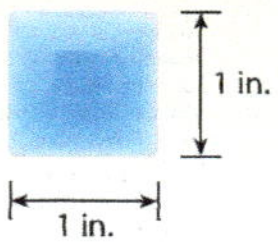

Area 4 in.^{2} Area 8 in.^{2} Area 9 in.^{2} Area 12 in.^{2}

TRY IT Math Toolkit grid paper, paper squares, unit tiles

Possible work:

SAMPLE A

Area 4 in.^{2}

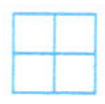

Side length 2 in.

Area 8 in.^{2}

Not possible

Area 9 in.^{2}

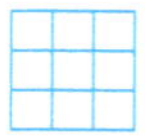

Side length 3 in.

Area 12 in.^{2}

Not possible

SAMPLE B

Area of a square: $A = s^2$

Miguel can make a 2-by-2 square: $2^2 = 4$

Miguel can make a 3-by-3 square: $3^2 = 9$

So, Miguel can make a square with area 4 in.^{2} (side length 2 in.) and a square with area 9 in.^{2} (side length 3 in.) He cannot make squares with areas of 8 in.^{2} or 12 in.^{2}.

DISCUSS IT

Ask: What strategy did you use to decide which areas are possible?

Share: My strategy was . . .

Learning Target SMP 1, SMP 2, SMP 3, SMP 4, SMP 5, SMP 6, SMP 7

Use square root and cube root symbols to represent solutions to equations of the form $x^2 = p$ and $x^3 = p$, where p is a positive rational number. Evaluate square roots of small perfect squares and cube roots of small perfect cubes. Know that $\sqrt{2}$ is irrational.

559

Error Alert If students think a square with area 8 in.^{2} or a square with area 12 in.^{2} can be made with unit tiles, ask them to read the problem again. Have them note that Miguel does not want to make just any rectangles, he wants to make squares. Be sure students understand that for a rectangle to be a square, all four of its sides must be the same length, and because Miguel is making the squares with 1 in.^{2} unit tiles, the sides must have a whole-number length.

Select and Sequence Student Strategies

Select 2–3 samples that represent the range of student thinking in your classroom. Here is one possible order for class discussion:

- unit tiles used to build the squares
- grid paper used to draw the squares
- table of side lengths and corresponding areas used to determine which squares can be made
- relationship between side length and areas of squares used to determine which squares can be made

Facilitate Whole Class Discussion

Call on students to share selected strategies. Ask students to come up with a way to test whether a strategy makes sense.

Guide students to **Compare and Connect** the representations. Reword any unclear statements, or ask a student to do so, so that others understand. Confirm with the speaker that the rewording is accurate.

ASK *How did each strategy show that squares with area 8 in.^{2} or 12 in.^{2} could not be built?*

LISTEN FOR It was not possible to build a square with 8 or 12 tiles or to draw one with exactly 8 or 12 grid squares. There is no whole number that can be multiplied by itself to get 8 or 12.

CONNECT IT

SMP 2, 4, 5

1 Look Back Look for understanding that to make a square with a given area, the total number of tiles used must be equal to the area of the square. It is possible to make squares with 4 tiles and with 9 tiles, but it is not possible to make squares with 8 tiles or with 12 tiles.

DIFFERENTIATION | RETEACH or REINFORCE

Hands-On Activity

Use tiles to make squares.

If students are unsure about what areas can be areas of a square, then use this activity to help them explore making squares from unit tiles.

Materials For each pair: 16 unit tiles

- Have students make a table with columns labeled *Area* and *Side Length*. The *Area* column should be numbered from 1 square unit to 16 square units.
- Instruct students to make a square out of 1 unit tile. Ask: *Can you make a square with 1 unit tile?* [Yes] Ask: *What is the area of the square?* [1 square unit] Ask: *What is the side length of the square?* [1 unit] Have students write the area, 1, in the *Area* column of the table and the side length, 1, in the *Side Length* column.
- Instruct students to make a square out of 2 unit tiles. Ask: *Can you make a square with 2 unit tiles?* [No] Have students skip the row in the table for an area of 2 square units.
- Instruct students to continue to try to make squares with 3 tiles up to 16 tiles and complete the table.
- Ask: *What do you observe about the relationship between the area and the side length of a square?* [Each area is equal to the side length times itself.]

LESSON 23 | SESSION 1

CONNECT IT

1 Look Back Which areas in the list are possible areas of the larger squares Miguel can make? What side lengths do these larger squares have? How do you know?
Miguel can make a square with area 4 in.^{2} and side length 2 in. He can also make a square with area 9 in.^{2} and side length 3 in. I used square tiles to make larger squares and counted how many tiles I used.

2 Look Ahead A **perfect square** is the product of an integer and itself.

a. Complete the table at the right. Which numbers in the table are perfect squares? Why?
The numbers in the right column are perfect squares. You can multiply an integer by itself to get these numbers.

x	x^2
1	1
2	4
3	9
4	16
5	25
6	36
7	49
8	64
9	81
10	100
11	121
12	144

b. The inverse operation of squaring is finding a square root. A **square root of x** is a number that when multiplied by itself is equal to x. So, a square root of 9 is 3 because $3 \cdot 3 = 9$. Another square root of 9 is -3. Why?
$(-3)(-3) = 9$, so -3 is a square root of 9.

c. A square root can be positive or negative. The symbol $\sqrt{}$ means the *positive* square root. So, $\sqrt{9} = 3$, but not -3. Complete the following.

$\sqrt{81} =$ 9 $\qquad \sqrt{144} =$ 12

To solve an equation like $x^2 = 17$, note that the variable is squared. To find the value of the variable, perform the inverse of squaring. Take the square root of both sides of the equation.

$x^2 = 17$

$x = \pm\sqrt{17}$

When you take a square root, both the positive and the negative square root are possible answers. Since 17 is not a perfect square, you cannot write $\sqrt{17}$ or $-\sqrt{17}$ as integers. Write the solution as $\pm\sqrt{17}$.

3 Reflect Explain how to find all the square roots of 16.
16 is a perfect square, so find an integer that when multiplied by itself equals 16. $4^2 = 16$ and $(-4)^2 = 16$, so the square roots are 4 and -4.

560

2 Look Ahead Point out that every perfect square has two square roots. The square root symbol means the positive square root. When solving an equation by taking the square root of both sides, both the positive and negative square root are possible solutions. For example, both 3 and -3 are solutions of $x^2 = 9$. Explain that the $\pm$ symbol is a shorthand way to express both solutions: ±3 means $+3$ and -3. In problem 2c, although 17 is not a perfect square, it has two square roots. In fact, any non-negative number has two square roots.

Ask a volunteer to rephrase the definitions of *perfect square* and *square root of x*. Support student understanding by reminding them that the areas they found are the perfect squares and the side lengths are the positive square roots.

CLOSE EXIT TICKET

3 Reflect Look for understanding of how to find the numbers that when multiplied by themselves yield a product of 16.

Common Misconception Listen for students who list the factors of 16 such as 2 and 8 or 1 and 16. As students share their strategies, point out that the square root of a number is a number that *when multiplied by itself* results in the given number.

Prepare for Finding Square Roots and Cube Roots to Solve Problems

Support Vocabulary Development

Assign **Prepare for Finding Square Roots and Cube Roots to Solve Problems** as extra practice in class or as homework.

If you have students complete this in class, then use the guidance below.

Ask students to consider the term *product*. As they consider the word, have them think of ways they have shown products of two numbers in the past.

Have students work individually to complete the graphic organizer. Invite students to share their completed organizers, and prompt a whole-class comparative discussion of the definitions, illustrations, examples, and non-examples they have generated.

Have students look at the expressions in problem 2 and discuss with a partner the ways that multiplication is shown. Students may describe each expression in words to help them decide which show products.

Problem Notes

1. Students should understand that a product is the result of multiplication. Student illustrations might include unit tiles arranged to form a rectangle, or an array of counters. Students should recognize that whole numbers, integers, fractions, decimals, variables, and expressions can all be multiplied to obtain products. Non-examples might include the results of other operations, such as addition, subtraction, and division.

2. The first expression shows 2 times a sum. The second expression shows a variable used as a factor 4 times. The third expression shows a coefficient times a variable. The fourth expression shows the product of a sum and a difference.

LESSON 23 | SESSION 1 Name:

Prepare for Finding Square Roots and Cube Roots to Solve Problems

1. Think about what you know about operations with rational numbers. Fill in each box. Use words, numbers, and pictures. Show as many ideas as you can.
Possible answers:

In My Own Words
A product is the result of multiplication.

My Illustrations
The product of 3 and 6 is 18.

product

Examples
The product of $\frac{2}{9}$ and $\frac{5}{7}$ is $\frac{2}{9} \times \frac{5}{7} = \frac{10}{63}$.
3^5 is the product of $3 \times 3 \times 3 \times 3 \times 3$.
The expression xy is the product of x and y.

Non-Examples
$5 + 12$ is a sum, not a product.
$8 - 4$ is a difference, not a product.
$24 \div 6$ is a quotient, not a product.

2. Which of the expressions at the right are examples of a product? Explain.

$2(10 + y)$

x^4

$-7a$

$(3 + 4)(3 - 4)$

All of the expressions are products; $2(10 + y)$ is the product of 2 and $10 + y$; x^4 is the product of x used as a factor 4 times; $-7a$ is the product of -7 and a; $(3 + 4)(3 - 4)$ is the product of $3 + 4$ and $3 - 4$.

561

REAL-WORLD CONNECTION

The relationship between the area of a square object and the square root of the area are used in many home projects. For example, suppose a homeowner wants to install a rectangular pen for her dog to cover an area of 400 square feet. To do this as economically as possible, the homeowner should purchase the least possible amount of fencing. A square pen would produce the least perimeter for the given area. To find the side length of the pen, the owner would take the square root of the area of the pen. Then, she would multiply the side length by 4 to find the total amount of fencing needed to build the pen. Ask students to think of when other real-world examples of finding square roots or cube roots would be useful.

Additional Practice

3 See ***Connect to Culture*** to support student engagement. Problem 3 provides another look at recognizing perfect squares. This problem is similar to the problem where Miguel is building larger squares from smaller square tiles. In both problems, various areas are given and students need to decide whether squares can be made with those areas. This problem asks which areas are possible for a square quilt made from 1 ft^2 fabric squares.

Students may want to use square tiles or grid paper to solve.

Suggest that students use **Three Reads** to help them make sense of the problem.

3 Garrett is cutting square patches from old sports jerseys. Each patch has an area of 1 ft^2. He wants to put some of the patches together to make square quilts.

a. Which areas listed below are possible areas of the square quilts Garrett can make? What side length will each of those square quilts have? Show your work.

Area 5 ft^2 Area 16 ft^2 Area 18 ft^2 Area 25 ft^2

Possible work:

Area 5 ft^2
Not possible

Area 16 ft^2

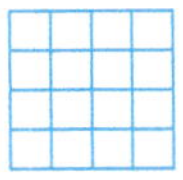

Side length 4 ft

Area 18 ft^2
Not possible

Area 25 ft^2

Side length 5 ft

SOLUTION Garrett can make a square quilt with area 16 ft^2 and side length 4 ft and with area 25 ft^2 and side length 5 ft.

b. Check your answer to problem 3a. Show your work.

Possible work:

$4^2 = 16$, so Garrett can make a square quilt with area 16 ft^2.

$5^2 = 25$, so Garrett can make a square quilt with area 25 ft^2.

5 and 18 are not perfect squares, so Garrett cannot make square quilts with areas 5 ft^2 or 18 ft^2.

DIFFERENTIATION | ENGLISH LANGUAGE LEARNERS

Use with **Session 2** Connect It

Levels 1–3: Listening/Speaking

Help students make sense of Connect It problem 4. Display the first Model It, then write problem 4's equation next to the last equation. Read problem 4 as students follow along. Ask: *What does the variable t represent?* Provide this frame:

- *The variable t represents* ____.

Help students make the connection between *t* and *time*. Have students look at a clock and count seconds. Ask: *Can time be a negative number? What can you use to find a square root? Is 47 in the table? Is the solution an integer?* Help students write responses using:

- *I know the solution will be* ____*. One reason is* ____*. Another reason is* ____.

Levels 2–4: Listening/Speaking

Help students make sense of Connect It problem 4. Read the problem with students and display the two Model Its. Call on students to paraphrase the key points of Model It. Ensure students connect the variable *t* with *time* and *seconds*. Ask: *Can the value of t be negative? Why or why not?* If needed, have students look at a clock and count seconds. Next, draw students' attention to the table of perfect squares. Ask: *Is 47 in the table? Why not?*

Ask students to write responses to the problem and call on volunteers to share. Model how to connect ideas and sentences using words like *because, so,* and *also.*

Levels 3–5: Listening/Speaking

Help students make sense of Connect It problem 4. Ask students to read the problem individually and then refer back to the Model It as an example. Ask questions to help students think about the problem: *How would the solution be the same as in Model It? How would it be different?* Have students turn and talk with partners. Reinforce that they should justify their solutions by providing reasons the solution is reasonable in the context of the problem. Remind students to listen to their partners and try to understand their thinking.

After partner discussions, have students write responses. Remind them to justify by explaining their reasoning.

Develop Finding a Square Root to Solve Problems

Purpose

- **Develop** strategies for solving real-world problems involving squares and square roots.
- **Recognize** that you can solve an equation with a squared term by taking the square root of both sides of the equation.

START CONNECT TO PRIOR KNOWLEDGE

Which One Doesn't Belong?

A: 1	B: 8
C: 25	D: 36

Possible Solutions

All are positive integers.

A is the only number that is its own square root.

B the only number that is not a perfect square.

C is the only odd number whose square root is not itself.

D is the only even-number perfect square.

WHY? Support students' recognition of whole numbers that are perfect squares.

DEVELOP ACADEMIC LANGUAGE

WHY? Practice using *If . . . then . . .* sentences to explain possible solutions.

HOW? Direct students to the first Model It. Ask students to share what d is in the situation. Explain that students can use *If d is ____,* *then ____* to explain the problem. Have students turn to partners and practice using the frame to fill in the sentence. Then have partners consider other ways they could use *If . . . then . . .* sentences to explain solution strategies.

TRY IT

SMP 1, 2, 4, 5, 6

Make Sense of the Problem

See ***Connect to Culture*** to support student engagement. Before students work on Try It, use **Three Reads** to help them make sense of the problem. After the first read, ask *What is the problem about?* After the second read, ask *What are you being asked to find?* After the third read, ask *What are the important quantities and relationships in the problem?*

LESSON 23 | SESSION 2

Develop Finding a Square Root to Solve Problems

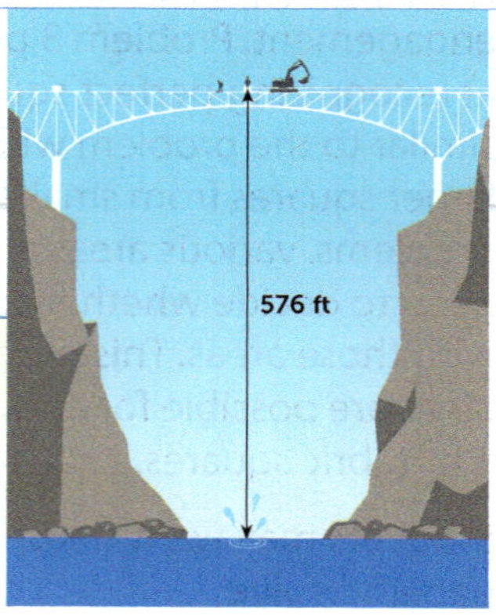

➤ **Read and try to solve the problem below.**

A worker on the Rio Grande Gorge Bridge in New Mexico drops a bolt that lands in the water 576 feet below. The equation $\frac{d}{16} = t^2$ represents the distance in feet, d, that an object falls in t seconds. How long does it take the bolt to hit the water?

TRY IT

Math Toolkit grid paper, paper squares, unit tiles

Possible work:

SAMPLE A

Try values for t to get a distance of 576 ft. Try $t = 2$.

$t = 2$ $\quad \frac{d}{16} = 2^2 \quad d = 2^2 \cdot 16 = 64$; too low

Try $t = 5$.

$t = 5$ $\quad \frac{d}{16} = 5^2 \quad d = 5^2 \cdot 16 = 400$; too low

$t = 6$ $\quad \frac{d}{16} = 6^2 \quad d = 6^2 \cdot 16 = 576$

So, $t = 6$. It takes 6 s for the bolt to fall 576 ft.

SAMPLE B

In the equation, $d = 576$. $\quad \frac{576}{16} = t^2$

$36 = t^2$

Guess and check solutions.

$t = 5 \rightarrow 36 = 5^2 \rightarrow 36 = 25$ False

$t = 6 \rightarrow 36 = 6^2 \rightarrow 36 = 36$ True

It takes 6 s for the bolt to hit the water.

DISCUSS IT

Ask: How can you check your answer?

Share: I can check my answer by . . .

563

DISCUSS IT

SMP 2, 3, 4, 5, 6

Support Partner Discussion

After students work on Try It, have them explain their work and then respond to Discuss It with a partner.

If students need support in getting started, prompt them to ask each other questions such as:

- *What do you notice about t in the equation?*
- *How can you tell if your answer is reasonable?*

Common Misconception Listen for students who get $36 = t^2$, but then divide 36 by 2 instead of taking the square root of both sides of the equation. As students share their strategies, remind them that the square root of a given number is a value that when multiplied by itself is equal to the given number.

Select and Sequence Student Strategies

Select 2–3 samples that represent the range of student thinking in your classroom. Here is one possible order for class discussion:

- guess and check used to test possible values of t
- (misconception) time incorrectly found by dividing 36 by 2, rather than by taking the square root
- equation written and solved by taking the square root of both sides of the equation

Facilitate Whole Class Discussion

Call on students to share selected strategies. As students share their strategies, remind them that a good explanation describes what was done and why it was done.

Guide students to **Compare and Connect** the representations. Allow individual think time for students to process the different ideas.

ASK *How did each strategy use the equation given in the problem?*

LISTEN FOR Some strategies used guess and check, substituting values for t. Others substituted 576 into the equation for d and then solved by taking the square root of both sides of the equation.

Model It

If students presented these models, have students connect these models to those presented in class.

If no student presented at least one of these models, have students first analyze key features of the models, and then connect them to the models presented in class.

ASK *How are the two Model Its related?*

LISTEN FOR The first one shows the solutions of the equation using the square root symbol. The second takes it a step further and considers which solutions make sense in the problem context and finds the square root.

For the equation, prompt students to think about the plus/minus symbol in the last equation.

- *What does the plus/minus symbol mean?*
- *Why does it not make sense for time to be negative?*

For the table of perfect squares, prompt students to note how the table helps to keep the integers and their squares organized.

- *How do you use the table to find the value of t?*
- *When might this approach not be practical?*

LESSON 23 | SESSION 2

Explore different ways to find a square root to solve a problem.

A worker on the Rio Grande Gorge Bridge in New Mexico drops a bolt that lands in the water 576 feet below. The equation $\frac{d}{16} = t^2$ represents the distance in feet, d, that an object falls in t seconds. How long does it take the bolt to hit the water?

Model It

You can solve the given equation for t.

The distance the bolt falls is 576 feet.

Substitute 576 for d in the equation.

$$\frac{d}{16} = t^2$$

$$\frac{576}{16} = t^2$$

$$36 = t^2$$

Take the square root of both sides of the equation.

$$\pm\sqrt{36} = t$$

Model It

You can check a list of perfect squares to try to find the value of t.

The value of t cannot be negative, so $t = \sqrt{36}$.

Look for 36 in a table of perfect squares.

t	1	2	3	4	5	6	7	8	9
t^2	1	4	9	16	25	36	49	64	81

564

DIFFERENTIATION | EXTEND

SMP 2

Deepen Understanding

Reasoning Quantitatively with Problems Involving Square Roots

Prompt students to think about how the distance after 3 seconds compares to the distance after 6 seconds.

ASK *It takes 6 seconds for the bolt to fall 576 feet. After 3 seconds, had the bolt fallen half this distance? Explain.*

LISTEN FOR No; substitute 3 for t in the formula $\frac{d}{16} = t^2$ and solve for d. The result is 144 feet, which is less than half of 576 feet.

ASK *How do the distances after 3 seconds and after 6 seconds compare? Explain.*

LISTEN FOR The distance after 3 seconds is $\frac{1}{4}$ the distance after 6 seconds. $\frac{1}{4} \cdot 576 = 144$

ASK *How can you use the formula to show why the distance the bolt falls after 3 seconds is $\frac{1}{4}$ the distance it falls after 6 seconds?*

LISTEN FOR Rewrite the formula as $d = 16t^2$ by multiplying each side by 16. Substitute $\frac{1}{2} \cdot 6$ for t to get $d = 16\left(\frac{1}{2} \cdot 6\right)^2 = 16 \cdot \frac{1}{4} \cdot 36 = \frac{1}{4} \cdot 576$.

Develop Finding a Square Root to Solve Problems

CONNECT IT

SMP 2, 4, 5, 6

Remind students that the quantities and the relationships between them are the same in each representation. Explain that they will now use those representations to reason about how to find a square root to solve a problem.

Before students begin to record and expand on their work in Model It, tell them that problems 1 and 4 will prepare them to provide the explanation asked for in problem 5.

Monitor and Confirm Understanding 1 – 3

- When taking the square root of both sides of an equation, both the positive and negative square roots need to be considered.
- There are two solutions to the equation, 6 and –6. However, because *t* represents a number of seconds, only 6 makes sense in the problem context.

Facilitate Whole Class Discussion

4 Look for understanding that there will be occasions when the number under the square root symbol is not a perfect square.

ASK *What does $\pm\sqrt{47}$ mean?*

LISTEN FOR It represents the two numbers, one positive and one negative, that can be multiplied by themselves to get a product of 47.

5 Look for understanding of what to do when solving an equation leads to an equation of the form $x^2 = a$.

ASK *When a solution leads to an equation that shows a variable squared equal to a number, what should the next step be? If the number is greater than zero, how many solutions will the equation have?*

LISTEN FOR Take the square root of both sides of the equation. There will be two solutions, the positive and negative square roots of the number.

6 **Reflect** Have all students focus on the strategies used to solve the Try It. If time allows, have students discuss their ideas with a partner.

CONNECT IT

➤ **Use the problem from the previous page to help you understand how to find a square root to solve a problem.**

1. Look at the steps taken to solve the equation in the first **Model It**. Why do you write $\pm\sqrt{36}$ after you take the square root of both sides of the equation?
   There is a positive square root and a negative square root. So, you write $\pm\sqrt{36}$ to show both values.

2. Look at the second **Model It**. How do you know that the value of *t* cannot be negative?
   The variable *t* represents the number of seconds it takes the bolt to hit the water. Time cannot be negative.

3. How long does it take the bolt to hit the water? 6 seconds

4. Suppose the first **Model It** ended with $t = \pm\sqrt{47}$. What would the solution to the problem be in this case? Why?
   The solution would be $\sqrt{47}$ seconds. Time cannot be negative. Also, 47 does not appear in the table of perfect squares, so you cannot write the answer as an integer.

5. When you solve a real-world problem, you may get an equation of the form $x^2 = a$. How do you use this equation to solve the problem?
   Possible answer: You solve the equation by taking the square root of both sides of the equation to get $x = \pm\sqrt{a}$. Then, determine if the positive and/or negative square root makes sense in the situation. Write the answer as an integer if *a* is a perfect square.

6. **Reflect** Think about all the models and strategies you have discussed today. Describe how one of them helped you better understand how to solve the **Try It** problem.
   Responses will vary. Check student responses.

565

DIFFERENTIATION | RETEACH or REINFORCE

Hands-On Activity

Use unit tiles to find perfect squares.

If students are unsure about recognizing perfect squares, then use this activity to reinforce the concept.

Materials For each group: 100 unit tiles

- Make a table with column titles *Number, Rectangle(s),* and *Square(s).*
- Write 24, 25, 36, 41 in the first column.
- Ask groups to investigate whether each number of tiles can form one or more rectangles or squares. Remind students that any number can be written as the product of 1 and itself, which can be represented by a rectangle.
- Have groups make as many rectangles and squares as they can with each number of tiles.
- Have students record the dimensions of all the rectangles and squares they are able to form for each number in the correct columns of the table.
- Ask: *Which numbers are perfect squares? Why?* [25 and 36; These numbers can form squares. Also, both are products of an integer times itself: $5 \cdot 5 = 25$ and $6 \cdot 6 = 36$.]

Apply It

For all problems, encourage students to use a model to support their thinking.

7 Students may recognize that the square roots of 36 are ± 6 and the square roots of 121 are ± 11, so $\pm \frac{6}{11}$ are the square roots of the fraction.

8 **A is correct.** The answer is the positive square root of 400, which is 20 because $20^2 = 400$.

B is not correct. This is the result of dividing 400 by 2 rather than taking its square root.

C is not correct. This is the result of finding the square of 40 instead of finding the square root of 400.

D is not correct. This answer involves finding the square of 400, not its square root.

Apply It

➤ **Use what you learned to solve these problems.**

7 Brianna is solving the equation $t^2 = \frac{36}{121}$. Her work is shown at the right. Is Brianna correct? Explain.

Brianna's work:

$t^2 = \frac{36}{121}$

$t = \pm\sqrt{\frac{36}{121}}$

$t = \pm\frac{6}{11}$

Yes; Possible explanation: When you take the square root, you must consider both the positive and the negative square root. Because $\frac{6}{11} \cdot \frac{6}{11} = \frac{36}{121}$ and $-\frac{6}{11} \cdot -\frac{6}{11} = \frac{36}{121}$, $t = \pm\frac{6}{11}$.

8 Yesterday, there were b mg of bacteria in a lab experiment. Today, there are b^2 mg of bacteria. There are 400 mg of bacteria today. How many milligrams of bacteria were there yesterday?

- **(A)** 20 mg
- **B** 200 mg
- **C** 1,600 mg
- **D** 160,000 mg

9 The equation $P^2 = 16A$ represents the perimeter, P, of a square with area, A. A square stained-glass window has an area of 4 ft². What is the perimeter of the window? Show your work.

$A = 4\text{ ft}^2$

Possible work:

$A = 4$

$P^2 = 16(4)$

$P^2 = 64$

$P = \pm\sqrt{64}$

The perimeter cannot be negative.

$P = \sqrt{64}$. $8^2 = 64$, so $P = 8$.

SOLUTION The perimeter of the window is 8 ft.

CLOSE EXIT TICKET

9 Students' solutions should show an understanding of:

- solving an equation of the form $x^2 = a$ by taking the square root of both sides of the equation.
- the fact that an equation of the form $x^2 = a$ has two solutions, $\pm\sqrt{a}$.
- interpreting the solution of an equation in the context of the problem.
- finding the square root of a perfect square.

Error Alert If students disregard the variable A in the equation and state the solution is $P = \sqrt{16}$ or 4, then ask them to look back at the equation and explain how they accounted for the area, A, in their solution.

Practice Finding a Square Root to Solve Problems

Problem Notes

Assign **Practice Finding a Square Root to Solve Problems** as extra practice in class or as homework.

1. Students may recognize that 486 is a multiple of 6 and rewrite $\frac{486}{6}$ as the perfect square, 81. If they do not realize this, then they may state the answer as $\sqrt{\frac{486}{6}}$. ***Medium***

2. Students should give both possible solutions either separately or using the $\pm$ symbol. Because in some of the previous problems only the positive solution has been applicable, they may forget to include the negative solution. ***Medium***

LESSON 23 | SESSION 2 Name:

Practice Finding a Square Root to Solve Problems

➤ **Study the Example showing how to find a square root to solve a problem. Then solve problems 1–5.**

Example

The equation $e^2 = \frac{S}{6}$ represents the edge length, e, of a cube with surface area, S. What is the edge length of a cube with surface area 90 cm²?

Substitute 90 for S in the equation.

$$e^2 = \frac{90}{6}$$

$$e^2 = 15$$

Take the square root of both sides of the equation.

$$e = \pm\sqrt{15}$$

The edge length cannot be negative, so $e = \sqrt{15}$. 15 is not a perfect square.

The edge length is $\sqrt{15}$ cm.

1. Suppose the cube in the Example has surface area 486 cm². What is the edge length in this case? Show your work.

   Possible work: $S = 486$, so $e^2 = \frac{486}{6}$

   $$e^2 = 81$$

   $$e = \pm\sqrt{81}$$

   Edge length cannot be negative, and $9^2 = 81$, so $e = 9$.

   SOLUTION The edge length is 9 cm.

2. What is the solution of the equation $w^2 = \frac{4}{9}$? Show your work.

   Possible work: $w^2 = \frac{4}{9}$

   $$w = \pm\sqrt{\frac{4}{9}}$$

   $\frac{2}{3} \cdot \frac{2}{3} = \frac{4}{9}$ and $-\frac{2}{3} \cdot -\frac{2}{3} = \frac{4}{9}$

   SOLUTION $\pm\frac{2}{3}$

Vocabulary

square root of x
the number that when multiplied by itself is equal to x.

perfect square
the product of an integer and itself.

567

Fluency & Skills Practice

Finding a Square Root to Solve Problems

In this activity, students solve equations in the form $x^2 = p$ and $x^2 + b = p$ by finding the square root.

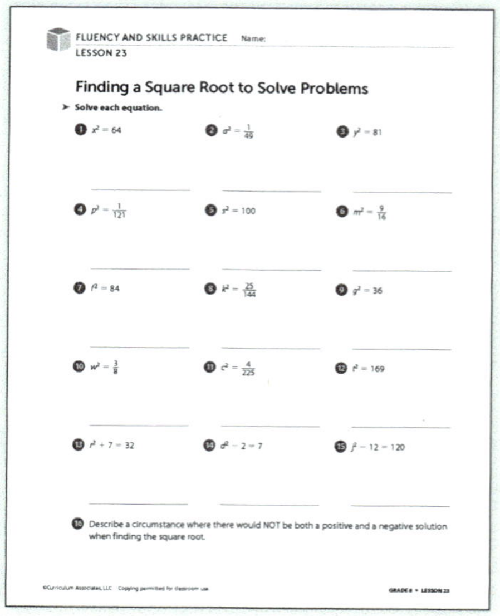
FLUENCY AND SKILLS PRACTICE Name:
LESSON 23

Finding a Square Root to Solve Problems

➤ Solve each equation.

Additional Practice

3 Students may incorrectly state that the answer is 3 because they took the square root of the area without first multiplying it by 2. ***Medium***

4 Students may reason that, just as when they solved linear equations in one variable, they should isolate the variable term on one side of the equation. Then, they can take the square root of both sides of the equation. ***Challenge***

5 Students may use guess and check to find the positive number that can be squared to get 10,000. ***Basic***

3 The equation $s^2 = 2A$ represents the area, A, of an isosceles right triangle with two short sides of length, s. A model sailboat has a sail that is an isosceles right triangle. The sail's area is 9 in.^{2}. What is the length of a short side of the sail? Show your work.

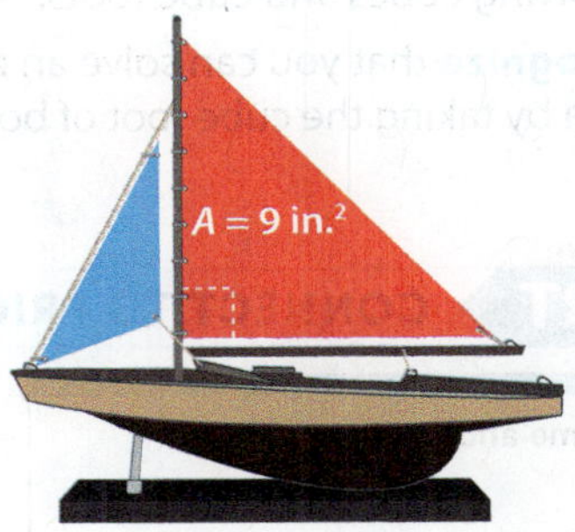

Possible work:

$s^2 = 2(9)$

$s^2 = 18$

$s = \pm\sqrt{18}$

Length cannot be negative, and 18 is not a perfect square.

SOLUTION The length of a short side of the sail is $\sqrt{18}$ in.

4 What is the solution of the equation $x^2 - 7 = 42$? Show your work.

Possible work:

$x^2 - 7 = 42$

$x^2 - 7 + 7 = 42 + 7$

$x^2 = 49$

$x = \pm\sqrt{49}$

49 is a perfect square.

SOLUTION ± 7

5 A square playground has an area of 10,000 ft^2. What is the side length of the playground? Show your work.

Possible work:

$A = s^2$

$10{,}000 = s^2$

$\pm\sqrt{10{,}000} = s$

Length cannot be negative, so $s = \sqrt{10{,}000}$.

$100^2 = 10{,}000$, so $s = 100$.

SOLUTION The side length is 100 ft.

DIFFERENTIATION | ENGLISH LANGUAGE LEARNERS

Use with **Session 3** Connect It

Levels 1–3: Listening/Writing

Help students interpret Connect It problem 3 and then write responses. Display the first Model It and point to the cube root as you read aloud problem 3 sentence 1. Then say: *You know s must be positive. How do you know?* Provide time for students to reason about the value s. Call on volunteers to share their ideas. Record statements, models, and diagrams. Then help students describe the models and diagrams in simple sentences using terms like *factors, product, positive, negative,* and *integer.* Then say: *You know a side length must be positive. How do you know?* Help students write what they know and what it helps them understand. Have them support their ideas using a model or diagram.

Levels 2–4: Listening/Writing

Help students interpret Connect It problem 3. Read the problem with students and rephrase the question: *Edge length cannot be negative. What is another reason that s must be positive?* Allow think time before students turn and talk with partners.

Next, prepare students to respond in writing. Review that an effective explanation gives reasons for, or justifies, ideas. Reinforce that students can justify using models, diagrams, definitions, or properties. Ask: *What rules or properties do you know about negative and positive integers?* List key words and phrases students can use in their responses, such as *product* and *factors*. Then have students write responses.

Levels 3–5: Listening/Writing

Support students as they read and interpret Connect It problem 3. Ask partners to confirm understanding by rephrasing the problem. Ask: *How can you justify your explanation?* If needed, suggest that students support their ideas using the definition of *perfect cube*, properties of integers, or other information they already know. Then remind students to write in a way that helps readers understand their ideas. Ask students to list words that show connections between ideas, such as *if, then, since,* and *so.*

Have students draft responses. Ask partners to read the responses together and discuss if reasons are clearly stated and justified. Have students revise their writing as needed.

Develop Finding a Cube Root to Solve Problems

Purpose

- **Develop** strategies for solving real-world problems involving cubes and cube roots.
- **Recognize** that you can solve an equation with a cubed term by taking the cube root of both sides of the equation.

START CONNECT TO PRIOR KNOWLEDGE

Same and Different

A: 25 m^2	B: 8 cm^3
C: 16 mi	D: 64 ft^2

Possible Solutions

All represent measurements.

A and D are area measurements with square units.

B is a volume measurement with a cubic unit.

C and D have U.S. customary units. A and B have metric units.

A, C, and D have numeric parts that are perfect squares.

WHY? Support students' facility with recognizing U.S. customary and metric units of length, area, and volume.

DEVELOP ACADEMIC LANGUAGE

WHY? Understand sentences that describe events that happen at different times.

HOW? Read Connect It problem 3. Explain that the question describes two events. Ask students to identify the order in which events happen. [Knowing *s* must be positive happens before realizing that a negative edge length does not make sense.] Discuss the difference between *even before* and *before* and encourage students to use *even* for emphasis when they are making a point during discussion or in writing.

TRY IT SMP 1, 2, 4, 5, 6

Make Sense of the Problem

See ***Connect to Culture*** to support student engagement. Before students work on Try It, use **Three Reads** to help them make sense of the problem. Remind students to look for key words, such as *cube* and *volume*, and key numbers, such as 27.

LESSON 23 | SESSION 3

Develop Finding a Cube Root to Solve Problems

➤ **Read and try to solve the problem below.**

Carolina works at a museum. She is looking online for a storage case for some large fossils. She wants the case to have a volume of 27 ft^3. Carolina would like the case to be a cube. What edge length should the case have?

TRY IT Math Toolkit unit cubes

Possible work:

SAMPLE A

I let a centimeter cube represent 1 ft^3.

27 cubes represent a volume of 27 ft^3.

I can arrange 27 small cubes into a 3-by-3-by-3 cube.

So, each edge length should be 3 ft.

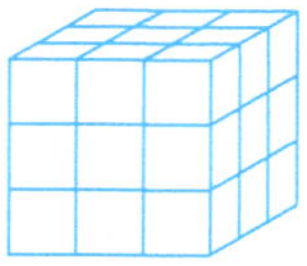

SAMPLE B

$V = s^3$ and $V = 27$.

Guess $s = 2$.

$V = s^3 = 2^3 = 8$; too small

Guess $s = 4$.

$V = s^3 = 4^3 = 64$; too big

Guess $s = 3$.

$V = s^3 = 3^3 = 27$

The case should have an edge length of 3 ft.

DISCUSS IT

Ask: How did you get started solving the problem?

Share: The first thing I did was . . .

569

DISCUSS IT SMP 1, 2, 3, 4, 5, 6

Support Partner Discussion

After students work on Try It, encourage them to respond to Discuss It with a partner. If students need support in getting started, prompt them to ask each other questions such as:

- *How is a case that is a cube different from cases that are not cubes?*
- *How is finding the volume of a cube case different from finding the volume of a case that is not a cube?*

Common Misconception Listen for students who think that the edge length of a cube can be found by dividing its volume by 3. As students share their strategies, ask them to check their answer by substituting the edge length they found into the volume formula. Help students understand that dividing by 3 is not the inverse of cubing a number.

Select and Sequence Student Strategies

Select 2–3 samples that represent the range of student thinking in your classroom. Here is one possible order for class discussion:

- unit cubes used to model the box
- (misconception) volume divided by 3 to find the (incorrect) edge length
- guess and check used to test possible edge lengths
- equation written and solved

Facilitate Whole Class Discussion

Call on students to share selected strategies. Use turn and talk to help students think through their responses before sharing with the group.

Guide students to **Compare and Connect** the representations. Prompt students to connect two different strategies by explaining how each gives the same solution.

ASK *How did the strategies use the idea that the case had to be a cube?*

LISTEN FOR The 27 unit cubes were used to form a prism with all edge lengths the same. The idea that the volume of a cube with edge length s is s^3 was used to guess and check possible edge lengths or to write an equation.

Model It

If students presented these models, have students connect these models to those presented in class.

If no student presented at least one of these models, have students first analyze key features of the models, and then connect them to the models presented in class.

ASK *How are the two Model Its related?*

LISTEN FOR The first one writes an equation and shows the solution using the cube root symbol. The second uses a table of perfect cubes to find the cube root.

For the equation, prompt students to recognize how the symbol for cube root differs from the symbol for square root.

- *How is the cube root symbol the same as the square root symbol? How is it different?*
- *How do you determine the cube root of a number?*

For the table, prompt students to note how the table shows each whole number and its cube. Ask: *How can you use this table to find the cube root of a perfect cube?*

Explore different ways to find a cube root to solve a problem.

Carolina works at a museum. She is looking online for a storage case for some large fossils. She wants the case to have a volume of 27 ft^3. Carolina would like the case to be a cube. What edge length should the case have?

Model It

You can write and solve an equation.

The volume, V, of a cube with edge length, s, is given by $V = s^3$.

Substitute 27 for V in the equation.

$27 = s^3$

Take the cube root of both sides of the equation. The **cube root of x** is the number that when cubed, or raised to the third power, is equal to x.

The symbol for cube root is $\sqrt[3]{}$.

$\sqrt[3]{27} = s$

Model It

You can check a list of perfect cubes to try to find the value of s.

A **perfect cube** is the product when an integer is used as a factor three times.

Look for 27 in a table of perfect cubes.

s	1	2	3	4	5	6	7	8	9
s^3	1	8	27	64	125	216	343	512	729

DIFFERENTIATION | EXTEND

SMP 7

Deepen Understanding

Making Use of the Structure in the Perfect Cube Table

Prompt students to think about how doubling or tripling a number affects its cube.

ASK *In the table, compare the s^3 values for s values of 2 and 4 and for s values of 3 and 6. Make a conjecture for how the value of s^3 changes when the value of s doubles.*

LISTEN FOR s^3 is 8 when $s = 2$ and 64 when $s = 4$. s^3 is 27 when $s = 3$ and 216 when $s = 6$. The s^3 value is multiplied by 8 when s is doubled.

ASK *Test your conjecture using the s values 4 and 8.*

LISTEN FOR s^3 is 64 when $s = 4$ and 512 when $s = 8$, and $512 = 8 \cdot 64$.

ASK *How can you show that when any number n is doubled, its cube is multiplied by 8?*

LISTEN FOR Cube the expression $2n$: $(2n)^3 = 2^3 \cdot n^3 = 8 \cdot n^3$, so $2n^3$ is 8 times n^3.

If time allows, ask students to consider how the value of s^3 changes when the value of s is tripled. They can start by comparing the s^3 values for $s = 1$ and $s = 3$ and for $s = 2$ and $s = 6$. They should find that tripling the value of s multiplies the value of s^3 by 3^3, or 27.

Develop Finding a Cube Root to Solve Problems

CONNECT IT

SMP 2, 4, 5, 6

Remind students that the quantities and the relationships between them are the same in each representation. Explain that they will now use those representations to reason about how to find a cube root.

Before students begin to record and expand on their work in Model It, tell them that problems 1 and 4 will prepare them to provide the explanation asked for in problem 5.

Monitor and Confirm Understanding 1 – 3

- To solve the equation, an operation must be used to isolate *s*. To undo the process of cubing a number, find the cube root.
- The table shows that the cube of 3 is 27, so 3 ft is the edge length of a box with volume 27 ft^3.
- Because the product of three negative factors is negative, the cube of a negative number must be negative. So, it is not possible for a positive number to have a negative cube root.

Facilitate Whole Class Discussion

4 Students should realize that 50 is not a perfect cube, so the edge length of the cube cannot be an integer.

ASK *What do you do if the number you are taking the cube root of is not a perfect cube?*

LISTEN FOR Write the answer using the cube root symbol or estimate the answer.

5 Look for understanding of what to do when solving an equation leads to an equation of the form $x^3 = a$.

ASK *When a solution leads to an equation that shows a variable cubed equal to a number, what should the next step be? How many solutions will the equation have?*

LISTEN FOR Take the cube root of both sides of the equation. If the cube root of the number is a perfect cube, write the solution as an integer. If it is not, write it with a cube root symbol. There will be one solution.

6 **Reflect** Have all students focus on the strategies used to solve the Try It. If time allows, have students discuss their ideas with a partner.

CONNECT IT

➤ **Use the problem from the previous page to help you understand how to find a cube root to solve a problem.**

1 Look at the steps taken to solve the equation in the first **Model It**. Why do you take the cube root of both sides of the equation?
The variable is cubed. To find the value of the variable, you do the inverse of cubing the variable; you take the cube root of both sides of the equation.

2 Look at the table in the second **Model It**. What edge length should the case have? 3 ft

3 In the first **Model It**, the ± symbol was not used when taking the cube root of both sides of the equation. How do you know that *s* must be positive even before you realize that a negative edge length does not make sense?
Possible answer: If *s* is −3, then $(-3)(-3)(-3) = -27$, not 27. Three negative factors will always give you a negative product, so the cube root of a positive number must always be positive.

4 Suppose Carolina wants a box with a volume of 50 ft^3. How would you write the edge length of the box? Why?
The edge length would be $\sqrt[3]{50}$ ft. Since 50 does not appear in a table of perfect cubes, you cannot write the answer as an integer.

5 How do you solve an equation of the form $x^3 = a$?
Possible answer: You solve the equation by taking the cube root of both sides of the equation to get $x = \sqrt[3]{a}$. Write the answer as an integer if *a* is a perfect cube.

6 **Reflect** Think about all the models and strategies you have discussed today. Describe how one of them helped you better understand how to find a cube root to solve a problem.
Responses will vary. Check student responses.

571

DIFFERENTIATION | RETEACH or REINFORCE

Hands-On Activity

Build with cubes to find perfect cubes.

If students are unsure about the relationship between cube roots and perfect cubes, then use this activity to reinforce this relationship.

Materials For each group: 125 unit cubes

- Make a table with columns labeled *Number, Rectangular Prism(s),* and *Cube(s).*
- Write 8, 12, 25, 27, and 64 in the first column.
- Have students try to build rectangular prisms or cubes with each number of unit cubes from the list. Have them record the dimensions of all of the rectangular prisms and cubes they are able to build for each number in the table.
- Have students discuss their findings. Remind them that for numbers that have many factors (such as 12), there may be more than one possible rectangular prism.
- Ask: *Which numbers are perfect cubes? Why?* [8, 27, and 64; These numbers can form cubes. Also, $2^3 = 8$, $3^3 = 27$, and $4^3 = 64$.]
- If time allows, repeat the activity using the numbers 24, 36, 81, and 125.

Apply It

For all problems, encourage students to use a model to support their thinking.

7 Students may make a list of whole numbers and their cubes or refer to the table in the second Model It to find that the cube root of 8 is 2 and the cube root of 27 is 3, so $\frac{2}{3}$ is the cube root of the fraction.

8 **D is correct.** Students may refer to a table of whole numbers and their cubes, locate 216 among the perfect cubes, and note that its cube root, 6, is within the required range.

A is not correct. This answer may have resulted from thinking that the cube of the number, 8, rather than its cube root, should be within the required range.

B is not correct. This answer may have resulted from thinking that the number, 8, rather than its cube root, should be within the required range.

C is not correct. This answer may have resulted from incorrectly attempting to find the cube root of the number by dividing by 3.

Apply It

➤ **Use what you learned to solve these problems.**

7 What is the solution of the equation $m^3 = \frac{8}{27}$? Show your work.

Possible work: $m^3 = \frac{8}{27}$

$m = \sqrt[3]{\frac{8}{27}}$

$\frac{2}{3} \cdot \frac{2}{3} \cdot \frac{2}{3} = \frac{8}{27}$, so $\sqrt[3]{\frac{8}{27}} = \frac{2}{3}$.

SOLUTION $\frac{2}{3}$

8 For which value of x is $5 < \sqrt[3]{x} < 10$?

A 2

B 8

C 27

(D) 216

9 The equation $P^3 = 64V$ represents the perimeter, P, of one face of a cube with volume, V. A sculpture in the shape of a cube has a volume of 3 m³. What is the perimeter of one face of the cube? Show your work.

Possible work:

$V = 3$

$P^3 = 64(3)$

$P^3 = 192$

$P = \sqrt[3]{192}$

192 is not in a table of perfect cubes.

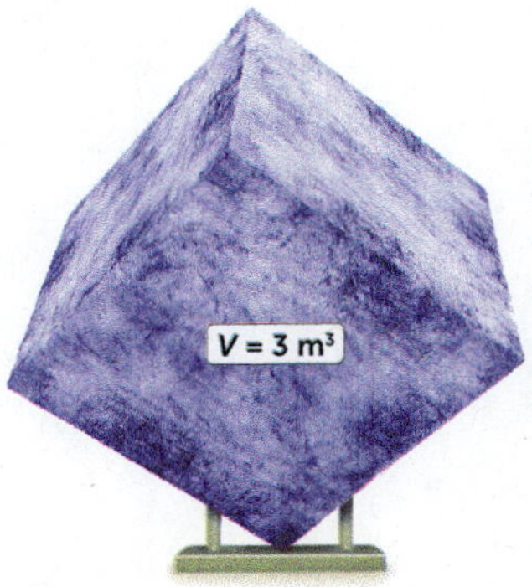

SOLUTION The perimeter of one face is $\sqrt[3]{192}$ m.

CLOSE **EXIT TICKET**

9 Students' solutions should show an understanding of:

- solving an equation of the form $x^3 = a$ by taking the cube root of both sides of the equation.
- the fact that not all numbers are perfect cubes, so it may be necessary to write an answer with a cube root symbol.
- interpreting the solution of an equation in the context of a problem.

Error Alert If students disregard the variable V in the equation and state the solution is $P = \sqrt[3]{64}$, or 4, then ask them to look back at the equation and explain how they accounted for the volume, V, in their solution.

Practice Finding a Cube Root to Solve Problems

Problem Notes

Assign **Practice Finding a Cube Root to Solve Problems** as extra practice in class or as homework.

1. Students may say that because there is no integer that can be cubed to get 344, the cube root of 344 is not an integer. So, the solution should be written with a cube root symbol. ***Medium***

2. Students may use the definition of cube root and reason that since cubing $\frac{6}{5}$ equals $\frac{216}{125}$, the cube root of $\frac{216}{125}$ is $\frac{6}{5}$. ***Medium***

LESSON 23 | SESSION 3 Name:

Practice Finding a Cube Root to Solve Problems

➤ **Study the Example showing how to find a cube root to solve a problem. Then solve problems 1–5.**

Example

What is the solution of the equation $x^3 = 343$?

Take the cube root of both sides of the equation.

$x^3 = 343$

$x = \sqrt[3]{343}$

Look for 343 in a table of perfect cubes.

x	1	2	3	4	5	6	7	8	9
x^3	1	8	27	64	125	216	343	512	729

The cube root of 343 is 7.

The solution of the equation is $x = 7$.

1. Suppose the equation in the Example was $x^3 = 344$. How would the solution be different? Explain.

   The solution would be $x = \sqrt[3]{344}$. Possible explanation: When you take the cube root of both sides of the equation, you get $x = \sqrt[3]{344}$. Since 344 is not in the table of perfect cubes, you cannot write the answer as an integer.

2. Tyler knows that $\frac{6}{5} \cdot \frac{6}{5} \cdot \frac{6}{5} = \frac{216}{125}$. Explain how he can use this to find the solution of the equation $c^3 = \frac{216}{125}$.

   Possible explanation: To solve $c^3 = \frac{216}{125}$, take the cube root of both sides of the equation. This gives you $c = \sqrt[3]{\frac{216}{125}}$. Since $\frac{6}{5} \cdot \frac{6}{5} \cdot \frac{6}{5} = \frac{216}{125}$, you know that $\sqrt[3]{\frac{216}{125}} = \frac{6}{5}$. So, $c = \frac{6}{5}$.

Vocabulary

cube root of *x*
the number that when cubed is equal to *x*.

perfect cube
the product when an integer is used as a factor three times.

Fluency & Skills Practice

Finding a Cube Root to Solve Problems

In this activity, students solve equations in the form $x^3 = p$ and $x^3 + b = p$ by finding the cube root.

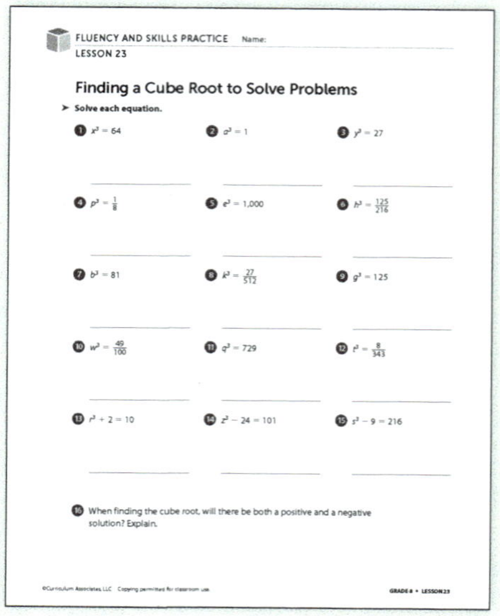
FLUENCY AND SKILLS PRACTICE Name:
LESSON 23

Finding a Cube Root to Solve Problems

➤ **Solve each equation.**

1. $x^3 = 64$
2. $a^3 = 1$
3. $y^3 = 27$
4. $p^3 = \frac{1}{8}$
5. $e^3 = 1{,}000$
6. $h^3 = \frac{125}{216}$
7. $b^3 = 81$
8. $k^3 = \frac{27}{512}$
9. $g^3 = 125$
10. $w^3 = \frac{49}{100}$
11. $q^3 = 729$
12. $t^3 = \frac{8}{343}$
13. $r^3 + 2 = 10$
14. $z^3 - 24 = 101$
15. $s^3 - 9 = 216$
16. When finding the cube root, will there be both a positive and a negative solution? Explain.

©Curriculum Associates, LLC Copying permitted for classroom use. GRADE 8 • LESSON 23

Additional Practice

3 Students may use guess and check until they arrive at $9^3 = 729$. ***Medium***

4 Students may reason that, just as when they solved linear equations in one variable, they should isolate the variable term on one side of the equation. Then, they can take the cube root of both sides of the equation. ***Challenge***

5 ***Basic***

LESSON 23 | SESSION 3

3 In 2018, there were z zebra mussels in a section of a river. In 2019, there were z^3 zebra mussels in that same section. There were 729 zebra mussels in 2019. How many zebra mussels were there in 2018? Show your work.

Possible work:

$z^3 = 729$

$z = \sqrt[3]{729}$

729 is a perfect cube since $9^3 = 729$.

zebra mussel

SOLUTION There were 9 zebra mussels in 2018.

4 What is the solution of the equation $y^3 + 15 = 140$? Show your work.

Possible work:

$y^3 + 15 = 140$

$y^3 + 15 - 15 = 140 - 15$

$y^3 = 125$

$y = \sqrt[3]{125}$

Since $5^3 = 125$, $y = 5$.

SOLUTION 5

5 Complete the following.

$\sqrt{0} =$ 0 $\qquad \sqrt{1} =$ 1

$\sqrt[3]{0} =$ 0 $\qquad \sqrt[3]{1} =$ 1

574

DIFFERENTIATION | ENGLISH LANGUAGE LEARNERS

Use with **Session 4** Apply It

MATH TERM

A *face* is a flat surface of a solid shape.

ACADEMIC VOCABULARY

Except for means *not including.* *Except for* is used to identify things not included in a group.

Levels 1–3: Reading/Speaking

Support Apply It problem 4 using **Act It Out** with geometric solids. Read the problem as students follow along. Have students circle *cube, volume, face, bottom,* and *area.* Ask students to use the solids to tell what they know about cubes, volume, and area. Define *face* for students. Guide students to count the faces of solids and identify the bottom. Ask students to count the faces without the bottom.

Reread the problem with students. Have them use *cube, volume, face, bottom,* and *area* to tell what they know and what they need to find out.

Levels 2–4: Reading/Speaking

Help students prepare for Apply It problem 4 by previewing the problem using a **Co-Constructed Word Bank.** As students review the words they identified, guide them to discuss multi-meaning words, related words, and word parts. For example, *face* can be a noun or verb and has different meanings in math and everyday language. *Except* has the prefix *ex-*, meaning *out*, and is related to the word *exception.*

Use **Three Reads** to help students read and interpret the problem. Encourage students to use terms from the Word Bank as they discuss the problem.

Levels 3–5: Reading/Speaking

Support Apply It problem 4 using an adaptation of **Three Reads.** Display the questions for each read and have students identify the sentence(s) in the problem that will help them answer the questions. Then have students use a **Co-Constructed Word Bank** to identify and discuss key terms in the sentences. For example:

- **Read 1:** sentence 1: *candle, cube*
- **Read 2:** sentence 4: *area*
- **Read 3:** sentences 2–3: *volume, each face, except for the bottom*

Have partners discuss the problem before writing their responses.

Refine Finding Square Roots and Cube Roots to Solve Problems

Purpose

- **Refine** strategies for finding square roots and cube roots.
- **Refine** understanding of how to find square roots and cube roots of fractions with numerators and denominators that are perfect squares or perfect cubes.

START CHECK FOR UNDERSTANDING

Solve the equation for x.
$x^3 = 216$

Solution

$x = 6$

WHY? Confirm students' understanding of finding a cube root to solve an equation, identifying common errors to address as needed.

MONITOR & GUIDE

Before students begin to work, use their responses to the **Start** to determine those who will benefit from additional support. Use the **Error Analysis** table below to guide remediation.

Have all students complete the Example and problems 1–3, using Consider This and Pair/Share as appropriate. Observe and monitor their reasoning and guide or redirect students as needed.

LESSON 23 | SESSION 4

Refine Finding Square Roots and Cube Roots to Solve Problems

➤ **Complete the Example below. Then solve problems 1–9.**

Example

The expression $4\sqrt{2}$ means $4 \cdot \sqrt{2}$. Use this information to write $(4\sqrt{2})^2$ without using a square root symbol.

Look at how you could use what you know about squares and square roots to rewrite the expression.

An expression squared means that the expression is multiplied by itself.

$$(4\sqrt{2})^2 = (4 \cdot \sqrt{2})(4 \cdot \sqrt{2})$$
$$= 4 \cdot 4 \cdot \sqrt{2} \cdot \sqrt{2}$$
$$= 16 \cdot 2$$

SOLUTION 32

CONSIDER THIS . . . The commutative and associative properties say that you can change the order and the grouping of the factors in a product.

PAIR/SHARE How do you know that your answer makes sense?

Apply It

1 A square window has an area of $\frac{16}{25}$ m^2. What is the perimeter of the window? Show your work.

Possible work:

Use s for the length of a side of the square window.

$$A = s^2$$
$$\frac{16}{25} = s^2$$
$$\pm\sqrt{\frac{16}{25}} = s$$

The side length is positive, so $s = \frac{4}{5}$.

$P = 4s = 4\left(\frac{4}{5}\right)$, or $\frac{16}{5}$

SOLUTION The perimeter of the window is $\frac{16}{5}$ m.

CONSIDER THIS . . . The perimeter of a square is 4 times the length of a side.

PAIR/SHARE What is a different way that you could solve the problem?

575

START ERROR ANALYSIS

If the error is . . .	Students may . . .	To support understanding . . .
$x = 72$	have divided 216 by 3 instead of taking the cube root.	Prompt students to check a list of perfect cubes to try to find the value of x.
$x = -6$ and 6	have thought that there are two solutions since the equation $x^2 = 216$ has two solutions.	Prompt students to check their solution by substituting the solution back in the original equation. They should see that -6 cubed equals -216, not 216.
$x = \sqrt{216}$	have taken the square root of 216 instead of the cube root.	Ask students how to isolate the variable x on one side of the equation. Elicit that they can solve the equation by taking the cube root of each side of the equation because the inverse of cubing a value is taking the cube root.

Example

Guide students in understanding the Example. Ask:

- *How can you use the definition of the square of a number to write $(4\sqrt{2})^2$ as a product of two factors?*
- *Can you multiply numbers in any order?*
- *What do you get when you square the square root of a number?*

Help all students focus on the Example and responses to the questions by asking them to provide reasons to explain how they know their solutions are correct.

Look for understanding that the result of squaring the square root of a number is that number. Also, look for understanding that when a product is squared, each factor in the expression is squared.

Apply It

1 Students should recall that the area of a square is given by $A = s^2$, and the perimeter of a square is given by $P = 4s$. To find the side length of the window, students may find the square root of $\frac{16}{25}$. Then they may use the formula for the perimeter of a square to find the perimeter of the window. *DOK 2*

2 Students may rewrite the expression as a product of three factors of $5 \cdot \sqrt[3]{3}$ and then group the three factors of 5 together and the three factors of $\sqrt[3]{3}$ together. Students should recognize that because the cube root of 3 is the number you multiply by itself 3 times to get 3, $\sqrt[3]{3} \cdot \sqrt[3]{3} \cdot \sqrt[3]{3}$ is equal to 3. *DOK 2*

3 **C is correct.** Students may solve the equation by taking the cube root of both sides of the equation.

A is not correct. This answer is the result of solving $x^2 = \frac{1}{64}$ without considering the negative root.

B is not correct. This answer is the result of solving $x^2 = \frac{1}{64}$.

D is not correct. This answer incorrectly includes the negative cube root as a solution.

DOK 3

LESSON 23 | SESSION 4

2 Write $(5\sqrt[3]{3})^3$ without using a cube root symbol. Show your work.

Possible work:

$(5\sqrt[3]{3})^3 = (5 \cdot \sqrt[3]{3})(5 \cdot \sqrt[3]{3})(5 \cdot \sqrt[3]{3})$

$= 5 \cdot 5 \cdot 5 \cdot \sqrt[3]{3} \cdot \sqrt[3]{3} \cdot \sqrt[3]{3}$

$= 125 \cdot 3$

$= 375$

CONSIDER THIS . . .
Note that $\sqrt[3]{3} \cdot \sqrt[3]{3} \cdot \sqrt[3]{3} = 3$.

PAIR/SHARE
How do you know the answer has to be greater than 125?

SOLUTION 375

3 What are all the solutions of the equation $x^3 = \frac{1}{64}$?

A $x = \frac{1}{8}$

B $x = \pm\frac{1}{8}$

C $x = \frac{1}{4}$

D $x = \pm\frac{1}{4}$

Magdalena chose B as the correct answer. How might she have gotten that answer?

Possible answer: Magdalena may have solved the equation $x^2 = \frac{1}{64}$ instead of the given equation.

CONSIDER THIS . . .
You can test a solution by substituting the value for the variable in the equation. Then check whether the equation results in a true statement.

PAIR/SHARE
How can you eliminate some answer choices without calculating?

576

GROUP & DIFFERENTIATE

Identify groupings for differentiation based on the **Start** and problems 1–3. A recommended sequence of activities for each group is suggested below. Use the resources on the next page to differentiate and close the lesson.

Approaching Proficiency

- **RETEACH** Hands-On Activity
- **REINFORCE** Problems 5, 6

Meeting Proficiency

- **REINFORCE** Problems 4–8

Extending Beyond Proficiency

- **REINFORCE** Problems 4–8
- **EXTEND** Challenge

Have all students complete the **Close: Exit Ticket.**

Resources for Differentiation are found on the next page.

Refine Finding Square Roots and Cube Roots to Solve Problems

Apply It

4 See ***Connect to Culture*** to support student engagement. Students should recall that the volume of a cube is $V = s^3$, and the area of a square is $A = s^2$. Students may write and solve an equation using the formula for volume of a cube to find the edge length of the candle, and then use the formula for the area of a square to find the area of each face of the candle. Because 5 faces will be painted, they should multiply the area by 5. ***DOK 3***

5 Students may cube the values in each answer choice to check if the result is 250.

B is correct.
$(\sqrt[3]{250})^3 = \sqrt[3]{250} \cdot \sqrt[3]{250} \cdot \sqrt[3]{250} = 250$

C is correct. $(5\sqrt[3]{2})^3 = 5\sqrt[3]{2} \cdot 5\sqrt[3]{2} \cdot 5\sqrt[3]{2} =$
$5 \cdot 5 \cdot 5 \cdot \sqrt[3]{2} \cdot \sqrt[3]{2} \cdot \sqrt[3]{2} = 125 \cdot 2 = 250$

A is not correct. Cubing this answer gives −250.

D is not correct. Cubing this answer gives −250.

E is not correct. Cubing this answer gives 1,250.

F is not correct. Cubing this answer gives −1,250.

DOK 2

6 Students may substitute each *y*-value into each equation to check if it is a solution. If the *y*-value does not make either equation true, then it is not a solution to either equation. ***DOK 1***

---

4 Manuel makes a candle in the shape of a cube. The candle has a volume of $\frac{8}{125}$ ft³. Manuel wants to paint each face of the candle, except for the bottom. What is the area he will paint? Show your work.

Possible work: Use *e* for the length of an edge of the candle.

$V = e^3$

$\frac{8}{125} = e^3$

$\sqrt[3]{\frac{8}{125}} = e$

So, $e = \frac{2}{5}$ and the area of each face is $\left(\frac{2}{5}\right)^2$ or $\frac{4}{25}$ ft².

Manuel will paint 5 faces: $5\left(\frac{4}{25}\right) = \frac{4}{5}$.

SOLUTION The area Manuel will paint is $\frac{4}{5}$ ft².

5 Which of the following can be the value of *x* in the equation $x^3 = 250$? Select all that apply.

A $-\sqrt[3]{250}$
(B) $\sqrt[3]{250}$
(C) $5\sqrt[3]{2}$
D $-5\sqrt[3]{2}$
E $5\sqrt[3]{10}$
F $-5\sqrt[3]{10}$

6 Tell whether each value of *y* in the table is a solution of $y^2 = 18$, a solution of $y^3 = 18$, or a solution of neither equation.

	$y^2 = 18$	$y^3 = 18$	Neither
a. $y = -\sqrt{18}$	●	○	○
b. $y = \sqrt{18}$	●	○	○
c. $y = -\sqrt[3]{18}$	○	○	●
d. $y = \sqrt[3]{18}$	○	●	○

577

DIFFERENTIATION

RETEACH

Hands-On Activity

Use the volume of a cube to find the cube root of a number.

Students approaching proficiency with finding cube roots will benefit from building models to find the relationship between the edge length and volume of a cube.

Materials For each pair: 64 unit cubes

- Remind students that *volume* is computed with three dimensions: length, width, and height. Explain that the length, width, and height of a cube are the same. Similarly, a cubed number has three identical factors.
- Have pairs count out 8 unit cubes. Ask them to build a cube with the unit cubes. Ask: *What is the volume of the cube?* [8 cubic units] *What is the edge length of the cube?* [2 units] *What is the cube root of 8?* [2] *What is 2 cubed?* [8]
- Next have pairs count out 27 units cubes and use them to build a cube. Ask: *What is the volume of the cube?* [27 cubic units] *What is the edge length of the cube?* [3 units] *What is the cube root of 27?* [3] *What is 3 cubed?* [27]
- Have pairs count out 64 unit cubes and use them to build a cube. Ask: *What is the volume of the cube?* [64 cubic units] *What is the edge length of the cube?* [4 units] *What is the cube root of 64?* [4] *What is 4 cubed?* [64]
- Ask: *How are the volume and edge length of a cube related to cubes and cube roots?* [The edge length of a cube is the cube root of the volume. The volume of a cube is the cube of its edge length.]

7 The area of a rectangle is $A = \ell \times w$. Students may use guess and check to find the length of the square rug. *DOK 3*

8 To solve the equation $x^3 = 25$, students should take the cube root of both sides of the equation to get $x = \sqrt[3]{25}$. Because 25 is not a perfect cube, the solution is written with the cube root symbol. *DOK 3*

CLOSE **EXIT TICKET**

9 **Math Journal** Look for understanding that to solve $x^2 = p$, you take the square root of both sides of the equation and get two solutions, and to solve $x^3 = p$, you take the cube root of both sides of the equation and get one solution.

Error Alert If students give the positive square root as the only solution to the square equation or give both a positive and negative solution to the cube equation, then encourage them to substitute their answers into the original equation to check.

End of Lesson Checklist

INTERACTIVE GLOSSARY Support students by suggesting they draw a square, labeling the side length with an integer. Then have them find its area. The side length is the *square root of* the area.

SELF CHECK Have students review and check off any new skills on the Unit 6 Opener.

7 The area of a square rug is the same as the area of a rectangular rug that is 9 ft long and 4 ft wide. Write and solve an equation to find the side length of the square rug. Show your work.

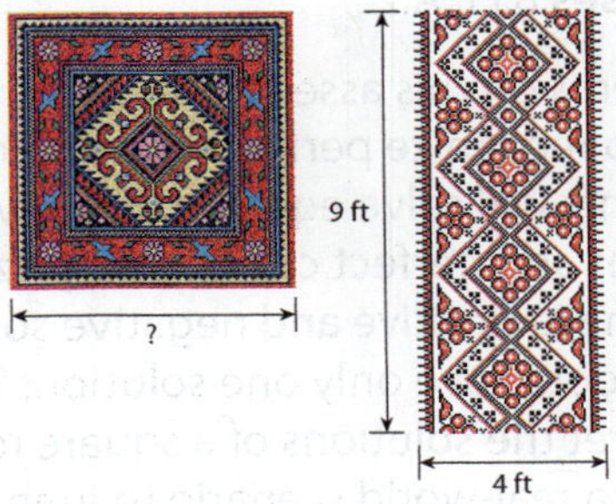

Possible work:

The area of the rectangular rug is $A = (9)(4) = 36$; 36 ft^2.

Use s for the side length of the square rug.

$s^2 = 36$

$s = \pm\sqrt{36}$

The length cannot be negative, so $s = \sqrt{36}$, or 6.

SOLUTION The side length of the square rug is 6 ft.

8 Lucía says that 25 is a perfect square, but not a perfect cube. She says this means the equation $x^2 = 25$ has two solutions, but the equation $x^3 = 25$ has no solutions. Do you agree? Explain.

No; Possible explanation: It is true that $x^2 = 25$ has two solutions, $x = 5$ and $x = -5$, but $x^3 = 25$ also has a solution. The solution is $x = \sqrt[3]{25}$.

9 **Math Journal** Choose a two-digit number, p. Write the equations $x^2 = p$ and $x^3 = p$. Explain how to solve the two equations you wrote.

Possible answer: I chose $p = 45$. The equations are $x^2 = 45$ and $x^3 = 45$. Solve the equation $x^2 = 45$ by taking the square root of both sides of the equation. There are two solutions, $x = \pm\sqrt{45}$. Solve the equation $x^3 = 45$ by taking the cube root of both sides of the equation. There is one solution, $x = \sqrt[3]{45}$.

End of Lesson Checklist

- [ ] **INTERACTIVE GLOSSARY** Find the entry for *square root of x*. Write a definition for a younger student. Show an example.
- [ ] **SELF CHECK** Go back to the Unit 6 Opener and see what you can check off.

578

REINFORCE

Problems 4–8

Solve square root and cube root problems.

Students meeting proficiency will benefit from additional work with square roots and cube roots by solving problems in a variety of formats.

- Have students work on their own or with a partner to solve the problems.
- Encourage students to show their work.

EXTEND

Challenge

Find numbers that are both perfect squares and perfect cubes.

Students extending beyond proficiency will benefit from finding numbers that are both perfect squares and perfect cubes.

- Have students work with a partner to solve this problem: *Find three numbers that are both perfect squares and perfect cubes.*
- Some students may use a list of perfect squares and a list of perfect cubes to identify one number in both lists. They may then look for a pattern in the factors that they can use to identify other perfect squares and perfect cubes.

PERSONALIZE

i-Ready

Provide students with opportunities to work on their personalized instruction path with *i-Ready* Online Instruction to:

- fill prerequisite gaps.
- build up grade-level skills.

Lesson Quiz

TESTED SKILLS

Assesses 8.EE.A.2

Problems on this assessment require students to be able to recognize perfect squares and perfect cubes. Students will solve equations involving perfect squares and perfect cubes, recognizing that square roots have positive and negative solutions while cube roots have only one solution. Students interpret the solutions of a square root equation within a real-world scenario to identify reasonable solutions. Students will also need to be familiar with exponents and using properties of equality to simplify expressions and solve equations.

Alternately, teachers may assign the **Digital Comprehension Check** online to assess student understanding of this material.

Error Alert Errors may result if students:

- model a real-world application with an incorrect equation.
- confuse square roots and cube roots.
- believe the cube root of a number will have both a negative and a positive solution.
- forget the negative square root.

Problem Notes

1 Students could solve the problem by setting x^3 equal to 512 and then recognizing that 512 is a perfect cube with a root of 8.

(2 points)

DOK 2 | **8.EE.A.2**

2 Students could solve the problem by taking the square root of the numerator and the denominator.

(2 points)

DOK 1 | **8.EE.A.2**

LESSON 23 • QUIZ | Name:

➤ Solve the problems.

1 In 2016, a school started its own aquarium with x fish. In 2019, there were x^3 fish in the same aquarium. There were 512 fish in 2019. How many fish were there in 2016? Show your work. *(2 points)*

Possible student work:

$x^3 = 512$

$x = \sqrt[3]{512}$ 512 is a perfect cube since $8^3 = 512$.

SOLUTION 8 fish

2 What are all the solutions of the equation $p^2 = \frac{9}{36}$? Show your work. *(2 points)*

Possible student work:

$p^2 = \frac{9}{36}$

$p = \pm\sqrt{\frac{9}{36}}$

$p = \pm\frac{3}{6}$

$p = \pm\frac{1}{2}$

SOLUTION $p = \pm\frac{3}{6}$ or $p = \pm\frac{1}{2}$

3 Which of the following could be the value of x in the equation $x^3 - 9 = 55$? Choose all the correct answers. *(2 points)*

A −8

B −4

C $\sqrt{64}$

(D) $\sqrt[3]{64}$

(E) 4

F 8

Choice Matrix and Multiple Select Scoring Rubric

Points	Expectations
2	All answers are correct
1	1 incorrect answer
0	2 or more incorrect answers

Short Response Scoring Rubric

Points	Expectations
2	Response has the correct solution(s) and includes well-organized, clear, and concise work demonstrating thorough understanding of mathematical concepts and/or procedures.
1	Response contains mostly correct solution(s) and shows partial understanding of mathematical concepts and/or procedures.
0	Response shows no attempt at finding a solution and no effort to demonstrate an understanding of mathematical concepts and/or procedures.

3 **D, E are correct.** Students could solve the problem by using the properties of equality to find the cube root of 64.

A is not correct. This answer is the result of finding the negative square root of 64.

B is not correct. This answer is the result of thinking that 64 has a negative cube root.

C is not correct. This answer is the result of confusing square roots and cube roots.

F is not correct. This answer is the result of finding the positive square root of 64.

(2 points)

DOK 2 | 8.EE.A.2

4 Students could also solve the problem by checking a list of perfect squares to determine that the square root of 100 is ± 10. Then they should recognize that the side length of the garden must be positive.

(2 points)

DOK 1 | 8.EE.A.2

5 **a.** The value $y = -\sqrt[3]{27}$ is a solution of $y^3 = -27$, not $y^3 = 27$.

b. The value $y = 9$ is not a solution of either equation because $9^2 = 81$ and $9^3 = 729$.

c. The value $y = -3\sqrt{3}$ is a solution of $y^2 = 27$ because $(-3\sqrt{3})^2 = 9 \cdot 3 = 27$.

d. The value $y = 3$ is a solution of $y^3 = 27$ because $3^3 = 27$.

(2 points)

DOK 2 | 8.EE.A.2

LESSON 23 • QUIZ Name:

4 A square garden has an area of 100 ft². What is the perimeter of the garden? Show your work. *(2 points)*

Possible student work:

Use s for the length of a side of the square garden.

$A = s^2$

$100 = s^2$

$\pm\sqrt{100} = s$

$\pm 10 = s$

The side length is positive, so $s = 10$.

$P = 4s = 4(10)$, or 40

SOLUTION The perimeter of the garden is 40 ft.

5 Determine whether each value of y in the table is a solution of $y^2 = 27$, is a solution of $y^3 = 27$, or is a solution of neither equation.

Choose *Solution of $y^2 = 27$*, *Solution of $y^3 = 27$*, or *Solution of Neither Equation*. *(2 points)*

	Solution of $y^2 = 27$	Solution of $y^3 = 27$	Solution of Neither Equation
a. $y = -\sqrt[3]{27}$	○	○	●
b. $y = 9$	○	○	●
c. $y = -3\sqrt{3}$	●	○	○
d. $y = 3$	○	●	○

DIFFERENTIATION

RETEACH Tools for Instruction

Students who require additional support for prerequisite or on-level skills will benefit from activities that provide targeted skills instruction.

GRADE 8

- **Lesson 23** Solve Equations Using Square and Cube Roots

REINFORCE Math Center Activity

Students who require practice to reinforce concepts and skills and deepen understanding will benefit from small group collaborative games and activities (available in on-level, below-level, and above-level versions).

GRADE 8

- **Lesson 23** Four Square Roots and Cube Roots in a Row

EXTEND Enrichment Activity

Students who have achieved proficiency with concepts and skills and are ready for additional challenges will benefit from group collaborative games and activities that extend understanding.

GRADE 8

- **Lesson 23** The Root of It

Overview | Express Rational Numbers as Fractions and Decimals

MATH FOCUS

Focus Standard

8.NS.A.1 Know that numbers that are not rational are called irrational. Understand informally that every number has a decimal expansion; for rational numbers show that the decimal expansion repeats eventually, and convert a decimal expansion which repeats eventually into a rational number.

See Unit 6 Overview for developing and applied standards.

STANDARDS FOR MATHEMATICAL PRACTICE (SMP)

SMP 1, 2, 3, 4, 5, and 6 are integrated into the Try-Discuss-Connect routine.*

This lesson provides additional support for:

7 Look for and make use of structure.

8 Look for and express regularity in repeated reasoning.

* See page 1o to learn how every lesson includes these SMP.

Objectives

Content Objectives

- Understand that every rational number has a decimal expansion.
- Recognize that the decimal expansion of a rational number repeats eventually.
- Write a repeating decimal as a fraction.

Language Objectives

- Explain why a decimal expansion is a rational number using the definition of *rational number* in writing.
- Demonstrate understanding of the terms *rational number, repeating decimal,* and *eventually* and use them to describe the decimal expansion of a rational number.
- Ask or respond to clarifying questions about strategies for writing a repeating decimal as a fraction during partner and class discussions.
- Make connections during discussion by explaining how a problem is similar to or different from another problem.

Prior Knowledge

- Write fractions as terminating or repeating decimals.
- Write terminating decimals as fractions.
- Classify numbers as counting numbers, whole numbers, integers, and rational numbers.

Vocabulary

Math Vocabulary

There is no new vocabulary. Review the following key terms.

rational number a number that can be expressed as the fraction $\frac{a}{b}$ where a and b are integers and $b \neq 0$. Rational numbers include integers, fractions, repeating decimals, and terminating decimals.

repeating decimals decimals that repeat the same digit or sequence of digits forever. A repeating decimal can be written with a bar over the repeating digits.

terminating decimals decimals that end, or end in repeated zeros.

Academic Vocabulary

eventually at some later time.

Learning Progression

In Grade 6, students learned the meaning of *rational number*.

In Grade 7, students used long division to write a fraction as a decimal and learned that the decimal form of a rational number terminates or eventually repeats.

In this lesson, students find decimal expansions for rational numbers and recognize that every rational number has a decimal expansion that repeats eventually. They also learn strategies for writing repeating decimals as fractions.

Later in Grade 8, students will be introduced to irrational numbers. They will distinguish between rational and irrational numbers and find rational approximations for irrational numbers. Students will see that, together, rational and irrational numbers make up the set of real numbers.

Pacing Guide

Items marked with ★ are available on the **Teacher Toolbox**.

	MATERIALS	DIFFERENTIATION
SESSION 1 **Explore** Writing Fractions as Decimals (35–50 min)		
• **Start** (5 min) • **Try It** (5–10 min) • **Discuss It** (10–15 min) • **Connect It** (10–15 min) • **Close: Exit Ticket** (5 min) **Additional Practice** (pages 583–584)	**Math Toolkit** grid paper Presentation Slides ★	**PREPARE** Interactive Tutorial ★ **RETEACH or REINFORCE** Visual Model
SESSION 2 **Develop** Writing a Repeating Decimal as a Fraction (45–60 min)		
• **Start** (5 min) • **Try It** (10–15 min) • **Discuss It** (10–15 min) • **Connect It** (15–20 min) • **Close: Exit Ticket** (5 min) **Additional Practice** (pages 589–590)	**Math Toolkit** grid paper Presentation Slides ★	**RETEACH or REINFORCE** Visual Model **REINFORCE** Fluency & Skills Practice ★ **EXTEND** Deepen Understanding
SESSION 3 **Refine** Expressing Rational Numbers as Fractions and Decimals (45–60 min)		
• **Start** (5 min) • **Monitor & Guide** (15–10 min) • **Group & Differentiate** (20–30 min) • **Close: Exit Ticket** (5 min)	**Math Toolkit** Have items from previous sessions available for students. Presentation Slides ★	**RETEACH** Visual Model **REINFORCE** Problems 4–8 **EXTEND** Challenge **PERSONALIZE** i-Ready
Lesson 24 Quiz ★ or **Digital Comprehension Check**		**RETEACH** Tools for Instruction ★ **REINFORCE** Math Center Activity ★ **EXTEND** Enrichment Activity ★

Overview | Express Rational Numbers as Fractions and Decimals

Connect to Culture

➤ **Use these activities to connect with and leverage the diverse backgrounds and experiences of all students. Engage students in sharing what they know about contexts before you add the information given here.**

SESSION 1 ■ □ □

Try It Ask students to share what they know about hip-hop music. Hip hop is a style of music that dates back as far as the 1960s. However, it made a breakthrough and gained vast popularity in the 1980s and 1990s. The two most significant elements of hip hop are *turntabling* and *rhyming*. A Jamaican immigrant is credited with much of the creation of hip hop. Today, the popularity of hip hop is widespread, and there are numerous renowned hip-hop artists.

SESSION 2 ■ ■ □

Try It Many people love cheese in one form or another. Popular uses are as a slice on a burger, a shredded Italian blend atop a pizza, or a delectable liquid drizzled over nachos. However, there are some cheeses in a league of their own due to their horrendous smell. The smell of Vieux Boulogne, a soft cheese from northern France, has been compared to the odor of a pair of socks that has been worn for a month and never washed! In fact, its fragrance is so repulsive that it was banned from being brought onto the public transportation system in France. Ask students if they are familiar with other types of cheese that have a distinct smell.

SESSION 3 ■ ■ ■

Apply It **Problem 4** Ask students who have explored a cave to describe what they saw and experienced. They may have seen icicle-like formations that hang from the ceiling and mounds that grow up from the floor. The two common types of mineral formations are called stalactites and stalagmites. They are formed from water that drips from cracks in a cave over a period of many years. Stalactites hang downward from cave ceilings, while stalagmites grow upward from the cave floors.

CULTURAL CONNECTION

Alternate Notation In Mexico, repeating decimals may be written slightly differently. Instead of using a bar over the repeating digit or group of digits, an arc is used. Encourage students who have experience with this notation for repeating decimals to share what they know with the class.

$0.1212... = 0.\overline{12}$

OR

$0.1212... = 0.\overset{\frown}{12}$

Connect to Family and Community

➤ **After the Explore session, have students use the Family Letter to let their families know what they are learning and to encourage family involvement.**

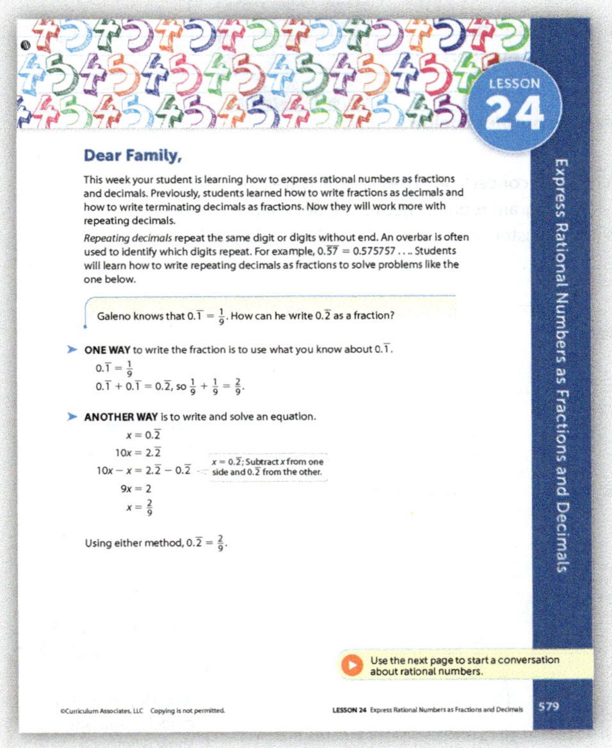

LESSON 24

Dear Family,

This week your student is learning how to express rational numbers as fractions and decimals. Previously, students learned how to write fractions as decimals and how to write terminating decimals as fractions. Now they will work more with repeating decimals.

Repeating decimals repeat the same digit or digits without end. An overbar is often used to identify which digits repeat. For example, $0.\overline{57} = 0.575757\ldots$. Students will learn how to write repeating decimals as fractions to solve problems like the one below.

Galeno knows that $0.\overline{1} = \frac{1}{9}$. How can he write $0.\overline{2}$ as a fraction?

➤ **ONE WAY** to write the fraction is to use what you know about $0.\overline{1}$.

$0.\overline{1} = \frac{1}{9}$

$0.\overline{1} + 0.\overline{1} = 0.\overline{2}$, so $\frac{1}{9} + \frac{1}{9} = \frac{2}{9}$.

➤ **ANOTHER WAY** is to write and solve an equation.

$x = 0.\overline{2}$

$10x = 2.\overline{2}$

$10x - x = 2.\overline{2} - 0.\overline{2}$ — $x = 0.\overline{2}$; Subtract x from one side and $0.\overline{2}$ from the other.

$9x = 2$

$x = \frac{2}{9}$

Using either method, $0.\overline{2} = \frac{2}{9}$.

Use the next page to start a conversation about rational numbers.

Express Rational Numbers as Fractions and Decimals

©Curriculum Associates, LLC Copying is not permitted. LESSON 24 Express Rational Numbers as Fractions and Decimals 579

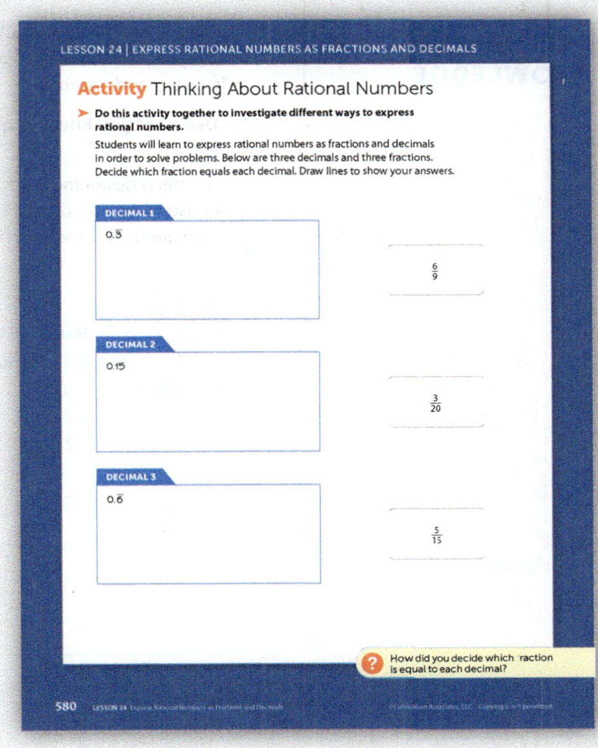

LESSON 24 | EXPRESS RATIONAL NUMBERS AS FRACTIONS AND DECIMALS

Activity Thinking About Rational Numbers

➤ **Do this activity together to investigate different ways to express rational numbers.**

Students will learn to express rational numbers as fractions and decimals in order to solve problems. Below are three decimals and three fractions. Decide which fraction equals each decimal. Draw lines to show your answers.

DECIMAL 1: $0.\overline{3}$ — $\frac{6}{9}$

DECIMAL 2: 0.15 — $\frac{3}{20}$

DECIMAL 3: $0.\overline{6}$ — $\frac{5}{15}$

How did you decide which raction is equal to each decimal?

580

Connect to Language

➤ **For English language learners, use the Differentiation chart to scaffold the language in each session. Use the Academic Vocabulary routine for academic terms before Session 1.**

DIFFERENTIATION | ENGLISH LANGUAGE LEARNERS — Use with **Session 1** **Connect It**

Levels 1–3: Reading/Writing

Help students read Connect It problem 2 and make sense of *repeating, repeat, terminating, terminate, fraction,* and *decimal.* If appropriate, ask students to identify the Spanish cognates *repetir, terminar, fracción,* and *decimal.* Guide students to identify the base words of *terminating* and *repeating.* Ask students to identify rational numbers using *fraction, decimal, terminating,* and *repeating.* Then use **Act It Out** to show the meaning of problem 2a sentence 2 and label *remainder* and *quotient*.

Next, help students write responses for problem 2b using:

- *A terminating decimal can be a* ____ *decimal.*
- *The digit* ____ *can repeat again and again.*

Levels 2–4: Reading/Writing

Help students read Connect It problem 2. Use a **Co-Constructed Word Bank**. If needed, suggest *without, remainders, repeat, repeating, terminating, recall, quotient*. Ask for models or examples to show the meaning of math terms. Explain that the prefix *re-* means again or back. Ask for words with *re-* and help students use the prefix to talk about the meanings of *repeat* and *recall*. Ask students to sort and discuss terms with the other word parts, like the ending *-ing*.

Next, help students write responses for problem 2b. Ask partners to discuss ways that repeating and terminating decimals are the same or different and write responses using:

- *I know repeating decimals* ____.
- *A terminating decimal can repeat* ____.

Levels 3–5: Reading/Writing

Help students read Connect It problem 2 by supporting their understanding of precise mathematical language, like *terminating* and *repeating*. Encourage students to use their knowledge of base words and word parts to make sense of the terms. Provide time for students to think about the similarities and differences between the types of decimals. Encourage them to identify other math terms they can use to describe and compare them. Then have students turn and talk with partners.

Have students prepare explanations for problem 2b. Reinforce that a clear explanation provides reasons using precise language. Have students write responses and compare answers with partners.

Explore Writing Fractions as Decimals

Purpose

- **Explore** the idea that every fraction can be written as a decimal using the division algorithm.
- **Understand** that the decimal expansion for every fraction eventually repeats.

START CONNECT TO PRIOR KNOWLEDGE

Same and Different

A: $\frac{1}{3}$	B: $\frac{6}{8}$
C: 0.75	D: $0.\overline{3}$

Possible Solutions

All are values less than 1.

A and B are fractions.

C and D are decimals. C is a terminating decimal, but D is not.

A and D have the same value.

B and C have the same value.

WHY? Support students' facility with recognizing terminating and repeating decimals.

TRY IT SMP 1, 2, 3, 4, 5, 6, 7, 8

Make Sense of the Problem

See ***Connect to Culture*** to support student engagement. Before students work on Try It, use **Say It Another Way** to help them make sense of the problem. Have them state which fractions they are analyzing.

DISCUSS IT SMP 2, 3, 6, 7, 8

Support Partner Discussion

After students work on Try It, have them respond to Discuss It with a partner. Listen for understanding that:

- if the division process leads to a step where there is no remainder or a remainder of 0, then the decimal is a terminating decimal.
- if, in the division process, the same digits appear in a repeating pattern in the quotient, then the decimal is a repeating decimal.

Explore Writing Fractions as Decimals

Previously, you learned about rational numbers. In this lesson, you will learn about expressing rational numbers as fractions and decimals.

➤ **Use what you know to try to solve the problem below.**

Chantel is designing a poster for a hip-hop concert. She uses art software to create a poster from her sketch. The software program requires her to use decimal measurements. Are both fractions in the poster repeating decimals? How do you know?

TRY IT

Math Toolkit grid paper

Possible work:

SAMPLE A

$$\begin{array}{r} 0.375 \\ 8\overline{)3.000} \\ -\,2\,4 \\ \hline 60 \\ -\,56 \\ \hline 40 \\ -\,40 \\ \hline 0 \end{array} \qquad \begin{array}{r} 0.4545\ldots \\ 33\overline{)15.0000} \\ -\,13\,2 \\ \hline 1\,80 \\ -\,1\,65 \\ \hline 150 \\ -\,132 \\ \hline 180 \\ -\,165 \\ \hline 15 \end{array}$$

$\frac{3}{8}$ is a terminating decimal: 0.375. $\frac{15}{33}$ is a repeating decimal because 45 continues forever: 0.4545 . . . .

SAMPLE B

$\frac{3}{8} = \frac{x}{10}$ $\qquad$ $\frac{15}{33} = \frac{x}{10}$

$\frac{30}{8} = x$ $\qquad$ $\frac{150}{33} = x$

$x = 3.75;\ x \div 10 = 0.375$ $\qquad$ $x = 4.545\ldots;\ x \div 10 = 0.4545\ldots$

$\frac{3}{8}$ is a repeating decimal because 0s repeat at the end: 0.37500 . . . . $\frac{15}{33}$ is a repeating decimal because 45 repeats forever: 0.4545 . . . .

DISCUSS IT

Ask: How does your model or strategy show whether a decimal is a repeating decimal?

Share: I can tell a decimal is a repeating decimal by . . .

Learning Target SMP 1, SMP 2, SMP 3, SMP 4, SMP 5, SMP 6, SMP 7, SMP 8

Know that numbers that are not rational are called irrational. Understand informally that every number has a decimal expansion; for rational numbers show that the decimal expansion repeats eventually, and convert a decimal expansion which repeats eventually into a rational number.

Error Alert If students think that $\frac{3}{8}$ is a repeating decimal equal to $2.\overline{6}$ and that $\frac{15}{33}$ is a terminating decimal equal to 2.2, then they have reversed the divisor and dividend when performing their long division. Ensure that they know the numerator is the dividend (inside the long division bracket) and the denominator is the divisor (outside the long division bracket).

Select and Sequence Student Strategies

Select 2–3 samples that represent the range of student thinking in your classroom. Here is one possible order for class discussion:

- long division with the numerator as the dividend and the denominator as the divisor
- equation setting the fraction equal to x over 10

Facilitate Whole Class Discussion

Call on students to share selected strategies. Students can use sentence starters such as:
I know that _____, so _____.

Guide students to **Compare and Connect** the representations. Call on several students to rephrase important ideas so that everyone hears them more than once and in more than one way.

ASK *How do you know the digits in the decimal form of $\frac{15}{33}$ will not eventually terminate?*

LISTEN FOR The remainders will keep alternating between 18 and 15, and so you will keep dividing 33 into 180 and then 150, over and over. So, the digits in the quotient will just keep repeating.

CONNECT IT

SMP 2, 4, 5

1 **Look Back** Look for understanding that the digits in the decimal equivalent of $\frac{3}{8}$ terminate, or end. The digits in the decimal equivalent of $\frac{15}{33}$ show a repeating pattern.

DIFFERENTIATION | RETEACH or REINFORCE

Visual Model
Write fractions as repeating decimals.

If students are unsure about how to write a fraction as a repeating decimal, then use this activity to help them understand the process.

- Display the fraction $\frac{5}{6}$.
- Ask: *When setting up a long division problem to write the fraction as a decimal, what is the dividend?* [5] *What is the divisor?* [6]
- Write a long division statement with 5 as the dividend and 6 as the divisor.
- Ask: *How many groups of 6 in 5?* [0]
- Write a decimal point and a 0 after the 5.
- Ask: *How many groups of 6 in 50?* [8]
- Demonstrate how to move up the decimal point in the quotient, write 8 in the quotient above 0, multiply 8 by 6, and write 48 under 50.
- Demonstrate how to subtract 48 from 50, write another 0 in the dividend, and bring down the 0.
- Ask: *How many groups of 6 in 20?* [3]
- Demonstrate how to write 3 in the quotient after 8, multiply 3 by 6, and write 18 under 20.
- Continue a few more steps until students are convinced the 3 will continue to repeat.
- Ask: *How can this quotient be written using an overbar?* [$0.8\overline{3}$]

CONNECT IT

1 **Look Back** How did you decide if the decimals are repeating?

Possible answer: I used long division to show that the fraction $\frac{3}{8}$ is a terminating decimal, 0.375, and $\frac{15}{33}$ is a repeating decimal, 0.4545 . . . .

2 **Look Ahead** You have already worked with rational numbers. A *rational number* is a number that can be expressed as the fraction $\frac{a}{b}$ where *a* and *b* are integers and $b \neq 0$.

a. Recall that repeating decimals repeat the same digit or digits without end. When you use long division to write a fraction as a decimal, how are the remainders related to the repeating digits in the quotient?

Possible answer: The same remainders keep repeating in a pattern, so the same digits keep repeating in the quotient.

b. The fraction $\frac{1}{2}$ can be written as the terminating decimal 0.5. What digit will repeat in the quotient when you use division to write $\frac{1}{2}$ as a decimal? Explain why terminating decimals are also considered repeating decimals.

0; Terminating decimals repeat the digit 0 without end.

c. An overbar is often used to identify which digits repeat in a repeating decimal. For example, $0.\overline{3}$ means 0.333 . . . and $0.\overline{45}$ means 0.454545 . . . .

Write the repeating decimals using an overbar.

0.777 . . . = $0.\overline{7}$ 0.358358358 . . . = $0.\overline{358}$

How could you write the terminating decimal using an overbar?

0.58 = $0.58\overline{0}$

3 **Reflect** Explain why you can think of every rational number as a number whose decimal expansion repeats eventually.

Any rational number can be written as a fraction $\frac{a}{b}$, where *a* and *b* are integers and $b \neq 0$. Such fractions can be written as repeating decimals using long division. If the repeating digit is 0, then the repeating decimal is called a terminating decimal.

582

---

2 **Look Ahead** Point out that all rational numbers have decimal expansions. These decimal expansions have digits that either terminate or repeat. Students should recognize that a decimal that terminates can also be thought of as a decimal that repeats 0s after the last nonzero digit. Students should understand that the digits under the bar are the digits that repeat.

CLOSE EXIT TICKET

3 **Reflect** Look for understanding that any rational number can be expressed as a repeating decimal, even if the repeating digit in the decimal is 0.

Common Misconception If students do not think a terminating decimal is also a repeating decimal, then show them that the numbers 0.5, 0.50, 0.500, 0.5000, and 0.50000 all represent the same amount, which is $\frac{1}{2}$. Encourage them to write each of those decimals as a fraction and then rewrite the fractions in simplest form.

Prepare for Expressing Rational Numbers as Fractions and Decimals

Support Vocabulary Development

Assign **Prepare for Expressing Rational Numbers as Fractions and Decimals** as extra practice in class or as homework.

If you have students complete this in class, then use the guidance below.

Ask students to consider the term *rational number*. Ensure they do not interchange the terms *rational number* and *fraction*. Every fraction is a rational number, but not every rational number is presented as a fraction. For example, 3 and 0.25 are rational numbers. They are not fractions, although they can be written in fraction form.

Have students work in pairs to complete the graphic organizer. Invite pairs to share their completed organizers, and prompt a whole-class comparative discussion of the definitions, known facts, and examples generated.

Have students look at the statement in problem 2 and discuss with a partner whether the mixed number can take on other forms.

Problem Notes

1. Students should understand that a rational number can be written as a quotient of two integers, $\frac{a}{b}$, where $b \neq 0$. Student examples might include fractions, decimals, and integers.

2. Students may reason that because 5 is a rational number and $\frac{1}{3}$ is a rational number, their sum is also a rational number.

LESSON 24 | SESSION 1 Name:

Prepare for Expressing Rational Numbers as Fractions and Decimals

1. Think about what you know about different types of numbers. Fill in each box. Use words, numbers, and pictures. Show as many ideas as you can.

Possible answers:

What Is It?
A rational number can be written as a quotient of two integers, $\frac{a}{b}$, where $b \neq 0$.

What I Know About It
Rational numbers can be written as fractions, decimals, whole numbers, and integers.

rational number

Examples
6 is a rational number because $6 = \frac{6}{1}$.

Examples
0.25 is a rational number because $0.25 = \frac{1}{4}$.

Examples
-3 is a rational number because $-3 = \frac{-3}{1}$.

2. Ana says $5\frac{1}{3}$ is not a rational number because it is not a fraction of the form $\frac{a}{b}$, where a and b are integers and $b \neq 0$. Do you agree? Explain.

No; Possible explanation: The number $5\frac{1}{3}$ can be written in the required form: $5\frac{1}{3} = 5 + \frac{1}{3} = \frac{15}{3} + \frac{1}{3} = \frac{16}{3}$. This shows that the number is a rational number.

583

REAL-WORLD CONNECTION

Sports statisticians often report statistics in decimal form. It is easier for many people to compare decimals than to compare fractions, which could have different denominators. For example, if one baseball player gets 23 hits in 65 at-bats and another gets 17 hits in 49 at-bats, their batting averages are reported as 0.354 and 0.347, respectively. These decimals are much easier to compare than the fractions $\frac{23}{65}$ and $\frac{17}{49}$. Ask students to think of other real-world examples when expressing rational numbers as fractions or decimals might be useful.

Additional Practice

3 Problem 3 provides another look at determining whether given fractions are equivalent to repeating decimals or terminating decimals. This problem is similar to the problem about the numbers representing poster dimensions. In both problems, two rational numbers are given, and students need to determine whether the numbers have decimal parts that repeat or terminate. This problem asks whether the numbers representing the fraction of rabbits in two groups that gained weight are repeating decimals.

Students may want to use long division to solve.

Suggest that students use **Say It Another Way** to ensure they understand what is being asked in the problem.

LESSON 24 | SESSION 1

3 Deyvi is comparing the weights of two groups of rabbits on different diets. In Group A, $\frac{7}{11}$ of the rabbits gained weight. In Group B, $\frac{7}{8}$ of the rabbits gained weight. He needs to record this information in a spreadsheet, which requires him to use decimals.

Rabbits	Weight Gain
Group A	$\frac{7}{11}$
Group B	$\frac{7}{8}$

a. Are both fractions in the table repeating decimals? Show your work.

Group A:

$$11\overline{)7.0000} = 0.6363\ldots$$
$$-66,\ 40,\ -33,\ 70,\ -66,\ 40,\ -33,\ 7$$

Group B:

$$8\overline{)7.000} = 0.875$$
$$-64,\ 60,\ -56,\ 40,\ -40,\ 0$$

SOLUTION Yes, $\frac{7}{11} = 0.\overline{63}$ and $\frac{7}{8} = 0.875$.

b. Check your answer to problem 3a. Show your work.

I double-checked my long division work. Both are repeating decimals because $0.\overline{63}$ repeats 63 and 0.875 is a terminating decimal and so repeats 0 at the end.

584

DIFFERENTIATION | ENGLISH LANGUAGE LEARNERS

Use with **Session 2** Apply It

Levels 1–3: Speaking/Writing

Help students read and make sense of Apply It problem 9. Read sentences 1–2 aloud, and use **Act It Out** to model the situation. For example, show a scale and fill it with cubes. Record the total weight. Select a cube from the scale. Ask: *What is the average weight of one avocado?*

Then read sentences 3–5 as students follow along. Ask: *What kind of number do you see? What do you need to do?* Help students summarize the task using the number in the problem, the terms *repeating decimal, fraction,* and *equation,* and these sentence frames:

- *The number* ____ *is a* ____.
- *I need to find the* ____. *I can use a* ____.

Levels 2–4: Speaking/Writing

Have students read and make sense of Apply It problem 9. Read the problem aloud as students listen. Invite volunteers to use **Act It Out** to role play weighing avocados, finding the total weight, and calculating the average weight. Ask: *What result is given in the problem? What does the result represent?* Provide time for students to reread the problem before turning to talk with partners. Check understanding of *average weight.*

Next, have students summarize the task and discuss their solution strategies with partners. Provide these sentence starters as a guide:

- *The problem says I need to* ____.
- *One strategy I can use is* ____.
- *I think that make sense because* ____.

Levels 3–5: Speaking/Writing

Have students read Apply It problem 9 with partners and make sense of the problem situation. Display the image and ask: *How does this image help you understand the problem?* Have partners share their responses.

Next, ask: *What is the result in the problem? What does the problem ask you to do? What can you use to find the solution?* Provide time for students to reread and think about solution strategies before turning to talk with partners. Ask students to take turns to listen and explain their strategies. If strategies differ, encourage partners to come up with a way to test the strategy or solution and see if it is correct.

Develop Writing a Repeating Decimal as a Fraction

Purpose

- **Develop** strategies for writing a repeating decimal as a fraction.
- **Recognize** that you can write and solve an equation to write a repeating decimal as a fraction.

START CONNECT TO PRIOR KNOWLEDGE

Same and Different

A: 0.25	B: $0.\overline{6}$
C: 0.6	D: $\frac{1}{4}$

Possible Solutions

All are rational numbers.

A, B, and C are decimals.

A and C are terminating decimals.

A and D are equivalent. B and C are not.

WHY? Support students' facility with recognizing types of rational numbers.

DEVELOP ACADEMIC LANGUAGE

WHY? Unpack sentences that explain a task.

HOW? Read Connect It problem 4. Tell students that the first sentence explains how to perform a task. Point out how the comma divides the sentence into two parts. Explain that the word *to* introduces the explanation and that this type of sentence opener is common in academic language. Have students identify the explanation and then the task. Encourage students to use similar structures when they share their work in the session.

- *To* ____, *I* ____.

TRY IT SMP 1, 2, 4, 5, 6, 7, 8

Make Sense of the Problem

See ***Connect to Culture*** to support student engagement. Before students work on Try It, have partners use **Say It Another Way** to help them make sense of the problem. Prompt students to consider the information in both the text and the picture when paraphrasing.

LESSON 24 | SESSION 2

Develop Writing a Repeating Decimal as a Fraction

Read and try to solve the problem below.

A grocery store has large wheels of cheese. The owner keeps track of the portion of each wheel that has been sold.

Write $\frac{1}{9}$ as a decimal. Then use your answer to write $0.\overline{4}$ as a fraction.

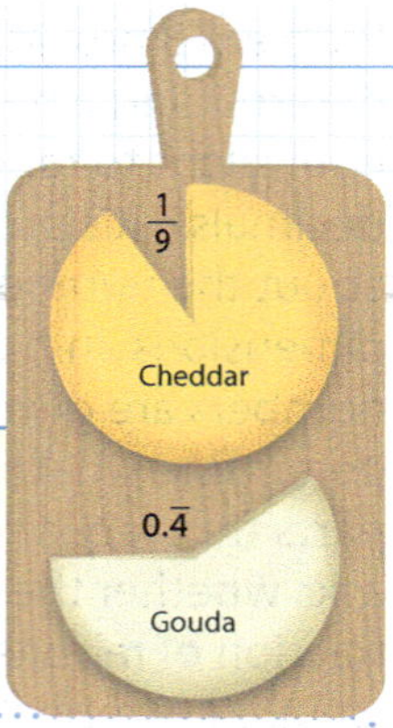

TRY IT Math Toolkit grid paper

Possible work:

SAMPLE A

$\frac{1}{9} = \frac{x}{10}$

$\frac{10}{9} = x$

$x = 1.\overline{1}$

$1.\overline{1} \div 10 = 0.\overline{1}$

So, $\frac{1}{9} = 0.\overline{1}$.

$0.\overline{4}$ is $4 \cdot 0.\overline{1}$, so multiply both sides by 4.

$4 \cdot \frac{1}{9} = 4 \cdot 0.\overline{1}$

$\frac{4}{9} = 0.\overline{4}$

So, $\frac{1}{9} = 0.\overline{1}$ and $0.\overline{4} = \frac{4}{9}$.

SAMPLE B

$$\begin{array}{r} 0.111\ldots \\ 9\overline{)1.000} \\ -9 \\ \hline 10 \\ -9 \\ \hline 10 \\ -9 \\ \hline 1 \end{array}$$

$\frac{1}{9} = 0.\overline{1}$

$0.\overline{1} = \frac{1}{9}$

$0.\overline{1} = \frac{1}{9}$

$0.\overline{1} = \frac{1}{9}$

$+\ 0.\overline{1} = \frac{1}{9}$

$0.\overline{4} = \frac{4}{9}$

DISCUSS IT

Ask: How do you know your answers make sense?

Share: My answers make sense because . . .

585

DISCUSS IT SMP 2, 3, 6

Support Partner Discussion

After students work on Try It, have them explain their work and then respond to Discuss It with a partner. To support students in extending the conversation, prompt them to discuss these questions:

- *What whole number is $\frac{1}{9}$ close to? What fraction is $0.\overline{4}$ close to?*
- *How would the results be the same or different if the quantities in this problem were negative numbers?*

Common Misconception Listen for students who think the overbar means that the decimal terminates. As students share their strategies, be sure they understand the difference between the meaning of 0.4 and $0.\overline{4}$. Have them turn and talk with a partner to discuss what the overbar indicates.

Select and Sequence Student Strategies

Select 2–3 samples that represent the range of student thinking in your classroom. Here is one possible order for class discussion:

- long division used to write $\frac{1}{9}$ as $0.\overline{1}$, then the fact that $0.\overline{4} = 4(0.\overline{1})$ used to write $0.\overline{4}$ as $\frac{4}{9}$
- (misconception) overbar thought to mean that the decimal terminates, so $0.\overline{4}$ written as $\frac{4}{10}$
- both sides of $x = 0.\overline{4}$ multiplied by 10, x subtracted from left side and $0.\overline{4}$ subtracted from right side, and the resulting equation solved for x to write the decimal as a fraction

Facilitate Whole Class Discussion

Call on students to share selected strategies. Remind students that they can ask questions about ideas that are not clear.

Guide students to **Compare and Connect** the representations. To engage all students, ask them to turn and talk to answer the question: *Which strategy made you think about the problem in a new way? Explain.*

ASK *How did each strategy relate $\frac{1}{9}$ and $0.\overline{4}$?*

LISTEN FOR Each used a relationship between the unit fraction, $\frac{1}{9}$, and the decimal, $0.\overline{1}$. Each also used the fact that $\frac{4}{9}$ is a multiple of $\frac{1}{9}$.

Model It

If students presented these models, have students connect these models to those presented in class.

If no student presented at least one of these models, have students first analyze key features of the models, and then connect them to the models presented in class.

ASK *How does each Model It result in a fraction?*

LISTEN FOR The first finds that $0.\overline{1}$ is equivalent to $\frac{1}{9}$ and uses this fact to write $0.\overline{4}$ as a decimal. The second multiplies $x = 0.\overline{4}$ by 10, subtracts the original equation to eliminate the repeating part, and solves for x to get a fraction.

For the long division, prompt students to consider how the decimal equivalent of $\frac{1}{9}$ is related to $0.\overline{4}$.

Ask: *How does knowing that $\frac{1}{9}$ is equivalent to $0.\overline{1}$ help you write $0.\overline{4}$ as a fraction?*

For the equation model, prompt students to look for structure in the solution.

- *Why multiply by 10, and not by 100 or 1,000?*
- *How does subtracting x from one side and $0.\overline{4}$ from the other help you write x as a fraction?*

➤ **Explore different ways to write a repeating decimal as a fraction.**

A grocery store has large wheels of cheese. The owner keeps track of the portion of each wheel that has been sold.

Write $\frac{1}{9}$ as a decimal. Then use your answer to write $0.\overline{4}$ as a fraction.

Model It

You can use long division to write a fraction as a decimal.

$$\begin{array}{r} 0.111\ldots \\ 9\overline{)1.000} \\ -9 \\ 10 \\ -9 \\ 10 \\ -9 \\ 1 \end{array}$$

You can use this result to write $0.\overline{4}$ as a fraction.

Model It

You can also use an equation to write a repeating decimal as a fraction.

$x = 0.\overline{4}$

Multiply both sides of the equation by a power of 10 to get a new equation. The number on the right side of the new equation should have the same repeating part as the number in the original equation. For $0.\overline{4}$, the repeating part of the decimal ends at the tenths place. So multiply both sides of the equation by 10. The number $4.\overline{4}$ has the same repeating part as $0.\overline{4}$.

$10 \cdot x = 10 \cdot 0.\overline{4}$

$10x = 4.\overline{4}$

Now subtract x from the left side and $0.\overline{4}$ from the right side of the equation.

$10x - x = 4.\overline{4} - 0.\overline{4}$

$9x = 4$

DIFFERENTIATION | EXTEND

SMP 7

Deepen Understanding

Looking for Structure in the Form of a Repeating Decimal

Lead the following discussion to help students see how to use the decimal form of a unit fraction to write other repeating decimals in fraction form.

ASK *What is the decimal form of $\frac{1}{99}$?*

LISTEN FOR The decimal form of $\frac{1}{99}$ is $0.\overline{01}$.

ASK *How can you use the decimal form of $\frac{1}{99}$ to write $\frac{2}{99}$ in decimal form?*

LISTEN FOR Since $\frac{2}{99}$ is 2 times as much as $\frac{1}{99}$, multiply $0.\overline{01}$ by 2 to get $0.\overline{02}$.

ASK *What are some other repeating decimals you can write in fraction form using the decimal form of $\frac{1}{99}$?*

LISTEN FOR Any multiple of $0.\overline{01}$ is a repeating decimal that can be written in fraction form using the decimal form of $\frac{1}{99}$. So, $0.\overline{03}$, $0.\overline{05}$, or $0.\overline{12}$ can be written in fraction form using the decimal form of $\frac{1}{99}$.

Develop Writing a Repeating Decimal as a Fraction

CONNECT IT

SMP 2, 4, 5, 6, 7, 8

Remind students that the quantities and the relationships between them are the same in each representation. Explain that they will now use those representations to reason about strategies for writing repeating decimals as fractions.

Before students begin to record and expand on their work in Model It, tell them that problems 2, 3, and 4 will prepare them to provide the explanation asked for in problem 5.

Monitor and Confirm Understanding 1 – 3

- $0.\overline{4}$ is equal to 4 times $0.\overline{1}$, so multiply $\frac{1}{9}$ by 4 to get a fraction equivalent to $0.\overline{4}$.
- Because $x = 0.\overline{4}$, you can subtract x from one side of the equation and $0.\overline{4}$ from the other, and the equation will stay balanced.
- Subtracting $0.\overline{4}$ from $4.\overline{4}$ eliminates the repeating part of the decimal.

Facilitate Whole Class Discussion

4 Look for understanding of how the power of 10 you multiply by is related to the place where the repeating part of the decimal ends. Have students consider what would happen if you multiplied by a lesser power of 10.

> **ASK** *What do you get if you multiply $0.\overline{36}$ by 10 instead of 100? Does subtracting $0.\overline{36}$ from that number eliminate the repeating decimal?*
>
> **LISTEN FOR** You get $3.6\overline{36}$. Subtracting $0.\overline{36}$ does not eliminate the repeating decimal.

5 Look for understanding of how the equation strategy eliminates the repeating decimal, leaving you with an equation you can solve to get a fraction.

> **ASK** *After you have subtracted to eliminate the repeating decimal, how do you know the fraction solution to the equation is equivalent to the repeating decimal?*
>
> **LISTEN FOR** The equation strategy starts by setting x equal to the repeating decimal. So, the fraction value you get for x must also be equal to the repeating decimal.

6 **Reflect** Have all students focus on the strategies used to solve the Try It. If time allows, have students discuss their ideas with a partner.

CONNECT IT

➤ **Use the problem from the previous page to help you understand how to write a repeating decimal as a fraction.**

1 Look at the first **Model It**. What is the decimal form of $\frac{1}{9}$? How can you use this answer to help you write $0.\overline{4}$ as a fraction?

$0.\overline{1}$; Possible answer: $0.\overline{4} = 4 \cdot 0.\overline{1}$, so $0.\overline{4} = 4 \cdot \frac{1}{9} = \frac{4}{9}$.

2 Look at the second **Model It**. Why can you subtract x from the left side and $0.\overline{4}$ from the right side of the equation $10x = 4.\overline{4}$? What does this step eliminate from the equation?

Possible answer: Since $x = 0.\overline{4}$, you can subtract x from one side and $0.\overline{4}$ from the other side and keep the equation balanced. This step eliminates the repeating part of the decimal.

3 What is $0.\overline{4}$ written as a fraction? $\frac{4}{9}$

4 **a.** To use an equation to write $0.\overline{36}$ as a fraction, multiply both sides of the equation by 100. Show how to write $0.\overline{36}$ as a fraction.

$x = 0.\overline{36}$, so $100x = 36.\overline{36}$. $100x - x = 36.\overline{36} - 0.\overline{36}$; $99x = 36$; $x = \frac{36}{99}$

b. What power of 10 would you use to find a fraction for $0.\overline{123}$? Why?

1,000; Possible answer: The repeating part of the decimal ends at the thousandths place.

5 How can you use an equation to write a repeating decimal as a fraction?

Possible answer: Set x equal to the decimal. Multiply both sides by a power of 10 based on the place value where the repeating part ends. Subtract x from the left side and the original decimal from the right side of the equation to eliminate the repeating decimal. Then solve for x.

6 **Reflect** Think about all the models and strategies you have discussed today. Describe how one of them helped you better understand how to solve the **Try It** problem.

Responses will vary. Check student responses.

587

DIFFERENTIATION | REETEACH or REINFORCE

Visual Model

Use a model to write repeating decimals as fractions.

If students are unsure about the equation strategy for writing repeating decimals as fractions, then use this activity to guide them through each step of the strategy.

- Display the repeating decimal $0.\overline{35}$.
- Ask: *What equation can be used to write this number as a fraction?* [$x = 0.\overline{35}$]
- Ask: *What should each side of the equation be multiplied by? Why? What is the resulting equation?* [100; Because the repeating decimal part ends in the hundredths place, multiply each side of the equation by 100; $100x = 35.\overline{35}$]
- Have volunteers display each step in solving the equation for x. Ask: *What should be subtracted from the left side of the equation?* [x]
- Ask: *What should be subtracted from the right side of the equation?* [$0.\overline{35}$]
- Ask: *What is the resulting equation?* [$99x = 35$]
- Ask: *What is the next step in solving the equation for x?* [Divide each side by 99.]
- Ask: *What fraction Is equivalent to $0.\overline{35}$?* [$\frac{35}{99}$] Have a volunteer display the fraction.

Apply It

For all problems, encourage students to use a model to support their thinking.

7 Students should understand that in order to show that the decimal is a rational number, they need to write it in the form of a fraction with an integer numerator and an integer denominator. They can use the equation strategy to do this.

8 **D is correct.** Students may solve this by using the equation strategy or by using the fact that $\frac{1}{9} = 0.\overline{1}$, so $1.\overline{1} = 1 + \frac{1}{9} = \frac{10}{9}$.

A is not correct. This answer is the fraction form of just the decimal portion of $1.\overline{1}$. Some students may immediately eliminate this answer because it is less than 1.

B is not correct. This answer results from multiplying the right side of $x = 1.\overline{1}$ by 10, but then adding x to the left side of the resulting equation instead of subtracting it. Some students may immediately eliminate this answer because it is less than 1.

C is not correct. This answer results from multiplying both sides by 100 but incorrectly writing the product on the right as $101.\overline{1}$ rather than $111.\overline{1}$.

Apply It

➤ **Use what you learned to solve these problems.**

7 Show that $0.\overline{47}$ is a rational number.

Possible work:

$$x = 0.\overline{47}$$
$$100x = 47.\overline{47}$$
$$100x - x = 47.\overline{47} - 0.\overline{47}$$
$$99x = 47$$
$$x = \frac{47}{99}$$

Since $0.\overline{47}$ can be written as a fraction $\frac{a}{b}$, where a and b are integers and $b \neq 0$, it is a rational number.

8 Which fraction is equivalent to $1.\overline{1}$?

A $\frac{1}{9}$

B $\frac{10}{11}$

C $\frac{100}{99}$

(D) $\frac{10}{9}$

9 Tiffany weighs a bunch of avocados. She divides their total weight by the number of avocados to find the average weight of one avocado. The result is $0.\overline{23}$ lb. Write $0.\overline{23}$ as a fraction. Show your work.

Possible work:

$$x = 0.\overline{23}$$
$$100x = 23.\overline{23}$$
$$100x - x = 23.\overline{23} - 0.\overline{23}$$
$$99x = 23$$
$$x = \frac{23}{99}$$

SOLUTION $\frac{23}{99}$

CLOSE EXIT TICKET

9 Students' solutions should show an understanding that:

- the equation strategy starts by setting x equal to the repeating decimal.
- the place where the repeating part of the decimal ends determines the power of 10 that both sides should be multiplied by.
- subtracting x from the left side and the original decimal from the right side of the resulting equation eliminates the repeating decimal.
- solving the final equation for x gives the fraction form of the repeating decimal.

Error Alert If students write $0.\overline{23}$ as $\frac{23}{9}$, then they moved the decimal point to get $23.\overline{23}$ on the left side of the equation but only multiplied the left side of the equation by 10. Ask students if it makes sense for the fraction equivalent to $0.\overline{23}$ to be greater than 1. Remind students that moving the decimal point two places to the left is equivalent to multiplying by 100, so they must multiply the left side of the equation by 100 as well.

Practice Writing a Repeating Decimal as a Fraction

Problem Notes

Assign **Practice Writing a Repeating Decimal as a Fraction** as extra practice in class or as homework.

1. Students should recognize that they need to multiply by 1,000 because the repeating part of the decimal ends in the thousandths place. ***Medium***

2. Students should understand that multiplying by a power of 10 greater than what is necessary to eliminate the repeated digits will result in a correct answer, but the fraction will not be in simplest form. ***Challenge***

LESSON 24 | SESSION 2 Name:

Practice Writing a Repeating Decimal as a Fraction

➤ **Study the Example showing how to write a repeating decimal as a fraction. Then solve problems 1–5.**

Example

Write $0.\overline{348}$ as a fraction.

$$x = 0.\overline{348}$$

The repeating part of the decimal ends at the thousandths place, so multiply both sides of the equation by 1,000.

$$1{,}000x = 348.\overline{348}$$

$$1{,}000x - x = 348.\overline{348} - 0.\overline{348}$$

$$999x = 348$$

$$x = \frac{348}{999} \text{ or } \frac{116}{333}$$

1. Write $0.\overline{721}$ as a fraction. Show your work. Possible work:

$$x = 0.\overline{721}$$

$$1{,}000x = 721.\overline{721}$$

$$1{,}000x - x = 721.\overline{721} - 0.\overline{721}$$

$$999x = 721$$

$$x = \frac{721}{999}$$

SOLUTION $\frac{721}{999}$

2. Jacob wrote $0.\overline{8}$ as a fraction by first writing $x = 0.\overline{8}$. Then he multiplied both sides of the equation by 100. Will this method work? If it will work, complete the calculation. If it will not work, explain why not.

Yes; Possible work:

$$x = 0.\overline{8}$$

$$100x = 88.\overline{8}$$

$$100x - x = 88.\overline{8} - 0.\overline{8}$$

$$99x = 88$$

$$x = \frac{88}{99}, \text{ or } \frac{8}{9}$$

Vocabulary

repeating decimals
decimals that repeat the same digit or sequence of digits forever.

589

Fluency & Skills Practice

Writing a Repeating Decimal as a Fraction

In this activity, students write repeating decimals as fractions.

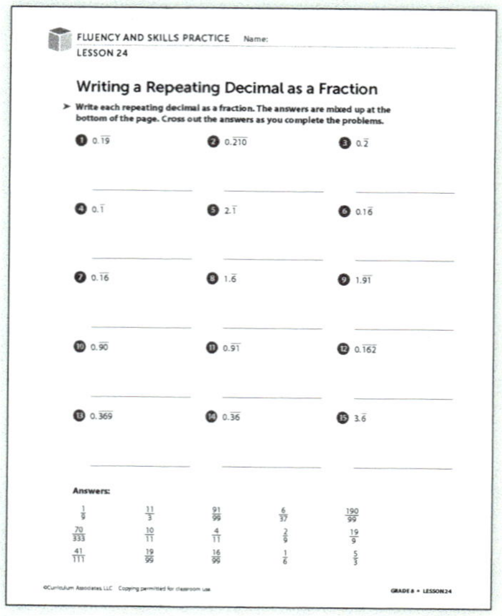

Additional Practice

3 **a.** Students should recognize that they need to multiply by 100 because the repeating part of the decimal ends in the hundredths place. ***Medium***

b. ***Basic***

4 ***Basic***

5 Students should recognize that they need to multiply by 10,000 because the repeating part of the decimal ends in the ten-thousandths place. ***Medium***

LESSON 24 | SESSION 2

3 The mass of a crystal is $0.\overline{49}$ kg.

a. Write $0.\overline{49}$ as a fraction. Show your work.

Possible work:

$$x = 0.\overline{49}$$
$$100x = 49.\overline{49}$$
$$100x - x = 49.\overline{49} - 0.\overline{49}$$
$$99x = 49$$
$$x = \frac{49}{99}$$

mass = $0.\overline{49}$ kg

SOLUTION $\frac{49}{99}$

b. Use your answer from problem 3a to write $9.\overline{49}$ as a fraction.

Possible answer: $9.\overline{49} = 9 + 0.\overline{49}$

$$= 9 + \frac{49}{99} \text{ or } 9\frac{49}{99}$$

4 Use the fact that $0.\overline{1} = \frac{1}{9}$ and $0.\overline{4} = \frac{4}{9}$ to write $0.\overline{5}$ as a fraction. Show your work.

Possible work: $0.\overline{5} = 0.\overline{1} + 0.\overline{4}$

$$= \frac{1}{9} + \frac{4}{9}$$
$$= \frac{5}{9}$$

SOLUTION $\frac{5}{9}$

5 Inés finds the population density of a county. She divides the population by the area in square miles. The result is $0.\overline{3648}$ people per square mile. Write $0.\overline{3648}$ as a fraction. Show your work.

Possible work:

$$x = 0.\overline{3648}$$
$$10{,}000x = 3{,}648.\overline{3648}$$
$$10{,}000x - x = 3648.\overline{3648} - 0.\overline{3648}$$
$$9{,}999x = 3{,}648$$
$$x = \frac{3{,}648}{9{,}999}$$

SOLUTION $\frac{3{,}648}{9{,}999}$, or $\frac{1{,}216}{3{,}333}$

590

DIFFERENTIATION | ENGLISH LANGUAGE LEARNERS

Use with **Session 3** **Apply It**

Levels 1–3: Reading/Writing

Help students interpret Apply It problem 3. Read the first sentence as students follow along. Clarify *decimal expansion* by pointing to the answer choices. Read Consider This and have students circle *long division*. Provide time for students to find the correct answer. Then help students read the second sentence and begin writing using these sentence frames:

- *The correct answer is* ____.
- *I got my answer using* ____.

Next, ask students to use models or equations to show how Rolando might have found his answer. Have students turn to partners and show how their answer is different from Rolando's answer. Help students write short sentences to show their ideas.

Levels 2–4: Reading/Writing

Help students interpret Apply It problem 3. Read sentence 1 with students and have them discuss the vocabulary term *eventually*. Display a place-value chart and model pronunciation. Emphasize the end sound of words like *tenths* and ask students to repeat. Then have partners talk about the answer choices using *repeats, does not repeat, eventually repeats, overbar, tenths,* and *hundredths*. Have students solve the problem. Suggest they read Consider This for possible solution strategies, if needed.

Next, prepare students to write. Have partners discuss reasons Rolando might have gotten C. Call on volunteers to share and ask students to reword ideas. Prompt students to write explanations using precise language.

Levels 3–5: Reading/Writing

Have students read and interpret Apply It problem 3. Ask students to discuss the meanings of *decimal expansion* and *eventually*. Provide time for students to compare the decimal expansions. Call on students to share. Have students reword statements using precise terms like *repeating decimal, overbar, tenths,* and *hundredths*.

Next, have students solve the problem. Suggest they read Consider This for extra support. Then have students use **Stronger and Clearer Each Time** to draft, discuss, and revise explanations of Rolando's mistake. Prompt students to write explanations with clear reasons and precise terminology.

Refine Expressing Rational Numbers as Fractions and Decimals

Purpose

- **Refine** strategies for expressing rational numbers as fractions and decimals.
- **Refine** understanding of how to write a fraction for a repeating decimal when the decimal has a nonrepeating part.

START CONNECT TO PRIOR KNOWLEDGE

Write $0.\overline{56}$ as a fraction.

Solution

$\frac{56}{99}$

WHY? Confirm students' understanding of expressing a repeating decimal as a fraction, identifying common errors to address as needed.

MONITOR & GUIDE

Before students begin to work, use their responses to the **Start** to determine those who will benefit from additional support. Use the **Error Analysis** table below to guide remediation.

Have all students complete the Example and problems 1–3, using Consider This and Pair/Share as appropriate. Observe and monitor their reasoning and guide or redirect students as needed.

Refine Expressing Rational Numbers as Fractions and Decimals

➤ **Complete the Example below. Then solve problems 1–9.**

Example

Write $0.2\overline{5}$ as a fraction.

Look at how you could multiply by two different powers of 10 to get numbers that will help you eliminate the repeating part of the decimal.

$x = 0.2\overline{5}$

$10x = 2.\overline{5}$

$100x = 25.\overline{5}$

$100x - 10x = 25.\overline{5} - 2.\overline{5}$

$90x = 23$

SOLUTION $\frac{23}{90}$

CONSIDER THIS . . . You can multiply by two different powers of 10 to get two different numbers with repeating 5s to the right of the decimal point.

PAIR/SHARE How can you check that the fraction you wrote is correct?

Apply It

1 Write $0.\overline{9}$ as a fraction. Show your work. (*Hint*: The result may surprise you.)

Possible work:

$x = 0.\overline{9}$

$10x = 9.\overline{9}$

$10x - x = 9.\overline{9} - 0.\overline{9}$

$9x = 9$

$x = \frac{9}{9}$, or 1

SOLUTION 1

CONSIDER THIS . . . $0.\overline{9}$ is greater than 0.9, greater than 0.99, greater than 0.999, and so on.

PAIR/SHARE What do you think is another way to write $5.\overline{9}$?

START ERROR ANALYSIS

If the error is . . .	Students may . . .	To support understanding . . .
$\frac{5}{9}$	have written $0.\overline{5}$ as a fraction.	Prompt students to use an equation to write the repeated decimal as a fraction. Remind them of the process. Set x equal to the decimal. Multiply both sides by a power of 10 based on the place value where the repeating part ends. Subtract x from the left side and the original decimal from the right side of the equation to eliminate the repeating decimal. Then solve for x.
$\frac{56}{101}$	have multiplied both sides of $x = 0.\overline{56}$ by 100, but then added on the left side of the equation.	Remind students that they should subtract x from the left side and the original decimal from the right side of the equation to eliminate the repeating decimal.
$\frac{56}{9}$	have multiplied the left side of $x = 0.\overline{56}$ by 10 and the right side by 100.	Remind students that they should multiply *both* sides of the equation by the *same* power of 10 so the number on the right side has the same repeating part, and to keep the equation balanced.

Refine

Example

Guide students in understanding the Example. Ask:

- *When you multiply both sides by 10, what digits are to the right of the decimal point in the resulting number?*
- *When you multiply both sides by 100, what digits are to the right of the decimal point in the resulting number?*
- *Why can you subtract 10x from the left side of $100x = 25.\overline{5}$ and subtract $2.\overline{5}$ from the right side? Why does this eliminate the repeating decimal?*
- *Would you get the same solution if you had used the usual fraction strategy, multiplying both sides by 100 and then subtracting x from the left side and $0.2\overline{5}$ from the right side?*

Help all students focus on the Example and responses to the questions by asking questions to clarify something you do not understand or to ask for more information.

Look for understanding that multiplying the equation by 10 and then multiplying it by 100 gives two equations that have decimals with the same repeating part starting right after the decimal point. Subtracting corresponding sides of the equations will eliminate the repeating decimal.

Apply It

1. Because students have already found that $0.\overline{1} = \frac{1}{9}$, they may use the idea that $0.\overline{9} = 9(0.\overline{1}) = 9\left(\frac{1}{9}\right)$. *DOK 1*

2. Students may follow the model in the Example and use two different powers of 10 to solve. *DOK 2*

3. **B is correct.** Students may use long division to find the quotient of $16 \div 33$.

   A is not correct. This answer is the result of stopping division at the hundredths place or rounding to the hundredths place.

   C is not correct. This answer is the result of stopping division at the hundredths place and assuming the 8s repeat.

   D is not correct. This answer is the result of thinking the decimal is terminating and using 0s to show it as a repeating decimal.

   DOK 3

---

2 Write $0.33\overline{4}$ as a fraction. Show your work.

Possible work:

$$x = 0.33\overline{4}$$
$$100x = 33.\overline{4}$$
$$1{,}000x = 334.\overline{4}$$
$$1{,}000x - 100x = 334.\overline{4} - 33.\overline{4}$$
$$900x = 301$$
$$x = \frac{301}{900}$$

SOLUTION $\frac{301}{900}$

CONSIDER THIS . . . Multiplying by what powers of 10 will give answers where only the repeating part of the number is to the right of the decimal point?

PAIR/SHARE How can you use your work to predict the fraction form of $0.33\overline{5}$?

3 Which of the following shows that the decimal expansion of $\frac{16}{33}$ eventually repeats?

A 0.48

(B) $0.\overline{48}$

C $0.4\overline{8}$

D $0.48\overline{0}$

Rolando chose C as the correct answer. How might he have gotten that answer?

Possible answer: Rolando may have used long division to find the quotient $16 \div 33$. Then, when he got 8 in the hundredths place, he stopped dividing, and assumed that the 8s repeat.

CONSIDER THIS . . . How might long division help you find the decimal expansion for $\frac{16}{33}$?

PAIR/SHARE What is an example of another fraction that has the same decimal expansion as $\frac{16}{33}$?

GROUP & DIFFERENTIATE

Identify groupings for differentiation based on the **Start** and problems 1–3. A recommended sequence of activities for each group is suggested below. Use the resources on the next page to differentiate and close the lesson.

Approaching Proficiency
- **RETEACH** Visual Model
- **REINFORCE** Problems 5, 6

Meeting Proficiency
- **REINFORCE** Problems 4–8

Extending Beyond Proficiency
- **REINFORCE** Problems 4–8
- **EXTEND** Challenge

Have all students complete the **Close: Exit Ticket.**

Resources for Differentiation are found on the next page.

Refine Expressing Rational Numbers as Fractions and Decimals

Apply It

4 See ***Connect to Culture*** to support student engagement. Students may follow the model in the Example and use two different powers of 10 to solve. *DOK 3*

5 For each of the first three repeating decimals, students may set x equal to the decimal, multiply both sides by a power of 10 based on the place value where the repeating part ends, subtract x from the left side and the original decimal from the right side to eliminate the repeating decimal, and then solve for x. After writing all three decimals as fractions, they should see a pattern that allows them to make a prediction about the fourth repeating decimal. *DOK 2*

6 **a.** 0.4 is less than $0.\overline{4}$.

b. There is no sequence of digits that repeats without end.

c. If long division is used to divide 1 by 7, a repeating pattern of digits will emerge in the quotient.

d. Long division shows that $\frac{5}{8}$ is equal to 0.625.

DOK 2

4 Stalagmites are rock and mineral formations that build up on a cave floor. A geologist finds that the average rate of growth of a stalagmite in a cave is $0.00\overline{35}$ inch per year. Write $0.00\overline{35}$ as a fraction. Show your work.

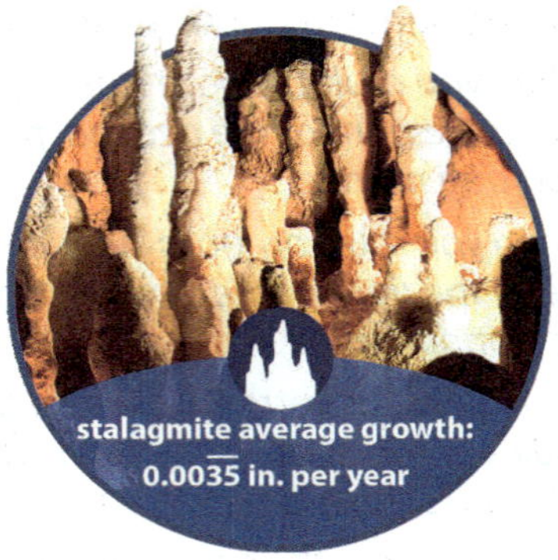

Possible work:

$$x = 0.00\overline{35}$$
$$100x = 0.\overline{35}$$
$$10{,}000x = 35.\overline{35}$$
$$10{,}000x - 100x = 35.\overline{35} - 0.\overline{35}$$
$$9{,}900x = 35$$
$$x = \frac{35}{9{,}900}$$

SOLUTION $\frac{35}{9{,}900}$, or $\frac{7}{1{,}980}$

5 Write $0.\overline{1}$, $0.\overline{01}$, and $0.\overline{001}$ as fractions. Then explain how you can use the results to predict how to write $0.\overline{0001}$ as a fraction.

Possible answer: $0.\overline{1} = \frac{1}{9}$, $0.\overline{01} = \frac{1}{99}$, and $0.\overline{001} = \frac{1}{999}$. So, $0.\overline{0001} = \frac{1}{9{,}999}$ because the pattern shows that the number of repeating digits is equal to the number of 9s in the denominator.

6 Tell whether each statement is *True* or *False*.

	True	False
a. The numbers 0.4 and $0.\overline{4}$ are equal to the same fraction.	○	●
b. The number 0.101100111000 . . . is a repeating decimal.	○	●
c. The fraction $\frac{1}{7}$ is equal to a repeating decimal.	●	○
d. The fraction $\frac{5}{8}$ is equal to $0.\overline{625}$.	○	●

593

DIFFERENTIATION

RETEACH

Visual Model

Write a repeating decimal with a nonrepeating digit as a fraction.

Students approaching proficiency with writing a repeating decimal as a fraction will benefit from walking through the steps of another example.

- Display $0.2\overline{7}$ and tell students you want to write this number as a fraction. Point out that the repeating part, 7, does not start right after the decimal point.
- Walk through the following steps to write the decimal as a fraction. Explain, or have a volunteer explain, the reason for each step.
  1. Write the equation $x = 0.2\overline{7}$.
  2. Multiply both sides by 10 to get a new equation with a repeating part that starts right after the decimal point.
  3. Multiply both sides of the original equation by 100 to get *another* equation with a repeating part that starts right after the decimal point.
  4. Subtract the Step 2 equation from the Step 3 equation to eliminate the repeating decimal.
  5. Solve the equation for x.

$$x = 0.2\overline{7}$$
$$10x = 2.\overline{7}$$
$$100x = 27.\overline{7}$$
$$100x - 10x = 27.\overline{7} - 2.\overline{7}$$
$$90x = 25$$
$$x = \frac{25}{90} \text{ or } \frac{5}{18}$$

- Ask: *Why did you need to write two equations?* [Sample answer: I needed two equations with decimals that had the same repeating part. This allowed the repeating parts to be eliminated.]

7. Students may rewrite both fractions in simplest form to show they are equivalent. *DOK 3*

8. Students may first analyze the decimal 0.12112111211112 . . . to determine whether it is a repeating decimal. Although there is a pattern in the digits, there is no fixed sequence of digits that repeats. So, the decimal is not a repeating decimal. *DOK 2*

CLOSE EXIT TICKET

9. **Math Journal** Look for understanding of how to use an equation to write a repeating decimal as a fraction.

Error Alert If students write the repeating decimal as $0.\overline{78}$ and get the fraction $\frac{78}{9}$, then they multiplied the left side of $x = 0.\overline{78}$ by 10 and the right side by 100. Reinforce that *both* sides of the equation must be multiplied by the same power of 10 in order to keep the equation balanced.

End of Lesson Checklist

INTERACTIVE GLOSSARY Support students by suggesting they use the word *eventually* in a story in a nonmathematical context. Then ask them to relate this to the idea that a repeating decimal has a pattern of digits that repeats eventually.

SELF CHECK Have students review and check off any new skills on the Unit 6 Opener.

LESSON 24 | SESSION 3

7. Quinn picks lemons from a tree. He finds the average weight of a lemon is 0.275 lb. He reads this as *275 thousandths* and writes the fraction as $\frac{275}{1,000}$. Hasina uses the strategies from this lesson to write a fraction as shown below. Who is correct? Explain.

$$x = 0.275$$
$$1{,}000x = 275.0$$
$$10{,}000x = 2{,}750.0$$
$$10{,}000x - 1{,}000x = 2{,}750.0 - 275.0$$
$$9{,}000x = 2{,}475$$
$$x = \frac{2{,}475}{9{,}000}$$

Both are correct; Possible explanation: Both methods work, and both fractions that they wrote are equivalent to $\frac{11}{40}$.

8. Do the strategies you learned for writing a repeating decimal as a fraction work for the decimal 0.12112111211112 . . .? Why or why not?

No; This is not a repeating decimal because there is no fixed sequence of digits that repeat. The strategies from this lesson will not work since it is not possible to multiply by a power of 10 to get only repeating digits to the right of the decimal point.

9. **Math Journal** Write a repeating decimal that includes the digits 7 and 8. Then show how to write the decimal as a fraction.

Possible answer and work: $0.\overline{78}$

$$x = 0.\overline{78}$$
$$100x = 78.\overline{78}$$
$$100x - x = 78.\overline{78} - 0.\overline{78}$$
$$99x = 78$$
$$x = \frac{78}{99}$$

End of Lesson Checklist

- [ ] **INTERACTIVE GLOSSARY** Write a new entry for *eventually*. Write at least one synonym for *eventually*.
- [ ] **SELF CHECK** Go back to the Unit 6 Opener and see what you can check off.

594

REINFORCE

Problems 4–8

Solve problems with repeating decimals.

Students meeting proficiency will benefit from additional work with writing a repeating decimal as a fraction by solving problems in a variety of formats.

- Have students work on their own or with a partner to solve the problems.
- Encourage students to show their work.

EXTEND

Challenge

Solve problems with repeating decimals that include a variable digit.

Students extending beyond proficiency will benefit from writing a repeating decimal with a variable digit as a fraction.

- Have students work with a partner to solve this problem: *Write* $0.01\overline{a}$ *as a fraction.* (Note that a represents the last digit of the number. The expression does not represent the product of 0.01 and $\overline{a}$.)
- Students may substitute different values for a to check to see if their answer is correct.

PERSONALIZE

i-Ready

Provide students with opportunities to work on their personalized instruction path with *i-Ready* Online Instruction to:

- fill prerequisite gaps.
- build up grade-level skills.

LESSON 24

Lesson Quiz

TESTED SKILLS

Assesses 8.NS.A.1

Problems on this assessment require students to be able to express rational numbers as fractions and decimals. Students will write repeating decimals as fractions and fractions as repeating decimals. Students will also need to be familiar with writing equivalent forms of fractions and nonrepeating decimals and using properties of equality to solve an equation.

Alternately, teachers may assign the **Digital Comprehension Check** online to assess student understanding of this material.

Error Alert Errors may result if students:

- stop dividing too soon before finding that a fraction has representation as a repeating decimal.
- place the bar over the incorrect digit or digits in the decimal representation of a rational number.
- incorrectly write or solve equations when converting a repeating decimal to a fraction.
- incorrectly calculate when performing division.

Problem Notes

1 **a.** The decimal 0.3 is equivalent to $\frac{3}{10}$, and $0.\overline{3}$ is equivalent to $\frac{1}{3}$.

b. The block of digits 111000 repeats.

c. The fraction $\frac{1}{9}$ is equivalent to $0.\overline{1}$.

d. The fraction $\frac{2}{11}$ is equivalent to $0.\overline{18}$.

(2 points)

DOK 1 | 8.NS.A.1

2 Students could solve the problem by writing the equation $x = 0.00\overline{22}$. Then they can multiply both sides by powers of 10 and eliminate the repeating part of the decimal to solve for x in a fraction form.

(2 points)

DOK 1 | 8.NS.A.1

LESSON 24 • QUIZ | Name:

➤ **Solve the problems.**

1 Choose *True* or *False* for each statement. *(2 points)*

	True	False
a. The numbers 0.3 and $0.\overline{3}$ are equal to the same fraction.	○	●
b. The number 0.111000111000 . . . is a repeating decimal.	●	○
c. The fraction $\frac{1}{9}$ is equal to a repeating decimal.	●	○
d. The fraction $\frac{2}{11}$ is equal to $0.\overline{18}$.	●	○

2 James finds the weight of a beetle to be $0.00\overline{22}$ lb. Write $0.00\overline{22}$ as a fraction. Show your work. *(2 points)*

Possible student work:

$$x = 0.00\overline{22}$$
$$100x = 0.\overline{22}$$
$$10{,}000x = 22.\overline{22}$$
$$10{,}000x - 100x = 22.\overline{22} - 0.\overline{22}$$
$$9{,}900x = 22$$
$$x = \frac{22}{9{,}900}$$

SOLUTION $\frac{22}{9{,}900}$

Choice Matrix Scoring Rubric

Points	Expectations
2	All answers are correct
1	1 incorrect answer
0	2 or more incorrect answers

Short Response Scoring Rubric

Points	Expectations
2	Response has the correct solution(s) and includes well-organized, clear, and concise work demonstrating thorough understanding of mathematical concepts and/or procedures.
1	Response contains mostly correct solution(s) and shows partial understanding of mathematical concepts and/or procedures.
0	Response shows no attempt at finding a solution and no effort to demonstrate an understanding of mathematical concepts and/or procedures.

3 Students could solve the problem by writing the equation $x = 0.11\overline{5}$. Then they can multiply both sides by powers of 10 and eliminate the repeating part of the decimal to solve for x in a fraction form.

(2 points)

DOK 1 | 8.NS.A.1

4 Students could solve the problem by writing the equation $x = 0.\overline{651}$. Then they can multiply both sides by powers of 10 and eliminate the repeating part of the decimal to solve for x in a fraction form.

(2 points)

DOK 1 | 8.NS.A.1

5 **B is correct.** Students could solve the problem by dividing 19 by 33 and finding that the digits 57 repeat.

A is not correct. This answer is the result of not understanding that the digits 57 repeat.

C is not correct. This answer is the result of not dividing correctly and not realizing that there are repeating digits.

D is not correct. This answer is the result of not dividing correctly.

(1 point)

DOK 1 | 8.NS.A.1

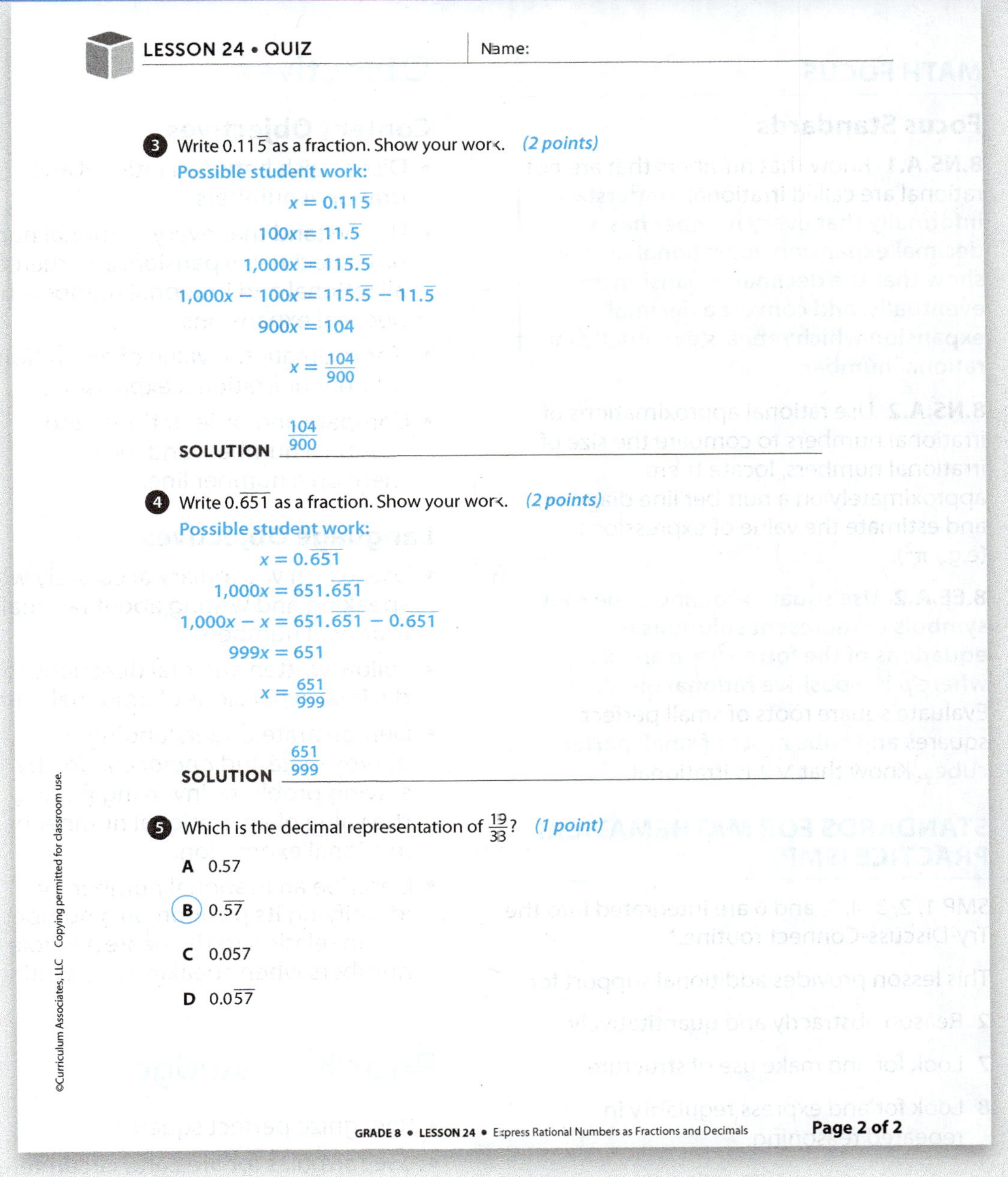

LESSON 24 • QUIZ Name:

3 Write $0.11\overline{5}$ as a fraction. Show your work. *(2 points)*

Possible student work:

$$x = 0.11\overline{5}$$
$$100x = 11.\overline{5}$$
$$1{,}000x = 115.\overline{5}$$
$$1{,}000x - 100x = 115.\overline{5} - 11.\overline{5}$$
$$900x = 104$$
$$x = \frac{104}{900}$$

SOLUTION $\frac{104}{900}$

4 Write $0.\overline{651}$ as a fraction. Show your work. *(2 points)*

Possible student work:

$$x = 0.\overline{651}$$
$$1{,}000x = 651.\overline{651}$$
$$1{,}000x - x = 651.\overline{651} - 0.\overline{651}$$
$$999x = 651$$
$$x = \frac{651}{999}$$

SOLUTION $\frac{651}{999}$

5 Which is the decimal representation of $\frac{19}{33}$? *(1 point)*

A 0.57

(B) $0.\overline{57}$

C 0.057

D $0.0\overline{57}$

©Curriculum Associates, LLC Copying permitted for classroom use.

GRADE 8 • LESSON 24 • Express Rational Numbers as Fractions and Decimals **Page 2 of 2**

DIFFERENTIATION

RETEACH Tools for Instruction

Students who require additional support for prerequisite or on-level skills will benefit from activities that provide targeted skills instruction.

GRADE 8

- **Lesson 24** Write a Repeating Decimal as a Fraction

REINFORCE Math Center Activity

Students who require practice to reinforce concepts and skills and deepen understanding will benefit from small group collaborative games and activities (available in on-level, below-level, and above-level versions).

GRADE 8

- **Lesson 24** Convert Repeating Decimals

EXTEND Enrichment Activity

Students who have achieved proficiency with concepts and skills and are ready for additional challenges will benefit from group collaborative games and activities that extend understanding.

GRADE 8

- **Lesson 24** Terminate or Repeat?

Overview | Find Rational Approximations of Irrational Numbers

MATH FOCUS

Focus Standards

8.NS.A.1 Know that numbers that are not rational are called irrational. Understand informally that every number has a decimal expansion; for rational numbers show that the decimal expansion repeats eventually, and convert a decimal expansion which repeats eventually into a rational number.

8.NS.A.2 Use rational approximations of irrational numbers to compare the size of irrational numbers, locate them approximately on a number line diagram, and estimate the value of expressions (e.g., π^2).

8.EE.A.2 Use square root and cube root symbols to represent solutions to equations of the form $x^2 = p$ and $x^3 = p$, where p is a positive rational number. Evaluate square roots of small perfect squares and cube roots of small perfect cubes. Know that $\sqrt{2}$ is irrational.

STANDARDS FOR MATHEMATICAL PRACTICE (SMP)

SMP 1, 2, 3, 4, 5, and 6 are integrated into the Try-Discuss-Connect routine.*

This lesson provides additional support for:

2 Reason abstractly and quantitatively.

7 Look for and make use of structure.

8 Look for and express regularity in repeated reasoning.

* See page 1o to learn how every lesson includes these SMP.

Objectives

Content Objectives

- Distinguish between rational and irrational numbers.
- Understand that every irrational number has a decimal expansion, and therefore all rational and irrational numbers have decimal expansions.
- Approximate the value of an irrational number or irrational expression.
- Compare and order rational and irrational numbers and locate them on a number line.

Language Objectives

- Use lesson vocabulary accurately when speaking and writing about rational and irrational numbers.
- Follow written and oral directions to find decimal expansions of irrational numbers.
- Demonstrate understanding of *approximate* and *approximation* by solving problems involving finding the value of an irrational number or irrational expression.
- Describe an irrational number by identifying its position on a number line in relation to the nearest whole numbers when speaking and writing.

Prior Knowledge

- Recognize perfect squares.
- Use formulas for area and circumference of a circle to find exact and approximate values.
- Write terminating and repeating decimals as fractions, and vice versa.
- Classify numbers as whole numbers, integers, and rational numbers.

Vocabulary

Math Vocabulary

irrational number a number that cannot be expressed as a quotient of two integers. The decimal expansion of an irrational number never repeats or terminates.

real numbers the set of rational and irrational numbers.

Review the following key terms.

perfect square the product of an integer and itself.

pi (π) in a circle, the quotient $\frac{\text{circumference}}{\text{diameter}}$. Common approximations are 3.14 and $\frac{22}{7}$.

rational number a number that can be expressed as the fraction $\frac{a}{b}$ where a and b are integers and $b \neq 0$.

repeating decimals decimals that repeat the same digit or sequence of digits forever. A repeating decimal can be written with a bar over the repeating digits.

square root of x the number that when multiplied by itself is equal to x.

terminating decimals decimals that end, or end in repeated zeros.

Academic Vocabulary

approximate (adjective) almost exact.

approximate (verb) to find a close position or almost exact value of something.

approximation value that is close to an exact value.

exact accurate and precise. An exact amount is not an estimate.

Learning Progression

In Grade 7, students wrote fractions as terminating or repeating decimals. They also learned formulas for area and circumference of a circle and applied those formulas to real-world problems.

Earlier in Grade 8, students identified perfect squares and found square roots of perfect squares. They also learned that rational numbers have decimal expansions that terminate or repeat.

➤

In this lesson, students distinguish between rational and irrational numbers and learn that irrational numbers have decimal expansions that do not terminate or repeat. They approximate values of irrational numbers and plot their locations on a number line, and they compare and order rational and irrational numbers.

➤

Later in Grade 8, students will work with the Pythagorean Theorem and its converse and apply the Pythagorean Theorem to real-world problems. Students will also use their knowledge of irrational numbers as they determine exact and approximate volumes of cylinders, cones, and spheres.

Pacing Guide

Items marked with ✦ are available on the **Teacher Toolbox**.

	MATERIALS	DIFFERENTIATION
SESSION 1 **Explore** Numbers That Are Not Rational (35–50 min)		
• **Start** (5 min) • **Try It** (5–10 min) • **Discuss It** (10–15 min) • **Connect It** (10–15 min) • **Close: Exit Ticket** (5 min) **Additional Practice** (pages 599–600)	**Math Toolkit** grid paper Presentation Slides ✦	**PREPARE** Interactive Tutorial ✦ **RETEACH or REINFORCE** Visual Model
SESSION 2 **Develop** Finding Rational Approximations and Locating Them on the Number Line (45–60 min)		
• **Start** (5 min) • **Try It** (10–15 min) • **Discuss It** (10–15 min) • **Connect It** (15–20 min) • **Close: Exit Ticket** (5 min) **Additional Practice** (pages 605–606)	**Math Toolkit** grid paper Presentation Slides ✦	**RETEACH or REINFORCE** Visual Model **REINFORCE** Fluency & Skills Practice ✦ **EXTEND** Deepen Understanding
SESSION 3 **Develop** Estimating the Value of Irrational Expressions (45–60 min)		
• **Start** (5 min) • **Try It** (10–15 min) • **Discuss It** (10–15 min) • **Connect It** (15–20 min) • **Close: Exit Ticket** (5 min) **Additional Practice** (pages 611–612)	**Math Toolkit** compasses, grid paper, rulers Presentation Slides ✦	**RETEACH or REINFORCE** Visual Model **Materials** For display: calculator **REINFORCE** Fluency & Skills Practice ✦ **EXTEND** Deepen Understanding
SESSION 4 **Refine** Finding Rational Approximations of Irrational Numbers (45–60 min)		
• **Start** (5 min) • **Monitor & Guide** (15–20 min) • **Group & Differentiate** (20–30 min) • **Close: Exit Ticket** (5 min)	**Math Toolkit** Have items from previous sessions available for students. Presentation Slides ✦	**RETEACH** Hands-On Activity **Materials** For each pair: ruler, Activity Sheet *1-Inch Grid Paper* ✦ **REINFORCE** Problems 4–8 **EXTEND** Challenge **PERSONALIZE** i-Ready
Lesson 25 Quiz ✦ or **Digital Comprehension Check**		**RETEACH** Tools for Instruction ✦ **REINFORCE** Math Center Activity ✦ **EXTEND** Enrichment Activity ✦

Overview | Find Rational Approximations of Irrational Numbers

Connect to Culture

➤ **Use these activities to connect with and leverage the diverse backgrounds and experiences of all students. Engage students in sharing what they know about contexts before you add the information given here.**

SESSION 2 ■ ■ □ □

Try It Ask students if they have ever had a vegetable garden. Have any gardeners describe what vegetables they grew and how well those vegetables did in their gardens. Along with tomatoes, lettuce is one of the simpler vegetables to grow in a garden. Lettuce can be planted alongside or even between flowers or other taller vegetables. The garden soil should be loose and have good drainage for the lettuce growth to have its best results.

SESSION 3 ■ ■ ■ □

Try It In Japan, *taiko* is the term used to refer to any kind of drum. Taiko drumming ensembles have been playing in Japan for more than 2,000 years. The drummers practice for many hours to perfect their choreographed routines. The routines are so intense that they not only showcase the musicianship of the drummers, they also display their athleticism. The drums are made in a variety of sizes. One specific type of drum is called an *odaiko*, which means *big, fat drum*. The world's largest odaiko drum is almost 10 feet in diameter. While the origins of taiko drumming are Japanese, it is an art form that is now practiced by groups around the world. Ask students whether they have ever heard a taiko drumming group play and what that experience was like.

SESSION 4 ■ ■ ■ ■

Try It **Problem 4** Ask students who have helped to build or renovate a playground in their community to share their experiences and describe what measures they took to help keep children safe. In many playgrounds, square rubber tiles are used to make a soft surface under play structures. These rubber tiles help prevent injuries, as they protect a falling child from concrete and blacktop. Rubber tiles do not require a lot of maintenance and typically last a long time. Many of these tiles are made from recycled materials.

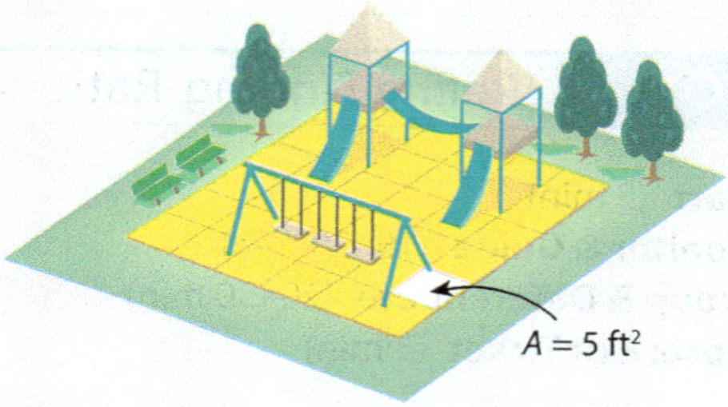

Connect to Family and Community

After the Explore session, have students use the Family Letter to let their families know what they are learning and to encourage family involvement.

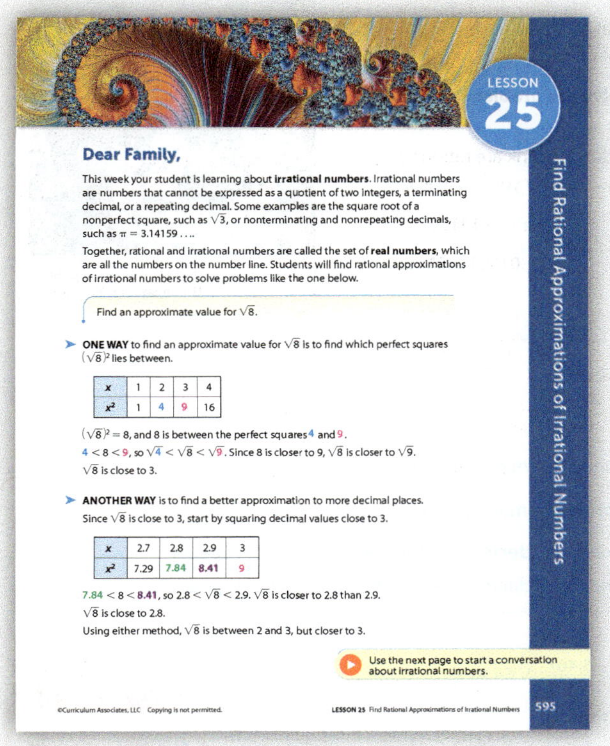

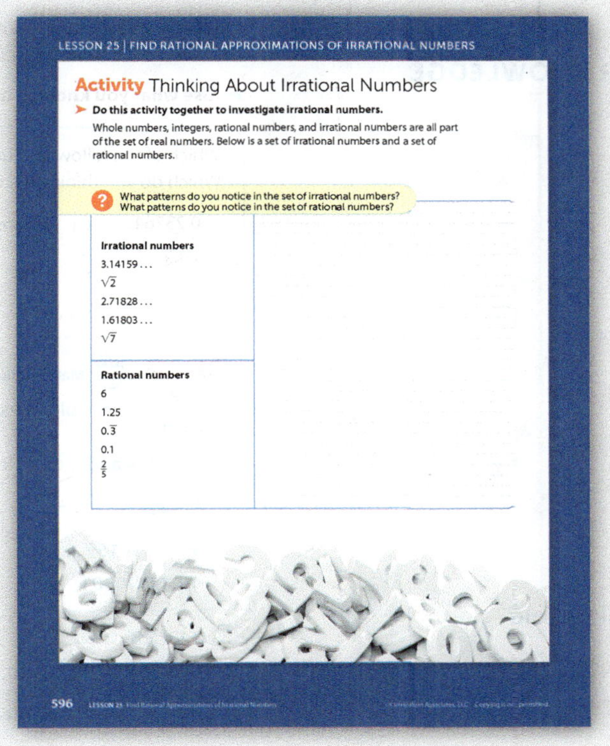

Connect to Language

For English language learners, use the Differentiation chart to scaffold the language in each session. Use the Academic Vocabulary routine for academic terms before Session 1.

DIFFERENTIATION | ENGLISH LANGUAGE LEARNERS

Use with **Session 1** **Connect It**

ACADEMIC VOCABULARY

An *overbar* is a bar placed over a digit or digits. It shows that the digit(s) repeat. For example, in $0.4\overline{9}$ the overbar shows that the digit 9 repeats.

An *ellipsis* (. . .) is a type of punctuation that shows a sentence or list will continue.

Levels 1–3: Reading/Listening

Help students read and make sense of Connect It problem 2. Display a table of perfect squares and the following frames. Have students circle *ir-* and *not* in the text and frames and complete the frames using *square root* and *perfect square*:

- *A rational number is a _____ of a _____.*
- *An **ir**rational number is a _____ of a number that is **not** a _____.*

Paraphrase problem 2b. Support students in describing irrational numbers:

- *An example of an irrational number is _____. The decimal does not _____ and it does not _____.*

Levels 2–4: Reading/Speaking

Help students with Connect It problem 2 by having them identify terms for numbers, such as *irrational number, quotient, integers,* and *perfect square.* Add the terms to a word bank, point out that *rational* and *irrational* have the same base, and explain that *ir-* means *not*. Ask: *What other prefix means* not? [*non-*] Have students identify terms with *non-* and discuss other words with *ir-* or *non-*.

Read the problem with students. Have students name the three types of decimals. Ask: *Which decimals have an overbar? Which have an ellipsis? Which have neither?*

Levels 3–5: Reading/Speaking

Help students with Connect It problem 2 by having them preview the problem and identify key terms using a **Co-Constructed Word Bank.** Suggest *irrational number; overbar; ellipsis;* and *nonterminating, nonrepeating decimal.* Compile and display terms. Then ask students to discuss different ways to group terms, like types of decimals, notation, and numbers; words with the same base; or words with prefixes. Ask: *What do* ir- *and* un- *mean?* [not]

Next, have students read the problem with partners. Have them take turns paraphrasing paragraphs. Ask students to pay attention to prefixes that change word meanings.

Explore Numbers That Are Not Rational

Purpose

- **Explore** the idea that some numbers are not rational.
- **Understand** that you can use what you know about rational numbers to determine whether a given number is rational or irrational.

START CONNECT TO PRIOR KNOWLEDGE

Which One Doesn't Belong?

A: $\sqrt{4}$	B: $0.\overline{6}$
C: 81	D: $\frac{7}{8}$

Possible Solutions

All are rational numbers.

A is the only square root.

B is the only repeating decimal.

C is the only perfect square and only whole number.

D is the only fraction and can be written as a terminating decimal.

WHY? Support students' facility with recognizing forms of numbers.

TRY IT SMP 1, 2, 3, 4, 5, 6, 7, 8

Make Sense of the Problem

Before students work on Try It, use **Co-Craft Questions** to help them make sense of the problem. Have students compare questions with a partner. They may revise their question(s) if they wish.

DISCUSS IT SMP 2, 3, 6, 7, 8

Support Partner Discussion

After students work on Try It, have them respond to Discuss It with a partner. Listen for understanding of:

- what makes a number a rational number.
- what it means for a number to be a terminating decimal.
- what it means for a number to be a repeating decimal.
- what an ellipsis at the end of a number means.
- what it means when digits are under an overbar.

Explore Numbers That Are Not Rational

"The Passage," part of *Metronome*, a public art installation in Union Square, New York City

Previously, you learned about rational numbers. In this lesson, you will learn about numbers that are not rational.

➤ **Use what you know to try to solve the problem below.**

Which of the following numbers do you think are rational? Which do you think are not rational? Justify your answers.

0.23764	$0.\overline{5467}$	$\pi = 3.14159\ldots$
$\sqrt{64}$	$\frac{2}{3}$	$1.010010001\ldots$

TRY IT Math Toolkit grid paper

Possible work:

SAMPLE A

0.23764 and $\sqrt{64} = 8$	rational; decimal terminates
$0.\overline{5467}$ and $\frac{2}{3} = 0.\overline{6}$	rational; decimal repeats
$\pi = 3.14159\ldots$	not rational; decimal neither terminates nor repeats
$1.010010001\ldots$	not rational; decimal neither terminates nor repeats

SAMPLE B

$0.23764 = \frac{23{,}764}{100{,}000}$; $0.\overline{5467} = \frac{5{,}467}{9{,}999}$; $\sqrt{64} = \frac{8}{1}$

rational; can be written as a fraction

$\pi = 3.14159\ldots$; $1.01001001\ldots$

not rational; cannot be written as a fraction

$\frac{2}{3}$

rational; already written as a fraction

DISCUSS IT

Ask: What strategy did you use to decide if a number is rational?

Share: The strategy I used was . . .

Learning Targets SMP 1, SMP 2, SMP 3, SMP 4, SMP 5, SMP 6, SMP 7, SMP 8

- Know that numbers that are not rational are called irrational.
- Use rational approximations of irrational numbers to compare the size of irrational numbers, locate them approximately on a number line diagram, and estimate the value of expressions.
- Know that $\sqrt{2}$ is irrational.

Common Misconception Listen for students who think 1.010010001. . . is a repeating decimal, and is therefore a rational number. As students share their strategies, ask them what the term *repeating decimal* means. If necessary, remind them that a repeating decimal has a digit or a sequence of digits that repeats without end. Ask students if 1.010010001. . . fits this definition. If students think it does, remind them that a repeating decimal can be written with a bar over the repeating digits. Ask students how they could write this number using that notation. They should see that this is impossible.

Select and Sequence Student Strategies

Select 2–3 samples that represent the range of student thinking in your classroom. Here is one possible order for class discussion:

- try to write each number as a fraction
- (misconception) 1.010010001. . . identified as a repeating decimal
- look for terminating and repeating decimals

Facilitate Whole Class Discussion

Call on students to share selected strategies. Remind students that one way to agree and build on ideas is to explain when they would use the strategy and when they might not.

Guide students to **Compare and Connect** the representations. To help students collect their ideas, ask them to turn and talk about what makes a number a rational number.

ASK *What are some ways to determine which numbers are rational?*

LISTEN FOR Try to write the number as a fraction with an integer numerator and denominator. See if the number is a terminating or repeating decimal or can be rewritten as one.

CONNECT IT

SMP 2, 3, 4, 5

1 Look Back Look for understanding that all rational numbers can be written as the quotient of two integers.

DIFFERENTIATION | RETEACH or REINFORCE

Visual Model

Classify numbers as rational or not rational.

If students are unsure about how to tell whether a number is rational, then show these examples.

- Display the decimal 0.965.
- Ask: *How can you tell whether this number is rational by its decimal form?* [It terminates.]
- Ask: *What is another way you can tell that it is a rational number?* [I can write it as a fraction with an integer numerator and denominator.]
- Invite a volunteer to write a fraction form of the number under the decimal form.
- Display the decimal $0.\overline{54}$.
- Ask: *How can you tell whether this number is rational by its decimal form?* [It repeats.]
- Ask: *Can this number be written as a fraction with an integer numerator and denominator?* [Yes]
- Invite a volunteer to show how to write the repeating decimal as a fraction. $\left[\frac{54}{99}\right]$
- Next, display the decimal 0.1211211121. . .
- Ask: *Is this a terminating decimal?* [No] *Is it a repeating decimal?* [No] *Why?* [Answers may vary.]
- If necessary, extend the decimal and underline the groups of 1 between the 2s. Point out that the number of 1s differs in each group, so there is no group of digits that repeats.
- Ask: *Do you think this number is rational?* [No]

LESSON 25 | SESSION 1

CONNECT IT

1 Look Back Which of the numbers do you think are rational? Which do you think are not rational? Justify your answers.

Possible answer: The rational numbers are 0.23764, $0.\overline{5467}$, $\sqrt{64}$, and $\frac{2}{3}$ because these can be written as fractions. π and 1.010010001. . . are not rational because I cannot write them as fractions.

2 Look Ahead An **irrational number** is a number that cannot be expressed as a quotient of two integers, a terminating decimal, or a repeating decimal.

a. The square root of any whole number that is not a perfect square is irrational. Write *rational* or *irrational* for each of the following.

$\sqrt{2}$ irrational $\sqrt{8}$ irrational

$\sqrt{4}$ rational $\sqrt{9}$ rational

$\sqrt{5}$ irrational $\sqrt{12}$ irrational

b. An irrational number can be expressed with a nonterminating, nonrepeating decimal. For example, 1.010010001 . . . is an irrational number.

Note that an overbar (for example, $0.\overline{1}$) indicates a repeating decimal. An ellipsis (. . .) indicates a nonterminating, nonrepeating decimal.

Together, the rational numbers and irrational numbers are called the **real numbers**. The real numbers are all the numbers on a number line. Write an example of each number in each region of the Venn diagram.

See diagram for possible answers.

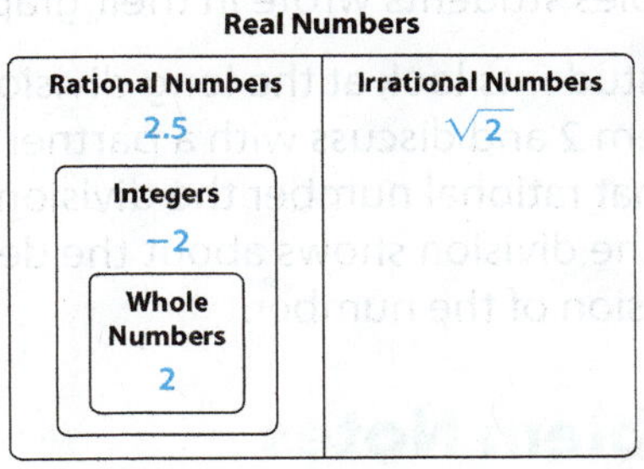

3 Reflect What is one way you can determine whether a number is rational or irrational?

Possible answer: Look at the decimal expansion. If it terminates or repeats, the number is rational. Otherwise, it is irrational.

598

---

2 Look Ahead Point out that a number that cannot be expressed as a quotient of integers, a terminating decimal, or a repeating decimal is *irrational*. Explain that the square root of any whole number that is not a perfect square is irrational. Tell students that moving forward, an overbar will indicate a repeating decimal, while an ellipsis will indicate a nonterminating, nonrepeating decimal.

Ask a volunteer to rephrase the definitions of *irrational number* and *real number*. Support student understanding by displaying a Venn diagram of real numbers, giving examples of real numbers and asking where each number belongs.

CLOSE EXIT TICKET

3 Reflect Look for understanding that you can determine whether a number is rational or irrational by trying to write it as a fraction with an integer numerator and denominator or by looking at its decimal expansion.

Common Misconception If students argue that an irrational number, such as π or $\sqrt{2}$, is rational because it can be written as a fraction, such as $\frac{\pi}{1}$ or $\frac{\sqrt{2}}{1}$, then remind them that the definition of rational number specifies that the numerator and denominator must both be *integers*.

Prepare for Finding Rational Approximations of Irrational Numbers

Support Vocabulary Development

Assign **Prepare for Finding Rational Approximations of Irrational Numbers** as extra practice in class or as homework.

If you have students complete this in class, then use the guidance below.

Ask students to consider the terms *rational number*, *repeating decimals*, and *terminating decimals*. Encourage them to think about the nonmathematical meanings of *terminate* and *repeat*.

Have students work individually to complete the graphic organizer. Invite students to share their completed organizers, and prompt a whole-class comparative discussion of the definitions and examples students wrote in their graphic organizers.

Have students look at the long division work in problem 2 and discuss with a partner how they can tell what rational number the division shows and what the division shows about the decimal expansion of the number.

Problem Notes

1. Students should understand that when a number is rational, it can be written as a quotient of two integers. Students should recognize that numbers that have decimal expansions that either terminate or repeat are rational numbers. Student examples might include repeating decimals with overbars or ellipses and terminating decimals that are whole numbers, integers, or that have a finite number of decimal places.

2. The divisor is 9 and the dividend is 4. This means the rational number is $\frac{4}{9}$. Students should recognize that the digit 4 will continue to repeat in the quotient. For problem 2c, note that even though the digit 4 is shown three times in the quotient, the most efficient way to write the repeating decimal is to write a single 4 under the overbar. The other 4s are redundant.

LESSON 25 | SESSION 1 Name:

Prepare for Finding Rational Approximations of Irrational Numbers

1. Think about what you know about rational numbers. Fill in each box. Use words, numbers, and pictures. Show as many ideas as you can. Possible answers:

Word	In My Own Words	Example
rational number	a number that can be written as a quotient of two integers, $\frac{a}{b}$, where $b \neq 0$	$\frac{3}{4}$ $-7 = \frac{-7}{1}$ $1.5 = \frac{3}{2}$
repeating decimals	decimals that repeat the same digit or sequence of digits forever	$0.\overline{1}$ $2.0\overline{5}$ $0.\overline{137}$
terminating decimals	decimals that end, or that end in repeating 0s	0.2 6.8 $0.75\overline{0}$

2. Look at the long division shown at the right.

$$\begin{array}{r} 0.444 \\ 9\overline{)4.000} \\ -\,3.6 \\ 40 \\ -\,36 \\ 40 \\ -\,36 \\ 4 \end{array}$$

a. What rational number of the form $\frac{a}{b}$ is shown by the long division?
$\frac{4}{9}$

b. Explain how you can use the long division to see that the rational number is equivalent to a repeating decimal.
Possible explanation: At every stage of the long division, the remainder is 4. This means the division process repeats over and over.

c. What is the repeating decimal?
$0.\overline{4}$

REAL-WORLD CONNECTION

When calculating areas of circular objects, irrational numbers typically are involved. Scientists at NASA use a formula including the irrational number π to calculate the length of time it takes the Dawn spacecraft to orbit the dwarf planet Ceres at any given altitude. Scientists can approximate the length of time by using rational approximations of the irrational number π in the formula. Ask students to think of other real-world examples of when using rational approximations of irrational numbers might be useful.

Additional Practice

3 Problem 3 provides another look at deciding whether numbers are rational or not. This problem is similar to the Try It problem. In both problems, students tell why they think given numbers are rational or not rational. This problem asks for students to decide which numbers from a different set of six numbers are rational.

Suggest that students use **Co-Craft Questions** before they begin. Their questions may involve asking which numbers can be written as terminating or repeating decimals or which numbers can be written as a quotient of two integers.

LESSON 25 | SESSION 1

3 Consider the numbers shown below.

$\sqrt{7} = 2.64575\ldots$	0.366	$1.0\overline{2}$
$0.151551555\ldots$	$\frac{2}{9}$	$\sqrt{100}$

a. Which of the numbers do you think are rational? Which do you think are not rational? Justify your answers.

$\sqrt{7} = 2.64575\ldots$	not rational; cannot be written as a fraction
$0.366 = \frac{366}{1{,}000}$	rational; can be written as a fraction
$1.0\overline{2} = \frac{101}{99}$	rational; can be written as a fraction
$0.151551555\ldots$	not rational; cannot be written as a fraction
$\frac{2}{9}$	rational; already written as a fraction
$\sqrt{100} = \frac{10}{1}$	rational; can be written as a fraction

b. Check your answer to problem 3a. Show your work.

$\sqrt{7} = 2.64575\ldots$	not rational; decimal neither terminates nor repeats
0.366	rational; decimal terminates
$1.0\overline{2}$	rational; decimal repeats
$0.151551555\ldots$	not rational; decimal neither terminates nor repeats
$\frac{2}{9} = 0.\overline{2}$	rational; decimal repeats
$\sqrt{100} = 10$	rational; decimal terminates

600

DIFFERENTIATION | ENGLISH LANGUAGE LEARNERS

Use with **Session 2** Connect It

Levels 1–3: Reading/Writing

Support Connect It problem 4 by displaying a decimal place-value chart and this paraphrase: *In problem 3, you squared decimals to find an approximate value of $\sqrt{2}$. You can square numbers to find the nearest hundredth (0.00), thousandth (0.000), and other decimal places. Can you continue forever? Will you find the exact value of $\sqrt{2}$? Why is this true?* Ask students to identify cognates, such as the Spanish cognates *aproximo, continua, decimales, exacto,* and *razón*. Clarify that *exact* is the opposite of *approximate* and *nearest*. Ask for examples of decimals that terminate, repeat, and neither terminate nor repeat. Ask which ones continue forever. Support written responses by helping students answer the questions in the paraphrase above.

Levels 2–4: Reading/Writing

Help students read and make sense of Connect It problem 4. First, display a decimal place-value chart, pronounce the places, and guide students to repeat. Ask: *Could you continue adding places to a decimal? For how long?* Display *continue, forever, eventually,* and *end* in a word bank. Ask students to identify the opposites *continue* and *end*. Have students discuss the compound word *forever* by discussing *for* and *ever*, and *eventually* by discussing the base word *event*. Next, ask for a word related to *forever* that has the opposite meaning; add *never* and *not ever* to the word bank. Prompt students to use the word bank as they discuss the question in the problem and write their responses.

Levels 3–5: Reading/Writing

Have students read and make sense of Connect It problem 4 by discussing the meanings of *continue forever* and *eventually end*. Encourage students to use a variety of strategies, such as identifying words with opposite meanings and analyzing word parts. Ask student to tell how these phrases relate to decimals, including the decimal expansions of rational and irrational numbers. Have students use **Say It Another Way** to confirm understanding of the problem.

Next, provide time for students to consider their responses before turning to partners to discuss which precise terms they will use to explain ideas clearly. Ask students to write responses independently.

Develop Finding Rational Approximations and Locating Them on the Number Line

Purpose

- **Develop** strategies for finding approximations of irrational numbers.
- **Recognize** that you can use successive approximations to estimate square roots of nonperfect squares and then locate these values on a number line.

START CONNECT TO PRIOR KNOWLEDGE

Same and Different

A: $\frac{1}{8}$	B: $0.\overline{12}$
C: $\sqrt{4}$	D: $\frac{1}{3}$

Possible Solutions

All are rational numbers.

A and C have decimal forms that terminate.

B and D have decimal forms that repeat.

A and D are in fraction form.

WHY? Support students' facility classifying numbers as rational, repeating decimals, or terminating decimals.

DEVELOP ACADEMIC LANGUAGE

WHY? Reinforce the meaning of *approximation* through suffixes and examples.

HOW? Have students tell what they do when they approximate. Then write *-tion* on the board. Explain that it forms a noun that names a condition or the result of an action. To help students form the noun, ask: *What do you get when you approximate?* Encourage students to find the words *solve, suppose,* and *discuss* in the session and use similar reasoning to form and explain the corresponding nouns *solution, supposition,* and *discussion.*

TRY IT SMP 1, 2, 4, 5, 6, 7, 8

Make Sense of the Problem

See ***Connect to Culture*** to support student engagement. Before students work on Try It, use **Three Reads** to help them make sense of the problem. Have students consider what they know about the concept of area and the meaning of *approximate.*

LESSON 25 | SESSION 2

Develop Finding Rational Approximations and Locating Them on the Number Line

➤ **Read and try to solve the problem below.**

Mei is building a raised bed in her garden to grow lettuce. She wants the base of the bed to be a square with an area of 2 square meters. Find an approximate side length of the base of the bed. Plot the value on the number line.

TRY IT Math Toolkit grid paper

Possible work:

SAMPLE A

A square with side length, s, has area, s^2.

If $s = 1$, then $1^2 = 1$. If $s = 2$, then $2^2 = 4$.

2 is between 1 and 4 and closer to 1. So, the side length is between 1 meter and 2 meters, closer to 1 meter.

SAMPLE B

Guess a side length of 1.7 meters.

$1.7^2 = 2.89$ Too high

Guess a side length of 1.4 meters.

$1.4^2 = 1.96$ This is close to the given area.

So, the side length is about 1.4 meters.

DISCUSS IT

Ask: What did you do first to solve the problem?

Share: The first thing I did was . . .

601

DISCUSS IT SMP 2, 3, 6

Support Partner Discussion

After students work on Try It, encourage them to respond to Discuss It with a partner. Listen for understanding that:

- the side length of the raised bed involves a number whose square is 2, or $\sqrt{2}$.
- because 2 is not a perfect square, the side length is expressed using an irrational number; the exact side length cannot be expressed using a decimal.

Common Misconception Listen for students who think a number line includes only numbers that are labeled or only numbers that are represented by tick marks. As students share their strategies, talk about the values of the tick marks between whole numbers and what they represent. Have students consider whether there are any other fractions or decimals between the tick marks. Have them identify these numbers, such as 1.25 and 1.75, and indicate where they would be on the number line.

Select and Sequence Student Strategies

Select 2–3 samples that represent the range of student thinking in your classroom. Here is one possible order for class discussion:

- reasoning that the side length is between $\sqrt{1}$ and $\sqrt{4}$, but closer to $\sqrt{1}$
- (misconception) approximation given as 1 because it is the closest labeled number
- guess and check used to find an approximation
- successive approximations used to find numbers whose squares are increasingly close to 2

Facilitate Whole Class Discussion

Call on students to share selected strategies. Remind students that one way to justify a solution is to tell why it is reasonable, given the problem context.

Guide students to **Compare and Connect** the representations. Call on students to rephrase important ideas so that everyone hears them more than once and in more than one way.

ASK *Did everyone get the same approximation? Why or why not?*

LISTEN FOR No. Some students approximated to more decimal places than others. Some guessed until they found an approximation whose square was close enough to 2. Others checked all numbers that were close and had the same number of decimal places to see which one had a square closest to 2.

Model It & Analyze It

If students presented these models, have students connect these models to those presented in class.

If no student presented at least one of these models, have students first analyze key features of the models, and then connect them to the models presented in class.

ASK *What is the connection between the Model It and Analyze It?*

LISTEN FOR Model It locates the value between two whole numbers. Analyze It improves the estimate by using values to the tenths place.

For the whole-number model, prompt students to look at the table.

- *How is the table of perfect squares used?*
- *Why is the side length between 1 and 2, not 1 and 4?*

For the decimal approximation, prompt students to consider if this model could be taken a step further. Ask: *How would you find an estimate to the hundredths place?*

LESSON 25 | SESSION 2

Explore different ways to find a rational approximation for an irrational number.

Mei is building a raised bed in her garden to grow lettuce. She wants the base of the bed to be a square with an area of 2 square meters. Find an approximate side length of the base of the bed. Plot the value on the number line.

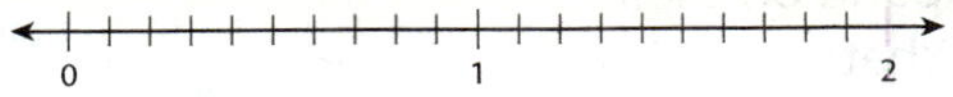

Model It

You can solve an area equation. You can find a rational approximation if the side length is irrational.

A square with side length, s, has area, s^2.

$s^2 = 2$ square meters, so $s = \sqrt{2}$ meters.

$\sqrt{2}$ is irrational, so you must find a rational approximation.

Look for the given area value in a table of perfect squares.

x	1	2	3
x^2	1	4	9

The given area value, 2, is between the perfect squares 1 and 4.

$1 < 2 < 4$

So, $\sqrt{1} < \sqrt{2} < \sqrt{4}$. This means $1 < \sqrt{2} < 2$.

The side length is between 1 and 2 meters.

Analyze It

You can improve your rational approximation by estimating to more decimal places.

You know the value of $\sqrt{2}$ is between 1 and 2. Now improve your approximation to the tenths place by squaring 1.1, 1.2, and so on.

x	1.1	1.2	1.3	1.4	1.5
x^2	1.21	1.44	1.69	1.96	2.25

602

DIFFERENTIATION | EXTEND

SMP 7

Deepen Understanding
Identifying Patterns Related to Irrational Roots

Use the table from Model It with a column added for $x = 4$ and $x^2 = 16$ to help students identify patterns related to irrational square roots and whole numbers.

ASK *Look at consecutive perfect squares. How many whole numbers are between 1^2 and 2^2? What are they? What about between 2^2 and 3^2? Between 3^2 and 4^2?*

LISTEN FOR There are two whole numbers, 2 and 3, between 1^2 and 2^2. There are four whole numbers, 5, 6, 7, and 8, between 2^2 and 3^2. There are six whole numbers, 10, 11, 12, 13, 14, and 15, between 3^2 and 4^2.

ASK *What do you notice about the number of whole numbers between perfect squares?*

LISTEN FOR The number of whole numbers increases by 2 each time.

ASK *Will the square roots of these whole numbers be rational or irrational? Why?*

LISTEN FOR irrational; The whole numbers are not perfect squares.

ASK *Are there more whole numbers with rational square roots or irrational square roots?*

LISTEN FOR There are many more whole numbers with irrational square roots.

Develop Finding Rational Approximations and Locating Them on the Number Line

CONNECT IT

SMP 2, 3, 4, 5, 6, 7, 8

Remind students that the area in each representation is the same, but the approximations of the side lengths are different. Explain that they will now use those representations to reason about how to find a rational approximation of an irrational number.

Before students begin to record and expand on their work in Model It & Analyze It, tell them that problems 3 and 4 will prepare them to provide the explanation asked for in problem 5.

Monitor and Confirm Understanding 1 – 2

- Because 2 is between 1.96 and 2.25 in the x^2 row of the table, $\sqrt{2}$ must be between the x-values corresponding to 1.96 and 2.25, which are 1.4 and 1.5.
- Because 2 is closer to 1.96 than to 2.25, $\sqrt{2}$ is closer to 1.4.
- The number line is divided to show tenths, so 1.4 corresponds to the fourth mark after 1.

Facilitate Whole Class Discussion

3 Look for understanding that, because $\sqrt{2}$ is between 1.4 and 1.5, but closer to 1.4, you can approximate $\sqrt{2}$ to the nearest hundredth by squaring successive hundredths starting at 1.41.

4 Look for understanding that since $\sqrt{2}$ is irrational, the approximation process can go on forever.

ASK *How do you know that you can continue finding decimal approximations closer and closer to $\sqrt{2}$ but never find the exact value?*

LISTEN FOR If I could find an exact decimal value, that would mean $\sqrt{2}$ would be a terminating or repeating decimal. This is not possible because it is an irrational number.

5 Look for the idea that every number, rational or irrational, can be located on the number line.

ASK *How is plotting an irrational number on the number line different from plotting a rational number?*

LISTEN FOR By using small intervals, you can plot any rational number exactly. Because you can only find a decimal approximation of an irrational number, you cannot plot its exact location.

6 **Reflect** Have all students focus on the strategies used to solve the Try It. If time allows, have students discuss their ideas with a partner.

CONNECT IT

➤ **Use the problem from the previous page to help you understand how to find a rational approximation for an irrational number.**

1 Look at **Analyze It**. How do you use the table to find the approximate value of $\sqrt{2}$ to the nearest tenth?
Since 2 is between 1.96 and 2.25, $\sqrt{2}$ is between 1.4 and 1.5. Also, 2 is closer to 1.96, so $\sqrt{2}$ is closer to 1.4.

2 What is the side length of the base of the garden bed to the nearest tenth? Plot the value on the number line. 1.4 meters

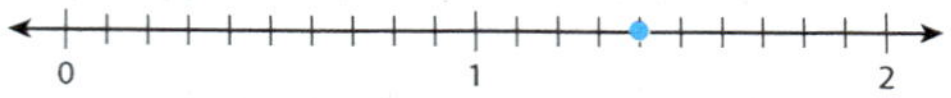

3 Suppose you want to find the approximate value of $\sqrt{2}$ to the nearest hundredth. What would you do next?
Make a table of values by squaring 1.41, 1.42, 1.43, etc. Find the two squared values that 2 lies between.

4 Suppose you continue to approximate the value of $\sqrt{2}$ to the nearest hundredth, then nearest thousandth, and so on. Could you continue this process forever or would it eventually end? Why?
You could continue forever. Since $\sqrt{2}$ is irrational, you can never get a terminating decimal that is equal to it.

5 All real numbers can be plotted on a number line. Why does it make sense that any rational or irrational number can be plotted on a number line?
Since rational and irrational numbers together make up the set of real numbers, they must have a location on the number line.

6 **Reflect** Think about all the models and strategies you have discussed today. Describe how one of them helped you better understand how to solve the **Try It** problem.
Responses will vary. Check student responses.

603

DIFFERENTIATION | RETEACH or REINFORCE

Visual Model

Use a table to approximate $\sqrt{8}$.

If students are unsure about how to use successive approximations to estimate irrational square roots, then use this model to help students understand the process.

- Display two horizontal tables with 6 columns and 2 rows. Label the rows x and x^2.
- Tell students you want to approximate $\sqrt{8}$, the length of the side of a square of area 8.
- Write 1–5 in the x row of the first table. Have a student complete the x^2 row.
- Point to the x^2 row. Ask: *Which two perfect squares is 8 between?* [4 and 9]
- Ask: *Which two whole numbers is $\sqrt{8}$ between? Which one is it closer to?* [2 and 3; 3]
- Move to the second table. Explain that now you want to approximate $\sqrt{8}$ to tenths.
- Ask: *Which tenths values should I write in the x row? Why?* [2.5 to 2.9 because $\sqrt{8}$ is between 2 and 3, but it is closer to 3.]
- Fill in the x-values and then work with students to complete the x^2 row.
- Point to the x^2 row. Ask: *Which numbers in the x^2 row is 8 between?* [7.84 and 8.41]
- Point to the x row. Ask: *Which two tenths is $\sqrt{8}$ between? Which is it closer to?* [2.8 and 2.9; 2.8]

Apply It

For all problems, encourage students to use a model to support their thinking.

7 First, students may eliminate the square roots of perfect squares 81 and 144. Then they may find the perfect squares above and below 151, and evaluate tenths values between the square roots of those two numbers to find the tenths value whose square is closest to 151.

8 **C is correct.** Students may rewrite 8 as $\sqrt{64}$ and then compare the numbers under the square root sign to determine that $\sqrt{65}$ is greatest.

A is not correct. This answer is equal to $\sqrt{64}$, which is less than $\sqrt{65}$.

B is not correct. This answer is the least value.

D is not correct. This answer is less than $\sqrt{65}$.

Apply It

➤ Use what you learned to solve these problems.

7 A park has three square-shaped fountains. The side lengths of the fountains, in feet, are $\sqrt{81}$, $\sqrt{144}$, and $\sqrt{151}$. Identify the side length that is an irrational number. Then approximate that value to the nearest tenth. Show your work.

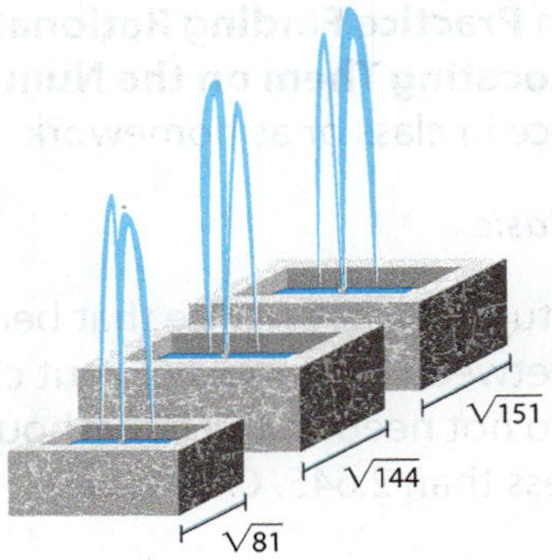

Possible work:

151 is not a perfect square, so $\sqrt{151}$ is irrational.

$144 < 151 < 169$

So, $12 < \sqrt{151} < 13$.

$12.1^2 = 146.41$ $12.2^2 = 148.84$ $12.3^2 = 151.29$

SOLUTION $\sqrt{151}$; the side length is about 12.3 ft.

8 Which of the following has the greatest value?

A 8

B $\sqrt{8}$

(C) $\sqrt{65}$

D $\sqrt{62}$

9 Elijah knows that $\sqrt{17}$ is between 4.1 and 4.2. He wants to find the approximate value of $\sqrt{17}$ to the nearest hundredth. Show how Elijah can find this value. Then plot the value on the number line.

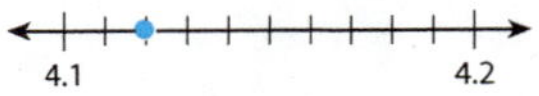

Possible work:

x	4.11	4.12	4.13
x^2	16.8921	16.9744	17.0569

$\sqrt{17}$ is closer to 4.12.

CLOSE EXIT TICKET

9 Students' solutions should show an understanding that:

- to approximate $\sqrt{17}$ to hundredths, you can square hundredths between 4.1 and 4.2 until you find the two squares 17 is between.
- of the two hundredths whose squares 17 is between, the one whose square is closer to 17 is closer to $\sqrt{17}$.

Error Alert If students give 4.13 as the approximation, then have them find the difference between 4.12^2 and 17 and between 4.13^2 and 17. Ask which number has a square that is closer to 17.

Practice Finding Rational Approximations and Locating Them on the Number Line

Problem Notes

Assign **Practice Finding Rational Approximations and Locating Them on the Number Line** as extra practice in class or as homework.

1. *Basic*
2. Students may realize that because $\sqrt{7}$ is between 2.64 and 2.65, but closer to 2.65, they do not need to consider thousandths values less than 2.645. ***Challenge***

LESSON 25 | SESSION 2 Name:

Practice Finding Rational Approximations and Locating Them on the Number Line

➤ **Study the Example showing how to find a rational approximation of an irrational number. Then solve problems 1–5.**

Example

Find the approximate value for $\sqrt{7}$ to the nearest hundredth.

7 is between the perfect squares 4 and 9, and closer to 9. So, $\sqrt{4} < \sqrt{7} < \sqrt{9}$.
$\sqrt{7}$ is between 2 and 3, and closer to 3.

x	2.5	2.6	2.7
x^2	6.25	6.76	7.29

$\sqrt{7}$ is between 2.6 and 2.7, and slightly closer to 2.6.

x	2.63	2.64	2.65
x^2	6.9169	6.9696	7.0225

$\sqrt{7}$ is between 2.64 and 2.65, and closer to 2.65.

So, $\sqrt{7}$ is approximately 2.65.

1 Plot the approximate value of $\sqrt{7}$ from the Example on the number line.

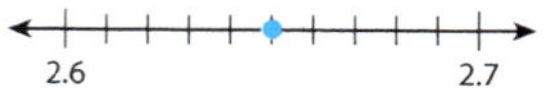

2 Explain how you could continue the work in the Example to approximate $\sqrt{7}$ to the nearest thousandth.

Possible answer: The table shows that $\sqrt{7}$ is between 2.64 and 2.65, and closer to 2.65. Since 2.65 is too large, try decimals with 4 in the hundredths place. So, find 2.645^2, 2.646^2, 2.647^2. Then look to see which of these squared values is closest to 7. The number that was squared to give you the value closest to 7 is the approximate value of $\sqrt{7}$ to the nearest thousandth.

605

Fluency & Skills Practice

Finding Rational Approximations and Locating Them on the Number Line

In this activity, students decide whether given square roots are rational or irrational. For irrational square roots, they write a rational approximation.

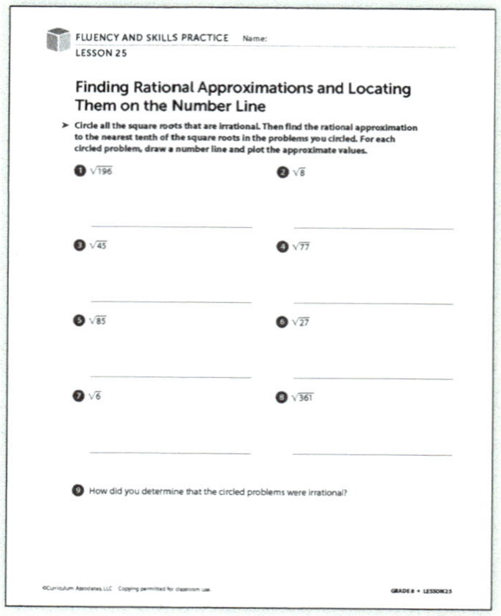

FLUENCY AND SKILLS PRACTICE Name:
LESSON 25

Finding Rational Approximations and Locating Them on the Number Line

➤ Circle all the square roots that are irrational. Then find the rational approximation to the nearest tenth of the square roots in the problems you circled. For each circled problem, draw a number line and plot the approximate values.

1 $\sqrt{196}$
2 $\sqrt{8}$
3 $\sqrt{45}$
4 $\sqrt{77}$
5 $\sqrt{85}$
6 $\sqrt{27}$
7 $\sqrt{6}$
8 $\sqrt{361}$
9 How did you determine that the circled problems were irrational?

©Curriculum Associates, LLC Copying permitted for classroom use. GRADE 8 • LESSON 25

Additional Practice

3 **a.** First find the perfect squares above and below 10. Then find the square roots of these perfect squares and determine which one $\sqrt{10}$ is closer to. Finally, square the tenths values close to the closer square root and find the one whose square is closest to 10. ***Medium***

b. ***Basic***

4 First find the perfect squares above and below 33. By comparing these perfect squares to 33, determine which one has a square root closer to $\sqrt{33}$. ***Medium***

5 Students may solve the problem by rewriting 3.8 as $\sqrt{14.44}$ and then comparing the numbers under the radical. ***Medium***

3 An outdoor square chessboard has an area of 10 m^2.

a. Find the approximate length of a side of the chessboard to the nearest tenth. Show your work.

Possible work:

10 is between the perfect squares 9 and 16, and closer to 9. So, $\sqrt{9} < \sqrt{10} < \sqrt{16}$. $\sqrt{10}$ is between 3 and 4, and closer to 3.

$3.1^2 = 9.61$ $3.2^2 = 10.24$

$\sqrt{10}$ is between 3.1 and 3.2, and closer to 3.2.

SOLUTION The side length is approximately 3.2 m.

b. Use your answer to problem 3a to plot the approximate value of $\sqrt{10}$ on the number line.

4 Ian wants to plot $\sqrt{33}$ on a number line that is only marked with whole numbers. Between which consecutive whole numbers should he plot the value? Which of those whole numbers should the value be closer to? Explain.

between 5 and 6, closer to 6; Possible explanation: 33 is between the perfect squares 25 and 36, and closer to 36.

$\sqrt{25} < \sqrt{33} < \sqrt{36}$, so $5 < \sqrt{33} < 6$

5 Order the following numbers from least to greatest: $\sqrt{16}$, $\sqrt{15}$, 3.8. Show your work.

Possible work:

$15 < 16$, so $\sqrt{15} < \sqrt{16}$.

$3.8^2 = 14.44$, so $3.8 < \sqrt{15}$.

SOLUTION 3.8, $\sqrt{15}$, $\sqrt{16}$

DIFFERENTIATION | ENGLISH LANGUAGE LEARNERS

Use with **Session 3** **Apply It**

Levels 1–3: Speaking/Listening

Help students interpret Apply It problem 9. Before reading, ask students to tell the height and length of the triangle. Ask: *Are the dimensions exact or approximate?* Display *exact* and *approximate*. Ask for cognates, such as *exacto* and *aproximo* in Spanish, and for examples of exact and approximate numbers. Point out the symbol ≈ for approximations. Then read the problem with students. Ask students to use *exact* and *approximate* to tell partners what they need to do to solve the problem:

- *I need to find the* ____ *area. Then I need to find the* ____ *area to the nearest* ____.

Levels 2–4: Speaking/Listening

Have students prepare for Apply It problem 9 by discussing the diagram and predicting what they will need to solve. Then read the problem aloud. Have students confirm or correct their prediction.

To help students make sense of the problem, ask: *How are the questions the same? How are they different?* Give students time to reread and study the words before discussing with partners.

- *Both questions ask for* ____.
- *One question asks for* ____, *while the other question asks for* ____.

Review *exact, approximate,* and *tenth* and have students solve the problem.

Levels 3–5: Speaking/Listening

Have students prepare for Apply It problem 9 by discussing the diagram with partners and predicting what they will need to solve. Read the problem aloud and ask partners to confirm or correct their predictions.

Next, give students time to consider their solution strategy before turning to discuss with partners. Have partners take turns asking and answering questions. If needed, have students use these questions and sentence frames:

- *What is your first step?*
- *What type of numbers will the exact area have? The approximation?*
- *How do you think you can use the hint?*

Develop Estimating the Value of Irrational Expressions

Purpose

- **Develop** strategies for estimating the value of an expression that includes an irrational number.
- **Recognize** that you can use a decimal approximation for an irrational number to get an estimate of the value of an irrational expression.

START CONNECT TO PRIOR KNOWLEDGE

Which One Doesn't Belong?

A $\sqrt{49}$	B $\sqrt{\frac{4}{9}}$
C $\sqrt{11}$	D $\sqrt{0.25}$

Possible Solutions

A is the only expression equal to a whole number.

B is the only expression with a fraction under the radical sign.

C is the only irrational number.

D is the only expression with a decimal under the radical sign.

WHY? Support students' facility with working with square roots.

DEVELOP ACADEMIC LANGUAGE

WHY? Reinforce language used to talk about estimates and calculations.

HOW? Make a two-column chart with *Almost exact* and *Exact* as headings. Have students brainstorm meanings, synonyms, and cognates. Then ask them to suggest related academic words, synonyms, and cognates they can use to talk about each action, for example *approximation, estimate, calculate,* and *precise*. Write suggestions in the correct columns on the table. Have students refer to the table as they talk about their work in the session.

TRY IT SMP 1, 2, 4, 5, 6

Make Sense of the Problem

See ***Connect to Culture*** to support student engagement. Before students work on Try It, use **Three Reads** to help them make sense of the problem. Before responding to each question, have students turn and talk about their responses.

Develop Estimating the Value of Irrational Expressions

Read and try to solve the problem below.

Jiro is a member of a taiko drumming group. He plays an odaiko drum that has a circular playing surface with a diameter of 6 feet. Jiro wants to paint the playing surface with a mitsudomoe symbol.

What is the exact area of the drum's playing surface? What is an approximation of the area? Round your approximation to the nearest hundredth of a square foot. ($A = \pi r^2$; $\pi \approx 3.14$, $\pi \approx \frac{22}{7}$)

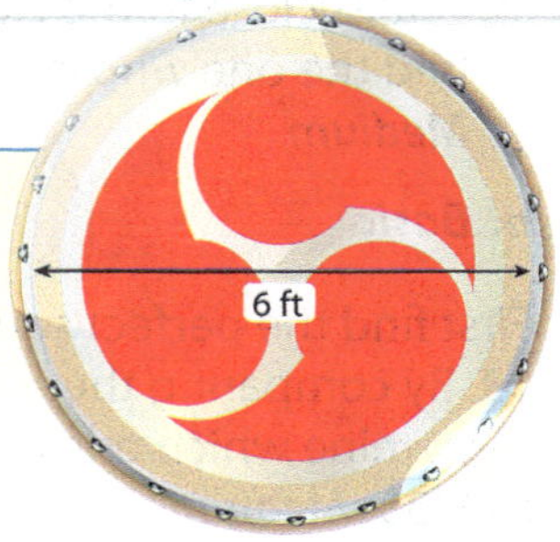

odaiko drum with mitsudomoe symbol

TRY IT Math Toolkit compasses, grid paper, rulers

Possible work:

SAMPLE A

The diameter is 6 ft, so the radius is 3 ft.

$A = \pi(3)^2$

$= 9\pi$

$\approx 9(3.14)$, or 28.26

The exact area is 9π ft^2. This is approximately 28.26 ft^2.

SAMPLE B

$d = 6$, so $r = 3$. $A = \pi r^2$ and $r^2 = 9$.

So, the exact value of the area is 9π ft^2.

Use $\frac{22}{7}$ to approximate π. $9\pi \approx 9\left(\frac{22}{7}\right)$

$= \frac{198}{7}$

≈ 28.29

An approximation of the area is 28.29 ft^2.

DISCUSS IT

Ask: How can you restate the problem in your own words?

Share: The problem is asking . . .

607

DISCUSS IT SMP 1, 2, 3, 4, 5, 6

Support Partner Discussion

After students work on Try It, have them explain their work and then respond to Discuss It with a partner. Look for understanding that:

- an exact area is written in terms of π.
- an approximate area is calculated using a fraction or decimal approximation of π.

Error Alert If students get an area of 36π, then they are using the diameter instead of the radius in the area formula. Have these students state the formula for the area of a circle and tell what the variables stand for. Then, have them reread the problem and note that 6 feet is the diameter, not the radius.

Select and Sequence Student Strategies

Select 2–3 samples that represent the range of student thinking in your classroom. Here is one possible order for class discussion:

- drum sketched on grid paper, then formula used
- decimal approximation of π, 3.14, used in calculation of approximate area
- fraction approximation of π, $\frac{22}{7}$, used in calculation of approximate area

Facilitate Whole Class Discussion

Call on students to share selected strategies. Prompt students to connect strategies by showing how they are alike and how they are different.

Guide students to **Compare and Connect** the representations. If a student's ideas are unclear, you might repeat the idea and reword it so that others understand.

ASK *Why are all the students' approximations not the same?*

LISTEN FOR Some students used a decimal approximation for π and some used a fraction. The different approximations lead to slightly different answers.

Picture It & Model It

If students presented these models, have students connect these models to those presented in class.

If no student presented at least one of these models, have students first analyze key features of the models, and then connect them to the models presented in class.

ASK *What do the models have in common?*

LISTEN FOR Each representation finds the length of the radius and then substitutes that length into the area formula.

For the exact solution, prompt students to consider the value of making a sketch.

- *Why is a sketch useful?*
- *What else could be labeled on the picture?*

For the approximate solution, prompt students to consider the structure of the equations.

- *What do the different symbols, = and ≈, tell about the solution?*
- *The instructions say to use 3.14 for π. How is the solution affected if 3.142, 3.1416, or 3.14159 is used as the decimal approximation for π?*

LESSON 25 | SESSION 3

➤ **Explore different ways to estimate the value of an irrational expression.**

Jiro is a member of a taiko drumming group. He plays an odaiko drum that has a circular playing surface with a diameter of 6 feet. Jiro wants to paint the playing surface with a mitsudomoe symbol.

What is the exact area of the drum's playing surface?

What is an approximation of the area? Round your approximation to the nearest hundredth of a square foot. ($A = \pi r^2$; $\pi \approx 3.14$, $\pi \approx \frac{22}{7}$)

Picture It

You can make a sketch and find the exact area using the formula for the area of a circle.

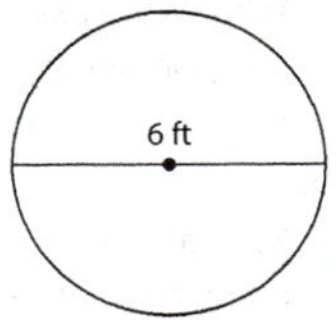

Since the diameter, d, is 6 ft, the radius, r, is $\frac{d}{2}$, or 3 ft.

$A = \pi r^2$

$= \pi(3)^2$

Model It

You can use an approximate value for π to find an approximate area.

Use $\pi \approx 3.14$.

$A = \pi(3)^2$

$\approx 3.14(3)^2$

608

DIFFERENTIATION | EXTEND

SMP 2

Deepen Understanding

Reasoning Abstractly and Quantitatively about Area of Circles

Have students consider how the area of the circle would change if the diameter were halved or doubled.

ASK *Imagine drawing a circle inside the circle in Picture It with half the diameter. Do you think its area would be half the original area? If not, would it be more or less than half?*

LISTEN FOR Its area would be much less than half the original area.

ASK *What is the exact area of a circle with diameter 3 ft? How does it compare to the original area?*

LISTEN FOR The area is 2.25π ft^2. This is $\frac{1}{4}$ of the original area, 9π ft^2.

ASK *Do you think a circle with double the diameter would have double the area?*

LISTEN FOR I think its area would be much more than double the original area.

ASK *What is the area of a circle with diameter 12 ft? How does it compare to the original area?*

LISTEN FOR The new area is 36π, which is 4 times the original area.

Develop Estimating the Value of Irrational Expressions

CONNECT IT

SMP 2, 3, 4, 5, 6

Remind students that the representations show how to find the exact area and the approximate area of the same circle. Explain that they will now use those representations to reason about estimating the value of an irrational expression.

Before students begin to record and expand on their work in Picture It & Model It, tell them that problems 1 and 4 will prepare them to provide the explanation asked for in problem 5.

Monitor and Confirm Understanding 1 – 3

- The symbol π represents an exact irrational number, and using it in the expression results in the exact area.
- Using 3.14 or $\frac{22}{7}$ as an approximation of π results in an approximate area.
- An approximation of the area can be more useful than the exact area in some situations.

Facilitate Whole Class Discussion

4 Look for understanding that more decimal digits in the approximation of π lead to a more precise answer.

> **ASK** *Why does using a value of π with more decimal places give a more accurate area?*
>
> **LISTEN FOR** Because π is an irrational number with digits that go on forever, the more decimal places used, the closer the approximation will be to the actual value of π. Calculating the area using a more accurate approximation of π will give a more accurate final answer.

5 Look for the idea that the symbolic form of irrational numbers is exact, and the numerical form is an approximation.

> **ASK** *When would it make sense to use an approximate value of an irrational number rather than the exact number in symbolic form?*
>
> **LISTEN FOR** You might want to find a length, area, or other measurement for some practical purpose. For example, you might want to know how much fencing to buy to enclose a square area or how much paint you need to cover a circular surface.

6 **Reflect** Have all students focus on the strategies used to solve the Try It. If time allows, have students discuss their ideas with a partner.

CONNECT IT

➤ **Use the problem from the previous page to help you understand how to estimate the value of an irrational expression.**

1 Look at **Picture It**. Why do you use π rather than 3.14 or $\frac{22}{7}$ in the calculation to find the exact area of the drum's surface?

Since π is an irrational number, 3.14 and $\frac{22}{7}$ are just approximations. To express the exact value, you have to use the symbol for the number.

2 Look at **Model It**. Why might you need a numerical value for the answer? Why use an approximation for π in this case?

Possible answer: You might need a numerical value if you need an estimate of the playing area to paint or replace it. To get a numerical value for the area of the playing surface, you need to use an approximate value of π.

3 What is the exact area of the drum's playing surface? Based on **Model It**, what is an approximation of the area to the nearest hundredth of a square foot?

9π ft^2; 28.26 ft^2

4 You can use a calculator to approximate some irrational numbers. For example, many calculators use 3.141592654 as an approximation for π. Would using this value for π give a more accurate final answer than using 3.14? Explain.

Yes; Possible explanation: The calculator approximates π to more decimal places and is therefore more accurate.

5 How do you write an exact value for an irrational expression? How do you write an approximate value?

If you need an exact value, use the symbolic form of the irrational number, such as π or $\sqrt{2}$. If you need an approximate value, replace the symbolic form with an approximate numerical value and evaluate as needed.

6 **Reflect** Think about all the models and strategies you have discussed today. Describe how one of them helped you better understand how to estimate the value of an irrational expression.

Responses will vary. Check student responses.

609

DIFFERENTIATION | RETEACH or REINFORCE

Visual Model

Demonstrate successive approximations of $\sqrt{2}$ to reinforce a symbolic form as an exact answer and other representations as approximations.

If students are unsure why symbolic forms like π and $\sqrt{2}$ represent exact values, then use this model to reinforce why representations other than symbolic forms are approximations.

Materials For display: calculator

- Display a two-column table with headers *Approximation* and *Approximation*^{2}.
- Fill in the left column with 1.4, 1.41, 1.414, 1.4142, 1.41421, and 1.414213.
- Tell students: *The numbers in the left column are approximations of $\sqrt{2}$.*
- Invite students to square the approximations and fill in the table. Discuss how close each square is to 2. [1.96, 1.9881, 1.999396, 1.99996164, 1.999989924, 1.999998409]
- Ask: *What pattern do you notice in the approximations?* [The more decimal places in the approximation, the closer to 2 its square is.]
- Ask: *How many decimal places do you need to get the exact value of $\sqrt{2}$?* [It is not possible. No matter how many places are shown, it will always be an approximation.] Explain that symbols, such as $\sqrt{2}$, are needed to write an exact value of an irrational number.

Apply It

For all problems, encourage students to use a model to support their thinking.

7 Students will need to find a decimal approximation of each value before plotting its location on the number line. Students may use methods learned in Session 2 to approximate the values of the square roots. They may use 3.14 as an approximation for π.

8 **A** **is correct**. Students may find a decimal approximation of each value and then compare the decimals to determine which is greatest.

B is not correct. This answer is less than 4π, which is about 12.56.

C is not correct. This answer is less than $\sqrt{16}$, which is 4, so it is less than 4π.

D is not correct. This answer has a value of about 7.14, which is less than 4π, which is about 12.56.

Apply It

➤ **Use what you learned to solve these problems.**

7 Consider the values $\sqrt{26}$, 2π, $-(\pi \times \frac{1}{3})$, and $-\sqrt{10}$. Plot and label the approximate location of each value on the number line. ($\pi \approx 3.14$)

Possible answers:

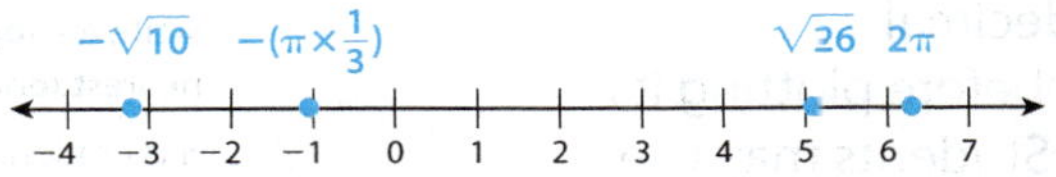

8 Which of the following has the greatest value? ($\pi \approx 3.14$)

A 4π (circled)

B 12

C $\sqrt{13}$

D $\sqrt{16} + \pi$

9 A yield sign on a highway has the shape of an equilateral triangle with sides that are 4 feet long. The height of this triangle is $2\sqrt{3}$ feet. What is the exact area of the triangle? What is an approximation of the area to the nearest tenth? Show your work. (*Hint*: $\sqrt{3} \approx 1.73$)

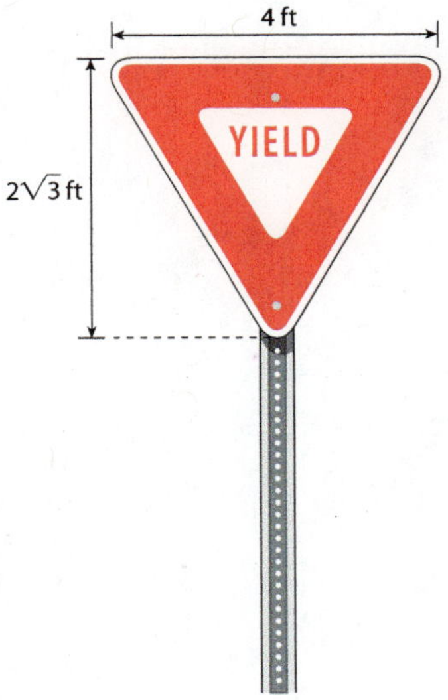

Possible work:

$A = \frac{1}{2}bh$

$= \frac{1}{2}(4)(2\sqrt{3})$

$= 4\sqrt{3}$

$\approx 4(1.73)$

$= 6.92$

SOLUTION The exact area is $4\sqrt{3}$ ft^2, which is ≈ 6.9 ft^2.

CLOSE EXIT TICKET

9 Students' solutions should show an understanding that:

- the exact answer should include a radical symbol.
- the approximation will involve a number to the tenths place.
- $2\sqrt{3}$ means $2 \cdot \sqrt{3}$.

Error Alert If students give 6.92 as the approximate answer, then ask them to reread the question, which asks for the answer to the nearest tenth. If students give the answer with the unit feet, rather than square feet, ask them whether the answer is a length or an area and whether feet is a unit of area.

Practice Estimating the Value of Irrational Expressions

Problem Notes

Assign **Practice Estimating the Value of Irrational Expressions** as extra practice in class or as homework.

1. Students may use 3.14 in their calculations and then round to the tenths place as the final step. ***Medium***
2. Students will need to find a decimal approximation of each value before plotting its location on the number line. Students may use methods learned in Session 2 to approximate the values of the square roots. They may use 3.14 as an approximation for π. ***Medium***

LESSON 25 | SESSION 3 Name:

Practice Estimating the Value of Irrational Expressions

➤ **Study the Example showing how to estimate the value of an irrational expression. Then solve problems 1–5.**

Example

Write an approximate value for the expression π^2 that is accurate to the nearest tenth.

π is irrational, but an approximate value is 3.14159 . . ..

Use $\pi \approx 3.14$ to get an answer accurate to the nearest tenth.

$\pi^2 \approx 3.14^2$

$= 9.8596$

Round to the nearest tenth.

$\pi^2 \approx 9.9$

1. Write an approximate value for π^3 that is accurate to the nearest tenth. Show your work. ($\pi \approx 3.14$)

   Possible work:

   $\pi \approx 3.14$

   $\pi^3 \approx 3.14^3$

   $= 30.959144$

   SOLUTION $\pi^3 \approx 31.0$

2. Consider the values $\pi - 3$, $-\sqrt{17}$, $\frac{\pi}{3}$, and $2\sqrt{2}$. Plot and label the approximate location of each value on the number line. ($\pi \approx 3.14$)

   Possible answers:

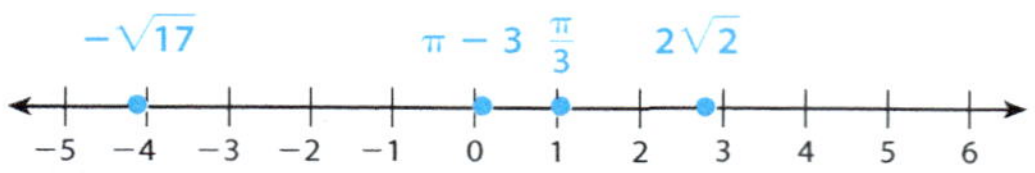

Vocabulary

irrational number
a number that cannot be expressed as a quotient of two integers.

611

Fluency & Skills Practice

Estimating the Value of Irrational Expressions

In this activity, students plot irrational numbers on a number line and write a comparison statement to order the irrational numbers from least to greatest.

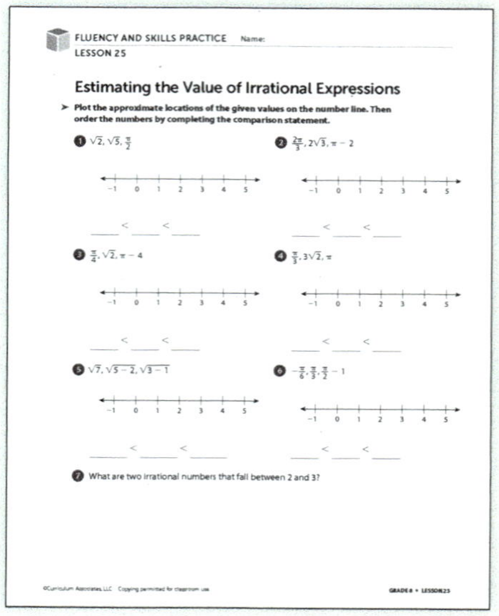
FLUENCY AND SKILLS PRACTICE Name:
LESSON 25

Estimating the Value of Irrational Expressions

➤ Plot the approximate locations of the given values on the number line. Then order the numbers by completing the comparison statement.

7 What are two irrational numbers that fall between 2 and 3?

Additional Practice

3 **a.** Students should recognize that since the problem asks for an exact answer, they should give the final answer with a square root symbol. ***Medium***

b. ***Basic***

4 Students may solve the problem by recognizing that Destiny uses an approximate value for π in her argument. ***Challenge***

5 ***Basic***

LESSON 25 | SESSION 3

3 Soledad wants to make a frame for a square painting. The area of the painting is 2 ft^2. Soledad wants to know the perimeter of the painting.

a. What is the exact perimeter? Show your work.

Possible work:

Use s for the side length. Then $s^2 = A$.

$s^2 = 2$

$s = \sqrt{2}$

The perimeter is $4s$, or $4\sqrt{2}$ ft.

SOLUTION The exact perimeter is $4\sqrt{2}$ ft.

b. What is an approximation of the perimeter to the nearest tenth of a foot? Show your work. (*Hint*: $\sqrt{2} \approx 1.414$)

Possible work:

$4\sqrt{2} \approx 4(1.414)$

$= 5.656$

SOLUTION The perimeter is approximately 5.7 ft.

4 Destiny says that 7π is a rational number because $7\left(\frac{22}{7}\right) = 22$, and 22 is a rational number. Do you agree or disagree with Destiny's reasoning? Explain.

Disagree; Possible explanation: Destiny used $\frac{22}{7}$ for π, but $\frac{22}{7}$ is just an approximate value of π and not the exact value. The exact value of 7π is irrational.

5 Which is greater, -9 or -3π? How do you know? ($\pi \approx 3.14$)

-9; Possible explanation: Since $\pi \approx 3.14$, $-3\pi \approx -9.42$, so -9 is greater.

612

DIFFERENTIATION | ENGLISH LANGUAGE LEARNERS

Use with **Session 4** **Apply It**

Levels 1–3: Speaking/Writing

Support Apply It problem 8 using **Notice and Wonder**. Display the quotient and ask students to tell what they notice and wonder using words, numbers, and/or number lines. Reword and record ideas using short sentences. If needed, prompt students to include the value of π and to tell whether π is a rational or irrational number.

Next, display and read the definition of *rational number*. Ask for examples of integers. Then point to the quotient and ask: *Is it a rational number? Why do you think that?* Have students connect to the notice and wonder statements. Then help students write using:

- *I know ____ is a(n) ____ number.*
- *One reason is ____. Another reason is ____.*

Levels 2–4: Speaking/Writing

Help students interpret Apply It problem 8. Ask them to review the definition of *rational number* using the Interactive Glossary and then confirm understanding using **Say It Another Way**. Ask for examples of rational numbers and integers.

Next, prompt students to tell what they know about π. Record statements for reference.

Help students write responses using the recorded statements and these frames:

- *I know a rational number is ____.*
- *I also know π is ____.*
- *This makes me think that ____.*

Levels 3–5: Speaking/Writing

Have partners read Apply It problem 8 and discuss ways to determine if Hugo is correct. Review that one way to justify or disprove a solution is to use definitions, properties, and what you already know to support or guide your strategy and thinking. Have students discuss the definitions, properties, and other information they might need. If students need guidance, suggest they use the definition of *rational number* and what they know about π.

After partners' discussions, have students write responses independently. Encourage them to write clear explanations by presenting ideas in a logical order with reasons to justify their thinking.

Refine Finding Rational Approximations of Irrational Numbers

Purpose

- **Refine** strategies for finding rational approximations for irrational numbers and expressions.
- **Refine** understanding of comparing and ordering rational and irrational numbers.

START CHECK FOR UNDERSTANDING

Find an approximate value of $\sqrt{22}$ to the nearest tenth.

Solution

4.7

WHY? Confirm students' understanding of finding a rational approximation for an irrational number, identifying common errors to address as needed.

MONITOR & GUIDE

Before students begin to work, use their responses to the **Start** to determine those who will benefit from additional support. Use the **Error Analysis** table below to guide remediation.

Have all students complete the Example and problems 1–3, using Consider This and Pair/Share as appropriate. Observe and monitor their reasoning and guide or redirect students as needed.

LESSON 25 | SESSION 4

Refine Finding Rational Approximations of Irrational Numbers

➤ **Complete the Example below. Then solve problems 1–9.**

Example

Is $\sqrt{2}$ greater than, less than, or equal to $1\frac{206}{500}$?

Look at how you could use a rational approximation for $\sqrt{2}$ to compare.

You can use a calculator to find that $\sqrt{2} \approx 1.414$.

Write a fraction for 1.414.

$$1.414 = 1 + 0.414$$
$$= 1 + \frac{414}{1{,}000}$$
$$= 1 + \frac{207}{500}$$
$$= 1\frac{207}{500}$$

SOLUTION $\sqrt{2}$ is greater than $1\frac{206}{500}$.

CONSIDER THIS . . . You can solve the problem by writing a fraction to approximate $\sqrt{2}$ or by writing $1\frac{206}{500}$ as a decimal.

PAIR/SHARE Without calculating, how do you know $\sqrt{2}$ cannot be equal to $1\frac{206}{500}$?

Apply It

1 Find an approximate value for $\sqrt{9} + \sqrt{10}$ to the nearest tenth. Show your work.

Possible work:

$\sqrt{9} = 3$

10 is between the perfect squares 9 and 16, and closer to 9.

So, $\sqrt{9} < \sqrt{10} < \sqrt{16}$. $\sqrt{10}$ is between 3 and 4, and closer to 3.

$3.1^2 = 9.61$ $3.2^2 = 10.24$

So, $\sqrt{10}$ is between 3.1 and 3.2, and closer to 3.2.

$$\sqrt{9} + \sqrt{10} \approx 3 + 3.2$$
$$= 6.2$$

SOLUTION $\sqrt{9} + \sqrt{10} \approx 6.2$

CONSIDER THIS . . . Only one of the addends is irrational.

PAIR/SHARE How do you know that your answer is reasonable?

613

START ERROR ANALYSIS

If the error is . . .	Students may . . .	To support understanding . . .
11	have divided 22 by 2.	Prompt students to think of the list of perfect squares. Ask: *Which two perfect squares is 22 between?* [16 and 25] Explain that they can improve their approximation by estimating to more decimal places.
5	have approximated the value to the nearest whole number.	Ask students to carefully read the question and calculate the approximation to the correct place value.
4.6	have thought 4.6^2, or 21.16, is closer to 22 than 4.7^2, or 22.09.	Prompt students to find and compare the differences between 22 and 21.16 and between 22.09 and 22 to see which value is closer to 22.

Example

Guide students in understanding the Example. Ask:

- *How can you estimate $\sqrt{2}$ without using a calculator?*
- *How can you write the decimal part of the approximation of $\sqrt{2}$ as a fraction? What denominator does this fraction need to have in order to compare it to $1\frac{206}{500}$?*
- *Could you write both $\sqrt{2}$ and $1\frac{206}{500}$ as decimals to compare? Why or why not?*

Help all students focus on the Example and responses to the questions by prompting students to check that their explanations are clear by pausing and asking classmates for questions or comments.

Look for understanding that students can write both $1\frac{206}{500}$ and an estimate of $\sqrt{2}$ as either fractions with the same denominator or as decimals to compare them.

Apply It

1 Students should know that $\sqrt{9} = 3$. Students may use a list of perfect squares to find that 10 is between perfect squares 9 and 16, and therefore $\sqrt{10}$ is between 3 and 4. Students may square 3.1, 3.2, 3.3, . . . to find the approximation of $\sqrt{10}$ to the nearest tenth, and then add this approximation to 3. *DOK 2*

2 Students may also rewrite $3\frac{6}{50}$, or $3\frac{12}{100}$, as the decimal 3.12 and then compare the decimal to 3.14, the decimal approximation of π. *DOK 2*

3 **D is correct.** Students may approximate each value and determine that $-(\pi + 2)$ is the farthest left on a number line, so it has the least value. It is important that students follow the order of operations.

A is not correct. This answer is equal to -5, which is greater than $-(\pi + 2)$, which is about -5.14.

B is not correct. This answer is positive, so it cannot be less than any of the negative choices.

C is not correct. This answer has a value of about -4.86, which is greater than $-(\pi + 2)$, which is about -5.14.

DOK 3

LESSON 25 | SESSION 4

2 Is π greater than, less than, or equal to $3\frac{6}{50}$? Show your work. ($\pi \approx 3.14$)

Possible work:

Write a fraction for 3.14.

$3.14 = 3 + 0.14$

$= 3 + \frac{14}{100}$

$= 3 + \frac{7}{50}$

$= 3\frac{7}{50}$

CONSIDER THIS . . . You can write an approximate decimal value for π to the nearest hundredth. Then write the decimal as a fraction.

PAIR/SHARE How does π compare to $3\frac{7}{50}$?

SOLUTION π is greater than $3\frac{6}{50}$.

3 Which of the following has the least value? ($\pi \approx 3.14$)

A $-\sqrt{25}$

B $\sqrt{37}$

C $\pi - 8$

(D) $-(\pi + 2)$

CONSIDER THIS . . . You can find the approximate value of the irrational numbers to the nearest tenth for this problem.

Adoncia chose C as the correct answer. How might she have gotten that answer?

Possible answer: Adoncia may have chosen the expression with the least absolute value: $|-4.86| < |-5.14|$. However, the value of $-(\pi + 2)$ is less than the value of $\pi - 8$.

PAIR/SHARE Can you eliminate any of the choices before doing any calculations or finding any approximate values?

614

GROUP & DIFFERENTIATE

Identify groupings for differentiation based on the **Start** and problems 1–3. A recommended sequence of activities for each group is suggested below. Use the resources on the next page to differentiate and close the lesson.

Approaching Proficiency
- **RETEACH** Hands-On Activity
- **REINFORCE** Problems 4, 6, 7

Meeting Proficiency
- **REINFORCE** Problems 4–8

Extending Beyond Proficiency
- **REINFORCE** Problems 4–8
- **EXTEND** Challenge

Have all students complete the **Close: Exit Ticket.**

Resources for Differentiation are found on the next page.

Refine Finding Rational Approximations of Irrational Numbers

Apply It

4 See ***Connect to Culture*** to support student engagement. Students may also use the fact that the area of the entire square play surface is $36 \cdot 5$ ft^2, or 180 ft^2, so each side of the play surface has a length of $\sqrt{180}$ ft. The perimeter is therefore $4\sqrt{180}$ ft. ***DOK 2***

5 Students may also write $\frac{22}{7}$ as $3\frac{1}{7}$, divide to rewrite $\frac{1}{7}$ as a decimal, and then compare the decimal to the decimal part of 3.14159 . . . ***DOK 3***

6 **a.** Multiplying a number by itself is the same as squaring that number. Squaring the square root of any number is that number.

b. If a decimal neither terminates nor repeats, it is an irrational number.

c. The square root of a number that is not a perfect square is irrational, and the opposite of that number is also irrational.

d. Any number minus itself is 0, which is rational.

DOK 1

---

4 A playground has square rubber tiles under a play structure. The tiles are arranged in 6 rows of 6 tiles each to make a large square play surface. The area of each tile is 5 ft^2.

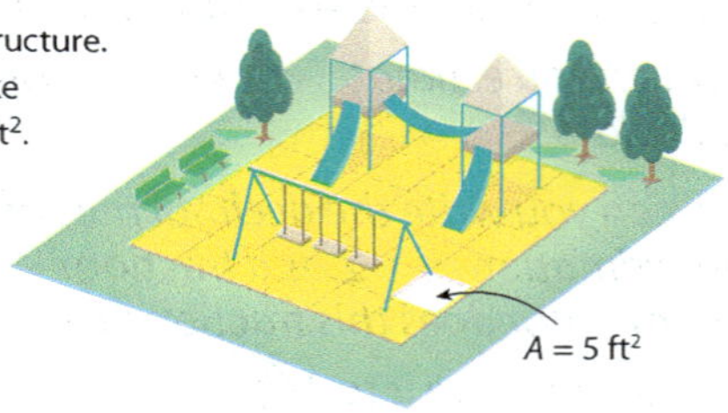

What is the exact perimeter of the play surface? What is an approximation of the perimeter to the nearest tenth of a foot? Show your work. (*Hint*: Use a calculator to get an approximation.)

Possible work:

Each square rubber tile has sides that are $\sqrt{5}$ ft long.

Each side of the square play surface is $6\sqrt{5}$ ft long.

The perimeter of the square play surface is $4(6\sqrt{5})$, or $24\sqrt{5}$ ft.

$24\sqrt{5} \approx 24(2.236)$

$= 53.664$

SOLUTION The perimeter is $24\sqrt{5}$ ft ≈ 53.7 ft.

5 The decimal expansion for π begins 3.14159 . . . . A common rational approximation for π is $\frac{22}{7}$. Is $\frac{22}{7}$ greater than or less than π? Explain.

Greater than; Possible explanation:

By long division, $\frac{22}{7} \approx 3.14286$

So, $\frac{22}{7} > \pi$.

6 Tell whether each value is *Rational* or *Irrational*.

	Rational	Irrational
a. $\sqrt{2} \cdot \sqrt{2}$	●	○
b. 0.20220222022220 . . .	○	●
c. $-\sqrt{11}$	○	●
d. $\pi - \pi$	●	○

615

DIFFERENTIATION

RETEACH

Hands-On Activity

Estimate the value of an irrational number.

Students approaching proficiency with finding the rational approximation of an irrational number will benefit from making a model of a square given the area, and then estimating the side lengths of the square using a ruler.

Materials For each pair: ruler, Activity Sheet *1-Inch Grid Paper*

- Display on inch grid paper a square with an area of 4 in.^{2}. Ask: *What is the area of this square?* [4 in.^{2}] *What is the side length of this square?* [2 in.] Repeat with squares with areas of 9 in.^{2} and 16 in.^{2}. [9 in.^{2}, 3 in.; 16 in.^{2}, 4 in.]
- Ask: *How can you use the side length of a square to find its area?* [Square the side length.]
- Have students draw a first-quadrant coordinate plane on their grid paper and draw a square with vertices at (0, 1), (1, 2), (2, 1), and (1, 0).
- Ask: *What is the area of the square? How do you know?* [The square covers four half-grid-squares, so the area of the square is 2 in.^{2}.]
- Remind students that the area formula for a square is $A = s^2$. In this case, the number that can be multiplied by itself to get 2 is $\sqrt{2}$. So the side length of the square is $\sqrt{2}$ in.
- Have students use an inch ruler to estimate the side length of the square.
- Ask: *What is the side length of the square to the nearest $\frac{1}{16}$ inch?* [$1\frac{6}{16}$ in. or $1\frac{7}{16}$ in.]
- Ask: *What is the side length of the square to the nearest tenth of an inch?* [about 1.4 in.]
- Ask: *What does this tell you about the value of $\sqrt{2}$?* [$\sqrt{2}$ is approximately equal to 1.4.]
- Repeat the activity with a square with vertices at (0, 4), (4, 8), (8, 4), and (4, 0).

7 Students may reason that each blade represents the radius of a circle, and the circumference of that circle is the distance the tip of the blade moves in one rotation. Students may use the formula $C = 2\pi r$ to find the number of feet the tip of the blade moves in one full rotation. *DOK 2*

8 A rational number can be written as a fraction in which the numerator and denominator are integers and the denominator is not 0. The numerator, 2π, is not an integer. *DOK 3*

CLOSE EXIT TICKET

9 **Math Journal** Look for understanding that students can identify the two perfect squares their two-digit number is between, and then square tenths between these square roots to get their estimate.

Error Alert If students determine the square root of their two-digit number is between the perfect squares, rather than between their square roots, then have students make a list of perfect squares and their square roots.

End of Lesson Checklist

INTERACTIVE GLOSSARY Support students by suggesting they work with a partner to make a list of 5 irrational numbers and 5 rational numbers.

SELF CHECK Have students review and check off any new skills on the Unit 6 Opener.

7 Wind turbines convert wind into energy. A wind turbine has blades that are each 116 feet long. To the nearest tenth of a foot, how many feet does the tip of one blade move in one full rotation? ($C = 2\pi r$; $\pi \approx 3.14$)

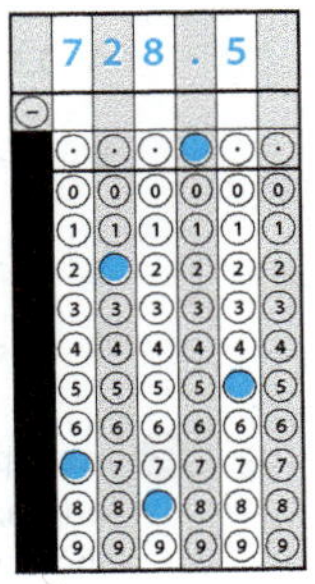

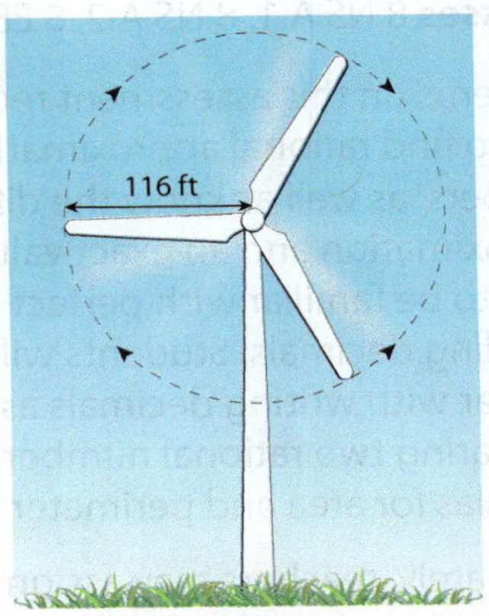

wind turbine

8 Hugo says that $\frac{2\pi}{3}$ is a rational number because it is expressed as a fraction.

Do you agree or disagree? Explain.

Disagree; Possible explanation: A rational number can be written as $\frac{a}{b}$, where a and b are integers and $b \neq 0$. The numerator, 2π, is not an integer, so this fraction does not show that the number is rational.

9 **Math Journal** Choose a two-digit number that is not a perfect square. Show how to find the approximate value of the square root of that number to the nearest tenth.

Possible answer: $\sqrt{18}$; 18 is between the perfect squares 16 and 25, and closer to 16. So $\sqrt{16} < \sqrt{18} < \sqrt{25}$. $\sqrt{18}$ is between 4 and 5, and closer to 4.

$4.1^2 = 16.81$ $4.2^2 = 17.64$ $4.3^2 = 18.49$

So, $\sqrt{18}$ is between 4.2 and 4.3, and closer to 4.2. $\sqrt{18} \approx 4.2$

End of Lesson Checklist

☐ **INTERACTIVE GLOSSARY** Find the entry for *irrational number*. Tell how irrational numbers and rational numbers are different.

☐ **SELF CHECK** Go back to the Unit 6 Opener and see what you can check off.

REINFORCE

Problems 4–8

Find rational approximations for irrational numbers.

Students meeting proficiency will benefit from additional work with finding rational approximations for irrational numbers by solving problems in a variety of formats.

- Have students work on their own or with a partner to solve the problems.
- Encourage students to show their work.

EXTEND

Challenge

Solve problems that involve rational approximations for an irrational number.

Students extending beyond proficiency will benefit from finding a rational approximation to solve an application problem.

- Have students work with a partner to solve this problem: *A square has an area of 6 ft^2. A semicircle, with one side of the square as its diameter, is cut out of the square. What is the perimeter of the resulting figure to the nearest hundredth?*
- Students may approximate the side length of the square using rational approximations and use that result for the diameter of the semicircle in calculations.

PERSONALIZE

i-Ready

Provide students with opportunities to work on their personalized instruction path with *i-Ready* Online Instruction to:

- fill prerequisite gaps.
- build up grade-level skills.

Lesson Quiz

TESTED SKILLS

Assesses 8.NS.A.1, 8.NS.A.2, 8.EE.A.2

Problems on this assessment require students to be able to find rational approximations of irrational numbers, as well as know the difference between an approximation and an exact value. Students will need to be familiar with perfect squares and rounding decimals. Students will also need to be familiar with writing decimals as fractions, comparing two rational numbers, and applying the formulas for area and perimeter of a square.

Alternately, teachers may assign the **Digital Comprehension Check** online to assess student understanding of this material.

Error Alert Errors may result if students:

- perform operations incorrectly when evaluating numbers.
- round numbers incorrectly.
- use an approximation instead of an exact value.
- incorrectly place the square root of an irrational number between two perfect squares.

Problem Notes

1 **C is correct.** Students could solve the problem by multiplying (3.14)(3.14) to get 9.8596, dividing by 2 to get 4.928, and then rounding to 4.93.

A is not correct. This answer is the result of dividing 3.14 by 2.

B is not correct. This answer is the result of adding 3.14 and 3.14 and then dividing by 2.

D is not correct. This answer is the result of multiplying (3.14)(3.14) and rounding to the nearest hundredth.

(1 point)

DOK 1 | **8.NS.A.1**

2 Students could also solve the problem by recognizing that $\sqrt{14}$ is between 3 and 4 and then finding the square of 3.1, 3.2, etc. to find the value closest to 14.

(2 points)

DOK 2 | **8.NS.A.2**

LESSON 25 • QUIZ | Name:

➤ **Solve the problems.**

1 What is the approximate value of $\frac{\pi^2}{2}$ rounded to the nearest hundredth? Use $\pi \approx 3.14$. *(1 point)*

A 1.57

B 3.14

(C) 4.93

D 9.86

2 Leslie paints on a square canvas that has an area of 14 ft^2. Plot the approximate length, to the nearest tenth, of one side of the canvas on the number line. Show your work. *(2 points)*

Possible student work:

14 is between the perfect squares 9 and 16, and closer to 16.
So, $\sqrt{9} < \sqrt{14} < \sqrt{16}$. $\sqrt{14}$ is between 3 and 4, and closer to 4.

$3.7^2 = 13.69$ $\quad$ $3.8^2 = 14.44$

$\sqrt{14}$ is between 3.7 and 3.8, and closer to 3.7. The side length is approximately 3.7 ft.

3 Marcus installs a square window in his house. The area of the window is 6 m^2. What is the exact perimeter of the window? Show your work. *(2 points)*

Possible student work:

Use s for the side length. Then $s^2 = A$.

$s^2 = 6$

$s = \sqrt{6}$

The perimeter is $4s = 4\sqrt{6}$ m.

SOLUTION The exact perimeter is $4\sqrt{6}$ m.

Short Response Scoring Rubric

Points	Expectations
2	Response has the correct solution(s) and includes well-organized, clear, and concise work demonstrating thorough understanding of mathematical concepts and/or procedures.
1	Response contains mostly correct solution(s) and shows partial understanding of mathematical concepts and/or procedures.
0	Response shows no attempt at finding a solution and no effort to demonstrate an understanding of mathematical concepts and/or procedures.

3 Students could solve the problem by recognizing that the side length of a square is the square root of the area of the square. Then multiply the side length by 4 to find the perimeter.

(2 points)

DOK 2 | 8.EE.A.2

4 Students could also solve the problem by recognizing that $\sqrt{19}$ is between 4 and 5 and then finding the square of 4.1, 4.2, etc., in order to find the value closest to 19. Similarly, they can place $\sqrt{11}$ between 3 and 4 and find the square of 3.1, 3.2, etc., in order to find the value closest to 11.

(2 points)

DOK 2 | 8.NS.A.2

5 (2 points)

DOK 1 | 8.EE.A.2

LESSON 25 • QUIZ Name:

4 What is the approximate value of $\sqrt{19} + \sqrt{11}$ to the nearest tenth? Show your work. *(2 points)*

Possible student work:

19 is between the perfect squares 16 and 25, and closer to 16.
So, $\sqrt{16} < \sqrt{19} < \sqrt{25}$. $\sqrt{19}$ is between 4 and 5, and closer to 4.
$4.3^2 = 18.49$ $4.4^2 = 19.36$
$\sqrt{19}$ is between 4.3 and 4.4, and closer to 4.4.
11 is between the perfect squares 9 and 16, and closer to 9.
So, $\sqrt{9} < \sqrt{11} < \sqrt{16}$. $\sqrt{11}$ is between 3 and 4, and closer to 3.
$3.3^2 = 10.89$ $3.4^2 = 11.56$
$\sqrt{11}$ is between 3.3 and 3.4, and closer to 3.3.
$\sqrt{19} + \sqrt{11} \approx 4.4 + 3.3 \approx 7.7$.

SOLUTION 7.7

5 Is π less than, greater than, or equal to $3\frac{29}{200}$? Use $\pi \approx 3.14$. Show your work. *(2 points)*

$3.14 = 3 + 0.14$
$= 3 + \frac{14}{100}$
$= 3 + \frac{28}{200}$
$= 3\frac{28}{200}$

SOLUTION π is less than $3\frac{29}{200}$.

DIFFERENTIATION

RETEACH Tools for Instruction

Students who require additional support for prerequisite or on-level skills will benefit from activities that provide targeted skills instruction.

GRADE 8
- **Lesson 25** Approximate and Order Irrational Numbers

REINFORCE Math Center Activity

Students who require practice to reinforce concepts and skills and deepen understanding will benefit from small group collaborative games and activities (available in on-level, below-level, and above-level versions).

GRADE 8
- **Lesson 25** Irrational Go Between

EXTEND Enrichment Activity

Students who have achieved proficiency with concepts and skills and are ready for additional challenges will benefit from group collaborative games and activities that extend understanding.

GRADE 8
- **Lesson 25** That's So Irrational

Overview | Understand the Pythagorean Theorem and Its Converse

UNDERSTAND: What is the Pythagorean Theorem?

MATH FOCUS

This Understand lesson extends students' understanding of triangles, including right triangles, as they explore the Pythagorean Theorem. Foundational understanding established in this lesson supports students in developing strategies to solve real-world problems using right triangle relationships.

Focus Standard

8.G.B.6 Explain a proof of the Pythagorean Theorem and its converse.

See Unit 6 Overview for developing and applied standards.

STANDARDS FOR MATHEMATICAL PRACTICE (SMP)

SMP 2, 3, and 7 are integrated into the Understand lesson structure.*

This lesson provides additional support for:

4 Model with mathematics.

5 Use appropriate tools strategically.

6 Attend to precision.

* See page 1o to learn how every lesson includes these SMP.

Objectives

Content Objectives

- Understand how the side lengths of a right triangle are related.
- Explain geometric and algebraic proofs of the Pythagorean Theorem.
- Explain a proof of the converse of the Pythagorean Theorem.
- Use the side lengths of a triangle to determine whether it is a right triangle.

Language Objectives

- Understand the lesson vocabulary and use it to describe relationships among the side lengths of right triangles in discussion and in writing.
- Respond to questions about proofs of the Pythagorean Theorem by referring to figures of congruent triangles in partner and class discussions.
- Explain in writing a proof of the converse of the Pythagorean Theorem by reasoning about angles in congruent triangles.

Prior Knowledge

- Determine whether three segments with given lengths can form a triangle.
- Understand that any triangle with a given set of three side lengths will be the same size and shape as any other triangle with those same three side lengths.
- Know that the sum of the measures of the angles in a triangle is 180°.
- Evaluate expressions with exponents.
- Understand the relationship between squares and square roots.

Vocabulary

Math Vocabulary

converse of the Pythagorean Theorem in a triangle, if the square of the length of the longest side is equal to the sum of the squares of the lengths of the other two sides, then the triangle is a right triangle.

hypotenuse the side of a right triangle opposite the right angle.

legs (of a right triangle) the two sides of a right triangle that form the right angle.

Pythagorean Theorem in any right triangle, the sum of the squares of the lengths of the legs, a and b, is equal to the square of the length of the hypotenuse, c. So, $a^2 + b^2 = c^2$.

Review the following key terms.

congruent (≅) same size and shape. Two figures are congruent if there is a sequence of rigid transformations that maps one figure onto the second.

right triangle a triangle with one right angle.

square a quadrilateral with 4 right angles and 4 sides of equal length.

square root of x the number that when multiplied by itself is equal to x.

Academic Vocabulary

proof evidence that something is true or false.

prove to use facts to show something is true or false.

Learning Progression

In Grade 6, students calculated the area of triangles and figures composed of triangles.

In Grade 7, students determined whether a given set of three measures determined no triangle, a unique triangle, or more than one triangle.

Earlier in Grade 8, students showed that the sum of the angle measures in a triangle is 180°.

In this lesson, students explore what the Pythagorean Theorem says about how the side lengths of a right triangle are related, and they explain geometric and algebraic proofs of the theorem. Students are also introduced to, and explain a proof of, the converse of the Pythagorean Theorem, which provides a way to tell whether a given triangle is a right triangle based on its side lengths.

In high school, students will develop criteria for triangle congruence. They will learn about trigonometric functions and the Law of Sines and Law of Cosines and use these concepts to find unknown measures in both right and nonright triangles.

Pacing Guide

Items marked with [Teacher Toolbox icon] are available on the **Teacher Toolbox**.

	MATERIALS	DIFFERENTIATION
SESSION 1 **Explore** The Pythagorean Theorem (35–50 min)		
• **Start** (5 min) • **Model It** (5 min) • **Discuss It** (5–10 min) • **Model It** (5–10 min) • **Discuss It** (10–15 min) • **Close: Exit Ticket** (5 min) **Additional Practice** (pages 621–622)	Presentation Slides	**PREPARE** Interactive Tutorial **RETEACH or REINFORCE** Hands-On Activity **Materials** For each student: ruler, scissors, Activity Sheet *1-Centimeter Grid Paper*
SESSION 2 **Develop** Understanding of the Pythagorean Theorem (45–60 min)		
• **Start** (5 min) • **Model It: Geometric Proof** (5 min) • **Discuss It** (5–10 min) • **Model It: Algebraic Proof** (5 min) • **Discuss It** (10–15 min) • **Connect It** (10–15 min) • **Close: Exit Ticket** (5 min) **Additional Practice** (pages 625–626)	Presentation Slides	**RETEACH or REINFORCE** Visual Model **Materials** For display: 4 congruent right triangles **REINFORCE** Fluency & Skills Practice
SESSION 3 **Refine** Ideas About the Pythagorean Theorem and Its Converse (45–60 min)		
• **Start** (5 min) • **Apply It** (35–50 min) • **Close: Exit Ticket** (5 min)	Presentation Slides	
Lesson 26 Quiz or **Digital Comprehension Check**		**RETEACH** Tools for Instruction **REINFORCE** Math Center Activity **EXTEND** Enrichment Activity

Connect to Culture

➤ **Use these activities to connect with and leverage the diverse backgrounds and experiences of all students.**

LESSON 26
The Pythagorean Theorem

Ask students if they have ever heard of the Pythagorean Theorem and if they know what it is about. The Pythagorean Theorem is one of the most famous theorems in mathematics. It involves the relationship between the side lengths of any right triangle. The theorem is named after the Greek mathematician and philosopher Pythagoras, who lived from about 570 to 490 BCE. However, the relationship described in the theorem was known long before Pythagoras was born. Ancient tablets dating back to 1900–1600 BCE show that the Babylonians understood the relationship.

People throughout history have been fascinated by the Pythagorean Theorem and have come up with many different ways to prove it. The ancient text *The Elements,* written by the Greek mathematician Euclid in about 300 BCE includes two proofs of the theorem. Since Euclid's time, over 350 more proofs of the theorem have been written, including proofs by Leonardo da Vinci and U.S. President James Garfield. Albert Einstein wrote a proof of the Pythagorean Theorem when he was 12 years old!

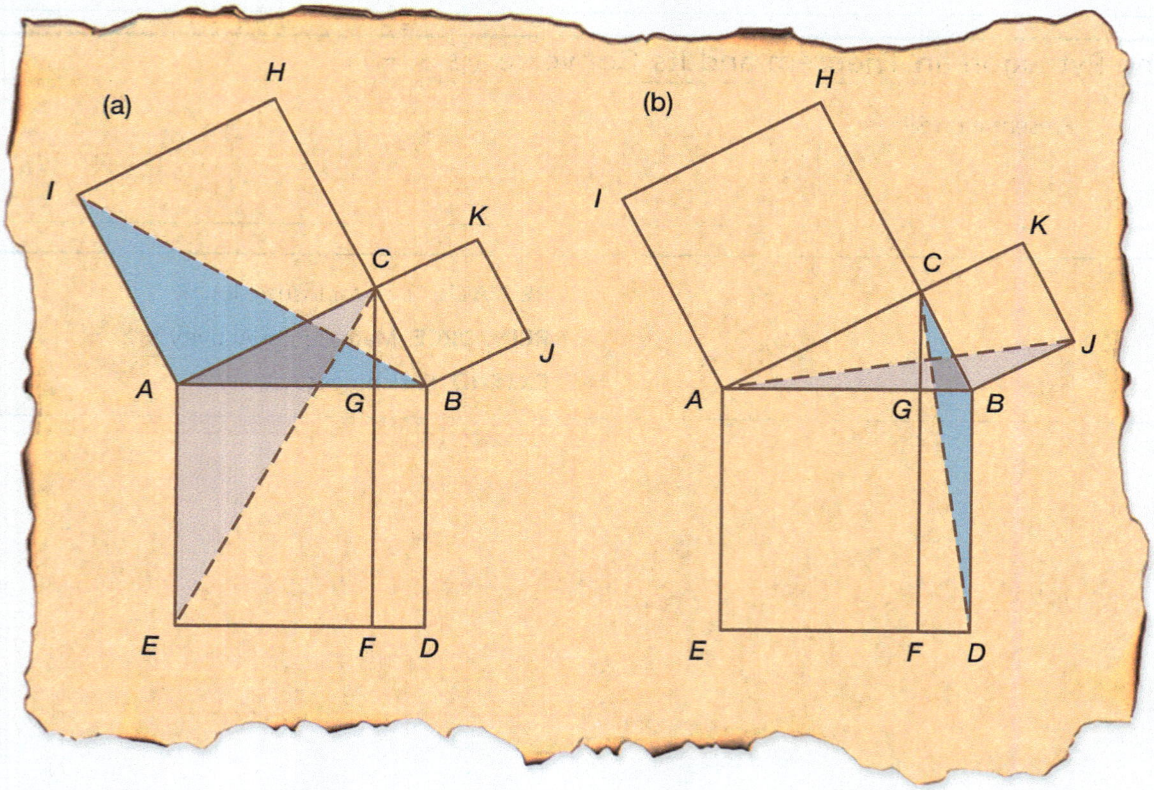

Connect to Family and Community

➤ **After the Explore session, have students use the Family Letter to let their families know what they are learning and to encourage family involvement.**

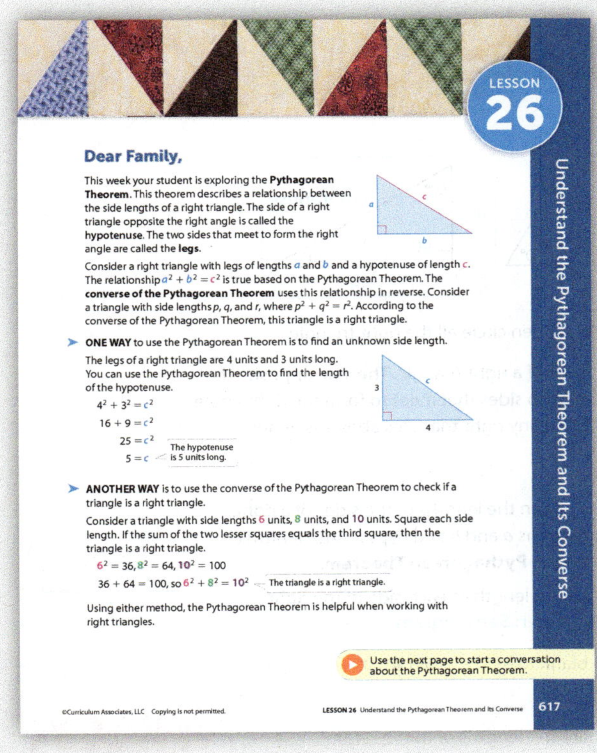

LESSON 26

Dear Family,

This week your student is exploring the **Pythagorean Theorem**. This theorem describes a relationship between the side lengths of a right triangle. The side of a right triangle opposite the right angle is called the **hypotenuse**. The two sides that meet to form the right angle are called the **legs**.

Consider a right triangle with legs of lengths a and b and a hypotenuse of length c. The relationship $a^2 + b^2 = c^2$ is true based on the Pythagorean Theorem. The **converse of the Pythagorean Theorem** uses this relationship in reverse. Consider a triangle with side lengths p, q, and r, where $p^2 + q^2 = r^2$. According to the converse of the Pythagorean Theorem, this triangle is a right triangle.

➤ **ONE WAY** to use the Pythagorean Theorem is to find an unknown side length.

The legs of a right triangle are 4 units and 3 units long. You can use the Pythagorean Theorem to find the length of the hypotenuse.

$4^2 + 3^2 = c^2$

$16 + 9 = c^2$

$25 = c^2$

$5 = c$ ← The hypotenuse is 5 units long.

➤ **ANOTHER WAY** is to use the converse of the Pythagorean Theorem to check if a triangle is a right triangle.

Consider a triangle with side lengths 6 units, 8 units, and 10 units. Square each side length. If the sum of the two lesser squares equals the third square, then the triangle is a right triangle.

$6^2 = 36, 8^2 = 64, 10^2 = 100$

$36 + 64 = 100$, so $6^2 + 8^2 = 10^2$ ← The triangle is a right triangle.

Using either method, the Pythagorean Theorem is helpful when working with right triangles.

Use the next page to start a conversation about the Pythagorean Theorem.

Understand the Pythagorean Theorem and Its Converse

©Curriculum Associates, LLC Copying is not permitted. LESSON 26 Understand the Pythagorean Theorem and Its Converse 617

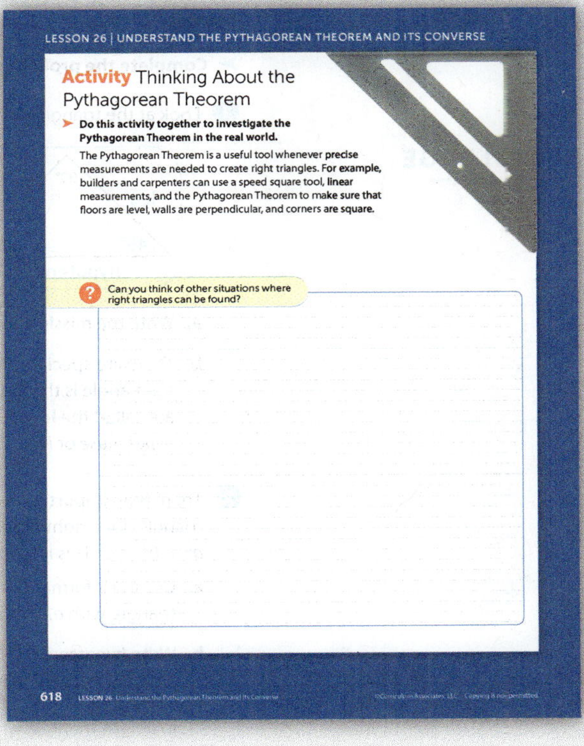

LESSON 26 | UNDERSTAND THE PYTHAGOREAN THEOREM AND ITS CONVERSE

Activity Thinking About the Pythagorean Theorem

➤ **Do this activity together to investigate the Pythagorean Theorem in the real world.**

The Pythagorean Theorem is a useful tool whenever precise measurements are needed to create right triangles. For example, builders and carpenters can use a speed square tool, linear measurements, and the Pythagorean Theorem to make sure that floors are level, walls are perpendicular, and corners are square.

Can you think of other situations where right triangles can be found?

618 LESSON 26 Understand the Pythagorean Theorem and Its Converse ©Curriculum Associates, LLC Copying is not permitted.

Connect to Language

➤ **For English language learners, use the Differentiation chart to scaffold the language in each session. Use the Academic Vocabulary routine for academic terms before Session 1.**

DIFFERENTIATION | ENGLISH LANGUAGE LEARNERS Use with **Session 1** **Model It**

ACADEMIC VOCABULARY

A *diagram* is a drawing that explains or shows the parts of something.

Relate means connect things in some way.

Support means provide facts, definitions, data, or other evidence to show that an argument or claim is true.

Levels 1–3: Speaking/Writing

Prepare students to write responses to Model It problem 4 by previewing the diagrams. Display the diagrams from problem 3 and problem 4. Review the term *relate* and ask for similar words, such as the Spanish cognate *relacionar*. Ask how the diagrams relate to each other and record students' responses.

Next, display the Pythagorean Theorem. Have students circle words in the responses you wrote down that relate to the theorem, like *sum* and *squares*. Help students use the words to draft written responses. Ask students to work with partners to read and revise their drafts.

Levels 2–4: Speaking/Writing

Prepare students to write responses to Model It problem 4. First, review the Academic Vocabulary with students. Explain that *relate* is the base word for common words and phrases. Ask for examples, like *relationship* and *related to*. Have students list math and academic terms that show how things relate. If needed, suggest *equal, product, sum, combine, same, similar,* and *different*.

Next, ask how Rodrigo's diagram relates to problem 3. Remind students to use precise terms. Then read problem 4 with students and use **Stronger and Clearer Each Time** to help them craft written responses.

Levels 3–5: Speaking/Writing

Prepare students to write responses to Model It problem 4. Have students read the problem and discuss the meaning of the Academic Vocabulary. Provide time for students to study the diagrams and decide how they are related. Have students share their ideas. Call on several students to rephrase important ideas so that everyone hears them more than once and in more than way.

Next, have students use **Stronger and Clearer Each Time** to draft, discuss, and revise written responses. Ask partners to discuss whether responses clearly show the connection between ideas and revise as needed.

Explore The Pythagorean Theorem

Purpose

- **Explore** the idea that, in a right triangle, the sum of the squares of the lengths of the legs is equal to the square of the length of the hypotenuse.
- **Understand** that the Pythagorean Theorem involves the relationship between the lengths of the sides of a right triangle and the areas of the squares drawn on the side lengths.

START CONNECT TO PRIOR KNOWLEDGE

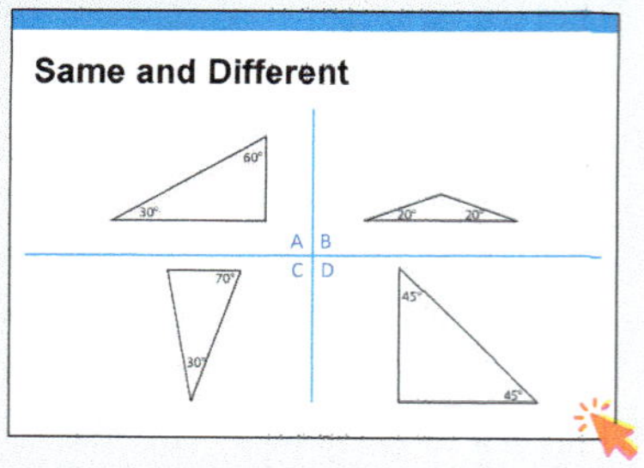

Possible Solutions

All are triangles.

A and D are both right triangles.

B and D are both isosceles triangles.

A and C are both scalene triangles.

B is the only obtuse triangle.

C is the only acute triangle.

WHY? Prepare students to think about the relationships between sides and angles in a triangle.

UNDERSTAND: What is the Pythagorean Theorem?

Explore the Pythagorean Theorem

Model It

➤ **Complete the problems about right triangles.**

1 Look at the triangles below.

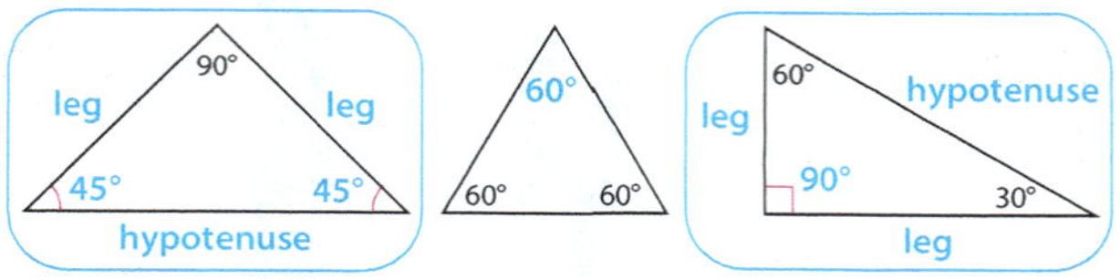

a. Write the missing angle measure(s). Then circle all the right triangles.

b. There are special names for the sides of a right triangle. The side opposite the right angle is the **hypotenuse**. The two sides that meet to form the right angle are called the **legs**. Label each side of any right triangles above as either *hypotenuse* or *leg*.

2 There is an important relationship between the lengths of the sides of a right triangle: for a right triangle with leg lengths a and b and hypotenuse length c, $a^2 + b^2 = c^2$. This relationship is called the **Pythagorean Theorem**.

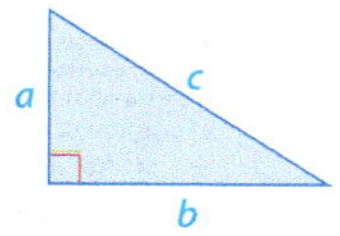

a. Use the information above to label the length of each side of the right triangle with a, b, or c. Possible answer: See diagram.

b. Write *hypotenuse* or *legs* in each blank to help explain what $a^2 + b^2 = c^2$ means in words:

In a right triangle, when you square the lengths of the <u>legs</u> and add these squares, the sum is equal to the square of the length of the <u>hypotenuse</u>.

DISCUSS IT

Ask: How is a hypotenuse similar to a leg? How is it different?

Share: I think the hypotenuse is the longest side in a right triangle because . . .

Learning Target SMP 2, SMP 3, SMP 4, SMP 5, SMP 6, SMP 7
Explain a proof of the Pythagorean Theorem and its converse.

619

MODEL IT SMP 2

Read the *Understand* question at the top of the page. Remind students that they know how to identify right triangles and that the sum of the angle measures of a triangle is 180°.

1 – 2 Tell students that they are going to use what they know about triangles and formulas to learn about a special property of right triangles. Read the problems. Have students explain the meaning of *hypotenuse* and *leg* in their own words.

Common Misconception If students think a triangle can have more than one hypotenuse, challenge them to draw a triangle with two right angles. Remind students that the sum of the measures of the angles in a triangle is 180°. If two angles each measure 90°, the third angle would have to measure 0°.

DISCUSS IT SMP 3, 7

Support Partner Discussion

After students complete problems 1 and 2, have them respond to Discuss It with a partner. Encourage them to think about the relationships between the angles of a triangle and the lengths of its sides.

Listen for understanding that:
- the longest side of a triangle is opposite the largest angle.
- the right angle is the largest angle in a right triangle, so the hypotenuse is the longest side.

Facilitate Whole Class Discussion

Prompt students to think about why it is important to identify the hypotenuse and the legs in a right triangle. Remind students to use precise language in their explanations.

ASK *Why are the sides given special names in a right triangle?*

LISTEN FOR The Pythagorean Theorem relates the lengths of the legs and the hypotenuse. You need to know which side is opposite the right angle.

MODEL IT

SMP 2

3 Tell students they will now think about how a model can help them understand the Pythagorean Theorem. Read the problem aloud and ask them to turn and talk about how the diagram relates to the italicized statement.

Common Misconception If students expect $a + b = c$ to be true, then review the wording of the Pythagorean Theorem. Using $a = 3$, $b = 4$, and $c = 5$, show that $a + b = c$ is not true, but $a^2 + b^2 = c^2$ is indeed true.

DISCUSS IT

SMP 3, 7

Support Partner Discussion

After students complete problem 3, have them respond to Discuss It with a partner. Encourage them to think about how the area of a square is related to its side length.

Listen for understanding that:

- squares drawn on the sides of lengths a, b, and c, have areas a^2, b^2, and c^2, respectively.
- the Pythagorean Theorem can be interpreted to mean that the combined areas of squares drawn on the legs of a right triangle is equal to the area of a square drawn on the hypotenuse.

DIFFERENTIATION | RETEACH or REINFORCE

Hands-On Activity

Make additional models of the Pythagorean Theorem.

If students are unsure about how the diagram supports the Pythagorean Theorem, then use this activity to provide additional examples.

Materials For each student: ruler, scissors, Activity Sheet *1-Centimeter Grid Paper*

- Assign each student one pair of leg lengths: 6 and 8; 5 and 12; 7 and 24; 9 and 12; 10 and 24.
- Have each student draw a right triangle with the assigned leg lengths on grid paper (with the legs on grid lines) and then cut out the triangle.
- Have students align one side of their triangle with a grid line and trace its length. Then, they should draw a square with that side length.
- Have students make squares for the other two sides of the triangle and cut out all their squares.
- Students should cut apart and rearrange pieces of the two smaller squares to cover the largest square without gaps or overlap.
- Discuss with students how this activity supports understanding of the Pythagorean Theorem.

LESSON 26 | SESSION 1

Model It

➤ **Complete the problems about the Pythagorean Theorem.**

3 Here is another way to think about the Pythagorean Theorem:

In a right triangle, the area of a square drawn on the hypotenuse is equal to the combined areas of the squares drawn on the two legs.

You can see an example of this in the diagram to the right.

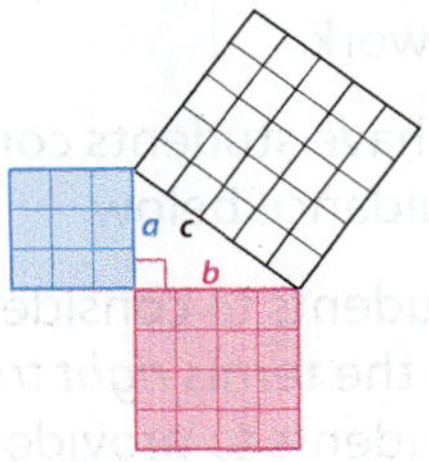

a. Write the length of each side of the right triangle.

a: 3 units

b: 4 units

c: 5 units

b. Write the area of each square.

Square with side length a: 9 square units

Square with side length b: 16 square units

Square with side length c: 25 square units

c. Use your answers from problems 3a and 3b to show that this diagram supports the Pythagorean Theorem. Identify which sides of the right triangle are the legs and which is the hypotenuse in your answer.

Possible answer: In the right triangle, a and b are the lengths of the legs and c is the length of the hypotenuse. The lengths are $a = 3$, $b = 4$, and $c = 5$, so $a^2 = 9$, $b^2 = 16$, and $c^2 = 25$. For the Pythagorean Theorem to be true, $a^2 + b^2 = c^2$. $9 + 16 = 25$ is a true statement, so this diagram supports the theorem.

DISCUSS IT

Ask: How does a square with side length a represent a^2?

Share: I think it is important to know which side of a right triangle is the hypotenuse because . . .

4 **Reflect** Rodrigo drew this diagram related to the diagram in problem 3. How does Rodrigo's diagram help to support understanding of the Pythagorean Theorem?

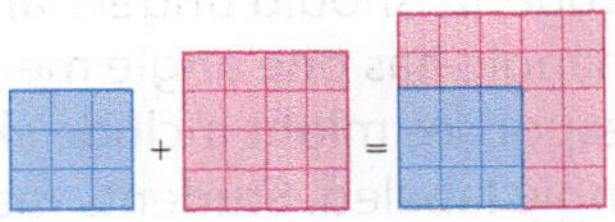

Possible answer: Rodrigo's diagram shows that combining the areas of the squares on the legs results in a square with the same area as the square on the hypotenuse. This supports the understanding that for a right triangle with legs of lengths a and b and hypotenuse of length c, $a^2 + b^2 = c^2$.

620

Facilitate Whole Class Discussion

Prompt students to think about the Pythagorean Theorem equation.

ASK *For a right triangle with side lengths a, b, and c, will the equation $a^2 + b^2 = c^2$ be true no matter which side lengths you substitute for a, b, and c? Explain.*

LISTEN FOR No. You need to substitute the leg lengths for a and b. It does not matter which length is a and which is b. The hypotenuse length must be c.

CLOSE **EXIT TICKET**

4 **Reflect** Look for understanding that the sum of the areas of the two smaller squares is equal to the area of the larger square.

Common Misconception If students do not see how the problem 4 diagram supports the Pythagorean Theorem, then have them look at the squares in problem 3. Students should see that the *addends* are the squares on the legs, and the *sum* is the square on the hypotenuse. By rearranging the pink squares around the blue square, the diagram shows that the combined area of the squares on the legs is equal to the area of the square on the hypotenuse.

Prepare for The Pythagorean Theorem and Its Converse

Support Vocabulary Development

Assign **Prepare for The Pythagorean Theorem and Its Converse** as extra practice in class or as homework.

If you have students complete this in class, then use the guidance below.

Ask students to consider the term *right triangle*. Relate the terms *right triangle* and *right angle*. Ask students to provide real-world examples of right triangles.

Have students work individually to complete the graphic organizer. Invite students to share their completed organizers and prompt a whole-class comparative discussion of examples and non-examples.

Have students look at the groups of angle measures in problem 2 and discuss how to determine whether a group of three angle measures can form a right triangle. Remind students that the sum of the angle measures in a triangle is 180°.

Problem Notes

1 Students should understand that a right triangle has one angle measuring 90°. Student responses might include sketches with the right angle labeled. Students may include sets of three possible angle measures for a right triangle. Students should recognize that the legs of a right triangle are perpendicular.

2 Students should recognize that the sum of the measures of the two smaller angles in a right triangle must equal 90°.

LESSON 26 | SESSION 1 Name:

Prepare for The Pythagorean Theorem and Its Converse

1 Think about what you know about triangles. Fill in each box. Use words, numbers, and pictures. Show as many ideas as you can.
Possible answers:

In My Own Words
a triangle with one right angle

My Illustrations

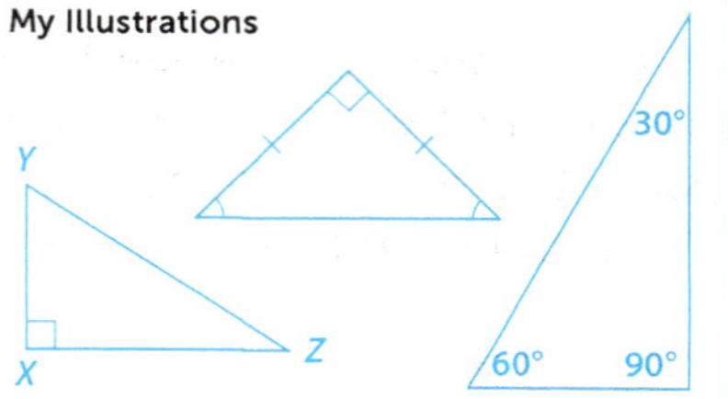

right triangle

Examples
a triangle with angle measures of 30°, 60°, and 90°
a triangle with angle measures of 45°, 45°, and 90°

Non-Examples

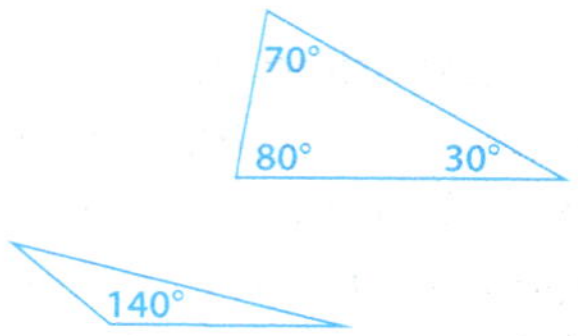

2 Circle the groups of angle measures that represent a right triangle.

25°, 90°, 75	(40°, 90°, 50°)
60°, 60°, 90°	(90°, 35°, 55°)

621

REAL-WORLD CONNECTION

Early film and TV had a screen ratio of width to height, called the *aspect ratio*, of 4 : 3. By the 1950s, many families had TVs, so film studios, in an attempt to get people into movie theaters, changed the aspect ratio of their films to about 12 : 5. This gave movie audiences a wide, panoramic view for a more dramatic presentation. In the late 1980s, TV customers wanted a theater experience at home. The standard aspect ratio for both films and TV was then changed to about 1.78 : 1, or 16 : 9. Now, when you buy a TV set, its size is reported only as the diagonal length of its screen. The aspect ratio and the Pythagorean Theorem allow you to calculate the length and width of the screen from its diagonal measurement. Ask students to think of other real-world examples when the Pythagorean Theorem might be useful.

3 **a.** Students should use the fact that the sum of the angle measures of a triangle is 180°. For the second triangle, students may reason that the two unknown angle measures are equal because the sides opposite them are the same length.

b. Students should recognize that only right triangles have sides that can be identified as legs or the hypotenuse.

4 Students should understand that the three squares are built onto the sides of a right triangle and that the combined areas of the squares on the legs is equal to the area of the square on the hypotenuse.

LESSON 26 | SESSION 1

Complete the problems 3–4.

3 Look at the triangles below.

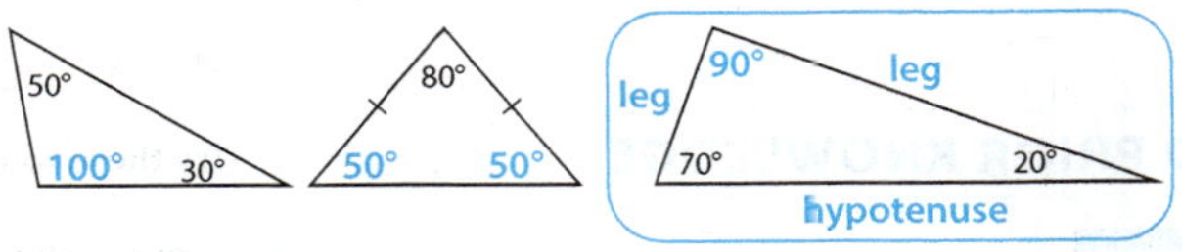

a. Write the missing angle measure(s) for each triangle. Then circle all of the right triangles. See diagram.

b. Label each side of any right triangles as either *hypotenuse* or *leg*. See diagram.

4 Explain how the diagram demonstrates the Pythagorean Theorem.

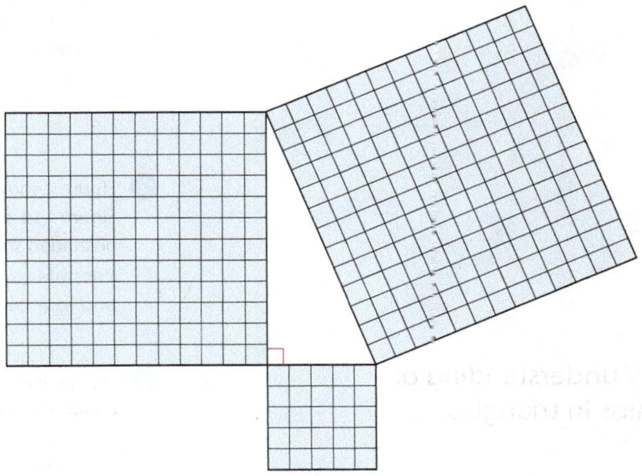

Possible answer: The diagram shows a right triangle with side lengths of 5, 12, and 13, with a square constructed on each side of the triangle. The diagram shows that the total area of the squares on the two legs ($5^2 + 12^2 = 25 + 144 = 169$) is equal to the area of the square on the hypotenuse ($13^2 = 169$).

622

DIFFERENTIATION | ENGLISH LANGUAGE LEARNERS

Use with **Session 2** Model It

Levels 1–3: Reading/Speaking

Help students make sense of Model It: Algebraic Proof problem 5. Read the problem and have students use **Co-Constructed Word Bank** to highlight key words such as *total, area, all, triangles, unshaded, shape, expression, square, sides,* and *length*. Display and review terms students selected. Ask students to identify any cognates they know, such as the Spanish cognates *total, área, triángulo,* and *expresión*. Then guide students to label the figure with terms from the Word Bank. Reread the problem and ask questions to help students make connections to the figure: *What number of triangles do you see? What is the area of one triangle? What is the area of all four triangles? Where is the unshaded shape? What is the side length? What is the area?*

Levels 2–4: Reading/Speaking

Help students make sense of Model It: Algebraic Proof problem 5. Have students read the problem and use a **Co-Constructed Word Bank** to highlight key words and phrases, such as *total area, all four triangles,* and *unshaded shape*. Help students review the terms and help them with related words. For example, explain that the prefix *un-* in *unshaded* means "not" and ask for the term without the prefix. Then encourage students to label the figure with terms from the Word Bank.

Next, have students reread the problem and discuss with partners using:

- *I noticed that* _____.
- *So, I decided to* _____ *because* _____.

Levels 3–5: Reading/Speaking

Have students make sense of Model It: Algebraic Proof problem 5 by discussing the figure with partners. Before reading the problem, have students describe what they notice about the figure. To emphasize key mathematical ideas in students' descriptions, ask others to repeat and rephrase statements related to the area, side lengths, and Pythagorean Theorem.

Next, have students read the problem and take turns explaining their thinking to partners. Remind students that a clear explanation will tell what they noticed about the figure and what they decided to do as a result.

Develop Understanding of the Pythagorean Theorem

Purpose

- **Develop** the idea that the Pythagorean Theorem applies to all right triangles.
- **Understand** that you can prove the Pythagorean Theorem using geometry or algebra.

START CONNECT TO PRIOR KNOWLEDGE

Always, Sometimes, Never

A The longest side of a triangle is called the hypotenuse.

B A right triangle can have side lengths n, n, and $2n$, where n is a whole number.

C A right triangle has an acute angle.

Solutions

A is sometimes true.

B is never true.

C is always true.

WHY? Reinforce students' understanding of side and angle relationships in triangles.

DEVELOP ACADEMIC LANGUAGE

WHY? Recognize the difference between *geometric* and *algebraic* proofs.

HOW? Before Model It, review that a proof in math is the group of steps that shows something is true or false. Help volunteers use word parts or origins to tell what *geometric* and *algebraic* describe. Ask: *What types of steps do you expect to see in a geometric proof? In an algebraic proof?* Then have students look at both Model Its and tell how the words connect to the steps.

MODEL IT

SMP 2, 6

1 – 4 As students complete the problems, have them explain the geometric properties used to justify each claim.

Common Misconception If students do not see why the unshaded area is the same in both figures, then help them see that both figures are squares with side length $a + b$, so the figures must have the same overall area. Then point out that for both figures, the area of the *same* four right triangles is subtracted to find the unshaded area. So, the unshaded area must be the same in both diagrams.

UNDERSTAND: What is the Pythagorean Theorem?

Develop Understanding of the Pythagorean Theorem

Model It: Geometric Proof

➤ **Try these four problems involving a proof of the Pythagorean Theorem.**

1 Figure 1 shows four congruent right triangles forming a square of side length $a + b$. You can prove that the unshaded shape is also a square.

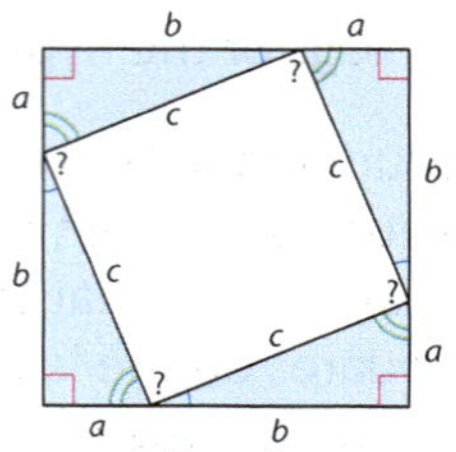

Figure 1

a. How do you know the sides of the unshaded shape are congruent?
All the sides have length c.

b. How can you prove that each angle of this shape measures 90°?
Possible answer: The measures of the two acute angles in each triangle add to 90° because the sum of the angle measures in a triangle is 180°. The two acute angles plus the angle labeled ? form a straight angle measuring 180°. So, the measure of each angle in the shape is 90°.

2 Figure 2 shows a different way to arrange the right triangles from Figure 1 to also form a square of side length $a + b$. Explain why each unshaded shape is also a square.
Possible explanation: They each have four right angles and four congruent sides.

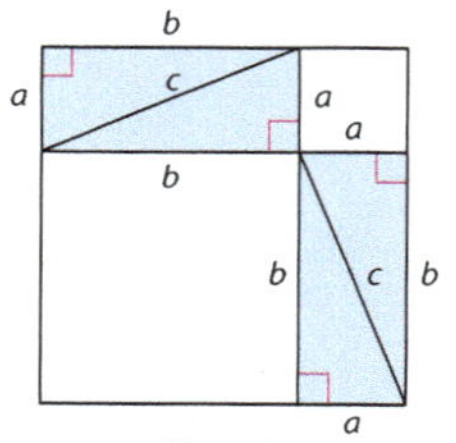

Figure 2

3 Explain why the total area of the two unshaded squares in Figure 2 equals the area of the unshaded square in Figure 1.
Possible answer: The large squares with side length $a + b$ in each figure have the same area. All triangles are the same size. So, the remaining areas are also the same size.

4 How do Figures 1 and 2 prove the Pythagorean Theorem?
Possible answer: The area of the unshaded square in Figure 1 is c^2. The combined area of the two small squares in Figure 2 is $a^2 + b^2$. These areas are equal, so $a^2 + b^2 = c^2$. a and b are the leg lengths and c is the hypotenuse length in each right triangle.

DISCUSS IT

Ask: How are the three unshaded squares important in this proof?

Share: Figures 1 and 2 are alike because . . .

DISCUSS IT

SMP 3, 6, 7

Support Partner Discussion

After students complete problems 1–4, have them respond to Discuss It with a partner. Support as needed with questions such as:

- *What is the side length of each unshaded square?*
- *How are these side lengths related to the side lengths of the right triangle?*

Facilitate Whole Class Discussion

Have students discuss whether problems 1–4 show a geometric proof that would work for *any* right triangle. Ask students to provide reasons to explain how they know their arguments are correct.

ASK *Do you think you could arrange copies of any right triangle to make figures like Figures 1 and 2?*

LISTEN FOR Yes. For any right triangle, you could put four copies of it together to get a figure like Figure 1, and the unshaded middle would be a square with sides the same length as the hypotenuse. You could also make a figure like Figure 2, where the unshaded parts are two squares with sides the same length as the legs.

MODEL IT

SMP 2

5 – 7 As students complete the problems, they will apply the distributive property, the commutative property of multiplication, and the subtraction property of equality. Review these properties, as needed. Challenge students to justify each step in their proof.

DISCUSS IT

SMP 3, 4, 5, 6, 7

Support Partner Discussion

After students complete problems 5–7, have them respond to Discuss It with a partner. Support as needed with questions such as:

- *Why do you need to use the distributive property twice to find $(a + b)(a + b)$?*
- *How does simplifying the area expression $(a + b)(a + b)$ help you compare it to the area expression you found in problem 5?*

Facilitate Whole Class Discussion

For each problem, have students explain their reasoning.

ASK *Why are you able to set the two algebraic expressions equal to each other?*

LISTEN FOR Each expression represents the same area, the area of the large square.

DIFFERENTIATION | RETEACH or REINFORCE

Visual Model

Present a dynamic version of the proof in the text.

If students are unsure about the geometric proof of the Pythagorean Theorem, then use this activity to show them how the figures used are related.

Materials For display: 4 congruent right triangles

- Before class begins, cut out 4 copies of the same right triangle, large enough for display. Label the legs a and b and label the hypotenuse c.
- Show students how to arrange the triangles so that the hypotenuses form the sides of a square as in Figure 1 on the previous page.
- Trace the large outer square that is formed.
- Elicit that the uncovered area of the small inner square is c^2.
- Rearrange the triangles inside the traced square to appear as they do in Figure 2 on the previous page. Point out that the outer square has not changed. The triangles have not changed, so the uncovered area is still c^2.
- Use the labels on the triangles to show that this area is also equal to $a^2 + b^2$.

Model It: Algebraic Proof

➤ **Try these three problems about a proof of the Pythagorean Theorem.**

5 What is the total area of all four triangles in Figure 1? What is the area of the unshaded shape? Use your answers to write an expression for the area of the square with side length $a + b$. $2ab$; c^2; $2ab + c^2$

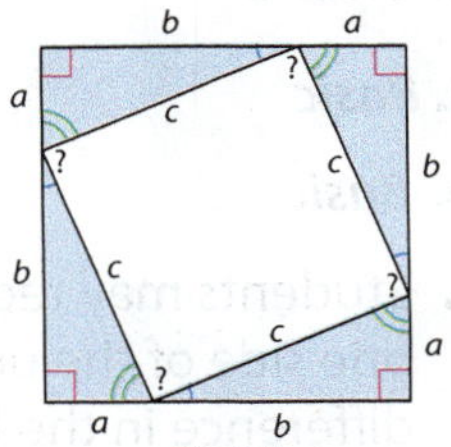

Figure 1

6 **a.** Why can the area of the large square be written as $(a + b) \cdot (a + b)$?
The side length is $a + b$, so the area is $(a + b)^2 = (a + b) \cdot (a + b)$.

b. The distributive property shows that $(a + b) \cdot (a + b) = a^2 + 2ab + b^2$:

$$(a + b) \cdot (a + b) = a(a + b) + b(a + b)$$
$$= a^2 + ab + ab + b^2$$
$$= a^2 + 2ab + b^2$$

Look at your answers to problem 5. Why is $a^2 + 2ab + b^2 = 2ab + c^2$?
Possible answer: Both sides of the equation are expressions for the area of the square with side length $a + b$.

7 Simplify the last equation in problem 6b by subtracting $2ab$ from both sides. How does this prove the Pythagorean Theorem?
$a^2 + b^2 = c^2$; Possible answer: It shows that in a right triangle, the sum of the squares of the leg lengths is equal to the square of the hypotenuse length.

DISCUSS IT

Ask: How does the distributive property help you to find the area of a square with side length $a + b$?

Share: Simplifying the area expressions is important because . . .

CONNECT IT

➤ **Complete the problems below.**

8 What do the geometric proof and the algebraic proof have in common?
Possible answer: Both proofs use Figure 1 to show that $a^2 + b^2 = c^2$.

9 How do both the geometric proof and the algebraic proof show that the Pythagorean Theorem applies to all right triangles?
Possible answer: The proofs do not use specific side lengths for a right triangle, so the theorem will work for any right triangle.

624

CONNECT IT

SMP 2, 3, 7

8 Student responses should show understanding that there is more than one way to prove a mathematical claim. Students should recognize that both proofs rely on the same figure.

CLOSE EXIT TICKET

9 Look for understanding that proofs use variables and examples use specific values. By using variables, students are proving that the Pythagorean Theorem is true for all right triangles.

Error Alert If students' work on the algebraic proof does not confirm the Pythagorean Theorem, then have them work with a partner to find their error. Two sets of eyes are often better than one, and both students will benefit from the discussion and recognition of what went wrong.

Practice Understanding of the Pythagorean Theorem

Problem Notes

Assign **Practice Understanding of the Pythagorean Theorem** as extra practice in class or as homework.

1. **a.** *Basic*

   b. *Basic*

   c. Students may recognize that the length of one side of the unshaded square is the difference in the lengths of the legs of the shaded triangles. ***Medium***

2. Students may replace the parts of the given word equation with the expressions they wrote in problem 1 and then simplify. ***Medium***

LESSON 26 | SESSION 2 Name:

Practice Understanding of the Pythagorean Theorem

➤ **Study how the Example shows how to begin a proof of the Pythagorean Theorem. Then solve problems 1–5.**

Example

Four congruent right triangles are arranged to form a large quadrilateral as shown. The unshaded shape formed in the middle of this figure is also a quadrilateral. Explain how you know both quadrilaterals are squares.

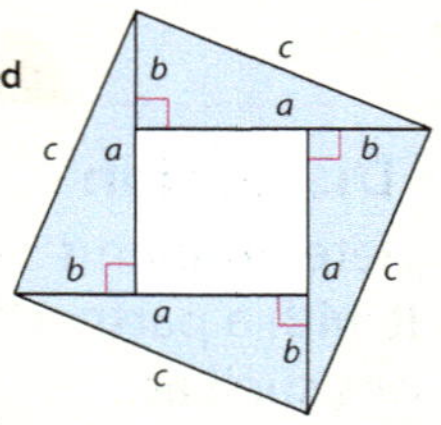

In the large quadrilateral, all sides are the same length, c. Each angle is made up of the two acute angles of a right triangle whose measures sum to 90°.

In the small quadrilateral, all sides are the same length, $a - b$. Each of the right triangles has a 90° angle that forms a linear pair with the angle in the small quadrilateral. So, each angle in the small quadrilateral is also 90°.

Both figures have four congruent sides and four right angles, so they are both squares.

1. Refer to the diagram in the Example to answer these questions.

   a. Write an expression for the area of the large square. $c \cdot c$ or c^2

   b. Write an expression for the total area of the 4 triangles. $4\left(\frac{1}{2}ab\right)$ or $2ab$

   c. Write an expression for the area of the small square. $(a - b)^2$

2. The diagram in the Example shows:

   area of large square = area of four triangles + area of small square

   Use your answers to problem 1 to write an equation to show this relationship. Then simplify the equation. (*Hint*: $(a - b)^2 = a^2 - 2ab + b^2$)

   $c^2 = 2ab + (a - b)^2$

   $c^2 = 2ab + a^2 - 2ab + b^2$

   $c^2 = 2ab - 2ab + a^2 + b^2$

   $c^2 = a^2 + b^2$

Fluency & Skills Practice

Understanding the Pythagorean Theorem

In this activity, students draw right triangles and label the sides to match Pythagorean Theorem equations. They also label the legs and hypotenuses of right triangles.

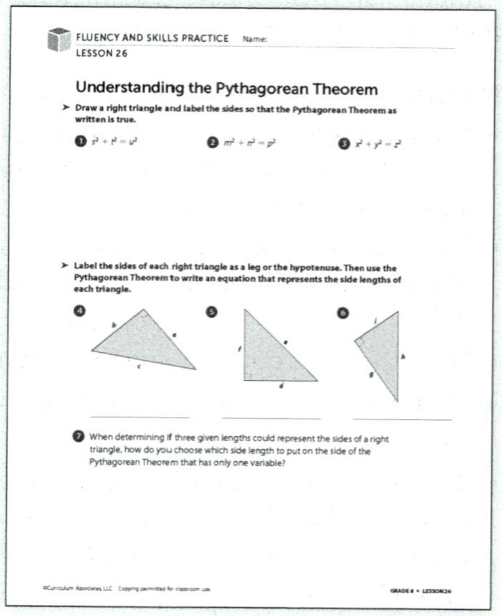

FLUENCY AND SKILLS PRACTICE Name:
LESSON 26

Understanding the Pythagorean Theorem

➤ **Draw a right triangle and label the sides so that the Pythagorean Theorem as written is true.**

1. $s^2 + t^2 = u^2$
2. $m^2 + n^2 = p^2$
3. $x^2 + y^2 = z^2$

➤ **Label the sides of each right triangle as a leg or the hypotenuse. Then use the Pythagorean Theorem to write an equation that represents the side lengths of each triangle.**

4.
5.
6.

7. When determining if three given lengths could represent the sides of a right triangle, how do you choose which side length to put on the side of the Pythagorean Theorem that has only one variable?

©Curriculum Associates, LLC Copying permitted for classroom use. GRADE 8 • LESSON 26

Additional Practice

UNDERSTAND LESSON

3 Students may reason that the role of the variables in the Pythagorean Theorem is not determined by alphabetical order. It is important to use the relationships shown in the equation to identify the legs and hypotenuse. ***Medium***

4 Students may start with the equation $a^2 + b^2 = c^2$ then substitute k for both a and b, and j for c. ***Medium***

5 Students may identify the legs and the hypotenuse of the given triangle, write an equation using the Pythagorean Theorem, and then compare their equation to the one presented in the problem. Students should not only write a correct equation; they should try to identify Andrew's error. ***Medium***

LESSON 26 | SESSION 2

3 Suppose you have a right triangle with sides of length x, y, and z where $y^2 = z^2 + x^2$. Which sides are the legs and which is the hypotenuse in the triangle? How do you know?

The sides with lengths z and x are the legs and the side with the length y is the hypotenuse; Possible explanation: I know from the Pythagorean Theorem that for a right triangle, the sum of the squares of the leg lengths equals the square of the hypotenuse length. Since $y^2 = z^2 + x^2$, y^2 must represent the square of the hypotenuse length and $z^2 + x^2$ must represent the sum of the squares of the leg lengths.

4 Damita uses the Pythagorean Theorem to write the equation $2k^2 = j^2$ to represent the triangle shown. Is she correct? Explain.

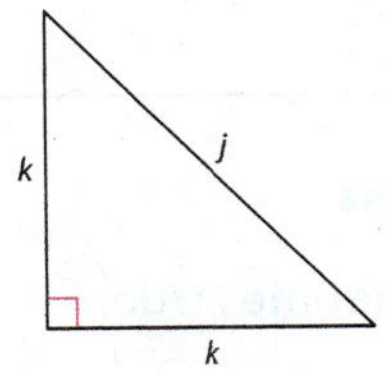

Yes; Possible explanation: The lengths of the legs are both k and the length of the hypotenuse is j. By the Pythagorean Theorem, $k^2 + k^2 = j^2$. This simplifies to $2k^2 = j^2$.

5 Andrew sketches a right triangle with side lengths p, q, and r as shown. He uses the Pythagorean Theorem to write the equation $p^2 + q^2 = r^2$ to represent the triangle. What is a correct equation for the triangle? What mistake might Andrew have made?

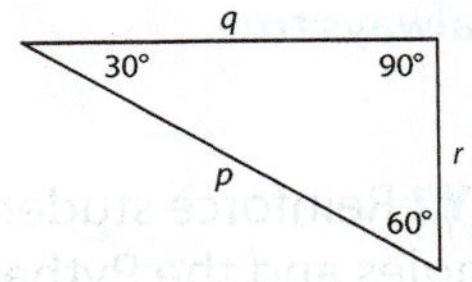

$q^2 + r^2 = p^2$ or $r^2 + q^2 = p^2$; Possible answer: Andrew might have assumed that the variables in the Pythagorean Theorem equation have to be in alphabetical order, as in $a^2 + b^2 = c^2$, instead of checking and using the actual lengths of the sides.

626

DIFFERENTIATION | ENGLISH LANGUAGE LEARNERS

Use with **Session 3** Apply It

Levels 1–3: Reading/Listening

Prepare students for Apply It problem 4 by reviewing the Pythagorean Theorem. Ask students to use words, diagrams, and equations to tell what they know about the theorem. Have students discuss using:

- *The Pythagorean Theorem is about _____.*
- *It helps us find the _____ of the _____.*

Next, read aloud paragraph 1 and ask students to highlight details about side lengths. Help them summarize the converse using:

- *The _____ show when a triangle is a _____.*

Read paragraph 2 and check understanding with Wh- questions such as: *What are the side lengths?* Ask students to use $\triangle XYZ$ to answer.

Levels 2–4: Reading/Listening

Prepare students for Apply It problem 4 by reviewing the Pythagorean Theorem. Have students tell what they know about the theorem. Ask: *What facts does the Pythagorean Theorem give about a right triangle?* Display the facts for reference. Then read problem 4 paragraph 1 and ask: *How is the order of the facts different in the theorem and in the converse?* Review the term *prove.* Ask: *What can we use to prove the converse?* Remind students that they proved the Pythagorean Theorem with 4 congruent triangles. Next, help students read and interpret paragraph 2. Ask: *What do we know about $\triangle XYZ$? What is unknown?*

Levels 3–5: Reading/Listening

Help students make sense of Apply It problem 4 by supporting their understanding of sentence structures. Read paragraph 1 with students and have them circle *if* and *then.* Remind students that sentences with *if/then* present a possible condition and the resulting situation. Have students identify the conditions and the result. Then guide students to compare the converse with the Pythagorean Theorem and to compare the order of conditions in each. Next, have students read paragraph 2 and underline the phrases with *that.* Explain that these phrases connect ideas in the sentences. Confirm understanding by asking: *What do we know about $\triangle XYZ$? What will the steps prove? How will they prove it?*

Refine Ideas About the Pythagorean Theorem and Its Converse

Purpose

- **Refine** understanding of the Pythagorean Theorem and prove the converse of the Pythagorean Theorem.

START CONNECT TO PRIOR KNOWLEDGE

Always, Sometimes, Never

A If a triangle has side lengths a, b, and c, then $a^2 + b^2 = c^2$.

B A leg of a right triangle is longer than the hypotenuse.

C The Pythagorean Theorem is true for an isosceles right triangle.

Solutions

A is sometimes true.

B is never true.

C is always true.

WHY? Reinforce students' understanding of triangles and the Pythagorean Theorem.

UNDERSTAND: What is the Pythagorean Theorem?

Refine Ideas About the Pythagorean Theorem and Its Converse

Apply It

➤ **Complete problems 1–5.**

1 Apply Sketch a right triangle with legs of lengths f and g and hypotenuse of length h. Write an equation relating the lengths of f, g, and h. Now use what you know about squares and square roots to write an expression for the length of the hypotenuse, h. Then choose values for f and g so that h is not a whole number. Find an approximate value for h.

$f^2 + g^2 = h^2 \longrightarrow h = \pm\sqrt{f^2 + g^2}$

h must be positive, so $h = \sqrt{f^2 + g^2}$.

Possible answer:

If $f = 5$ and $g = 6$, then $h = \sqrt{5^2 + 6^2} = \sqrt{61} \approx 7.8$

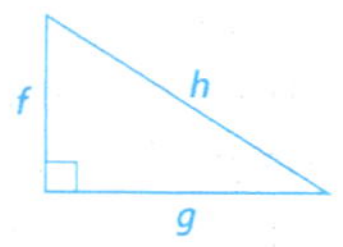

2 Generalize What is the length of the hypotenuse for each isosceles right triangle?

$\triangle A$: $\sqrt{2}$;

$\triangle B$: $\sqrt{18}$;

$\triangle C$: $\sqrt{2x^2}$

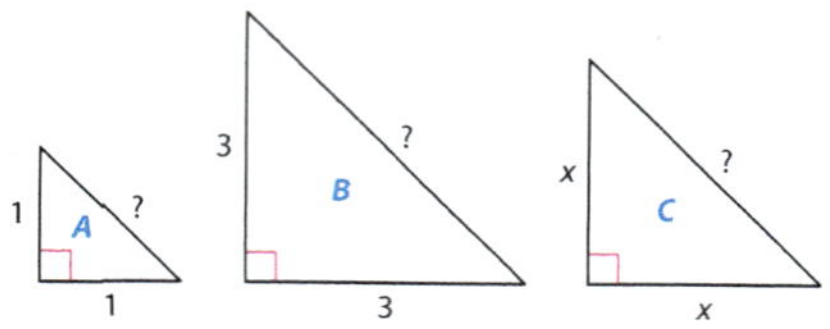

3 Analyze A right triangle with leg lengths of 5 and 12 has a hypotenuse of length 13. Show that a triangle with side lengths $5p$, $12p$, and $13p$ is also a right triangle. Explain your reasoning, using what you know about similar triangles.

Possible answer: A triangle with side lengths $5p$, $12p$, and $13p$ is similar to the triangle with side lengths 5, 12, and 13 because corresponding side lengths are proportional. In similar triangles, corresponding angles are congruent. So, the angle between the legs with lengths $5p$ and $12p$ is a right angle, and the triangle is a right triangle.

627

APPLY IT SMP 2, 3, 4, 5, 6, 7

Have students work independently or with a partner for problems 1–3.

1 Apply Look for understanding that solving for h involves taking the square root of both sides of the equation. Students should recognize that, although a square root may be positive or negative, h represents a length, so it must be positive.

Error Alert If students think that $\sqrt{f^2 + g^2} = f + g$, then challenge them to test this relationship with numerical values, such as $f = 3$ and $g = 4$.

2 Generalize Look for understanding that the Pythagorean Theorem can be used to solve for the unknown hypotenuse length in each figure. For example, for the first figure, if c is the hypotenuse length, then $1^2 + 1^2 = c^2$. So $c^2 = 2$, and $c = \sqrt{2}$. For the triangle with side length x, students can generalize the pattern from the first two triangles or use the Pythagorean Theorem to find the hypotenuse length algebraically: $x^2 + x^2 = c^2$, $2x^2 = c^2$, $c = \sqrt{2x^2}$.

3 Analyze Look for understanding that similar triangles have corresponding angles with equal measures.

4 Before students begin, read the first part of the problem aloud and discuss how the converse of the Pythagorean Theorem is related to, but different from, the Pythagorean Theorem. Point out that the Pythagorean Theorem applies when you *know* you have a right triangle. The converse of the Pythagorean Theorem gives you a way to figure out *whether* a given triangle is a right triangle or not. Then have students read the directions for Parts A, B, and C, and have them rephrase to confirm that they understand each part of the task.

As students work on their own, walk around to check their sketches of $\triangle DEF$ and help them explain their thinking.

Have students share their sketch with a partner and explain how they know the two triangles are congruent and that $\angle Z$ is a right angle.

CLOSE EXIT TICKET

5 **Math Journal** Look for understanding that if the side lengths of a triangle satisfy the equation $a^2 + b^2 = c^2$, then it is a right triangle, and if the side lengths of the triangle do not satisfy the equation, then it is NOT a right triangle.

Error Alert If students multiply the squares of the side lengths by 2 when testing statement B, then ask them to read the statement again. Ignacio multiplies the side lengths by 2. He is then squaring the product. So, for example, he is squaring (2×3), not multiplying 3^2 by 2.

End of Lesson Checklist

INTERACTIVE GLOSSARY Support students by suggesting they work with a partner to review the lesson and identify important things about the theorem. Encourage them to include sketches with their descriptions.

LESSON 26 | SESSION 3

4 A triangle is a right triangle if the square of one side length equals the sum of the squares of the other two side lengths. This relationship is called the **converse of the Pythagorean Theorem**. You can use congruent triangles to prove this converse.

Start with $\triangle XYZ$ with side lengths a, b, and c as shown. The triangle is drawn so that $a^2 + b^2 = c^2$. The angle measures are unknown. Follow the steps below to show that $\triangle XYZ$ must be a right triangle by proving that $\angle Z$ must be a right angle.

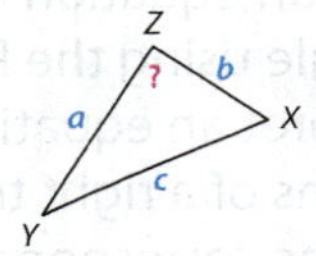

PART A Sketch $\triangle DEF$ with a right angle at F such that $FE = ZY = a$ and $FD = ZX = b$. What is DE, the length of the hypotenuse? Explain.

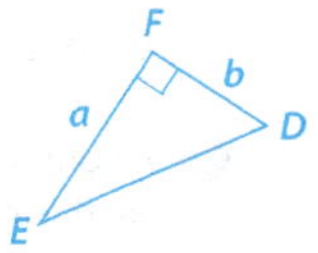

$DE = c$; Possible explanation: $\triangle DEF$ is a right triangle, so $a^2 + b^2 = DE^2$. I know from $\triangle XYZ$ that $a^2 + b^2 = c^2$, so $c^2 = DE^2$ and $c = DE$.

PART B How do you know that $\triangle XYZ$ and $\triangle DEF$ are congruent triangles?

Possible answer: When you know the three side lengths of a triangle, there is only one possible triangle you can make. $\triangle XYZ$ and $\triangle DEF$ have the same side lengths, a, b, and c, so the triangles are congruent.

PART C Explain how you know that $\angle Z$ is a right angle.

Possible answer: If two triangles are congruent, corresponding angles are congruent. $\angle Z \cong \angle F$ and $m\angle F = 90°$, so $m\angle Z = 90°$.

5 **Math Journal** Ignacio draws a right triangle with side lengths of 3, 4, and 5. He claims: A) If you add 2 to the length of each side, the new triangle will be a right triangle. B) If you multiply each side length by 2, the new triangle will be a right triangle. Use words and numbers to explain if each claim is true.

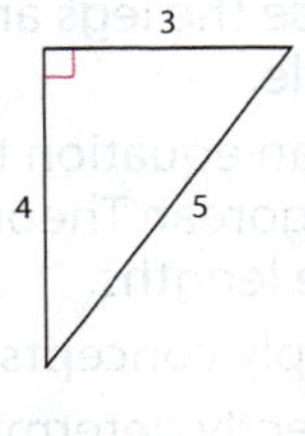

Possible answer: Claim A: Side lengths are 5, 6, 7. By the Pythagorean Theorem, $5^2 + 6^2$ should equal 7^2. $25 + 36 \neq 49$, so the triangle is not a right triangle and A is false. Claim B: Side lengths are 6, 8, 10. By the Pythagorean Theorem, $6^2 + 8^2$ should equal 10^2. $36 + 64 = 100$, so the triangle is a right triangle and B is true.

End of Lesson Checklist

☐ **INTERACTIVE GLOSSARY** Find the entry for *Pythagorean Theorem*. Add two important things you learned about the Pythagorean Theorem in this lesson.

628

Short Response Scoring Rubric (2 points) — Problem 4

Points	Expectations
PART A	
2	The length of the hypotenuse, $\overline{DE}$, is correctly identified AND student's reasoning is explained.
1	The length of the hypotenuse, $\overline{DE}$, is correctly identified without justification.
PART B	
2	The explanation states that the corresponding sides of the triangles are congruent and that only one triangle is possible with the given side lengths.
1	The explanation recognizes that the corresponding sides of the triangles are congruent.
PART C	
2	The explanation notes that corresponding angles of congruent triangles are congruent AND that angles Z and F are congruent.
1	The explanation notes that corresponding angles of congruent triangles are congruent but does not connect that fact to angles Z and F.

Lesson Quiz

TESTED SKILLS

Assesses 8.G.B.6

Problems on this assessment require students to write an equation relating the side lengths of a right triangle using the Pythagorean Theorem. They will interpret an equation that represents the side lengths of a right triangle to determine which lengths correspond to the legs and which length corresponds to the hypotenuse. Students will use the Pythagorean Theorem to find the exact value of the length of the hypotenuse of a right triangle as well as an algebraic expression for the length of the hypotenuse. They will analyze an equation to determine if it correctly applies the Pythagorean Theorem for a given triangle. Students will also need to be familiar with similar triangles and square roots.

Alternately, teachers may assign the **Digital Comprehension Check** online to assess student understanding of this material.

Error Alert Errors may result if students:

- confuse the legs and hypotenuse of a right triangle.
- write an equation that does not model the Pythagorean Theorem, such as forgetting squares on the lengths.
- misapply concepts of similar triangles.
- incorrectly determine the length of the missing side or inaccurately evaluate a square root.

Problem Notes

1 **D is correct.** Students could solve the problem by writing the equation $4^2 + 4^2 = c^2$ and solving for *c*.

A is incorrect. This answer is the result of taking the square root of one leg length.

B is incorrect. This answer is the result of adding the leg lengths and then taking the square root of the sum.

C is incorrect. This answer is the result of squaring one leg length and then taking the square root.

(1 point)

DOK 2 | 8.G.B.6

LESSON 26 • QUIZ | Name:

➤ **Solve the problems.**

1 The figure shows an isosceles right triangle. What is the length of the hypotenuse? *(1 point)*

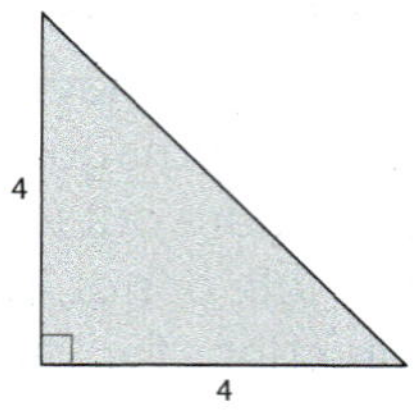

A 2

B $2\sqrt{2}$

C 4

(D) $4\sqrt{2}$

2 A right triangle has sides of length *a*, *b*, and *c* such that $b^2 = a^2 + c^2$. Which sides are the legs and hypotenuse in the triangle? Explain your reasoning. *(2 points)*

SOLUTION *a* and *c* are the legs, and *b* is the hypotenuse; Possible explanation: The Pythagorean Theorem states that for a right triangle the sum of the squares of the leg lengths equals the square of the hypotenuse length. Since $b^2 = a^2 + c^2$, b^2 represents the square of the hypotenuse length and $a^2 + c^2$ represents the sum of the squares of the leg lengths.

3 A right triangle with legs of lengths *x* and *y* has a hypotenuse of length *z*. Write an expression for the length of the hypotenuse, *z*. Show your work. *(2 points)*

Possible student work: Make a sketch of a right triangle with legs labeled *x* and *y*, and hypotenuse labeled *z*.

$x^2 + y^2 = z^2 \longrightarrow z = \pm\sqrt{x^2 + y^2}$

z must be positive, so $z = \sqrt{x^2 + y^2}$.

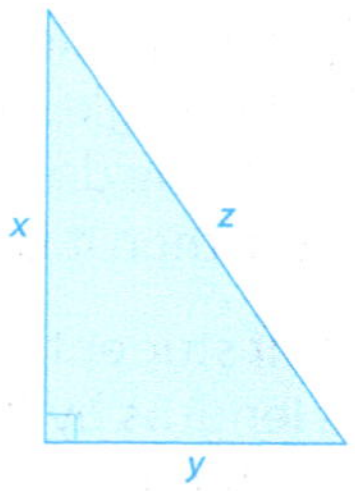

SOLUTION $z = \sqrt{x^2 + y^2}$

Short Response Scoring Rubric

Points	Expectations
2	Response has the correct solution(s) and includes well-organized, clear, and concise work demonstrating thorough understanding of mathematical concepts and/or procedures.
1	Response contains mostly correct solution(s) and shows partial understanding of mathematical concepts and/or procedures.
0	Response shows no attempt at finding a solution and no effort to demonstrate an understanding of mathematical concepts and/or procedures.

2 Students could solve the problem by recognizing that the sum of the squares of the leg lengths of a right triangle is equal to the square of the hypotenuse length.

(2 points)

DOK 2 | 8.G.B.6

3 Students could solve the problem by using the Pythagorean Theorem to write an equation and then solve for *z*.

(2 points)

DOK 2 | 8.G.B.6

4 Students could solve the problem by recognizing that the two described triangles are similar, and similar triangles have congruent angles.

(2 points)

DOK 2 | 8.G.B.6

5 Students could solve the problem by identifying the legs of the right triangle from the diagram and then writing the correct equation to apply the Pythagorean Theorem.

(2 points)

DOK 3 | 8.G.B.6

LESSON 26 • QUIZ | Name:

4 A right triangle with leg lengths of 3 and 4 has a hypotenuse of length 5. Show that a triangle with side lengths 3*h*, 4*h*, and 5*h* is also a right triangle. Explain your reasoning. *(2 points)*

SOLUTION Possible explanation: A triangle with side lengths 3*h*, 4*h*, and 5*h* is similar to a triangle with side lengths 3, 4, and 5 because corresponding side lengths are proportional. In similar triangles, corresponding angles are congruent. So, the angle between the legs with lengths 3*h* and 4*h* is a right angle, and the triangle is a right triangle.

5 Lindsay sketches a right triangle with lengths *f*, *g*, and *h* as shown. She uses the Pythagorean Theorem to write the equation $f^2 + g^2 = h^2$ to represent the triangle. How can Lindsay correct her error? Explain your reasoning. *(2 points)*

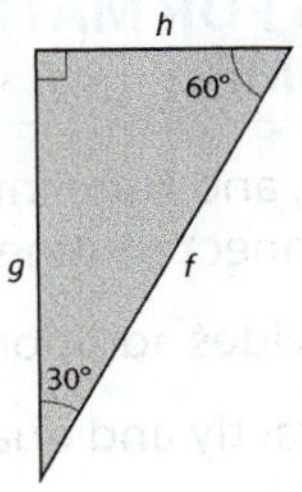

SOLUTION $h^2 + g^2 = f^2$; Possible explanation: Lindsay might have assumed that the variables in the Pythagorean Theorem equation have to be in alphabetical order with the hypotenuse represented on the right side of the equation.

DIFFERENTIATION

RETEACH Tools for Instruction

Students who require additional support for prerequisite or on-level skills will benefit from activities that provide targeted skills instruction.

GRADE 8

- **Lesson 26** Proof of the Pythagorean Theorem

REINFORCE Math Center Activity

Students who require practice to reinforce concepts and skills and deepen understanding will benefit from small group collaborative games and activities (available in on-level, below-level, and above-level versions).

GRADE 8

- **Lesson 26** Use Pythagorean Theorem Vocabulary

EXTEND Enrichment Activity

Students who have achieved proficiency with concepts and skills and are ready for additional challenges will benefit from group collaborative games and activities that extend understanding.

GRADE 8

- **Lesson 26** Semicircles Instead of Squares

Overview | Apply the Pythagorean Theorem

MATH FOCUS

Focus Standards

8.G.B.7 Apply the Pythagorean Theorem to determine unknown side lengths in right triangles in real-world and mathematical problems in two and three dimensions.

8.G.B.8 Apply the Pythagorean Theorem to find the distance between two points in a coordinate system.

See Unit 6 Overview for developing and applied standards.

STANDARDS FOR MATHEMATICAL PRACTICE (SMP)

SMP 1, 2, 3, 4, 5, and 6 are integrated into the Try-Discuss-Connect routine.*

This lesson provides additional support for:

2 Reason abstractly and quantitatively.

4 Model with mathematics.

7 Look for and make use of structure.

* See page 1o to learn how every lesson includes these SMP.

Objectives

Content Objectives

- Apply the Pythagorean Theorem to determine unknown side lengths in right triangles in real-world and mathematical problems, in two and three dimensions.
- Identify and use Pythagorean triples.
- Use the Pythagorean Theorem to find the distance between two points in the coordinate plane.

Language Objectives

- Provide reasons to explain in speaking and writing whether a set of numbers is a Pythagorean triple.
- Ask and answer questions about solution strategies for finding the distance between two points in the coordinate plane during partner and class discussion.
- Justify solutions to problems using the Pythagorean Theorem and the lesson vocabulary in speaking and in writing.

Prior Knowledge

- Find the square of a number.
- Find or estimate the square root of a number.
- Understand the Pythagorean Theorem and be able to explain geometric and algebraic proofs of it.

Vocabulary

Math Vocabulary

There is no new vocabulary. Review the following key terms.

multiple the product of a given number and any other whole number.

Pythagorean Theorem in any right triangle, the sum of the squares of the lengths of the legs, a and b, is equal to the square of the length of the hypotenuse, c. So, $a^2 + b^2 = c^2$.

right rectangular prism a right prism where the bases and other faces are all rectangles.

Academic Vocabulary

consider to think carefully.

Learning Progression

In Grades 6 and 7, students found areas of triangles and calculated distances between points on the same horizontal or vertical line in the coordinate plane.

Earlier in Grade 8, students evaluated expressions with exponents and found square roots of positive rational numbers.

In the previous lesson, students were introduced to the Pythagorean Theorem, and they explained proofs of the Pythagorean Theorem and its converse.

In this lesson, students use the Pythagorean Theorem to find unknown lengths and distances in mathematical and real-world problems. The problems require them to find unknown side lengths in triangles, unknown diagonal lengths in rectangles and rectangular prisms, and distances between points in the coordinate plane.

Later in Grade 8, students will apply the Pythagorean Theorem to find unknown dimensions in cylinders, cones, or spheres.

In high school, students will continue to use the Pythagorean Theorem to prove other theorems and solve applied problems involving triangles.

Pacing Guide

Items marked with ⭐ are available on the **Teacher Toolbox.**

	MATERIALS	DIFFERENTIATION
SESSION 1 Explore Applying the Pythagorean Theorem (35–50 min)		
• **Start** (5 min) • **Try It** (5–10 min) • **Discuss It** (10–15 min) • **Connect It** (10–15 min) • **Close: Exit Ticket** (5 min) **Additional Practice** (pages 633–634)	**Math Toolkit** grid paper, rulers, unit tiles Presentation Slides ⭐	**PREPARE** Interactive Tutorial ⭐ **RETEACH or REINFORCE** Hands-On Activity **Materials** For each group: 169 unit tiles
SESSION 2 Develop Finding an Unknown Length in a Right Triangle (45–60 min)		
• **Start** (5 min) • **Try It** (10–15 min) • **Discuss It** (10–15 min) • **Connect It** (15–20 min) • **Close: Exit Ticket** (5 min) **Additional Practice** (pages 639–640)	**Math Toolkit** centimeter grid paper, centimeter rulers, unit cubes Presentation Slides ⭐	**RETEACH or REINFORCE** Hands-On Activity **Materials** For each pair: tape measure, yard stick, or meter stick **REINFORCE** Fluency & Skills Practice ⭐ **EXTEND** Deepen Understanding
SESSION 3 Develop Finding an Unknown Length in a Three-Dimensional Figure (45–60 min)		
• **Start** (5 min) • **Try It** (10–15 min) • **Discuss It** (10–15 min) • **Connect It** (15–20 min) • **Close: Exit Ticket** (5 min) **Additional Practice** (pages 645–646)	**Math Toolkit** grid paper, rulers Presentation Slides ⭐	**RETEACH or REINFORCE** Visual Model **Materials** For display: an open box, tape measure, string, tape **REINFORCE** Fluency & Skills Practice ⭐ **EXTEND** Deepen Understanding
SESSION 4 Develop Finding Distance in the Coordinate Plane (45–60 min)		
• **Start** (5 min) • **Try It** (10–15 min) • **Discuss It** (10–15 min) • **Connect It** (15–20 min) • **Close: Exit Ticket** (5 min) **Additional Practice** (pages 651–652)	**Math Toolkit** compasses, graph paper, rulers, tracing paper Presentation Slides ⭐	**RETEACH or REINFORCE** Visual Model **Materials** For display: large first-quadrant coordinate plane **REINFORCE** Fluency & Skills Practice ⭐ **EXTEND** Deepen Understanding
SESSION 5 Refine Applying the Pythagorean Theorem (45–60 min)		
• **Start** (5 min) • **Monitor & Guide** (15–20 min) • **Group & Differentiate** (20–30 min) • **Close: Exit Ticket** (5 min)	**Math Toolkit** Have items from previous sessions available for students. Presentation Slides ⭐	**RETEACH** Visual Model **Materials** For display: large four-quadrant coordinate plane **REINFORCE** Problems 4–7 **EXTEND** Challenge **PERSONALIZE** i-Ready
Lesson 27 Quiz ⭐ or **Digital Comprehension Check**		**RETEACH** Tools for Instruction ⭐ **REINFORCE** Math Center Activity ⭐ **EXTEND** Enrichment Activity ⭐

Overview | Apply the Pythagorean Theorem

Connect to Culture

➤ **Use these activities to connect with and leverage the diverse backgrounds and experiences of all students. Engage students in sharing what they know about contexts before you add the information given here.**

SESSION 1 ■ □ □ □ □

Try It Living primarily in the northeast United States and eastern Canada, the Mi'kmaq people are one of the largest groups of indigenous people in North America. Historically, the Mi'kmaq traveled from season to season as they hunted and fished for their food. Mi'kmaq clothing was made of deer and moose skin, with fur robes for winter. Clothing was often decorated with colored porcupine quills. Ask students to share anything else they know about the Mi'kmaq people.

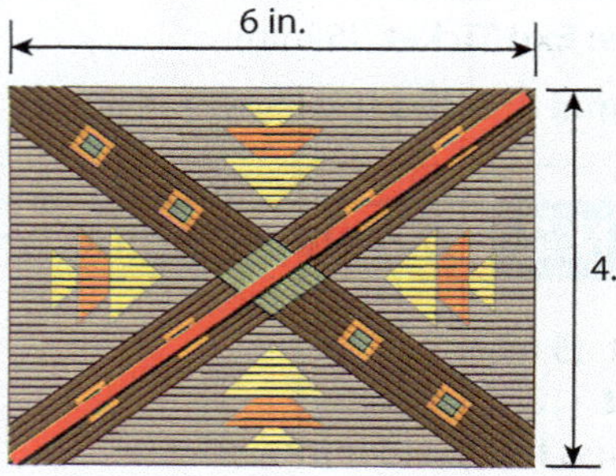

SESSION 2 ■ ■ □ □ □

Try It Ask students whether they have ever seen a cat stuck in a tree. If so, how did the cat get down? Because their claws curve toward the back, cats are good at climbing up, but many cats do not know how to climb down. When a cat tries to climb down, its claws point up and cannot hold the cat's body against the tree. This makes the cat think it is going to fall, so it stops trying. To be able to climb down, the cat must do so backward, with its tail to the ground.

SESSION 3 ■ ■ ■ □ □

Try It Ask students if they have ever used a paintbrush to paint a craft. Have students describe the different sizes of paintbrushes and explain why someone making a craft might want to use a larger or a smaller brush. Each paintbrush size is associated with a number, with greater numbers representing larger brushes. A paintbrush numbered *0* is very small and a paintbrush numbered *40* is large. The numbering system was invented before scale modeling became popular, so now brushes smaller than size *0* exist, down to size *00000*.

SESSION 5 ■ ■ ■ ■ ■

Apply It **Problem 5** Ask students who keep jewelry or other items in plastic storage cubes to describe what they like about these cubes and what they wish was different about the cubes. A storage cube with an edge length of 6 inches can also serve as a decoration on a nightstand or other shelf. Small items can fit in a storage cube this size, but putting too much in a small cube makes items hard to remove. Other advantages of a small storage cube are the ease of moving it to another location and packing it in luggage when needed.

Connect to Family and Community

➤ **After the Explore session, have students use the Family Letter to let their families know what they are learning and to encourage family involvement.**

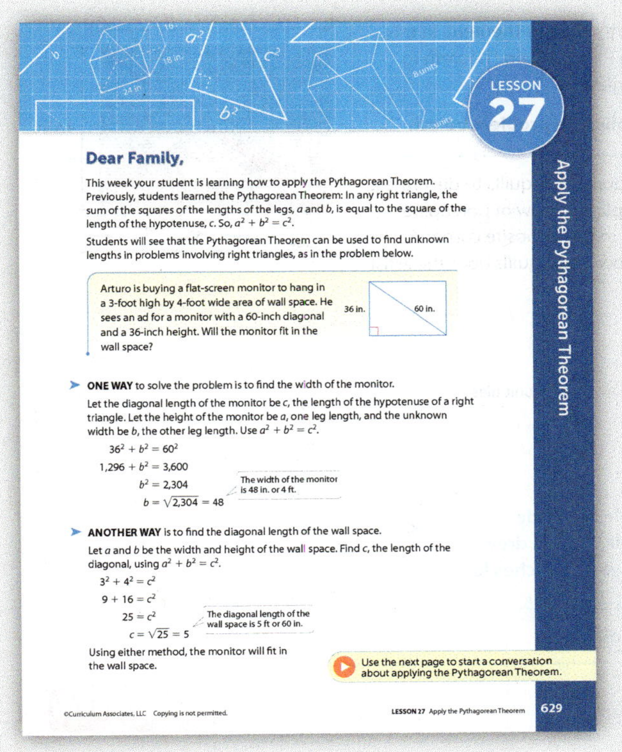

LESSON 27

Apply the Pythagorean Theorem

Dear Family,

This week your student is learning how to apply the Pythagorean Theorem. Previously, students learned the Pythagorean Theorem: In any right triangle, the sum of the squares of the lengths of the legs, *a* and *b*, is equal to the square of the length of the hypotenuse, *c*. So, $a^2 + b^2 = c^2$.

Students will see that the Pythagorean Theorem can be used to find unknown lengths in problems involving right triangles, as in the problem below.

Arturo is buying a flat-screen monitor to hang in a 3-foot high by 4-foot wide area of wall space. He sees an ad for a monitor with a 60-inch diagonal and a 36-inch height. Will the monitor fit in the wall space?

36 in. 60 in.

➤ **ONE WAY** to solve the problem is to find the width of the monitor.

Let the diagonal length of the monitor be *c*, the length of the hypotenuse of a right triangle. Let the height of the monitor be *a*, one leg length, and the unknown width be *b*, the other leg length. Use $a^2 + b^2 = c^2$.

$36^2 + b^2 = 60^2$

$1{,}296 + b^2 = 3{,}600$

$b^2 = 2{,}304$

$b = \sqrt{2{,}304} = 48$

The width of the monitor is 48 in. or 4 ft.

➤ **ANOTHER WAY** is to find the diagonal length of the wall space.

Let *a* and *b* be the width and height of the wall space. Find *c*, the length of the diagonal, using $a^2 + b^2 = c^2$.

$3^2 + 4^2 = c^2$

$9 + 16 = c^2$

$25 = c^2$

$c = \sqrt{25} = 5$

The diagonal length of the wall space is 5 ft or 60 in.

Using either method, the monitor will fit in the wall space.

Use the next page to start a conversation about applying the Pythagorean Theorem.

©Curriculum Associates, LLC Copying is not permitted. LESSON 27 Apply the Pythagorean Theorem 629

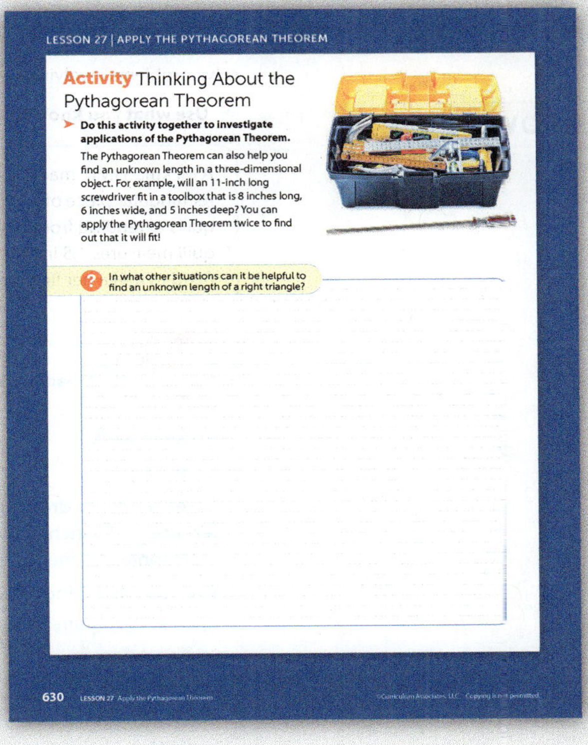

LESSON 27 | APPLY THE PYTHAGOREAN THEOREM

Activity Thinking About the Pythagorean Theorem

➤ **Do this activity together to investigate applications of the Pythagorean Theorem.**

The Pythagorean Theorem can also help you find an unknown length in a three-dimensional object. For example, will an 11-inch long screwdriver fit in a toolbox that is 8 inches long, 6 inches wide, and 5 inches deep? You can apply the Pythagorean Theorem twice to find out that it will fit!

In what other situations can it be helpful to find an unknown length of a right triangle?

630 LESSON 27 Apply the Pythagorean Theorem ©Curriculum Associates, LLC Copying is not permitted.

Connect to Language

➤ **For English language learners, use the Differentiation chart to scaffold the language in each session. Use the Academic Vocabulary routine for academic terms before Session 1.**

DIFFERENTIATION | ENGLISH LANGUAGE LEARNERS — Use with **Session 1** **Connect It**

MATH TERM

A *theorem* is an idea that can be proved using a chain of logic and reasoning.

ACADEMIC VOCABULARY

A *set* is a group or collection of things.

A *triple* is made up of three units or things.

Levels 1–3: Reading/Speaking

Help students interpret Connect It problem 2. Read problem 2a with students. Guide them to circle the equation and *Pythagorean Theorem*. Display the theorem and say: *This theorem is named after the Greek mathematician Pythagoras.* Help students summarize the theorem:

- *The Pythagorean* _____ *describes properties of* _____ *triangles.*

Next, read problem 2b with students and have them circle *Pythagorean triple*. Then use **Act It Out** to guide partners to draw a 3, 4, 5 right triangle and show that the equation is true. Then ask students to identify the Pythagorean triples.

Levels 2–4: Reading/Speaking

Prepare students to interpret Connect It problem 2. Display *theorem, triple,* and *set,* and have students discuss meanings. Point out the Latin prefix *tri-*, meaning 3. Ask students to list related words, like *triangle* and *tripod,* and to tell the word for 3 in other languages (e.g., *tres, trois*).

Next, help students make sense of problems 2a and 2b. Clarify that the capital P in Pythagorean refers to the name of a mathematician. Have them use **Act It Out** to draw the 3, 4, 5 right triangle described in problem 2b and summarize:

- *Three whole-number* _____ *of a right triangle are called a* _____.

Levels 3–5: Reading/Speaking

Have students prepare for Connect It problem 2 by reviewing the terms *theorem* and *triple.* Ask students to discuss meanings and generate words with the same prefixes (e.g., *theorem, theory, triple, triangle, tripod*).

Next, have students work in pairs to make sense of problems 2a and 2b. Have partners discuss how Pythagorean triples relate to the theorem. Encourage students to identify math terms in both parts, like *lengths* and *right triangle.* For extra support, have students use **Act It Out** to draw the 3, 4, 5 right triangle described in problem 2b.

Explore Applying the Pythagorean Theorem

Purpose

- **Explore** the idea that you can use the Pythagorean Theorem to find the length of the hypotenuse of a right triangle when you are given the lengths of the legs.
- **Understand** that you can apply the Pythagorean Theorem in real-world situations to find unknown lengths in a right triangle.

START CONNECT TO PRIOR KNOWLEDGE

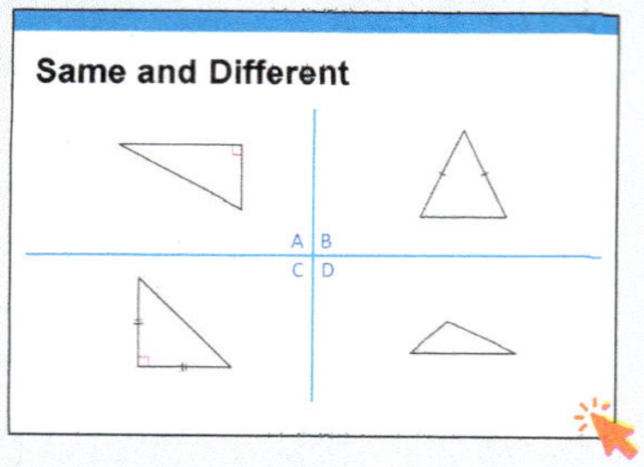

Possible Solutions

All are triangles.

A and D are scalene triangles.

A and C are right triangles.

B and C are isosceles triangles.

WHY? Support students' facility with recognizing types of triangles.

Explore Applying the Pythagorean Theorem

Previously, you learned about the Pythagorean Theorem. In this lesson, you will learn how to use the Pythagorean Theorem to solve problems involving right triangles.

➤ **Use what you know to try to solve the problem below.**

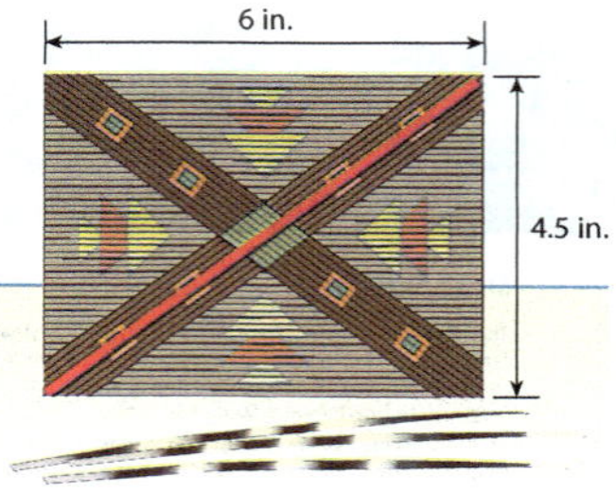

A Mi'kmaq (Mic-mac) artist uses porcupine quills to decorate a rectangular piece of leather. She places a row of porcupine quills extending from one corner to the opposite corner. Each quill measures 1.5 inches long. How many quills does the artist need to make her first diagonal?

TRY IT Math Toolkit grid paper, rulers, unit tiles

Possible work:

SAMPLE A

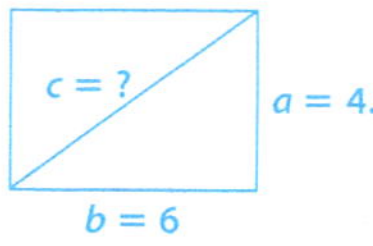

I used a ruler to draw a rectangle with side lengths of 4.5 inches and 6 inches. I then drew a diagonal and measured it. It was 7.5 inches long.

Each quill is 1.5 inches long: $7.5 \div 1.5 = 5$.

She needs 5 quills to make the diagonal.

SAMPLE B

$(4.5)^2 + 6^2 = c^2$

$20.25 + 36 = 56.25$

$c^2 = 56.25$, so $c = \pm\sqrt{56.25}$. Length cannot be negative, so $c = 7.5$.

Each quill is 1.5 in. long, so she needs $7.5 \div 1.5 = 5$ quills.

DISCUSS IT

Ask: What did you do first to find the number of quills? Why?

Share: I knew . . . so I . . .

Learning Targets SMP 1, SMP 2, SMP 3, SMP 4, SMP 5, SMP 6, SMP 7

- Apply the Pythagorean Theorem to determine unknown side lengths in right triangles in real-world and mathematical problems in two and three dimensions.
- Apply the Pythagorean Theorem to find the distance between two points in a coordinate system.

TRY IT SMP 1, 2, 4, 5, 6

Make Sense of the Problem

See ***Connect to Culture*** to support student engagement. Before students work on Try It, use **Say It Another Way** to help them make sense of the problem.

DISCUSS IT SMP 1, 2, 3, 6

Support Partner Discussion

After students work on Try It, have them respond to Discuss It with a partner. Listen for understanding of:

- the relationship between the side lengths and the length of the diagonal of the piece of leather.
- the relationship between the length of the diagonal of the piece of leather and the length of each quill.

Error Alert If students think the number of quills needed is 7.5, then they neglected to divide the length of the diagonal by 1.5, the length of each quill. Make sure students understand that the problem is asking for the number of quills needed to make the diagonal, rather than the length of the diagonal in inches.

Select and Sequence Student Strategies

Select 2–3 samples that represent the range of student thinking in your classroom. Here is one possible order for class discussion:

- rectangle with side lengths 4.5 in. and 6 in. drawn and diagonal measured
- sides of drawing measured and proportion solved to find diagonal length of actual rectangle
- Pythagorean Theorem used to find diagonal length

Facilitate Whole Class Discussion

Call on students to share selected strategies. Encourage students to speak clearly and loudly so that everyone can hear.

Guide students to **Compare and Connect** the representations. Prompt students to ask for more information as needed during the discussion.

ASK *How did these strategies use math that you learned in earlier lessons?*

LISTEN FOR Some strategies used the Pythagorean Theorem, or squaring and finding square roots, and others used proportions.

CONNECT IT

SMP 2, 4, 5

1 Look Back Look for understanding that the length of the diagonal is 7.5 inches, and it takes 5 quills to form that length.

DIFFERENTIATION | RETEACH

Hands-On Activity

Use unit tiles to find the hypotenuse of a right triangle, given the leg lengths.

If students are unsure about finding the length of the hypotenuse of a right triangle if they know the lengths of the legs, then use this activity to help them visualize the relationship.

Materials For each group: 169 unit tiles

- Display a triangle with legs of length 5 and 12.
- Tell students to model the 5-unit leg with 5 unit tiles. Then tell them to make a square out of tiles with side length 5 units.
- Ask: *How many unit tiles are in the square?* [25]
- Tell students to model the 12-unit leg with 12 unit tiles. Then tell them to make a square out of tiles with side length 12 units.
- Ask: *How many unit tiles are in the square?* [144]
- Ask: *How many unit tiles are used in all?* [169]
- Have students take apart their squares and use the combined tiles to make one larger square.
- Ask: *What is the side length of the new large square?* [13]
- Ask: *How is this length related to the triangle?* [13 units is the length of the hypotenuse.]
- Discuss with students how this activity shows the steps in finding the length of the hypotenuse when you know the lengths of the legs: 1) Square the length of each leg; 2) add the squares of the leg lengths; 3) take the square root of the sum.

LESSON 27 | SESSION 1

CONNECT IT

1 Look Back How many quills are in the diagonal? How do you know?

5; Possible answer: I drew a right triangle and used the Pythagorean Theorem to find the length of the hypotenuse. Then, I divided this length by 1.5 to find the number of quills.

2 Look Ahead

a. Fill in the blanks to restate the Pythagorean Theorem.

In any __right__ triangle, the sum of the squares of the lengths of the __legs__ is equal to the square of the length of the __hypotenuse__.

If *a* and *b* are the lengths of the legs of a right triangle and *c* is the length of the hypotenuse, then the theorem can be represented by the equation $a^2 + b^2 = c^2$.

b. When the side lengths of a right triangle are whole numbers, the lengths are known as *Pythagorean triples*. For example, the set of lengths 3, 4, 5 is a Pythagorean triple because $3^2 + 4^2 = 5^2$. Look at each set of three numbers shown on the right. Circle each set that is a Pythagorean triple. See diagram.

2, 3, 4
4, 5, 6
(5, 12, 13)
(6, 8, 10)
(8, 15, 17)
9, 16, 25

c. Jason says that if you multiply each length in a Pythagorean triple by the same factor, you will get another Pythagorean triple. Explain why Jason is correct.

Possible explanation: Let the set of lengths *a*, *b*, *c* be a Pythagorean triple such that $a^2 + b^2 = c^2$. If 2*a*, 2*b*, 2*c* is also a Pythagorean triple, then $(2a)^2 + (2b)^2 = (2c)^2$ or $4a^2 + 4b^2 = 4c^2$. If you divide both sides of this equation by 4, you get $a^2 + b^2 = c^2$, so 2*a*, 2*b*, 2*c* is a Pythagorean triple. Any multiple will work the same way.

3 Reflect Give an example to show that a multiple of a Pythagorean triple is also a Pythagorean triple.

Possible answer: If you multiply the lengths in the Pythagorean triple 3, 4, 5 by 3, you get the lengths 9, 12, 15 which is also a Pythagorean triple: $9^2 + 12^2 = 15^2 \longrightarrow 81 + 144 = 225$.

632

2 Look Ahead Students should recognize that the Pythagorean Theorem applies only to right triangles and that, in a right triangle, the legs are the two shorter sides and the hypotenuse is the longest side.

Ask a volunteer to rephrase the information about *Pythagorean triples*. Support student understanding by having a volunteer explain why 6, 8, 10 is a Pythagorean triple, while 4, 5, 6 is not.

CLOSE EXIT TICKET

3 Reflect Look for understanding of generating a new Pythagorean triple by multiplying each length in a Pythagorean triple by the same factor. Note that the new lengths must also be whole numbers.

Error Alert If students find an example where multiplying a Pythagorean triple by a factor does not produce another Pythagorean triple, then have them work with a partner to check their work. They should check their original Pythagorean triple, their multiplication, that they correctly squared each new number, and that they correctly compared the sum of the two smaller squares to the largest square.

Prepare for Applying the Pythagorean Theorem

Support Vocabulary Development

Assign **Prepare for Applying the Pythagorean Theorem** as extra practice in class or as homework.

If you have students complete this in class, then use the guidance below.

Ask students to consider the term *Pythagorean Theorem*. Ensure that students understand when the theorem can be used and when it cannot be used.

Have students work individually to complete the graphic organizer. Invite students to share their completed organizers, and prompt a whole-class comparative discussion of the definitions, illustrations, examples, and non-examples they used in their graphic organizers.

Have students look at the question in problem 2 and discuss with a partner what the triangle might look like. Have students draw a diagram to support their thinking.

Problem Notes

1. Students should understand that the Pythagorean Theorem states that in a right triangle, the sum of the squares of the two leg lengths is equal to the square of the hypotenuse length. Student illustrations might include an image of a right triangle with legs labeled a and b and hypotenuse labeled c and the equation $a^2 + b^2 = c^2$. Students should recognize this theorem applies to right triangles, so if a triangle is acute or obtuse, the Pythagorean Theorem cannot be used.

2. Students may reason that the hypotenuse is always the longest side in a right triangle.

LESSON 27 | SESSION 1 Name:

Prepare for Applying the Pythagorean Theorem

1. Think about what you know about right triangles. Fill in each box. Use words, numbers, and pictures. Show as many ideas as you can. Possible answers:

Pythagorean Theorem

In My Own Words

In a right triangle, the sum of the squares of the two leg lengths is equal to the square of the hypotenuse length.

My Illustrations

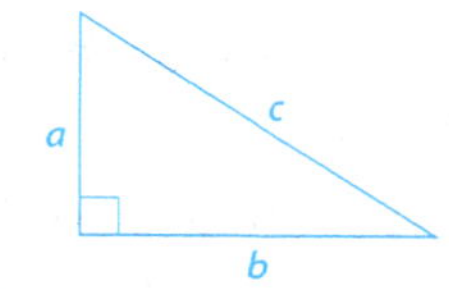

$a^2 + b^2 = c^2$

Examples

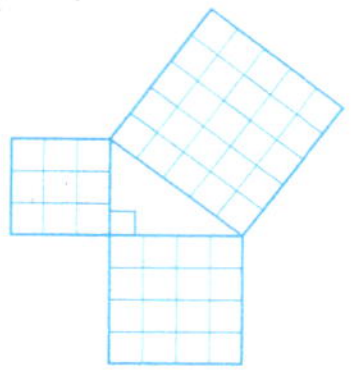

$3^2 + 4^2 = 5^2$

Non-Examples

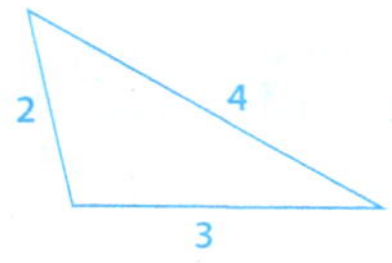

$2^2 + 3^2 \neq 4^2$

2. Suppose you have a right triangle with side lengths 26, 24, and 10. Which lengths represent the legs and which length represents the hypotenuse of the triangle? Use the Pythagorean Theorem to explain how you know.

leg lengths: 10, 24; hypotenuse length: 26; Possible explanation: If a triangle is a right triangle, then according to the Pythagorean Theorem, the sum of the squares of the leg lengths equals the square of the hypotenuse length. $10^2 + 24^2 = 26^2 = 100 + 576 = 676$, so 26 is the length of the hypotenuse.

633

REAL-WORLD CONNECTION

Carpenters use the Pythagorean Theorem in their constructions. Suppose a shed is being built such that its front shape is a rectangle with two congruent right triangles on top. The right angles of the triangles are back to back, and the hypotenuses lie along the angles of the roof. To help calculate the amount of roofing material needed, a carpenter will need to know the length of the hypotenuse for each of the right triangles. She can use the height of the triangle and half of the width of the shed along with the Pythagorean Theorem to find the length of each triangle's hypotenuse. Ask students to think of other real-world examples when applying the Pythagorean Theorem might be useful.

Additional Practice

3 Problem 3 provides another look at applying the Pythagorean Theorem. This problem is similar to the problem about an artist using porcupine quills to decorate a rectangular piece of leather. In both problems, two side lengths of a right triangle are given, and students use the Pythagorean Theorem to find the length of the hypotenuse. This problem asks for the length of ribbon needed to make two diagonals of a flag. Note that since we are finding an approximate length, there is no need to worry about the area of overlap of the ribbons.

Students may want to use unit tiles or grid paper to solve.

Suggest that students use **Three Reads** to help them understand what the problem is about, what is being asked, and what information they are given.

LESSON 27 | SESSION 1

3 The flag of Scotland consists of a blue rectangular background with two white diagonals.

a. The dimensions of a Scottish flag are shown. If the flag's diagonals are made of white ribbon, what length of ribbon is needed for both diagonals? Show your work. Round your answer to the nearest foot.

Possible work:

$3^2 + 5^2 = c^2$

$9 + 25 = c^2$

$34 = c^2$

$\pm\sqrt{34} = c$

c must be positive, so $\sqrt{34} \approx 6$.

About 6 ft are needed for one ribbon, so about 12 ft are needed for two.

SOLUTION The total length of ribbon needed is about 12 ft.

b. Check your answer to problem 3a. Show your work.

Possible work:

Check that $\sqrt{34}$ is the correct diagonal length.

$(\sqrt{34})^2 = 3^2 + 5^2$

$34 = 9 + 25$

$34 = 34$

$\sqrt{34} \approx 6$ is the length of one diagonal, so double it for two diagonals.

About 12 ft is correct.

634

DIFFERENTIATION | ENGLISH LANGUAGE LEARNERS

Use with **Session 2** Apply It

Levels 1–3: Reading/Speaking

Help students make sense of Apply It problem 6. First, help students understand the problem context by reading aloud sentence 1 and using **Act It Out**. Guide students to label the banner, roof, and fence on the diagram. Then provide a string or rope and ask students to show what it means to string it from the top of one thing to another. Next, ask students to study the diagram and underline the question in the problem. Rephrase: *What is the height of the roof?* Have students trace the line on the diagram to show what they need to find. Encourage them to use math terms like *height, right triangle,* and *side length* to answer. Before having them solve the problem, read each sentence aloud and ask partners to find measurements on the diagram.

Levels 2–4: Reading/Speaking

Help students make sense of Apply It problem 6 by previewing the diagram. Give students time to study and label things in the diagram. [Possible terms: *roof, fence, banner, height, side lengths, distance, right triangle*] Then call on students to describe the diagram.

Next, help students read and make sense of the problem by discussing the meaning of compound and open compound words, such as *salesman, fence pole, banner rope,* and *rooftop.* Then have students use **Say It Another Way** to confirm understanding. Afterwards, ask students to identify the question and to tell how they can use the diagram to solve the problem.

Levels 3–5: Reading/Speaking

Have students read and interpret Apply It problem 6 using an adaptation of **Three Reads**. After each read, have students discuss the focus question with partners. Then prompt students to make connections between the problem and the diagram. Give students time to think about their answers before sharing. Provide sentence starters to guide discussions:

- *The diagram shows* ____.
- *The diagram helps me understand* ____.
- *How does* ____ *connect to the problem?*
- *Can you show me how* ____ *connects to the diagram?*
- *That makes sense. I also think* ____.

Develop Finding an Unknown Length in a Right Triangle

Purpose

- **Develop** strategies for finding an unknown leg length in a right triangle.
- **Recognize** that the Pythagorean Theorem can be used to find any unknown side length in a right triangle if the other two side lengths are known.

START CONNECT TO PRIOR KNOWLEDGE

Which One Doesn't Belong?

A	B
3 cm, 4 cm, 5 cm	7.5 m, 7.5 m, 22.5 m
C	**D**
1 in., 1 in., $\sqrt{2}$ in.	3.2 ft, 3.2 ft, 3.2 ft

Possible Solutions

A is the only set that involves a Pythagorean triple.

B is the only set that cannot be side lengths of a triangle.

C is the only set with an irrational length value.

D is the only set that can be side lengths of an equilateral triangle.

WHY? Support students' facility with recognizing side lengths that can represent different types of triangles, as well as those that cannot represent the side lengths of a triangle.

DEVELOP ACADEMIC LANGUAGE

WHY? Support understanding of the academic word *consider* with synonyms and antonyms.

HOW? Write the following words and phrases in random order on the board: *disregard, mind, note, take into account, think about, ignore, neglect, examine, evaluate, pay no attention*. Have students think about the meaning of *consider* and tell how they can sort the words. Then read Connect It problem 2. Invite students to use synonyms or antonyms to talk about their answers. (Ex. *I can disregard . . . .*)

TRY IT SMP 1, 2, 4, 5, 6

Make Sense of the Problem

See ***Connect to Culture*** to support student engagement. Before students work on Try It, use **Notice and Wonder** to help them make sense of the problem.

Develop Finding an Unknown Length in a Right Triangle

➤ **Read and try to solve the problem below.**

A firefighter is trying to rescue a kitten from a tree. He leans a 13-foot ladder so its top touches the tree. The base of the ladder is 5 feet from the base of the tree. The tree forms a right angle with the ground. How high up the tree does the ladder reach?

TRY IT **Math Toolkit** centimeter grid paper, centimeter ruler, unit cubes

Possible work:

SAMPLE A

On cm grid paper, I let each grid square represent a square foot. I used 13 unit cubes to make a ladder, tilting it against my tree so it starts 5 grid squares away from the tree. The top of ladder hits the tree 12 grid squares up.

The ladder reaches 12 feet up the tree.

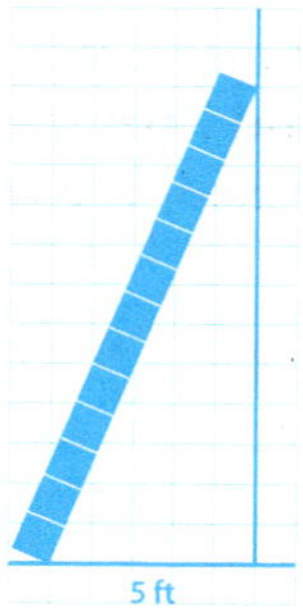

SAMPLE B

I know one leg of the right triangle formed by the ladder, ground, and the tree is 5 ft long. I also know the hypotenuse is 13 ft. I am looking for the length of the other leg. I know the leg must be less than 13 ft because the hypotenuse is always the longest side in a right triangle.

I think that 5, 12, 13 is a Pythagorean triple.

$5^2 + 12^2 = 25 + 144 = 169 = 13^2$, so the unknown leg must be 12 ft.

The ladder reaches 12 feet up the tree.

DISCUSS IT

Ask: Where does your model show the leg and the hypotenuse of the right triangle formed by the ground, tree, and ladder?

Share: In my model, . . . represents . . .

DISCUSS IT SMP 2, 3, 4, 5, 6

Support Partner Discussion

After students work on Try It, encourage them to respond to Discuss It with a partner. If students need support in getting started, prompt them to ask each other questions such as:

- *Where is the right angle in your model?*
- *What object represents the hypotenuse?*
- *What does the tree represent?*
- *Which lengths do you know, and which length is unknown?*

Common Misconception Listen for students who think that the unknown length can be found by adding the squares of the known lengths and taking the square root of the sum. As students share their strategies, have them identify the legs and the hypotenuse in a labeled drawing of the situation. Elicit the fact that the unknown length is a leg of a right triangle, not the hypotenuse, so it is the value of b in $5^2 + b^2 = 13^2$. Discuss how to solve this equation.

Select and Sequence Student Strategies

Select 2–3 samples that represent the range of student thinking in your classroom. Here is one possible order for class discussion:

- model drawn on grid paper and cubes or a ruler used to find unknown length
- (misconception) squares of known lengths added and square root of the sum taken to find the unknown length
- Pythagorean Theorem correctly used to find the unknown leg length

Facilitate Whole Class Discussion

Call on students to share selected strategies. Prompt students to describe what they assumed about the problem and what they decided to do as a result.

Guide students to **Compare and Connect** the representations. Allow individual think time for students to consider the different ideas.

ASK *How do these strategies use right triangles?*

LISTEN FOR The drawings show a right triangle with the ladder as the hypotenuse, the distance from the base of the ladder to the tree as one leg and the distance from the bottom of the tree to the top of the ladder as the other. The known and unknown lengths form a right triangle, so the Pythagorean Theorem can be used.

Picture It & Model It

If students presented these models, have students connect these models to those presented in class.

If no student presented at least one of these models, have students first analyze key features of the models, and then connect them to the models presented in class.

ASK *How are the strategies in Picture It and Model It related?*

LISTEN FOR The picture shows the right triangle that is formed and what the known and unknown lengths are. The model applies the Pythagorean Theorem to find the unknown length.

For the drawing, prompt students to compare the parts of the sketch to the key information provided in the problem. Ask: *How do you determine which length in the drawing is unknown?*

For the Pythagorean Theorem, prompt students to notice where the information from the description is substituted into the equation.

- *What does b represent in the drawing?*
- *Why is 13^2 the sum in the equation?*

➤ Explore different ways to find how to use the Pythagorean Theorem to find an unknown length.

A firefighter is trying to rescue a kitten from a tree. He leans a 13-foot ladder so its top touches the tree. The base of the ladder is 5 feet from the base of the tree. The tree forms a right angle with the ground. How high up the tree does the ladder reach?

Picture It

You can draw a picture to show the information you are given and what you still need to find.

Model It

You can use the Pythagorean Theorem.

The ladder represents the hypotenuse of the right triangle formed by the ladder, tree, and ground. Let b be the length you need to find.

$5^2 + b^2 = 13^2$

$25 + b^2 = 169$

$b^2 = 169 - 25$

$b^2 = 144$

$b = \pm\sqrt{144}$

DIFFERENTIATION | EXTEND

SMP 4

Deepen Understanding

Modeling a Problem to Help Understand How to Solve It

Prompt students to consider this scenario: *The firefighter knows the kitten in the tree is 12 feet from the ground. He wants to ensure that he can reach the kitten with the 13-foot ladder. How far from the base of the tree should he place the ladder?*

ASK *How would the drawing for this scenario be different?*

LISTEN FOR It would look the same, but the length of the vertical leg would be labeled 12 ft, and the length of the horizontal leg would be unknown.

ASK *How would it change the computation?*

LISTEN FOR If a is the unknown length, you need to solve $a^2 + 12^2 = 13^2$, or $a^2 + 144 = 169$. You would subtract 144 from both sides of the equation to get $a^2 = 25$, and then take the square root of both sides of the equation.

Ask students to consider another related scenario: *The firefighter has an extension ladder. The kitten in the tree is 12 feet from the ground. If the firefighter puts the base of the ladder 5 feet from the tree, how long will he need to make the ladder to reach the kitten?* Discuss how the drawing and computation would change. In this scenario, the unknown length is the hypotenuse and the equation is $5^2 + 12^2 = c^2$.

Develop Finding an Unknown Length in a Right Triangle

CONNECT IT SMP 2, 3, 4, 5, 6

Remind students that the quantities and the relationships between them are the same in each representation. Explain that they will now use those representations to reason about how to use the Pythagorean Theorem to find an unknown length.

Before students begin to record and expand on their work in Picture It & Model It, tell them that problem 3 will prepare them to provide the explanation asked for in problem 4.

Monitor and Confirm Understanding 1 – 2

- The tree, the ground, and the ladder form a right triangle.
- The length of the hypotenuse is 13 ft, the length of the ladder. The length of one leg is 5 ft, the distance from the base of the ladder to the base of the tree. The length of the other leg is the unknown distance, b ft.
- The unknown distance can be found by solving $5^2 + b^2 = 13^2$.
- The solution of the equation is $b = \pm 12$. Because b represents a length, only the positive solution, 12, makes sense.

Facilitate Whole Class Discussion

3 Students should begin with the formula for the Pythagorean Theorem, $a^2 + b^2 = c^2$, where a and b are the leg lengths and c is the hypotenuse length of a right triangle.

> **ASK** *Why does this problem specify subtraction equations?*
>
> **LISTEN FOR** To isolate either the a^2 or b^2 term, you have to subtract the other from each side of the equation.

4 Look for the idea that the Pythagorean Theorem can be used to find an unknown leg length when the lengths of the other leg and the hypotenuse are known.

> **ASK** *What do you need to know in order to apply the Pythagorean Theorem to find an unknown side length of a triangle?*
>
> **LISTEN FOR** You need to know that the triangle is a right triangle, and you need to know two of the side lengths.

5 **Reflect** Have all students focus on the strategies used to solve the Try It. If time allows, have students discuss their ideas with a partner.

CONNECT IT

➤ **Use the problem from the previous page to help you understand how to use the Pythagorean Theorem to find an unknown length.**

1 Look at **Picture It** and **Model It**. Explain how the picture and the equation $5^2 + b^2 = 13^2$ represent this situation.

Possible explanation: The ground meets the tree at a right angle, so you can draw a right triangle with the ground and tree as the legs and the ladder as the hypotenuse. The ground leg is 5 ft and the ladder hypotenuse is 13 ft. So, you can use the Pythagorean Theorem to find the unknown tree leg, b.

2 **a.** How high up the tree does the ladder reach? Why do you not need to consider the negative square root of b?

12 ft; b is a length and cannot be negative.

b. When using the Pythagorean Theorem to find an unknown length, do you ever need to consider a negative square root? Explain.

No; Possible explanation: You are always finding the length of a side of a triangle, and length can never be negative.

3 A right triangle has leg lengths a and b and hypotenuse length c. Write a subtraction equation that you could use to solve for b. Write a subtraction equation that you could use to solve for a.

$b^2 = c^2 - a^2$; $a^2 = c^2 - b^2$

4 When might you use one of the equations in problem 3? Why?

Possible answer: Use one of the equations when you are trying to find the length of a leg in a right triangle. These equations will need fewer solving steps and can also remind you that you are solving for a leg.

5 **Reflect** Think about all the models and strategies you have discussed today. Describe how one of them helped you better understand how to solve the **Try It** problem.

Responses will vary. Check student responses.

637

DIFFERENTIATION | RETEACH or REINFORCE

Hands-On Activity

Use the Pythagorean Theorem to find an unknown leg length.

If students are unsure about how to apply the Pythagorean Theorem to find an unknown leg length, then use this activity to reinforce the concept.

Materials For each pair: tape measure, yard stick, or meter stick

- Have each pair find a rectangular object in the room to measure. Some suggestions include a window, door, bookshelf, book, desktop, cabinet door, or drawer face.
- Encourage students to make a sketch of the object and label it as they work.
- Instruct students to measure and record the length and width of the object.
- Have students use the Pythagorean Theorem to calculate the length of the diagonal of the object to the nearest whole unit and then check by measuring its length.
- Ask students to choose another rectangular object and measure its width and the length of a diagonal.
- Have students use the Pythagorean Theorem to calculate the length of the object to the nearest whole unit, and then check by measuring its length.

Apply It

For all problems, encourage students to use a model to support their thinking.

6 First, students must use the Pythagorean Theorem to solve for the unknown length of the right triangle. Then they need to add this value to 8 ft, the height of the fence pole, to get the height of the building.

7 Students may substitute the given sets of numbers into $a^2 + b^2 = c^2$. The set of side lengths that do not make the equation true do not form a right triangle.

D is correct. $12^2 + 15^2 \neq 18^2$, or $144 + 225 \neq 324$.

A is not correct. $5^2 + 6^2 = (\sqrt{61})^2$, or $25 + 36 = 61$.

B is not correct. $24^2 + 7^2 = 25^2$, or $576 + 49 = 625$.

C is not correct. $14^2 + 7^2 = (\sqrt{245})^2$, or $196 + 49 = 245$.

Apply It

➤ **Use what you learned to solve these problems.**

6 A car salesman is stringing banners from the top of the roof to a fence pole 20 feet away. The fence pole is 8 feet high. He uses 29 feet of banner rope to reach from the rooftop to the fence pole. How tall is the roof? Show your work.

Possible work:

$b^2 = 29^2 - 20^2$

$b^2 = 841 - 400$

$b^2 = 441$

$b = \sqrt{441} = 21$

$21 + 8 = 29$

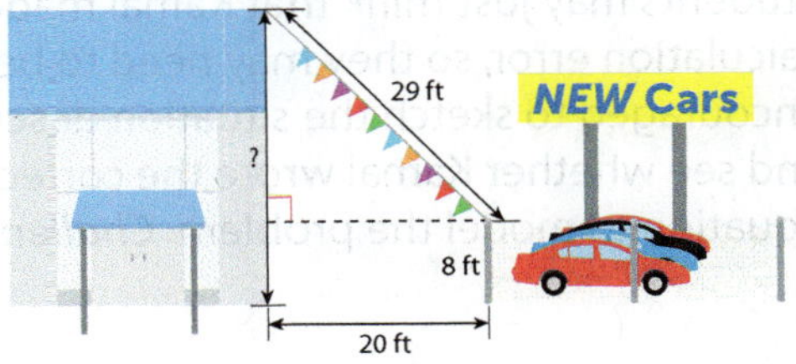

SOLUTION The roof is 29 feet tall.

7 Which set of side lengths do not form a right triangle?

A $5, 6, \sqrt{61}$

B 24, 7, 25

C $14, 7, \sqrt{245}$

(D) 12, 15, 18

8 The perimeter of an equilateral triangle is 48 cm. Find the height of the triangle to the nearest whole number. Show your work.

Possible work: The sides of the triangle are all the same length. $48 \div 3 = 16$; each side length is 16 cm.

$h^2 = 16^2 - 8^2$

$h^2 = 256 - 64$

$h^2 = 192$

$h = \sqrt{192}$

192 is between 13 and 14, but it is closer to 14

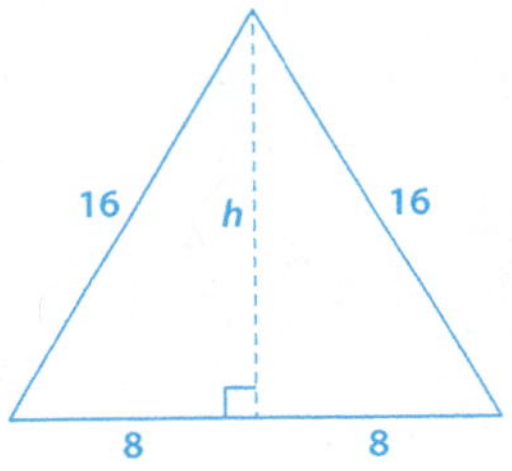

SOLUTION The height of the triangle is about 14 cm.

CLOSE EXIT TICKET

8 Students' solutions should show an understanding that:

- the side length of the equilateral triangle is 16 cm, one third of its perimeter.
- the height segment splits the equilateral triangle into two congruent right triangles.
- the length of the hypotenuse of each right triangle is 16 cm, and the lengths of the legs are 8 cm and the unknown height.
- the height can be found by solving $h^2 = 16^2 - 8^2$.
- the height, $\sqrt{192}$, is about 14 cm.

Error Alert If students find that the height is 18 cm, then they are mistakenly treating the unknown length as a hypotenuse and solving $8^2 + 16^2 = h^2$. Encourage them to draw a sketch of the situation. They should see that the unknown height is the length of a leg, not the hypotenuse.

Practice Finding an Unknown Length in a Right Triangle

Problem Notes

Assign **Practice Finding an Unknown Length in a Right Triangle** as extra practice in class or as homework.

1. *Basic*
2. Students may just think that Kamal made a calculation error, so they may need to be encouraged to sketch the situation described and see whether Kamal wrote the correct equation to model the problem. ***Challenge***

Practice Finding an Unknown Length in a Right Triangle

➤ **Study the Example showing how to find an unknown length in a right triangle. Then solve problems 1–4.**

Example

A meteorologist ties a spherical balloon that is 2 feet in diameter to a stake in the ground. The string is 15 feet long. The wind blows the balloon so that the top of it is 8 feet to the right of the stake. What is the distance, *b*, from the top of the balloon to the ground?

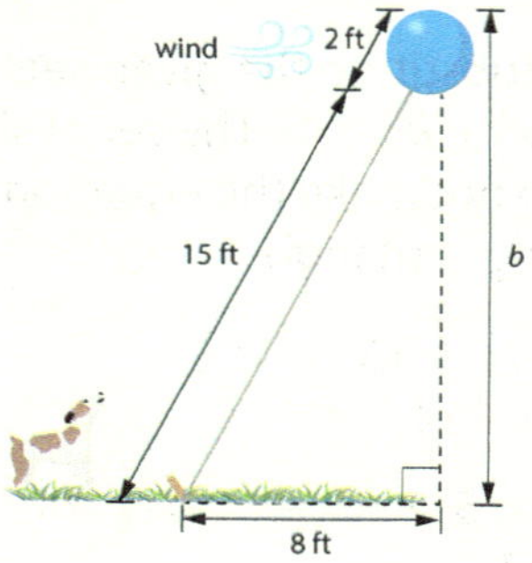

Use a right triangle. The lengths of the hypotenuse and one leg are known. Use the Pythagorean Theorem to find the length of the other leg.

$b^2 = c^2 - a^2$

$b^2 = 17^2 - 8^2$

$b^2 = 289 - 64$

$b^2 = 225$

$b = \sqrt{225}$ or 15

The distance from the top of the balloon to the ground is 15 ft.

1. Imani used the equation $8^2 + b^2 = 17^2$ to find the distance from the top of the balloon to the ground in the Example. Why does this equation also work?

   Possible explanation: Imani's equation shows the same three terms, but the terms are rearranged. Both equations correctly use the Pythagorean Theorem, so either can be used to find the unknown distance.

2. Kamal said the distance from the top of the balloon to the ground in the Example is $\sqrt{353}$ ft. What mistake might Kamal have made?

   Possible answer: Kamal may have used 17 ft as a leg length of the right triangle instead of as the hypotenuse length when applying the Pythagorean Theorem.

Fluency & Skills Practice

Finding an Unknown Length in a Right Triangle

In this activity, students use the Pythagorean Theorem to find unknown side lengths of right triangles.

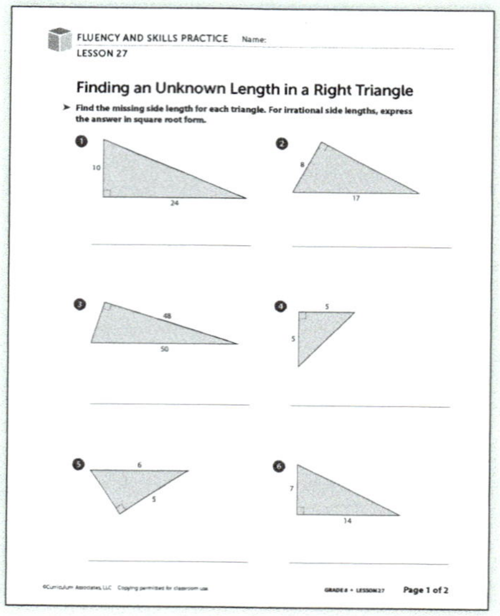
FLUENCY AND SKILLS PRACTICE Name:
LESSON 27
Finding an Unknown Length in a Right Triangle
Page 1 of 2

Additional Practice

3 **a.** Students should recognize that the height of $\triangle ABC$ is a leg of right $\triangle ABD$. Substitute the known leg length, *AD*, and the known hypotenuse length, *AB*, into the Pythagorean Theorem to find the height of the triangle. Note, the height is the length of $\overline{BD}$, not the length of $\overline{BC}$. ***Medium***

b. To find *BC*, students apply the Pythagorean Theorem to find the hypotenuse length of right $\triangle BCD$ using the length of $\overline{BD}$ found in problem 3a. ***Medium***

4 Students might find $c = 1.5$ and record 1.5 yd as their final answer. Students must read carefully to see that the problem is asking for the perimeter of the deck, rather than just the side length, *c*. ***Medium***

LESSON 27 | SESSION 2

3 The diagram shows $\triangle ABC$.

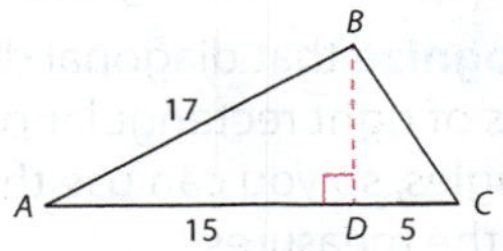

a. What is the height of $\triangle ABC$? Show your work.

Possible work:

$a^2 = c^2 - b^2$

$a^2 = 17^2 - 15^2$

$a^2 = 289 - 225$

$a^2 = 64$

$a = \sqrt{64} = 8$

SOLUTION The height of $\triangle ABC$ is 8.

b. What is the length of $\overline{BC}$ in $\triangle ABC$? Show your work.

Possible work:

$5^2 + 8^2 = c^2$

$25 + 64 = c^2$

$89 = c^2$

$c = \sqrt{89}$

SOLUTION The length of $\overline{BC}$ is $\sqrt{89}$.

4 Alyssa is designing a square wooden deck with side length *c* yards. She will build the deck over her square patio, as shown in the diagram. Find the perimeter of the deck. Show your work.

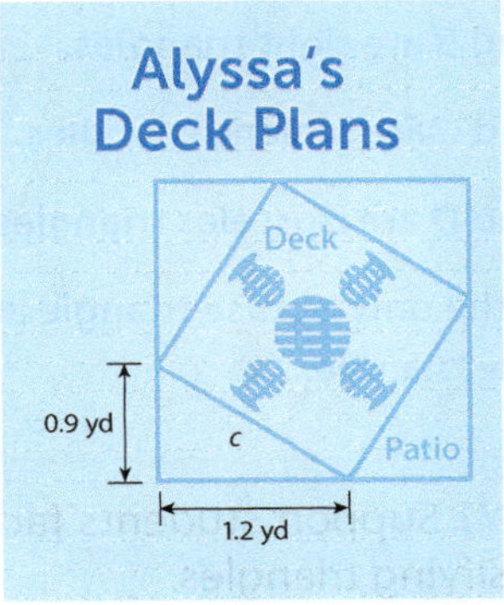

Possible work: The length of one side of the deck is the hypotenuse of a right triangle with leg lengths of 0.9 yard and 1.2 yards.

$0.9^2 + 1.2^2 = c^2$

$0.81 + 1.44 = c^2$

$2.25 = c^2$

$\sqrt{2.25} = c$

$1.5 = c$

The perimeter of the deck is 4c.

$4 \times 1.5 = 6$

SOLUTION The perimeter of the deck is 6 yards.

640

DIFFERENTIATION | ENGLISH LANGUAGE LEARNERS

Use with **Session 3** **Connect It**

Levels 1–3: Reading/Writing

Prepare students for Connect It problem 4 by helping them generate a word bank of terms related to right rectangular prisms and right triangles. Provide right rectangular prisms and right triangles from the Math Toolkit. Guide students to point to and name different parts of the shapes as you record them. [Possible terms: *side, edge, face, base, diagonal, length, leg, hypotenuse, angle, right angle*]

Next, read the problem aloud and display the Pythagorean Theorem. Have partners identify a strategy that uses the Pythagorean Theorem. Ask: *What can you use the theorem to find? What do you need to know?* Allow partners to point to the models or shapes and help them write responses.

Levels 1–3: Reading/Writing

Read Connect It problem 4 with students. Prepare for written responses by helping students with key terms like *unknown.* Next, ask students to review the Pythagorean theorem and use **Co-Constructed Word Bank** to identify words and phrases they might use in their written responses. If needed, suggest *side length* and *right triangle.* Then ask students to add terms related to right rectangular prisms, like *face, base,* and *diagonal.*

Use **Stronger and Clearer Each Time** to help with written responses. Encourage students to use models or diagrams to develop their ideas and then explain to partners. After discussing, have students write responses using the Word Bank.

Levels 1–3: Reading/Writing

Have students read Connect It problem 4 and confirm understanding using **Say It Another Way.** If needed, help students make sense of *unknown* by identifying the prefix *un-* and discussing how it changes the meaning of the base.

Next, have students use **Stronger and Clearer Each Time** to craft their written explanations. If needed, prompt students to develop their ideas using models or diagrams before drafting responses. Then have partners meet to explain their ideas. Encourage partner feedback on the use of precise language, like math terms describing a prism. After sufficient partner discussion, ask students to revise their writing.

Develop Finding an Unknown Length in a Three-Dimensional Figure

Purpose

- **Develop** strategies for finding unknown lengths in three-dimensional figures.
- **Recognize** that diagonal distances inside and on the faces of right rectangular prisms are hypotenuses of right triangles, so you can use the Pythagorean Theorem to find the measures.

START CONNECT TO PRIOR KNOWLEDGE

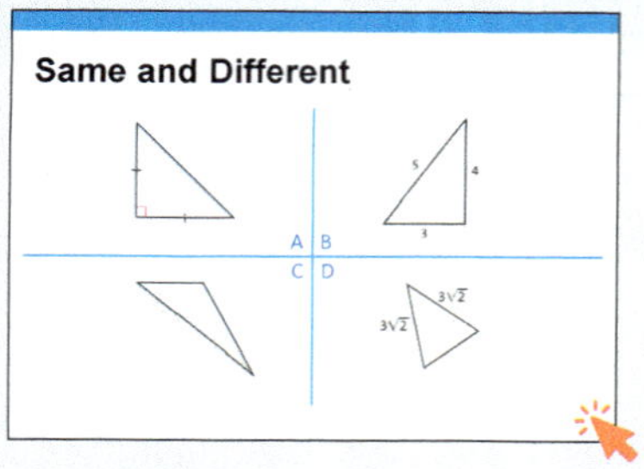

Possible Solutions

All of the figures are triangles.

A and B are right triangles.

B and C are scalene triangles.

A and D are isosceles triangles.

C is the only obtuse triangle and D is the only acute triangle.

WHY? Support students' facility with classifying triangles.

DEVELOP ACADEMIC LANGUAGE

WHY? Unpack dense sentences.

HOW? Ask a student to read Apply It problem 7 aloud. Point out that academic sentences can be long and dense in order to convey precise information. Have students consult the diagram and find parts of the sentence that describe the distance exactly. Encourage students to be precise as they identify parts of figures in other problems.

TRY IT

SMP 1, 2, 4, 5, 6

Make Sense of the Problem

See ***Connect to Culture*** to support student engagement. Before students work on Try It, use **Three Reads** to help them make sense of the problem. After the first read, ask: *What is the problem about?* After the second read, ask: *What are you trying to find?* After the third read, ask: *What are the important quantities and relationships in the problem?*

LESSON 27 | SESSION 3

Develop Finding an Unknown Length in a Three-Dimensional Figure

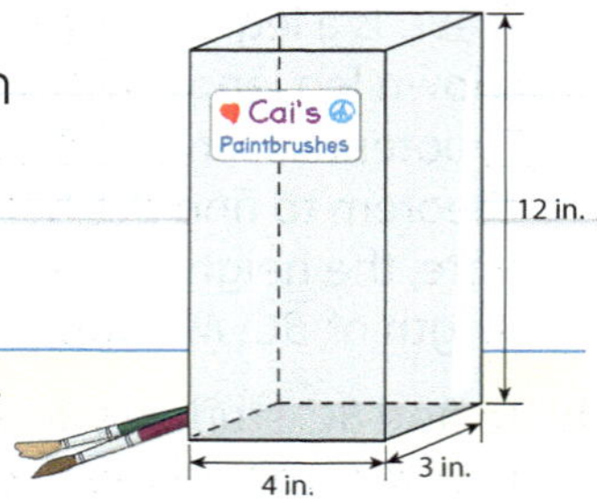

Read and try to solve the problem below.

Cai has a box for her paintbrushes. The box is a right rectangular prism. What is the longest paintbrush that will fit in the box?

TRY IT

Math Toolkit grid paper, rulers

Possible work:

SAMPLE A

I want to find length y. There are two right triangles I can use. I need to find x and then find y.

$3^2 + 4^2 = x^2$

$9 + 16 = x^2$

$25 = x^2$

$5 = x$

$5^2 + 12^2 = y^2$

$25 + 144 = y^2$

$169 = y^2$

$13 = y$

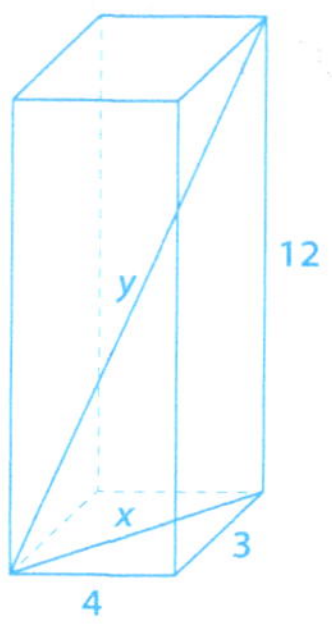

The longest paintbrush that will fit in the box is 13 inches.

SAMPLE B

I can use the Pythagorean Theorem to find the diagonal of the base, and then use it again to find the diagonal of the box.

3, 4, 5 is a Pythagorean triple, so the diagonal of the base is 5.

5, 12, 13 is also a Pythagorean triple, so the diagonal of the box is 13.

The longest paintbrush that will fit in the box is 13 in.

DISCUSS IT

Ask: Why did you choose that strategy to find the longest paintbrush that will fit?

Share: The problem is asking . . .

641

DISCUSS IT

SMP 1, 2, 3, 4, 5, 6

Support Partner Discussion

After students work on Try It, encourage them to respond to Discuss It with a partner. If students need support in getting started, prompt them to ask each other questions such as:

- *How did you know where to begin?*
- *Did a sketch of the box help you visualize its dimensions?*
- *Why does the Pythagorean Theorem have to be applied twice?*

Common Misconception Listen for students who think the length of the longest paintbrush is the length of the diagonal of the 4 in.-by-12 in. face of the box. As students share their strategies, ask them to compare the length of the diagonal from one corner of the box to the opposite corner to the length of the diagonal of this face. If you have a real box available, you might have students measure and compare the length of the diagonal of the largest face to the length of the diagonal of the box. You could also use the classroom as an example.

Select and Sequence Student Strategies

Select 2–3 samples that represent the range of student thinking in your classroom. Here is one possible order for class discussion:

- draws diagram and applies Pythagorean Theorem twice to solve
- **(misconception)** thinks that length of diagonal of 4-by-12 face is the solution
- uses Pythagorean triples to find solution

Facilitate Whole Class Discussion

Call on students to share selected strategies. Prompt students to justify their solutions by providing reasons they are reasonable in the problem context.

Guide students to **Compare and Connect** the representations. Have students turn and talk with a partner to discuss ways they can check to be sure their answer is reasonable.

ASK *How is the Pythagorean Theorem used in these strategies?*

LISTEN FOR The theorem is used to find the length of the diagonal of the 3-by-4 face and then the diagonal of the box. Some strategies used Pythagorean triples.

Picture It & Model It

If students presented these models, have students connect these models to those presented in class.

If no student presented at least one of these models, have students first analyze key features of the models, and then connect them to the models presented in class.

ASK *How are the strategies in Picture It and Model It related?*

LISTEN FOR Picture It shows labeled diagrams of the two right triangles involved in the problem. Model It applies the Pythagorean Theorem to those triangles to find the unknown length.

For the diagrams, prompt students to compare the parts of each diagram to the key information provided in the problem. Ask: *What do the variables c and e represent?*

For the equations, prompt students to note how the expression $3^2 + 4^2$ is substituted for c^2 in the last equation.

- *How is this strategy different from finding the diagonal of the 3-by-4 face first and then finding the diagonal of the box?*
- *Which approach do you prefer, doing two calculations or combining the steps and doing only one? Why?*

➤ **Explore different ways to find an unknown length in a right rectangular prism.**

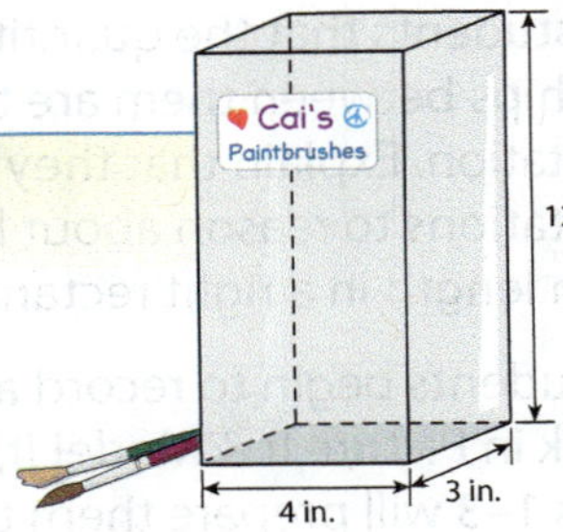

Cai has a box for her paintbrushes. The box is a right rectangular prism. What is the longest paintbrush that will fit in the box?

Picture It

You can draw a diagram to represent the problem.

Look for right triangles that can help you find the length you need.

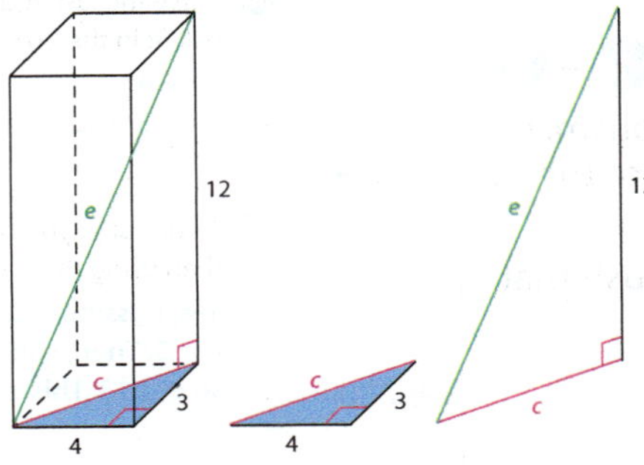

You can use the diagonal length of the base, c, to find the diagonal length of the box, e.

Model It

You can use the Pythagorean Theorem to write equations.

To find the diagonal length of the base: $3^2 + 4^2 = c^2$

To find the diagonal length of the box: $c^2 + 12^2 = e^2$

Substitute to get one equation: $3^2 + 4^2 + 12^2 = e^2$

DIFFERENTIATION | EXTEND

SMP 7

Deepen Understanding
Applying the Structure of the Pythagorean Theorem to Cylinders

Prompt students to consider how the Pythagorean Theorem can be used to determine the diagonal length of a cylinder. Suppose Cai's box is a cylinder with height 12 inches and diameter 4 inches. What is the longest paintbrush that will fit in the cylinder?

ASK *How would the diagram change?*

LISTEN FOR There would be only one right triangle. The diameter of the base and the height of the cylinder are the two legs of a right triangle. The hypotenuse of the right triangle will be the diagonal of the cylinder.

ASK *How will the solution change?*

LISTEN FOR You would need only one equation. You would need to solve $4^2 + 12^2 = c^2$, where c is the diagonal of the cylinder.

ASK *The dimension values are not a Pythagorean triple. How can you find c?*

LISTEN FOR Evaluate the squares to get $16 + 144 = c^2$, simplify to get $160 = c^2$, and take the square root of both sides of the equation to get $c = \sqrt{160}$. Use a calculator or successive approximations to get $c \approx 12.6$ in.

Develop Finding an Unknown Length in a Three-Dimensional Figure

CONNECT IT

SMP 2, 3, 4, 5, 6

Remind students that the quantities and the relationships between them are the same in each representation. Explain that they will now use those representations to reason about how to find an unknown length in a right rectangular prism.

Before students begin to record and expand on their work in Picture It & Model It, tell them that problems 1–3 will prepare them to provide the explanation asked for in problem 4.

Monitor and Confirm Understanding 1 – 2

- Finding the length of the diagonal of the prism, *e*, is dependent upon knowing *c*, the length of the diagonal of the 3-by-4 face.
- The value of *e* is 13, so the longest paintbrush that will fit has a length of 13 in.

Facilitate Whole Class Discussion

3 Look for understanding that finding the value of *c* first and then using that value in the calculation of *e* gives the same solution as the method in Model It.

4 Look for understanding that you can use the Pythagorean Theorem to find a diagonal length in a right rectangular prism when the dimensions of the prism are given.

ASK *If you knew only the height of the right rectangular prism and the length of the diagonal of the prism, would you be able to find the prism's dimensions?*

LISTEN FOR No, the diagonal length and the height could be used to find the length of the diagonal of the base. However, you would need to know either the length or width of the base in order to find the other dimension.

5 **Reflect** Have all students focus on the strategies used to solve the Try It. If time allows, have students discuss their ideas with a partner.

CONNECT IT

➤ **Use the problem from the previous page to help you understand how to find an unknown length in a right rectangular prism.**

1 Look at **Picture It** and **Model It**. How does finding the length of diagonal *c* help you find the length of diagonal *e*?

Possible answer: The diagonal *c* is both the hypotenuse of the right triangle in the base and a leg of the right triangle with hypotenuse *e*.

2 Solve the last equation in **Model It** to find *e*. What is the longest paintbrush that will fit in the box?

$3^2 + 4^2 + 12^2 = e^2 \longrightarrow 9 + 16 + 144 = e^2 \longrightarrow 169 = e^2 \longrightarrow \sqrt{169} = e \longrightarrow$ $e = 13$; The longest paintbrush that will fit in the box is 13 in.

3 Tyrone says you can also solve the problem by first solving $3^2 + 4^2 = c^2$ for *c* and then using this value of *c* to solve $c^2 + 12^2 = e^2$ for *e*. Is Tyrone correct? Explain.

Yes; Possible explanation: Solve $3^2 + 4^2 = c^2$ for *c* to get $9 + 16 = 25 = c^2$, so $c = 5$. Then, substitute $c = 5$ into $c^2 + 12^2 = e^2$ to get $25 + 144 = 169 = e^2$, so $e = 13$. This is the same value for *e* as in problem 2.

4 When can you use the Pythagorean Theorem to find an unknown length in a right rectangular prism?

Possible answer: You can use the Pythagorean Theorem to find a side length of a right triangle when you know the other two side lengths. So, you could find an unknown length of a side or a diagonal of one of the faces, or the length of a diagonal of the prism.

5 **Reflect** Think about all the models and strategies you have discussed today. Describe how one of them helped you better understand how to solve the **Try It** problem.

Responses will vary. Check student responses.

643

DIFFERENTIATION | RETEACH or REINFORCE

Visual Model

Find the diagonal length of a rectangular prism.

If students are unsure about finding the length of a diagonal of a rectangular prism, then use this model to help them visualize the concept.

Materials For display: an open box, tape measure, string, tape

- Stretch a piece of string from one corner of the box to the opposite corner to form a diagonal, secure it with tape, and select a face of the box to be the base.
- Ask a student to point to the edge length that will represent the height.
- Invite a student to measure and record the length, width, and height of the box.
- Point out that the string is the diagonal and that you want to find its length. Discuss why it is necessary to first find the length of the diagonal of the base.
- Sketch the base and ask a student to calculate the length of its diagonal.
- Using the diagonal of the base as one leg, sketch a right triangle with the height of the box as the other leg length. Help students see how this triangle relates to the box.
- Invite a student to calculate the length of the diagonal of the box. Use a tape measure to verify the calculations.

Apply It

For all problems, encourage students to use a model to support their thinking.

6 Students may use the expression $9^2 + 12^2$ for the length of one leg and use the Pythagorean Theorem: $a^2 + b^2 = PR^2 \rightarrow 9^2 + 12^2 + 8^2 = PR^2$.

7 **D is correct.** Students may solve the problem by first finding the hypotenuse of the base of the prism by substituting 3 for a and 5 for b, into $a^2 + b^2 = c^2$ to find $c = \sqrt{34}$. They may then find the diagonal of the prism by using $\sqrt{34}$ and 8 for leg lengths to find the hypotenuse length of $\sqrt{98}$ units.

A is not correct. This answer is the hypotenuse of the base of the rectangular prism.

B is not correct. This answer is the result of using 4 for the diagonal of the base to then calculate the diagonal of the prism as $4^2 + 8^2 = e^2$.

C is not correct. This answer is the hypotenuse of one of the 5-by-8 faces of the prism.

Apply It

➤ **Use what you learned to solve these problems.**

6 Find the length of the diagonal from P to Q in this right rectangular prism. Show your work. Possible work:

$PR = \sqrt{9^2 + 12^2}$

$PR = \sqrt{225}$

$PR = 15$

$PQ = \sqrt{8^2 + 15^2}$

$PQ = \sqrt{289}$

$PQ = 17$

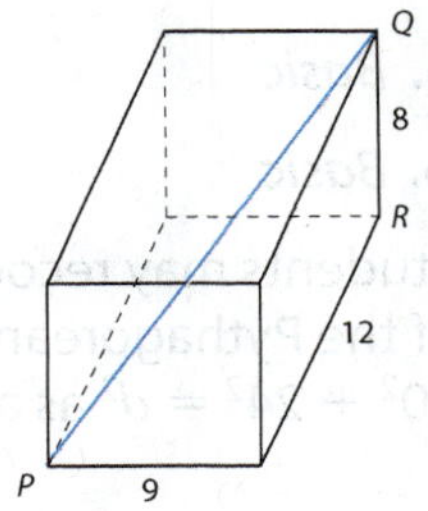

SOLUTION The length of the diagonal from P to Q is 17.

7 What is the distance from one corner of the bottom base to the opposite corner of the top base in this right rectangular prism?

A $\sqrt{34}$ units

B $\sqrt{80}$ units

C $\sqrt{89}$ units

(D) $\sqrt{98}$ units

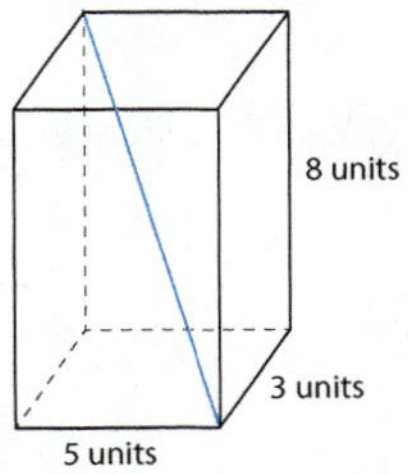

8 Anica is shipping a poster to a customer. When the poster is rolled up, it measures 6 feet long. She will use a box that is a right rectangular prism with a base that is 3 feet by 4 feet. What whole number could be the shortest height of the box that will hold the poster? Show your work.

Possible work:

$6^2 - (3^2 + 4^2) = h^2$

$36 - (9 + 16) = h^2$

$11 = h^2$

$\sqrt{11} = h$

$\sqrt{11}$ is between 3 and 4.

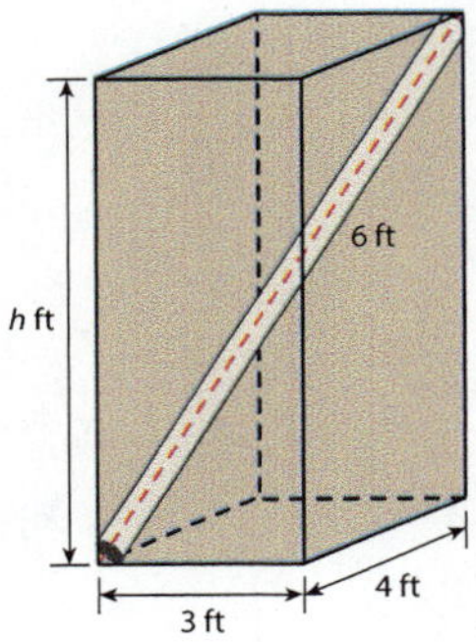

SOLUTION The box must be at least 4 ft tall.

CLOSE EXIT TICKET

8 Students' solutions should show an understanding that:

- the length of the rolled-up poster, 6 ft, is the shortest possible diagonal length of the prism.
- the unknown height is the length of a leg of a right triangle with hypotenuse length 6 ft and its other leg length as the diagonal of the base.
- the diagonal length of the base is $\sqrt{3^2 + 4^2}$ or 5.
- the unknown height can be found by solving $5^2 + h^2 = 6^2$ for h.

Error Alert If students mistakenly solve this problem as they did the previous examples, by using 6 ft to represent the height of the prism and calculating the diagonal length of the prism, then encourage them to reread the problem to see what they are being asked to find. Ask students to note which dimension is labeled with a variable.

Practice Finding an Unknown Length in a Three-Dimensional Figure

Problem Notes

Assign **Practice Finding an Unknown Length in a Three-Dimensional Figure** as extra practice in class or as homework.

1. **a.** *Basic*

   b. *Basic*

2. Students may recognize 6 and 8 as leg lengths of the Pythagorean triple 6, 8, 10 and write $10^2 + 24^2 = d^2$ as a first step. ***Medium***

LESSON 27 | SESSION 3 Name:

Practice Finding an Unknown Length in a Three-Dimensional Figure

➤ **Study the Example explaining how to find the length of a diagonal in a right rectangular prism. Then solve problems 1–4.**

Example

The diagram shows a diagonal drawn in a right rectangular prism. Explain how you can find *d*, the length of this diagonal.

Look for right triangles. Side length *d* is the hypotenuse of the right triangle with leg lengths *c* and 24. Side length *c* is the hypotenuse of the right triangle in the base of the prism with leg lengths 6 and 8. Use the Pythagorean Theorem to find *c*. Then use it again to find *d*.

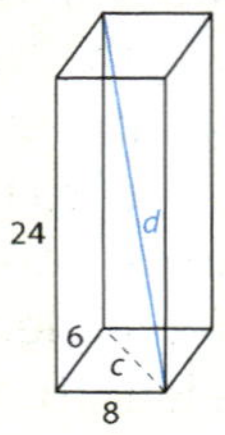

1. **a.** How do you know that the triangle with side lengths 6, 8, and *c* in the Example is a right triangle?

   Possible answer: All the faces of a right rectangular prism have four right angles. The base is a face of the prism, so the angle between the sides of lengths 6 and 8 is a right angle.

   b. How do you know that the triangle with side lengths *c*, 24, and *d* in the Example is a right triangle?

   Possible answer: In a right rectangular prism, vertical faces meet the bases at right angles. Side length *c* is on a base and side length 24 is on a vertical face, so the angle between them is a right angle.

2. What is the length of the diagonal *d* in the Example? Show your work.

   Possible work:

$$(6^2 + 8^2) + 24^2 = d^2$$
$$100 + 576 = d^2$$
$$676 = d^2$$
$$\sqrt{676} = d$$
$$d = 26$$

SOLUTION The length of the diagonal is 26.

Fluency & Skills Practice

Finding an Unknown Length in a Three-Dimensional Figure

In this activity, students use the Pythagorean Theorem to find the length of the diagonals of rectangular prisms.

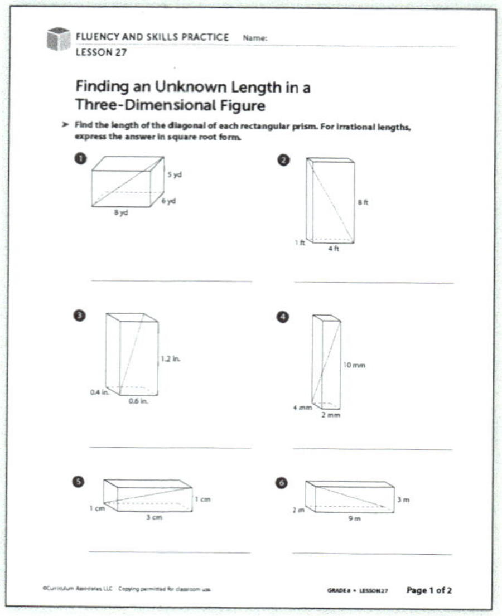

Additional Practice

3 Students may use a calculator to find the approximation of $\sqrt{134} \approx 11.6$ to determine that since $11.6 < 12$, the ruler will not fit. ***Medium***

4 Students may substitute the expression $0.8^2 + 1.2^2$ for d and write the equation $0.8^2 + 1.2^2 + 0.6^2 = d^2$. ***Challenge***

3 Will a 12-inch ruler fit in a box that is a right rectangular prism with a width of 5 inches, a length of 10 inches, and a height of 3 inches? Explain your answer.

No; Possible explanation:

Let c be the diagonal of the base.

$3^2 + 5^2 = c^2$

$9 + 25 = c^2$

$34 = c^2$

Let d be the diagonal of the box.

$34 + 10^2 = d^2$

$34 + 100 = d^2$

$134 = d^2$

$\sqrt{134} = d$

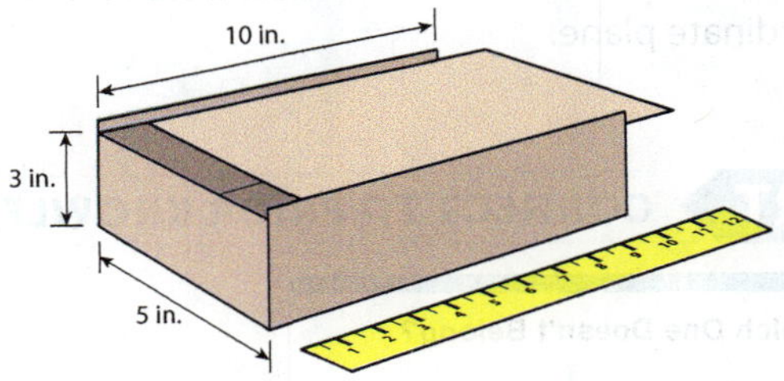

$\sqrt{134}$ is less than $\sqrt{144}$, so it is less than 12. The ruler will not fit.

4 In the right rectangular prism, what is the length of the diagonal from M to N to the nearest tenth of a meter? Show your work.

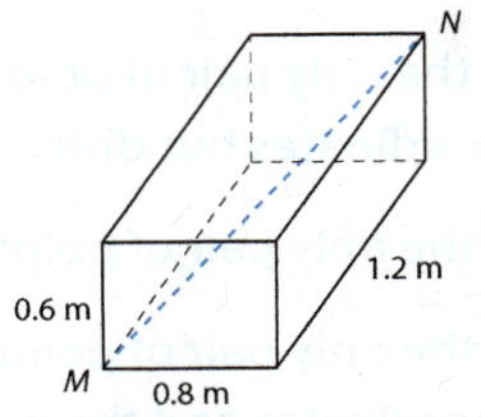

Possible work:

Let c be the diagonal of the base.

$0.8^2 + 1.2^2 = c^2$

$0.64 + 1.44 = c^2$

$2.08 = c^2$

Let d be the diagonal from M to N.

$2.08 + 0.6^2 = d^2$

$2.08 + 0.36 = d^2$

$2.44 = d^2$

$d = \sqrt{2.44} \approx 1.562$

SOLUTION The diagonal from M to N is about 1.6 m.

DIFFERENTIATION | ENGLISH LANGUAGE LEARNERS

Use with **Session 4 Connect It**

ACADEMIC VOCABULARY

Distance is the linear space between two things.

Horizontal describes something that goes side to side instead of up and down.

Vertical describes something that goes up and down instead of side to side.

Levels 1–3: Speaking/Writing

Prepare for Connect It problem 5 by reviewing the Academic Vocabulary. Help students connect to other words in English or home languages, such as *horizon* or *horizonte* in Spanish. Ask students to draw a horizontal and a vertical line on a coordinate plane. Then have them draw one that is not horizontal or vertical. Help students read and interpret the problem using:

- *I want to find the* ____ *between* ____ *points on a line. I know the line is not* ____. *The line is also not* ____.

Ask students to use graphs or models to show how to solve the problem. Help partners write responses.

Levels 2–4: Speaking/Writing

Help students read and interpret Connect It problem 5. Ask students to circle the Academic Vocabulary and use a coordinate plane to show their meanings.

Help students use **Say It Another Way** to paraphrase the problem. If needed, clarify that the verb phrase *to lie on*, in this context, means "to be (set) on."

Ask students to use **Stronger and Clearer Each Time** to craft explanations. Have students explain ideas to partners. Encourage partners to discuss the order of the steps and work together to revise their writing.

Levels 3–5: Speaking/Writing

Have students read and interpret Connect It problem 5. Ask students to plot possible points in a coordinate plane and then explain to partners how they know the points accurately represent the problem. Encourage students to use terms like *horizontal* and *vertical* in their explanations.

Next, have students draft responses by describing a possible solution strategy. Remind students to start with the first step and to explain why the strategy works. Have students use **Stronger and Clearer Each Time** to discuss their ideas with partners and then revise their writing.

Develop Finding Distance in the Coordinate Plane

Purpose

- **Develop** strategies for finding the shortest distance between two points in the coordinate plane.
- **Recognize** that you can use the Pythagorean Theorem to find nonhorizontal and nonvertical distances in the coordinate plane.

START CONNECT TO PRIOR KNOWLEDGE

Which One Doesn't Belong?

A (2, 5) and (9, 5)	B (−10, 3) and (−10, 3)
C (2, −2) and (4, −8)	D (−4, −3) and (−4, −8)

Possible Solutions

A is the only pair of points with the same *y*-coordinates but different *x*-coordinates.

B is the only pair of points that are the same.

C is the only pair of points where both the *x*-coordinates and the *y*-coordinates are different.

D is the only pair of points with the same *x*-coordinates but different *y*-coordinates.

WHY? Support students' facility with determining the similarities and differences for two ordered pairs.

DEVELOP ACADEMIC LANGUAGE

WHY? Reinforce understanding of *hypotenuse* through word origins.

HOW? Explain that *hypotenuse* comes from the Greek word *hypoteinousa* that means "stretching under." Have students look at the triangle in Picture It. Ask: *Under what part does the hypotenuse stretch?* [the right angle] Next, review the math definition of the word. Have students discuss whether the hypotenuse of a right triangle always *stretches under* the right angle.

TRY IT SMP 1, 2, 4, 5, 6

Make Sense of the Problem

Before students work on Try It, use **Co-Craft Questions** to help them make sense of the problem. Have students turn and talk with a partner to write questions they can ask about this problem before beginning to solve it.

LESSON 27 | SESSION 4

Develop Finding Distance in the Coordinate Plane

➤ **Read and try to solve the problem below.**

Find the shortest distance between the points (0, −6) and (−8, 0).

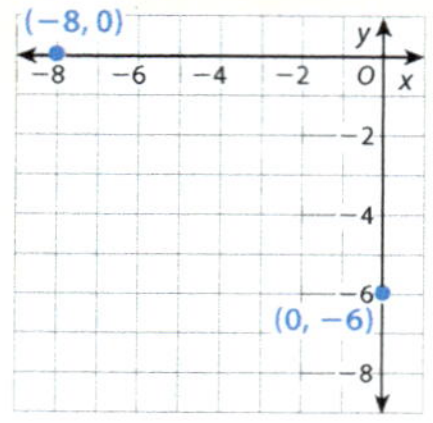

TRY IT Math Toolkit compasses, graph paper, rulers, tracing paper

Possible work:

SAMPLE A

I used the edge of a piece of paper to mark the distance between the two points. Then, I placed the edge of the paper along a horizontal grid line to see how many grid squares it measures, which is about 10.

The distance between (−8, 0) and (0, −6) is about 10 units.

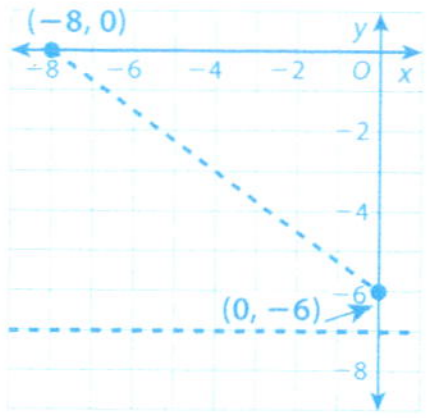

SAMPLE B

The distance between these points could be the hypotenuse of a right triangle with the right angle at the origin. The length of the side on the *x*-axis is 8 units and the length of the side on the *y*-axis is 6 units.

6, 8, 10 is a multiple of the Pythagorean triple 3, 4, 5.

So, the distance between the two points is 10 units.

DISCUSS IT

Ask: How did you get started?

Share: I started by . . .

647

DISCUSS IT SMP 1, 2, 3, 4, 5, 6

Support Partner Discussion

After students work on Try It, encourage them to respond to Discuss It with a partner. If students need support in getting started, prompt them to ask each other questions such as:

- *Did you draw a segment connecting the points? How did this help you?*
- *Did you use a ruler or other tool?*

Common Misconception Listen for students who think that to find the distance, they can find the number of units each point is from the origin and then add those values. As students share their strategies, remind them that the shortest distance between the points is the distance along the segment that connects them.

Develop

Select and Sequence Student Strategies

Select 2–3 samples that represent the range of student thinking in your classroom. Here is one possible order for class discussion:

- marks distance between points on a piece of paper, then measures the distance in grid units
- (misconception) adds the horizontal distance between $(-8, 0)$ and the origin to the vertical distance between $(0, -6)$ and the origin
- draws segment to connect points, creating a right triangle with legs along the axes, and uses the Pythagorean Theorem to find distance

Facilitate Whole Class Discussion

Call on students to share selected strategies. As students share their strategies, remind them that one way to agree and build on ideas is to give reasons that explain why the strategy makes sense.

Guide students to **Compare and Connect** the representations. Remind students that good listeners ask questions to clarify ideas or ask for more information during math discussions.

ASK *Which strategy would work best in cases where finding an exact distance between two points is important? Why?*

LISTEN FOR A strategy that uses the Pythagorean Theorem will always give an exact answer if you find the exact horizontal and vertical distance. Measuring the distance only gives an estimate.

Picture It & Model It

If students presented these models, have students connect these models to those presented in class.

If no student presented at least one of these models, have students first analyze key features of the models, and then connect them to the models presented in class.

ASK *How are the strategies in Picture It and Model It related?*

LISTEN FOR Picture It shows the right triangle formed when the points are connected and labels the legs *a* and *b* and the hypotenuse *c*. Model It applies the Pythagorean Theorem to the triangle.

For the drawing, prompt students to think about how the right triangle is formed. Ask: *If the two points were not on the axes, could you still draw a right triangle with the segment connecting the points as the hypotenuse?*

For the equation, prompt students to note the values each variable represents. Ask: *Do you think the values of a and b could be used interchangeably? Why or why not?*

➤ **Explore different ways to find the distance between points in the coordinate plane.**

Find the shortest distance between the points $(0, -6)$ and $(-8, 0)$.

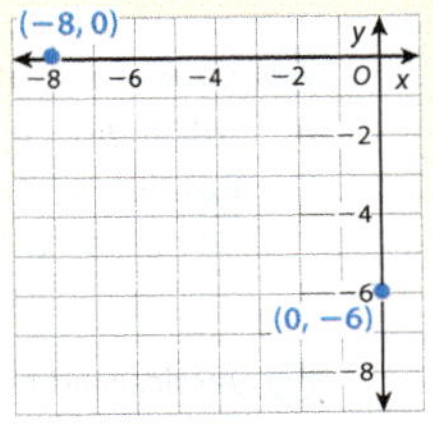

Picture It

You can draw a right triangle.

Draw a line segment between the points. Then draw a right triangle so the distance between the points is the hypotenuse.

In the right triangle, *a* and *b* are the lengths of the legs and *c* is the length of the hypotenuse.

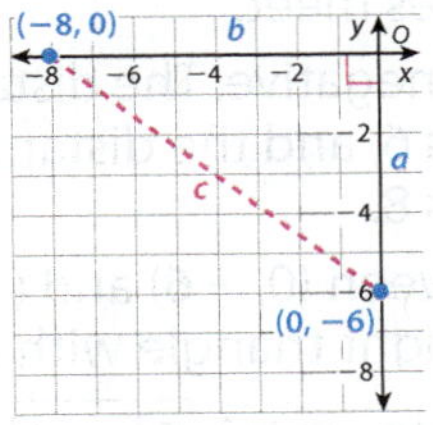

Model It

You can use the Pythagorean Theorem to find the unknown distance.

$a^2 + b^2 = c^2$

$6^2 + 8^2 = c^2$

DIFFERENTIATION | EXTEND

SMP 2

Deepen Understanding

Generalizing the Distance from $(x, 0)$ to $(0, y)$

Prompt students to think about general points $(x, 0)$ and $(0, y)$ on the *x*- and *y*-axes. Ask them to imagine connecting the points to form a right triangle with its legs on the axes, as in Picture It. Establish that the distance between the points is the hypotenuse.

ASK *What would be the leg lengths? Remember that x and y can be positive or negative.*

LISTEN FOR $|x|$ and $|y|$

ASK *Apply the Pythagorean Theorem using $|x|$ and $|y|$ for the leg lengths and c for the hypotenuse length. What do you get when you solve for c?*

LISTEN FOR $|x|^2 + |y|^2 = c^2$; You get $c = \sqrt{|x|^2 + |y|^2}$ because only the positive square root makes sense for the length.

ASK *Are the absolute value symbols under the square root symbol needed? Explain.*

LISTEN FOR No; whether *x* and *y* are positive or negative, you get a positive number when you square them.

Generalize Have students rewrite the equation as $c = \sqrt{x^2 + y^2}$. Discuss the fact that this is a formula for the distance between any two points of the form $(x, 0)$ and $(0, y)$.

Develop Finding Distance in the Coordinate Plane

CONNECT IT

SMP 2, 4, 5, 6

Remind students that the points and the distance between them are the same in each representation. Explain that they will now use those representations to reason about finding the distance between two points in the coordinate plane.

Before students begin to record and expand on their work in Picture It & Model It, tell them that problems 3 and 4 will prepare them to provide the explanation asked for in problem 5.

Monitor and Confirm Understanding 1 – 3

- Because the two points lie on the *x*- and *y*-axes, the right angle of the triangle is at the origin where the two axes meet.
- Distance is never negative. The distance from the origin to $(0, -6)$ is 6, and the distance from the origin to $(-8, 0)$ is 8.
- The distance between $(0, -6)$ and $(-8, 0)$ is the hypotenuse of a right triangle with legs of length 6 and 8. So, the distance is $\sqrt{6^2 + 8^2} = \sqrt{100} = 10$.

Facilitate Whole Class Discussion

4 Look for an understanding that you can count each grid square on a horizontal or vertical line as 1 unit, but you cannot count grid squares on a diagonal line as 1 unit each.

> **ASK** *Why is it not possible to count the number of grid spaces/squares along the line segment between the two points?*
>
> **LISTEN FOR** The diagonal length or other interior slant-line lengths of a square with side length 1 do not also equal 1.

5 Look for the idea that you can use the Pythagorean Theorem to find nonvertical and nonhorizontal distances between points in the coordinate plane.

> **ASK** *Once you connect the given points to form the hypotenuse of the right triangle, how do you draw its legs?*
>
> **LISTEN FOR** Draw a horizontal line through one of the points and a vertical line through the other point. The point where the two lines intersect represents the vertex of the right angle.

6 **Reflect** Have all students focus on the strategies used to solve the Try It. If time allows, have students discuss their ideas with a partner.

CONNECT IT

➤ **Use the problem from the previous page to help you understand how to find the distance between two points in the coordinate plane.**

1 Look at **Picture It**. How do you know the triangle formed by the two points and the origin is a right triangle?

Possible answer: The *x*-axis and the *y*-axis are perpendicular, so the angle formed at the origin is a right angle.

2 Jessica said the lengths of the legs are -6 units and -8 units. What mistake did Jessica make? What are the correct lengths of the legs?

Distance, or length, is never negative; 6 units and 8 units

3 Look at **Model It**. What is the distance between $(0, -6)$ and $(-8, 0)$? Why can you use the Pythagorean Theorem to find this distance?

10 units; Possible explanation: The distance between $(0, -6)$ and $(-8, 0)$ is the length of the hypotenuse of a right triangle with known leg lengths.

4 Why is it important that the distance between $(0, -6)$ and $(-8, 0)$ be the hypotenuse of the right triangle and not a leg?

Possible answer: If the distance is a leg, then the right angle must be at one end of this leg. This means at least one of the other sides will not be horizontal or vertical and so you cannot easily find its length.

5 Explain how to find the distance between any two points in the coordinate plane that do not lie on the same horizontal or vertical line.

Possible answer: Draw a line segment between the points. Draw horizontal and vertical legs so that this segment is the hypotenuse of a right triangle. Use the Pythagorean Theorem to find the length of the segment.

6 **Reflect** Think about all the models and strategies you have discussed today. Describe how one of them helped you better understand how to find the distance between two points in the coordinate plane.

Responses will vary. Check student responses.

649

DIFFERENTIATION | RETEACH or REINFORCE

Visual Model

Use the Pythagorean Theorem to find distance.

If students are unsure about how to use the Pythagorean Theorem to find the distance between two points on the coordinate plane, then use this activity as reinforcement.

Materials For display: large first-quadrant coordinate plane

- Invite students to plot points at (4, 6), (10, 6), and (10, 2) and label them *School, Park,* and *Home*, respectively. Connect the points. Tell students each grid unit is 1 mile.
- Explain that Raj plans to bike from school to the park, and then from the park home. Ask: *How far is it from school to the park? From the park to home?* [6 mi; 4 mi]
- Ask: *How did you find the distances?* [Subtract 4 from 10, or count over 6 units; Subtract 2 from 6, or count up 4 units] Label these lengths on the diagram.
- Ask: *What if Raj decides to bike straight home from school? How can you find that distance?* [Draw a right triangle and use the Pythagorean Theorem.]
- Ask volunteers to show their solution. [$4^2 + 6^2 = c^2$; $c = \sqrt{52} \approx 7.2$; 7.2 mi.]
- Ask: *How much farther is Raj's trip if he stops at the park?* [2.8 miles]

Apply It

For all problems, encourage students to use a model to support their thinking.

7 Students may plot each point to find the one that meets the requirement.

D is correct. One leg is already known to be 4 units. This point makes the other leg 3 units, so the side lengths of the right triangle are a 3, 4, 5 Pythagorean triple.

A is not correct. This answer will make one of the right triangle's legs 5 units long. The hypotenuse and a leg cannot have the same length.

B is not correct. This answer will make both legs 4 units long, so the hypotenuse would have a length of $4\sqrt{2}$ units rather than 5.

C is not correct. It is not possible to draw a right triangle using this point.

8 Students may work backwards to come up with leg lengths for which the hypotenuse length is 20. Students should look for two numbers whose squares add to 20 and draw legs with those lengths.

Apply It

➤ **Use what you learned to solve these problems.**

7 Hailey plots the first two vertices of a right triangle in the coordinate plane. Where could she plot the third point so the hypotenuse of the triangle has a length of 5 units?

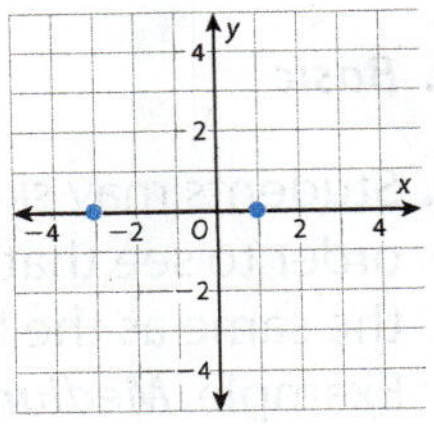

A (1, 5)

B (−3, 4)

C (0, −5)

(D) (1, −3)

8 Draw a line segment from the origin (0, 0) with length $\sqrt{20}$. Show your work. See graph for possible line segment. Possible work:

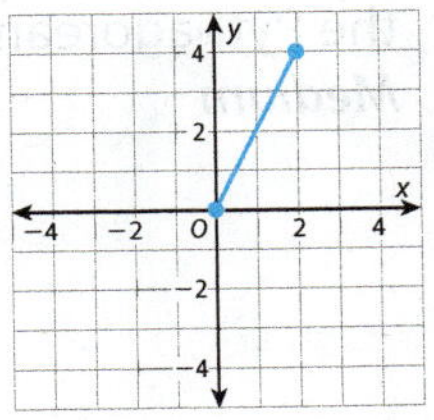

Let a and b be the lengths of the legs and c be the length of the hypotenuse of a right triangle. Let $c = \sqrt{20}$.

$a^2 + b^2 = c^2$

$a^2 + b^2 = (\sqrt{20})^2$

$a^2 + b^2 = 20$

$4 + 16 = 20$

$2^2 + 4^2 = 20$

The leg lengths of this triangle are 2 and 4.

9 Find the distance between the points shown. Show your work.

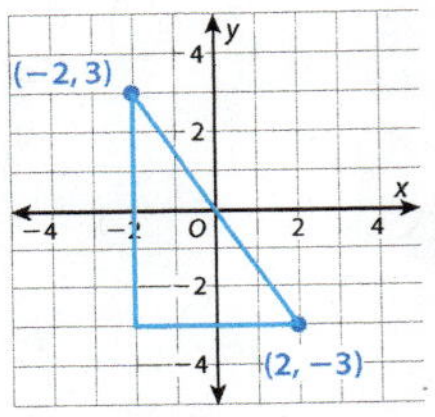

Possible work: See graph.

The vertical leg length is 6 units. The horizontal leg length is 4 units. Use the Pythagorean Theorem where c is the distance between the two points.

$6^2 + 4^2 = c^2$

$36 + 16 = c^2$

$52 = c^2$

$\sqrt{52} = c$

SOLUTION The distance is $\sqrt{52}$ units.

CLOSE EXIT TICKET

9 Students' solutions should show an understanding of:

- how to draw a right triangle with the segment between the given points as the hypotenuse.
- how to find the lengths of the horizontal and vertical legs.
- how to use the Pythagorean Theorem or a known Pythagorean triple to find the hypotenuse length, which is the distance between the points.

Error Alert If students try to find the length of the hypotenuse of the triangle by counting the number of intervals or grid squares through which the segment passes, then remind them that you can only count grid units when the segments are horizontal or vertical. You can use the Pythagorean Theorem to show that the diagonal of a square with side length 1 is not 1.

Practice Finding Distance in the Coordinate Plane

Problem Notes

Assign **Practice Finding Distance in the Coordinate Plane** as extra practice in class or as homework.

1 a. *Basic*

b. Students may sketch this other triangle in order to see that the lengths of its legs are the same as the lengths of the legs in the Example. ***Medium***

c. Students should understand that, if the points are not vertices of a right triangle, the Pythagorean Theorem cannot be used. ***Medium***

LESSON 27 | SESSION 4 Name:

Practice Finding Distance in the Coordinate Plane

➤ **Study the Example showing how to find the distance between two points in the coordinate plane. Then solve problems 1–3.**

Example

What is the distance between $P(-1, 3)$ and $Q(3, -2)$ in the coordinate plane?

Draw a right triangle with $R(-1, -2)$ as the vertex of the right angle. Then use the Pythagorean Theorem to find the length of the hypotenuse, which is the distance between P and Q.

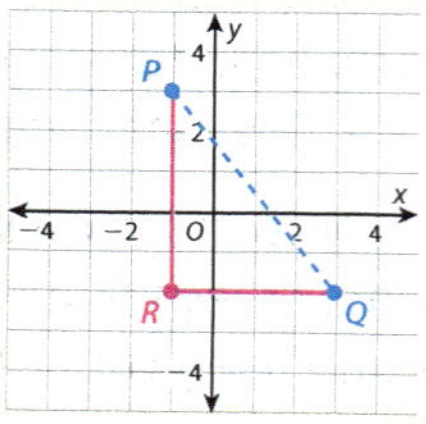

$QR = 4$ units, $RP = 5$ units, $PQ = c$ units

$$4^2 + 5^2 = c^2$$
$$16 + 25 = c^2$$
$$41 = c^2$$
$$\sqrt{41} = c$$

The distance between $P(-1, 3)$ and $Q(3, -2)$ is $\sqrt{41}$ units.

1 Look at the Example.

a. Describe another right triangle you could draw from points $P(-1, 3)$ and $Q(3, -2)$.

Draw a right triangle with (3, 3) as the vertex of the right angle.

b. Will your triangle from problem 1a give you the same distance between points P and Q? Explain.

Yes; Possible explanation: The leg lengths I would use in the Pythagorean Theorem are the same: 4 units and 5 units.

c. Would drawing a triangle with points $(-1, 3)$, $(3, -2)$, and $(3, 2)$ as vertices help you find the distance between the points? Explain.

No; Possible explanation: These vertices will not form a right triangle. You can only use the Pythagorean Theorem if you draw a right triangle.

651

Fluency & Skills Practice

Finding Distance in the Coordinate Plane

In this activity, students use the Pythagorean Theorem to find the distance between two points in the coordinate plane.

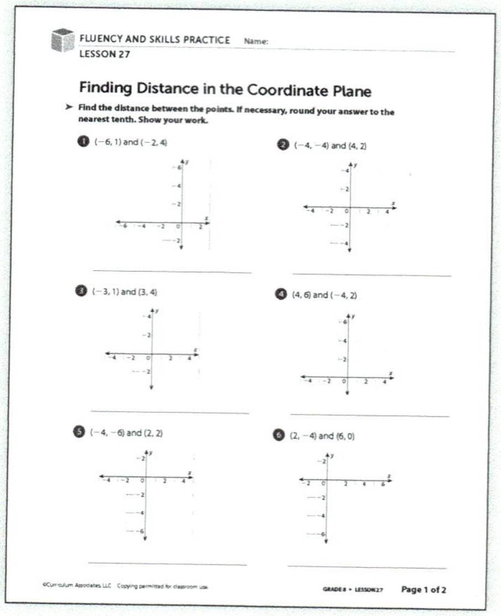

FLUENCY AND SKILLS PRACTICE Name:
LESSON 27

Finding Distance in the Coordinate Plane

➤ Find the distance between the points. If necessary, round your answer to the nearest tenth. Show your work.

1 $(-6, 1)$ and $(-2, 4)$

2 $(-4, -4)$ and $(4, 2)$

3 $(-3, 1)$ and $(3, 4)$

4 $(4, 6)$ and $(-4, 2)$

5 $(-4, -6)$ and $(2, 2)$

6 $(2, -4)$ and $(6, 0)$

©Curriculum Associates, LLC Copying permitted for classroom use. GRADE 8 • LESSON 27 Page 1 of 2

Additional Practice

2 Students will need to subtract negative coordinates that are not integers or count partial units to find the side lengths. ***Challenge***

3 **a.** Students may recognize the side lengths are a multiple of a Pythagorean triple or may calculate the distance using the Pythagorean Theorem. Also, students may correctly choose the point $(1, -3)$ instead of $(-5, 5)$ to construct their right triangle. ***Medium***

b. Students may correctly use the point $(1, -3)$ instead of $(7, 5)$ to construct their right triangle. Also, students may sketch both triangles used to find the distances in each part of the problem in order to visualize their congruence. ***Medium***

c. Students need to find JL to answer this question: $JL = 7 - (-5) = 12$. ***Medium***

LESSON 27 | SESSION 4

2 What is the distance between the points shown? Show your work. Round your answer to the nearest tenth.

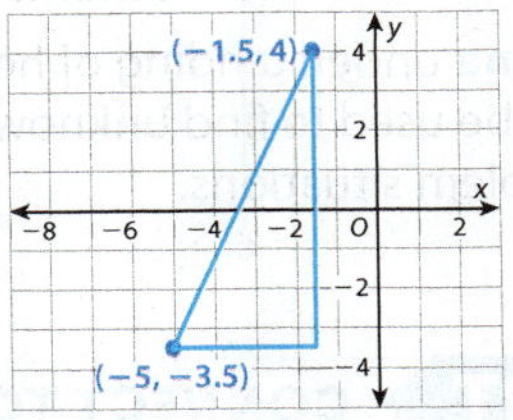

Possible work: See graph.

leg lengths: 3.5 units, 7.5 units; hypotenuse length: c units

$3.5^2 + 7.5^2 = c^2$

$12.25 + 56.25 = c^2$

$68.5 = c^2$

$c = \sqrt{68.5} \approx 8.3$

SOLUTION about 8.3 units

3 Dr. Patel plots points J, K, and L in the coordinate plane.

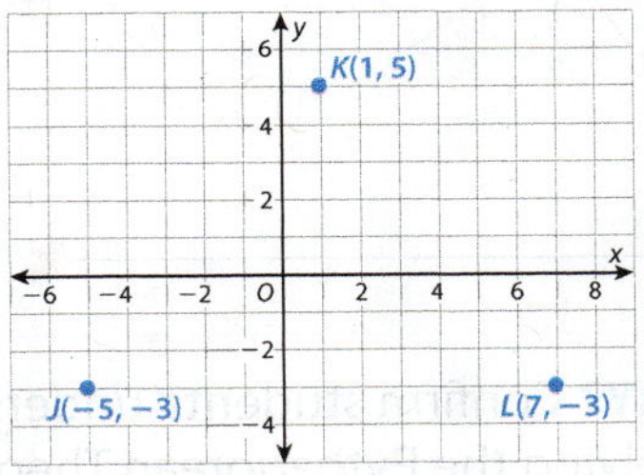

a. What is the distance between points J and K? Show your work.

Possible work: Plot a point at $(-5, 5)$.

The leg lengths are 6 units and 8 units.

I recognize this as a multiple of the 3, 4, 5 Pythagorean triple: 6, 8, 10. The length of the hypotenuse is 10 units.

SOLUTION 10 units

b. What is the distance between points K and L? Show your work.

Possible work: Plot a point at $(7, 5)$.

The leg lengths are 6 units and 8 units.

This is a multiple of the 3, 4, 5 Pythagorean triple: 6, 8, 10. The length of the hypotenuse is 10 units.

SOLUTION 10 units

c. Is $\triangle JKL$ an equilateral triangle? Explain.

No; Possible explanation: $\triangle JKL$ has only two congruent sides. An equilateral triangle has three congruent sides. $\overline{JK}$ and $\overline{KL}$ are each 10 units long and $\overline{JL}$ is 12 units long.

652

DIFFERENTIATION | ENGLISH LANGUAGE LEARNERS

Use with Session 5 **Apply It**

Levels 1–3: Speaking/Listening

To prepare for written responses, help students describe solution strategies for Apply It problem 3. Read Consider This aloud and prompt students to draw right triangles. Have partners describe the solution strategies:

- *This triangle can help us find ____.*
- *We can use the triangle to ____.*

Call on volunteers to share in their own words. Reword and record statements for reference. Then paraphrase Pair/Share: *We can find the solution using right triangles. Is there one or more than one possible triangle?* Encourage partners to draw other possibilities and use the recorded statements to describe the solution strategies.

Levels 2–4: Speaking/Listening

Have students read and interpret Apply It problem 3. Prompt students to tell what they need to solve. Ask students to read Consider This and discuss *useful* before they solve the problem.

To prepare for written responses, have students take turns describing their solution strategies to partners. Then ask partners to read and discuss Pair/Share and work together to describe other possible solution strategies. Ask: *What strategy do you think Ummi used to solve the problem? Do you think she used an incorrect strategy? Do you think she made a calculation error?* Give students time to think about Ummi's mistake before turning to discuss with partners.

Levels 3–5: Speaking/Listening

Have students make sense of Apply It problem 3 through partner discussion. Ask students to read the problem independently. Provide think time for students to consider solution strategies. Then have partners compare and discuss their strategies. If students need help getting started, have them read and discuss Consider This. Then ask students to solve the problem independently.

To prepare for written responses, ask students to read and discuss Pair/Share. Have partners describe other possible solution strategies. Ask: *What strategy do you think Ummi might have used?* Ask partners to discuss how Ummi might have gotten her answer and suggest how she might correct her mistake.

Refine Applying the Pythagorean Theorem

Purpose

- **Refine** strategies for applying the Pythagorean Theorem in real-world and mathematical contexts.
- **Refine** understanding of how the Pythagorean Theorem can be used to find unknown side lengths in a variety of problem situations.

START CONNECT TO PRIOR KNOWLEDGE

What is the height of $\triangle ABC$?

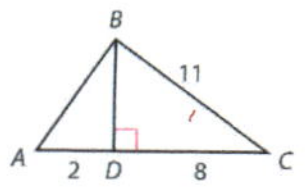

Solution

$\sqrt{57}$

WHY? Confirm students' understanding of applying the Pythagorean Theorem, identifying common errors to address as needed.

MONITOR & GUIDE

Before students begin to work, use their responses to the **Start** to determine those who will benefit from additional support. Use the **Error Analysis** table below to guide remediation.

Have all students complete the Example and problems 1–3, using Consider This and Pair/Share as appropriate. Observe and monitor their reasoning and guide or redirect students as needed.

Refine Applying the Pythagorean Theorem

➤ **Complete the Example below. Then solve problems 1–8.**

Example

Chase drew a triangle with vertices at (−2, −1), (−1, 2), and (1, −1). Classify Chase's triangle as scalene, isosceles, or equilateral.

Look at how you could use the Pythagorean Theorem.

Draw a right triangle at each nonvertical and nonhorizontal side of the original triangle.

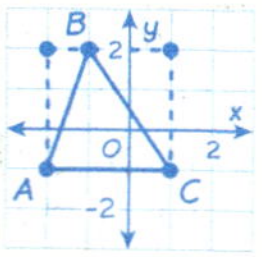

$\overline{AB}$: $1^2 + 3^2 = AB^2$

$AB^2 = 10$, so $AB = \sqrt{10}$.

$\overline{BC}$: $2^2 + 3^2 = BC^2$

$BC^2 = 13$, so $BC = \sqrt{13}$.

$\overline{AC}$: $AC = 3$

SOLUTION Chase's triangle is scalene.

CONSIDER THIS . . . An isosceles triangle has at least two congruent sides. A scalene triangle has no congruent sides.

PAIR/SHARE How else could you solve this?

Apply It

1 Mr. Gaspar wants to store a 12-foot-long pipe in a tool closet. The closet has the shape of a right rectangular prism with the dimensions shown. Will the pipe fit? Show your work.

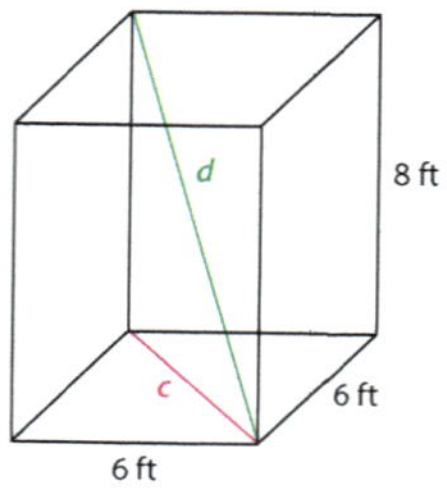

Possible work:

$6^2 + 6^2 = c^2$

$c^2 + 8^2 = d^2$

$6^2 + 6^2 + 8^2 = d^2$

$d = \sqrt{136} \approx 11.66$

$11.66 \text{ ft} < 12 \text{ ft}$

SOLUTION No, the diagonal length is less than 12 feet.

CONSIDER THIS . . . This problem takes more than one step to solve.

PAIR/SHARE Can you find two different paths to the solution? Explain.

START ERROR ANALYSIS

If the error is . . .	Students may . . .	To support understanding . . .
57	have forgotten to take the square root of b^2 and used $c^2 - a^2 = b$.	Review with students that $c^2 - a^2 = b^2$ can be used to find the unknown leg length in a right triangle, not $c^2 - a^2 = b$.
$\sqrt{21}$	have used $2 + 8 = 10$ as the length of a leg in $\triangle BCD$ instead of using 8 as the leg length.	Prompt students to draw a picture of a triangle to show the information they are given and what they still need to find.
$\sqrt{185}$	have solved the equation $11^2 + 8^2 = c^2$.	Ask students to identify the legs and hypotenuse of $\triangle BCD$. They should realize that $\overline{CD}$ and $\overline{BD}$ are legs and $\overline{BC}$ is the hypotenuse of $\triangle BCD$.

Example

Guide students in understanding the Example. Ask:

- *What measurements do you need to classify triangles as scalene, isosceles, or equilateral?*
- *How can you draw a right triangle and use the Pythagorean Theorem to find the length of $\overline{AB}$?*
- *How can you draw a right triangle and use the Pythagorean Theorem to find the length of $\overline{BC}$?*
- *How can you find the length of a horizontal segment, such as $\overline{AC}$?*

Help all students focus on the Example and responses to the questions by prompting students to refer to a diagram as they answer the questions.

Look for understanding that the Pythagorean Theorem is used to find nonhorizontal and nonvertical distances in the coordinate plane.

Apply It

1. Students may solve the problem by using the Pythagorean Theorem twice, first to find the diagonal of the base and then to find the diagonal of the prism. *DOK 2*

2. Students may also draw a point E at (2, 3) to make a right triangle. Then from point A, they might go left 2 units and down 4 units to find point C at (−4, −1). From point B, they might go left 2 units and down 4 units to find point D at (0, −3). *DOK 3*

3. **B is correct.** This problem can be solved by drawing a right triangle with hypotenuse length w ft and leg lengths 30 − 14, or 16, ft and 50 − 20, or 30, ft. Applying the Pythagorean Theorem gives
$w = \sqrt{16^2 + 30^2} = \sqrt{1{,}156} = 34.$
Or, students may find the length of the diagonal of the whole yard and subtract the length of the hypotenuse of the garden.

A is not correct. This answer is the approximate length of the diagonal of the garden.

C is not correct. In this answer, the two leg lengths were added instead of adding the squares of the leg lengths and then finding the square root.

D is not correct. This answer is the approximate length of the diagonal of the entire yard.

DOK 3

LESSON 27 | SESSION 5

2 $\overline{AB}$ is one side of a square. Find the coordinates of the other two vertices of the square and draw the square. Explain your reasoning.

Possible answer: Plot point E at (−2, 1) to make a right triangle. $\triangle ABE$ has legs of lengths 2 and 4 and hypotenuse of length AB.

To draw other segments the same length as $\overline{AB}$, I can draw a right triangle with the same leg lengths as $\triangle ABE$.

From point A, I went up 4 and right 2 to get point C at (0, 7). From point B, I went right 2 and up 4 to get point D at (4, 5).

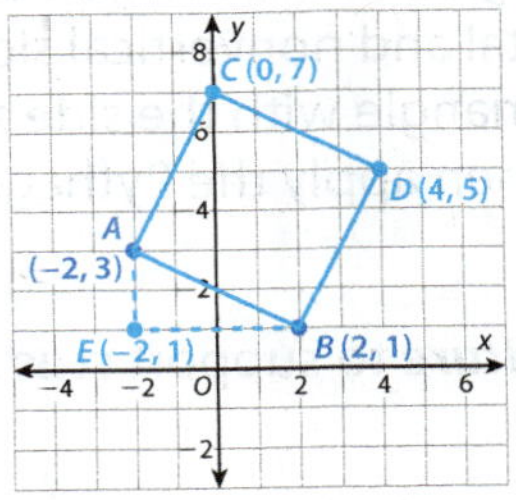

CONSIDER THIS . . . How could a right triangle help you find the side length of the square?

PAIR/SHARE How else could you solve this?

3 Mr. Shaw is building a walkway from the corner of his house out to his vegetable garden in the corner of the yard. The dimensions of the yard and the garden are shown. What is the length of the walkway, w, to the nearest foot?

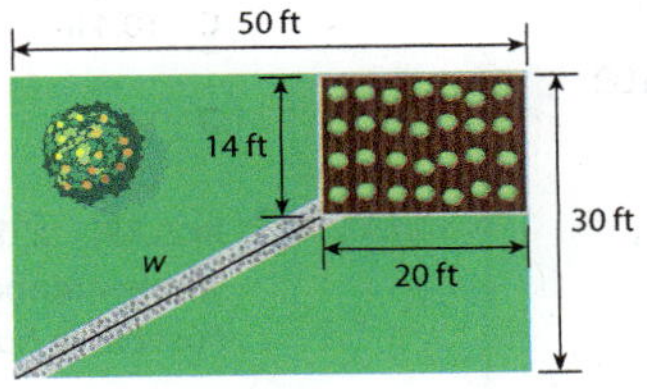

A 24 ft

(B) 34 ft

C 46 ft

D 58 ft

Ummi chose C as the correct answer. How might she have gotten that answer?

Possible answer: Ummi may have added the two leg lengths of the right triangle she drew instead of adding the squares of the lengths and then finding the square root.

CONSIDER THIS . . . Where can you draw a useful right triangle?

PAIR/SHARE Was there more than one helpful right triangle that would lead to the solution?

654

GROUP & DIFFERENTIATE

Identify groupings for differentiation based on the **Start** and problems 1–3. A recommended sequence of activities for each group is suggested below. Use the resources on the next page to differentiate and close the lesson.

Approaching Proficiency
- **RETEACH** Visual Model
- **REINFORCE** Problems 5, 7

Meeting Proficiency
- **REINFORCE** Problems 4–7

Extending Beyond Proficiency
- **REINFORCE** Problems 4–7
- **EXTEND** Challenge

Have all students complete the **Close: Exit Ticket.**

Resources for Differentiation are found on the next page.

Refine Applying the Pythagorean Theorem

Apply It

4 After reflecting triangle *ABC*, students will need to find the side lengths of the image. For each of the nonhorizontal and nonvertical sides, they may draw a right triangle with the side as the hypotenuse, and then apply the Pythagorean Theorem. *DOK 3*

5 See ***Connect to Culture*** to support student engagement.

C is correct. The length of the diagonal of the base is $\sqrt{6^2 + 6^2}$, or $\sqrt{72}$. The length of the diagonal of the cube can be found using $d^2 = 6^2 + (\sqrt{72})^2 = 108$. $d = \sqrt{108} \approx 10.4$

A is not correct. This answer is the length of an edge of the cube.

B is not correct. This answer is the approximate length of a diagonal of the base.

D is not correct. This answer is the sum of two edge lengths.

DOK 2

6 **a.** $CA = \sqrt{7^2 + 24^2}$, or 25.

b. $CA = \sqrt{9^2 + 24^2}$, or $\sqrt{657}$ and $\sqrt{657}$ is not a whole-number length.

c. $CA = \sqrt{10^2 + 24^2}$, or 26.

d. $AB = \sqrt{25^2 - 24^2}$, or 7.

DOK 3

4 Draw the reflection of $\triangle ABC$ across the *y*-axis. Then show that the corresponding sides of the two triangles are congruent.

Possible work:

$AB = 3$

$A'B' = 3$

$AC = \sqrt{4^2 + 2^2} = \sqrt{20}$

$A'C' = \sqrt{4^2 + 2^2} = \sqrt{20}$

$BC = \sqrt{4^2 + 1^2} = \sqrt{17}$

$B'C' = \sqrt{4^2 + 1^2} = \sqrt{17}$

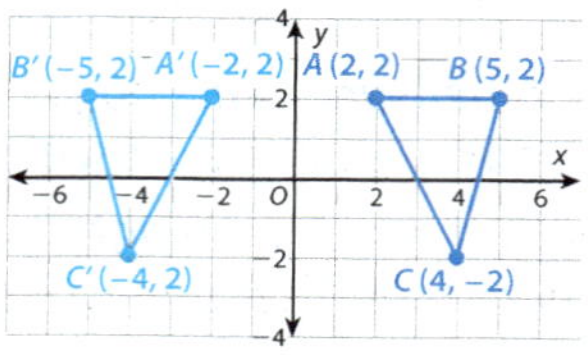

5 A small plastic storage cube has a side length of 6 inches. What is the length of $\overline{AB}$ to the nearest tenth of an inch?

A 6 in.

B 8.5 in.

(C) 10.4 in.

D 12 in.

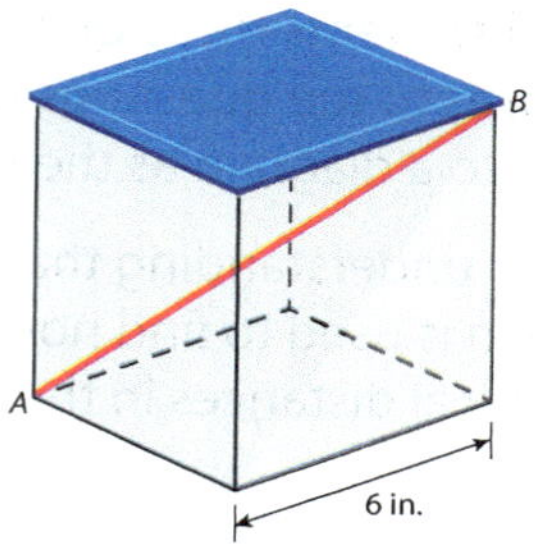

6 In $\triangle ABC$, $\overline{BC}$ is longer than $\overline{AB}$, and $BC = 24$. $\overline{AB}$ and $\overline{CA}$ have whole-number lengths. Tell whether each side length is *Possible* or *Not Possible*.

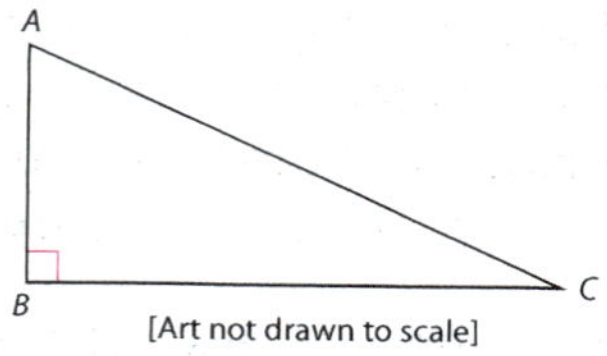

	Possible	Not Possible
a. $AB = 7$	●	○
b. $AB = 9$	○	●
c. $AB = 10$	●	○
d. $CA = 25$	●	○

655

DIFFERENTIATION

RETEACH

Visual Model

Use the Pythagorean Theorem to find perimeter.

Students approaching proficiency with using the Pythagorean Theorem to find the distance between two points will benefit from this model.

Materials For display: large four-quadrant coordinate plane

- Tell students that the distance between grid lines represents 1 inch. Ask a student to plot the quadrilateral with vertices $A(-2, 6)$, $B(6, -1)$, $C(-4, -4)$, and $D(-6, 0)$.
- Ask: *Do you think it is possible to find the perimeter without a ruler or other measuring tool? If so, how?* [Yes; draw a right triangle along each of the 4 sides of the quadrilateral and find the length of each hypotenuse/side of the quadrilateral. Then add the side lengths.]
- Have a student show how to use horizontal and vertical grid lines to construct a right triangle with $\overline{AB}$ as the hypotenuse. Have another student state the leg lengths in inches.
- Ask a student to substitute these lengths into the Pythagorean Theorem to find *AB*. Ask: *What is the length of $\overline{AB}$?* [$\sqrt{8^2 + 7^2} = \sqrt{113}$; $\sqrt{113}$ in.]
- Have students work in pairs to find the lengths of the other sides.
- Have student volunteers demonstrate how they found the following: $BC = \sqrt{10^2 + 3^2}$, or $\sqrt{26}$, in.; $CD = \sqrt{2^2 + 4^2}$, or $\sqrt{20}$, in.; $DA = \sqrt{4^2 + 6^2}$, or $\sqrt{52}$, in.
- Ask: *What will you have to do next to find the perimeter of the quadrilateral?* [Add the four side lengths.]
- Ask: *What is the perimeter to the nearest inch?* [33 in.]

7 Students may count units to find the length of $\overline{AB}$, which is 6. The length of the opposite side, $\overline{CD}$, is also 6. Students may use the Pythagorean Theorem to find the length of $\overline{AD}$ by drawing a right triangle with $\overline{AD}$ as the hypotenuse and applying the Pythagorean Theorem. The length is 5. The length of the opposite side, $\overline{BC}$, is also 5. The perimeter is the sum of the four side lengths, which is 22. ***DOK 2***

CLOSE EXIT TICKET

8 **Math Journal** Look for understanding that the length and width of the base of the box and the Pythagorean Theorem can be used to find the diagonal length of the base of the box. Then the diagonal length of the base of the box, the height of the box, and the Pythagorean Theorem can be used to find the diagonal length of the box.

Error Alert If students do not think the baseball bat will fit in the box, then have them review Session 3 Picture It to reinforce using the Pythagorean Theorem twice to find the diagonal length of the box.

End of Lesson Checklist

INTERACTIVE GLOSSARY Support students by suggesting they make a list of things they will *consider* doing this upcoming weekend.

SELF CHECK Have students review and check off any new skills on the Unit 6 Opener.

7 What is the perimeter of parallelogram *ABCD*?

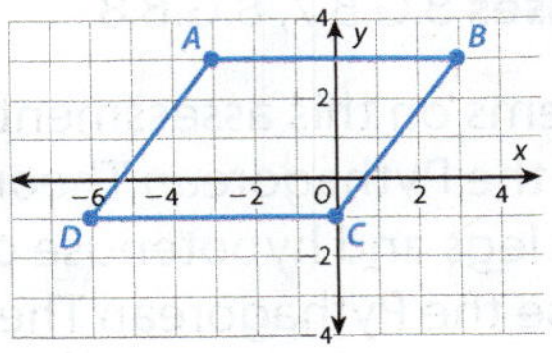

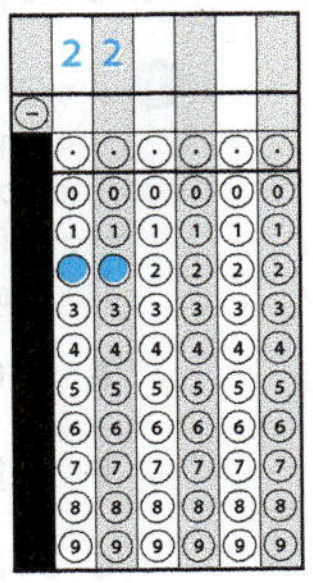

8 **Math Journal** José is mailing some baseball equipment to his cousin. He wants to include a baseball bat that is 33 in. long. Will the baseball bat fit completely in the box? Explain your reasoning.

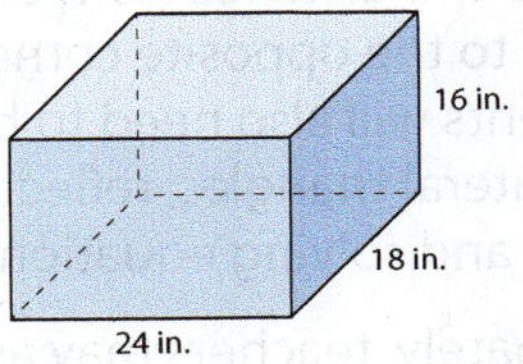

Yes; Possible explanation: You can use the Pythagorean Theorem twice to find the maximum length that can fit along the longest diagonal of the box. The diagonal of the bottom face of the box is $\sqrt{24^2 + 18^2} = \sqrt{900} = 30$; 30 in. Then, the length of the longest diagonal is $\sqrt{30^2 + 16^2} = \sqrt{1{,}156} = 34$; 34 in. Because the bat is only 33 in. long, it wil fit in the box.

End of Lesson Checklist

☐ **INTERACTIVE GLOSSARY** Write a new entry for *consider*. Tell what you do when you consider something.

☐ **SELF CHECK** Go back to the Unit 6 Opener and see what you can check off.

REINFORCE

Problems 4–7
Solve problems using the Pythagorean Theorem.

Students meeting proficiency will benefit from additional work with the Pythagorean Theorem by solving problems in a variety of formats.

- Have students work on their own or with a partner to solve the problems.
- Encourage students to show their work.

EXTEND

Challenge
Find the area of a circle using the Pythagorean Theorem.

Students extending beyond proficiency will benefit from using the Pythagorean Theorem to help them calculate the area of a circle from an inscribed rectangle.

- Have students work with a partner to solve this problem: *What is the area of the circle?*
- Students may first use the Pythagorean Theorem to find the diagonal of the rectangle, which is a diameter of the circle.

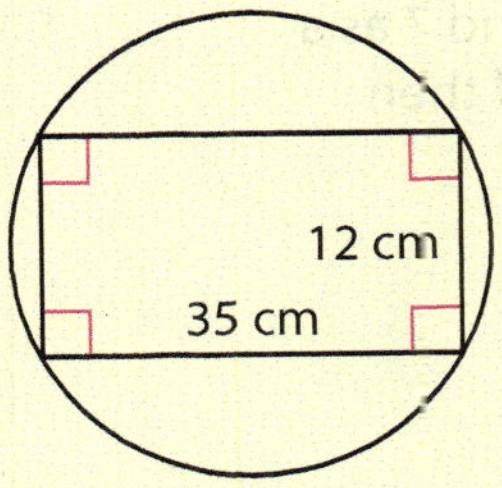

PERSONALIZE

i-Ready

Provide students with opportunities to work on their personalized instruction path with *i-Ready* Online Instruction to:

- fill prerequisite gaps.
- build up grade-level skills.

LESSON 27
Lesson Quiz

TESTED SKILLS

Assesses 8.G.B.7, 8.G.B.8

Problems on this assessment require students to apply the Pythagorean Theorem to find the lengths of the legs and hypotenuse of a right triangle. They will use the Pythagorean Theorem to find missing side lengths of triangles, including problems involving real-world situations. Students will use the lengths of the sides of a triangle to determine whether it is an equilateral triangle and to show that the side lengths of a triangle and its reflection are congruent. They will use the Pythagorean Theorem to find the distance from one corner of a rectangular prism to the opposite corner on the opposite base. Students will also need to be familiar with equilateral triangles, reflection of points, square roots, and solving equations.

Alternately, teachers may assign the **Digital Comprehension Check** online to assess student understanding of this material.

Error Alert Errors may result if students:

- confuse the length of the hypotenuse with the length of one of the legs.
- incorrectly reflect a point in the coordinate plane.
- incorrectly write an equation when using the Pythagorean Theorem to find a side length.
- apply the Pythagorean Theorem when the triangle is not a right triangle.
- incorrectly solve for a side length of a right triangle.

Problem Notes

1 **C is correct.** Students could solve the problem by substituting 7 for one leg length and 25 for the hypotenuse in the Pythagorean Theorem, finding the unknown side, and then adding the height of the pole.

A is incorrect. This answer is the result of finding the missing side of the triangle but not adding 10 to find the height of the school.

B is incorrect. This answer is the result of subtracting 7 from 25 and then adding 10 to find the height of the school.

D is incorrect. This answer is the result of substituting 10 as the hypotenuse and 7 as a leg in the Pythagorean Theorem and then adding 10.

(1 point)

DOK 2 | 8.G.B.7

LESSON 27 • QUIZ | Name:

➤ **Solve the problems.**

1 A worker is connecting a cable from the rooftop of a school to a fence pole 7 ft away. The pole is 10 ft high. He uses 25 ft of cable to reach from the rooftop to the fence pole. How tall is the school? *(1 point)*

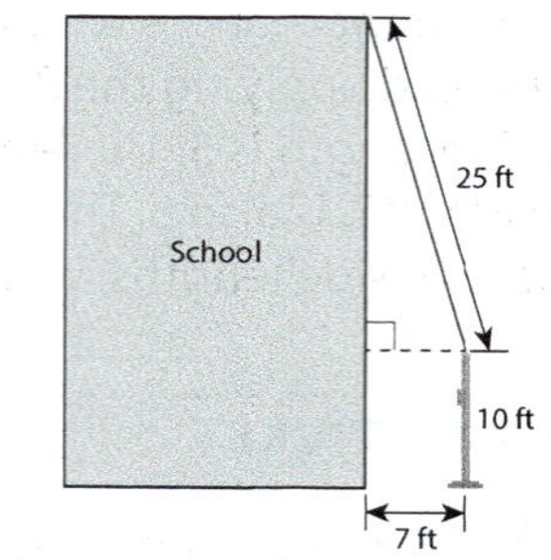

A 24 ft

B 28 ft

(C) 34 ft

D 61 ft

2 Miguel plots points *A*, *B*, and *C* in the coordinate plane.

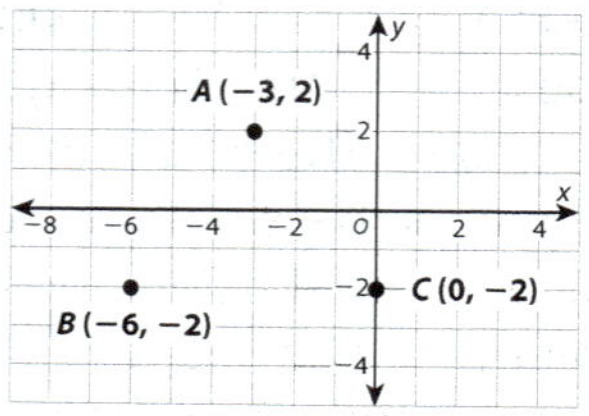

PART A What is the distance between points *A* and *B*? Explain your reasoning. *(2 points)*

SOLUTION 5 units; Possible explanation: The leg lengths are 3 units and 4 units. This is a 3–4–5 Pythagorean triple. The length of the hypotenuse is 5 units. So, the distance between *A* and *B* is also 5 units.

PART B Is △*ABC* an equilateral triangle? Explain your reasoning. *(2 points)*

SOLUTION No; Possible explanation: The triangle has only two congruent sides. $\overline{AB}$ and $\overline{AC}$ are each 5 units long, and $\overline{BC}$ is 6 units long.

Short Response Scoring Rubric

Points	Expectations
2	Response has the correct solution(s) and includes well-organized, clear, and concise work demonstrating thorough understanding of mathematical concepts and/or procedures.
1	Response contains mostly correct solution(s) and shows partial understanding of mathematical concepts and/or procedures.
0	Response shows no attempt at finding a solution and no effort to demonstrate an understanding of mathematical concepts and/or procedures.

2 **Part A**

(2 points)

DOK 2 | 8.G.B.8

Part B

Students could solve the problem by determining the length of each side of the triangle and finding that one side is not the same length as the other two sides.

(2 points)

DOK 2 | 8.G.B.8

3 Students could solve the problem by reflecting triangle *RST* across the *y*-axis. Then calculate the side lengths of each triangle to show that the corresponding sides are congruent.

(2 points)

DOK 2 | 8.G.B.8

4 **C is correct.** Students could solve the problem by finding the diagonal length of the base and then calculating the diagonal length from one corner of the prism's bottom base to the opposite corner of its top base. The length of the diagonal is $\sqrt{31}$.

A is incorrect. This answer is the result of estimating $\sqrt{31}$ between 4 and 5 and rounding to 4.

B is incorrect. This answer is the result of estimating $\sqrt{31}$ between 5 and 6 and rounding to 5.

D is incorrect. This answer is the result of estimating $\sqrt{31}$ between 6 and 7 and rounding to 7.

(1 point)

DOK 2 | 8.G.B.7

LESSON 27 • QUIZ   Name:

3 Triangle *RST* is given in the coordinate plane. If triangle *RST* is reflected across the *y*-axis, will the corresponding sides of the two triangles be congruent? Show your work. *(2 points)*

Possible student work: Draw the reflection R'S'T' in the coordinate plane.

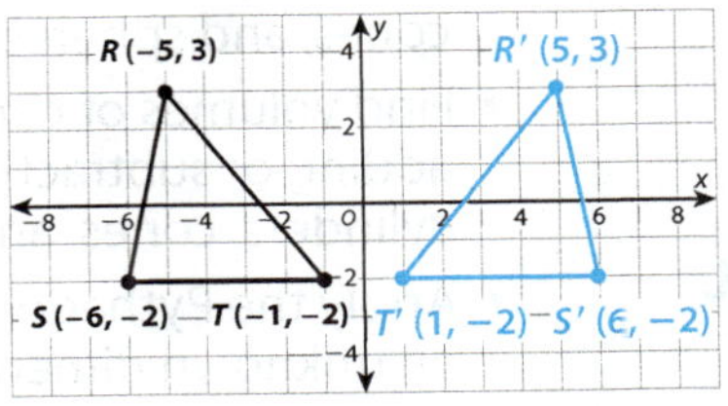

$ST = 5$

$S'T' = 5$

$RS = \sqrt{5^2 + 1^2} = \sqrt{26}$

$R'S' = \sqrt{5^2 + 1^2} = \sqrt{26}$

$RT = \sqrt{4^2 + 5^2} = \sqrt{41}$

$R'T' = \sqrt{4^2 + 5^2} = \sqrt{41}$

SOLUTION Yes, the corresponding sides of the two triangles are congruent.

4 Dina is shipping a wall map to a collector. When the map is rolled up, it measures 7 ft long. She will use a box that is a right rectangular prism with a base that is 3 ft by 3 ft. Which whole number could be the shortest height of the box that will hold the map? *(1 point)*

A 4 ft

B 5 ft

C 6 ft (circled)

D 7 ft

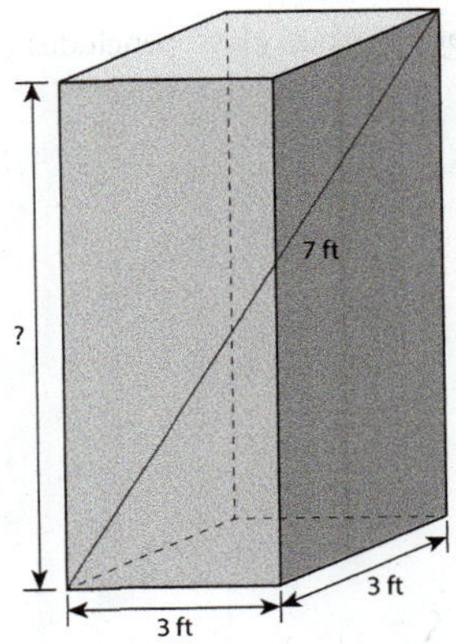

DIFFERENTIATION

RETEACH Tools for Instruction

Students who require additional support for prerequisite or on-level skills will benefit from activities that provide targeted skills instruction.

GRADE 8

- **Lesson 27** Pythagorean Theorem and Rectangular Prisms

REINFORCE Math Center Activity

Students who require practice to reinforce concepts and skills and deepen understanding will benefit from small group collaborative games and activities (available in on-level, below-level, and above-level versions).

GRADE 8

- **Lesson 27** Find Pythagorean Triples

EXTEND Enrichment Activity

Students who have achieved proficiency with concepts and skills and are ready for additional challenges will benefit from group collaborative games and activities that extend understanding.

GRADE 8

- **Lesson 27** Spiral of Theodorus

Overview | Solve Problems with Volumes of Cylinders, Cones, and Spheres

MATH FOCUS

Focus Standard

8.G.C.9 Know the formulas for the volumes of cones, cylinders, and spheres and use them to solve real-world and mathematical problems.

See Unit 6 Overview for developing and applied standards.

STANDARDS FOR MATHEMATICAL PRACTICE (SMP)

SMP 1, 2, 3, 4, 5, and 6 are integrated into the Try-Discuss-Connect routine.*

This lesson provides additional support for:

2 Reason abstractly and quantitatively.

7 Look for and make use of structure.

* See page 1o to learn how every lesson includes these SMP.

Objectives

Content Objectives

- Understand relationships between the volumes of cylinders, cones, and spheres.
- Use formulas to find volumes of cylinders, cones, and spheres.
- Find volumes of composite solids by adding or subtracting volumes of cylinders, cones, and spheres.
- Apply the Pythagorean Theorem to find an unknown dimension of a cone.
- Use formulas for the circumference and area of a circle to find the unknown radius of a cone or cylinder.
- Use a given volume and the appropriate volume formula to find the radius or height of a cylinder, cone, or sphere.

Language Objectives

- Use lesson vocabulary accurately when speaking and writing about volumes of cylinders, cones, and spheres.
- Interpret problems involving composite solids by referring to figures and describing relationships between parts.
- Justify dimensions of figures by using the Pythagorean Theorem and definitions when speaking and writing.
- Connect strategies for finding and using volume by listening during class discussion and explaining how the strategies give the same solution.

Prior Knowledge

- Find the volume of right prisms.
- Find the area of circles.

Vocabulary

Math Vocabulary

cone a three-dimensional figure with one circular base and one vertex, connected by a curved surface.

sphere a three-dimensional figure in which every point is the same distance from the center.

Review the following key terms.

cylinder a three-dimensional figure with two parallel curved bases that are the same size. The bases are connected by a curved surface.

prism a three-dimensional figure with two parallel bases that are the same size and shape. The other faces are parallelograms. A prism is named by the shape of the base.

radius (of a circle) a line segment from the center of a circle to any point on the circle. Also, the distance from the center to any point on a circle.

vertex the point where two rays, lines, or line segments meet to form an angle.

volume the amount of space inside a solid figure. Volume is measured in cubic units such as cubic inches.

Academic Vocabulary

circular in the shape of a circle; round.

cylindrical in the shape of a cylinder or can.

spherical in the shape of a sphere or ball.

Learning Progression

In Grade 7, students found areas and circumferences of circles and solved problems involving volumes of right prisms.

Earlier in Grade 8, students learned about irrational numbers, found square roots and cube roots, and applied the Pythagorean Theorem to find unknown lengths.

In this lesson, students explore the relationship between the volume of a cylinder and the volume of a cone, and between the volume of a cylinder and the volume of a sphere. They use volume formulas to solve problems about cylinders, cones, and spheres and about composite solids made from these figures. They use the Pythagorean Theorem and area and circumference formulas to find unknown dimensions in cones and cylinders that they can then use to find volume.

In high school, students will derive volume formulas using dissection, Cavalieri's principle, and informal limit arguments. They continue to solve more complex problems involving the volume of cylinders, pyramids, cones, and spheres.

Pacing Guide

Items marked with ✱ are available on the **Teacher Toolbox.**

	MATERIALS	DIFFERENTIATION
SESSION 1 **Explore** Volumes of Cylinders, Cones, and Spheres (35–50 min)		
• **Start** (5 min) • **Try It** (5–10 min) • **Discuss It** (10–15 min) • **Connect It** (10–15 min) • **Close: Exit Ticket** (5 min) **Additional Practice** (pages 661–662)	Presentation Slides ✱	**PREPARE** Interactive Tutorial ✱ **RETEACH or REINFORCE** Hands-On Activity **Materials** For each group: scissors, tape, uncooked rice, Activity Sheet *Nets: Open Cylinder and Cone* ✱
SESSION 2 **Develop** Finding Volume (45–60 min)		
• **Start** (5 min) • **Try It** (10–15 min) • **Discuss It** (10–15 min) • **Connect It** (15–20 min) • **Close: Exit Ticket** (5 min) **Additional Practice** (pages 667–668)	Presentation Slides ✱	**RETEACH or REINFORCE** Visual Model **REINFORCE** Fluency & Skills Practice ✱ **EXTEND** Deepen Understanding
SESSION 3 **Develop** Finding an Unknown Dimension (45–60 min)		
• **Start** (5 min) • **Try It** (10–15 min) • **Discuss It** (10–15 min) • **Connect It** (15–20 min) • **Close: Exit Ticket** (5 min) **Additional Practice** (pages 673–674)	Presentation Slides ✱	**RETEACH or REINFORCE** Visual Model **REINFORCE** Fluency & Skills Practice ✱ **EXTEND** Deepen Understanding
SESSION 4 **Refine** Solving Problems with Volumes of Cylinders, Cones, and Spheres (45–60 min)		
• **Start** (5 min) • **Monitor & Guide** (15–20 min) • **Group & Differentiate** (20–30 min) • **Close: Exit Ticket** (5 min)	Presentation Slides ✱	**RETEACH** Visual Model **Materials** For display: 2 empty soup cans of different sizes, ruler, water **REINFORCE** Problems 4–8 **EXTEND** Challenge **PERSONALIZE** i-Ready
Lesson 28 Quiz ✱ or **Digital Comprehension Check**		**RETEACH** Tools for Instruction ✱ **REINFORCE** Math Center Activity ✱ **EXTEND** Enrichment Activity ✱

Overview | Solve Problems with Volumes of Cylinders, Cones, and Spheres

Connect to Culture

➤ **Use these activities to connect with and leverage the diverse backgrounds and experiences of all students. Engage students in sharing what they know about contexts before you add the information given here.**

SESSION 2 ■ ■ □ □

Try It Ask students if they have ever seen or learned about a yurt. Have students with experience describe what a yurt looks like. A yurt is a portable circular shelter made of poles and usually covered in felted wool from sheep, goats, or even yaks! Yurts have been used in central Asia for over 2,500 years. They were originally designed by nomadic people as temporary structures. They are light and easy to set up and dismantle. The round shape is ideal for the high winds of the Siberian steppe. More than half the population of Mongolia lives in yurts.

SESSION 3 ■ ■ ■ □

Try It If any students have worked on a farm, ask them to share what they know about harvesting corn. Corn grows inside an outer layer called a husk. Inside, on the cob, is where the kernels of corn grow. Each kernel produces one strand of silk that sticks out of the end of the husk. If pollen lands on the silk's sticky end, the corn kernel can develop. This means that there is at least one strand of silk for every kernel on the cob! The best time to pick corn is when the silk has turned brown on the end, but the husk is still green. Before picking their corn, farmers puncture sample kernels to see if a milky liquid is produced. If the liquid is clear and not milky, the corn is not ready to be picked.

SESSION 4 ■ ■ ■ ■

Apply It **Problem 4** Ask students if they have ever used a test tube for a science experiment. Ask them to describe what a test tube looks like and why they think a test tube is shaped the way it is. Test tubes are used to contain, mix, and heat liquid or solid chemicals. The half-sphere shape at the bottom of a test tube helps the chemicals mix together as temperature changes occur. The cylinder part of a test tube helps when pouring the chemical into another container. Test tubes are typically clear so scientists can observe color changes as chemicals react.

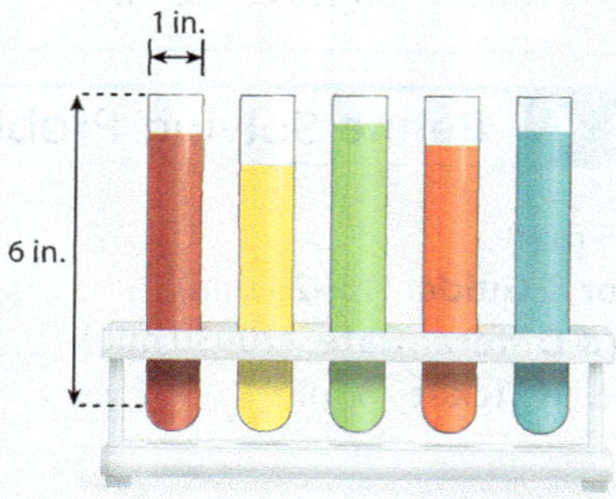

Connect to Family and Community

➤ **After the Explore session, have students use the Family Letter to let their families know what they are learning and to encourage family involvement.**

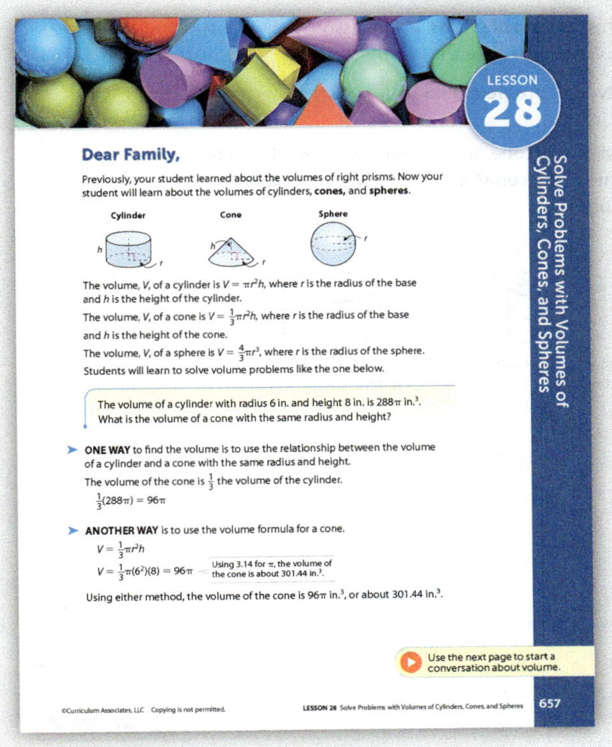

LESSON 28

Dear Family,

Previously, your student learned about the volumes of right prisms. Now your student will learn about the volumes of cylinders, **cones,** and **spheres**.

The volume, V, of a cylinder is $V = \pi r^2 h$, where r is the radius of the base and h is the height of the cylinder.

The volume, V, of a cone is $V = \frac{1}{3}\pi r^2 h$, where r is the radius of the base and h is the height of the cone.

The volume, V, of a sphere is $V = \frac{4}{3}\pi r^3$, where r is the radius of the sphere.

Students will learn to solve volume problems like the one below.

The volume of a cylinder with radius 6 in. and height 8 in. is 288π in.^{3}. What is the volume of a cone with the same radius and height?

➤ **ONE WAY** to find the volume is to use the relationship between the volume of a cylinder and a cone with the same radius and height.

The volume of the cone is $\frac{1}{3}$ the volume of the cylinder.

$\frac{1}{3}(288\pi) = 96\pi$

➤ **ANOTHER WAY** is to use the volume formula for a cone.

$V = \frac{1}{3}\pi r^2 h$

$V = \frac{1}{3}\pi(6^2)(8) = 96\pi$ — Using 3.14 for π, the volume of the cone is about 301.44 in.^{3}.

Using either method, the volume of the cone is 96π in.^{3}, or about 301.44 in.^{3}.

Use the next page to start a conversation about volume.

Solve Problems with Volumes of Cylinders, Cones, and Spheres

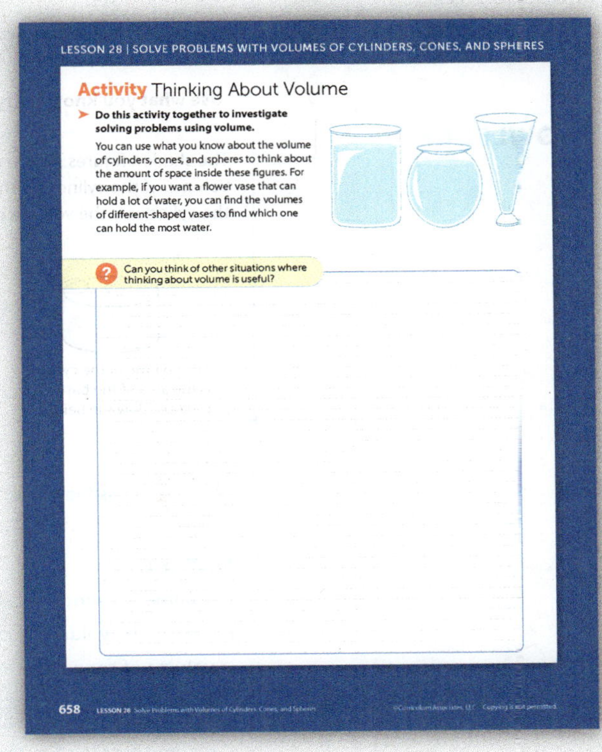

LESSON 28 | SOLVE PROBLEMS WITH VOLUMES OF CYLINDERS, CONES, AND SPHERES

Activity Thinking About Volume

➤ **Do this activity together to investigate solving problems using volume.**

You can use what you know about the volume of cylinders, cones, and spheres to think about the amount of space inside these figures. For example, if you want a flower vase that can hold a lot of water, you can find the volumes of different-shaped vases to find which one can hold the most water.

Can you think of other situations where thinking about volume is useful?

Connect to Language

➤ **For English language learners, use the Differentiation chart to scaffold the language in each session. Use the Academic Vocabulary routine for academic terms before Session 1.**

DIFFERENTIATION | ENGLISH LANGUAGE LEARNERS Use with **Session 1** **Connect It**

Levels 1–3: Reading/Listening

Have students prepare for Connect It problem 2 by using **Act It Out** to sort and describe geometric solids. Distribute sets of assorted geometric solids to partners and give them time to sort the solids into groups. Ask students to tell how they sorted the solids. Display *curved surface* and *flat base.* Ask students to identify and count curved surfaces and flat bases on the solids. Then read aloud sentence 1 of problems 2a–c as you point to the corresponding solids.

Next, review *volume* and *area*. If appropriate, point out the Spanish cognates *volumen* and *area*. Read each part as students follow along. Ask students to circle any variables or fractions and connect to the figures. Have students work with partners to write formulas.

Levels 2–4: Reading/Listening

Have students prepare for Connect It problem 2 by sorting and describing geometric solids. Have students work with partners to discuss different ways they can sort the solids. Call on volunteers to share their ideas. Call on several students to rephrase important ideas so that everyone hears them many times and in many ways.

To help students interpret the problem, first focus on sentence 1 of each problem part and read the full text. Ask students to repeat and use solids to show the meanings. Help students with the math terms *volume, area, radius,* and *height*. Read the problem and ask: *What can you use to write the formula?* Have students discuss with partners.

Levels 3–5: Reading/Listening

Have students make sense of Connect It problem 2 by building on what they already know about two- and three-dimensional figures. After reading the first sentence of the problem aloud, have students identify the curved surfaces on each of the figures and tell what the figures have in common. Then use **Say It Another Way** to confirm understanding of each description. Remind students that one way to solve a problem is by connecting it to other information they already know. Ask these questions to help students make connections: *How is the figure related to another figure? What is the relationship between a ____ and a ____? What formula do you already know and how can it help you?*

Explore Volumes of Cylinders, Cones, and Spheres

Purpose

- **Explore** the idea that volumes of cones and spheres are related to the volume of a cylinder with the same dimensions.
- **Understand** that volume relationships can be used to derive the volume formulas for cones and spheres based on the volume formula for a cylinder.

START CONNECT TO PRIOR KNOWLEDGE

Same and Different

A: $V = Bh$	B: $A = \pi r^2$
C: $V = \ell wh$	D: $A = \ell w$

Possible Solutions

All are mathematical formulas.

A and C are formulas for volume of a rectangular prism.

B and D are formulas for area.

B has π and an exponent in the formula.

C and D use length and width in the formulas.

WHY? Support students' facility for understanding area and volume formulas.

Explore Volumes of Cylinders, Cones, and Spheres

Previously, you learned how to find the volumes of prisms. In this lesson, you will learn how to find the volumes of cylinders, cones, and spheres.

➤ **Use what you know to try to solve the problem below.**

The shaded figures shown are a cylinder, a cone, and a sphere. What fraction of the volume of the cylinder is the volume of the cone? What fraction of the volume of the cylinder is the volume of the sphere?

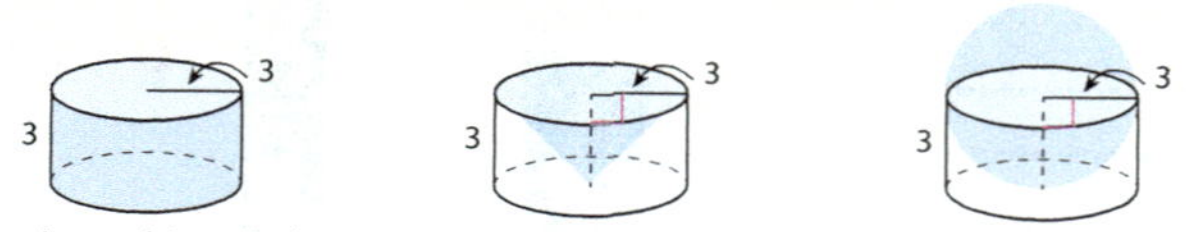

The volume of the cylinder is the area of the base multiplied by the height.

The volume of the cone is 9π.

The volume of the sphere is 36π.

TRY IT Possible work:

SAMPLE A

volume of cylinder $= \pi(3^2) \cdot 3$, or 27π

For $\pi \approx 3.14$, volume of cylinder ≈ 84.78.

volume of cone $= 9\pi \approx 28.26$

$\frac{\text{volume of cone}}{\text{volume of cylinder}} \approx \frac{28.26}{84.78} = \frac{1}{3}$

volume of sphere $= 36\pi \approx 113.04$

$\frac{\text{volume of sphere}}{\text{volume of cylinder}} \approx \frac{113.04}{84.78} = \frac{4}{3}$

SAMPLE B

$V(\text{cylinder}) = (3^2 \cdot \pi) \cdot 3$, or 27π

$\frac{V(\text{cone})}{V(\text{cylinder})} = \frac{9\pi}{27\pi} = \frac{1}{3}$

$\frac{V(\text{sphere})}{V(\text{cylinder})} = \frac{36\pi}{27\pi} = \frac{4}{3}$

DISCUSS IT

Ask: How did you find the volume of the cylinder?

Share: I found the volume by . . .

Learning Target SMP 1, SMP 2, SMP 3, SMP 4, SMP 5, SMP 6, SMP 7
Know the formulas for the volumes of cones, cylinders, and spheres and use them to solve real-world and mathematical problems.

659

TRY IT SMP 1, 2, 4, 5, 6

Make Sense of the Problem

Before students work on Try It, use **Notice and Wonder** to help them make sense of the problem. Have students work in pairs to study the images in the Try It problem. Have them discuss the questions: *How are the images the same? How are they different?* Debrief by displaying the problem and discussing what the students noticed and wondered about that relates to the problem.

DISCUSS IT SMP 2, 3, 6

Support Partner Discussion

After students work on Try It, have them respond to Discuss It with a partner. Listen for understanding of:

- finding the area of the base of the cylinder.
- multiplying the area of the base of the cylinder by the height of the cylinder.

Error Alert If students say that the volume of the cylinder is 18π, they may be calculating the circumference of the base rather than its area. Ask students what the formula for area and the formula for circumference of a circle are and then ask them which one they should use to find the volume of the cylinder.

Select and Sequence Student Strategies

Select 2–3 samples that represent the range of student thinking in your classroom. Here is one possible order for class discussion:

- find the approximate volume of each solid and write fractions comparing approximate volumes
- find the exact volume of each solid and write fractions comparing exact volumes

Facilitate Whole Class Discussion

Call on students to share selected strategies. After each strategy, allow individual think time for students to process the ideas.

Guide students to **Compare and Connect** the representations. Review that one way to connect two strategies is to show why each method gives the same solution.

ASK *Does it matter whether you compare the exact volumes or the approximate volumes? Why?*

LISTEN FOR No, as long as you use the same approximation for π for both figures, the approximations will divide to 1, just as π divides to 1 when you use exact volumes.

CONNECT IT

SMP 2, 4, 5

1 Look Back Look for understanding that the volume of a cone is $\frac{1}{3}$ the volume of the cylinder, and the volume of the sphere is $\frac{4}{3}$ the volume of the cylinder.

DIFFERENTIATION | RETEACH or REINFORCE

Hands-On Activity

Relate volumes of cylinders and cones.

If students are unsure about the relationship between the volume of cones and cylinders, then use this activity to visually reinforce the connection.

Materials For each group: scissors, tape, uncooked rice, Activity Sheet *Nets: Open Cylinder and Cone*

- Have students cut out the nets and tape them to form the two solids.
- Ask: *Do the cone and the cylinder have the same radius? How can you tell?* [Yes; Place the bases on top of each other and compare the bases.]
- Ask: *Do they have the same height? How can you tell?* [Yes; Stand the solids next to each other and place a ruler on the top base of the cylinder to compare the heights.]
- Instruct students to fill the cone with rice and dump the contents into the cylinder. Repeat this until the cylinder is full.
- Ask: *How many cones of rice does it take to fill the cylinder?* [3]
- Ask: *What does this show about how the volume of a cone is related to the volume of a cylinder with the same radius and same height?* [The volume of the cone is $\frac{1}{3}$ the volume of the cylinder.]

LESSON 28 | SESSION 1

CONNECT IT

1 Look Back What fraction of the volume of the cylinder is the volume of the cone? What fraction of the volume of the cylinder is the volume of the sphere? How did you get your answers?

$\frac{1}{3}$; $\frac{4}{3}$; Possible answer: First, I found the volume of the cylinder. Then I divided the volume of the cone by the volume of the cylinder, and I divided the volume of the sphere by the volume of the cylinder.

2 Look Ahead The figures in this lesson all have curved surfaces.

a. A cylinder has two parallel circular bases that are the same size. The volume of a cylinder is the area of the base multiplied by the height. Complete the volume formula for a cylinder with radius, *r*, and height, *h*.

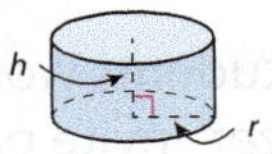

$V =$ $\pi r^2 h$

b. A **cone** has one circular base and one vertex. The volume of a cone is $\frac{1}{3}$ the volume of a cylinder with the same radius and height. Complete the volume formula for a cone with radius, *r*, and height, *h*.

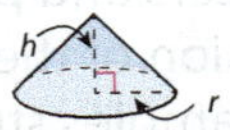

$V =$ $\frac{1}{3}\pi r^2 h$

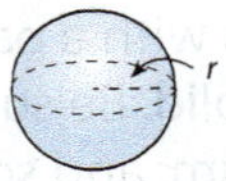

c. Every point on the surface of a **sphere** is the same distance from the center. The volume of a sphere with radius, *r*, is $\frac{4}{3}$ the volume of a cylinder with radius and height both equal to *r*. Complete the volume formula for a cylinder with radius, *r*, and height, *h*. $V =$ πr^3

Complete the volume formula for a sphere with radius, *r*.

$V =$ $\frac{4}{3}\pi r^3$

3 Reflect How is the volume formula for a cylinder like the volume formula for a rectangular prism? How are the formulas different?

Possible answer: The volume formula for both is the area of the base multiplied by the height. The volume formula for a cylinder is different from the volume formula for a prism because there are only two dimensions needed, the radius and height.

660

---

2 Look Ahead Point out that there are relationships between the volume of a cylinder and the volumes of a cone with the same radius and height and a sphere with the same radius. Explain that these relationships can be used to write volume formulas. The formula for volume of a cylinder is $V = \pi r^2 h$, the formula for volume of a cone is $V = \frac{1}{3}\pi r^2 h$, and the formula for volume of a sphere is $V = \frac{4}{3}\pi r^3$.

Ask a volunteer to rephrase the definitions of *cone* and *sphere*. Support student understanding by pointing out that a cylinder has two parallel circular bases, a cone has one circular base, and a sphere does not have a base.

CLOSE **EXIT TICKET**

3 Reflect Look for understanding that both the formula for the volume of a rectangular prism and the formula for the volume of a cylinder multiply the area of the base of the solid by its height.

Common Misconception If students do not see how the formulas are similar, then write $V = Bh$ and substitute ℓw as the area of the base for the prism and πr^2 as the area of the base for the cylinder.

Prepare for Solving Problems with Volumes of Cylinders, Cones, and Spheres

Support Vocabulary Development

Assign **Prepare for Solving Problems with Volumes of Cylinders, Cones, and Spheres** as extra practice in class or as homework.

If you have students complete this in class, then use the guidance below.

Ask students to consider the term *volume*. Remind them of the previous work they did with volumes of prisms.

Have students work in pairs to complete the graphic organizer. Invite pairs to share their completed organizers and prompt a whole-class comparative discussion of the definitions, known information, and examples students generated in their work.

Have students look at the solids in problem 2 and discuss with a partner how to find the volume of each solid. Be sure students understand each figure is a prism, and so the volume of each is equal to the area of the base times the height.

Problem Notes

1. Students should understand that volume is the amount of space inside a solid figure. Student responses might include that volume can only be found for three-dimensional figures and is measured in cubic units. Students may include the general volume formula for a prism or formulas for specific types of prisms, such as a cube.

2. **a.** The base of the prism can either be a 3-by-3 rectangle or a 3-by-13 rectangle. When a 3-by-3 base is used, the area of the base is 9 in.^{2} and the height is 13 in. When a 3-by-13 base is used, the area of the base is 39 in.^{2} and the height is 3 in.

   b. The base of the triangular prism is a right triangle. The Pythagorean Theorem must be used to find the missing dimension in the base, which is 12 cm. So, the area of the base is 30 cm^2 and the height of the prism is 2 cm.

LESSON 28 | SESSION 1 Name:

Prepare for Solving Problems with Volumes of Cylinders, Cones, and Spheres

1. Think about what you know about three-dimensional figures and volume. Fill in each box. Use words, numbers, and pictures. Show as many ideas as you can.
Possible answers:

volume

What Is It?
Volume is the amount of space inside a solid figure.

What I Know About It
Volume is measured in cubic units, like in.^{3}, ft^3, or m^3. Three-dimensional figures, like cubes and prisms, have volume. Two-dimensional figures, like squares and circles, do not have volume.

Examples

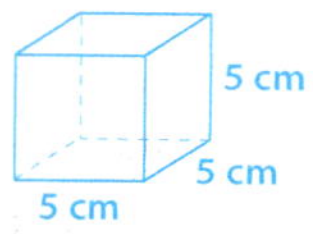

$V = s^3$
$= 125$ cm^3

Examples

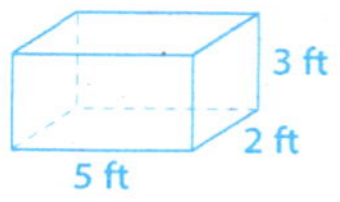

$V = \ell \times w \times h$
$= 30$ ft^3

Examples

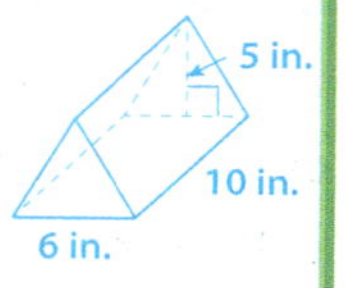

$V = \frac{1}{2}Bh$
$= 150$ in.^{3}

2. Find the volume of each figure.

a.

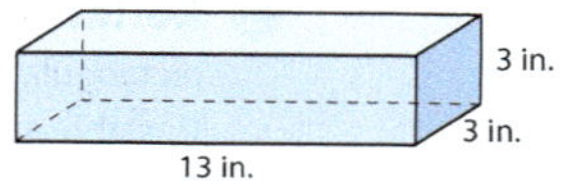

117 in.^{3}

b.

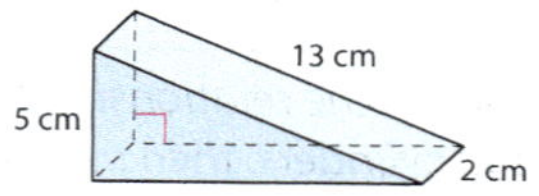

60 cm^2

661

REAL-WORLD CONNECTION

Structural engineers are responsible for the creative designs of water slides seen at water parks all over the world. Trying to satisfy thrill-seekers while providing a safe experience is a challenging job. In their quest to gratify riders, structural engineers have designed water slides with forms composed not only from cylinders, but also from cones and spheres. By incorporating these geometric shapes in their designs, it is important that the engineers understand how to calculate volumes of these solids to know how much space the water, rafts, and riders will take up within the structures.

Additional Practice

3 Problem 3 provides another look at comparing the volume of a cylinder to the volume of a cone with the same radius and height and to the volume of a sphere with the same radius. This problem is similar to the Try It problem, but a different radius and height are given. In both problems, the radius of the base of the cylinder is equal to the height of the cylinder.

Students may want to use exact measures or approximations to make the comparisons.

Suggest that students use **Three Reads** to make sure they understand what the problem is about and what is being asked.

3 The shaded figures shown are a cylinder, a cone, and a sphere.

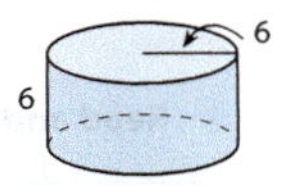

The volume of the cylinder is the area of the base multiplied by the height.

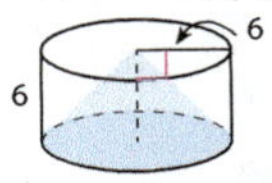

The volume of the cone is 72π.

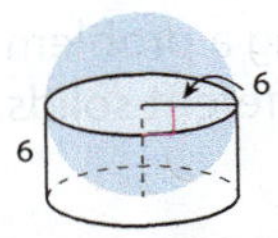

The volume of the sphere is 288π.

a. What fraction of the volume of the cylinder is the volume of the cone? What fraction of the volume of the cylinder is the volume of the sphere? Show your work.

Possible work:

$$\text{volume of cylinder} = \pi(6^2) \cdot 6$$
$$= 36\pi \cdot 6$$
$$= 216\pi$$

For $\pi \approx 3.14$, volume of cylinder ≈ 678.24.

$$\text{volume of cone} = 72\pi \approx 226.08$$

$$\frac{\text{volume of cone}}{\text{volume of cylinder}} = \frac{226.08}{678.24} = \frac{1}{3}$$

$$\text{volume of sphere} = 288\pi \approx 904.32$$

$$\frac{\text{volume of sphere}}{\text{volume of cylinder}} = \frac{904.32}{678.24} = \frac{4}{3}$$

SOLUTION The volume of the cone is $\frac{1}{3}$ the volume of the cylinder. The volume of the sphere is $\frac{4}{3}$ the volume of the cylinder.

b. Check your answer to problem 3a. Show your work.

Possible work:

$$\text{volume of cylinder} = (6^2 \cdot \pi) \cdot 6$$
$$= 216\pi$$

$$\frac{\text{volume of cone}}{\text{volume of cylinder}} = \frac{72\pi}{216\pi} = \frac{1}{3}$$

$$\frac{\text{volume of sphere}}{\text{volume of cylinder}} = \frac{288\pi}{216\pi} = \frac{4}{3}$$

DIFFERENTIATION | ENGLISH LANGUAGE LEARNERS

Use with **Session 2** **Connect It**

ACADEMIC VOCABULARY

To *combine* is to form by joining things together. We can combine two or more figures or amounts.

Whole is used to describe something that is in one piece. It means entire, complete, or total.

Levels 1–3: Speaking/Listening

To help students interpret Connect It problem 4, review the Academic Vocabulary. Ask: *What operation can we use to combine? What other word means whole?* [total]

Read the problem as students follow along. Help them connect Bridget's work to the figures in Picture It and the formulas in Model It. Ask: *How many parts are in Bridget's work? In the yurt? Is Bridget's idea correct?* Provide think time. Then call on students to share their ideas using words or sketches, or by pointing to the figures. Reword ideas using short sentences and record for students to refer to as they write.

Levels 2–4: Speaking/Listening

To help students interpret Connect It problem 4, ask them to discuss the Academic Vocabulary. Then explain that one way to understand more about Bridget's strategy is to connect it to Model It. Ask: *What did Bridget combine? Is this a useful strategy? How do you know?* Provide time for students to study Bridget's work and connect it to the figures before students discuss.

To prepare for written responses, ask students to explain to partners what they noticed about the problem and/or figures and what it helped them understand.

Levels 3–5: Speaking/Listening

Have students interpret Connect It problem 4 by reading the problem with partners and discussing what Bridget combined. Review that one way to understand more about a strategy is by analyzing how it is similar to or different from other strategies. Encourage students to take turns asking and answering questions as they discuss how Bridget's strategy connects to other strategies. If needed, provide these questions to support discussions:

- *How does Bridget's strategy compare to Picture It?*
- *How is the strategy similar to Model It? How is it different?*

Develop Finding Volume

Purpose

- **Develop** strategies for using formulas to find the volumes of cylinders, cones, spheres, and composite solids composed of these figures.
- **Recognize** whether solving a problem requires adding or subtracting volumes of different solids.

START CONNECT TO PRIOR KNOWLEDGE

Same and Different

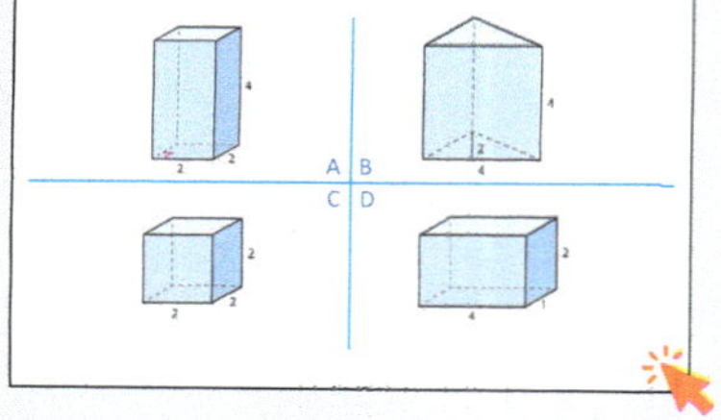

Possible Solutions

All are right prisms and have the same base area using the bottom face as the base.

A and B have the same volume.

C and D have the same volume.

A, C, and D are rectangular prisms.

WHY? Support students' facility identifying and comparing volume of prisms and areas of their faces.

DEVELOP ACADEMIC LANGUAGE

WHY? Use prefixes to confirm word meanings.

HOW? Write these word pairs: *medicine – medical, category – categorical, technology – technical, rectangle – rectangular*, and *cell – cellular* and ask students to discuss how the suffixes *-ical* and *-ular* affect the meanings of the base word or root. [makes an adjective; means *related to* or *like*] Ask students to use the information to explain the meanings of *cylindrical, circular*, and *spherical* in their own words.

TRY IT SMP 1, 2, 4, 5, 6

Make Sense of the Problem

See ***Connect to Culture*** to support student engagement. Before students work on Try It, use **Notice and Wonder** to help them make sense of the problem. After showing students the question, return to students' notice and wonder ideas to determine which are relevant for this problem.

Develop Finding Volume

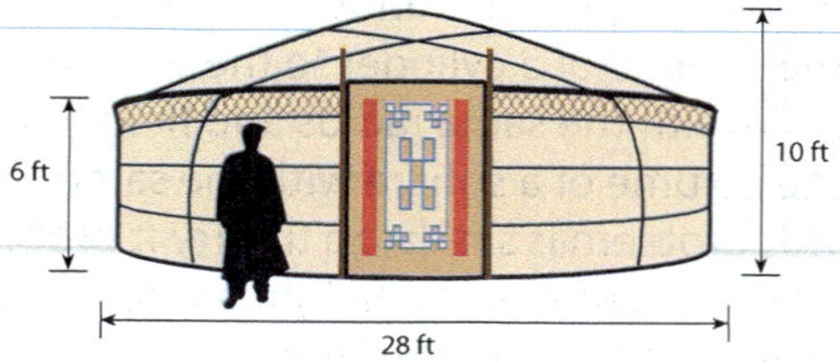

➤ **Read and try to solve the problem below.**

A yurt is a one-room home shaped like a cone on top of a cylinder. The yurt shown above is 10 feet tall with a diameter of 28 feet. Its walls are 6 feet high. What is the total volume of the yurt? Use 3.14 for π.

TRY IT Possible work:

SAMPLE A

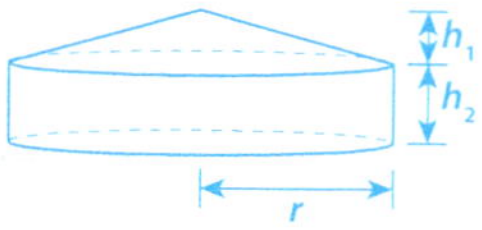

$r = 28 \div 2 = 14$

h_1 (cone) $= 10 - 6 = 4$

h_2 (cylinder) $= 6$

$V = \frac{1}{3}\pi r^2 h_1 + \pi r^2 h_2$

$= \left(\frac{1}{3}\pi \cdot 14^2 \cdot 4\right) + (\pi \cdot 14^2 \cdot 6)$

$= \left(261\frac{1}{3}\pi\right) + 1{,}176\pi$

$\approx 4{,}513.23$

The volume is about 4,513.23 ft^3.

SAMPLE B

If the top was a cylinder, its volume would be $V = \pi(14)^2 \cdot 4 = 784\pi$. But the top is a cone, so its volume is $\frac{1}{3}(784\pi) = 261\frac{1}{3} \cdot \pi$.

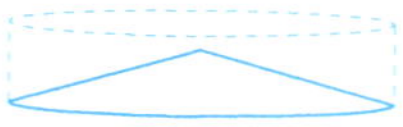

The volume of the bottom is:

$V = \pi(14)^2 \cdot 6 = 1{,}176\pi$

The volume of the entire yurt is:

$261\frac{1}{3} \cdot \pi + 1{,}176\pi = 1{,}437\frac{1}{3} \cdot \pi \approx 4{,}513.23$

The total volume is about 4,513.23 ft^3.

DISCUSS IT

Ask: How did you find the volume of each part of the yurt?

Share: I found the volume by . . .

663

DISCUSS IT SMP 2, 3, 6

Support Partner Discussion

After students work on Try It, encourage them to respond to Discuss It with a partner. Listen for understanding that:

- the height of the cone is the height of the yurt, 10 ft, minus the height of the walls, 6 ft.
- the volume of the cone can be found by using the volume formula for a cone or by finding the volume of a cylinder with radius 14 and height 4 and calculating one-third of the result.

Common Misconception Listen for students who think the volume of the cone on the top is $\frac{1}{3}$ the volume of the cylinder on the bottom. As students share their strategies, ask them whether the two solids have the same radius and height. Have students label the radius and height of each figure to recognize that, while the radii are the same, the heights are different. Point out that the volume of a cone is $\frac{1}{3}$ the volume of a cylinder only when they have both the same radius *and* the same height.

Select and Sequence Student Strategies

Select 2–3 samples that represent the range of student thinking in your classroom. Here is one possible order for class discussion:

- formulas used to find the volume of the cylinder and cone, and then volumes added
- (misconception) volume of cone assumed to be one-third the volume of the cylinder even though heights differ
- equation written for combined volume of two figures, and then substitution used to solve

Facilitate Whole Class Discussion

Call on students to share selected strategies. Have students turn and talk about how their solution was the same or different from those presented before continuing the discussion.

Guide students to **Compare and Connect** the representations. Prompt students to connect two different strategies by explaining how each gives the same solution.

ASK *What key ideas did you take away from comparing solution strategies?*

LISTEN FOR When solving real-world problems, I may connect the words and numbers given to a picture. I can label the picture and use it to determine the mathematical concepts or formulas I can use to solve the problem.

Picture It & Model It

If students presented these models, have students connect these models to those presented in class.

If no student presented at least one of these models, have students first analyze key features of the models, and then connect them to the models presented in class.

ASK *How are Picture It and Model It related?*

LISTEN FOR Picture It separates the figure into a cone and a cylinder and labels key dimensions. Model It uses formulas to find the volumes.

For the diagrams of the cone and cylinder, prompt students to think about the dimensions.

- *How can you tell from the problem and original diagram what the height of the cone is?*
- *How are the original dimensions from the problem used to find the radius?*

For the model with formulas, prompt students to consider the solutions.

- *Are the values of r and h the same for the cone and the cylinder?*
- *What must be done to finish solving the problem?*

➤ **Explore different ways to find the volumes of cylinders and cones.**

A yurt is a one-room home shaped like a cone on top of a cylinder. The yurt shown is 10 feet tall with a diameter of 28 feet. Its walls are 6 feet high. What is the total volume of the yurt? Use 3.14 for π.

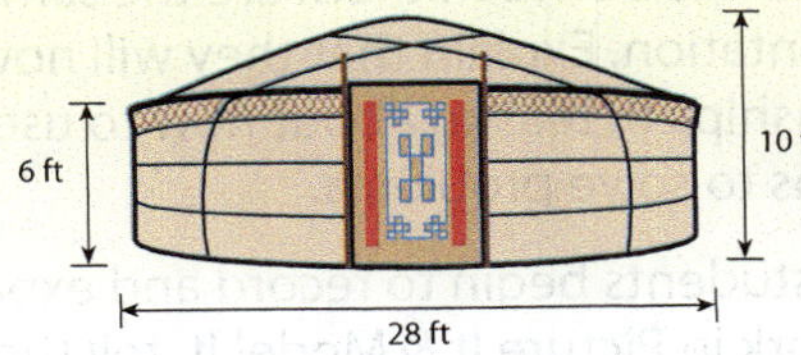

Picture It

You can separate the figure into two parts.

The top is a cone.

$r = 14$ and $h = 4$

The bottom is a cylinder.

$r = 14$ and $h = 6$

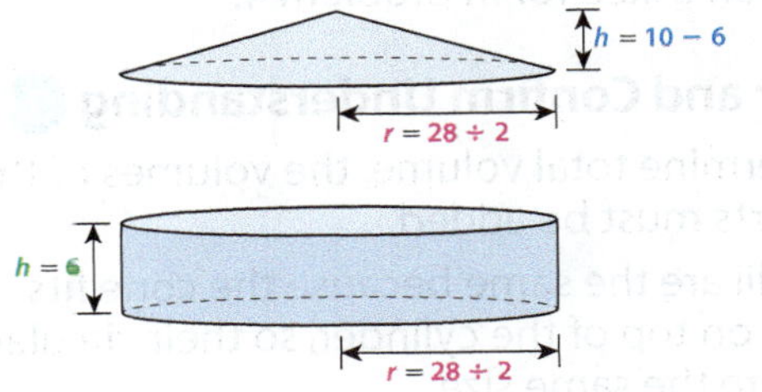

Model It

You can find the volume of each part of the figure.

volume of cone $= \frac{1}{3}\pi r^2 h$

$= \frac{1}{3}\pi \cdot 14^2 \cdot 4$

$= 261\frac{1}{3} \cdot \pi$

volume of cylinder $= \pi r^2 h$

$= \pi \cdot 14^2 \cdot 6$

$= 1{,}176 \cdot \pi$

664

DIFFERENTIATION | EXTEND

SMP 2

Deepen Understanding
Reasoning Quantitatively with Formulas for Volume

Prompt students to consider equivalent forms of the sum of the formulas.

ASK *Suppose you want to write one expression for the combined volume. What expression do you get if you simply add the two volume expressions?*

LISTEN FOR $\frac{1}{3}\pi r^2 h + \pi r^2 h$

ASK *What does h represent? Is it the same in both addends? Explain.*

LISTEN FOR the height of the cone and the height of the cylinder; No; The heights are not the same, so they must be represented differently somehow.

ASK *How could you rewrite the sum using subscripts for each h to make them different?*

LISTEN FOR $\frac{1}{3}\pi r^2 h_{cone} + \pi r^2 h_{cylinder}$

ASK *Are there any common factors? What is an equivalent factored expression? What does the factored form of the expression show that the figures have in common?*

LISTEN FOR $\pi r^2\left(\frac{1}{3}h_{cone} + h_{cylinder}\right)$; The area of the circular base is the same for both the cone and cylinder.

Develop Finding Volume

CONNECT IT

SMP 2, 4, 5, 6

Remind students that the quantities and the relationships between them are the same in each representation. Explain that they will now use those relationships to reason about how to use volume formulas to solve problems.

Before students begin to record and expand on their work in Picture It & Model It, tell them that problem 3 will prepare them to provide the explanation asked for in problem 4.

Monitor and Confirm Understanding 1 – 2

- To determine total volume, the volumes of the two parts must be added.
- The radii are the same because the cone fits exactly on top of the cylinder, so their circular bases are the same size.

Facilitate Whole Class Discussion

3 Look for understanding that the volume of the cone is not $\frac{1}{3}$ the volume of the cylinder because the heights of the figures are different.

ASK *What must be true for the volume of a cone to be $\frac{1}{3}$ the volume of a cylinder?*

LISTEN FOR Both the radius and the height of the two figures must be the same.

4 Look for understanding that the volume formulas cannot be combined because *h* does not represent the same value in each expression.

ASK *What does each addend in Bridget's formula represent? Can the same variable represent two different values?*

LISTEN FOR The first addend represents the volume of the cone and the second addend represents the volume of the cylinder. No; A variable represents the same value each time it appears in a single expression.

5 **Reflect** Have all students focus on the strategies used to solve the Try It. If time allows, have students discuss their ideas with a partner.

CONNECT IT

➤ **Use the problem from the previous page to help you understand how to use volume formulas to solve problems.**

1 Look at **Model It**. What is the total volume of the yurt? How did you get your answer? Use 3.14 for π.

about 4,513.23 ft^3; I found the approximate volume of each part of the yurt and then found their sum.

2 Look at the figures in **Picture It**. How do you know that the cone and the cylinder have the same radius?

Possible answer: The base of the cone and the base of the cylinder are the same-size circle.

3 Is the volume of the cone $\frac{1}{3}$ the volume of the cylinder? Explain.

No; Possible answer: The volume of the cone would have $\frac{1}{3}$ the volume of the cylinder if both had the same radius and the same height. They have the same radius, but not the same height.

4 Bridget combines the volume formulas for the parts of the yurt to write a volume formula for the whole yurt. Her work is shown.

$$V = \frac{1}{3}\pi r^2h + \pi r^2h$$
$$= \frac{4}{3}\pi r^2h$$

Is Bridget correct? Explain.

No; Possible answer: The variable *h* represents a different height in each formula, so $\frac{1}{3}\pi r^2h$ and πr^2h are not like terms that can be combined.

5 **Reflect** Think about all the models and strategies you have discussed today. Describe how one of them helped you better understand how to solve the **Try It** problem.

Responses will vary. Check student responses.

665

DIFFERENTIATION | RETEACH or REINFORCE

Visual Model

Connect dimensions of solids to volume relationships.

If students are unsure about the how to use the volume formulas for cones and cylinders, then use this activity to help them practice.

- Display the following word problem: *A grain silo is shaped like a cone on top of a cylinder. The walls of the silo are 12 ft high and the height of the cone on top is one-fourth the height of the walls. The diameter of the cone is 16 ft. What is the total volume of the grain silo?*
- Invite a student to sketch a drawing with dimensions labeled. Encourage others in the class to critique the drawing to ensure it is accurate.
- Ask: *What formula is used for the cylindrical part of the silo?* [$V = \pi r^2h$] *What does that formula look like with the cylinder dimensions substituted?* [$V = \pi(8)^2(12)$] *What is the exact volume of the cylindrical part of the silo?* [$V = 768\pi$]
- Ask: *What formula is used for the conical top of the silo?* $\left[V = \frac{1}{3}\pi r^2h\right]$ *What does that formula look like with the cone dimensions substituted?* $\left[V = \frac{1}{3}\pi(8)^2(3)\right]$ *What is the exact volume of the conical part of the silo?* [$V = 64\pi$]
- Ask: *What is the total volume of the silo?* [$V = 768\pi + 64\pi = 832\pi$]

Apply It

For all problems, encourage students to use a model to support their thinking.

6 Students may solve the problem by using the volume formula to find the volume of the pool filled to 4 ft and then divide the result by 72 to get an answer in hours.

7 Students may reason that to find the height in terms of r, they will need to set the formulas equal to each other and solve for h.

Apply It

➤ **Use what you learned to solve these problems.**

6 A cylindrical swimming pool has a radius of 9 feet. Daniel fills the pool with water at a rate of 72 cubic feet per hour. How long will it take for the depth of water in the pool to reach 4 feet? Show your work. Use 3.14 for π. Possible work:

volume of pool $= \pi r^2 h$

$= \pi \cdot 9^2 \cdot 4$

$\approx 1{,}017.36$

$1{,}017.36 \div 72 = 14.13$

SOLUTION It will take a little more than 14 hours.

7 A sphere and a cylinder have the same radius, r, and the same volume. What is the height of the cylinder in terms of r? Show your work. Possible work:

volume of sphere = volume of cylinder

$\frac{4}{3}\pi r^3 = \pi r^2 h$

$\frac{4}{3}r = h$

SOLUTION $h = \frac{4}{3}r$

8 A tennis ball has a diameter of 2.7 inches. A cylindrical container for tennis balls is shown. When there are three tennis balls in the container, how much empty space is in the container? Show your work. Use 3.14 for π.

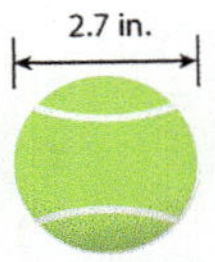

Possible work:

volume of can $= \pi(1.5)^2 \cdot 8.5$

≈ 60.05

volume of 3 balls $= 3 \times \frac{4}{3}\pi \cdot (1.35)^3$

$\approx 4\pi(2.46)$

≈ 30.9

$60.05 - 30.9 = 29.15$

SOLUTION There is about 29 in.^{3} of empty space.

CLOSE EXIT TICKET

8 Students' solutions should show an understanding that:

- the amount of empty space is the volume of the container minus the combined volume of the three balls.
- the volume of the container is the area of its base times its height, or $\pi r^2 h$.
- the volume of each ball is $\frac{4}{3}\pi r^3$.

Error Alert If students get a volume for the three balls of less than 30.9 in.^{3}, then they may have squared the radius rather than cubing it. Have students review the formulas for volumes of a cylinder and a sphere and redo their calculations.

Practice Finding Volume

Problem Notes

Assign **Practice Finding Volume** as extra practice in class or as homework.

1. Students may also solve the problem by writing one combined equation for the volume. They may then substitute for the variables and solve. ***Medium***

2. **a.** Students may solve the problem by writing the formula for a cylinder, substituting the given values and simplifying. ***Basic***

   b. Students may solve the problem by writing the formula for a cone, substituting the given values and simplifying. ***Basic***

   c. Students may solve the problem by writing the formula for a sphere, substituting the given values and simplifying. ***Basic***

LESSON 28 | SESSION 2 Name:

Practice Finding Volume

➤ **Study the Example showing how to use formulas to find the volume of a figure. Then solve problems 1–5.**

Example

The figure shows a cone shape removed from a solid cylinder. What is the volume of the figure without the cone? Use 3.14 for π.

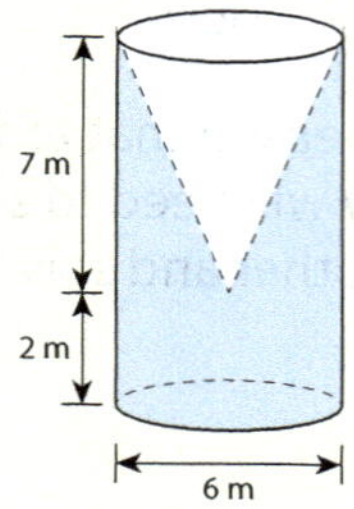

cylinder:

$V = \pi r^2 h$

$= \pi \cdot \left(\frac{6}{2}\right)^2 \cdot (7 + 2)$

$= \pi \cdot 3^2 \cdot 9$

$= 81\pi$

cone:

$V = \frac{1}{3}\pi r^2 h$

$= \frac{1}{3} \cdot \pi \cdot \left(\frac{6}{2}\right)^2 \cdot 7$

$= \frac{1}{3} \cdot \pi \cdot 3^2 \cdot 7$

$= 21\pi$

difference in volumes: $81\pi - 21\pi = 60\pi \approx 188.4$

The volume of the figure is about 188.4 m^3.

1. The figure shown is made up of two identical cones and a cylinder. What is the volume of the figure? Show your work. Use 3.14 for π. Possible work:

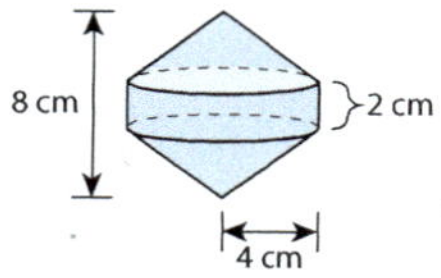

cone: $V = \frac{1}{3}\pi r^2 h$

$= \frac{1}{3} \cdot \pi \cdot 4^2 \cdot 3$

$= 16\pi$

cylinder: $V = \pi r^2 h$

$= \pi \cdot 4^2 \cdot 2$

$= 32\pi$

add volumes: $16\pi + 16\pi + 32\pi = 64\pi \approx 200.96$

SOLUTION about 200.96 cm^3

2. What is the volume of each figure? Use 3.14 for π.

   a. a cylinder with diameter 20 m and height 7 m about 2,198 m^3

   b. a cone with radius 3 yd and height 11 yd about 103.62 yd^3

   c. a sphere with radius 9 cm about 3,052 cm^3

667

Fluency & Skills Practice

Finding Volume

In this activity, students use formulas to find the volume of cylinders, cones, spheres, and composite figures.

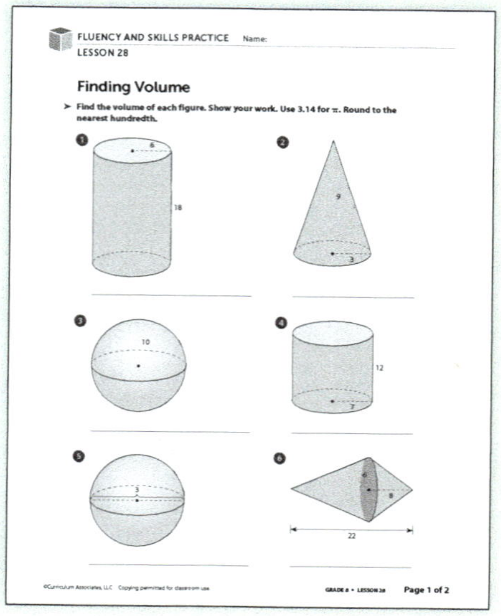
FLUENCY AND SKILLS PRACTICE Name:
LESSON 28

Finding Volume

➤ Find the volume of each figure. Show your work. Use 3.14 for π. Round to the nearest hundredth.

Page 1 of 2

Additional Practice

Additional Practice

3 Students may also solve the problem by first finding the volume of each mold and then dividing to find that the 5-cm diameter mold holds 1.95 times as much as the 4-cm diameter mold. They could then divide 12 by 1.95 to see how many 5-cm diameter molds they could fill. ***Challenge***

4 Students may also solve the problem by writing one combined equation of the spherical volume formula minus the cone volume formula. They may then substitute for the variables and solve. ***Medium***

5 **a.** ***Medium***

b. ***Medium***

c. Students may find the volume of the entire sphere and then divide that volume by 2. ***Challenge***

LESSON 28 | SESSION 2

3 Carmen is packing moisturizing bath powder into spherical molds. She has enough powder to fill about 12 spherical molds with a diameter of 4 cm. How many spherical molds with a diameter of 5 cm could she fill with the same amount of powder? Show your work. Possible work:

volume of twelve 4-cm diameter molds $= 12\left(\frac{4}{3}\pi \cdot 2^3\right)$

$= 128\pi$

volume of a 5-cm diameter mold $= \frac{4}{3}\pi \cdot (2.5)^3$

$\approx 20.833\pi$

$128\pi \div 20.833\pi \approx 6.144$

SOLUTION She could fill up to 6 molds.

4 A sphere has a radius of 4 feet. A cone has a radius of 5 feet and a height of 7 feet. What is the difference in the volumes of the cone and sphere, to the nearest cubic foot? Show your work. Use 3.14 for π. Possible work:

volume of sphere $= \frac{4}{3}\pi r^3$

$= \frac{4}{3}\pi \cdot 4^3$

$= 85\frac{1}{3}\pi$

volume of cone $= \frac{1}{3}\pi r^2 h$

$= \frac{1}{3}\pi \cdot 5^2 \cdot 7$

$= 58\frac{1}{3}\pi$

difference in volumes $= 85\frac{1}{3}\pi - 58\frac{1}{3}\pi = 27\pi \approx 84.78$

SOLUTION about 85 ft^3

5 How many cubic inches of soil would it take to fill each planter? Use 3.14 for π.

a.

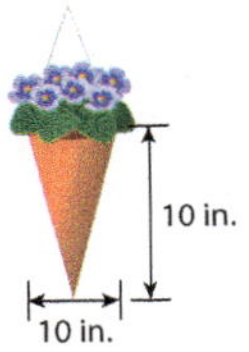

about 262 $in.^3$

b.

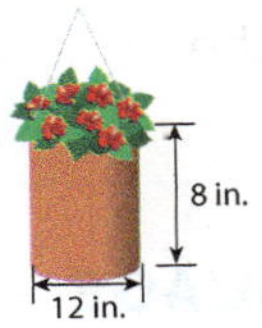

about 904 $in.^3$

c.

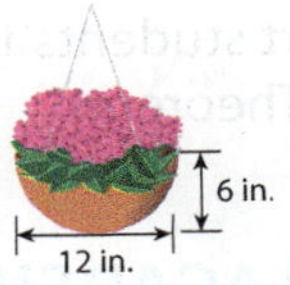

about 452 $in.^3$

668

DIFFERENTIATION | ENGLISH LANGUAGE LEARNERS

Use with **Session 3** Connect It

ACADEMIC VOCABULARY

To *suppose* means to believe to be true. The word *suppose* may be used to present new information or situations that are different from the original.

Levels 1–3: Speaking/Writing

To help students interpret Connect It problem 3, ask them to circle *radius*, *cone*, *height*, and *volume*. Ask students to use the words as they tell what they know about a cone.

Help students respond by connecting to Picture It. Ask them to write what they knew and to identify the strategy:

- *In Picture It, we knew the* ____.
- *We did not know the* ____.
- *We used* ____ *to* ____. *Then we* ____.

Next, help students adjust the frames to write about the new problem.

Levels 2–4: Speaking/Writing

To support Connect It problem 3, help students read the problem and discuss the meaning of *suppose*. Ask them to discuss why *knew* is in the past tense. Ensure students connect the past tense verb to the problem already solved. Next, have students prepare to write responses. Ask them to describe the strategies used for the original problem and tell how the new problem is different using:

- *In the original problem, we knew* ____ *and not* ____.
- *In* ____, *we used* ____ *to* ____. *Then we used* ____ *to* ____.
- *In the new problem,* ____.

Levels 3–5: Speaking/Writing

Have students interpret Connect It problem 3 by discussing the meaning of *suppose*. Then ask: *How is the information in this problem different than in the original word problem?* Provide think time before having students discuss ideas with partners.

Have students prepare to write by first discussing their ideas with partners. Remind students that one way to connect is by thinking about previously used strategies. After discussions, have students write responses. Remind them to connect to the original problem and to start with the first step of the strategy.

Develop Finding an Unknown Dimension

Purpose

- **Develop** strategies for determining an unknown dimension of a cylinder, cone, or sphere.
- **Recognize** that the Pythagorean Theorem can be used to find an unknown dimension of a cone.

START CONNECT TO PRIOR KNOWLEDGE

Which One Doesn't Belong?

Triangle with the side lengths:

A: 0.3, 0.4, 0.5	B: 8, 15, 17
C: 7, 12, 13	D: 1, 1, $\sqrt{2}$

Possible Solutions

A is the only right triangle with three decimal side lengths.

B is the only triangle whose side lengths are a Pythagorean triple.

C is the only triangle that is not a right triangle.

D is the only isosceles triangle.

WHY? Support students' facility with the Pythagorean Theorem.

DEVELOP ACADEMIC LANGUAGE

WHY? Support students as they craft clear explanations using precise language.

HOW? Remind students that using precise mathematical language and complete sentences makes explanations clearer and easier to understand. Prior to Discuss It, work with students to develop a list of precise terms from Try It such as *height, radius, distance, triangle,* and *edge*. During Discuss It, collect and display students' explanations.

TRY IT SMP 1, 2, 4, 5, 6

Make Sense of the Problem

See ***Connect to Culture*** to support student engagement. Before students work on Try It, use **Three Reads** to help them make sense of the problem. Have students turn and talk before responding to each question.

Develop Finding an Unknown Dimension

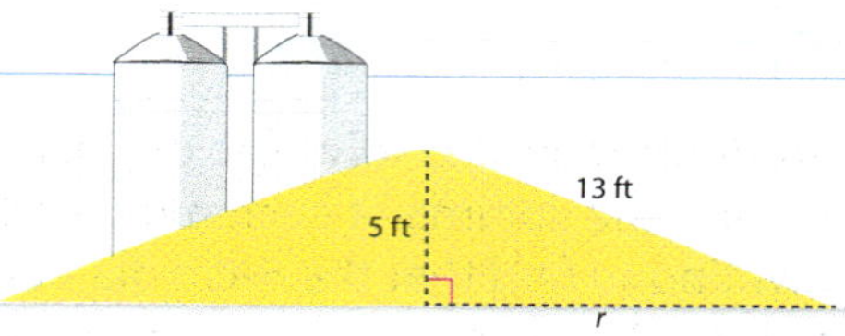

➤ **Read and try to solve the problem below.**

A cone-shaped pile of corn in a field has a height of 5 feet. The distance from the top of the pile to the edge is 13 feet. What is the volume of the pile of corn? Use 3.14 for π.

TRY IT

Possible work:

SAMPLE A

The height, radius, and distance from top to edge form a 5, 12, 13 right triangle.

$h = 5, r = 12$

$V = \frac{1}{3}\pi r^2 h$

$= \frac{1}{3}\pi \cdot 12^2 \cdot 5$

$= 240\pi$

≈ 753.6

The volume is about 753.6 ft³.

SAMPLE B

The lengths labeled r, 5, and 13 form a right triangle.

$r^2 + 5^2 = 13^2$

$r^2 + 25 = 169$

$r^2 = 144$

$V = \frac{1}{3}\pi r^2 h$

$= \frac{1}{3}\pi \cdot 144 \cdot 5 \quad (h = 5, r^2 = 144)$

$= 240\pi$

≈ 753.6

The volume is about 753.6 ft³.

DISCUSS IT

Ask: What was your first step?

Share: The first thing I did was . . .

DISCUSS IT SMP 2, 3, 6

Support Partner Discussion

After students work on Try It, encourage them to respond to Discuss It with a partner. If students need support in getting started, prompt them to ask each other questions such as:

- *What information is needed to find the volume of a cone?*
- *Is all the needed information given in the problem? If not, how did you find it?*

Error Alert If students use the side length of 13 ft as the radius, then ask them to look at the labels on the given figure. Point out that 13 ft is the distance from the vertex of the cone to the edge of the base. The radius of the cone is labeled r. It is unknown, so students need to find this distance.

Select and Sequence Student Strategies

Select 2–3 samples that represent the range of student thinking in your classroom. Here is one possible order for class discussion:

- Pythagorean Theorem used to find the radius; then volume formula used
- Pythagorean triple identified to find the radius; then volume formula used
- r^2 identified using Pythagorean Theorem and substituted into volume formula

Facilitate Whole Class Discussion

Call on students to share selected strategies. Prompt students to build on ideas they agree with by giving reasons that a strategy will always work or will sometimes work.

Guide students to **Compare and Connect** the representations. Allow time for students to think by themselves before starting the discussion.

ASK *What information in the problem text or image led most students to their first step?*

LISTEN FOR The labeled image helps show that the radius is unknown, but that it will be needed to find the volume. It also shows that the radius is the leg of a right triangle, so its length can be found using the Pythagorean Theorem.

Picture It & Model It

If students presented these models, have students connect these models to those presented in class.

If no student presented at least one of these models, have students first analyze key features of the models, and then connect them to the models presented in class.

ASK *How is Model It related to Picture It?*

LISTEN FOR Picture It shows a right triangle with the radius labeled and uses the Pythagorean Theorem to find its value. Model It uses the radius found in Picture It to find the volume of the cone.

For the Pythagorean Theorem, prompt students to consider why this method was chosen. Ask: *How does drawing a picture help you see that the Pythagorean Theorem can be used?*

For the volume formula, prompt students to think about the structure of the formula.

- *How can you break the formula into parts that represent the base and height of the cone?*
- *Why is it important to understand the meaning of the quantities in a formula?*

➤ Explore different ways to find an unknown dimension.

A cone-shaped pile of corn in a field has a height of 5 feet. The distance from the top of the pile to the edge is 13 feet. What is the volume of the pile of corn? Use 3.14 for π.

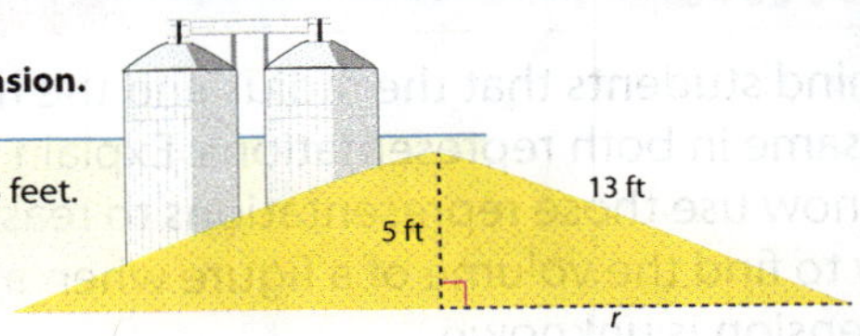

Picture It

You can use the Pythagorean Theorem to find the radius of the cone.

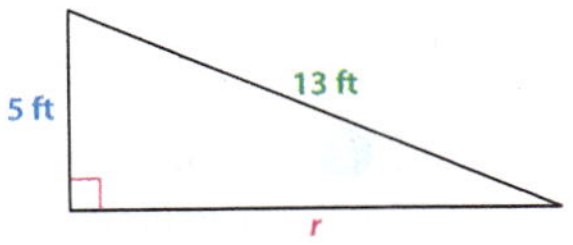

$r^2 + 5^2 = 13^2$

$r^2 + 25 = 169$

$r^2 = 144$

$r = 12$

Model It

You can use the formula for the volume of the cone.

$V = \frac{1}{3}\pi r^2 h$

$= \frac{1}{3}\pi \cdot 12^2 \cdot 5$

$= \frac{1}{3}\pi \cdot 144 \cdot 5$

670

DIFFERENTIATION | EXTEND SMP 7

Deepen Understanding
Using Structure to Extend Understanding of Surface Area

Prompt students to consider which pieces of information in Picture It are needed to find volume and whether the other information can be used for anything else.

ASK *What information is necessary to calculate the volume of a cone?*

LISTEN FOR the radius and the height or the area of the base and the height

ASK *Which piece of information in the triangle is not needed in the formula for volume?*

LISTEN FOR the hypotenuse of the right triangle

Explain that the hypotenuse of the right triangle is the distance along the surface of the cone from the vertex to the base and is called the *slant height* of the cone. The slant height is not needed to find the volume, but is needed to find surface area. Explain that surface area of a cone is the area of the base plus $\pi r\ell$, where ℓ is the slant height.

ASK *What is the surface area of the conical corn pile?*

LISTEN FOR The formula would be the area of the base plus the slanted surface of the cone. This is represented by $\pi r2 + \pi r\ell = 144\pi + 156\pi = 300\pi$, or about 942.5 square feet.

Develop Finding an Unknown Dimension

CONNECT IT

SMP 2, 4, 5, 6

Remind students that the radius and the height are the same in both representations. Explain that they will now use those representations to reason about how to find the volume of a figure when a dimension is unknown.

Before students begin to record and expand on their work in Picture It & Model It, tell them that problems 3 and 4 will prepare them to provide the explanation asked for in problem 5.

Monitor and Confirm Understanding 1 – 2

- Only r^2 needs to be found in order to use the volume formula, so once you know $r^2 = 144$, there is no need to solve for *r*.

Facilitate Whole Class Discussion

3 Look for understanding that the Pythagorean Theorem can also be used to find the height of the cone.

ASK *Could you stop once you know the value of h^2, or do you need to find h? Why?*

LISTEN FOR No, you could not stop. You need to find *h* because the volume formula uses *h* not h^2.

4 Look for understanding that because the circumference of a circle is $2\pi r$ or πd, you could find the radius or diameter of the cylinder. If you find the diameter, you then need to divide by 2 to get the radius, which is needed in the volume formula.

5 Look for understanding that the Pythagorean Theorem can be used to find an unknown dimension when a right triangle is involved.

ASK *How does the fact that the radius, the height, and the distance from the vertex to the edge form a right triangle help you find an unknown radius or height?*

LISTEN FOR If two of these lengths are known, then you can use the Pythagorean Theorem to find the third length.

6 **Reflect** Have all students focus on the strategies used to solve the Try It. If time allows, have students discuss their ideas with a partner.

CONNECT IT

➤ **Use the problem from the previous page to help you understand how to find the volume of a figure when a dimension is unknown.**

1 Look at **Picture It**. The third step shows $r^2 = 144$. Do you need to solve this equation for *r* to find the volume of the cone? Explain.
No; Possible explanation: The radius is squared in the volume formula, so you could substitute r^2 directly into the volume formula instead of finding *r* and then squaring it again.

2 Look at **Model It**. What is the volume of the pile of corn?
The volume of the pile of corn is about 753.6 ft^3.

3 Suppose you knew the radius of the cone and not the height. How could you find the volume of the cone?
Possible answer: I could use the Pythagorean Theorem to find the height and then substitute the height and radius into the volume formula.

4 What dimension of a cylinder or cone could you find if you know the circumference or area of a base? Explain.
The radius; Possible explanation: The circumference of a circle is $2\pi r$, so you can find *r* by dividing *C* by 2π. The area of a circle is πr^2, so you can find *r* by dividing *A* by π and then take the square root.

5 How can you use the distance from the vertex of a cone to the edge of its base to help you find an unknown radius or height?
Possible answer: If you know the distance from the vertex to the edge of the base and the radius (or the height), then you can use the Pythagorean Theorem to find the height (or the radius).

6 **Reflect** Think about all the models and strategies you have discussed today. Describe how one of them helped you better understand how to solve the **Try It** problem.
Responses will vary. Check student responses.

671

DIFFERENTIATION | RETEACH or REINFORCE

Visual Model

Use mathematical relationships to solve problems.

If students are unsure about finding the unknown information needed to find the volume of a cone, then use this visual to help them understand.

- Display a diagram of a cone showing the right triangle formed by its radius, *r*, height, *h*, and surface distance from the vertex to the base, ℓ. Explain that the distance ℓ is called the *slant height*.
- Ask: *What is the relationship between the right triangle and the cone?* [The right triangle is a partial slice of the cone with leg lengths *r* and *h* and hypotenuse length ℓ.]
- Ask: *How can you use the Pythagorean Theorem to find the radius or height if only one is known and the slant height is known?* [Substitute the known values and solve.]
- Ask: *After using the Pythagorean Theorem, how could you find the volume of a cone?* [The volume formula uses both radius and height, so after finding the unknown value, I can substitute *r* and *h* into the volume formula and solve for *V*.]
- Ask: *Suppose you know the area of the base and the height of a cone. Can you find the volume? Do you need to find the radius first? Explain.* [I can find the volume without finding the radius by substituting the area of the base for πr^2 in the formula.]

Apply It

For all problems, encourage students to use a model to support their thinking.

7 Students may reason that because the only known values are shown for the cone, they must first find the volume of the cone and then equate this result to the volume formula for a sphere.

8 Students may reason that because a combined volume is given, they will need a combined volume formula for a cylinder and a cone.

Apply It

➤ **Use what you learned to solve these problems.**

7 The cone and sphere have equal volumes. What is the radius of the sphere? Show your work.

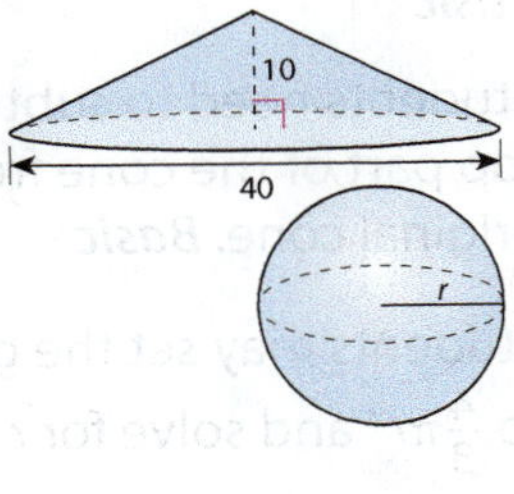

Possible work:

cone: $V = \frac{1}{3}\pi r^2 h$

$= \frac{1}{3}\pi \cdot 20^2 \cdot 10$

$= \frac{4{,}000}{3}\pi$

$\frac{4{,}000}{3}\pi = \frac{4}{3}\pi r^3$

$1{,}000 = r^3$

$10 = r$

SOLUTION $r = 10$

8 The volume of the figure is 138π m³. What is the radius? Show your work. Use 3.14 for π. Possible work:

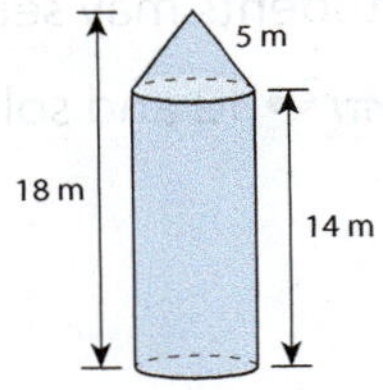

height of cone: $18 - 14 = 4$

volume of cone $= \frac{1}{3}\pi r^2 h$

$= \frac{4}{3}\pi r^2$

volume of cylinder $= \pi r^2 h$

$= 14\pi r^2$

$138\pi = \frac{4}{3}\pi r^2 + 14\pi r^2$

$138\pi = 15\frac{1}{3}\pi r^2$

$9 = r^2$

$3 = r$

SOLUTION $r = 3$ m

9 The circumference of a globe is 16π inches. What is the volume of the globe? Show your work. Use 3.14 for π.

Possible work:

$2\pi r = 16\pi$

$r = 8$

$V = \frac{4}{3}\pi r^3$

$= \frac{4}{3}\pi \cdot 8^3$

$\approx 2{,}143.57$

SOLUTION The volume is about 2,144 in.³.

672

CLOSE EXIT TICKET

9 Students' solutions should show an understanding that:

- the circumference formula must be used to find the radius of the sphere before the volume of the sphere can be found.
- the volume formula for a sphere is $V = \frac{4}{3}\pi r^3$.

Error Alert If students get an answer greater than 2,144 in.³, then they may have found and used the diameter instead of the radius in the volume formula. Review the two circumference formulas, $C = \pi d$ and $C = 2\pi r$, and the relationship between diameter and radius.

Practice Finding an Unknown Dimension

Problem Notes

Assign **Practice Finding an Unknown Dimension** as extra practice in class or as homework.

1. **a.** ***Basic***

   b. Students need to subtract the volume of the top part of the cone from the volume of the original cone. ***Basic***

2. **a.** Students may set the given volume equal to $\frac{4}{3}\pi r^3$ and solve for r. ***Medium***

   b. Students may set the given volume equal to $3\pi r^2$ and solve for r. ***Medium***

   c. Students may set the given volume equal to $\frac{1}{3}\pi r^2 \bullet 12$ and solve for r. ***Medium***

LESSON 28 | SESSION 3 Name:

Practice Finding an Unknown Dimension

➤ **Study the Example showing how to find an unknown dimension to find volume. Then solve problems 1–4.**

Example

A cone is divided into two parts, as shown. The original cone has a height of 14 and a radius of 6. The top part of the divided figure is a cone with a height of 7. Use similar triangles to find the radius of the top part. Then find the volume of the top part. Use 3.14 for π.

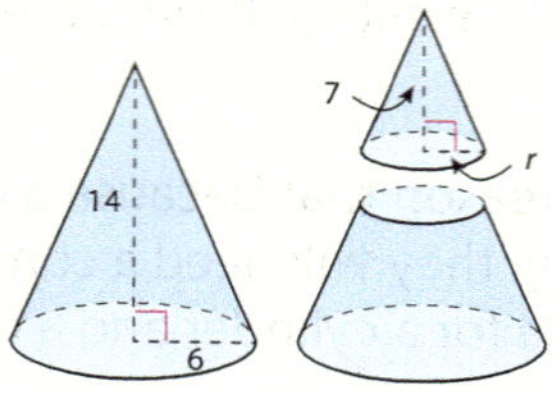

$\frac{r}{6} = \frac{7}{14} \longrightarrow r = 3$

$V = \frac{1}{3}\pi r^2 h$

$= \frac{1}{3}\pi \cdot 3^2 \cdot 7$

$= 21\pi$

$21(3.14) = 65.94$

The volume is about 65.94 cubic units.

1. **a.** What is the volume of the original cone in the Example before it is divided? Use 3.14 for π.

   $\frac{1}{3}(3.14)(6^2)(14) = 527.52$; about 527.52 cubic units

   b. What is the volume of the bottom part of the cone after it is divided?

   $527.52 - 65.94 = 461.58$; about 461.58 cubic units

2. What is the radius of each figure described?

   a. a sphere with a volume of $\frac{500\pi}{3}$ cm^3

   5 cm

   b. a cylinder with a height of 3 m and a volume of 147π m^3

   7 m

   c. a cone with a height of 12 in. and a volume of 16π in.^{3}

   2 in.

Vocabulary

cone
a three-dimensional figure with one circular base and one vertex, connected by a curved surface.

cylinder
a three-dimensional figure with two parallel curved bases that are the same size.

sphere
a three-dimensional figure in which every point is the same distance from the center.

673

Fluency & Skills Practice

Finding an Unknown Dimension

In this activity, students use volume formulas and given information to find unknown dimensions or volumes of cylinders, cones, and spheres.

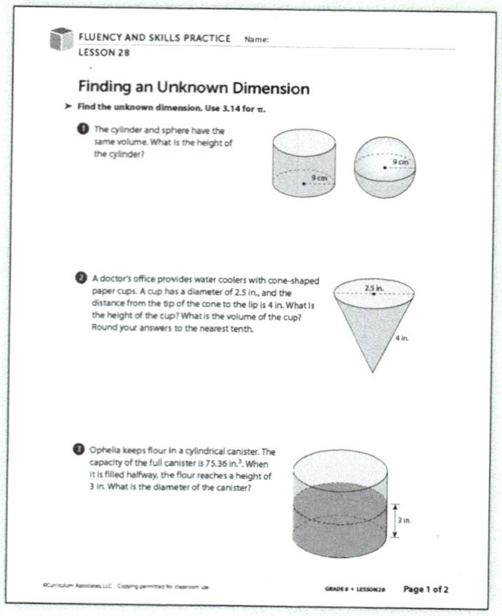

FLUENCY AND SKILLS PRACTICE Name:
LESSON 28

Finding an Unknown Dimension

➤ **Find the unknown dimension. Use 3.14 for π.**

1. The cylinder and sphere have the same volume. What is the height of the cylinder? (9 cm, 9 cm)

2. A doctor's office provides water coolers with cone-shaped paper cups. A cup has a diameter of 2.5 in., and the distance from the tip of the cone to the lip is 4 in. What is the height of the cup? What is the volume of the cup? Round your answers to the nearest tenth. (2.5 in., 4 in.)

3. Ophelia keeps flour in a cylindrical canister. The capacity of the full canister is 75.36 in.^{3}. When it is filled halfway, the flour reaches a height of 3 in. What is the diameter of the canister? (3 in.)

©Curriculum Associates, LLC Copying permitted for classroom use. GRADE 8 • LESSON 28 Page 1 of 2

Additional Practice

3 Both the radius and height are unknown. The circumference formula may be used to find the radius. Then the radius and the distance from the vertex to the edge can be used in the Pythagorean Theorem to find the height. Once the height and radius are known, students may use the volume formula to solve. ***Challenge***

4 The height of the cone is unknown. The radius of the cone is the same as the radius of the cylinder. The Pythagorean Theorem can be used to find the height of the cone. Then the volume formulas may be used to find total volume. ***Medium***

LESSON 28 | SESSION 3

3 The circumference of the base of the cone shown is 8π mm. What is the volume of the cone? Show your work. Use 3.14 for π.

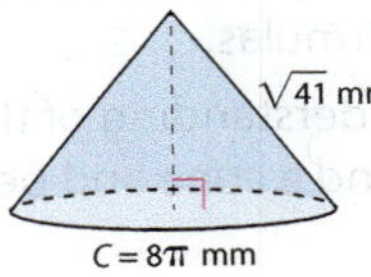

Possible work:

$2\pi r = 8\pi$ $\qquad$ $4^2 + h^2 = (\sqrt{41})^2$ $\qquad$ $V = \frac{1}{3}\pi r^2 h$

$\frac{2\pi r}{2\pi} = \frac{8\pi}{2\pi}$ $\qquad$ $16 + h^2 = 41$ $\qquad$ $= \frac{1}{3}\pi \cdot 4^2 \cdot 5$

$r = 4$ $\qquad$ $h^2 = 25$ $\qquad$ $= \frac{80\pi}{3}$

$h = 5$ $\qquad$ ≈ 83.7

SOLUTION $V \approx 83.7$ mm^3

4 A cylindrical storage bin is filled with sunflower seeds. The seeds form a cone-shaped pile above the bin. How many cubic feet of sunflower seeds are in the bin? Show your work. Use 3.14 for π.

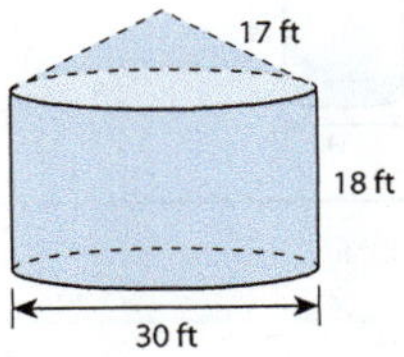

Possible work:

height of cone:

$h^2 + 15^2 = 17^2$

$h^2 + 225 = 289$

$h^2 = 64$

$h = 8$

volume of cone:

$V = \frac{1}{3}\pi r^2 h$

$= \frac{1}{3}\pi \cdot 15^2 \cdot 8$

$= 600\pi$

volume of cylinder:

$V = \pi r^2 h$

$= \pi \cdot 15^2 \cdot 18$

$= 4{,}050\pi$

total volume $= 600\pi + 4{,}050\pi = 4{,}650\pi \approx 14{,}601$

SOLUTION There are about 14,601 ft^3 of sunflower seeds.

674

DIFFERENTIATION | ENGLISH LANGUAGE LEARNERS

Use with **Session 4** **Apply It**

MATH TERM

Diameter is the distance across a circle that goes through the center of the circle.

Cylindrical describes the shape of a cylinder.

Spherical describes the shape of a sphere.

Levels 1–3: Reading/Speaking

Help students make sense of Apply It problem 6. Use an adaptation of **Three Reads**. For Read 1, read aloud sentences 1–2. Ask students to label the candle, pitcher, wax, and mold. Ask Wh- questions for understanding. (e.g., *What shape is ____? What does Geraldo do first? What does he do next?*)

For Read 2, help students read the question and craft a sentence frame they can use for their solutions.

For Read 3, read the full problem as students follow along and circle the quantities. Ask students to identify the shape of each figure, its diameter and radius, and the height of the pitcher.

Levels 2–4: Reading/Speaking

Help students make sense of Apply It problem 6 using an adaptation of **Three Reads**. After Read 1, prompt students to use words from the problem to label the image. Ask: *How does the image help you understand the problem situation?* Ask others to repeat and rephrase. Then present sentence starters to help with Read 2:

- *We are trying to figure out ____.*
- *First we need to know ____. Then we need to figure out ____.*

After Read 3, have students discuss *diameter*. Ask: *How will the quantities help you solve the problem?*

Levels 3–5: Reading/Speaking

To prepare for Apply It problem 6, have students use **Notice and Wonder** to preview the image with partners and share their ideas. If appropriate, encourage students to reword their ideas with precise math terms, such as *cylinder* and *sphere*. Record statements for reference. Ask students to read the problem and discuss how it connects to the statements. Next, have students discuss math terms in the problem, such as *diameter* and the lesson vocabulary *cylindrical* and *spherical*. Then ask: *What is the problem about? What might you do first? Next?* Have students discuss with partners.

Refine Solving Problems with Volumes of Cylinders, Cones, and Spheres

Purpose

- **Refine** strategies for finding unknown dimensions and volumes of cylinders, cones, and spheres, including using volume formulas.
- **Refine** understanding of the relationship between a cylinder and a cone and between a cylinder and a sphere.

START CONNECT TO PRIOR KNOWLEDGE

What is the volume of the figure?
Use 3.14 for π.

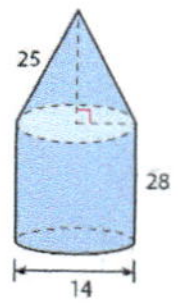

Solution

5,538.96 units^3

WHY? Confirm students' understanding of calculating volumes of cylinders and cones, identifying common errors to address as needed.

MONITOR & GUIDE

Before students begin to work, use their responses to the **Start** to determine those who will benefit from additional support. Use the **Error Analysis** table below to guide remediation.

Have all students complete the Example and problems 1–3, using Consider This and Pair/Share as appropriate. Observe and monitor their reasoning and guide or redirect students as needed.

Refine Solving Problems with Volumes of Cylinders, Cones, and Spheres

➤ **Complete the Example below. Then solve problems 1–9.**

Example

The volume formula for a cone is the same whether or not the vertex is directly above the center of the base. What is the volume of this cone?

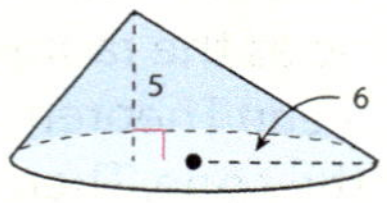

Look at how you could use a volume formula.

$r = 6, h = 5$

$V = \frac{1}{3}\pi r^2 h$

$V = \frac{1}{3}\pi \cdot 6^2 \cdot 5$

SOLUTION 60π, or about 188.4 cubic units

CONSIDER THIS . . . Which volume formula can you use?

PAIR/SHARE If you knew the distance from the vertex to the edge and the height of the cone, would you be able to find the volume? Explain.

Apply It

1 The figure shown is made up of a cone and a half sphere. What is the volume of the figure? Show your work. Use 3.14 for π.

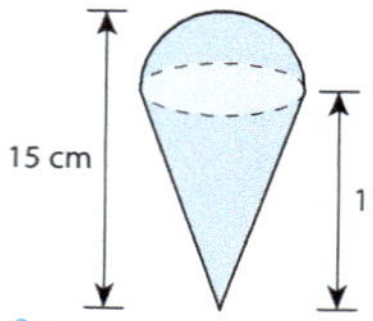

Possible work:

$r = 15 - 11 = 4$

half sphere: $V = \frac{1}{2} \cdot \frac{4}{3}\pi r^3$

$= \frac{1}{2} \cdot \frac{4}{3}\pi \cdot 4^3$

$= 42\frac{2}{3}\pi$

cone: $V = \frac{1}{3}\pi r^2 h$

$= \frac{1}{3}\pi \cdot 4^2 \cdot 11$

$= 58\frac{2}{3}\pi$

volume of figure $= 42\frac{2}{3}\pi + 58\frac{2}{3}\pi = 101\frac{1}{3}\pi \approx 318.19$

SOLUTION $V \approx 318$ cm^3

CONSIDER THIS . . . The radius of the half sphere is also the radius of the cone.

PAIR/SHARE Could you solve the problem by adding the volumes of the cone and full sphere, then dividing the sum by 2? Explain.

675

START ERROR ANALYSIS

If the error is . . .	Students may . . .	To support understanding . . .
1,230.88 units^3	have found only the volume of the cone.	Prompt students to break the figure into parts. Then find the volumes of the parts and add.
4,308.08 units^3	have found only the volume of the cylinder.	Ask students to carefully analyze the figure. They should notice the figure can be broken into two parts. Have them calculate the volume of each part and then add.
5,590.25 units^3	have used 25 as the height of the cone when finding the volume.	Prompt students to separate the figure into two parts. Elicit from students that the top is a cone and the bottom is a cylinder. Students should notice they will need to use the Pythagorean Theorem to find the height of the cone.

Example

Guide students in understanding the Example. Ask:

- *How is this cone different from other cones?*
- *What is the radius of the cone? What is the height of the cone?*
- *How can you use the formula for the volume of a cone to solve this problem? How could you use the volume of a cylinder to solve this problem?*

Help all students focus on the Example and responses to the questions by prompting students to paraphrase the speaker's ideas. They can ask questions about ideas that are unclear.

Look for understanding that even though the vertex is not directly above the center of the base, the height of the cone is still 5, and therefore the formula for the volume of a cone can be used.

Apply It

1 Students may subtract the height of the cone from the total height of the figure to find the radius of the cone and half sphere. Then they may use formulas to find the volume of each part. The volume of the half sphere is $\frac{1}{2}$ the volume of a sphere with the given radius. *DOK 2*

2 Students may use the given information to find the volume of the half sphere and subtract the volume of half sphere from the volume of the figure. Then they may substitute the new volume and the radius of 5 m into the formula for the volume of a cylinder to calculate the height. *DOK 2*

3 **A is correct.** When a cylinder and cone each have the same radius and volume, the ratio of the heights is 1 : 3.

B is not correct. This answer is the result of subtracting 3 from the height of the cone instead of dividing by 3.

C is not correct. When a cylinder and cone have the same radius and volume, the ratio of the heights is 1 : 3, not 3 : 4 as with a cylinder and sphere.

D is not correct. This answer is the result of multiplying the height of the cone by 3 instead of dividing by 3.

DOK 3

LESSON 28 | SESSION 4

2 The figure shown is made up of a half sphere and a cylinder. The volume of the figure is about 497 cubic meters. What is the height of the cylinder? Show your work. Use 3.14 for π.

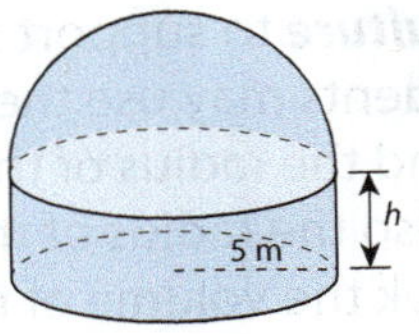

Possible work:

$$V = \frac{1}{2} \cdot \frac{4}{3}\pi r^3 + \pi r^2 h$$

$$497 = \frac{1}{2} \cdot \frac{4}{3}\pi \cdot 5^3 + \pi \cdot 5^2 \cdot h$$

$$497 \approx 261.67 + 78.5h$$

$$235.33 \approx 78.5h$$

$$3 \approx h$$

CONSIDER THIS . . . Remember to find the volume of half a sphere, not a whole one.

PAIR/SHARE If another half sphere was attached to the bottom of the figure, what would the new volume be?

SOLUTION about 3 m

3 A cylinder and a cone have the same radius and the same volume. The height of the cone is 12 cm. What is the height of the cylinder?

(A) 4 cm

B 9 cm

C 16 cm

D 36 cm

David chose D as the correct answer. How might he have gotten that answer?

Possible answer: David might have multiplied by 3 instead of dividing by 3.

CONSIDER THIS . . . The variable *r* can represent both the radius of the cone and the radius of the cylinder.

PAIR/SHARE How can you answer the question without knowing the radius or volume?

676

GROUP & DIFFERENTIATE

Identify groupings for differentiation based on the **Start** and problems 1–3. A recommended sequence of activities for each group is suggested below. Use the resources on the next page to differentiate and close the lesson.

Approaching Proficiency

- **RETEACH** Visual Model
- **REINFORCE** Problems 4, 5, 7

Meeting Proficiency

- **REINFORCE** Problems 4–8

Extending Beyond Proficiency

- **REINFORCE** Problems 4–8
- **EXTEND** Challenge

Have all students complete the **Close: Exit Ticket**.

Resources for Differentiation are found on the next page.

Refine Solving Problems with Volumes of Cylinders, Cones, and Spheres

Apply It

4 See ***Connect to Culture*** to support student engagement. Students may use the diameter of the test tube to find the radius of the half sphere, which is also the radius of the cylinder. Students may break the volume of the test tube into two parts and use formulas to find the volume of each part. The volume of the half sphere is $\frac{1}{2}$ the volume of a sphere. ***DOK 2***

5 **a.** $V(\text{fig. I}) = \frac{1}{3}\pi(6)^2(6) + \frac{1}{3}\pi(6)^2(6) = 144\pi$ and $V(\text{fig. II}) = \frac{1}{2} \cdot \frac{4}{3}\pi(6)^3 + \pi(6)^2(6) = 360\pi$. 360π is $2.5 \cdot 144\pi$.

b. $V(\text{fig. IV}) = \frac{1}{3}\pi(6)^2(6) + \pi(6)^2(6) = 288\pi$ and $V(\text{sphere with radius 6}) = \frac{4}{3}\pi(6)^3 = 288\pi$.

c. $V(\text{sphere with radius 6}) = \frac{4}{3}\pi(6)^3 = 288\pi$ and $V(\text{fig. I}) = \frac{1}{3}\pi(6)^2(6) + \frac{1}{3}\pi(6)^2(6) = 144\pi$. 288π is $2 \cdot 144\pi$.

d. $V(\text{fig. III}) = \frac{1}{3}\pi(6)^2(6) + \frac{1}{2} \cdot \frac{4}{3}\pi(6)^3 = 216\pi$ and $V(\text{fig. II}) = \frac{1}{2} \cdot \frac{4}{3}\pi(6)^3 + \pi(6)^2(6) = 360\pi$. 216π is $\frac{3}{5} \cdot 360\pi$.

e. $V(\text{fig. III}) = \frac{1}{3}\pi(6)^2(6) + \frac{1}{2} \cdot \frac{4}{3}\pi(6)^3 = 216\pi$ and $V(\text{cylinder with radius 6 and height 12}) = \pi(6)^2(12) = 432\pi$.

DOK 2

4 A laboratory test tube is cylindrical with a half-sphere bottom. The height of the cylindrical part is 6 inches. What is the volume of the test tube? Show your work. Use 3.14 for π.

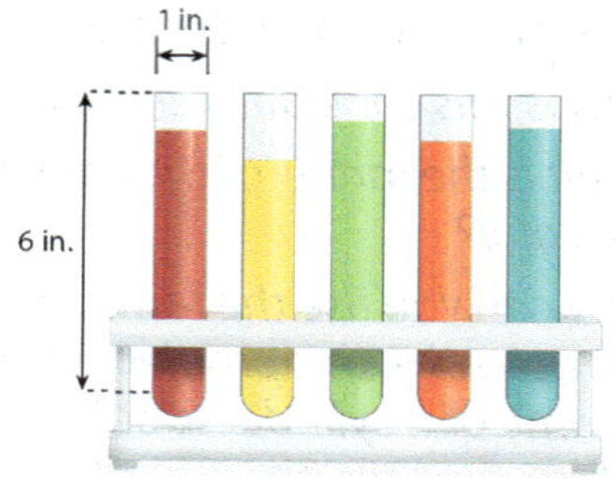

Possible work:

volume of cylinder $= \pi r^2 h = \pi(0.5)^2 \cdot 6 \approx 4.71$

volume of half sphere $= \frac{1}{2} \cdot \frac{4}{3}\pi r^3 = \frac{2 \cdot \pi \cdot (0.5)^3}{3} \approx 0.26$

volume of test tube $= 4.71 + 0.26 = 4.97$

SOLUTION The volume is about 4.97 in.^{3}.

5 Tell whether each statement is *True* or *False*.

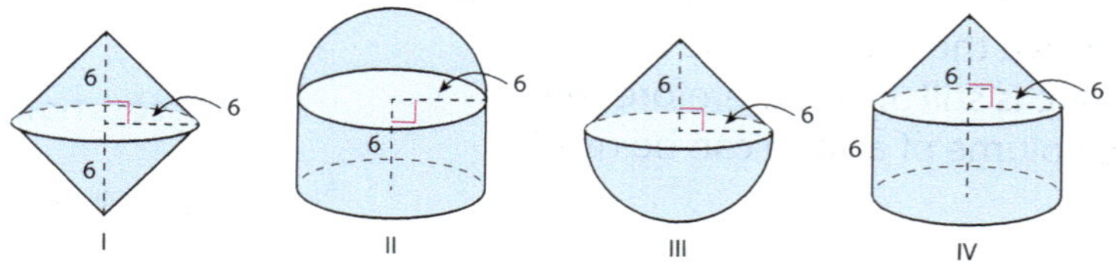

	True	False
a. The volume of Figure II is exactly twice the volume of Figure I.	○	●
b. The volume of Figure IV is equal to the volume of a sphere with radius 6.	●	○
c. The volume of a sphere with radius 6 is exactly twice the volume of Figure I.	●	○
d. The volume of Figure III is exactly one-third the volume of Figure II.	○	●
e. The volume of Figure III is equal to the volume of a cylinder with radius 6 and height 12.	○	●

677

DIFFERENTIATION

RETEACH

Visual Model

Find an unknown measure.

Students approaching proficiency with calculating the volume of cylinders will benefit from using the volume of one cylinder to find the height of another cylinder with a different radius.

Materials For display: 2 empty soup cans of different sizes, ruler, water

[Answers are based on a can of soup with a radius of 4 cm and height of 12 cm and a soup can with a radius of 5.5 cm and height of 15.5 cm.]

- Choose two students to find the radius and height of each can. Work with the class to calculate the volume of the smaller can, using the formula $V = \pi r^2 h$. Use 3.14 for π. [Sample answer: small can: 4 cm, 12 cm; large can: 5.5 cm, 15.5 cm; small can volume: about 602.88 cm^3]
- Ask: *Will the second can have the same volume as the first? How do you know?* [Sample answer: No; The radius and height are different.]
- Fill the smaller can with water.
- Ask: *If I pour the water from the first can into the second, how will the height of the water in the second can compare to the first? Why?* [Sample answer: The water will not go up as high in the second can. Since the radius is greater, the water gets more spread out and the height will be less.]
- Ask: *Which measure will stay the same when I pour the water from one can to another: radius, height, or volume?* [volume]
- Instruct students to do the following: Using the formula $V = \pi r^2 h$, substitute the volume of the first can (which is the same as the volume of the water) for V, the radius of the second can for r, and 3.14 for π. Then have them solve for h to find the height of the water in the second can.
- Ask: *What will be the height of the water in the second can?* [Sample answer: about 6.35 cm]
- Pour the water and confirm by measuring.

6 Students may use the given information to calculate the volume of wax in the cylindrical pitcher and the volume of a spherical candle. Then they may divide to calculate the number of spherical candles that can be made. *DOK 2*

7 The volume of a cone is given by $V = \frac{1}{3}\pi r^2 h$. *DOK 1*

8 Substitute 36π for V in the formula for the volume of a sphere and solve for r. Multiply the radius by 2 to find the diameter. *DOK 2*

CLOSE EXIT TICKET

9 **Math Journal** Look for understanding that the dimensions, r and h, must be whole numbers such that $\pi r^2 h$ is between 200 and 250.

Error Alert If students choose dimensions that do not give a volume between 200 ft^3 and 250 ft^3, then review the volume formula for a cylinder with them. Suggest they make a table with possible values for r and h and the corresponding V values and use guess-and-check to find r and h values that give V values in the correct range.

End of Lesson Checklist

INTERACTIVE GLOSSARY Support students by suggesting they work with a partner to give a verbal description of a cylinder, cone, and sphere.

SELF CHECK Have students review and check off any new skills on the Unit 6 Opener.

LESSON 28 | SESSION 4

6 Geraldo is making candles. He melts wax in a cylindrical pitcher and then pours the wax into spherical molds. The pitcher has a diameter of 6 in. The wax in the pitcher is 7 in. deep. How many spherical candles can he make if each mold has a diameter of 4 in.?

He can make 5 candles.

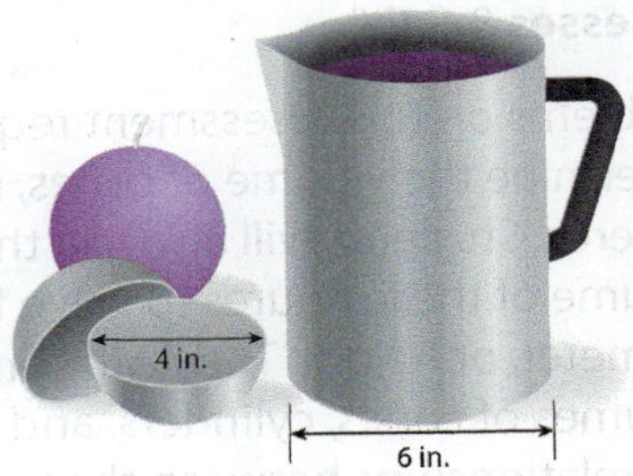

7 The volume of a cone with radius r and height h is $V = \frac{1}{3}\pi r^2 h$.

8 The volume of a sphere is 36π. What is the diameter of the sphere?

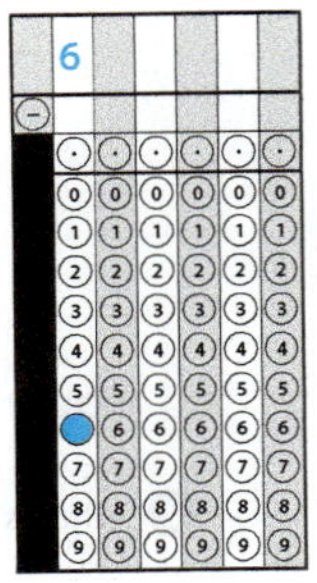

9 **Math Journal** You are designing a cylindrical tank that holds between 200 and 250 cubic feet of water. If the radius and height must be whole numbers, what could the dimensions of the tank be?

Possible work and answer:

$\pi r^2 h = 225$ $\quad V = \pi r^2 h$

$r^2 h \approx 72$ $\quad = \pi \cdot 3^2 \cdot 8$

$9 \cdot 8 = 72$ $\quad = 72\pi$

$3^2 \cdot 8 = 72$ $\quad \approx 226$

The dimensions could be $r = 3$ and $h = 8$.

End of Lesson Checklist

- [ ] **INTERACTIVE GLOSSARY** Find the entries for *cylinder, cone,* and *sphere*. For each entry, sketch an example of the figure.
- [ ] **SELF CHECK** Go back to the Unit 6 Opener and see what you can check off.

678

REINFORCE

Problems 4–8

Solve problems with calculating volumes of cylinders, cones, and spheres.

Students meeting proficiency will benefit from additional work with calculating volumes of cylinders, cones, and spheres by solving problems in a variety of formats.

- Have students work on their own or with a partner to solve the problems.
- Encourage students to show their work.

EXTEND

Challenge

Find the volume of a sphere using the Pythagorean Theorem.

Students extending beyond proficiency will benefit from using the Pythagorean Theorem to help them calculate the volume of a sphere.

- Have students work with a partner to solve this problem: *The cylinder has a height of 24 cm and a base area of 25π cm^2. What is the volume of the sphere?*

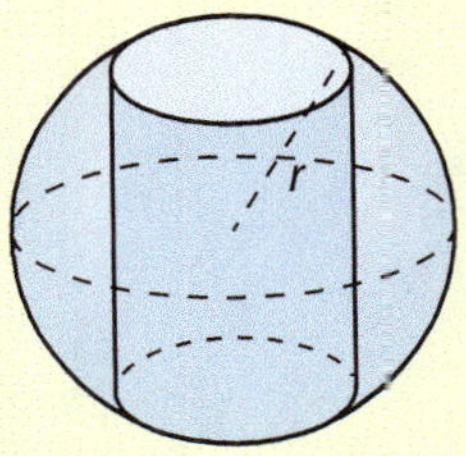

- Students may first use the formula for the area of a circle to find the radius of the base of the cylinder. They can then use the Pythagorean Theorem to find the radius of the sphere.

PERSONALIZE

i-Ready

Provide students with opportunities to work on their personalized instruction path with *i-Ready* Online Instruction to:

- fill prerequisite gaps.
- build up grade-level skills.

LESSON 28

Lesson Quiz

TESTED SKILLS

Assesses 8.G.C.9

Problems on this assessment require students to determine the volume of cones, cylinders, and spheres. Students will also use the formulas for volume of these figures to solve for the radius, diameter, or height. They will compare the volumes of cones, cylinders, and spheres and use the relationships between the volumes of the figures to solve for unknown measurements. Students will also need to be familiar with squaring and cubing numbers and solving equations.

Alternately, teachers may assign the **Digital Comprehension Check** online to assess student understanding of this material.

Error Alert Errors may result if students:

- apply the incorrect volume formula for a figure.
- incorrectly substitute values into a formula.
- assume that figures with the same volume always have the same height, radius, or diameter.
- make a computation error.

Problem Notes

1. Students could solve the problem by finding the radius of the cylinder by dividing 10 by 2 to get 5, then substituting values into the formula for volume of a cylinder, $V = \pi r^2 h$.

   (2 points)

   DOK 1 | **8.G.C.9**

2. Students could solve the problem by substituting the given values into the formula for volume of a cone, $V = \frac{1}{3}\pi r^2 h$.

   (2 points)

   DOK 1 | **8.G.C.9**

LESSON 28 • QUIZ   Name:

➤ **Solve the problems.**

1. What is the volume of a cylinder with a diameter of 10 m and a height of 3 m? Use 3.14 for π. Show your work. *(2 points)*

Possible student work:

$V = \pi r^2 h$

$= \pi \cdot \left(\frac{10}{2}\right)^2 \cdot 3$

$= \pi \cdot 5^2 \cdot 3$

$= 75\pi$

≈ 235.5

SOLUTION 235.5 m^3

2. What is the volume of a cone with a radius of 2 ft and a height of 9 ft? Use 3.14 for π. Show your work. *(2 points)*

Possible student work:

$V = \frac{1}{3}\pi r^2 h$

$= \frac{1}{3} \cdot \pi \cdot 2^2 \cdot 9$

$= 12\pi$

≈ 37.68

SOLUTION 37.68 ft^3

Short Response Scoring Rubric

Points	Expectations
2	Response has the correct solution(s) and includes well-organized, clear, and concise work demonstrating thorough understanding of mathematical concepts and/or procedures.
1	Response contains mostly correct solution(s) and shows partial understanding of mathematical concepts and/or procedures.
0	Response shows no attempt at finding a solution and no effort to demonstrate an understanding of mathematical concepts and/or procedures.

3 **B is correct.** Students could solve the problem by setting the formula for the volume of a cone equal to the formula for the volume of a cylinder, $\frac{1}{3}\pi r^2 18 = \pi r^2 h$, substituting the known value, and then solving for the height of the cylinder.

A is not correct. This answer is the result of dividing 18 by 3 incorrectly.

C is not correct. This answer is the result of forgetting $\frac{1}{3}$ in the formula for the volume of a cone or assuming that the two figures have the same height.

D is not correct. This answer is the result of using a factor of 3 in the formula for volume of a cone instead of a factor of $\frac{1}{3}$.

(1 point)

DOK 2 | 8.G.C.9

4 Students could solve the problem by finding the volume of each figure and then subtracting the volumes.

(2 points)

DOK 2 | 8.G.C.9

5 (1 point)

DOK 2 | 8.G.C.9

LESSON 28 • QUIZ Name:

3 A cylinder and a cone have the same radius and the same volume. The height of the cone is 18 cm. What is the height of the cylinder? *(1 point)*

A 3 cm

(B) 6 cm

C 18 cm

D 27 cm

4 A sphere has a radius of 5 in. A cone has a radius of 6 in. and a height of 8 in. What is the difference in the volumes of the cone and the sphere, to the nearest cubic inch? Use 3.14 for π. Show your work. *(2 points)*

Possible student work:

volume of sphere:

$= \frac{4}{3}\pi r^3$

$= \frac{4}{3} \cdot \pi \cdot 5^3$

$= 166\frac{2}{3}\pi$

volume of cone:

$= \frac{1}{3}\pi r^2 h$

$= \frac{1}{3} \cdot \pi \cdot 6^2 \cdot 8$

$= 96\pi$

difference in volumes $= 166\frac{2}{3}\pi - 96\pi = 70\frac{2}{3}\pi \approx 221.89$

SOLUTION about 222 in.^{3}

5 The volume of a sphere is 288π. What is the diameter of the sphere? Record your answer on the grid. Then fill in the bubbles. *(1 point)*

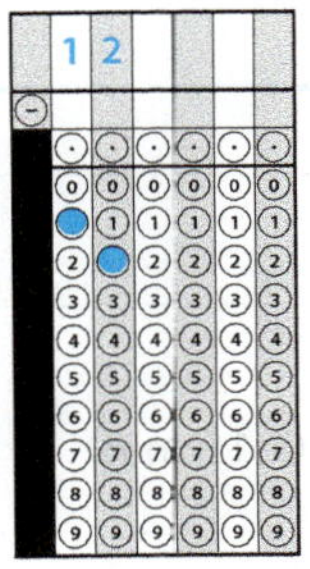

DIFFERENTIATION

RETEACH Tools for Instruction

Students who require additional support for prerequisite or on-level skills will benefit from activities that provide targeted skills instruction.

GRADE 8

- **Lesson 28** Volume of Cylinders and Cones

REINFORCE Math Center Activity

Students who require practice to reinforce concepts and skills and deepen understanding will benefit from small group collaborative games and activities (available in on-level, below-level, and above-level versions).

GRADE 8

- **Lesson 28** Use Volume Vocabulary for Cylinders, Cones, and Spheres

EXTEND Enrichment Activity

Students who have achieved proficiency with concepts and skills and are ready for additional challenges will benefit from group collaborative games and activities that extend understanding.

GRADE 8

- **Lesson 28** Double Up

Overview | Irrational Numbers, the Pythagorean Theorem, and Volume

MATH FOCUS

Focus Standards

8.NS.A.2, 8.EE.A.2, 8.G.B.7, 8.G.C.9

STANDARDS FOR MATHEMATICAL PRACTICE (SMP)

This lesson provides support for:

1 Make sense of problems and persevere in solving them.

3 Construct viable arguments and critique the reasoning of others.

6 Attend to precision.

Additional SMP

2, 4, 5, 7, 8

Lesson at a Glance

In this lesson, students apply multiple skills from the unit to solve real-world problems related to using renewable energy sources in farming. Problems involve finding square roots, using fractions and decimals to express rational numbers, understanding and applying the Pythagorean Theorem, and using the formulas for the volume of a cylinder and the volume of a cone.

Key Skills

- Use the Pythagorean Theorem to find unknown side lengths of right triangles.
- Find rational approximations for irrational numbers.
- Use volume formulas for a cylinder and a cone.
- Calculate with rational numbers that are expressed as fractions and decimals.
- Apply the perimeter and area formulas for a square to solve problems.

Pacing Guide

Items marked with ✦ are available on the **Teacher Toolbox**.

	MATERIALS
SESSION 1 (45–60 min)	
Installing a Wind Turbine	
Study an Example Problem and Solution (20–30 min) Example Problem (10–15 min) | One Student's Solution (10–15 min) **Try Another Approach** (25–30 min) Plan It (5 min) | Solve It (15–20 min) | Reflect (5 min)	**Math Toolkit** grid paper, ruler, unit cubes For each student: Activity Sheet *Solution Sheet* ✦
SESSION 2 (45–60 min)	
Designing a Food-Waste Digester	
Discuss Models and Strategies (20–30 min) Plan It and Solve It (15–25 min) | Reflect (5 min)	**Math Toolkit** compass, grid paper, ruler For each student: Activity Sheet *Solution Sheet* ✦
Fencing a Solar Farm	
Persevere On Your Own (25–30 min) Solve It (20–25 min) | Reflect (5 min)	**Math Toolkit** grid paper For each student: Activity Sheet *Solution Sheet* ✦

DIFFERENTIATION

RETEACH Extra Support
Materials For each student: grid paper

EXTEND Challenge

Purpose

- **Examine** a problem that involves the Pythagorean Theorem and irrational numbers.
- **Analyze** a sample solution to identify what makes it a good solution.
- **Demonstrate** that the problem has more than one approach and more than one solution.

Study an Example Problem and Solution

Installing a Wind Turbine

Make Sense of the Problem

Present the Installing a Wind Turbine problem and use **Three Reads** to help students make sense of it. For each read, have a different volunteer read aloud each section of information.

After the first read, be sure students understand the terms *anchor point* and *guy wire* and how the guy wires support the tower.

> **ASK** *How do the side view and top view help you understand the parts of the wind turbine and how it is installed?*
>
> **LISTEN FOR** The side view shows that the anchor points are on the ground and that three guy wires extend from each anchor point and attach to the tower at three different heights. The top view shows that there are three anchor points spaced evenly around the tower.

After the second read, listen for students to articulate that they need to find the total length of steel cable Adnan will need for the guy wires.

After the third read, have students identify the important quantities and relationships in the problem, including any quantities that involve student choice. Ensure that students understand that student choice means there can be multiple correct solutions to the problem.

> **ASK** *What are the important numbers and relationships?*
>
> **LISTEN FOR** The important numbers are the tower heights and the heights to *A*, *B*, and *C*. An important relationship is that distance from the base of the tower to the anchor point is $\frac{1}{2}$ to $\frac{3}{4}$ of the tower height.

Invite students to share their ideas about how they might use concepts from the unit to solve this problem. Allow them to describe different approaches, but do not implement any strategies.

Math in Action | SESSION 1

Irrational Numbers, the Pythagorean Theorem, and Volume

Math IN Action

SMP 1 Make sense of problems and persevere in solving them.

Study an Example Problem and Solution

➤ **Read this problem involving the Pythagorean Theorem and irrational numbers. Then look at one student's solution to this problem on the following pages.**

Installing a Wind Turbine

Adnan plans to install a wind turbine to help generate electricity for his farm. Steel cables called guy wires will support the tower for the wind turbine. Read the information about the guy wires.

Choose a tower height, and decide how far the anchor points for the guy wires will be from the base of the tower. What is the total length of steel cable Adnan will need for the guy wires?

Guy Wires for the Turbine Tower

- **Use 3 anchor points.** All should be the same distance from the base of the tower.
- **Use 3 guy wires** to connect each anchor point to the tower at three different heights.
- **Plan for an extra 5 feet** of length for attaching each wire to the anchor point and tower.

Tower Height (ft)	Height to *A* (ft)	Height to *B* (ft)	Height to *C* (ft)
70	65	44	22
80	75	50	25
90	85	57	28

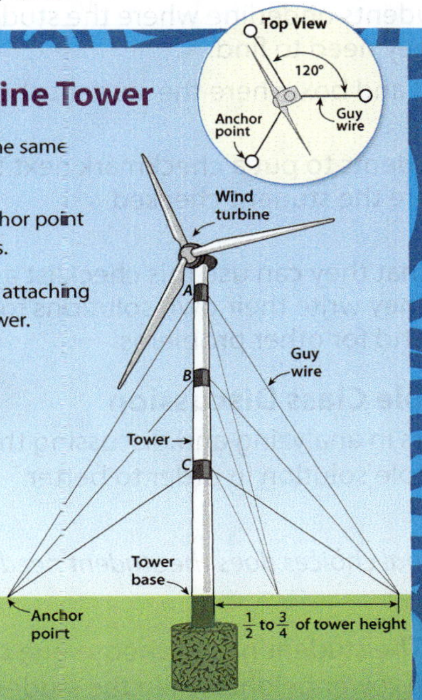

679

CONNECT TO CONTEXT

Installing a Wind Turbine Ask students whether they have ever seen a wind turbine or a wind farm. Wind turbines are used to generate energy. The wind blows the turbine blades, which causes them to turn. This turning motion is transferred to a generator to produce electricity. Wind turbines are usually placed where there is a lot of wind and open space. In the United States, there are over 57,000 wind turbines. As of 2018, wind turbines were responsible for producing enough electricity to power 30 million homes. Wind farms are a group of wind turbines in the same area. One of the benefits of wind farms is that they leave 98% of the farmland undisturbed, making it possible to use the land for farming or ranching.

Assumption Alert Point out that it is sometimes necessary to make assumptions as part of modeling with mathematics. For this problem, it is assumed that the tower makes a right angle with the ground.

One Student's Solution

Read through the sample solution to the Installing a Wind Turbine problem together, one section at a time. Point out that the Notice That boxes provide important information about this student's solution.

Problem-Solving Checklist

Explain to students that they will use the Problem-Solving Checklist on this page to identify what makes this a good solution.

- Have students look at the sample solution to find and circle where the student wrote known, or given, information.
- Then have students underline where the student wrote what they need to find.
- As a class, find and box where the student showed their work.
- Finally, ask students to put a checkmark next to the place where the student checked their solution.
- Tell students that they can use this checklist as a model when they write their own solutions for this problem and for other problems.

Facilitate Whole Class Discussion

Support students in analyzing and discussing the steps of the sample solution in order to better understand it.

ASK *What initial choices does the student need to make?*

LISTEN FOR The student has to choose one of the three given tower heights. Then the student has to choose the distance between the anchor points and the base of the tower from a range of $\frac{1}{2}$ to $\frac{3}{4}$ of the tower height chosen.

ASK *Why does the student draw three different right triangles?*

LISTEN FOR The student assumes the tower makes a right angle with the ground. So, when each guy wire is attached to the tower, a right triangle is formed. Each anchor point holds three guy wires that attach to the tower at three different heights, *A*, *B*, and *C*. Each of the three right triangles corresponds to one of the three heights.

One Student's Solution

NOTICE THAT . . . The side view of the tower shows that the distance between the anchor points and the base of the tower should be $\frac{1}{2}$ to $\frac{3}{4}$ of the tower height.

First, I have to choose a tower height and decide how far the anchor points will be from the base of the tower.

I will choose the shortest tower height from the table, 70 feet.

I will make the distance between the anchor points and the base of the tower $\frac{1}{2}$ of the tower height, or 35 feet.

Next, I will draw pictures to show the given information about the three guy wires from an anchor point.

I know the heights to points *A*, *B*, and *C* for a 70-foot tower.

NOTICE THAT . . . Each guy wire forms the hypotenuse of a right triangle with vertices at the base of the tower, the anchor point, and point *A*, *B*, or *C*.

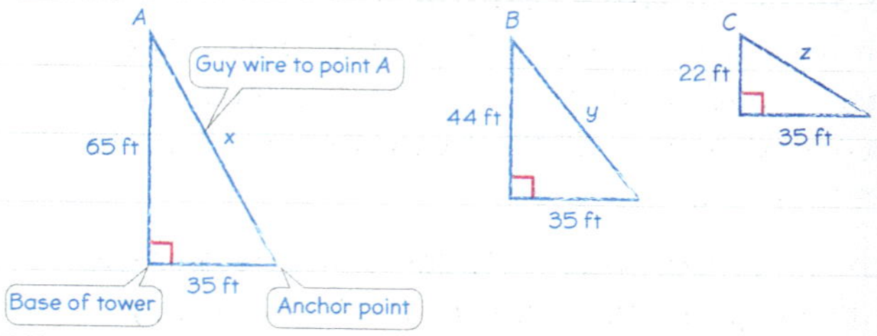

Then, I can use the Pythagorean Theorem to calculate the exact length of each guy wire.

Wire to point *A*:	Wire to point *B*:	Wire to point *C*:
$65^2 + 35^2 = x^2$	$44^2 + 35^2 = y^2$	$22^2 + 35^2 = z^2$
$4{,}225 + 1{,}225 = x^2$	$1{,}936 + 1{,}225 = y^2$	$484 + 1{,}225 = z^2$
$5{,}450 = x^2$	$3{,}161 = y^2$	$1{,}709 = z^2$
$\sqrt{5{,}450} = x$	$\sqrt{3{,}161} = y$	$\sqrt{1{,}709} = z$

Problem-Solving Checklist

- ☐ Tell what is known.
- ☐ Tell what the problem is asking.
- ☐ Show all your work.
- ☐ Show that the solution works.

Prompt students to think about how the Pythagorean Theorem is used in this situation.

ASK *Why can the student use the Pythagorean Theorem to calculate the length of each guy wire?*

LISTEN FOR The student knows the distance from the base of the tower to the anchor point and the heights to *A*, *B*, and *C*. These are the lengths of the legs of the right triangles. The student can use the Pythagorean Theorem to solve for the length of each hypotenuse, which is the length of the guy wire.

ASK *Why are only the positive square roots given as the answers?*

LISTEN FOR The variables *x*, *y*, and *z* represent the distances from the points *A*, *B*, and *C* to the anchor points. Distance cannot be negative.

Discuss the fact that the student can only find decimal approximations of the square roots, not exact values.

ASK *Why can't the student find the exact lengths of the cables?*

LISTEN FOR These lengths are square roots of whole numbers that are not perfect squares. Square roots of whole numbers that are not perfect squares are irrational numbers. This means they cannot be expressed as terminating or repeating decimals.

ASK *Why do you think the student used tables in the solution?*

LISTEN FOR The tables were used to stay organized and keep track of which values the square roots lie between.

Have students discuss the use of estimation and appropriate precision from the sample solution.

ASK *Why is rounding up to the next whole number appropriate in this context?*

LISTEN FOR The guy wires attach to the tower. Rounding down could result in a length of guy wire that is too short to connect.

ASK *Why does the student add 5 feet to each length of guy wire?*

LISTEN FOR The requirements for the problem state to plan for an extra 5 feet to attach the guy wires to the anchor point and tower.

Have students review the final step of the solution.

ASK *Why does the student multiply the length of each guy wire by 3 to find the total length of cable needed?*

LISTEN FOR There are three anchor points. The three lengths the student found are for just one anchor point, so the student has to multiply each length by 3.

Math in Action

Now, I can find a rational approximation of each irrational number.

To make sure there is enough cable, I will round up.

Wire to point A: $x = \sqrt{5{,}450}$

The length of the wire to point A is between 73 feet and 74 feet.

x	70	72	73	74
x^2	4,900	5,184	5,329	5,476

Wire to point B: $y = \sqrt{3{,}161}$

The length of the wire to point B is between 56 feet and 57 feet.

y	50	52	54	56	57
y^2	2,500	2,704	2,916	3,136	3,249

Wire to point C: $z = \sqrt{1{,}709}$

The length of the wire to point C is between 41 feet and 42 feet.

z	40	41	42
z^2	1,600	1,681	1,764

Next, I will add an extra 5 feet to each length to account for attaching the guy wires to the anchor point and tower.

Wire to point A: $74 + 5 = 79$

Wire to point B: $57 + 5 = 62$

Wire to point C: $42 + 5 = 47$

Finally, I will find the total length of the guy wires.

There are 3 anchor points, so I can multiply each of the different lengths by 3 and then add.

$3(79) + 3(62) + 3(47) = 237 + 186 + 141 = 564$

Adnan will need about 564 feet of steel cable if he chooses a 70-foot tower and places the anchor points 35 feet from the base.

NOTICE THAT . . . You can start to estimate each square root by approximating to the nearest ten. Because $70^2 = 4{,}900$ and $80^2 = 6{,}400$, you know that $70 < \sqrt{5{,}450} < 80$.

NOTICE THAT . . . You could also add to find the total length of the guy wires to one anchor point and then multiply the sum by 3.

681

After discussing the sample solution, have a volunteer summarize the steps taken to solve the problem.

ASK *How can you summarize the steps in the sample solution?*

LISTEN FOR Choose a tower height and decide how far the anchor points will be from the base of the tower. Draw three right triangles whose hypotenuses represent the lengths of the guy wires from the anchor point to each of the points A, B, and C on the tower. Use the Pythagorean Theorem to find the exact length of the hypotenuse of each triangle. Then find a rational approximation of each square root. Add 5 feet to each guy wire length to allow enough cable to attach the wires to the anchor point and tower. Multiply each length by 3 and add the results to find the total length of guy wire needed for the chosen tower.

Try Another Approach

Installing a Wind Turbine

Materials For each student: Activity Sheet *Solution Sheet*

Facilitate Whole Class Discussion

After reviewing the sample student solution on the previous pages, prompt students to look for different approaches to solve the problem.

ASK *What are some different steps you could use to solve the problem?*

LISTEN FOR Select a different tower height. This makes the values for the heights *A*, *B*, and *C* where the guy wires attach to the tower different, too. It also changes the range of allowable distances from the base of the tower to the anchor points. Scale drawings of the triangles can be made on grid paper and the distances measured with a ruler.

Plan It

Facilitate Whole Class Discussion

Read the Plan It questions from the next page aloud. Prompt students to discuss how they will approach and solve this problem in another way.

ASK *How will the solution be different if you use a greater tower height?*

LISTEN FOR A greater tower height has greater heights for points *A*, *B*, and *C*, where the guy wires are attached to the tower. Therefore, the hypotenuses of the right triangles will be longer and more steel cable will be required for the guy wires.

ASK *How will you be able to show that the distance from the base of the tower to the anchor points is $\frac{1}{2}$ to $\frac{3}{4}$ of the tower height?*

LISTEN FOR I can multiply the tower height by $\frac{1}{2}$ and then by $\frac{3}{4}$ and show that the distance is between the two results.

Try Another Approach

➤ **There are many ways to solve problems. Think about how you might solve the Installing a Wind Turbine problem in a different way.**

Problem-Solving Checklist

- ☐ Tell what is known.
- ☐ Tell what the problem is asking.
- ☐ Show all your work.
- ☐ Show that the solution works.

Installing a Wind Turbine

Adnan plans to install a wind turbine to help generate electricity for his farm. Steel cables called guy wires will support the tower for the wind turbine. Read the information about the guy wires.

Choose a tower height, and decide how far the anchor points for the guy wires will be from the base of the tower. What is the total length of steel cable Adnan will need for the guy wires?

Guy Wires for the Turbine Tower

- **Use 3 anchor points.** All should be the same distance from the base of the tower.
- **Use 3 guy wires** to connect each anchor point to the tower at three different heights.
- **Plan for an extra 5 feet** of length for attaching each wire to the anchor point and tower.

Tower Height (ft)	Height to *A* (ft)	Height to *B* (ft)	Height to *C* (ft)
70	65	44	22
80	75	50	25
90	85	57	28

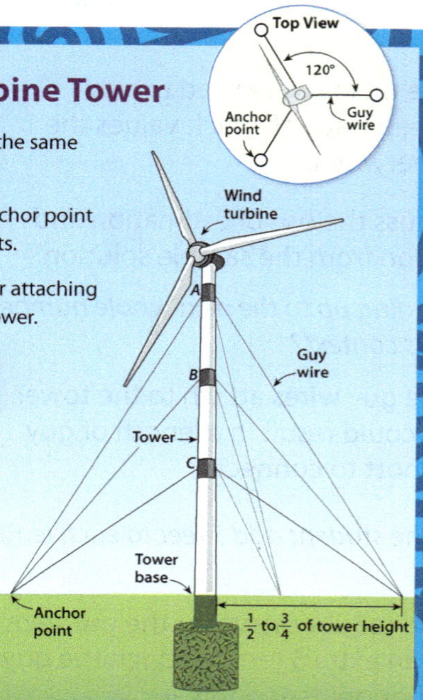

Solve It

Problem-Solving Tips

Introduce the Problem-Solving Tips as ideas students may use to explain their thinking. Remind them to also use the Problem-Solving Checklist to make sure their answer is complete.

Have students write their own complete solutions on a copy of Activity Sheet *Solution Sheet* or a blank sheet of paper.

Reflect

As they work, have students share their thinking with a partner and discuss the Reflect questions.

As time permits, have students explain their solutions to the class.

Possible Solution

I will choose the 80-ft tower and make the distance between the anchor points and the base of the tower $\frac{1}{2}$ of the tower height, or 40 ft.

I will make scale drawings of the right triangles corresponding to the heights *A*, *B*, and *C* on centimeter grid paper. I will let 1 cm in the drawings represent 5 ft.

Wire to *A*: The distance to the anchor point is 40 ft, which is 8 cm on the grid. The distance to *A* is 75 ft, which is 15 cm on the grid. So, I drew a right triangle with legs of lengths 8 cm and 15 cm, measured along grid lines. I used a ruler to measure the hypotenuse and found that it was 17 cm long. Each centimeter represents 5 ft, so 17 cm represents 17(5), or 85 ft.

Wire to *B*: The distance to *B* is 50 ft, which is 10 cm on the grid. So, I drew a right triangle with legs of lengths 8 cm and 10 cm, measured along grid lines. I measured the hypotenuse and found that it was a little less than 13 cm long. This represents about 13(5), or 65 ft.

Wire to *C*: The distance to *C* is 25 ft, which is 5 cm on the grid. So, I drew a right triangle with legs of lengths 8 cm and 5 cm, measured along grid lines. I measured the hypotenuse and found that it was about 9.5 cm long. This represents about 9.5(5), or 47.5 ft. I rounded up to 48 ft.

Now, I can add 5 ft to each guy wire length and multiply the sum of the lengths by 3:

$$3(90 + 70 + 53) = 639$$

Adnan will need approximately 639 ft of cable for the guy wires if he chooses the 80-ft tower and places anchor points 40 ft from the base.

Math in Action

Plan It

➤ **Answer these questions to help you start thinking about a plan.**

a. What height will you use for the tower of the wind turbine?

b. How far from the base of the turbine will the anchor points be? How can you show that this distance is between $\frac{1}{2}$ and $\frac{3}{4}$ of the tower height?

Solve It

➤ **Find a different solution for the Installing a Wind Turbine problem. Show all your work on a separate sheet of paper. You may want to use the Problem-Solving Tips to get started.**

PROBLEM-SOLVING TIPS

Math Toolkit grid paper, ruler, unit cubes

Key Terms

right triangle	hypotenuse	Pythagorean Theorem
square root of *x*	leg	rational number
perfect square	approximation	irrational number

Models You may want to use . . .

- a picture or diagram to organize the information you are given.
- the Pythagorean Theorem to find unknown side lengths of right triangles.
- perfect squares to help you find rational approximations of irrational numbers.

Reflect

Use Mathematical Practices As you work through the problem, discuss these questions with a partner.

- **Make Sense of Problems** How can you tell whether the lengths you calculate for the guy wires are reasonable?
- **Repeated Reasoning** What steps can you use to estimate the square root of a 4-digit number that is not a perfect square?

683

Scoring Rubric (4 points)

Points	Expectations
4	The solution and explanation are clear and complete. The hypotenuse lengths are reasonable, and the calculations for the total amount of steel cable required are correct.
3	The solution is complete, with minor errors in either one of the hypotenuse lengths or in the calculation of the total amount of steel cable required.
2	All parts of the task were attempted. One or more errors were made in calculating hypotenuse lengths. These errors may have caused the total amount of steel cable required to be unreasonable.
1	Some parts of the task were not attempted. Explanations are missing or incomplete, and there are several signficant calculation errors.

Math in Action

Purpose

- **Understand** two new open-ended, multi-step problems involving volume of cylinders and cones and finding the side length and perimeter of a square with a given area.
- **Choose** appropriate models and strategies to plan for and solve the problems.

Discuss Models and Strategies

Designing a Food-Waste Digester

Materials For each student: Activity Sheet *Solution Sheet*

Make Sense of the Problem

Present the Designing a Food-Waste Digester problem and use **Three Reads** to help students make sense of it. Have different volunteers take turns reading aloud each section of information.

ASK *What are some clarifying questions you could ask about the details of the problem?*

LISTEN FOR Student responses may include questions about the requirements for the measurements of the digester.

Invite volunteers to point out what is known and what they need to figure out.

ASK *What do you need to include in your solution?*

LISTEN FOR I need to include a design that shows the diameter of the digester and the heights of the cylinder and cone. I also must show that the volume and diameter of the digester, the height of the cylinder, and the diameter-to-height ratio for the cylinder are all in the specified ranges and that the height of the cone is about $\frac{1}{12}$ of the diameter.

Ensure that students understand the requirements for the diameter-to-height ratio for the cylinder.

ASK *How can you verify that your choices for the diameter and the height of the cylinder meet the ratio requirements in the last row of the table?*

LISTEN FOR Students may point out that the ratios indicate that the diameter must be between 2 and 4 times the height. So, when they divide the diameter by the height, the result should be between 2 and 4.

Discuss Models and Strategies

Problem-Solving Checklist

- ☐ Tell what is known.
- ☐ Tell what the problem is asking.
- ☐ Show all your work.
- ☐ Show that the solution works.

➤ **Read the problem. Write a solution on a separate sheet of paper. Remember, there can be lots of ways to solve a problem.**

Designing a Food-Waste Digester

A city near Adnan's farm is planning to build a biogas plant. At the plant, food waste from the city and feed waste from local farms, including Adnan's, will be loaded into tanks called digesters. Inside the digesters, bacteria will break down the waste and produce a combination of gases called biogas—a renewable energy source.

A team of engineers is designing the digesters at the biogas plant. Read through their notes, and then help them make a design for the digesters.

Design for Food-Waste Digesters

The digesters will have a cone-shaped portion below ground, a cylinder-shaped portion above ground, and a dome-shaped top.

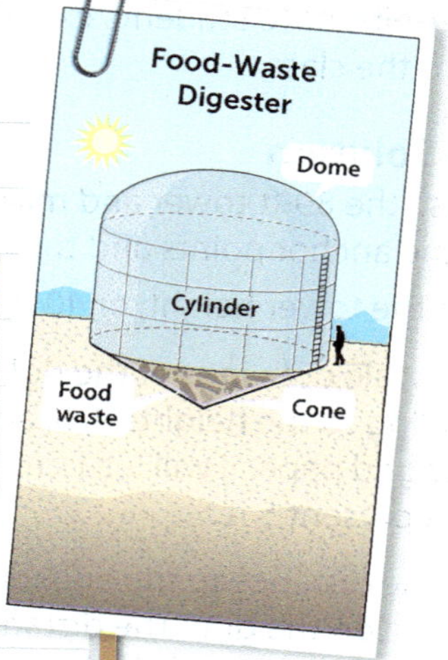

Requirements:

Measurement	Minimum	Maximum
Volume (not including dome)	1,400 m^3	2,000 m^3
Diameter of digester	10 m	22 m
Height of cylinder	5 m	12 m
Diameter-to-height ratio for cylinder	2 : 1	4 : 1

Also, the height of the cone should be about $\frac{1}{12}$ of the diameter.

WHAT WE NEED TO DO:

- Provide a design that shows the diameter of the digester and the heights of the cylinder and cone. Do not worry about the height of the dome for now.
- Show that the design meets all of the requirements.

684

Discuss possible steps, ways to organize the information, and techniques that might be helpful. Invite students to take notes.

ASK *What are some ways that you can organize your work?*

LISTEN FOR Students may suggest making a table or a labeled diagram to show the combinations of measurements they choose and to verify the requirements have been met.

CONNECT TO CONTEXT

Designing a Food-Waste Digester Ask students whether they have ever heard of biogas or seen a biogas plant. Biogas plants produce a renewable energy source called biogas by implementing a process known as anaerobic digestion. In biogas plants, organic matter, such as municipal food waste and farm feed waste, is converted to biogas as it decomposes. Not only do biogas plants make a source of renewable energy, but they also reduce the amount of waste being placed in landfills and decrease our dependence on fossil fuels.

Appropriate Precision Point out to students that the problem states that the height of the cone should be *about* $\frac{1}{12}$ of the diameter. It does not need to be exactly $\frac{1}{12}$ of the diameter.

Plan It and Solve It

Problem-Solving Checklist & Tips

Have students use various resources, including the Problem-Solving Checklist and the Problem-Solving Tips, as they begin to plan a solution.

Support Student Work

Have students work in pairs to discuss their preliminary solution strategies and the Reflect questions. Discuss a variety of approaches as a class. Let students revise their plans and discuss again with a partner.

When students are confident that their plans make sense, have them write a complete solution on a copy of Activity Sheet *Solution Sheet* or a blank sheet of paper.

Reflect

As they work, have students share their thinking with a partner and discuss the Reflect questions.

As time permits, have students explain their solutions to the class.

Possible Solution

My table of values is shown with calculations below.

Measurement	Choice
Volume (not including dome)	1,697 m^3
Diameter of digester	16 m
Height of cylinder	8 m
Diameter-to-height ratio for cylinder	16 : 8, or 2 : 1

I used $\frac{1}{12}(16) = \frac{4}{3}$ m as the height of the cone.

Cylinder: $V = \pi r^2 h = \pi(8)^2 \cdot 8 \approx 1{,}608$

Cone: $V = \frac{1}{3}\pi r^2 h = \frac{1}{3}\pi(8)^2 \cdot \frac{4}{3} \approx 89$

The volume of the cylinder is about 1,608 m^3. The volume of the cone is about 89 m^3. The total volume is about 1,608 m^3 + 89 m^3, or 1,697 m^3.

I checked each value to verify all criteria are met.

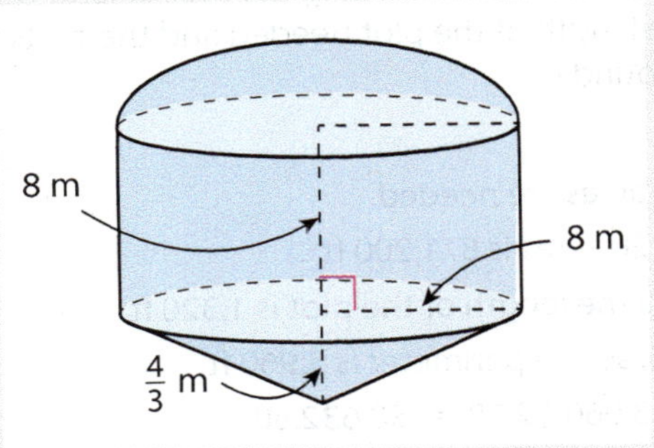

Math in Action

Plan It and Solve It

➤ **Find a solution to the Designing a Food-Waste Digester problem.**

Write a detailed plan and support your answer. Be sure to include:

- a design for the food-waste digester that includes its diameter and the heights of the cylinder and cone.
- evidence that your design meets all of the requirements listed in the notes.

PROBLEM-SOLVING TIPS

Math Toolkit compass, grid paper, ruler

Key Terms

cylinder	cone	diameter
radius	volume	irrational number
π	approximation	sum

Sentence Starters

- If I choose . . . for the diameter of the digester, then the height of the cylinder should be between . . . and . . .
- If I choose . . . for the diameter of the digester, then the height of the cone should be about . . .

Reflect

Use Mathematical Practices As you work through the problem, discuss these questions with a partner.

- **Persevere** Does your first design meet all of the requirements? If not, how can you adjust your design?
- **Use Structure** Which dimension has the greatest effect on the volume of the digester—the diameter, the height of the cylinder, or the height of the cone? Explain.

In the United States, the second largest municipal solid waste sent to landfills is food.

685

Scoring Rubric (4 points)

Points	Expectations
4	The solution is complete. It includes a detailed plan that specifies the diameter and the heights of the cylinder and cone. Evidence that the design meets all of the requirements is given. A design is provided, and the measurements are correctly labeled.
3	The solution is complete, with minor errors. All dimensions are given and meet the problem requirements. Minor errors were made in calculating the volume. A design is provided, and measurements are correctly labeled.
2	All parts of the problem were attempted. Some of the dimensions do not meet the problem requirements. Correct volume formulas were used, but there are errors in the calculations. A design is provided but includes several errors.
1	The solution is incomplete. Some of the dimensions do not meet the problem requirements. Volume calculations are missing or incorrect. The design is missing or incorrect.

Persevere On Your Own

Fencing a Solar Farm

Materials For each student: Activity Sheet *Solution Sheet*

Make Sense of the Problem

Present the Fencing a Solar Farm problem and use **Three Reads** to help students make sense of it. Have different volunteers take turns reading aloud each section of information. Be sure students understand that any number between 770 and 850 can be chosen as the number of solar panels per acre.

CONNECT TO CONTEXT

Fencing a Solar Farm Ask students whether they have seen a home with solar panels on the roof. These solar panels provide energy to the home. Solar farms do the same thing on a much larger scale. By using thousands of solar panels, a solar farm can generate electricity to power thousands of homes and businesses. Energy companies place their solar panels on land rented from farmers. Many energy companies are turning to sheep farmers to rent land because the sheep can graze on the grass both under and in between the rows of panels.

UNIT 6 Math in Action | SESSION 2

Persevere On Your Own

➤ **Read the problem. Write a solution on a separate sheet of paper.**

Problem-Solving Checklist

- ☐ Tell what is known.
- ☐ Tell what the problem is asking.
- ☐ Show all your work.
- ☐ Show that the solution works.

Fencing a Solar Farm

An energy company is planning to rent part of Adnan's farm. The company will install solar panels on the land to help produce electricity for a nearby city. Read this email between two employees of the energy company, and help complete the assignment.

Delete Archive Reply Reply All Forward

To: Emily
Subject: Fencing for New Solar Farm

Hi Emily,

We are planning to install 16,000 solar panels on Adnan's farm. We estimate that we can install between 770 and 850 solar panels per acre.

Our rental agreement allows Adnan to graze his sheep underneath the panels, which means we'll need to build a fence suitable for sheep around the land we rent. To keep the cost of fencing down, we are planning to rent a square piece of land. We can spend up to $8,000 for fencing.

Fencing for Sheep

Fencing Type	Cost per Linear Foot
Eight-strand wire	$2.18
Woven wire	$1.40

YOUR ASSIGNMENT:
- Estimate the number of acres of land we need to rent.
- Estimate our cost to fence the land with each type of fencing.
- Determine which type or types of fencing we can afford.

Thank you!

Kimani

P.S. One acre is equal to 43,560 square feet. You might need this fact for your calculations.

686

DIFFERENTIATION | Use with Fencing a Solar Farm

RETEACH

Extra Support
Learning about acres.

Some students may need help understanding what an acre represents in terms of measuring land.

- Ask: *What is an acre?* [a unit used to represent area, usually of land]
- Explain that an acre is a unit of area even though it is not the square of a linear unit, like square feet or square meters.
- Ask: *Does an acre of land have a particular shape?* [No; an acre can be any shape.]
- Ask. *How many square feet are equal to 1 acre?* [43,560 ft^2]
- Ask: *If an acre of land is shaped like a square, then what do you know about the length and width of the land?* [They are the same.]
- Ask: *If an acre of land is a square, what mathematical operation can be used to find the length of the sides in feet?* [square root]

EXTEND

Challenge
Solve a different problem.

The energy company is planning to install 16,000 solar panels, with 800 panels per acre. They plan to rent a rectangular plot of land with a width of 660 ft. Find the length of the plot needed and the costs to build both fence types around it.

Possible Solution:

16,000 ÷ 800 = 20, so 20 acres are needed.

20 • 43,560 = 871,200, so 20 acres is 871,200 ft^2.

871,200 ÷ 660 = 1,320, so the length of the plot is 1,320 ft.

2(660) + 2(1,320) = 3,960, so the perimeter is 3,960 ft.

Cost of eight-strand wire: 3,960($2.18) = $8,632.80

Cost of woven wire: 3,960($1.40) = $5,544.00

Solve It

Remind students that there are many different ways to solve a problem.

Invite them to look back at the Problem-Solving Checklist to help them get started. They might also want to look at the Problem-Solving Tips on other pages to get some ideas for how to start.

Have students write their complete solution on a copy of Activity Sheet *Solution Sheet* or a blank sheet of paper.

Reflect

Have students work with a partner to share their thinking and discuss the Reflect questions.

As time permits, have students explain their solutions to the class.

Possible Solution

I will use the average of the least and greatest possible numbers of solar panels per acre: $850 + 770 = 1{,}620$ and $1{,}620 \div 2 = 810$.

So, there will be 810 solar panels in each acre. To find the number of acres needed, I can divide the total number of solar panels, 16,000, by 810:

$16{,}000 \div 810 \approx 19.75$

So, about 20 acres are needed.

There are 43,560 ft^2 in each acre, so there are 20(43,560), or 871,200 ft^2 in 20 acres.

I can estimate the square root of 871,200 to find the side length of the square piece of land.

x	933	934	935
x^2	870,489	872,356	874,225

I will round up the side length to 934 ft.

The perimeter of the square is $(4)(934) = 3{,}736$ ft.

I can multiply the perimeter by the cost per foot to find the total cost of each type of fencing.

Eight-strand wire: $(3{,}736)(\$2.18) = \$8{,}144.48$

Woven wire: $(3{,}736)(\$1.40) = \$5{,}230.40$

With the spending limit of up to $8,000, the energy company can afford the woven wire fencing using 810 solar panels per acre.

Math in Action

Solve It

➤ **Find a solution to the Fencing a Solar Farm problem.**

- Estimate how many acres of land the energy company needs to rent to have enough space for 16,000 solar panels.
- Estimate the energy company's cost to fence the land with each type of fencing.
- Determine which type or types of fencing the company can afford with their fencing budget of $8,000.

Reflect

Use Mathematical Practices After you complete the problem, choose one of these questions to discuss with a partner.

- **Reason Mathematically** How did you estimate the side length of the square piece of land?
- **Critique Reasoning** How many feet of fencing does your partner suggest the company buy? Will this amount of fencing be enough to enclose the land needed for the solar panels? Explain.

Sheep have rectangular shaped pupils. This helps them have better peripheral vision to view their surroundings.

687

Scoring Rubric (4 points)

Points	Expectations
4	The solution is complete, and all work is shown. Estimates for the number of acres of land and the cost to fence the land with each type of fencing are correctly calculated. An explanation of the affordability of the fencing is complete and accurate.
3	The solution is complete. Minor errors were made in calculating the number of acres of land and the cost to fence that land with each type of fencing. An explanation of the affordability of the fencing is complete and reasonable.
2	All parts of the task were attempted. Several errors were made in calculating the number of acres of land and the cost to fence that land with each type of fencing. An explanation of the affordability of the fencing may have errors in reasoning.
1	Some parts of the task were not attempted. The estimates, cost, and explanation are missing or inaccurate.

Self Reflection

Have students review the skills on the **Self Reflection** page and work in pairs to respond to the prompts. Encourage students to revisit the work they did in each lesson in order to help develop growth mindset.

- Remind students that this is the same list of skills that they saw on the **Self Check** page at the beginning of the unit.
- Tell students that revisiting the list of skills is an opportunity for them to reflect on their learning and progress during the unit.
- Have students read through the list of skills independently and then work in pairs to respond to the prompts. Encourage students to revisit the work they did in each lesson as they think about how to respond to the prompts.
- Discuss students' responses to the prompts as a class if time permits. Tell students that they will build on these skills in later lessons during the year and/or in other grade levels.

UNIT 6 Self Reflection

In this unit you learned to . . .

Skill	Lesson
Recognize numbers as perfect squares and perfect cubes.	23
Take the square root or cube root of a number to solve problems.	23
Know every rational number can be written as a repeating or a terminating decimal.	24
Write repeating decimals as fractions.	24
Find rational approximations of irrational numbers and locate them on the number line.	25
Explain the Pythagorean Theorem and its converse.	26
Apply the Pythagorean Theorem to find an unknown length in a figure or distance between two points in the coordinate plane.	27, 28
Know the volume formulas for cones, cylinders, and spheres and use them to solve problems.	28
Actively participate in discussions by asking questions and rephrasing or building on your classmates' ideas.	23–28

Think about what you have learned.

➤ **Use words, numbers, and drawings.**

1. The most important topic I learned is __________ because . . .

2. The hardest thing I learned to do is __________ because . . .

3. I could use more practice with . . .

688

Vocabulary Self-Assessment

- Students have interacted with and used unit math and academic vocabulary throughout the unit in listening, speaking, reading, and writing. Use this activity to review the terms and help students check their understanding of the definitions.
- Have students read the vocabulary terms and put a check mark by the terms they can use in speaking and writing. Students can look up words they do not know in the Interactive Glossary or the Academic Glossary in the Teacher Toolbox.

Problem Notes

1. Students may also identify an integer or the cube root of a perfect cube as an example of a rational number. Encourage students to use complete sentences in their responses.
3. Check that students have not confused *perfect cube* and *perfect square* by encouraging students to provide examples of both.
4. Students may also identify the question as, "I know the lengths of the two legs of a right triangle. How can I find the length of the hypotenuse?"

If time allows, this is a good opportunity to have students work in pairs to read and provide feedback on responses. Feedback should focus on the word meaning, accuracy, and clarity of the response.

UNIT 6 Vocabulary Review

➤ **Review the unit vocabulary. Put a check mark by items you can use in speaking and writing. Look up the meaning of any terms you do not know.**

Math Vocabulary		Academic Vocabulary
☐ cone	☐ perfect cube	☐ approximate (verb)
☐ converse of the Pythagorean Theorem	☐ perfect square	☐ exact
☐ cube root of x	☐ Pythagorean Theorem	☐ integer
☐ irrational number	☐ real numbers	☐ product
☐ legs (of a right triangle)	☐ square root of x	☐ prove

➤ **Use the unit vocabulary to complete the problems.**

1. How are rational numbers and irrational numbers alike and different? Use at least three math or academic vocabulary terms in your explanation. Underline each term you use. Give an example of each type of number.
   Possible explanation: Rational and irrational numbers are alike because they are both real numbers. They are different because irrational numbers cannot be written as a fraction or repeating decimal. You can find a rational approximation for an irrational number. $0.\overline{33}$ is a rational number, and the square root of 2 is an irrational number.

2. Is -5 a square root of 25? Explain.
   Yes; Possible explanation: The product of -5 and -5 is 25.

3. Describe a perfect cube. Use two math or academic vocabulary terms in your answer. Underline each term you use.
   Possible answer: A perfect cube is the product when an integer is used as a factor three times. For example, $4 \times 4 \times 4 = 4^3 = 64$. This means 64 is a perfect cube and the cube root of 64 is 4.

4. The answer to a question is *Use the Pythagorean Theorem*. What might the question be?
   Possible answer: The question might be, "I know the lengths of the hypotenuse and one leg of a right triangle. How can I find the length of the other leg?"

Unit Review

Problem Notes

1. Students could also solve the problem by adding to find perimeter:
$P = \frac{7}{8} + \frac{7}{8} + \frac{7}{8} + \frac{7}{8} = \frac{28}{8}$, or $3\frac{1}{2}$, m.
DOK 1 | 8.EE.A.2

2. **a.** $\frac{1}{9} = 0.\overline{1}$ and $\frac{11}{99} = 0.\overline{1}$
b. $\frac{3}{8} = 0.375$
c. $0.3 = \frac{3}{10}$ and $0.\overline{3} = \frac{1}{3}$
d. $\frac{2}{11} = 0.\overline{18}$
DOK 1 | 8.NS.A.1

3. $-\sqrt{19} \approx -4.36$;
$\pi - 7 \approx -3.86$;
$-\sqrt{2} \approx -1.41$;
$\frac{\pi}{5} \approx 0.63$
DOK 2 | 8.NS.A.2

UNIT 6 Unit Review

➤ **Use what you have learned to complete these problems.**

1. A square table has an area of $\frac{49}{64}$ m². What is the perimeter of the table? Show your work.

Possible student work:

Use s for the length of a side of the square table.

$A = s^2$

$\frac{49}{64} = s^2$

$\pm\sqrt{\frac{49}{64}} = s$

The side length is positive, so $s = \frac{7}{8}$; $P = 4s = 4\left(\frac{7}{8}\right) = \frac{28}{8} = \frac{7}{2}$, or 3.5.

SOLUTION 3.5 m

2. Decide if each statement about decimals or fractions is true or false.

Choose *True* or *False* for each statement.

	True	False
a. The fractions $\frac{1}{9}$ and $\frac{11}{99}$ are equal to the same repeating decimal.	●	○
b. The fraction $\frac{3}{8}$ is equal to a repeating decimal.	○	●
c. The numbers 0.3 and $0.\overline{3}$ are equal to the same fraction.	○	●
d. The fraction $\frac{2}{11}$ is equal to a repeating decimal.	●	○

3. Consider the values $\frac{\pi}{5}$, $-\sqrt{2}$, $-\sqrt{19}$, and $\pi - 7$. Plot and label the approximate location of each value on the number line. ($\pi \approx 3.14$)

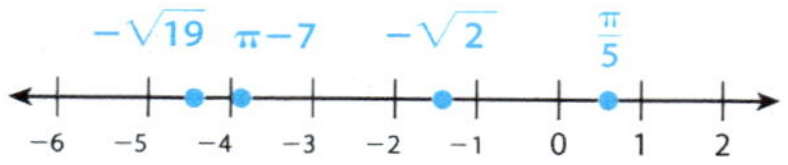

690

SMP 1, 2, 4, 5, 6, 7

Unit Game

8.G.B.8

Pythagorean Puzzler

Materials For each player: Recording Sheet, ruler or straightedge, calculator; For each pair: 2 sets of Integer Cards

WHY Reinforce using the Pythagorean Theorem to find the distance between two points in the coordinate plane.

HOW Players use Integer Cards to make ordered pairs and then use the Pythagorean Theorem to find the distance between the graphed points.

- Have students check each other's calculations for each round before finding the total length.
- After students finish the game, ask them to share strategies they used. Ask questions such as: *What did you do to create ordered pairs that would give the greatest lengths? How did you use the Pythagorean Theorem to find the length of your segments?*

Vary the Game Twice during the game, a player may choose to return one card to the bottom of the pile and draw a new card.

Challenge Instead of finding the total length at the end of the game, players pick three of the points on their grid to make a triangle. They find the perimeter of their triangle. The player with the greatest perimeter wins.

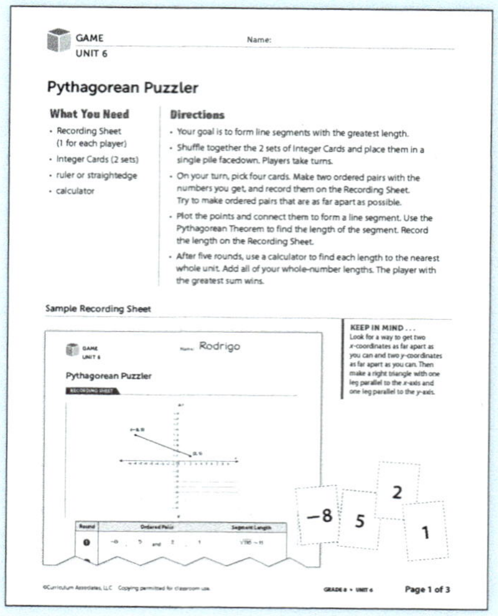

4 Students could also solve the problem by using the decimal form of the lengths: $2.25^2 + 3^2 = 3.75^2$; $14.0625 = 14.0625$.

DOK 3 | **8.G.B.6**

5 *DOK 2* | **8.G.B.7**

6 **C is correct.** Students could solve the problem by comparing the formula for volume of a cylinder, $\pi r^2 h$, to the formula for volume of a cone, $\frac{1}{3}\pi r^2 h$, when the height of the cylinder is 9 cm. The volume of the cylinder is $\pi r^2(9)$, or $9\pi r^2$. Since the volumes are the same, set the two volumes equal to each other: $9\pi r^2 = \frac{1}{3}\pi r^2 h$. The height of the cone must be 27 for both sides of the equation to be the same.

A is not correct. This answer represents dividing 9 by 3 instead of multiplying 9 and 3.

B is not correct. This answer represents the height of the cylinder.

D is not correct. This answer represents multiplying 9 and 9 instead of 9 and 3.

DOK 2 | **8.G.C.9**

7 *DOK 2* | **8.G.B.8**

4 Raymond draws a right triangle with side lengths 9, 12, and 15. He says that if he divides each side length by 4, the new triangle will be a right triangle. Is Raymond correct? Explain your reasoning.

SOLUTION Yes; Possible explanation: By the Pythagorean Theorem, $\left(\frac{9}{4}\right)^2 + \left(\frac{12}{4}\right)^2$ should equal $\left(\frac{15}{4}\right)^2$. The triangle is a right triangle because $\frac{81}{16} + \frac{144}{16} = \frac{225}{16}$, so Raymond is correct.

5 Maddie is mailing some field hockey equipment to her sister. She wants to use the box shown. Can she close the box with a 30-in. field hockey stick inside it? Explain your reasoning.

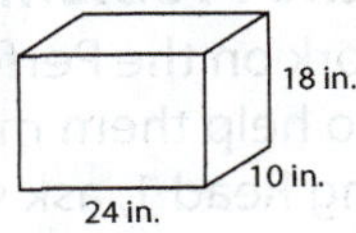

Possible student work:

Diagonal on bottom of box:
$24^2 + 10^2 = c^2$
$676 = c^2$
$c = \sqrt{676} = 26$

Diagonal of box:
$26^2 + 18^2 = g^2$
$1{,}000 = g^2$
$g = \sqrt{1{,}000} \approx 31.6$

SOLUTION Yes; Possible explanation: The length of the hockey stick is less than the diagonal of the box, so it will fit in the box.

6 A cylinder and a cone have the same radius and the same volume. The height of the cylinder is 9 cm. What is the height of the cone?

A 3 cm **B** 9 cm **(C)** 27 cm **D** 81 cm

7 What is the distance between the points (3, −3) and (−1, 2)? Round your answer to the nearest tenth. Record your answer on the grid. Then fill in the bubbles.

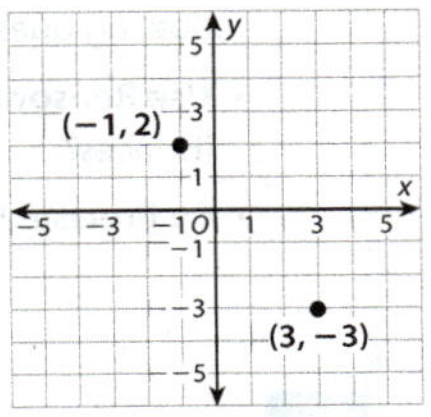

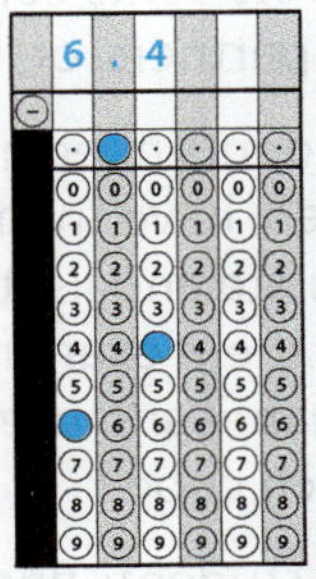

691

Literacy Connection

Lyric Poetry

Materials "The Lighthouse," Literacy Connection Problems

Summary In "The Lighthouse," students read a poem about ships and sailors from the perspective of a lighthouse.

Math Connection This poem uses figurative language to express admiration for the reliability and importance of a lighthouse. After reading the poem, students solve problems about building a lighthouse model and calculating the distance traveled near a lighthouse's beam.

- Have students read the passage.
- Distribute the literacy connection problems. After reading the directions aloud, direct students to turn and talk about problem 1. Check for understanding.
- Have students work independently to complete the remaining problems. Encourage them to use manipulatives or to draw pictures to solve each problem.
- Circulate and monitor while students work.
- Ask volunteers to share and discuss their solutions with the class.

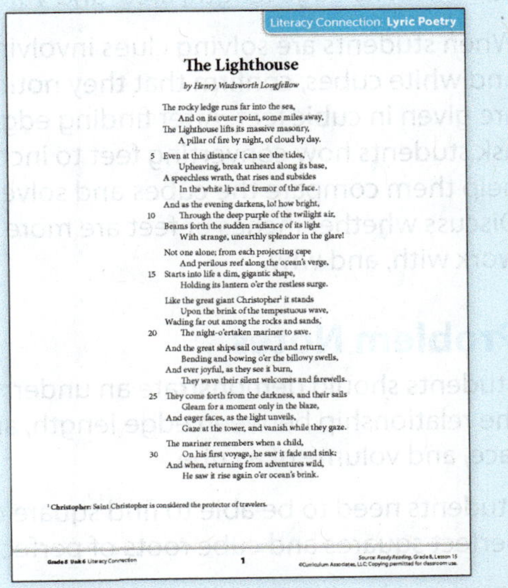

Literacy Connection: Lyric Poetry

The Lighthouse

by Henry Wadsworth Longfellow

The rocky ledge runs far into the sea,
And on its outer point, some miles away,
The Lighthouse lifts its massive masonry,
A pillar of fire by night, of cloud by day.

Even at this distance I can see the tides,
Upheaving, break unheard along its base,
A speechless wrath, that rises and subsides
In the white lip and tremor of the face.

And as the evening darkens, lo! how bright,
Through the deep purple of the twilight air,
Beams forth the sudden radiance of its light
With strange, unearthly splendor in the glare!

Not one alone; from each projecting cape
And perilous reef along the ocean's verge,
Starts into life a dim, gigantic shape,
Holding its lantern o'er the restless surge.

Like the great giant Christopher[1] it stands
Upon the brink of the tempestuous wave,
Wading far out among the rocks and sands,
The night-o'ertaken mariner to save.

And the great ships sail outward and return,
Bending and bowing o'er the billowy swells,
And ever joyful, as they see it burn,
They wave their silent welcomes and farewells.

They come forth from the darkness, and their sails
Gleam for a moment only in the blaze,
And eager faces, as the light unveils,
Gaze at the tower, and vanish while they gaze.

The mariner remembers when a child,
On his first voyage, he saw it fade and sink;
And when, returning from adventures wild,
He saw it rise again o'er ocean's brink.

[1] **Christopher:** Saint Christopher is considered the protector of travelers.

Grade 8 Unit 6 Literacy Connection 1 Source: Ready Reading, Grade 8, Lesson 15 ©Curriculum Associates, LLC Copying permitted for classroom use.

Unit Review

Purpose

Apply equations of the form $x^2 = p$ and $x^3 = p$ in order to solve puzzles for a game.

MATH FOCUS

DOK 3

Standards 8.EE.A.2

MONITOR & GUIDE SMP 1, 2, 4, 5, 6

Make Sense of the Problem

Before students work on the Performance Task, use **Three Reads** to help them make sense of the problem. During Read 1, ask students to focus on the context of the problem. Collect student responses, such as *solving puzzles to unlock doors* and *using cubes*. On Read 2, emphasize how the clues relate to square roots and cube roots. On Read 3, encourage students to identify the important quantities and how they relate to solving the problem. For instance, point out that the volume of each cube is given, but some clues refer to area and edge length.

Facilitate Problem Solving

Have students complete the task independently, with partners, or in small groups.

If students need additional support as they get started, have them use the equation $v = e^3$ to calculate and list the first 10 perfect cubes. Then have them examine the volumes of the cubes in the game and use the list to find the edge length of each cube.

After students find edge lengths, have them find the area of one face of each cube. Encourage students to sketch the cubes in each color and label each cube with its edge length, area, and volume.

When students are solving clues involving the black and white cubes, confirm that they notice volumes are given in cubic feet. After finding edge lengths, ask students how converting feet to inches could help them compare the cubes and solve the puzzles. Discuss whether inches or feet are more efficient to work with, and why.

Problem Notes

Students should demonstrate an understanding of the relationship between edge length, area of one face, and volume of a cube.

Students need to be able to find square roots of perfect squares and cube roots of perfect cubes.

Students should understand that the root of a fraction is the root of the numerator divided by the root of the denominator.

Performance Task

Answer the questions and show all your work on separate paper.

In an adventure video game, players collect cubes. Each cube is labeled with its volume:

Red cube: 64 in.^{3}	Gold cube: $\frac{729}{64}$ in.^{3}
Blue cube: 343 in.^{3}	White cube: $\frac{8}{27}$ ft^3
Green cube: $\frac{125}{8}$ in.^{3}	Black cube: $\frac{125}{216}$ ft^3

Players use cubes to solve puzzles to unlock doors to new levels. First, write and solve an equation to find the edge length of each cube. Then solve the puzzles to unlock Doors One and Two. Identify the cubes that will open each door. Explain your reasoning.

At Door One, players have red, blue, green, and gold cubes.

- Two different cubes unlock Door One.
- One of the cubes has a face with an area of $\frac{25}{4}$ in.^{2}.
- The sum of the edge lengths of the cubes is $\frac{13}{2}$ in.

At Door Two, players have blue, green, gold, white, and black cubes.

- Three different cubes unlock Door Two.
- The cubes must be used in order from greatest to least volume.
- The first cube has a volume of 1,000 in.^{3}.
- The last cube has a face with an area of 49 in.^{2}.

Checklist

Did you . . .

- ☐ use an equation to find the edge length of each cube?
- ☐ explain which cubes are used to unlock the doors?
- ☐ check your puzzle solutions for accuracy?

Reflect

Use Mathematical Practices After you complete the task, choose one of the following questions to answer.

- **Use Reasoning** How are a cube's edge lengths related to its volume and area of its faces?
- **Be Precise** How could you test your solutions to prove that they solve the puzzles?

Students may convert feet to inches to help them solve puzzles involving the black and white cubes.

Students should recognize that volume is measured in cubic units, area is measured in square units, and edge length is measured in linear units.

Student responses should include the set of cubes that solves each puzzle with an explanation for each.

Reflect

Use Reasoning Look for understanding that the edge length is the cube root of the volume of the cube, and that squaring the edge length results in the area of one face of the cube.

Be Precise Look for explanations that include checking the selected cubes against each clue in the puzzle.

4-Point Solution

First, I found the edge length of each cube using the equation $v = e^3$. Because the volume is given, I used the cube root to solve for e:

Red cube: $e = 4$ in.	Gold cube: $e = \frac{9}{4}$ in.
Blue cube: $e = 7$ in.	White cube: $e = \frac{2}{3}$ ft
Green cube: $e = \frac{5}{2}$ in.	Black cube: $e = \frac{5}{6}$ ft

Door One: green and red cubes; One of the cubes has a face with an area of $\frac{25}{4}$ in.^{2}, so I used the equation $e^2 = \frac{25}{4}$ and solved for e by taking the square root. The edge length of the green cube is $\frac{5}{2}$ in. The sum of the edge lengths of the cubes is $\frac{13}{2}$ in. The edge length of the first cube is $\frac{5}{2}$ in., so I subtracted to find the edge length of the second cube: $\frac{13}{2} - \frac{5}{2} = \frac{8}{2} = 4$ in.

This means that the second cube is the red cube.

Door Two: black, white, and blue cubes; The last cube has a face with an area of 49 in.^{2}, so I used the equation $e^2 = 49$ and solved for e by taking the square root. The edge length of the blue cube is 7 in. Because the cubes must be used in order from largest to smallest, the other two cubes must have an edge length greater than 7, so the cubes to open Door Two cannot be green or gold.

To compare the black and white cubes, I multiplied each edge length by 12 to convert to inches. The white cube's edge length is 8 inches, and the black cube's edge length is 10 inches. Then I used the equation $v = e^3$ to find the volume of each cube in cubic inches. The white cube's volume is 512 in.^{3}: $512 = 8^3$. The black cube's volume is 1,000 in.^{3}: $1{,}000 = 10^3$. Finally, I ordered the cubes from greatest to least volume: black (1,000 in.^{3}), white (512 in.^{3}), and blue (343 in.^{3}).

Scoring Rubric

Points	Expectations
4	The student's response is accurate and complete. All calculations are correct. The student clearly explains how the chosen cubes satisfy each clue.
3	The student's strategy and process are correct, but there are minor errors in calculating edge lengths or areas of the faces of one or more cubes. All requirements have been addressed.
2	The response contains several mistakes in calculations. The student may have attempted to find all edge lengths and solve each puzzle, but the response is incorrect and/or incomplete.
1	The student's response is incorrect and incomplete. One or more edge lengths may not have been calculated, and clues may have been skipped. The response does not address all requirements of the problem.

DIFFERENTIATION | EXTEND

If students have more time to spend on this problem or require an additional challenge, then use this extension to have them write a set of clues to open a third door.

Game designers are writing the puzzle for players to open Door Three. They want players to use three different cubes. One clue must use the cube that has the least volume. Another clue must be based on area of a cube's face. And a clue must be based on edge length of a cube. Help designers write a puzzle. Then identify which cubes solve the puzzle.

Solution

- Puzzle: Three different cubes unlock Door Three. The first cube has the least possible volume. The second cube has a face with an area that is $\frac{19}{16}$ in.^{2} greater than the area of a face of another cube. The third cube has an edge length that is 4 times greater than the edge length of another cube.
- Cubes: The gold cube has the least volume: $\frac{729}{64}$ in.^{3}. The area of a gold cube's face is $\left(\frac{9}{4}\right)^2 = \frac{81}{16}$ in.^{2}. The area of a green cube's face is $\left(\frac{5}{2}\right)^2 = \frac{25}{4}$ in.^{2}, or $\frac{100}{16}$ in.^{2}. The difference between the faces is $\frac{100}{16} - \frac{81}{16} = \frac{19}{16}$. A face of the green cube has an area that is $\frac{19}{16}$ in.^{2} greater than the area of a face of the gold cube. The edge of the green cube multiplied by 4 is $\frac{5}{2} \times 4 = \frac{20}{2} = 10$. Since the edge length of the black cube is 10 in., the edge length of the black cube is 4 times greater than the edge length of the green cube. The gold, green, and black cubes open Door Three.

Problem Notes

Form A is shown. *See* ***Teacher Toolbox*** *for Form B.*

1 Students could solve the problem by first finding the area of the rectangular window using the formula $A = \ell w$. Next, recognize that the area of the square window must also be 64 in.^{2}, and each side length will have the same measure. Then take the square root of 64 to find the side length. The side length will be the positive square root of 64, which is 8.

(2 points)

DOK 1 | 8.EE.A.2

2 **D is correct.** Students could solve the problem by dividing and recognizing that the quotient has repeating digits, $0.\overline{54}$.

A is not correct. This answer represents 0.540000… with the 0 repeating instead of the digits 54 repeating.

B is not correct. This answer represents the correct digits, but the digits are not repeating.

C is not correct. This answer represents a single digit repeating (0.544444…) instead of both digits repeating.

(1 point)

DOK 1 | 8.NS.A.1

3 Students could also solve the problem by creating a table of squares to estimate the perfect squares close to 2. $\sqrt{3}$ is between 1.7 and 1.8, so use 1.7 to approximate $\sqrt{3}$.

x	1.5	1.6	1.7	1.8
x^2	2.25	2.56	2.89	3.24

(2 points)

DOK 1 | 8.EE.A.2

4 Students could solve the problem by finding the value of the hypotenuse, z, of a right triangle with legs of lengths x and y by using the Pythagorean Theorem that states that $x^2 + y^2 = z^2$. Then take the square root of both sides and consider the positive value only. Accept all values of x and y that give an accurate approximate of z that is not a whole number.

(2 points)

DOK 2 | 8.G.B.6

5 (1 point)

DOK 2 | 8.G.B.7

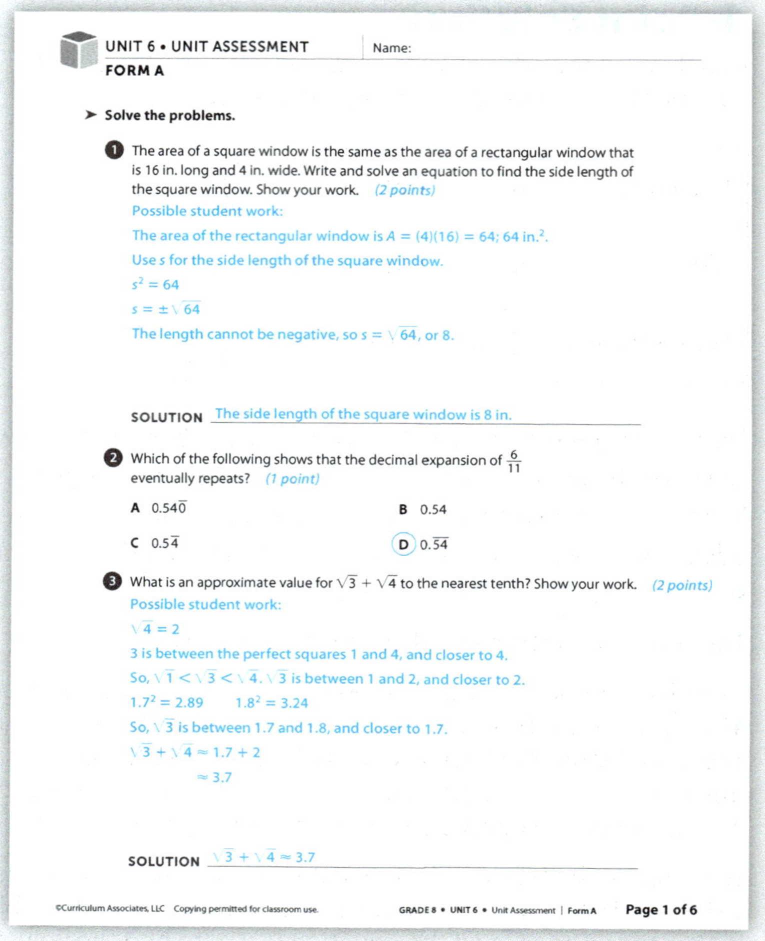
UNIT 6 • UNIT ASSESSMENT Name:
FORM A

➤ **Solve the problems.**

1 The area of a square window is the same as the area of a rectangular window that is 16 in. long and 4 in. wide. Write and solve an equation to find the side length of the square window. Show your work. *(2 points)*

Possible student work:

The area of the rectangular window is $A = (4)(16) = 64$; 64 in.^{2}.

Use s for the side length of the square window.

$s^2 = 64$

$s = \pm\sqrt{64}$

The length cannot be negative, so $s = \sqrt{64}$, or 8.

SOLUTION The side length of the square window is 8 in.

2 Which of the following shows that the decimal expansion of $\frac{6}{11}$ eventually repeats? *(1 point)*

A $0.54\overline{0}$

B 0.54

C $0.5\overline{4}$

D $0.\overline{54}$

3 What is an approximate value for $\sqrt{3} + \sqrt{4}$ to the nearest tenth? Show your work. *(2 points)*

Possible student work:

$\sqrt{4} = 2$

3 is between the perfect squares 1 and 4, and closer to 4.

So, $\sqrt{1} < \sqrt{3} < \sqrt{4}$. $\sqrt{3}$ is between 1 and 2, and closer to 2.

$1.7^2 = 2.89$ $1.8^2 = 3.24$

So, $\sqrt{3}$ is between 1.7 and 1.8, and closer to 1.7.

$\sqrt{3} + \sqrt{4} \approx 1.7 + 2$

≈ 3.7

SOLUTION $\sqrt{3} + \sqrt{4} \approx 3.7$

©Curriculum Associates, LLC Copying permitted for classroom use. GRADE 8 • UNIT 6 • Unit Assessment | Form A Page 1 of 6

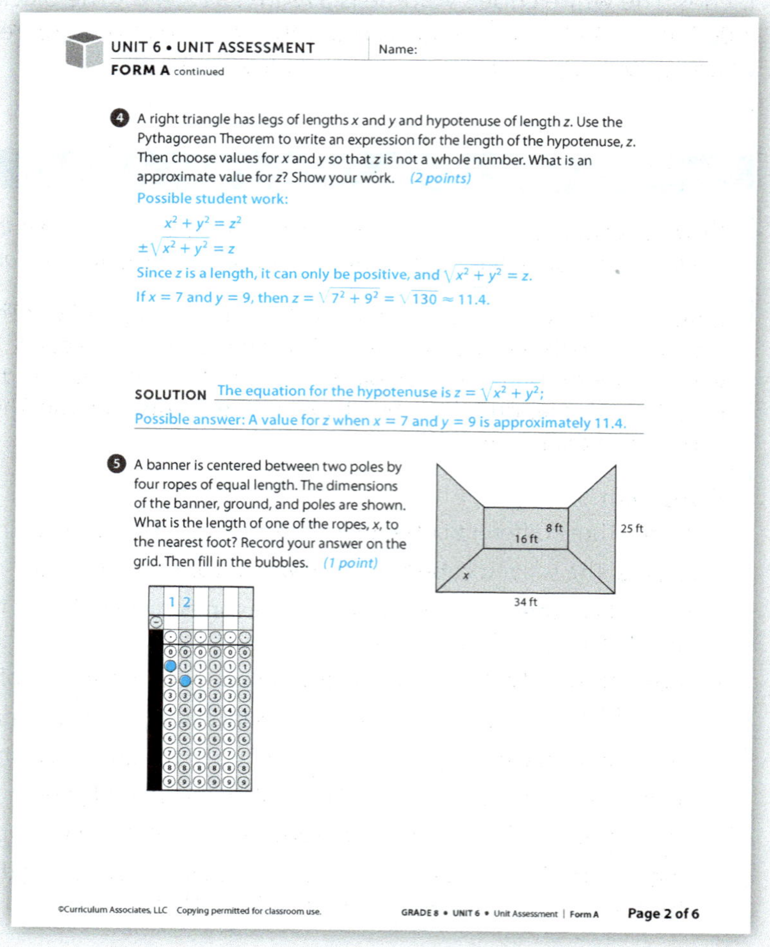
UNIT 6 • UNIT ASSESSMENT Name:
FORM A continued

4 A right triangle has legs of lengths x and y and hypotenuse of length z. Use the Pythagorean Theorem to write an expression for the length of the hypotenuse, z. Then choose values for x and y so that z is not a whole number. What is an approximate value for z? Show your work. *(2 points)*

Possible student work:

$x^2 + y^2 = z^2$

$\pm\sqrt{x^2 + y^2} = z$

Since z is a length, it can only be positive, and $\sqrt{x^2 + y^2} = z$.

If $x = 7$ and $y = 9$, then $z = \sqrt{7^2 + 9^2} = \sqrt{130} \approx 11.4$.

SOLUTION The equation for the hypotenuse is $z = \sqrt{x^2 + y^2}$;
Possible answer: A value for z when $x = 7$ and $y = 9$ is approximately 11.4.

5 A banner is centered between two poles by four ropes of equal length. The dimensions of the banner, ground, and poles are shown. What is the length of one of the ropes, x, to the nearest foot? Record your answer on the grid. Then fill in the bubbles. *(1 point)*

©Curriculum Associates, LLC Copying permitted for classroom use. GRADE 8 • UNIT 6 • Unit Assessment | Form A Page 2 of 6

6 Students could check their work and verify the fraction is a repeating decimal by using long division.

(2 points)

DOK 1 | **8.NS.A.1**

7 **a.** $\sqrt{256} = 16$

b. $3\pi - \pi = 2\pi = 6.2831\ldots$

c. The value $0.903846153\ldots$ does not terminate nor repeat.

d. $-\sqrt{8} \times \sqrt{8} = -8$

e. The value $\sqrt{11} = 0.4145\ldots$ does not terminate nor repeat.

f. $4\sqrt{3} - 4\sqrt{3} = 0$

(2 points)

DOK 1 | **8.NS.A.1**

8 Students could also solve the problem by using the Pythagorean Theorem to show that $\left(\frac{15}{k}\right)^2 + \left(\frac{8}{k}\right)^2$ is equal to $\left(\frac{17}{k}\right)^2$: $\frac{225}{k^2} + \frac{64}{k^2} = \frac{289}{k^2}$.

(2 points)

DOK 3 | **8.G.B.6**

9 **A, C, E are correct.** Students could solve the problem by substituting the given measurements into the appropriate volume formula. The volume of a cone is $\frac{1}{3}\pi r^2 h$, the volume of a sphere is $\frac{4}{3}\pi r^3$, and the volume of a cylinder is $\pi r^2 h$.

B is not correct. This answer represents a volume of 288π:
$\frac{4}{3}\pi r^3 = \frac{4}{3}\pi(6)^3 = 288\pi$.

D is not correct. This answer represents a volume of 162π:
$\frac{1}{3}\pi r^2 h = \frac{1}{3}\pi(9)^2(6) = 162\pi$.

F is not correct. This answer represents a volume of 18π:
$\frac{1}{2} \cdot \frac{4}{3}\pi r^3 = \frac{2}{3}\pi(3)^3 = 18\pi$.

(2 points)

DOK 2 | **8.G.C.9**

10 (2 points)

DOK 1 | **8.EE.A.2**

UNIT 6 • UNIT ASSESSMENT Name:

FORM A continued

6 How is $0.55\overline{6}$ written as a fraction? Show your work. *(2 points)*

Possible student work:

$x = 0.55\overline{6}$

$100x = 55.\overline{6}$

$1{,}000x = 556.\overline{6}$

$1{,}000x - 100x = 556.\overline{6} - 55.\overline{6}$

$900x = 501$

$x = \frac{501}{900}$

$= \frac{167}{300}$

SOLUTION $\frac{167}{300}$

7 Decide if each value is rational or irrational.

Choose *Rational* or *Irrational* for each expression. *(2 points)*

	Rational	Irrational
a. $\sqrt{256}$	●	○
b. $3\pi - \pi$	○	●
c. 0.903846153…	○	●
d. $-\sqrt{8} \times \sqrt{8}$	●	○
e. $\frac{\sqrt{11}}{8}$	○	●
f. $4\sqrt{3} - 4\sqrt{3}$	●	○

UNIT 6 • UNIT ASSESSMENT Name:

FORM A continued

8 A right triangle with leg lengths of 8 and 15 has a hypotenuse of length 17. Show that a triangle with side lengths $\frac{8}{k}$, $\frac{15}{k}$, and $\frac{17}{k}$ is also a right triangle. Explain your reasoning. *(2 points)*

SOLUTION Possible explanation: A triangle with side lengths $\frac{8}{k}$, $\frac{15}{k}$, and $\frac{17}{k}$ is similar to the triangle with side lengths 8, 15, and 17 because corresponding side lengths are proportional. In similar triangles, corresponding angles are congruent. So, the angle between the legs with lengths $\frac{8}{k}$ and $\frac{15}{k}$ is a right angle, and the triangle is a right triangle.

9 Which figures have a volume of 216π cubic units? Choose all that apply. *(2 points)*

(A) A cone with a radius of 6 units and a height of 18 units.

B A sphere with a radius of 6 units.

(C) A cylinder with radius of 3 units and a height of 24 units.

D A cone with a radius of 9 units and a height of 6 units.

(E) A cylinder with a radius of 6 units and a height of 6 units.

F A half sphere with radius of 3 units.

10 Kayla is surrounding a square mosaic with tiles. The area of the mosaic is 17 ft^2. What is the exact perimeter of the mosaic? Use s for the side length and P for perimeter. Write your answers in the blanks. *(2 points)*

$s^2 =$ 17

$s =$ $\sqrt{17}$

$P =$ 4 $\sqrt{17}$

Problem Notes

11 Students could also draw a different square by moving 3 units down and 2 units right from S to plot a point at $(1, -7)$ and moving 3 units down and 2 units right from T to plot a point at $(4, -5)$.

(2 points)

DOK 2 | **8.G.B.8**

12 **a.** Three times the volume of figure A is $3 \cdot 2 \cdot \frac{1}{3}\pi r^2 h$, or $2\pi(4)^3$. The volume of figure B is $\pi r^2 h + \frac{1}{3}\pi r^2 h$, or $\frac{4}{3}\pi(4)^3$.

b. The volume of figure C is $\frac{4}{3}\pi(r)^3$, or $\frac{4}{3}\pi(4)^3$. Twice the volume of figure A is $2 \cdot 2 \cdot \frac{1}{3}\pi r^2 h$, or $\frac{4}{3}\pi(4)^3$.

c. The volume of figure B is $\pi r^2 h + \frac{1}{3}\pi r^2 h$, or $\frac{4}{3}\pi(4)^3$. The volume of figure C is $\frac{4}{3}\pi(r)^3$, or $\frac{4}{3}\pi(4)^3$.

d. The sum of the volumes of figure B and figure C is $\frac{4}{3}\pi(r)^3 + \frac{4}{3}\pi(r)^3$, or $\frac{8}{3}\pi(4)^3$. Four times the volume of figure A is $4 \cdot 2 \cdot \frac{1}{3}\pi(r)^3$, or $\frac{8}{3}\pi(4)^3$.

(2 points)

DOK 2 | **8.G.C.9**

13 Students could also solve the problem by creating a table of squares to estimate the perfect squares close to 4 and 2. The closest square to $\sqrt{15}$ is 15.21, so use 3.9. The closest square to $\sqrt{6}$ is 5.76, so use 2.4.

x	3.7	3.8	3.9
x^2	13.69	14.44	15.21

x	2.3	2.4	2.5
x^2	5.29	5.76	6.25

(2 points)

DOK 2 | **8.NS.A.2**

14 Students could also solve the problem by first making a sketch of the container to help visualize how the marker could fit. Next, using the Pythagorean Theorem, find the hypotenuse of the base, approximately 5.7 in. Then find the diagonal formed from the top corner to the opposite bottom corner. The legs of this triangle will be 4 and 5.7 in., so the hypotenuse is approximately 6.9 in.

(2 points)

DOK 2 | **8.G.B.7**

15 **A is correct.** Students could solve the problem by using approximation strategies or a calculator. Then compare the values to identify the expression with the least value as $-\sqrt{9}$, which is equal to -3.

B is not correct. This answer is $-(\pi - 1) \approx -(3.14 - 1) \approx -2.14$.

C is not correct. This answer is $\sqrt{8} \approx 2.82$.

D is not correct. This answer is $\pi - 3 \approx 3.14 - 3 \approx 0.14$.

(1 point)

DOK 1 | **8.NS.A.2**

UNIT 6 • UNIT ASSESSMENT Name:
FORM A continued

11 In the coordinate plane, $\overline{ST}$ is labeled as one side of a square. What are the coordinates of the other two vertices of the square? Draw the square. Explain your reasoning. *(2 points)*

Possible student work:

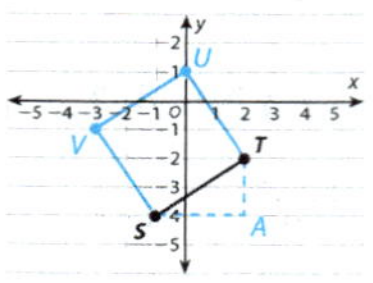

SOLUTION point U (0, 1) and point V (−3, −1); Possible explanation: Draw point A at (2, −4) to make a right triangle. $\triangle AST$ has legs of lengths 3 and 2 and hypotenuse of length ST. To draw other segments the same length as $\overline{ST}$, draw a right triangle with the same leg lengths as $\triangle AST$. From point T, move up 3 units and left 2 units to get point U at (0, 1). From point S, move left 2 units and up 3 units to get point V at (−3, −1).

12 Decide if each statement about figures A, B, and C is true or false.

Choose *True* or *False* for each statement. *(2 points)*

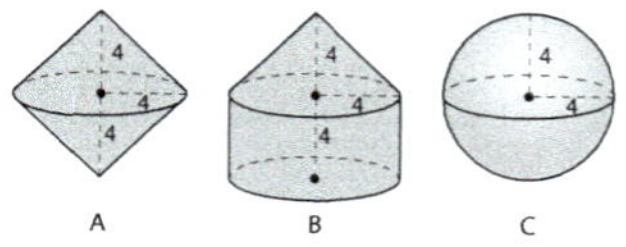

	True	False
a. Three times the volume of A is equal to the volume of B.	○	●
b. The volume of C is equal to twice the volume of A.	●	○
c. The volume of B is equal to the volume of C.	●	○
d. The sum of the volume of B and C is equal to four times the volume of A.	●	○

UNIT 6 • UNIT ASSESSMENT Name:
FORM A continued

13 Is $\sqrt{15}$ greater than, less than, or equal to $\sqrt{6} + \sqrt{6}$? Show your work. *(2 points)*

Possible student work:

15 is between the perfect squares 3 and 4, and closer to 4.

$3.8^2 = 14.44$, and $3.9^2 = 15.21$. So, $\sqrt{15} \approx 3.9$.

6 is between the perfect squares 2 and 3, and closer to 2.

$2.4^2 = 5.76$, and $2.5^2 = 6.25$. So, $\sqrt{6} \approx 2.4$.

Since $\sqrt{15} \approx 3.9$ and $\sqrt{6} + \sqrt{6} \approx 2.4 + 2.4 \approx 4.8$, $\sqrt{15}$ is less than $\sqrt{6} + \sqrt{6}$.

SOLUTION $\sqrt{15}$ is less than $\sqrt{6} + \sqrt{6}$.

14 Sean has a plastic container in the shape of a cube with side lengths of 4 in. Can he close the lid on the container with a 6-in. marker inside it? Explain your reasoning. *(2 points)*

Possible student work:

Find the length of the diagonal on the bottom of the box.

$4^2 + 4^2 = c^2$

$32 = c^2$

$c = \sqrt{32} \approx 5.7$

Then find the diagonal of the rectangle with side lengths $\sqrt{32}$ and 4.

$\sqrt{32}^2 + 4^2 = g^2$

$48 = g^2$

$g = \sqrt{48} \approx 6.9$

SOLUTION Yes; Possible explanation: Since the length of the marker, 6 inches, is less than the maximum diagonal of the box, 6.9 in., the marker will fit inside the container with the lid closed.

15 Which of the following has the least value? ($\pi \approx 3.14$) *(1 point)*

(A) $-\sqrt{9}$ **B** $-(\pi - 1)$

C $\sqrt{8}$ **D** $\pi - 3$

Scoring Guide

For the problems in the Unit 6 Unit Assessments (Forms A and B), the table shows:

- depth of knowledge (DOK) level
- points for scoring
- lesson assessed by each problem
- standard addressed

Problem	DOK	Points	Lesson	Standard
1	1	2	23	8.EE.A.2
2	1	1	24	8.NS.A.1
3	1	2	25	8.EE.A.2
4	2	2	26	8.G.B.6
5	2	1	27	8.G.B.7
6	1	2	24	8.NS.A.1
7	1	2	25	8.NS.A.1
8	3	2	26	8.G.B.6
9	2	2	28	8.G.C.9
10	1	2	25	8.EE.A.2
11	2	2	27	8.G.B.8
12	2	2	28	8.G.C.9
13	2	2	25	8.NS.A.2
14	2	2	27	8.G.B.7
15	1	1	25	8.NS.A.2

Scoring Rubrics

Short Response Scoring Rubric

Points	Expectations
2	Response has the correct solution(s) and includes well-organized, clear, and concise work demonstrating thorough understanding of mathematical concepts and/or procedures.
1	Response contains mostly correct solution(s) and shows partial understanding of mathematical concepts and/or procedures.
0	Response shows no attempt at finding a solution and no effort to demonstrate an understanding of mathematical concepts and/or procedures.

Fill-in-the-Blank, Multiple Select, and Choice Matrix Scoring Rubric

Points	Expectations
2	All answers are correct
1	1 incorrect answer
0	2 or more incorrect answers

Print Resources

Reach all students using these print resources that support instruction, practice, assessment, and differentiation.

Resources can be found in the Student Worktext or Teacher's Guide or downloaded from the Teacher Toolbox section in the Teacher Digital Experience.

In-Class Instruction and Practice

Teacher's Guide

- Learning Progression
- ELL Language Expectations
- Connect to Culture
- Discussion Prompts and Instructional Support

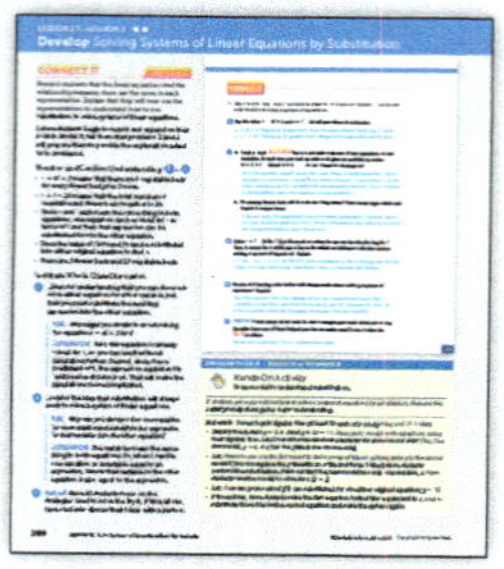

Student Worktext

Use the blue pages for in-class instruction and practice.

Instruction Page

Independent Practice for School or Home

Teacher's Guide

- Additional Practice
- Cumulative Practice

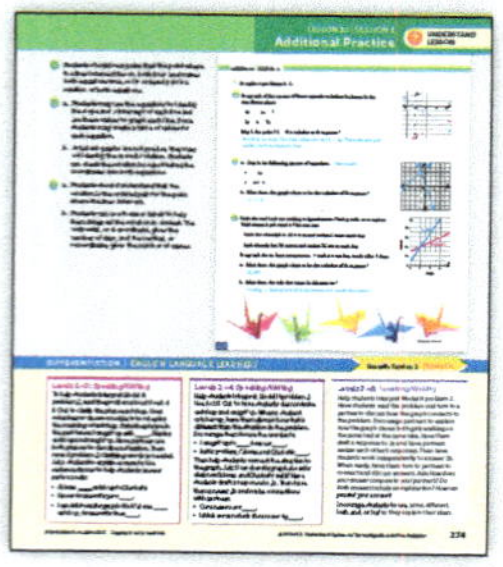

Student Worktext

Use the green pages for independent practice.

- Additional Practice
- Cumulative Practice

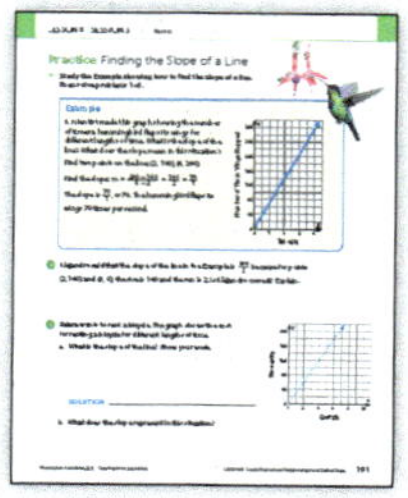

Additional Practice Page

Teacher Toolbox

- Fluency and Skills Practice
- Unit Game
- Cumulative Practice

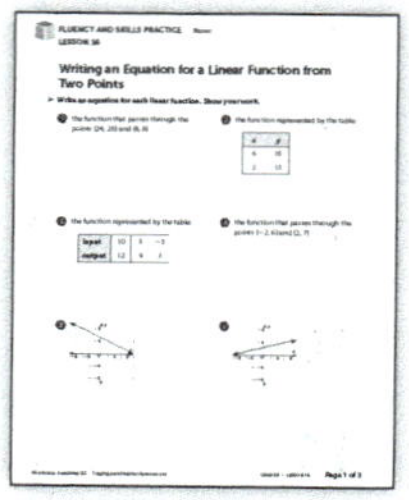

Fluency and Skills Practice

Assessments and Reports

Teacher's Guide

- Starts
- Support Whole Group/Partner Discussion
- Ask/Listen Fors
- Common Misconceptions
- Error Alerts
- Close: Exit Ticket

Student Worktext

- Self Checks
- Apply It
- Reflect Questions
- Self Reflection
- Math Journal Questions
- Unit Review

Self Check

Teacher Toolbox

- Editable Lesson Quizzes
- Editable Unit Assessments

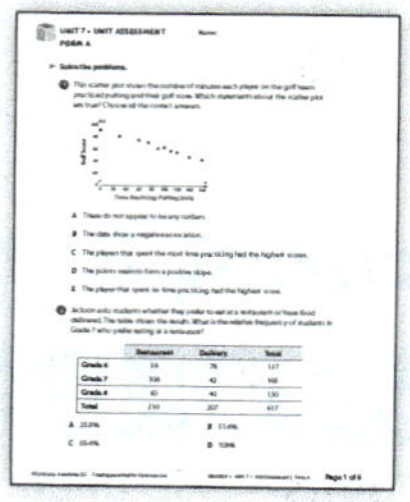

Unit Assessment

Differentiation

Before the Unit/Lesson: Prerequisites Report

Recommended resources to support students' learning needs are highlighted in the Prerequisites report.

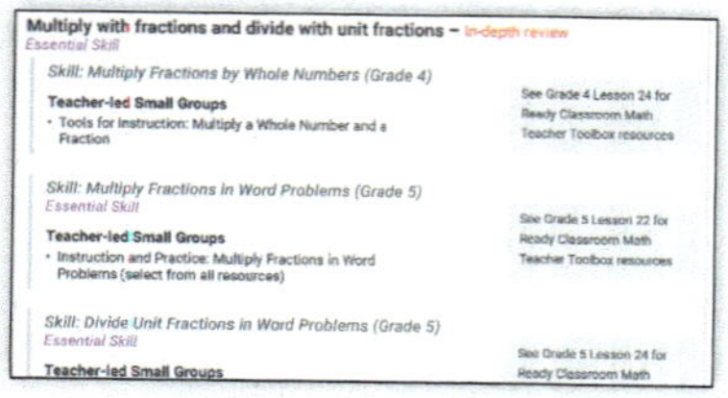

Prerequisites Report: Resources

During the Lesson: Teacher's Guide

- Hands-On Activities or Visual Models
- Deepen Understanding
- ELL Differentiated Instruction
- Refine Sessions

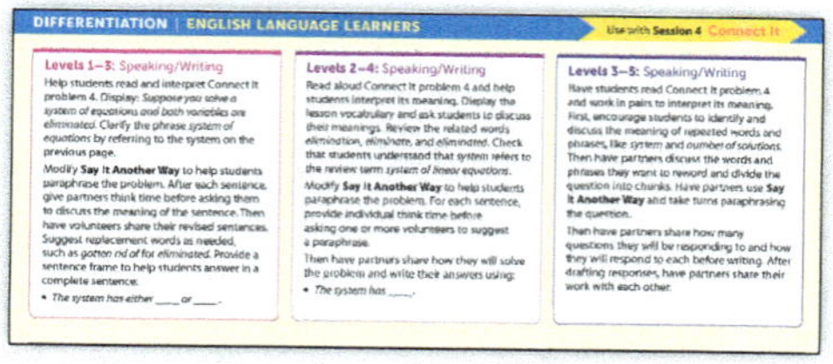

ELL Differentiated Instruction

After the Lesson: Teacher Toolbox

- Reteach: Tools for Instruction
- Reinforce: Math Center Activities
- Extend: Enrichment Activities

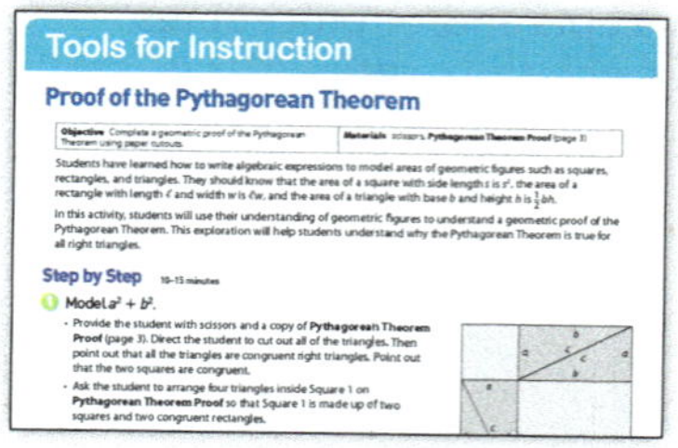

Reteach: Tools for Instruction

Digital Resources

Engage students with digital resources that provide interactive instruction, practice, assessment, and differentiation.

Resources can be found in the Student Digital Experience and the Teacher Digital Experience.

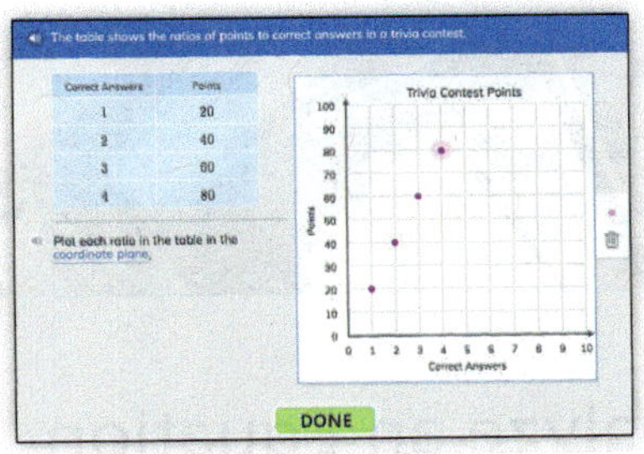

Interactive Tutorials

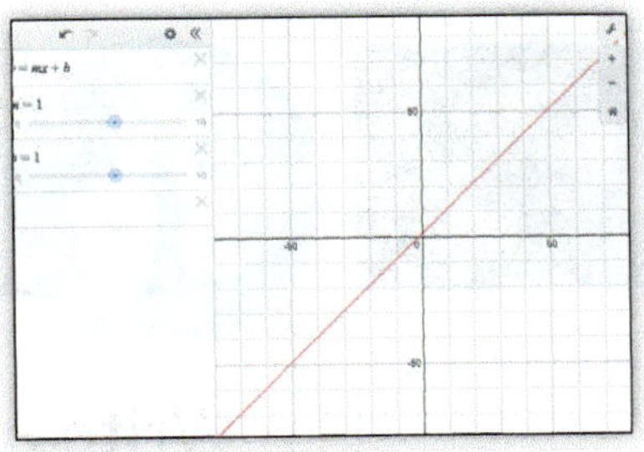

Digital Math Tools powered by Desmos

PowerPoint® Slides

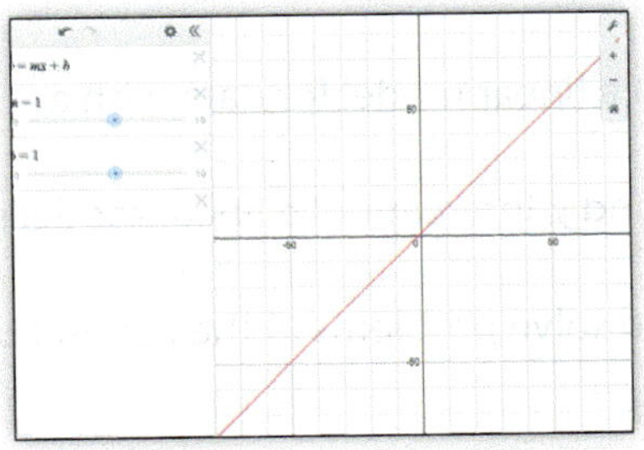

Digital Math Tools powered by Desmos

Learning Games

Digital Practice

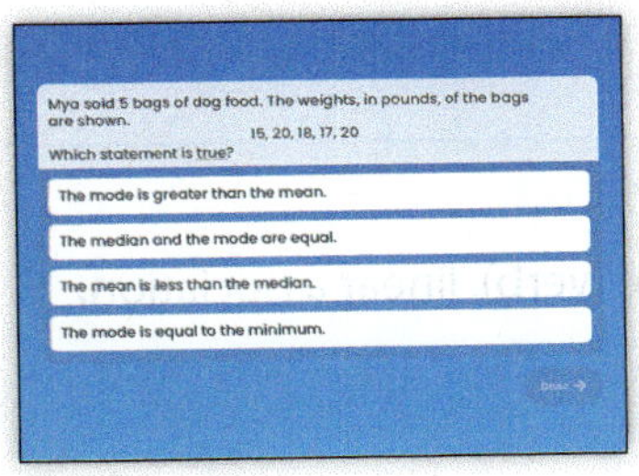

Diagnostic

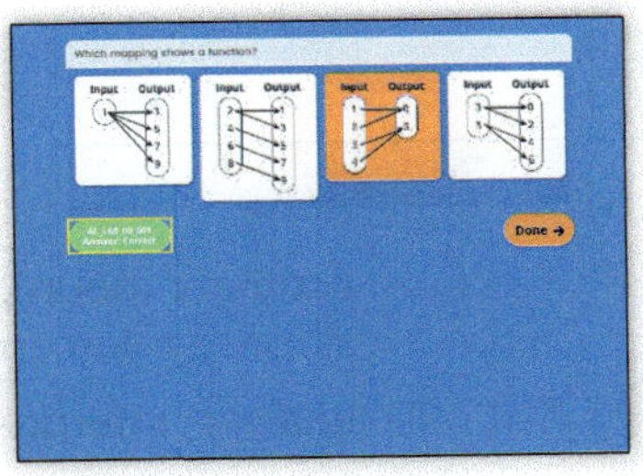

Lesson and Unit Comprehension Checks

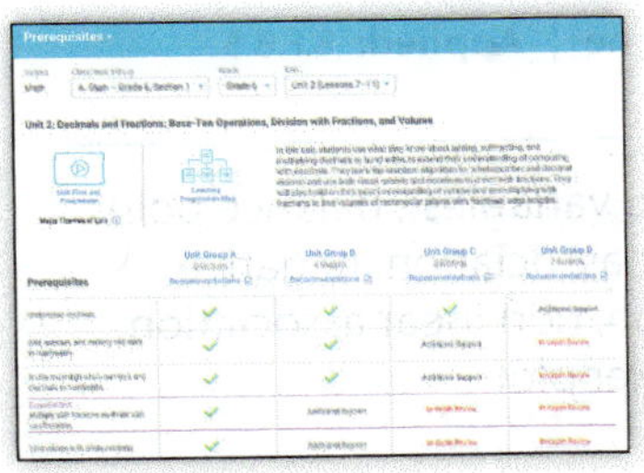

Prerequisites Report

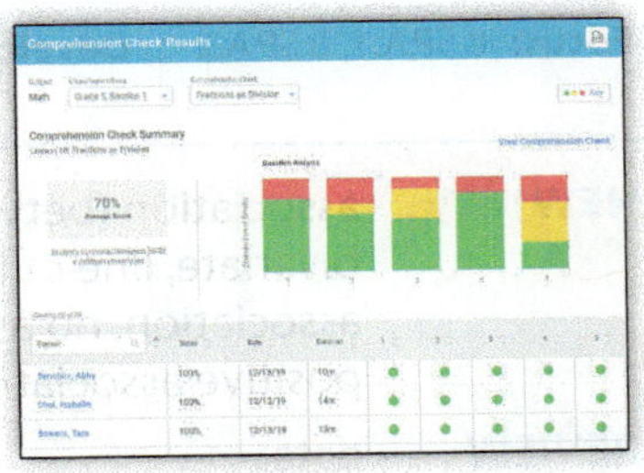

Comprehension Check Reports

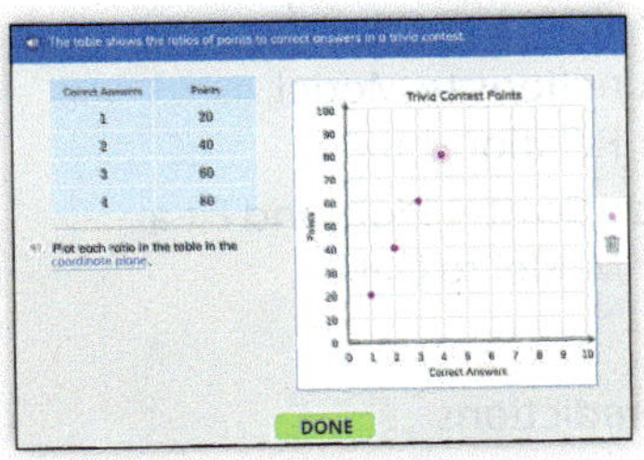

Interactive Tutorials

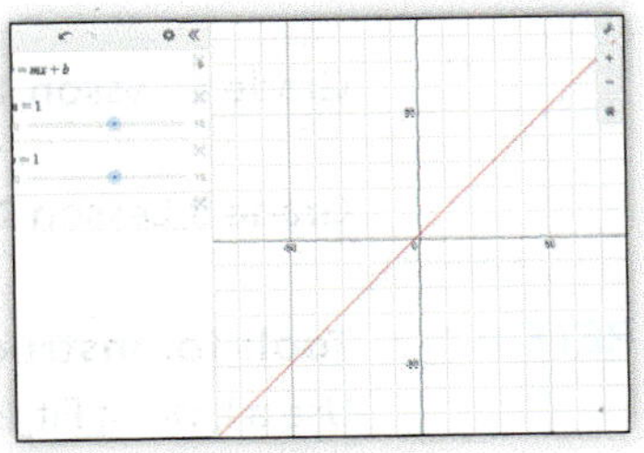

Digital Math Tools powered by Desmos

Learning Games

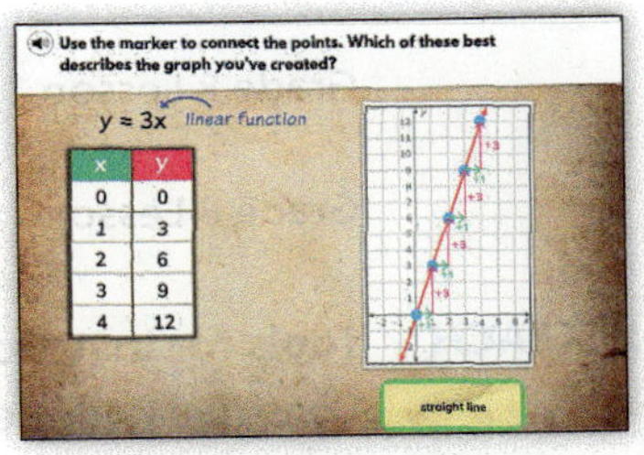

Optional Add-On: *i-Ready Personalized Instruction*

Microsoft PowerPoint® is a registered trademark of Microsoft Corporation.

UNIT 7

Statistics

Two-Variable Data and Fitting a Linear Model

Before the Unit

- Self Check
- Prepare for Two-Variable Data and Fitting a Linear Model

After the Unit

- Math in Action
- Self Reflection
- Vocabulary Review
- Unit Review & Performance Task
- Unit Assessment, Forms A and B
- Digital Comprehension Checks

LESSON 29

Analyze Scatter Plots and Fit a Linear Model to Data

PACING: 5 sessions

OBJECTIVES

- Construct scatter plots for sets of bivariate data.
- Interpret scatter plots to determine the association between two quantities.
- Interpret the meaning of an association between two quantities, in context.
- Determine, informally by visual inspection, whether a line is a good fit for data that show a linear association.
- Informally determine a line of fit for data that show a linear association.

STANDARDS

Focus: 8.SP.A.1, 8.SP.A.2 | **Developing:** none | **Applied:** 8.F.B.5

VOCABULARY

NEW association (between two variables), balance point, bivariate, line of fit, linear association, negative association, no association, nonlinear association, positive association, scatter plot

REVIEW data

ACADEMIC shape (of data)

LESSON-LEVEL DIFFERENTIATION

PREPARE **Ready Prerequisite Lessons**

Grade 6 Lesson 28 Solve Problems in the Coordinate Plane

Grade 8 Lesson 16 Use Functions to Model Linear Relationships

Grade 8 Lesson 18 Analyze Functional Relationships Qualitatively

RETEACH **Tools for Instruction**

Construct and Use Scatter Plots

REINFORCE **Center Activity**

Use Vocabulary for Scatter Plots

EXTEND **Enrichment Activity**

Geometric Associations

See the Lesson Overview for additional session-level differentiation.

LESSON 30

Write and Analyze an Equation for Fitting a Linear Model to Data

PACING: 4 sessions

OBJECTIVES

- Write an equation of a linear model for data with a linear association.
- Interpret the slope and *y*-intercept of a linear model in the context of the data.
- Use a linear model to solve problems in the context of the data.

STANDARDS

Focus: 8.SP.A.3 | **Developing:** none | **Applied:** 8.F.A.3, 8.F.B.4, 8.SP.A.1, 8.SP.A.2

NEW none

REVIEW estimate (noun), estimate (verb), linear association, slope, *y*-intercept

ACADEMIC analyze, interpret, predict

PREPARE **Ready Prerequisite Lessons**

Grade 8 Lesson 9 Derive and Graph Linear Equations of the Form $y = mx + b$

Grade 8 Lesson 16 Use Functions to Model Linear Relationships

Grade 8 Lesson 29 Analyze Scatter Plots and Fit a Linear Model to Data

RETEACH **Tools for Instruction**

Use a Line of Fit to Make Predictions

REINFORCE **Center Activity**

Scatter Plot Predictions

EXTEND **Enrichment Activity**

Elephant Pics

See the Lesson Overview for additional session-level differentiation.

LESSON 31

Understand Two-Way Tables

PACING: 3 sessions

OBJECTIVES

- Understand how to read, interpret, and build two-way tables that show frequencies.
- Understand the distinction between measurement data and categorical data.
- Understand how patterns of association can be seen by using a two-way table.

STANDARDS

Focus: 8.SP.A.4 | **Developing:** none | **Applied:** none

NEW categorical data, two-way table

REVIEW association (between two variables), data

ACADEMIC category, cell, survey

PREPARE **Ready Prerequisite Lesson**
Grade 6 Lesson 14 Use Part-to-Part and Part-to-Whole Ratios

RETEACH **Tools for Instruction**
Reading Two-Way Tables

REINFORCE **Center Activity**
Complete Two-Way Tables

EXTEND **Enrichment Activity**
To Dance or Not to Dance . . .

See the Lesson Overview for additional session-level differentiation.

NOTES

. . . continued

Two-Variable Data and Fitting a Linear Model

LESSON 32

Construct and Interpret Two-Way Tables

PACING: 4 sessions

OBJECTIVES

- Construct two-way tables of relative frequencies using row totals, column totals, or the overall total.
- Interpret two-way tables of relative frequencies.
- Analyze patterns of association in two-way tables of relative frequencies.

STANDARDS

Focus: 8.SP.A.4 | **Developing:** none | **Applied:** none

VOCABULARY

NEW	relative frequency
REVIEW	association (between two variables), frequency, percent, random sample, two-way table
ACADEMIC	likelihood, random

LESSON-LEVEL DIFFERENTIATION

PREPARE — **Ready Prerequisite Lessons**

- **Grade 6 Lesson 14** Use Part-to-Part and Part-to-Whole Ratios
- **Grade 6 Lesson 18** Use Percents to Solve Problems
- **Grade 8 Lesson 31** Understand Two-Way Tables

RETEACH — **Tools for Instruction**
Two-Way Tables

REINFORCE — **Center Activity**
Match Relative Frequency

EXTEND — **Enrichment Activity**
Trees Under Attack

See the Lesson Overview for additional session-level differentiation.

Math IN Action

Math Lessons from the Real World

Internet Users | Age Groups | Emissions, GDP, and Urban Population

PACING: 2 sessions

KEY SKILLS

- Make and interpret scatter plots.
- Make two-way tables showing frequencies and relative frequencies.
- Describe the association between two variables.
- Use a scatter plot to make predictions about missing data.

STANDARDS

Focus: 8.SP.A.1, 8.SP.A.2, 8.SP.A.3, 8.SP.A.4

Digital Resources

- Unit and Lesson Comprehension Checks
- Comprehension Check Reports
- Prerequisites Report
- Digital Tools powered by Desmos®
- Interactive Tutorials
- Learning Games (available 2020)
- Digital Practice (available 2021)

i-Ready

A personalized instruction path helps students fill prerequisite gaps and build up grade-level skills.

NOTES

Two-Variable Data and Fitting a Linear Model

Which lessons are students building upon?

Grade 6, Lesson 28
Solve Problems in the Coordinate Plane
6.NS.C.8, 6.G.A.3

→

Grade 8, Lesson 16
Use Functions to Model Linear Relationships
8.F.B.4

→

Grade 8, Lesson 18
Analyze Functional Relationships Qualitatively
8.F.B.5

Grade 8, Lesson 9
Derive and Graph Linear Equations of the Form $y = mx + b$
8.EE.B.6

→

Grade 8, Lesson 16
Use Functions to Model Linear Relationships
8.F.B.4

→

Grade 8, Lesson 29
Analyze Scatter Plots and Fit a Linear Model to Data
8.SP.A.1, 8.SP.A.2

Grade 6, Lesson 14
Use Part-to-Part and Part-to-Whole Ratios
6.RP.A.3a

Grade 6, Lesson 14
Use Part-to-Part and Part-to-Whole Ratios
6.RP.A.3a

→

Grade 6, Lesson 18
Use Percents to Solve Problems
6.RP.A.3c

→

Grade 8, Lesson 31
Understand Two-Way Tables
8.SP.A.4

In this unit . . .

Lesson 29
Analyze Scatter Plots and Fit a Linear Model to Data
8.SP.A.1, 8.SP.A.2

Lesson 30
Write and Analyze an Equation for Fitting a Linear Model to Data
8.SP.A.3

Lesson 31
Understand Two-Way Tables
8.SP.A.4

Lesson 32
Construct and Interpret Two-Way Tables
8.SP.A.4

Which lessons are students preparing for?

In this unit		
Lesson 29: Analyze Scatter Plots and Fit a Linear Model to Data (8.SP.A.1, 8.SP.A.2)	Statistics and Probability: Interpreting Categorical and Quantitative Data, HSS.ID.B.6b	Statistics and Probability: Interpreting Categorical and Quantitative Data, HSS.ID.B.6c
Lesson 30: Write and Analyze an Equation for Fitting a Linear Model to Data (8.SP.A.3)	Statistics and Probability: Interpreting Categorical and Quantitative Data, HSS.ID.C.7	Statistics and Probability: Interpreting Categorical and Quantitative Data, HSS.ID.C.8
Lesson 31: Understand Two-Way Tables (8.SP.A.4)	Grade 8, Lesson 32: Construct and Interpret Two-Way Tables, 8.SP.A.4	Statistics and Probability: Conditional Probability and the Rules of Probability, HSS.CP.A.4
Lesson 32: Construct and Interpret Two-Way Tables (8.SP.A.4)	Statistics and Probability: Interpreting Categorical and Quantitative Data, HSS.ID.B.5	Statistics and Probability: Interpreting Categorical and Quantitative Data, HSS.ID.C.9

Professional Learning

Discourse as a Tool for Learning the Language of Mathematics

Adapted from *Teaching Mathematics to English Language Learners,* by Dr. Gladis Kersaint

Gladis Kersaint, Ph.D.
Dr. Kersaint is the Dean of the Neag School of Education at the University of Connecticut and a respected scholar in mathematics education whose research focuses on equity, mathematical discourse, and effective teaching and learning of at-risk students.

All students are mathematics language learners, regardless of their level of English language proficiency and whether they are English language learners or proficient speakers of English (Thompson et al., 2008).

Although it is important to build scaffolds to support students who are learning English and mathematics at the same time, it is essential to recognize that mathematics is a technical language that *all* students must learn. Students who are proficient English speakers also require support as they learn the language of mathematics. Mathematical discourse allows all students to develop mathematical language.

As indicated in the Standards for Mathematical Practice, students should attend to precision by using correct mathematical language, including vocabulary, symbolic representations, syntax, semantics, and linguistic features (Kersaint, Thompson, and Petkova, 2013). In addition, they must have **ample opportunities to use the language of mathematics** as they engage in various forms of communication.

Discourse allows students to practice precision in multiple areas, including:

Vocabulary

- English words with a different meaning in mathematics, such as *negative, table,* or *rational.*
- Specialized terms, such as *hypotenuse* or *trapezoid.*
- Terms with multiple meanings in mathematics, such as *median* or *base.*

Symbols

- Ways to read and interpret symbolic representations; for example, $a \times b$ can be expressed as *a times* b, *the product of* a *and* b, or *multiply* a *and* b.

Syntax

- Understanding the rules that govern the structure of sentences; for example, *A number y is 4 more than a number x* is translated symbolically to $y = x + 4$.

Semantics

- The process of making meaning from language.
- The same mathematics word may be interpreted differently depending on the context. For example: *the median of a set of numbers* versus *the median of a triangle.*

Try-Discuss-Connect

The *Try-Discuss-Connect* routine offers regular opportunities for students to use the language of mathematics as they share ideas with partners or the class. In addition, language routines such as Three Reads support students in making meaning from academic and mathematical language.

Develop Academic Language

Develop Academic Language guides students in interpreting academic language and using it in discourse during each lesson. Students build vocabulary with academic or mathematical words and phrases, and they take apart precise academic sentences to extract meaning. Conversation tips offer practical ways for students to express and connect mathematical ideas in partner or class discussion.

DEVELOP ACADEMIC LANGUAGE

WHY? Unpack meaning of dense sentences.

HOW? Read Connect It problem 5. Chunk the second sentence: *Describe how one of them/ helped you better understand/ solving linear equations in one variable/ with the variable on both sides of the equation.* Say: *Think about a strategy.* Point to relevant chunks and ask: *What did the strategy help you understand? What type of linear equations? Where is the variable in the equations?*

Differentiation for English Language Learners

Language Expectations

The chart below shows examples of what English learners at different levels of English language proficiency can do in connection with one of the Common Core State Standards (CCSS) addressed in this unit. As you plan for this unit, use these examples of language expectations to help you differentiate instruction to meet the needs of English learners.

Standard 8.SP.A.2 Know that straight lines are widely used to model relationships between two quantitative variables. For scatter plots that suggest a linear association, informally fit a straight line, and informally assess the model fit by judging the closeness of the data points to the line.

LANGUAGE DOMAINS	BEGINNING Level 1	INTERMEDIATE Level 2	Level 3	ADVANCED/ADVANCED HIGH Level 4	Level 5
LISTENING	Listen to a paraphrase of a multi-step word problem involving bivariate data. Connect the problem to pictures and to the axis labels of scatter plots with teacher support.	Listen to a paraphrase of a multi-step word problem involving bivariate data. Connect the problem to pictures and to the axis labels of scatter plots with peer support.	Listen to a paraphrase of a multi-step word problem involving bivariate data. Connect the problem to pictures and to the axis labels of scatter plots with peer support.	Listen to a multi-step word problem involving bivariate data. Connect the problem to the axis labels of scatter plots with peer support.	Listen to a multi-step word problem involving bivariate data. Connect the problem to the axis labels of scatter plots.
SPEAKING	With a partner, use sentence frames to tell whether a line is or is not a good fit for bivariate data on a scatter plot. Justify that opinion by selecting from an illustrated list of sentences. (e.g., *The line is near the data points.*)	With a partner, use sentence frames to tell whether a line is or is not a good fit for bivariate data on a scatter plot and to justify that opinion using sentence frames.	In small-group discussions, express opinions about whether or not a line is a good fit for bivariate data on a scatter plot. Justify opinions by completing sentence starters.	Express opinions about whether or not a line is a good fit for bivariate data on a scatter plot. Justify opinions by using a list of descriptive phrases and a dictionary if needed.	Express opinions about whether or not a line is a good fit for bivariate data on a scatter plot. Justify opinions by using a list of descriptive phrases.
READING	Follow a series of one-step written instructions to draw a good line of fit for data with a linear association by connecting each step to illustrated examples with teacher modeling.	Follow a series of one-step written instructions to draw a good line of fit for data with a linear association by connecting each step to illustrated examples with teacher guidance.	Follow multi-step written instructions to draw a good line of fit for data with a linear association by working with teacher support to make sense of key terms and connect them to illustrated examples.	Follow multi-step written instructions to draw a good line of fit for data with a linear association by working with a partner to identify math terms and connect them to illustrated examples.	Follow multi-step written instructions to draw a good line of fit for data with a linear association by working with a partner to connect the steps to illustrated examples.
WRITING	With an illustrated word bank, determine whether data show a linear association and, if so, describe a good line of fit with peer support.	With a partner, determine whether data show a linear association and, if so, describe a good line of fit by using a word bank.	With a partner, determine whether data show a linear association and, if so, describe a good line of fit by using the Interactive Glossary.	Determine whether data show a linear association and, if so, describe a good line of fit by using lesson vocabulary.	Determine whether data show a linear association and, if so, describe a good line of fit.

Models, Progressions, and Teaching Tips

As you plan lessons, use this information to unpack the learning progressions and make connections between key concepts.

Unit Themes

The major themes of this unit are:

- You will build on what you know about one-variable data displays by constructing and analyzing two-variable data displays.
- Knowing about linear equations will help you model a linear pattern in a two-variable data set and use your model to make predictions.
- You will organize and interpret two-variable categorical data and describe possible associations between the variables using relative frequencies.

Prior Knowledge

Students will build on prior understandings of two-variable relationships.

Students should:

- be able to write an equation for a linear function.
- be able to plot points in the coordinate plane.
- be able to identify and interpret rate of change and initial value in context.
- understand the significance of clusters and outliers in a data display.

Watch the video
See the flow and progression of math concepts in this unit come to life with tips and insights on using models and making connections.

Bivariate Data

INSIGHTS ON . . .

Two-Variable Data

✔ In Grades 6 and 7, students explored univariate, or one-variable, data and used plots and measures of center and variability to describe data distributions. In Grade 8, students will explore bivariate, or two-variable, data and look for relationships, or associations, between the variables.

✔ Bivariate data can be *quantitative* or *categorical*. Quantitative data are numbers or measurements. Categorical data are data that are divided into groups or categories, such as characteristics of a population. Categorical data are often words.

EXAMPLE A data set that lists the number of hours slept and the test score for each student in a class is bivariate quantitative data. A data set that lists the grade and answer to a yes or no question for each student is bivariate categorical data.

Students learn that **bivariate data** are data for two paired variables collected from the same subjects.

Bivariate Quantitative Data

Hours Slept	6	8	8	7	9
Test Score	68	75	90	60	88

Bivariate Categorical Data

Grade	11	12	12	10
Like horseback riding?	yes	no	yes	no

Bivariate Quantitative Data

INSIGHTS ON . . .

Understanding Scatter Plots

✔ In Grade 6, students used dot plots, histograms, and box plots to display univariate data and described and interpreted gaps, clusters, and outliers. In Grade 8, they use scatter plots to display bivariate data and look for possible associations between the two variables.

✔ Each point on a scatter plot represents a pair of values for the two variables. Students see that a scatter plot can provide a picture of an association between the variables that is not obvious when the data are presented in lists.

✔ When using a scatter plot to analyze associations, students ask themselves: *Is there an association? Is the association linear? Is the association positive or negative?*

- Linear associations look roughly like a straight path of dots across the graph.
- Nonlinear associations look like a curved path across the graph.
- For positive associations, the path of points goes up from left to right. For negative associations, it goes down.
- When there is no association, the points make no path.

✔ Help students to recognize that an association between two variables does not imply that a change in one variable *causes* a change in the other.

EXAMPLE Suppose a scatter plot shows a positive association between the number of miles students live from school and the number of minutes it takes them to get ready in the morning. This does not mean that living farther from school causes students to take longer to get ready in the morning.

✔ Students must attend to precision when constructing scatter plots. Plotting points accurately can take time. To avoid getting bogged down, have students use digital tools for larger data sets.

✔ Common Misconception Students may not realize they can choose the scale of the axes or use a break in an axis when constructing a scatter plot. Ask: *If you used a different scale, what would look the same? What would look different?*

Students construct and analyze **scatter plots** to explore **associations** between variables in a bivariate data set.

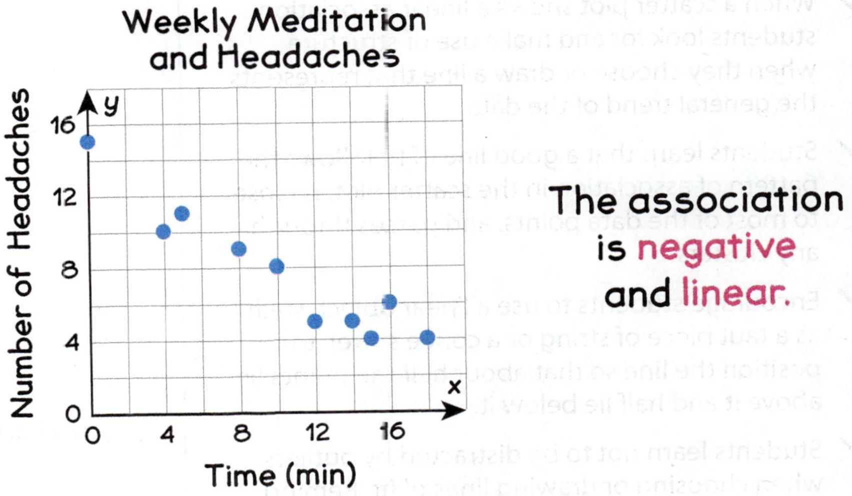

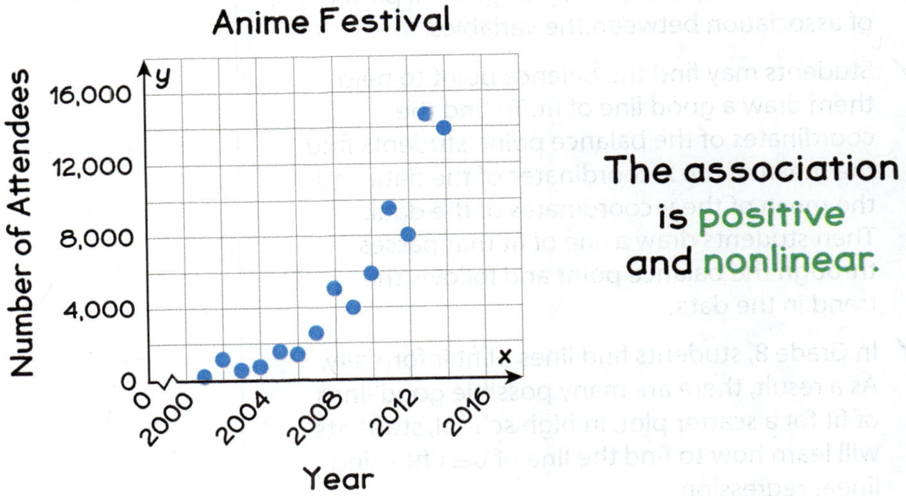

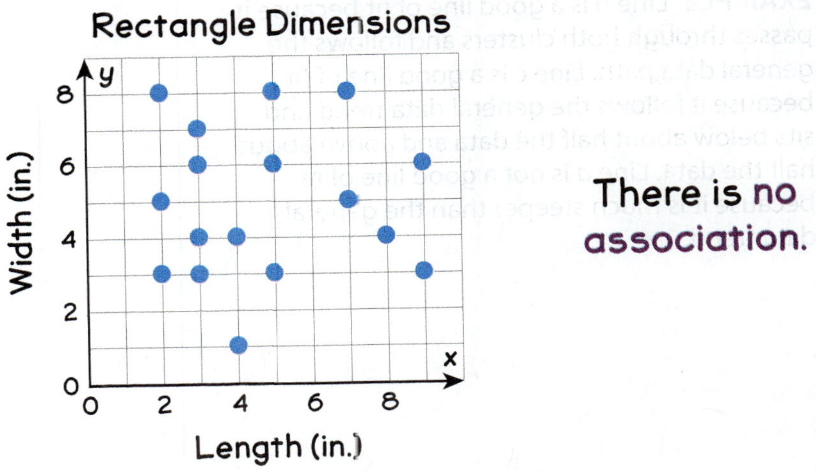

Bivariate Quantitative Data *(continued)*

INSIGHTS ON . . .

Informally Fitting a Line to a Scatter Plot

- ✔ When a scatter plot shows a linear association, students look for and make use of structure when they choose or draw a line that represents the general trend of the data.
- ✔ Students learn that a good line of fit follows the pattern of association in the scatter plot, is close to most of the data points, and passes through any clusters.
- ✔ Encourage students to use a linear object, such as a taut piece of string or a coffee stirrer, to position the line so that about half the points lie above it and half lie below it.
- ✔ Students learn not to be distracted by outliers when choosing or drawing lines of fit. Remind them that they are looking for general patterns of association between the variables.
- ✔ Students may find the balance point to help them draw a good line of fit. To find the coordinates of the balance point, students find the mean of the *x*-coordinates of the data and the mean of the *y*-coordinates of the data. Then students draw a line of fit that passes through the balance point and follows the trend in the data.
- ✔ In Grade 8, students find lines of fit informally. As a result, there are many possible good lines of fit for a scatter plot. In high school, students will learn how to find the line of best fit using linear regression.

EXAMPLE Line *b* is a good line of fit because it passes through both clusters and follows the general data path. Line *c* is a good line of fit because it follows the general data trend and sits below about half the data and above about half the data. Line *a* is not a good line of fit because it is much steeper than the general data trend.

Students **fit a line** to a scatter plot visually . . .

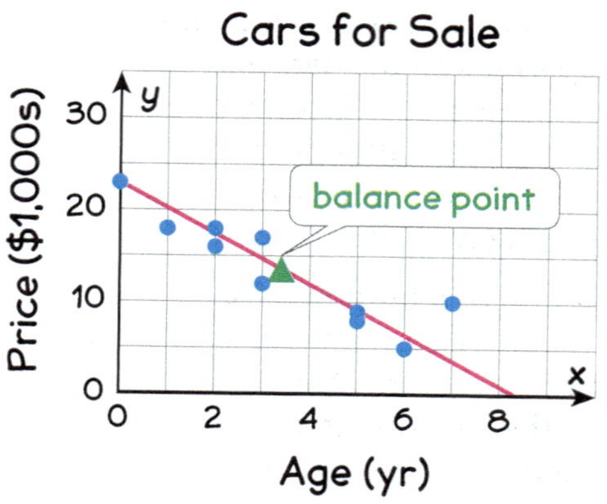

. . . and see that there can be more than one **good line of fit**.

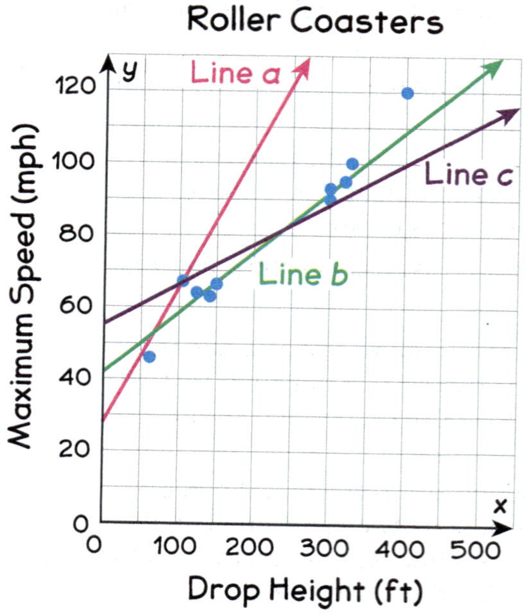

Line *b* and Line *c* fit the data well. Line *a* is not a good fit because it lies above most of the points.

Bivariate Quantitative Data *(continued)*

INSIGHTS ON . . .

Equations of a Good Line of Fit

✔ By using what they know about linear functions, students write an equation that models the line of fit for the data. To write the equation, students determine the *y*-intercept and slope and substitute these values into $y = mx + b$.

✔ It is not always possible to estimate the *y*-intercept of a line of fit from a graph, for example, when there is a break in the *x*-axis. In these cases, students will need to find the *y*-intercept algebraically.

✔ Students make sense of an equation for a line of fit by interpreting the slope and *y*-intercept in context. Encourage students to attend to precision when interpreting the rate of change and initial value and to check their answers for reasonableness.

EXAMPLE The *y*-intercept 118 means that, even with no money spent on online advertising, the company can expect sales of about $118,000. The slope 5.7 means that, for every additional thousand dollars spent on online advertising, the company can expect sales to increase by $5,700.

✔ Once students write an equation for a line of fit, they can use it to make predictions. Have students keep in mind that predictions found using a line of fit are estimates, not exact values.

✔ **Common Misconception** Watch for students who use a line of fit to make predictions far beyond the values in the data set. For example, predicting that spending $1,000,000 on advertising will result in sales of $5,818,000 might be unreasonable since the data set only includes *x*-values up to $6,000.

✔ Students also use the graph of a fit line (rather than its equation) to visually make predictions about the data. It is important to use points *on the line* and not points *from the data set*, since individual data points may stray from the path of the fit line.

EXAMPLE Since the line of fit passes through (4, 140), you could predict sales of $140,000 for $4,000 spent on online advertising.

Students **write an equation** for the line of fit . . .

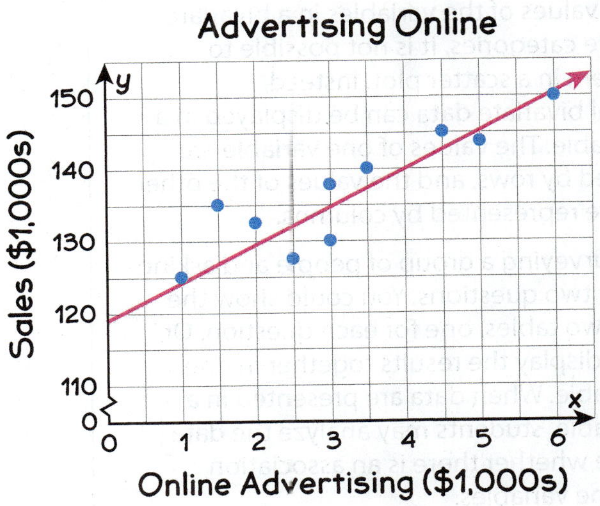

The *y*-intercept is about 118.

The line of fit appears to go through (0, 118) and (3, 135).

Slope: $\frac{135 - 118}{3 - 0} = \frac{17}{3} \approx 5.7$

The equation of the line of fit is $y = 5.7x + 118$.

. . . and use the equation to **interpret trends** in context and **make predictions**.

When the company spends $4,000 for online advertising, what might sales be?

$y = 5.7x + 118$

$y = 5.7(4) + 118$

$y = 140.8$

For $4,000 spent on online advertising, sales might reach $140,800.

Bivariate Categorical Data

INSIGHTS ON . . .

Understanding Two-Way Tables

- ✔ When the values of the variables in a bivariate data set are categories, it is not possible to display them in a scatter plot. Instead, categorical bivariate data can be displayed in a two-way table. The values of one variable are represented by rows, and the values of the other variable are represented by columns.
- ✔ Imagine surveying a group of people and asking them each two questions. You could show the results in two tables, one for each question. Or, you could display the results together in one two-way table. When data are presented in a two-way table, students may analyze the data and decide whether there is an association between the variables.
- ✔ Students see that it is sometimes possible to display *quantitative* data in a two-way table. First, the data values have to be separated into intervals. Each interval can then be represented as a category in a table.

  EXAMPLE The variable age could be separated into categories for children (ages less than 18 years) and adults (ages 18 years or greater).
- ✔ Error Alert If students calculate totals and write 240 in the bottom right cell, they may have added 36 + 42 + 42 + 72 + 48. Point out that the number in the bottom right cell can be found by adding the values above it in the Total column *or* by adding the values to the left of it in the Total row. These totals will be the same. It is not the sum of all numbers in that row *and* column.
- ✔ To help students understand how two-way tables are constructed and used, give them an opportunity to collect bivariate categorical data and display their results in a two-way table. For example, they might ask their classmates whether or not they have pets and whether or not they have siblings.

Students use **bivariate categorical data** to construct **two-way tables** . . .

What grade are you in?

Do you like to play board games?

	G6	G7	G8	Total
Yes	12	24	36	72
No	24	18	6	48
Total	36	42	42	120

total number of G6 students surveyed

G8 students who do not like board games

total number of students surveyed

. . . and use them to **identify and describe associations.**

Is there an association between the grade level and the number of students who like board games?

Since there are about the same number of students in each grade, compare the number of students who replied *yes*.

Board games are more popular with Grade 8 students than with students in Grade 6 or Grade 7.

Bivariate Categorial Data *(continued)*

INSIGHTS ON . . .

Relative Frequency Two-Way Tables

✔ When the number of responses is nearly evenly divided between categories, students may compare frequencies to look for associations in the data. When the number of responses is not evenly divided, students learn to calculate and compare relative frequencies.

✔ A relative frequency is the quotient of the number of times a response occurs and the total number of responses in a single category or in a whole survey.

✔ Two-way tables show relative frequencies by row or by column. Students find that the totals to use depend on the *whole* in the question they are trying to answer.

EXAMPLE The first question asks about the percent of Grade 8 students. So, the totals used to compute the relative frequencies should be the grade-level totals. The second question asks about the percent of students who like board games. So, the totals used to compute the relative frequencies should be the totals of the Yes and No rows.

Students analyze patterns in **two-way tables** of **relative frequencies** using **column totals** . . .

What percent of Grade 8 students like board games?

	G6	G7	G8	Total
Yes	$\frac{12}{36} \approx 33\%$	$\frac{24}{42} \approx 57\%$	$\frac{36}{42} \approx 86\%$	$\frac{72}{120} = 60\%$
No	$\frac{24}{36} \approx 67\%$	$\frac{18}{42} \approx 43\%$	$\frac{6}{42} \approx 14\%$	$\frac{48}{120} = 40\%$
Total	100%	100%	100%	

. . . and **row totals.**

What percent of students who like board games are in Grade 6?

	G6	G7	G8	Total
Yes	$\frac{12}{72} \approx 17\%$	$\frac{24}{72} \approx 33\%$	$\frac{36}{72} = 50\%$	100%
No	$\frac{24}{48} = 50\%$	$\frac{18}{48} \approx 38\%$	$\frac{6}{48} \approx 12\%$	100%
Total	$\frac{36}{120} = 30\%$	$\frac{42}{120} = 35\%$	$\frac{42}{120} = 35\%$	

Future Learning

Students will move on to extend their knowledge of bivariate data.

Students will:

- learn about linear regression to find the line of best fit for a data set.
- informally assess the fit of a function by plotting and analyzing residuals.
- use technology to interpret the correlation coefficient of a linear model.
- use two-way tables as a sample space to approximate conditional probability.

Unit Big Ideas

This unit introduces students to bivariate data. This includes quantitative data displayed in scatter plots and analyzed with lines of fit, and categorical data displayed in two-way tables and analyzed with relative frequencies. Students preview the skills they will be learning in this unit and assess what they know and do not know about them. Students record their progress after completing each lesson and reflect on their learning at the end of the unit.

The major themes of this unit are:

- You will build on what you know about one-variable data displays by constructing and analyzing two-variable data displays.
- Knowing about linear equations will help you model a linear pattern in a two-variable data set and use your model to make predictions.
- You will organize and interpret two-variable categorical data and describe possible associations between the variables using relative frequencies.

Self Check

- Take a few minutes to have each student independently read through the list of skills. Ask students to consider each skill and check the box if it is a skill they think they already have.
- Remind students that these skills are likely to all be new to them and that over time, they will be able to check off more and more skills.

Support Whole Class Discussion

Engage students in a discussion about the skills with questions such as:

- *Which skills seem related to something you already know?*
- *Which skills do you think you would use in your everyday life? Why?*

Support Growth Mindset

At the end of the unit, have students review the skills on the **Student Book Self Reflection** page and work in pairs to respond to the prompts. Encourage students to revisit the work they did in each lesson.

Unit 7

Statistics

Two-Variable Data and Fitting a Linear Model

Self Check Before starting this unit, check off the skills you know below. As you complete each lesson, see how many more skills you can check off!

I can . . .	Before	After
Make and use scatter plots to recognize and describe patterns and associations in two-variable data.	☐	☐
Assess linear models for good fit to a set of data.	☐	☐
Write and interpret equations for linear models that are good lines of fit for data.	☐	☐
Understand and identify associations in two-variable categorical data by displaying frequencies in two-way tables.	☐	☐
Construct and interpret two-way tables with relative frequencies.	☐	☐
Explain my ideas about two-variable data clearly by using models to show why the ideas make sense for the problem.	☐	☐

Unit Skills	Lesson
Make and use scatter plots to recognize and describe patterns and associations in two-variable data.	29
Assess linear models for good fit to a set of data.	29
Write and interpret equations for linear models that are good lines of fit for data.	30
Understand and identify associations in two-variable categorical data by displaying frequencies in two-way tables.	31, 32
Construct and interpret two-way tables with relative frequencies.	32
Explain your ideas about two-variable data clearly by using models to show why the ideas make sense for the problem.	29–32

Prepare for Unit 7

- Read the directions and the labels in the box, or have a student do so. Call on volunteers to explain the task in their own words.
- Have students label each graph using the labels in the box.
- Have students work with a partner to share their ideas and explain their thinking. Encourage students to revise their work if needed.
- Circulate and validate responses and clarify any misconceptions.
- After most students have finished, debrief with a whole class discussion.

Build Academic Vocabulary

- Display academic terms that will be used throughout this unit when discussing word problems and possible solutions: *analyze* and *model*. Students will likely have some prior knowledge of the terms from math learning in previous grade levels. Use the **Academic Vocabulary** routine described in Unit 1 Professional Learning to provide explicit instruction and active engagement.
- Additional academic vocabulary for each lesson is listed in the Lesson Overview. The cognate chart below includes the Spanish cognates for academic vocabulary introduced in the unit and in each lesson. To support students whose primary language is Spanish, use the **Cognate Support** routine described in Unit 1 Professional Learning
- Support students as they move from informal language to formal academic language by using the **Collect and Display** routine. Have students refer to the chart during discussion and writing.

UNIT 7

Prepare for Two-Variable Data and Fitting a Linear Model

➤ **You have learned about functions, relationships, and rates of change. Label each graph of a function with the labels below. You may use the same graph of a function for more than one label.**

increasing function	decreasing function	linear function
constant rate of change	varying rate of change	nonlinear function

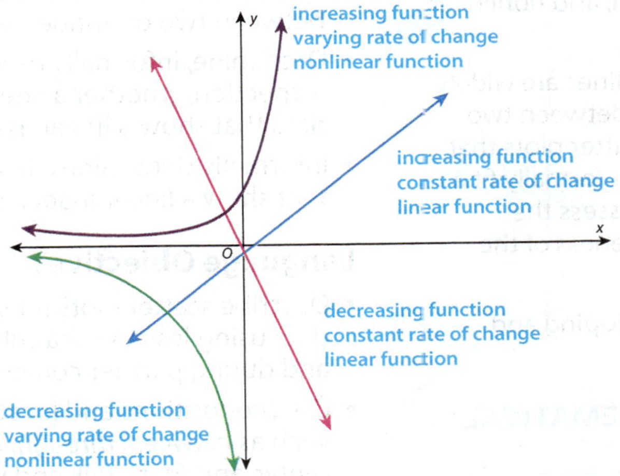

Compare your answers with a partner and explain your thinking. Discuss the answers on which you disagree. You may revise or add to your work.

Answers will vary. Check student work on the graph.

694

Cognates for Academic Vocabulary in Unit 7

ACADEMIC WORD	SPANISH COGNATE	ACADEMIC WORD	SPANISH COGNATE
analyze	*analizar*	interpret	*interpretar*
category	*categoría*	model	*modelo*
cell	*célula*	predict	*predecer*

Overview | Analyze Scatter Plots and Fit a Linear Model to Data

MATH FOCUS

Focus Standards

8.SP.A.1 Construct and interpret scatter plots for bivariate measurement data to investigate patterns of association between two quantities. Describe patterns such as clustering, outliers, positive or negative association, linear association, and nonlinear association.

8.SP.A.2 Know that straight lines are widely used to model relationships between two quantitative variables. For scatter plots that suggest a linear association, informally fit a straight line, and informally assess the model fit by judging the closeness of the data points to the line.

See Unit 7 Overview for developing and applied standards.

STANDARDS FOR MATHEMATICAL PRACTICE (SMP)

SMP 1, 2, 3, 4, 5, and 6 are integrated into the Try-Discuss-Connect routine.*

This lesson provides additional support for:

2 Reason abstractly and quantitatively.

3 Construct viable arguments and critique the reasoning of others.

5 Use appropriate tools strategically.

* See page 1o to learn how every lesson includes these SMP.

Objectives

Content Objectives

- Construct scatter plots for sets of bivariate data.
- Interpret scatter plots to determine the association between two quantities.
- Interpret the meaning of an association between two quantities, in context.
- Determine, informally by visual inspection, whether a line is a good fit for data that show a linear association.
- Informally determine a line of fit for data that show a linear association.

Language Objectives

- Describe scatter plots for sets of bivariate data using lesson vocabulary in writing and during partner conversations.
- Use prepositions and location words, such as *between, through, to, close, center,* and *far* to talk and write about relationships between two quantities.
- Use lesson vocabulary to explain whether lines on a scatter plot are good lines of fit for the data.

Prior Knowledge

- Plotting and reading points on the coordinate plane.
- Analyzing one-variable data.
- Finding, understanding, and comparing measures of center and variability.
- Writing linear functions.

Vocabulary

Math Vocabulary

association (between two variables) a relationship between two variables.

balance point the point that represents the center of a data set. In a two-variable data set, the coordinates of the balance point are the mean of each variable.

bivariate involving two variables.

line of fit a line drawn on a scatter plot to approximately model the relationship between the two sets of data.

linear association an association in which the relationship between the two variables can be generally approximated using a line.

negative association a linear association in which as the value of one variable increases, generally the value of the other variable decreases.

no association when two variables have no relationship or association.

nonlinear association an association in which no line can reasonably describe the relationship between two variables.

positive association a linear association in which as the value of one variable increases, generally the value of the other variable increases.

scatter plot a graph of two-variable data displayed as ordered pairs.

Review the following key term.

data a set of collected information.

Academic Vocabulary

shape (of data) a description of the way the lines on a graph or dots on a scatter plot are arranged.

Learning Progression

In Grade 6, students calculated measures of center.

In Grade 7, students wrote equations to model proportional relationships between two variables.

Earlier in Grade 8, students worked with linear functions and interpreted slopes and *y*-intercepts in context.

In this lesson, students work with two-variable data. They use scatter plots to determine whether there is an association between the variables. In cases where there is a linear association, students learn to informally fit a line to model the data and to evaluate a given line to determine whether it is a good fit.

Later in Grade 8, students will explore linear associations in more depth, writing and analyzing equations for lines of fit. In later lessons, they will consider and analyze two-variable categorical data.

Pacing Guide

Items marked with ✱ are available on the **Teacher Toolbox**.

SESSION 1 **Explore** Scatter Plots (35–50 min)

- **Start** (5 min)
- **Try It** (5–10 min)
- **Discuss It** (10–15 min)
- **Connect It** (10–15 min)
- **Close: Exit Ticket** (5 min)

Additional Practice (pages 699–700)

Math Toolkit graph paper, graphing calculator

Presentation Slides ✱

PREPARE Interactive Tutorial ✱

RETEACH or REINFORCE Hands-On Activity
Materials For each pair: stopwatch

SESSION 2 **Develop** Using a Scatter Plot to Analyze Data (45–60 min)

- **Start** (5 min)
- **Try It** (10–15 min)
- **Discuss It** (10–15 min)
- **Connect It** (15–20 min)
- **Close: Exit Ticket** (5 min)

Additional Practice (pages 705–706)

Math Toolkit calculator, graph paper, graphing calculator

Presentation Slides ✱

RETEACH or REINFORCE Visual Model

REINFORCE Fluency & Skills Practice ✱

EXTEND Deepen Understanding

SESSION 3 **Develop** Assessing Linear Models for Good Fit (45–60 min)

- **Start** (5 min)
- **Try It** (10–15 min)
- **Discuss It** (10–15 min)
- **Connect It** (15–20 min)
- **Close: Exit Ticket** (5 min)

Additional Practice (pages 711–712)

Presentation Slides ✱

RETEACH or REINFORCE Visual Model
Materials For display: 4 scatter plots, string

REINFORCE Fluency & Skills Practice ✱

EXTEND Deepen Understanding

SESSION 4 **Develop** Fitting a Linear Model Informally (45–60 min)

- **Start** (5 min)
- **Try It** (10–15 min)
- **Discuss It** (10–15 min)
- **Connect It** (15–20 min)
- **Close: Exit Ticket** (5 min)

Additional Practice (pages 717–718)

Math Toolkit calculator, straightedges, string

Presentation Slides ✱

RETEACH or REINFORCE Hands-On Activity
Materials For each student: chenille stem, tape, Activity Sheet *Scatter Plot with Linear Association* ✱

REINFORCE Fluency & Skills Practice ✱

EXTEND Deepen Understanding

SESSION 5 **Refine** Analyzing Scatter Plots and Fitting a Linear Model to Data (45–60 min)

- **Start** (5 min)
- **Monitor & Guide** (15–20 min)
- **Group & Differentiate** (20–30 min)
- **Close: Exit Ticket** (5 min)

Math Toolkit Have items from previous sessions available for students.

Presentation Slides ✱

RETEACH Hands-On Activity
Materials For each student: chenille stem, tape, Activity Sheet *Coordinate Plane: First Quadrant* ✱

REINFORCE Problems 4–7

EXTEND Challenge

PERSONALIZE i-Ready

Lesson 29 Quiz ✱ or **Digital Comprehension Check**

RETEACH Tools for Instruction ✱

REINFORCE Math Center Activity ✱

EXTEND Enrichment Activity ✱

Overview | Analyze Scatter Plots and Fit a Linear Model to Data

Connect to Culture

➤ **Use these activities to connect with and leverage the diverse backgrounds and experiences of all students. Engage students in sharing what they know about contexts before you add the information given here.**

SESSION 1 ■□□□□

Try It Take a survey on how much screen time students spend, on average, per day. Screen time can include time spent looking at any screen, such as a television, computer, phone, or game console. While some screen time is educational, studies show that too much screen time can result in several health problems. With some careful self-monitoring, healthy screen-time habits can be developed.

SESSION 2 ■■□□□

Try It Invite students to share their experiences with watching anime. *Anime* is a Japanese word referring to animation. Anime can be seen in television shows, games, and movies. Anime productions try to emotionally involve the viewer by using brilliant colors, emphasized facial expressions, and engaging narratives. Anime festivals take place all over the world and allow those with this common interest to network and learn about new anime media.

Year	Number of Attendees	Year	Number of Attendees
2001	149	2009	3,996
2002	1,015	2010	5,894
2003	449	2011	9,771
2004	755	2012	7,999
2005	1,476	2013	14,875
2006	1,390	2014	13,877
2007	2,697	2015	22,312
2008	5,001		

SESSION 3 ■■■□□

Apply It **Problem 7** Invite students who have been on a roller coaster to explain what it felt like and describe any unique features of the roller coaster. Most roller coasters have tracks made of steel or wood. Roller coasters have various twists, turns, and speeds. One of the fastest and highest roller coasters in the United States is Top Thrill Dragster at Cedar Point in Sandusky, Ohio. This roller coaster has a height of 420 feet and drops riders 400 feet at a speed of 120 miles per hour.

SESSION 4 ■■■■□

Try It Buying a house is the largest investment many Americans will make. House prices fluctuate with the economy, but are typically driven by inflation and the age and location of the house. Supply and demand as well as ability to obtain mortgages or other loans also play a part in the cost of a house. Ask students to brainstorm what might increase or decrease costs of houses in their area.

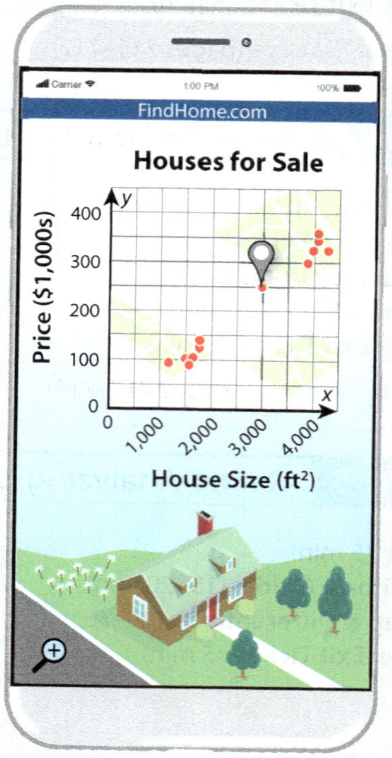

SESSION 5 ■■■■■

Apply It **Problem 2** Ask students to share which social media sites they use the most. Social media allows users to share pictures, post updates on their lives, watch videos, stay in touch with relatives and friends from a distance, and much more. Young adults were the first users of social media, but now people of all ages are involved in various platforms. In 2008, an estimated 1% of the U.S. population used social media. That number has since grown to around 80%.

Connect to Family and Community

➤ **After the Explore session, have students use the Family Letter to let their families know what they are learning and to encourage family involvement.**

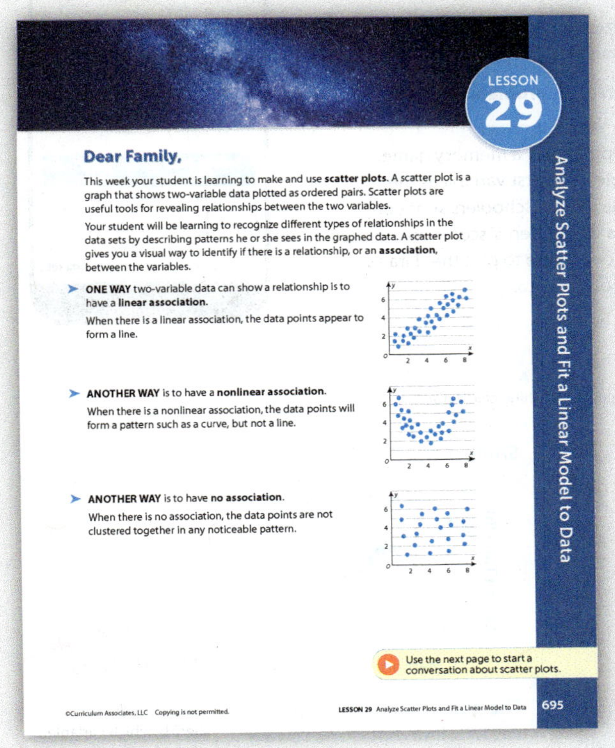
LESSON 29

Dear Family,

This week your student is learning to make and use **scatter plots.** A scatter plot is a graph that shows two-variable data plotted as ordered pairs. Scatter plots are useful tools for revealing relationships between the two variables.

Your student will be learning to recognize different types of relationships in the data sets by describing patterns he or she sees in the graphed data. A scatter plot gives you a visual way to identify if there is a relationship, or an **association,** between the variables.

➤ **ONE WAY** two-variable data can show a relationship is to have a **linear association.**

When there is a linear association, the data points appear to form a line.

➤ **ANOTHER WAY** is to have a **nonlinear association.**

When there is a nonlinear association, the data points will form a pattern such as a curve, but not a line.

➤ **ANOTHER WAY** is to have **no association.**

When there is no association, the data points are not clustered together in any noticeable pattern.

Use the next page to start a conversation about scatter plots.

Analyze Scatter Plots and Fit a Linear Model to Data

©Curriculum Associates, LLC Copying is not permitted. LESSON 29 Analyze Scatter Plots and Fit a Linear Model to Data 695

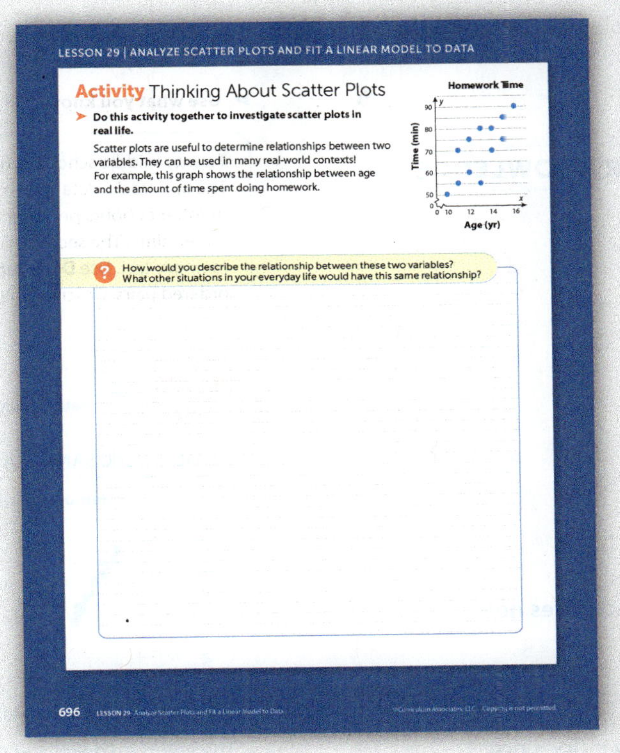
LESSON 29 | ANALYZE SCATTER PLOTS AND FIT A LINEAR MODEL TO DATA

Activity Thinking About Scatter Plots

➤ **Do this activity together to investigate scatter plots in real life.**

Scatter plots are useful to determine relationships between two variables. They can be used in many real-world contexts! For example, this graph shows the relationship between age and the amount of time spent doing homework.

How would you describe the relationship between these two variables? What other situations in your everyday life would have this same relationship?

696

Connect to Language

➤ **For English language learners, use the Differentiation chart to scaffold the language in each session. Use the Academic Vocabulary routine for academic terms before Session 1.**

DIFFERENTIATION | ENGLISH LANGUAGE LEARNERS — Use with **Session 1** **Connect It**

Levels 1–3: Reading/Speaking

Modify **Three Reads** to help students understand Connect It problems 2a and 2b. Read the first paragraph. Have students circle the words in bold. Begin a **Co-Constructed Word Bank** with the terms. Then reread the paragraph and have students circle words that can help them understand the words in bold. Add the words to the bank. Have students read a third time and discuss the words they learned. Repeat with the second paragraph. Explain that *modeled by* means *represented with*. Have students refer to the bank as they answer problems 2a and 2b. Ask: *Do the points follow a pattern? What pattern? What does this mean?*

Levels 2–4: Reading/Speaking

Modify **Three Reads** to help students make sense of Connect It problems 2a and 2b. Have students read the first paragraph with a partner and discuss the words in bold. Have them add the terms to a **Co-Constructed Word Bank.**

Then have partners reread the paragraph and circle words that define the words in bold. Have students add those words to the bank. Have partners read a third time and take turns defining the terms in bold. Repeat for the second paragraph. Call on volunteers to explain the meaning of *modeled by*. Then have students refer to the bank as they answer problems 2a and 2b. Ask: *What do you notice about the points on the graph? What does this mean?*

Levels 3–5: Reading/Speaking

Modify **Three Reads** to help students discuss and use the information in Connect It problems 2a and 2b. Have students read the first two paragraphs and discuss the meaning of the words in bold.

Have students read a second time and refer to the graph to provide examples of each term. Then have students read problems 2a and 2b and use **Say It Another Way to** explain what they need to find out. Encourage them to include terms from the problem and data from the scatter plot in their explanations. Have students extend discourse by adding on to a volunteer's explanation.

Explore Scatter Plots

Purpose

- **Explore** the idea that scatter plots can show an association between two variables.
- **Understand** that the association between variables is linear if the points follow a straight-line pattern, positive if one variable tends to increase while the other increases, and negative if one variable tends to decrease while the other increases.

START CONNECT TO PRIOR KNOWLEDGE

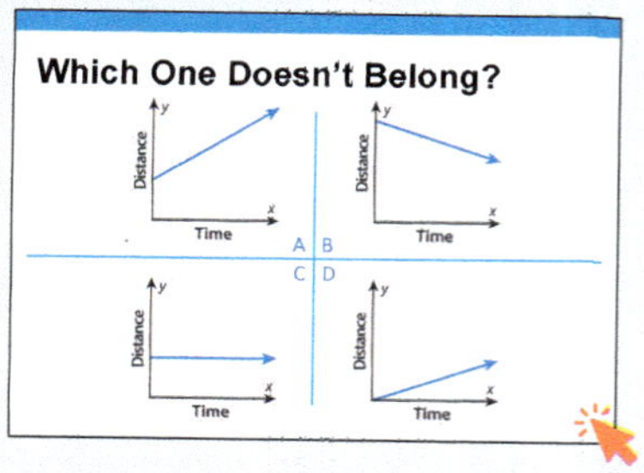

Possible Solutions

All are linear functions.

A is the only function where distance does not start at 0 and increases.

B is the only function where distance is decreasing.

C is the only function where distance does not change.

D is the only function where distance starts at 0.

WHY? Support students' facility with comparing and describing linear functions.

Explore Scatter Plots

Previously, you learned how to analyze one-variable data in dot plots. In this lesson, you will learn about analyzing two-variable data.

➤ **Use what you know to try to solve the problem below.**

Twenty middle schoolers use an app to play a memory game. The app tracks data for two variables. The first variable is the number of hours per week that the middle schoolers spent on screen time. The second variable is the students' scores on a memory test. Use **Data Set: Memory Game** to plot the data as ordered pairs. Describe the shape of the data.

Screen Time (h)	Memory Test Score
10	97
11	94
11	96

See page DS1 for the complete data set.

TRY IT Math Toolkit graph paper, graphing calculator

Possible work: SAMPLE A

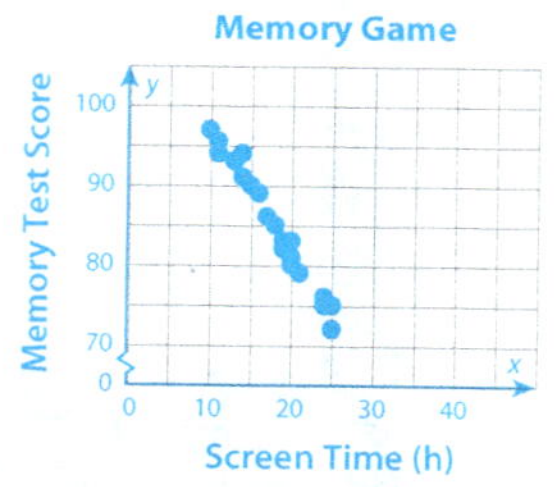

The points go down and to the right. They appear to follow a straight-line pattern.

SAMPLE B

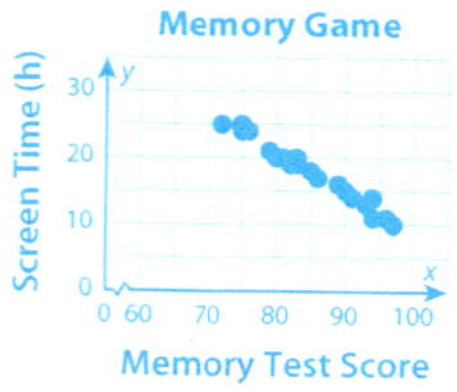

The points almost form a straight line that slopes down to the right.

DISCUSS IT

Ask: How did you decide which variable should go on the *x*-axis and which variable should go on the *y*-axis?

Share: I started by . . .

Learning Targets SMP 1, SMP 2, SMP 3, SMP 4, SMP 5, SMP 6

- Construct and interpret scatter plots for bivariate measurement data to investigate patterns such as clustering, outliers, positive or negative association, linear association, and nonlinear association.
- For scatter plots that suggest a linear association, informally fit a straight line, and informally assess the model fit by judging the closeness of the data points to the line.

697

TRY IT SMP 1, 2, 4, 5, 6

Make Sense of the Problem

See ***Connect to Culture*** to support student engagement. Before students work on Try It, use **Notice and Wonder** to help them make sense of the problem. Ask students what they notice about the data and what they might predict based on the problem.

DISCUSS IT SMP 2, 3, 4, 6

Support Partner Discussion

After students work on Try It, have them respond to Discuss It with a partner. Listen for understanding that:

- either variable can go on either axis, but usually, the independent variable goes on the *x*-axis.
- the test score depends on the screen time, so screen time is the independent variable.

Common Misconception Listen for students who think the scale on both axes must be the same. As students share their strategies, have students who used a different scale on the *x*-axis than on the *y*-axis, or who used a "break" in the scale to show a skip in numbers, explain their process.

Select and Sequence Student Strategies

Select 2–3 samples that represent the range of student thinking in your classroom. Here is one possible order for class discussion:

- scatter plot with memory test score on the *x*-axis
- (misconception) scatter plot with same scale on each axis
- scatter plot with screen time on the *x*-axis
- scatter plot using a "broken scale" on one or more axes

Facilitate Whole Class Discussion

Call on students to share selected strategies. Reinforce with students that clear explanations use complete sentences and precise vocabulary.

Guide students to **Compare and Connect** the representations. To emphasize key mathematical ideas in students' explanations, ask others to repeat and rephrase the statements. Record the ideas for reference during the lesson.

ASK *Do the points on the scatter plots that were presented show any particular pattern?*

LISTEN FOR The points are in a straight-line pattern that slants downward from left to right.

CONNECT IT

SMP 2, 4, 5

1 Look Back Look for understanding that as screen time increases, the memory score decreases.

DIFFERENTIATION | RETEACH or REINFORCE

Hands-On Activity

Gather data and make a scatter plot.

If students are unsure about how to make a scatter plot and look for a pattern in the data, then use this activity for another example of making a scatter plot using real-world data.

Materials For each pair: stopwatch

- Assign each pair a number of seconds between 5 and 20.
- Have one partner use the stopwatch and another partner sit in a chair and tap his or her foot and count the number of taps.
- When the partner with the stopwatch says *go*, the foot-tapping partner should tap one foot and count the number of taps until the partner with the stopwatch says *stop* after the assigned number of seconds.
- Display a two-column table with one column labeled *Time (s)* and the other *Taps*.
- Pairs should record their time and number of taps in this table.
- Make a scatter plot of the data with time on the *x*-axis and number of taps on the *y*-axis.
- Ask: *What is the pattern in the data?* [linear; As time increases, the number of taps increases.]
- Now make a scatter plot with number of taps on the *x*-axis and time on the *y*-axis. Ask: *What is the pattern in the data?* [linear; As the number of taps increases, the time increases.]
- Point out that the overall shape of the data does not change when you switch axis variables.

CONNECT IT

1 Look Back Describe the shape of the data. What do you notice about the relationship between the two variables?

The data have a linear shape. Possible answer: I noticed that when screen time is high, the memory test score is low. When screen time is low, the memory test score is high.

2 Look Ahead The graph shows data for two variables. Two-variable data sets are also called **bivariate** data sets. When you plot the data points from a bivariate data set, you make a **scatter plot**.

Scatter plots can visually show an **association**, or relationship, between the variables. When the points follow a linear pattern, they can be *modeled* by a straight line and have a **linear association**.

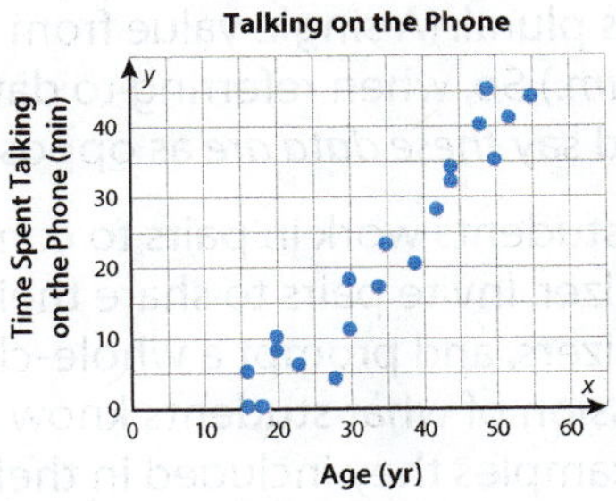

a. How does the scatter plot show that age and time spent talking on the phone have a linear association?

Possible answer: The points follow a straight-line pattern, moving upward from left to right.

b. Is it possible to draw a line that includes every data point? Explain.

No; Possible explanation: The data follow a linear pattern, but there is not one line that could connect every data point.

c. Linear association can be positive or negative. A **positive association** occurs when one variable tends to increase while the other increases. A **negative association** occurs when one variable tends to decrease while the other increases. Is there a positive or negative association between age and time spent talking on the phone? Explain.

A positive association. The data show that as age increases, the amount of time spent talking on the phone increases.

3 Reflect What do you think a scatter plot that does not have a linear association might look like?

Possible answer: The scatter plot might have points that seem randomly placed or the points might seem arranged in a shape other than a line.

2 Look Ahead Point out that the scatter plot shows a relationship, or association, between age and time spent talking on the phone. Although the points on the scatter plot do not fall exactly on a line, they do form a linear pattern. Discuss the fact that the pattern of points increases from left to right, which shows that as age increases, time spent talking on the phone tends to increase as well.

Ask volunteers to rephrase the definitions of *bivariate, scatter plot, association, linear association, positive association,* and *negative association*.

CLOSE EXIT TICKET

3 Reflect Look for understanding that points on a scatter plot that does not have a linear association do not have a linear pattern. They could have a curved pattern or no pattern at all.

Common Misconception If students think that a scatter plot must have a linear association, provide them with a data set that has no association and have them make a scatter plot. One possible data set is (1, 5), (2, 8), (3, 0), (4, 3), (5, 9), (6, 2), (7, 6), (8, 0), (9, 3).

Prepare for Analyzing Scatter Plots and Fitting a Linear Model to Data

Support Vocabulary Development

Assign **Prepare for Analyzing Scatter Plots and Fitting a Linear Model to Data** as extra practice in class or as homework.

If you have students complete this in class, then use the guidance below.

Ask students to consider the term *data*. Explain that *data* is plural. (A single value from a data set is called a *datum*.) So, when referring to data, students should say *these data are* as opposed to *this data is*.

Have students work in pairs to complete the graphic organizer. Invite pairs to share their completed organizers, and prompt a whole-class comparative discussion of what students know about data from the examples they included in their organizers.

Have students look at the statements in problem 2 and brainstorm with a partner some types of data displays. For each display, have partners discuss when that particular display would be used.

Problem Notes

1. Students should understand that data is a set of collected information. Students may mention data from surveys or scientific research. Students may also mention that data can be numbers or categories and can be given in a list or table or displayed in a graph.

2. Students should list various ways they have seen data presented. Students may say that tables are useful for seeing exact values, while graphs are useful for identifying patterns and trends in the data.

LESSON 29 | SESSION 1 Name:

Prepare for Analyzing Scatter Plots and Fitting a Linear Model to Data

1. Think about what you know about data and statistics. Fill in each box. Use words, numbers, and pictures. Show as many ideas as you can.
Possible answers:

What Is It?
a set of collected information, such as a list of measurements

What I Know About It
Data can be numbers like ages or not numbers like types of animals.
Data can be displayed in tables or graphs.
You can analyze data to answer questions and make decisions.

data

Examples

Text Messages Sent per Day	Number of Teens
0–20	8
21–40	1
41–60	3

Examples
test scores, salaries, time spent outside each day, daily temperatures, first names of students in my class, colors of markers, etc.

2. Name some ways data can be displayed. Explain when each display might be more useful.
Possible answer: I can display data in tables, line plots, and bar graphs. Tables are useful when I need exact numbers, but line plots or bar graphs can be more useful when I need to see trends or patterns in the data.

699

REAL-WORLD CONNECTION

A volcanologist is a scientist who studies volcanos. Volcanologists collect data on the intensity and duration of volcanic eruptions, the time between eruptions, and the frequency of underlying earthquakes. By plotting these data for a particular volcano and analyzing patterns or trends, they can try to predict the next time the volcano will erupt. Ask students to think of other real-world examples when plotting data and looking for patterns might be useful.

Additional Practice

3 Problem 3 provides another look at making a scatter plot and analyzing the shape of its data. This problem is similar to the problem about hours of screen time and memory test scores. In both problems, a scatter plot is made, and the plot is examined to see if a pattern in the data exists. This problem has students make a scatter plot of weights and life expectancies for various dog breeds.

Students may want to use graph paper to make their scatter plots.

Suggest that students use **Notice and Wonder** to help them make sense of the problem before they make their scatter plots.

LESSON 29 | SESSION 1

3 The table shows the average adult weight and average life expectancy for 12 dog breeds.

Average Weight (lb)	Life Expectancy (yr)
115	6.5
125	7
90	8.9
57.5	10.3
62.5	12.3
45	12
70	11
4.9	12.4
25	12.7
12	13.4
16	11
5	14.7

a. Plot the data as ordered pairs. Describe the shape of the data. Show your work.

Possible work and graph:

(115, 6.5), (125, 7), (90, 8.9), (57.5, 10.3), (62.5 12.3), (45, 12), (70, 11), (4.9, 12.4), (25, 12.7), (12, 13 4), (16, 11), (5, 14.7)

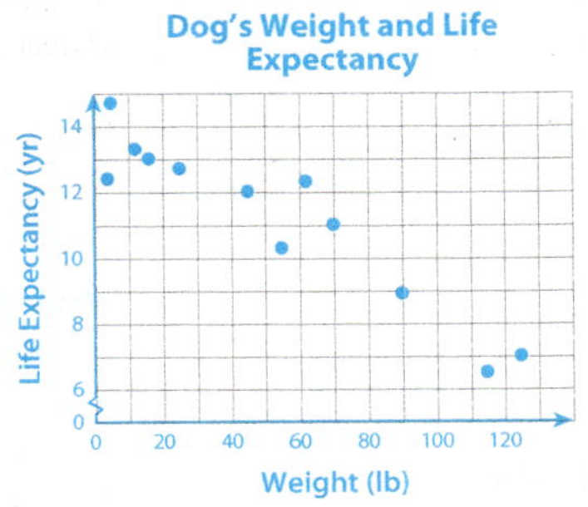

SOLUTION The points go down and to the right. The points appear to follow a linear pattern.

b. Check your answer to problem 3a. Show your work.

Possible answer: I double-checked the points I plotted and they fall in a straight-line pattern.

700

DIFFERENTIATION | ENGLISH LANGUAGE LEARNERS

Use with **Session 2** **Analyze It**

ACADEMIC VOCABULARY

To approximate means to come close to something.

To analyze means to observe and examine in detail.

Levels 1–3: Reading/Speaking

To reinforce students' understanding of associations between variables, display and discuss the Academic Vocabulary. Then read Analyze It as students follow along. Pause after each sentence and ask questions to help students talk about the process: *What do you need to examine or analyze? What will you look for? What do you know after analyzing the points?* Provide sentence frames:

- *I need to analyze* ____.
- *I will look for* ____.
- *After analyzing, I know that* ____.

Levels 2–4: Reading/Speaking

To reinforce students' understanding of Analyze It, first read the Academic Vocabulary. Then read Analyze It with students. Have students tell what they need to analyze. Create a T-chart with the headings *From the Text* and *My Observations.* In the left column, summarize sentences 2 to 4 from the text. Then guide students to analyze the points and share their observations. Record their observations in the right column next to the summaries of sentences 2 to 4.

Have students meet with partners to discuss their observations.

Levels 3–5: Reading/Speaking

To reinforce students' understanding of analyzing associations between variables, display and read the Academic Vocabulary. Have students read Analyze It and turn to partners to discuss what they need to analyze. Then have them compare each sentence in Analyze It to the points in the plot.

Have students work through each sentence and take turns stating their observations. Call the class back together and have partners share their observations with the class.

Develop Using a Scatter Plot to Analyze Data

Purpose

- **Develop** strategies for analyzing data in a scatter plot.
- **Recognize** that an association between two variables can be linear or nonlinear, or there can be no association.

START CONNECT TO PRIOR KNOWLEDGE

Which One Doesn't Belong?

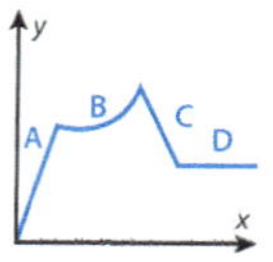

Possible Solutions

A is the only section increasing at a constant rate.

B is the only curved section.

C is the only section with a negative slope.

D is the only section with a slope of 0.

WHY? Support students' facility with recognizing lines, curves, and slope.

DEVELOP ACADEMIC LANGUAGE

WHY? Reinforce the meaning and use of *association* through word origins and synonyms.

HOW? Write *association* on the board. Explain that it comes from the Latin word *associare* (to unite) and is often used in academic language. Have students brainstorm synonyms and cognates for the word (*connection, relation, relationship, link, union, asociación* in Spanish, *asosyasyon* in Haitian Creole). Have students discuss the use of the word in the session. Ask: *What are the two things connected or related in a linear association?*

TRY IT SMP 1, 2, 4, 5, 6

Make Sense of the Problem

See ***Connect to Culture*** to support student engagement. Before students work on Try It, have them use **Say It Another Way** with a partner to help them make sense of the problem. Ask several pairs to tell how they paraphrased the problem.

Develop Using a Scatter Plot to Analyze Data

➤ **Read and try to solve the problem below.**

A city hosts an anime festival every year. The number of attendees over a span of 15 years is shown in the table. Describe any relationship between the variables. Is there a linear association between the variables?

Year	Number of Attendees	Year	Number of Attendees
2001	149	2009	3,996
2002	1,015	2010	5,894
2003	449	2011	9,771
2004	755	2012	7,999
2005	1,476	2013	14,875
2006	1,390	2014	13,877
2007	2,697	2015	22,312
2008	5,001		

TRY IT Math Toolkit calculator, graph paper, graphing calculator

Possible work:

SAMPLE A

The number of attendees increases each year, but the data pattern is curved, not straight. There is not a linear association.

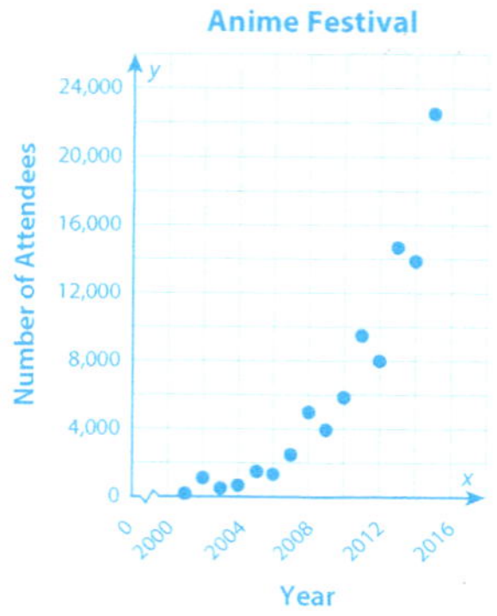

SAMPLE B

As the year increases, the number of attendees also increases. The data points are in a curve pattern, not a straight line. There is not a linear association between the variables.

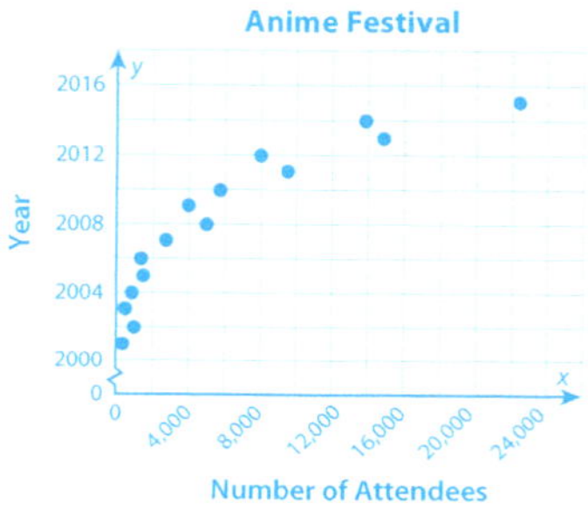

DISCUSS IT

Ask: How did you determine if there was a linear association?

Share: The strategy I used was . . .

DISCUSS IT SMP 2, 3, 6

Support Partner Discussion

After students work on Try It, have them explain their work and then respond to Discuss It with a partner. Listen for understanding that:

- points in a straight line or close to a straight line indicate that the association is linear.
- a curved pattern of data points means the association is not linear.

Common Misconception Look for students who say that the variables have a linear association. As students share their thinking, have them explain the parts of the scatter plot that led them to their conclusion. Remind them that the type of association must reflect the entire data set, not just a portion.

Select and Sequence Student Strategies

Select 2–3 samples that represent the range of student thinking in your classroom. Here is one possible order for class discussion:

- table used to conclude association is nonlinear
- (misconception) table or scatter plot used to incorrectly conclude association is linear
- scatter plot with number of attendees on the *x*-axis used to conclude association is nonlinear
- scatter plot with year on the *x*-axis used to conclude association is nonlinear

Facilitate Whole Class Discussion

Call on students to share selected strategies. Remind students to use complete sentences to help their listeners understand the explanations.

Guide students to **Compare and Connect** the representations. Call on several students to rephrase important ideas so that everyone hears them more than once and in more than one way.

ASK *What do the scatter plots that were presented show about how the variables are related?*

LISTEN FOR The points follow a pattern, so there is an association. The pattern is a curve, so the association is nonlinear.

Picture It & Analyze It

If students presented these models, have students connect these models to those presented in class.

If no student presented at least one of these models, have students first analyze key features of the models, and then connect them to the models presented in class.

ASK *Which of the descriptions in Analyze It describe the scatter plot in Picture It?*

LISTEN FOR The data do not follow a linear pattern, so the association is nonlinear.

For the scatter plot, prompt students to consider how the scatter plot shows the relationship between the variables.

- *Do the data show an increasing or decreasing pattern?*
- *Does the number of attendees change at a constant rate over time?*

For the verbal descriptions of associations, prompt students to think about how the variables might be connected in each situation.

- *How do the data appear in a linear association?*
- *What would a scatter plot look like if there were no association?*

Explore different ways to understand analyzing data in scatter plots.

A city hosts an anime festival every year. The number of attendees over a span of 15 years is shown in the table. Describe any relationship between the variables. Is there a linear association between the variables?

Year	Number of Attendees	Year	Number of Attendees
2001	149	2009	3,996
2002	1,015	2010	5,894
2003	449	2011	9,771
2004	755	2012	7,999
2005	1,476	2013	14,875
2006	1,390	2014	13,877
2007	2,697	2015	22,312
2008	5,001		

Picture It

You can make a scatter plot.

Choose the variable for each axis. Plot the data as ordered pairs.

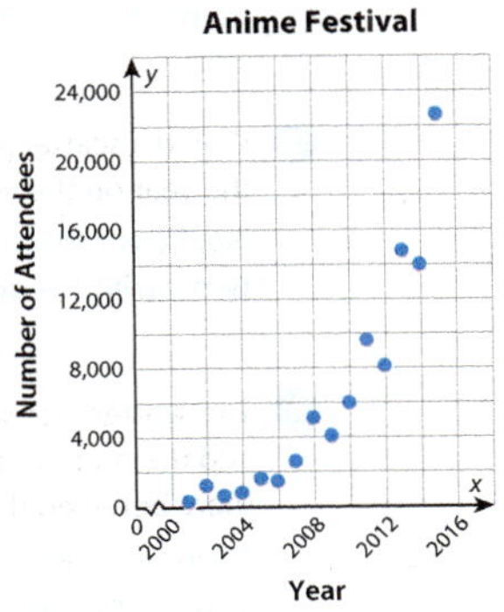

Analyze It

You can analyze the scatter plot to look for patterns in the data.

A data pattern with points that approximate a straight line shows a linear association between the variables.

A data pattern that is not linear shows a **nonlinear association** between the variables.

If there is no pattern at all in the data points, there is **no association** between the variables.

702

DIFFERENTIATION | EXTEND

SMP 2

Deepen Understanding
Reasoning About One- and Two-Variable Data Displays

Have students think about one-variable data displays, such as dot plots, box plots, and histograms, and compare them to a scatter plot.

ASK *What types of data display could you use for the number of attendees only?*

LISTEN FOR A dot plot or box plot could show these data. A histogram could show the data if they were grouped into intervals.

ASK *What information would these displays reveal about the number of attendees?*

LISTEN FOR A dot plot or histogram would show how often each number of attendees occurred. A box plot would show the median, interquartile range, and range of values.

ASK *What does this scatter plot show about the number of attendees that a one-variable data display would not show?*

LISTEN FOR The scatter plot shows how the number of attendees increases in a nonlinear pattern as time passes.

Develop Using a Scatter Plot to Analyze Data

CONNECT IT

SMP 2, 4, 5, 6

Remind students that the association between the two variables is the same in each representation. Explain that they will now use those representations to reason about how to use scatter plots to analyze bivariate data.

Before students begin to record and expand on their work in Picture It & Analyze It, tell them that problems 3 and 4 will prepare them to provide the explanation asked for in problem 5.

Monitor and Confirm Understanding 1 – 3

- The general shape of the data points is a curve, which indicates a nonlinear association.
- In general, as the year increases, the number of attendees increases.
- Switching the axes for the variables does not change the type of association.

Facilitate Whole Class Discussion

4 Look for understanding that there is no pattern to the data points, so there is no association between the two variables.

ASK *How is this scatter plot different from the other scatter plots you have seen so far in this lesson?*

LISTEN FOR The points in this scatter plot do not follow a linear or curved pattern.

5 Look for the idea that a linear or nonlinear pattern in the data points means there is an association between the variables. No pattern means no association.

ASK *Why is it easier to see an association between variables when the data are displayed in a scatter plot rather than in a table?*

LISTEN FOR In a scatter plot, I can see whether the points fall in some type of regular pattern, like a line or a curve.

6 **Reflect** Have all students focus on the strategies used to solve the Try It. If time allows, have students discuss their ideas with a partner.

CONNECT IT

➤ **Use the problem from the previous page to help you understand how to use scatter plots to analyze data.**

1 Look at **Picture It** and **Analyze It**. Describe the pattern of the data points in the scatter plot. What association is there between the variables?

The data points form a curve, not a straight line. The variables have a nonlinear association.

2 Describe the relationship between the year and the number of attendees.

As the year increases, the number of attendees tends to increase. In most years, more people attend the festival than the year before.

3 Would a scatter plot showing the number of attendees on the horizontal axis and the year on the vertical axis show a different association? Explain.

No; Possible explanation: The data would still follow a curve. Switching the two variables does not change the type of association.

4 The scatter plot shows the ages of 10 attendees at the anime festival and the number of action figures they bought. What association is there between the variables? How do you know?

There is no association between the age of the attendees and the number of figures bought. The points do not follow a line or a curve.

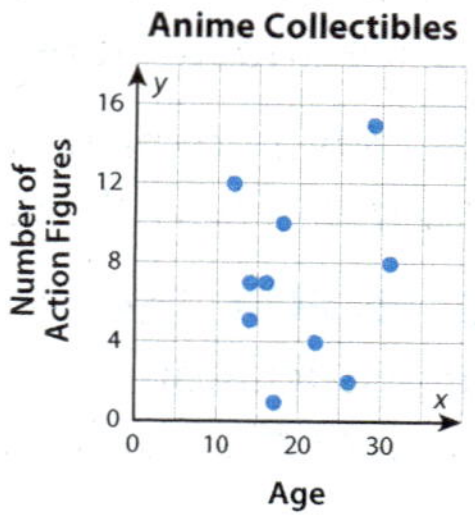

5 How does a scatter plot help you identify the association between the variables in a bivariate data set?

Scatter plots can show patterns in the data points. If there is no pattern, then there is no association between the two variables.

6 **Reflect** Think about all the models and strategies you have discussed today. Describe how one of them helped you better understand how to solve the **Try It** problem.

Responses will vary. Check student responses.

703

DIFFERENTIATION | RETEACH or REINFORCE

Visual Model

Construct scatter plots that show different types of associations.

If students are unsure about identifying associations using a scatter plot, then use this activity to help them make graphs with linear, nonlinear, and no association.

- Display a scatter plot that has a clear linear association.
- Ask: *Does this scatter plot have a linear or a nonlinear association? How do you know?* [linear; The points follow a pattern that resembles a straight line.]
- Ask: *How can the graph be changed so that it shows a nonlinear association?* [Add more points or remove some points until the points form a curved pattern.]
- Invite students to alter the scatter plot so that it shows a nonlinear pattern.
- Ask: *Does this scatter plot have a linear or a nonlinear association? How do you know?* [nonlinear; The points follow a pattern that resembles a curve.]
- Ask: *How can the graph be changed so that it shows no association?* [Add more points until the points do not form a pattern.]
- Invite students to add points to the scatter plot until it shows no association.

Apply It

Remind students that the points do not have to fall exactly on a line or curve for a scatter plot to show an association between the variables.

7 Students may want to try to draw a smooth curve that follows the pattern and comes close to the points.

8 **D is correct.** These points do not exactly form a line, but they follow a linear pattern.

A is incorrect. The scatter plot shows no association.

B is incorrect. The scatter plot shows a nonlinear association.

C is incorrect. The points do not form a linear pattern.

Apply It

➤ **Use what you learned to solve these problems.**

7 Does the scatter plot show a *linear association*, a *nonlinear association*, or *no association* between the variables? Explain.

The scatter plot shows a nonlinear association. The points follow a pattern, but the pattern is not linear.

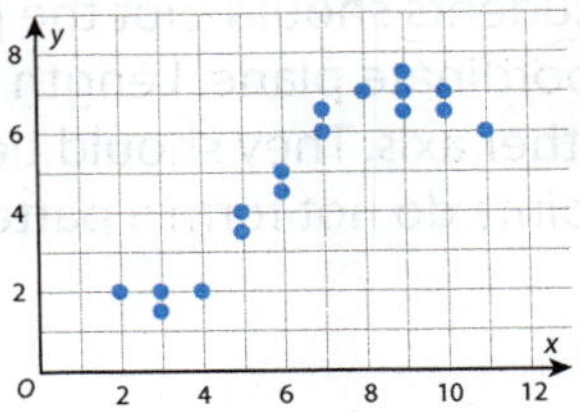

8 Which scatter plot shows a linear association?

A
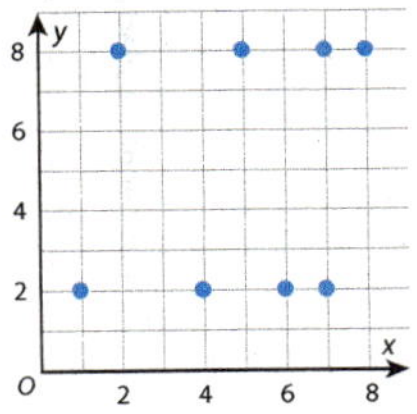

B
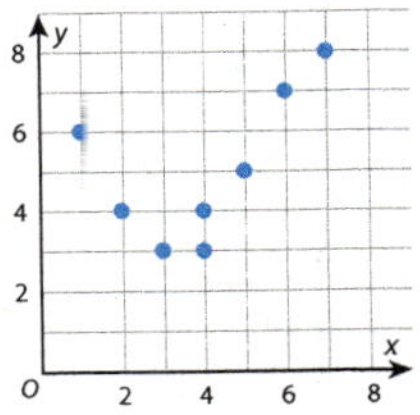

C
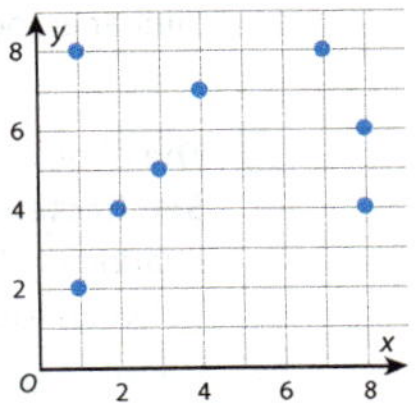

(D)
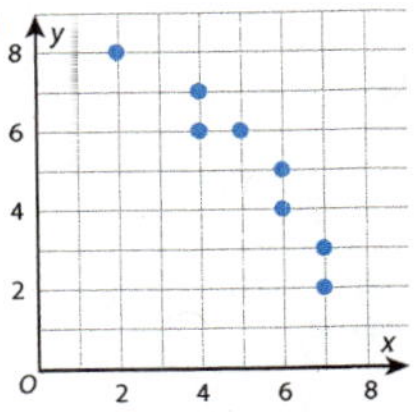

9 The scatter plot shows the gold medal times for the men's Olympic 100-meter dash for several years. Is there a *linear association*, a *nonlinear association*, or *no association* between the year and the winning time? Describe any relationship you see between the variables.

There is a linear association. Possible answer: As the years increase, the winning times decrease. Winning times are getting shorter.

100-Meter Dash
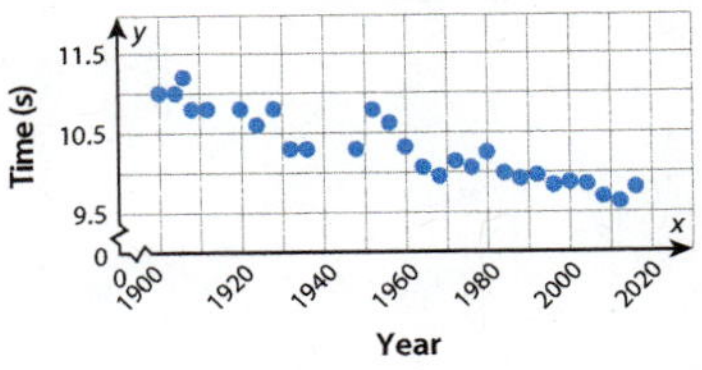

CLOSE EXIT TICKET

9 Students' descriptions should show an understanding that:

- the association represented by the scatter plot is linear.
- all the points in the scatter plot do not have to lie exactly on a line for the association to be linear.
- as the years increase, the winning times decrease.

Error Alert If students identify the association as nonlinear, then have them use a string or a chenille stem to see that they can find a line that follows the general path of most of the points.

Practice Using a Scatter Plot to Analyze Data

Problem Notes

Assign **Practice Using a Scatter Plot to Analyze Data** as extra practice in class or as homework.

1 Students should plot the points on the coordinate plane. Length and width can be on either axis. They should determine that the points do not form a pattern. ***Medium***

Practice Using a Scatter Plot to Analyze Data

➤ **Study the Example showing how to describe an association between two variables. Then solve problems 1–4.**

Example

The data compare the amount of time people spent meditating and the number of headaches they got over a one-week period. Describe any association between these two variables.

Meditation (min)	Number of Headaches
14	5
18	4
0	15
5	11
12	5
10	8
15	4
8	9
4	10
16	6

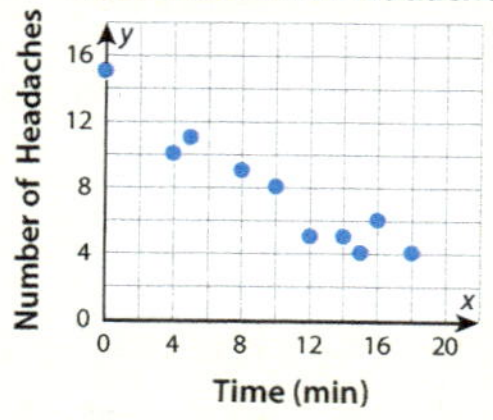

The points follow a linear pattern. There is a linear association between the two variables.

1 The dimension data for 15 rectangles are recorded. Use **Data Set: Rectangle Dimensions** to make a scatter plot of the data relating each length to its width. Describe any association between the lengths and widths.

Rectangle Dimensions

Length (in.)	Width (in.)
3	3
2	3
4	1

See page DS1 for the complete data set.

Possible graph and answer:

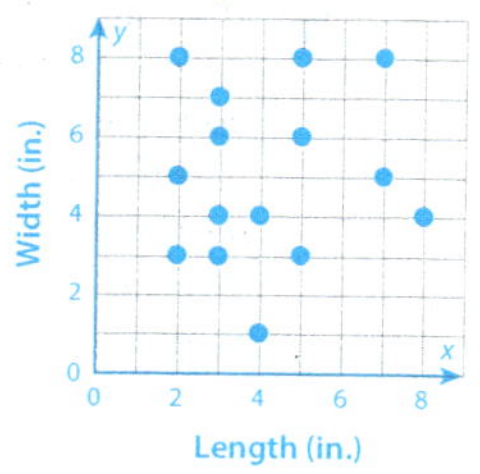

The data points do not show a pattern. There is no association between the lengths and widths.

Fluency & Skills Practice

Using a Scatter Plot to Analyze Data

In this activity, students construct scatter plots from data tables and determine whether there is a linear association, nonlinear association, or no association between the two variables.

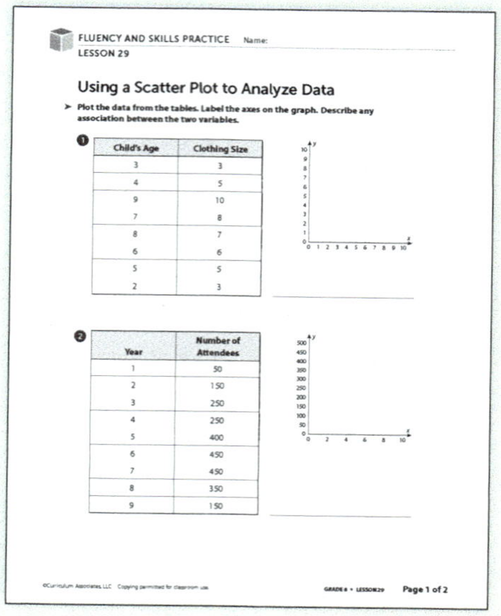

Additional Practice

2 a. ***Basic***

b. Students may reason that the overall pattern of points indicates that as the pitch speed increases, the hit speed increases as well. So, a pitch with a higher speed will also have a higher hit speed. ***Medium***

3 Students may reason that rate of change is the same as slope. A line has constant slope, but a curve does not. ***Challenge***

4 **C is correct.** How far a person lives from school should not affect how often they visit the doctor.

A is incorrect. Not completing assignments is likely related to test scores.

B is incorrect. When a person is absent, they miss assignments.

D is incorrect. The further someone lives from school, the longer it will take to drive to school.

Medium

2 The scatter plot shows the pitch speed and hit speed for 10 swings by a certain baseball player. *Pitch speed* is the speed at which a baseball is thrown by the pitcher. *Hit speed* is the speed at which a ball travels after the batter hits it.

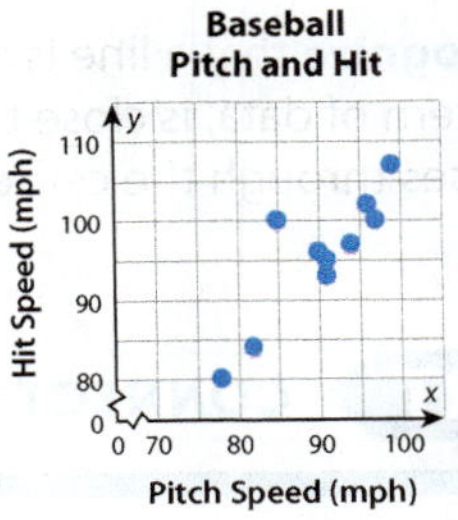

a. Describe any association between these two variables. Explain your reasoning.

linear association; The data follow a pattern that can be approximated by a straight line.

b. Would you expect a pitch of 80 mph or a pitch of 90 mph to have a higher hit speed? Explain.

A pitch of 90 mph would have a higher hit speed. As the pitch speed of a ball increases, the hit speed also increases.

3 How would the rate of change between two variables with a linear association differ from the rate of change between two variables with a nonlinear association?

Possible answer: The rate of change would be constant or close to constant for a linear association. The rate of change would not be constant for a nonlinear association.

4 Students at Central Middle School survey their classmates on a number of different topics. Which pair of variables from the survey would be most likely to have no association?

A test scores and number of missing assignments

B number of absences and number of missing assignments

(C) distance from home to school and number of visits to the doctor's office in one year

D distance from home to school and driving time

DIFFERENTIATION | ENGLISH LANGUAGE LEARNERS

Use with **Session 3** Try It

Levels 1–3: Speaking/Writing

To help students write their answers to Try It, read the problem. Explain the meaning of *model*. Guide students to tell what *good model* means in this context:

- *A good model is a line that represents _____.*

Have students work in pairs to discuss line *a* and decide whether it is a good model:

- *Line a _____ a good model because _____.*

Repeat for lines *b*, *c*, and *d*. Help students add to their explanation by telling how many points or groups of points surround the lines. Once students discuss, have them choose a line that is a good model and write their explanations.

Levels 2–4: Speaking/Writing

To help students write their answers to Try It, read the problem. Have students explain the meaning of "good model" in this context. Ask students to turn to a partner to discuss each of the four lines on the scatter plot. As they discuss, encourage them to tell whether the line is a good model and why. Then have partners tell whether they selected the same line. If not, encourage them to explain the differences. If students selected the same line, encourage them to explain why. Then have students write their answers:

- *I chose _____ as a good model for the data because _____.*

Levels 3–5: Speaking/Writing

To help students write their answers to Try It, have them read the problem. Allow think time for them to analyze the lines in the scatter plot. Encourage them to talk about the lines and tell how they represent or do not represent the data. Then, have students choose a line and write their answers.

Have students turn to partners to share and explain their choices. Encourage them to use the word *choice* to comment on their partner's answers. Remind students to be respectful when they disagree with their partners and to provide reasons or drawings to explain. Ask: *Do you think your partner's line is a good choice? Why?*

Develop Assessing Linear Models for Good Fit

Purpose

- **Develop** strategies for assessing whether a line is a good fit for a set of data on a scatter plot.
- **Recognize** that a line is a good fit if it closely follows the pattern of data, is close to most of the data points, and passes through the centers of clusters of data points.

START CONNECT TO PRIOR KNOWLEDGE

Which One Doesn't Belong?

A: $-2x + y = 4$	B: $y = -3x + 1$
C: $y = \frac{1}{2}x - 2$	D: $y = 3x$

Possible Solutions

A is the only equation not in slope-intercept form.

B is the only equation whose line has a negative slope.

C is the only equation whose line has a negative *y*-intercept.

D is the only equation whose line passes through the origin.

WHY? Support students' facility with recognizing characteristics of linear equations and their lines.

DEVELOP ACADEMIC LANGUAGE

WHY? Clarify the meaning of *good fit* in math.

HOW? Read Connect It problem 1. Explain that *good fit* in this context means *good model or representation*. Have students use the words *model* or *representation* to paraphrase the questions. Then have them select and describe a good line of fit:

Line ___ is a good line of fit because ___.

TRY IT

SMP 1, 2, 3, 4, 5, 6

Make Sense of the Problem

Before students work on Try It, use **Notice and Wonder** to help them make sense of the problem. Be sure they consider both the graph and the problem statement. Record what students say. Then have students discuss which observations are relevant to solving the problem.

LESSON 29 | SESSION 3

Develop Assessing Linear Models for Good Fit

➤ **Read and try to solve the problem below.**

Avery is saving money to buy her first car. A used car lot nearby has 15 cars for sale. The scatter plot shows a linear association between the price and the age of the 15 cars. Drawing a line that models or follows the pattern of the data can help Avery determine the age of a car she can afford.

Four lines are drawn on the scatter plot. Which line do you think is a good model for the data? Explain your choice.

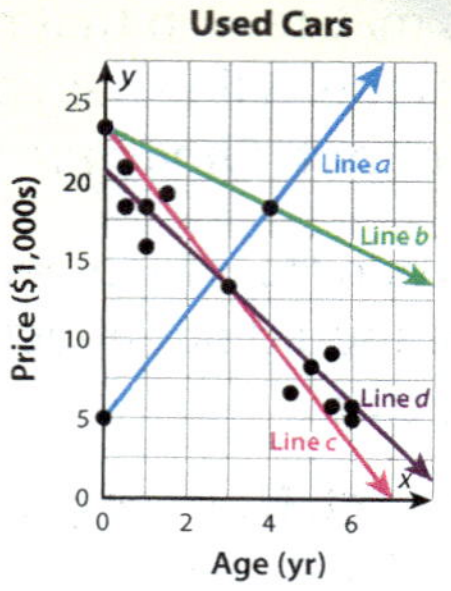

TRY IT

Possible work:

SAMPLE A

Line *d* is a good model for the data because it goes through or near most data points or groups of points.

SAMPLE B

Line *c* seems to be a good model for the data because it goes through two points that line up well with the rest of the data.

DISCUSS IT

Ask: How did you choose which line you thought was a good model?

Share: At first, I thought . . .

707

DISCUSS IT

SMP 2, 3, 4, 6

Support Partner Discussion

After students work on Try It, encourage them to respond to Discuss It with a partner. To support students in extending the conversation, prompt them to discuss these questions:

- *What characteristics of the data did you use to choose a line that is a good model?*
- *What about the lines made them a good choice or a poor choice for a good model?*

Common Misconception Look for students who chose line *a* as a good model because it has almost as many points above it as below it. As students share their strategies, ensure they consider whether the data points have a positive or negative association and choose a line that matches the association.

Select and Sequence Student Strategies

Select 2–3 samples that represent the range of student thinking in your classroom. Here is one possible order for class discussion:

- line chosen because it goes through or near most data points
- (misconception) line *a* chosen because it has half the points above and half below the line
- line chosen because it goes through two representative points

Facilitate Whole Class Discussion

Call on students to share selected strategies. Prompt students to justify their solutions by explaining why they are reasonable.

Guide students to **Compare and Connect** the representations. Allow individual think time for students to process the strategies before starting this discussion.

ASK *Did everyone choose the same line? Do you think there is more than one correct solution to this problem? Why?*

LISTEN FOR There are two lines that come close to most of the data points and follow the pattern in the data. Either could be a good model.

Analyze It

If students presented these models, have students connect these models to those presented in class.

If no student presented at least one of these models, have students first analyze key features of the models, and then connect them to the models presented in class.

ASK *What does each good line of fit have in common?*

LISTEN FOR Each comes close to most of the points and has a negative slope to show the negative association.

For the graph with lines *a* and *c*, prompt students to think about the direction of most of the data points.

- *How are the data points near line a similar to or different from the majority of data points?*
- *How are the data points near line c similar to or different from the majority of data points?*

For the graph with lines *b* and *d*, prompt students to consider groups of data with close values. Ask: *Why might a line that goes through clusters of data be representative of the data set?*

LESSON 29 | SESSION 3

Explore different ways to decide whether a line is a good fit for data.

Avery is saving money to buy her first car. A used car lot nearby has 15 cars for sale. The scatter plot shows a linear association between the price and the age of the 15 cars. Drawing a line that models or follows the pattern of the data can help Avery determine the age of a car she can afford.

Four lines are drawn on the scatter plot. Which line do you think is a good fit for the data? Explain your choice.

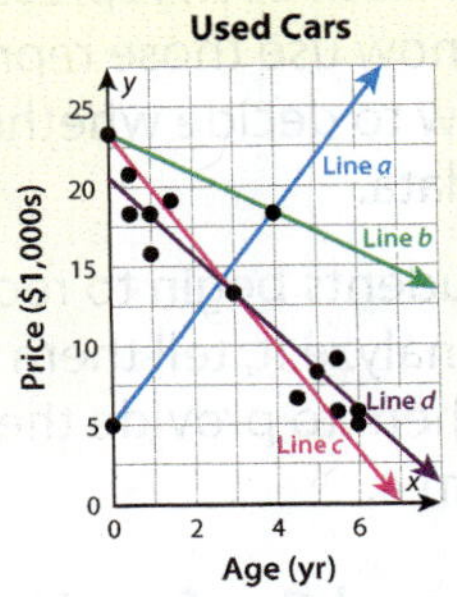

Analyze It

You can look for lines that follow the pattern of most of the data points.

A good **line of fit** closely follows the pattern of the data and models the type of linear association.

The data have a negative association. Line *a* does not follow the pattern of most of the data points. The line passes through a point that is far away from the rest of the data. This point is an outlier.

Line *c* follows the pattern of data.

Make sure a scatter plot shows a linear association before thinking about lines of fit.

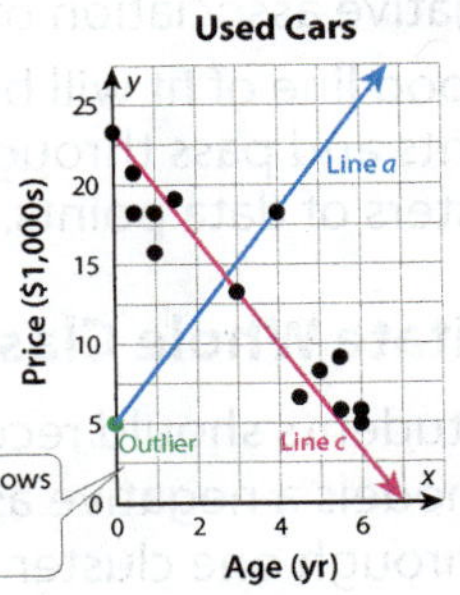

Analyze It

You can look for lines that go through groups of data points.

Data points grouped close together form a cluster. A good line of fit often passes through the center of clusters.

Line *b* passes through two data points above the clusters.

Line *d* passes through both clusters.

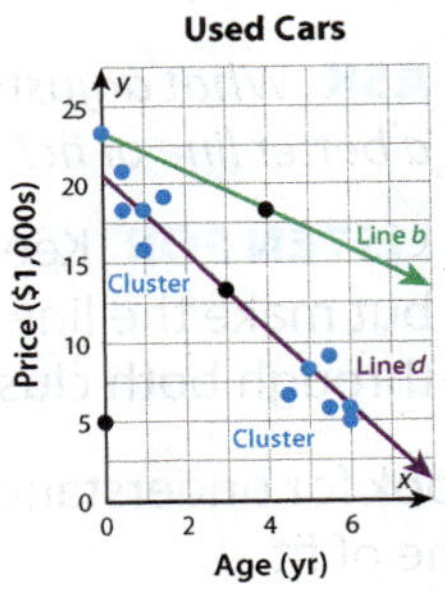

708

DIFFERENTIATION | EXTEND SMP 5

Deepen Understanding
Using Lines of Fit to Make Predictions

Have students consider the relationship between the data points and a line of fit.

ASK *What is the actual price for the 5-year-old car on the lot? How does this compare to the price predicted by line c?*

LISTEN FOR The actual price is about \$8,000. The value predicted by line *c* is about \$7,000. The values are not the same but are close.

ASK *What is the actual price for the 4-year-old car on the lot? How does this compare to the price predicted by line c?*

LISTEN FOR The actual price is about \$18,000. Line *c* predicts a price of about \$10,000. The actual price is almost double the predicted price.

ASK *What would you predict for the price of a 2-year-old car using line c?*

LISTEN FOR A 2-year-old car would cost about \$16,500.

Generalize Encourage students to discuss the idea that a line of fit can be used to make predictions. However, the line only approximates the pattern followed by *most* of the data points. So, in some cases, the prediction may not be close to the actual value.

Develop Assessing Linear Models for Good Fit

CONNECT IT

SMP 2, 4, 5, 6

Remind students that the data and the scatter plot are the same in each representation. Explain that they will now use those representations to reason about how to decide whether a line is a good line of fit for data.

Before students begin to record and expand on their work in Analyze It, tell them that problems 1–3 will prepare them to provide the explanation asked for in problem 4.

Monitor and Confirm Understanding 1 – 2

- A good line of fit will model the positive or negative association of the data.
- A good line of fit will be close to most of the data points and pass through or near the centers of clusters of data points.

Facilitate Whole Class Discussion

3 Students should recognize that, although line *e* models a negative association and goes through one cluster of data, it does not go through both clusters and is not as close to the majority of points as it could be.

> **ASK** *What adjustment would make line e a better line of fit?*
>
> **LISTEN FOR** Keep the *y*-intercept the same, but make the line steeper, so it passes through both clusters of points.

4 Look for understanding of what makes a good line of fit.

> **ASK** *Although there can be more than one good line of fit, how can you generalize what is true about good lines of fit?*
>
> **LISTEN FOR** A good line of fit will follow the overall pattern of the data and model the same type of linear association. It should also be close to most of the data points and pass through most or all clusters.

5 **Reflect** Have all students focus on the strategies used to solve the Try It. If time allows, have students discuss their ideas with a partner.

CONNECT IT

➤ **Use the problem from the previous page to help you understand how to decide whether a line is a good fit for data.**

1 Look at the first **Analyze It**. Is line *a* a good line of fit for the data? Is line *c* a good line of fit? Explain.

No; Yes; Possible explanation: The data show a negative association. Line *a* does not model a negative association. Line *c* models a negative association and is close to most of the data points.

2 Look at the second **Analyze It**. Is line *b* a good line of fit for the data? Is line *d* a good line of fit? Explain.

No; Yes; Possible explanation: Line *b* models a negative association but is above most of the points. It does not pass through either cluster. Line *d* models a negative association and passes through both data clusters.

3 A new line *e* is drawn on the scatter plot as shown. Is line *e* a good line of fit for the data? Explain.

No; Possible explanation: Line *e* models a negative association, but it passes through only one of the clusters. It is not as close to many of the data points as it could be.

Used Cars

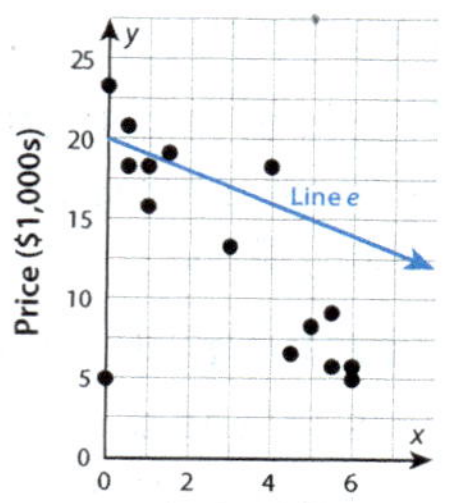

4 How can you tell if a line is a good line of fit for data with a linear association?

Possible answer: The line should follow the overall pattern of the data and model the type of linear association. It should also pass through most or all clusters and be close to most of the data points.

5 **Reflect** Think about all the models and strategies you have discussed today. Describe how one of them helped you understand how to decide whether a line is a good fit for data.

Responses will vary. Check student responses.

709

DIFFERENTIATION | RETEACH or REINFORCE

Visual Model

Model evaluating lines of fit.

If students are unsure about why data on a scatter plot can have multiple good lines of fit, then use this activity to help them evaluate lines of fit.

Materials For display: 4 scatter plots, string

- Display the graph of a scatter plot showing a positive linear association with one cluster.
- Ask: *What type of association is modeled by the data points?* [positive, linear]
- Hold the string taut where one possible good line of fit would be located. Ask: *Is this a good line of fit? Why?* [Yes; Possible answer: It follows the direction of data and there are about the same number of data points above and below the line.]
- Ask: *Are there other lines that could be good lines of fit? Why?* [Yes; Possible answer: Many lines could go through the cluster and be close to most of the data points.]
- Place the string on the graph in a spot that would not be a good line of fit. Ask: *Is this a good line of fit? Why?* [No; Possible answer: The line is below (or above) most of the points.]
- Repeat the steps above for graphs showing clusters or other linear associations.

Apply It

For all problems, remind students that there can be more than one good line of fit for a data set.

6 Students should understand that an outlier is not representative of the data set as a whole. Given that, it should not be used as one of the points to determine whether a line is a good line of fit.

7 See ***Connect to Culture*** to support student engagement.

D and E are correct. Both lines model a positive association. Line *d* goes through both clusters, and line *e* is close to both clusters and has roughly the same number of data points above and below it.

A is incorrect. This line models a positive association, but most of the data points are below the line.

B is incorrect. This line models a negative association.

C is incorrect. This line models a positive association but has most of the data points below the line.

Apply It

Use what you learned to solve these problems.

6 Describe how to determine whether a point in a data set is an outlier. How does a good line of fit take an outlier into account?
Possible answer: An outlier is far away from most of the data points and does not fit into the general pattern. A good line of fit follows the pattern of the data points, excluding any outliers.

7 This scatter plot shows a linear association between the drop height and the maximum speed for 12 steel roller coasters. Which is a good line of fit for the data? Select all that apply.

A Line *a*

B Line *b*

C Line *c*

(D) Line *d*

(E) Line *e*

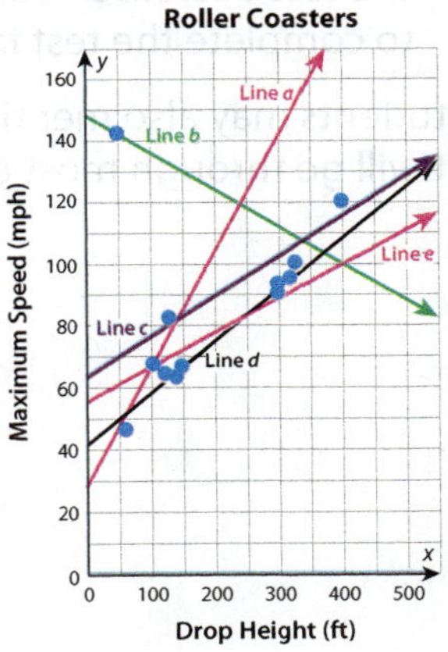

8 Look at the scatter plot in problem 7.

a. Does the scatter plot show a positive or negative association?
a positive association

b. What does the association suggest about drop height and the maximum speed of the steel roller coasters?
As the drop height increases, the maximum speed of the roller coaster also increases.

c. Choose one of the data clusters. Explain what the cluster suggests about roller coasters.
Possible answer: Several roller coasters in the data set have a maximum speed of 60–80 miles per hour from a drop of 100–150 feet.

CLOSE EXIT TICKET

8 Students' solutions should show an understanding that:
- the data have a positive association.
- as the drop height increases, the maximum speed of the roller coaster also increases.
- each data point or cluster can be interpreted in context.

Error Alert If students incorrectly interpret the clusters, then have them write the range of values on the *x*- and *y*-axes for the cluster they chose. Have them use the labels from the graph and the values they wrote to describe the cluster.

Practice Assessing Linear Models for Good Fit

Problem Notes

Assign **Practice Assessing Linear Models for Good Fit** as extra practice in class or as homework.

1. **a.** Students should recognize that, because all the data are closely bunched together, there are no outliers. ***Basic***

   b. Students should recognize that the data show that as age increases, time to complete the test decreases. So, an older child is likely to complete the test faster. ***Medium***

2. Students may also mention that a good line of fit will go through most or all clusters. ***Medium***

LESSON 29 | SESSION 3 Name:

Practice Assessing Linear Models for Good Fit

➤ **Study the Example showing possible good lines of fit. Then solve problems 1–5.**

Example

Researchers timed 20 children who placed pegs into a peg board. The task tested the children's ability to grasp and manipulate objects. The scatter plot shows the linear association between the age of the child and the time spent to complete the task. Decide whether each line is a good fit for the data. Explain your reasoning.

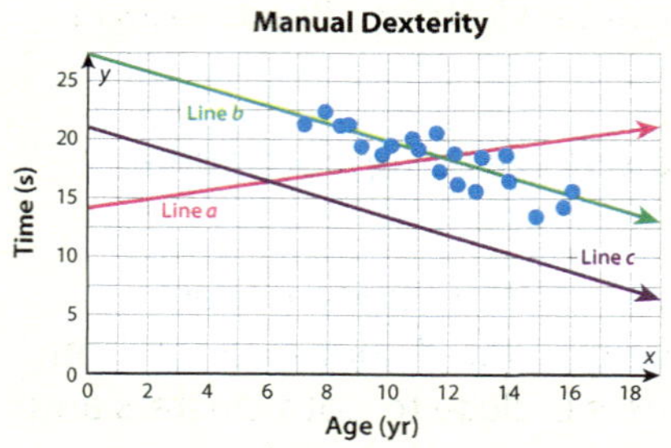

Line *a* is not a good fit because it models a positive association. The data show a negative association.

Line *b* is a good fit because it models a negative association and is close to all the data points.

Line *c* is not a good fit. Although it models a negative association, the line is below all of the data points.

1. Analyze the data in the scatter plot from the Example.

   a. Identify any outliers. There are no outliers.

   b. What does the association suggest about a child's age and his or her ability to complete the test?

   The older the child, the less time it takes to complete the test.

2. How can you decide whether a line is a good line of fit for data on a scatter plot?

   Possible answer: A good line of fit follows the pattern and direction of most of the data and models the type of linear association. It should be as close to as many points as possible.

Vocabulary

line of fit
a line drawn on a scatter plot to approximately model the relationship between two sets of data.

outlier
a data value that is much greater or much less than most of the other values in the data set.

711

Fluency & Skills Practice

Assessing Linear Models for Good Fit

In this activity, students are given scatter plots, and they identify the best line of fit for each scatter plot from several choices. Students also identify any outliers and desribe whether there is a positive or negative association in the data.

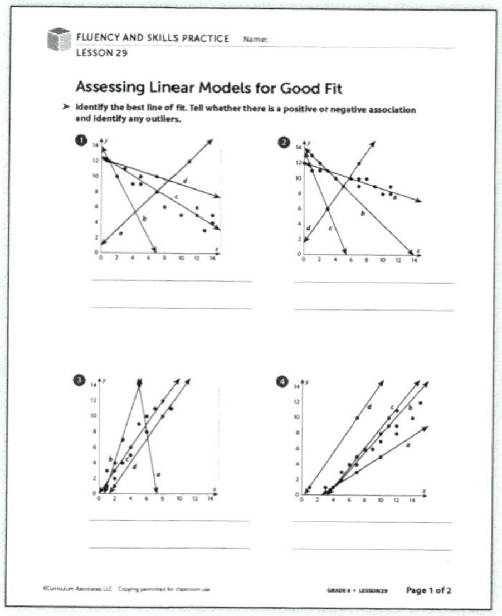
FLUENCY AND SKILLS PRACTICE Name:
LESSON 29

Assessing Linear Models for Good Fit

➤ Identify the best line of fit. Tell whether there is a positive or negative association and identify any outliers.

Page 1 of 2

Additional Practice

3 Students may also mention that the line is not close to most of the data points. ***Medium***

4 ***Basic***

5 Since (6, 4) follows the overall pattern of the data points, it is not an outlier. ***Medium***

LESSON 29 | SESSION 3

3 Ten adults were asked their age and the amount of time they watch cable television news each week. The scatter plot shows the data from the survey. Is line *a* a good line of fit for the data? Explain.

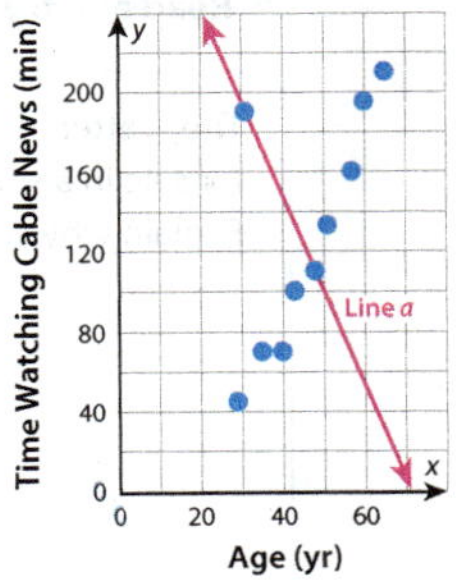

No; Possible explanation: Line *a* goes through a point that is an outlier, and it does not model the positive association of the data.

4 Which line is a good line of fit? Explain your choice

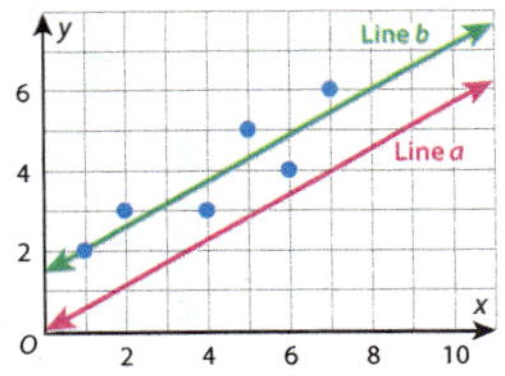

Line *b*; Possible explanation: Both lines follow the pattern and direction of data. Line *b* passes through or near all the data points. Line *a* passes under all the data points.

5 Alison says that (6, 4) is an outlier in the scatter plot in problem 4. Do you agree with Alison? Explain.

No; Possible explanation: The point (6, 4) is not an outlier because it is near the other data points and follows the same pattern. An outlier is a point that is far away from the rest of the data.

712

DIFFERENTIATION | ENGLISH LANGUAGE LEARNERS

Use with **Session 4** **Connect It**

Levels 1–3: Speaking/Writing

Help students prepare to answer Connect It problem 2. Write *consider* on the board. Provide examples with context clues: *I will consider all the options before I make a decision. It is time to consider which college to attend.* Then invite students to tell the meaning of the phrase *think about*. Help students paraphrase the examples using *think about*. Then, read the problem and ask: *Are all lines that pass through the balance point good lines of fit? What else do you need to consider?* Allow students to discuss other characteristics that the lines should have:

- *A good line of fit should* ____.

Levels 2–4: Speaking/Writing

Help students prepare to answer Connect It problem 2. Write the word *consider* on the board and ask students to share with their partner a time they had to consider or think about something. Call on volunteers to share their experiences. Ask other students to paraphrase. Help students read the problem. Have them consider and list characteristics of a good line of fit. Then have them use *should* to write their answers.

Help students connect with previous knowledge by recalling examples where they had to consider something before solving a problem.

Levels 3–5: Speaking/Writing

Help students prepare to answer Connect It problem 2. Call on volunteers to tell the meaning of *consider*. Then have students tell what they know about the lines and what else they need to consider. Allow think time for students to write their answers. Encourage them to use *should* in their answers. Then have them meet with partners and ask each other questions about their considerations.

Have students connect with previous knowledge by asking for examples when they had to consider something before writing an answer.

Develop Fitting a Linear Model Informally

Purpose

- **Develop** strategies for informally fitting a line of good fit.
- **Recognize** that there are multiple lines of good fit and multiple options for fitting them.

START CONNECT TO PRIOR KNOWLEDGE

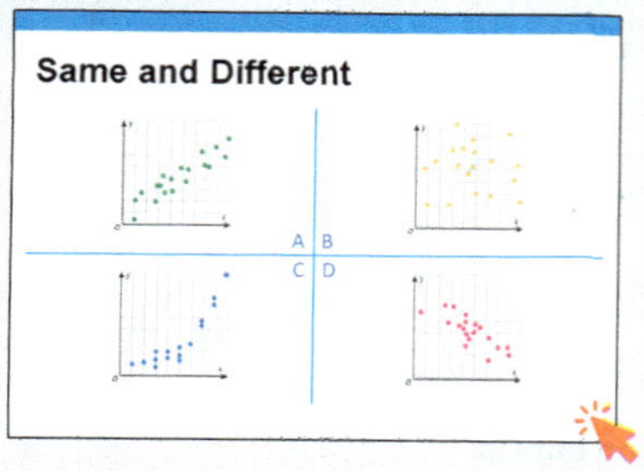

Possible Solutions

All are scatter plots.

A, C, and D show a data pattern.

A and D have a linear association.

B has no association.

C has a nonlinear association.

WHY? Support students' facility with recognizing data associations.

DEVELOP ACADEMIC LANGUAGE

WHY? Discuss language used to explain reasoning.

HOW? Read Apply It 7. Ask: *What do you need to do after you draw the line of fit?* Call on volunteers to tell the meaning of *Explain your reasoning*. Then have students turn to partners to discuss language they can use to explain reasoning. Ask: *Do you talk about actions in the past or the present? Do you use the phrase "for example"? How?*

TRY IT SMP 1, 2, 4, 5, 6

Make Sense of the Problem

See ***Connect to Culture*** to support student engagement. Before students work on Try It, use **Three Reads** to help them make sense of the problem. During each read of the problem, have students answer questions as they relate to both the problem stem and the scatter plot: *What is the problem about? What are you trying to find out? What are the important quantities and relationships?*

LESSON 29 | SESSION 4

Develop Fitting a Linear Model Informally

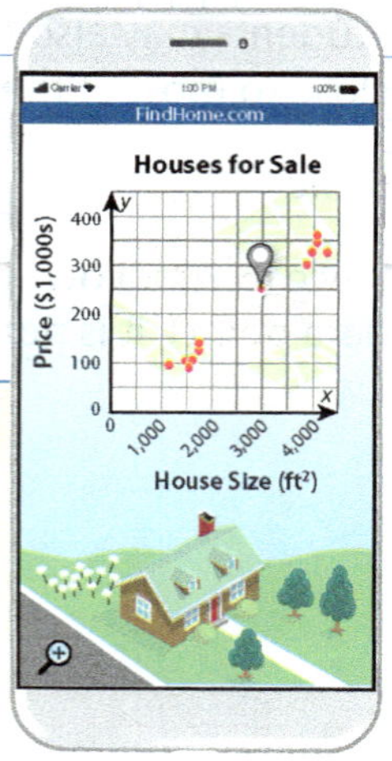

➤ **Read and try to solve the problem below.**

The scatter plot shows data for the size and price of 12 houses for sale in a small town. Draw a good line of fit for these data. Explain why you think it is a good fit.

TRY IT Math Toolkit calculator, straightedges, string

Possible work: SAMPLE A

I picked two points that followed the data pattern and drew a line through them. This line is a good fit because it is close to almost all the data.

SAMPLE B

The line I drew is a good fit because it goes through the middle of the data and follows the general pattern of the data.

DISCUSS IT

Ask: What did you do first to draw your line of fit? Why?

Share: First, I . . .

713

DISCUSS IT SMP 2, 3, 6

Support Partner Discussion

After students work on Try It, encourage them to respond to Discuss It with a partner. Listen for understanding that:

- a good line of fit represents the overall data pattern.
- a good line of fit often goes through the middle of any data clusters.

Common Misconception Look for students who think the line of fit must always pass through the leftmost and rightmost data points. Although this might give a good line of fit in some situations, have students discuss what happens if one (or both) of these "end" data points is an outlier, or if both were above or below most of the data points. You might also point out that there may be more than one leftmost or rightmost data point.

Select and Sequence Student Strategies

Select 2–3 samples that represent the range of student thinking in your classroom. Here is one possible order for class discussion:

- string used to identify a line through the "middle" of the data points
- (misconception) line automatically drawn through the leftmost and rightmost data points
- line through the middle of the two clusters
- line drawn that follows the pattern of data and comes close to most of the points

Facilitate Whole Class Discussion

Call on students to share selected strategies. Prompt students to connect this problem to problems they solved in the last session, where they figured out which of a set of given lines was a good fit.

Guide students to **Compare and Connect** the representations. Have students turn and talk with a partner to discuss why there are many possible good lines of fit.

ASK *How are [student's name]'s and [student's name]'s lines different? How are they the same?*

LISTEN FOR Some were drawn using two points, some were drawn by thinking about clusters, and some were drawn by just trying to come close to as many points as possible. All the lines considered the association of the data.

Picture It & Model It

If students presented these models, have students connect these models to those presented in class.

If no student presented at least one of these models, have students first analyze key features of the models, and then connect them to the models presented in class.

ASK *Do you prefer the line-fitting strategy in Picture It or Model It?*

LISTEN FOR I prefer the Picture It strategy because it does not require calculations, but you might prefer the Model It strategy because it gives you a definite point to draw the line through.

For the line that goes through the clusters, prompt students to consider the clusters. Ask: *How do you decide which point in the cluster to draw the line of good fit through?*

For the balance point model, prompt students to consider the two different lines of fit drawn. Ask: *Why are both lines good lines of fit?*

➤ **Explore different ways to informally fit a line to data.**

The scatter plot shows data for the size and price of 12 houses for sale in a small town. Draw a good line of fit for these data. Explain why you think it is a good fit.

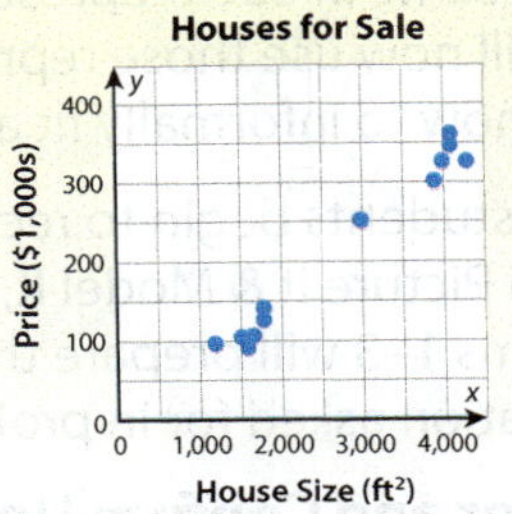

Picture It

You can use data clusters to draw a good line of fit.

If the data have clusters, a good line of fit is likely to pass through the center of the clusters. Use a straightedge to draw a line that goes through the centers of the clusters.

Model It

You can calculate the mean of the data for each variable to find the **balance point**.

Recall that the mean of a data set is the sum of all the data points divided by the number of data points.

mean size of home: $\frac{33,000}{12} = 2,750$

mean price of home: $\frac{2,563}{12} \approx 213.6$

Good lines of fit often pass through or near the balance point. The balance point is usually not a data point.

The balance point for these data is (2750, 213.6).

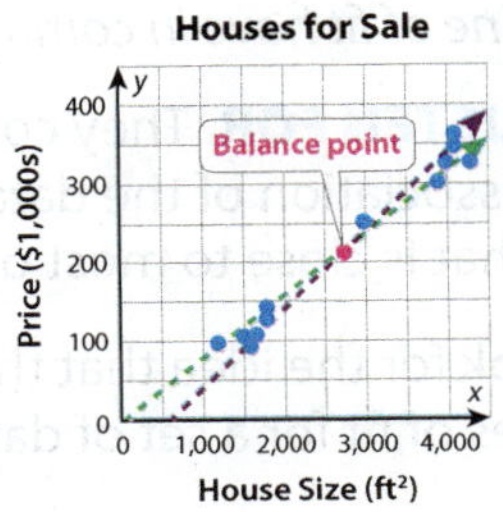

DIFFERENTIATION | EXTEND

SMP 3

Deepen Understanding

Reasoning About the Balance-Point Method for Data with Outliers

Prompt students to think about how the balance point is calculated and how it might be affected by outliers.

ASK *How is the mean of a one-variable data set affected by outliers?*

LISTEN FOR Outliers can significantly increase or decrease the mean, so the mean may not be a good measure of center.

ASK *How do you think adding outliers to this plot would affect the balance point?*

LISTEN FOR It might pull the balance point away from the overall pattern of points.

ASK *Find the balance point if the outlier (500, 450) is added to the plot. Do you think a good line of fit would pass through this new balance point?*

LISTEN FOR The new balance point is (2577, 232). This point is a little above the overall pattern of points, so it might not be a good point to draw the line of fit through.

Generalize Have a discussion about using the balance-point method when a data set has outliers. Students may suggest ignoring the outliers when calculating the balance point.

Develop Fitting a Linear Model Informally

CONNECT IT

SMP 2, 4, 5, 6

Remind students that the data and the scatter plot are the same in each representation. Explain that they will now use those representations to reason about how to informally fit a line to data.

Before students begin to record and expand on their work in Picture It & Model It, tell them that problems 1–3 will prepare them to provide the explanation asked for in problem 4.

Monitor and Confirm Understanding 1 – 2

- Data clusters, especially when there are two, create anchors for a line that will follow the shape of the data.
- The balance point alone is not enough to determine a good line of fit. The line must follow the association and be near most points.

Facilitate Whole Class Discussion

3 Look for understanding that there are many strategies for determining a good line of fit.

ASK *What do the strategies that find a good line of fit have in common?*

LISTEN FOR They consider the pattern or association of the data and try to find a line that is close to most of the data points.

4 Look for the idea that there are multiple good lines of fit for a set of data.

ASK *What are the characteristics of any good line of fit?*

LISTEN FOR It follows the pattern in the data and comes close to most of the points.

5 **Reflect** Have all students focus on the strategies used to solve the Try It. If time allows, have students discuss their ideas with a partner.

CONNECT IT

Use the problem from the previous page to help you understand how to informally fit a line to data.

1 Look at **Picture It**. Explain why data clusters can be used to determine a line of fit for the data.

Possible answer: Lines that go through the centers of clustered data will likely follow the pattern of most of the data.

2 Look at **Model It**. You can draw many different lines that would pass through the balance point. Not all would make good lines of fit. What else would you need to consider to draw a good line of fit that passes through the balance point?

Possible answer: The line should also follow the pattern or association of the data and be close to most of the data points.

3 Did you or any of your classmates use a different method to draw a good line of fit? Explain.

Possible answer: Yes. I chose two data points that followed the pattern of points closely and drew a line through them.

4 Think about data with linear association. Is it possible to draw more than one good line of fit for a scatter plot? Explain.

Yes; Possible explanation: There are multiple good lines of fit. Different lines that are good fits can result from different methods, such as using the balance point, using clusters of data, or using two data points that follow the pattern of data.

5 **Reflect** Think about all the models and strategies you have discussed today. Describe how one of them helped you better understand how to solve the **Try It** problem.

Responses will vary. Check student responses.

715

DIFFERENTIATION | RETEACH or REINFORCE

Hands-On Activity

Identify and justify good lines of fit.

If students have difficulty using a straightedge to locate and draw a line of fit because it covers up some of the points, then use this activity so they can see all the data points as they try to fit a line.

Materials For each student: chenille stem, tape, Activity Sheet *Scatter Plot with Linear Association*

- Each student should use the chenille stem to identify a good line of fit for the scatter plot.
- As students work, encourage them to find a line that is close to most of the points and that follows the association of the data.
- When students are satisfied with the position of their line, they should tape the chenille stem in place.
- Have students compare their lines of fit with a partner. Each partner should explain why they positioned the line as they did and why it is a good fit for the data.
- Allow partners to give feedback about each other's lines.
- After the partner discussion, allow students to adjust the positions of their lines if they wish.

Apply It

For all problems, encourage students to use a model to support their thinking. Allow some leeway in precision of lines of fit since there are multiple correct answers.

6 **a.** Students should recognize that speed is represented on the *x*-axis and gas mileage is represented on the *y*-axis and plot points appropriately.

b. Students may add the speed values and divide the sum by 6 to find the *x*-coordinate of the balance point. They may add the gas mileage values and divide the sum by 6 to find the *y*-coordinate of the balance point.

c. Students' lines will likely be different from the one on the student page, but should go through the balance point and be a good representation of the pattern in the data.

Apply It

➤ **Use what you learned to solve these problems.**

6 The table shows average speed and gas mileage for 6 cars.

a. Complete the scatter plot for the data. See graph.

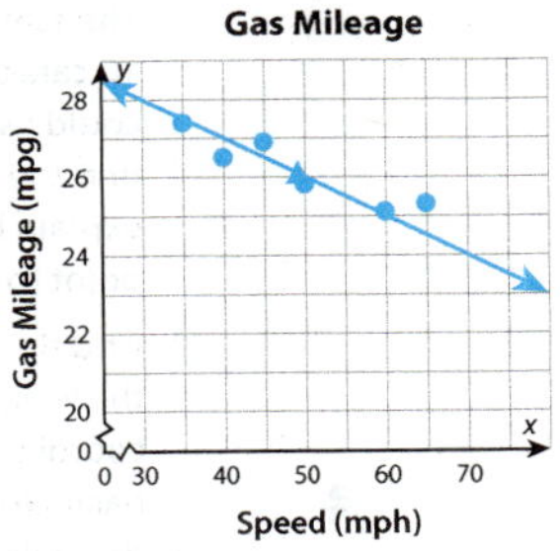

Speed (miles per hour)	Gas Mileage (miles per gallon)
35	27.1
65	25.3
60	25.4
40	26.2
45	26.9
50	25.6

b. Calculate the balance point of the data. Plot the point as a triangle on the scatter plot. Show your work.

See graph. Possible student work:

Mean speed = $\frac{295}{6} \approx 49.2$; Mean gas mileage = $\frac{156.5}{6} \approx 26.1$

SOLUTION (49.2, 26.1)

c. Draw a good line of fit for the data on the scatter plot. Explain your reasoning.

See graph for possible line. Possible explanation: I used a ruler and drew a line through the balance point that best followed the pattern of the rest of the data points.

7 The scatter plot shows the standing long jump distances and heights for 15 middle school students. Draw a good line of fit for the data. Explain your reasoning.

See graph for possible line. Possible explanation: I drew a line in the direction of the data pattern that passed through the centers of two clusters.

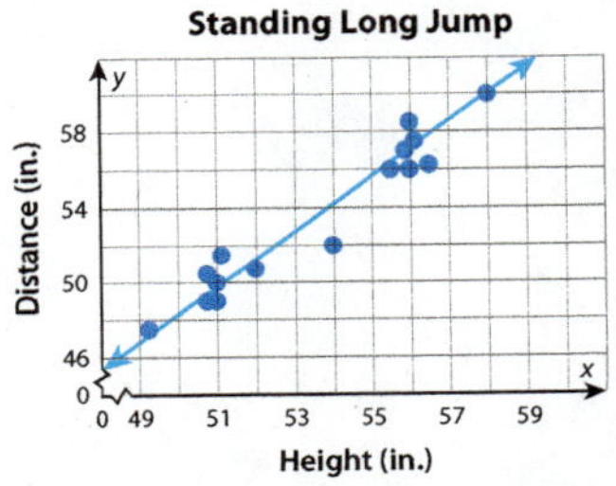

CLOSE **EXIT TICKET**

7 Students' solutions should show an understanding that:

- a good line of fit should follow the pattern of the association.
- a good line of fit should go through the middle of the data or be close to most of the data points.

Error Alert If students draw a line of fit that does not fit the data well, then have them compare their line with a good line of fit drawn by another student. Have the other student explain how they reasoned about how to position the line.

Practice Fitting a Linear Model Informally

Problem Notes

Assign **Practice Fitting a Linear Model Informally** as extra practice in class or as homework.

1. *Basic*
2. Students should calculate and plot the balance point and then may reason how to draw the line through this point. ***Medium***

 Name:

Practice Fitting a Linear Model Informally

➤ **Study the Example showing how to informally fit a line to data with a linear association. Then solve problems 1–5.**

Example

The scatter plot shows the age and price of 10 cars at a car dealership. Explain how you could use the data set of the scatter plot to find the balance point of the data. Then explain how you could use the balance point to draw a good line of fit for the data.

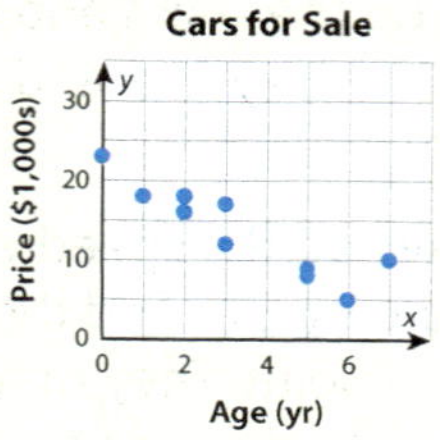

Find the mean of the *x*-values and the mean of the *y*-values in the data set. These means are the coordinates of the balance point. Then plot the balance point on the scatter plot. Draw a line through the balance point that follows the general pattern of the data. It should be close to most of the data points. Ignore any outliers.

1. Is the linear association in the Example data positive or negative? Describe the relationship between the variables.

   Negative; The points go down and to the right. As the age of a car increases, the price decreases.

2. The scatter plot from the Example is repeated below. The data for the scatter plot are given in the table. Find and plot the balance point as a triangle. Use the balance point to draw a good line of fit for the data.

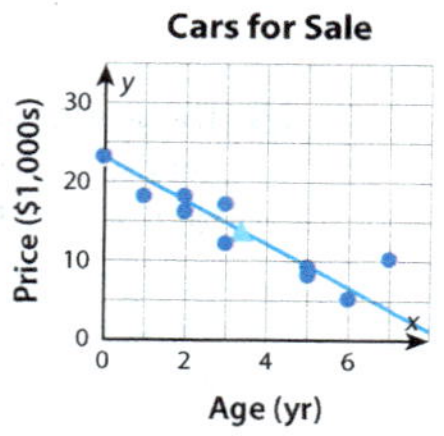

(3.4, 13.6); See graph for possible line.

Age (yr)	Price ($1,000s)
0	23
1	18
2	18
2	16
3	17
3	12
5	9
5	8
6	5
7	10

Fluency & Skills Practice

Fitting a Linear Model Informally

In this activity, students construct scatter plots from data tables. For each problem, they calculate and plot the balance point and draw a good line of fit.

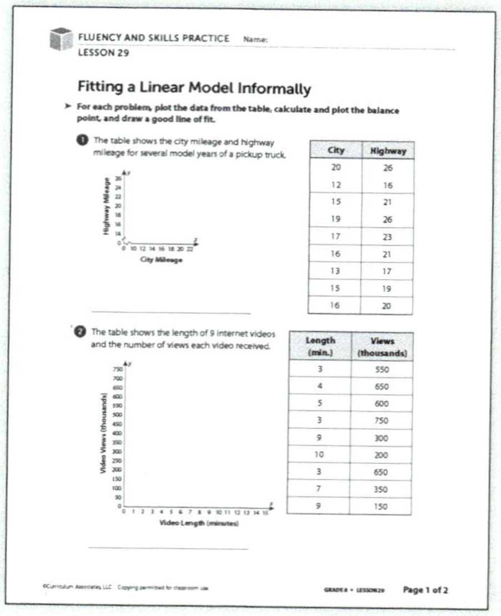
FLUENCY AND SKILLS PRACTICE Name:
LESSON 29

Fitting a Linear Model Informally

➤ **For each problem, plot the data from the table, calculate and plot the balance point, and draw a good line of fit.**

1. The table shows the city mileage and highway mileage for several model years of a pickup truck.

City	Highway
20	26
12	16
15	21
19	26
17	23
16	21
13	17
15	19
16	20

2. The table shows the length of 9 internet videos and the number of views each video received.

Length (min.)	Views (thousands)
3	550
4	650
5	600
3	750
9	300
10	200
3	650
7	350
9	150

©Curriculum Associates, LLC Copying permitted for classroom use. GRADE 8 • LESSON 29 Page 1 of 2

Additional Practice

3 Students should understand that it is possible that a good line of fit will not pass through any data points. It only needs to be *close to* most of the points. ***Medium***

4 Students may draw a line of fit that goes through both clusters and is close to most data points. ***Medium***

5 Students should understand that the outlier should not be considered because it will pull the line of fit away from most of the data points. A good line of fit should be representative of the data as a whole, not one point. ***Challenge***

LESSON 29 | SESSION 4

3 Alanna says that a good line of fit has to include at least one data point that lies on the line. Explain why Alanna is not correct.

Possible explanation: A good line of fit can be close to all of the data points without going through any of them.

4 Draw a good line of fit for the data in the scatter plot. Describe any clusters or outliers that you notice.

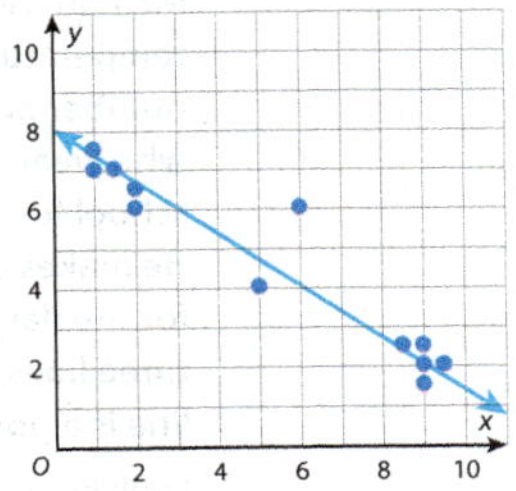

See graph for possible line. There is a cluster of data in the top left, gathered around (1.5, 7) and a cluster of data in the lower right, gathered around (9, 2). There are no outliers.

5 The scatter plot compares 10 daily high temperatures and the number of frozen fruit bars sold at a snack stand. The line of fit shown takes into account the outlier at (91, 10). Explain why it is not a good line of fit. Then draw a good line of fit.

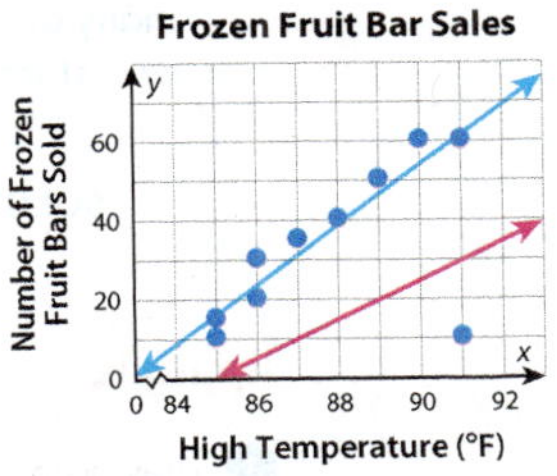

See graph for possible line. Possible explanation: The original line lies below all of the points except the outlier. A good line of fit will be close to most data points and ignore the outlier.

718

DIFFERENTIATION | ENGLISH LANGUAGE LEARNERS

Use with **Session 5** **Apply It**

Levels 1–3: Speaking/Writing

To help students write an answer to the question in Consider This (Apply It 3), provide a word bank with *data points, clusters of data, linear patterns*. Have them discuss the question with a partner. Guide students to look at the scatter plot and select a good line of fit. Then have them explain their answer using the terms in the word bank. Ask: *How did the clusters of data help you find a good line of fit?* Provide sentence starters for partners to complete:

- *If there is one cluster of data, I can* ____.
- *If there are two clusters of data, I can* ____.
- *There are* ____ *clusters of data, so I* ____.

Levels 2–4: Speaking/Writing

To help students write an answer to the question in Consider This (Apply It 3), have them brainstorm a list of math words that could be used to describe a good line of fit. Elicit *data points, clusters of data, balance point, linear patterns*.

Provide sentence starters to help students tell what they would do for different scenarios, what they noticed in the problem, and what they did based on that observation.

- *If there were two clusters, I would* ____.
- *If there was one cluster, I would* ____.
- *I noticed that* ____, *so I* ____.

Levels 3–5: Speaking/Writing

To help students write an answer to the question in Consider This (Apply It 3), have students draft a response that considers different scenarios, such as one cluster and two clusters. Encourage students to use *If* ____ *then* ____ sentences and the conditional to explain what they would do in each case. Allow think time for students to work individually. Then have them meet with partners to review.

Encourage partners to review the drafts for correct use of *would* in the sentences. Ask: *What would you do if there were* ____? Then have partners tell what they did based on the information in the problem.

Refine Analyzing Scatter Plots and Fitting a Linear Model to Data

Purpose

- **Refine** strategies for constructing and interpreting scatter plots.
- **Refine** understanding of how to informally fit a line to a scatter plot that shows a linear association between the variables and of how to informally assess the fit of a given modeling line.

START CHECK FOR UNDERSTANDING

Which line is a good line of fit for the data?

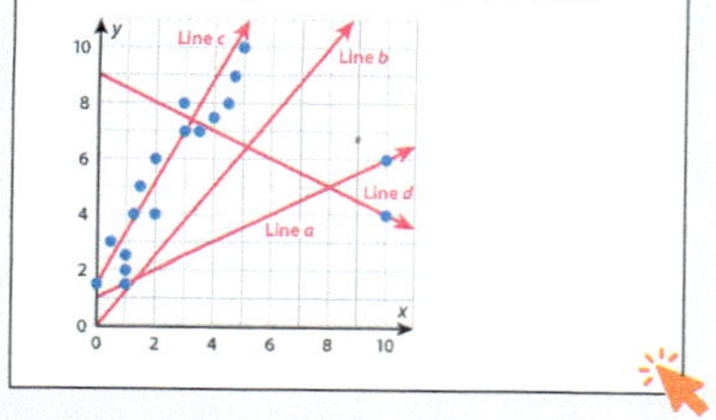

Solution

Line c

WHY? Confirm students' understanding of assessing the fit of a modeling line by judging the closeness of the data points to the line, identifying common errors to address as needed.

MONITOR & GUIDE

Before students begin to work, use their responses to the **Start** to determine those who will benefit from additional support. Use the **Error Analysis** table below to guide remediation.

Have all students complete the Example and problems 1–3, using Consider This and Pair/Share as appropriate. Observe and monitor their reasoning and guide or redirect students as needed.

LESSON 29 | SESSION 5

Refine Analyzing Scatter Plots and Fitting a Linear Model to Data

➤ **Complete the Example below. Then solve problems 1–8.**

Example

Mr. Ramírez records the temperature and the number of students who wear a coat to school for 12 Mondays. He makes a scatter plot for the data and draws three lines of fit. Which line is a good line of fit?

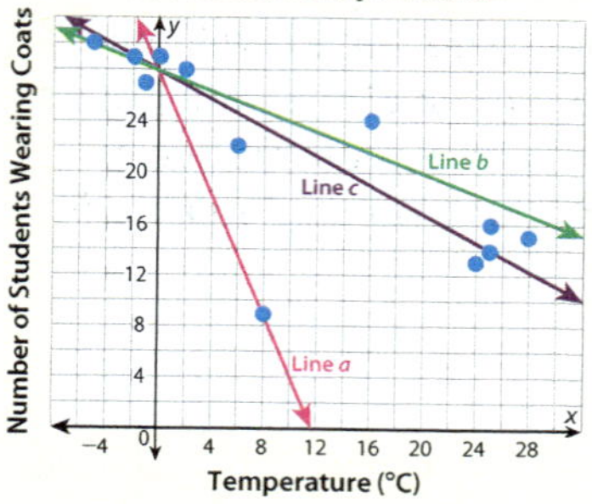

Look how you could use clusters and outliers.

Line *c* passes through both clusters and is close to all the data points except the outlier. Line *a* goes through the outlier and is far away from many other data points. Line *b* passes through only one cluster and starts to rise away from the data pattern.

SOLUTION Line *c*

CONSIDER THIS . . . Sometimes it is possible to draw more than one good line of fit.

PAIR/SHARE How does the line change when the outlier is considered?

Apply It

1 Draw a good line of fit for the scatter plot. Why is it a good fit for the data?

See graph for possible line. Possible explanation: I drew a line that is close to all the data points and follows the direction of the data.

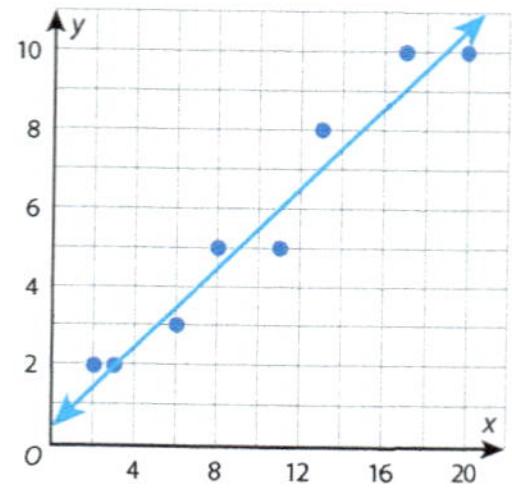

CONSIDER THIS . . . Does a good line of fit have to pass through any data points?

PAIR/SHARE Are there situations in which there is no good line of fit?

START ERROR ANALYSIS

If the error is . . .	Students may . . .	To support understanding . . .
Line *a*	have thought a good line of fit must pass through an outlier.	Ask students to define *outlier*. Elicit from students that a line passing through an outlier is probably not a good line of fit.
Line *b*	have thought any line that models the association of the data points is a good line of fit.	Ask students to review the characteristics of a good line of fit. Elicit from students that line *b* models a positive association but is below most of the points.
Line *d*	have thought a line that goes through a cluster of data points is a good line of fit.	Ask students to review how to determine a good line of fit using clusters. Elicit from students that trends in the data indicate a positive or negative association, which then informs the general direction of good fit lines.

Example

Guide students in understanding the Example. Ask:

- *Where are the two clusters of data?*
- *How can the location of clusters help you identify a good line of fit?*
- *Does a good line of fit generally pass through an outlier? Explain why or why not.*

Help all students focus on the Example and responses to the questions. As students respond to the questions, encourage others to ask follow-up questions to clarify the answers.

Look for understanding that a good line of fit will usually pass through both clusters of data.

Apply It

1. Students should draw a line that follows the general pattern of points and that passes through the "middle" of all the points, where roughly half of the points are above the line and half of the points are below the line. *DOK 2*

2. See ***Connect to Culture*** to support student engagement. Students may solve the problem by making a scatter plot of the data and then analyzing the pattern of points. When there is a linear association, the data points are in a straight-line pattern. *DOK 2*

3. **C is correct.** Line *c* is close to most of the points and passes through both clusters of data.

   A is not correct. Line *a* passes through two data points but is above most of the points.

   B is not correct. Line *b* passes though one cluster of data instead of both clusters of data.

   D is not correct. Only line *c* fits the data.

   DOK 3

2 The percent of U.S. adults who use at least one social media platform was recorded for each of several years. Use **Data Set: Social Media Users** to determine what type of association the data show. How are the variables related? Show your work.

Social Media Users

Year	U.S. Adults (%)
2005	7
2006	11
2008	25

See page DS1 for the complete data set.

CONSIDER THIS . . . Data can show a linear association, a nonlinear association, or no association.

Possible work:

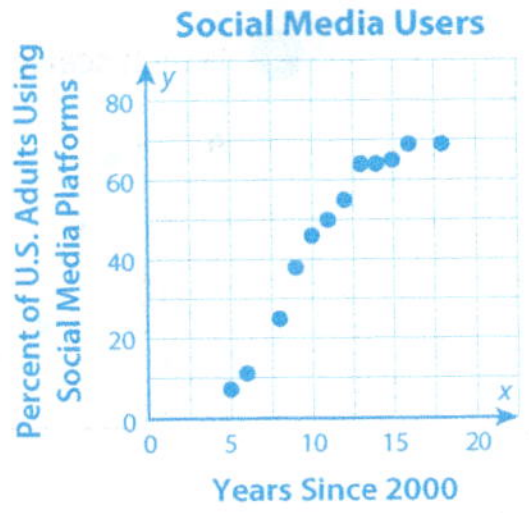

SOLUTION a positive linear association; The percentage of social media users is increasing each year.

PAIR/SHARE How many different ways can you describe a linear association?

3 Which line on the scatter plot is a good line of fit for the data?

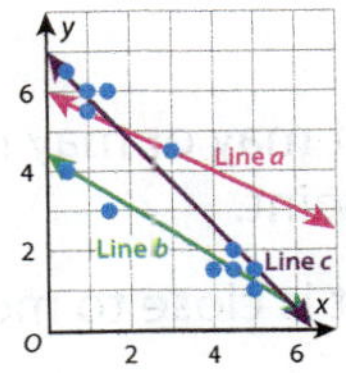

A Line *a*

B Line *b*

(C) Line *c*

D All three lines

CONSIDER THIS . . . How can clusters of data help determine a good line of fit?

Isabella chose B as the correct answer. How might she have gotten that answer?

Possible answer: She chose the line that passes through one cluster of data, but there are two clusters. A good line of fit would pass through both clusters, not just one.

PAIR/SHARE What do you look for in a good line of fit?

720

GROUP & DIFFERENTIATE

Identify groupings for differentiation based on the **Start** and problems 1–3. A recommended sequence of activities for each group is suggested below. Use the resources on the next page to differentiate and close the lesson.

Approaching Proficiency
- **RETEACH** Hands-On Activity
- **REINFORCE** Problems 5, 7

Meeting Proficiency
- **REINFORCE** Problems 4–7

Extending Beyond Proficiency
- **REINFORCE** Problems 4–7
- **EXTEND** Challenge

Have all students complete the **Close: Exit Ticket**.

Resources for Differentiation are found on the next page.

Refine Analyzing Scatter Plots and Fitting a Linear Model to Data

Apply It

4 Students should realize that not all scatter plots have a line of fit. A line of fit is appropriate only when the data have a linear association. The data on this plot have no association. *DOK 3*

5 **D** **is correct.** The data points follow a straight-line pattern.

A is not correct. This scatter plot has a nonlinear association because the data points form a curve, not a line.

B is not correct. This scatter plot has no association because the data points do not follow any pattern.

C is not correct. This scatter plot has a nonlinear association because the data points form a curve, not a line.

DOK 1

6 **a.** A good line of fit may or may not include at least one data point.

b. A good line of fit is close to most of the data points.

c. A good line of fit may or may not include the origin.

d. If the data points do not have a linear association, then there is not a line of fit that models the data.

DOK 2

---

4 Xavier says that the line shown on the scatter plot is a good line of fit because the number of data points above and below the line is the same. Do you agree? Explain.

No; Possible explanation: For there to be a good line of fit, the data must have a linear association. The data on the scatter plot have no association, so no line is a good line of fit.

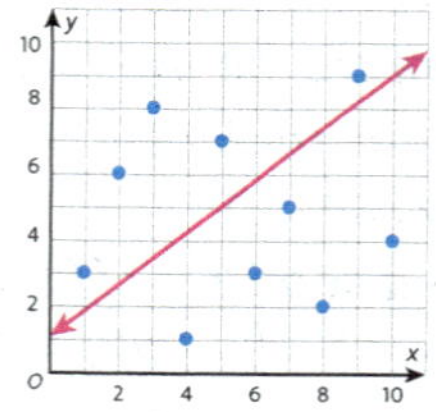

5 Which scatter plot has a linear association?

A
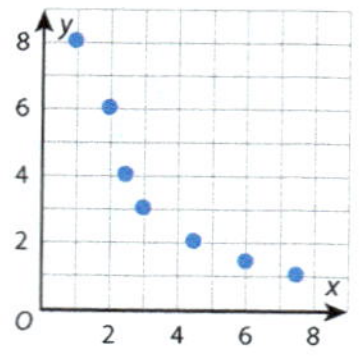

B
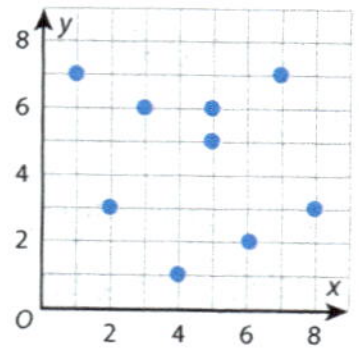

C
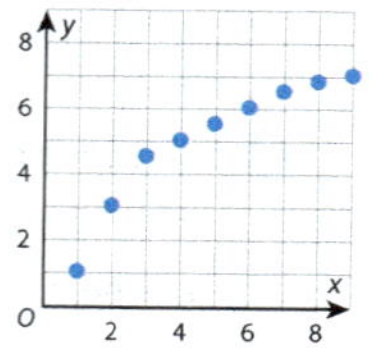

(D)
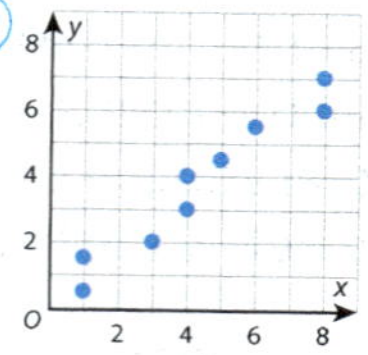

6 Tell whether each statement is *True* or *False*.

	True	False
a. A good line of fit must go through at least one data point.	○	●
b. A line of fit is good if all of the data points are fairly close to it.	●	○
c. A good line of fit almost always goes through the origin (0, 0).	○	●
d. There is always a line of fit for any set of data points.	○	●

721

DIFFERENTIATION

RETEACH

Hands-On Activity

Assess lines of fit.

Students approaching proficiency with assessing a line of fit will benefit from modeling a good line of fit.

Materials For each student: chenille stem, tape, Activity Sheet *Coordinate Plane: First Quadrant*

- Instruct students to plot 15 points that show a linear association (either positive or negative). One of the points should be an outlier.
- Verify each student's scatter plot shows a linear association.
- Ask: *What type of association does your line of fit represent? How do you know?* [linear; The points follow a straight-line pattern.]
- Instruct students to trade scatter plots with a partner.
- Have students tape a chenille stem on the graph they were given to model a good line of fit.
- Instruct partners to discuss and assess the line of fit.
- Ask: *What makes a good line of fit?* [A line of fit is good when it follows the direction of data and most of the points are close to it.]
- Ask: *How does the outlier impact the line of fit?* [Because there is only one outlier out of 15 points, the outlier can be ignored when placing line of fit.]

7 **a.** The data have a linear association because the points form a straight-line pattern. *DOK 1*

b. Students should recall that, for a positive association, as one variable increases, the other variable increases. For a negative association, as one variable increases, the other variable decreases. *DOK 2*

c. Students may fit a line by using the balance point, clusters of data, or two data points that follow the overall pattern of data. *DOK 2*

CLOSE EXIT TICKET

8 **Math Journal** Look for understanding of the different types of association and that only scatter plots with a linear association can have a line of fit.

Error Alert If students think a line of fit can be drawn for the nonlinear association, then have them sketch a line they think fits the nonlinear data. Ask students if the line is close to most of the data points.

End of Lesson Checklist

INTERACTIVE GLOSSARY Support students by suggesting they work with a partner to look for examples of types of association and lines of fit in the Student Worktext.

SELF CHECK Have students review and check off any new skills on the Unit 7 Opener.

LESSON 29 | SESSION 5

7 The scatter plot shows the approximate number of adults and number of voters in the 10 most populous U.S. states in 2016.

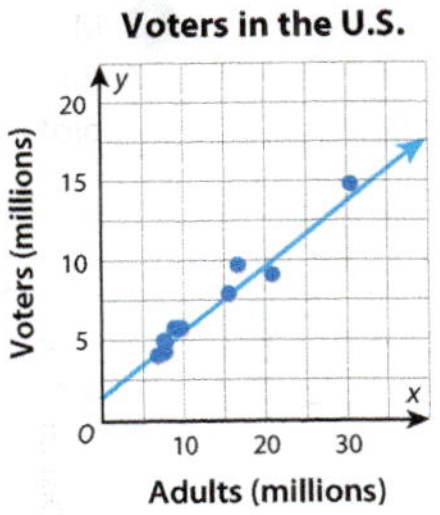

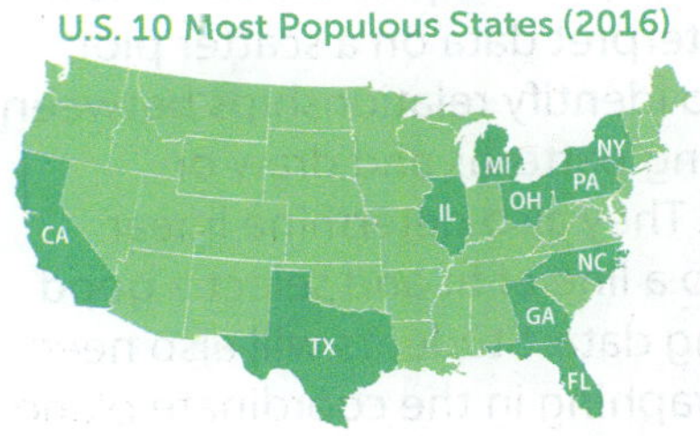

a. Explain how you know that the data have a linear association.
The data have a linear association because the data roughly follow a straight line.

b. Do the data have a positive or negative association? Describe the relationship between the variables.
The data have a positive association. As the number of adults increases, the number of voters increases.

c. Draw a good line of fit for the data. See graph for possible line.

8 **Math Journal** Draw four scatter plots: one showing a positive linear association, one showing a negative linear association, one showing a nonlinear association, and one showing no association. Which of your four scatter plots can have good lines of fit for their data? Explain.
Plots will vary; check student plots. Possible explanation: Only scatter plots with a linear association can have a good line of fit.

End of Lesson Checklist

- [ ] **INTERACTIVE GLOSSARY** Find the entries for *association* and *line of fit*. Rewrite the definitions in your own words.
- [ ] **SELF CHECK** Go back to the Unit 7 Opener and see what you can check off.

722

REINFORCE

Problems 4–7
Solve problems involving scatter plots.

Students meeting proficiency will benefit from additional work with exploring scatter plots by solving problems in a variety of formats.

- Have students work on their own or with a partner to solve the problems.
- Encourage students to show their work.

EXTEND

Challenge
Conduct an experiment to make a scatter plot.

Students extending beyond proficiency will benefit from collecting data to make a scatter plot.

- Have students work with a partner to solve this problem: *Collect data by asking 10 students their shoe size and height. Convert all the heights to inches. Use the data to make a scatter plot. Describe the association, if any, between shoe size and height. If there is a linear association, draw a good line of fit.*
- Once the scatter plot is made, have students write 2–3 questions that can be answered by using the scatter plot.

PERSONALIZE

i-Ready

Provide students with opportunities to work on their personalized instruction path with *i-Ready* Online Instruction to:

- fill prerequisite gaps.
- build up grade-level skills.

LESSON 29

Lesson Quiz

TESTED SKILLS

Assesses 8.SP.A.1, 8.SP.A.2

Problems on this assessment require students to be able to graph and interpret data on a scatter plot. Students will need to identify relationships between variables by describing patterns and draw or recognize lines of fit. They also determine linear association related to a line of fit and select a good line of fit representing data. Students will also need to be familiar with graphing in the coordinate plane.

Alternately, teachers may assign the **Digital Comprehension Check** online to assess student understanding of this material.

Error Alert Errors may result if students:

- confuse positive association and negative association.
- attempt to model data using a line when there is no association.
- assume that a line of fit must pass through most of the data points on the scatter plot.
- identify a line of fit without counting the number of points above and below the line.

Problem Notes

1 Students could solve this problem by plotting ordered pairs for the values shown in the table. The *x*-value is the time in minutes, and the *y*-value is the distance in miles.

(2 points)

DOK 2 | **8.SP.A.1**

2 **Part A**

Students could solve this problem by analyzing the scatter plot and recognizing that the points go down and to the right.

(2 points)

DOK 1 | **8.SP.A.1**

Part B

Students could solve this problem by drawing a line that goes through the center of the points, has a negative slope, and has approximately the same number of points above and below the line. One possible line is shown; accept other reasonable possibilities.

(2 points)

DOK 2 | **8.SP.A.2**

LESSON 29 • QUIZ   Name:

➤ **Solve the problems.**

1 Maryanne walks on nature trails. The table shows her time and distance for 5 different walks. Make a scatter plot of the data. *(2 points)*

Time (min)	Distance (mi)
6	0.5
12	1
21	1.5
27	2
30	3

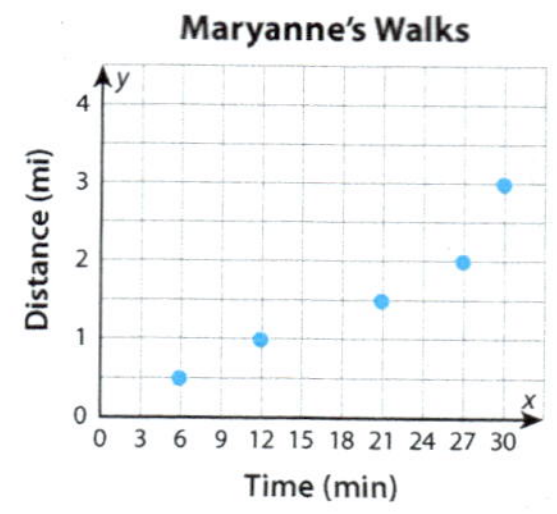

2 The scatter plot shows the approximate number of dogs available for adoption during a 10-month period at an animal rescue center.

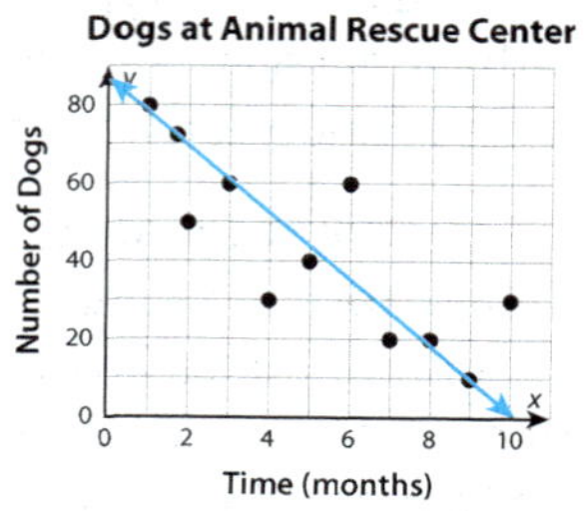

PART A

Do the data have a positive or negative association? Explain your reasoning. *(2 points)*

SOLUTION Negative association; Possible explanation: As the time increases, the number of dogs in the shelter decreases.

PART B

Graph a good line of fit for the data in the coordinate plane above. *(2 points)*

Graphing Coordinate Grid Scoring Rubric

Points	Expectations
2	Response has good line of fit or scatter plot with all points correctly placed.
1	Response has a line of fit with negative slope that is not in the middle of the data. Scatter plot contains 1 point that is incorrectly placed.
0	Response has a line of fit that does not follow the general trend of the data. Scatter plot has 2 or more points that are incorrectly placed.

Short Response Scoring Rubric

Points	Expectations
2	Response has the correct solution and includes well-organized, clear, and concise work demonstrating thorough understanding of concepts.
1	Response contains a mostly correct solution and shows partial understanding of concepts.
0	Response shows no attempt at finding a solution and no effort to demonstrate an understanding of concepts.

3 Students could solve this problem by analyzing the scatter plot to recognize that the data points are not clustered together in any noticeable pattern, so there is no association.

(2 points)

DOK 3 | **8.SP.A.2**

4 **C is correct.** Students could solve this problem by recognizing that line *c* follows the pattern of the data points and that there are the same number of points above and below the line.

A is not correct. This answer is a line that is above most of the data points despite showing a positive association.

B is not correct. This answer is a line that does not follow the pattern of the data points; it shows a constant association instead of a positive association.

D is not correct. This answer is a line that does not follow the pattern of the data points; although it passes directly through two data points, it shows a negative association instead of a positive association.

(1 point)

DOK 1 | **8.SP.A.2**

LESSON 29 • QUIZ Name:

3 Louis says that the line shown on the scatter plot is a good line of fit for the data because there are two points that lie on the line. Is Louis correct? Explain your reasoning. *(2 points)*

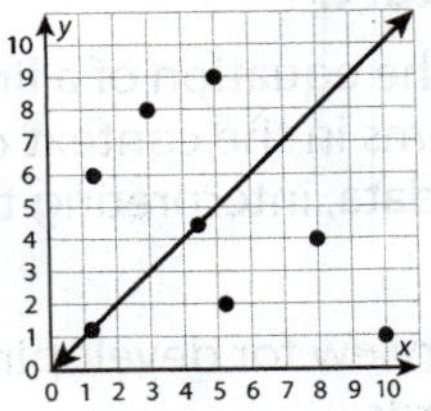

SOLUTION No; Possible explanation: For there to be a good line of fit, the data must have a linear association. The data on the scatter plot has no association, so no line is a good line of fit.

4 Which line on the scatter plot is a good line of fit for the data? *(1 point)*

A Line *a*

B Line *b*

C Line *c*

D Line *d*

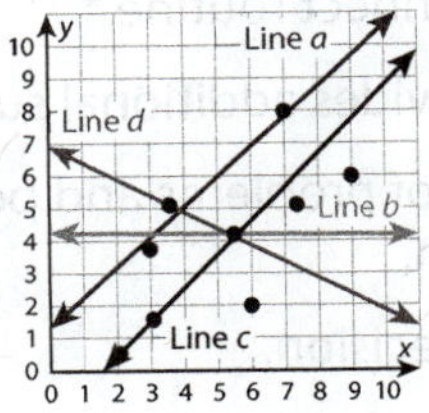

DIFFERENTIATION

RETEACH Tools for Instruction

Students who require additional support for prerequisite or on-level skills will benefit from activities that provide targeted skills instruction.

GRADE 8

- **Lesson 29** Construct and Use Scatter Plots

REINFORCE Math Center Activity

Students who require practice to reinforce concepts and skills and deepen understanding will benefit from small group collaborative games and activities (available in on-level, below-level, and above-level versions).

GRADE 8

- **Lesson 29** Use Vocabulary for Scatter Plots

EXTEND Enrichment Activity

Students who have achieved proficiency with concepts and skills and are ready for additional challenges will benefit from group collaborative games and activities that extend understanding.

GRADE 8

- **Lesson 29** Geometric Associations

Overview | Write and Analyze an Equation for Fitting a Linear Model to Data

MATH FOCUS

Focus Standard

8.SP.A.3 Use the equation of a linear model to solve problems in the context of bivariate measurement data, interpreting the slope and intercept.

See Unit 7 Overview for developing and applied standards.

STANDARDS FOR MATHEMATICAL PRACTICE (SMP)

SMP 1, 2, 3, 4, 5, and 6 are integrated into the Try-Discuss-Connect routine.*

This lesson provides additional support for:

1 Make sense of problems and persevere in solving them.

6 Attend to precision.

* See page 1o to learn how every lesson includes these SMP.

Objectives

Content Objectives

- Write an equation of a linear model for data with a linear association.
- Interpret the slope and *y*-intercept of a linear model in the context of the data.
- Use a linear model to solve problems in the context of the data.

Language Objectives

- Read and interpret word problems to write equations that represent linear models for data with linear associations.
- Use the terms *slope* and *y-intercept* to describe linear models.
- Understand the Academic Vocabulary and use it to read problems, analyze models, share strategies, and make predictions.
- Discuss ideas about linear models using lesson vocabulary.

Prior Knowledge

- Interpret slope and *y*-intercept of a line in context.
- Build scatter plots.
- Describe the relationship between two variables represented in a scatter plot.
- Identify outliers, clusters, and associations in bivariate data.

Vocabulary

Math Vocabulary

There is no new vocabulary. Review the following key terms.

estimate (noun) a close guess made using mathematical thinking.

estimate (verb) to give an approximate number or answer based on mathematical thinking.

linear association an association in which the relationship between the two variables can be generally approximated using a line.

slope for any two points on a line, the $\frac{\text{rise}}{\text{run}}$ or $\frac{\text{change in } y}{\text{change in } x}$. It is a measure of the steepness of a line. It is also called the rate of change of a linear function.

***y*-intercept** the *y*-coordinate of the point where a line, or graph of a function, intersects the *y*-axis.

Academic Vocabulary

analyze to examine details and patterns in order to draw conclusions or make estimates.

interpret to explain the meaning of something.

predict to make a guess, estimate, or conjecture based on data.

Learning Progression

Earlier in Grade 8, students graphed, wrote equations for, and interpreted linear functions. In the previous lesson, students made scatter plots for bivariate data and informally fit a line to data that showed a linear association.

In this lesson, students continue to work with bivariate data and scatter plots, focusing on finding equations for linear models. They interpret the slopes and *y*-intercepts of the linear models in context and use the models to make predictions.

In high school algebra, students will formalize the analysis of lines of best fit. They will also work with nonlinear functions that model data.

Pacing Guide

Items marked with are available on the **Teacher Toolbox**.

	MATERIALS	DIFFERENTIATION
SESSION 1 **Explore** Writing an Equation of a Linear Model (35–50 min)		
• **Start** (5 min) • **Try It** (5–10 min) • **Discuss It** (10–15 min) • **Connect It** (10–15 min) • **Close: Exit Ticket** (5 min) **Additional Practice** (pages 727–728)	**Math Toolkit** graph paper, graphing calculator Presentation Slides	**PREPARE** Interactive Tutorial **RETEACH or REINFORCE** Visual Model **Materials** For display: First quadrant grid with *x*-axis labeled *Study Time (min)* and a scale from 0 to 50 by 10s and *y*-axis labeled *Quiz Score* and a scale from 0 to 100 by 10s
SESSION 2 **Develop** Writing and Interpreting an Equation of a Linear Model (45–60 min)		
• **Start** (5 min) • **Try It** (10–15 min) • **Discuss It** (10–15 min) • **Connect It** (15–20 min) • **Close: Exit Ticket** (5 min) **Additional Practice** (pages 733–734)	**Math Toolkit** calculator, graph paper Presentation Slides	**RETEACH or REINFORCE** Visual Model **Materials** For display: Activity Sheet *Coordinate Plane: First Quadrant* **REINFORCE** Fluency & Skills Practice **EXTEND** Deepen Understanding
SESSION 3 **Develop** Analyzing a Linear Model to Make Predictions (45–60 min)		
• **Start** (5 min) • **Try It** (10–15 min) • **Discuss It** (10–15 min) • **Connect It** (10–15 min) • **Close: Exit Ticket** (5 min) **Additional Practice** (pages 739–740)	**Math Toolkit** calculator, graph paper Presentation Slides	**RETEACH or REINFORCE** Visual Model **Materials** For display: Try It scatter plot with line of fit **REINFORCE** Fluency & Skills Practice **EXTEND** Deepen Understanding
SESSION 4 **Refine** Writing and Analyzing an Equation for Fitting a Linear Model to Data (45–60 min)		
• **Start** (5 min) • **Monitor & Guide** (15–20 min) • **Group & Differentiate It** (20–30 min) • **Close: Exit Ticket** (5 min)	**Math Toolkit** Have items from previous sessions available for students. Presentation Slides	**RETEACH** Hands-On Activity **Materials** For each pair: straightedge, chenille stem, Activity Sheet *Coordinate Plane: First Quadrant* **REINFORCE** Problems 4–7 **EXTEND** Challenge **PERSONALIZE** i-Ready
Lesson 30 Quiz or **Digital Comprehension Check**		**RETEACH** Tools for Instruction **REINFORCE** Math Center Activity **EXTEND** Enrichment Activity

Overview | Write and Analyze an Equation for Fitting a Linear Model to Data

Connect to Culture

➤ **Use these activities to connect with and leverage the diverse backgrounds and experiences of all students. Engage students in sharing what they know about contexts before you add the information given here.**

SESSION 1 ■ □ □ □

Try It In 2010, President Barack Obama started an annual tradition of holding a science fair at the White House. Students are invited to present projects related to biotechnology. Their projects must use biological concepts to produce goods or services. Various awards are given at this prestigious event. Ask students to share what they might present if invited to a science fair similar to the one held at the White House.

SESSION 2 ■ ■ □ □

Try It Invite students to describe their favorite kinds of exercise. Why do they feel it is important to exercise? The American Heart Association recommends that adults get at least 2.5 hours of aerobic exercise per week, preferably spread out during the week. They should also attempt some sort of muscle-strengthening activity, such as weightlifting at least 2 days per week. The association also recommends that children of ages 6–17 get at least 60 minutes of exercise per day.

SESSION 3 ■ ■ ■ □

Apply It **Problem 7** Have students who have been on interesting hikes in unique areas share their experiences with the class. One of the most dangerous hikes in the world is on a trail at Huayna Picchu in Peru. This trail has both an upper path and a lower path. The upper path involves strenuous climbs that lead to a view of the famous Inca ruins at Machu Picchu. In the United States, The Maze in Utah's Canyonlands National Park is considered to be one of the toughest trails to hike. Trails in The Maze lead to various canyons and rivers. Hiking in The Maze requires a permit.

SESSION 4 ■ ■ ■ ■

Example Ask whether any students have had a pet snake and, if they have, to describe what it was like, and what was needed to feed and care for the snake. Corn snakes like the one shown are named for the pattern and color of the scales on their skin, which resemble corn kernels. These snakes are primarily found in the southeastern and eastern United States. They do not all live in the wild. Corn snakes also make good pets. They can live up to 20 years with proper care and grow to be about 4 to 6 feet long. Corn snakes eat every few days. Adults swallow their food, which consists mainly of rats, mice, and bats, whole.

Connect to Family and Community

➤ **After the Explore session, have students use the Family Letter to let their families know what they are learning and to encourage family involvement.**

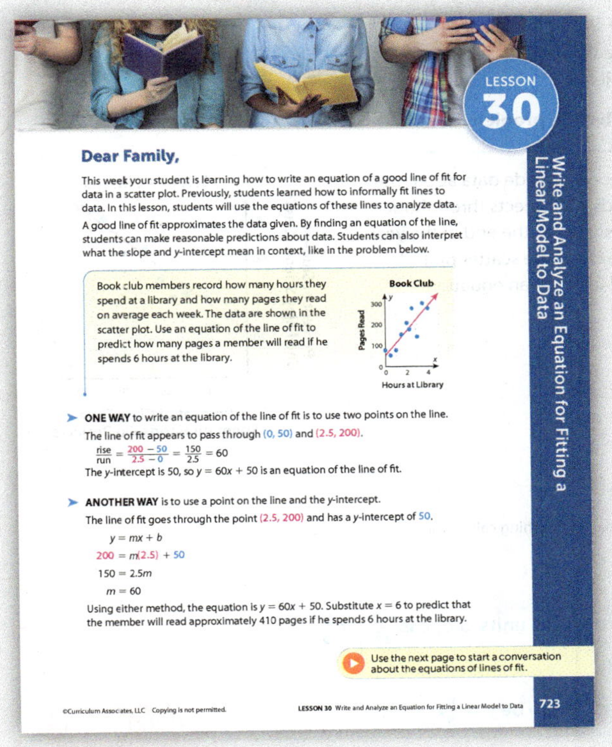

LESSON 30

Write and Analyze an Equation for Fitting a Linear Model to Data

Dear Family,

This week your student is learning how to write an equation of a good line of fit for data in a scatter plot. Previously, students learned how to informally fit lines to data. In this lesson, students will use the equations of these lines to analyze data.

A good line of fit approximates the data given. By finding an equation of the line, students can make reasonable predictions about data. Students can also interpret what the slope and y-intercept mean in context, like in the problem below.

Book club members record how many hours they spend at a library and how many pages they read on average each week. The data are shown in the scatter plot. Use an equation of the line of fit to predict how many pages a member will read if he spends 6 hours at the library.

➤ **ONE WAY** to write an equation of the line of fit is to use two points on the line.

The line of fit appears to pass through (0, 50) and (2.5, 200).

$\frac{\text{rise}}{\text{run}} = \frac{200 - 50}{2.5 - 0} = \frac{150}{2.5} = 60$

The y-intercept is 50, so $y = 60x + 50$ is an equation of the line of fit.

➤ **ANOTHER WAY** is to use a point on the line and the y-intercept.

The line of fit goes through the point (2.5, 200) and has a y-intercept of 50.

$$y = mx + b$$
$$200 = m(2.5) + 50$$
$$150 = 2.5m$$
$$m = 60$$

Using either method, the equation is $y = 60x + 50$. Substitute $x = 6$ to predict that the member will read approximately 410 pages if he spends 6 hours at the library.

Use the next page to start a conversation about the equations of lines of fit.

©Curriculum Associates, LLC Copying is not permitted. LESSON 30 Write and Analyze an Equation for Fitting a Linear Model to Data 723

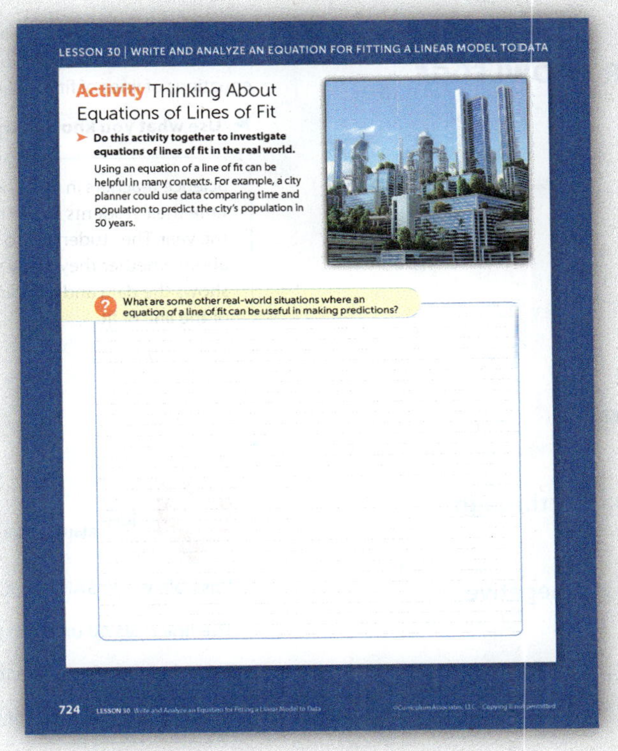

LESSON 30 | WRITE AND ANALYZE AN EQUATION FOR FITTING A LINEAR MODEL TO DATA

Activity Thinking About Equations of Lines of Fit

➤ **Do this activity together to investigate equations of lines of fit in the real world.**

Using an equation of a line of fit can be helpful in many contexts. For example, a city planner could use data comparing time and population to predict the city's population in 50 years.

What are some other real-world situations where an equation of a line of fit can be useful in making predictions?

724 LESSON 30 Write and Analyze an Equation for Fitting a Linear Model to Data ©Curriculum Associates, LLC Copying is not permitted.

Connect to Language

➤ **For English language learners, use the Differentiation chart to scaffold the language in each session. Use the Academic Vocabulary routine for academic terms before Session 1.**

DIFFERENTIATION | ENGLISH LANGUAGE LEARNERS

Use with **Session 1** **Connect It**

ACADEMIC VOCABULARY

A *reasonable prediction* is a guess that is based on data and makes sense.

To *suggest* means to demonstrate, point to, or give an idea about something.

Levels 1–3: Speaking/Writing

Help students make reasonable predictions when solving Connect It problem 2. Display the Academic Vocabulary. Model making a reasonable prediction about the weather and suggesting what to wear. Read the Look Ahead paragraph. Ask questions after each sentence to check for comprehension. Read problem 2a. Think aloud about the plot and ask partners to discuss. Then help them write their answers:

- *The slope of the line is _____, so the rate is _____.*
- *When the percent of time doing projects increases, the percent of students who enjoy science _____.*

Levels 2–4: Speaking/Writing

Help students make reasonable predictions when solving Connect It problem 2. Display the Academic Vocabulary. Call on volunteers to take turns making a reasonable prediction about the weather and suggesting what to wear. Read the Look Ahead paragraph. Ask questions after each sentence to check for comprehension. Then read problem 2a. Allow think time for partners to discuss. Then have them write their answers:

The relationship between _____ and _____ is _____. This suggests that when the percent of time _____, the percent of students who enjoy science will _____.

Levels 3–5: Speaking/Writing

Help students make reasonable predictions when solving Connect It problem 2. Display the Academic Vocabulary. Have students share examples of reasonable predictions and suggestions based on those predictions. Then have students read the Look Ahead paragraph and **Say It Another Way**. Have other students show thumbs up if the paraphrase is accurate and thumbs down if the paraphrase is incomplete or incorrect. Allow students time to revise, as needed. Then have students complete problem 2a using the Academic Vocabulary.

Explore Writing an Equation of a Linear Model

Purpose

- **Explore** the idea that an equation can be written for a line of fit.
- **Understand** that the equation for the line of fit can be used to make predictions.

START CONNECT TO PRIOR KNOWLEDGE

Which One Doesn't Belong?

A	B
$y = 4x + 1$	$y = -2x$
C	**D**
$y = -3 - x$	$6 = y$

A is the only equation whose line has a positive slope.

B is the only equation whose line passes through the origin.

C is the only equation whose line has a negative *y*-intercept.

D is the only equation with no *x*-term and whose line is horizontal.

WHY? Support students' facility with identifying slopes and *y*-intercepts of lines based on their equations.

TRY IT SMP 1, 2, 4, 5, 6

Make Sense of the Problem

See ***Connect to Culture*** to support student engagement. Before students work on Try It, use **Co-Craft Questions** to help them make sense of the problem. Have students turn and talk to discuss what it means to find the equation for the line of fit. If time allows at the end of the session, return to the list of student-generated questions and choose a few to attempt to answer.

DISCUSS IT SMP 2, 3, 6

Support Partner Discussion

After students work on Try It, have them respond to Discuss It with a partner. Listen for understanding of:

- how to find the slope of the line.
- how to find the *y*-intercept of the line.

LESSON 30 | SESSION 1

Explore Writing an Equation of a Linear Model

Previously, you learned how to make scatter plots and fit lines to data. In this lesson, you will learn about using the equations of lines of fit to solve problems.

➤ **Use what you know to try to solve the problem below.**

Science teachers in 10 middle schools provide data about the time their students spend on hands-on projects throughout the year. The students also take a survey at the end of the year about whether they enjoy science class. The scatter plot shows the data and a good line of fit. Write an equation of the line of fit.

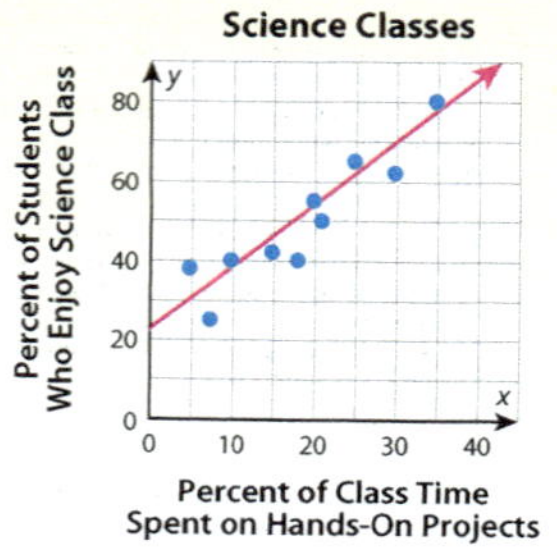

TRY IT Math Toolkit graph paper, graphing calculator

Possible work: SAMPLE A

The line rises 40 units for every run of 25 units. Slope is $\frac{40}{25}$, or $\frac{8}{5}$.

The *y*-intercept appears to be 23.

I estimate an equation of the line of fit to be $y = \frac{8}{5}x + 23$.

SAMPLE B

I used points (5, 30) and (30, 70) to find the slope: $\frac{70 - 30}{30 - 5} = \frac{40}{25} = \frac{8}{5}$.

Down 8 and left 5 from (5, 30) is (0, 22). So, the *y*-intercept is 22.

An equation of the line of fit is $y = \frac{8}{5}x + 22$.

DISCUSS IT

Ask: What did you do first to find an equation of the line of fit?

Share: I started by . . .

Learning Target SMP 1, SMP 2, SMP 3, SMP 4, SMP 5, SMP 6

Use the equation of a linear model to solve problems in the context of bivariate measurement data, interpreting the slope and intercept.

725

Common Misconception Listen for students who think that the slope is calculated using two data points, rather than two points on the line of best fit. As students share their strategies, discuss the fact that the slope measures the rate of change for the line, so it is calculated using two points on the line.

Select and Sequence Student Strategies

Select 2–3 samples that represent the range of student thinking in your classroom. Here is one possible order for class discussion:

- rise over run used to find slope; *y*-intercept found by inspection
- (misconception) two data points used to find slope
- formula used to find slope; *y*-intercept found by inspection
- formula used to find slope; *y*-intercept found by using a point on the line and solving $y = mx + b$ for b

Facilitate Whole Class Discussion

Call on students to share selected strategies. Prompt students to check their understanding by trying to paraphrase the speaker's ideas. They can ask questions about ideas that are unclear.

Guide students to **Compare and Connect** the representations. If discussion lags, ask students to turn and talk about what is needed to find the equation of the line of fit.

ASK *How does [student name]'s way of finding the equation compare to [student name]'s way?*

LISTEN FOR Each student determined the slope and y-intercept. There were different ways to find the changes in x and y and different ways to identify y when $x = 0$.

CONNECT IT

SMP 2, 4, 5

1 Look Back Look for understanding that the slope of the line of fit is $\frac{8}{5}$ and that the y-intercept is about 22.

DIFFERENTIATION | RETEACH or REINFORCE

Visual Model

Understand the line of fit.

If students are unsure of how to generate the equation of the line of fit from the graph, then use this activity to help them understand the process.

Materials For display: First quadrant grid with x-axis labeled *Study Time (min)* and a scale from 0 to 60 by 10s and y-axis labeled *Quiz Score* and a scale from 0 to 100 by 10s

- Before starting the activity, draw (but do not label) the line $y = \frac{3}{2}x + 50$, plot and label the point (10, 65) on the line, and plot several points close to, but not on, the line.
- Explain to students that you want to find the equation for the line of fit.
- Ask: *How many points are needed to find slope?* [2]
- Ask: *You know one point. What is a point on the line of fit that lies where the gridlines intersect?* [(20, 80)]
- Invite a student to demonstrate using the slope formula with (10, 65) and (20, 80) to find $\frac{3}{2}$.
- Ask: *What is the meaning of the slope and y-intercept in the context of the situation?* [slope: A score would increase by 3 points for every 2 additional minutes of study time; y-intercept: A student who did not study should expect to score 50.]
- Ask: *What is the equation of the line of best fit?* [$y = \frac{3}{2}x + 50$]

CONNECT IT

1 Look Back What is an equation of the line of fit? How did you find the equation?

Possible answer: $y = \frac{8}{5}x + 22$; I found two points on the line and used them to calculate the slope. Then I estimated that the line crosses the y-axis at the point (0, 22), so the y-intercept is 22.

2 Look Ahead A good line of fit represents the data. The equation of the line models the association between the variables. You can use the equation to make reasonable predictions.

a. What is the relationship between the slope of the line of fit and the rate of change in the equation? What does this suggest about hands-on projects in science classes?

Possible answer: The slope of the line of fit equation is positive, so the rate of change between the variables is positive. This matches the positive association shown in the data. As the percent of time doing hands-on projects increases, the percent of students who enjoy science class also increases.

b. Suppose you know the percent of time a science class spends doing hands-on projects. How could you use your equation to predict the percent of students who enjoy science class?

Possible answer: I could substitute the percent of time spent doing hands-on projects for x and then solve the equation for y, which is the percent of students who enjoy science class.

3 Reflect Use your equation to predict the percent of students who will say they enjoy science class if the class does hands-on projects 15% of the time. Is it the same value as the actual data? Explain.

Possible answer: Using $y = \frac{8}{5}x + 22$, I get 46%. The actual data value is about 42%, which is a close estimate.

726

---

2 Look Ahead Point out that a line of fit can be used to make predictions for the data. Students should recognize that once an equation is obtained, they can substitute x-values to predict y-values. In this case, they can substitute the percent of time a class spends doing online projects for x. The resulting y-value will be a prediction of the percent of students who enjoy science class. The result may not be an actual data value but will be a reasonable prediction based on the pattern in the data.

CLOSE | EXIT TICKET

3 Reflect Look for understanding that a reasonable prediction is 46% and that this value is an estimate of the actual value. Allow some leeway in accuracy because some students may have a slightly different equation, which would result in a different prediction.

Common Misconception If students think that there is only one correct prediction, then record all student answers for the class. Circle answers that seem to be reasonable predictions.

Prepare for Writing and Analyzing an Equation for Fitting a Linear Model to Data

Support Vocabulary Development

Assign **Prepare for Writing and Analyzing an Equation for Fitting a Linear Model to Data** as extra practice in class or as homework.

If you have students complete this in class, then use the guidance below.

Ask students to consider the term *linear association*. Encourage them to think about their prior work identifying *associations* and what the term *linear* means.

Have students work in pairs to complete the graphic organizer. Invite pairs to share their completed organizers, and prompt a whole-class comparative discussion of the definitions, examples, and non-examples.

Have students look at the scatter plot in problem 2 and discuss with a partner how the points on the scatter plot are arranged. Encourage them to debate whether or not a straight line can be drawn that is near most of the data points.

Problem Notes

1 Students should understand that when points in a scatter plot have a linear association, there is a relationship between two variables that can be modeled by a straight line. Students should recognize that when a linear association is positive, the points on a scatter plot rise from left to right, and when a linear association is negative, the points on a scatter plot fall from left to right.

2 Students should observe that although the points form a pattern, it is a curve and not a line. So, the data show a nonlinear association.

LESSON 30 | SESSION 1 Name:

Prepare for Writing and Analyzing an Equation for Fitting a Linear Model to Data

1 Think about what you know about scatter plots that show linear associations. Fill in each box. Use words, numbers, and pictures. Show as many ideas as you can.

Possible answers:

What Is It?

a relationship between two variables that can be modeled by a straight line

What I Know About It

A linear association is positive if the data rise from left to right. A linear association is negative if the data fall from left to right.

linear association

Examples

Non-Examples

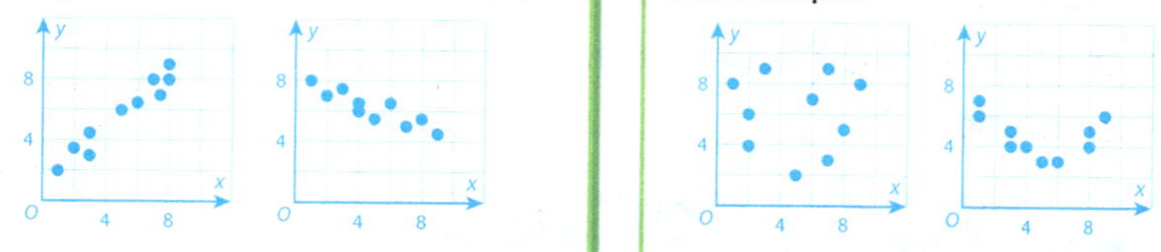

2 Do these data show a linear association? Explain.

No; Possible explanation: The data do not follow a pattern that can be modeled by a straight line. The pattern of data is curved, not straight.

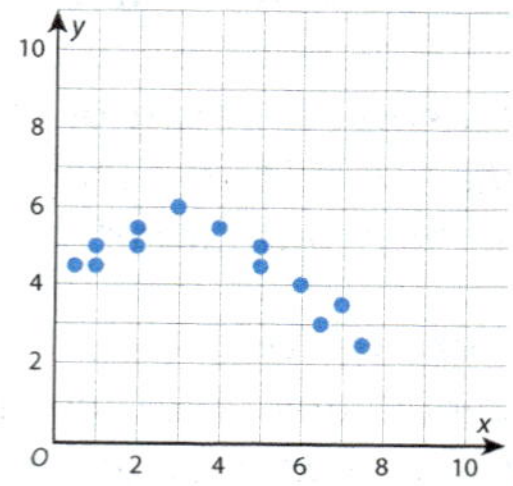

727

REAL-WORLD CONNECTION

Concession stand managers at an amusement park might use scatter plots to show temperature and daily attendance. They could use these scatter plots along with a line of fit to predict the daily attendance based on the forecasted temperatures. This will help the managers determine how many employees to schedule on a given day or how much food to have at the concession stands. Ask students to think of other real-world examples when using a line of fit for a scatter plot might be useful.

3 Problem 3 provides another look at writing the equation of a line of fit for data shown in a scatter plot. This problem is similar to the problem about the amount of time students spend on hands-on science projects. In both problems, a scatter plot and a good line of fit is shown. This problem asks for the equation of a line of fit for data relating the number of hours students spend playing outside on a Sunday to the number of hours they spend playing video games.

Students may want to use graph paper or a graphing calculator to solve.

Suggest that students use **Three Reads**, asking themselves one of the following questions each time:

- *What is this problem about?*
- *What is the question I am trying to answer?*
- *What information is important?*

3 This scatter plot shows the number of hours students spend playing outside and playing video games on a Sunday. A good line of fit is drawn through the data

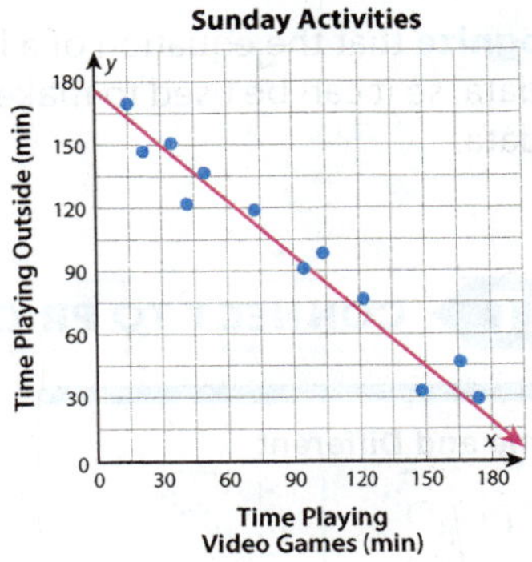

a. Write an equation of the line of fit. Show your work.

Possible work:

The line of fit seems to pass through (0, 177), so the *y*-intercept is 177.

The rise is −105 and the run is 120, so the slope is $-\frac{105}{120}$, or $-\frac{7}{8}$.

SOLUTION An equation of the line of fit is $y = -\frac{7}{8}x + 177$.

b. Check your answer to problem 3a. Show your work.

The line of fit passes through (30, 150) and (150, 45).

slope: $m = \frac{45 - 150}{150 - 30} = \frac{-105}{120} = -\frac{7}{8}$

(0, 177) seems to be on the line, so the *y*-intercept is 177.

Using $y = mx + b$, an equation of the line of fit is $y = -\frac{7}{8}x + 177$.

DIFFERENTIATION | ENGLISH LANGUAGE LEARNERS

Use with **Session 2** **Apply It**

Levels 1–3: Reading/Listening

Help students interpret Apply It problem 7. Divide the argument in parts: *the line of fit for problem 6/ is not a good fit/ because the rates of change between different pairs of data points/ do not always match the slope/ of the line of fit.* Discuss each part of the argument.

Have students point to the line of fit. Ask: *Does Kazuko think this is a good line of fit?* Point out that *because* introduces an explanation. Ask: *Why does he think that?* Help students point to pairs of data and discuss the rates. Then ask: *What is a good line of fit? Do you agree with Kazuko? Why?*

- *A good line of fit ____.*
- *I ____ with Kazuko because the line still represents/does not represent the data.*

Levels 2–4: Reading/Listening

Help students prepare to write their responses to Apply It problem 7. Divide the argument in parts and discuss each part. Have students turn to a partner to tell what Kazuko thinks about the line of fit in problem 6. Ask students to write what they know about good lines of fit. Provide the sentence starter:

- *A good line of fit should ____.*

Help students reread Kazuko's argument and compare it with their ideas. Then, have them write whether they agree or disagree with Kazuko using:

- *I agree/disagree with Kazuko because ____.*

Levels 3–5: Reading/Listening

Help students prepare to write their responses to Apply It problem 7. Have students turn and talk to discuss the argument and interpret its meaning. Call on several students to **Say It Another Way** to confirm understanding and give students time to process the ideas.

Have students write one or two sentences to describe a good line of fit. Ask them to compare their descriptions with the line of fit in problem 6. Ask: *Is this an example of a good line of fit? Why?* Then have students compare their ideas with Kazuko's argument. Allow time for students to draft their answers. Then have them review with partners.

Develop Writing and Interpreting an Equation of a Linear Model

Purpose

- **Develop** strategies for writing and interpreting an equation for a line of fit.
- **Recognize** that the equation of a line of fit represents the data, so it can be used to make predictions about the data.

START CONNECT TO PRIOR KNOWLEDGE

Same and Different

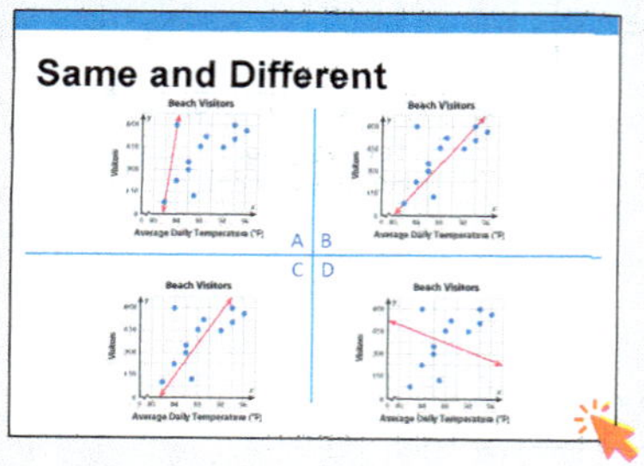

Possible Solutions

B and C show good lines of fit.

A and D show lines that are not good lines of fit.

A and B show lines that pass through data points.

D shows a line with a negative slope.

WHY? Support students' facility with identifying good lines of fit.

DEVELOP ACADEMIC LANGUAGE

WHY? Reinforce understanding of *appears to* through synonyms and context.

HOW? Read Model It. Have students brainstorm synonyms for the phrase (*seems, looks like*). If students suggest *becomes visible*, ask questions to provide context and highlight the difference: *Did the line become visible all of a sudden? Does it look like the line goes through the points (0, 82) and (1, 78)?* Then have students use the phrase to describe the line.

TRY IT SMP 1, 2, 4, 5, 6

Make Sense of the Problem

See ***Connect to Culture*** to support student engagement. Before students work on Try It, use **Three Reads** to help them make sense of the problem. Encourage students to consider both the problem statement and the graph. Have students turn and talk with a partner before responding to each question with the whole class.

LESSON 30 | SESSION 2

Develop Writing and Interpreting an Equation of a Linear Model

Read and try to solve the problem below.

The scatter plot shows data for 14 women ages 18–25. The graph shows their average resting heart rates and number of hours of physical activity each week. A good line of fit is drawn through the data.

A 20-year-old woman decides to exercise 2 more hours each week. How might this affect her average resting heart rate?

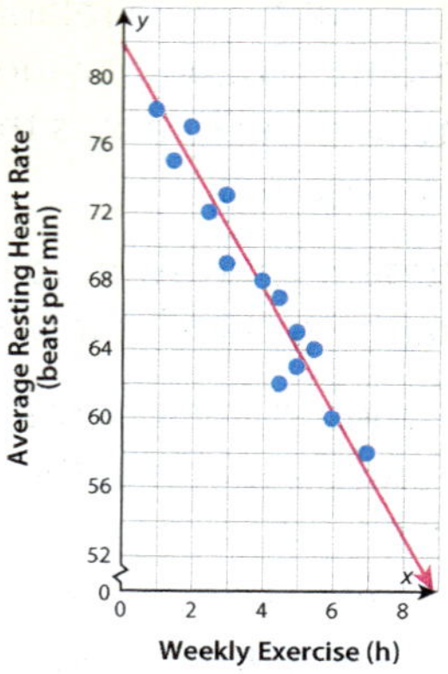

TRY IT Math Toolkit calculator, graph paper

Possible work: SAMPLE A

Using points (2, 75) and (5, 64):

slope: $\frac{75 - 64}{2 - 5} = -\frac{11}{3}$; y-intercept: 82; line of fit: $y = -\frac{11}{3}x + 82$

When $x = 0$: $y = 82$; when $x = 2$: $y = -\frac{11}{3}(2) + 82 \approx 74.7$; $74.7 - 82 = -7.3$

Her resting heart rate will decrease by about 7.3 beats per minute.

SAMPLE B

y-intercept: 82; Start at (0, 82) and count down 18 and right 5 to (5, 64).

Slope: $-\frac{18}{5}$, or -3.6; Heart rate decreases about 3.6 beats a minute for every hour of exercise, so for 2 hours it will decrease by about 7.2 beats per minute.

DISCUSS IT

Ask: Why did you choose that strategy to find the heart rate?

Share: I started by . . .

729

DISCUSS IT SMP 2, 3, 6

Support Partner Discussion

After students work on Try It, have them explain their work and then respond to Discuss It with a partner. If students need support in getting started, prompt them to ask each other questions such as:

- *Did you find the equation of the line? If so, how did you use it to find the answer?*
- *Do you need to know how many hours the woman exercises now in order to answer the question?*

Error Alert If students give the slope as the answer, stating that her heart rate will decrease by about 3.7 beats per minute, then ask them what the slope means in this situation. Students should recognize that the slope is the change in heart rate for every increase of *one* hour of exercise. Point out that the problem states that the woman will be increasing her weekly exercise by *two* hours.

Select and Sequence Student Strategies

Select 2–3 samples that represent the range of student thinking in your classroom. Here is one possible order for class discussion:

- use graph of line to determine *y*-values for *x*-values 2 units apart and then subtract
- use rise and run to estimate slope of fit line and multiply by 2
- use slope formula to find slope and multiply by 2
- write an equation, substitute *x*-values 2 units apart, and find difference in *y*-values

Facilitate Whole Class Discussion

Call on students to share selected strategies. Ask students to use precise language, such as *slope*, *y-intercept*, and *rate of change*, in their explanations.

Guide students to **Compare and Connect** the representations. Allow students individual think time after each strategy to process the ideas and consider how to verbalize their connections.

ASK *How does each strategy use the line of fit?*

LISTEN FOR Some use the line to find *y*-values for *x*-values that are 2 units apart. Some find the slope, or rate of change, of the line. Some find the slope and *y*-intercept and use it to write an equation.

Picture It & Model It

If students presented these models, have students connect these models to those presented in class.

If no student presented at least one of these models, have students first analyze key features of the models, and then connect them to the models presented in class.

ASK *What is the same and what is and different about the models presented?*

LISTEN FOR One estimates slope using rise over run. The other uses the slope formula. The slope estimates are different, but close. The *y*-intercepts are the same.

For the model that finds rise over run, prompt students to consider which points on the line were chosen. Ask: *Could two other points on the line be chosen to determine slope?*

For the model that estimates the slope using a formula, prompt students to think about what happens after the slope is determined. Ask: *Once the slope is found, what else needs to be done to find the equation of the line of fit?*

➤ Explore different ways to write and interpret an equation of a linear model.

The scatter plot shows data for 14 women ages 18–25. The graph shows their average resting heart rates and number of hours of physical activity each week. A good line of fit is drawn through the data.

A 20-year-old woman decides to exercise 2 more hours each week. How might this affect her average resting heart rate?

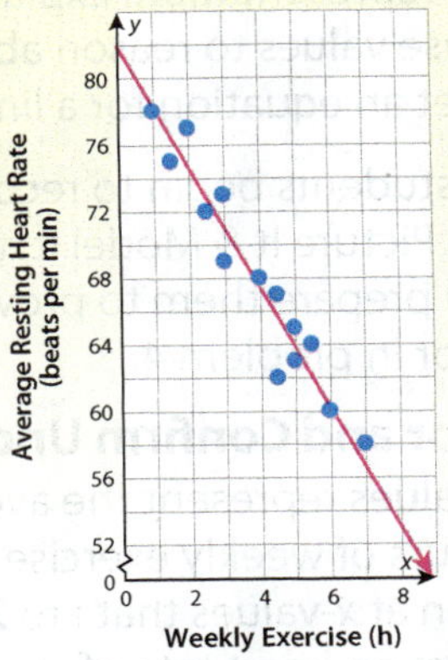

Picture It

You can estimate the slope of the line of fit using $\frac{\text{rise}}{\text{run}}$.

$\frac{\text{rise}}{\text{run}} = -\frac{11}{3} \approx -3.7$

The estimated slope of the line of fit is $-\frac{11}{3}$.

The *y*-intercept is about 82.

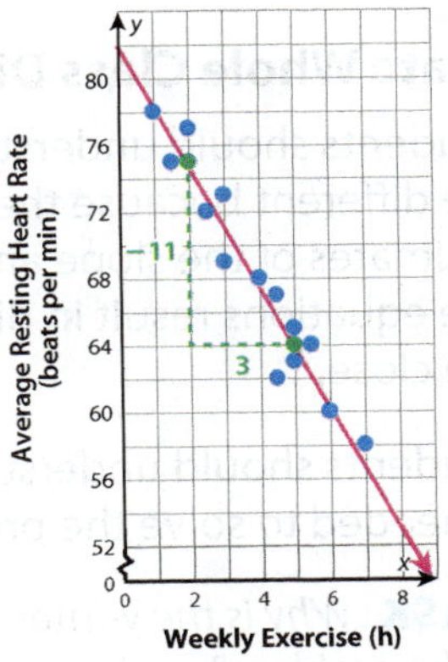

Model It

You can estimate the slope of the line of fit using the slope formula.

The line of fit appears to go through the points (0, 82) and (1, 78).

Slope: $\frac{78-82}{1-0} = \frac{-4}{1} = -4$

The estimated slope of the line of fit is −4. The *y*-intercept is 82.

730

DIFFERENTIATION | EXTEND

SMP 1

Deepen Understanding
Making Sense of the "Reversed" Graph

Prompt students to consider how "reversing" the graph would affect the slope of the line of fit and what the slope would mean in the context of the situation.

ASK *What does the slope of the line of fit, −4, represent in this situation?*

LISTEN FOR It is the change in the average resting heart rate for each additional hour of weekly exercise.

ASK *Suppose the axes are reversed. Using the points from Model It, what two points would lie on the line of fit for the reversed graph?*

LISTEN FOR Because (0, 82) and (1, 78) are on the original line, (82, 0) and (78, 1) would be on the line for the reversed graph.

ASK *Use these points to find the slope of the line of fit for the reversed graph. How does it compare to the slope of the original line? What does the slope mean in this situation?*

LISTEN FOR The slope, $-\frac{1}{4}$, is the reciprocal of the original slope. It is the average change in the hours of weekly exercise for each change of 1 beat per minute in the resting heart rate.

Develop Writing and Interpreting an Equation of a Linear Model

CONNECT IT

SMP 2, 4, 5, 6

Remind students that the data points are the same in each representation. Explain that they will now use those values to reason about how to write and interpret an equation for a linear model.

Before students begin to record and expand on their work in Picture It & Model It, tell them that problems 1–3 will prepare them to provide the explanation asked for in problem 4.

Monitor and Confirm Understanding 1

The y-values represent the average resting heart rate for x hours of weekly exercise. So, evaluating each equation at x-values that are 2 hours apart will show the effect on heart rate of exercising 2 more hours each week.

Facilitate Whole Class Discussion

2 Students should understand that the equations are different because they are written based on estimates of the slope and y-intercept. While the equations result in different answers, they are close.

3 Students should understand that only the slope is needed to solve the problem.

ASK *Why is the y-intercept not needed to solve the problem?*

LISTEN FOR You need to know only how much the heart rate changes for each additional hour of weekly exercise. This is the slope. Knowing the y-intercept, which is the heart rate for 0 hours of weekly exercise, is unnecessary.

4 Look for the idea that the whole line is needed when the question relates to more than just the slope or just the y-intercept.

ASK *What types of questions could you answer using the whole equation?*

LISTEN FOR You could predict the heart rate for a given number of hours of exercise, or you could predict the number of hours of exercise needed to get a certain heart rate.

5 **Reflect** Have all students focus on the strategies used to solve the Try It. If time allows, have students discuss their ideas with a partner.

CONNECT IT

➤ **Use the problem from the previous page to help you understand how to write and interpret an equation of a linear model.**

1 Write the equations of the lines of fit for **Picture It** and for **Model It**. Use each equation to determine how exercising 2 more hours per week will affect the resting heart rate of a 20-year-old woman.

Picture It: $y = -3.7x + 82$; Possible answer: Using (0, 82) and (2, 74.6), heart rate decreases by about 7.4 beats per minute. Model It: $y = -4x + 82$; Possible answer: Using (0, 82) and (2, 74), heart rate decreases by about 8 beats per minute.

2 The equations of the lines of fit in problem 1 give different answers to the problem. Does this mean that one of the answers is wrong? Explain.

No; Possible explanation: The answers are different but close. The equations are estimates because they are found by estimating the coordinates of points on the line. As long as estimates are reasonable, small differences in the calculations from the equations should be expected.

3 Would it be possible to answer the **Try It** problem without using an equation of the line of fit? Explain.

Yes; Possible explanation: I could use the slope as the rate of change and set up a proportion.

4 For what kinds of data questions would you need to find and use the whole equation of the line of fit?

Possible answer: Questions that have to do with more than the rate of change between variables, such as predicting the value of one variable when given a value for the other variable.

5 **Reflect** Think about all the models and strategies you have discussed today. Describe how one of them helped you better understand how to write and interpret an equation of a linear model.

Responses will vary. Check student responses.

731

DIFFERENTIATION | RETEACH or REINFORCE

Visual Model

Use a model to investigate slope of a line of fit.

If students are unsure how to find an equation of a line of fit, then use this activity to demonstrate the process.

Materials For display: Activity Sheet *Coordinate Plane: First Quadrant*

- Display a scatter plot with the points (1, 2), (2, 5), (3, 4), (4, 7), (5, 5), (6, 6), (7, 8), (8, 6), (9, 7), and (10, 9). Then draw a line through the points (0, 3), (4, 5), and (8, 7).
- Ask: *Does the line of fit pass through any data points?* [No.]
- Ask: *How can you find the slope of the line of fit?* [Choose two places where the line intersects gridlines on the graph and find the slope between those two points.]
- Ask: *What is the slope?* $\left[\frac{1}{2}\right]$
- Ask: *How can you find the y-intercept of the line of fit?* [Estimate where the line intersects the y-axis.] *What is the y-intercept?* [3]
- Ask: *What is the equation for this line of fit?* $\left[y = \frac{1}{2}x + 3\right]$
- Point out that finding an equation of a line of fit is the same as finding the equation of any line.

Apply It

For all problems, encourage students to use a model to support their thinking.

6 Students may solve the problem by using the slope formula and then reason that the slope represents a unit rate. So, it is the change in stride length for each 1-inch increase in height.

7 Students may explain that the line of fit is an estimate used to model the association for all the data points, so the slope should not be expected to exactly match the rate of change between any two data points.

Apply It

➤ **Use what you learned to solve these problems.**

6 The scatter plot shows the stride lengths and heights for 10 middle school students. A good line of fit is drawn through data points (57.5, 22.8) and (63, 25). What is the slope of the line of fit? What does the slope say about how stride length changes when height is increased by 1 in.?

0.4; The slope tells me that for each height increase of 1 in., stride length increases by about 0.4 in.

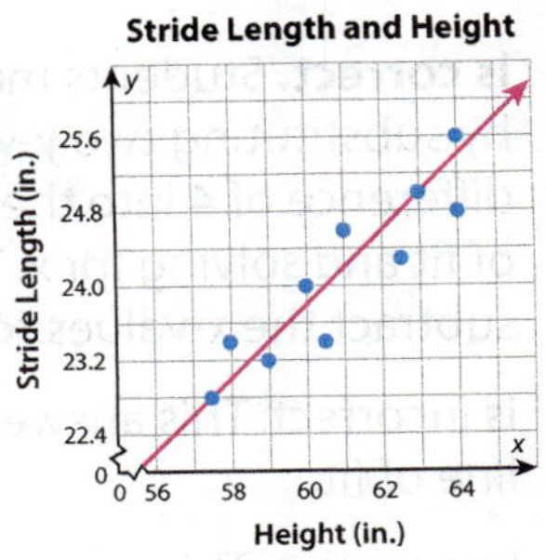

7 Kazuko says that the line of fit for problem 6 is not a good fit because the rates of change between different pairs of data points do not always match the slope of the line of fit. Do you agree with Kazuko? Why or why not?

Disagree; Possible explanation: The line of fit is a model for the data. The slope of the line of fit is a good model of what happens to stride length when height increases, but it is not exact.

8 A teacher asks 12 students in his public speaking course the percent of time they feel anxious in class. This scatter plot shows the percent of time a student feels anxious and their current grade. Write an equation of the line of fit. Show your work.

Possible work:

The line of fit appears to go through the points (30, 90) and (85, 70).

$m = \frac{90 - 70}{30 - 85} = -\frac{20}{55} = -\frac{4}{11}$

The y-intercept appears to be 100.

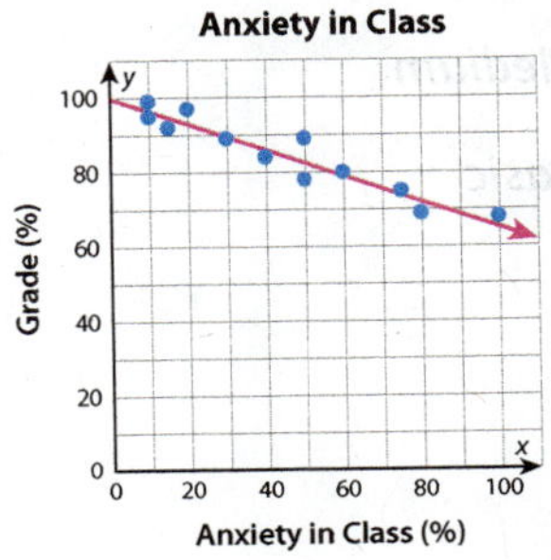

SOLUTION Possible equation: $y = -\frac{4}{11}x + 100$

CLOSE **EXIT TICKET**

8 Students' solutions should show an understanding that:

- the slope can be found by identifying two points on the line and using the slope formula or by finding rise over run.
- the y-intercept can be read from the graph of the line of fit or found by substituting the slope and a point on the line into the slope-intercept form of a line.

Error Alert If students find a slope of $\frac{4}{11}$, then ask them whether the line increases or decreases from left to right and what this indicates about the sign of the slope. Have these students recalculate the slope, making sure they subtract the y-coordinates and the x-coordinates of the points they choose in the same order.

Practice Writing and Interpreting an Equation of a Linear Model

Problem Notes

Assign **Practice Writing and Interpreting an Equation of a Linear Model** as extra practice in class or as homework.

1 **B is correct.** Students may solve the problem by substituting two y-values with a difference of 4 into the equation of the line of fit and solving for x. Then they may subtract the x-values to get the result.

A is incorrect. This answer uses the slope of the line of fit.

C is incorrect. This answer results from substituting $x = 4$ into the equation of the line of fit.

D is incorrect. This answer results from substituting two x-values with a difference of 4 into the equation of the line of fit instead of two y-values.

Medium

2 *Basic*

LESSON 30 | SESSION 2 Name:

Practice Writing and Interpreting an Equation of a Linear Model

➤ **Study the Example showing how to write and interpret an equation of a linear model. Then solve problems 1–3.**

Example

The scatter plot shows the foot lengths and the hand lengths of 20 students. The foot length of Student A is 5 cm more than the foot length of Student B. About how much longer would you expect Student A's hand to be than Student B's?

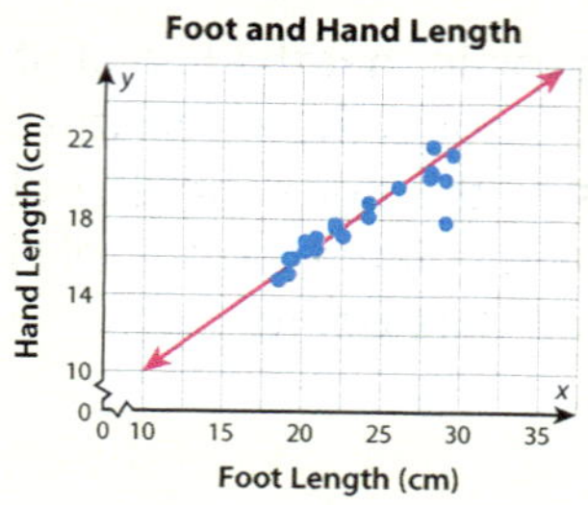

The line of fit seems to go through (30, 22) and (20, 16).

Slope: $\frac{22-16}{30-20} = \frac{6}{10} = 0.6$

There is a break in the x-axis. Use $y = mx + b$ to find the y-intercept.

$16 = 0.6(20) + b \longrightarrow 16 = 12 + b \longrightarrow 4 = b$

An equation of the line of fit is $y = 0.6x + 4$.

10 cm foot length: $y = 0.6(10) + 4 = 10$ cm hand length

15 cm foot length: $y = 0.6(15) + 4 = 13$ cm hand length

$13 - 10 = 3$

Student A's hand length should be about 3 cm longer than Student B's.

1 In the Example, suppose Student A's hand length was 4 cm longer than Student B's. About how much longer would you expect Student A's foot to be?

A 0.6 cm

B 6.7 cm

C 6.4 cm

D 2.4 cm

2 What does the y-intercept of the line of fit in the Example mean in terms of the problem? Does it make sense?

If a student's foot length is 0 cm, the hand length will be 4 cm; No.

733

Fluency & Skills Practice

Writing and Interpreting an Equation of a Linear Model

In this activity, students are given a scatter plot with a good line of fit for each data set, and they write an equation of the line of fit.

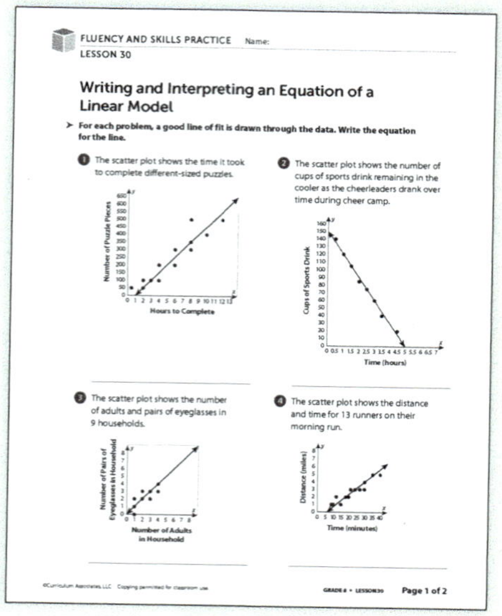

FLUENCY AND SKILLS PRACTICE Name:
LESSON 30

Writing and Interpreting an Equation of a Linear Model

➤ For each problem, a good line of fit is drawn through the data. Write the equation for the line.

1 The scatter plot shows the time it took to complete different-sized puzzles.

2 The scatter plot shows the number of cups of sports drink remaining in the cooler as the cheerleaders drank over time during cheer camp.

3 The scatter plot shows the number of adults and pairs of eyeglasses in 9 households.

4 The scatter plot shows the distance and time for 13 runners on their morning run.

©Curriculum Associates, LLC Copying permitted for classroom use

GRADE 8 • LESSON 30 Page 1 of 2

3 **a.** Students may estimate the coordinates of two points to find the slope, so the values they find for the slope and y-intercept may vary. However, the slope should be close to 1.25, and the y-intercept should be close to 22.5. Note that students should not estimate the y-intercept from the graph because of the break in the scale for the x-axis. ***Medium***

b. Students may also solve the problem by substituting $x = 0$ and $x = 5$ (or any two x-values that are 5 units apart) into the equation for the line of fit and then subtracting to find the change in y-values. Note that since the slope was found using estimated coordinates, answers to this problem may vary. ***Challenge***

c. Because students' equations may vary, the results may vary when 48 is substituted for y. Students may also solve this problem by drawing a horizontal line from 48 on the y-axis across to the line of fit, and then a vertical line down to the x-axis to estimate the x-value. ***Medium***

LESSON 30 | SESSION 2

3 A middle school basketball team records the number of minutes they practice free throws before games. Then they record the percent of free throws they make during each game. The scatter plot shows the results. A good line of fit is drawn through the data.

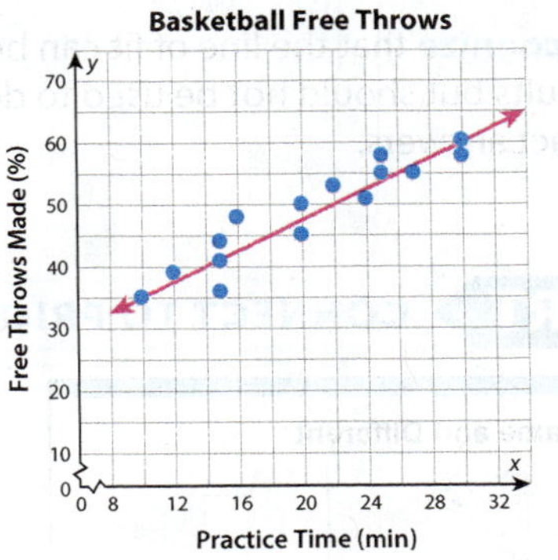

a. Write an equation of the line. Show your work.

Possible work:

The line appears to go through (10, 35) and (18, 45).

The estimated slope is $\frac{45 - 35}{18 - 10} = \frac{10}{8} = 1.25$.

$35 = 1.25(10) + b$

$35 = 12.5 + b$

$22.5 = b$

SOLUTION Possible equation: $y = 1.25x + 22.5$

b. What can the team expect to happen to the percent of free throws they make during a game if they practice an additional 5 minutes before the game? Explain.

The team can expect the percent of free throws they make to go up by 6.25%; Possible explanation: The slope is 1.25, so for each additional minute practiced, the percent of free throws made increases by 1.25%. For 5 extra minutes, the percentage can be expected to go up by $5(1.25) = 6.25\%$.

c. The basketball team makes 48% of free throws during a game. Based on the data, about how many minutes would you estimate they practiced before the game? Show your work.

Possible work:

$y = 1.25x + 22.5$

$48 = 1.25x + 22.5$

$25.5 = 1.25x$

$20.4 = x$

SOLUTION They practiced about 20.4 min before the game.

734

DIFFERENTIATION | ENGLISH LANGUAGE LEARNERS

Use with **Session 3** **Apply It**

Levels 1–3: Speaking/Writing

Help students interpret Apply It problem 7. Read the first paragraph and create a **Co-Constructed Word Bank**. Discuss unfamiliar words or terms students can use to talk about the problem, such as *scatter plot, data, distance, time*, and *statements*. Review the scatter plot and the equation to check understanding. Then read the answer choices and add more words to the bank, as needed. Point out *farther* and *longer* and clarify as needed. Then explain *about* and *exact*. Ask: *Do these words mean the same? Which word means* more or less? Guide students to read each answer choice and discuss with a partner whether they are true or not.

Levels 2–4: Speaking/Writing

Help students interpret Apply It problem 7. Use **Notice and Wonder** to help students think and talk about the scatter plot. Have students tell what they notice about the line and what they wonder about the data. Then read the first paragraph and create a **Co-Constructed Word Bank**. Discuss unfamiliar words or terms students can use to talk about the problem. After discussing meanings, encourage students to suggest synonyms, cognates, or examples. Then have students read the answer choices. Check to see whether students want to add words to the bank. Call on volunteers to explain *about* and *exact*. Have students read each choice, decide whether they are true or not, and share their responses with a partner.

Levels 3–5: Speaking/Writing

Help students interpret Apply It problem 7. Use **Notice and Wonder** to help students think and talk about the scatter plot. Have students tell what they notice about the line and what they wonder about the data. Then read the first paragraph. Have students turn to partners to discuss unfamiliar words or words they could use to talk about the problem. Encourage them to use synonyms, cognates, or examples as they talk about the words. Then have students quickly scan the answer choices. Have them tell which choices describe estimates and which describe exact distances. Ask them to read each choice and decide whether they are true or not.

Develop Analyzing a Linear Model to Make Predictions

Purpose

- **Develop** strategies for analyzing a linear model to make predictions.
- **Recognize** that the line of fit can be used to predict results but should not be used to determine exact answers.

START CONNECT TO PRIOR KNOWLEDGE

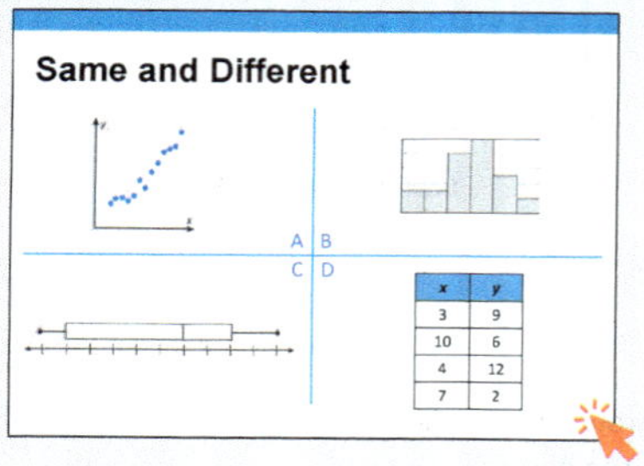

Possible Solutions

All of the displays show data.

A and D show two-variable data.

B and C show single-variable data.

WHY? Support students' understanding of one- and two-variable data displays.

DEVELOP ACADEMIC LANGUAGE

WHY? Develop understanding of sentences with passive voice.

HOW? Read the question in Connect It 2. Discuss active and passive voice. Have students identify the action in the question (*predicted*). Ask: *What does the action affect?* [the value of sales] Then have students use active voice to tell what predicts the value of sales:

The ____ predicts the value of sales.

Then have students tell the predicted value.

TRY IT

SMP 1, 2, 4, 5, 6

Make Sense of the Problem

Before students work on Try It, have students read the problem with a partner and use **Say It Another Way** to help them make sense of the problem.

LESSON 30 | SESSION 3

Develop Analyzing a Linear Model to Make Predictions

➤ **Read and try to solve the problem below.**

The scatter plot shows the average amount several companies spend on online advertising and their average monthly sales. A good line of fit is drawn through the data. Suppose a company spends an average of $4,000 on advertising. What would you predict their average monthly sales to be?

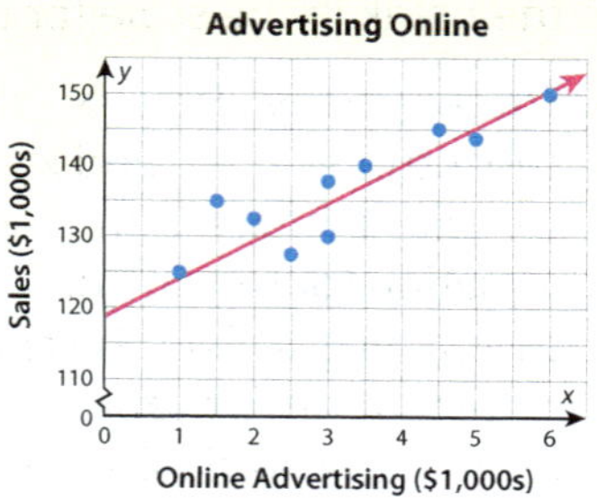

TRY IT Math Toolkit calculator, graph paper

Possible work:

SAMPLE A

The *y*-values of the data points with advertising closest to $4,000 (or $x = 4$) are 140 and 145. The average of 140 and 145 is 142.5.

The average monthly sales would be about $142,500.

SAMPLE B

The *y*-intercept is about 118 and the line seems to go through (2, 130).

slope: $\frac{130 - 118}{2 - 0} = \frac{12}{2} = 6$

For each increase of 1 in *x*, the value of *y* increases by 6.

Add 6 to 118 four times for an increase of 4 in *x*.

$118 + 6 + 6 + 6 + 6 = 142$

Average monthly sales would be about $142,000.

DISCUSS IT

Ask: How do you know your answer is reasonable?

Share: The problem is asking . . .

735

DISCUSS IT

SMP 2, 3, 6

Support Partner Discussion

After students work on Try It, have them explain their work and then respond to Discuss It with a partner. Listen for understanding that:

- the prediction is reasonable if the predicted sales amount is more than the amount when $3,000 is spent but less than when $5,000 is spent.
- the prediction is reasonable if, when the data point is plotted on the scatter plot, it follows the trend of the rest of the data.

Error Alert If students share an answer in the hundreds of dollars, such as $140, then ask them to read the label on the *y*-axis. Point out that the sales are in thousands of dollars, and ask what a scale value of 140 means. If students find an equation for a line of fit and substitute 4,000 for *x* instead of 4, then have them read the label on the *x*-axis. Point out that the *x* in their equation is the number of *thousands* of dollars in advertising, so $4,000 is represented by the *x*-value 4.

Select and Sequence Student Strategies

Select 2–3 samples that represent the range of student thinking in your classroom. Here is one possible order for class discussion:

- average the two y-values for data points with x-values closest to \$4,000
- draw a vertical line up from 4 to the line of fit and, from there, a horizontal line to the y-axis
- find the slope and increase the y-intercept value by that amount four times
- find the equation for the line of fit and substitute $x = 4$

Facilitate Whole Class Discussion

Call on students to share selected strategies. Prompt students to check their understanding by trying to paraphrase the speaker's ideas. They can ask questions about ideas that are unclear.

Guide students to **Compare and Connect** the representations. If discussion lags, ask students to turn and talk about how to use a line of fit to make predictions before continuing the discussion.

ASK *How did the way [student name] made the prediction compare to the way [student name] made the prediction?*

LISTEN FOR Students used the trend in the data to find a reasonable value when $x = 4$. Students may have used data points near the line, the line itself, or an equation to make their predictions.

Picture It & Model It

If students presented these models, have students connect these models to those presented in class.

If no student presented at least one of these models, have students first analyze key features of the models, and then connect them to the models presented in class.

ASK *How are the models the same? How are they different?*

LISTEN FOR Both models use the line of fit to make the prediction. Picture It uses the graph, while Model It uses an equation.

For the solution that uses the graph, prompt students to consider how the line of fit and data points are related.

- *Is there a data point where $x = 4$?*
- *Why can the line of fit be used to make a prediction in this case?*

For the model that uses the equation, prompt students to consider what value to substitute for x.

- *What does each x-value represent?*
- *Why is 4 substituted for x, instead of 4,000?*

➤ **Explore different ways to analyze a linear model to make predictions.**

The scatter plot shows the average amount several companies spend on online advertising and their average monthly sales. A good line of fit is drawn through the data. Suppose a company spends an average of \$4,000 on advertising. What would you predict their average monthly sales to be?

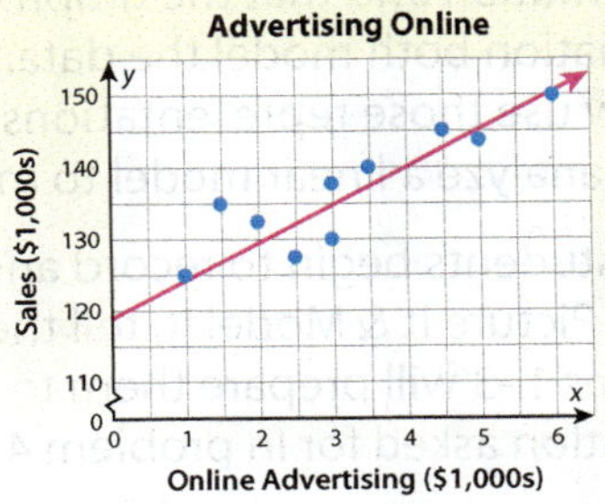

Picture It

You can analyze the line of fit at $x = 4$.

Draw a vertical line from $x = 4$ to the line of fit. Then draw a horizontal line from the intersection of the vertical line and the line of fit to the y-axis.

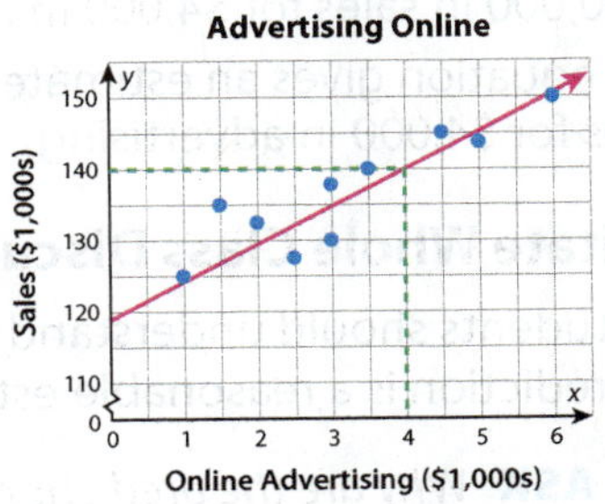

Model It

You can write an equation of the line of fit and substitute $x = 4$.

The y-intercept is about 118.

The line appears to go through (0, 118) and (3, 135).

slope: $\frac{135 - 118}{3 - 0} = \frac{17}{3} \approx 5.7$

An equation of the line of fit is $y = 5.7x + 118$.

$y = 5.7(4) + 118$

DIFFERENTIATION | EXTEND SMP 6

Deepen Understanding
Understanding Precision of a Line of Fit

Prompt students to think about how the data provide actual results in certain instances, but the line of fit only gives predictions.

ASK *Based on the line of fit, what is the predicted amount of sales when \$6,000 is spent for online advertising? What is the actual sales value for \$6,000 in online advertising?*

LISTEN FOR Each sales value is about \$150,000.

ASK *Based on the line of fit, what is the predicted amount of sales when \$2,000 is spent for online advertising? What is the actual sales value for \$2,000 in online advertising?*

LISTEN FOR Predicted sales are about \$129,000. Actual sales are about \$132,000.

ASK *Why might a value predicted by a line of fit and an actual value differ?*

LISTEN FOR A line of fit comes close to most of the data values, but, unless the points are exactly on the line, the line predictions will not exactly match.

Generalize Ask students why a line of fit is useful. Students should see that a line of fit models the general association of the data. Point out that Picture It demonstrates that a line of fit is useful for making predictions about values that are not in the data set.

Develop Analyzing a Linear Model to Make Predictions

CONNECT IT

SMP 2, 4, 5, 6

Remind students that the data are the same in each representation and that the graph of the line and the equation both model the data. Explain that they will now use those representations to reason about how to analyze a linear model to make predictions.

Before students begin to record and expand on their work in Picture It & Model It, tell them that problems 1–3 will prepare them to provide the explanation asked for in problem 4.

Monitor and Confirm Understanding 1 – 2

- $x = 4$ means spending $4,000 on advertising.
- The graph of the line of fit shows an estimate of $140,000 in sales for $4,000 in advertising.
- The equation gives an estimate of $140,800 in sales for $4,000 in advertising.

Facilitate Whole Class Discussion

3 Students should understand that either prediction is a reasonable estimate.

ASK *Why are the predictions different?*

LISTEN FOR Both are just estimates. One is found by looking at the graph. The other is found by using an equation that was found using estimated values from the graph.

4 Look for the idea that the equation is a model of the overall pattern of data. It does not represent exact data values but can be used to make reasonable predictions.

ASK *Why do you think the Try It asked you to* predict *the sales for $4,000 in advertising rather than to find the sales?*

LISTEN FOR There is no way to know the exact value from the graph. The data are not precisely linear, and the line of fit is just a model for the overall association between the variables. It can only be used to make predictions.

5 Students should realize that the line of fit can extend beyond the boundaries of the graph.

6 **Reflect** Have all students focus on the strategies used to solve the Try It. If time allows, have students discuss their ideas with a partner.

CONNECT IT

➤ **Use the problem from the previous page to help you understand how to analyze a linear model to make predictions.**

1 Look at **Picture It**. Why analyze the line of fit at $x = 4$? What value of sales is predicted for $4,000 in advertising?
$x = 4$ represents spending $4,000 in advertising. The line of fit predicts about $140,000 in sales for $4,000 in advertising.

2 Look at **Model It**. What value of sales is predicted for $4,000 in advertising?
The equation predicts $140,800 in sales for $4,000 in advertising.

3 Are the predictions from **Picture It** and **Model It** far apart? Is one prediction better than the other?
No, they are close in value. Possible answer: No, both predictions are based on the line of fit that reasonably models the data.

4 Does the **Model It** prediction mean that spending an average of $4,000 on online advertising will definitely result in average monthly sales of $140,800? Explain.
No; Possible explanation: The line of fit estimates the data. Actual data points are not always on the line of fit.

5 Suppose an average of more than $6,000 is spent on online advertising. Can the equation of the line of fit still be used to predict average monthly sales? Explain.
Yes; Possible explanation: The line of fit continues on past what is shown in the scatter plot. You can predict unknown or future outcomes by substituting values of one variable into the equation of the line of fit to predict the value of the other variable.

6 **Reflect** Think about all the models and strategies you have discussed today. Describe how one of them helped you better understand how to analyze a linear model to make predictions.
Responses will vary. Check student responses.

737

DIFFERENTIATION | RETEACH or REINFORCE

Visual Model

Make predictions for values outside the scatter plot.

If students are unsure how a line of fit can be used to predict future values, then use this activity to have students make predictions.

Materials For display: Try It scatter plot with line of fit

- Ask: *Based on the line of fit, what value of sales is predicted if $5,500 is spent on online advertising?* [about $148,000] *How could you use the line of fit to predict sales if $7,500 is spent on online advertising?* [Extend the line of fit or use an equation of the line and find the corresponding y-value for an x-value of $7,500.]
- Ask: *Based on the equation of the line of fit, what value of sales is predicted if $7,500 is spent on online advertising?* [$160,750]
- Invite a student to extend the x-axis to 10 and y-axis to 200, and then extend the line of fit to where their new graph stops. Ask: *Is your predicted value reasonable? Explain.* [Yes; the line falls between the y-values $160,000 and $165,000 when x is $7,500.]
- Point out how it is worth finding an equation that can be used to predict *any* future value, whereas a graph may be limited by space, etc.

Apply It

For all problems, encourage students to use a model to support their thinking.

7 See ***Connect to Culture*** to support student engagement.

B, D, and E are correct. Students may verify B and D by substituting the distance in the equation and solving for the time. They may verify E by inspection because the line of fit goes up and to the right.

A is incorrect. Using the equation, a 3.25-mile hike will take about 102.4 minutes.

C is incorrect. Both the line and the equation predict a hike slightly shorter than 4 miles.

8 Students should understand that the line of fit is an estimate and will not align exactly with every data point. However, it still generally represents the data.

LESSON 30 | SESSION 3

Apply It

➤ **Use what you learned to solve these problems.**

7 A hiking club goes on 10 different hikes. The scatter plot shows the data for the distance of each hike and the time it takes to complete it. The equation of the line of fit is $y = 30.9x + 2$. Which statements are true about the data? Select all that apply.

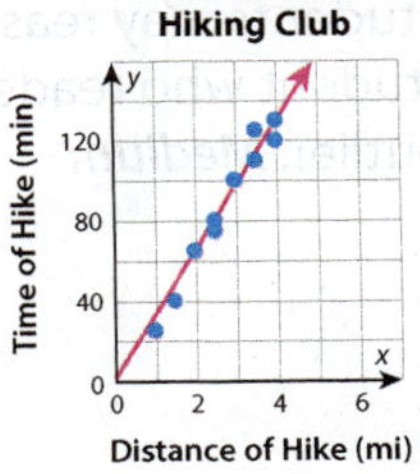

A The line of fit predicts that a 3.25-mile hike will take about 30.9 minutes to complete.

(B) The line of fit predicts that a 2.75-mile hike will take about 87 minutes to complete.

C If it takes 120 minutes to complete the hike, the line of fit predicts the distance of the hike as exactly 4 miles.

(D) The line of fit predicts that a hike that takes 45 minutes to complete is about 1.4 miles long.

(E) In general, the farther the hike, the longer it takes to complete.

8 The hiking club in problem 7 completes a 4-mile hike in 140 min. The equation of the line of fit predicts that the hike will take 125.6 min. Why are the two values different? Is the line of fit a good representation of the data? Explain.

The line of fit is an estimation of the data and may not match up with exact data points. The line of fit can still be a good representation even if it doesn't exactly match the data points.

9 The scatter plot shows employees' hourly pay and years of employment at a water park. A good line of fit represented by $y = 0.75x + 7$ is drawn through the data. Aiden predicts that an employee who makes \$8.50 an hour has been working at the water park for 2 years. Is Aiden's prediction correct? Show your work.

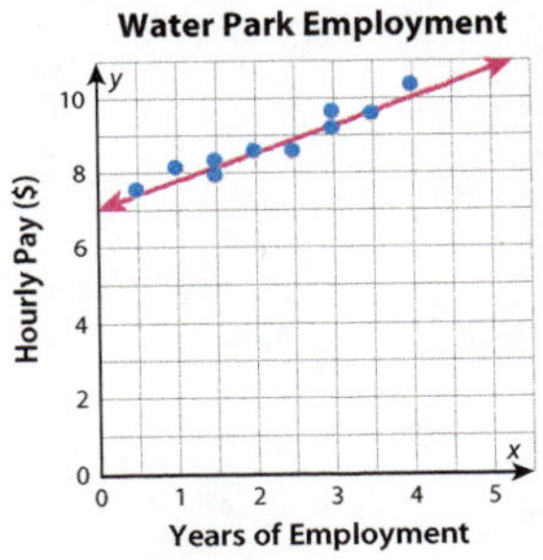

Possible work:

$8.50 = 0.75x + 7$

$1.50 = 0.75x$

$2 = x$

SOLUTION Yes, Aiden's prediction is correct.

738

CLOSE EXIT TICKET

9 Students' solutions should show an understanding that:

- Aiden's prediction can be confirmed using the equation of the line of fit: either substitute 2 for x and solve for y, or substitute 8.50 for y and solve for x.
- when $x = 2$, the value of y is 8.5.

Error Alert If students answer no, then have them check which variable is represented by the x-axis and which is represented by the y-axis because they may have reversed the values when substituting.

Practice Analyzing a Linear Model to Make Predictions

Problem Notes

Assign **Practice Analyzing a Linear Model to Make Predictions** as extra practice in class or as homework.

1 Students may reason that the data point for the student who reads 8.6 hours a week is an outlier. ***Medium***

 Name:

Practice Analyzing a Linear Model to Make Predictions

➤ **Study the Example showing how to use a linear model to make predictions. Then solve problems 1–3.**

Example

Ten students record the time they spend reading each week. At the end of the year, they take a spelling test. The scatter plot shows the average weekly hours of reading time for each student and his or her score on the test. The equation of the line of fit is $y = 3.5x + 53$. Use the equation to predict the test score for a student who reads an average of 2 hours per week.

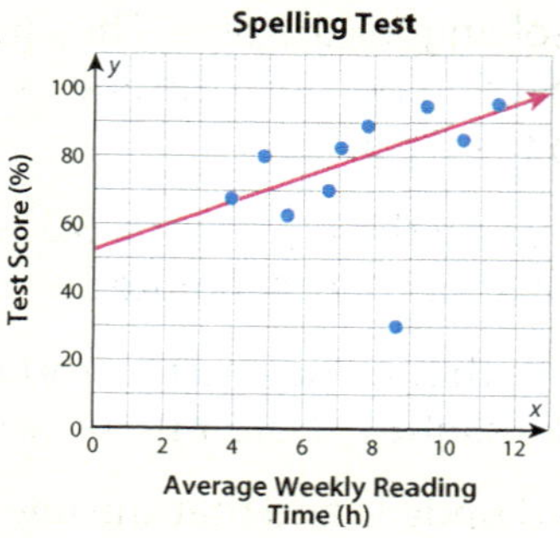

Substitute 2 for x in the equation of the line of fit.

$y = 3.5(2) + 53$

$y = 7 + 53$

$y = 60$

A student who reads 2 hours per week can expect a test score of about 60%.

1 One student in the Example reads an average of 8.6 hours a week outside of class and gets a 30% on the spelling test. The prediction from the line of fit is that the student would get an 83.1%. How can the prediction be so far away from its value?

Possible answer: The student's test score is an outlier, so it is not surprising that the prediction is inaccurate.

Fluency & Skills Practice

Analyzing a Linear Model to Make Predictions

In this activity, for each problem, students calculate the equation of a given line of fit and then use the equation to make predictions.

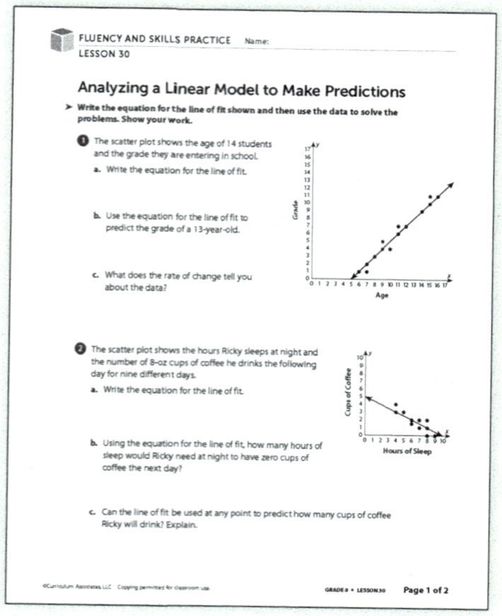
FLUENCY AND SKILLS PRACTICE Name:
LESSON 30

Analyzing a Linear Model to Make Predictions

➤ **Write the equation for the line of fit shown and then use the data to solve the problems. Show your work.**

1 The scatter plot shows the age of 14 students and the grade they are entering in school.

a. Write the equation for the line of fit.

b. Use the equation for the line of fit to predict the grade of a 13-year-old.

c. What does the rate of change tell you about the data?

2 The scatter plot shows the hours Ricky sleeps at night and the number of 8-oz cups of coffee he drinks the following day for nine different days.

a. Write the equation for the line of fit.

b. Using the equation for the line of fit, how many hours of sleep would Ricky need at night to have zero cups of coffee the next day?

c. Can the line of fit be used at any point to predict how many cups of coffee Ricky will drink? Explain.

©Curriculum Associates, LLC Copying permitted for classroom use. GRADE 8 • LESSON 30 Page 1 of 2

Additional Practice

2 **a.** Students may solve the problem by substituting 80 for x in the equation of the line of fit and solving for y. ***Medium***

b. Students may substitute $y = 70$ into the equation of the line of fit and solve for x. Note that this problem cannot be solved by using the graph because the point on the line where $y = 70$ is beyond the part of the graph that is shown. ***Medium***

3 **a.** Students may use a different pair of points to calculate the slope. For example, the line passes through (0, 5) and (10, 15). Using these points also gives a slope of 1. ***Medium***

b. Students may substitute 0 for x to get a wait time of 5 minutes, and then use reasoning skills to determine whether this result is reasonable for the situation. ***Challenge***

LESSON 30 | SESSION 3

2 A math teacher asks 20 of her middle school students how much time they spend on a computer after school. This scatter plot shows the amount of time in minutes each student spends on a computer and his or her math grade. The equation of the line of fit is $y = -0.13x + 92$.

Computer Use and Math Grades

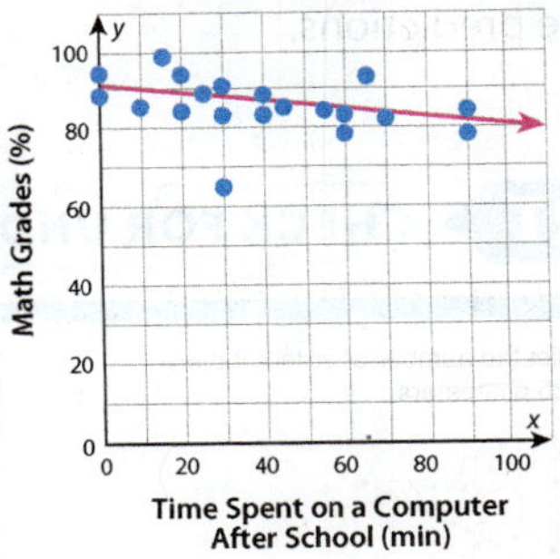

a. A student spends 80 min on a computer after school. What do you predict the student's math grade to be?

81.6%

b. A student's math grade is 70%. What do you predict for the number of minutes the student spends on a computer after school? Show your work. Possible answer:

$(70) = -0.13x + 92$

$-22 = -0.13x$

$169 \approx x$

SOLUTION The student spent about 169 minutes on a computer.

3 This scatter plot shows the wait time for a roller coaster at an amusement park on a weekday and the outside temperature.

Temperature and Roller Coaster Wait Times

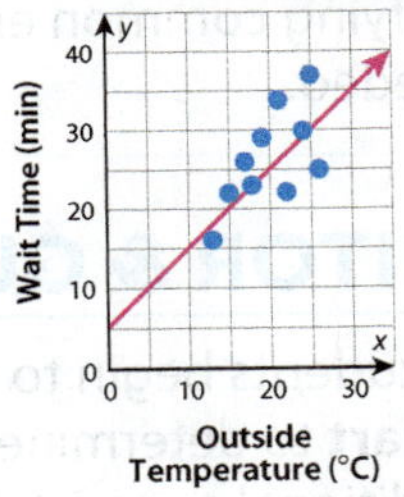

a. Write an equation of the line of fit. Show your work.

Possible work:

The line appears to cross the y-axis at (0, 5), so the y-intercept is 5. The line appears to go through the points (25, 30) and (30, 35).

Slope: $\frac{35 - 30}{30 - 25} = \frac{5}{5} = 1$

SOLUTION Possible equation: $y = x + 5$

b. Suppose the outside temperature is 0°C. Would you use the equation of the line of fit to predict the waiting time of a roller coaster? Explain.

Possible answer: No. The value of 0°C is freezing and amusement parks would most likely not be open. Also, the value of 0 is far away from all the other x-values, so the equation might not be valid.

740

DIFFERENTIATION | ENGLISH LANGUAGE LEARNERS

Use with **Session 4** **Apply It**

ACADEMIC VOCABULARY

Predictions are guesses or estimates based on data and information.

To *convince* is to cause someone to believe or do something.

If something is *useful*, it can help.

Levels 1–3: Speaking/Writing

Help students understand Apply It problem 7 and create convincing arguments. Display and discuss the Academic Vocabulary. Then read Fernando's statement. Help students use the words *estimates* and *help* to tell what Fernando believes:

- *Fernando says that* ____ *do not* ____.

Ask: *What can you tell Fernando to change his mind?* Have partners turn and discuss. Then help them write their responses using this sentence starter:

- *Predictions from good lines of fit are helpful because* ____.

Levels 2–4: Speaking/Writing

Help students understand Apply It problem 7 and create convincing arguments. Display and discuss the Academic Vocabulary. Then read Fernando's statement. Have students turn to partners to discuss how they can convince Fernando to change his mind. Then use **Act It Out** to have students role play: one student represents Fernando and the other tries to convince "him" to change his mind. Students switch roles and repeat. Then guide students to write and review their arguments with a partner.

Levels 3–5: Speaking/Writing

Help students understand Apply It problem 7 and create convincing arguments. Display and discuss the Academic Vocabulary. Then have students read and explain Fernando's statement. Use **Act It Out** to have students role play: one student represents Fernando and the other tries to convince "him" to change his mind. Call on volunteers to comment on the arguments:

- *I think your argument is/is not convincing because* ____.

Then have students write their arguments using reasons to convince Fernando.

Refine Writing and Analyzing an Equation for Fitting a Linear Model to Data

Purpose

- **Refine** strategies for writing and interpreting an equation for a linear model.
- **Refine** understanding of analyzing a linear model to make predictions.

START CHECK FOR UNDERSTANDING

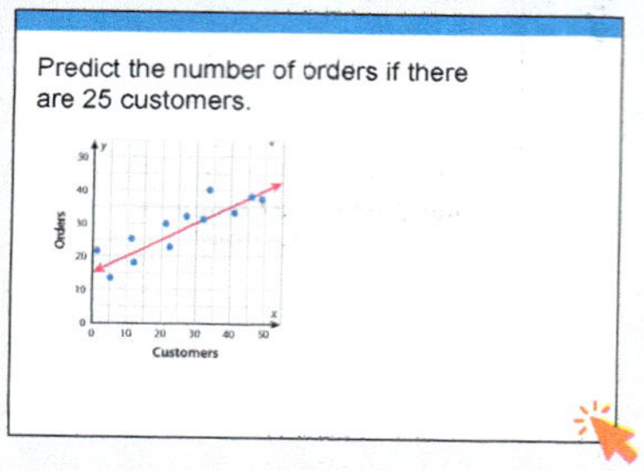

Solution

27 (or 28)

WHY? Confirm students' understanding of using a line of fit to make a prediction, identifying common errors to address as needed.

MONITOR & GUIDE

Before students begin to work, use their responses to the **Start** to determine those who will benefit from additional support. Use the **Error Analysis** table below to guide remediation.

Have all students complete the Example and problems 1–3, using Consider This and Pair/Share as appropriate. Observe and monitor their reasoning and guide or redirect students as needed.

LESSON 30 | SESSION 4 ■ ■ ■ ■

Refine Writing and Analyzing an Equation for Fitting a Linear Model to Data

➤ **Complete the Example below. Then solve problems 1–8.**

Example

The scatter plot shows the lengths and weights of 10 adult corn snakes. A good line of fit passes through (1.4, 28) and (2.4, 36). Predict the likely weight of an adult corn snake that is 38 in. long.

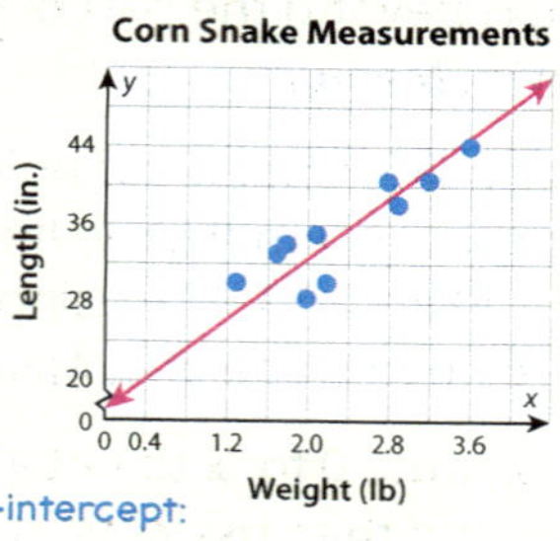

Look at how you could show your work using the slope and y-intercept.

Slope:

$m = \frac{36-28}{2.4-1.4} = \frac{8}{1} = 8$

y-intercept:

$36 = 8(2.4) + b$

$36 = 19.2 + b$

$b = 16.8$

An equation of the line of fit is $y = 8x + 16.8$. Substitute 38 for y and solve for x.

$38 = 8x + 16.8$

$x = 2.65$

SOLUTION The snake would likely weigh about 2.65 lb.

CONSIDER THIS . . . Finding the slope of the line of fit can help you write its equation.

PAIR/SHARE How else can you use the scatter plot to make a prediction for the weight of a snake that is 38 in. long?

Apply It

1. Use the information in the Example to predict the length of a corn snake that weighs 1.6 lb. Show your work.

Possible work:

$y = 8x + 16.8$

$y = 8(1.6) + 16.8$

$y = 12.8 + 16.8$

$y = 29.6$

SOLUTION The snake would be about 29.6 in. long.

CONSIDER THIS . . . The equation of a line of fit can be used to make predictions about either variable.

PAIR/SHARE Will the predicted values from a line of fit always match real data? Why or why not?

741

START ERROR ANALYSIS

If the error is . . .	Students may . . .	To support understanding . . .
20	have found the y-value of 25 and looked at the corresponding x-value to make a prediction.	Prompt students to look at the labels on the axes and explain what the values along the x-axis represent and what the values along the y-axis represent. Have students make a new prediction based on that understanding.
32	have looked at the data point that has an x-value of 26 and used that to make the prediction.	Explain that the line of fit should be used to make predictions. Students can estimate the y-value at $x = 25$. They can also estimate the coordinates of two ordered pairs on the line of fit to write an equation and then substitute $x = 25$.
65	have found the slope as $\frac{run}{rise}$ and therefore used an incorrect equation for the line of fit to make a prediction.	Prompt students to recall that slope is $\frac{rise}{run}$. Elicit from students that *rise* is the change in y-values and *run* is the change in x-values. Have students write a new equation for the line of fit and make a prediction.

Example

See ***Connect to Culture*** to support student engagement. Guide students in understanding the Example. Ask:

- *What does the slope of the line of fit represent?*
- *What does the y-intercept represent?*
- *Why is it not possible to estimate the y-intercept by looking at the graph?*
- *Does the line of fit give the exact weight of an adult corn snake that is 38 inches long? Explain how you know.*

Help all students focus on the Example and responses to the questions by reinforcing that good listeners ask questions to clarify ideas or ask for more information during math discussions.

Look for understanding that in order to predict the weight of an adult corn snake that is 38 inches long, students must substitute 38 for y in the equation for the line of fit and solve for x.

Apply It

1 Students may also predict the length using the graph of the line of fit. *DOK 1*

2 The slopes and y-intercepts that students find may vary slightly, depending on the two points they choose. *DOK 2*

3 **D is correct.** Students may solve the problem by using the axis labels to interpret the slope, or $\frac{\text{rise}}{\text{run}}$.

A is not correct. This answer gives the value of the y-intercept, not the slope.

B is not correct. This answer is an incorrect interpretation of slope as $\frac{\text{run}}{\text{rise}}$, which in this case is the change in temperature for each dollar change in sales.

C is not correct. This answer gives the value of the y-intercept, not the slope.

DOK 3

LESSON 30 | SESSION 4

2 A food truck vendor records the sales of cups of hot cocoa over a 10-day period. She also records each day's high temperature. The scatter plot shows the data and a good line of fit. Write an equation of the line of fit. Show your work.

Possible work:

The line of fit appears to go through the points (28, 850) and (40, 650).

$m = \frac{850-650}{28-40} = \frac{200}{-12} \approx -16.7$

$850 = -16.7(28) + b$

$1{,}317.6 = b$

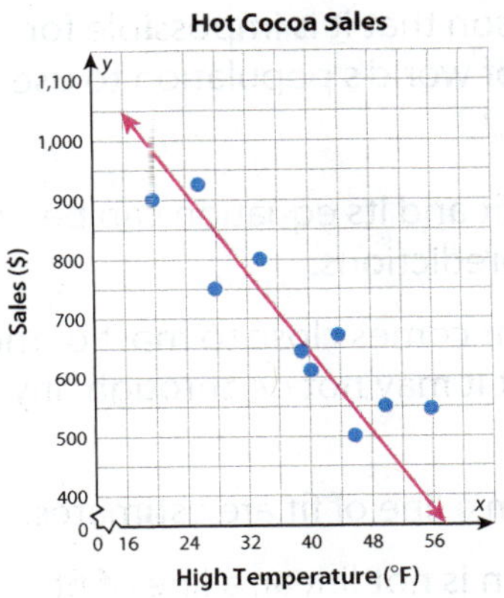

CONSIDER THIS . . . Some points on the line of fit are easier to estimate than others.

PAIR/SHARE What other good line of fit could be drawn through the data?

SOLUTION Possible equation: $y = -16.7x + 1{,}317.6$

3 The equation $y = -14.6x + 1{,}259.2$ is another possible equation of the line of fit in problem 2. What is the slope of the equation and what does it mean?

A The slope is 1,259.2. A temperature rise of 1°F means sales will increase by $1,259.2.

B The slope is −14.6. A temperature decrease of 14.6°F means sales will decrease by $1.00.

C The slope is 1,259.2. A sales increase of $1,259.2 means the temperature will decrease by 14.6°F.

D The slope is −14.6. A temperature increase of 1°F means sales will decrease by $14.60.

Issay chose B as the correct answer. How might he have gotten that answer?

Possible answer: Issay interpreted slope as the quotient of change in temperature to sales instead of change in sales to temperature.

CONSIDER THIS . . . The slope of a line of fit estimates a rate of change between the variables.

PAIR/SHARE Is the y-intercept meaningful for these data? Why or why not?

742

GROUP & DIFFERENTIATE

Identify groupings for differentiation based on the **Start** and problems 1–3. A recommended sequence of activities for each group is suggested below. Use the resources on the next page to differentiate and close the lesson.

Approaching Proficiency

- **RETEACH** Hands-On Activity
- **REINFORCE** Problems 5, 6

Meeting Proficiency

- **REINFORCE** Problems 4–7

Extending Beyond Proficiency

- **REINFORCE** Problems 4–7
- **EXTEND** Challenge

Have all students complete the **Close: Exit Ticket**.

Resources for Differentiation are found on the next page.

Refine Writing and Analyzing an Equation for Fitting a Linear Model to Data

Apply It

4 Students may reason that it is impossible for more than 100% of world's population to use the internet. *DOK 3*

5 **a.** A good line of fit and its equation can be used to make predictions.

b. A good line of fit comes close to most of the data points, but it may not go through any data points.

c. Predictions from a line of fit are estimates.

d. If the association is not linear, a line of fit cannot be drawn. A line cannot be used to model a nonlinear situation.

e. The same strategies for finding slope and *y*-intercept work for any line, including a line of fit.

DOK 1

6 **a.** Students may solve the problem by substituting $2025 - 2008 = 17$ for *x* in the equation of the line of fit and solving for *y*. *DOK 2*

b. Students may solve the problem by using the axis labels to interpret the slope, or $\frac{\text{rise}}{\text{run}}$. *DOK 2*

---

4 The scatter plot shows the percentage of the world's population that used the internet each year between 2008 and 2016. A good line of fit is drawn through the data. Estimate the slope of the line of fit. Can the rate of change indicated by the slope continue forever? Explain.

$m \approx 3$; No; Possible explanation: The rate of change cannot increase forever because eventually the internet usage will reach 100%.

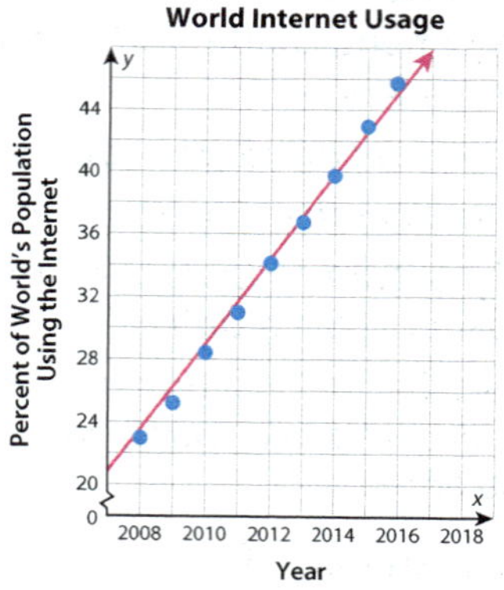

5 Tell whether each statement is *True* or *False*.

	True	False
a. A good line of fit can be used to make predictions.	●	○
b. A good line of fit always goes through at least two data points.	○	●
c. The predictions from a good line of fit are exact.	○	●
d. If there is an association between two variables, a good line of fit can always be drawn.	○	●
e. The slope and the *y*-intercept of a line of fit can be found using the same strategies as other graphed lines.	●	○

6 The scatter plot shows the weight in pounds of the world's heaviest giant pumpkin each year since 2008. The equation of the line of fit is $y = 90x + 1{,}629$.

a. Based on the equation, the heaviest pumpkin in 2025 will weigh 3,159 pounds.

b. What does the slope of the line of fit tell you about the giant pumpkins in the problem?

The weight of the world's heaviest giant pumpkins is increasing by 90 lb each year.

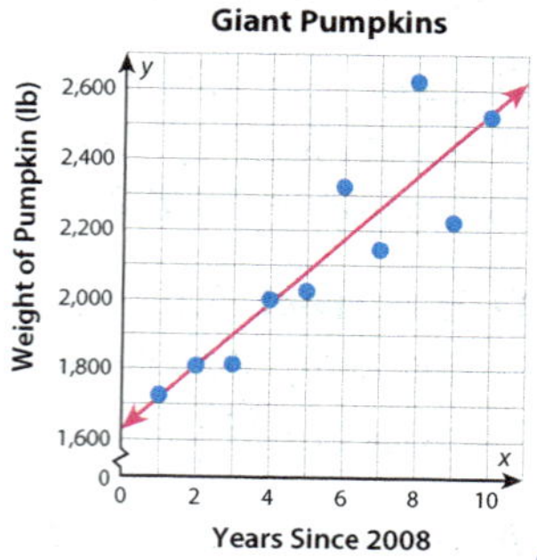

743

DIFFERENTIATION

RETEACH

Hands-On Activity

Use a line of fit to make a prediction.

Students approaching proficiency with using a line of fit to make a prediction will benefit from finding a line of fit and using its graph and equation to make predictions.

Materials For each pair: straightedge, chenille stem, Activity Sheet *Coordinate Plane: First Quadrant*

- Instruct students to label the *x*-axis *Time (days)* and the *y*-axis *Height of Plant (cm)*.
- Have students plot the points (1, 0), (2, 1), (3, 1), (4, 3), (5, 4), (6, 4), (7, 5), and (8, 6).
- Have students place their chenille stem on the coordinate plane to model a good line of fit. Then have them use the placement of the chenille stem and a straightedge to draw a line of fit. Ask: *What is the equation of your line of fit? Explain how you found it.* [Possible answer: $y = 0.7x$; I used two points from my line of fit, (0, 0) and (5, 3.5), to find the slope. I analyzed the line of fit to identify that the *y*-intercept is 0.]
- Ask: *What is the predicted height of the plant after 15 days? Explain how to use the equation of your line of fit to make the prediction.* [Possible answer: 10.5 cm; Substitute 15 for *x* into the equation of the line of fit.]
- Ask: *What is the predicted height of the plant after 15 days? Explain how to use the line of fit to make the prediction.* Remind students that they may extend the line if needed. [Possible answer: 10.5 cm; I can find the *y*-coordinate of the point on the line with *x*-coordinate 15.]

7 A good line of fit represents the overall pattern in the data. So, a line of fit can still be a good representation even if it does not give exact data values. *DOK 2*

CLOSE EXIT TICKET

8 **Math Journal** Look for understanding that two points on the line can be used to estimate the slope and y-intercept. Then, after the equation is written, it can be used to make the prediction. Students should also understand that the x-values are years since 2010, so the year 2020 corresponds to an x-value of 10.

Error Alert If students write an equation for the line of fit that has a slope of $-\frac{4}{15}$, then remind them that slope is $\frac{\text{rise}}{\text{run}}$, not $\frac{\text{run}}{\text{rise}}$.

End of Lesson Checklist

INTERACTIVE GLOSSARY Support students by suggesting they tell a partner what they know about the word *interpret*. Have partners discuss the meaning in a nonmathematical context first. For example, what does it mean to interpret a book or a speech that is in another language? Then have them relate this to the idea of interpreting the slope and y-intercept of a linear model.

SELF CHECK Have students review and check off any new skills on the Unit 7 Opener.

LESSON 30 | SESSION 4

7 Fernando says that the predictions from good lines of fit are not useful because they are guesses. What could you say to Fernando to convince him that you can make useful predictions from good lines of fit?

Possible answer: The predictions that come from good lines of fit may not be exact, but they are educated guesses that provide close estimates. These estimates can be used to make predictions and can therefore help to make long-term plans. Good lines of fit can also be used to determine whether new data follow the existing data trend or are outliers.

8 **Math Journal** A middle school science teacher surveys his students each year. He asks how many families have a landline telephone. This scatter plot shows the percent of families with a landline in each year since 2010. A good line of fit is drawn through the data. Write an equation of the line. Then predict the percent of families that will have a landline in 2020.

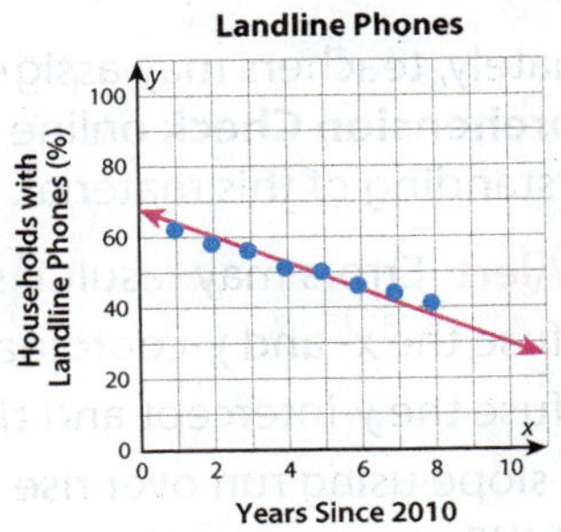

Possible work: The line of fit appears to pass through (2, 60) and (6, 45).

$m = \frac{60 - 45}{2 - 6} = \frac{15}{-4} = -3.75$

$y = -3.75x + b$

$45 = -3.75(6) + b$

$67.5 = b$

$y = -3.75x + 67.5$

$y = -3.75(10) + 67.5$

$y = 30$

About 30% of families will have landlines in 2020.

End of Lesson Checklist

- [ ] **INTERACTIVE GLOSSARY** Write a new entry for *interpret*. Tell what you do when you *interpret* the meaning of the slope and y-intercept of a linear model.
- [ ] **SELF CHECK** Go back to the Unit 7 Opener and see what you can check off.

744

REINFORCE

Problems 4–7

Solve problems using a line of fit.

Students meeting proficiency will benefit from additional work with using a line of fit to make predictions by solving problems in a variety of formats.

- Have students work on their own or with a partner to solve the problems.
- Encourage students to show their work.

EXTEND

Challenge

Make predictions.

Students extending beyond proficiency will benefit from using a line of fit to make a prediction.

- Have students work with a partner to solve this problem: *The water level of a river is changing during a rainstorm. Make a scatter plot and draw a line of fit. Predict when the water level will surpass flood stage of 10 feet.*
- Some students may incorrectly base their response on the number of hours rather than the water level in feet.

Hours	Feet
0	6.5
1	6.7
2	7.2
3	6.8
4	7.5
5	7.9
6	8.3
7	8.8
8	9.1
9	8.6
10	9.3

PERSONALIZE

i-Ready

Provide students with opportunities to work on their personalized instruction path with *i-Ready* Online Instruction to:

- fill prerequisite gaps.
- build up grade-level skills.

Lesson Quiz

TESTED SKILLS

Assesses 8.SP.A.3

Problems on this assessment require students to write an equation of a good line of fit for data in a scatter plot. Students must be able to make reasonable predictions about the data in a scatter plot and interpret what the slope and *y*-intercept mean in context. Students will also need to be familiar with graphing in the coordinate plane, writing equations, finding slope, and interpreting data given in a scatter plot.

Alternately, teachers may assign the **Digital Comprehension Check** online to assess student understanding of this material.

Error Alert Errors may result if students:

- confuse the *x*- and *y*-coordinates of a graph.
- confuse the *y*-intercept and the slope of a line.
- find slope using run over rise instead of rise over run.
- miscalculate the equation of a line of fit.

Problem Notes

1 **D is correct.** Students could solve this problem by recognizing that the *y*-intercept is the *y*-coordinate where the line of fit crosses the *y*-axis, or the value of *y* when *x* is 0. The point (0, 122) indicates that at a temperature of 0°F, the store can expect to sell 122 pairs of gloves.

A is not correct. This answer represents the slope of the line instead of the *y*-intercept.

B is not correct. This answer represents the *y*-intercept, but the values of 0 and 122 are reversed when describing the meaning of the *y*-intercept.

C is not correct. This answer represents the slope of the line instead of the *y*-intercept.

(1 point)

DOK 1 | 8.SP.A.3

LESSON 30 • QUIZ Name:

➤ **Solve the problems.**

1 A sporting goods store records the sales of gloves over a 10-day period. They also record each day's low temperature. The scatter plot shows the data and a good line of fit. The equation for the line of fit shown is $y = -1.2x + 122$. What is the *y*-intercept of the equation, and what does it mean? *(1 point)*

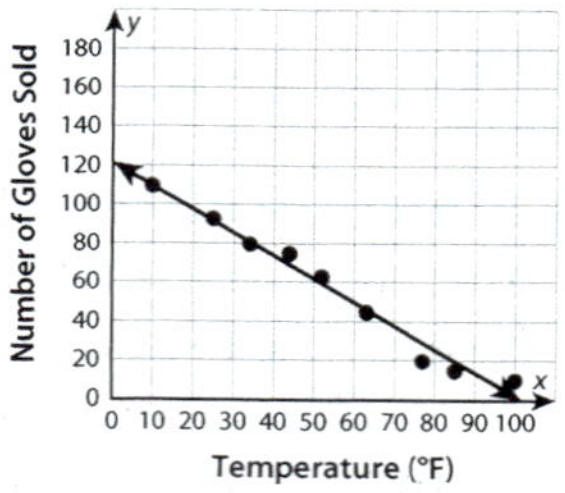

A The *y*-intercept is −1.2. The store will sell 1 fewer pair of gloves for every decrease of −1.2°F.

B The *y*-intercept is 122. The store will sell 0 pairs of gloves when the temperature is 122°F.

C The *y*-intercept is −1.2. The store will sell 1.2 fewer pairs of gloves for every decrease of 1°F.

(D) The *y*-intercept is 122. The store will sell 122 pairs of gloves when the temperature is 0°F.

2 A ski park features skiing in winter and hiking in summer. They record attendance at the park and temperature, in degrees Fahrenheit. The scatter plot shows the data and a good line of fit. Decide if each statement about a line of fit is true.

Choose *True* or *False* for each statement. *(2 points)*

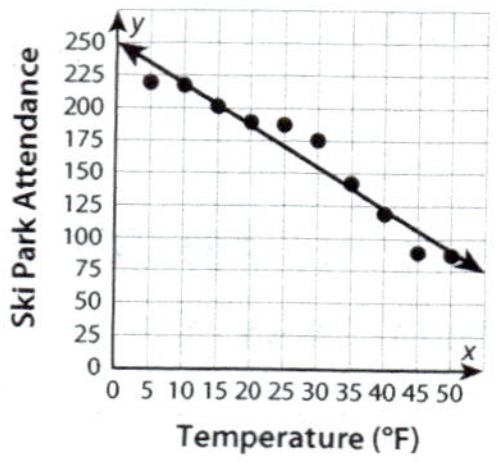

	True	False
a. The line of fit could be used to predict the attendance when the temperature is 60°F.	●	○
b. The line of fit shows a positive association.	○	●
c. If the temperature is greater than 70°F, the estimated ski park attendance will be fewer than 75 people.	●	○
d. A possible equation for the line of fit is $y = -3.1x + 250$.	●	○

Choice Matrix Scoring Rubric

Points	Expectations
2	All answers are correct
1	1 incorrect answer
0	2 or more incorrect answers

Short Response Scoring Rubric

Points	Expectations
2	Response has the correct solution(s) and includes well-organized, clear, and concise work demonstrating thorough understanding of mathematical concepts and/or procedures.
1	Response contains mostly correct solution(s) and shows partial understanding of mathematical concepts and/or procedures.
0	Response shows no attempt at finding a solution and no effort to demonstrate an understanding of mathematical concepts and/or procedures.

2 **a.** An equation for the line of fit can be written using two points on the line or a point on the line and the y-intercept. Let x represent the temperature and y represent the ski park attendance. Substitute 60 for the temperature, x, to find the predicted ski park attendance, y.

b. As the temperature increases, the ski park attendance decreases. So, the line of fit shows a negative association.

c. It can be estimated from the line of fit that when the x-values are greater than 70, the y-values will be less than 75.

d. A point on the line and the y-intercept can be used to write an equation for the line of fit. The line has a y-intercept of 250. The line of fit goes through the point (8, 225). So, using $225 = m(8) + 250$, m is approximately -3.125.

(2 points)

DOK 2 | 8.SP.A.3

3 Students could solve this problem by recognizing that a line of fit gives an estimation.

(2 points)

DOK 2 | 8.SP.A.3

4 (2 points)

DOK 1 | 8.SP.A.3

5 Students could solve this problem by selecting any two points on the line to write the equation, resulting in variances in prediction. Accept minor variations with supporting work.

(2 points)

DOK 2 | 8.SP.A.3

LESSON 30 • QUIZ | Name:

3 Gia uses a good line of fit to predict how much her coin collection will be worth in 20 years. Gia finds a good line of fit for her data. She says that the good line of fit gives exact values for predictions. Is Gia correct? Explain your reasoning. *(2 points)*

SOLUTION Gia is incorrect; Possible explanation: A prediction that comes from a good line of fit is a close estimate but not an exact value.

4 The scatter plot shows the weights and age of a puppy and a good line of fit. The equation for the line of fit shown is $y = 2x + 1.5$, where x represents the puppy's age in weeks and y represents the puppy's weight. Predict the weight of a 12-week-old puppy in pounds. Show your work. *(2 points)*

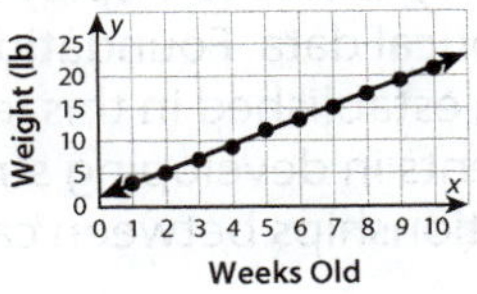

Possible student work:

$y = 2x + 1.5$

$y = 2(12) + 1.5$

$y = 25.5$

SOLUTION 25.5 pounds

5 A company introduces a customer service app. They track the number of customers who use it over an 8-month period. The scatter plot shows the data and a good line of fit. Write an equation of the line. Then predict the number of customers that will use the app after 12 months. Show your work. *(2 points)*

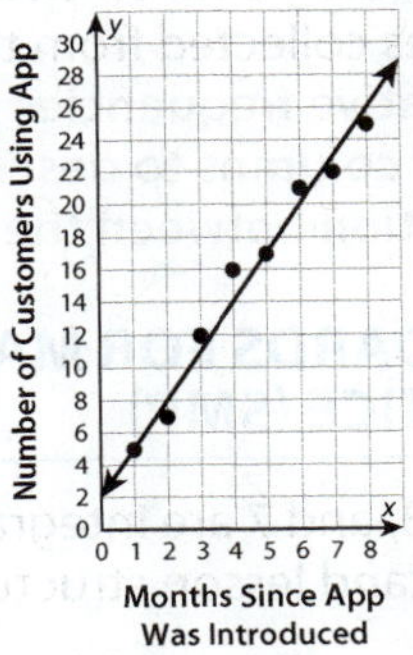

Possible student work:

The line of fit appears to pass through (1, 5) and (5, 17).

$m = \frac{17 - 5}{5 - 1} = \frac{12}{4} = 3$

$y = 3x + b$ | $y = 3x + 2$

$5 = 3(1) + b$ | $y = 3(12) + 2$

$2 = b$ | $y = 38$

SOLUTION Possible answer: $y = 3x + 2$; 38 customers

DIFFERENTIATION

RETEACH Tools for Instruction

Students who require additional support for prerequisite or on-level skills will benefit from activities that provide targeted skills instruction.

GRADE 8

- **Lesson 30** Use a Line of Fit to Make Predictions

REINFORCE Math Center Activity

Students who require practice to reinforce concepts and skills and deepen understanding will benefit from small group collaborative games and activities (available in on-level, below-level, and above-level versions).

GRADE 8

- **Lesson 30** Scatter Plot Predictions

EXTEND Enrichment Activity

Students who have achieved proficiency with concepts and skills and are ready for additional challenges will benefit from group collaborative games and activities that extend understanding.

GRADE 8

- **Lesson 30** Elephant Pics

Overview | Understand Two-Way Tables

UNDERSTAND: Why are two-way tables useful?

MATH FOCUS

This Understand lesson extends students' understanding of ways to organize data by using two-way tables to display and analyze categorical data. Foundational understanding established in this lesson supports students in developing strategies to identify relationships between categorical variables.

Focus Standard

8.SP.A.4 Understand that patterns of association can also be seen in bivariate categorical data by displaying frequencies and relative frequencies in a two-way table. Construct and interpret a two-way table summarizing data on two categorical variables collected from the same subjects. Use relative frequencies calculated for rows or columns to describe possible association between the two variables.

STANDARDS FOR MATHEMATICAL PRACTICE (SMP)

SMP 2, 3, and 7 are integrated into the Understand lesson structure.*

This lesson also provides additional support for:

1 Make sense of problems and persevere in solving them.

5 Use appropriate tools strategically.

* See page 1o to learn how every lesson includes these SMP.

Objectives

Content Objectives

- Understand how to read, interpret, and build two-way tables that show frequencies.
- Understand the distinction between measurement data and categorical data.
- Understand how patterns of association can be seen by using a two-way table.

Language Objectives

- Use adverbs and prepositions such as *across* and *down* and the words *center, cell, row,* and *column* to analyze, write, and talk about two-way tables that show frequencies.
- Read measurement data in a two-way table and analyze the data in writing.
- Use lesson vocabulary to analyze and describe two-way tables and patterns of association.

Prior Knowledge

- Understand that frequency is a count of items with a given property.
- Use frequencies to show the distribution of data in categories.
- Recognize that variables may or may not be related and that patterns in data can be used to understand relationships between variables.

Vocabulary

Math Vocabulary

categorical data data that are divided into categories, such as characteristics of the population. Categorical data values are often words.

two-way table a table that displays two-variable categorical data. One variable is shown along the top, the other down the side. Each entry in the table gives information about the frequency or relative frequency for the paired data.

Review the following key terms.

association (between two variables) a relationship between two variables. Two variables can be described as having a *linear association*, a *nonlinear association*, or *no association*. Linear associations can be described as *positive* or *negative*.

data a set of collected information. Often numerical information such as a list of measurements.

Academic Vocabulary

category a collection of objects grouped together based on attributes they have in common.

cell the area in a table where a column and row meet.

survey to collect data by asking people questions.

Learning Progression

In Grade 6, students learned about variability in statistical data, and they learned how to summarize and describe distributions of measurement data.

In Grade 7, students compared data sets to one another.

Earlier in Grade 8, students used scatter plots to investigate associations in bivariate measurement data.

In this lesson, students extend their work with data patterns to investigate associations between categorical variables. They see how data for two categorical variables can be organized into a two-way table that shows how the categories interact so that associations can be identified. Students also see how measurement data can be grouped so that they can be displayed in two-way tables.

In the next lesson, students will learn how to use two-way tables to calculate relative frequencies and use relative frequencies to interpret data and examine associations.

In high school, students will use relative frequencies and probability, including conditional probability, to analyze relationships displayed in two-way tables.

Pacing Guide

Items marked with are available on the **Teacher Toolbox**.

	MATERIALS	DIFFERENTIATION
SESSION 1 Explore Two-Way Tables (35–50 min)		
• **Start** (5 min) • **Model It** (5 min) • **Discuss It** (5–10 min) • **Model It** (5–10 min) • **Discuss It** (10–15 min) • **Close: Exit Ticket** (5 min) **Additional Practice** (pages 749–750)	Presentation Slides	**PREPARE** Interactive Tutorial **RETEACH or REINFORCE** Hands-On Activity **Materials** For each pair: 5–20 two-color counters and 5–20 unit cubes in red and yellow
SESSION 2 Develop Understanding of Two-Way Tables (45–60 min)		
• **Start** (5 min) • **Model It: Data on the Edges of the Table** (5 min) • **Discuss It** (5–10 min) • **Model It: Data in the Center of the Table** (5 min) • **Discuss It** (10–15 min) • **Connect It** (10–15 min) • **Close: Exit Ticket** (5 min) **Additional Practice** (pages 753–754)	Presentation Slides	**RETEACH or REINFORCE** Hands-On Activity **Materials** For each pair: cards displaying numbers 1, 2, 3, 3, 4, 4, 6, 7, 10 **REINFORCE** Fluency & Skills Practice
SESSION 3 Refine Ideas About Two-Way Tables (45–60 min)		
• **Start** (5 min) • **Apply It** (35–50 min) • **Close: Exit Ticket** (5 min)	Presentation Slides	
Lesson 31 Quiz or **Digital Comprehension Check**		**RETEACH** Tools for Instruction **REINFORCE** Math Center Activity **EXTEND** Enrichment Activity

Overview | Understand Two-Way Tables

Connect to Culture

➤ **Use these activities to connect with and leverage the diverse backgrounds and experiences of all students. Engage students in sharing what they know about contexts before you add the information given here.**

SESSION 1 ■ □ □

Model It Invite students to share their favorite games and their experiences with fantasy gaming. Fantasy board games became popular in the 1980s. These games revolve around role-play as participants send their characters on adventures, following a main theme. The game sets guidelines for play instead of strict rules. Players make choices about their characters' behaviors and responses to different situations, making each game different.

SESSION 2 ■ ■ □

Model It Government leaders often use surveys to learn what their constituents think about important issues facing the community. These surveys help leaders prioritize tasks to best meet the needs of the people. Ask students to suggest the types of questions that city councils, governors, or school administrators might ask their citizens or students. Invite students to suggest ways they can share their opinions with people making decisions for their community.

SESSION 3 ■ ■ ■

Apply It **Problem 4** Invite students to talk about the types of food they have purchased from a food truck. Food trucks bring fresh, delicious food to people. They make it possible for workers to eat lunch without traveling long distances and for people to try new foods. Street vendors have sold food at portable stands for many years. On the streets of the original colonies, people bought roasted ears of corn, fruit, oysters, and sweets. Ice cream trucks first brought frozen treats to neighborhoods in the 1920s. In 1974, an entrepreneur converted an ice cream truck into the country's first taco truck. Today, these small businesses are thriving, bringing new tastes directly to their customers.

Connect to Family and Community

After the Explore session, have students use the Family Letter to let their families know what they are learning and to encourage family involvement.

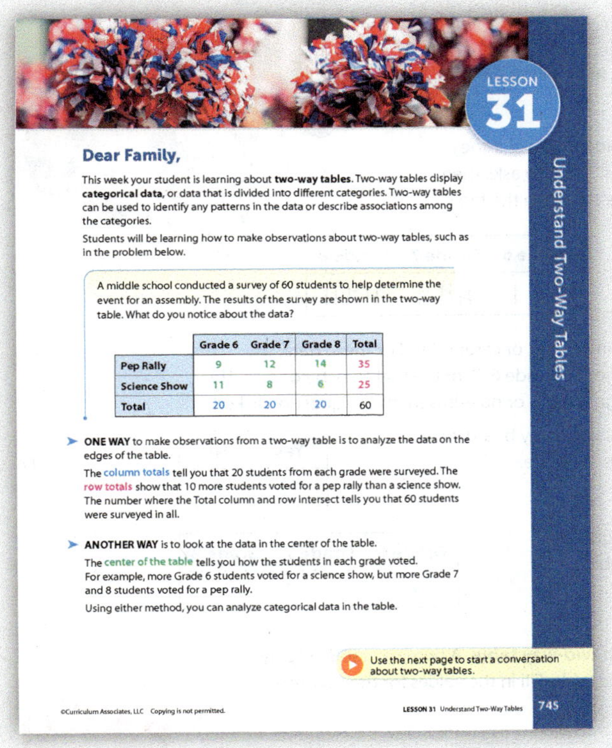
LESSON 31

Understand Two-Way Tables

Dear Family,

This week your student is learning about **two-way tables.** Two-way tables display **categorical data,** or data that is divided into different categories. Two-way tables can be used to identify any patterns in the data or describe associations among the categories.

Students will be learning how to make observations about two-way tables, such as in the problem below.

A middle school conducted a survey of 60 students to help determine the event for an assembly. The results of the survey are shown in the two-way table. What do you notice about the data?

	Grade 6	Grade 7	Grade 8	Total
Pep Rally	9	12	14	35
Science Show	11	8	6	25
Total	20	20	20	60

ONE WAY to make observations from a two-way table is to analyze the data on the edges of the table.

The column totals tell you that 20 students from each grade were surveyed. The row totals show that 10 more students voted for a pep rally than a science show. The number where the Total column and row intersect tells you that 60 students were surveyed in all.

ANOTHER WAY is to look at the data in the center of the table.

The center of the table tells you how the students in each grade voted. For example, more Grade 6 students voted for a science show, but more Grade 7 and 8 students voted for a pep rally.

Using either method, you can analyze categorical data in the table.

Use the next page to start a conversation about two-way tables.

©Curriculum Associates, LLC Copying is not permitted. LESSON 31 Understand Two-Way Tables 745

LESSON 31 | UNDERSTAND TWO-WAY TABLES

Activity Thinking About Two-Way Tables

Do this activity together to investigate two-way tables in the real world.

Two-way tables can be useful in making decisions based on patterns in data. For example, a local theater can conduct a survey to see how many people in different age groups like different types of movies. One category in the table would be the ages of the people surveyed. The other category would be the types of movies. The survey results can help the theater plan movie festivals that will appeal to different age groups.

Action Comedy Scifi Drama
Kind of Movie
Age
11–14 15–18 19+

What are some other categories of data that could be used in a survey?

746

Connect to Language

For English language learners, use the Differentiation chart to scaffold the language in each session. Use the Academic Vocabulary routine for academic terms before Session 1.

DIFFERENTIATION | ENGLISH LANGUAGE LEARNERS Use with **Session 1** **Model It**

Levels 1–3: Reading/Speaking

To help students interpret information from a two-way table, read Model It problem 3b as students follow along. Help students create a **Co-Constructed Word Bank** with words that name or refer to parts of the table, such as *cell, row, column, center, across,* and *down.* Discuss the meaning of the words. Then have students take turns pointing to examples in the table. Reread the problem and ask: *What cells do you need to fill in? What row? How many columns are missing one value?* Allow think time, then help students complete the table and describe their answers:

- *The value in row "No" and column "Grade 6" tells how many ____.*

Levels 2–4: Reading/Speaking

To help students interpret information from a two-way table, read Model It problem 3b as students follow along. Help students create a **Co-Constructed Word Bank** with words that name or refer to parts of the table. Suggest *cell* and *across.* Have students suggest other words and discuss their meanings. Then have students take turns using the words to identify examples in the table. Have students reread the problem. Ask: *What parts of the table do you need to fill in?* Encourage students to use words from the bank to answer. Then have them complete the table and describe their answers:

- *The value in row ____ and column ____ tells ____.*

Levels 3–5: Reading/Speaking

To help students interpret information from a two-way table, ask them to read Model It problem 3b. Have students create a **Co-Constructed Word Bank** with words that name or refer to parts of the table. Then have students reread the problem and tell what they need to complete and how they will do it. Suggest they refer to the word bank as they explain. Allow time for students to complete the problem, then ask: *How did you find the value in the third row and the third column? What does that value mean?* Repeat for other rows and columns.

Explore Two-Way Tables

Purpose

- **Explore** the idea that two-way tables are a way to organize two-variable data sets.
- **Understand** that two-way tables can be used to organize categorical data.

START CONNECT TO PRIOR KNOWLEDGE

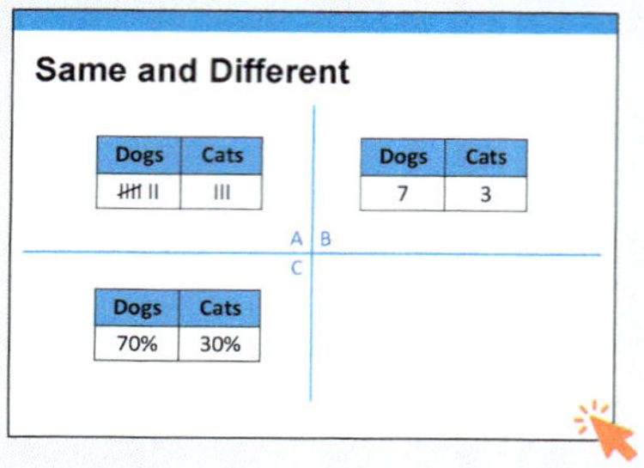

Possible Solutions

All are tables of data about dogs and cats.

All show the same ratio of dogs to cats.

A and B show the numbers of dogs and cats.

C cannot be used to find the number of dogs or cats.

WHY? Prepare students to understand that relationships cannot be identified when values are summarized individually.

MODEL IT SMP 2, 5

Read the Understand question at the top of the page. Remind students that they know how to use tally marks and tables to record data.

1 – 2 See ***Connect to Culture*** to support student engagement. Tell students that they are going to use what they know about tables that show frequencies to think about how to display data for two categories in a single table. Read the problems aloud. To confirm understanding, ask a student to rephrase each problem.

When discussing problem 2, direct students' attention to the cell that lies in both the total row and the total column. Ask students to explain what the number in that cell represents.

Common Misconception If students do not understand why numbers can be used to record categorical data, then ask them to identify the categories and think about what the numbers represent. Challenge students to identify examples of measurement data to compare with categorical data.

LESSON 31 | SESSION 1 ■ □ □

Explore Two-Way Tables

UNDERSTAND: Why are two-way tables useful?

Model It

➤ **Complete the problems about organizing data into tables.**

1 Yukio asks 20 students at her middle school if they like to play fantasy board games. She also asks them their current grade. Her data are shown in the tables.

Yes	No
𝍸 𝍸 ||	𝍸 |||

Grade 6	Grade 7	Grade 8
𝍸 |	𝍸 ||	𝍸 ||

Categorical data are collected in groups, or categories. For these data, the students choose from one category—Grade 6, 7, or 8—that they belong to. They then choose from another category—yes or no—based on the question asked.

a. How many students like to play fantasy board games? How many do not? Complete the table.

Yes	No
12	8

b. How many students in each grade responded? Complete the table.

Grade 6	Grade 7	Grade 8
6	7	7

2 Yukio's data can be displayed in a **two-way table**. A two-way table displays data for two categories in a single table. Fill in the values for the row and column totals.

	Grade 6	Grade 7	Grade 8	Total
Yes				12
No				8
Total	6	7	7	20

DISCUSS IT

Ask: Does it matter which category is placed in the rows and which is placed in the columns? Explain.

Share: I cannot fill in all cells in the problem 2 table because . . .

Learning Target SMP 1, SMP 2, SMP 3, SMP 5, SMP 7
Understand that patterns of association can also be seen in bivariate categorical data by displaying frequencies and relative frequencies in a two-way table. Construct and interpret a two-way table summarizing data on two categorical variables collected from the same subjects.

747

DISCUSS IT SMP 3, 7

Support Partner Discussion

After students complete problems 1 and 2, have them respond to Discuss It with a partner. Listen for understanding that:

- the rows represent the answer choices for one question, and the columns represent the answer choices for the other.
- it does not matter which category is placed in the rows and which is placed in the columns; the information will be the same.
- there is not enough information to complete the table started in problem 2.

Facilitate Whole Class Discussion

Prompt students to talk about why a two-way table is valuable.

ASK *What can the two-way table tell you that the two one-way tables cannot?*

LISTEN FOR Each one-way table shows data for just one question. The two-way table can tell you how the data for both questions are related.

MODEL IT

SMP 2, 3, 5

3 Tell students that they will now think about how to complete a two-way table. For problem 3b, ask students to explain how they know their table entries are correct.

Common Misconception If students do not understand how to complete the table, suggest they cover everything but the row or column they are working on. Ask them to use the numbers in that row or column to write a subtraction sentence.

4 Ask students to think about what each number in a two-way table means and how the values in the total column and row are related to the data in the center cells and to each other.

DISCUSS IT

SMP 3, 7

Support Partner Discussion

After students complete problem 4, have them respond to Discuss It with a partner. Encourage them to think about how the numbers in the center cells are related to the numbers in the edge cells.

Listen for understanding that:

- each value in the total row (column) shows the sum of the values above it (to the left of it).
- a subtraction sentence helps find missing values.

DIFFERENTIATION | RETEACH or REINFORCE

Hands-On Activity

Use counters and cubes to complete a two-way table.

If students are unsure about how to complete a two-way table, then use this activity to help them see how the values are related.

Materials For each pair: 5–20 two-color counters and 5–20 unit cubes in red and yellow

- Distribute a collection of counters and cubes to each pair. Direct each pair to decide how many counters will show red and how many yellow.
- Display this table and have pairs copy it.

	Red	Yellow	Total
Counters			
Cubes			
Total			

- Have pairs sort the cubes and counters into the proper categories and then complete the table.
- To ensure understanding, have pairs explain the meaning of the numbers in different cells of another pairs' table.

LESSON 31 | SESSION 1

Model It

➤ **Complete the problems about two-way tables.**

3 Below is the two-way table displaying data Yukio collected when she asked 20 students if they like to play fantasy board games. The *Yes* data have been added to Yukio's table.

	Grade 6	Grade 7	Grade 8	Total
Yes	2	6	4	12
No	4	1	3	8
Total	6	7	7	20

a. What does the data value 4 mean in the table?
4 of the Grade 8 students who were surveyed like to play fantasy board games.

b. The values in the center cells of a two-way table must add across to equal the row totals, as shown for the *Yes* response. They must also add down to equal the column totals. Complete the table to find how many Grade 6, Grade 7, and Grade 8 students do not like to play fantasy board games.
See table.

4 Is it possible for a number in one of the center cells of a two-way table to be greater than the total for that row or column? Explain.
No. If a number in a center cell was greater than its row or column total, then at least one other number in the row or column would have to be negative. You cannot have a negative number of responses to a question.

DISCUSS IT

Ask: How did the row and column totals help you complete the table?

Share: I know my values in the table are correct because . . .

5 **Reflect** Think about the information you get from separate one-way tables and the information you get from a two-way table. What is different? What is the advantage of a two-way table?
Possible answer: Separate one-way tables only give totals for each choice within a category. Two-way tables break the totals down by the choices within the other category. Two-way tables make it easier to see patterns and draw conclusions.

748

Facilitate Whole Class Discussion

Prompt students to think about how the values in a single row or column of a table are related.

ASK *What does the total value in a row represent? A column?*

LISTEN FOR It represents the number of times that answer was given.

CLOSE EXIT TICKET

5 **Reflect** Look for understanding that a two-way table contains more information than two one-way tables. It categorizes the responses to both questions and shows how they are related.

Common Misconception If students do not understand the advantages of a two-way table over two one-way tables, then ask them specific questions about the tables in this session: *Can you use both a one-way table and a two-way table to find the number of students who answered yes? What if you wanted to know how many students who answered yes are in Grade 7? Can you use both a one-way table and a two-way table to find the number of Grade 8 students? What if you wanted to know how many Grade 8 students answered no?*

Prepare for Two-Way Tables

Support Vocabulary Development

Assign **Prepare for Two-Way Tables** as extra practice in class or as homework.

If you have students complete this in class, then use the guidance below.

Ask students to consider the term *association*. Invite students to share how they use the word *association* or *associate* in conversation. Then encourage them to talk to a partner about how these meanings are related to the mathematical term.

Have students work in pairs to complete the graphic organizer. Invite pairs to share their completed organizers and prompt a whole-class comparative discussion of students' examples.

Have students look at the scatter plot in problem 2 and discuss with a partner the pattern shown by the plotted data values.

Problem Notes

1. Students should understand that *association* describes a relationship between two variables. Student responses may include sketches of scatter plots. Students should recognize that associations may be linear or nonlinear and that two variables may have no association at all. They might also write that linear associations can be positive or negative.

2. Students should understand that each point on the scatter plot shows a related pair of temperature and sales values. The pattern of points shows the association between the variables.

LESSON 31 | SESSION 1 Name:

Prepare for Two-Way Tables

1. Think about what you know about associations among data. Fill in each box. Use words, numbers, and pictures. Show as many ideas as you can.
Possible answers:

association

What Is It?
a relationship between two variables

What I Know About It
- Scatter plots can show associations between two variables.
- Associations between two variables can be linear or nonlinear.
- Data may have no association if the data do not relate in any way.

Examples

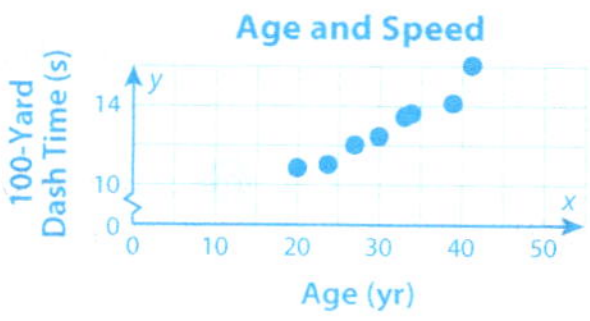

positive linear association

Examples

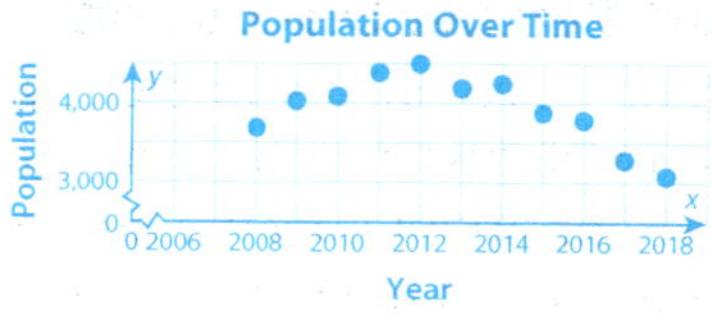

nonlinear association

2. The scatter plot shows the outside temperature and coffee sales for a small cafe. Does there appear to be any association between temperature and sales? Explain.
Yes. Temperature and sales have a negative linear association. As temperature increases, sales decrease.

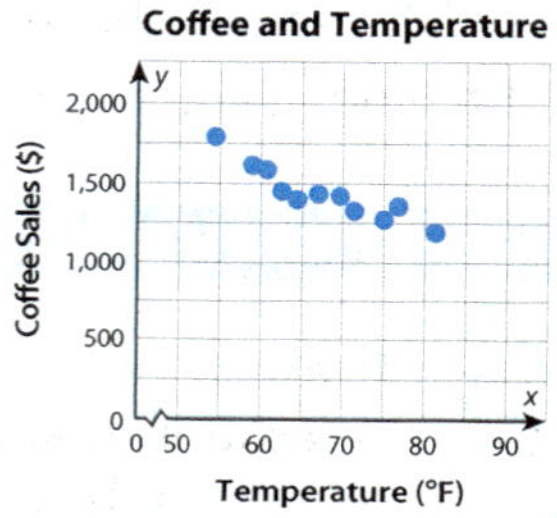

749

REAL-WORLD CONNECTION

National surveys often report their findings using two-way tables to show the relationship between categories. For example, the rows of a two-way table might represent regions of the country while the columns represent opinions on a particular political issue. Each cell in the table would show the percent of people in a particular region who have a particular opinion. The table as a whole would show how opinions about the issue vary by region. Ask students to think of other real-world examples when two-way tables might be useful.

3 **a.** Students should recognize that each tally mark represents one person.

b. Students may complete the table by counting tally marks in the second table.

c. Students may recognize that they do not have enough information to fill in the center cells in the table. The number in the bottom-right cell is the total number of people surveyed. It is equal to both the total of the numbers above it and the total of the numbers to the left of it.

4 Students should recognize that each value in the total row is the sum of the values in the cells above it. Also, each value in the total column is the sum of the values in the cells to the left of it.

LESSON 31 | SESSION 1

Complete problems 3 and 4.

3 A school district is thinking of having their students wear uniforms. Morgan surveys teachers and students to see whether they are in favor of school uniforms. Morgan shows the data she collected in two tables.

Student	Teacher
HHT HHT III	HHT II

In Favor	Not in Favor
IIII	HHT HHT HHT I

a. How many students did Morgan survey? How many teachers? Complete the table.

Student	Teacher
13	7

b. How many of those surveyed are in favor of uniforms? How many are not? Complete the table.

In Favor	Not in Favor
4	16

c. Fill in the values for the row totals and column totals.

	In Favor	Not in Favor	Total
Student			13
Teacher			7
Total	4	16	20

4 A student collects data about cars in the teachers' parking lot. The student fills in most of the two-way table. Complete the table to find how many of each type of car in the teachers' parking lot are non-hybrid.

	Hybrid	Non-Hybrid	Total
Sedan	6	11	17
Hatchback	4	8	12
SUV	3	9	12
Total	13	28	41

750

DIFFERENTIATION | ENGLISH LANGUAGE LEARNERS

Use with **Session 2** **Connect It**

ACADEMIC VOCABULARY

To *recommend* means to suggest something to do.

A *recommendation* is what you suggest.

Levels 1–3: Reading/Speaking

To help students write a response to Connect It problem 4, display the Academic Vocabulary. Help students use the words to talk about their responses to problem 1b. Ask: *What did you recommend?*

- *I ____ that the city build the ____.*
- *My ____ was to build the ____.*

Allow time for students to review their first recommendations. Then reword problem 4. Ask: *Do you recommend the same thing?* Have students use:

- *Yes, I ____ the same thing.*
- *No, I do not ____ the same thing. My new ____ is ____.*

Levels 2–4: Reading/Speaking

To help students write a response to Connect It problem 4, display the Academic Vocabulary. Help students use the words to talk about their responses to problem 1b. Ask: *What did you recommend?* Make sure students use the past tense. Have students look at the table in problem 3a. Allow time for them to think about their previous recommendations.

Ask: *Do you recommend the same thing or do you want to change your recommendation?* Help students use *recommend* and *recommendation* to answer verbally, then in writing.

Levels 2–4: Reading/Speaking

To help students write a response to Connect It problem 4, display the Academic Vocabulary. Have students use the words to talk about their responses to problem 1b. Ask: *What did you recommend?*

Have students look at the table in problem 3a. Then have them turn to partners to discuss previous and new recommendations. Allow time for students to discuss and write their answers. If students use the present tense to write about new recommendations, encourage them to rewrite using *would*. Ask: *What would you recommend this time?*

Develop Understanding of Two-Way Tables

Purpose

- **Develop** the idea that patterns of association can be seen in two-way tables.
- **Understand** why constructing two-way tables with frequencies is helpful when analyzing categorical data.

START CONNECT TO PRIOR KNOWLEDGE

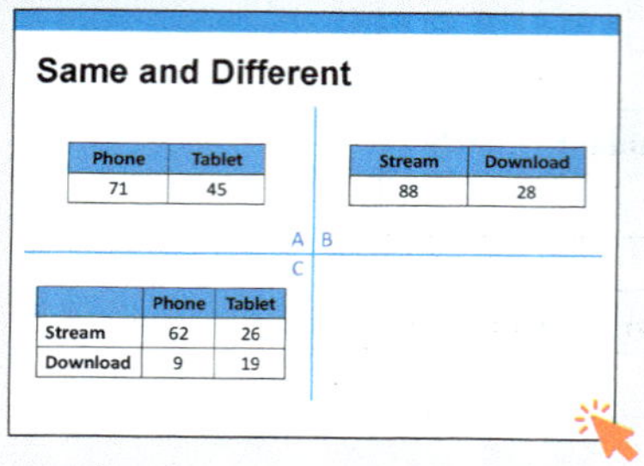

Possible Solutions

A and B are one-way tables.

A and C show data for devices.

B and C show data for delivery methods.

C is the only two-way table and relates the data in A and B.

WHY? Support students' understanding of the difference between one-way and two-way tables.

DEVELOP ACADEMIC LANGUAGE

WHY? Unpack meaning in dense sentences.

HOW? Display this sentence from Model It 1: *The city planning committee surveys people/ who/ rent a home in the city,/ own a home in the city,/ or commute from the surrounding area to the city.* Explain that *who* signals that the next part of the sentence describes *people*. Ask: *What kind of people are surveyed?* Ask students to use the conjunction *or* to tell who was surveyed.

MODEL IT

SMP 1, 2, 5

1 – 2 See ***Connect to Culture*** to support student engagement. As students complete the problems, use turn and talk to help them think through their responses before sharing with the group.

Common Misconception If students are not able to describe the information that would be provided by the center cells of the two-way table, then circle one of the center cells. Have students identify the row label and column label for that cell. Then ask them what a number in that cell would tell them.

UNDERSTAND: Why are two-way tables useful?

Develop Understanding of Two-Way Tables

Model It: Data on the Edges of the Table

➤ **Try these two problems involving two-way tables.**

1 A city considers building a theater, a small park, or a library on an empty lot. The city planning committee surveys people who rent a home in the city, own a home in the city, or commute from the surrounding area to the city each day. The results of the survey are shown.

Library	Park	Theater
卌 卌 卌 卌 ||	卌 卌 卌 卌 卌 ||||	卌 卌 卌 卌 卌 卌 卌 ||||

Renter	Owner	Commuter
卌 卌 卌 卌 卌 卌 ||||	卌 卌 卌 卌 卌 卌 卌 |	卌 卌 卌 卌

a. Fill in the values for the row totals and column totals. See table.

	Library	Park	Theater	Total
Renter				34
Owner				36
Commuter				20
Total	22	29	39	90

b. Which would you recommend building on the lot? Why? Possible answer: a theater; The table columns show how many votes were given for each option. The greatest column total is for a theater.

c. Which group of people surveyed had the fewest responses? Explain. commuters; The table rows show how many people in each group were surveyed. The lowest row total is for commuters.

2 What information would the data in the unfilled center cells of the table in problem 1a provide? Why might the committee want to consider these data?
These data would break down the total responses by the choices in each category. Possible answer: The committee might be interested to know how the people who live in the city feel versus commuters.

DISCUSS IT

Ask: How are row and column totals in two-way tables useful for examining categorical data?

Share: The row totals and column totals let you consider . . .

DISCUSS IT

SMP 3, 7

Support Partner Discussion

After students complete problems 1 and 2, have them respond to Discuss It with a partner. Support as needed with questions such as:

- *What do the row totals of this two-way table tell you?*
- *What do the column totals of this two-way table tell you?*
- *What does the value in the bottom-right corner cell tell you?*

Facilitate Whole Class Discussion

Have students talk about how to use the two-way table to organize and find the information they need.

ASK *How are the numbers in the Total row and Total column alike?*

LISTEN FOR Each is the total number of people who gave a certain answer. The corner number is the total number of people in the survey.

ASK *How are cells in the Total row and Total column different from the cells in the center of the table?*

LISTEN FOR Cells in the center tell how many people gave a specific pair of answers.

MODEL IT
SMP 2

3 As students complete the problem, have them discuss with a partner what each number in the table means in context.

DISCUSS IT
SMP 3, 5, 7

Support Partner Discussion

After students complete problem 3, have them respond to Discuss It with a partner. As partners are talking, remind them to use complete sentences to explain what they did and why. Suggest students use sentence frames such as *I did ____ first because ____,* and *Then I ____ because ____.*

Facilitate Whole Class Discussion

Have students talk about how to find missing values in a two-way table.

ASK *What information do you need to find a missing value in a two-way table?*

LISTEN FOR I need to know the other values in the same row or column as the empty cell.

DIFFERENTIATION | RETEACH or REINFORCE

Hands-On Activity
Build a two-way table.

If students are unsure about how the values in a two-way table are related, then use this activity to help them find connections.

Materials For each pair: small cards displaying the numbers 1, 2, 3, 3, 4, 4, 6, 7, 10

- Display a two-way table template on the board and have students copy it on their paper. Each cell should be large enough to fit a number card.

	Answer A	Answer B	Total
Answer C			
Answer D			
Total			

- Tell students to use the cards to fill in the table.
- There will be more than one correct solution. If students have trouble getting started, suggest that they start with the least and greatest values.
- Monitor students' work to ensure that their table is reasonable.
- Discuss students' solutions to help illustrate possible different strategies. Ask: *Which card did you place first? Did you start with the center cells or the total cells? How did you know when an arrangement did not work?*

LESSON 31 | SESSION 2

Model It: Data in the Center of the Table

➤ **Try this problem about frequencies in two-way tables.**

3 **a.** Complete the table for the city planning committee's survey data.

	Library	Park	Theater	Total
Renter	10	15	9	34
Owner	12	14	10	36
Commuter	0	0	20	20
Total	22	29	39	90

b. Which group of people will be most unhappy if the planning committee recommends building a library? How do you know?
commuters; None of the commuters surveyed voted for a library.

DISCUSS IT

Ask: How did you know which numbers to use to complete the table?

Share: I know that 90 represents . . . because . . .

CONNECT IT

➤ **Complete the problems below.**

4 Look at the data in the center cells of the table in problem 3a above. Do these data change your recommendation for which facility the city should build on the lot from problem 1b? Explain.
Possible answer: Yes, I would now recommend building a park. Even though a theater got the most votes overall, more than half of those votes came from commuters. For the people who live in the city, a park was the most popular option.

5 Brownstown Middle School's principal asks students the language they plan to study in high school. Complete the two-way table. Describe any association between grade and the language students plan to study.
Possible answer: Students in Grade 6 are much less likely to choose Spanish than students in Grade 7 or Grade 8.

	Spanish	German	French	Total
Grade 6	18	22	24	64
Grade 7	37	20	18	75
Grade 8	46	15	12	73
Total	101	57	54	212

752

CONNECT IT
SMP 1, 2, 3, 7

4 Student responses should show understanding that the choice of library, park, or theater is related to whether people rent, own, or commute. Looking at this relationship provides more useful information for the committee to use in making its decision. Have students share their responses and justify their reasoning. There is more than one possible reasonable response.

CLOSE EXIT TICKET

5 Look for understanding that the values in some cells can only be found after other cells are filled in. Students may recognize that Spanish is the most popular choice for students in Grades 7 and 8, but it is the least popular choice for students in Grade 6. They may also notice that French is the least popular overall, but it is the most popular choice for Grade 6 students.

Common Misconception If students do not think they have enough information to complete the table, then have them start with a cell that represents the only missing value in its row or column.

Practice Understanding of Two-Way Tables

Problem Notes

Assign **Practice Understanding of Two-Way Tables** as extra practice in class or as homework.

1 **a.** Students may find it helpful to cover the part-time and total rows to identify the most common mode of transportation for full-time workers. They can then hide the part-time and full-time rows to focus on the overall results. ***Medium***

b. Students should look at the most popular response in each row. ***Medium***

LESSON 31 | SESSION 2 Name:

Practice Understanding of Two-Way Tables

➤ **Study how the Example shows how to analyze data in a two-way table. Then solve problems 1–4.**

Example

Residents of a city answer a question about how they get to work. They also answer a question about whether they work full time or part time. The two-way table shows the data collected. City leaders want to advertise to increase the number of bus riders. What type of worker should the ads target? Explain.

	Bus	Walk	Car	Subway	Other	Total
Part Time	43	37	12	47	3	142
Full Time	25	31	57	28	44	185
Total	68	68	69	75	47	327

Fewer full-time workers ride the bus, so the program should target them.

1 Use the table in the Example to answer the following questions.

a. Is the most common form of transportation for the full-time workers the same as the most common form of transportation overall? Why or why not?

No. The most common form of transportation for full-time workers is a car. The most common form of transportation overall is the subway, but it is the second lowest for full-time workers. The total number of workers who use the subway is high because that is the most common form of transportation for part-time workers.

b. Is there an association between the type of worker and the form of transportation? Explain.

Yes. Possible explanation: A car is more likely to be used by a full-time worker while the subway is more likely to be used by a part-time worker.

Vocabulary
two-way table
a table that displays two-variable categorical data.

753

Fluency & Skills Practice

Understanding Two-Way Tables

In this activity, students solve problems using two-way tables, and they complete two-way tables based on given information.

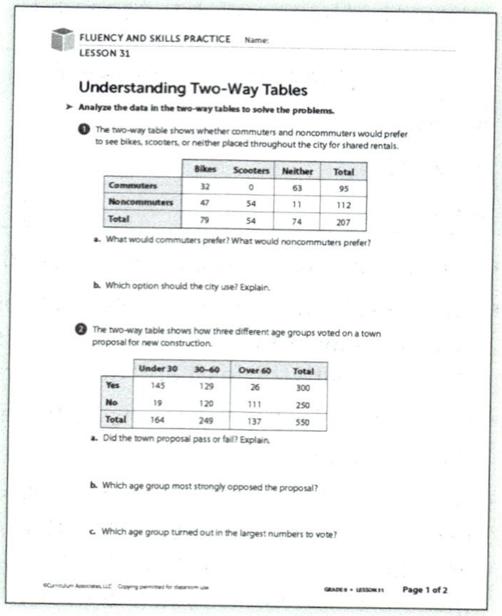
FLUENCY AND SKILLS PRACTICE Name:
LESSON 31

Understanding Two-Way Tables

➤ **Analyze the data in the two-way tables to solve the problems.**

1 The two-way table shows whether commuters and noncommuters would prefer to see bikes, scooters, or neither placed throughout the city for shared rentals.

	Bikes	Scooters	Neither	Total
Commuters	32	0	63	95
Noncommuters	47	54	11	112
Total	79	54	74	207

a. What would commuters prefer? What would noncommuters prefer?

b. Which option should the city use? Explain.

2 The two-way table shows how three different age groups voted on a town proposal for new construction.

	Under 30	30–60	Over 60	Total
Yes	145	129	26	300
No	19	120	111	250
Total	164	249	137	550

a. Did the town proposal pass or fail? Explain.

b. Which age group most strongly opposed the proposal?

c. Which age group turned out in the largest numbers to vote?

©Curriculum Associates, LLC Copying permitted for classroom use

GRADE 8 • LESSON 31 Page 1 of 2

Additional Practice

2 Students should recognize that a sibling can be a brother *or* sister, so the answer to this question is not completely determined. They need to think about likelihood rather than certainty. ***Medium***

3 **a.** Students may start with either the first or second column. ***Basic***

b. There is more than one reasonable conclusion. It is important that students justify their analysis using information from the table. ***Medium***

4 Students have no way to challenge the information in the center cells. To find the error, they must check the totals. ***Challenge***

2 Thirty middle school students are asked if they have at least one sibling. The data collected are shown in the table. In which grade would you expect the fewest students to have a sister? Explain.

	Grade 6	Grade 7	Grade 8	Total
Sibling(s)	3	9	7	19
No Siblings	7	2	2	11
Total	10	11	9	30

Grade 6. The number of Grade 6 students who have no siblings is more than twice the number of students who have at least one sibling.

3 A swimming pool manager is planning an activity for the Fourth of July. He surveys some of the kids at the pool to see what they would prefer.

	Cannonball Contest	Coin Dive	Relay Races	Total
8–10 Years Old	8	25	13	46
11–13 Years Old	14	8	18	40
Total	22	33	31	86

a. Complete the table. See table.

b. Which activity should the manager choose? Explain.

Possible answer: relay races; The coin dive has the most votes overall, but it is the least popular for 11- to 13-year-olds. The relay races got the second most votes overall. It is the most popular for 11- to 13-year-olds and the second most popular for 8- to 10-year-olds.

4 Platon makes a two-way table that shows the favorite activities at a summer camp. He sorts the data for different age groups. Jordan says Platon made an error. Do you agree with Jordan? Explain

Yes; Possible explanation: The age 6–8 row total is not the sum of the numbers in the row. The row total should be 41.

	Art	Swimming	Kickball	Total
6–8	15	18	8	31
9–11	9	21	12	42
12–14	12	24	6	42
Total	36	63	26	125

754

DIFFERENTIATION | ENGLISH LANGUAGE LEARNERS

Use with Session 3 **Apply It**

Levels 1–3: Listening/Speaking

To help students interpret Apply It problem 2, read the problem aloud. Reword the first two sentences using active voice, for example: *Someone gives a survey to 120 people . . . . The question asks how many packages they ____.* Then have students turn to partners to review the table and decide whether there is an association or relationship between the number of packages and age. Help students compare the totals for each age range. Use *older* and *younger* to explain the ranges. Then ask: *What age receives more packages? What age receives fewer? What is the association between packages and age?*

- *The totals show that ____ people receive ____ packages than ____ people.*

Levels 2–4: Listening/Speaking

To help students interpret Apply It problem 2, read the problem with students. Reword the first sentence using active voice. Then have students reread the second sentence and **Say It Another Way**. Guide them as they change from passive to active voice. Then have students turn to partners to review the table and decide whether there is an association between the number of packages and age. Have students compare the totals for each range. Ask them to use *older* and *younger* to explain the ranges. Then ask: *What age receives more packages? What age receives fewer? What is the association between packages and age?*

- *The totals show that ____.*

Levels 3–5: Listening/Speaking

To help students interpret Apply It problem 2, use **Say It Another Way.** Guide students to tell the difference between active and passive voice. Then have them paraphrase the first two sentences using active voice. Have students turn to partners to review the table and decide whether there is an association between the number of packages and the age. Have students use *older* and *younger* to explain the ranges. Then have them describe the association between packages and age. Ask: *What can you tell from the totals shown on the table? Did you use passive or active voice in your answer? How do you know?*

Refine Ideas About Two-Way Tables

Purpose

- **Refine** understanding of two-way tables as a way of interpreting categories of data.

START CONNECT TO PRIOR KNOWLEDGE

Which Would You Rather?

Based on the survey of favorite games, which video game would you choose to play?

	Game A	Game B	Game C
Grade 7	14	6	10
Grade 8	8	12	10

Possible Solutions

Game B is the most popular game in Grade 8 and I am in Grade 8, so I would choose B.

Game C is equally popular across both grades, so I would choose it.

Game A is preferred by 22, Game B by 18, and Game C by 20, so I would choose Game A.

I would play all three games and see which I like.

WHY? Reinforce students' abilities to analyze data in a two-way table.

APPLY IT

SMP 2, 3, 7

Have students work independently or with a partner for problems 1–3.

1 **Translate** Look for understanding that the measurement data are being grouped to make categories. There are two categories for the number of bags sold (0–25 bags and 26–50 bags) and two categories for the number of hours (0–5 hours and 6–10 hours).

Encourage students to think about the difference between displaying measurement data in a scatter plot versus in a two-way table. A scatter plot is built using individual responses, with a point for each pair of related values. A two-way table is constructed by dividing values of the two variables into categories and recording the number of data pairs in each pair of related categories.

UNDERSTAND: Why are two-way tables useful?

Refine Ideas About Two-Way Tables

Apply It

➤ Complete problems 1–5.

1 **Translate** Measurement data can also be separated into categories and displayed in two-way tables. The Spanish club is selling bags of trail mix to raise money for a trip. The number of hours each member works and the bags of trail mix they sell are recorded. Use **Data Set: Trail Mix Sales** to complete the two-way table.

Trail Mix Sales

Hours	Bags Sold
1	13
1	15
1	21

See page DS2 for the complete data set.

	0–25 Bags Sold	26–50 Bags Sold	Total
0–5 Hours	11	2	13
6–10 Hours	2	5	7
Total	13	7	20

2 **Interpret** A survey is given to 120 people ages 21–60. The people are asked how many packages they received in the past month. The table shows the results. Is there an association between the number of packages and age? Explain.

	1–2 Packages	3–4 Packages	5+ Packages	Total
Age 21–40	22	26	9	57
Age 41–60	41	14	8	63
Total	63	40	17	120

Yes. Older people seem to receive fewer packages than younger people.

3 **Analyze** Based on this incomplete table, Badru says 47 students do not have pets. Is Badru correct? How do you know?

	Summer Job	No Summer Job	Total
No Pets		34	
Pets	103		180
Total	150		

No. $150 - 103 = 47$, the number of students with a summer job and no pets. There are also 34 students with no summer job and no pets. $47 + 34 = 81$

755

Common Misconception If students do not understand how to complete the table, suggest they first go through the data set and make a tally mark in the appropriate cell for each pair of values. For example, a sale of 28 bags in 3 hours would be recorded as a tally mark in the cell for 0–5 hours and 26–50 bags sold. After students have gone through the whole data set, they can replace the tally marks with numbers.

2 **Interpret** Look for understanding that values in the center cells, rather than the totals, should be used for comparisons. Direct students' attention to the Total column. Ask them to explain why these numbers do not show that older people get more packages. Students should recognize that the totals in this column are the number of people in each age category and do not include information about the number of packages. Looking across the rows, students can see that most older people receive only 1–2 packages, while most younger people receive 3 or more packages.

3 **Analyze** Look for understanding that the number of students with no pets can be found in the Total column. Ask students to explain why it would be helpful to complete the entire table before answering the question.

4 See ***Connect to Culture*** to support student engagement. Before students begin, read the first part of the problem aloud and ask students what they should look for in the table. Then have students read the directions for Part A and Part B and have them rephrase to confirm that they understand each part of the task.

As students work on their own, walk around to ensure that they are completing their tables correctly.

Have students share their conclusions with a partner. Suggest students try to build on their partner's ideas that they agree with by adding details or explanations.

CLOSE EXIT TICKET

5 **Math Journal** Look for understanding that the values in the center allow students to identify associations between variables.

Error Alert If students have trouble seeing an association in the data, have them cover the Total column and Total row. Ask, *Which column shows the students who practice less? Do they make fewer mistakes than students in the other column?*

End of Lesson Checklist

INTERACTIVE GLOSSARY Support students by suggesting that they explain what each cell in a specific table represents. Then have students think of two types of data they could display in a two-way table, such as pizza or salad and olives or no olives.

4 Francisca owns a food truck that serves Mexican food. She wants to know whether she should include rice with a taco or burrito order. One Saturday, she records whether customers who buy a taco or burrito also order rice.

PART A Complete the two-way table for the data.

	Rice	No Rice	Total
Taco	47	88	135
Burrito	97	31	128
Total	144	119	263

PART B Should Francisca include rice with a taco or burrito order? Explain.

Possible answer: She should include rice only with a burrito order. Less than half of taco customers order rice. But over three times as many burrito customers order rice than do not.

5 **Math Journal** A piano teacher asks her students the amount of time they spend practicing each day. She then notes the number of mistakes they make in a recital. What association can you see from the data in the table? What might the piano teacher recommend to her students?

	0–30 Minutes	31–60 Minutes	Total
0–25 Mistakes	1	8	9
26–60 Mistakes	13	2	15
Total	14	10	24

Possible answer: More students who practiced less made more mistakes. Students who practiced longer tended to make fewer mistakes. The teacher should point this out to her students and suggest they practice more if they want to make fewer mistakes.

End of Lesson Checklist

☐ **INTERACTIVE GLOSSARY** Find the entry for *two-way table*. Rewrite the definition in your own words.

Short Response Scoring Rubric (2 points) — Problem 4

Points	Expectations
PART A	
2	Each entry in the table is correct.
1	Three or four of the entries in the table are correct.
PART B	
2	Student recognizes that rice is more popular with burritos **AND** provides a justification of the reasoning.
1	Student does not recognize that rice is more popular with burritos **OR** does not provide a justification of the reasoning.

LESSON 31
Lesson Quiz

TESTED SKILLS

Assesses 8.SP.A.4

Problems on this assessment require students to be able to interpret data in two-way tables. Students will draw conclusions and make associations based on data in a completed two-way table and compare results for one group to the overall results of the population. They will also complete a two-way table with missing values and interpret the meaning of a value in the table. Students will also need to be familiar with reading data in one-way tables and using operations to find missing table values.

Alternately, teachers may assign the **Digital Comprehension Check** online to assess student understanding of this material.

Error Alert Errors may result if students:

- misinterpret the meaning of data in a row or column.
- confuse interpreting the categorical data in a column for a row and vice versa.
- compare column or row totals when data in the center of the table are required.

Problem Notes

1 **A is correct.** Students could solve this problem by recognizing that the number of Grade 9 students who enjoy drawing, 7, is more than the number of students in the other grades that enjoy drawing. A person who enjoys drawing is more likely to take art classes.

B is incorrect. In Grade 10, 4 students enjoy drawing, which is less than 7 students.

C is incorrect. In Grade 11, 2 students enjoy drawing, which is less than 7 students.

D is incorrect. In Grade 12, 4 students enjoy drawing, which is less than 7 students.

(1 point)

DOK 1 | **8.SP.A.4**

2 Students could solve the problem by noting that 20 out of 35 high school students prefer eating out, so this category of people prefer eating out over cooking at home. Then they could compare the data for the preference overall. Seventy-nine people preferred cooking at home, and 61 people preferred eating out. So, the preference overall was cooking at home.

(2 points)

DOK 2 | **8.SP.A.4**

LESSON 31 • QUIZ Name:

➤ **Solve the problems.**

1 Forty high school students are asked what kind of hobbies they enjoy. The data collected are shown in the table. In which grade could the greatest number of students taking art classes be expected? *(1 point)*

	Grade 9	Grade 10	Grade 11	Grade 12	Total
Sports	3	8	6	6	22
Drawing	7	4	2	4	18
Total	10	12	8	10	40

(A) Grade 9

B Grade 10

C Grade 11

D Grade 12

2 One hundred forty people were surveyed to see if they like to eat out or cook at home. Is the most common preference of high schoolers the same as the most common preference overall? Use the table to answer the question. Explain your reasoning. *(2 points)*

	High School	College	Young Adult	Seniors	Total
Eat Out	20	16	15	10	61
Cook at Home	15	14	30	20	79
Total	35	30	45	30	140

SOLUTION No; Possible explanation: High schoolers prefer to eat out, but the overall population that was surveyed prefers to cook at home.

 GRADE 8 • LESSON 31 • Understand Two-Way Tables **Page 1 of 2**

Fill-in-the-Blank Scoring Rubric

Points	Expectations
2	All answers are correct
1	1 incorrect answer
0	2 or more incorrect answers

Short Response Scoring Rubric

Points	Expectations
2	Response has the correct solution(s) and includes well-organized, clear, and concise work demonstrating thorough understanding of mathematical concepts and/or procedures.
1	Response contains mostly correct solution(s) and shows partial understanding of mathematical concepts and/or procedures.
0	Response shows no attempt at finding a solution and no effort to demonstrate an understanding of mathematical concepts and/or procedures.

3 (2 points)

DOK 1 | **8.SP.A.4**

4 Students could solve this problem by reviewing each category of number of visits to the grocery store. The data are almost evenly divided among the two age groups, so no association can be made between age and number of visits.

(2 points)

DOK 2 | **8.SP.A.4**

5 Students could solve the problem by first completing the missing data in the two-way table. In the swimming column, subtract 13 left-handed swimmers from the total of 89 to get 76 right-handed swimmers. The total of right-handed students is the sum of the students who run track and are right-handed and students who swim and are right-handed. So, the row total for right-handed, 158, will be the number of all right-handed students.

(2 points)

DOK 3 | **8.SP.A.4**

LESSON 31 • QUIZ Name:

3 A survey is given to pet owners living in apartments, townhouses, and houses to determine the pet they own. Complete the table. Write your answers in the blanks. *(2 points)*

	Apartment	Townhouse	House	Total
Dog	3	10	24	37
Cat	8	20	8	36
Total	11	30	32	73

4 A survey is given to 96 people ages 20–60. They are asked about the number of times they went to the grocery store in the past month. The table shows the results. Is there an association between the number of visits and age? Explain your reasoning. *(2 points)*

	0–1 visit	2–3 visits	4 or more visits	Total
Ages 20–40	5	38	5	48
Ages 41–60	5	39	4	48
Total	10	77	9	96

SOLUTION No; Possible explanation: The number of visits to the grocery store is about the same across the age groups.

5 Based on this incomplete table of student athletes, Noah says 76 students are right-handed. Is Noah correct? Explain your reasoning. *(2 points)*

	Track	Swimming	Total
Left-Handed Students	9	13	22
Right-Handed Students	82	76	158
Total	91	89	180

SOLUTION No; Possible explanation: 76 is the number of students who swim and are right-handed: 89 − 13 = 76. There are also 82 students who run track and are right-handed; 76 + 82 = 158.

DIFFERENTIATION

RETEACH Tools for Instruction

Students who require additional support for prerequisite or on-level skills will benefit from activities that provide targeted skills instruction.

GRADE 8
- **Lesson 31** Reading Two-Way Tables

REINFORCE Math Center Activity

Students who require practice to reinforce concepts and skills and deepen understanding will benefit from small group collaborative games and activities (available in on-level, below-level, and above-level versions).

GRADE 8
- **Lesson 31** Complete Two-Way Tables

EXTEND Enrichment Activity

Students who have achieved proficiency with concepts and skills and are ready for additional challenges will benefit from group collaborative games and activities that extend understanding.

GRADE 8
- **Lesson 31** To Dance or Not to Dance...

Overview | Construct and Interpret Two-Way Tables

MATH FOCUS

Focus Standard

8.SP.A.4 Understand that patterns of association can also be seen in bivariate categorical data by displaying frequencies and relative frequencies in a two-way table. Construct and interpret a two-way table summarizing data on two categorical variables collected from the same subjects. Use relative frequencies calculated for rows or columns to describe possible association between the two variables.

STANDARDS FOR MATHEMATICAL PRACTICE (SMP)

SMP 1, 2, 3, 4, 5, and 6 are integrated into the Try-Discuss-Connect routine.*

This lesson provides additional support for:

1 Make sense of problems and persevere in solving them.

7 Look for and make use of structure.

* See page 1o to learn how every lesson includes these SMP.

Objectives

Content Objectives

- Construct two-way tables of relative frequencies using row totals, column totals, or the overall total.
- Interpret two-way tables of relative frequencies.
- Analyze patterns of association in two-way tables of relative frequencies.

Language Objectives

- Use lesson vocabulary and the words *row, column, overall, average,* and *whole* to describe two-way tables with relative frequencies in writing.
- Use the Academic Vocabulary and related words such as *likely* and *randomly* to discuss and write about patterns of association in two-way tables with frequencies.

Prior Knowledge

- Construct and interpret two-way tables showing frequencies.
- Analyze patterns of association in two-way tables with frequencies.

Vocabulary

Math Vocabulary

relative frequency the quotient that compares the number of times a data value occurs and the total number of data values. This can be expressed as a fraction, decimal, or percent.

Review the following key terms.

association (between two variables) a relationship between two variables. Two variables can be described as having a *linear association*, a *nonlinear association*, or *no association*. Linear associations can be described as *positive* or *negative*.

frequency a numerical count of how many times a data value occurs in a data set.

percent per 100. A percent is a rate per 100. A percent can be written using the percent symbol (%) and represented as a fraction or decimal. For example, 15% can be represented as $\frac{15}{100}$ or as 0.15.

random sample a sample in which every element in the population has an equal chance of being selected.

two-way table a table that displays two-variable categorical data. One variable is shown along the top, the other down the side. Each entry in the table gives information about the frequency or relative frequency for the paired data.

Academic Vocabulary

likelihood the chance that something will happen.

random chosen without a reason or decision.

Learning Progression

In Grade 7, students made tables of frequencies for single-variable data.

In the previous lesson, students built two-way tables with frequencies and analyzed patterns of association between variables by using two-way tables with frequencies.

In this lesson, students construct two-way tables with relative frequencies using row totals, column totals, or the overall total. They also analyze two-way tables with relative frequencies to identify and describe associations between variables.

In high school courses, students will build on their understanding of two-way tables of relative frequencies and analyzing bivariate data. They will use their understanding of association to express strong and weak associations using correlation coefficients.

Pacing Guide

Items marked with are available on the **Teacher Toolbox**.

	MATERIALS	**DIFFERENTIATION**
SESSION 1 **Explore** Whole-Table Relative Frequencies (35–50 min) • **Start** (5 min) • **Try It** (5–10 min) • **Discuss It** (10–15 min) • **Connect It** (10–15 min) • **Close: Exit Ticket** (5 min) **Additional Practice** (pages 761–762)	Presentation Slides	**PREPARE** Interactive Tutorial **RETEACH or REINFORCE** Hands-On Activity **Materials** For each pair: 30 two-color counters
SESSION 2 **Develop** Constructing Two-Way Tables with Relative Frequencies (45–60 min) • **Start** (5 min) • **Try It** (10–15 min) • **Discuss It** (10–15 min) • **Connect It** (15–20 min) • **Close: Exit Ticket** (5 min) **Additional Practice** (pages 767–768)	Presentation Slides	**RETEACH or REINFORCE** Visual Model **REINFORCE** Fluency & Skills Practice **EXTEND** Deepen Understanding
SESSION 3 **Develop** Interpreting and Analyzing Two-Way Tables (45–60 min) • **Start** (5 min) • **Try It** (10–15 min) • **Discuss It** (10–15 min) • **Connect It** (15–20 min) • **Close: Exit Ticket** (5 min) **Additional Practice** (pages 773–774)	Presentation Slides	**RETEACH or REINFORCE** Visual Model **REINFORCE** Fluency & Skills Practice **EXTEND** Deepen Understanding
SESSION 4 **Refine** Constructing and Interpreting Two-Way Tables (45–60 min) • **Start** (5 min) • **Monitor & Guide** (15–20 min) • **Group & Differentiate** (20–30 min) • **Close: Exit Ticket** (5 min)	Presentation Slides	**RETEACH** Visual Model **REINFORCE** Problems 4–6 **EXTEND** Challenge **PERSONALIZE** i-Ready
Lesson 32 Quiz or **Digital Comprehension Check**		**RETEACH** Tools for Instruction **REINFORCE** Math Center Activity **EXTEND** Enrichment Activity

Overview | Construct and Interpret Two-Way Tables

Connect to Culture

➤ **Use these activities to connect with and leverage the diverse backgrounds and experiences of all students. Engage students in sharing what they know about contexts before you add the information given here.**

SESSION 1 ■ □ □ □

Try It Ask if any students have been to the Library of Congress. If so, have them describe their experience. The Library of Congress, which occupies three buildings on Capitol Hill in Washington, DC, is the largest library in the world. Each day, the library adds around 10,000 items to its millions of books, recordings, photographs, maps, sheet music scores, and other manuscripts. The library has over 800 miles of bookshelves. Have students discuss how the Library of Congress might be the same or different from their local library.

SESSION 2 ■ ■ □ □

Apply It **Problem 5** Ask for a show of hands of students who listen to podcasts regularly. Choose some students to talk about the subjects of their favorite podcasts. There are currently about 750,000 podcasts to which subscribers listen. About 51% of people in the United States have listened to a podcast, and about 16 million listen to podcasts regularly. About half of these people listen while at home and one-fourth listen while driving. The most popular podcast genres include comedy, education, and current events.

SESSION 3 ■ ■ ■ □

Try It Ask students to state an opinion on cell phone use in schools and to support their side of the issue. While some schools allow students to use cell phones in class, others do not. Proponents of cell phone use say that students will have access to phones their entire lives and need to get used to multitasking at an early age. They also argue that cell phones have applications that can be beneficial for student success. Those against cell phone use say it use is a distraction to students. They claim students will use social media or play games instead of learning.

SESSION 4 ■ ■ ■ ■

Apply It **Problem 4** Ask students who have raised puppies to share their experiences. Allow time for other students to ask questions. The ideal birth weight for a puppy depends on its breed. During the first month of life, a newborn puppy's weight may double or triple. Gaining up to 15% of birth weight daily may be considered healthy. Puppies start out by feeding on only their mother's milk. They may eat solid food at the age of 4 weeks and be weaned off their mother's milk at the age of 6 weeks.

Connect to Family and Community

After the Explore session, have students use the Family Letter to let their families know what they are learning and to encourage family involvement.

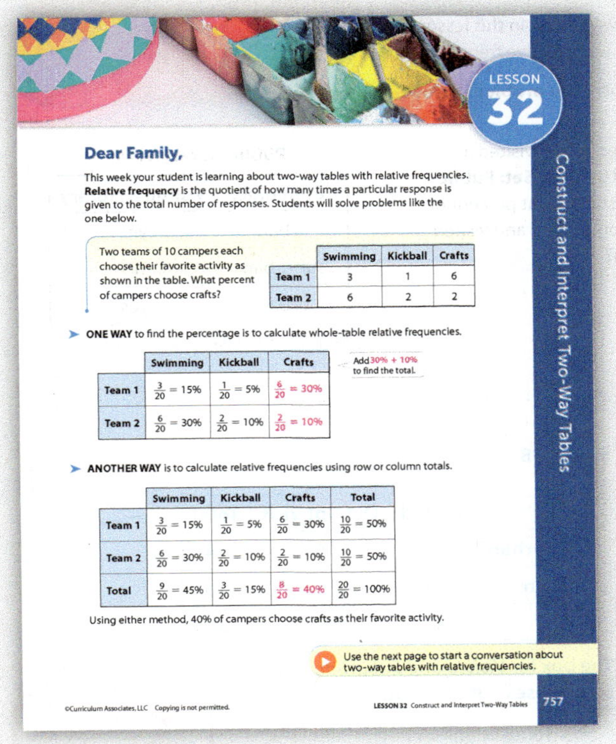

LESSON 32

Construct and Interpret Two-Way Tables

Dear Family,

This week your student is learning about two-way tables with relative frequencies. **Relative frequency** is the quotient of how many times a particular response is given to the total number of responses. Students will solve problems like the one below.

Two teams of 10 campers each choose their favorite activity as shown in the table. What percent of campers choose crafts?

	Swimming	Kickball	Crafts
Team 1	3	1	6
Team 2	6	2	2

ONE WAY to find the percentage is to calculate whole-table relative frequencies.

	Swimming	Kickball	Crafts
Team 1	$\frac{3}{20} = 15\%$	$\frac{1}{20} = 5\%$	$\frac{6}{20} = 30\%$
Team 2	$\frac{6}{20} = 30\%$	$\frac{2}{20} = 10\%$	$\frac{2}{20} = 10\%$

Add 30% + 10% to find the total.

ANOTHER WAY is to calculate relative frequencies using row or column totals.

	Swimming	Kickball	Crafts	Total
Team 1	$\frac{3}{20} = 15\%$	$\frac{1}{20} = 5\%$	$\frac{6}{20} = 30\%$	$\frac{10}{20} = 50\%$
Team 2	$\frac{6}{20} = 30\%$	$\frac{2}{20} = 10\%$	$\frac{2}{20} = 10\%$	$\frac{10}{20} = 50\%$
Total	$\frac{9}{20} = 45\%$	$\frac{3}{20} = 15\%$	$\frac{8}{20} = 40\%$	$\frac{20}{20} = 100\%$

Using either method, 40% of campers choose crafts as their favorite activity.

Use the next page to start a conversation about two-way tables with relative frequencies.

©Curriculum Associates, LLC Copying is not permitted. LESSON 32 Construct and Interpret Two-Way Tables 757

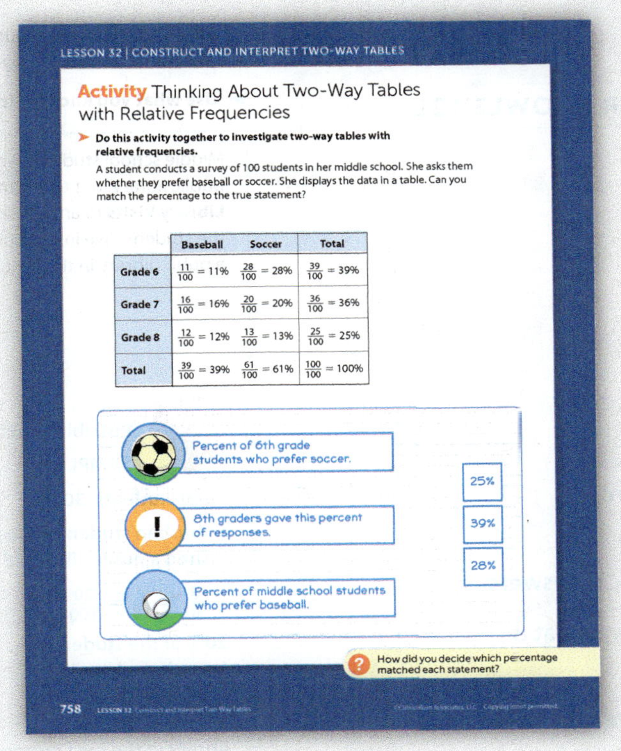

LESSON 32 | CONSTRUCT AND INTERPRET TWO-WAY TABLES

Activity Thinking About Two-Way Tables with Relative Frequencies

Do this activity together to investigate two-way tables with relative frequencies.

A student conducts a survey of 100 students in her middle school. She asks them whether they prefer baseball or soccer. She displays the data in a table. Can you match the percentage to the true statement?

	Baseball	Soccer	Total
Grade 6	$\frac{11}{100} = 11\%$	$\frac{28}{100} = 28\%$	$\frac{39}{100} = 39\%$
Grade 7	$\frac{16}{100} = 16\%$	$\frac{20}{100} = 20\%$	$\frac{36}{100} = 36\%$
Grade 8	$\frac{12}{100} = 12\%$	$\frac{13}{100} = 13\%$	$\frac{25}{100} = 25\%$
Total	$\frac{39}{100} = 39\%$	$\frac{61}{100} = 61\%$	$\frac{100}{100} = 100\%$

How did you decide which percentage matched each statement?

758 LESSON 32 Construct and Interpret Two-Way Tables

Connect to Language

For English language learners, use the Differentiation chart to scaffold the language in each session. Use the Academic Vocabulary routine for academic terms before Session 1.

DIFFERENTIATION | ENGLISH LANGUAGE LEARNERS Use with **Session 1** **Connect It**

Levels 1–3: Reading/Speaking

Help students understand the information in Connect It problem 2. Divide the definition: *A relative frequency/ is/ the quotient of/ the number of times a response occurs/ to/ the total number of responses . . . .* Explain that *is* tells that something will be explained or defined. Ask: *What does the sentence define?* Help students find words that express a relationship. [*quotient, to*] Then help them identify the quantities in the relationship:

- *Number of times a response occurs*
- *Total number of responses*

Read the remaining sentences and create a **Co-Constructed Word Bank**. Then have students complete the problem.

Levels 2–4: Reading/Speaking

Help students understand the information in Connect It problem 2. Divide the definition: *A relative frequency/ is/ the quotient of/ the number of times a response occurs/ to/ the total number of responses . . . .* Explain that *is* tells that something will be explained or defined. Help students discuss the first three parts. Ask: *What do you know about relative frequency so far?* [It is a quotient.] Then help students find the word *to* and identify the quantities in the relationship:

- *Number of times a response occurs*
- *Total number of responses*

Read the remaining sentences and create a **Co-Constructed Word Bank**. Have students work on the problem and discuss their answers.

Levels 3–5: Reading/Speaking

Help students understand the information in Connect It problem 2. Have students divide the definition into parts and consider the meaning of each part. Ask students to turn to partners to discuss the first three parts. Ask: *What is this sentence about? How do you know? What are some details in the sentence? What do the words* is *and* to *tell about the sentence?* Then have students express the relationship.

Have students read the remaining sentences and discuss words or numbers they can use to solve the problem. Then have students work on the problem and talk about their answers.

Explore Whole-Table Relative Frequencies

Purpose

- **Explore** the idea of using percent to express the relative frequencies of survey responses.
- **Understand** that two-way tables with frequencies are useful for finding the information needed to calculate relative frequencies.

START CONNECT TO PRIOR KNOWLEDGE

Which One Doesn't Belong?

A: Do you have a passport?	B: What is your age?
C: What is your favorite color?	D: What kinds of pets do you have?

Possible Solutions

A is the only question with only two possible answers.

B is the only question with numerical answers.

C is the only question with an answer that is an opinion.

D is the only question that can have more than one answer.

WHY? Support students' facility in understanding categorical data.

TRY IT SMP 1, 2, 4, 5, 6

Make Sense of the Problem

See ***Connect to Culture*** to support student engagement. Before students work on Try It, use **Three Reads** to help them make sense of the problem. After the first read, ask students to describe what the problem is about. After the second read, ask students to paraphrase what the question is asking. After the third read, ask students to list the important quantities and relationships in the problem.

DISCUSS IT SMP 2, 3, 4, 5, 6

Support Partner Discussion

After students work on Try It, have them respond to Discuss It with a partner. Listen for understanding that:

- there are 6 students who live in a suburban community and have visited a public library.
- there are 30 total students in the data set.
- a percent is a part out of 100.

LESSON 32 | SESSION 1

Explore Whole-Table Relative Frequencies

Johnson City Public Library
books, programs, classes, and more

Previously, you learned about two-way tables. In this lesson, you will learn to use two-way tables with relative frequencies.

➤ **Use what you know to try to solve the problem below.**

Middle school students were asked if they visited a public library in the past month. Use **Data Set: Public Library Visits** to answer this question. What percent of the students live in a suburban community and visited a public library in the past month?

Public Library Visits

Community	Visited a Library
urban	yes
suburban	no
urban	yes

See page DS2 for the complete data set.

TRY IT

Possible work:

SAMPLE A

Total students: 30

Suburban students who visited a public library: 6

$\frac{6}{30} = \frac{2}{10} = \frac{20}{100}$

20% of the students interviewed live in a suburban community and visited a public library in the past month.

SAMPLE B

	Visited	Did Not Visit	Total
Suburban	6	8	14
Urban	11	5	16
Total	17	13	30

The box for *Visited* and *Suburban* shows 6 responses out of 30 total responses.

$\frac{6}{30} \cdot 100\% = 20\%$

20% of the middle school students polled are from a suburban community and visited a library in the past month.

DISCUSS IT

Ask: Why did you choose that strategy to find the percentage?

Share: I knew . . . so I . . .

Learning Target SMP 1, SMP 2, SMP 3, SMP 4, SMP 5, SMP 6, SMP 7
Understand that patterns of association can also be seen in bivariate categorical data by displaying frequencies and relative frequencies in a two-way table. Construct and interpret a two-way table summarizing data on two categorical variables collected from the same subjects. Use relative frequencies calculated for rows or columns to describe possible association between the two variables.

759

Common Misconception Listen for students who divide the number of students who live in a suburban community and have visited a public library by the number of students who have visited a public library or by the number of students who live in a suburban community. As students share their strategies, lead a discussion about why the total number of students must be used when finding the percent and how this total can be determined.

Select and Sequence Student Strategies

Select 2–3 samples that represent the range of student thinking in your classroom. Here is one possible order for class discussion:

- tally chart made and used to find percent
- (misconception) division using a subtotal for the denominator instead of the total number of students
- number of rows in data set with both *suburban* and *yes* and total number of rows used to find percent
- two-way table with frequencies constructed and used to find percent

Facilitate Whole Class Discussion

Call on students to share selected strategies. Prompt students to better understand the problem by connecting it with others they have solved.

Guide students to **Compare and Connect** the representations. To prompt students to use precise academic language, call on volunteers to reword vague or unclear statements.

ASK *What information did each of these strategies use to find the percent? What were the different ways this information was found?*

LISTEN FOR The strategies used the number of students who live in a suburban community and visited a public library, and the total number of students who were surveyed. These numbers were found by organizing the given data using tally charts or two-way tables or just by counting.

CONNECT IT

SMP 2, 4, 5

1 **Look Back** Look for understanding that there are 6 students who live in a suburban community *and* have visited the library, and there are 30 students in all. So, the percent can be found by dividing 6 by 30.

DIFFERENTIATION | RETEACH or REINFORCE

Hands-On Activity

Use counters to understand data.

If students are unsure how to find the percent, then use this activity to help them solve the problem.

Materials For each pair: 30 two-color counters

- Present the data set to students. Ask: *How many students are in the data set?* [30]
- Have pairs place 30 counters on their table. Each counter should have the yellow side up.
- Tell one partner to place a finger on the first counter and the other partner to place a finger on the first entry row of the data set. If the row represents a student who has *suburban* for community and *yes* for visited a library, then the counter should be flipped to red. If not, students move to the next counter and next row.
- Once all the data rows have been examined, ask: *How many students live in a suburban community and have visited a public library?* [6]
- Have students place their counters in 3 rows with 2 red counters and 8 yellow counters in each row.
- Ask: *What fraction of the columns have red counters?* $\left[\frac{2}{10}\right]$ *What is this as a percent?* [20%] *What does this represent?* [20% live in a suburban community and have visited a public library.]

LESSON 32 | SESSION 1

CONNECT IT

1 **Look Back** What percent of the students live in a suburban community and visited a public library in the past month? Explain how you know.

20%; Possible explanation: In the data set, I counted 6 students who live in a suburban community and visited a library. Then I counted 30 students in all and divided to find the percentage.

2 **Look Ahead** A **relative frequency** is the quotient of the number of times a response occurs to the total number of responses in a category or in a whole survey. You have seen two-way tables showing frequencies, or counts. A two-way table can also show relative frequencies. Relative frequencies can be shown as fractions, decimals, or percentages. Consider this two-way table with frequencies.

	Prefer Reading	Prefer Playing Outside	Total
Grade 6	6	18	24
Grade 8	22	4	26
Total	28	22	50

The relative frequency of students surveyed who are in Grade 8 and prefer reading is $\frac{22}{50}$, or 44%.

a. What is the relative frequency of all the students surveyed who are in Grade 6 and prefer playing outside?

$\frac{18}{50} = 0.36$

$= 36\%$

b. What is the relative frequency of all the students surveyed who prefer reading?

$\frac{28}{50} = 0.56$

$= 56\%$

3 **Reflect** How can relative frequencies be helpful when looking at data?

Possible answer: Relative frequencies use percentages, which are helpful when the sizes of surveys are different.

760

2 **Look Ahead** Point out that relative frequency is calculated by dividing the number of times a response occurs by the total in a category or the overall total. Students should recognize that there are several totals in the table and that the row totals sum to the overall total, as do the column totals.

Ask a volunteer to rephrase the definition of *relative frequency*. Support students by pointing out that in problems 2a and 2b, the relative frequency is found by dividing the frequency by the overall total. Tell students that a relative frequency is sometimes found by dividing by a row or column total.

CLOSE EXIT TICKET

3 **Reflect** Look for understanding that relative frequencies can be expressed as fractions, decimals, or percents. Relative frequencies compare parts of the data to a whole.

Common Misconception Listen for students who do not realize that a completed two-way table with frequencies has enough information to find relative frequencies. Challenge these students to explain what information is still needed.

Prepare for Constructing and Interpreting Two-Way Tables

Support Vocabulary Development

Assign **Prepare for Constructing and Interpreting Two-Way Tables** as extra practice in class or as homework.

If you have students complete this in class, then use the guidance below.

Ask students to consider the term *percent*. You might point out that *per* means *for each* and *cent* means *100*, so *percent* means *for each 100*. Have them brainstorm what kinds of things should go in each box of the graphic organizer.

Have students work individually to complete the graphic organizer. Invite students to share their completed organizers and prompt a whole-class comparative discussion of the illustrations, examples, and non-examples given.

Have students look at the question in problem 2 and discuss with a partner what information is given. Partners should discuss how they can take that information and generate a percent.

Problem Notes

1. Students should understand that a percent is a rate per 100. Student responses might include a hundreds grid showing a percent, a tape diagram, or numbers written with a percent symbol. Students should recognize that fractions and decimals can be converted to percents using division or a proportion.

2. Students should understand that 18 is the part and 25 is the whole. They can divide 18 by 25 or set up a proportion to find that 72% is the correct answer.

LESSON 32 | SESSION 1 Name:

Prepare for Constructing and Interpreting Two-Way Tables

1. Think about what you know about ratios and percentages. Fill in each box. Use words, numbers, and pictures. Show as many ideas as you can.

Possible answers:

In My Own Words

a rate per 100; can be written with a % after the number

My Illustrations

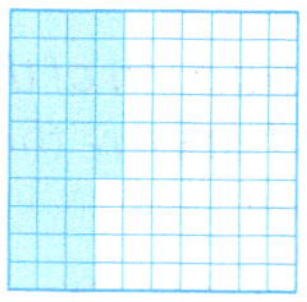

36% of the grid is shaded.

percent

Examples

There are 20 students in a class and 3 are left-handed.

$\frac{3}{20} \times \frac{5}{5} = \frac{15}{100}$

15% of the students are left-handed.

Non-Examples

$\frac{1}{5}$

6

3 : 2

0.23

7 of 10 kittens are female

2. Teenagers were asked what type of book they prefer to read. There were 18 teenagers who prefer e-books and 7 teenagers who prefer paperback or hardcover books. Anne says 72% of the teenagers prefer to read an e-book. Is Anne correct? Explain.

Yes; There are 25 teenagers in the poll. The number who prefer an e-book is 18, and $\frac{18}{25} = \frac{72}{100}$. So, 72% prefer to read an e-book.

761

REAL-WORLD CONNECTION

An actuary is a person who works for a health insurance company and analyzes data to calculate insurance premiums. As part of their work, actuaries construct and analyze two-way tables to determine likelihoods of risk based on certain criteria. For example, they may look at data related to age and exercise rates. This may factor in with other data as the actuaries decide on costs for insurance fees. Ask students to think of other real-world examples when constructing and interpreting two-way tables of data might be useful.

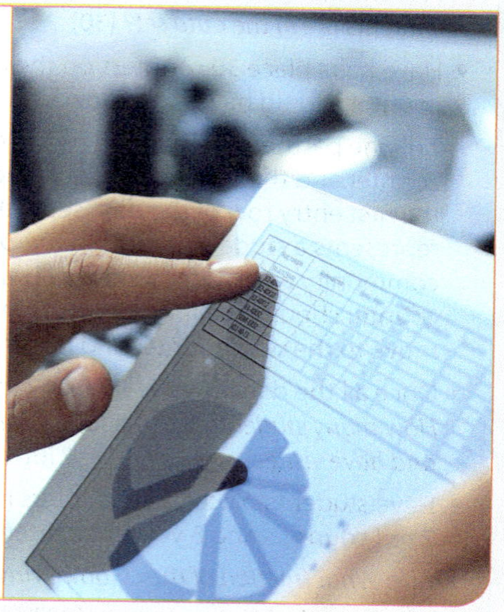

3 Problem 3 provides another look at finding a percent given a data set. This problem is similar to the problem about students who live in a suburban community and have visited a public library. In both problems, survey data are provided, and students must identify the number of students who gave a particular pair of responses and the total number of students in order to calculate a percent. This problem asks for the percent of all students who are in Grade 11 and have gone horseback riding.

Students may want to use a table with frequencies to solve.

Suggest that students use **Three Reads** to help them make sense of the problem. They should determine what the problem is about, what they are trying to find out, and the important quantities and relationships in the problem.

LESSON 32 | SESSION 1

3 Students at a high school take a survey. One question asks if they have ever gone horseback riding. Use **Data Set: Horseback Riding** to answer problem 3a.

Horseback Riding

Grade	Horseback
11	yes
11	yes
12	no

See page DS3 for the complete data set.

a. What percent of the students surveyed are in Grade 11 and have gone horseback riding? Show your work.

Possible work:

	Horseback	No Horseback	Total
Grade 11	12	4	16
Grade 12	5	9	14
Total	17	13	30

Students in Grade 11 who have gone horseback riding: 12

Total surveyed: 30

$\frac{12}{30} \times 100\% = 40\%$

SOLUTION 40% of the students surveyed are in Grade 11 and have gone horseback riding.

b. Check your answer to problem 3a. Show your work.

Possible work:

Total number of students in survey: 30

Number of Grade 11 students who have gone horseback riding: 12

$\frac{12}{30} = 0.4$

$0.40 \cdot 100\% = 40\%$

762

DIFFERENTIATION | ENGLISH LANGUAGE LEARNERS

Use with **Session 2** **Connect It**

MATH TERM

An *average* is a number that describes the center or typical value of a set of data.

Levels 1–3: Reading/Writing

Help students prepare to solve Connect It problem 1. Display the Math Term and its definition. Share examples of how *average* may be used in everyday language. Write *above average*, *average*, and *below average*.

Say: *An average grade is 85. What is a grade above average? What is a grade below average?* Write students' answers. Review the math symbols for *above*, *at*, *below*. Then help students use the terms in their responses:

- *Ten students have ____. Two of them have ____.*

Levels 2–4: Reading/Writing

Help students prepare to solve Connect It problem 1. Display the Math Term and ask students to discuss how they have heard *average* used before. Write the terms *above average*, *average*, and *below average*.

Suggest a topic, such as grades, and have students brainstorm examples of how *average* would be used. Write students' ideas. Review the math symbols for *above*, *at*, and *below*. Then help students use the terms in their answers: *How many students out of 10 also have at- or below-average foot length?*

Levels 3–5: Reading/Writing

Help students solve Connect It problem 1. Display the Math Term. Ask students to demonstrate understanding of *above average*, *average*, and *below average*. Have students work with two partners. Ask partners to consider a context that uses averages, such as sports or grades. Have partners take turns discussing averages, quantities above average, and quantities below average. Ask volunteers to use math symbols to express their examples. Have students work on the problem individually and then meet again to tell how they used the terms in their answers.

Develop Constructing Two-Way Tables with Relative Frequencies

Purpose

- **Develop** strategies for constructing two-way tables with relative frequencies based on either row or column totals.
- **Recognize** that two-way tables showing relative frequencies can be constructed by rows or by columns when given data or a two-way table with frequencies.

START CONNECT TO PRIOR KNOWLEDGE

Same and Different

A: 75%	B: $\frac{3}{4}$
C: 0.75	D: $\frac{27}{36}$

Possible Solutions

All values are equivalent.

A is the only percent.

C is the only decimal.

B is the only fraction in simplest form.

C is the only fraction not in simplest form.

A and C both contain the quantity 75.

WHY? Support students' facility with recognizing equivalent ways of expressing the same part of a whole.

DEVELOP ACADEMIC LANGUAGE

WHY? Understand the meaning of *target*.

HOW? Read Apply It problem 5. Have students find the word *target* and explain its multiple meanings as a noun and a verb. Share that some companies survey people to identify who would buy their products and which products they prefer to buy. Companies then decide how to offer the product or advertise to these people. Companies target these potential customers. Have students look at the table and tell what age group the audiobook company should target.

TRY IT SMP 1, 2, 4, 5, 6

Make Sense of the Problem

Before students work on Try It, use **Say It Another Way** to help them make sense of the problem. Listen for understanding that the whole is the number of students with above-average height.

Develop Constructing Two-Way Tables with Relative Frequencies

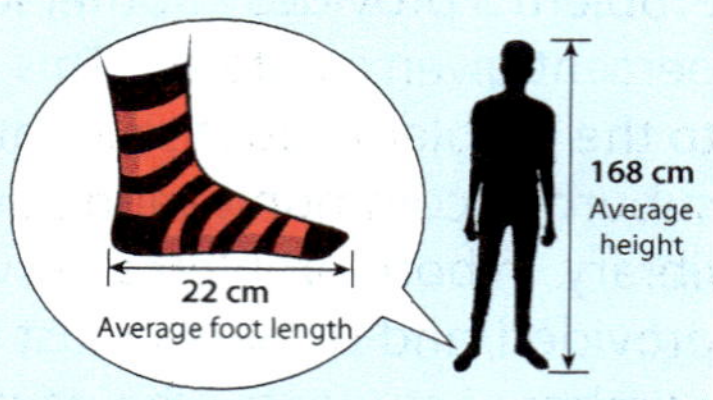

➤ **Read and try to solve the problem below.**

The scatter plot shows the heights and foot lengths of 30 male students at a middle school. Their average foot length is 22 cm. Their average height is 168 cm.

What percent of the students with above-average height have at- or below-average foot length?

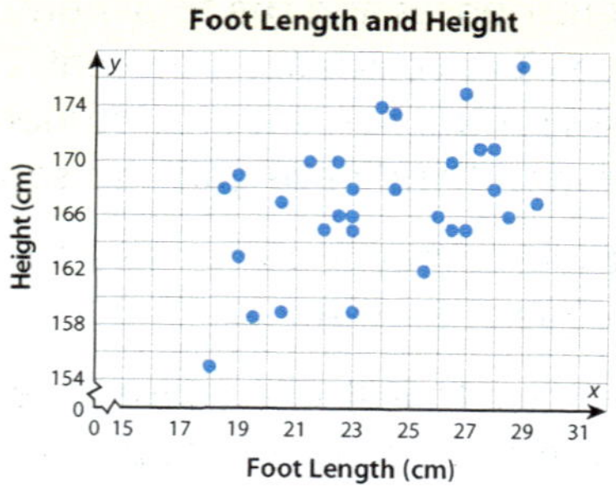

TRY IT Possible work:

SAMPLE A

10 students have height greater than 168 cm. Of these 10, 2 have foot lengths less than or equal to 22 cm. $\frac{2}{10} \cdot 100\% = 20\%$

So, 20% of students with above-average height have at- or below-average foot length.

SAMPLE B

I drew a vertical line at $x = 22$ and a horizontal line at $y = 168$ on the graph to make it easier to count points. There are 10 points above the 168 cm height line. Two of them are to the left of the 22 cm foot length line. $\frac{2}{10} \cdot 100\% = 20\%$.

20% of students with height greater than 168 cm have a foot length less than or equal to 22 cm.

DISCUSS IT

Ask: How did you determine the percentage from the scatter plot?

Share: I determined the percentage by . . .

DISCUSS IT SMP 2, 3, 5, 6

Support Partner Discussion

After students work on Try It, encourage them to respond to Discuss It with a partner. If students need support in getting started, prompt them to ask each other questions such as:

- *Which points on the scatter plot represent students with above-average height?*
- *Which points represent students with foot length at or below average?*
- *Which points show students in both categories?*

Common Misconception Look for students who think the whole is the total number of students (data points), rather than the number of students who are taller than 168 cm. As students share their strategies, remind them of their previous work with calculating percent. Ensure they understand that the word(s) following *of* generally represent the *whole* that should be placed in the denominator.

Select and Sequence Student Strategies

Select 2–3 samples that represent the range of student thinking in your classroom. Here is one possible order for class discussion:

- data points counted to find part and whole used to calculate percent
- (misconception) total number of students incorrectly used as whole in calculating percent
- lines drawn through average values to help count part and whole used to calculate percent
- two-way table with frequencies to find part and whole used to calculate percent

Facilitate Whole Class Discussion

Call on students to share selected strategies. Reinforce with students that clear explanations use complete sentences and precise vocabulary.

Guide students to **Compare and Connect** the representations. Prompt students to check their understanding by trying to rephrase the speaker's ideas and ask questions if they are unclear.

ASK *What similarities do the strategies share?*

LISTEN FOR A part (number of students with at- or below-average foot length and above-average height) and a whole (students with above-average height) are found before the percent is calculated.

Model It

If students presented these models, have students connect these models to those presented in class.

If no student presented at least one of these models, have students first analyze key features of the models, and then connect them to the models presented in class.

ASK *How do the tables in the Model Its differ?*

LISTEN FOR The two-way table in the first Model It shows frequencies, and the two-way table in the second Model It shows relative frequencies.

For the two-way table with frequencies, prompt students to make the connection between the scatter plot and the data values in the table. Ask: *The point (22, 165) is plotted in the scatter plot. Where is this data value reflected in the table?*

For the two-way table with relative frequencies, prompt students to understand that the whole used in the percent calculation is a row total.

- *What do the row totals represent?*
- *What do the column totals represent?*

LESSON 32 | SESSION 2

➤ **Explore different ways to understand constructing two-way tables with relative frequencies.**

The scatter plot shows the heights and foot lengths of 30 male students at a middle school. Their average foot length is 22 cm. Their average height is 168 cm.

What percent of the students with above-average height have at- or below-average foot length?

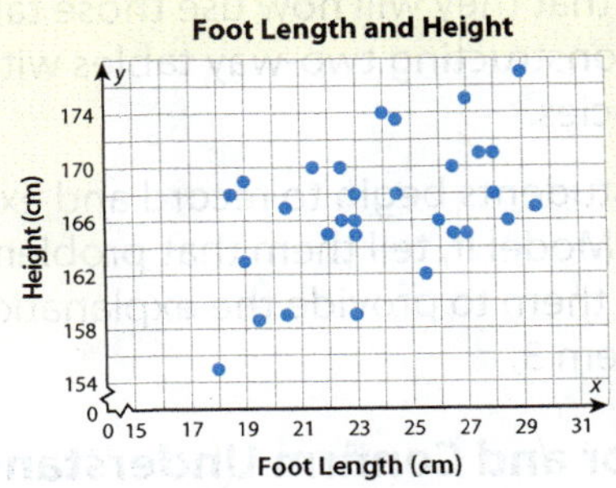

Model It

You can start by making a two-way table with frequencies.

	Foot Length ≤ 22 cm	Foot Length > 22 cm	Total
Height ≤ 168 cm	7	13	20
Height > 168 cm	2	8	10
Total	9	21	30

Model It

You can then make a two-way table with relative frequencies using row totals.

The rows represent the categories for height. The question is asking about a percentage of students in one of the height categories. The row totals are height totals and are the *wholes* in your relative frequencies.

	Foot Length ≤ 22 cm	Foot Length > 22 cm	Total
Height ≤ 168 cm	$\frac{7}{20} = 0.35 = 35\%$	$\frac{13}{20} = 0.65 = 65\%$	$\frac{20}{20} = 1.00 = 100\%$
Height > 168 cm	$\frac{2}{10} = 0.20 = 20\%$	$\frac{8}{10} = 0.80 = 80\%$	$\frac{10}{10} = 1.00 = 100\%$
Total	$\frac{9}{30} = 0.30 = 30\%$	$\frac{21}{30} = 0.70 = 70\%$	

764

DIFFERENTIATION | EXTEND

SMP 7

Deepen Understanding

Comparing Tables with Frequencies and Relative Frequencies

Prompt students to consider the different information each table provides. Ask them to imagine that the table with relative frequencies shows percents without calculations.

ASK *How are the two tables different?*

LISTEN FOR The table of frequencies shows the number of students in each category. The table of relative frequencies shows the percent of students in each category.

ASK *There are 7 shorter people who have foot lengths at or below average compared to 2 taller people. Why is the difference in percent only 15%?*

LISTEN FOR The table with relative frequencies compares data for the height categories even though the number of taller people is much less than the number of shorter people. There are more short people compared to tall people.

ASK *Can the table with relative frequencies be used to make the table with frequencies?*

LISTEN FOR No. The table with relative frequencies does not give the total number of students or the total in each height category, so you could not find the number in each category.

Develop Constructing Two-Way Tables with Relative Frequencies

CONNECT IT

SMP 2, 4, 5, 6

Remind students that each table represents the same bivariate set of data from the scatter plot. Explain that they will now use those tables to reason about constructing two-way tables with relative frequencies.

Before students begin to record and expand on their work in Model It, tell them that problem 2 will prepare them to provide the explanation asked for in problem 3.

Monitor and Confirm Understanding 1

The percent of students with above-average height who have foot length at or below average is 20%. This can be found by dividing 2, the number of students with above-average height and below-average foot length, by 10, the number of students with above-average height. This percent can be found at the intersection of the second row and first column of the two-way table with relative frequencies.

Facilitate Whole Class Discussion

2 Look for understanding that the *parts* used to calculate the percents are the same for both the table with row totals and the table with column totals. The *wholes*, however, change from row (height) totals to column (foot length) totals.

ASK *Why should your question in problem 2c be about the percent of students in one of the foot-length categories?*

LISTEN FOR The table uses the column totals, which are the foot-length categories. So, the center cells show the percent of students in each foot-length category that have above- or below-average height.

3 Look for understanding that the *whole* amount determines how the relative frequencies in a two-way table should be calculated.

ASK *How do you know what the whole amount is in a problem?*

LISTEN FOR You need to carefully consider the wording of the question. Look for which category follows the word *of* in the question.

4 **Reflect** Have all students focus on the strategies used to solve the Try It. If time allows, have students discuss their ideas with a partner.

CONNECT IT

➤ **Use the problem from the previous page to help you understand how to construct two-way tables with relative frequencies.**

1 Look at the second **Model It**. What percent of the students with above-average height have at- or below-average foot length? Explain.

20%; Possible explanation: In the table, of the 10 total students with above-average height, 2 also have at- or below-average foot length.

2 **a.** Complete the two-way table with relative frequencies using column totals.

	Foot Length ≤ 22 cm	Foot Length > 22 cm	Total
Height ≤ 168 cm	$\frac{7}{9} \approx 0.78 = 78\%$	$\frac{13}{21} \approx 0.62 = 62\%$	$\frac{20}{30} \approx 0.67 = 67\%$
Height > 168 cm	$\frac{2}{9} \approx 0.22 = 22\%$	$\frac{8}{21} \approx 0.38 = 38\%$	$\frac{10}{30} \approx 0.33 = 33\%$
Total	$\frac{9}{9} = 1.00 = 100\%$	$\frac{21}{21} = 1.00 = 100\%$	

b. The column totals are the *wholes* in your relative frequencies. What do the column totals represent? the categories for foot length

c. Write and answer a question that can be answered using the table you completed in problem 2a.

Possible answer: What percent of the students with above-average foot length have above-average height? About 38%

3 You can calculate relative frequencies using row totals, column totals, or the entire table total. What determines which method you should use?

The *whole* amount in the question.

4 **Reflect** Think about all the models and strategies you have discussed today. Describe how one of them helped you better understand how to solve the **Try It** problem.

Answers may vary. Check student responses.

765

DIFFERENTIATION | RETEACH or REINFORCE

Visual Model

Model making a two-way table with relative frequencies.

If students are unsure about how to use a two-way table with frequencies to make a two-way table with relative frequencies, then use this activity to guide them through the process.

- Display the table with frequencies from the Session 1 Look Ahead.
- Display a second table with the same row and column headings, but with blank cells in the interior of the table. This will be used to make a table with relative frequencies using the information from the table with frequencies displayed.
- Ask: *Which whole should be used to answer the question: What percent of 8th graders prefer reading?* [row totals]
- For each entry in the table, have students decide what numbers from the table with frequencies to use in the calculation. Then have them calculate the corresponding relative frequency.
- Have students tell what each relative frequency in the table represents in context.
- If time permits, ask students to come up with a question that could be answered using column totals. Then complete the table using column totals.

Apply It

For all problems, encourage students to use the tables to support their thinking. Allow some leeway with precision when rounding with percents.

5 See ***Connect to Culture*** to support student engagement. Students should recognize that since the audiobook company is the driving force behind this study, the relative frequencies should be *column* totals, since *Audiobook* is one of the column headers.

6 Students should understand that in this problem, the focus consists of people 30 and older. Since the categories that refer to the ages of people are row labels, the relative frequencies for this problem should be *row* totals.

Apply It

➤ **Use what you learned to solve these problems.**

5 One hundred adults are asked whether they prefer listening to podcasts or audiobooks. The table shows the results. An audiobook company needs to know what age group to target in advertising. What method should the company use to calculate relative frequencies? Explain.

	Podcast	Audiobook	Total
Younger than 30	39	12	51
30 and Older	22	27	49
Total	61	39	100

They should calculate using column totals. The question is about audiobook listeners, which is a column category.

6 A company specializes in online content for people 30 and older. Should they use the same relative frequencies used by the company in problem 5? Explain.

No; Possible explanation: Since the company is concerned with the ages of customers, they should use relative frequencies calculated by row totals.

7 Amata counts the number of jumping jacks each of 25 high school students do in one minute. Her data are shown in the table. What percent of high school students younger than 17 did more than 50 jumping jacks in a minute? Show your work.

	Younger than 17	17 and Older	Total
≤ 50 Jumping Jacks	11	7	18
> 50 Jumping Jacks	3	4	7
Total	14	11	25

Possible work:

There are 14 high school students younger than 17. Three did more than 50 jumping jacks in one minute.

$\frac{3}{14} \approx 0.21 = 21\%$

SOLUTION About 21%

CLOSE EXIT TICKET

7 Students' solutions should show an understanding that:

- the problem represents a column-totals situation because it asks about the percent of students *younger than 17*, which is a column head.
- the number in the cell where the *Younger than 17* column and the *> 50 Jumping Jacks* row intersect, 3, is the *part* in the relative-frequency calculation.
- the total of the *Younger than 17* column, 14, is the *whole* in the relative-frequency calculation.

Error Alert If students use the total number of students, 25, as the whole when calculating the relative frequency, then remind them that this problem is focused on the group of students who are younger than 17. These students are represented by the first column, for which the total is 14.

Practice Constructing Two-Way Tables with Relative Frequencies

Problem Notes

Assign **Practice Constructing Two-Way Tables with Relative Frequencies** as extra practice in class or as homework.

1 Students may also write:

- What percent of patients who wear helmets are 10 and older? [about 61%]
- What percent of patients who do not wear helmets are younger than 10? [about 18%]
- What percent of patients who do not wear helmets are 10 and older? [about 82%]

Students should understand that the *of* group in their question has to be one of the two rows, since this is a row-totals table. ***Medium***

 Name:

Practice Constructing Two-Way Tables with Relative Frequencies

➤ **Study the Example showing how to construct a two-way table with relative frequencies. Then solve problems 1–3.**

Example

A doctor collects the data below on 50 patients involved in bicycle accidents. Which age group may need a stronger reminder to wear helmets?

	Younger than 10	10 and Older	Total
Helmet	13	20	33
No Helmet	3	14	17
Total	16	34	50

Calculate relative frequencies using column totals.

	Younger than 10	10 and Older	Total
Helmet	$\frac{13}{16} \approx 0.81 = 81\%$	$\frac{20}{34} \approx 0.59 = 59\%$	$\frac{33}{50} \approx 0.66 = 66\%$
No Helmet	$\frac{3}{16} \approx 0.19 = 19\%$	$\frac{14}{34} \approx 0.41 = 41\%$	$\frac{17}{50} = 0.34 = 34\%$
Total	$\frac{16}{16} = 1.00 = 100\%$	$\frac{34}{34} = 1.00 = 100\%$	

patients ages 10 and older; About 41% of patients 10 and older did not wear a helmet compared to 19% of patients younger than 10.

1 The relative frequencies in the table below are calculated by row using the Example data. Write and answer a question that can be answered using this table.

	Younger than 10	10 and Older	Total
Helmet	0.39	0.61	1.00
No Helmet	0.18	0.82	1.00
Total	0.32	0.68	

Possible answer: What percent of patients who wear helmets are younger than 10? About 39%

Vocabulary
relative frequency
the quotient that compares the number of times a data value occurs and the total number of data values.

Fluency & Skills Practice

Constructing Two-Way Tables with Relative Frequencies

In this activity, students complete two-way tables with relative frequencies based on the data given in two-way tables with frequencies.

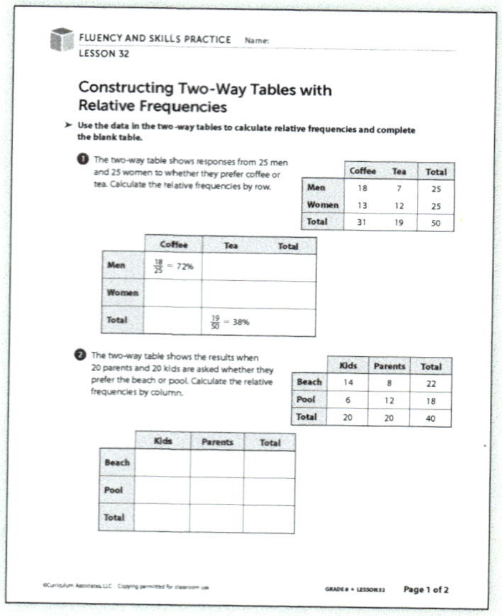
FLUENCY AND SKILLS PRACTICE Name:
LESSON 32

Constructing Two-Way Tables with Relative Frequencies

➤ **Use the data in the two-way tables to calculate relative frequencies and complete the blank table.**

1 The two-way table shows responses from 25 men and 25 women to whether they prefer coffee or tea. Calculate the relative frequencies by row.

	Coffee	Tea	Total
Men	18	7	25
Women	13	12	25
Total	31	19	50

	Coffee	Tea	Total
Men	$\frac{18}{25} = 72\%$		
Women			
Total		$\frac{19}{50} = 38\%$	

2 The two-way table shows the results when 20 parents and 20 kids are asked whether they prefer the beach or pool. Calculate the relative frequencies by column.

	Kids	Parents	Total
Beach	14	8	22
Pool	6	12	18
Total	20	20	40

	Kids	Parents	Total
Beach			
Pool			
Total			

©Curriculum Associates, LLC Copying permitted for classroom use. GRADE 8 • LESSON 32 Page 1 of 2

2 Students should recognize the percent of Grade 6 students who prefer to watch basketball is being compared to the percent of Grade 7 students who prefer to watch basketball. Because the rows represent grade levels, the calculations should be based on row totals. ***Challenge***

3 **a.** If students calculate the relative frequencies by rows, then they should know to use 41 and 140 as the denominators. If students calculate the relative frequencies by columns, then they should know to use 87 and 94 as their denominators. ***Medium***

b. If students use row totals, then the question should be of the form *What percent of students who do/do not plan to go to college do/do not play a musical instrument?*

If students use column totals, then the question should be of the form *What percent of students who do/do not play a musical instrument do/do not plan to go to college?* ***Medium***

LESSON 32 | SESSION 2

2 Hiroaki asked students whether they prefer to watch football, basketball, or soccer. The table shows the results. Hiroaki thinks that basketball is more popular for seventh graders than for sixth graders. To show this, he makes a table with relative frequencies calculated using column totals. Do you agree with Hiroaki? Explain.

	Football	Basketball	Soccer	Total
Grade 6	44	35	13	92
Grade 7	37	41	18	96
Grade 8	32	48	15	95
Total	113	124	46	283

No; Possible explanation: The number of students in each grade is represented by the row totals. So, to find the percentage of students in Grades 6 and 7 who prefer watching basketball, the relative frequencies should be calculated by row totals.

3 High school seniors are asked two questions. Do you plan to go to college? Do you play a musical instrument? The table shows the data.

	No Instrument	Instrument	Total
No College	24	17	41
College	63	77	140
Total	87	94	181

a. Complete the two-way table with relative frequencies, either by row or by column. Round to hundredths.

Possible table:

	No Instrument	Instrument	Total
No College	$\frac{24}{41} \approx 0.59$	$\frac{17}{41} \approx 0.41$	$\frac{41}{41} = 1.00$
College	$\frac{63}{140} = 0.45$	$\frac{77}{140} = 0.55$	$\frac{140}{140} = 1.00$
Total	$\frac{87}{181} \approx 0.48$	$\frac{94}{181} \approx 0.52$	

b. Write and answer a question that can be answered by your table.

Possible answer: What percent of students who do not plan to go to college play a musical instrument? Approximately 41%

768

DIFFERENTIATION | ENGLISH LANGUAGE LEARNERS

Use with Session 3 **Connect It**

Levels 1–3: Reading/Speaking

Help students understand and respond to Connect It problem 4. Read the problem and create a **Co-Constructed Word Bank** with definitions for *interpret, associations, categorical*, and *data*. Help students use the meanings to talk about the problem. Ask: *What do you need to interpret? What associations do you look for?*

- *I need to interpret* _____.
- *I have to look for associations between* _____.

Use a two-way table to discuss responses that are nearly evenly divided compared to responses that vary. Then have students turn to partners to share their responses before writing.

Levels 2–4: Reading/Speaking

Help students to understand and respond to Connect It problem 4. Read the problem with students. Create a **Co-Constructed Word Bank** with definitions for *interpret, associations, categorical*, and *data*. Have students use the meanings to say the problem another way. Ask: *What do you need to interpret? What associations do you look for?*

- *I have to* _____.
- *I have to look for* _____.

Use a two-way table to discuss responses that are nearly evenly divided compared to responses that vary. Have students write their responses and share with a partner to get feedback and revise accordingly.

Levels 3–5: Reading/Speaking

Help students to understand and respond to Connect It problem 4. Have students read the problem and discuss definitions for *interpret, associations, categorical*, and *data*. Then have students reread the problem and **Say It Another Way**.

Use a two-way table to have students discuss responses that are nearly evenly divided compared to responses that vary. Call on volunteers to explain *nearly* and *evenly*.

Have students respond to the problem and exchange answers with a partner. Encourage them to review and explain whether and how they used *nearly* and *evenly* in their answers.

Develop Interpreting and Analyzing Two-Way Tables

Purpose

- **Develop** strategies for interpreting and analyzing table with relative frequencies.
- **Recognize** that tables with relative frequencies can be used to describe possible associations in a set of data.

START CONNECT TO PRIOR KNOWLEDGE

Always, Sometimes, Never

	Grade 11	Grade 12
Job	11	29
No Job	22	15

A 40% of the students surveyed have a job.

B A third of students in a grade have a job.

C Use row totals to find the percent of students with a job that are in Grade 12.

Solutions

A is never true.

B is sometimes true.

C is always true.

WHY? Support students' ability to calculate appropriate relative frequencies using row, column, or overall totals when answering questions about a table with frequencies.

DEVELOP ACADEMIC LANGUAGE

WHY? Reinforce understanding and correct use of *either, or,* and *neither.*

HOW? Write the words on the board. Use objects and gestures as you say: *I will have **either** water **or** milk. I like **either of** the two drinks. I will not have water **or** milk. I like **neither** water **nor** milk.* Point out how the words are used in affirmative and negative statements. Read Connect It problem 3. Have students use *or* instead of *either of* to paraphrase the first sentence.

TRY IT SMP 1, 2, 4, 5, 6

Make Sense of the Problem

See ***Connect to Culture*** to support student engagement. Before students work on Try It, use **Three Reads** to help them make sense of the problem. After the first read, ask: *What is the problem about?* After the second read, ask: *What are you trying to find out?* And after the third read, ask: *What are the important quantities and relationships in the problem?* Use turn and talk to help students think through their responses.

LESSON 32 | SESSION 3

Develop Interpreting and Analyzing Two-Way Tables

➤ **Read and try to solve the problem below.**

Twenty middle school students are asked whether they own cell phones. The table shows their responses and grade levels. Which grade has the highest percentage of students who own cell phones?

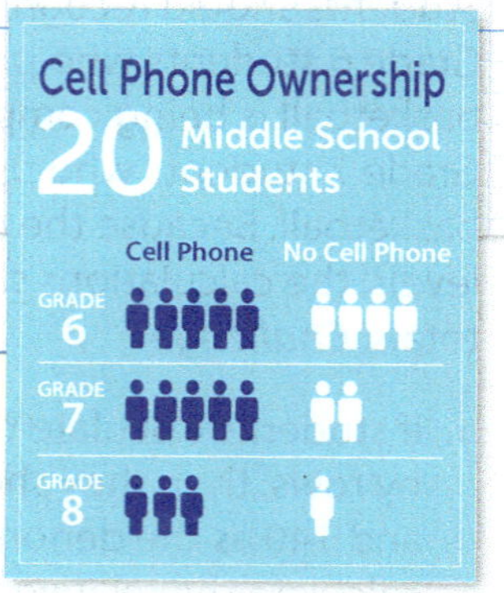

TRY IT

Possible work:

SAMPLE A

Grade 6: $\frac{5}{9} \approx 0.56 \approx 56\%$

Grade 7: $\frac{5}{7} \approx 0.71 \approx 71\%$

Grade 8: $\frac{3}{4} = 0.75 = 75\%$ Grade 8

SAMPLE B

	Phone	No Phone	Total
Grade 6	5	4	9
Grade 7	5	2	7
Grade 8	3	1	4
Total	13	7	20

Grade 6: $\frac{5}{9} \times 100\% \approx 56\%$

Grade 7: $\frac{5}{7} \times 100\% \approx 71\%$

Grade 8: $\frac{3}{4} \times 100\% = 75\%$

Grade 8 has the highest percentage.

DISCUSS IT

Ask: How is your strategy similar to mine? How is it different?

Share: My strategy shows . . .

769

DISCUSS IT SMP 2, 3, 6

Support Partner Discussion

After students work on Try It, encourage them to respond to Discuss It with a partner. If students need support in getting started, prompt them to ask each other questions such as:

- *How did you determine the whole for each calculation?*
- *Do you have to make a table to answer this question?*
- *How did you perform your calculations?*

Common Misconception Listen for students who calculate their frequencies based on cell phone totals instead of grade-level totals. As students share their strategies, ensure they discuss that the intent of the question is to calculate which grade has the highest percent of students who own cell phones. So, to find the percent for a specific grade level, they should divide number of students with cell phones by the number of students in that grade level.

Select and Sequence Student Strategies

Select 2–3 samples that represent the range of student thinking in your classroom. Here is one possible order for class discussion:

- percent computed directly from the image data
- (misconception) percent calculated using column totals as the whole
- two-way table with frequencies made and used to find percent
- two-way table with relative frequencies calculated using row totals made to find percent

Facilitate Whole Class Discussion

Call on students to share selected strategies. Prompt students to build on ideas they agree with by adding details to help classmates understand more about the strategy or solution.

Guide students to **Compare and Connect** the representations. To prompt students to use precise academic language, call on volunteers to reword vague or unclear statements.

ASK *What did [student name] and [student name] use to figure out the percents?*

LISTEN FOR [Student name] used the image to determine what fraction should be used to calculate each grade's percent. [Student name] made a table with frequencies to organize the data to determine what fraction should be used to calculate each grade's percent.

Model It & Analyze It

If students presented these models, have students connect these models to those presented in class.

If no student presented at least one of these models, have students first analyze key features of the models, and then connect them to the models presented in class.

ASK *How are Model It and Analyze It related?*

LISTEN FOR Analyze It uses the relative frequencies in the Model It table to compare the data for each grade.

For the two-way table with relative frequencies, prompt students to think about how the table was built.

- *What do the rows and columns represent?*
- *Why were row totals used to calculate the relative frequencies?*

For the comparison of relative frequencies, prompt students to focus on the percent.

- *What do the percents mean in this context?*
- *Why is the total percent greater than 100%?*

➤ **Explore different ways to understand interpreting and analyzing two-way tables.**

Twenty middle school students are asked whether they own cell phones. The table shows their responses and grade levels. Which grade has the highest percent of students who own cell phones?

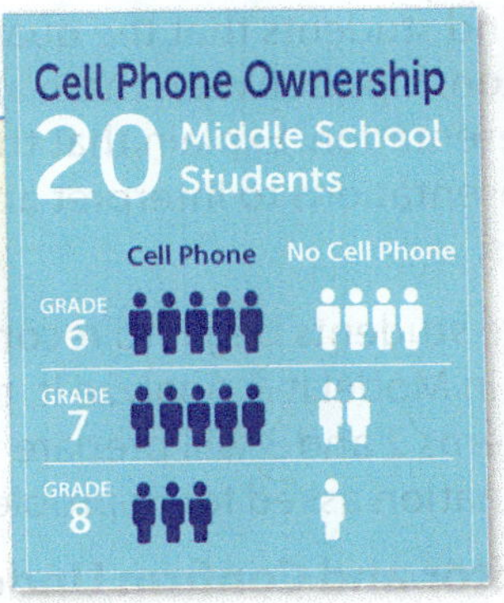

Model It

You can make a two-way table with relative frequencies calculated using row totals.

	Cell Phone	No Cell Phone	Total
Grade 6	$\frac{5}{9} \approx 0.56$	$\frac{4}{9} \approx 0.44$	$\frac{9}{9} = 1.00$
Grade 7	$\frac{5}{7} \approx 0.71$	$\frac{2}{7} \approx 0.29$	$\frac{7}{7} = 1.00$
Grade 8	$\frac{3}{4} = 0.75$	$\frac{1}{4} = 0.25$	$\frac{4}{4} = 1.00$
Total	$\frac{13}{20} = 0.65$	$\frac{7}{20} = 0.35$	

Analyze It

You can analyze the relative frequencies in the table.

Look at the *Cell Phone* column. Compare the decimals for each grade.

Grade 6: 0.56 = 56%

Grade 7: 0.71 = 71%

Grade 8: 0.75 = 75%

DIFFERENTIATION | EXTEND

SMP 1

Deepen Understanding

Making Sense of Information in a Two-Way Table with Frequencies

Prompt students to think about the comparison shown in the Model It table.

ASK *This table uses row totals. What comparisons can you make using this table?*

LISTEN FOR Because row totals show the number of students in each grade, you can compare the percent of students within each grade who do or do not own cell phones.

ASK *If the table calculations used column totals, what comparisons could you make?*

LISTEN FOR Because column totals show the total numbers of students who own or do not own cell phones, you could compare the percent of cell phone owners who are in each grade or the percent of non-cell phone owners who are in each grade.

ASK *If the table just showed the decimals, and not fractions, how could you determine whether row totals or column totals were used?*

LISTEN FOR When row totals are used, the row relative frequencies sum to 1.00, or 100%. When column totals are used, the column relative frequencies sum to 1.00, or 100%.

Develop Interpreting and Analyzing Two-Way Tables

CONNECT IT

SMP 2, 4, 5, 6

Remind students that the quantities and the relationships between them are the same in each representation. Explain that they will now use those representations to interpret and analyze two-way tables.

Before students begin to record and expand on their work in Model It & Analyze It, tell them that problems 2 and 3 will prepare them to provide the explanation asked for in problem 4.

Monitor and Confirm Understanding 1 – 2

- Grade 8 had the greatest percent of students with cell phones.
- Each row represents a grade. Since percents per grade are being compared, row totals should be used to calculate the relative frequencies.

Facilitate Whole Class Discussion

3 Look for understanding that relative frequencies can be used to compare parts of different wholes.

ASK *Which grade had the greatest number of students with cell phones? Which grade had the greatest percent of students with cell phones? Why are these answers different?*

LISTEN FOR Grades 6 and 7 both had the greatest number, 5. Grade 8 had the greatest percent, 75%. The answers are different because the total is different for each grade. Even though Grade 8 had the smallest number of students with cell phones, that number is compared to the smallest total to find the relative frequency. For Grade 8, the greatest part of the total has cell phones.

4 Look for the idea that two-way tables can be used to find associations in categorical data, just as scatter plots are used to find associations in measurement data.

ASK *When is a two-way table with frequencies sufficient for interpreting associations, and when is it better to use a two-way table with relative frequencies?*

LISTEN FOR If the totals for the categories you are comparing are close, a two-way table with frequencies can be used. If the totals are very different, then it is better to use a two-way table with relative frequencies.

5 **Reflect** Have all students focus on the strategies used to solve the Try It. If time allows, have students discuss their ideas with a partner.

CONNECT IT

➤ **Use the problem from the previous page to help you understand how to interpret and analyze two-way tables.**

1 Look at **Analyze It**. Which grade has the highest percent of students who own cell phones? How do you know?

Grade 8; 75% of eighth graders own cell phones. Only 56% of sixth graders and 71% of seventh graders own cell phones.

2 Look at the table in **Model It**. Why are the relative frequencies calculated by row?

Responses per grade are given in the rows. So, to compare relative frequencies based on grade, the relative frequencies should be calculated by row.

3 The tallies in the original table show that fewer students in Grade 8 have cell phones than in either of the other two grades. Why do you use relative frequencies to make a comparison?

Possible answer: A comparison of frequencies is misleading because each grade has a different number of students. Relative frequencies are quotients and can be used to compare parts of different wholes.

4 How can you find and interpret associations in categorical data using a two-way table?

Possible answer: When the number of responses is nearly evenly divided within categories, I can use frequencies to look for associations in the data. When the number of responses vary, I can use relative frequencies.

5 **Reflect** Think about all the models and strategies you have discussed today. Describe how one of them helped you better understand how to interpret and analyze two-way tables.

Answers may vary. Check student responses.

771

DIFFERENTIATION | RETEACH or REINFORCE

Visual Model

Construct and analyze a two-way table with frequencies.

If students are unsure about analyzing categorical data, then use this visual model to help reinforce the concept and solidify their understanding.

- Display a blank two-way table with column headings *Pets*, *No Pets*, and row headings *Pet Allergies*, *No Pet Allergies*.
- Ask students if they have pets, and if they have pet allergies. Using a show of hands, complete the table.
- Pose the following question to students: *How should a table with relative frequencies be made to answer the question: Are people with pet allergies more or less likely to have pets than people without allergies?* [Use row totals to make the table.]
- Construct the table with relative frequencies using student input.
- Ask: *Are people with pet allergies more or less likely to have pets than people without allergies?* [Answers will vary based on original data.]
- Have students brainstorm additional questions that could be answered with the data in the table with relative frequencies.

Apply It

For all problems, encourage students to use data to support their thinking.

6 **a.** Students may reason that because the decision the manager is considering is based on guacamole, the relative frequencies are based on row totals. Then they should compare guacamole vs. no guacamole for each taco type.

b. Students should demonstrate understanding that the relative frequencies being compared to answer this question are based on the total number of tacos ordered.

LESSON 32 | SESSION 3

Apply It

➤ **Use what you learned to solve these problems.**

6 A restaurant manager collects data from 350 diners who order tacos. She records the type of taco each diner orders. She also notes whether diners add guacamole to their tacos. The table shows her data.

	Steak Taco	Chicken Taco	Total
Guacamole	$\frac{92}{179} \approx 51.4\%$	$\frac{87}{179} \approx 48.6\%$	$\frac{179}{179} = 100\%$
No Guacamole	$\frac{86}{171} \approx 50.3\%$	$\frac{85}{171} \approx 49.7\%$	$\frac{171}{171} = 100\%$
Total	$\frac{178}{350} \approx 50.9\%$	$\frac{172}{350} \approx 49.1\%$	

a. The manager is considering adding guacamole to all tacos. Do you think this is a good plan? Explain your reasoning.

Possible answer: No; only about half of the customers who ordered each kind of taco added guacamole.

b. Did the diners prefer steak tacos or chicken tacos overall? Explain.

The diners preferred steak tacos by a slight percentage. The total percent of diners who preferred steak tacos was about 50.9%, while the total percent of diners who preferred chicken tacos was about 49.1%.

7 Tamera asks 500 people in her town if they recycle. The table shows her data. Of those who recycle, which age group tends to recycle the least? Show your work.

	30 and Younger	31–50	Older than 50	Total
Recycle	176	168	57	401
Do Not Recycle	13	38	48	99
Total	189	206	105	500

Possible work: Relative column frequencies for recycles:

≤ 30: $\frac{176}{189} \approx 0.931 \approx 93.1\%$; 31–50: $\frac{168}{206} \approx 0.816 \approx 81.6\%$;

> 50: $\frac{57}{105} \approx 0.543 \approx 54.3\%$

SOLUTION People older than 50 recycle the least.

772

CLOSE EXIT TICKET

7 Students' solutions should show an understanding that:

- responses of different age groups are being compared. Since age groups are column heads, the relative frequency calculations will be based on column totals.
- if the percent of each age group that recycles is calculated, then the group with the least percent is the answer; if the percent of each age group that does not recycle is calculated, then the group with the greatest percent is the answer.

Error Alert If students perform their calculations based on row totals, then have them discuss with a partner that the focus is on comparing the actions among the different age groups.

Practice Interpreting and Analyzing Two-Way Tables

Problem Notes

Assign **Practice Interpreting and Analyzing Two-Way Tables** as extra practice in class or as homework.

1. **a.** The table in the Example reveals that the *35 and Older* age group has a greater percent of people who still have cable TV. ***Basic***

   b. ***Basic***

Practice Interpreting and Analyzing Two-Way Tables

➤ **Study the Example showing how to interpret and analyze a two-way table. Then solve problems 1–3.**

Example

A random sample of adults is asked whether they have cable TV. The table shows the responses. Explain how to use the table to determine if there is an association between age and having cable TV.

	Cable TV	No Cable TV	Total
Younger than 35	66	247	313
35 and Older	59	72	131
Total	125	319	444

You can make a two-way table with relative frequencies calculated by rows to determine if there is an association.

	Cable TV	No Cable TV	Total
Younger than 35	$\frac{66}{313} \approx 0.21$	$\frac{247}{313} \approx 0.79$	$\frac{313}{313} = 1.00$
35 and Older	$\frac{59}{131} \approx 0.45$	$\frac{72}{131} \approx 0.55$	$\frac{131}{131} = 1.00$
Total	$\frac{125}{444} \approx 0.28$	$\frac{319}{444} \approx 0.72$	

1. Use the data from the tables in the Example.

   a. A video subscription service is running a *cut the cord* campaign to get people to give up cable. What age group should they target? Explain.

   They should target people 35 and older. About 45% of people in that age group still have cable, while only about 21% of people younger than 35 do.

   b. Which age group has the higher percentage of people with no cable TV? Explain.

   Younger than 35; About 79% of those younger than 35 have no cable TV.

Fluency & Skills Practice

Interpreting and Analyzing Two-Way Tables

In this activity, students analyze data in two-way tables and calculate relatve frequencies to solve problems about the data.

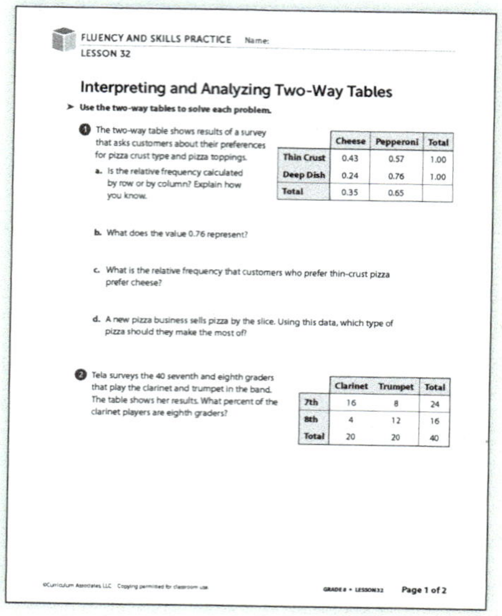
FLUENCY AND SKILLS PRACTICE   Name:
LESSON 32

Interpreting and Analyzing Two-Way Tables

➤ **Use the two-way tables to solve each problem.**

1. The two-way table shows results of a survey that asks customers about their preferences for pizza crust type and pizza toppings.

	Cheese	Pepperoni	Total
Thin Crust	0.43	0.57	1.00
Deep Dish	0.24	0.76	1.00
Total	0.35	0.65	

   a. Is the relative frequency calculated by row or by column? Explain how you know.

   b. What does the value 0.76 represent?

   c. What is the relative frequency that customers who prefer thin-crust pizza prefer cheese?

   d. A new pizza business sells pizza by the slice. Using this data, which type of pizza should they make the most of?

2. Tela surveys the 40 seventh and eighth graders that play the clarinet and trumpet in the band. The table shows her results. What percent of the clarinet players are eighth graders?

	Clarinet	Trumpet	Total
7th	16	8	24
8th	4	12	16
Total	20	20	40

Additional Practice

2 Students need to add the number of *45 and Older* customers who received a paper-only receipt and the number of *45 and Older* customers who received both types of receipt. Then they need to divide that sum by the total number of people who received a paper-only receipt or both types of receipt. ***Challenge***

3 **a.** Students should realize Nathan is only correct if you look at the counts, or frequencies, shown in the table. ***Medium***

b. If they compute relative frequencies using row totals, students will see that only $\frac{15}{55}$, or 27%, of beginners prefer performing the Heelflip trick, compared to 60% of veterans. ***Medium***

2 A store recorded whether 100 customers requested paper receipts, email receipts, or both. What percent of people who received paper receipts were 45 and older? Explain.

	Paper Only	Email Only	Both	Total
Younger than 45	10	25	5	40
45 and Older	40	5	15	60
Total	50	30	20	100

approximately 79%; People who requested both kinds of receipt also received a paper receipt, so the total receiving paper receipts was 70. Of these, 55 were 45 or older. $\frac{55}{70} \approx 78.6\%$

3 The table shows the results of a survey of skateboarders at a skate park. Nathan thinks that more beginner skateboarders than veteran skateboarders prefer doing a Heelflip trick.

	Prefer Ollie Trick	Prefer Heelflip Trick	Total
Beginner	40	15	55
Veteran	6	9	15
Total	46	24	70

a. Explain how Nathan can be correct.
Possible explanation: Nathan is correct if you just look at frequencies. Of those who prefer doing a Heelflip trick, 15 are beginner and 9 are veteran.

b. Explain how Nathan can be incorrect.
Possible explanation: When relative frequencies are calculated by row, only about 27% of beginners prefer doing a Heelflip trick, but 60% of veterans do.

Heelflip Trick

DIFFERENTIATION | ENGLISH LANGUAGE LEARNERS

Use with **Session 4** **Apply It**

Levels 1–3: Listening/Speaking

Prepare students to discuss the table in Apply It problem 6a. Write the words *athlete* and *nonathlete* in a T-chart. Share the Spanish cognate *atleta*. Invite students to share other cognates. Say: *Athletes are good at sports or exercises. They usually compete.* Call on volunteers to give examples of athletes and write them in the chart. Next, underline and explain *non* in *nonathletes*. Ask for examples. Read the problem and ask: *How many students are there? How many students are athletes? What do they say about lunch?* Repeat with similar questions for nonathletes. Then help students talk about the rows and columns and complete the table.

Levels 2–4: Listening/Speaking

Prepare students to discuss the table in Apply It problem 6a. Write the words *athlete* and *nonathlete* in a T-chart. Invite students to share cognates. Ask students to share what they know about athletes and call on volunteers to give examples of athletes and write them in the chart. Next, underline *non* and call on volunteers to explain *nonathletes* and provide examples.

Read the problem with students and ask: *How many students are there? What types of students are surveyed? What do they say about lunch?* Have students turn to partners to discuss. Then have them talk about the rows and columns and complete the table.

Levels 3–5: Listening/Speaking

Prepare students to discuss the table in Apply It problem 6a. Write the words *athlete* and *nonathlete* in a T-chart. Invite students to share cognates and examples. Call on volunteers to explain the difference between athletes and nonathletes.

Have students read the problem and use *athletes* and *nonathletes* to explain how the text connects to the rows and columns in the table. Allow time for students to complete the table. Then have them turn to partners to compare and discuss their work.

Refine Constructing and Interpreting Two-Way Tables

Purpose

- **Refine** strategies for building and interpreting two-way tables.
- **Refine** understanding of using tables with relative frequencies to describe and interpret associations in the data.

START CHECK FOR UNDERSTANDING

What percent of players younger than 12 made more than 10 free throws?

	< 12	≥ 12	Total
≤ 10 Free Throws	5	12	17
> 10 Free Throws	2	6	8
Total	7	18	25

Solution

about 29%

WHY? Confirm students' understanding of interpreting two-way tables, identifying common errors to address as needed.

MONITOR & GUIDE

Before students begin to work, use their responses to the **Start** to determine those who will benefit from additional support. Use the **Error Analysis** table below to guide remediation.

Have all students complete the Example and problems 1–3, using Consider This and Pair/Share as appropriate. Observe and monitor their reasoning and guide or redirect students as needed.

Refine Constructing and Interpreting Two-Way Tables

➤ **Complete the Example below. Then solve problems 1–7.**

Example

Students at a middle school are asked whether they prefer an individual project, a partner project, or a group project. The table shows the results. What is the likelihood that a randomly selected student in Grade 7 will prefer a partner project?

	Individual Project	Partner Project	Group Project	Total
Grade 6	32	20	40	92
Grade 7	22	24	31	77
Grade 8	20	15	46	81
Total	74	59	117	250

Look at how you could show your work using relative frequency.

There are 77 students in Grade 7. There are 24 students in Grade 7 who prefer a partner project. $\frac{24}{77} \approx 0.312$

SOLUTION The likelihood is about 31%.

CONSIDER THIS . . .
Rows in the table for Grade 6, Grade 8, and the total can be covered up so that only the row for Grade 7 is showing.

PAIR/SHARE
Explain why the denominator is 77.

Apply It

1 Look at the table in the Example. What is the likelihood that a student who prefers a group project is in Grade 8? Show your work.

Possible work:

$\frac{46}{117} \approx 0.393$

SOLUTION The likelihood is about 39.3%.

CONSIDER THIS . . .
The column totals are for the different types of projects that the students prefer.

PAIR/SHARE
What is the likelihood a student who is in Grade 8 will prefer a group project?

START ERROR ANALYSIS

If the error is . . .	Students may . . .	To support understanding . . .
25%	have calculated the relative frequency by rows.	Ask students to explain how they decide whether to calculate relative frequencies by rows or by columns.
8%	have calculated the relative frequency by the grand total.	Help students break up the question stem. Ask: *How many players are younger than 12? Of these, how many players made more than 10 free throws?*
about 33%	have calculated the percent of players 12 or older who made more than 10 free throws.	Prompt students to review what the question is asking. Elicit from students that they need to analyze the table using the column "< 12."

Example

Guide students in understanding the Example. Ask:

- *What is the question asking?*
- *Will a column total or a row total be used to answer this question?*
- *How does understanding the question help you decide what total to use to compute the relative frequency?*

Help all students focus on the Example and responses to the questions by having students describe what they noticed or assumed about the problem. Then have them explain how they used those observations or assumptions.

Look for understanding that the relative frequency is found using the total for the Grade 7 row.

Apply It

1 Students may solve the problem by finding the relative frequency by columns because the question is asking about group projects, which is a column category. *DOK 2*

2 Students may find relative frequencies using the total number of students in the school because the question does not ask about the percent from a particular group. *DOK 2*

3 **B is correct.** Divide the number of Grade 8 students who wear glasses, 5, by the total number of students in Grade 8, 56.

A is not correct. This answer is the number of students in Grade 8 who wear glasses, written with a percent symbol.

C is not correct. This answer is the number of students who wear glasses, written with a percent symbol.

D is not correct. This answer is the number of students in Grade 8 who wear glasses divided by the total number of students who wear glasses.

DOK 3

2 There are 255 students at Brownsville Middle School. The students are asked whether they prefer art or music class and whether they prefer science or math class. The table shows the results. Which is greater: the percent of students who prefer science and art classes or the percent of students who prefer math and music classes? Show your work.

	Art Class	Music Class	Total
Science Class	51	56	107
Math Class	73	75	143
Total	124	131	255

Possible work:

Find relative frequencies using the total number of students in the school as a whole.

prefer science and art: $\frac{51}{255} = 0.20 = 20\%$

prefer math and music: $\frac{75}{255} \approx 0.29 \approx 29\%$

SOLUTION The percent who prefer math and music is greater.

CONSIDER THIS . . . What is the *whole* here?

PAIR/SHARE What calculations did you use to make your conclusion?

3 The table shows data for students at a middle school. What is the relative frequency of students in Grade 8 who wear glasses?

	Glasses	Contacts	Neither	Total
Grade 7	11	21	12	44
Grade 8	5	29	22	56
Total	16	50	34	100

A 5%

B 8.93%

C 16%

D 31.25%

Angela chose D as the correct answer. How might she have gotten that answer?

Possible answer: Angela used the column total of 16. Her answer represents the relative frequency of students who wear glasses that are in Grade 8.

CONSIDER THIS . . . The question is asking only about the data for Grade 8 students.

PAIR/SHARE How did you know what column or row to use?

776

GROUP & DIFFERENTIATE

Identify groupings for differentiation based on the **Start** and problems 1–3. A recommended sequence of activities for each group is suggested below. Use the resources on the next page to differentiate and close the lesson.

Approaching Proficiency

- **RETEACH** Visual Model
- **REINFORCE** Problems 4, 5

Meeting Proficiency

- **REINFORCE** Problems 4–6

Extending Beyond Proficiency

- **REINFORCE** Problems 4–6
- **EXTEND** Challenge

Have all students complete the **Close: Exit Ticket**.

Resources for Differentiation are found on the next page.

Refine Constructing and Interpreting Two-Way Tables

Apply It

4 **a.** See ***Connect to Culture*** to support student engagement. Students may reason that because the column totals are 1, the columns were used to calculate the relative frequencies. ***DOK 1***

b. The number 0.56 is in the column for the smallest puppies and the row for female puppies. Because the column totals were used to calculate the relative frequencies, 0.56 represents the fraction of the smallest puppies that were female. ***DOK 2***

5 **a.** For the statement to be true, the percent for the school bus being on time should be greater than 50% for both rainy days and sunny days.

b. The row totals were used to calculate the relative frequencies.

c. In the *School Bus Early* column, compare the percent for rainy days to the percent for sunny days. The percent for sunny days is greater.

d. The percents for the row totals are 100%, which indicates that row totals were used to calculate the relative frequencies.

DOK 1

4 A veterinarian collects data on the weights of newborn puppies in several litters. The table shows her data.

	Smallest	Not the Smallest	Total
Male	0.44	0.61	0.58
Female	0.56	0.39	0.42
Total	1.00	1.00	1.00

a. What method was used to calculate the relative frequencies in the table? How do you know?

Possible answer: The relative frequencies were calculated by column because the column totals are 1.

b. What does 0.56 represent? Explain.

Possible answer: Because the frequencies are column frequencies, 0.56 indicates that 56% of the smallest puppies of the litters were female.

5 Tell whether each statement about the table is *True* or *False*.

	School Bus Early	School Bus on Time	School Bus Late	Total
Rainy Day	11.6%	36.2%	52.2%	100%
Sunny Day	33.3%	36.4%	30.3%	100%
Total	22.2%	36.3%	41.5%	

	True	False
a. The school bus is mostly on time.	○	●
b. The relative frequencies are for the whole table.	○	●
c. The school bus tends to be early on sunny days more so than on rainy days.	●	○
d. The relative frequencies are by row.	●	○

777

DIFFERENTIATION

RETEACH

Visual Model

Construct a two-way table with relative frequencies.

Students approaching proficiency with building and interpreting two-way tables will benefit from constructing and analyzing two-way tables with frequencies and relative frequencies.

- Display two blank two-way tables, each with two columns and two rows, plus a total column and a total row. One of these tables will be a table for frequencies and one will be a table for relative frequencies.
- Tell students you want to compare those students who play an instrument and those who play a sport. Ask students to provide the labels for the rows and columns. [Plays Instrument, Does Not Play Instrument; Plays Sports, Does Not Play Sports]
- Using a show of hands, collect the data and record it in the first table.
- Working with students, use the data in the first table to make a table with relative frequencies using totals for the sports categories.
- Ask: *What is the relative frequency of students who play a sport who also play an instrument?* [Answers will vary.] Ask: *What is another question that can be asked about this table with relative frequencies?* [Sample answer: What is the relative frequency of students who do not play a sport who also play an instrument?]
- If time permits, repeat for a table with relative frequencies using totals for the instrument categories or using overall totals.

6 **a.** Students may first use the given information to make a two-way table with frequencies and then use this table to make a table with relative frequencies. *DOK 2*

b. Students may compare the relative frequency of athletes who prefer an early lunch to athletes who prefer a late lunch. *DOK 3*

CLOSE EXIT TICKET

7 **Math Journal** Look for understanding of how to construct a two-way table with relative frequencies using row, column, or overall totals. Look for understanding of how to interpret the table in order to write an appropriate question.

Error Alert If students calculate relative frequencies by rows but ask a question about the relative frequency of students in a certain grade who do or do not play chess, then ask them what the row totals represent and what this means about the percents in the table with relative frequencies. Have students rewrite their question.

End of Lesson Checklist

INTERACTIVE GLOSSARY Support students by suggesting they look up *relative* in a dictionary and explain how this definition can help them better understand *relative frequency*.

SELF CHECK Have students review and check off any new skills on the Unit 7 Opener.

LESSON 32 | SESSION 4

6 Neva asks 50 students at her school whether they prefer an early or a late lunch. She surveys 27 athletes and 21 of them prefer a late lunch. The remaining students she surveys are nonathletes. 16 of the nonathletes prefer an early lunch.

a. Complete the two-way table with the relative frequencies calculated by row.

	Early Lunch	Late Lunch	Total
Athlete	0.22	0.78	1.00
Nonathlete	0.70	0.30	1.00
Total	0.44	0.56	

b. Currently, most of the students in the first lunch period are athletes. Should the school consider changing schedules? Explain.

Yes; A much higher percentage of athletes prefer a late lunch. A much higher percentage of nonathletes prefer an early lunch.

7 **Math Journal** Make a two-way table with relative frequencies for the data shown. Write and answer a question that can be answered using your table.

	Grade 6	Grade 7	Grade 8	Total
Plays Chess	35	45	68	148
Does Not Play Chess	56	86	59	201
Total	91	131	127	349

Possible work:

	Grade 6	Grade 7	Grade 8	Total
Plays Chess	38.5%	34.4%	53.5%	42.4%
Does Not Play Chess	61.5%	65.6%	46.5%	57.6%
Total	100%	100%	100%	

How likely is it that a random Grade 7 student will play chess? Explain.

Not very likely. Almost 66% of Grade 7 students do not play chess.

End of Lesson Checklist

☐ **INTERACTIVE GLOSSARY** Find the entry for *relative frequency*. Tell how relative frequency is different from frequency.

☐ **SELF CHECK** Go back to the Unit 7 Opener and see what you can check off.

778

REINFORCE

Problems 4–6

Solve problems using two-way tables with relative frequencies.

Students meeting proficiency will benefit from additional work with building and interpreting two-way tables with relative frequencies by solving problems in a variety of formats.

- Have students work on their own or with a partner to solve the problems.
- Encourage students to show their work.

EXTEND

Challenge

Construct and analyze two-way tables with frequencies with missing data.

Students extending beyond proficiency will benefit from making and analyzing a two-way table with frequencies with missing data.

- Have students work with a partner to solve this problem: *Nia asks 80 students whether they are in choir or not in choir. Of the 32 in choir, 8 like dramas and 11 like comedies. In all, there are 33 students who like action movies and 24 students who like dramas. Determine the percent of students not in choir who like comedies.*
- Repeat, this time having students make a two-way table with relative frequencies to determine the percent of students who are in choir who like action movies.

PERSONALIZE

i-Ready

Provide students with opportunities to work on their personalized instruction path with *i-Ready* Online Instruction to:

- fill prerequisite gaps.
- build up grade-level skills.

Lesson Quiz

TESTED SKILLS

Assesses 8.SP.A.4

Problems on this assessment require students to be able to interpret two-way tables and use data to calculate relative frequencies. They will use relative frequencies to compare preferences among different populations, calculate likelihoods, and determine which group is best targeted by a membership campaign. Students will also need to be familiar with reading two-way tables and calculating percents.

Alternately, teachers may assign the **Digital Comprehension Check** online to assess student understanding of this material.

Error Alert Errors may result if students:

- miscalculate percents, such as dividing the whole by the part.
- misrepresent or miscalculate fractions and decimals.
- misread columns or rows.
- calculate relative frequencies using the whole table when using row or column totals is required, or vice versa.
- misinterpret values in a two-way table.

Problem Notes

1 Students could solve this problem by dividing the number of family members who prefer each option by the total number of family members surveyed and then comparing the percents.

(2 points)

DOK 2 | 8.SP.A.4

2 Students could solve this problem by dividing 8, the number of students in Grade 6 surveyed who prefer piano, by 22, the total number of students surveyed who prefer piano.

(2 points)

DOK 1 | 8.SP.A.4

LESSON 32 • QUIZ Name:

➤ **Solve the problems.**

1 Marie surveys her extended family to see if they would prefer a family reunion to be held in the country or in the city, and if they would prefer Mexican or Italian food to be served. Which is greater: the percentage of family members who would prefer the reunion be held in the country with Mexican food, or those who would prefer the reunion be held in the city with Italian food? Show your work. *(2 points)*

	Country	City	Total
Mexican Food	6	12	18
Italian Food	6	6	12
Total	12	18	30

Possible student work: country with Mexican food: $\frac{6}{30}$ = 20%; city with Italian food: $\frac{6}{30}$ = 20%

SOLUTION Possible answer: The same percentage of family members would prefer the reunion be held in the city with Italian food as prefer the country with Mexican food.

2 A group of students are surveyed and asked if they would prefer to play piano, guitar, or violin. The table shows the results. What is the likelihood that a randomly selected student who prefers to play piano will be in Grade 6? Round your answer to the nearest tenth. Show your work. *(2 points)*

	Piano	Guitar	Violin	Total
Grade 6	8	7	4	19
Grade 7	10	12	5	27
Grade 8	4	7	9	20
Total	22	26	18	66

Possible student work: $\frac{8}{22} \approx$ 36.4%.

SOLUTION The likelihood is about 36.4%.

Short Response Scoring Rubric

Points	Expectations
2	Response has the correct solution(s) and includes well-organized, clear, and concise work demonstrating thorough understanding of mathematical concepts and/or procedures.
1	Response contains mostly correct solution(s) and shows partial understanding of mathematical concepts and/or procedures.
0	Response shows no attempt at finding a solution and no effort to demonstrate an understanding of mathematical concepts and/or procedures.

3 **D is correct.** Students could solve the problem by dividing 7, the number of students in Grade 7 surveyed who prefer math, by 15, the total number of students in Grade 7 surveyed.

A is incorrect. This answer represents the number of students in Grade 7 who prefer math.

B is incorrect. This answer represents dividing 7 by 42, the total number of middle school students surveyed, instead of dividing 7 by the total number of students in Grade 7 surveyed.

C is incorrect. This answer represents dividing 7 by 23, the number surveyed who prefer math, instead of the total number of students in Grade 7 surveyed.

(1 point)

DOK 1 | **8.SP.A.4**

4 Students could solve this problem by dividing the number of people in each age group who have a gym membership by the total number of people in that age group and then comparing the percents.

(2 points)

DOK 3 | **8.SP.A.4**

LESSON 32 • QUIZ Name:

3 Middle school students are asked whether they prefer math or science. The table shows the results. What is the approximate relative frequency of students in Grade 7 who prefer math? *(1 point)*

	Math	Science	Total
Grade 6	5	5	10
Grade 7	7	8	15
Grade 8	11	6	17
Total	23	19	42

A 7.0% **B** 16.7% **C** 30.4% **(D)** 46.7%

4 A random sample of adults is asked whether they have a gym membership. The table shows the responses. A gym holds a campaign to encourage people to buy a membership. What age group should they target? Explain your reasoning. *(2 points)*

	Membership	No Membership	Total
Younger than 40	56	23	79
40 and Older	33	48	81
Total	89	71	160

Possible student work:

Younger than 40: $\frac{56}{79} \approx 71\%$

40 and Older: $\frac{33}{81} \approx 41\%$

SOLUTION 40 and older; Possible explanation: About 71% of people younger than 40 already have a gym membership, while only about 41% in the older age group have a membership.

DIFFERENTIATION

RETEACH Tools for Instruction

Students who require additional support for prerequisite or on-level skills will benefit from activities that provide targeted skills instruction.

GRADE 8
- **Lesson 32** Two-Way Tables

REINFORCE Math Center Activity

Students who require practice to reinforce concepts and skills and deepen understanding will benefit from small group collaborative games and activities (available in on-level, below-level, and above-level versions).

GRADE 8
- **Lesson 32** Match Relative Frequency

EXTEND Enrichment Activity

Students who have achieved proficiency with concepts and skills and are ready for additional challenges will benefit from group collaborative games and activities that extend understanding.

GRADE 8
- **Lesson 32** Trees Under Attack

Overview | Representing Data

MATH FOCUS

Focus Standards

8.SP.A.1, 8.SP.A.2, 8.SP.A.3, 8.SP.A.4

STANDARDS FOR MATHEMATICAL PRACTICE (SMP)

This lesson provides support for:

1 Make sense of problems and persevere in solving them.

3 Construct viable arguments and critique the reasoning of others.

6 Attend to precision.

Additional SMP

2, 4, 5, 7

Lesson at a Glance

In this lesson, students apply multiple skills from the unit to solve real-world problems related to data displays for a research project. Problems involve making and interpreting scatter plots, making two-way tables showing frequencies or relative frequencies, describing the association between variables, and using a scatter plot to make predictions about missing data.

Key Skills

- Make and interpret scatter plots.
- Make two-way tables showing frequencies and relative frequencies.
- Describe the association between two variables.
- Use a scatter plot to make predictions about missing data.

Pacing Guide

Items marked with are available on the **Teacher Toolbox**.

MATERIALS

SESSION 1 (45–60 min)

Internet Users

Study an Example Problem and Solution (20–30 min)

Example Problem (10–15 min) | One Student's Solution (10–15 min)

Try Another Approach (25–30 min)

Plan It (5 min) | Solve It (15–20 min) | Reflect (5 min)

Math Toolkit graph paper, graphing calculator, straightedge, string

For each student: Activity Sheet *Solution Sheet*

SESSION 2 (45–60 min)

Age Groups

Discuss Models and Strategies (20–30 min)

Plan It and Solve It (15–25 min) | Reflect (5 min)

Math Toolkit calculator, graph paper, straightedge

For each student: Activity Sheet *Solution Sheet*

Emissions, GDP, and Urban Population

Persevere On Your Own (25–30 min)

Solve It (20–25 min) | Reflect (5 min)

Math Toolkit graph paper, graphing calculator, straightedge, string

For each student: Activity Sheet *Solution Sheet*

DIFFERENTIATION

RETEACH Extra Support

Materials For display: graph paper, string

EXTEND Challenge

Purpose

- **Examine** a problem that involves scatter plots and two-way tables.
- **Analyze** a sample solution to identify what makes it a good solution.
- **Demonstrate** that the problem has more than one approach and more than one solution.

Study an Example Problem and Solution

Internet Users

Make Sense of the Problem

Present the Internet Users problem and use **Three Reads** to help students make sense of it. For each read, have a different volunteer read aloud each section of information.

After the first read, be sure students recognize that the goal of the problem is to look for and display relationships between population using the internet and one of the other variables in Darius's table.

ASK *What are the other variables Darius has given Brett data for?*

LISTEN FOR The other variables shown in the table Darius attached are CO_2 emissions per capita, total population, life expectancy at birth, and population under age 15.

After the second read, listen for students to say that they need to make a scatter plot to show the relationship between the population using the internet and another variable they choose, make a two-way table showing the percent of countries in the project that have above-average values for both variables, and describe any association they see.

After the third read, have students identify the important quantities and relationships in the problem, including any quantities that involve student choice. Ensure that students understand that student choice means there can be multiple correct solutions to the problem.

Invite students to share their ideas about how they might use concepts from the unit to solve this problem. Allow them to describe different approaches but do not implement any strategies.

ASK *How can you use scatter plots and two-way tables to interpret and analyze data?*

LISTEN FOR A scatter plot may show an association between two variables. A two-way table showing relative frequencies can help compare parts of different wholes.

Math in Action

SMP 1 Make sense of problems and persevere in solving them.

Study an Example Problem and Solution

➤ **Read this problem involving scatter plots and two-way tables. Then look at one student's solution to this problem on the following pages.**

Internet Users

Brett and Darius are working together on a research project involving several different countries. They have collected data on several variables for each country. Read the email from Darius. Then complete Brett's deliverables.

Delete Archive Reply Reply All Forward

To: Brett
Subject: Data displays for research project

Hi Brett,

There are 25 countries in our project. I wonder if the percent of the population using the internet is related to any of the other variables. I have attached data for the population using the internet and data for several other variables.

DELIVERABLES:
- Choose a variable to analyze along with the population using the internet.
- Make a scatter plot to show the relationship.
- Make a two-way table to show the percent of the countries in our project that have above-average usage of the internet and an above-average value for the variable you chose.
- Describe any association between the variables.

Thanks, Darius

Attachments:

Country	Population using the internet (%)	CO_2 Emissions per capita (metric tons)	Total population (thousands)	Life expectancy at birth (years)	Population under age 15 (%)
Afghanistan	11.4	0.3	32,358	62.3	47.42
Argentina	69.7	4.7	40,765	75.7	24.42
Australia	86.5	15.3	22,606	82.4	18.95

See page DS4 for the complete data set.

Be sure to place your router away from fish tanks! Water can block WiFi signals and slow down your internet connection.

CONNECT TO CONTEXT

Internet Users Students may not be familiar with *demographics*. Explain that demographics are statistical data about the characteristics of a population, such as the age, gender, and income of the people within the population. Governments collect statistical data related to many subjects including economics, demographics, and social classes. This information is used to aid in decision-making. For this problem, the data gathered include population using the internet, CO_2 emissions, total population, life expectancy at birth, and population under age 15. CO_2 emissions, or carbon dioxide emissions into the atmosphere, are often associated with the burning of fossil fuels, like natural gas, crude oil, and coal. Total population is all the inhabitants of a particular town, area, or country. Life expectancy at birth is the average number of years that a newborn is expected to live based on current mortality rates. Population under age 15 is the percent of the population younger than 15 years old.

Appropriate Precision Notice that each column in the table indicates the units used for that variable. Often, data values for an entire population can be large. In that case, numbers may be written in the thousands, millions, or billions so the data values will fit in the table and be easier to read.

One Student's Solution

Read through the sample solution to the Internet Users problem together, one section at a time. Point out that the Notice That boxes provide important information about this student's solution.

Problem-Solving Checklist

Explain to students that they will use the Problem-Solving Checklist on this page to identify what makes this a good solution.

- Have students look at the sample solution to find and circle where the student wrote known, or given, information.
- Then have students underline where the student wrote what they need to find.
- As a class, find and box where the student showed their work.
- Finally, ask students to put a checkmark next to the place where the student checked their solution.
- Tell students that they can use this checklist as a model when they write their own solutions for this problem and for other problems.

Facilitate Whole Class Discussion

Support students in analyzing and discussing the steps of the sample solution in order to better understand it.

ASK *How does making a scatter plot of the data help the student to identify the positive, linear association?*

LISTEN FOR It is difficult to see the patterns of the data set in a table. Plotting all the points in a scatter plot makes it easier to see that the data tend to lie along a line with positive slope, going up and to the right.

ASK *What do the vertical and horizontal average lines tell the student about the data that fall into each of the four sections?*

LISTEN FOR Data in the bottom left section are below average for both population using the internet and life expectancy. Data that fall in the bottom right section are above average for population using the internet, but below average for life expectancy. Data that fall in the top left section are above average for life expectancy, but below average for population using the internet. Data that fall in the top right section are above average for both population using the internet and life expectancy.

UNIT 7 Math in Action | SESSION 1

One Student's Solution

NOTICE THAT . . . The averages for each variable in the data table are located in the last row of the table. See the full data set on page DS4.

First, I have to choose a variable to analyze.

I think that countries that have a higher percent of the population using the internet may also have higher life expectancy. So, I will investigate the relationship between those two variables.

Next, I need to make a scatter plot.

There is no clear independent or dependent variable. I will put population using the internet on the *x*-axis and life expectancy on the *y*-axis.

The average percent of the population using the internet is 52.8%. I can draw a vertical line through this value. The average life expectancy is 70.8 years. I can draw a horizontal line through this value.

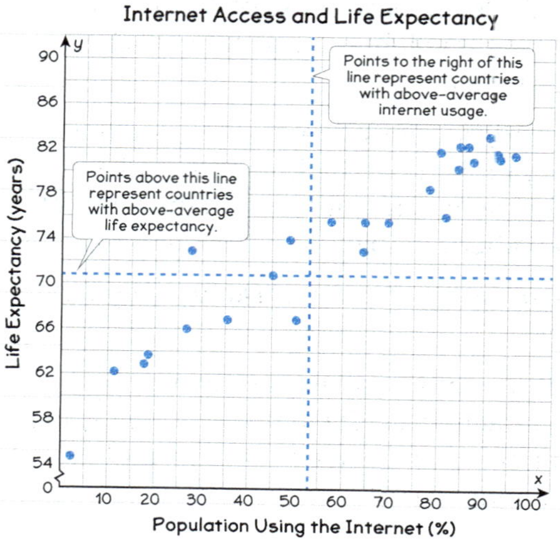

Problem-Solving Checklist

- ☐ Tell what is known.
- ☐ Tell what the problem is asking.
- ☐ Show all your work.
- ☐ Show that the solution works.

I could model the pattern in the data with a straight line with a positive slope, so the variables have a positive, linear association.

780

Prompt students to discuss the similarities and differences between a two-way table showing frequencies and a two-way table showing relative frequencies.

ASK *How does making a two-way table showing frequencies help the student think through the problem?*

LISTEN FOR The two-way table showing frequencies gives the student a way to organize the data from the graph and summarize the data.

ASK *Why do you think the student calculates whole-table relative frequencies?*

LISTEN FOR The student needs to compare the combination of the two variables to the whole group of countries to see if there is any association.

Have students discuss the benefits of using both a scatter plot and two-way tables in this solution.

ASK *How did the student benefit from displaying the data in multiple ways?*

LISTEN FOR The scatter plot helped the student see the association like a picture. The two-way tables made two different types of summaries of the data and confirmed the association identified in the scatterplot.

After discussing the sample solution, have a volunteer summarize the steps taken to solve the problem.

ASK *How can you summarize the steps in the sample solution?*

LISTEN FOR Choose a variable to analyze. Make a scatter plot of the chosen variable and the population using the internet. Add lines to show the average for each variable. Analyze the scatter plot and describe any association between the variables. Make a two-way table showing frequencies, or the numbers of countries with above- and below-average values for each variable. Then, make another two-way table showing whole-table relative frequencies. Describe any association in the data shown in the two-way tables and compare it to the association shown in the scatter plot.

Math IN Action

Then, I can count the number of points in each section of the graph to make a two-way table showing frequencies.

	Life expectancy ≤ 70.8	Life expectancy > 70.8	Total
Population using the internet ≤ 52.8%	8	2	10
Population using the internet > 52.8%	0	15	15
Total	8	17	25

NOTICE THAT . . . There are no countries in Brett and Darius's project that have above-average internet usage and below-average life expectancy.

Now, I can calculate whole-table relative frequencies to show the percent of countries in our project with above-average internet usage and above-average life expectancy.

	Life expectancy ≤ 70.8	Life expectancy > 70.8	Total
Population using the internet ≤ 52.8%	$\frac{8}{25} = 32\%$	$\frac{2}{25} = 8\%$	40%
Population using the internet > 52.8%	$\frac{0}{25} = 0\%$	$\frac{15}{25} = 60\%$	60%
Total	32%	68%	100%

I can see that there is association between population using the internet and life expectancy. 60% of countries in the project have above-average internet usage and have above-average life expectancy.

Finally, I can check my solution by comparing the scatter plot and the two-way table.

Both data displays show association: as the percent of the population using the internet increases, life expectancy increases.

781

Try Another Approach

Internet Users

Materials For each student: Activity Sheet *Solution Sheet*

Facilitate Whole Class Discussion

After reviewing the sample student solution on the previous pages, prompt students to look for different approaches to solve the problem.

ASK *What are some different steps you could use to solve the problem?*

LISTEN FOR Choose a different variable. Switch which variables are on the *x*- and *y*-axes. The table showing frequencies is not required, so it is not needed for the solution. The two-way table showing whole-table relative frequencies is required, so I will make that two-way table.

Plan It

Facilitate Whole Class Discussion

Read the Plan It questions from the next page aloud. Prompt students to discuss how they will approach and solve this problem in another way.

ASK *What are some relationships you might expect to see for each variable related to internet use? How will this help you choose a variable to analyze?*

LISTEN FOR If I think there will be an association, I might choose that variable so I can see if I am right. I do not expect to see an association between total population and population using the internet. Because the population using the internet is given as a percent, it is unlikely to be related to the total population as a number. I would expect countries with a greater percent of their population under age 15 to also have a greater percent of their population using the internet because younger people tend to focus more on technology. I would expect to see countries with higher CO_2 emissions have a smaller population using the internet because their focus is on manufacturing not technology.

Try Another Approach

Problem-Solving Checklist

- ☐ Tell what is known.
- ☐ Tell what the problem is asking.
- ☐ Show all your work.
- ☐ Show that the solution works.

➤ **There are many ways to solve problems. Think about how you might solve the Internet Users problem in a different way.**

Internet Users

Brett and Darius are working together on a research project involving several different countries. They have collected data on several variables for each country. Read the email from Darius. Then complete Brett's deliverables.

Delete Archive Reply Reply All Forward

To: Brett
Subject: Data displays for research project

Hi Brett,

There are 25 countries in our project. I wonder if the percent of the population using the internet is related to any of the other variables. I have attached data for the population using the internet and data for several other variables.

DELIVERABLES:
- Choose a variable to analyze along with the population using the internet.
- Make a scatter plot to show the relationship.
- Make a two-way table to show the percent of the countries in our project that have above-average usage of the internet and an above-average value for the variable you chose.
- Describe any association between the variables.

Thanks, Darius

Attachments:

Country	Population using the internet (%)	CO_2 Emissions per capita (metric tons)	Total population (thousands)	Life expectancy at birth (years)	Population under age 15 (%)
Afghanistan	11.4	0.3	32,358	62.3	47.42
Argentina	69.7	4.7	40,765	75.7	24.42
Australia	86.5	15.3	22,606	82.4	18.95

See page DS4 for the complete data set.

ASK *What is the purpose of using a two-way table showing frequencies as well as a two-way table showing relative frequencies?*

LISTEN FOR Two-way tables that show frequencies help you organize the given information. A two-way table showing frequencies could be misleading if the number of countries in each of the categories is different. Two-way tables that show relative frequencies compare the parts to the whole, so if the number of responses varies among the categories, the comparison still makes sense.

Solve It

Problem-Solving Tips

Introduce the Problem-Solving Tips as ideas students may use to explain their thinking. Remind them to also use the Problem-Solving Checklist to make sure their answer is complete.

Have students write their own complete solutions on a copy of Activity Sheet *Solution Sheet* or a blank sheet of paper.

Reflect

As they work, have students share their thinking with a partner and discuss the Reflect questions.

As time permits, have students explain their solutions to the class.

Possible Solution

Countries with a greater percent of the population using the internet may have greater populations.

First, I will make a table showing whole-table relative frequencies.

	Pop. using the internet ≤ 52.8%	Pop. using the internet > 52.8%	Total
Total pop. ≤ 16,348	$\frac{5}{25} = 20\%$	$\frac{5}{25} = 20\%$	$\frac{10}{25} = 40\%$
Total pop. > 16,348	$\frac{5}{25} = 20\%$	$\frac{10}{25} = 40\%$	$\frac{15}{25} = 60\%$
Total	$\frac{10}{25} = 40\%$	$\frac{15}{25} = 60\%$	100%

A country with a greater population is more likely to have a greater percent using the internet, but a country with a lesser population is not more likely to have a lesser percent using the internet.

Then, I will make a scatter plot to show the data.

Population Using Internet and Total Population

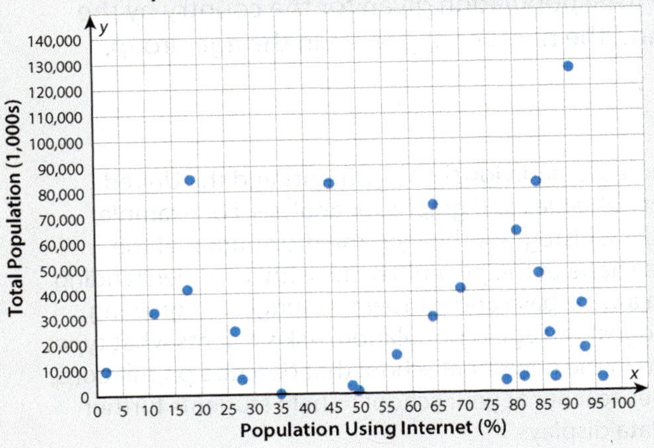

The scatter plot does not appear to show an association. This disagreed with my hypothesis.

Math in Action

Plan It

➤ **Answer these questions to help you start thinking about a plan.**

a. Which variable do you think will be interesting to analyze along with the population using the internet? Why?

b. Will your two-way table show frequencies or relative frequencies? Why?

Solve It

➤ **Find a different solution for the Internet Users problem. Show all your work on a separate sheet of paper. You may want to use the Problem-Solving Tips to get started.**

PROBLEM-SOLVING TIPS

Math Toolkit graph paper, graphing calculator, straightedge, string

Key Terms

scatter plot	relative frequency	nonlinear association
bivariate	no association	positive association
two-way table	linear association	negative association

Sentence Starters

- As the percent of the population using the internet increases . . .
- The percent of countries with above-average internet usage . . .

Reflect

Use Mathematical Practices As you work through the problem, discuss these questions with a partner.

- **Be Precise** How will you scale the axes for your scatter plot? Why?
- **Make Sense of Problems** How is the information in the "Worldwide Average" row of the data table different from the information in the other rows? How will you use this information in your scatter plot and in your two-way table?

783

Scoring Rubric (4 points)

Points	Expectations
4	The solution and explanation are clear and complete, with no errors. The scatter plot and two-way table are included and correct. The description of the association agrees with the scatter plot and table.
3	All parts of the task were completed. Solution steps are correct, but parts of the scatter plot and/or two-way table may be inaccurate. The association described is reasonable for the scatter plot and table.
2	All parts of the task were attempted. Parts of the scatter plot and/or two-way table are missing or inaccurate. The description of the association may be incorrect or disagree with the scatter plot and table.
1	Some parts of the task were not attempted. The scatter plot, two-way table, and the description of the association are incomplete or inaccurate.

Math in Action

Purpose

- **Understand** two new open-ended, multi-step problems involving two-way tables and association.
- **Choose** appropriate models and strategies to plan for and solve the problems.

Discuss Models and Strategies

Age Groups

Materials For each student: Activity Sheet *Solution Sheet*

Make Sense of the Problem

Present the Age Groups problem and use **Three Reads** to help students make sense of it. Have different volunteers take turns reading aloud each section of information.

ASK *What are some clarifying questions you could ask about the details of the problem?*

LISTEN FOR Student responses may include questions about whether the population between ages 15 and 60 is important. Students might ask about why the table uses decimals to describe population or why the values in the total population column are so much bigger than the values in the population under age 15 and population over age 60 columns.

Invite volunteers to point out what is known and what they need to figure out.

ASK *What do you need to include in your solution?*

LISTEN FOR The solution needs to include two-way tables showing data about two or three countries in Brett and Darius's project. One two-way table should display the percent of the population in each age group. Another two-way table should display the number of people in each age group. The solution also needs to include descriptions of any associations identified.

Ensure that students understand that one two-way table will display relative frequencies and the other two-way table will display frequencies.

ASK *What type of information is given in the data set provided by Brett for the population under age 15 and the population over age 60? How do you know?*

LISTEN FOR The data set gives relative frequencies for those two age groups because they are expressed as a percent.

Discuss Models and Strategies

Problem-Solving Checklist
- ☐ Tell what is known.
- ☐ Tell what the problem is asking.
- ☐ Show all your work.
- ☐ Show that the solution works.

➤ **Read the problem. Write a solution on a separate sheet of paper. Remember, there can be lots of ways to solve a problem.**

Age Groups

Brett and Darius have collected data on the size of two age groups in each country in their project. Read an email from Brett. Then complete Darius's deliverables.

Delete Archive Reply Reply All Forward

To: Darius
Subject: Two-way tables for research project

Hi Darius,

I would like to include two-way tables showing some of our data in our report. I have attached data on populations for different age groups for each country in our project.

DELIVERABLES:
- Choose two or three countries from our project.
- Make a two-way table to display the percent of the population in each age group.
- Make a second two-way table to display the number of people in each age group.
- Describe any association you see in the tables.

Thanks!

Brett

Attachments:

Country	Total Population (thousands)	Population under age 15 (%)	Population over age 60 (%)
Afghanistan	32,358	47.42	3.82
Argentina	40,765	24.42	14.97
Australia	22,606	18.95	19.46

See page DS5 for the complete data set.

Population growth is caused by more children being born and by individuals living longer lives.

Discuss possible steps, ways to organize the information, and techniques that might be helpful. Invite students to take notes.

ASK *How will you determine the number of people in each age group?*

LISTEN FOR I will multiply the total population given for the country by the percent for each age group to find the number of people in the age group.

CONNECT TO CONTEXT

Age Groups Population data collected by individual governments and the United Nations can be displayed in a variety of tables and graphs for analysis. For example, a population pyramid for the world is a histogram showing the distribution of the population among age groups. The shape of the pyramid helps with an understanding of growth patterns. A pyramid with a wide base and narrow top suggests a growing population while a narrow base suggests an aging population. Ask students what types of data displays they may have seen in the news or at school that describe populations. Optionally, work with a social studies teacher at your school to help students further explore population statistics and data displays.

Plan It and Solve It

Problem-Solving Checklist & Tips

Have students use various resources, including the Problem-Solving Checklist and the Problem-Solving Tips, as they begin to plan a solution.

Support Student Work

Have students work in pairs to discuss their preliminary solution strategies and the Reflect questions. Discuss a variety of approaches as a class. Let students revise their plans and discuss again with a partner.

When students are confident that their plans make sense, have them write a complete solution on a copy of Activity Sheet *Solution Sheet* or a blank sheet of paper.

Reflect

As they work, have students share their thinking with a partner and discuss the Reflect questions.

As time permits, have students explain their solutions to the class.

Possible Solution

I will choose Ecuador, Venezuela, and Argentina because they are three different countries on the same continent with different-size populations.

I will make a two-way table displaying relative frequencies by age group.

	Pop. < 15	Pop. ages 15–60	Pop. > 60	Total
Ecuador	30.29%	60.5%	9.21%	100%
Venezuela	28.84%	61.99%	9.17%	100%
Argentina	24.42%	60.61%	14.97%	100%
Total	26.97%	61.07%	11.96%	100%

I will make a two-way table displaying frequencies by age group. Frequencies are found by multiplying the percent for each age group by the total population for each country.

	Pop. < 15	Pop. ages 15–60	Pop. > 60	Total
Ecuador	4,442	8,873	1,351	14,666
Venezuela	8,490	18,248	2,699	29,437
Argentina	9,955	24,708	6,103	40,766
Total	22,887	51,829	10,153	84,869

There is an association. Each of the countries has about the same percent of the population in the same age group.

Math in Action

Plan It and Solve It

➤ **Find a solution to the Age Groups problem.**

Write a detailed plan and support your answer. Be sure to include:

- two or three countries from the project.
- a two-way table displaying relative frequencies.
- a two-way table displaying frequencies, or counts.
- a description of any association you see in the tables.

PROBLEM-SOLVING TIPS

Math Toolkit calculator, graph paper, straightedge

Key Terms

relative frequency	two-way table	bivariate
percent	data	association
column	row	frequency

Questions

- How many people are under age 15 in each of the countries you have chosen? How many total people are under age 15 in these countries?
- What percent of people are between ages 15 and 60 in each of the countries you have chosen?

Reflect

Use Mathematical Practices As you work through the problem, discuss these questions with a partner.

- **Make Sense of Problems** Which two-way table will you make first? Why?
- **Use Structure** Write a question that could be answered using a table showing frequencies. Write a question that could be answered using a table showing relative frequencies.

The oldest documented human lived to be 122 years and 164 days old!

785

Scoring Rubric (4 points)

Points	Expectations
4	The solution and explanation are clear and complete, with no errors. A two-way table showing relative frequencies and a two-way table showing frequencies are provided. The association is correctly described.
3	All parts of the task were completed. The two-way tables showing frequencies and relative frequencies are provided but may have minor calculation errors. The association is correctly described.
2	All parts of the task were attempted. The two-way tables showing frequencies and relative frequencies are provided but may have calculation errors. The association may not be correctly described.
1	Some parts of the task were not attempted. The two-way table showing relative frequencies, the two-way table showing frequencies, and the association are either missing, incomplete, or inaccurate.

Persevere On Your Own

Emissions, GDP, and Urban Population

Materials For each student: Activity Sheet
Solution Sheet

Make Sense of the Problem

Present the Emissions, GDP, and Urban Population problem and use **Three Reads** to help students make sense of it. Have different volunteers take turns reading aloud each section of information. Make sure students recognize they will need to use a line of fit to make predictions about the missing data.

CONNECT TO CONTEXT

Emissions, GDP, and Urban Population Students may not have any familiarity with CO_2 emissions, GDP, or urban population. Tell students that CO_2 emissions, or carbon dioxide emissions into the atmosphere, are often associated with the burning of fossil fuels, like natural gas, crude oil, and coal. Remind students that the Internet Users problem also provided information about CO_2 emissions, and point out that this problem shows total CO_2 emissions, instead of per capita emissions. GDP, or gross domestic product, is the total value of goods and services produced in a country in one year. It is used as an indicator of the general health of a country's economy. *Urban population* refers to the population living in areas that have greater population density and can be an indicator of the development and wealth of a country.

UNIT 7 Math in Action | SESSION 2

Persevere On Your Own

➤ **Read the problem. Write a solution on a separate sheet of paper.**

Emissions, GDP, and Urban Population

Brett wonders if there are any relationships among the following for the countries in his project: CO_2 emissions, GDP (gross domestic product, or the total value of goods and services produced in one year), and urban population. Look at the data and read his notes. Then make and use a scatter plot to predict as many missing values as you can.

Problem-Solving Checklist

- ☐ Tell what is known.
- ☐ Tell what the problem is asking.
- ☐ Show all your work.
- ☐ Show that the solution works.

We are missing three values:

Ecuador: GDP →

Finland: Urban Population →

Lebanon: CO_2 Emissions →

I could use a line of fit to predict these values.

Country	Total CO_2 Emissions (million metric tons)	GDP (billions of U.S. dollars)	Urban Population (millions)
Afghanistan	10	22.0	8
Argentina	204	637.5	37
Australia	361	1,408.7	19
Canada	537	1,647.1	28
Ecuador	44		9
Egypt	202	195.1	35
Ethiopia	12	75.6	18
Fiji	1	4.9	0.488
Finland	47	252.2	
France	303	2,582.5	51
Germany	720	3,693.2	64
Jamaica	7	14.8	2
Japan	1,214	4,872.4	116
Kenya	14	74.9	11
Lebanon		53.4	4
Micronesia	0.15	0.3	0.025
Netherlands	167	830.6	15
Nicaragua	5	13.8	3
Norway	48	399.5	4
Slovakia	31	95.6	3
Somalia	0.6	1.5	4
Spain	234	1,314.3	37
Turkey	346	851.5	55
Venezuela	185	255.1	26
Yemen	23	28.0	9

786

DIFFERENTIATION | Use with Emissions, GDP, and Urban Population

RETEACH

Extra Support

Make and interpret a line of fit.

Materials: For display: graph paper, string

- Display any student's scatter plot that shows a linear association.
- Ask: *Do you observe any patterns in the data?* [The data rise from left to right. As the *x*-values increase, the *y*-values also increase.]
- Ask: *How could you decide where to draw a good line of fit?* [The line of fit should follow the pattern of the data, and it should have about the same number of points above and below the line.]
- Ask: *Is there more than one good line of fit? Why?* [Yes; because it is an approximate model of the data.]
- Have volunteers place the string to model different lines of fit. After each student, discuss why each line is (or is not) a good line of fit.
- Ask: *What does a good line of fit show about the data?* [A good line of fit models the association between the variables.]

EXTEND

Challenge

Solve a different problem.

Brett wonders whether the line of fit for the countries in his project will also make sense for other countries. He finds the data shown. Does the line of fit you found make sense for these countries? Explain your answer.

Country	Total CO_2 Emissions (million metric tons)	GDP (billions of U.S. dollars)	Urban Population (millions)
China	10,291	11,218	838
Russia	1,705	1,246	107

Possible Solution

No; I predicted GDP, *y*, by substituting urban population for *x* in the equation of my line of fit, $y = \frac{250}{6}x - 166$. For China, $y \approx 34{,}751$. For Russia, $y \approx 4{,}292$. Both preditions are much higher than the actual values.

Solve It

Remind students that there are many different ways to solve a problem.

Invite them to look back at the Problem-Solving Checklist to help them get started. They might also want to look at the Problem-Solving Tips on other pages to get some ideas for how to start.

Have students write their complete solution on a copy of Activity Sheet *Solution Sheet* or a blank sheet of paper.

Reflect

Have students work with a partner to share their thinking and discuss the Reflect questions.

As time permits, have students explain their solutions to the class.

Possible Solution

I will make a scatter plot of GDP and urban population, with urban population on the x-axis and GDP on the y-axis. My scatter plot shows a positive linear association, so I will draw a line of fit.

GDP (billions of U.S. dollars) and Urban Population (millions)

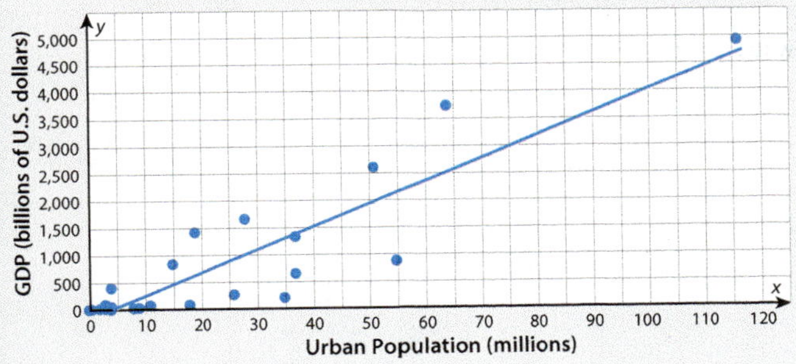

My line of fit intersects the points (40, 1,500) and (100, 4,000). The slope for my line of fit is $\frac{2,500}{60}$.

The equation is: $y = \frac{2,500}{60}x + b$. Solving for b using (40, 1,500) gives $1,500 = \frac{250}{6}(40) + b$. So, b is -167.

The equation of the line of fit is $y = \frac{250}{6}x - 167$.

I will substitute known values into the equation to predict the missing values for Ecuador and Finland.

Ecuador: $y = \frac{250}{6}(9) - 167 = 208$

Finland: $252.2 = \frac{250}{6}x - 167$

$419.2 = \frac{250}{6}x$

$10.0608 = x$

I estimate that the GDP for Ecuador is about $208 billion, and the urban population of Finland is about 10 million.

Math in Action

Solve It

➤ **Find a solution to the Emissions, GDP, and Urban Population problem.**

- Make a scatter plot to show the relationship between the two variables you selected.
- Describe any association shown in the scatter plot.
- Draw a line of fit and write an equation for your line.
- Use your line of fit to predict two of the values that are missing in the table.

Reflect

Use Mathematical Practices After you complete the problem, choose one of these questions to discuss with a partner.

- **Critique Reasoning** Do you agree with your partner's placement of the line of fit and the equation your partner wrote to model it? Explain.
- **Reason Mathematically** What does the slope of your line of fit suggest about the data?

787

Points	Expectations
Scoring Rubric (4 points)	
4	The solution and explanation are clear and complete, with no errors. The scatter plot, line of fit, and missing values are provided. The association is correctly described.
3	All parts of the task were completed. The scatter plot includes a reasonable line of fit, but may have minor errors. The association is correctly described. The equation of the line of fit is a reasonable approximation of the line drawn. Missing values are provided and are reasonable.
2	All parts of the task were attempted. The scatter plot may have errors and a line of fit is drawn. The equation of the line of fit and missing values are provided but may be incorrect. The association may not be correctly described.
1	Some parts of the task were not attempted. The scatter plot, line of fit, missing values, and the association are either missing, incomplete, or inaccurate.

Self Reflection

Have students review the skills on the **Self Reflection** page and work in pairs to respond to the prompts. Encourage students to revisit the work they did in each lesson in order to help develop growth mindset.

- Remind students that this is the same list of skills that they saw on the **Self Check** page at the beginning of the unit.
- Tell students that revisiting the list of skills is an opportunity for them to reflect on their learning and progress during the unit.
- Have students read through the list of skills independently and then work in pairs to respond to the prompts. Encourage students to revisit the work they did in each lesson as they think about how to respond to the prompts.
- Discuss students' responses to the prompts as a class if time permits. Tell students that they will build on these skills in later lessons during the year and/or in other grade levels.

UNIT 7 Self Reflection

In this unit you learned to . . .

Skill	Lesson
Make and use scatter plots to recognize and describe patterns and associations in two-variable data.	29
Assess linear models for good fit to a set of data.	29
Write and interpret equations for linear models that are good lines of fit for data.	30
Understand and identify associations in two-variable categorical data by displaying frequencies in two-way tables.	31, 32
Construct and interpret two-way tables with relative frequencies.	32
Explain your ideas about two-variable data clearly by using models to show why the ideas make sense for the problem.	29–32

Think about what you have learned.

➤ **Use words, numbers, and drawings.**

1. The most important math I learned was __________ because . . .

2. I am proud that I can . . .

3. I would like to learn more about how to . . .

788

Vocabulary Self-Assessment

- Students have interacted with and used unit math and academic vocabulary throughout the unit in listening, speaking, reading, and writing. Use this activity to review the terms and help students check their understanding of the definitions.
- Have students read the vocabulary terms and put a check mark by the terms they can use in speaking and writing. Students can look up words they do not know in the Interactive Glossary or the Academic Glossary in the Teacher Toolbox.

Problem Notes

1. Students may also draw and label a line of fit on the first graph. Check that students understand the terms they used to describe each graph by encouraging them to sketch additional examples of each that do not look exactly like the ones on the page.
2. Students may also identify calculating relative frequencies as a way to analyze two-way tables by explaining that a relative frequency is the ratio of the number of times a response occurs to the total number of responses in a category or in a whole survey.

If time allows, this is a good opportunity to have students work in pairs to read and provide feedback on responses. Feedback should focus on the word meaning, accuracy, and clarity of the response.

UNIT 7 Vocabulary Review

Review the unit vocabulary. Put a check mark by items you can use in speaking and writing. Look up the meaning of any terms you do not know.

Math Vocabulary

- ☐ categorical data
- ☐ cluster
- ☐ line of fit
- ☐ linear association
- ☐ no association
- ☐ nonlinear association
- ☐ outlier
- ☐ relative frequency
- ☐ scatter plot
- ☐ two-way table

Academic Vocabulary

- ☐ analyze
- ☐ likelihood
- ☐ random
- ☐ survey (verb)

Use the unit vocabulary to complete the problems.

1 Use as many math vocabulary terms as you can to describe each graph.

Possible answers:

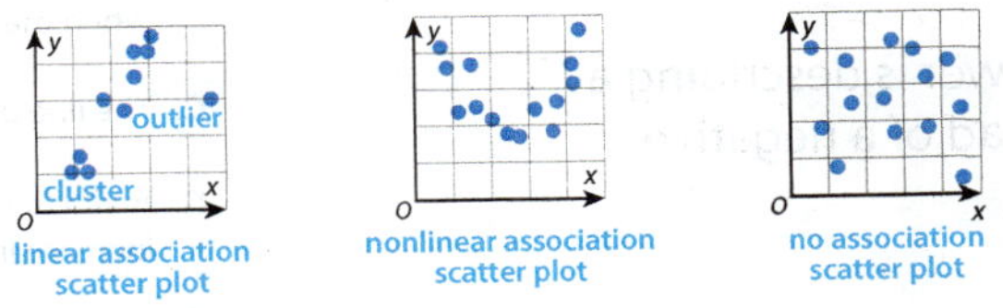

2 Use at least three math or academic vocabulary terms to describe the display of data below. Underline each term you use.

	Grade 6	Grade 7	Grade 8
Buy Lunch	23	45	76
Bring Lunch	72	56	16
Total	95	101	92

Possible answer: This is a two-way table displaying categorial data. The columns tell you that students from three different grades were surveyed on whether they buy lunch or bring lunch. When I analyze the data, I can see that a greater number of the older students tend to buy lunch and a greater number of the younger students tend to bring lunch.

789

Unit Review

Problem Notes

1. Students could also draw a line of fit that passes through the points (5, 27), (8, 21), (9, 19), and (14, 9). This line is a good fit because it models a negative association and is close to all the data points.

   DOK 3 | 8.SP.A.1

2. **B, C, E are correct.** Students could solve the problem by writing an equation for the line of fit and using the equation and the scatter plot to determine whether the statements are true or false.

   A is not correct. This answer represents a line with a positive slope instead of a negative slope.

   D is not correct. This answer is describing a positive association instead of a negative association.

   DOK 2 | 8.SP.A.3

3. Students could determine and explain any associations or lack of associations between age groups and the way they read a book by creating a relative frequency table and interpreting the data for the age groups. About 87% of those surveyed aged 11–30 most commonly read books on an electronic device.

   DOK 2 | 8.SP.A.4

UNIT 7 **Unit Review**

➤ **Use what you have learned to complete these problems.**

1. Researchers timed 20 children reading a page of text. The scatter plot shows the age of the child and the total time spent reading the page. Draw a good line of fit. Explain your reasoning.

   Possible student work:

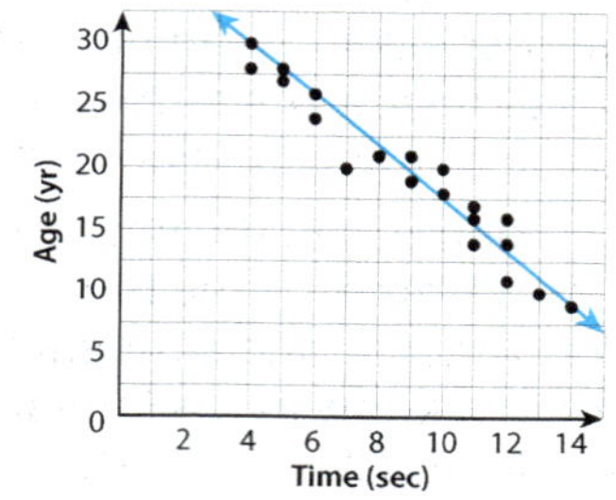

   SOLUTION Possible answer: The line is a good fit because it models a negative association and is close to all the data points.

2. This scatter plot shows sales of winter coats at a store and the outside temperature. Which statements describe the scatter plot and line of fit? Choose all the correct answers.

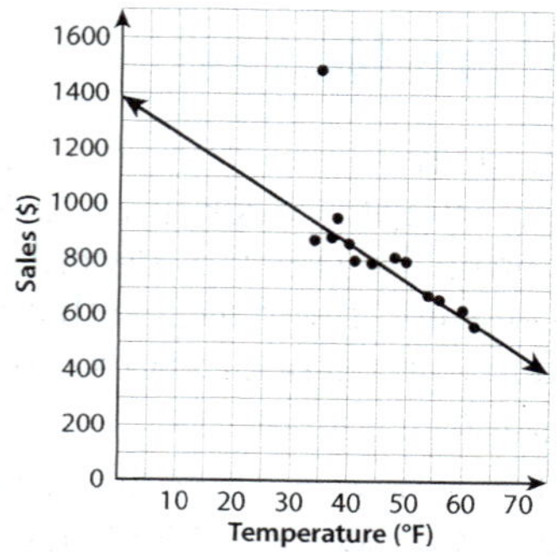

   A A possible equation of the line of fit is $y = 13x + 1{,}382$.

   (B) The line of fit can be used to predict winter coat sales when the temperature is 70°F.

   (C) The line of fit shows a negative association.

   D An increase in temperature most likely means an increase in sales.

   (E) If the temperature is less than 40°F, then the estimated sales will be over $800.

3. A survey is given to 228 people aged 11–70. The people are asked how they most commonly read a book. The table shows the results. Is there an association between the method of reading a book and age? Explain your reasoning.

	Audiobook	Electronic Device	Paperback/Hardcover	Total
Ages 11–30	4	76	7	87
Ages 31–50	21	25	24	70
Ages 51–70	24	21	26	71

   SOLUTION Yes; Possible explanation: An electronic device is most likely for ages 11–30. No method is more likely than the others for ages 31–70.

790

Unit Game

8.SP.A.1, 8.SP.A.2

SMP 1, 2, 3, 4, 5, 6, 7

Scatter Plot Association

Materials For each player: Recording Sheet, ruler or straightedge (optional); For each pair: 1 set of Grid Section Cards

WHY Reinforce constructing a scatter plot to model a linear association, a nonlinear association, or no association. Also, reinforce using a line of fit to analyze and describe scatter plots.

HOW Players use Grid Section Cards to plot points on a coordinate grid to create scatter plots that show a positive linear assocation, a negative linear association, a nonlinear association, and no association. Players compare their plots to determine the best representation.

- Clarify that students may add 0, 1, or 3 data points to each section, but only 4 times each.
- After students finish the game, ask them to share strategies they used. Ask questions such as: *How did you decide how many points to use in a section of the grid? How did you decide where to place the points to create each association?*

Challenge Have students find the balance point of the data for each plot.

ELL Support Ask students to discuss the differences between the terms *negative linear association, nonlinear association,* and *no association.* Ask students to draw a sketch of each type of association for reference.

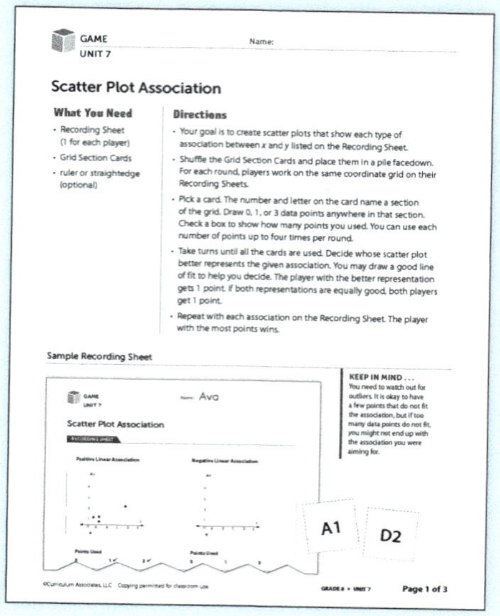

4 *DOK 1* | 8.SP.A.4

5 **A, C, D are correct.** Students could solve the problem by checking each line to determine if it follows the pattern of the data points and if about half the data points are on either side of the line.

B is not correct. This answer represents a horizontal line that has a 0 slope.

E is not correct. Although Line *d* has a positive slope and passes through four points, all the other points are below the line. So, it is not as good a fit as Line *a*, which has about half the points on either side of the line.

DOK 1 | 8.SP.A.2

6 *DOK 2* | 8.SP.A.4

4 Students in Grades 7 and 8 are asked whether they prefer earning money completing indoor chores, completing outdoor chores, or babysitting. The table shows the results. What is the likelihood that a randomly selected student in Grade 8 prefers babysitting? Record your answer on the grid. Then fill in the bubbles.

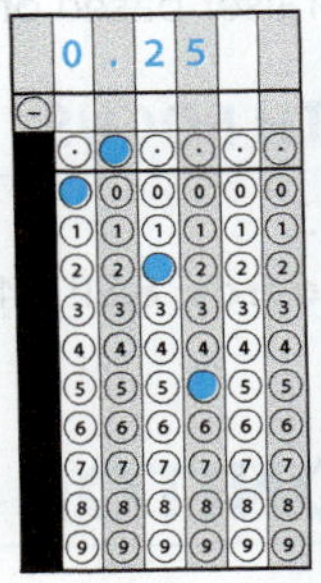

	Indoor Chores	Outdoor Chores	Babysitting	Total
Grade 7	22	60	16	98
Grade 8	32	46	26	104
Total	54	106	42	202

5 Which statements are true about the scatter plot? Choose all the correct answers.

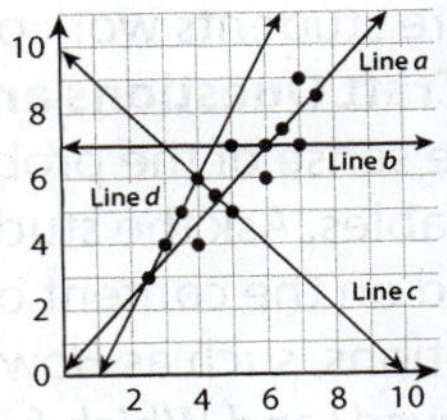

(A) Line *a* is a good fit because it models a positive association and is close to all the data points.

B Line *b* is a good fit because it goes through three of the data points.

(C) Line *c* is not a good fit because it models a negative association.

(D) Line *d* is not a good fit; although it models a positive association, it is above most of the data points.

E Lines *a* and *d* are equally good lines of fit for the data.

6 A survey is given to 189 people aged 11–30. The people are asked how they prefer to watch a movie. The incomplete table shows the results. Complete the table to show how to find how many people aged 11–20 prefer going to the movie theater. Write your answers in the blanks.

	Movie Theater	At Home	Total
Ages 11–20	56	31	87
Ages 21–30	18	84	102
Total	74	115	189

791

Literacy Connection

Social Studies Article

Materials "Language Change," Literacy Connection Problems

Summary In "Language Change," students learn about the reasons languages change over time and the types of changes that may occur.

Math Connection This social studies article introduces students to some of the research that linguists carry out. After reading the passage, students will use statistical tools and models that they have learned about, such as scatter plots and two-way tables, to analyze data about language evolution.

- Have students read the passage.
- Distribute the literacy connection problems. After reading the directions aloud, direct students to turn and talk about problem 1. Check for understanding.
- Have students work independently to complete the remaining problems. Encourage them to use manipulatives or to draw pictures to solve each problem.
- Circulate and monitor while students work.
- Ask volunteers to share and discuss their solutions with the class.

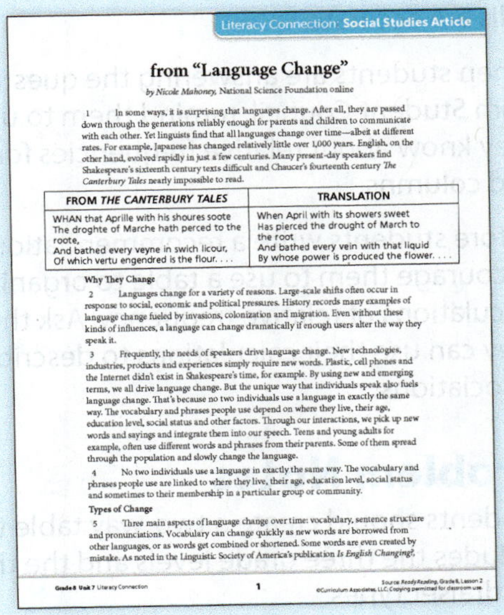
Literacy Connection: **Social Studies Article**

from "Language Change"

by Nicole Mahoney, National Science Foundation online

1 In some ways, it is surprising that languages change. After all, they are passed down through the generations reliably enough for parents and children to communicate with each other. Yet linguists find that all languages change over time—albeit at different rates. For example, Japanese has changed relatively little over 1,000 years. English, on the other hand, evolved rapidly in just a few centuries. Many present-day speakers find Shakespeare's sixteenth century texts difficult and Chaucer's fourteenth century *The Canterbury Tales* nearly impossible to read.

FROM *THE CANTERBURY TALES*	TRANSLATION
WHAN that Aprille with his shoures soote The droghte of Marche hath perced to the roote, And bathed every veyne in swich licour, Of which vertu engendred is the flour. . . .	When April with its showers sweet Has pierced the drought of March to the root And bathed every vein with that liquid By whose power is produced the flower. . . .

Why They Change

2 Languages change for a variety of reasons. Large-scale shifts often occur in response to social, economic and political pressures. History records many examples of language change fueled by invasions, colonization and migration. Even without these kinds of influences, a language can change dramatically if enough users alter the way they speak it.

3 Frequently, the needs of speakers drive language change. New technologies, industries, products and experiences simply require new words. Plastic, cell phones and the Internet didn't exist in Shakespeare's time, for example. By using new and emerging terms, we all drive language change. But the unique way that individuals speak also fuels language change. That's because no two individuals use a language in exactly the same way. The vocabulary and phrases people use depend on where they live, their age, education level, social status and other factors. Through our interactions, we pick up new words and sayings and integrate them into our speech. Teens and young adults for example, often use different words and phrases from their parents. Some of them spread through the population and slowly change the language.

4 No two individuals use a language in exactly the same way. The vocabulary and phrases people use are linked to where they live, their age, education level, social status and sometimes to their membership in a particular group or community.

Types of Change

5 Three main aspects of language change over time: vocabulary, sentence structure and pronunciations. Vocabulary can change quickly as new words are borrowed from other languages, or as words get combined or shortened. Some words are even created by mistake. As noted in the Linguistic Society of America's publication *Is English Changing?*,

Grade 8 Unit 7 Literacy Connection 1 Source: *Ready Reading*, Grade 8, Lesson 2 ©Curriculum Associates, LLC Copying permitted for classroom use.

Unit Review

Purpose

Apply knowledge of constructing and interpreting a two-way table in order to use relative frequencies and possible associations to determine the best possible fundraiser based on student preferences.

MATH FOCUS

DOK 3

Standards 8.SP.A.4

MONITOR & GUIDE SMP 2, 3, 4, 5, 6

Make Sense of the Problem

Before students work on the Performance Task, use **Co-Craft Questions and Problems** to help them make sense of the problem. Draw their attention to the tables. Ask the students to write questions based on the content of the tables. Collect student questions, such as *How many total students were surveyed?* and *Which fundraiser is most preferred?* Point out the goal of the Performance Task, analyzing data to choose the best fundraiser. Confirm that students understand they will create a two-way table to answer the questions from Student Council.

Facilitate Problem Solving

Have students complete the task independently, with partners, or in small groups.

If students need additional support as they get started, guide them to create the two-way table by asking what the column and row headers should be and what data they know from the given information. Ask them how they can use what they know to determine the missing information.

After students have completed their tables, ask how they can prove that the totals and individual data cells are accurate.

When students are answering the questions from Student Council, remind them to use what they know about relative frequencies for rows and columns.

Before students write a recommendation, encourage them to use a table to organize their calculations of relative frequency. Ask them how they can use their calculations to describe any associations.

Problem Notes

Students should create a two-way table that includes the three grade levels and the three fundraiser types.

Students should demonstrate ability to calculate relative frequencies, row or column.

UNIT 7 Unit Review

Performance Task

➤ **Answer the questions and show all your work on separate paper.**

Student Council gave a survey to middle school students. The table shows how many students in each grade were surveyed.

Grade 6	Grade 7	Grade 8
50	52	54

The students were asked how they prefer to raise money for a new school garden. The table below shows how many students preferred each possible fundraiser.

Dance-a-thon	Walkathon	Swim-a-thon
68	51	37

Of the students surveyed:

- 22 Grade 6 students prefer a dance-a-thon.
- 18 Grade 7 students prefer a walkathon.
- 32 Grade 8 students prefer a dance-a-thon
- 5 Grade 8 students prefer a swim-a-thon.

Student Council asks you to analyze the data to help them choose the fundraiser that will have the greatest participation so the most money will be raised. Create a two-way table that includes the information gathered from the survey. Then answer the following questions submitted by Student Council:

- What percent of Grade 8 students surveyed prefer a walkathon?
- What percent of students surveyed who prefer a dance-a-thon are Grade 6 students?
- What percent of students surveyed prefer a swim-a-thon?
- Which fundraiser do you recommend? Explain your reasoning.

Checklist

Did you . . .

- ☐ create an accurate two-way table?
- ☐ check that your calculations of relative frequency match the given information?
- ☐ use data and associations from your two-way table to make a reasonable recommendation for a fundraiser?

Reflect

Use Mathematical Practices After you complete the task, choose one of the following questions to answer.

- **Be Precise** Will calculating relative frequencies by rows or columns influence your data?
- **Argue and Critique** What mathematical evidence supports your recommendation?

792

Students should be able to accurately answer the questions and use their responses to help frame their recommendation and identify associations between number of students and preferred fundraisers.

Students should recognize when associations are strong enough to base their recommendations on them. Associations are *strong enough* when there are clear relationships and significant data support the recommendation.

Student responses should include a two-way table, responses to the questions from Student Council, and a fundraiser recommendation. Students should defend their recommendation using data from their table and relative frequencies.

Reflect

Be Precise Look for understanding that the students know the difference between overall relative frequencies, row frequencies, and column frequencies.

Argue and Critique Look for explanations that show students supporting their fundraiser recommendation with a relative frequency indicating a reasonably strong association.

4-Point Solution

I used a two-way table to organize the totals and data I knew from the given information. Then I used what I knew to find the missing information.

	Dance-a-thon	Walkathon	Swim-a-thon	Total
Grade 6	22	16	12	50
Grade 7	14	18	20	52
Grade 8	32	17	5	54
Total	68	51	37	156

There were 54 Grade 8 students surveyed, and 17 prefer a walkathon, which is about 31%.

There were 68 students surveyed who prefer a dance-a-thon, and 22 are Grade 6 students, which is about 32%.

There were 156 students surveyed, and 37 prefer a swim-a-thon, which is about 24%.

The dance-a-thon was preferred the most, with an overall relative frequency of about 44% (68 out of 156 students). This is not over half of those surveyed, so I created a relative frequency table using row totals that shows the percent of students in each grade who prefer each type of fundraiser to see if the percents for dance-a-thon are greater for each grade.

	Dance-a-thon	Walkathon	Swim-a-thon	Total
Grade 6	44%	32%	24%	100%
Grade 7	27%	35%	38%	100%
Grade 8	59%	31%	9%	≈100%

I recommend the dance-a-thon because it is preferred by 44% of Grade 6 students, 27% of Grade 7 students, and 59% of Grade 8 students surveyed.

Scoring Rubric

Points	Expectations
4	The student's response is accurate and complete. The student created a two-way table, answered Student Council's questions, and used mathematical reasoning to describe which fundraiser might raise the most money.
3	The student's strategy and process are correct, but there are minor errors in calculations. All questions have been answered. A recommendation has been written.
2	The response contains several mistakes in the calculations. The student may have attempted to address all parts of the problem, but the response is incorrect and/or incomplete.
1	The student's response is incorrect and incomplete. The response does not address all the questions or provide a recommendation.

DIFFERENTIATION | EXTEND

If students have more time to spend on this problem or require an additional challenge, then use this extension to have them revisit their recommendation based on new information about the students.

Student Council was given the following updated information regarding the school garden fundraiser. The information provides new data about the participation plans of the middle school students.

- Fewer than half of the Grade 6 students plan to participate.
- About half of the Grade 7 students plan to participate.
- Almost all of the Grade 8 students plan to participate.

Does your fundraiser recommendation change based on this new information?

Solution

No. It does not change my recommendation because 59% of the Grade 8 students chose a dance-a-thon. Since most of the Grade 8 students will attend and only half of the Grade 7 students will attend, the dance-a-thon continues to be the fundraiser that will make the most money for the new school garden. Also, since fewer than half of the Grade 6 students will attend and most of those surveyed preferred the dance-a-thon, it's safe to assume that the students will participate in a dance-a-thon.

Unit Assessment

Problem Notes

Form A is shown. *See* ***Teacher Toolbox*** *for Form B.*

1 **A, B, E are correct.** Students could solve the problem by drawing a line through the data and interpreting the slope of the line as negative. Then determine the type of linear association and describe the relationship between the variables.

C is not correct. This answer represents data points that would appear higher than other data points when moving from left to right.

D is not correct. This answer describes points that would move upward from left to right.

(2 points)

DOK 2 | **8.SP.A.1**

2 **C is correct.** Students could solve the problem by finding the relative frequency, $\frac{108}{165}$.

A is not correct. This answer represents dividing the number of Grade 7 students by the total number of students surveyed, $\frac{108}{417}$.

B is not correct. This answer represents the relative frequency of students who prefer eating in a restaurant that are in Grade 7, $\frac{108}{210}$.

D is not correct. This answer represents the number of Grade 7 students who prefer eating at a restaurant.

(1 point)

DOK 1 | **8.SP.A.4**

3 **a.** There are 25 students who go home by car and are participants in after-school programs compared to 6 students going home by car who do not participate in after-school programs.

b. The most common form of transportation for participants is car, and the most common form of transportation for nonparticipants is bike.

c. Walking is almost evenly split among 16 participants and 15 nonparticipants.

d. Participants are least likely to ride a bike.

(2 points)

DOK 2 | **8.SP.A.4**

4 (1 point)

DOK 1 | **8.SP.A.3**

UNIT 7 • UNIT ASSESSMENT   Name:
FORM A

➤ **Solve the problems.**

1 This scatter plot shows the number of minutes each player on the golf team practiced putting and their golf score. Which statements about the scatter plot are true? Choose all the correct answers. *(2 points)*

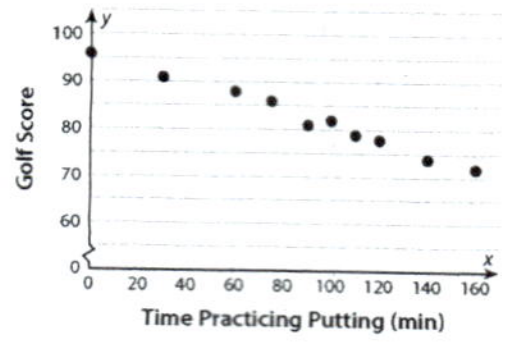

(A) There do not appear to be any outliers.

(B) The data show a negative association.

C The players that spent the most time practicing had the highest scores.

D The points seem to form a positive slope.

(E) The player that spent no time practicing had the highest score.

2 Jackson asks students whether they prefer to eat at a restaurant or have food delivered. The table shows the results. What is the relative frequency of students in Grade 7 who prefer eating at a restaurant? *(1 point)*

	Restaurant	Delivery	Total
Grade 6	59	78	137
Grade 7	108	42	165
Grade 8	90	40	130
Total	210	207	417

A 25.8%
B 51.4%
(C) 65.4%
D 108%

©Curriculum Associates, LLC Copying permitted for classroom use. GRADE 8 • UNIT 7 • Unit Assessment | Form A **Page 1 of 6**

UNIT 7 • UNIT ASSESSMENT   Name:
FORM A continued

3 The table shows the results of a survey of students. The students are asked if they participate in after-school programs and how they get home from school. The administration wants to know if a student's form of transportation affects whether they participate in after-school programs. Decide if each statement about the two-way table is true. Choose *True* or *False* for each statement. *(2 points)*

	Bike	Walk	Car	Bus	Total
Participants	8	16	25	14	63
Nonparticipants	24	15	6	17	62
Total	32	31	31	31	125

	True	False
a. Students who go home in a car are more likely to participate in an after-school program.	●	○
b. The most common form of transportation for participants and nonparticipants is the same.	○	●
c. Walking does not appear to affect participation.	●	○
d. Participants are least likely to take a bus home.	○	●

4 The scatter plot shows the number of apples Aniyah picked from her apple trees each year. The equation of the line of fit is $y = 15.2x + 111$. What is the predicted number of apples picked in year 5? Record your answer on the grid. Then fill in the bubbles. *(1 point)*

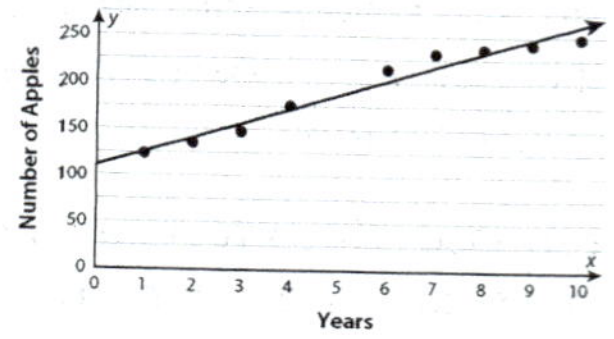

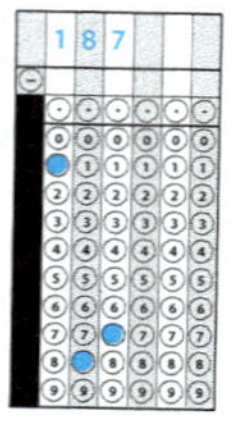

©Curriculum Associates, LLC Copying permitted for classroom use. GRADE 8 • UNIT 7 • Unit Assessment | Form A **Page 2 of 6**

5 Students can ignore the outlier and draw a line that passes through most of the points and has an equal number of points above and below the line.

(2 points)

DOK 3 | **8.SP.A.1**

6 Students could recognize that slope is the constant before *x* in the equation of the line of fit.

(2 points)

DOK 2 | **8.SP.A.3**

UNIT 7 • UNIT ASSESSMENT Name:
FORM A continued

5 This scatter plot shows the years since 2010 and the number of coding club members at the library. The line of fit shown takes into account the outlier at (9, 5). Explain why it is not a good line of fit. Then draw a good line of fit. *(2 points)*

Possible student work:

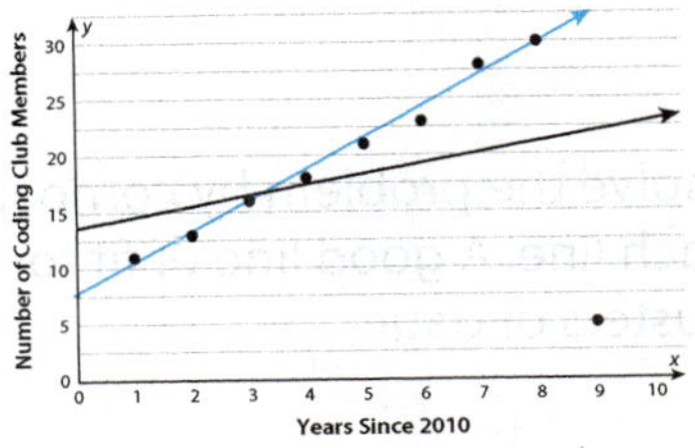

SOLUTION Possible explanation: The original line only lies close to two of the points. A good line of fit will be close to most of the data points and ignore the outlier.

6 This scatter plot shows the amount of time, in hours, 12 students spent on their science project and their project grade. The equation of the line of fit is $y = 9.5x + 52$. What is the slope of the equation, and what does it mean? Explain your reasoning. *(2 points)*

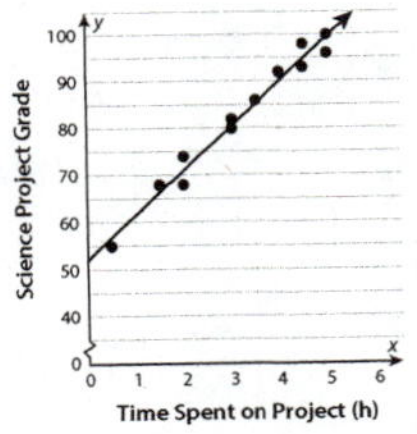

SOLUTION 9.5; Possible explanation: The slope of 9.5 means that for every hour spent working on the project, the grade increases by 9.5 points.

©Curriculum Associates, LLC Copying permitted for classroom use. GRADE 8 • UNIT 7 • Unit Assessment | Form A Page 3 of 6

7 Students could recognize that another possible association is a song over 3 minutes long will most likely have fewer than 100 purchases.

(2 points)

DOK 2 | **8.SP.A.4**

8 **a.** A line of fit could pass through data points with some points above the line and some below the line.

b. A good line of fit indicates linear association.

c. There can be only one good line of fit, or else the slope is not constant and the data do not follow a straight line.

d. A line of good fit indicates the data follow a straight line.

(2 points)

DOK 1 | **8.SP.A.2**

9 (2 points)

DOK 2 | **8.SP.A.4**

UNIT 7 • UNIT ASSESSMENT Name:
FORM A continued

7 A songwriter records the length, in minutes, of her songs. She then notes the number of her songs that were bought online. What association can be observed from the data in the table? Explain your reasoning. *(2 points)*

	0–100 Bought	Over 100 Bought	Total
Less Than 3 Minutes	5	26	31
3 Minutes or More	31	8	39
Total	36	34	70

SOLUTION Possible explanation: A song less than 3 minutes is more likely to be bought. A song more than 3 minutes is less likely to be bought.

8 Decide if each statement about a line of fit is true. Choose *True* or *False* for each statement. *(2 points)*

	True	False
a. Sometimes a line of fit will not pass through any of the data points.	●	○
b. A line of fit does not necessarily indicate a linear association.	○	●
c. Sometimes more than one line of fit is needed to model a data set.	○	●
d. A set of data has to show a linear pattern in order for a line to be a good fit.	●	○

9 A school asks students what type of sports they play. Complete the two-way table for the survey data. Write your answers in the blanks. *(2 points)*

	Plays Team Sports	Plays Individual Sports	Does Not Play Sports	Total
Grade 7	22	57	9	88
Grade 8	36	62	25	123
Total	58	119	34	211

©Curriculum Associates, LLC Copying permitted for classroom use. GRADE 8 • UNIT 7 • Unit Assessment | Form A Page 4 of 6

Problem Notes

10 Students could select and reasonably estimate any two points on the line to find slope and write the equation. Accept minor variations with supporting work.

(2 points)

DOK 2 | 8.SP.A.3

11 Students could solve the problem by comparing the proximity of the data points to each line. A good line of fit for this scatter plot will go through both clusters of data.

(2 points)

DOK 2 | 8.SP.A.2

12 The data pattern is curved instead of a straight line. So, a linear association cannot be made, and a good line of fit cannot be drawn.

(2 points)

DOK 2 | 8.SP.A.1

13 **B, C, E are correct.** Students could solve the problem by comparing the cell values and interpreting the data to determine which statements are true.

A is not correct. This answer represents the Grade 8 total instead of Grade 8 students who chose football.

D is not correct. This answer represents looking at the soccer balls column instead of the Grade 7 row. Kickballs were the most popular choice for Grade 7 students.

(2 points)

DOK 2 | 8.SP.A.4

UNIT 7 • UNIT ASSESSMENT Name:
FORM A continued

10 A record keeper records the distance from the scorer to the goal, in feet, and how long, in minutes, into the game they scored. The scatter plot shows the data and a good line of fit. Write an equation for the line of fit. Show your work. *(2 points)*

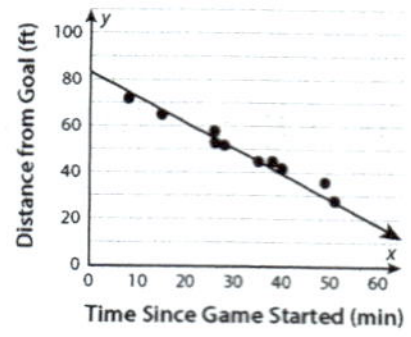

Possible student work:
The line of fit appears to go through points (30, 50) and (40, 40).

$m = \frac{40 - 50}{40 - 30} = \frac{-10}{10} = -1$

$y = -1x + b$

$40 = -1(40) + b$

$40 = -40 + b$

$80 = b$

$y = -x + 80$

SOLUTION Possible answer: $y = -x + 80$

11 Which line on the scatter plot is a good line of fit for the data? Explain your reasoning. *(2 points)*

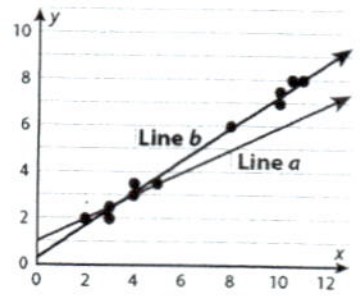

SOLUTION Line b; Possible explanation: The line passes through the points with half the points above the line and half the points below the line.

UNIT 7 • UNIT ASSESSMENT Name:
FORM A continued

12 Alfred says that the line shown on the scatter plot is a good line of fit because the line goes through the middle of all the data points. Do you agree? Explain your reasoning. *(2 points)*

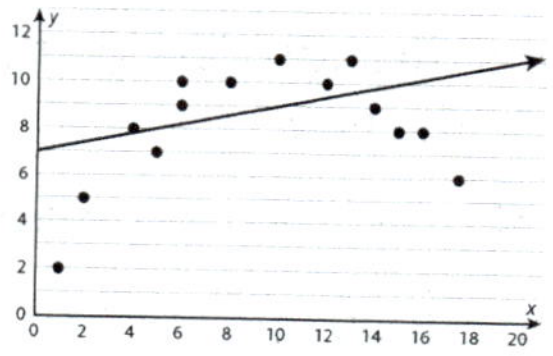

SOLUTION No; Possible explanation: For there to be a good line fit, the data must have a linear association. The data on the scatter plot are not in the shape of a straight line but instead in the shape of a curve.

13 A physical education teacher asks her students which type of sports ball she should buy for the gym. The results of the survey are shown in the table. Which statements are true for the data? Choose all the correct answers. *(2 points)*

	Basketballs	Soccer Balls	Footballs	Kickballs	Total
Grade 6	9	18	14	36	77
Grade 7	5	29	16	58	108
Grade 8	26	12	5	12	55
Total	40	59	35	106	240

A Fifty-five Grade 8 students chose kickballs.

(B) Kickballs got the most votes.

(C) A Grade 8 student would most likely choose basketballs.

D Soccer balls were the most popular choice for Grade 7 students.

(E) Seventy-seven Grade 6 students were surveyed.

Scoring Guide

For the problems in the Unit 7 Unit Assessments (Forms A and B), the table shows:

- depth of knowledge (DOK) level
- points for scoring
- lesson assessed by each problem
- standard addressed

Problem	DOK	Points	Lesson	Standard
1	2	2	29	8.SP.A.1
2	1	1	32	8.SP.A.4
3	2	2	32	8.SP.A.4
4	1	1	30	8.SP.A.3
5	3	2	29	8.SP.A.1
6	2	2	30	8.SP.A.3
7	2	2	31	8.SP.A.4
8	1	2	29	8.SP.A.2
9	2	2	31	8.SP.A.4
10	2	2	30	8.SP.A.3
11	2	2	29	8.SP.A.2
12	2	2	29	8.SP.A.1
13	2	2	31	8.SP.A.4

Scoring Rubrics

Short Response Scoring Rubric

Points	Expectations
2	Response has the correct solution(s) and includes well-organized, clear, and concise work demonstrating thorough understanding of mathematical concepts and/or procedures.
1	Response contains mostly correct solution(s) and shows partial understanding of mathematical concepts and/or procedures.
0	Response shows no attempt at finding a solution and no effort to demonstrate an understanding of mathematical concepts and/or procedures.

Choice Matrix, Fill-in-the-Blank, and Multiple Select Scoring Rubric

Points	Expectations
2	All answers are correct
1	1 incorrect answer
0	2 or more incorrect answers

Data Sets

Unit 7

LESSON 29 | SESSION 1

Try It

Memory Game	
Screen Time (h)	**Memory Test Score**
10	97
11	94
11	96
13	93
14	94
14	91
15	90
16	89
17	86
18	85
19	82
19	83
20	80
20	81
20	83
21	79
24	75
24	76
25	75
25	72

LESSON 29 | SESSION 2

Practice 1

Rectangle Dimensions	
Length (in.)	**Width (in.)**
3	3
2	3
4	1
3	4
4	4
2	5
5	3
3	6
5	6
3	7
7	5
2	8
8	4
7	8
5	8

LESSON 29 | SESSION 5

Refine 2

Social Media Users	
Year	**U.S. Adults (%)**
2005	7
2006	11
2008	25
2009	38
2010	46
2011	50
2012	55
2013	62
2014	62
2015	65
2016	69
2018	69

Data Sets

Data Sets

Unit 7

LESSON 31 | SESSION 3

Apply It 1

Trail Mix Sales

Hours	Bags Sold
1	13
1	15
1	21
2	20
2	24
3	11
3	23
3	28
4	22
4	28
5	11
5	15
5	19
6	34
7	28
7	43
8	20
8	28
9	15
9	49

LESSON 32 | SESSION 1

Try It

Public Library Visit

Community	Visited a Library
urban	yes
suburban	no
urban	yes
urban	no
urban	yes
suburban	no
suburban	yes
urban	no
suburban	yes
urban	yes
urban	yes
suburban	yes
suburban	no
suburban	no
urban	yes
urban	no
suburban	yes
urban	yes
urban	yes
suburban	no
suburban	yes
suburban	no
urban	yes
suburban	no
urban	yes
suburban	no
urban	yes
urban	no
urban	no
suburban	yes

Data Sets

Unit 7

LESSON 32 | SESSION 1

Prepare for 3

Horseback Riding	
Grade	**Horseback**
11	yes
11	yes
12	no
12	yes
12	no
12	no
11	yes
11	no
12	yes
11	yes
11	yes
12	no
11	no
12	yes
11	yes
11	yes
12	no
11	yes
12	no
11	yes
11	no
11	yes
11	yes
12	yes
12	no
11	no
12	yes
12	no
12	no
11	yes

Data Sets

Unit 7

MATH IN ACTION | SESSION 1

Internet Users

Country	Population using the internet (%)	CO_2 Emissions per capita (metric tons)	Total Population (thousands)	Population under age 15 (%)	Life expectancy at birth (years)
Afghanistan	11.4	0.3	32,358	47.42	62.3
Argentina	69.7	4.7	40,765	24.42	75.7
Australia	86.5	15.3	22,606	18.95	82.4
Canada	92.7	15.1	34,350	16.37	81.8
Ecuador	57.3	2.8	14,666	30.29	75.6
Egypt	45.0	2.2	82,537	31.25	70.8
Ethiopia	18.6	0.1	84,734	43.29	63.7
Fiji	50.0	1.3	868	28.88	66.9
Finland	87.5	8.6	5,385	16.42	80.7
France	80.5	4.7	63,126	18.26	81.9
Germany	84.4	8.9	82,163	13.17	80.4
Jamaica	48.8	2.7	2,751	27.78	74.0
Japan	90.9	9.6	126,497	13.12	83.3
Kenya	17.8	0.3	41,610	42.37	62.9
Lebanon	78.2	4.3	4,259	21.64	78.6
Micronesia	35.3	1.4	112	35.81	66.9
Netherlands	93.2	9.9	16,665	17.21	81.3
Nicaragua	27.9	0.8	5,870	33.37	73.1
Norway	96.5	9.2	4,925	18.64	81.6
Slovakia	81.6	5.6	5,472	15.00	76.2
Somalia	2.0	0.1	9,557	47.35	54.9
Spain	84.6	5.1	46,455	15.20	82.5
Turkey	64.7	4.5	73,640	26.00	75.6
Venezuela	64.3	6.1	29,437	28.84	73.1
Yemen	26.7	0.9	24,800	40.72	66.0
Worldwide Average	52.8	5.1	16,348	28.80	70.8

Data Sets

Unit 7

MATH IN ACTION | SESSION 2

Age Groups

Country	Total Population (thousands)	Population under age 15 (%)	Population over age 60 (%)
Afghanistan	32,358	47.42	3.82
Argentina	40,765	24.42	14.97
Australia	22,606	18.95	19.46
Canada	34,350	16.37	20.82
Ecuador	14,666	30.29	9.21
Egypt	82,537	31.25	8.62
Ethiopia	84,734	43.29	5.17
Fiji	868	28.88	8.38
Finland	5,385	16.42	25.90
France	63,126	18.26	23.82
Germany	82,163	13.17	26.72
Jamaica	2,751	27.78	10.98
Japan	126,497	13.12	31.92
Kenya	41,610	42.37	4.25
Lebanon	4,259	21.64	12.03
Micronesia	112	35.81	6.67
Netherlands	16,665	17.21	23.02
Nicaragua	5,870	33.37	6.59
Norway	4,925	18.64	21.41
Slovakia	5,472	15.00	18.60
Somalia	9,557	47.35	4.46
Spain	46,455	15.20	22.86
Turkey	73,640	26.00	10.56
Venezuela	29,437	28.84	9.17
Yemen	24,800	40.72	4.54

Data Sets

NOTES

UNIT 5

Cumulative Practice

Purpose

Sets 1–3 of the cumulative practice are designed to practice determining if the relationship between two quantities is a function, identifying linear and nonlinear functions, and using functions to model linear relationships.

Problem Notes

Set 1 Functions

Review: Grade 8 Lesson 15

Standard: **8.F.A.1**

Error Alert If students write that *y* is not a function of *x* in problem 1 then ask them how the inputs and outputs of a function are related. Have them graph the values in the table to see that there is only one point above or below each input value.

Set 2 Linear and Nonlinear Functions

Review: Grade 8 Lesson 15

Standard: **8.F.A.3**

UNIT 5 Cumulative Practice Name:

Cumulative Practice

Set 1 Functions

➤ **Fill in the blanks for problem 1.**

1. The table shows inputs and outputs.

Input (x)	1	2	3	4	5
Output (y)	1	1	2	2	3

In the table, y __is__ a function of x, because each __input__ has only one __output__.

➤ **Solve problem 2.**

2. Complete the graph by plotting the (input, output) pairs in the table. Use the graph to explain why y is not a function of x.

Input (x)	−2	1	0	−1	2	0
Output (y)	0	2	1	0	4	3

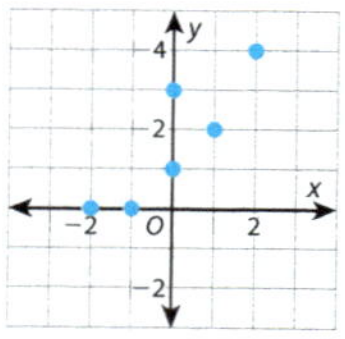

The point (0, 3) is directly above (0, 1). This means the input 0 has two outputs, 1 and 3, so y is not a function of x.

Set 2 Linear and Nonlinear Functions

➤ **Tell whether each function is *linear* or *nonlinear*.**

1. $y = 2x + 4$ __linear__

2. $y = \frac{x}{2} - 3$ __linear__

3. $y = x^2 + 2$ __nonlinear__

4. $y = 2$ __linear__

5. 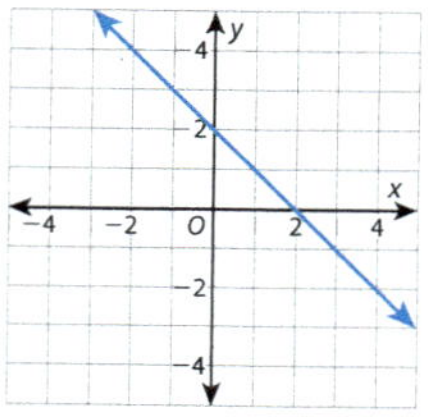

__linear__

6. 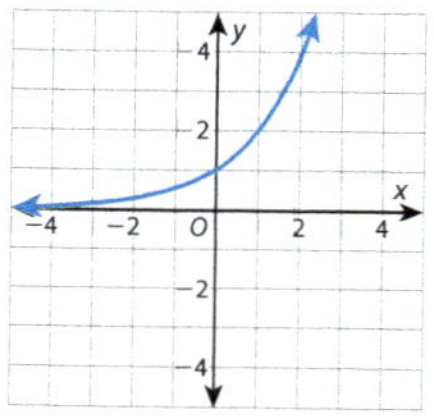

__nonlinear__

Cumulative Practice

CP17

Set 3 Use Functions to Model Linear Relationships

Review: Grade 8 Lesson 16

Standard: **8.F.B.4**

Error Alert If students find that the rate of change is $-\frac{4}{3}$ in problem 4 because they think the function is decreasing, then have them plot (2, −3) and then use $\frac{\text{rise}}{\text{run}}$ to plot the next point. Ask them whether the slope is positive or negative.

Set 3 Use Functions to Model Linear Relationships

➤ **Solve the problems. Show your work.** Possible work:

1. The total cost of an order of custom jackets is a function of the number of jackets. The table shows the cost of ordering different numbers of jackets. Write an equation for the linear function that models this situation.

Jackets	Cost
10	$350
40	$1,100
50	$1,350

Rate of change $= \frac{1{,}350 - 350}{50 - 10}$ $350 = 25(10) + b$

$= \frac{1{,}000}{40}$ $100 = b$

$= 25$ So, $y = 25x + 100$.

2. Rafael is biking home from work. The graph shows Rafael's distance from home as a function of time.

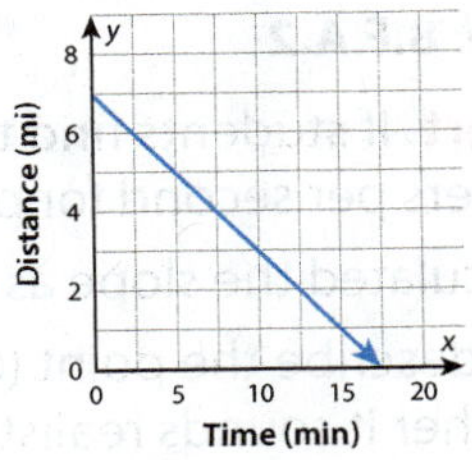

Find the initial value and rate of change for the function and describe what each quantity means in this situation.

The initial value is 7, which means Rafael works 7 miles from home.

Rate of change $= \frac{7 - 5}{0 - 5}$

$= -\frac{2}{5}$ or -0.4

The rate of change is −0.4, which means his distance from home decreases by 0.4 mile per minute of travel.

3. Diana observes a snail moving away from herself. The snail moves 2 inches in 4 seconds. The snail is 9 inches away from Diana after 3 seconds. Write an equation for the snail's distance from Diana, y, as a function of time, x.

Rate of change $= \frac{2}{4} = 0.5$ $9 = 0.5(3) + b$

$9 = 1.5 + b$

$b = 7.5$ So, $y = 0.5x + 7.5$

4. The graph of a linear function passes through the point (2, −3). The value of the function decreases by 4 when the input decreases by 3. Write the equation that models the function.

Rate of change $= \frac{-4}{-3} = \frac{4}{3}$

$-3 = \frac{4}{3}(2) + b$

$-5\frac{2}{3} = b$ So, $y = \frac{4}{3}x - 5\frac{2}{3}$.

CP18

Cumulative Practice

Purpose

Sets 4–7 of the cumulative practice are designed to practice comparing functions that have different representations, analyzing graphs of functional relationships, graphing proportional relationships and calculating slope, and solving systems of linear equations.

Problem Notes

Set 4 Compare Functions

Review: Grade 8 Lesson 17

Standard: **8.F.A.2**

Error Alert If students find that the dog's speed is 0.06 meters per second for problem 1, then they have calculated the slope as $\frac{\text{run}}{\text{rise}}$ instead of $\frac{\text{rise}}{\text{run}}$. Ask them to describe the point (6, 100) in words. Then ask whether it sounds realistic that a dog running 100 meters in 6 seconds is running at a speed of 0.06 meters per second.

Set 5 Analyze Graphs of Functional Relationships

Review: Grade 8 Lesson 18

Standard: **8.F.B.5**

UNIT 5 Cumulative Practice Name:

Set 4 Compare Functions

➤ **Solve the problem. Show your work.** Possible work:

1. The graph shows the distance a dog runs over time. The equation $d = 13t$ gives the distance a cat runs in meters as a function of time in seconds. Which animal is faster, and by how much?

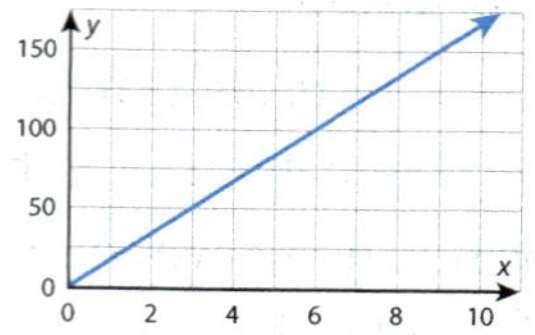

Slope of dog graph: $\frac{100}{6} = 16\frac{2}{3}$

Equation for cat: $d = 13t$

Equation for dog: $d = 16\frac{2}{3}t$

$16\frac{2}{3} > 13$ and $16\frac{2}{3} - 13 = 3\frac{2}{3}$, so the dog is faster by $3\frac{2}{3}$ meters per second.

Set 5 Analyze Graphs of Functional Relationships

➤ **Use the graph at the right for problems 1–3. For each section, tell whether the graph is *increasing, decreasing,* or *neither,* and whether it is *linear* or *nonlinear.***

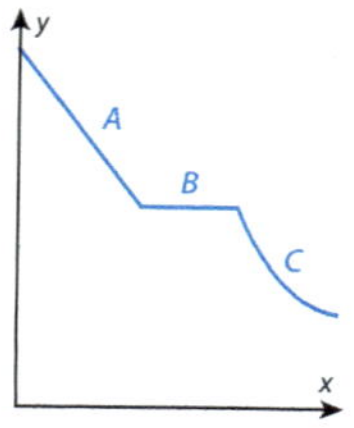

1. Section *A* decreasing; linear
2. Section *B* neither; linear
3. Section *C* decreasing; nonlinear

➤ **Use the graph at the right for problems 4–6. Identify the entire interval for which each statement is true.**

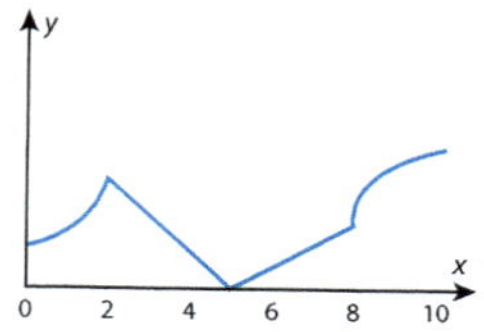

4. For 5 $< x <$ 8, the function increases at a constant rate.
5. For 0 $< x <$ 2, the function increases slowly at first and then starts to speed up.
6. For 8 $< x <$ 10, the function increases quickly at first and then starts to slow down.

Cumulative Practice

CP19

Set 6 Graph Proportional Relationships and Calculate Slope

Review: Grade 8 Lesson 8

Standard: **8.EE.B.5**

Set 7 Solve Systems of Linear Equations

Review: Grade 8 Lessons 12, 13, 14

Standards: **8.EE.C.8a, 8.EE.C.8b, and 8.EE.C.8c**

Error Alert If students find an incorrect solution for problem 2 or 3, then have them check their solution by evaluating the original system of equations at that point. Encourage them to always check their answers.

Set 6 Graph Proportional Relationships and Calculate Slope

➤ **Solve the problems. Show your work.** Possible work:

1. A train travels at a constant speed for 15 minutes and covers 20 miles in that time. Complete the graph to show the change in the train's distance over time. What is the slope of the line?

(0, 0) and (15, 20) are points on the line.

So, the slope is $\frac{20-0}{15-0} = \frac{4}{3}$.

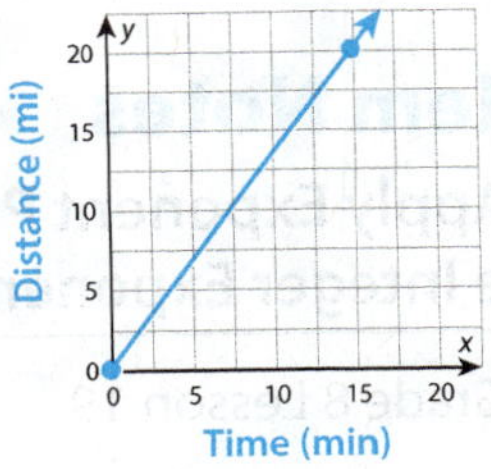

2. What is the slope of the line in the graph below?

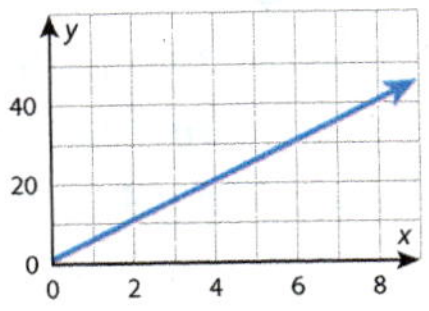

(0, 0) and (8, 40) are points on the line so, the slope is $\frac{40-0}{8-0} = 5$.

Set 7 Solve Systems of Linear Equations

➤ **Solve the systems of linear equations. Show your work** Possible work:

1.

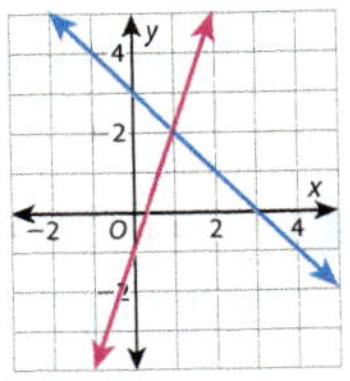

The lines intersect at (1, 2).

Solution: (1, 2)

2. $y = 2x$

$y + 4x = 9$

$2x + 4x = 9$

$6x = 9$

$x = 1.5$

$y = 2x$

$y = 2(1.5)$

$y = 3$

Solution: (1.5, 3)

3. $3x + 2y = 0$

$x + y = 1$

$3x + 2y = 0$

$+ -2x - 2y = -2$

$x + 0y = -2$

$x = -2$

$y = 1 - x$

$y = 1 - (-2)$

$y = 3$

Solution: (−2, 3)

CP20

Cumulative Practice

Purpose

Sets 1–4 of the cumulative practice are designed to practice applying exponent properties for integer exponents, expressing numbers using integer powers of 10, and performing operations with numbers in scientific notation.

Problem Notes

Set 1 Apply Exponent Properties for Positive Integer Exponents

Review: Grade 8 Lesson 19

Standard: **8.EE.A.1**

Error Alert If students write 6^{10} for problem 4 because they think they can always add the exponents of factors they are multiplying, then have them write out $(-3)^5 \cdot (-2)^5$ as repeated multiplication and then simplify it to see that it is equal to 6^5, not 6^{10}. Encourage students to express the conclusion that they cannot add the exponents unless the bases are the same.

Set 2 Apply Exponent Properties for All Integer Exponents

Review: Grade 8 Lesson 20

Standard: **8.EE.A.1**

UNIT 6 Cumulative Practice Name:

Set 1 Apply Exponent Properties for Positive Integer Exponents

Rewrite each expression as a single power for problems 1–6. Show your work. Possible work:

1. $2^6 \cdot 2^5 \cdot 2^2$
   $2^{6+5+2} = 2^{13}$
2. $\frac{(5^3 \cdot 5^2)}{5}$
   $5^{3+2-1} = 5^4$
3. $(-3)^4 \cdot (-3)^3$
   $(-3)^{4+3} = (-3)^7$
4. $(-3)^5 \cdot (-2)^5$
   $(-3 \cdot -2)^5 = 6^5$
5. $\frac{(7 \cdot 7^2)^4}{7}$
   $\frac{(7^3)^4}{7^1} = 7^{3 \cdot 4 - 1}$
   $= 7^{11}$
6. $\frac{3^2 \cdot 15^7}{5^7}$
   $3^2 \cdot \left(\frac{15}{5}\right)^7 = 3^2 \cdot 3^7$
   $= 3^9$

Solve problem 7. Show your work.

7. What value of n makes the equation $\frac{(3^n)^3}{3} = (3)^6(3)^5$ true? Possible work:
   $3n - 1 = 6 + 5$
   $3n = 12$
   $n = 4$

Set 2 Apply Exponent Properties for All Integer Exponents

Evaluate the expressions for problems 1–6. Show your work. Possible work:

1. $\frac{5^{-2}}{5 \cdot 3^0}$
   $5^{-2} \cdot 5^{-1} \cdot 3^0 = 5^{-3} \cdot 1$
   $= \frac{1}{125}$
2. $3^{-2} \cdot 3^0$
   $\frac{1}{9} \cdot 1 = \frac{1}{9}$
3. $\left(\frac{4}{3}\right)^{-2}$
   $\frac{4^{-2}}{3^{-2}} = \frac{3^2}{4^2}$
   $= \frac{9}{16}$
4. $(3^{-2} \cdot 4^{-1}\ 2^0)^{-2}$
   $3^{-2(-2)} \cdot 4^{-1(-2)} \cdot 2^{0(-2)}$
   $= 3^4 \cdot 4^2 \cdot 1$
   $= 81 \cdot 16$
   $= 1{,}296$
5. $42^{-3} \cdot 7^5$
   $(6 \cdot 7)^{-3} \cdot 7^5 = 6^{-3} \cdot 7^{-3} \cdot 7^5$
   $= 6^{-3} \cdot 7^2$
   $= \frac{49}{216}$
6. $\frac{(4^{-2})^2}{(2^{-3})^2}$
   $\frac{4^{(-4)}}{2^{(-6)}} = \frac{2^6}{4^4}$
   $= \frac{2^6}{2^8}$
   $= 2^{-2}$
   $= \frac{1}{4}$

Solve problem 7. Show your work.

7. What value of n makes the equation $8^{-n} = \frac{1}{2^3}$ true? Possible work:
   $\frac{1}{2^3} = \frac{1}{8}$ and $8^{-1} = \frac{1}{8}$ so $n = 1$.

Cumulative Practice

CP21

Set 3 Express Numbers Using Integer Powers of 10

Review: Grade 8 Lesson 21

Standard: **8.EE.A.3**

Set 4 Scientific Notation

Review: Grade 8 Lesson 22

Standard: **8.EE.A.4**

Error Alert If students write 7.8×10^5 or 7.8×10^6 for problem 1 because they subtracted $7.25 - 6.47$, then have them write the problem and their solution in standard form so they can see their mistake. Remind them that to subtract two numbers in scientific notation, they must rewrite one or both numbers so that their powers of 10 are equal before they subtract.

Set 3 Express Numbers Using Integer Powers of 10

➤ **Write an estimate for each number as a single digit times an integer power of 10 for problems 1–3.**

1. 7.549 8×10^0
2. 0.00061 6×10^{-4}
3. 9486 9×10^3

➤ **Write each number in standard form for problems 4–6.**

4. $4 \times 10^6 =$ 4,000,000
5. $7 \times 10^1 =$ 70
6. $3 \times 10^{-5} =$ 0.00003

➤ **Fill in the blanks to compare the numbers for problems 7 and 8.**

7. 6×10^6 is 20 times as great as 3×10^5.
8. 2×10^2 is 4,000 times as great as 5×10^{-2}.

Set 4 Scientific Notation

➤ **Solve the problems. Write your answers in scientific notation. Show your work.** Possible work:

1. $(7.25 \times 10^6) - (6.47 \times 10^5)$
$(72.5 \times 10^5) - (6.47 \times 10^5) = 66.03 \times 10^5$
$= 6.603 \times 10^6$

2. $6.2 \times 10^{-4} + 0.0025$
$0.00062 + 0.0025 = 0.00312$
$= 3.12 \times 10^{-3}$

3. $(900{,}000) \times (2.2 \times 10^{-3})$
$(9 \times 10^5) \times (2.2 \times 10^{-3}) = (9 \times 2.2) \times (10^5 \times 10^{-3})$
$= 19.8 \times 10^2$
$= 1.98 \times 10^3$

4. $(6.5 \times 10^9) + (1.2 \times 10^{10}) \times (3.4 \times 10^8)$
$(65 \times 10^8) + (120 \times 10^8) - (3.4 \times 10^8)$
$= (65 + 120 - 3.4) \times 10^8$
$= 181.6 \times 10^8$
$= 1.816 \times 10^{10}$

5. $(3.6 \times 10^4) \div (6 \times 10^3)$
$36{,}000 \div 6{,}000 = 6$
$= 6 \times 10^0$

6. $(3.1 \times 10^{-3}) \times (0.0025)$
$(3.1 \times 10^{-3}) \times (2.5 \times 10^{-3})$
$= (3.1 \times 2.5) \times (10^{-3} \times 10^{-3})$
$= 7.75 \times 10^{-6}$

Cumulative Practice

Purpose

Sets 5–8 of the cumulative practice are designed to practice identifying linear functions, comparing functions, determining the number of solutions to one-variable equations, and performing transformations involving dilations.

Problem Notes

Set 5 Functions

Review: Grade 8 Lesson 15

Standard: **8.F.A.3**

Error Alert If students incorrectly identify a linear function as nonlinear, or a nonlinear function as linear, then have them draw a graph of the function. Remind them that the graph of a linear function is always a straight line.

Set 6 Compare Functions

Review: Grade 8 Lesson 17

Standard: **8.F.A.2**

Set 5 Functions

➤ **Tell whether each function is *linear* or *nonlinear*.**

1. $y = 2x$ linear
2. $y = \frac{3}{x}$ nonlinear
3. $2y - 1 = 4x + 2$ linear
4.

Input (x)	1	3	5	7	9
Output (y)	1	9	25	49	81

nonlinear

5.

Input (x)	1	3	5	7	9
Output (y)	0	1	2	3	4

linear

Set 6 Compare Functions

➤ **Solve the problems. Show your work.** Possible work:

1. A used bookstore sells hardcover and paperback books. The equation $C = 4b$ gives the cost in dollars for buying paperback books. The cost is a function of the number of books. The table shows the cost for buying hardcover books.

Books	2	4	6	8	10
Cost ($)	12	24	36	48	60

What is the difference in cost of the two types of books?

The cost of one paperback book is $C = 4(1) = 4$.

The cost of one hardcover book is $\frac{60 - 12}{10 - 2} = 6$.

$6 - 4 = 2$; The difference in cost is $2.

2. Jada and Tom are racing to a finish line. The equation $d = 400 - 4.4t$ gives Jada's distance in meters from the finish line after t seconds. The graph shows Tom's distance from the finish line over time. Who is closer to the finish line at $t = 0$? Who is running faster?

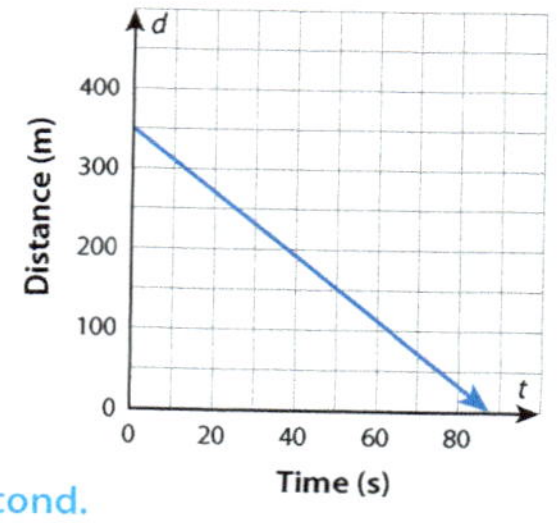

At $t = 0$, Jada is $400 - 4.4(0) = 400$ m from the finish line. Tom is 350 m from the finish line at $t = 0$, so Tom is closer.

Jada's rate of change is -4.4 meters per second.

Tom's rate of change is $\frac{350 - 150}{0 - 50} = -\frac{200}{50}$ or -4 meters per second.

$|-4.4| > |-4|$, so Jada is running faster.

Set 7 Solutions to One-Variable Equations

Review: Grade 8 Lesson 11

Standard: **8.EE.C.7a**

Error Alert If students find $x = -4.5$ for problem 3, then they may not have distributed properly when multiplying $2(x + 4)$. Have them evaluate the given equation for $x = -4.5$ to see that their answer is incorrect, and then encourage them to find their mistake.

Set 8 Transformations Involving Dilations

Review: Grade 8 Lesson 5

Standard: **8.G.A.3**

Set 7 Solutions to One-Variable Equations

➤ **Solve each equation for *x* and tell how many solutions it has. Show your work.** Possible work:

1. $15 - 3x = 12 + 3x$
   $3 = 6x$
   $x = \frac{1}{2}$; one solution

2. $4x + 6 = 4x + 9$
   $6 = 9$ is a false statement
   There is no solution.

3. $3x + 8 = 2(x + 4) - x - 5$
   $3x + 8 = 2x + 8 - x - 5$
   $3x = x - 5$
   $2x = -5$
   $x = -2.5$; one solution

4. $3(3x - 2) = 2(5x + 3) - x$
   $9x - 6 = 10x + 6 - x$
   $9x - 6 = 9x + 6$
   $-6 = 6$ is a false statement
   There is no solution.

5. $3(x + 4) = 2(2x + 3)$
   $3x + 12 = 4x + 6$
   $6 = x$; one solution

6. $4x - 1 = 3(2x + 1) - 2x - 4$
   $4x - 1 = 6x + 3 - 2x - 4$
   $4x - 1 = 4x - 1$
   $-1 = -1$; infinitely many solutions

Set 8 Transformations Involving Dilations

➤ **Perform each sequence of transformations. Draw the image.**

1. Rotate $\triangle ABC$ 180° clockwise around the origin. Then dilate the image by a scale factor of 2 with a center of dilation at the origin.

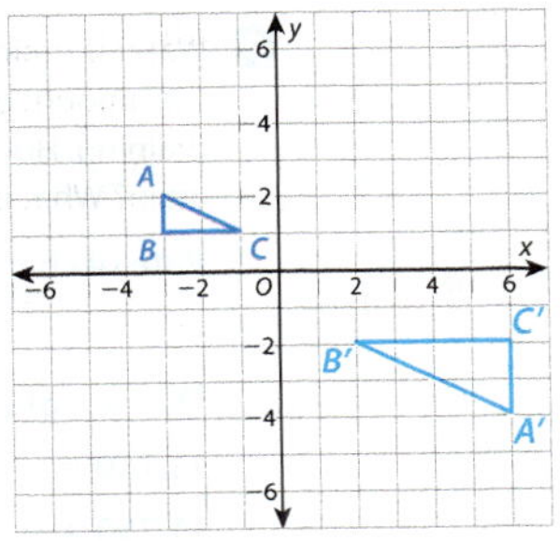

2. Dilate $\triangle ABC$ by a scale factor of $\frac{1}{3}$ with a center of dilation at the origin. Then reflect the image across the *y*-axis.

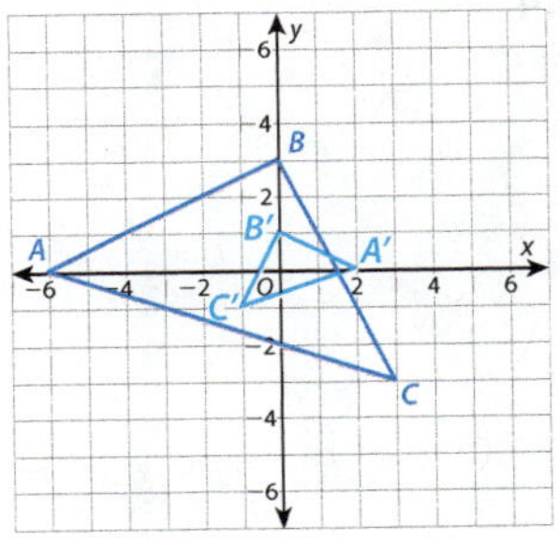

CP24

Cumulative Practice

Purpose

Sets 1–4 of the cumulative practice are designed to practice finding square roots and cube roots to solve problems, using functions to model linear relationships, and applying the Pythagorean Theorem and its converse.

Problem Notes

Set 1 Square Roots and Cube Roots

Review: Grade 8 Lesson 23

Standard: **8.EE.A.2**

Error Alert If students answer $\pm\frac{3}{4}$ for problem 1, then have them evaluate the original equation for both $\frac{3}{4}$ and $-\frac{3}{4}$ to see that it is only true when $s = \frac{3}{4}$. Remind students that a positive number must have a positive cube root, because the product of three negative numbers is negative.

Set 2 Use Functions to Model Linear Relationships

Review: Grade 8 Lesson 16

Standard: **8.F.B.4**

UNIT 7 Cumulative Practice Name:

Set 1 Square Roots and Cube Roots

➤ **Solve the equations. Show your work.** Possible work:

1. $s^3 = \frac{27}{64}$
   $s = \sqrt[3]{\frac{27}{64}}$
   $s = \frac{3}{4}$

2. $x^2 - 29 = 4$
   $x^2 = 33$
   $x = \pm\sqrt{33}$

3. $x^3 = 729$
   $x = \sqrt[3]{729}$
   $x = 9$

4. $y^2 + 16 = 25$
   $y^2 = 9$
   $y = \pm\sqrt{9}$
   $y = \pm 3$

5. $m^3 + 4 = 12$
   $m^3 = 8$
   $m = \sqrt[3]{8}$
   $m = 2$

6. $x^2 - 5 = -4$
   $x^2 = 1$
   $x = \pm\sqrt{1}$
   $x = \pm 1$

Set 2 Use Functions to Model Linear Relationships

➤ **Solve the problems. Show your work.** Possible work:

1. A plane flies toward an airport at a constant speed. After 40 minutes, it is 1,300 miles from the airport. After 1 hour, it is 1,100 miles from the airport. Write an equation for the plane's distance from the airport, *y*, as a function of flying time in hours, *x*.

   Rate of change: $\frac{1,100 - 1,300}{1 - \frac{2}{3}} = \frac{-200}{\frac{1}{3}}$
   $= -600$

   $1,100 = -600(1) + b$
   $1,700 = b$ So, $y = -600x + 1,700$.

2. Water is drained from a pool at a constant rate. The table shows the amount of water remaining in the pool as a function of time draining. How much water was in the pool when it started to drain? What is the rate of change?

Time (min)	Water (gal)
30	11,750
60	11,000
120	9,500

   Rate of change: $\frac{9,500 - 11,750}{120 - 30} = \frac{-2,250}{90}$
   $= -25$

   The rate of change is -25; the pool is draining 25 gallons per minute.
   $11,750 = -25(30) + b$
   $11,750 = -750 + b$
   $12,500 = b$, so there were 12,500 gallons of water in the pool at the start.

Cumulative Practice

CP25

Set 3 The Pythagorean Theorem and Its Converse

Review: Grade 8 Lesson 26

Standard: **8.G.B.6**

Set 4 Apply the Pythagorean Theorem in a Geometric Figure

Review: Grade 8 Lesson 27

Standard: **8.G.B.7**

Error Alert If students answer 8.6 ft for problem 1, then they may have calculated the length of the diagonal of the base of the prism, not of the entire prism. Have students draw and label the two right triangles they need to use to find the length of the diagonal from *D* to *E* and encourage them to try the problem again.

Set 3 The Pythagorean Theorem and Its Converse

➤ **Fill in the blank to describe the converse of the Pythagorean Theorem for problem 1.**

1. In a triangle, if the square of the length of one side of the triangle is equal to the sum of the squares of the lengths of the other two sides, then the triangle is a right triangle.

➤ **Solve problems 2 and 3.**

2. A right triangle has sides of length *e*, *f*, and *g* where $f^2 - g^2 = e^2$. Which side is the hypotenuse?
   The side with length *f*.

3. What is the length of the hypotenuse of the right triangle? Show your work. Possible work:

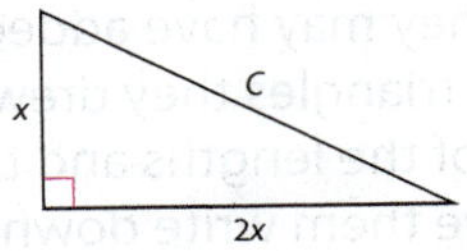

   $c^2 = x^2 + (2x)^2$
   $c^2 = 5x^2$, so $c = \sqrt{5x^2}$. The length of the hypotenuse is $\sqrt{5x^2}$.

Set 4 Apply the Pythagorean Theorem in a Geometric Figure

➤ **Solve the problems. Show your work.**

1. The figure is a right rectangular prism. To the nearest tenth of a foot, what is the length of the diagonal from *D* to *E*? Possible work:

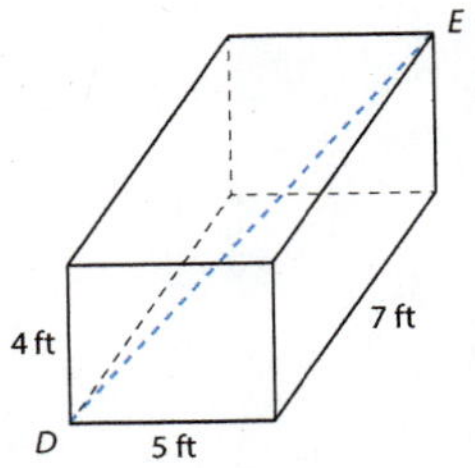

   Let *c* be the length of the diagonal of the base.
   $c^2 = 7^2 + 5^2$; $c^2 = 49 + 25$; $c^2 = 74$
   Let *d* be the length of the diagonal from *D* to *E*.
   $d^2 = 74 + 4^2$; $d^2 = 74 + 16$; $d^2 = 90$
   $d = \sqrt{90} \approx 9.5$, so the length of the diagonal from *D* to *E* is about 9.5 ft.

2. What is the height of $\triangle RST$? Possible work:

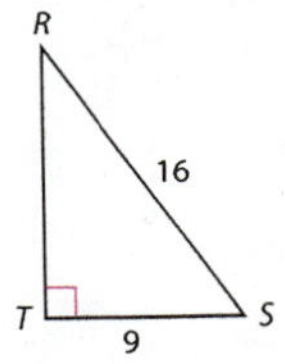

   $a^2 = 16^2 - 9$
   $a^2 = 256 - 81$
   $a^2 = 175$; $a = \sqrt{175}$, so the height of $\triangle RST$ is $\sqrt{175}$.

CP26

Cumulative Practice

Purpose

Sets 5–7 of the cumulative practice are designed to practice applying the Pythagorean Theorem in the coordinate plane, analyzing graphs of functional relationships, and solving linear equations in one variable.

Problem Notes

Set 5 Apply the Pythagorean Theorem in the Coordinate Plane

Review: Grade 8 Lesson 27

Standard: **8.G.B.8**

Error Alert If students answer 24 units for problem 3, then they may have added the two leg lengths of the right triangles they drew instead of adding the squares of the lengths and then finding the square root. Have them write down the Pythagorean Theorem and identify the lengths of the legs and the hypotenuse in this context.

UNIT 7 Cumulative Practice Name:

Set 5 Apply the Pythagorean Theorem in the Coordinate Plane

➤ **Use the figure at the right to solve problems 1 and 2. Show your work.** Possible work:

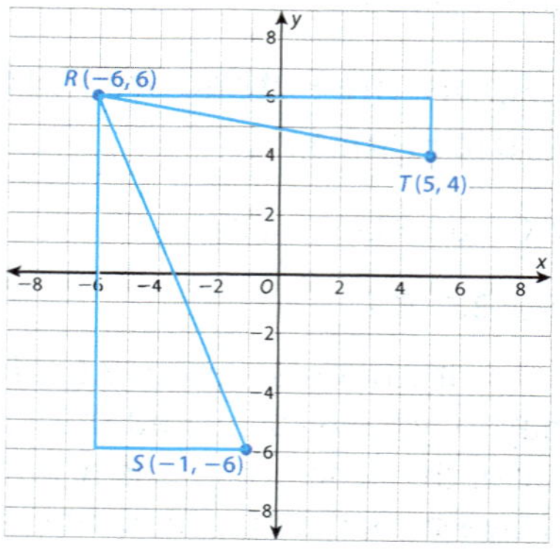

1 What is the distance between points R and S?

Leg lengths: 12 units, 5 units; hypotenuse length c units

$12^2 + 5^2 = c^2$

$169 = c^2$

$c = \sqrt{169} = 13$, so $RS = 13$ units.

2 What is the distance between points R and T?

Leg lengths: 11 units, 2 units; hypotenuse length c units

$11^2 + 2^2 = c^2$

$125 = c^2$

$c = \sqrt{125} \approx 11.2$, so RT is about 11.2 units.

➤ **Solve problem 3. Show your work.** Possible work:

3 What is the perimeter of trapezoid $ABCD$?

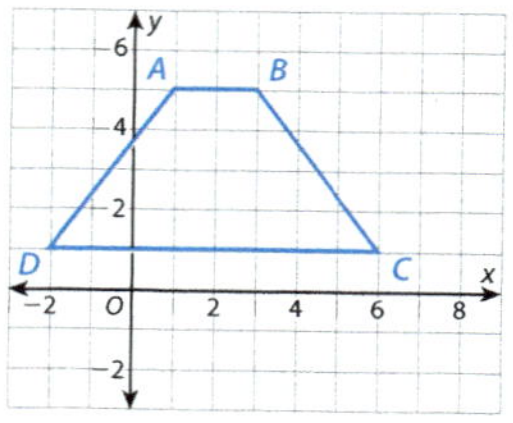

$AB = 2$ units; $DC = 8$ units

AD: $AD^2 = 3^2 + 4^2$, so $AD = \sqrt{25} = 5$ units

$BC = AD$ so $BC = 5$ units

$2 + 8 + 5 + 5 = 20$, so the perimeter of trapezoid $ABCD$ is 20 units.

Set 6 Analyze Graphs of Functional Relationships

Review: Grade 8 Lesson 18

Standard: **8.F.B.5**

Error Alert If students write that the function is constant for sections *A*, *B*, *D*, and *F* in problem 2, then they may have confused a constant function with a function that changes at a constant rate. Have them draw a function that changes at a constant rate and ask them how it is different from a constant function.

Set 7 Solve Linear Equations in One Variable

Review: Grade 8 Lesson 10

Standard: **8.EE.C.7b**

Set 6 Analyze Graphs of Functional Relationships

➤ **Use the figure at the right for problems 1–6. Identify the section(s) for which each statement is true.**

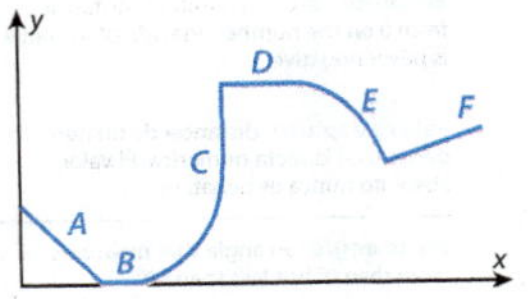

1. The function is increasing. C, F
2. The function is constant. B, D
3. The function is changing at a varying rate. C, E
4. The function changes slowly at first and then speeds up. C, E
5. The function is decreasing. A, E
6. The function is linear. A, B, D, F

➤ **Use the figure at the right for problem 7. Fill in the blanks.**

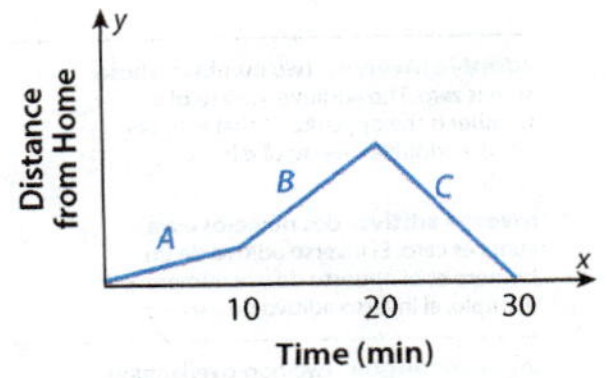

7. The graph represents Riley's walk.

She walks fastest over the interval 20 $< x <$ 30.

She walks slowest over the interval 0 $< x <$ 10.

She walks away from home over the interval 0 $< x <$ 20.

Set 7 Solve Linear Equations in One Variable

➤ **Solve the equations. Show your work.** Possible work:

1. $5t - \frac{2}{3} = 4\left(\frac{1}{2}t - \frac{1}{4}\right)$

   $5t - \frac{2}{3} = 2t - 4$

   $3t = -\frac{1}{3}$

   $t = -\frac{1}{9}$

2. $5(m + 1) - \frac{5}{3} = 4\left(m - \frac{2}{3}\right)$

   $15(m + 1) - 5 = 4(3m - 2)$

   $15m + 15 - 5 = 12m - 8$

   $3m = -18$

   $m = -6$

3. $0.5(2.5 - 5x) = 3.5 - 4x$

   $2.5 - 5x = 7 - 8x$

   $3x = 4.5$

   $x = 1.5$

Interactive Glossary

See Teacher Toolbox for online Multilingual Glossary.

Interactive Glossary/Glosario interactivo

English/Español	Example/Ejemplo	Notes/Notas
Aa		
absolute value a number's distance from 0 on the number line. Absolute value is never negative. **valor absoluto** distancia de un número desde 0 en la recta numérica. El valor absoluto nunca es negativo.	$\lvert -3 \rvert = 3$ $\lvert 3 \rvert = 3$	
acute angle an angle that measures more than 0° but less than 90°. **ángulo agudo** ángulo que mide más de 0° pero menos de 90°.		
acute triangle a triangle that has three acute angles. **triángulo acutángulo** triángulo que tiene tres ángulos agudos.		
additive inverses two numbers whose sum is zero. The additive inverse of a number is the opposite of that number, i.e., the additive inverse of *a* is −*a*. **inverso aditivo** dos números cuya suma es cero. El inverso aditivo de un número es el opuesto de ese número; por ejemplo, el inverso aditivo de *a* es −*a*.	−2 and 2 $\frac{1}{2}$ and $-\frac{1}{2}$	
adjacent angles two non-overlapping angles that share a vertex and a side. **ángulos adyacentes** dos ángulos que no se superponen y que comparten un vértice y un lado.	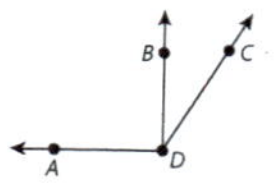 ∠*ADB* and ∠*BDC* are adjacent angles.	
algorithm a set of routine steps used to solve problems. **algoritmo** conjunto de pasos rutinarios que se siguen para resolver problemas.	17 R 19 31)546 − 31 236 − 217 19	

English/Español	Example/Ejemplo	Notes/Notas
alternate exterior angles when two lines are cut by a transversal, a pair of angles on opposite sides of the transversal and outside the two lines. When the two lines are parallel, alternate exterior angles are congruent. **ángulos alternos externos** cuando a dos rectas se cortan con una transversal, par de ángulos en lados opuestos de la transversal y fuera de las dos rectas. Cuando las dos rectas son paralelas, los ángulos alternos externos son congruentes.	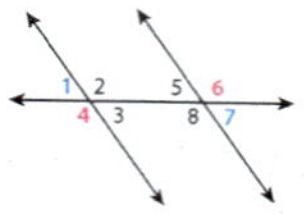 ∠1 and ∠7 ∠4 and ∠6	
alternate interior angles when two lines are cut by a transversal, a pair of angles on opposite sides of the transversal and between the two lines. When the two lines are parallel, alternate interior angles are congruent. **ángulos alternos internos** cuando a dos rectas se cortan con una transversal, par de ángulos en lados opuestos de la transversal y entre las dos rectas. Cuando las dos rectas son paralelas, los ángulos alternos internos son congruentes.	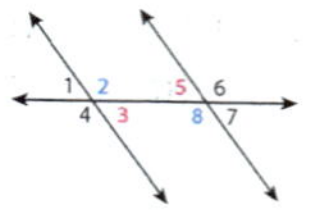 ∠2 and ∠8 ∠3 and ∠5	
angle a geometric shape formed by two rays, lines, or line segments that meet at a common point. **ángulo** figura geométrica formada por dos semirrectas, rectas o segmentos de recta que se encuentran en un punto común.	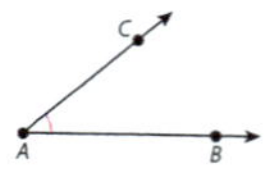	
area the amount of space inside a closed two-dimensional figure. Area is measured in square units such as square centimeters. **área** cantidad de espacio dentro de una figura bidimensional cerrada. El área se mide en unidades cuadradas, como los centímetros cuadrados.	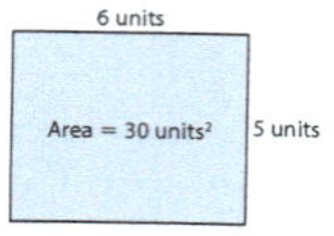	

English/Español	Example/Ejemplo	Notes/Notas
association (between two variables) a relationship between two variables. Two variables can be described as having a *linear association*, a *nonlinear association*, or *no association*. Linear associations can be described as *positive* or *negative*. **asociación (entre dos variables)** relación que existe entre dos variables. Dos variables se pueden describir como que tienen una *asociación lineal*, *no lineal*, o *ninguna asociación*. Las asociaciones lineales se pueden describir como *positivas* o *negativas*.	There is a positive association between *x* and *y*. 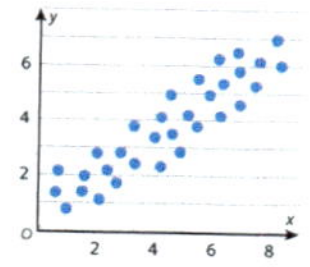	
associative property of addition regrouping the terms does not change the value of the expression. **propiedad asociativa de la suma** reagrupar los términos no cambia el valor de la expresión.	$(a + b) + c = a + (b + c)$ $(2 + 3) + 4 = 2 + (3 + 4)$	
associative property of multiplication regrouping the terms does not change the value of the expression. **propiedad asociativa de la multiplicación** reagrupar los términos no cambia el valor de la expresión.	$(a \cdot b) \cdot c = a \cdot (b \cdot c)$ $(2 \cdot 3) \cdot 4 = 2 \cdot (3 \cdot 4)$	
axis a horizontal or vertical number line that determines a coordinate plane. The plural form is *axes*. **eje** recta numérica horizontal o vertical que determina un plano de coordenadas.	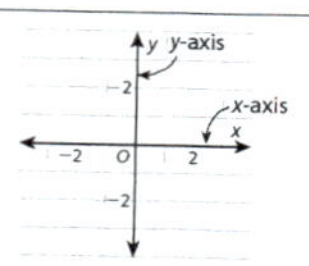	

English/Español	Example/Ejemplo	Notes/Notas
Bb		
balance point the point that represents the center of a data set. In a two-variable data set, the coordinates of the balance point are the mean of each variable. **punto de equilibrio** punto que representa el centro de un conjunto de datos. En un conjunto de datos de dos variables, las coordenadas del punto de equilibrio son la media de cada variable.	Data set: (1, 1), (3, 4), (5, 6), (7, 8) $\frac{1+3+5+7}{4} = 4$ $\frac{1+4+6+8}{4} = 4.75$ Balance point: (4, 4.75)	
base (of a parallelogram) a side of a parallelogram from which the height is measured. **base (de un paralelogramo)** lado de un paralelogramo desde el que se mide la altura.	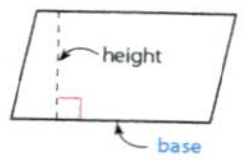	
base (of a power) in a power, the number that is used as a repeated factor. **base (de una potencia)** en una potencia, el número que se usa como factor que se repite.	8^2 base	
base (of a three-dimensional figure) a face of a three-dimensional figure from which the height is measured. **base (de una figura tridimensional)** cara de una figura tridimensional desde la que se mide la altura.	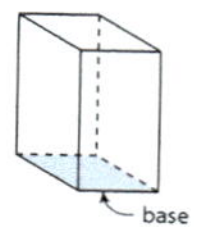	
base (of a triangle) a side of a triangle from which the height is measured. **base (de un triángulo)** lado de un triángulo desde el que se mide la altura.	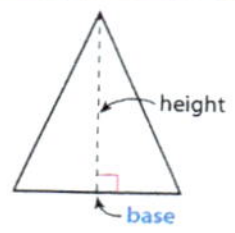	

English/Español	Example/Ejemplo	Notes/Notas

bivariate involving two variables.

bivariante que tiene dos variables.

Car Data	
Years Old	Color
3	Red
4	Blue

box plot a visual display of a data set on a number line that shows the minimum, the lower quartile, the median, the upper quartile, and the maximum. The sides of the box show the lower and upper quartiles and the line inside the box shows the median. Lines connect the box to the minimum and maximum values.

diagrama de caja representación visual de un conjunto de datos en una recta numérica que muestra el mínimo, el cuartil inferior, la mediana, el cuartil superior y el máximo. Los lados de la caja muestran los cuartiles inferior y superior y la recta del centro muestra la mediana. Las rectas conectan la caja con los valores mínimo y máximo.

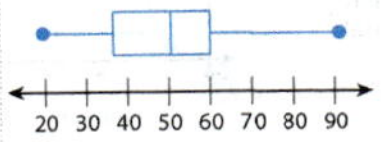

English/Español	Example/Ejemplo	Notes/Notas

Cc

categorical data data that are divided into categories, such as characteristics of the population.

datos por categorías datos que se dividen en categorías, como las características de la población.

Car color: red, blue, white, black

center (of a circle) the point inside a circle that is the same distance from every point on the circle.

centro (de un círculo) punto dentro de un círculo que está a la misma distancia de todos los puntos del círculo.

center of dilation a fixed point from which a figure is dilated.

centro de dilatación punto fijo desde el que se dilata una figura.

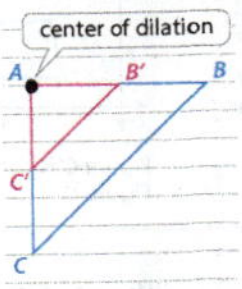

center of rotation a fixed point around which a figure is rotated.

centro de rotación punto fijo alrededor del que se rota una figura.

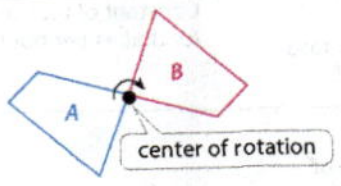

circle a two-dimensional shape in which every point is the same distance from the center.

círculo figura bidimensional en que todos los puntos están a la misma distancia del centro.

circumference the distance around the outside of a circle. It can be thought of as the perimeter of the circle.

circunferencia distancia alrededor del exterior de un círculo. Se puede considerar como el perímetro del círculo.

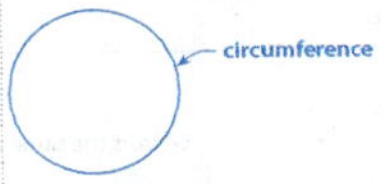

English/Español	Example/Ejemplo	Notes/Notas

closed figure a two-dimensional figure that begins and ends at the same point.

figura cerrada figura bidimensional que comienza y termina en el mismo punto.

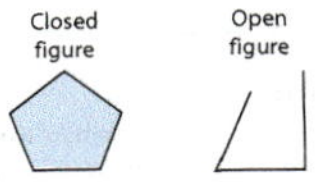

cluster a group of data points that are close to each other.

agrupación conjunto de datos que están cerca unos de otros.

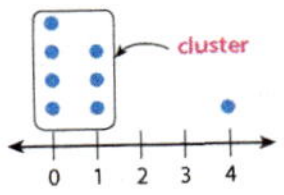

coefficient a number that is multiplied by a variable.

coeficiente número que se multiplica por una variable.

$5x + 3$

coefficient

commission a fee paid for services, often a percent of the total cost. A salesperson who earns a commission often gets a percent of the total sale.

comisión tarifa que se paga por servicios, que suele ser un porcentaje del costo total. Un vendedor que gana una comisión por lo general recibe un porcentaje de la venta total.

A 5% commission on \$4,000 is 0.05(\$4,000), or \$200.

common denominator a number that is a common multiple of the denominators of two or more fractions.

denominador común número que es múltiplo común de los denominadores de dos o más fracciones.

A common denominator for $\frac{1}{2}$ and $\frac{3}{5}$ is 10 because $2 \cdot 5 = 10$.

commutative property of addition changing the order of the addends does not change the sum.

propiedad conmutativa de la suma cambiar el orden de los sumandos no cambia el total.

$a + b = b + a$

$4.1 + 7.5 = 7.5 + 4.1$

English/Español	Example/Ejemplo	Notes/Notas

commutative property of multiplication changing the order of the factors does not change the product.

propiedad conmutativa de la multiplicación cambiar el orden de los factores no cambia el producto.

$ab = ba$

$4(7.5) = 7.5(4)$

compare to describe the relationship between the value or size of two numbers or quantities.

comparar describir la relación que hay entre el valor o el tamaño de dos números o cantidades.

$-4 < 8.5$

complementary angles two angles whose measures sum to 90°.

ángulos complementarios dos ángulos cuyas medidas suman 90°.

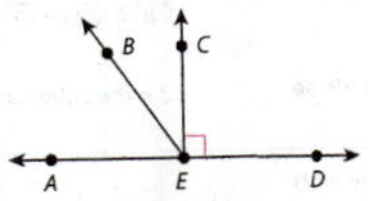

$\angle AEB$ and $\angle BEC$

complex fraction a fraction in which the numerator is a fraction, the denominator is a fraction, or both the numerator and the denominator are fractions.

fracción compleja fracción en la que el numerador es una fracción, el denominador es una fracción, o tanto el numerador como el denominador son fracciones.

$$\frac{\frac{1}{2}}{\frac{3}{4}}$$

compose to make by combining parts. You can put together numbers to make a greater number or put together shapes to make a new shape.

componer formar al combinar partes. Se pueden unir números para hacer un número mayor o unir figuras para formar una figura nueva.

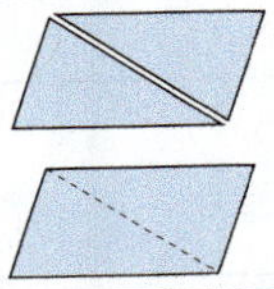

composite number a number that has more than one pair of whole number factors.

número compuesto número que tiene más de un par de números enteros como factores.

16 is a composite number because $1 \cdot 16$, $2 \cdot 8$, and $4 \cdot 4$ all equal 16.

Interactive Glossary

English/Español	Example/Ejemplo	Notes/Notas
compound event an event that consists of two or more simple events. **evento compuesto** evento que consiste en dos o más eventos simples.	Rolling a number cube twice	
cone a three-dimensional figure with one circular base and one vertex, connected by a curved surface. **cono** figura tridimensional que tiene una base circular y un vértice, conectados por una superficie curva.		
congruent (≅) same size and shape. Two figures are congruent if there is a sequence of rigid transformations that maps one figure onto the second. **congruente (≅)** del mismo tamaño y forma. Dos figuras son congruentes si hay una secuencia de transformaciones rígidas que hace coincidir una figura con la segunda.	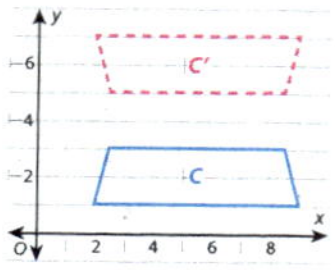 Figure *C′* is congruent to Figure *C*.	
constant of proportionality the unit rate in a proportional relationship. **constante de proporcionalidad** tasa unitaria en una relación proporcional.	Unit rate: $10 per hour Constant of proportionality for dollars per hours: 10.	
converse of the Pythagorean Theorem in a triangle, if the square of the length of the longest side is equal to the sum of the squares of the lengths of the other two sides, then the triangle is a right triangle. **recíproco del teorema de Pitágoras** en un triángulo, si el cuadrado de la longitud del lado más largo es igual a la suma de los cuadrados de las longitudes de los otros dos lados, entonces el triángulo es un triángulo rectángulo.	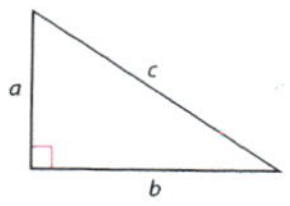 If $c^2 = a^2 + b^2$, the triangle is a right triangle.	
convert to write an equivalent measurement using a different unit. **convertir** escribir una medida equivalente usando una unidad diferente.	60 in. is the same as 5 ft.	

English/Español	Example/Ejemplo	Notes/Notas
coordinate plane a two-dimensional space formed by two perpendicular number lines called *axes*. **plano de coordenadas** espacio bidimensional formado por dos rectas numéricas perpendiculares llamadas ejes.	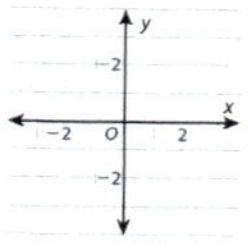	
corresponding angles (1) angles in the same relative position in figures. When figures are similar or congruent, corresponding angles are congruent. (2) angles in the same relative position when two lines are cut by a transversal. When the two lines are parallel, corresponding angles are congruent. **ángulos correspondientes** (1) ángulos que están en la misma posición relativa en las figuras. Cuando las figuras son semejantes o congruentes, los ángulos correspondientes son congruentes. (2) ángulos que están en la misma posición relativa cuando se cortan dos rectas con una transversal. Cuando las dos rectas son paralelas, los ángulos correspondientes son congruentes.	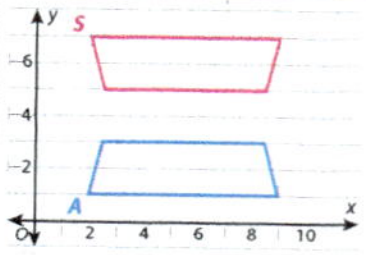 $\angle A$ and $\angle S$ 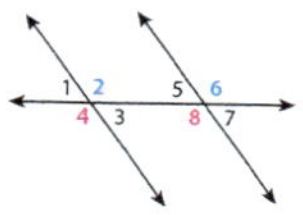 $\angle 2$ and $\angle 6$ $\angle 4$ and $\angle 8$	
corresponding sides sides in the same relative position in figures. When figures are congruent, corresponding sides are the same length. **lados correspondientes** lados que están en la misma posición relativa en las figuras. Cuando las figuras son congruentes, los lados correspondientes tienen la misma longitud.	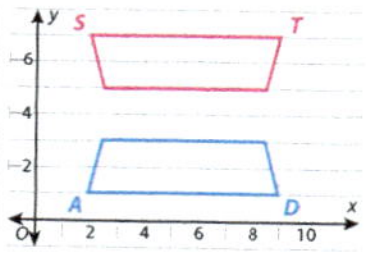 $\overline{AD}$ and $\overline{ST}$	
corresponding terms terms that have the same position in two related patterns. For example, the second term in one pattern and the second term in a related pattern are corresponding terms. **términos correspondientes** términos que tienen la misma posición en dos patrones relacionados. Por ejemplo, el segundo término en un patrón y el segundo término en un patrón relacionado son términos correspondientes.	Pattern A: 12, 18, 24, 30 Pattern B: 6, 9, 12, 15	

English/Español	Example/Ejemplo	Notes/Notas
cross-section a two-dimensional shape that is exposed by making a straight cut through a three-dimensional figure. **sección transversal** figura bidimensional que se forma al hacer un corte recto a través de una figura tridimensional.	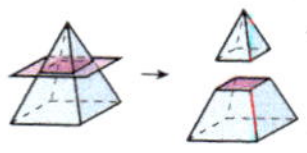	
cube a rectangular prism in which each face of the prism is a square. **cubo** prisma rectangular en el que cada cara del prisma es un cuadrado.	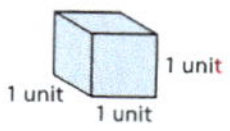	
cube root of *x* the number that when cubed is equal to *x*. **raíz cúbica de *x*** número que cuando se eleva al cubo es igual a *x*.	$\sqrt[3]{8} = \sqrt[3]{2 \cdot 2 \cdot 2}$ $= 2$ 2 is the cube root of 8.	
cylinder a three-dimensional figure with two parallel curved bases that are the same size. The bases are connected by a curved surface. **cilindro** figura tridimensional que tiene dos bases curvas paralelas que tienen el mismo tamaño. Las bases están conectadas por una superficie curva.	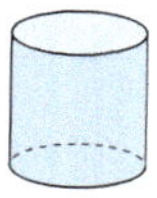	

English/Español	Example/Ejemplo	Notes/Notas
Dd		
data a set of collected information. Often numerical information such as a list of measurements. **datos** conjunto de información reunida. Con frecuencia, información numérica como una lista de medidas.	Commute length (mi): 15, 22, 10.5, 21, 9.5	
decimal a number containing a decimal point that separates a whole from fractional place values (tenths, hundredths, thousandths, and so on). **decimal** número que tiene un punto decimal que separa un entero de los valores posicionales fraccionarios (décimas, centésimas, milésimas, etc.).	1.293	
decompose to break into parts. You can break apart numbers and shapes. **descomponer** separar en partes. Se puede separar en partes números y figuras.	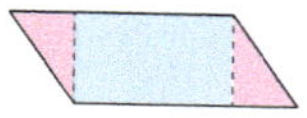	
degree (°) a unit used to measure angles. **grado (°)** unidad que se usa para medir ángulos.	There are 360° in a circle.	
denominator the number below the line in a fraction that tells the number of equal parts in the whole. **denominador** número debajo de la línea en una fracción que indica el número de partes iguales que hay en el entero.	$\frac{3}{4}$	
dependent variable a variable whose value depends on the value of a related independent variable. **variable dependiente** variable cuyo valor depende del valor de una variable independiente relacionada.	$y = 5x$ The value of *y* depends on the value of *x*.	

English/Español	Example/Ejemplo	Notes/Notas
diameter a line segment that goes through the center of a circle and has endpoints on the circle. Also, the distance across a circle through the center. **diámetro** segmento de recta que pasa por el centro de un círculo y tiene extremos en el círculo. También, la distancia de un lado al otro del círculo a través del centro.	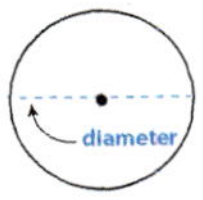	
difference the result of subtraction. **diferencia** resultado de la resta.	16.75 − 15.70 1.05	
digit a symbol used to write numbers. **dígito** símbolo que se usa para escribir números.	The digits are 0, 1, 2, 3, 4, 5, 6, 7, 8, and 9.	
dilation a transformation that makes a scale copy of a figure. A dilation is a proportional shrinking or enlargement of a figure. **dilatación** transformación que produce una copia a escala de una figura. Una dilatación es una reducción o ampliación proporcional de una figura.	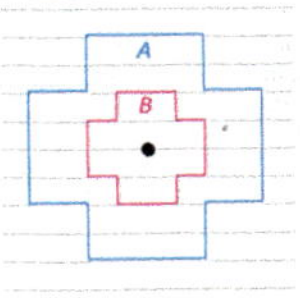 Figure *B* is a dilation of Figure *A*.	
dimension length in one direction. A figure may have one, two, or three dimensions. **dimensión** longitud en una dirección. Una figura puede tener una, dos o tres dimensiones.	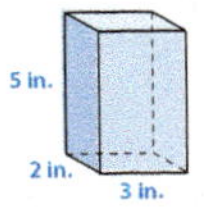	
distribution a representation that shows how often values in a data set occur. **distribución** representación que muestra la frecuencia con la que ocurren los valores en un conjunto de datos.	Pet: Bird 7; Cat 12; Dog 8; Snake 3 (see table below)	

Pet	Frequency
Bird	7
Cat	12
Dog	8
Snake	3

English/Español	Example/Ejemplo	Notes/Notas
distributive property multiplying each term in a sum or difference by a common factor does not change the value of the expression. **propiedad distributiva** multiplicar cada término de una suma o diferencia por un factor común no cambia el valor de la expresión.	$a(b + c) = ab + ac$ $5(4 + 2) = 5(4) + 5(2)$	
dividend the number that is divided by another number. **dividendo** número que se divide por otro número.	$22.5 \div 3 = 7.5$	
divisor the number by which another number is divided. **divisor** número por el que se divide otro número.	$22.5 \div 3 = 7.5$	
dot plot a data display that shows data as dots above a number line. A dot plot may also be called a *line plot*. **diagrama de puntos** representación de datos que muestra datos como puntos sobre una *recta numérica*.	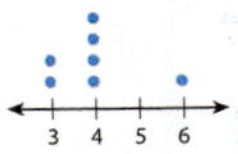	

Ee

English/Español	Example/Ejemplo	Notes/Notas
edge a line segment where two faces meet in a three-dimensional shape. **arista** segmento de recta en el que dos caras se unen en una figura tridimensional.	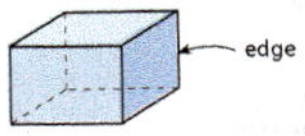	
equal having the same value, same size, or same amount. **igual** que tiene el mismo valor, el mismo tamaño o la misma cantidad.	$50 - 20 = 30$ $50 - 20$ is equal to 30.	
equation a mathematical statement that uses an equal sign (=) to show that two expressions have the same value. **ecuación** enunciado matemático que tiene un signo de igual (=) para mostrar que dos expresiones tienen el mismo valor.	$x + 4 = 15$	
equilateral triangle a triangle that has all three sides the same length. **triángulo equilátero** triángulo que tiene los tres lados de la misma longitud.	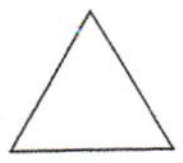	
equivalent having the same value. **equivalente** que tiene el mismo valor.	4 is equivalent to $\frac{8}{2}$.	
equivalent expressions two or more expressions in different forms that always name the same value. **expresiones equivalentes** dos o más expresiones en diferentes formas que siempre nombran el mismo valor.	$2(x + 4)$ is equivalent to $2x + 2(4)$ and $2x + 8$.	

English/Español	Example/Ejemplo	Notes/Notas
equivalent fractions two or more different fractions that name the same part of a whole or the same point on the number line. **fracciones equivalentes** dos o más fracciones diferentes que nombran la misma parte de un entero o el mismo punto en la recta numérica.	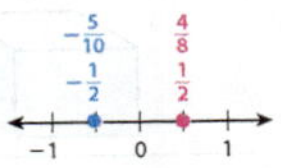	
equivalent ratios two ratios that express the same comparison. Multiplying both numbers in the ratio $a : b$ by a nonzero number n results in the equivalent ratio $na : nb$. **razones equivalentes** dos razones que expresan la misma comparación. Multiplicar ambos números en la razón $a : b$ por un número distinto de cero n da como resultado la razón equivalente $na : nb$.	6 : 8 is equivalent to 3 : 4	
estimate (noun) a close guess made using mathematical thinking. **estimación** suposición aproximada que se hace por medio del razonamiento matemático.	$28 + 21 = ?$ $30 + 20 = 50$ 50 is an estimate of $28 + 21$.	
estimate (verb) to give an approximate number or answer based on mathematical thinking. **estimar** dar un número o respuesta aproximada basados en el razonamiento matemático.	$28 + 21$ is about 50.	
evaluate to find the value of an expression. **evaluar** hallar el valor de una expresión.	The expression $4.5 \div (1 + 8)$ has a value of 0.5.	

Interactive Glossary

English/Español	Example/Ejemplo	Notes/Notas
event a set of one or more outcomes of an experiment. **evento** conjunto de uno o más resultados de un experimento.	Experiment: rolling a number cube once Possible events: rolling an even number, rolling a 1	
experiment a repeatable procedure involving chance that results in one or more possible outcomes. **experimento** procedimiento repetible en el que se hacen pruebas y da uno o más resultados posibles.	Experiment: rolling a number cube once	
experimental probability the probability of an event occurring based on the results from an experiment. **probabilidad experimental** probabilidad de que un evento ocurra con base en los resultados de un experimento.	A coin is flipped 30 times and lands heads up 17 times. The experimental probability of the coin landing heads up is $\frac{17}{30}$.	
exponent in a power, the number that shows how many times the base is used as a factor. **exponente** en una potencia, el número que muestra cuántas veces se usa la base como factor.	8^2 (exponent)	
exponential expression an expression that includes an exponent. **expresión exponencial** expresión que tiene un exponente.	$3x^3$	

English/Español	Example/Ejemplo	Notes/Notas
expression a group of numbers, variables, and/or operation symbols that represents a mathematical relationship. An expression without variables, such as 3 + 4, is called a *numerical expression*. An expression with variables, such as $5b^2$, is called an *algebraic expression*. **expresión** grupo de números, variables y/o símbolos de operaciones que representa una relación matemática. Una expresión sin variables, como 3 + 4, se llama *expresión numérica*. Una expresión con variables, como $5b^2$, se llama *expresión algebraica*.	$\frac{32-4}{7}$ $3x + y - 9$	
exterior angle when you extend one side of a polygon, the angle between the extended side and the adjacent side. This angle forms a linear pair with the adjacent interior angle of the polygon. **ángulo externo** cuando se amplía un lado de un polígono, se forma un ángulo entre el lado ampliado y el lado adyacente. Este ángulo forma un par lineal con el ángulo interno adyacente del polígono.	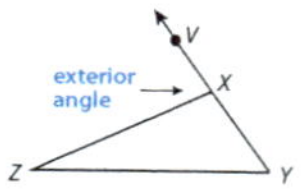	

English/Español	Example/Ejemplo	Notes/Notas
Ff		
face a flat surface of a solid shape. **cara** superficie plana de una figura sólida.	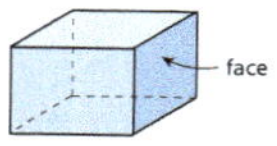	
factor (noun) a number, or expression with parentheses, that is multiplied. **factor** número, o expresión entre paréntesis, que se multiplica.	4 × 5 = 20 (factors)	
factor (verb) to rewrite an expression as a product of factors. **descomponer** volver a escribir una expresión como producto de factores.	$12x + 42 = 6(2x + 7)$	
factor pair two numbers that are multiplied together to give a product. **par de factores** dos números que se multiplican para dar un producto.	4 × 5 = 20 (factor pair)	
factors of a number whole numbers that multiply together to get the given number. **factores de un número** números enteros que se multiplican para obtener el número dado.	4 × 5 = 20 4 and 5 are factors of 20.	
formula a mathematical relationship that is expressed in the form of an equation. **fórmula** relación matemática que se expresa en forma de ecuación.	$A = \ell w$	

English/Español	Example/Ejemplo	Notes/Notas
fraction a number that names equal parts of a whole. A fraction names a point on the number line and can also represent the division of two numbers. **fracción** número que nombra partes iguales de un entero. Una fracción nombra un punto en la recta numérica y también puede representar la división de dos números.		
frequency a numerical count of how many times a data value occurs in a data set. **frecuencia** conteo numérico de cuántas veces ocurre un valor en un conjunto de datos.	Data set: 12, 13, 12, 15, 12, 13, 15, 14, 12, 12	
function a rule in which each input results in exactly one output. **función** regla en la que cada entrada resulta en exactamente una salida.	Rule: $y = \frac{3}{2}x$ 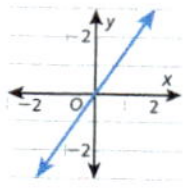	

Data Value	Frequency
12	5
13	2
14	1
15	2

English/Español	Example/Ejemplo	Notes/Notas

Gg

gap an interval of the number line for which a distribution has no data values.

espacio intervalo de la recta numérica para el que una distribución no tiene valores.

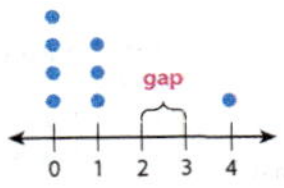

gratuity an amount added on to the cost of a service, often a percent of the total cost. Gratuity is often referred to as a *tip*.

propina cantidad que se suma al costo de un servicio; suele ser un porcentaje del costo total.

A gratuity of 18% on a \$20 bill is 0.18(\$20), or \$3.60.

greatest common factor (GCF) the greatest factor two or more numbers have in common.

máximo común divisor (M.C.D.) el mayor factor que dos o más números tienen en común.

GCF of 20 and 30: $2 \cdot 5$, or 10

$20 = 2 \cdot 2 \cdot 5$

$30 = 2 \cdot 3 \cdot 5$

grouping symbol a symbol, such as braces {}, brackets [], or parentheses (), used to group parts of an expression that should be evaluated before others.

símbolo de agrupación símbolo, como las llaves {}, los corchetes [] o los paréntesis (), que se usa para agrupar partes de una expresión que deben evaluarse antes que otras.

$3 \div (7 - 2) = 3 \div 5$

$\frac{3}{7-2} = \frac{3}{5}$

English/Español	Example/Ejemplo	Notes/Notas

Hh

height (of a parallelogram) the perpendicular distance from a base to the opposite side.

altura (de un paralelogramo) distancia perpendicular desde una base hasta el lado opuesto.

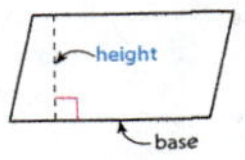

height (of a prism) the perpendicular distance from a base to the opposite base.

altura (de un prisma) distancia perpendicular desde una base hasta la base opuesta.

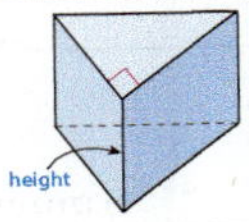

height (of a triangle) the perpendicular distance from a base to the opposite vertex.

altura (de un triángulo) distancia perpendicular desde una base hasta el vértice opuesto.

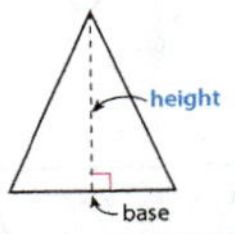

hexagon a polygon with exactly 6 sides and 6 angles.

hexágono polígono que tiene exactamente 6 lados y 6 ángulos.

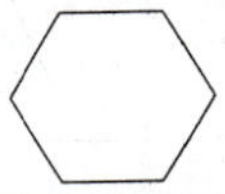

histogram a data display similar to a bar graph. A histogram groups the data into equal-size intervals. The height of each bar represents the number of data points in that group.

histograma presentación de datos parecida a una gráfica de barras. Un histograma agrupa los datos en intervalos de igual tamaño. La altura de cada barra representa el número de datos que hay en ese grupo.

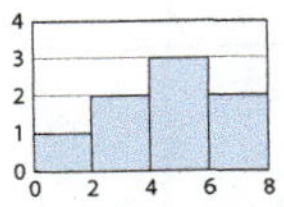

English/Español	Example/Ejemplo	Notes/Notas

hypotenuse the side of a right triangle opposite the right angle.

hipotenusa lado de un triángulo rectángulo opuesto al ángulo recto.

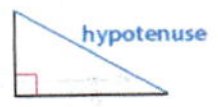

Ii

identity property of multiplication any number multiplied by 1 is itself.

propiedad de identidad de la multiplicación cualquier número multiplicado por 1 es el mismo número.

$3 \cdot 1 = 3$

image a figure that results from a transformation or sequence of transformations.

imagen figura que resulta de una transformación o secuencia de transformaciones.

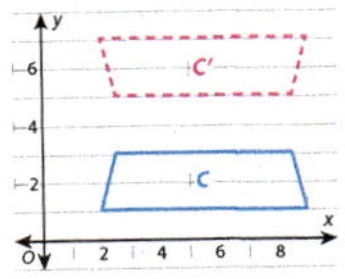

Figure *C′* is the image of Figure *C* after a reflection.

English/Español	Example/Ejemplo	Notes/Notas

independent variable a variable whose value is used to find the value of another variable. An independent variable determines the value of a dependent variable.

variable independiente variable cuyo valor se usa para hallar el valor de otra variable. Una variable independiente determina el valor de una variable dependiente.

$y = 5x$

The value of x is used to find the value of y.

inequality a mathematical statement that uses an inequality symbol (<, >, ≤, ≥) to show the relationship between values of expressions.

desigualdad enunciado matemático que muestra con un símbolo de desigualdad (<, >, ≤, ≥) la relación que existe entre los valores de las expresiones.

$4{,}384 > 3{,}448$

$x \geq -2$

initial value in a linear function, the value of the output when the input is 0.

valor inicial en una función lineal, el valor de la salida cuando la entrada es 0.

$y = \frac{1}{2}x + 25$ (initial value: 25)

input (of a function) the independent variable of a function.

entrada (de una función) variable independiente de una función.

$y = 2x + 1$

Input (x)	0	2	3
Output (y)	1	5	7

integers the set of whole numbers and their opposites.

enteros (positivos y negativos) conjunto de números enteros y sus opuestos.

−3, −1, 0, 2, 3

interquartile range (IQR) the difference between the upper quartile and lower quartile.

rango entre cuartiles (REC) diferencia entre el cuartil superior y el cuartil inferior.

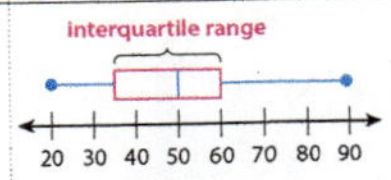

IQR: 60 − 35 = 25

Interactive Glossary

English/Español	Example/Ejemplo	Notes/Notas
inverse operations operations that undo each other. For example, addition and subtraction are inverse operations, and multiplication and division are inverse operations. **operaciones inversas** operaciones que se cancelan entre sí. Por ejemplo, la suma y la resta son operaciones inversas, y la multiplicación y la división son operaciones inversas.	$300 \div 10 = 30$ $30 \times 10 = 300$	
irrational number a number that cannot be expressed as a quotient of two integers. The decimal expansion of an irrational number never repeats or terminates. **número irracional** número que no se puede expresar como el cociente de dos enteros. La expansión decimal de un número irracional nunca se repite o termina.	1.12112111211112 . . . $\sqrt{2}$	
isosceles triangle a triangle that has at least two sides the same length. **triángulo isósceles** triángulo que tiene al menos dos lados de la misma longitud.	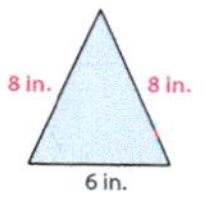	

English/Español	Example/Ejemplo	Notes/Notas
Ll		
least common multiple (LCM) the least multiple shared by two or more numbers. **mínimo común múltiplo (m.c.m.)** el menor múltiplo que comparten dos o más números.	LCM of 20 and 30: $2 \cdot 2 \cdot 3 \cdot 5$, or 60 $20 = 2 \cdot 2 \cdot 5$ $30 = 2 \cdot 3 \cdot 5$	
legs (of a right triangle) the two sides of a right triangle that form the right angle. **catetos (de un triángulo rectángulo)** los dos lados de un triángulo rectángulo que forman el ángulo recto.	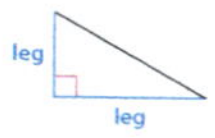	
like terms two or more terms that have the same variable factors. **términos semejantes** dos o más términos que tienen los mismos factores variables.	$2x^2$ and $4x^2$ 1.2 and 5.1 $6xy$ and xy	
line a straight row of points that goes on forever in both directions. **recta** línea recta de puntos que continúa infinitamente en ambas direcciones.		
line of fit a line drawn on a scatter plot to approximately model the relationship between the two sets of data. **recta de aproximación** línea que se dibuja en un diagrama de dispersión para representar de manera aproximada la relación que existe entre los dos conjuntos de datos.	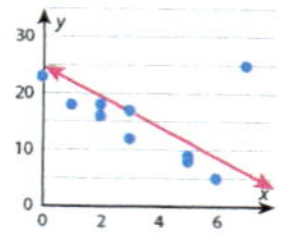	
line of reflection a line across which a figure is reflected. **eje de reflexión** línea a través de la que se refleja una figura.	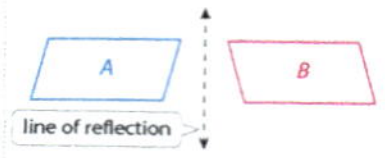	

English/Español	Example/Ejemplo	Notes/Notas
line of symmetry a line that divides a shape into two mirror images. **eje de simetría** línea que divide a una figura en dos imágenes reflejadas.		
line segment a straight row of points between two endpoints. **segmento de recta** fila recta de puntos entre dos extremos.		
linear association an association in which the relationship between the two variables can be generally approximated using a line. **asociación lineal** asociación en la que la relación que existe entre las dos variables se puede aproximar de manera general usando una recta.	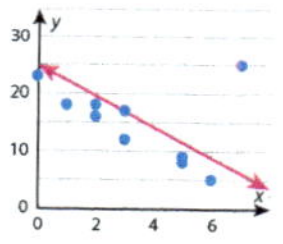	
linear equation an equation whose graph is a straight line. **ecuación lineal** ecuación cuya gráfica es una línea recta.	Equation: $y = \frac{3}{2}x$ 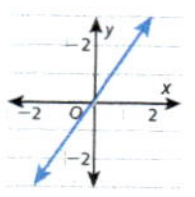	
linear function a function that can be represented by a linear equation. The graph of a linear function is a nonvertical straight line. **función lineal** función que se puede representar con una ecuación lineal. La gráfica de una función lineal es una recta no vertical.	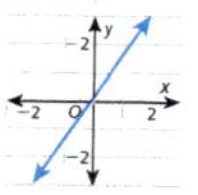	

English/Español	Example/Ejemplo	Notes/Notas
linear pair two angles that are adjacent and supplementary. **par lineal** dos ángulos que son adyacentes y suplementarios.	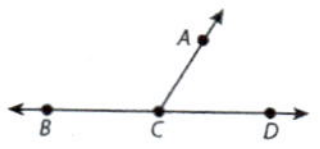$\angle BCA$ and $\angle ACD$ form a linear pair.	
lower quartile the middle number between the minimum and the median in an ordered set of numbers. The lower quartile is also called the 1st quartile or Q1. **cuartil inferior** el número del medio entre el mínimo y la mediana en un conjunto ordenado de números. El cuartil inferior también se llama primer cuartil, o Q1.	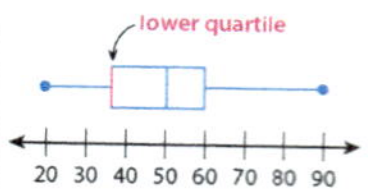	

Mm

English/Español	Example/Ejemplo	Notes/Notas
markdown an amount subtracted from the cost of an item to determine the final price. The amount subtracted is often a percent of the cost. **reducción de precio** cantidad que se resta al costo de un artículo para determinar el precio final. La cantidad que se resta suele ser un porcentaje del costo.	A discount of $20 is the same as a markdown of $20.	
markup an amount added to the cost of an item to determine the final price. The amount added is often a percent of the cost. **margen de ganancia** cantidad que se suma al costo de un artículo para determinar el precio final. La cantidad que se suma suele ser un porcentaje del costo.	A price increase of $25 is the same as a markup of $25.	
maximum (of a data set) the greatest value in a data set. **máximo (de un conjunto de datos)** mayor valor en un conjunto de datos.	Data set: 9, 10, 8, 9, 7	
mean the sum of a set of values divided by the number of values. This is often called the *average*. **media** suma de un conjunto de valores dividida por el número de valores. Suele llamarse *promedio*.	Data set: 9, 10, 8, 9, 7 Mean: $\frac{9 + 10 + 8 + 9 + 7}{5} = 8.6$	
mean absolute deviation (MAD) the sum of the distances of each data point from the mean of the data set divided by the number of data points. It is always positive. **desviación media absoluta (DMA)** suma de las distancias de cada dato desde la media del conjunto de datos dividido por el número de datos. Siempre es positiva.	Data set: 9, 10, 8, 9, 7 Mean: 8.6 MAD: $\frac{0.4 + 1.4 + 0.6 + 0.4 + 1.7}{5} = 0.9$	

English/Español	Example/Ejemplo	Notes/Notas
measure of center a single number that summarizes what is typical for all the values in a data set. Mean and median are measures of center. **medida de tendencia central** único número que resume qué es típico para todos los valores en un conjunto de datos. La media y la mediana son medidas de tendecia central.	Data set: 9, 10, 8, 9, 7 Mean: 8.6 Median: 9	
measure of variability a single number that summarizes how much the values in a data set vary. Mean absolute deviation and interquartile range are measures of variability. **medida de variabilidad** único número que resume cuánto varían los valores en un conjunto de datos. La desviación media absoluta y el rango entre cuartiles son medidas de variabilidad.	Data set: 9, 10, 8, 9, 7 MAD: 0.9 IQR: 1	
median the middle number, or the halfway point between the two middle numbers, in an ordered set of values. **mediana** el número del medio, o punto intermedio entre los dos números del medio, de un conjunto ordenado de valores.	Data set: 9, 10, 8, 9, 7 7, 8, 9, 9, 10	
minimum (of a data set) the least value in a data set. **mínimo (de un conjunto de datos)** valor mínimo en un conjunto de datos.	Data set: 9, 10, 8, 9, 7	
multiple the product of a given number and any other whole number. **múltiplo** producto de un número dado y cualquier otro número entero.	4, 8, 12, 16 are multiples of 4.	

English/Español	Example/Ejemplo	Notes/Notas
multiplicative comparison a comparison that tells how many times as many. **comparación multiplicativa** comparación que indica cuántas veces más.	$\frac{1}{2} \times 6 = 3$ tells that 3 is $\frac{1}{2}$ times as many as 6 and that 3 is 6 times as many as $\frac{1}{2}$.	
multiplicative inverse a number is the multiplicative inverse of another number if the product of the two numbers is 1. **inverso multiplicativo** un número es el inverso multiplicativo de otro número si el producto de los dos números es 1.	3 and $\frac{1}{3}$	

Nn

English/Español	Example/Ejemplo	Notes/Notas
negative association a linear association in which as the value of one variable increases, generally the other variable decreases. **asociación negativa** asociación lineal en la que el valor de una variable por lo incrementa, generalmente cuando el valor de la otra variable disminuye.	Cars for Sale 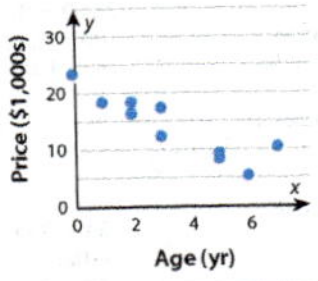	

English/Español	Example/Ejemplo	Notes/Notas
negative numbers numbers that are less than 0. They are located to the left of 0 on a horizontal number line and below 0 on a vertical number line. **números negativos** números que son menores que 0. Se ubican a la izquierda del 0 en una recta numérica horizontal y debajo del 0 en una recta numérica vertical.	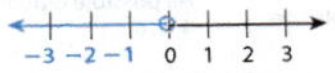	
net a flat, "unfolded" representation of a three-dimensional shape. **modelo plano** representación plana "desplegada" de una figura tridimensional.	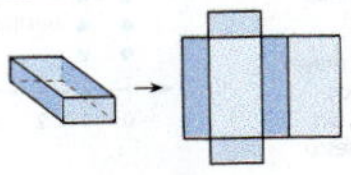	
no association when two variables have no relationship or association. **sin asociación** cuando dos variables no tienen relación o asociación.	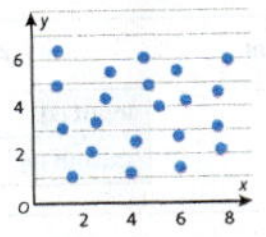	
nonlinear association an association in which no line can reasonably describe the relationship between two variables. **asociación no lineal** asociación en la que ninguna recta puede describir razonablemente la relación que existe entre dos variables.	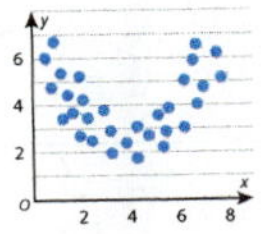	
nonlinear function a function with a graph that is not a straight line. **función no lineal** función que tiene una gráfica que no es una línea recta.	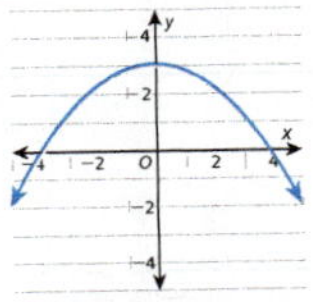	

Interactive Glossary

English/Español	Example/Ejemplo	Notes/Notas
numerator the number above the line in a fraction that tells the number of equal parts that are being described. **numerador** número que está sobre la línea en una fracción y que indica el número de partes iguales que se describen.	$\frac{3}{4}$	

Oo

English/Español	Example/Ejemplo	Notes/Notas
obtuse angle an angle that measures more than 90° but less than 180°. **ángulo obtuso** ángulo que mide más de 90° pero menos de 180°.	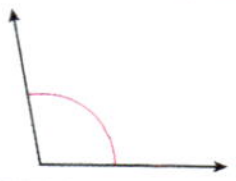	
obtuse triangle a triangle that has one obtuse angle. **triángulo obtusángulo** triángulo que tiene un ángulo obtuso.	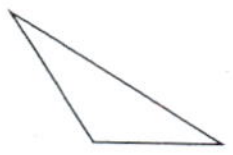	

English/Español	Example/Ejemplo	Notes/Notas
opposite numbers numbers that are the same distance from 0 on the number line but in opposite directions. Opposite numbers have the same numeral, but opposite signs. The opposite of a number is also called the *additive inverse* of that number. **números opuestos** números que están a la misma distancia del 0 en la recta numérica pero en direcciones opuestas. Los números opuestos son el mismo número, pero con el signo opuesto. El opuesto de un número también se llama *inverso de suma* de ese número.	−3 and 3 $-\frac{8}{15}$ and $\frac{8}{15}$	
Order of Operations a set of rules that state the order in which operations should be performed to evaluate an expression. **orden de las operaciones** conjunto de reglas que establecen el orden en el que deben hacerse las operaciones para evaluar una expresión.	Working from left to right: 1. Grouping symbols 2. Exponents 3. Multiplication/Division 4. Addition/Subtraction	
ordered pair a pair of numbers, (*x*, *y*), that describes the location of a point in the coordinate plane. The *x*-coordinate gives the point's horizontal distance from the *y*-axis, and the *y*-coordinate gives the point's vertical distance from the *x*-axis. **par ordenado** par de números, (*x*, *y*), que describen la ubicación de un punto en el plano de coordenadas. La coordenada *x* da la distancia horizontal del punto desde el eje *y*, y la coordenada *y* da la distancia vertical del punto desde el eje *x*.	(*x*, *y*) *x*-coordinate *y*-coordinate	
origin the point (0, 0) in the coordinate plane where the *x*-axis and *y*-axis intersect. **origen** el punto (0, 0) en el plano de coordenadas donde el eje *x* y el eje *y* se intersecan.	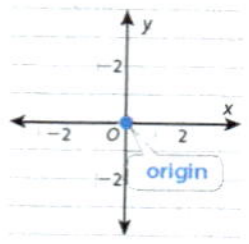	

English/Español	Example/Ejemplo	Notes/Notas
outcome one of the possible results of a chance experiment. **resultado** uno de los efectos posibles de un experimento aleatorio.	Experiment: Rolling a number cube once All possible outcomes: 1, 2, 3, 4, 5, 6	
outlier a data value that is much greater or much less than most of the other values in the data set. An outlier seems to not quite fit with the rest of the data points. **valor atípico** dato que es mucho mayor o mucho menor que la mayoría de los otros valores del conjunto de datos. Un valor atípico parece no ajustarse al resto de los datos.		
output (of a function) the dependent variable of a function. **salida (de una función)** variable dependiente de una función.	$y = 2x + 1$ Input (*x*): 0, 2, 3 Output (*y*): 1, 5, 7	

Pp

English/Español	Example/Ejemplo	Notes/Notas
parallel (‖) always the same distance apart and never meeting. **paralelos** (‖) que están siempre a la misma distancia y nunca se encuentran.	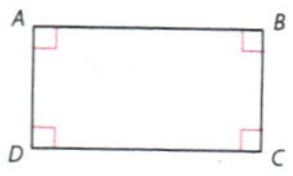 $\overline{AB} \parallel \overline{CD}$ and $\overline{AD} \parallel \overline{BC}$	
parallel lines lines that are always the same distance apart and never intersect. **rectas paralelas** rectas que siempre están a la misma distancia y nunca se intersecan.	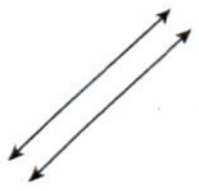	
parallelogram a quadrilateral with opposite sides parallel and equal in length. **paralelogramo** cuadrilátero que tiene lados opuestos paralelos y de la misma longitud.		
partial products the products you get in each step of the partial-products strategy. You use place value to find partial products. **productos parciales** productos que se obtienen en cada paso de la estrategia de productos parciales. Se usa el valor posicional para hallar productos parciales.	218 × 6 Partial products: 6 × 200, or 1,200, 6 × 10, or 60, and 6 × 8, or 48	
partial quotients the quotients you get in each step of the partial-quotient strategy. You use place value to find partial quotients. **cocientes parciales** cocientes que se obtienen en cada paso de la estrategia de cocientes parciales. Se usa el valor posicional para hallar cocientes parciales.	2,124 ÷ 4 Partial quotients: 2,000 ÷ 4, or 500, 100 ÷ 4, or 25, and 24 ÷ 4, or 6	
partial sums the sums you get in each step of the partial-sums strategy. You use place value to find partial sums. **sumas parciales** totales que se obtienen en cada paso de la estrategia de sumas parciales. Se usa el valor posicional para hallar sumas parciales.	124 + 234 Partial sums: 100 + 200, or 300, 20 + 30, or 50, and 4 + 4, or 8	

English/Español | Example/Ejemplo | Notes/Notas

partial-products strategy a strategy used to multiply multi-digit numbers.

estrategia de productos parciales estrategia que se usa para multiplicar números de varios dígitos.

Example:
218
× 6
48 (6 × 8 ones)
60 (6 × 1 ten)
+ 1,200 (6 × 2 hundreds)
1,308

partial-quotients strategy a strategy used to divide multi-digit numbers.

estrategia de cocientes parciales estrategia que se usa para dividir números de varios dígitos.

Example:
6
25
500
4)2,125
− 2,000
125
− 100
25
− 24
1

The quotient 531 is the sum of partial quotients (6, 25, and 500) and the remainder (1).

partial-sums strategy a strategy used to add multi-digit numbers.

estrategia de sumas parciales estrategia que se usa para sumar números de varios dígitos.

Example:
312
+ 235
Add the hundreds. 500
Add the tens. 40
Add the ones. + 7
547

peak in a distribution, the shape formed when many data points are at one value or group of values.

pico en una distribución, la figura que se forma cuando los puntos de muchos datos están en un valor o grupo de valores.

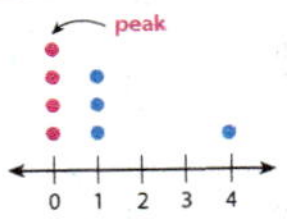

pentagon a polygon with exactly 5 sides and 5 angles.

pentágono polígono que tiene exactamente 5 lados y 5 ángulos.

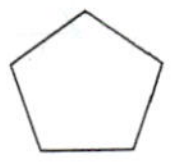

per *for each* or *for every*. The word *per* can be used to express a rate, such as \$2 per pound.

por *por cada*. La palabra *por* se puede usar para expresar una tasa, como \$2 por libra.

Example: A price of \$2 per pound means for every pound, you pay \$2.

English/Español | Example/Ejemplo | Notes/Notas

percent per 100. A percent is a rate per 100. A percent can be written using the percent symbol (%) and represented as a fraction or decimal.

porcentaje por cada 100. Un porcentaje es una tasa por cada 100. Un porcentaje se puede escribir usando el símbolo de porcentaje (%) y se representa como fracción o decimal.

Example: 15% can be represented as $\frac{15}{100}$ or 0.15.

percent change the amount of change compared to the original (or starting) amount, expressed as a percent.

Percent change = $\frac{\text{amount of change}}{\text{original amount}} \times 100$

cambio porcentual cantidad de cambio en comparación con la cantidad original (o inicial) que se expresa como porcentaje.

Cambio porcentual =

$\frac{\text{cantidad de cambio}}{\text{cantidad original}} \times 100$

Example:
Saturday: 250 people
Sunday: 300 people
Change from Saturday to Sunday: 300 − 250 = 50
Percent change:
$\frac{50}{250} \times 100 = 20\%$

percent decrease the percent change when a quantity decreases from its original amount.

Percent decrease =

$\frac{\text{amount of decrease}}{\text{original amount}} \times 100$

disminución porcentual cambio porcentual cuando una cantidad disminuye desde su cantidad original.

Disminución porcentual =

$\frac{\text{cantidad de disminución}}{\text{cantidad original}} \times 100$

Example:
Saturday: 250 people
Sunday: 200 people
Change from Saturday to Sunday: 250 − 200 = 50
Percent change:
$\frac{50}{250} \times 100 = 20\%$
There is a 20% decrease from Saturday to Sunday.

percent error the difference between the correct value and the incorrect value compared to the correct value, expressed as a percent.

Percent error = $\frac{\text{amount of error}}{\text{correct value}} \times 100$

error porcentual diferencia que hay entre el valor correcto y el valor incorrecto en comparación con el valor correcto, expresada como porcentaje.

Error porcentual = $\frac{\text{cantidad de error}}{\text{valor correcto}} \times 100$

Example:
A bag of flour weighs 4.5 lb. It should weigh 5 lb.
Percent error:
$\frac{5 - 4.5}{5} \times 100 = 10\%$

English/Español | Example/Ejemplo | Notes/Notas

percent increase the percent change when a quantity increases from its original amount.

Percent increase =

$\frac{\text{amount of increase}}{\text{original amount}} \times 100$

incremento porcentual cambio porcentual cuando una cantidad se incrementa desde su cantidad original.

Aumento porcentual =

$\frac{\text{cantidad de incremento}}{\text{cantidad original}} \times 100$

Example:
Saturday: 250 people
Sunday: 300 people
Change from Saturday to Sunday: 300 − 250 = 50
Percent change:
$\frac{50}{250} \times 100 = 20\%$
There is a 20% increase from Saturday to Sunday.

perfect cube the product when an integer is used as a factor three times.

cubo perfecto producto cuando se usa un entero como factor tres veces.

Example: $27 = 3^3$

perfect square the product of an integer and itself.

cuadrado perfecto producto de un entero por sí mismo.

Example: $9 = 3^2$

perimeter the distance around a two-dimensional shape. The perimeter is equal to the sum of the lengths of the sides.

perímetro distancia alrededor de una figura bidimensional. El perímetro es igual a la suma de las longitudes de los lados.

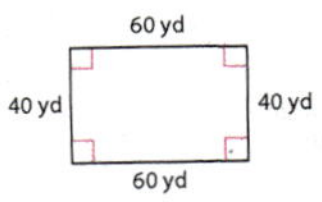

Perimeter: 200 yd
(60 yd + 40 yd + 60 yd + 40 yd)

perpendicular (⊥) meeting to form right angles.

perpendicular (⊥) unión donde se forman ángulos rectos.

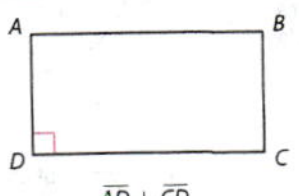

$\overline{AD} \perp \overline{CD}$

perpendicular lines two lines that meet to form a right angle, or a 90° angle.

rectas perpendiculares dos rectas que se encuentran y forman un ángulo recto, o ángulo de 90°.

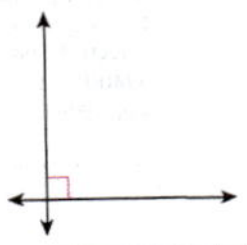

English/Español | Example/Ejemplo | Notes/Notas

pi (π) in a circle, the quotient $\frac{\text{circumference}}{\text{diameter}}$. Common approximations are 3.14 and $\frac{22}{7}$.

pi (π) en un círculo, el cociente de $\frac{\text{circumferencia}}{\text{diámetro}}$. Las aproximaciones comunes son 3.14 y $\frac{22}{7}$.

Example: $\pi \approx 3.14$ or $\frac{22}{7}$

place value the value of a digit based on its position in a number.

valor posicional valor de un dígito que se basa en su posición en un número. Por ejemplo, el 2 en 3.52 está en la posición de las centésimas y tiene un valor de 2 centésimas, o 0.02.

Example: The 2 in 3.52 is in the hundredths place and has a value of 2 hundredths or 0.02.

plane figure a two-dimensional figure, such as a circle, triangle, or rectangle.

figura plana figura bidimensional, como un círculo, un triángulo o un rectángulo.

plane section a two-dimensional shape that is exposed by making a straight cut through a three-dimensional figure.

sección plana figura bidimensional que se expone al hacer un corte recto a través de una figura tridimensional.

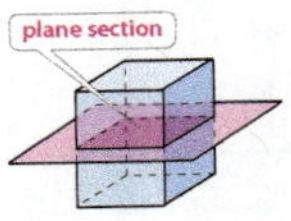

point a single location in space.

punto ubicación única en el espacio.

polygon a two-dimensional closed figure made with three or more straight line segments that meet only at their endpoints.

polígono figura bidimensional cerrada formada por tres o más segmentos de recta que se encuentran solo en sus extremos.

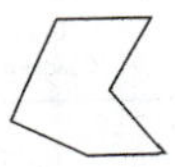

Interactive Glossary

English/Español	Example/Ejemplo	Notes/Notas
population the entire group of interest. Samples are drawn from populations. **población** grupo entero de interés. Las muestras se obtienen de las poblaciones.	Sample: 10 students from each Grade 8 homeroom in a school Population: All Grade 8 students in the school	
positive association a linear association in which as the value of one variable increases, generally the value of the other variable increases. **asociación positiva** asociación lineal en la que el valor de una variable aumenta, generalmente cuando el valor de la otra variable aumenta.	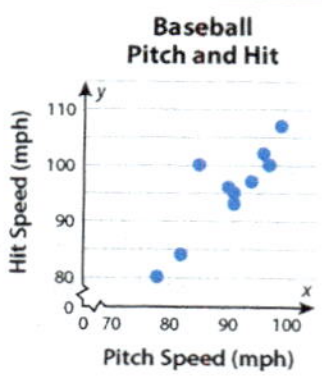	
positive numbers numbers that are greater than 0. They are located to the right of 0 on a horizontal number line and above 0 on a vertical number line. **números positivos** números que son mayores que 0. Se ubican a la derecha del 0 en una recta numérica horizontal y sobre el 0 en una recta numérica vertical.		
power an expression with a base and an exponent. **potencia** expresión que tiene una base y un exponente.	8^2	
power of 10 a number that can be written as a product of 10s. **potencia de 10** número que se puede escribir como el producto de 10.	100 and 1,000 are powers of 10 because $100 = 10 \times 10$ and $1{,}000 = 10 \times 10 \times 10$.	
prime number a whole number greater than 1 whose only factors are 1 and itself. **número primo** número entero mayor que 1 cuyos únicos factores son 1 y sí mismo.	2, 3, 5, 7, 11, 13	

English/Español	Example/Ejemplo	Notes/Notas
prism a three-dimensional figure with two parallel bases that are the same size and shape. The other faces are parallelograms. A prism is named by the shape of the base. **prisma** figura tridimensional que tiene dos bases paralelas que tienen el mismo tamaño y la misma forma. Las otras caras son paralelogramos. La base determina el nombre del prisma.	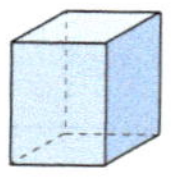	
probability a number between 0 and 1 that expresses the likelihood of an event occurring. **probabilidad** número entre 0 y 1 que expresa la posibilidad de que ocurra un evento.	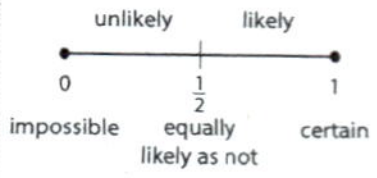	
product the result of multiplication. **producto** resultado de la multiplicación.	$3 \cdot 5 = 15$	
proportional relationship the relationship between two quantities where one quantity is a constant multiple of the other quantity. If the quantities x and y are in a proportional relationship, you can represent that relationship with the equation $y = kx$, where the value of k is constant (unchanging). **relación proporcional** relación que existe entre dos cantidades en la que una cantidad es un múltiplo constante de la otra. Si las cantidades x y y están en una relación proporcional, esa relación se puede representar con la ecuación $y = kx$, en la que el valor de k es constante (no cambia).	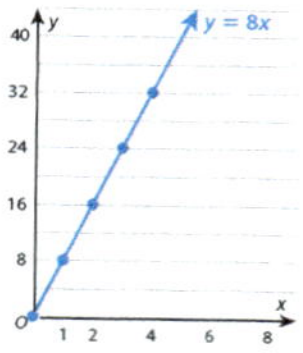	
pyramid a three-dimensional figure whose base is a polygon and whose other faces are triangles. A pyramid is named by the shape of its base. **pirámide** figura tridimensional cuya base es un polígono y cuyas otras caras son triángulos. La base determina el nombre de la pirámide.	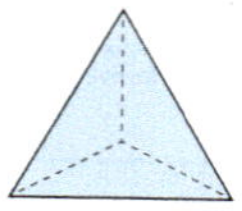	

English/Español	Example/Ejemplo	Notes/Notas
Pythagorean Theorem in any right triangle, the sum of the squares of the lengths of the legs, a and b, is equal to the square of the length of the hypotenuse, c. So, $a^2 + b^2 = c^2$. **Teorema de Pitágoras** en un triángulo rectángulo cualquiera, la suma del cuadrado de las longitudes de los catetos, a y b, es igual al cuadrado de la longitud de la hipotenusa, c. Por lo tanto, $a^2 + b^2 = c^2$.	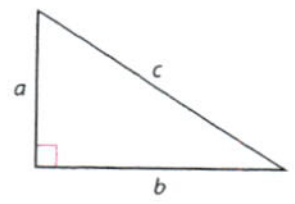If the triangle is a right triangle, then $a^2 + b^2 = c^2$	

Qq

English/Español	Example/Ejemplo	Notes/Notas
quadrants the four regions of the coordinate plane that are formed when the x-axis and y-axis intersect at the origin. **cuadrantes** las cuatro regiones del plano de coordenadas que se forman cuando los ejes x y y se intersecan en el origen.	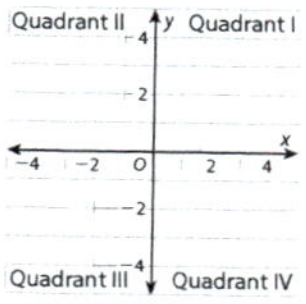	
quadrilateral a polygon with exactly 4 sides and 4 angles. **cuadrilátero** polígono que tiene exactamente 4 lados y 4 ángulos.	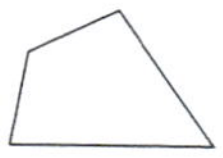	

English/Español	Example/Ejemplo	Notes/Notas
qualitative description a description that focuses on the general relationship between quantities, often without using specific values. **descripción cualitativa** descripción que se enfoca en la relación general que existe entre las cantidades, con frecuencia sin usar valores específicos.	Gas prices stay steady, then drop, then increase.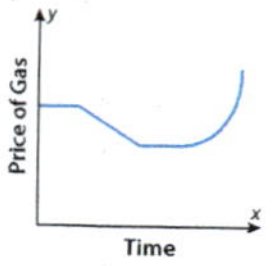	
quotient the result of division. **cociente** resultado de la división.	$22.5 \div 3 = 7.5$	

Rr

English/Español	Example/Ejemplo	Notes/Notas
radius (of a circle) a line segment from the center of a circle to any point on the circle. Also, the distance from the center to any point on a circle. **radio (de un círculo)** segmento de recta desde el centro de un círculo hasta cualquier punto en el círculo. Además, la distancia desde el centro hasta cualquier punto en un círculo.	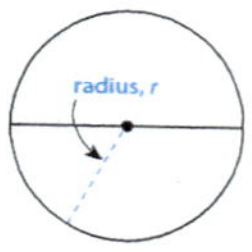	
random sample a sample in which every element in the population has an equal chance of being selected. **muestra aleatoria** muestra en la que todos los elementos de la población tienen la misma probabilidad de ser elegidos.	The names of all of the students in the school are placed in a hat. Without looking, 30 names are selected. The 30 students are a random sample of the population.	

English/Español	Example/Ejemplo	Notes/Notas
range the difference between the greatest value (maximum) and the least value (minimum) in a data set. **rango** diferencia entre el mayor valor (máximo) y el menor valor (mínimo) en un conjunto de datos.	Data set: 9, 10, 8, 9, 7 Range: $10 - 7 = 3$	
rate a ratio tells the number of units of one quantity for 1 unit of another quantity. Rates are often expressed using the word *per*. **tasa** razón que indica el número de unidades de una cantidad para 1 unidad de otra cantidad. Las razones suelen expresarse usando la palabra *por*.	5 miles per hour 2 cups for every 1 serving	
rate of change in a linear relationship between *x* and *y*, it tells how much *y* changes when *x* changes by 1. **tasa de cambio** en una relación lineal entre *x* y *y*, indica cuánto cambia *y* cuando *x* cambia en 1.	$y = \frac{1}{2}x + 25$ rate of change	
ratio a way to compare two quantities when there are *a* units of one quantity for every *b* units of the other quantity. You can write the ratio in symbols as *a* : *b* and in words as *a to b*. **razón** manera de comparar dos cantidades cuando hay *a* unidades de una cantidad por cada *b* unidades de la otra cantidad. Se puede escribir la razón en símbolos como *a* : *b* y en palabras como *a a b*.	 4 circles : 2 triangles	
rational number a number that can be expressed as the fraction $\frac{a}{b}$ where *a* and *b* are integers and $b \neq 0$. Rational numbers include integers, fractions, repeating decimals, and terminating decimals. **número racional** número que se puede expresar como la fracción $\frac{a}{b}$ en la que *a* y *b* son enteros y $b \neq 0$. Los números racionales incluyen los enteros, las fracciones, los decimales periódicos y los decimales finitos.	$\frac{3}{4}, -\frac{1}{8}, -3, 0, 1.2$	

English/Español	Example/Ejemplo	Notes/Notas
ray a part of a line that has one endpoint and goes on forever in one direction. **semirrecta** parte de una recta que tiene un extremo y continúa infinitamente en una dirección.		
real numbers the set of rational and irrational numbers. **números reales** conjunto de números racionales e irracionales.	Real Numbers Rational Numbers: 27, 0.25, $\frac{1}{3}$ Irrational Numbers: $\sqrt{8}$, π, 1.46829903...	
reciprocal for any nonzero number *a*, the reciprocal is $\frac{1}{a}$. The reciprocal of any fraction $\frac{a}{b}$ is $\frac{b}{a}$. Zero does not have a reciprocal. The reciprocal of a number is also called the *multiplicative inverse* of that number. **recíproco** para cualquier número *a* distinto de cero, el recíproco es $\frac{1}{a}$. El recíproco de cualquier fracción $\frac{a}{b}$ es $\frac{b}{a}$. El cero no tiene recíproco. El recíproco de un número también se llama *inverso multiplicativo* de ese número.	The reciprocal of $\frac{4}{5}$ is $\frac{5}{4}$. The reciprocal of $\frac{1}{6}$ is 6. The reciprocal of -8 is $-\frac{1}{8}$.	
rectangle a quadrilateral with 4 right angles. Opposite sides of a rectangle are the same length. **rectángulo** cuadrilátero que tiene 4 ángulos rectos. Los lados opuestos de un rectángulo tienen la misma longitud.		
rectangular prism a prism where the bases are rectangles. **prisma rectangular** prisma en el que las bases son rectángulos.	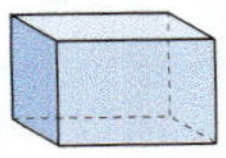	

English/Español	Example/Ejemplo	Notes/Notas
reflection a transformation that flips (reflects) a figure across a line to form a mirror image. This line is called the *line of reflection*. **reflexión** transformación que gira (refleja) una figura del otro lado de una línea para formar una imagen reflejada. Esta línea se llama *eje de reflexión*.	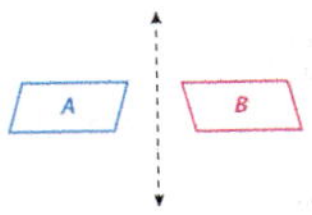 	
relative frequency the quotient that compares the number of times a data value occurs and the total number of data values. This can be expressed as a fraction, decimal, or percent. **frecuencia relativa** cociente que compara el número de veces que ocurre un valor y el número total de valores. Esto se puede expresar como fracción, decimal o porcentaje.	Data set: red, green, red, red, blue, yellow, blue, white Frequency of *blue*: 2 Total data values: 8 Relative frequency of *blue*: $\frac{2}{8}$, or $\frac{1}{4}$, or 0.25, or 25%	
remainder the amount left over when one number does not divide another number a whole number of times. **residuo** cantidad que queda cuando un número no divide a otro un número entero de veces.	$7 \div 2 = 3 \text{ R } 1$ 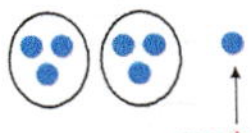 	
repeating decimals decimals that repeat the same digit or sequence of digits forever. A repeating decimal can be written with a bar over the repeating digits. **decimal periódico** decimales que repiten el mismo dígito o secuencia de dígitos infinitamente. Un decimal periódico se puede escribir con una barra sobre los dígitos que se repiten.	$0.\overline{3}$ $2.\overline{51}$	
rhombus a quadrilateral with all sides the same length. **rombo** cuadrilátero que tiene todos los lados de la misma longitud.	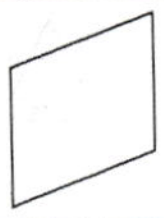	

English/Español	Example/Ejemplo	Notes/Notas
right angle an angle that measures 90°. **ángulo recto** ángulo que mide 90°.	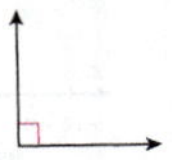	
right prism a prism where each base is perpendicular to the other faces. In a right prism, the faces that are not bases are rectangles. **prisma recto** prisma en el que cada base es perpendicular a las otras caras. En un prisma recto, las caras que no son bases son rectángulos.	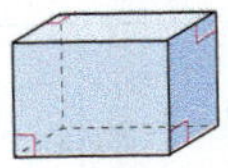	
right rectangular prism a right prism where the bases and other faces are all rectangles. **prisma rectangular recto** prisma recto en el que las bases y las otras caras son rectángulos.	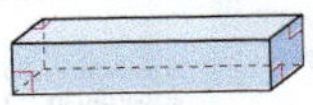	
right triangle a triangle with one right angle. **triángulo rectángulo** triángulo que tiene un ángulo recto.	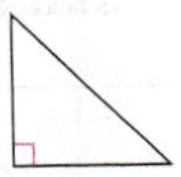	
right triangular prism a right prism where the bases are triangles and the other faces are rectangles. **prisma triangular recto** prisma recto en el que las bases son triángulos y las otras caras son rectángulos.	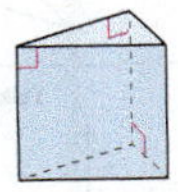	

Interactive Glossary

English/Español	Example/Ejemplo	Notes/Notas
rigid transformation a transformation in which the size and the shape of the figure does not change. *Translations*, *reflections*, and *rotations* are examples of rigid transformations. **transformación rígida** transformación en la que el tamaño y la forma de la figura no cambian. Las *traslaciones*, las *reflexiones* y las *rotaciones* son ejemplos de transformaciones rígidas.	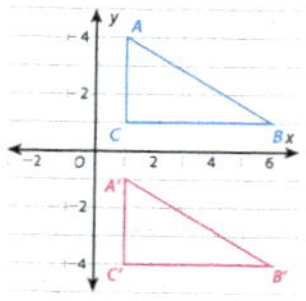 $\triangle A'B'C'$ is a rigid transformation of $\triangle ABC$.	
rotation a transformation that turns (rotates) a figure through a given angle and in a given direction around a fixed point. This point is called the center of rotation. **rotación** transformación que gira (rota) una figura a través de un ángulo dado y en una dirección dada alrededor de un punto fijo. Este punto se llama centro de rotación.	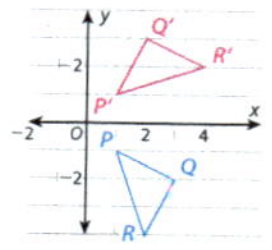 $\triangle P'Q'R'$ is a rotation of $\triangle PQR$.	
round to approximate the value of a number by finding the nearest ten, hundred, or other place value. **redondear** aproximar el valor de un número hallando la decena, la centena u otro valor posicional más cercano.	48 rounded to the nearest ten is 50.	

English/Español	Example/Ejemplo	Notes/Notas
Ss		
same-side exterior angles when two lines are cut by a transversal, a pair of angles on the same side of the transversal and outside the two lines. When the two lines are parallel, same-side exterior angles are supplementary. **ángulos externos del mismo lado** cuando dos rectas se cortan con una transversal, par de ángulos del mismo lado de la transversal y fuera de las dos rectas. Cuando las dos rectas son paralelas, los ángulos externos del mismo lado son suplementarios.	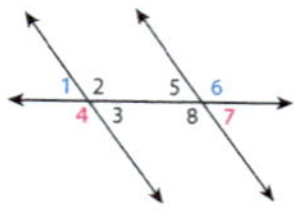 $\angle 1$ and $\angle 6$ $\angle 4$ and $\angle 7$	
same-side interior angles when two lines are cut by a transversal, a pair of angles on the same side of the transversal and between the two lines. When the two lines are parallel, same-side interior angles are supplementary. **ángulos internos del mismo lado** cuando dos rectas se cortan con una transversal, par de ángulos del mismo lado de la transversal y entre de las dos rectas. Cuando las dos rectas son paralelas, los ángulos internos del mismo lado son suplementarios.	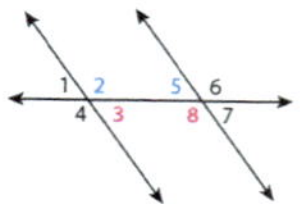 $\angle 2$ and $\angle 5$ $\angle 3$ and $\angle 8$	
sample a part of a population. **muestra** parte de una población.	Population: All students in the school Sample: Three students in each homeroom	
sample space the set of all possible unique outcomes for an experiment. **espacio muestral** conjunto de todos los resultados posibles de un experimento.	Experiment: Rolling a number cube Sample space: 1, 2, 3, 4, 5, 6	
scale tells the relationship between a length in a drawing, map, or model to the actual length. **escala** indica la relación que hay entre una longitud en un dibujo, un mapa o un modelo y la longitud real.	Scale from a map to actual distances in a town: 1 in. to 20 mi	

English/Español	Example/Ejemplo	Notes/Notas
scale (on a graph) the value represented by the distance between one tick mark and the next on a number line. **escala (en una gráfica)** valor representado por la distancia que hay entre una marca y la siguiente en una recta numérica.	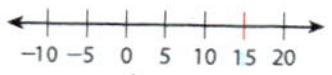 scale = 5	
scale drawing a drawing in which the measurements correspond to the measurements of the actual object by the same scale. **dibujo a escala** dibujo en el que las medidas se corresponden con las medidas del objeto real según la misma escala.	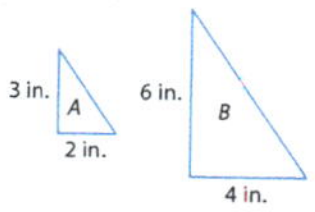 $\triangle A : \triangle B$ is 1 : 2.	
scale factor the factor you multiply all the side lengths in a figure by to make a scale copy. **factor de escala** factor por el que se multiplican todas las longitudes laterales en una figura para hacer una copia a escala.	Scale from a map to the actual distance: 1 in. to 20 mi Scale factor from distances on the map to the actual distances: 20	
scalene triangle a triangle that has no sides the same length. **triángulo escaleno** triángulo que no tiene lados de la misma longitud.		
scatter plot a graph of two-variable data displayed as ordered pairs. **diagrama de dispersión** gráfica de datos de dos variables que se muestran como pares ordenados.	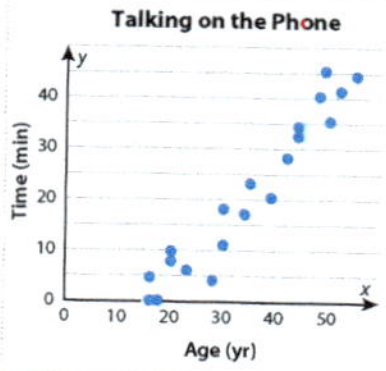	

English/Español	Example/Ejemplo	Notes/Notas
scientific notation a way of expressing a number as a product in the form $n \times 10^a$, where a is an integer and n is a decimal number such that $1 \le n < 10$. **notación científica** manera de expresar un número como producto con la forma $n \times 10^a$, en la que a es un entero y n es un número decimal tal que $1 \le n < 10$.	$5{,}900{,}000 = 5.9 \times 10^6$	
sequence of transformations one or more transformations performed in a certain order. **secuencia de transformaciones** una o más transformaciones llevadas a cabo en un orden determinado.	A reflection followed by a rotation	
side a line segment that forms part of a two-dimensional shape. **lado** segmento de recta que forma parte de una figura bidimensional	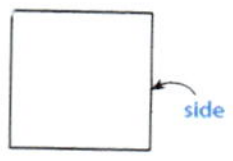	
similar (~) having the same shape. Two figures are similar if there is a sequence of rigid transformations and/or dilations that maps one figure onto the second. **semejante (~)** que tienen la misma forma. Dos figuras son semejantes si hay una secuencia de transformaciones rígidas y/o dilataciones que hacen coincidir una figura con la segunda.	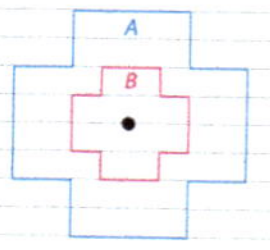 Figures *A* and *B* are similar.	
similar triangles triangles that are scale drawings of one another. Similar triangles have the same shape but may have a different size. **triángulos semejantes** triángulos que son dibujos a escala unos de otros. Los triángulos semejantes tienen la misma forma pero pueden tener diferente tamaño.	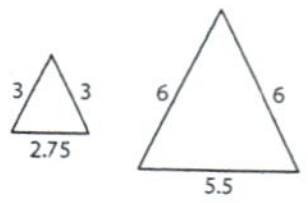	

English/Español	**Example/Ejemplo**	**Notes/Notas**
simple interest a percent of an amount that is borrowed or invested. **interés simple** porcentaje de una cantidad que se toma prestada o se invierte.	$I = Prt$ I = interest P = principal (amount borrowed or invested) r = interest rate t = time	
skewed left when most of the data points of a distribution are clustered near the greater values. **asimétrica a la izquierda** cuando la mayoría de los datos de una distribución se agrupan cerca de los valores más altos.	Skewed Left 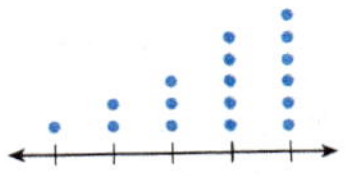	
skewed right when most of the data points of a distribution are clustered near the lesser values. **asimétrica a la derecha** cuando la mayoría de los datos de una distribución se agrupan cerca de los valores más bajos.	Skewed Right 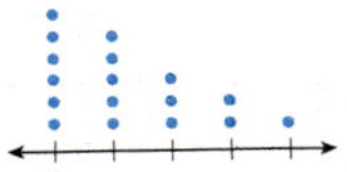	
slope for any two points on a line, the $\frac{\text{rise}}{\text{run}}$ or $\frac{\text{change in } y}{\text{change in } x}$. It is a measure of the steepness of a line. It is also called the *rate of change* of a linear function. **pendiente** para dos puntos cualesquiera en una recta, la $\frac{\text{distancia vertical}}{\text{distancia horizontal}}$ o $\frac{\text{cambio en } y}{\text{cambio en } x}$. Es una medida de la inclinación de una recta. También se llama *tasa de cambio* de una función lineal.	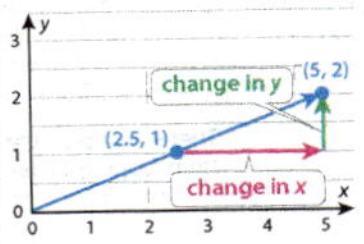 Slope: $\frac{1}{2.5} = 0.4$	
slope-intercept form a linear equation in the form $y = mx + b$, where m is the slope and b is the y-intercept. **forma pendiente-intercepto** ecuación lineal en la forma $y = mx + b$, en la que m es la pendiente y b es el intercepto en y.	equation: $y = 2x + 1$ slope: 2 y-intercept: (0, 1)	

English/Español	**Example/Ejemplo**	**Notes/Notas**
solution of an equation a value that can be substituted for a variable to make an equation true. **solución de una ecuación** valor que puede sustituir a una variable para hacer que una ecuación sea verdadera.	The value 5 is the solution of the equation $19 = 4x - 1$ because $19 = 4(5) - 1$.	
solution of an inequality a value that can be substituted for a variable to make an inequality true. **solución de una desigualdad** valor que puede sustituir a una variable para hacer que una desigualdad sea verdadera.	All values of x less than 5 ($x < 5$) are solutions of the inequality $5x < 25$.	
sphere a three-dimensional figure in which every point is the same distance from the center. **esfera** figura tridimensional en la que todos los puntos están a la misma distancia del centro.	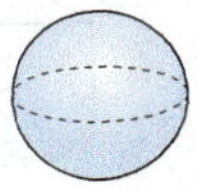	
square a quadrilateral with 4 right angles and 4 sides of equal length. **cuadrado** cuadrilátero que tiene 4 ángulos rectos y 4 lados de la misma longitud.		
square root of x the number that when multiplied by itself is equal to x. **raíz cuadrada de x** número que cuando se multiplica por sí mismo es igual a x.	$\sqrt{16} = \sqrt{4 \cdot 4}$ $= 4$ 4 is the square root of 16.	
statistical question a question that can be answered by collecting data that are expected to vary. **pregunta estadística** pregunta que se puede responder reuniendo datos que se espera que varíen.	What is the typical amount of rain in April?	

English/Español	**Example/Ejemplo**	**Notes/Notas**
straight angle an angle that measures 180°. The sides of a straight angle form a straight line. **ángulo llano** ángulo que mide 180°. Los lados de un ángulo llano forman una línea recta.	 $\angle ABC$ is a straight angle.	
sum the result of addition. **total** resultado de la suma.	24 + 35 = 59	
supplementary angles two angles whose measures sum to 180°. **ángulos suplementarios** dos ángulos cuyas medidas suman 180°.	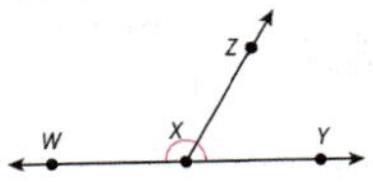 $\angle WXZ$ and $\angle ZXY$ are supplementary angles.	
surface area the sum of the areas of all the faces of a three-dimensional figure. **área total** suma de las áreas de todas las caras de una figura tridimensional.	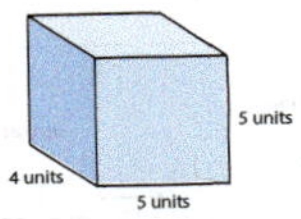 Surface Area: 2(4)(5) + 2(4)(5) + 2(5)(5) = 130 units^2	
symmetric when a distribution has the same shape on both sides of a middle point. **simétrico** cuando una distribución tiene la misma forma en ambos lados de un punto que está en el medio.	Symmetric 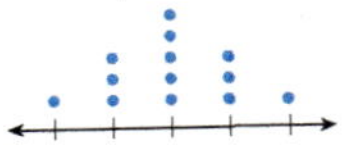	

English/Español	**Example/Ejemplo**	**Notes/Notas**
system of linear equations a group of related linear equations in which a solution makes all the equations true at the same time. A system of equations can have zero, one, or infinitely many solutions. **sistema de ecuaciones lineales** grupo de ecuaciones lineales relacionadas en el que una solución hace que todas las ecuaciones sean verdaderas al mismo tiempo. Un sistema de ecuaciones puede tener cero, una o infinitas soluciones.	$y = 4x + 8$ $y = 3x + 8$	

Tt

tax a percent of income or of the cost of goods or services paid to the government. **impuesto** porcentaje del ingreso o del costo de bienes o servicios que se paga al gobierno.	A 7% sales tax on a purchase of $40 is $2.80	
term a number, a variable, or a product of numbers, variables, and/or expressions. A term may include an exponent. **término** número, variable o el producto de números, variables y/o expresiones. Un término puede tener un exponente.	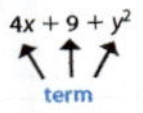	

English/Español	Example/Ejemplo	Notes/Notas
terminating decimals decimals that end, or end in repeated zeros. **decimal finito** decimal en el que termina un número, o que termina en ceros repetidos.	0.25 5.6 −7.125	
theoretical probability the probability of an event occurring based on what is expected to happen. **probabilidad teórica** probabilidad de que ocurra un evento según lo que se espera que suceda.	There are two equally likely outcomes to flipping a coin: heads up or tails up. The theoretical probability of the outcome heads up is $\frac{1}{2}$, or 50%.	
three-dimensional solid, or having length, width, and height. For example, a cube is three-dimensional. **tridimensional** sólido, o que tiene longitud, ancho y altura. Por ejemplo, un cubo es tridimensional.	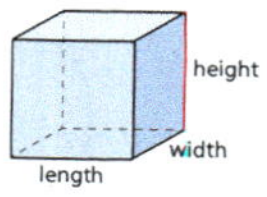	
transformation a change in location, orientation, or size of a figure. **transformación** cambio de ubicación, orientación o tamaño de una figura.	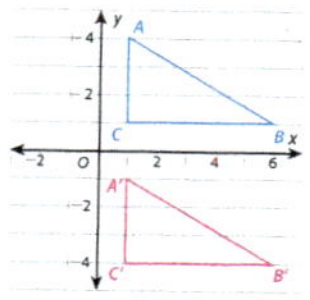 △A′B′C′ is a transformation of △ABC.	
translation a transformation that moves (slides) each point of a figure the same distance and in the same direction. **traslación** transformación que mueve (desplaza) cada punto de una figura la misma distancia y en la misma dirección.	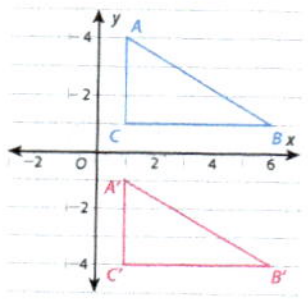 △A′B′C′ is a translation of △ABC 5 units down.	

English/Español	Example/Ejemplo	Notes/Notas
transversal a line that cuts two or more lines. The lines cut by the transversal may or may not be parallel. **transversal** línea que corta dos o más rectas. Las rectas cortadas por la transversal pueden ser o no ser paralelas.	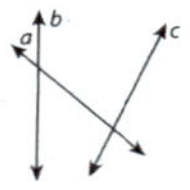 Line *a* is a transversal that cuts lines *b* and *c*.	
trapezoid (exclusive) a quadrilateral with exactly one pair of parallel sides. **trapecio (exclusivo)** cuadrilátero que tiene exactamente un par de lados paralelos.	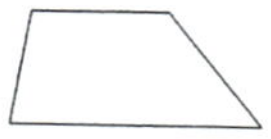	
trapezoid (inclusive) a quadrilateral with at least one pair of parallel sides. **trapecio (inclusivo)** cuadrilátero que tiene al menos un par de lados paralelos.		
tree diagram a visual that shows all possible outcomes of an experiment. **diagrama de árbol** representación visual que muestra todos los resultados posibles de un experimento.	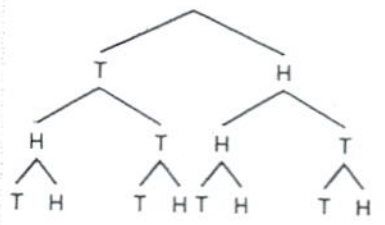 There are 8 possible outcomes from flipping a coin 3 times.	
trial a single performance of an experiment. **ensayo** ejecución única de un experimento.	Rolling a number cube once	
triangle a polygon with exactly 3 sides and 3 angles. **triángulo** polígono que tiene exactamente 3 lados y 3 ángulos.	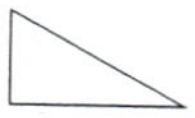	
triangular prism a prism where the bases are triangles. **prisma triangular** prisma en el que las bases son triángulos.	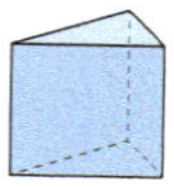	

English/Español	Example/Ejemplo	Notes/Notas
two-dimensional flat, or having measurement in two directions, like length and width. For example, a rectangle is two-dimensional. **bidimensional** plano, o que tiene medidas en dos direcciones, como longitud y ancho. Por ejemplo, un rectángulo es bidimensional.	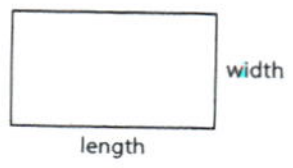	
two-way table a table that displays two-variable categorical data. One variable is shown along the top, the other down the side. Each entry in the table gives information about the frequency or relative frequency for the paired data. **tabla de doble entrada** tabla que muestra datos categóricos de dos variables. Una variable se muestra arriba y la otra abajo al costado. Cada entrada en la tabla da información acerca de la frecuencia o frecuencia relativa para los pares de datos.	see table below	

	Red Car	Black Car
New Car	16	22
Used Car	23	14

Uu

English/Español	Example/Ejemplo	Notes/Notas
unit fraction a fraction with a numerator of 1. Other fractions are built from unit fractions. **fracción unitaria** fracción que tiene un numerador de 1. Otras fracciones se construyen a partir de fracciones unitarias.	$\frac{1}{5}$	
unit rate the numerical part of a rate. For the ratio $a : b$, the unit rate is the quotient $\frac{a}{b}$. **tasa por unidad** parte numérica de una tasa. Para la razón $a : b$, la tasa por unidad es el cociente $\frac{a}{b}$.	Rate: 3 miles per hour Unit rate: 3	
unknown the value you need to find to solve a problem. **incógnita** valor que hay que hallar para resolver un problema.	$20.5 + x = 30$	
upper quartile the middle number between the median and the maximum in an ordered set of numbers. The upper quartile is also called the 3rd quartile or Q3. **cuartil superior** número del medio entre la mediana y el máximo en un conjunto ordenado de números. El cuartil superior también se llama tercer cuartil, o Q3.	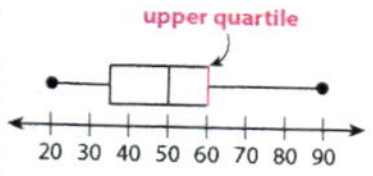	

English/Español | **Example/Ejemplo** | **Notes/Notas**

Vv

variability how spread out or close together values in a data set are.

variabilidad la dispersión o cercanía de los valores en un conjunto de datos.

Gavin's Handstand Times

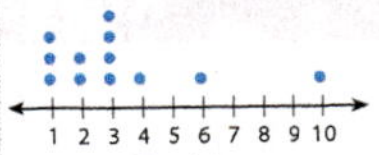

There is high variability in Gavin's handstand times.

variable a letter that represents an unknown number. In some cases, a variable may represent more than one number.

variable letra que representa un número desconocido. En algunos casos, una variable puede representar más de un número.

$3x + 9 = 90$

vertex the point where two rays, lines, or line segments meet to form an angle.

vértice punto en el que dos semirrectas, rectas o segmentos de recta se encuentran y forman un ángulo.

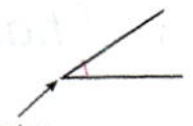

vertical angles opposite angles formed when two lines intersect. Vertical angles are congruent.

ángulos opuestos por el vértice ángulos opuestos que se forman cuando se intersecan dos rectas. Los ángulos opuestos por el vértice son congruentes.

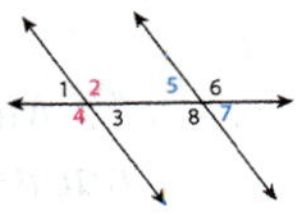

∠5 and ∠7
∠2 and ∠4

volume the amount of space inside a solid figure. Volume is measured in cubic units such as cubic inches.

volumen cantidad de espacio dentro de una figura sólida. El volumen se mide en unidades cúbicas como las pulgadas cúbicas.

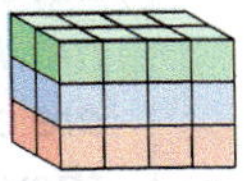

volume: 24 units^3

English/Español | **Example/Ejemplo** | **Notes/Notas**

Ww

whole numbers the numbers 0, 1, 2, 3, 4, . . . Whole numbers are nonnegative and have no fractional part.

números enteros los números 0, 1, 2, 3, 4, . . . Los números enteros no son negativos y no tienen partes fraccionarias.

0, 8, 187

Xx

x-axis the horizontal number line in the coordinate plane.

eje x recta numérica horizontal en el plano de coordenadas.

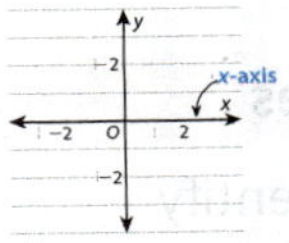

x-coordinate the first number in an ordered pair. It tells the point's horizontal distance from the y-axis.

coordenada x primer número en un par ordenado. Indica la distancia horizontal del punto al eje y.

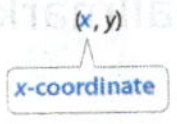

English/Español | **Example/Ejemplo** | **Notes/Notas**

x-intercept the x-coordinate of the point where a line, or graph of a function, intersects the x-axis.

intercepto en x coordenada x del punto en el que una recta, o gráfica de una función, interseca al eje x.

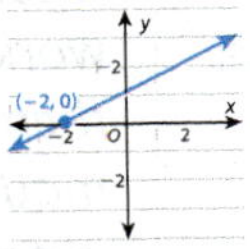

The x-intercept is −2.

Yy

y-axis the vertical number line in the coordinate plane.

eje y recta numérica vertical en el plano de coordenadas.

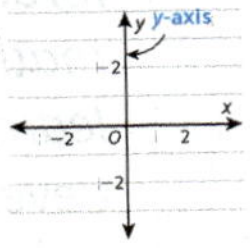

y-coordinate the second number in an ordered pair. It tells the point's vertical distance from the x-axis.

coordenada y el segundo número en un par ordenado. Indica la distancia vertical del punto al eje x.

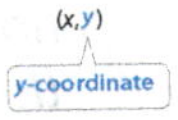

English/Español | **Example/Ejemplo** | **Notes/Notas**

y-intercept the y-coordinate of the point where a line, or graph of a function, intersects the y-axis.

intercepto en y coordenada y del punto en el que una recta, o gráfica de una función, interseca al eje y.

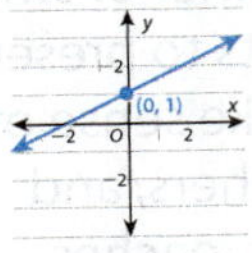

The y-intercept is 1.

Zz

zero pair two numbers whose sum is zero. Opposite numbers form a zero pair.

par cero dos números cuya suma es cero. Los números opuestos forman un par cero.

−3 and 3 form a zero pair.
1.2 and −1.2 form a zero pair.

Supporting Research

i-Ready® Classroom Mathematics is built on research from a variety of federal initiatives, national mathematics organizations, and experts in mathematics.

i-Ready Classroom Mathematics Uses . . .	Examples	Research Says . . .
Instructional Routines		
An instructional routine supports students in achieving mathematical proficiency and rigor within a collaborative structure to develop greater understanding of how to reason mathematically.	*i-Ready Classroom Mathematics* lessons follow a Try-Discuss-Connect instructional routine in which students make sense of a problem, discuss and connect strategies and models, reflect on their learning, and apply that learning to new problems in **Try It**, **Discuss It**, **Picture It & Model It**, **Connect It**, and **Apply It**.	*". . . [I]nstructional routines are situated in the learning opportunity itself, providing students with a predictable frame for engaging with the content. . . . They allow for a greater focus on learning . . . [and] help teachers and students build crucial thinking habits."* —Kelemanik, Lucenta, & Creighton, 2016
Mathematical Practices		
Mathematical Practices identify habits of mind and everyday ways of approaching math that are hallmarks of successful math students.	Mathematical Practices are an integral part of *i-Ready Classroom Mathematics* instruction. • The **Mathematical Practices** section of the Student Handbook in the Student Worktext serves as reference for students. • Mathematical Practices are built into the instruction and problems throughout each session. • **Deepen Understanding** features in the Teacher's Guide provide rigorous discourse questions for specific Practices.	*". . . Mathematical Practice[s] describe eight habits of mind teachers must incorporate into classroom instruction to help students develop depth of understanding of critical mathematical concepts. . . . If students are engaged in using the eight Practices, they are learning rigorous, meaningful mathematics."* —Gojak and Miles, 2016
Collaborative Learning		
Collaborative learning (partner or small group) encourages students to present and defend their ideas, make sense of and critique the ideas of others, and refine and amend their approaches.	*i-Ready Classroom Mathematics* lessons provide multiple opportunities for collaborative learning, such as: • **Discuss It** prompts where students explain and justify their strategies to each other. • **Consider This** prompts where students compare problem-solving approaches, solutions, and reasoning.	*"Research tells us that when students work collaboratively, which also gives them opportunities to see and understand mathematics connections, equitable outcomes result."* —Boaler, 2016
Mathematical Discourse		
Mathematical discourse in instruction uses questioning, listening, reading, writing, interpreting information, and reflection to communicate mathematical knowledge.	*i-Ready Classroom Mathematics* lessons include predictable opportunities for sharing of ideas and understandings. • **Discuss It** prompts students to explain and justify their strategies. • In **Consider This**, students compare problem-solving approaches, solutions, and reasoning. • **Ask-Listen** for questioning in the Teacher's Guide provides discussion prompts and expectations for possible student responses. • **Deepen Understanding** features in the Teacher's Guide provide math discourse for specific Practices.	*"Mathematical discourse serves as a forum in which to exchange and record mathematics ideas, document evidence of learning, and monitor growth in knowledge development. Teachers gain insights not only about what students know but also about the approaches they use, how—and how well—they understand the ideas, and the ways they present their knowledge."* —Kersaint, 2016

i-Ready Classroom Mathematics Uses . . .	Examples	Research Says . . .
Connection to Prior Knowledge		
Connection to prior learning encourages students to draw on their experiences and knowledge and leads to coherence of mathematical understanding.	*i-Ready Classroom Mathematics* lessons routinely provide opportunities for students to connect to prior knowledge. • Each **Explore** session introduces a new concept by having students make sense of and solve a problem based on applying prior knowledge. • **Start** slides establish a clear entry point by activating and/or connecting to prior learning related to the content of the session.	*"Mathematical knowledge and understanding cannot be transferred directly from teacher to student. Students must be provided with opportunities to construct their own knowledge and understanding that reflect, refine, and extend their prior knowledge, skills, and experiences."* — Ellis, Yeh, and Hurdato, 2017
Productive Struggle		
Productive struggle occurs when students are allowed critical processing time to reason about and make sense of mathematical situations on their own.	*i-Ready Classroom Mathematics* lessons are structured so that students work independently in the **Try It** to persevere in making sense of a given problem and starting their own solution strategy.	*"Effective teaching of mathematics consistently provides students, individually and collectively, with opportunities and supports to engage in productive struggle as they grapple with mathematical ideas and relationships."* — NCTM, 2014
Select and Sequence		
Selecting and sequencing is an instructional practice where teachers identify students and specific approaches to focus on during whole class discussion and make a purposeful decision about the order of student presentations.	The *i-Ready Classroom Mathematics* Teacher's Guide includes a **Select and Sequence Student Solutions** section that provides an order of possible student approaches ranging from concrete to representational to abstract that teachers can use to make decisions about the structure of whole-class discussions.	*"Through planning, teachers can anticipate likely student contributions, prepare responses that they might make to them, and make decisions about how to structure students' presentations to further their mathematical agenda for the lesson."* — Smith and Stein, 2011
Making Connections		
Making connections occurs when students compare approaches, strategies, tools, and representations, then generalize their understanding.	The *i-Ready Classroom Mathematics* Try-Discuss-Connect instructional routine actively engages students in making connections. • **Discuss It** whole-class discourse focuses on comparing and connecting student representations and approaches identified by the teacher during select and sequencing. • **Picture It** & **Model It** representations are compared and connected to student representations. • In **Connect It**, students record their learning, articulate their approaches, and demonstrate understanding of mathematical learning goals.	*"Effective teaching of mathematics engages students in making connections among mathematical representations to deepen understanding of mathematics concepts and procedure, and as tools for problem-solving."* — NCTM, 2014

Supporting Research

<table>
<tr><th>i-Ready Classroom Mathematics Uses . . .</th><th>Examples</th><th>Research Says . . .</th></tr>
<tr><td colspan="3">CRA Model</td></tr>
<tr><td>The Concrete-Representational-Abstract (CRA) Model is a three-part instructional model that enhances students' mathematical learning.</td><td>The CRA Model is built into all i-Ready Classroom Mathematics lessons.<ul><li>In Try It, students analyze a problem in a very focused way to help them begin to develop concrete solutions. Students may use concrete, representational, or abstract strategies to solve the problem, based on their understanding of the problem or mathematical concept.</li><li>In Discuss It, as teachers sequence student strategies, they have students share concrete approaches before discussing other mathematical representations and more abstract strategies.</li><li>Through the Connect It questions, students connect concrete and representational approaches to more abstract understanding as they formalize their learning.</li><li>Hands-On Activities at point of use and at the end of each lesson in the Teacher's Guide support students needing additional work on a concept or skill.</li></ul></td><td>"Using and connecting representations leads students to deeper understanding. Different representations, including concrete models, pictures, words, and numbers, should be introduced, discussed, and connected to support students in explaining their thinking and reasoning."
—Clements and Sarama, 2014</td></tr>
<tr><td colspan="3">Conceptual Understanding</td></tr>
<tr><td>Conceptual understanding is meaningful knowledge of mathematical concepts and relations and understanding of why math processes and rules work.</td><td>All i-Ready Classroom Mathematics lessons lay a foundation for conceptual understanding of the mathematical principles underlying strategies and skills being addressed.<ul><li>Understand lessons put a special emphasis on these principles.</li><li>Deepen Understanding features in the Teacher's Guide provide further support for conceptual understanding.</li></ul></td><td>"To prepare students for Algebra, the curriculum must simultaneously develop conceptual understanding, computational fluency, and problem-solving skills."
—National Mathematics Advisory Panel, 2008</td></tr>
<tr><td colspan="3">Reasoning and Problem Solving</td></tr>
<tr><td>Reasoning about mathematical ideas and approaches to problem solving contributes to the development of foundational conceptual understanding and procedural fluency.</td><td>Problem solving and reasoning about mathematics are at the heart of i-Ready Classroom Mathematics.<ul><li>Try It, Discuss It, Picture It & Model It, and Connect It engage students in active problem solving and support reasoning through productive struggle, peer discussion, and whole-class discourse.</li><li>Apply It problems are an opportunity for students to independently apply flexible use of strategies to solve new problems and reflect on their learning.</li></ul></td><td>"Effective teaching of mathematics engages students in solving and discussing tasks that promote mathematical reasoning and problem solving and allow multiple entry points and varied solution strategies."
—NCTM, 2014</td></tr>
</table>

i-Ready Classroom Mathematics Uses . . .	Examples	Research Says . . .
Procedural Fluency and Skills		
Procedural fluency and skills are the ways students use their knowledge to accurately, flexibly, and efficiently apply mathematical procedures and operations.	*i-Ready Classroom Mathematics* directly addresses the development of procedural skills connected to conceptual understanding. • **Additional Practice** encourages students to demonstrate flexible use of strategies, explain their thinking about procedures, and apply procedures appropriately and efficiently. • **Fluency & Skills Practice** are ongoing opportunities for students to accurately, flexibly, and efficiently practice mathematical procedures and operations.	*"Effective teaching of mathematics builds fluency with procedures on a foundation of conceptual understanding so that students, over time, become skillful in using procedures flexibly as they solve contextual and mathematical problems."* —NCTM, 2014
Formative Assessment		
Formative assessment is a strategy that involves frequent, in-classroom progress checks of students' understanding and mastery of math concepts and skills.	*i-Ready Classroom Mathematics* lessons are structured so teachers can monitor understanding throughout. • **Common Misconceptions** and **Error Alerts** in the Teacher's Guide are ongoing formative assessment opportunities, with support for correcting misconceptions and errors. • Refine sessions include a **Check for Understanding** in the Teacher's Guide to help assess students' progress toward mastery of skills, identify specific misconceptions, and provide support on the spot.	*"Teachers' regular use of formative assessment improves their students' learning, especially if teachers have additional guidance on using the assessment to design and to individualize instruction."* —National Mathematics Advisory Panel, 2008
Support for All: Differentiated Instruction		
Differentiated Instruction is an approach to teaching that gives students multiple ways to access and make sense of mathematical ideas.	*i-Ready Classroom Mathematics* lessons provide a full range of support for differentiating instruction. • **Hands-On Activities**, **Visual Models**, **Deepen Understanding**, and **Challenge Activities** in the Teacher's Guide provide differentiation options for use during lessons. • Recommendations in the Teacher's Guide for **prerequisite lessons**, **Tools for Instruction**, **Center Activities**, and **Enrichment Activities** provide differentiation options for use after lessons.	*"Differentiation is a teacher's proactive response to learner needs shaped by mindset and guided by general principles of differentiation: an environment that encourages and supports learning, quality curriculum, [and] assessment that informs teaching. . . ."* —Tomlinson & Moon, 2013

Supporting Research

i-Ready Classroom Mathematics Uses . . .	Examples	Research Says . . .
Support for All: Culturally Responsive		
Being culturally and linguistically responsive (CLR) entails the validation, affirmation, building and bridging of students' cultural and linguistic behaviors through instructional practices.	Support for a culturally responsive classroom is woven into every lesson in *i-Ready Classroom Mathematics*. • Lessons follow the Universal Design for Learning (UDL), ensuring that all students can access the mathematics by providing multiple ways of representing information for engagement, action, and expression. • **Connect to Culture** at the beginning of each lesson in the Teacher's Guide provides ideas for promoting cultural responsiveness throughout the sessions. • In each unit, **Connect Language Development to Mathematics** gives strategies on establishing a classroom environment supporting mathematical discourse for all learners.	*"CLR is the validation and affirmation of the home (indigenous) culture and home language for the purpose of building and bridging the student to success in the culture of academia and mainstream society."* —Hollie, 2011
Support for All: ELL		
i-Ready Classroom Mathematics helps teachers scaffold language so that students can access and express understanding of rigorous grade-level mathematics.	All *i-Ready Classroom Mathematics* lessons use many approaches to support English Language Learners (ELL). • The Student Worktext has pictoral and visual representations combined with direct simple text to clearly present concepts. • **ELL Differentiated Instruction** in every session provides scaffolds for the different levels of language proficiency and language domains so teacher can address students' language needs. • Additional ELL and language support in the Teacher's Guide includes **Language Objectives** and a **Develop Academic Language** feature in every session and vocabulary development for both mathematical terms and academic language.	*"The framework [is] . . . a new vision for mathematics instruction that explicitly attends to the needs of ELLs, addressing the interdependence of language and mathematics."* —Council of the Great City Schools, 2016

References

Ball, D. L., Ferrini-Mundy, J., Kilpatrick, J., Milgram, R. J., Schmid, W., and Schaar, R. (2005). Reaching for common ground in K–12 mathematics education. *Notices of the American Mathematical Society*, 52(9)

Beed, P. L., Hawkins, E. M., & Roller, C. M. (1991). Moving learners toward independence: The power of scaffolded instruction. *The Reading Teacher*, 44(9), 648–655

Boaler, J. (2008, 2015). *What's Math Got to Do with It?*. New York, NY: Penguin Group

Boaler, Jo (2016). *Mathematical Mindsets*. San Francisco, CA: Jossey-Bass

Clements, D., Sarama, J. (2014). *Learning and Teaching Early Math: The Learning Trajectories Approach*. New York, NY: Routledge

Council of the Great City Schools. (2016). A Framework for Re-Envisioning Mathematics Instruction for English Language Learners

Eastburn, J. A. (2011). The effects of a concrete, representational, abstract (CRA) instructional model on tier 2 first-grade math students in a response to intervention model: Educational implications for number sense and computational fluency. Dissertation. *ProQuest Information & Learning*, AAI3408708

Ellis, M., Yeh, C., Hurtado, C. (2017). *Reimaging the Mathematics Classroom*. Reston, VA: National Council of Teachers of Mathematics

Furner, J. M., Yahya, N., & Duffy, M. L. (2005). 20 Ways to teach mathematics: strategies to reach all students. *Intervention in School and Clinic*, 41(1)

Gojak, L. M., Miles, R. H. (2016). *The Common Core Mathematics Companion: The Standards Decoded*. Thousand Oaks, CA: Corwin

Hall, T., Vue, G., Strangman, N., & Meyer, A. (2003). *Differentiated instruction and implications for UDL implementation*. Wakefield, MA: National Center on Accessing the General Curriculum. (Links updated 2014). Accessed at http://aem.cast.org/about/publications/2003/ncacdifferentiatedinstruction-udl.html

Hess, K. K., Carlock, D., Jones, B., & Walkup, J. R. (2009). *What exactly do "fewer, clearer, and higher standards" really look like in the classroom? Using a cognitive rigor matrix to analyze curriculum, plan lessons, and implement assessments*. Accessed at: https://www.csai-online.org/resources/what-exactly-do-fewer-clearer-and-higher-standards-really-lookclassroom-using-cognitive

Hollie, S. (2011). *Culturally and Linguistically Responsive Teaching and Learning*. Huntington Beach, CA: Shell Education

Kazemi, E. and Hintz, A. (2014). Intentional Talk. Portland, ME: Stenhouse Publishers

Kelemanik, G., Lucenta, A., Creighton, S. (2016). *Routines for Reasoning*. Dover, NH: Heinemann

Kersaint, G. (2016). Orchestrating Mathematical Discourse to Enhance Student Learning, Curriculum Associates. Accessed at: http://readycentral.com/articles/using-discourse-effectively-in-the-ready-classroom/

Kersaint, G. (2017). Selecting and Sequencing Student Solutions. Accessed at: http://readycentral.com/articles/using-discourse-effectively-in-theready-classroom/

Kersaint, G., Thompson, D. R., Petkova, M. (2013). Teaching Mathematics to English Language Learners. New York, NY: Routledge

National Council of Supervisors of Mathematics. (2013). Improving student achievement in mathematics by using manipulatives with classroom instruction. National Council of Supervisors of Mathematics Improving Student Achievement Series. No. 11

National Council of Teachers of Mathematics (2010). *Teaching and Learning Mathematics*

National Council of Teachers of Mathematics (2014). *Principles to Action*

National Council of Teachers of Mathematics (2014). *Using Research to Improve Instruction*

National Council of Teachers of Mathematics (2017). *Enhancing Classroom Practice*

National Council of Teachers of Mathematics. (2007). Effective Strategies for Teaching Students with Difficulties in Mathematics

National Mathematics Advisory Panel. (2008). Foundations for success: *The final report of the National Mathematics Advisory Panel*. Accessed at: http://www2.ed.gov/about/bdscomm/list/ mathpanel/index.html

National Research Council. (2001). *Adding it Up: Helping Children Learn Mathematics*. Mathematics Learning Study Committee: Kilpatrick, J., Swafford, J., & Findell, B. (eds.). Washington, D.C.: National Academy Press

Pashler, H., Bain, P., Bottge, B., Graesser, A., Koedinger, K., McDaniel, M., & Metcalfe, J. (2007). *Organizing instruction and study to improve student learning* (NCER 2007–2004)

Richhart, R. (2015). *Creating Cultures of Thinking*. San Francisco, CA: Jossey-Bass

Robertson, K. (2009). Math instruction for English language learners. *Colorin Colorado!* Accessed at: http://www.colorincolorado.org/article/30570/

Schmidt, W., Houang, R., & Cogan, L. (2002). A coherent curriculum, *American Educator*, Summer, 2002

Seethaler, P. M., Fuchs, L. S., Fuchs, D., & Compton, D. L. (2012). Predicting first graders' development of calculation versus word-problem performance: the role of dynamic assessment. *Journal of Educational Psychology* 104(1), 224–234

Smith, M. S., Stein, M. K. (2011). 5 *Practices for Orchestrating Productive Mathematics Discussions*. Reston, VA: The National Council of Teachers of Mathematics, Inc.

Tomlinson, C. A., Moon, T. R. (2013). Assessment and Student Success in a Differentiated Classroom. Association for Supervision & Curriculum Development

Washington, D.C.: National Center for Education Research, Institute of Education Sciences, U.S. Department of Education. Retrieved from http://ncer.ed.gov

Content Focus in the Common Core State Standards (CCSS)

The correlations on these two pages identify the Major, Supporting, and Additional Clusters described by the Common Core State Standards (CCSS). Use the tables to help inform *i-Ready® Classroom Mathematics* instructional pacing so that students spend the majority of their time on the work of the major clusters, with time spent on supporting and additional clusters used to enhance that work.

Major Areas of Focus

The Common Core State Standards (CCSS) require that the instructional focus of each grade be on the major clusters of that grade. This means that some clusters of the standards require greater emphasis than others. This greater emphasis may be based on the depth of the ideas, the time that students need to master the concepts, the content's importance to future mathematics topics, or a combination of some or all of these. A greater focus on the most critical material at each grade ensures that students develop deep conceptual understanding, strong procedural skill and fluency, and the ability to apply their learning to solve problems in the mathematics classroom and their everyday lives.

The table below indicates the clusters of Major focus in the Common Core State Standards (CCSS).

Standard Clusters with Major Focus	Standard(s)	Lesson(s)
Expressions & Equations		
Work with radicals and integer exponents.	8.EE.A.1, 8.EE.A.2, 8.EE.A.3, 8.EE.A.4	19, 20, 21, 22, 23, 25
Understand the connections between proportional relationships, lines, and linear equations.	8.EE.B.5, 8.EE.B.6	8, 9, 17
Analyze and solve linear equations and pairs of simultaneous linear equations.	8.EE.C.7, 8.EE.C.7a, 8.EE.C.7b, 8.EE.C.8, 8.EE.C.8a, 8.EE.C.8b, 8.EE.C.8c	10, 11, 12, 13, 14
Functions		
Define, evaluate, and compare functions.	8.F.A.1, 8.F.A.2, 8.F.A.3	15, 17
Use functions to model relationships between quantities.	8.F.B.4, 8.F.B.5	16, 18
Geometry		
Understand congruence and similarity using physical models, transparencies, or geometry software.	8.G.A.1, 8.G.A.1a, 8.G.A.1b, 8.G.A.1c, 8.G.A.2, 8.G.A.3, 8.G.A.4, 8.G.A.5	1, 2, 3, 4, 5, 6, 7
Understand and apply the Pythagorean Theorem.	8.G.B.6, 8.G.B.7, 8.G.B.8	26, 27

Supporting and Additional Areas of Focus

Although some clusters have greater focus in the Common Core State Standards (CCSS), this does not mean that standards within the clusters identified as Supporting or Additional can be neglected during instruction. Neglecting material will leave gaps in students' skills and understanding and may leave students unprepared for the challenges of a later grade. Standards for topics that are not a major focus are written in such a way as to support and strengthen the areas of major focus. This allows for valuable connections that add coherence to the grade.

The table below indicates the clusters with Supporting or Additional focus in the Common Core State Standards (CCSS).

Standard Clusters with Supporting or Additional Focus	Standard(s)	Lesson(s)
The Number System		
Know that there are numbers that are not rational, and approximate them by rational numbers.	8.NS.A.1, 8.NS.A.2	24, 25
Geometry		
Solve real-world and mathematical problems involving volume of cylinders, cones, and spheres.	8.G.C.9	28
Statistics & Probability		
Investigate patterns of association in bivariate data.	8.SP.A.1, 8.SP.A.2, 8.SP.A.3, 8.SP.A.4	29, 30, 31, 32

Common Core State Standards (CCSS) Correlations

i-Ready® Classroom Mathematics lessons reflect the same focus as the major clusters of the Common Core State Standards (CCSS). To better ensure the lessons reflect the major work of the grade, the standards are further classified as *Focus*, *Developing*, or *Applied*.

- Focus standards indicate the instructional goal of the lesson and the content assessed on the Lesson Quiz or Comprehension Check.
- Developing standards indicate concepts and skills that are being introduced and developed but will be the focus of a future lesson. These standards will be assessed in a future Lesson Quiz or Comprehension Check.
- Applied standards indicate skills and concepts that were the focus of a previous lesson that have already been assessed. These standards are now considered part of a student's toolkit and will be applied in this lesson.

The tables below correlate the standards to lessons, and the lessons to standards.

Correlation by Common Core State Standard

Standard	Emphasis	Lesson(s)
The Number System		
Know that there are numbers that are not rational, and approximate them by rational numbers.		
8.NS.A.1 Know that numbers that are not rational are called irrational. Understand informally that every number has a decimal expansion; for rational numbers show that the decimal expansion repeats eventually, and convert a decimal expansion which repeats eventually into a rational number.	Supporting	**Focus:** 24, 25
8.NS.A.2 Use rational approximations of irrational numbers to compare the size of irrational numbers, locate them approximately on a number line diagram, and estimate the value of expressions (e.g., π^2). *For example, by truncating the decimal expansion of* $\sqrt{2}$*, show that* $\sqrt{2}$ *is between 1 and 2, then between 1.4 and 1.5, and explain how to continue on to get better approximations.*	Supporting	**Focus:** 25 Applied: 27, 28

Standard	Emphasis	Lesson(s)
Expressions & Equations		
Work with radicals and integer exponents.		
8.EE.A.1 Know and apply the properties of integer exponents to generate equivalent numerical expressions. *For example,* $3^2 \times 3^{-5} = 3^{-3} = \frac{1^3}{3} = \frac{1}{27}$.	Major	**Focus:** 19, 20 Applied: 21, 22
8.EE.A.2 Use square root and cube root symbols to represent solutions to equations of the form $x^2 = p$ and $x^3 = p$, where p is a positive rational number. Evaluate square roots of small perfect squares and cube roots of small perfect cubes. Know that $\sqrt{2}$ is irrational.	Major	**Focus:** 23, 25 Applied: 26, 27
8.EE.A.3 Use numbers expressed in the form of a single digit times an integer power of 10 to estimate very large or very small quantities, and to express how many times as much one is than the other. *For example, estimate the population of the United States as 3 times* 10^8 *and the population of the world as 7 times* 10^9*, and determine that the world population is more than 20 times larger.*	Major	**Focus:** 21 Applied: 22
8.EE.A.4 Perform operations with numbers expressed in scientific notation, including problems where both decimal and scientific notation are used. Use scientific notation and choose units of appropriate size for measurements of very large or very small quantities (e.g., use millimeters per year for seafloor spreading). Interpret scientific notation that has been generated by technology.	Major	**Focus:** 22 Developing: 21
Understand the connections between proportional relationships, lines, and linear equations.		
8.EE.B.5 Graph proportional relationships, interpreting the unit rate as the slope of the graph. Compare two different proportional relationships represented in different ways. For example, compare a distance-time graph to a distance-time equation to determine which of two moving objects has greater speed.	Major	**Focus:** 8, 17 Applied: 9
8.EE.B.6 Use similar triangles to explain why the slope m is the same between any two distinct points on a non-vertical line in the coordinate plane; derive the equation $y = mx$ for a line through the origin and the equation $y = mx + b$ for a line intercepting the vertical axis at b.	Major	**Focus:** 8, 9 Applied: 15, 16
Analyze and solve linear equations and pairs of simultaneous linear equations.		
8.EE.C.7 Solve linear equations in one variable.		
a. Give examples of linear equations in one variable with one solution, infinitely many solutions, or no solutions. Show which of these possibilities is the case by successively transforming the given equation into simpler forms, until an equivalent equation of the form $x = a$, $a = a$, or $a = b$ results (where a and b are different numbers).	Major	**Focus:** 11 Applied: 12, 13
b. Solve linear equations with rational number coefficients, including equations whose solutions require expanding expressions using the distributive property and collecting like terms.	Major	**Focus:** 10 Developing: 9 Applied: 11, 12, 13, 14, 24
8.EE.C.8 Analyze and solve pairs of simultaneous linear equations.		
a. Understand that solutions to a system of two linear equations in two variables correspond to points of intersection of their graphs, because points of intersection satisfy both equations simultaneously.	Major	**Focus:** 12 Applied: 13, 14
b. Solve systems of two linear equations in two variables algebraically, and estimate solutions by graphing the equations. Solve simple cases by inspection. *For example,* $3x + 2y = 5$ *and* $3x + 2y = 6$ *have no solution because* $3x + 2y$ *cannot simultaneously be 5 and 6.*	Major	**Focus:** 12, 13 Applied: 14
c. Solve real-world and mathematical problems leading to two linear equations in two variables. *For example, given coordinates for two pairs of points, determine whether the line through the first pair of points intersects the line through the second pair.*	Major	**Focus:** 14 Developing: 12, 13

Correlation by Common Core State Standard *(continued)*

Standard	Emphasis	Lesson(s)
Functions		
Define, evaluate, and compare functions.		
8.F.A.1 Understand that a function is a rule that assigns to each input exactly one output. The graph of a function is the set of ordered pairs consisting of an input and the corresponding output.	Major	**Focus:** 15 Applied: 17
8.F.A.2 Compare properties of two functions each represented in a different way (algebraically, graphically, numerically in tables, or by verbal descriptions). *For example, given a linear function represented by a table of values and a linear function represented by an algebraic expression, determine which function has the greater rate of change.*	Major	**Focus:** 17 Developing: 16
8.F.A.3 Interpret the equation $y = mx + b$ as defining a linear function, whose graph is a straight line; give examples of functions that are not linear. *For example, the function $A = s^2$ giving the area of a square as a function of its side length is not linear because its graph contains the points (1, 1), (2, 4) and (3, 9), which are not on a straight line.*	Major	**Focus:** 15 Developing: 9 Applied: 17, 30
Use functions to model relationships between quantities.		
8.F.B.4 Construct a function to model a linear relationship between two quantities. Determine the rate of change and initial value of the function from a description of a relationship or from two (x, y) values, including reading these from a table or from a graph. Interpret the rate of change and initial value of a linear function in terms of the situation it models, and in terms of its graph or a table of values.	Major	**Focus:** 16 Developing: 12, 13, 14 Applied: 17, 18, 30
8.F.B.5 Describe qualitatively the functional relationship between two quantities by analyzing a graph (e.g., where the function is increasing or decreasing, linear or nonlinear). Sketch a graph that exhibits the qualitative features of a function that has been described verbally.	Major	**Focus:** 18 Developing: 16, 17 Applied: 29

Standard	Emphasis	Lesson(s)
Geometry		
Understand congruence and similarity using physical models, transparencies, or geometry software.		
8.G.A.1 Verify experimentally the properties of rotations, reflections, and translations:		
a. Lines are taken to lines, and line segments to line segments of the same length.	Major	**Focus:** 1 Applied: 2, 3
b. Angles are taken to angles of the same measure.	Major	**Focus:** 1 Applied: 2, 3
c. Parallel lines are taken to parallel lines.	Major	**Focus:** 1 Applied: 2, 3
8.G.A.2 Understand that a two-dimensional figure is congruent to another if the second can be obtained from the first by a sequence of rotations, reflections, and translations; given two congruent figures, describe a sequence that exhibits the congruence between them.	Major	**Focus:** 3 Developing: 1, 2 Applied: 6, 7
8.G.A.3 Describe the effect of dilations, translations, rotations, and reflections on two-dimensional figures using coordinates.	Major	**Focus:** 2, 3
8.G.A.4 Understand that a two-dimensional figure is similar to another if the second can be obtained from the first by a sequence of rotations, reflections, translations, and dilations; given two similar two-dimensional figures, describe a sequence that exhibits the similarity between them.	Major	**Focus:** 4, 5 Applied: 7, 8
8.G.A.5 Use informal arguments to establish facts about the angle sum and exterior angle of triangles, about the angles created when parallel lines are cut by a transversal, and the angle-angle criterion for similarity of triangles. *For example, arrange three copies of the same triangle so that the sum of the three angles appears to form a line, and give an argument in terms of transversals why this is so.*	Major	**Focus:** 6, 7 Applied: 8, 10
Understand and apply the Pythagorean Theorem.		
8.G.B.6 Explain a proof of the Pythagorean Theorem and its converse.	Major	**Focus:** 26 Applied: 27
8.G.B.7 Apply the Pythagorean Theorem to determine unknown side lengths in right triangles in real-world and mathematical problems in two and three dimensions.	Major	**Focus:** 27 Applied: 28
8.G.B.8 Apply the Pythagorean Theorem to find the distance between two points in a coordinate system.	Major	**Focus:** 27
Solve real-world and mathematical problems involving volume of cylinders, cones, and spheres.		
8.G.C.9 Know the formulas for the volumes of cones, cylinders, and spheres and use them to solve real-world and mathematical problems.	Additional	**Focus:** 28

Correlation by Common Core State Standard *(continued)*

Standard	Emphasis	Lesson(s)
Statistics & Probability		
Investigate patterns of association in bivariate data.		
8.SP.A.1 Construct and interpret scatter plots for bivariate measurement data to investigate patterns of association between two quantities. Describe patterns such as clustering, outliers, positive or negative association, linear association, and nonlinear association.	Supporting	**Focus:** 29 Applied: 30
8.SP.A.2 Know that straight lines are widely used to model relationships between two quantitative variables. For scatter plots that suggest a linear association, informally fit a straight line, and informally assess the model fit by judging the closeness of the data points to the line.	Supporting	**Focus:** 29 Applied: 30
8.SP.A.3 Use the equation of a linear model to solve problems in the context of bivariate measurement data, interpreting the slope and intercept. *For example, in a linear model for a biology experiment, interpret a slope of 1.5 cm/hr as meaning that an additional hour of sunlight each day is associated with an additional 1.5 cm in mature plant height.*	Supporting	**Focus:** 30 Developing: 16
8.SP.A.4 Understand that patterns of association can also be seen in bivariate categorical data by displaying frequencies and relative frequencies in a two-way table. Construct and interpret a two-way table summarizing data on two categorical variables collected from the same subjects. Use relative frequencies calculated for rows or columns to describe possible association between the two variables. *For example, collect data from students in your class on whether or not they have a curfew on school nights and whether or not they have assigned chores at home. Is there evidence that those who have a curfew also tend to have chores?*	Supporting	**Focus:** 31, 32

Correlation by *i-Ready Classroom Mathematics* Lesson

Lesson	Standard(s)	Emphasis
Unit 1 Geometric Figures: Rigid Transformations and Congruence		
Lesson 1 Understand Rigid Transformations and Their Properties	**Focus:** 8.G.A.1, 8.G.A.1a, 8.G.A.1b, 8.G.A.1c Developing: 8.G.A.2	Major Major
Lesson 2 Work with Single Rigid Transformations in the Coordinate Plane	**Focus:** 8.G.A.3 Developing: 8.G.A.2 Applied: 8.G.A.1a, 8.G.A.1b, 8.G.A.1c	Major Major Major
Lesson 3 Work with Sequences of Transformations and Congruence	**Focus:** 8.G.A.2, 8.G.A.3 Applied: 8.G.A.1a, 8.G.A.1b, 8.G.A.1c	Major Major
Unit 2 Geometric Figures: Transformations, Similarity, and Angle Relationships		
Lesson 4 Understand Dilations and Similarity	**Focus:** 8.G.A.4	Major
Lesson 5 Perform and Describe Transformations Involving Dilations	**Focus:** 8.G.A.3, 8.G.A.4	Major
Lesson 6 Describe Angle Relationships	**Focus:** 8.G.A.5 Applied: 8.G.A.2	Major Major
Lesson 7 Describe Angle Relationships in Triangles	**Focus:** 8.G.A.5 Applied: 8.G.A.2, 8.G.A.4	Major Major
Unit 3 Linear Relationships: Slope, Linear Equations, and Systems		
Lesson 8 Graph Proportional Relationships and Define Slope	**Focus:** 8.EE.B.5, 8.EE.B.6 Applied: 8.G.A.4, 8.G.A.5	Major Major
Lesson 9 Derive and Graph Linear Equations of the Form $y = mx + b$	**Focus:** 8.EE.B.6 Developing: 8.EE.C.7b, 8.F.A.3 Applied: 8.EE.B.5	Major Major Major
Lesson 10 Solve Linear Equations in One Variable	**Focus:** 8.EE.C.7, 8.EE.C.7b Applied: 8.G.A.5	Major Major
Lesson 11 Determine the Number of Solutions to One-Variable Equations	**Focus:** 8.EE.C.7, 8.EE.C.7a Applied: 8.EE.C.7b	Major Major
Lesson 12 Understand Systems of Linear Equations in Two Variables	**Focus:** 8.EE.C.8, 8.EE.C.8a, 8.EE.C.8b Developing: 8.EE.C.8c, 8.F.B.4 Applied: 8.EE.C.7a, 8.EE.C.7b	Major Major Major
Lesson 13 Solve Systems of Linear Equations Algebraically	**Focus:** 8.EE.C.8, 8.EE.C.8b Developing: 8.EE.C.8c, 8.F.B.4 Applied: 8.EE.C.7a, 8.EE.C.7b, 8.EE.C.8a	Major Major Major
Lesson 14 Represent and Solve Problems with Systems of Linear Equations	**Focus:** 8.EE.C.8, 8.EE.C.8c Developing: 8.F.B.4 Applied: 8.EE.C.7b, 8.EE.C.8a, 8.EE.C.8b	Major Major Major

Correlation by *i-Ready Classroom Mathematics* Lesson (continued)

Lesson	Standard(s)	Emphasis
Unit 4 Functions: Linear and Nonlinear Relationships		
Lesson 15 Understand Functions	**Focus:** 8.F.A.1, 8.F.A.3 Applied: 8.EE.B.6	Major Major
Lesson 16 Use Functions to Model Linear Relationships	**Focus:** 8.F.B.4 Developing: 8.F.A.2, 8.F.B.5 Developing: 8.SP.A.3 Applied: 8.EE.B.6, 8.F.A.3	Major Major Supporting Major
Lesson 17 Compare Different Representations of Functions	**Focus:** 8.EE.B.5, 8.F.A.2 Developing: 8.F.B.5 Applied: 8.F.A.1, 8.F.A.3, 8.F.B.4	Major Major Major
Lesson 18 Analyze Functional Relationships Qualitatively	**Focus:** 8.F.B.5 Applied: 8.F.B.4	Major Major
Unit 5 Integer Exponents: Properties and Scientific Notation		
Lesson 19 Apply Exponent Properties for Positive Integer Exponents	**Focus:** 8.EE.A.1	Major
Lesson 20 Apply Exponent Properties for All Integer Exponents	**Focus:** 8.EE.A.1	Major
Lesson 21 Express Numbers Using Integer Powers of 10	**Focus:** 8.EE.A.3 Developing: 8.EE.A.4 Applied: 8.EE.A.1	Major Major Major
Lesson 22 Work with Scientific Notation	**Focus:** 8.EE.A.4 Applied: 8.EE.A.1, 8.EE.A.3	Major Major
Unit 6 Real Numbers: Rational Numbers, Irrational Numbers, and the Pythagorean Theorem		
Lesson 23 Find Square Roots and Cube Roots to Solve Problems	**Focus:** 8.EE.A.2	Major
Lesson 24 Express Rational Numbers as Fractions and Decimals	**Focus:** 8.NS.A.1 Applied: 8.EE.C.7b	Supporting Major
Lesson 25 Find Rational Approximations of Irrational Numbers	**Focus:** 8.EE.A.2 **Focus:** 8.NS.A.1, 8.NS.A.2	Major Supporting
Lesson 26 Understand the Pythagorean Theorem and Its Converse	**Focus:** 8.G.B.6 Applied: 8.EE.A.2	Major Major
Lesson 27 Apply the Pythagorean Theorem	**Focus:** 8.G.B.7, 8.G.B.8 Applied: 8.EE.A.2, 8.G.B.6 Applied: 8.NS.A.2	Major Major Supporting
Lesson 28 Solve Problems with Volumes of Cylinders, Cones, and Spheres	**Focus:** 8.G.C.9 Applied: 8.G.B.7 Applied: 8.NS.A.2	Additional Major Supporting

Lesson	Standard(s)	Emphasis
Unit 7 Statistics: Two-Variable Data and Fitting a Linear Model		
Lesson 29 Analyze Scatter Plots and Fit a Linear Model to Data	**Focus:** 8.SP.A.1, 8.SP.A.2 Additional: 8.F.B.5	Supporting Major
Lesson 30 Write and Analyze an Equation for Fitting a Linear Model to Data	**Focus:** 8.SP.A.3 Applied: 8.F.A.3, 8.F.B.4 Applied: 8.SP.A.1, 8.SP.A.2	Supporting Major Supporting
Lesson 31 Understand Two-Way Tables	**Focus:** 8.SP.A.4	Supporting
Lesson 32 Construct and Interpret Two-Way Tables	**Focus:** 8.SP.A.4	Supporting

Math in Action Correlation

Math in Action Lesson	Common Core State Standards (CCSS)
Unit 1 Rigid Transformations in the Coordinate Plane	8.G.A.1a, 8.G.A.2, 8.G.A.3
Unit 2 Dilations, Similarity, and Angle Relationships	8.G.A.3, 8.G.A.4, 8.G.A.5
Unit 3 Linear Relationships and Systems of Equations	8.EE.B.5, 8.EE.C.7a, 8.EE.C.7b, 8.EE.C.8a, 8.EE.C.8b, 8.EE.C.8c
Unit 4 Functional Relationships	8.EE.B.5, 8.F.A.1, 8.F.A.2, 8.F.A.3, 8.F.B.4, 8.F.B.5
Unit 5 Scientific Notation and Properties of Exponents	8.EE.A.1, 8.EE.A.3, 8.EE.A.4
Unit 6 Irrational Numbers, the Pythagorean Theorem, and Volume	8.NS.A.2, 8.EE.A.2, 8.G.B.7, 8.G.C.9
Unit 7 Representing Data	8.SP.A.1, 8.SP.A.2, 8.SP.A.3, 8.SP.A.4

Standards for Mathematical Practices (SMP) Correlations

i-Ready® Classroom Mathematics lessons utilize the Standards for Mathematical Practice (SMP) to foster deeper understanding of critical mathematical concepts during instruction. The following tables correlate the eight SMP to lessons and the lessons to SMP. Further description of how the SMP are integrated into the lessons and built into the routine can be found before the first unit of each volume.

Correlation by Standards for Mathematical Practice (SMP)

SMP	Wording	Lesson(s)
1	Make sense of problems and persevere in solving them.	2, 3, 5, 6, 7, 8, 9, 10, 11, 13, 14, 15, 16, 17, 18, 19, 20, 21, 22, 23, 24, 25, 27, 28, 29, 30, 31, 32, 33
2	Reason abstractly and quantitatively.	1–32
3	Construct viable arguments and critique the reasoning of others.	1–32
4	Model with mathematics.	2, 3, 5, 6, 7, 8, 9, 10, 11, 12, 13, 14, 16, 17, 18, 19, 20, 21, 22, 23, 24, 25, 26, 27, 28, 29, 30, 32
5	Use appropriate tools strategically.	1, 2, 3, 5, 6, 7, 8, 9, 10, 11, 13, 14, 16, 17, 18, 19, 20, 21, 22, 23, 24, 25, 26, 27, 28, 29, 30, 31, 32
6	Attend to precision.	1, 2, 3, 4, 5, 6, 7, 8, 9, 10, 11, 13, 14, 16, 17, 18, 19, 20, 21, 22, 23, 24, 25, 26, 27, 28, 29, 30, 32
7	Look for and make use of structure.	1, 2, 3, 4, 5, 8, 9, 11, 12, 13, 15, 16, 18, 19, 20, 21, 22, 23, 24, 25, 26, 27, 28, 31, 32
8	Look for and express regularity in repeated reasoning.	5, 11, 15, 19, 20, 21, 23, 24, 25

Correlation by *i-Ready Classroom Mathematics* Lesson

Lesson	SMP
Unit 1 Geometric Figures: Rigid Transformations and Congruence	
Lesson 1 Understand Rigid Transformations and Their Properties	2, 3, 5, 6, 7
Lesson 2 Work with Single Rigid Transformations in the Coordinate Plane	1, 2, 3, 4, 5, 6, 7
Lesson 3 Work with Sequences of Transformations and Congruence	1, 2, 3, 4, 5, 6, 7
Unit 2 Geometric Figures: Transformations, Similarity, and Angle Relationships	
Lesson 4 Understand Dilations and Similarity	2, 3, 6, 7
Lesson 5 Perform and Describe Transformations Involving Dilations	1, 2, 3, 4, 5, 6, 7, 8
Lesson 6 Describe Angle Relationships	1, 2, 3, 4, 5, 6
Lesson 7 Describe Angle Relationships in Triangles	1, 2, 3, 4, 5, 6

Lesson	SMP
Unit 3 Linear Relationships: Slope, Linear Equations, and Systems	
Lesson 8 Graph Proportional Relationships and Define Slope	1, 2, 3, 4, 5, 6, 7
Lesson 9 Derive and Graph Linear Equations of the Form $y = mx + b$	1, 2, 3, 4, 5, 6, 7
Lesson 10 Solve Linear Equations in One Variable	1, 2, 3, 4, 5, 6
Lesson 11 Determine the Number of Solutions to One-Variable Equations	1, 2, 3, 4, 5, 6, 7, 8
Lesson 12 Understand Systems of Linear Equations in Two Variables	2, 3, 4, 7
Lesson 13 Solve Systems of Linear Equations Algebraically	1, 2, 3, 4, 5, 6, 7
Lesson 14 Represent and Solve Problems with Systems of Linear Equations	1, 2, 3, 4, 5, 6
Unit 4 Functions: Linear and Nonlinear Relationships	
Lesson 15 Understand Functions	1, 2, 3, 7, 8
Lesson 16 Use Functions to Model Linear Relationships	1, 2, 3, 4, 5, 6, 7
Lesson 17 Compare Different Representations of Functions	1, 2, 3, 4, 5, 6
Lesson 18 Analyze Functional Relationships Qualitatively	1, 2, 3, 4, 5, 6, 7
Unit 5 Integer Exponents: Properties and Scientific Notation	
Lesson 19 Apply Exponent Properties for Positive Integer Exponents	1, 2, 3, 4, 5, 6, 7, 8
Lesson 20 Apply Exponent Properties for All Integer Exponents	1, 2, 3, 4, 5, 6, 7, 8
Lesson 21 Express Numbers Using Integer Powers of 10	1, 2, 3, 4, 5, 6, 7, 8
Lesson 22 Work with Scientific Notation	1, 2, 3, 4, 5, 6, 7
Unit 6 Real Numbers: Rational Numbers, Irrational Numbers, and the Pythagorean Theorem	
Lesson 23 Find Square Roots and Cube Roots to Solve Problems	1, 2, 3, 4 5, 6, 7, 8
Lesson 24 Express Rational Numbers as Fractions and Decimals	1, 2, 3, 4, 5, 6, 7, 8
Lesson 25 Find Rational Approximations of Irrational Numbers	1, 2, 3, 4, 5, 6, 7, 8
Lesson 26 Understand the Pythagorean Theorem and Its Converse	2, 3, 4, 5, 6, 7
Lesson 27 Apply the Pythagorean Theorem	1, 2, 3, 4, 5, 6, 7
Lesson 28 Solve Problems with Volumes of Cylinders, Cones, and Spheres	1, 2, 3, 4, 5, 6, 7
Unit 7 Statistics: Two-Variable Data and Fitting a Linear Model	
Lesson 29 Analyze Scatter Plots and Fit a Linear Model to Data	1, 2, 3, 4, 5, 6
Lesson 30 Write and Analyze an Equation for Fitting a Linear Model to Data	1, 2, 3, 4, 5, 6
Lesson 31 Understand Two-Way Tables	1, 2, 3, 5, 7
Lesson 32 Construct and Interpret Two-Way Tables	1, 2, 3, 4, 5, 6, 7

Unit Review Correlation

i-Ready® Classroom Mathematics Unit Reviews reflect balanced coverage of levels of Depth of Knowledge (DOK). The table below shows the levels of depth of knowledge for the items in the Unit Reviews, the standard(s) addressed, and the corresponding *i-Ready® Classroom Mathematics* lesson(s) assessed by each item.

Problem	DOK[1]	Standard(s)	Lesson(s)
Unit 1 Geometric Figures: Rigid Transformations and Congruence			
1	2	8.G.A.1a	1
2	2	8.G.A.1b	1
3	2	8.G.A.1c	1
4	2	8.G.A.2	3
5	2	8.G.A.2	3
6	2	8.G.A.3	2
7	2	8.G.A.3	3
PT	3	8.G.A.2, 8.G.A.3	2, 3
Unit 2 Geometric Figures: Transformations, Similarity, and Angle Relationships			
1	1	8.G.A.5	6
2	2	8.G.A.3	5
3	2	8.G.A.4	4
4	2	8.G.A.4	5
5	1	8.G.A.3	5
6	2	8.G.A.5	7
7	3	8.G.A.5	6
PT	3	8.G.A.5	6

[1]**Depth of Knowledge levels:**
1. The item requires recall of a one-step, well-defined, or straight algorithmic procedure.
2. The item requires mental processing beyond recall and observation.
3. The item requires reasoning, explanations, generalization, and connection to other ideas.

Problem	DOK[1]	Standard(s)	Lesson(s)
Unit 3 Linear Relationships: Slope, Linear Equations, and Systems			
1	1	8.EE.B.5	8
2	2	8.EE.C.7a	11
3	3	8.EE.C.8a	12
4	2	8.EE.C.8c	14
PT	3	8.EE.C.7, 8.EE.C.7b	10
Unit 4 Functions: Linear and Nonlinear Relationships			
1	1	8.F.A.1	15
2	1	8.F.A.2	17
3	2	8.F.B.4	16
4	3	8.F.B.5	18
5	2	8.F.A.3	15
6	2	8.F.B.4	16
7	2	8.EE.B.5	17
PT	3	8.F.A.2, 8.F.A.3, 8.F.B.4	15, 16, 17
Unit 5 Integer Exponents: Properties and Scientific Notation			
1	1	8.EE.A.1	19
2	1	8.EE.A.1	20
3	2	8.EE.A.3	21
4	2	8.EE.A.4	22
5	1	8.EE.A.1	20
6	2	8.EE.A.3	21
7	2	8.EE.A.4	22
PT	3	8.EE.A.3, 8.EE.A.4	21, 22

[1]**Depth of Knowledge levels:**
1. The item requires recall of a one-step, well-defined, or straight algorithmic procedure.
2. The item requires mental processing beyond recall and observation.
3. The item requires reasoning, explanations, generalization, and connection to other ideas.

Correlations

Problem	DOK[1]	Standard(s)	Lesson(s)
Unit 6 Real Numbers: Rational Numbers, Irrational Numbers, and the Pythagorean Theorem			
1	1	8.EE.A.2	23
2	1	8.NS.A.1	24
3	2	8.NS.A.2	25
4	3	8.G.B.6	26
5	2	8.G.B.7	27
6	2	8.G.C.9	28
7	2	8.G.B.8	27
PT	3	8.EE.A.2	23, 25
Unit 7 Statistics: Two-Variable Data and Fitting a Linear Model			
1	3	8.SP.A.1	29
2	2	8.SP.A.3	30
3	2	8.SP.A.4	31
4	1	8.SP.A.4	32
5	1	8.SP.A.2	29
6	2	8.SP.A.4	31
PT	3	8.SP.A.4	31, 32

[1]**Depth of Knowledge levels:**
1. The item requires recall of a one-step, well-defined, or straight algorithmic procedure.
2. The item requires mental processing beyond recall and observation.
3. The item requires reasoning, explanations, generalization, and connection to other ideas.

Acknowledgment

Common Core State Standards © 2010. National Governors Association Center for Best Practices and Council of Chief State School Officers. All rights reserved.

Photography Credits

3c Pictorial Press Ltd/Alamy Stock Photo; 7 Unholy Vault Designs/Shutterstock; 19 Aquarius Studio/Shutterstock; 47 sampono_art/Shutterstock; 85 ANRIR/Shutterstock; 97 Georgejmclittle/Shutterstock; 119 logoboom/Shutterstock; 141 zhengzaishuru/Shutterstock; 179 Baloncici/Shutterstock; 201 varandah/Shutterstock.com; 229 Suzanne Tucker/Shutterstock; 251 fizkes/Shutterstock; 273 Celiafoto/Shutterstock; 285 Andrey_Popov/Shutterstock; 313 Love Silhouette/Shutterstock; 351 nata-lunata/Shutterstock; 363 Gorondenkoff/Shutterstock; 391 Milan Ilic Photographer/Shutterstock; 413 Edgloris Marys/Shutterstock.com; 451 Lopolo/Shutterstock; 473 K_E_N/Shutterstock; 495 Nor Gal/Shutterstock; 517 muratart/Shutterstock; 561 Erikson Stock/Shutterstock; 583 Richard Paul Kane/Shutterstock.com; 599 NASA/JPL-Caltech; 617c Universal Images Group North America LLC/Alamy Stock Photo; 621 Viappy/Shutterstock; 633 Holmes846/Shutterstock; 661 Tooykrub/Shutterstock.com; 699 beboy/Shutterstock; 727 Gregory E. Clifford/Shutterstock.com; 749 Sergieiev/Shutterstock; 761 tsyhun/Shutterstock

Data Sets

541 https://nssdc.gsfc.nasa.gov/planetary/factsheet/; 700 https://www.akc.org/expert-advice/nutrition/breed-weight-chart/; 704 Rosenbaum, Mike. (2019, June 12). 100 Meter Men's Olympic Medalists. Retrieved from https://www.liveabout.com/100-meter-mens-olympic-medalists-3259179; 704 https://www.olympic.org/rio-2016/athletics/100m-men; 720 https://www.pewresearch.org/internet/fact-sheet/social-media/; 722 http://www.electproject.org/2016g; 743 https://data.worldbank.org/indicator/IT.NET.USER.ZS?end=2017&start=1960&view=chart; 743 https://en.wikipedia.org/wiki/Giant_pumpkin; 743 https://www.newsweek.com/world-record-pumpkin-mathias-willemijns-580566; 779 http://data.un.org/Default.aspx; 784 http://data.un.org/Default.aspx